Commercial Law

Third edition

Robert Bradgate MA (Cantab), Solicitor
Reader in Commercial Law
Sheffield University

Butterworths
LexisNexis™

Members of the LexisNexis Group worldwide

United Kingdom	LexisNexis Butterworths Tolley, a Division of Reed Elsevier (UK) Ltd, Halsbury House, 35 Chancery Lane, LONDON, WC2A 1EL, and 4 Hill Street, EDINBURGH EH2 3JZ
Argentina	LexisNexis Argentina, BUENOS AIRES
Australia	LexisNexis Butterworths, CHATSWOOD, New South Wales
Austria	LexisNexis Verlag ARD Orac GmbH & Co KG, VIENNA
Canada	LexisNexis Butterworths, MARKHAM, Ontario
Chile	LexisNexis Chile Ltda, SANTIAGO DE CHILE
Czech Republic	Nakladatelství Orac sro, PRAGUE
France	Editions du Juris-Classeur SA, PARIS
Hong Kong	LexisNexis Butterworths, HONG KONG
Hungary	HVG-Orac, BUDAPEST
India	LexisNexis Butterworths, NEW DELHI
Ireland	Butterworths (Ireland) Ltd, DUBLIN
Italy	Giuffrè Editore, MILAN
Malaysia	Malayan Law Journal Sdn Bhd, KUALA LUMPUR
New Zealand	LexisNexis Butterworths, WELLINGTON
Poland	Wydawnictwo Prawnicze LexisNexis, WARSAW
Singapore	LexisNexis Butterworths, SINGAPORE
South Africa	Butterworths SA, DURBAN
Switzerland	Stämpfli Verlag AG, BERNE
USA	LexisNexis, DAYTON, Ohio

© Reed Elsevier (UK) Ltd 2000
Reprinted 2003

A CIP Catalogue record for this book is available from the British Library.

ISBN 0 406 91603 9

Typeset by Doyle & Co, Colchester
Printed and bound in Great Britain by Antony Rowe Ltd, Chippenham, Wilts

Visit Butterworths LexisNexis *direct* at www.butterworths.com

Preface

It is a little over five years since the publication of the second edition of this book. The extent of the changes in the law during that time is indicated by the fact that this third edition is some 150 pages longer than its predecessor. This increase is in part a reflection of the fact that an increasing volume of material is now available through the proliferation of specialist series of law reports and electronic resources. It may be said that much of that new material involves merely illustration, or at best refinement, of existing principles rather than radical new developments, but, even where that is the case, the volume of new material indicates the increased volume of commercial litigation and the continuing growth in the significance of commercial law.

A sizeable proportion of the new material cannot be dismissed in this way, however, since it involves significant new developments. What is perhaps surprising is just how much of the new material is statutory, much of it exerting an influence throughout the book. The doctrine of privity has often proved a nuisance in relation to commercial operations. It is therefore hardly surprising that the Contracts (Rights of Third Parties) Act 1999 should recur throughout the book. There are other pervasive influences, too. The Financial Services and Markets Act 2000, although not central to the area covered by this book, crops up repeatedly. The growth of electronic commerce, and the legislation designed to facilitate it, including the Electronic Communications Act 2000, is another pervasive theme. The influence of EC law continues to grow, especially, but not solely, in the area of consumer protection.

I have tried to take account of all of this new material, whilst striving to keep the size of the book manageable. At the same time, I have taken the opportunity to re-write some parts of the book with which I was unhappy or which, with the benefit of hindsight, I now feel merit a different approach. Some indication of the main changes may be in order.

Part II (Agency) has been generally updated to take account, mainly, of various case law developments. The most important of those are undoubtedly the cases applying the Commercial Agents Regulations. The Regulations represent a significant step in the 'Europeanisation' of our commercial law. The approach of the courts to their interpretation has been instructive. They have shown a remarkable facility to adopt and apply concepts which might have been thought alien, including the requirement of 'good faith' between principal and agent, and have rapidly begun to develop the Regulations so as to provide commercial agents with significant protection in dealings with their principals. Elsewhere, there have been a number of significant developments in relation to agents' fiduciary duties, in part as a result of the general development of the law relating to fiduciaries.

Part III (Sale and Supply of Goods) takes account of a number of case law developments. Of these the most important are in Chapters 11 and 12. Despite the valiant efforts of the Court of Appeal in *Stevenson v Rogers* to reconcile their decision with that in *R & B Customs Brokers*, it is difficult to see how the two decisions can stand together. Whilst *Stevenson* is broadly to be welcomed, the existence of the two decisions leaves a number of questions unanswered. Similarly, the decision in *Bence Graphics* is difficult to reconcile with prior authority. The decision of the House of Lords in *Slater v Finning*, on the other hand, whilst important, is altogether easier to reconcile with its antecedents. Perhaps the most interesting cases in this area, however, are the first decisions applying the 1994 reforms to the statutory implied terms and the remedies for their breach. Those decisions tend to confirm the view, propounded in the previous edition, that the 1994 reforms would often produce little change to the outcomes of cases. The decision in *Thain v Anniesland Trade Centre* would, it is submitted, have been precisely the same under the pre-1994 law. The important decision in *Truk UK v Tokmakidis* suggests that some of the changes to the law on acceptance and rejection may also be less significant than might at first have been thought.

Elsewhere, other important cases, such as *Barber v NWS Bank* and *Atari Corpn v Electronics Boutique Stores* are discussed in some detail. In Chapter 8 I have re-written the section dealing with the status of computer software in the light of the decisions in *St Albans City and District Council v ICL* and *Beta Computers v Adobe Systems*. It must be said that neither of these decisions is entirely satisfactory; in particular the distinction drawn in *St Albans*, which depends on the medium via which software is supplied, seems unattractive. These cases are unlikely to be the last word on a subject which is set to grow in importance in coming years. The main developments in Part III, however, are again statutory. The EC Directive on consumer guarantees is now completed and we await its implementation. The 1995 Sale of Goods (Amendment) Act was passed too late to be dealt with satisfactorily in the second edition, and I have therefore re-written much of Chapter 15, and parts of Chapters 16 and 17, to take account of it. I have also included in Chapter 18 coverage of the Late Payment of Commercial Debts (Interest) Act 1998, which seems to me to represent a first, but significant, step in the development of protection for small businesses, whilst also perhaps indicating the way in which the general tone of our commercial law is changing.

There are many changes in Part IV. In the chapters on credit and security I have taken account, inter alia, of *Re Cosslett (Contractors)*, *Re BCCI (No 8)* (where Lord Hoffmann's remarks on 'conceptual impossibility' are a telling comment on the attitude of the courts to matters of commercial law) and the line of cases on guarantees and third party undue influence following from *Barclays Bank v O'Brien*. It must be questioned whether the line drawn in those cases is drawn in the right place and it may be that we have not yet had the last word on this subject. There are several new cases on consumer credit, including *Forthright Finance v Ingate* on s 75 and, of course, *Dimond v Lovell* on the meaning of credit. The single biggest body of case law in this part of the book, however, is concerned with aspects of banking law and related topics. Among the cases considered are *Novaknit Hellas v Kumar Bros International*; *HKSB v GD Trade Co*; *Kpohraror v Woolwich Building Society*; *Christofi v Barclays Bank*; and *Turner v Royal Bank of Scotland*. One reason for the proliferation of claims against banks, of course, is the availability of a 'deep pocket' to meet a liability. This is obviously a factor behind claims against banks for dishonest assistance in breach of trust and/or knowing receipt of trust funds. Whilst the law on dishonest assistance may be said to have been clarified by the decision in *Royal Brunei Airlines v Tan*, it must be said that recent cases such as *BCCI v Akindele* and *Twinsectra v Yardley* have not done the same for the law on knowing assistance. Perhaps the most interesting of the banking cases, however, does not involve a bank as litigant. The decision in *Esso v Milton* on the effect of payment by direct debit has been widely criticised and I am inclined to agree with the critics. At times it may be dangerous to extend established rules by analogy to new instruments. I have also sought in this section to take account of the Cruickshank report into banking services, which seems likely to produce some changes in the relationship between banks and their customers.

In Part V (International Trade) I have taken the opportunity to re-organise some of the material. The influence of e-commerce is starting to be felt in this area, with the development of the BOLERO project, and it seems likely that it will continue to grow. The main developments here, however, are in case law. We now have the first case law applying the Carriage of Goods by Sea Act 1992, in *The Berge Sisar* and *The Aegean Sea*, although it must be said that they are somewhat less then satisfactory. It is instructive to note that, notwithstanding the passing of the 1992 Act, some privity problems remain unresolved, and the common law will continue to have a role to play in this area even after the passing of the 1999 Third Parties Act, as demonstrated by the decisions in *The Pioneer Container* and *The Mahkutai*. Again, however, the biggest single body of new material relates to banking and deals with documentary credits. Amongst the cases considered in Chapter 34 are *Seaconsar v Markazi*; *Kredietbank v Midland Bank*; *Glencore v Bank of China*; *Banco Santander v Bayfern*; *Czarnikow-Rionda v Standard Bank*; *Cargill v Bangladesh Sugar and Food Industries*; and *Kvaerner John Brown v Midland Bank*. Quite why there should be this sudden proliferation in documentary credits litigation is unclear – unless it is simply that more cases are now being reported – but many of the decisions seem to have significance, in terms of what they say about the courts' approach to pure commercial contracts, beyond the narrow area of documentary credits.

Part VI deals with Insurance and Dispute Resolution. I was staggered by the volume of case law on insurance since the last edition, much of it significant. I have tried to take account of as much of it as seemed appropriate, whilst bearing in mind that this is not a specialist text on insurance. Among the cases considered are *Kausar v Eagle Star*; *Economides v Commercial Union*; *Norwich Union v Qureshi*; and *Galloway v Guardian Royal Exchange*. In the context of the debate about the role of 'good faith' in commercial law it is difficult to see how the concept of 'good faith' recognised in insurance law bears any relation to the notion of 'good faith' as generally understood. Perhaps the most interesting new case in this chapter, however, is the recent decision in *McAlpine v BAI (Run-Off)*. In the light of this decision it seems that insurance is not so far removed from the general law of contract, at least in some respects, as is sometimes thought.

Chapter 36, on dispute resolution, was extensively re-written for the last edition. The introduction of the Civil Procedure Rules following the Woolf Reforms and the passing of the Arbitration Act 1996 have necessitated its being re-written again for this.

I have said nothing, so far, about Part I of the book. This is in many ways where I have made the biggest changes for this new edition. Chapter 2 attempts a potted summary of the law of contract and, given its breadth, it is hardly surprising that there is much new material here. The most important is in the three areas which I regard as 'pervasive' of the book as a whole – exclusion clauses, privity and remedies. In relation to the first, I have taken account of the 1999 changes to the Unfair Terms in Consumer Contracts Regulations (it is greatly to be hoped that some attempt to consolidate the Regulations and the Unfair Contract Terms Act will be made in the near future) as well as *AEG v Logic Resource, Stevenson v Rogers* and the Court of Appeal decision in *Zockoll v Mercury* on s 3 of the Unfair Contract Terms Act. I am surprised that this decision has not been reported (so far as I am aware) in any of the mainstream series of law reports. The section on privity has been re-written (again) to take account of the Rights of Third Parties

Act 1999 as well as decisions following *Linden Gardens*. I have managed to incorporate some reference to the House of Lords' decision in *McAlpine v Panatown*, although it appeared too late to permit the consideration it deserves. *Panatown* straddles the line between privity and damages, of course. The decision in *Blake* was handed down at the same time and it, too, requires further consideration. The court now has power to award an account of profits as a remedy for breach of contract but quite when it will do so is unclear. Elsewhere, I have added sections on electronic commerce and on the interpretation of contracts in the light of the line of decisions culminating in *Investors Compensation Scheme v West Bromwich Building Society*. Given its importance, the neglect of contract interpretation by courses on contract and commercial law (including my own) is hard to justify.

And that leaves Chapter 1. I have extensively re-written and extended this chapter to reflect what I now see as the major themes running through the book and the issues with which commercial law must now deal. These include the Europeanisation and internationalisation of commercial law, the split between commercial and consumer law, e-commerce, the role of equity in commercial law, and the protection and promotion of good faith. To my surprise, and contrary to the view expressed in the last edition, codification of commercial law is back on the agenda – partly, no doubt, as a result of some of these questions.

As usual, I would like to thank colleagues, including both teachers and students, who have assisted me in various ways in the production of this edition. Special mention should go (in alphabetical order) to John Adams, Graham Battersby, John Birds, Roger Brownsword, Alexandra Ganotaki, Mirghazem Jafarzadeh, Gerard McCormack, Severine Saintier, Christian Twigg-Flesner, Fidelma White and Alison Williams, and to Professor Aubrey Diamond, who (gently) pointed out some errors in the previous edition. Singling these out is not intended to deny or denigrate the contributions of many others who have helped develop my ideas on various topics. It remains the case, of course, that the opinions expressed in the book are my own and that I am solely responsible for any errors which remain. Thanks are also due to all at Butterworths involved with the production of this edition, who did a sterling job and patiently tolerated my repeatedly missing deadlines and breaking assurance that 'I'm sure I can finish by . . .'. When I was asked to produce a new edition I willingly agreed. I hopelessly underestimated the sheer size of the task I had undertaken. One great regret is that work on this edition denied me the opportunity to see much of the last hurrah of those two cricketing giants, Curtley Ambrose and Courtney Walsh. It was not only my summer which was affected, however, and the biggest thanks of all must again go to Mags, who again not only read various chunks of the manuscript but provided help, encouragement and support, both moral and practical, and, above all, tolerated my disappearance behind a wall of books in my 'study' and my various eccentric working practices (and hours). Without her, I doubt I would have completed this.

The prefaces to the previous editions have drawn parallels between the book and Nottingham Forest FC. Readers will, I hope, understand if, in the light of their current plight, I prefer not to draw any such parallels on this occasion . . .

The law is stated as at 31 August 2000, although it has been possible to take account of some later developments at proof stage.

Robert Bradgate

Sheffield
October 2000

Bradgate: Commercial Law on the Internet

An Internet home page has been established for readers of this book. This home page has two main purposes:

- first, it provides links to websites containing important primary sources such as codes, consultation documents and reports which are not always easily accessible in law libraries;

- secondly, it will be used to provide periodic updating information on key developments in law and policy.

The first update will appear in April 2001. The site will then be updated periodically throughout the life of the book. Those who wish to receive notice of the updates can register on the website.

To access the website go to the Butterworths academic home page – **www.lawcampus.butterworths.co.uk/** – click on the Student Focus link, and then access the web-linked books by clicking on that item in the menu on the left-hand side of your screen. There you will find a link to Bradgate.

Contents

Contents

Table of statutes

Numbers in the right-hand column are to paragraph numbers. Those in **bold** type indicate where the material is set out in full or in part.

Table of cases

C

Part I

The legal framework

Chapter 1

The Nature and Sources of Commercial Law

1.0   What is commercial law?

Commercial law is notoriously difficult to define. At page 1205 of his authoritative text on the subject, Professor Goode asks 'Does commercial law exist?' and confesses that:

> 'The absence of anything resembling a commercial code makes this question harder to answer than might be imagined. If by commercial law we mean a relatively self-contained, integrated body of principles and rules peculiar to commercial transactions, then we are constrained to say that this is not to be found in England[1].'

Goode's initial question is, of course, rhetorical. Commercial law exists, even if its ambit cannot be precisely described. To quote another eminent English academic, although English lawyers are familiar with, and may use, the expression 'commercial law', 'if asked what it contrasted with rather than what it contained [an English lawyer] would have no answer at all'[2]. As Goode observes, unlike many civil law countries, and unlike the USA with its Uniform Commercial Code, English law has no recognisable coherent commercial code.

The absence of a clearly defined category of 'commercial law' is perhaps unsurprising: the strength of the common law has traditionally been its pragmatism: English law has been concerned with providing solutions to practical problems rather than with theoretical categorisation[3]. Even the assertion that English lawyers might be able to describe the 'content' of commercial law may be questioned. The content of academic courses and texts on 'commercial law' varies widely, and a practising lawyer might include within 'commercial law' a number of matters which would appear in none of the courses or books. Thus a commercial practitioner might deal with matters concerned with contracts; the supply of goods and services; finance, lending and security; insurance; property; tax; competition law and intellectual property; partnerships and companies. Many of those matters are dealt with separately from 'commercial law' in academic courses. Perhaps most curiously of all, company law is treated as a subject distinct from commercial law, despite the central role of companies in commercial activity, and that separation extends to the courts, where there are separate Companies and Commercial Courts[4]. This is in sharp contrast with the approach in many civilian jurisdictions where company law is regarded as part of the Commercial Code.

Clearly books, and courses, must be selective in the material they cover, so that the contents of a textbook on 'commercial law' (including this one) should not be regarded as attempting to provide an exhaustive list of the content of 'commercial law'; the separation of company law from commercial law can thus be justified for the purposes of exposition and teaching. However, it has been suggested that the two subjects are approached differently by the courts and legislature, and that separation is more difficult to justify[5].

In the absence of an agreed legal definition of 'commercial law' one turns to the dictionary, which defines commerce as the 'exchange of merchandise or services especially on a large scale; buying and selling'. 'Commercial law' can thus be defined as the law relating to commercial activity, especially transactions concerned with the supply of goods and services and the financing thereof. Similarly, Professor Goode defines 'commercial law as the totality of the law's response to the needs and practices of the mercantile community'[6]. On the basis of such definitions certain subjects clearly form part of commercial law: for instance, the law relating to the sale of goods. However, as these definitions recognise, 'commercial law' is essentially a pragmatic, fact-based, subject; and its content may change and develop as commercial practices and activities change from time to time.

This chapter seeks to identify the key principles and characteristics of commercial law. The first half of the chapter will trace the history and identify the main principles of modern English commercial law. The second half seeks to identify some key current issues in, and influences on, the development of commercial law.

1   Goode, *Commercial Law* (2nd edn, 1995) p 1205.
2   Weir, 'The Common Law System', *International Encyclopaedia of Comparative Law* Vol II ch 2 Part 3 para 135.
3   But see *Re State of Norway's Application* [1990] 1 AC 723, [1989] 1 All ER 745, HL, considering the Evidence (Proceedings in Other Jurisdictions) Act 1975, s 1, s 9(1) referring to 'proceedings in any civil or commercial matter'.
4   See 36.1.1.
5   See Sealy, *Company Law and Commercial Reality* (1984) p 3.
6   *Commercial Law* (2nd edn, 1995) p 1205.

1.1   The principles of commercial law

In order to accommodate commercial activities, commercial law draws on principles from a number of different areas of jurisprudence: the 'exchange of merchandise and services' is managed, legally, primarily through the mechanism of contract law, but principles from tort, property, equity and trusts[1] and even criminal law may be regarded as part of 'commercial law'. A definition of commercial law in terms of its content may therefore be doomed to failure. However, certain attitudes and approaches can be recognised and regarded as forming the 'ethos' of commercial law. Essentially, the purpose of commercial law has been regarded as the facilitation of commercial activity. Within this broad objective a number of principles can be identified: certainty and predictability; respect for party autonomy; recognition of the customs and practices of the mercantile community; and flexibility in order to accommodate changing practices. One might add more[2]. Some, for instance, would argue that the law should also promote values of fairness and good faith, especially if commercial law is defined widely to include consumer transactions. The role of good faith is considered further below.

Clearly, some of these principles overlap: recognition of market practices may, for instance, be seen as an aspect of respect for party autonomy, and both may be seen as tending to promote certainty. Others are in tension: flexibility, necessary to respond to changes in market practice, tends to be achieved only at the expense of certainty. Similarly, simple, 'bright line' rules tend to be more certain but may produce unfair results in individual cases, whereas flexible, discretionary principles may be productive of justice in individual cases but will tend to be less predictable in their operation. The key challenge for commercial law is therefore to strike the right balance between the competing principles, and it must be recognised that the balance may be struck in different places according to the circumstances. Thus, for instance, in relation to 'pure' commercial transactions, such as those involving multinational corporations in the commodity or shipping trades, the balance will generally favour certainty. On the other hand, where there is a significant imbalance between the parties, especially where one is a consumer, some measure of certainty may be sacrificed in favour of fairness or flexibility. Ultimately, these various principles all serve the one end, of facilitating commercial activity, or, as Lord Steyn, a leading commercial judge, has put it on a number of occasions, to give effect to the reasonable expectations of honest people.

1   The proper role of equitable principles in commercial law is currently the subject of much debate. This issue is considered further below.
2   Professor Goode has identified eight principles: see (1988) 14 Monash University LR 135 at 148ff.

1.1.1 *Certainty*

From early times, it has been recognised that commercial people require the law to deal speedily with their problems and to provide clear solutions, to enable costly and time-consuming litigation to be avoided if possible: 'it is better to lose by the application of a swift and certain rule than to win after long and uncertain delay'[1]. This need has been met in various ways. Special procedures have been developed to meet the needs of commercial people. Thus in medieval times special courts were provided for the resolution of commercial disputes; and today the Commercial Court aims to provide a procedure which is quick, simple and flexible[2], whilst the courts have been prepared to develop effective new remedies, such as Anton Piller and Mareva injunctions[3] to respond quickly and effectively to commercial disputes.

If the law is to be capable of dealing speedily with disputes, it must, so far as possible, be clear and certain. If the law is certain, the outcome of a dispute may be predicted and the parties may resolve it without resort to litigation. If litigation is necessary, disputes can be dealt with quickly. Certainty is especially at a premium in relation to market transactions, where speedy decisions may have to be made against the background of fluctuating prices[4].

There are several aspects to 'certainty'. Above all it means that the law should be clear. The law should also be capable of being applied in a predictable way. Thus, for instance, a rule giving courts a discretion to strike down contract terms as unreasonable may be a clear rule in the sense that it can be described simply, but its application in a particular case may be unpredictable. Certainty also requires that settled legal rules should not lightly be changed. Once a rule has been established, parties will contract on the basis of that rule. If the rule is then changed, settled contracts may be disturbed and the expectations of the contractors not fulfilled. So, for instance:

'once a court has put a construction on commercial documents in standard form, commercial men act on it. It should be followed in all subsequent cases. If the business community is not satisfied with the decision, they should alter the standard form[5].'

This approach is not restricted to rules of law established by court decision. In *The Giannis K*[6], the House of Lords was asked to hold that the interpretation of the Bills of Lading Act 1855, long favoured by leading practitioner texts, was incorrect. Stressing that insurance premiums would have been adjusted and claims settled on the basis of the interpretation favoured in the texts, Lord Lloyd indicated that he would be 'reluctant to disturb such a course of business unless convinced that the textbook writers are wrong'[7].

1   Street, *Foundations of Legal History* p 328.
2   See 36.1.1 below.
3   Now known as 'search orders' and 'freezing injunctions' respectively and awarded under statutory powers (Civil Procedure Act 1997, s 7 and Supreme Court Act 1981, s 37(3)): see 36.1.2.1 below.
4   See, for instance, the approach in *Bunge Corpn v Tradax SA* [1981] 2 All ER 513, qualifying the application of the *Hong Kong Fir* approach to the treatment of breach of contract (*Hong Kong Fir Shipping Co Ltd v Kawasaki Kisen Kaisha Ltd* [1962] 2 QB 26): see 2.5.6, 10.2.1.
5   Per Lord Denning MR in *The Annefield* [1971] 1 All ER 394 at 405. See also the comments of Lord Diplock in *Pioneer Shipping Ltd v BTP Tioxide, The Nema* [1982] AC 724 at 737.
6   *Effort Shipping Co Ltd v Linden Management SA* [1998] 1 All ER 495.
7   At 504. The courts are likely to be particularly reluctant to overturn settled rules of law now that, as a result of the House of Lords' decision in *Kleinwort Benson Ltd v Lincoln City Council* [1998] 4 All ER 513, a payment made on the basis of a settled understanding of the law may be recovered as a payment made under a mistake if that settled understanding is later held to be wrong.

1.1.2   *Party autonomy*

A second feature of commercial law is its respect for party autonomy. This can clearly be seen in the law of contract, with its central doctrines of freedom and sanctity of contract[1] and its refusal to question the adequacy of consideration or to intervene in contracts on the basis of 'fairness'. This non-interventionist approach is justified on the basis that it 'facilitates the conduct of trade'[2] by promoting certainty[3]. For the same reason the House of Lords refused to accept that there is a general power to intervene in contracts on the grounds of 'inequality of bargaining power'[4]. Respect for party autonomy is therefore closely connected to the promotion of certainty.

In recent years, with the development of the 'consumer society', legislation such as the Unfair Contract Terms Act 1977 and Consumer Credit Act 1974 has encouraged the courts to intervene in certain categories of contract, and the courts too have shown an increased willingness to adopt a more interventionist approach than has traditionally been the case[5]. However, what may be described as 'pure' commercial contracts are often excluded from the ambit of such interventionist legislation. Thus, for instance, the Consumer Credit Act has no application to contracts with companies, or where the amount of credit involved exceeds £25,000[6] and the Unfair Contract Terms Act has no application to a wide range of contracts including those for the international supply of goods, contracts of insurance, charterparties and so on[7].

1   See 2.0.1.
2   Per Lord Diplock in *Schroeder Music Publishing Co Ltd v Macaulay* [1974] 1 WLR 1308 at 1316, HL.

3   But see Hedley [1990] CLJ 209, who describes this view as 'naive' and contrasts it with the 'cynical' view that the judges refuse to intervene in business transactions because of their lack of knowledge of the business world.
4   *National Westminster Bank plc v Morgan* [1985] AC 686: see 2.4.3.
5   See 2.4.3 below.
6   Consumer Credit Act 1974, s 8; Consumer Credit (Increase of Monetary Limits) Amendment Order 1998, SI 1998/996; see ch 25.
7   Unfair Contract Terms Act 1977, s 26, Sch 1; see 2.6.4.

1.1.3   *Recognition of commercial practices and responsiveness to the needs of the commercial community*

In *Kleinwort Benson Ltd v Lincoln City Council* Lord Lloyd observed that 'In the field of commercial law . . . the custom of merchants has always been a fruitful source of law'[1]. There is a long history of the courts recognising and giving legal effect to the customs and practices of the mercantile community even, if necessary, at the expense of stretching legal concepts or even denying fundamental principles, for 'all kinds of legal magic can be worked by mercantile usage'[2].

The most common means by which effect is given to commercial custom or usage is by implying a term into a contract[3]. Thus if parties have contracted in a locality or trade where there is a settled custom or usage, a term giving effect to that custom or usage may be implied into their contract. Alternatively, evidence of a settled custom or usage may be admitted to assist in the interpretation of a contract. It is not enough, however, for a practice to be common. In order for a custom or usage to receive judicial recognition it must be shown to be certain, in the sense of being well established, notorious (ie well known), so that it may be assumed that the parties contracted on the basis of it, and reasonable, so that reasonable, honest people would accept it[4]. If these requirements are satisfied the court will, in effect, assume that the parties contracted on the basis of the custom or usage[5]. Even if a custom or usage satisfies these requirements, however, it cannot give rise to an implied term if that would contradict the express terms of the contract.

Where a court finds that a term is implied into a particular contract on the basis of custom or usage its judgment is effectively declaratory. If the contract is of a common type the custom/usage will, in effect, become a legal incident of all contracts of that type in the particular market or trade. By judicial recognition mercantile usage can become part of the common law. A bill of lading is recognised as a document of title to goods at common law[6]; a bill of exchange is a negotiable instrument, transfer of which can confer on the transferee a title free of any defects in the title of the transferee[7]. The status of the bill of lading as a document of title and of the bill of exchange as a negotiable instrument depends on judicial recognition of mercantile usage.

As commercial people find new ways of doing business, the law must respond. Commercial law must therefore adapt to and accommodate changing commercial practices: 'If old forms are now used to express different meanings from those read into them in earlier days the courts should be prompt to recognise the altered use if they are satisfied that there is in fact a change'[8]. New customs and usages may be established, and if they satisfy the requirements of certainty, notoriety and reasonableness, they may receive judicial recognition. So, for instance, there is no obstacle to new classes of instruments being recognised as negotiable if a commercial usage to that effect is established[9]. Even, however, where a practice is not so well established as to be regarded as a settled custom or usage, the courts

7

will often seek to give effect to it, in order to facilitate commerce and, we might say, give effect to the reasonable expectations of commercial people. The attitude of the courts was highlighted by Lord Hoffmann when he cautioned that 'the courts should be very slow to declare a practice of the commercial community to be conceptually impossible'[10].

In recent years the courts have had to consider the status and effect of retention of title clauses[11], letters of intent[12], letters of comfort[13], credit and cheque guarantee cards[14], direct debits[15] and numerous new financing arrangements[16] and financial instruments[17].

In order to adapt to such changes in practice the law must be flexible; but, as noted earlier, flexibility is often bought at the expense of certainty. One of the hallmarks of commercial law has been its willingness to accommodate new commercial practices by imaginative manipulation and adaptation of existing legal concepts such as agency and bailment. In seeking to respond to and facilitate commercial activity, commercial law is essentially pragmatic: 'concepts such as bailment and fiduciary duty must not be allowed to be our masters, but must rather be regarded as the tools of our trade'[18].

It is not only the courts who seek to respond to and accommodate the needs of the commercial community. Legislation takes the same approach. Thus, for instance, reform to commercial law will normally be preceded by consultation with the commercial community; and if the law is found to be out of step with commercial needs or expectations, reform may be swift[19].

At the dawn of the twenty-first century, information and communications technologies are leading to even greater changes in the way business is transacted. Perhaps the greatest challenge to commercial law as it enters the twenty-first century is the need to respond to the ever increasing pace of technological change and the use of technology in business. The special problems of e-commerce are considered further below as one of the factors influencing the development of commercial law.

1   [1998] 4 All ER 513 at 549.
2   Goode (1988) 14 Monash Univ LR 136 at 155.
3   Strictly speaking a 'custom' is a practice associated with a particular area, a 'usage' with a particular trade, but the terms tend now to be used almost interchangeably.
4   *Cunliffe-Owen v Teather and Greenwood* [1967] 3 All ER 561.
5   *Vitol SA v Phibro Energy AG, The Mathuraki* [1990] 2 Lloyd's Rep 84.
6   See 32.1.
7   See 27.3.3.
8   Atkin J in *Groom v Barber* [1915] 1 KB 316 at 325.
9   See *Goodwin v Robarts* (1875) LR 10 Exch 337; *Bechuanaland Exploration Co v London Trading Bank* [1898] 2 QB 658.
10 *Re BCCI SA (No 8)* [1997] 4 All ER 568 at 578.
11 See 18.4.
12 *British Steel Corpn v Cleveland Bridge and Engineering Co Ltd* [1984] 1 All ER 504: see 2.3.4; 8.1.
13 *Kleinwort Benson Ltd v Malaysian Mining Corpn Bhd* [1989] 1 All ER 785, [1989] 1 WLR 379, CA: see 2.3.5.
14 *Re Charge Card Services Ltd* [1989] Ch 497, [1988] 3 All ER 702, CA.
15 *Esso Petroleum Co Ltd v Milton* [1997] 2 All ER 593.
16 See eg *Welsh Development Agency v Export Finance Co* [1992] BCC 270; *Re Curtain Dream plc* [1990] BCLC 925: see 22.0.4.2; 22.2.2.1.
17 See eg the cases concerned with the effects of interest rate swaps such as: *Westdeutsche Landesbank Girozentrale v Islington London Borough Council* [1996] AC 669, [1996] 2 All ER 961; *Kleinwort Benson Ltd v Sandwell Borough Council* [1994] 4 All ER 890; *Barclays Bank plc v Glasgow City Council* [1994] QB 404; *Kleinwort Benson Ltd v Glasgow City Council* [1999] 1 AC 153; *Kleinwort Benson Ltd v South Tyneside Metropolitan Borough Council* [1994] 4 All ER 972.

18 Per Goff LJ in *Clough Mill Ltd v Martin* [1984] 3 All ER 982 at 987, CA.
19 See eg the reforms effected by the Carriage of Goods by Sea Act 1992 and the Sale of Goods (Amendment) Act 1995 discussed at 32.6.5 and 15.6.2. In each case legislation was preceded by a Law Commission report which involved extensive consultation with the commercial community affected.

1.2   The historical development of commercial law

Many of the principles of modern commercial law have their roots in the lex mercatoria (law merchant) developed in medieval times. At that time much trade was carried on at fairs; in addition, much of it was of an international character. Merchants from all over Europe would travel with their goods to fairs all over the continent. The importance of trade, and the need to respect the rights of foreign merchants, was acknowledged by Magna Carta, which provided that 'all merchants shall have safety and security in coming into England, and going out of England, and in staying and travelling through England . . .'. Merchants trading at the fairs would form a close-knit community; where disputes arose between merchants, they needed some means of settling those disputes quickly. Such disputes were therefore settled at special courts, including the courts of Piepowder (or Piepoudre)[1], which decided cases quickly and according to the customs and practices of merchants. Instead of lawyer-judges, cases were decided by juries composed of merchants, presided over by a 'judge' drawn from the mercantile community, and these courts may be regarded as similar to modern arbitration tribunals[2].

Since trade was international, and the courts decided disputes according to the customs of merchants, mercantile courts in different countries would decide cases according to the same principles. These came to be described as the 'lex mercatoria' which, by the fifteenth century, could be described as 'law universal throughout the world'[3]. Many of the principles of the lex mercatoria differed from those of the general common law[4]. The legal recognition of such important commercial documents as bills of lading[5] and bills of exchange[6] dates back to the lex mercatoria and this period.

In the seventeenth century, however, the competition between the courts for business ultimately led to the common law courts, and particularly the court of Kings Bench, taking over much of the business of the mercantile courts. In order to take over that business, the courts had to appeal to the mercantile community and so some of the principles of the lex mercatoria developed in the mercantile courts for use in mercantile disputes were absorbed into the common law. By 1628 Coke could write that 'the lex mercatoria is part of the law of the realm'[7]. However, in other ways the law administered in the common law courts differed from the lex mercatoria, and for some time the principles continued to diverge. Moreover, at about the same time, other European nation states were about to embark on codification of their laws, leading to the absorption of commercial law into national law. The international character of the lex mercatoria was therefore lost, and national laws began to diverge (although there is still a considerable degree of similarity in many areas).

In England the modification of the common law to meet mercantile needs was largely accomplished during the late seventeenth and eighteenth centuries, under Lords Chief Justices Holt and Mansfield. Under Holt, for example, the law of bailment[8] and of negotiable instruments[9] was largely developed, and under Mansfield the incorporation of commercial law into the common law was largely completed:

'It was due to Lord Mansfield's genius that the harmonisation of commercial custom and the common law was carried out with an almost complete understanding of the requirements of the commercial community, and the principles of the old law, and that that marriage of ideas proved acceptable to both merchants and lawyers[10]. '

1   Literally 'pieds poudres' – dusty feet – reflecting the fact that the courts were intended to provide speedy justice for travelling merchants.
2   See 36.2.
3   Yearbook 13 Edw IV 9 pl 5.
4   But see Baker [1979] CLJ 295, who argues that although the lex mercatoria offered separate, speedy procedures, there never was a body of substantive 'law merchant', as opposed to commercial custom, separate from the common law.
5   See ch 32.
6   See ch 28.
7   Coke, *Commentaries*.
8   In *Coggs v Bernard* (1703) 2 Ld Raym 909.
9   See ch 28.
10   Schmitthoff, 'International Business Law, A New Law Merchant' in *Current Law and Social Problems* (1961) p 129.

1.2.1   *Codification*

By the late nineteenth century many of the principles of modern commercial law were developed. However, having been developed by the common law, the principles were to be found scattered throughout the reports of a mass of decided cases and, as a result, were largely inaccessible. At the end of the century, therefore, largely at the instigation of the commercial community[1], many of the most important principles were codified in statutory form. Unlike some other jurisdictions, they were not incorporated into one single code, but were embodied in individual statutes dealing with individual areas, such as the Bills of Exchange Act 1882, Factors Act 1889, Partnership Act 1890, Sale of Goods Act 1893 and Marine Insurance Act 1906. As codifying Acts, these statutes were based on the existing common law (although in some areas the legislation, either intentionally or inadvertently, made important changes to the existing law), which in turn was based on recognition of mercantile custom and practice.

The strength of the codification is indicated by the fact that many of these statutes provided models for legislation in other parts of the common law world. In England, all but the 1893 Sale of Goods Act remain in force today; and, although the 1893 Act has been repealed and replaced, many of its provisions are repeated in the Sale of Goods Act 1979[2].

1   See Lord Rodger of Earlesferry, 'The Codification of Commercial Law in Victorian Britain' (1992) 108 LQR 570.
2   Significant amendments were made to the 1979 Act in 1994 and 1995 by the Sale and Supply of Goods Act 1994, the Sale of Goods (Amendment) Acts 1994 and 1995: see chs 11, 12, 15 and 17.

1.2.2   *Influences on modern commercial law*

Modern English commercial law may thus be said to be the product of mercantile practice, recognised by and filtered through the common law and statutory codification. The law is, however, constantly developing. Three main influences on the continuing development of the modern law can be identified: consumerism; international harmonisation, especially resulting from membership of the EU; and, increasingly, the need to respond to the technological revolution and development of electronic commerce. These influences are considered further below. There is considerable interplay between them. The EU responds to wider international developments, but also regards raising levels of consumer protection as a significant part of its brief, whilst e-commerce, in particular, demands both an international response and consideration of the special needs of consumers.

1.3   The rise of consumerism and the development of consumer law

The industrial revolution brought about profound changes in the social, economic and political life of the UK. It has been estimated that between 1860 and 1900 the real wages of urban workers increased by 60%[1]. The increased economic power of the general public and the mass production of consumer durables, such as bicycles, sewing machines and furniture, led to a massive increase in commercial activity. The process was further fuelled by the growth in the provision of credit and the continued increase in prosperity during the twentieth century. Together with the rise of welfare philosophies during the period after the Second World War, this led to a recognition that the existing contractual basis for the analysis of commercial activity, with its assumption of equality of bargaining power and doctrines of freedom and sanctity of contract, was inadequate to deal with the problems created by the increase in consumption and the increasing complexity of goods and sophistication of sales techniques. The courts developed the principles of negligence law to deal with problems caused by defective goods[2] and Parliament legislated to regulate the supply of credit[3].

Consumer protection law is not a wholly twentieth-century phenomenon. There has been legislation to control the content and adulteration of food since the Assize of Bread and Ale of 1266, and, as Atiyah points out:

> 'Consumer protection was a major legislative preoccupation throughout the nineteenth century and it was not by any means confined purely to the prevention of fraud . . . Since fraud was often difficult to prove, it was very common for Parliament to legislate on the principle of preventing modes of commercial behaviour which facilitated fraud'[4].

However, the greatest changes in the legal response to commercial activity have come since the Second World War, with the rise of consumer lobby groups. The period since the 1960s has seen a considerable increase in the volume of legislation designed to protect the interests of 'consumers', whilst, at the same time, the courts have shown an increasing willingness to abandon the concepts of freedom of contract and adopt an increasingly interventionist role in order to protect weaker parties to contracts. As a result it is possible now to recognise a separate category of consumer protection law within commercial law.

Many legal techniques have been used as means of consumer protection. They include:

(a) statutory control of contracts, either by stipulating implied terms, or by regulating the exercise of rights under contracts: for instance, non-excludable terms are implied into contracts for the supply of goods[5], whilst the Consumer

Credit Act 1974 restricts the right of a creditor to repossess goods supplied on hire-purchase;
(b) regulatory control, for instance by licensing, as under the Consumer Credit Act 1974[6];
(c) criminal law, for instance in the contexts of trade descriptions and product[7] and food safety[8]; and
(d) self regulation, for instance by the promotion and encouragement of codes of practice, often backed by the threat of legislation; thus, for instance, insurance and banking are largely free from statutory regulation, the industries having been encouraged from time to time to take steps themselves to correct practices perceived to be prejudicial to consumers[9].

1   Mathias, *The First Industrial Nation* (1878).
2   *Donoghue v Stevenson* [1932] AC 562.
3   Moneylenders Act 1927; Hire Purchase Act 1938.
4   *The Rise and Fall of Freedom of Contract* (1979) p 545.
5   Unfair Contract Terms Act 1977, ss 6–7, below 2.6.4.1.
6   See 24.3.
7   Consumer Protection Act 1987; General Product Safety Regulations 1994, SI 1994/2328.
8   Food Safety Act 1990.
9   There will be greater legal regulation of this sector when the Financial Services and Markets Act 2000 is brought into effect.

1.3.1   *Commercial and consumer law*

What is the relationship between 'consumer law' and 'commercial law'? Defining 'consumer law' is no easier than defining 'commercial law'. Many civil law jurisdictions draw a sharp distinction between the two with separate civil and commercial codes, the latter applying only to transactions between merchants, but no such distinction is drawn by the common law which applies many rules to both consumer and commercial transactions[1]. Thus, for instance, although the Sale of Goods Act is often perceived as a consumer protection measure, many of its principles are based on the common law recognition of mercantile practices during the eighteenth and nineteenth centuries. It is a prime example of commercial law, and, indeed, many of its provisions are at variance with consumer expectations and even their interests; it has had to be modified by the Supply of Goods (Implied Terms) Act 1973 and the Unfair Contract Terms Act 1977 and, more recently, the Sale and Supply of Goods Act 1994 in order to make it an effective consumer protection measure[2]. On the other hand, many commercial activities with a profound impact on 'consumer interests', such as insurance and banking, are often ignored by texts on consumer law and regarded as being aspects of pure commercial law. It may therefore be artificial, if not impossible, to draw a sharp distinction between 'commercial' and 'consumer' law. Where common rules are applied to both classes of transaction, a decision in a 'commercial' case may set a precedent for 'consumer' transactions and vice versa.

One reason for the difficulty in defining 'consumer law' is the difficulty in defining 'consumer'. To some extent all buyers and end-users of products and services can be regarded as 'consumers'. Perhaps the better view, then, is that consumers are simply a category of participants in commercial activity. As Samuels points out:

'In a world of self-service petrol stations and supermarkets we are all now, to an extent, business persons'[3].

On this view, consumer law is concerned with the modification of commercial law to protect those participants in the market who are seen to be at a disadvantage and to require protection, and the increased willingness of the courts in recent years to modify contract principles and intervene to prevent abuses of market power can be seen as an element of consumer protection law. The crucial question, then, is to decide who is in need of protection. Several modern statutes protect 'consumers', but often use different definitions of 'consumer'. In many cases businesses may be 'consumers'. Thus, for instance, the Consumer Protection Act 1987 protects any person who suffers injury, or damage to property, as a result of a defect in a product, although it limits compensation for property damage to property which was intended for private use or consumption[4]. The Consumer Credit Act 1974 protects all users of credit of up to £25,000, other than incorporated persons: thus an individual business person may be protected by the Act[5]. The Unfair Contract Terms Act 1977 defines a consumer as a person who neither makes, nor purports to make, a contract in the course of a business; however, it has been held that a business which buys goods can still be acting as a consumer for this purpose[6].

In those cases where consumer protection legislation allows the court to intervene in contractual relationships, it may be more important to decide which contracts should be excluded from the ambit of the legislation rather than which should be included, in order to avoid undermining certainty in commercial contracts. Thus the Consumer Credit Act makes clear that certain common trade situations are not regulated by the Act; and the Unfair Contract Terms Act specifically excludes a range of contracts from its control.

The function of consumer law may therefore be said to be regulatory, in contrast with the essentially facilitative function of commercial law. However, by providing consumers with a measure of legal protection, the law may give them confidence to participate in the market and thus, in effect, by providing a measure of regulation, further facilitate activity. One might therefore suggest that if 'commercial law' is defined broadly as all the law relating to commercial activity, 'consumer (protection) law' can be regarded as one component, albeit an increasingly important one, in the overall structure of commercial law. On the other hand, in so far as commercial law is concerned with the examination of the civil law relationships between parties to particular classes of commercial transaction, much of consumer protection law is outside its ambit. This book is primarily concerned with the private law consequences of commercial transactions involving the supply of goods and services, especially on a large scale. Thus although we will consider the implications of the law for consumers where it is appropriate, we will not examine the broader techniques of consumer protection law[7].

If consumer law is concerned with the protection of those who are at a disadvantage in the market, it becomes apparent that it is not enough simply to draw a line between 'commercial' and 'consumer' transactions. A small business may be at a market disadvantage when dealing with a larger one just as much as a consumer might be. On the whole, the common law has refused to intervene in contracts between businesses merely on account of inequality of bargaining power. On the other hand, there is growing recognition of the need to protect smaller businesses from abuse of power by their larger trading partners. As governments have become aware of the economic importance of 'small businesses', it is possible to identify an emerging strand of legislation concerned with the protection of smaller businesses[8].

1   For defence of this approach see Reynolds, 'The Applicability of General Rules of Private Law to Consumer Disputes' in Anderman et al (eds) *Law and the Weaker Party* (1982).

2   Further reform will be necessary to implement the EC Directive on Certain Aspects of the Sale of Consumer Goods and Associated Guarantees. See ch 11.
3   'Civil Law and Commercial Law: A Distinction Worth Making?' (1986) 102 LQR 569 at 572.
4   See 13.1.4.
5   See 25.0.1.
6   *R & B Customs Brokers Co Ltd v UDT Ltd* [1988] 1 All ER 847, [1988] 1 WLR 321, CA; cf *Stevenson v Rogers* [1999] 1 All ER 613: see 2.6.4.2.
7   The reader interested in those broader techniques is referred to one of the several excellent texts on the subject: see eg Harvey and Parry, *The Law of Consumer Protection and Fair Trading* (5th edn, 1996); Scott and Black *Cranston's Consumers and the Law* (3rd edn, 2000); Ramsay, *Consumer Protection, Text and Materials* (1989); Oughton, *Consumer Law: Text, Cases and Materials* (1991).
8   See eg the EC Directive on Self-employed (Commercial) Agents (86/653/EEC), below ch 6, and the Late Payment of Commercial Debts (Interest) Act 1998, below, 18.0.1.1.

1.4   The internationalisation of commercial law

There has been international commercial activity throughout recorded history. Traders have always sought out new markets and new opportunities. Today, however, the volume and importance of international commercial activity is greater than ever. We speak of a 'global economy'. Goods and services are traded not just locally but internationally, and through the Internet and e-commerce the advantages of an international market are available to even the smallest of traders and to consumers.

We have seen that although commercial law was originally 'international' in character, national laws diverged over time[1]. In recent years, however, it has been recognised that international trade needs an international legal response. Differences between national laws can pose an obstacle to trade. A trader may be reluctant to agree to subject his contract to the law of a foreign state, especially that of his trading partner. The negotiation of a contract may therefore be hindered by disagreement over which national law is to govern the contract. If such questions are not settled in advance, they may have to be resolved if and when a dispute arises. Conflict of law problems are notoriously difficult to resolve and their resolution can considerably increase the cost of and time taken in resolving the dispute.

In one sense it may be said that there is already an international law for international trade. One of the proudest claims of English commercial law is that it is the law of choice of the international commercial community. English commercial law, with its emphasis on certainty and speed and the facilitation of commerce, is felt to be particularly well adapted to the needs of commerce, and English commercial lawyers and judges are similarly highly regarded. Many international contracts, especially in the commodity and shipping trades, therefore include an express choice of English law as the law applicable to the contract, often coupled with an agreement for disputes to be resolved by litigation in the English Commercial Court or by arbitration in London, even when neither of the contracting parties is English.

A contract between two multinational commodity traders is one thing, however. An export contract between a small English seller and a similar German (for example) buyer, is another. It may be much more difficult to get the English seller to accept German law, or the German buyer to accept English law. A contract made over the Internet between an American seller and an English consumer is something different again. It will probably be quite impossible for the consumer, with little or no bargaining power, to insist on any law other than that of the supplier, even if the consumer considers the issue at all.

For various reasons, therefore – to reduce the potential for conflict of law problems, to facilitate the negotiation of contracts, and to try to establish minimum levels of international consumer protection – recent years have seen a growth in efforts to harmonise national laws applicable to commercial and consumer transactions. The development of the Internet and e-commerce has given an added impetus to such efforts, for the Internet recognises no national boundaries.

1   See 1.2.

1.4.1 *The influence of the European Union*

A number of international governmental and commercial agencies have been involved in the harmonisation process. An English reader may be forgiven for thinking first of the European Union. In fact the EU has, to date, had relatively little impact on pure commercial law. It has promulgated important directives on banking and insurance, concerned with such issues as the establishment and regulation of businesses[1]. It is also responsible for a Directive on Commercial Agency, which has already had a significant impact on English agency law[2]. Its main efforts, however, have so far been in the field of consumer protection[3], where it has issued directives on consumer credit, unfair contract terms[4], consumer guarantees in the sale of goods[5] and distance sales contracts[6], amongst other topics. These and other directives are an increasingly important source of rights for consumers.

The impact of these measures on English law should not be underestimated. Through the various directives, English lawyers are becoming introduced to concepts already familiar to civil lawyers, such as 'good faith' between contractors. The recent tendency of the UK government when implementing EU directives has been to transpose the text of the directive, often more or less verbatim, into regulations made under the European Communities Act 1972. This causes its own problems, for the directives often fit uncomfortably, at best, with existing domestic law. One side effect, however, is to require English lawyers to come to terms with the civilian style of legislative drafting. Based on early reported decisions on the Commercial Agents and Unfair Terms Directives, the English courts appear to be dealing with these alien concepts and drafting styles more easily than might have been feared. In coming years, the EU is likely to continue to exert an important influence on the development, especially, of English consumer law.

1   See 29.1.3.
2   Directive on Self-employed (Commercial) Agents (86/653/EEC): see ch 6.
3   The Treaty of Maastricht introduced a new article, art 129a, into the Treaty of Rome to allow the European Community to legislate to achieve a high level of consumer protection.
4   Directive 1993/13/EC on unfair terms in consumer contracts: see 2.6.5.
5   Directive 1999/44/EC on certain aspects of the sale of consumer goods and associated guarantees (1999) OJ L171/12, 7 July 1999. See 11.8, 12.5.
6   Directive 1997/7/EC on the protection of consumers in respect of distance contracts.

1.4.2 *International agencies and the harmonisation of commercial law*[1]

So far as pure commercial law is concerned, other international agencies involved in the harmonisation of laws are at least as important as the EU. The most important is perhaps the United Nations Commission on International Trade Law

(UNCITRAL)[2], which not only promulgates conventions, model laws and other instruments itself, but also seeks to co-ordinate the activities of the various organisations involved in harmonisation of international trade law. UNCITRAL is responsible for a number of important international instruments, but its most important 'product' is the Vienna Convention on Contracts for the International Sale of Goods, completed in 1980[3]. This is an attempt to harmonise the rules governing the formation of and the rights and duties of the parties under international sales contracts. UNCITRAL is also responsible, inter alia, for Model Laws on International Commercial Arbitration[4] and Electronic Commerce, which, as their names suggest, are intended to be used as models by states wishing to legislate on these topics.

Mention should also be made of the International Institute for the Unification of Private Law (UNIDROIT), which has produced a number of conventions designed to operate alongside the Vienna Sales Convention and covering such topics as international finance leasing, international factoring and agency in international sales contracts.

Views on the desirability, practicability and effectiveness of international harmonisation differ[5]. Many English lawyers remain deeply sceptical of, and even hostile to, such efforts. International conventions have no effect unless ratified by individual nations. Although the UK often plays a prominent role in the preparation of international instruments, it often then fails to ratify them. 'We seem unable to organise our affairs so as to reap the fruits of our own often arduous labours'[6]. The Vienna Convention is a case in point. It has been ratified by almost every major trading nation, with the exceptions of Japan and the UK.

There are various reasons for this attitude – inertia and apathy, in addition to a genuine, although possibly exaggerated, concern that ratification will introduce an unwelcome degree of uncertainty into English commercial law. In fact, many would argue that the Vienna Convention is better suited to international contracts than are the existing rules of English sales law. There, however, signs of a gradual change in attitude. The UK government has indicated that it intends to ratify the Vienna Convention when Parliamentary time can be found for the legislation which would be needed to give it effect in domestic law. When a new Arbitration Act for England and Wales was prepared it was decided not to adopt the UNCITRAL Model Law, but the Model Law was used as a basis for many of the new Act's provisions[7]. In an increasingly global commercial environment it seems unlikely that the UK can continue to stand aloof from the trend towards harmonisation.

1   See generally Goode, in Cranston and Goode (eds), *Commercial and Consumer Law – National and International Dimensions* (1993).
2   See 31.4.
3   See 33.3.
4   See 36.2.3.
5   See Hobhouse (1990) 106 LQR 530; cf Steyn, 'A Kind of Esperanto' in Birks (ed), *The Frontiers of Liability (Vol 2)* (1994); see 31.4.2.
6   Goode, *Commercial Law in the Next Millenium* (1997) p 94.
7   See 36.2.3.

1.4.3   *The International Chamber of Commerce*

The EU, UNCITRAL and UNIDROIT are governmental agencies. On the whole, the legal instruments they produce are addressed to governments. Whilst the UK government is often less than whole-hearted in its enthusiasm for harmonisation, the commercial community is sometimes a little more enthusiastic. The International Chamber of Commerce plays an important role in lobbying on behalf of business interests but also provides other services. In particular, it operates its own arbitration system, which is widely used by businesses. It is also responsible for the production of two of the most important international harmonising instruments.

INCOTERMS is a directory of trade terms used in international sales contracts, and sets out the rights and duties of buyer and seller under the most common forms of international contract[1]. As a result, parties can define their rights and obligations by simply adopting the appropriate shorthand formula from INCOTERMS.

The Uniform Customs and Practice for Documentary Credits is, in effect, a statement of banking practice in relation to documentary credit operations (a common method of financing international sale contracts)[2]. Like INCOTERMS, the Uniform Customs have no legal status as such. They derive their legal effect through contract. However, they are almost universally adopted by the international banking community and applied to documentary credit transactions, with the result that the law governing documentary credits is, in effect, largely the same the world over.

1   See 33.0.
2   See 34.1.1.

1.4.4 *Statements of principles*

One of the criticisms directed at attempts at harmonisation, whether at the EU or broader international level, is that attempts to legislate for specific topics, such as aspects of the law of sale or unfair contract terms, take no account of the fact that the treatment of such topics in domestic law may be rooted in the particular legal traditions of individual legal systems. Thus, for instance, both sale and unfair terms are part of the broader law of contract. The EU's Directives on Unfair Terms in Consumer Contracts and Consumer Guarantees respectively deal with those topics in ways which fit uneasily into the framework of English sale and general contract law. Partly in an attempt to address this difficulty, efforts have been made to identify more general principles of contract and commercial law shared by different legal systems. Two deserve special mention.

In 1995 the Lando Commission published its 'Principles of European Contract Law'[1]. The Commission is a group of European contract law academics. It began work in the 1970s with the objective of producing a European Commercial Code. The magnitude of such a task is indicated by the fact that the 'Principles' are far more limited in scope. They are nevertheless an important and immensely significant contribution to the development of European contract law. The initial volume covers the rights and obligations of contracting parties and remedies for non-performance. It is intended that future work of the Commission may cover contract formation, interpretation, validity and agency.

The 'Principles' have no legal force as such. In effect they contain a statement of the general principles which underpin the contract laws of the countries of Europe and to that extent they may provide a basis upon which future attempts to harmonise aspects of contract and commercial law within the EU may be based. At the individual level individual contracting parties may agree to contract subject to them and thus give them binding effect through their contracts.

At much the same time as the Lando 'Principles' were being prepared, UNIDROIT was engaged on a similar project, leading to the publication in 1994 of its 'Principles of International Commercial Contracts'[2]. Their preparation involved representatives of common law, civil law and socialist systems from countries around the world. The effort was prompted by recognition that:

> '[e]fforts towards the international unification of law have hitherto essentially taken the form of binding instruments, such as supranational legislation or international conventions, or of model laws. [T]hese instruments often risk remaining little more than a dead letter and tend to be rather fragmentary in character[3].'

To this end:

> 'the objective of the UNIDROIT Principles is to establish a balanced set of rules designed for use throughout the world irrespective of the legal traditions and the economic and political conditions of the countries in which they are to be applied'[4].

The Principles consist of a series of articles containing general propositions of contract law, accompanied by explanatory commentary. They are intended, in particular, to supplement the UNCITRAL Vienna Sales Convention, although they are capable of more general application. Like the Lando Principles, they have no independent legal force, but may have effect by virtue of individual contracts being made subject to them as an alternative to a particular national law. In addition, it is intended that they should be used to interpret other international legal instruments and as a model for national and international legislators[5].

There are a number of differences between the two sets of principles. The UNIDROIT Principles are wider in scope than the Lando Principles in that, first, they draw on a wider range of legal traditions and, second, they cover a wider area, including contract formation, validity and interpretation as well as contract contents and remedies for non-performance. On the other hand, the Lando Principles are intended to be generally applicable to non-commercial and to domestic as well as international contracts. However, the purpose of the two instruments is largely the same, as are many of the principles they identify. Like the Lando Principles, the UNIDROIT Principles seek to set out a broad international restatement of general principles of contract law applicable to international commercial contracts. Although both instruments seek to identify and state common principles, both seek in places to go beyond existing law. As the Introduction to the UNIDROIT Principles states, 'they . . . embody what are perceived to be the best solutions, even if they are still not yet generally adopted'[6].

Both sets of principles have already exerted considerable influence. In particular, the UNIDROIT Principles have influenced revisions to the laws of a number of countries[7]. It may be expected that, over time, both the Lando and UNIDROIT 'Principles' will come to exert an influence on the development of English contract and commercial law, both directly, by providing a model for domestic legislation, and indirectly by influencing the thinking of practitioners, judges and commentators as they become more familiar with them.

1   Lando and Beale (eds), *The Principles of European Contract Law (Part I: Performance, Non-performance and Remedies)* (1995).

2   See generally Furmston (1996) 10 JCL 11; Bonell (1997) 1 Uniform Law Rev 34; Goode, in
    Lomincka and Morse (eds), *Contemporary Issues in Commercial Law: Essays in Honour of
    Professor A. G. Guest* (1997).
3   UNIDROIT Principles of International Commercial Contracts p vii.
4   Ibid p viii.
5   Preamble to the Principles, pp 4–5.
6   Page viii.
7   See Bonell (1997) 1 Uniform Law Rev 34.

1.4.5 *Common law influences*

The point has been made earlier that English law has traditionally been the law of
choice of the international commercial community. We have noted, too, that English
law is increasingly exposed to influences from civil law systems. One of the
concerns of those who are worried by this development is that those influences
may undermine the certainty which has been the hallmark of English commercial
law and which has enabled it to meet the needs of the commercial community.
English law is, however, also exposed to another set of influences. It must not be
forgotten that English law is part of the broader common law family – indeed, the
mother of the family which includes the laws of the United States and of many
Commonwealth and other countries. Thus, for instance, the English Sale of Goods
Act 1893 provided a model for the sales laws of Australia, Canada, India, Ireland
and New Zealand, amongst others. In recent years those systems, too, have exerted
an influence on the development of English commercial law so that it is possible
to speak of a convergence of common law systems. Decisions of US and
Commonwealth courts have, of course, traditionally been persuasive authority in
English courts. In recent years there have been signs of a willingness to draw
more strongly on experience in other common law jurisdictions. This influence
can be seen in modern statutory reforms to commercial law. The Carriage of
Goods by Sea Act 1992, Sale of Goods (Amendment) Act 1995 and Contracts
(Rights of Third Parties) Act 1999 all resulted from Law Commission reports. In
each case the Law Commission undertook a comparative survey and
recommended reform because it was felt that English law dealt with the issues
under consideration less well than did the laws of other jurisdictions. Moreover,
the legislation in each case can be seen to have been influenced by the approaches
taken in other common law jurisdictions.

In a number of areas the courts of Australia, Canada and New Zealand, in
particular, have been more adventurous than those of England in developing the
common law. Thus, for instance, the courts of Canada and Australia have undertaken
judicial reform of the privity doctrine[1]. In Australia the courts have been prepared
to develop the doctrine of estoppel as a basis for the enforcement of promises not
supported by consideration[2]. The courts of Australia, Canada and New Zealand
have all been more adventurous than their English counterparts in using various
common law doctrines to promote good faith dealing between contractors[3].

These developments have, to date, had only limited impact on English law, which
is perhaps more constrained by its concern to satisfy the needs of the commercial
community. However, it seems fair to assume that, in a 'shrinking world', there
will continue to be mutual cross-fertilisation between the various common law
systems, leading to a closer convergence. If so, it may be that English law, standing,
as it were, with one foot in the common law world and the other in the civil law
based system of the EU, may be well placed to act as a bridge between the two
systems as they, too, converge.

19

1   *Trident General Insurance Co Ltd v McNiece Bros Pty Ltd* (1988) 80 ALJR 574; *London Drugs v Kuehne & Nagel* (1992) 97 DLR (4th) 261. The doctrine has now been modified in England by the Contracts (Rights of Third Parties) Act 1999. See 2.7.2.
2   *Waltons Stores (Interstate) Ltd v Maher* (1988) 164 CLR 387. See also the US case of *Hoffman v Red Owl Stores Inc* 133 NW 2d 167 (1965) where recovery was permitted on the similar basis of foreseeable detrimental reliance.
3   See generally Sir Anthony Mason (2000) 116 LQR 66.

1.4.6   *A new lex mercatoria?*

The process of harmonisation of international commercial law has led some to talk of the development of a 'new *lex mercatoria*'[1]. It is not uncommon to find arbitration clauses in commercial contracts which empower the arbitrator to decide disputes arising from the contract in accordance with lex mercatoria rather than any national law. It is, however, not clear of what this 'new' lex mercatoria consists. Indeed, whether it exists at all is hotly debated. If it is taken to include international harmonising legal instruments such as the Vienna Sales Convention, this is not lex mercatoria in the original sense, for that expression indicated an autonomous body of rules which existed independently of national law, whereas modern international conventions have no effect unless and until incorporated into, and given effect by, national law. It is therefore suggested that the new lex mercatoria might consist of international trade usages. It has been suggested that these might include concepts such as those reflected in the UNIDROIT Principles of International Commercial Contracts and the ICC's Uniform Customs and Practice for Documentary Credits. However, these too differ from lex mercatoria in that, first, they are codified and, second, they take effect by incorporation into a contract. Indeed, when uncodified trade usages are given legal effect it is done by their being incorporated, as express or implied terms, in contracts. Strictly speaking, therefore, the better view seems to be that there is no 'new' lex mercatoria in the original sense of that meaning[2]. Significantly, the UNIDROIT Principles recommend that contractors wishing to subject their contracts to the principles should do so by expressly referring to them rather than by using vague references to 'usages and customs of international trade' or 'lex mercatoria'[3]. One may perhaps be forgiven, however, for suggesting that this is largely a matter of semantics. Whilst there may technically be no new lex mercatoria, there is little doubt that there is emerging a new world legal order, based on a search for common principles and rooted in the practices and expectations of the commercial community.

1   See Lando (1985) 34 ICLQ 747.
2   See Goode (1997) 46 ICLQ 1.
3   UNIDROIT Principles of International Commercial Contracts p 4.

1.5   Electronic commerce

By changing the way in which goods were manufactured, marketed and sold, the industrial revolution posed new problems for commercial law. Now the technological revolution is bringing about changes just as great. It affects the way business is done, the way in which goods and services are marketed, the way in which contracts are made and performed and even the range and type of products which are sold. It therefore poses new challenges for the law, which must respond to these developments.

Perhaps the most significant aspect of the technological revolution is the development of e-commerce – the marketing and supply of goods and services through electronic media. E-commerce is not, however, new. In its widest sense it includes contracts made by telephone, telex and fax. Computer contracting via electronic data interchange has been possible since the mid 1980s. However, the growth of open access networks and especially of the Internet, has made computer marketing and contracting much more widely available than was previously the case.

E-commerce offers opportunities to both businesses and consumers. It offers businesses access to a wider, potentially global, customer base without the need to maintain an expensive infrastructure of physical outlets. It enables customers for both goods and services to choose from a much wider range of suppliers than is possible using traditional means. Governments, seeing this phenomenon as a potential wealth creator, are keen to encourage its growth. In evidence to a Select Committee in 1999 the UK government estimated that the global market for e-commerce was worth \$12bn and likely to grow to \$1 trillion by 2005[1]. It is recognised, however, that its potential will only be realised if its status is secure and certain. Potential users must be assured that messages sent and data stored electronically will have the same legal effect and value as messages sent and stored by traditional – paper based – methods. They must be assured of the confidentiality of messages, to protect sensitive information, payment details and so on.

The essential challenge for the law is thus to facilitate the use and development of e-commerce by creating a suitable legal environment in which it can develop. In particular, if consumers are to be encouraged to use e-commerce, some regulation of the environment may be required to give them the required degree of confidence to do so[2]. To an extent, therefore, the challenge e-commerce poses for the law is the challenge faced by commercial law generally – to strike the right balance between facilitation and regulation. E-commerce, however, raises other problems. Legal issues of data protection, confidentiality, copyright etc may have to be addressed. Moreover, public policy issues enter the equation. Security of data messages may be improved by use of encryption techniques, but encryption techniques may allow criminals and terrorists to escape the surveillance of law enforcement and security authorities. On the other hand, allowing such authorities to have access to data raises issues of privacy, civil liberties and human rights. There is a further problem. Legislation in this area must not be too technology-specific. The speed of technological development now is such that legislation directed specifically at existing technologies would risk freezing the law, making it likely to be quickly rendered obsolete by new developments.

1   See 'Building Confidence in Electronic Commerce': the Government's Proposals, Seventh Report of the Trade and Industry Select Committee, Session 1998-99, p xii.
2   See Brownsword and Howells (1999) 19 LS 1.

1.5.1 *The legal response*

A number of national and international legal instruments already contain specific provisions to deal with aspects of e-commerce[1]. It was recognised, however, that a more general legal framework was needed to create the required degree of confidence in e-commerce. Moreover, the global character of the Internet requires a global legal response. With these objectives in mind, in 1996 UNCITRAL produced a Model Law on Electronic Commerce[2]. This has been followed by a number of regional and national governments and legislative bodies producing texts, often based, at least in part, on the Model Law, although also covering other topics. At the European level providing a framework for e-commerce is seen as a vital aspect of the Single Market. It is recognised that the legal framework must be:

> 'clear and simple, predictable and consistent with the rules applicable at international level so that it does not adversely affect the competitiveness of European industry or impede innovation in that sector'[3].

The EU has therefore produced Directives on Electronic Commerce[4] and Electronic Signatures[5]. The UK government has stated that its objective is to make the UK the best environment in the world in which to trade electronically by 2002. To that end it has, after extensive consultation[6], passed the Electronic Communications Act 2000 to implement the Electronic Signatures Directive and to govern some aspects of e-commerce in the UK.

The underlying objective of the various legislative texts passed so far has been to create and bolster confidence in e-commerce by creating a secure legal foundation, and thus to facilitate its use. Consistent with the general ethos of commercial law, the emphasis has been on facilitation, rather than regulation. Legislation, taking a lead from the UNCITRAL Model Law, has therefore sought to create a broad legal framework, capable of flexible application as the technology develops. To this end, the key issues addressed so far have been the freedom to provide services, the liability of service providers such as those providing e-mail services and Internet access, and the legal validity and effect of electronic messages and digital signatures.

1 See eg Carriage of Goods by Sea Act 1992, s 1(5); UNCITRAL Model Law on International Commercial Arbitration 1985, art 7(2); UNIDROIT Convention on International Factoring 1988, art 1(4). Provision for the use of electronic media is also made in INCOTERMS 2000.
2 The text is available at the UNCITRAL website: www.un.or.at/uncitral/english/texts/electcom/ml-ec.htm.
3 Recital 60 to the Electronic Commerce Directive.
4 Directive 2000/31/EC, OJ L 178 17.7.2000, p 1.
5 Directive 1999/93/EC, OJ L 13 19.1.2000, p 12.
6 See 'Building Confidence in Electronic Commerce: A Consultation Document', 1999; the Trade and Industry Select Committee's report, 'Building Confidence in Electronic Commerce: The Government's Proposals', 1999; and 'Promoting Electronic Commerce' (1999, Cm 4417).

1.5.1.1 *Electronic documents*

Many established legal rules require the use of documents, paper, written notices etc. Such requirements can pose an obstacle to the development of e-commerce unless they can be satisfied by electronic equivalents. The Model Law addresses this problem by taking as its central principle the 'functional equivalence approach', according to which traditional requirements for writing, documents, signature and so on can be satisfied by electronic techniques which serve the same function. Its core provision states that 'information shall not be denied legal effect, validity or enforceability solely on the grounds that it is in the form of a data message'[1]. Subsequent articles then provide that legal requirements for writing[2], signature[3] and the use of originals[4] can be satisfied by the use of data messages in appropriate forms, and that rules of evidence should not deny the admissibility of data messages solely because of their form[5].

This approach is followed by the EC Directive. It requires member states to ensure that their laws allow contracts to be concluded electronically[6]. The UK Electronic Communications Act has the same objective. It recognises that requirements for writing and/or signature may hamper the use of e-commerce, but rather than simply stating that electronic documents are to have the same status as their paper equivalents, it contains power for the appropriate Secretary of State by statutory instrument to modify 'in such manner as he may think fit for the purpose of authorising or facilitating the use of electronic communications or electronic storage' the provisions of any existing primary or secondary legislation or scheme, licence or approval issued under any legislation which require anything to be done or evidenced in writing or by use of a document or by post or other specified means of delivery, or to be signed or sealed, records to be kept, etc[7].

1   Article 5.
2   Article 6.
3   Article 7.
4   Article 8.
5   Article 9.
6   Article 9.
7   Section 8.

1.5.1.2   *Electronic signatures and data encryption*

Even where there is no positive legal requirement that a document be signed in order to have legal validity, signature has an important evidential function. It may authenticate a document or message so as to identify the sender or validate its contents. If electronic messages are to be trusted in the same way as more traditional forms, some method has to be found of replicating the effect of manual signature of a paper document.

There are a number of methods by which electronic messages and documents might be signed, including by the use of biometric systems, such as finger print or voice recognition, or by retinal scanning. The most effective form of electronic signature currently available, however, depends on the use of encryption technology. A message, or part thereof, can be encrypted by use of a computer algorithm code or 'key'. The key algorithm is so long that the message can only be effectively decrypted by using a corresponding decoding algorithm. Each user of this technology would therefore be issued with a unique pair of matching keys. One would be kept private and the other made public. A message encrypted with a particular private key can only be decrypted with the corresponding public key. By encrypting part of a message or document using his own unique 'private key' a person can therefore effectively 'sign' it, identifying himself as the sender and/or indicating his assent to its contents. Should he dispute the authenticity of the message or document, it can be tested by decrypting the signature using his public key. Successful decryption will indicate that the original must have been encrypted with his private key and thus that he signed it.

The Model Law does not deal directly with these issues[1]. It states that positive legal requirements for a document to be signed can be satisfied by the use of an appropriate electronic method, and that 'information in the form of a data message shall be given due evidential weight', taking account of 'the manner in which its originator was identified'[2]. Within the EC the matter is addressed directly by the Electronic Signatures Directive, which is implemented in the UK by the Electronic Communications Act 2000. The Act provides for electronic signatures 'incorporated into or logically associated with' electronic communications to be admissible in evidence as to the authenticity and/or integrity of the communication[3]. However, signature by encryption raises special problems. First, there must be some means of connecting a particular 'key' with the individual to whom it belongs. Second, public/private key encryption systems can, of course, also be used to encrypt entire messages so as to keep their contents secret[4]. Whilst this meets the need to maintain the confidentiality of electronic data, it gives rise to law enforcement and security issues as described earlier.

The preferred solution to the first problem is to require some third party to certify the authenticity of a digital signature by confirming the identity of the holder of a particular key pair, as required. Thus if the authenticity of a signature should be questioned in any proceedings, a certificate from the relevant authority may be produced as evidence of the identity of the key holder and, therefore, the signatory. This is the approach taken in the EC directive, and the Electronic Communications Act makes such a certificate admissible in proceedings[5]. Striking the correct balance between individual privacy concerns and public law enforcement and security concerns was more difficult. At one stage the UK government proposed that all holders of encryption keys should be required to deposit a copy of their private key with a depository so as to allow access to it by law enforcement and security agencies if required. Ultimately, however, these proposals were abandoned and the Act simply creates a relatively unregulated framework for the provision of encryption services. Part I provides for the Secretary of State to establish a register of approved providers of cryptography support services. However, the Act does not make registration compulsory for those wishing to provide cryptography services; the purpose of approval is simply to give an indication to potential users that the provider meets certain standards, and the government has indicated that Part I will not be brought into force if industry can devise an acceptable regime for the approval of cryptography service providers[6].

1   UNCITRAL is working on a set of Uniform Rules on Electronic Signatures.
2   Article 9.
3   Section 7.
4   In this case the message will be encrypted using the intended recipient's public key so that only he will be able to decrypt it using his private key.
5   Section 7(1)(b).
6   Explanatory Notes to the Electronic Communications Bill, 26 January 2000, para 10. Powers for law enforcement and security agencies to obtain access to encrypted data and demand the production of appropriate 'keys' are contained in the Regulation of Investigatory Powers Act 2000.

1.5.1.3   *Provision of services and liability of service providers*

One of the most difficult legal issues arising out of the development of the Internet is the extent to which service providers should be liable for the content of messages transmitted over, and data stored on, their services, such as e-mail networks and bulletin boards. The EC directive seeks to establish a framework within which suppliers of information society services[1] will be free to supply services throughout the EU. It provides that member states may not make the provision of information society services subject to prior approval[2] and that a person who provides a service consisting of transmitting information, providing access to a communication network or storing information, shall not, without more, be liable for the information transmitted or stored[3]. Member states cannot require such service providers to monitor the information transmitted by or stored on their systems[4].

1   As defined in Directives 98/34/EC and 98/84/EC.
2   Article 4.
3   Articles 11–14.
4   Article 15.

1.5.2 *E-commerce and commercial law*

The main thrust of the various legislative instruments described is facilitative rather than regulatory. However, as mentioned above, measures to protect consumers can make an important contribution to the improving confidence in e-commerce. The EC Directive therefore contains provisions designed to provide a measure of consumer protection in order to enhance consumers' confidence in e-commerce. It requires that information service providers must acknowledge a customer's order, electronically, without undue delay, and provide certain information to the recipients of such services[1]. The Directive is intended to be read together with a number of other Directives dealing with consumer protection[2], especially in relation to the distance marketing of goods and services[3].

A legal framework for e-commerce is thus being established at national and international level. It will, however, be apparent that many of the legal issues raised, or likely to be raised, are not addressed in the legal texts described above. Even basic issues – such as where and when is a contract concluded in cyber-space[4], or when is a payment complete when made electronically – have not been addressed.

Some of these legal issues, such as data protection, for instance, are already the subject of detailed legislation[5]. Others may require specific legislation in due course. It is submitted, however, that on the whole specific legislation is not required. Many of the problems raised are not new, but are old problems raised in a novel form by the new technology. It may be that such questions are best left to be resolved by the courts as and when they arise. If it be objected that this fails to provide legal certainty, one may reply that the commercial community has not in the past been deterred from devising new practices before they have been given legal sanction. Indeed, some aspects of the use of established technology, such as fax and telephony, are still not definitively settled. It may be anticipated that the courts will respond to new developments in e-commerce as they have in the past responded to new developments in commerce generally, by seeking, so far as is appropriate, to facilitate commercial activity by giving effect to settled practices and reasonable expectations. And in so doing we may anticipate that the courts will use the familiar common law techniques of adapting existing concepts and doctrines to the new electronic environment.

1   Articles 5 and 6.
2   Listed in recital 11.
3   Specifically that on Distance Selling (Directive 97/7/EC) implemented by the Consumer Protection (Distance Selling) Regulations 2000, SI 2000/2334 which, inter alia, require consumers to be supplied with certain information at the time of contracting. See also the Commission's proposal for a Directive on Distance Selling of Financial Services: COM 98 0468, OJ L 385 11.12.98, p 11.

4   The UNCITRAL Model Law does include provisions (arts 14 and 15) dealing with the question
    when a data message shall be deemed to be received, but these would not necessarily determine
    such questions as whether an offer can be made via a web site or when an e-mailed acceptance
    takes effect. Similarly the provisions of the EC Directive requiring messages to be
    acknowledged are not directly concerned with the question when a contract is formed.
5   Data Protection Act 1998.

1.6   Good faith

In *Interfoto Picture Library Ltd v Stilletto Visual Programmes Ltd* Bingham LJ
observed that:

> 'In many civil law systems, and perhaps in most legal systems outside
> the common law world, the law of obligations recognises and enforces
> an overriding principle that in making and carrying out contracts parties
> should act in good faith. This does not simply mean that they should not
> deceive each other, a principle which any legal system must recognise;
> its effect is perhaps most aptly conveyed by such metaphorical
> colloquialisms as "playing fair", "coming clean" or "putting one's cards
> face upwards on the table". It is in essence a principle of fair and open
> dealing.'[1]

A general principle of good faith is a feature of French, German and Italian
law, but it is not confined to civil law systems. It features, too, in the United
States Uniform Commercial Code[2]. Both the Lando Principles of European
Contract Law[3] and the UNIDROIT Principles of International Commercial
Contracts[4] include a requirement for parties to act in good faith in the negotiation
and performance of contracts[5].

English law recognises no such general rule. Good faith is required by certain
statutory provisions. A person wishing to take advantage of the Sale of Goods
Act rules governing title disputes is generally required to have acted 'in good
faith'. However, good faith is defined for this purpose subjectively, in terms of
'honesty'[6]. It is clear that this is very different from the concept described by
Bingham LJ and recognised by other legal systems. A duty of good faith rather
closer to that concept is imposed at common law in the context of certain contracts
between a fiduciary and his principal, and a small category of contracts *uberrimae
fidei* – of the utmost good faith – is recognised, including contracts of partnership
and contracts of insurance[7]. In the latter context its most important feature is that
it imposes a duty of disclosure on the parties during negotiation and performance
of the contract. In fact, it seems that when Lord Mansfield propounded that duty
in the leading case of *Carter v Boehm*[8] he intended it to apply to contracts
generally. However, his broad notion of good faith never took root and was blown
away by the prevailing wind of laissez faire individualism of the nineteenth
century. Indeed, in its modern form the duty of disclosure in insurance impinges
much more on the insured than on the insurer and its application can often be
said to be contrary to good faith in any real sense[9].

This is not, however, to say that English law is not concerned with the
protection of good faith values. 'The aim of our commercial law ought to be to
encourage fair dealings between parties[10].' 'In dealings as between man and
man the English law does set up a high, but not too high, attainable standard of
honesty and fair dealing which, to my mind, is of the very greatest value to the

whole community and especially to the commercial community[11].' In *Interfoto* Bingham LJ explained the approach of English law as follows:

> 'English law has, characteristically, committed itself to no such overriding principle but has developed piecemeal solutions in response to demonstrated problems of unfairness. Many examples could be given. Thus equity has intervened to strike down unconscionable bargains. Parliament has stepped in to regulate the imposition of exemption clauses and the form of certain hire-purchase agreements. The common law also has made its contribution, by holding that certain classes of contract require the utmost good faith, by treating as irrecoverable what purport to be agreed estimates of damage but are in truth a disguised penalty for breach, and in many other ways.'

Other familiar contract doctrines could be cited. Thus the rules governing estoppel and the implication of terms into contracts, the concepts of duress and undue influence, the doctrines of mistake and misrepresentation, the principle of the objective interpretation of contractual statements and the rule requiring special notice to be given to unusual contract terms[12], can all be seen as being concerned with the protection of 'good faith'. So too can the reluctance of the courts to allow a buyer to reject goods where his conduct has led the seller to believe that he would not do so[13] or to terminate a contract on the grounds of a minor breach[14] or in order to escape from a bad bargain. English law, however, tends to be sceptical of broad, general principles. Thus, for instance, the existence of a general principle allowing the court to interfere in contracts on the grounds of 'inequality of bargaining power'[15] has been denied[16], as has that of a 'general principle of fair dealing negativing any liberty to blow hot and cold in commercial conduct'[17]. It is therefore hardly surprising that English law recognises no general duty of 'good faith'.

1 [1988] 1 All ER 348 at 352.
2 UCC, s 1–203. See also the *Second Restatement of Contracts*, s 205.
3 Article 1.106.
4 Article 1.7.
5 The Lando and UNIDROIT principles both contain a number of specific rules which may be regarded as particular aspects of the duty of good faith. The general principle underpins them, and operates to qualify each party's exercise of its rights and performance of its duties under the contract.
6 Sale of Goods Act, s 61(3). The Bills of Exchange Act 1882, s 90, is in identical terms. Under the Carriage of Goods by Sea Act 1992 a person can only be the lawful holder of a bill of lading if he acquired it 'in good faith'. Good faith is not defined for this purpose but it seems likely that it has the same meaning as in the Sale of Goods Act.
7 See 35.3.
8 (1766) 3 Burr 1905 at 1910.
9 See 35.3.
10 Steyn LJ in *CTN Cash and Carry Ltd v Gallaher Ltd* [1994] 4 All ER 714 at 719.
11 Lord Atkin, quoted in Harvey (ed), *The Lawyer and Justice* (1978) p 131.
12 As in *Interfoto* itself. See also the comment of Brooke LJ in *Lacey's Footwear Ltd v Bowler International Freight Ltd* [1997] 2 Lloyd's Rep 367 at 385.
13 See 12.2 below.
14 See eg *Hong Kong Fir Shipping Co Ltd v Kawasaki Kisen Kaisha Ltd* [1962] 2 QB 26, [1962] 1 All ER 474, CA; *The Hansa Nord* [1976] QB 44 [1975] 3 All ER 739, CA.
15 *Lloyds Bank Ltd v Bundy* [1975] QB 326, [1974] 3 All ER 757, CA.
16 Per Lord Scarman in *National Westminster Bank plc v Morgan* [1985] AC 686 at 708; see also *Pao On v Lau Yiu Long* [1980] AC 614 at 634. See 2.4.3.
17 *Panchaud Freres SA v Etablissements General Grain Co* [1970] 1 Lloyd's Rep 53 at 59, CA, per Winn LJ; see *Glencore Grain Rotterdam BV v Lebanese Organisation for International Commerce* [1997] 4 All ER 514: see 2.8.2.

1.6.1   *The rise of good faith*

In recent years, however, there has been growing interest in the concept of good faith, and there is now an extensive literature on the subject[1]. This is partly a result of English lawyers having been exposed to 'good faith' requirements in specific contractual contexts. Thus a general duty has been introduced by EC directives dealing with commercial agency[2] and unfair terms in consumer contracts[3]. These requirements have their roots in the civil law jurisdictions of continental Europe. Courts in several Commonwealth jurisdictions have also embraced the good faith concept without being directly exposed to these influences[4]. 'Good faith' has also provided a stimulus for legislation. Introducing the Second Reading Debate on the Late Payment of Commercial Debts (Interest) Bill in the House of Commons in 1998, the Minister for Small Firms, Trade and Industry observed that legislation to combat late payment was necessary because:

> 'Paying late is wrong and unfair. Any business that pays late as a matter of course is effectively saying that it is acceptable to abuse the provision of trade credit and the good faith of its suppliers[5].'

Many English commentators and judges, however, remain sceptical about the need for, or desirability of English law adopting, a general requirement of good faith. Some, following the line expounded by Bingham LJ in the passage from *Interfoto* quoted above, take the line that there is no need to introduce such a duty. Others positively object to its introduction. In *Walford v Miles* Lord Ackner took the view that a duty to negotiate in good faith would be too uncertain to be enforceable and, moreover, 'inherently repugnant to the adversarial position of the parties when involved in negotiations'[6]. It may be that it is easier for the common law to accept a duty of good faith once a contract has been concluded, when there will often be an implied term requiring the parties to co-operate, or at least not to hinder performance of the contract.

There are more fundamental objections, however. In so far as 'good faith' seems to set external standards of behaviour, it seems to be inconsistent with the traditional ethos of commercial law, which is facilitative rather than regulatory. It is feared that a general duty of good faith would introduce an undesirable degree of uncertainty into commercial law[7]. Certainty is one of the core requirements of commercial law. If a good faith requirement were to give unfettered discretion to judges to decide cases in accordance with subjective notions of morality or fairness, it would undermine that certainty[8]. 'In the case of commercial contracts, broad concepts of honesty and fair dealing, however laudable, are a somewhat uncertain guide when determining the existence or otherwise of an obligation which may arise even in the absence of any dishonest or unfair intent[9].' Similarly, in *CTN Cash and Carry Ltd v Gallagher Ltd* Steyn LJ counselled against introducing external standards of morality into commercial law, observing that 'it is a mistake for the law to set its sights too highly when the critical inquiry is not whether the conduct is lawful but whether it is morally or socially unacceptable'[10]. Underlying these and similar comments is a concern not to jeopardise the role of English law in international commercial dispute resolution. English law has long prided itself on being a major, possibly the leading, system for the resolution of international commercial disputes. Perhaps, too, there is a feeling that in a market economy a party should have the freedom to drive a hard bargain and, having done so, enjoy the fruit of it.

1 See eg Powell (1956) 9 CLP 16; Brownsword (1994) 8 JCL 197; Waddams (1995) 9 JCL 53; Stapleton (1999) 52 CLP 1; Beatson and Friedmann (eds) *Good Faith and Fairness in Contract Law* (1997); Harrison *Good Faith in Sales* (1997); Brownsword, Hird and Howells (eds): *Good Faith in Contract: Concept and Context* (1999); and see Furmston (ed) *Butterworths Law of Contract* (1999) paras 1.77–1.101.
2 86/653/EEC, implemented by the Commercial Agents (Council Directive) Regulations (SI 1993/3053); see 6.1.
3 93/13/EEC, implemented by the Unfair Terms in Consumer Contracts Regulations 1999, SI 1999/2083; see 2.6.5.
4 See generally Mason (2000) 116 LQR 66.
5 HC Debates 5 May 1998 Col 594.
6 [1992] 2 AC 128 at 138, [1992] 1 All ER 453 at 460.
7 See Goode, *Commercial Law in the Next Millennium* (1998) pp 19–20. Contrast Professor Goode's earlier enthusiasm for good faith: see (1988) 14 Monash LR 135 at 151.
8 See eg Bridge, in Brownsword, Hird and Howells (eds), *Good Faith: Content and Context* (1999).
9 Slade LJ in *Banque Financière de la Cite v Westgate Insurance Co Ltd* [1989] 2 All ER 952 at 990.
10 [1994] 4 All ER 714 at 719.

1.6.2 *A good faith requirement*

One of the difficulties facing advocates of a general good faith requirement is that they cannot define it. Most would agree that 'good faith' precludes dishonesty. Beyond that, it is unclear what it would require, or what, if anything, it would add to the 'piecemeal' doctrines by which English law protects similar values. If 'good faith' is based on some external moral or ethical standard, many of the fears voiced by its opponents are justified. References to 'playing fair', 'coming clean', 'putting one's cards face upwards on the table' and 'fair and open dealing' only reinforce the doubts.

One solution to this problem would be to define 'good faith' in any particular case by reference to the standards of the particular contractual context[1]. An alternative formulation would regard it as contrary to good faith for a contractor to act dishonestly or in a way contrary to the expectations of his contract partner, where he has created or knows, or may be taken to know, of those expectations. To put it another way, a contractor who acts contrary to the reasonable expectations of his contract partner may be said to act contrary to good faith. There may be little between these two formulations. 'Reasonable expectations' would depend, in part, on the practices of the particular market.

This comes close to a formula used by Lord Steyn, who has on several occasions referred to the role of contract law as being the protection of the reasonable expectations of honest people[2]. Many would see this as something close to a concept of good faith. Writing in 1997, Lord Steyn said 'I have no heroic suggestion for the introduction of a general duty of good faith in our contract law'. However, he continued:

> 'It is not necessary. As long as our courts always respect the reasonable expectations of parties our contract law can be left to develop in accordance with its own pragmatic traditions. And where in specific contexts duties of good faith are imposed on parties our legal system can readily accommodate such a well tried notion. After all, there is not a world of difference between the objective requirement of good faith and the reasonable expectations of parties.'

Few would disagree with the notion that the law of contract should seek to protect 'the reasonable expectations of honest people', albeit that some might be uncomfortable with it as a general legal principle. If, as Lord Steyn suggests, English law is already concerned with the protection of 'reasonable expectations' the introduction of a general requirement of good faith would probably make little difference to the great majority of cases. Nor would it generate any more uncertainty than exists at present, for instance when a court decides whether a term referred to as a 'condition' is properly so classified[3] or whether a breach of contract is sufficiently serious to justify termination of the contract applying the *Hong Kong Fir* test[4].

If English law already protects good faith by the 'piecemeal' doctrines by which it seeks to respect the 'reasonable expectations' of contractors, one might well ask what would be gained by admitting a general principle of 'good faith'? The answer is that, first, it would increase the transparency of the law. Where a contractor seeks to terminate a contract allegedly because of a trivial breach by the other party, but in fact to escape from a bad bargain, the court may be reluctant to allow him to do so. It may prevent him from terminating by holding that the term broken is not a condition and finding that the breach is insufficiently serious to justify termination. The underlying reason for the decision, however, may be that termination for such a breach would not accord with the reasonable expectations of the party in breach and would thus be contrary to 'good faith'. Second, it is argued, the general principle could be invoked to deal with cases not covered by existing discrete doctrines, and would thus facilitate development of the law.

The evidence of cases reported to date on the directives on commercial agency and unfair terms in consumer contracts suggests that English judges may find the concept less difficult to handle than some might expect. It may be, therefore, that there is less to fear from a concept of good faith than some might suggest. At any rate, it seems unavoidable that as English law is increasingly exposed to influences from other nations and legal traditions the role of 'good faith' in commercial law will continue to be the subject of much discussion.

1   See Brownsword, in Brownsword, Hird and Howells (eds), *Good Faith: Content and Context* (1999); Furmston (ed) *Butterworths Law of Contract* (1999) paras 1.77–1.101.
2   See *Associated Japanese Bank (International) Ltd v Crédit du Nord SA* [1988] 3 All ER 902 at 903; *G Percy Trentham Ltd v Archital Luxfer Ltd* [1993] 1 Lloyd's Rep 25 at 27; *First Energy (UK) Ltd v Hungarian International Bank Ltd* [1993] 2 Lloyd's Rep 194 at 196; [1991] Denning LJ 131; (1997) 113 LQR 432.
3   As in *Schuler v Wickman Machine Tool Sales Ltd* [1974] AC 235, [1973] 2 All ER 39: see 2.5.6.
4   *Hong Kong Fir Shipping Co Ltd v Kawasaki Kisen Kaisha* CA. See 2.5.6.

1.7   The role of equity in commercial law

In recent years there has been much discussion of the role of equity in commercial law[1]. Given the importance placed on certainty in commercial law, it might be thought that there is no place in it for equity, with its emphasis on discretion and conscience. Indeed:

> 'wise judges have often warned against the wholesale importation into commercial law of equitable principles inconsistent with the certainty and speed which are essential requirements for the orderly conduct of business affairs'[2].

Thus the courts have 'resolutely set their faces against . . . the extension of the equitable doctrines of constructive notice to commercial transactions' for fear of 'doing infinite mischief and paralyzing the trade of the country'[3]. Similarly, the courts have been circumspect about allowing equitable property concepts associated with trusts to infiltrate commercial law[4]. A successful claim to an equitable property interest will bind third parties and give the claimant priority over the trustee's other creditors in the event of the trustee's insolvency. But this may be the very reason why the court should be slow to find such an interest. The equitable property interest which exists behind a trust is invisible to creditors. It may thus act as an impediment to the free transfer of property with which commerce is concerned:

> 'a businessman who has entered into transactions relating to or dependent on property rights could find that assets which apparently belong to one person in fact belong to another; that there are "off balance sheet" liabilities of which he cannot be aware; that these property rights and liabilities arise from circumstances unknown not only to himself but also to anyone else who has been involved in the transactions'[5].

In the same way, in recent cases the courts have recognised that the imposition of fiduciary obligations of loyalty may be inappropriate in a commercial context[6].

This does not mean, however, that equitable concepts and doctrines have no place in commercial law. Quite the reverse is true. Equitable concepts have made a significant contribution to the development of commercial law. In the law of contract, since equity guards against unconscionable conduct, many of the 'piecemeal solutions' by which the law seeks to promote 'good faith' are equitable. They include the right to rescind for misrepresentation, the concept of undue influence and, of course, promissory estoppel, which tempers the rigour of the doctrine of consideration and, by preventing the revocation of a promise once relied on, prevents unconscionable behaviour. Specific performance (albeit rarely granted in relation to commercial contracts) is equitable. Even more significant is the contribution of equity to the law of secured lending. The floating charge, which provides companies with a convenient and flexible means of giving security and has thus made a major contribution to their ability to raise finance, is a creation of equity. So, too, is the equitable lien. Elsewhere, equitable concepts have been invoked by commercial lawyers from time to time in order to facilitate commercial activity[7]. Even the trust, in origin a device for controlling family property, is deployed in a commercial setting. Express trusts are the basis for investment devices, such as pension funds and unit trusts. Constructive and resulting trusts, too, have their place in commercial law. A constructive or resulting trust may protect a creditor who pays money to a business for a specific purpose[8], or customers who make advance payment for goods or services[9], if the business becomes insolvent. Even fiduciary concepts and duties may be imposed in an appropriate case.

> '[T]he growing complexity and professionalism of commercial life . . . have accompanied the change from an industrial to a service economy and the growth of the financial services industry. Much commerce today is based on trust; on each side of a commercial arms' length transaction there are likely to be relationships of trust and confidence . . . There has never been a greater need to impose on those who engage in commerce the high standards of conduct which equity demands . . . It exacts higher standards than those of the market place, where the end justifies the means and the old virtues of loyalty, fidelity and responsibility are admired less than the "success, self-interest, wealth, winning and not getting caught"[10].'

It has been said that fiduciary obligations are imposed to protect 'legitimate expectations'. On their face they look very like duties of good faith. In fact they go further. Whereas good faith requires a contractor to have regard to the interests and expectations of the other contracting party as well as his own, in a spirit of co-operation, fiduciary obligations require the fiduciary to prefer the interests of his principal to his own[11]. If 'good faith' is inconsistent with the adversarial self interest of commerce, fiduciary obligations may be thought to be even more so. The key is to bear in mind the flexibility of equity. Fiduciary obligations will not be imposed where they would be inappropriate in a commercial context. But fiduciary obligations are sufficiently flexible to be tailored to fit the context. Similarly, in the absence of an express declaration of trust, the courts should be slow to find that property is held on constructive or resulting trust in a commercial context where that would adversely affect the interests of third parties. Insolvency, where the concepts of trusts and fiduciary duties are frequently invoked, will often be the very situation in which they are inappropriate. Provided, though, that the courts remain vigilant to ensure that they are not invoked where they would be inappropriate, the concepts of equity, like those of the common law, may be invoked by the commercial law as tools to facilitate commercial activity as and where necessary[12].

1   See Goodhart and Jones (1980) 43 MLR 409; Millett (1998) 114 LQR 214.
2   Lord Browne-Wilkinson in *Westdeutsche Landesbank Girozentrale v Islington London Borough Council* [1996] AC 669 at 704, [1996] 2 All ER 961 at 987.
3   Per Lindley LJ in *Manchester Trust v Furness* [1895] 2 QB 539 at 545. See also *London Joint Stock Bank v Simmons* [1892] AC 201. See, eg, the comments of Lord Goff on the desirability of extending to commercial transactions the equitable jurisdiction to give relief against forfeiture: [1984] LMCLQ 382 at 392; see 2.10.1.
4   See eg *Re Wait* [1927] 1 Ch 606, [1926] All ER Rep 433, CA; *Re Goldcorp Exchange Ltd (in receivership)* [1994] 2 All ER 806, [1995] 1 AC 74, see 15.5.
5   Lord Browne-Wilkinson in *Westdeutsche Landesbank Girozentrale v Islington LBC* [1996] AC 669 at 705, [1996] 2 All ER 961 at 987.
6   *Kelly v Cooper* [1993] AC 205; *Arklow Developments v Maclean* [2000] 1 WLR 594. See 6.2.1.4.
7   See eg *Aluminium Industrie Vaassen BV v Romalpa Aluminium Ltd* [1976] 2 All ER 552.
8   *Barclays Bank Ltd v Quistclose Investments Ltd* [1970] AC 567, [1968] 3 All ER 651.
9   *Re Kayford Ltd* [1975] 1 All ER 604, [1975] 1 WLR 279; *Re Goldcorp Exchange Ltd (in receivership)* [1994] 2 All ER 806, [1995] 1 AC 74.
10 Millett (1998) 114 LQR 214 at 216, quoting from Sacks, *The Politics of Hope* (1997) p 179.
11 See Mason (2000) 116 LQR 66.
12 See the comments of Robert Goff LJ in *Clough Mill Ltd v Martin* [1984] 3 All ER 982 at 987, above 1.1.3.

1.8   A new codification?

Many civil law countries have a commercial code applying to all commercial transactions; similarly, in the US, commercial law is codified in the Uniform Commercial Code. In England the commercial law is contained in a number of individual statutes and in common law decisions, some dating back several hundred years. The nineteenth-century codification was only partial and the statutes are now subject to a considerable case law gloss interpreting the statutory provisions. In recent years further statutory modifications have been made, sometimes to protect consumers, often to implement European Directives. No links are made between different parts of commercial law. In the law of sale, for instance, the Sale of Goods Act 1979 was amended by three new statutes in 1994 and 1995. Even if the amendments are read into the 1979 Act, they provide only an incomplete picture of the law of sale which must take account of other legislation affecting consumer sales transactions. Further amendments are likely to be required to implement European Directives[1]. Controls on exclusion clauses in sale contracts are contained in the Unfair Contract Terms Act 1977, which itself is overlapped by the similar controls on unfair terms in the Unfair Terms in Consumer Contracts Regulations 1999[2].

As a result the law is often difficult to locate. Certainly there must be doubts about its accessibility to the ordinary business people and consumers who are affected by it. To some extent the great practitioner textbooks, such as *Benjamin's Sale of Goods*, *Bowstead and Reynolds on Agency* and *Scrutton on Charterparties*, fulfil the role of restatements of the law of the areas to which they relate. Such texts, containing statements of principle with detailed commentary, are immensely authoritative and are held in high regard by practitioners and the judiciary[3]. However, they are intended for legal specialists and, in any case, tend each to cover a particular area.

The law, then, may be said to be in much the same state as it was immediately before it was partly codified at the end of the nineteenth century. As a result, many commentators have, in recent years, argued that there is a need for a new codification of English commercial law in order to make its provisions accessible to business[4]. In the second edition of this book it was suggested that such a project was unlikely. The Law Commission had abandoned its attempt to codify the English law of contract, and had rejected the idea of a wholesale revision of the Sale of Goods Act[5]. Similarly, wholesale reform of the law of banking and negotiable instruments[6] and of security interests in moveable property[7] had been rejected. It seems, however, that the possibility of a new codification is now back on the agenda[8]. In June 1999 the Law Commission indicated that it was considering a Commercial Code for England and Wales[9]. It seems unlikely, however, that any such code would be a statement of detailed rules. Such a project would be a gargantuan task. Moreover, given the pace of change of commercial practice, it would run the risk of being obsolete before completion. If successful it might freeze the law, rendering it unable to adapt to new practices.

Such a code is not, however, what is envisaged. Rather, it seems, what is intended is a statement of the broad principles which underpin the detailed rules, which might not necessarily have statutory force[10]. Modern international instruments such as the UNIDROIT and Lando Principles might provide a model for such a project. Such a statement of principles would be accessible to non-specialists as well as specialists. It could be referred to by lawyers, judges and legislators as and when new issues, not provided for by existing rules, arise. It could be offered to countries without a developed commercial law as a model[11]. Moreover, it would require English lawyers to consider and identify the principles which underpin its rules, and might thus better equip them to participate in debates about the international development of commercial law. In the context of the international harmonisation of commercial law, emphasis on detailed rules tends to highlight differences between systems, obscuring the fact that there are often similarities between the problems addressed, and the solutions offered to those problems, by different legal systems. Identification of such principles would also better equip the law to respond to the challenge of changing practice and the problems of e-commerce.

Traditionally, English lawyers have been uncomfortable with broad principles. This has been the reason for the rejection of a concept of 'inequality of bargaining power' and is part of the reason for scepticism about the desirability of a general concept of good faith. English statutes have tended to be more detailed than their civilian counterparts and, it has been argued, the English judiciary are unfamiliar with such legislative drafting styles. This is, however, no longer true, if ever it was. Growing familiarity with legislation based on EU directives has increasingly brought the judiciary into contact with the civilian style of legislative drafting and such evidence as there is so far suggests that applying it causes them less difficulty than might at one time have been expected. Moreover, even domestic legislation now sometimes adopts this style, consisting of broad statements of principles, whose details are fleshed out by delegated legislation from time to time[12].

Even such a codification, or restatement of principles, would be an enormous task. Difficult questions, including some of the issues raised in this chapter, would have to be addressed. Should a requirement of 'good faith' be one of the principles included in such a code? Should the code apply to consumer and commercial transactions, or to commercial transactions only? From time to time calls have been made for a separate code for consumer transactions[13]. We have noted that, partly as a result of the impact of EU legislation, there is an increasing divergence between the detailed law relating to domestic, or consumer, transactions and large scale and/or international transactions. If a distinction between commercial and consumer transactions is to be made, where is the line between the two to be drawn?

What is clear, is that as the nature and volume of commercial activity continues to change, many of the detailed rules contained in statutes passed in the late nineteenth century seem increasingly inadequate to meet the needs of modern commercial activity. At the dawn of the twenty-first century the time is ripe for a re-evaluation of the content and structure of commercial law.

1   Directive 1999/44/EC on certain aspects of the sale of consumer goods and associated guarantees: see 11.8; Directive 97/7/EC (OJ 1997 L 144/19) on the protection of consumers in respect of distance contracts.
2   See 2.6.5.
3   See the comments of Lord Goff of Chieveley (1997) 46 ICLQ 745 at 750 and of Lord Lloyd in *The Giannis NK* [1998] 1 All ER 495 at 504.
4   See eg Goode, *Commercial Law* (2nd edn, 1995) p 1206 ff; *Commercial Law in the Next Millennium* (1998) p 100.
5   'Sale and Supply of Goods', LC Rep 160, para 1.11.
6   Report of the Review Committee on Banking Services Law and Practice 1989 Cmnd 622; see ch 28.
7   Diamond, 'A Review of Security Interests in Property', DTI 1989; see 22.3.
8   See Arden [1997] CLJ 510; Lord Goff of Chieveley (1997) 46 ICLQ 745.
9   Law Com 259 (1999) paras 1.12–1.16.
10 See Law Com 259 (1999).
11 Goode, *Commercial Law in the Next Millennium* (1998), p102; Lord Goff of Chieveley (1997) 46 ICLQ 745 at 751.
12 See eg the Consumer Protection Act 1987, Pt II and the Food Safety Act 1990.
13 See eg NCC 'Buying Problems' 1984; for the contrary view, see Reynolds, 'The Applicability of General Rules of Private Law to Consumer Disputes' in Anderman et al (eds), *Law and the Weaker Party* (1982).

Chapter 2

Principles of Contract Law

2.0 Contracts and commerce

Commerce is concerned with the exchange of goods and services, and the legal framework of 'exchange' is provided by the law of contract. Each of the commercial transactions examined in this book is a species of contract and some would see the study of commercial law as involving little more than the study of the rules governing those individual contracts. Although it was suggested in Chapter 1 that commercial law is more than simply the 'law of contracts', the law of contract is a central element. Each different type of transaction is governed by its own special rules; however, the general principles of contract law, such as those concerned with the formation of contracts, underpin those rules and apply to all the different classes of contract except in so far as modified by particular rules applying to the particular class of contract. Indeed, the general principles of contract law were developed primarily in cases concerned with the paradigm commercial transaction, the contract for sale of goods, and then extended by analogy to other classes of contract. Arguably, the essential 'rules' of contract law today can be most clearly recognised in what might be called 'pure commercial' cases[1]. In addition, 'contract' is a flexible concept which can be invoked by the courts in order to provide solutions to difficult fact situations. Thus the court may find an implied or collateral contract between parties where there is no formal agreement between them, in order to give one a remedy against the other. Such devices are not confined to disputes arising in a commercial context, but they are often used to good effect in that context[2].

---

1   This involves a narrow view of the scope of the law of contract; for a wider view see Collins, *The Law of Contract* (3rd edn, 1997).
2   See eg *Pyrene Co v Scandia Navigation Co* [1954] 2 QB 402, [1954] 2 All ER 158, below 33.1; *New Zealand Shipping Co Ltd v Satterthwaite & Co Ltd* [1975] AC 154, [1974] 1 All ER 1015, PC, below 32.5.3.2; *Shanklin Pier Ltd v Detel Products* [1951] 2 KB 854, [1951] 2 All ER 471, below 13.2.2.

2.0.1   *The philosophy of contract*

Many of the essential principles were developed during the eighteenth and early nineteenth centuries, and were profoundly influenced by the then prevailing economic philosophy of laissez-faire. It was believed that if individuals were left free to promote their own economic self-interest they would inevitably bargain to obtain the maximum benefit for themselves, and thus produce the maximum social wealth for society as a whole. Contract was the principal vehicle for the facilitation of exchange, and the developing law of contract came to embody those principles. It was assumed that if the parties to a contract entered into it voluntarily, its terms must be fair and be in their interests. Laissez-faire thus gave rise to the doctrines of freedom and sanctity of contract: individuals were free to choose whether or not to contract at all, and, if so, with whom and on what terms.

It is true that the courts refused to enforce certain categories of contracts: for instance, contracts whose objects are illegal, contrary to current morality, or otherwise contrary to public policy, such as agreements in restraint of trade or to oust the jurisdiction of the court, are void even today. It was also recognised from an early time that some categories of persons could not protect their own interests and so needed protection against exploitation by stronger contracting parties. Thus, for instance, minors and persons of unsound mind were, and still are, recognised as having reduced contractual capacity to enter into binding obligations.

However, these were exceptional cases. In most cases, freedom and sanctity of contract ruled. Contractual obligations were voluntarily undertaken, in contrast with those imposed by the courts in tort. The court should therefore interfere in contracts as little as possible: it would not make a contract for the parties and would normally restrict its role to the interpretation and enforcement of the agreed terms. The attitude of the courts is summed up in the words of Sir George Jessel:

> 'If there is one thing more than another which public policy requires, it is that men of full age and competent understanding shall have the utmost liberty of contracting and that their contracts, when entered into freely and voluntarily, shall be held sacred and shall be enforced by the Courts of Justice'[1].

Where the court was called upon to intervene, for example in order to deal with an event not provided for by the parties, it would seek to justify its intervention by claiming to be giving effect to the intentions of the parties. Thus terms could be implied into contracts only where necessary and where they must have been intended by the parties[2]; and even the doctrine of frustration and its effect on contracts was said to be dependent on the intentions of the parties[3].

Profound changes in social behaviour and in political and economic thinking during the late nineteenth and much of the twentieth century led to a gradual erosion of the classical doctrine of 'freedom of contract'. Laissez-faire individualism was replaced by more collectivist and welfare-based philosophies. At the same time, economic activity expanded, so that all groups in society became involved in contracting, whilst economic power came to be concentrated in the hands of large, often monopolistic, organisations, such as the utility and railway companies. It came to be recognised that the notion of 'freedom of contract' was often illusory for individuals wishing to obtain goods or services from such organisations, who would often do business only on their own terms. Gradually, therefore, the law came to intervene in contracts to protect the weaker party. The principal force for intervention was legislation designed to protect weaker contracting parties, such as tenants, employees and consumers, but the judges too, prompted by such legislation, became prepared to adopt a more interventionist role. They also became prepared to acknowledge their intervention; thus in 1956 it was acknowledged that the doctrine of frustration was based not on the intention of the parties to the contract, but on the court imposing a reasonable solution to deal with an unforeseen event[4], although even as late as 1976 the courts were still unwilling to acknowledge the same truth in relation to implied terms[5]. During this period contract itself declined in importance, as many goods and services which might otherwise have been provided under contract were supplied by the welfare agencies of the state. Even the concept of contract was reduced in significance, as the courts became increasingly willing to recognise their interventionist role and the law of tort expanded at the expense of contract.

By the 1970s it therefore became possible to talk of the death of 'freedom of contract'. Many contractual obligations were not voluntarily undertaken, but were imposed by the law. Thus, for instance, the Sale of Goods Act implied certain terms into contracts of sale, and the Unfair Contract Terms Act 1977 prevented their exclusion in certain situations. Since 1979 there has been a radical shift in political and economic thinking, which has seen a resurgence in laissez-faire thinking and has emphasised the role of the market in the provision of goods and services. Many of the services previously provided by the state have been replaced or supplemented by contract-based alternatives[6] and public authorities are required to put the provision of their services out to competitive tendering. Although not all the radical changes of the 1980s are universally accepted, all major political parties in Britain – and, indeed, in other countries – now seem to accept the importance of the market economy. The prevailing spirit is therefore in tune with the philosophy which inspired freedom of contract. However, the genie is out of the bottle: although in recent years the courts have sought to cut back the imposition of obligations in the law of tort, there are as yet no signs of them abandoning their willingness to intervene in contracts; indeed, they seem increasingly willing to intervene even in 'commercial' contracts[7] and it is unlikely that there will be any significant repeal of the substantial body of legislation designed to protect weaker contracting parties such as consumers. Indeed, there is likely to be an increasing volume of such legislation initiated by the European Community[8], especially as the Maastricht Treaty gave the Community new competence to act in the field of consumer protection in order to contribute to the attainment of a high level of consumer protection.

1 *Printing and Numerical Registering Co v Sampson* (1875) LR 19 Eq 462 at 465.
2 *The Moorcock* (1889) 14 PD 64, CA; *Southern Foundries (1926) Ltd v Shirlaw* [1939] 2 KB 206, CA.
3 See *Taylor v Caldwell* (1863) 3 B & S 826.
4 In *Davis Contractors Ltd v Fareham UDC* [1956] AC 696, [1956] 2 All ER 145, HL.
5 See *Liverpool City Council v Irwin* [1977] AC 239, [1976] 2 All ER 39, HL.
6 Eg the freedom to contract out of the state pension scheme under the Social Security Act 1986.
7 See eg the developing doctrine of economic duress; and for other examples see: *Interfoto Picture Library Ltd v Stiletto Visual Programmes Ltd* [1989] QB 433, [1988] 1 All ER 348, CA; *AEG (UK) Ltd v Logic Resource Ltd* [1996] CLC 265; and *R & B Customs Brokers Co Ltd v United Dominions Trust Ltd* [1988] 1 All ER 847, [1988] 1 WLR 321, CA.
8 For recent examples, see the Directives on Unfair Terms in Consumer Contracts (1993/13/EC), below 2.6.5; Protection of Consumers in Respect of Distance Contracts (1997/7/EC); and Certain Aspects of the Sale of Consumer Goods and Associated Guarantees (1999/44/EC), below 11.8, 12.5.

2.1 Contracts and business

The textbook analysis of contract law gives a misleading impression of the role of contracts in business. It is well known that business practices are often difficult to reconcile with the technical analysis of contract formation. Indeed, it has been suggested in the past that business personnel have often been largely ignorant of contract law, although there are indications that managers now have a greater awareness of legal principles than formerly[1]. More significantly, the law of contract is concerned with the pathology of failed contracts. Innumerable contracts are made each day, and the great majority of them are performed satisfactorily, without dispute. Even where disputes do arise, it is rare for the parties to resort to legal sanctions: businesspeople are generally anxious to avoid litigation for a number of reasons[2] and consumers can rarely afford to litigate. Instead, the parties may rely on self-help remedies or informally negotiated settlements, often without reference to their strict legal rights and duties, in order to maintain a trading relationship or general goodwill.

This is not to say that businesses do not use contracts. Indeed, most commercial exchanges are governed by extensive express terms; sometimes the terms are the result of lengthy negotiations between the parties. More often, contracts are made on standard terms, which may be prepared by bodies such as trade associations for use by all traders in a particular field, designed to balance the interests of the parties[3], or which may be standard conditions of sale or purchase prepared by one party to favour its own interests.

Businesses use contracts to plan their business relationships. Although some simple contracts involve no continuing relationship, most involve some degree of trust: the seller of goods who allows the buyer credit needs some assurance that the buyer will pay; the buyer wants some assurance that the goods will perform according to expectations, but the seller will not be prepared to accept open-ended liability. Where the contract creates a continuing relationship, as does a construction contract or a contract for the manufacture of a large piece of machinery, the need for trust is greater. Contracts can be used to plan the relationship, defining the obligations of the parties and allowing them to make financial, insurance and other arrangements in the knowledge that the contract will be performed. The commercial pressure to perform in the interests of goodwill will normally ensure performance. Indeed, many agreements which could not be enforced at law are made, and performed, simply because of the commercial pressure to perform[4]. However, where the relationship depends on a legally binding contract, the business can rely on the fact that, as a last resort, it can seek legal sanctions to enforce the agreement: the law 'is always in the background: . . . the parties know in general what the legal position is and may adjust their attitudes accordingly. As one sales manager put it: "it is an umbrella under which we operate" '[5].

1   See Beale and Dugdale, 'Contracts Between Businessmen' (1975) 2 BJ Law and Society 45.
2   See ch 36.
3   Examples include the standard forms used for construction and engineering contracts and for commodity dealing.
4   See the attitude of Lord Russel and Viscount Dilhorne in *Esso Petroleum Ltd v Customs and Excise Comrs* [1976] 1 All ER 117, [1976] 1 WLR 1, HL, below 8.1.
5   Beale and Dugdale, 'Contracts Between Businessmen' (1975) 2 BJ Law and Society 45 at 48. In a 1997 survey, Deakin, Lane and Wilkinson discovered that English businesses were more likely than German or Italian businesses to resort to litigation to enforce contracts: Deakin and Michie (eds) *Contract Law, Trust Relations and Incentives for Co-operation: A Comparative Study* in *Contracts, Co-operation and Competition: studies in economics and management* (1997).

2.1.1 *The courts, business and contracts*

The courts are not always oblivious to the difference between legal theory and commercial practice. The artificiality of the theoretical analysis of contracts was recognised by Lord Wilberforce when he said that:

'English law, having committed itself to a rather technical and schematic doctrine of contract, in application takes a practical approach, often at the cost of forcing the facts to fit uneasily into the marked slots of offer, acceptance and consideration'[1].

In another leading case, Lord Wright urged the courts not to impose unrealistic and legalistic technical requirements on business contracts, observing that:

'Businessmen often record the most important agreements in crude and summary fashion; modes of expression sufficient and clear to them in the course of their business may appear to those unfamiliar with the business far from complete or precise. It is accordingly the duty of the court to construe such documents fairly and broadly, without being too astute or subtle at finding defects'[2].

More recently, Lord Goff, commenting on the role of the judge in interpreting commercial contracts, said:

'[The judges'] only desire is to give sensible commercial effect to the transaction. We are there to help businessmen, not to hinder them: we are there to give effect to their transactions, not to frustrate them: we are there to oil the wheels of commerce, not to put a spanner in the works, or even grit in the oil'[3].

Lord Steyn put it more generally: 'A thread runs through our contract law that effect must be given to the reasonable expectations of honest men'[4]. A court considering a dispute arising out of a commercial transaction should therefore strive to give effect, so far as possible, to the commercial expectations of the parties. Thus, where the parties have acted on the basis that they have a contract, the court will normally seek to treat their agreement as contractual[5]. A court interpreting a contract will seek to give it 'commercial effect'[6]. In other contexts, too, the court deciding a commercial case may be influenced by its view of commercial expectations. Thus, for instance, where one party alleges a breach in order to escape from a bargain which has proved disadvantageous or uneconomic, the court will often strive to hold the parties to their bargain, even at the expense of strict legal doctrine[7].

1   In *New Zealand Shipping Co Ltd v Satterthwaite & Co Ltd* [1975] AC 154 at 167, PC.
2   In *Hillas v Arcos* [1932] All ER Rep 494 at 503–504, HL.
3   [1984] LMCLQ 382 at 391.
4   'Contract Law: Fulfilling the Reasonable Expectations of Honest Men' (1997) 113 LQR 433.
5   See eg *Foley v Classique Coaches Ltd* [1934] 2 KB 1, below 2.3.3.
6   See eg *Charter Reinsurance v Fagan* [1997] AC 313, [1996] 3 All ER 46; *Mannai Investment Co Ltd v Eagle Star Life Assurance Co Ltd* [1997] AC 749, [1997] 3 All ER 352; *Investors Compensation v West Bromwich Building Society* [1998] 1 All ER 98; see below 2.5.5.
7   See eg *Cehave NV v Bremer Handelsgesellschaft mbH* [1976] QB 44, [1975] 3 All ER 739, CA, below 9.2.3 for an example of this approach.

2.2   What is a contract?

Contracts are often defined as 'legally enforceable agreements', but it might be more accurate to speak of 'legally enforceable promises', for in a contractual dispute one party is normally seeking to enforce a promise made by the other; and some contracts do not involve agreements in any real sense of the word[1]. However, although recognising that it is morally desirable that promises should be kept, the law does not enforce all promises. It is therefore essential to distinguish between those promises which are legally enforceable and those which are not. The most important factor used by the law to draw the distinction is consideration: a promise supported by consideration moving from the promisee is enforceable by the promisee as a contract, whereas a bare promise is normally not enforceable as a contract, although in certain circumstances it may be binding on the promisor on some other basis. The only exceptional case where a promise is contractually enforceable in the absence of consideration is where the promise is contained in a deed, where the fact that the promisor went to the trouble of embodying his promise in a formal document can be taken as indicating that the promise was intended to have legal effect.

It seems that, historically, 'consideration' represented merely a reason which justified the court enforcing the promise. However, by the nineteenth century, a 'doctrine' of consideration had developed, according to which certain factors would, and others would not, be recognised as constituting consideration and it became established that 'consideration' must be something done or promised by the promisee which was either a benefit to the promisor or a detriment to the promisee[2]. In other words, promises would only be enforceable as contracts when the promisee supplied, or promised to supply, something in return for the promise: contract law was concerned with bargains or exchanges. The modern tendency to define consideration as 'the price of the promise'[3] underlines this fact. However, it should be borne in mind that provided the promisee supplies in exchange for the promise something which the law regards as sufficient consideration, the court will regard the promise as enforceable, regardless of the value of the consideration: 'consideration must be sufficient but need not be adequate'. Thus a lease at a peppercorn rent is a valid contract.

One result of this development of a 'doctrine' of consideration has been a loss of flexibility: promises which ought to be enforced cannot be enforced as contracts because they are unsupported by consideration, whilst other promises which it might be undesirable for the law to enforce are supported by consideration. As a result, the law has had to develop other concepts – such as estoppel and intention to create legal relations – to deal with these two situations[4]. In the modern law of contract it is possible to identify a shift of emphasis from consideration to intention. An agreement made in a commercial context, intended to be acted on, will not lightly be held unenforceable for lack of consideration. Thus the courts have been prepared to relax the classical doctrine of consideration[5], whilst developing other bases for the enforcement of promises, such as estoppel and waiver. Under these doctrines a promise may be enforceable even if unsupported by consideration, if the promisee has acted in reliance on it. At the present time, however, their ambit is limited. Whereas a promise supported by consideration may be enforced to the extent of the promisee's expectations, a promise enforceable on the basis of estoppel or waiver is normally only enforceable to the extent that the promisee has relied on it. More importantly, as English law currently stands, estoppel and waiver may be used defensively to prevent revocation of a promise, but may not provide the basis of a claim. In Australia the courts have gone further and have permitted a claim to be based on estoppel[6]. It may be that the English courts will in due course follow suit. Certainly the relaxation of the doctrine of consideration is likely to continue. Since it is now possible for a third party to enforce a contractual promise made for his benefit, without providing consideration[7], it may seem odd to maintain the requirement of consideration where it is the promisee who seeks to enforce a promise, and there are clear hints in recent cases that the courts may, in due course, wish to review the consideration doctrine[8].

1 Although they may be analysed in terms of 'agreement' in order to satisfy the theoretical requirements of contract law.
2 *Currie v Misa* (1875) LR 10 Exch 153.
3 *Dunlop v Selfridge* [1915] AC 847 at 855, HL.
4 See 2.8 and 2.3.5.
5 *Williams v Roffey Bros & Nicholls (Contractors) Ltd* [1991] 1 QB 1, [1990] 1 All ER 512, CA.
6 *Waltons Stores (Interstate) Ltd v Maher* (1988) 164 CLR 387.
7 Under the Contracts (Rights of Third Parties) Act 1999: see below 2.7.2.
8 See eg *The Pioneer Container: KH Enterprise (cargo owners) v Pioneer (owners)* [1994] 2 AC 324 at 335, [1994] 2 All ER 250 at 256, per Lord Goff; *Williams v Natural Life Health Foods Ltd* [1998] 2 All ER 577 at 584, per Lord Steyn.

2.2.1 *Consideration and commercial contracts*

Consideration is rarely a problem in commercial contracts for the supply of goods and services: businessmen tend not to promise something for nothing[1]. Business contracts are generally bilateral and each side's performance, or promise of performance, is consideration for the promise of the other. Thus if S agrees to deliver goods to B, the price to be paid on delivery, S's promise to deliver provides consideration for B's promise to pay, and vice versa. However, consideration becomes important in three situations.

First, it is well established that 'past consideration' is not sufficient consideration in law. Thus consideration must be provided in exchange for the promise being enforced: the consideration must be provided at the same time as, or after, the promise in question and an act done, or promise made, before the promise will be 'past consideration'. The practical importance of this is that terms cannot be incorporated into a contract after the contract is made, unless the promisee provides some new consideration to support the new term. It is not uncommon for businesses to make contracts by telephone and then later send out standard terms: if the contract was made on the telephone, those terms will not be part of the contract. Similarly, terms printed on an invoice sent after the contract has been performed will normally be ineffective; and if the seller of goods makes a promise about the goods after the contract has been made, that promise will not be enforceable[2].

Second, the performance of an existing duty may not be good consideration. If there is a contract between A and B, performance by A of his existing duties under that contract is generally no consideration for a fresh promise by B[3]. This is particularly important where contracts are varied. In recent years, however, the courts have been willing to find consideration in even a minimal variation by A of his existing duties, leaving the validity of the variation to be examined in the light of more flexible doctrines, such as the developing law of economic duress[4]. Indeed, in certain circumstances A's performance of his existing duties may provide consideration if that performance confers a practical benefit on B[5]. Performance by A of a duty owed to B under an existing contract has been held good consideration for a promise made by C[6].

Third, consideration may become important where a court discovers an implied contract between two parties who have not entered into a formal agreement. This is often done, for instance, to prevent a party to a contract containing an exclusion clause suing a stranger to the contract, such as a sub-contractor, to avoid the exclusion clause[7]. In such a case the court may imply a promise by the complainant to the sub-contractor to give the latter the protection of the exclusion clause; consideration for that promise may be found in the sub-contractor's performance of its duties under its contract with the main contractor[8].

1   *Olley v Marlborough Court Hotel Ltd* [1949] 1 KB 532, [1949] 1 All ER 127, CA.
2   *Roscorla v Thomas* (1842) 3 QB 234.
3   *Stilk v Myrick* (1809) 2 Camp 317.
4   See eg *The Atlantic Baron* [1979] QB 705, [1978] 3 All ER 1170.
5   See *Williams v Roffey Bros & Nicholls (Contractors) Ltd* [1991] 1 QB 1, [1990] 1 All ER 512, CA; contrast *Re Selectmove Ltd* [1995] 2 All ER 531; (1994) 110 LQR 353, below 2.8.1.
6   *New Zealand Shipping Co Ltd v Satterthwaite & Co Ltd* [1975] AC 154, [1974] 1 All ER 1015, PC.
7   As in *New Zealand Shipping Co Ltd v Satterthwaite & Co Ltd*, above.
8   The sub-contractor in such a case may now be able to take the benefit of the exclusion by virtue of the Contracts (Rights of Third Parties) Act 1999, so that it may no longer be necessary to imply a contract between complainant and sub-contractor.

2.3   Agreement

Contracts are normally defined as 'legally enforceable agreements'. The emphasis on 'agreement' has two aspects. First, a contract must be voluntarily entered into by the parties. 'A contract is essentially an agreement that is freely entered into on terms that are freely negotiated[1]'. Thus the arrangement between an electricity company and a customer for the supply of electricity was not a contract since the terms of the supply and the price of the electricity were fixed by statute[2]. Secondly, the parties must be in agreement with each other as to its terms. However, 'agreements' may be made in a wide variety of ways, from simple sales over the counter, to protracted negotiations resulting in formal contracts. In order to accommodate all such situations, the law has developed a simple and rational model of agreements, and analyses agreements, often artificially[3], in terms of 'offer' and 'acceptance'. However, despite the language of 'agreement' and 'consensus' which is often used, it should be borne in mind that the law of contract analyses the intentions of the parties objectively, by examining the outward appearance created by their words and actions. A person's words and actions are interpreted in the way in which they would be understood by a reasonable person in the position of the person to whom they are addressed[4]. Thus, if viewed objectively, the parties appear to be in agreement, they will be deemed to be in agreement, and will be bound, even if they intend different things. Equally, it may be that even though the parties are in agreement, they will be held not to have entered into a contract if there is no outward manifestation of their agreement[5]. The objective approach facilitates proof: a subjective approach would require parties to prove their actual intentions and would allow an unscrupulous person to escape from a contract by simply asserting that he did not actually mean what he appeared to mean. 'A contracting party cannot escape liability by saying that he had his fingers crossed behind his back'[6].

One advantage of the conceptual analysis of agreement is that it can be applied to new situations as they arise. The EC's directive on electronic commerce requires member states to 'ensure that their legal systems allow contracts to be concluded by electronic means'[7] but neither the directive nor the UK Electronic Communications Act 2000 contains specific rules to govern the formation of contracts. Problems of contract formation in an e-commerce environment will therefore fall to be resolved by application of the general principles governing contract formation.

1   *W v Essex County Council* [1998] 3 All ER 111 at 128 per Stuart Smith LJ.
2   *NORWEB plc v Dixon* [1995] 3 All ER 952.
3   As recognised by Lord Wilberforce in *New Zealand Shipping Co Ltd v Satterthwaite & Co Ltd* [1975] AC 154 at 167, PC, quoted above 2.1.1.
4   See *Bowerman v ABTA Ltd* [1996] CLC 451; *Carlyle Finance Ltd v Pallas Industrial Finance Ltd* [1999] 1 All ER (Comm) 659.
5   As in *Felthouse v Bindley* (1863) 1 New Rep 401.
6   Per Hobhouse LJ in *Bowerman v ABTA Ltd* [1996] CLC 451 at 463.
7   Article 9.

2.3.1   *Offer*

An offer is any statement, whether made by words or conduct, which unequivocally indicates that the person making it is willing to be legally bound by its terms if the other party accepts them. Thus if a person making a statement reserves the right to negotiate further, the statement cannot be regarded as an offer, but may be regarded as an 'invitation to treat', inviting offers. Certain common situations have been considered by the courts, and although each case must depend on its own facts, it seems that generally:

(a) estimates, to manufacture or supply goods or services, may be regarded as offers if the terms of supply are clear and complete;
(b) price lists[1], circulars, advertisements[2] etc are generally not regarded as offers, although this is not an absolute rule; and
(c) requests for tenders to supply or buy goods or services are generally invitations to treat, so that each person who submits a tender makes an offer, leaving the person who made the request to choose which to accept; however, in appropriate circumstances, the request may make clear that tenders satisfying certain criteria will be considered, or even that they will be successful; in such a case the person requesting tenders may be contractually bound to consider[3], or even award a contract to[4], a tender which satisfies the stated criteria.

Even where estimates, price lists or requests for tenders are not offers, they may be contractually significant. For instance, they may set out the terms on which any offer must be made and make clear that orders, or tenders, must incorporate those terms.

The status of web sites has not yet been considered by the courts. It is submitted that there can be no general rule that a web site is, or is not, an offer. Instead, the status of web sites will depend on the circumstances of the case and, in particular, on the nature of the goods or services to be supplied and the language used. A web site offering to supply goods or services should not automatically be treated as an invitation to treat. One of the reasons for generally treating price lists and advertisements of goods for sale as invitations to treat is that this accords with the presumed intention of the parties. The seller may have a limited, finite stock and cannot be understood to be committing himself to contract with everyone who might respond to the advertisement. The same analysis could apply to a web site 'offering' tangible items, such as books, for sale. On the other hand, where a web site 'offers' on line downloadable services, such as software, there is no problem of supply and demand, since such services can be infinitely reproduced. There is therefore no obstacle to treating such sites as offers in law, if the language used is consistent with such an interpretation[5].

An offer can be withdrawn at any time before it is accepted, even if the offeror has promised to keep it open, unless that promise is supported by consideration[6]. However, withdrawal will not be effective until it is communicated to the offeree.

1   *Grainger & Son v Gough* [1896] AC 325, HL.
2   *Partridge v Crittenden* [1968] 2 All ER 421, [1968] 1 WLR 1204.
3   *Blackpool and Fylde Aero Club Ltd v Blackpool Borough Council* [1990] 3 All ER 25, [1990] 1 WLR 1195, CA.
4   *Harvela Investments Ltd v Royal Trust Co of Canada (CI) Ltd* [1986] AC 207, [1985] 2 All ER 966, HL.
5   The EC directive on electronic commerce requires member states to ensure that in the case of the on-line supply of information society services the customer's order is acknowledged by the supplier without undue delay, and provides that order and acknowledgment are deemed to be received when they are accessible to the parties to whom they are addressed (art 11).
6   Contrast the position under the Vienna Convention on International Sales Law, art 16(2), under which an offer stated to be open for a fixed time would be irrevocable until expiry of the stated period, regardless of consideration. This reflects the position in civil law systems. The Convention is not part of English law at the present time: see 33.3. The position is similar under the UNIDROIT Principles of International Commercial Contracts, art 2.4.

2.3.2   *Acceptance*

An acceptance is any statement, by words or conduct, which clearly and unequivocally indicates that the person making it agrees to be bound by the terms of the offer. It must be an absolute and unconditional acceptance of all the terms of the offer; if it adds to or varies the terms of the offer, it will be regarded as a counter-offer, which may be accepted in its own right, but which rejects and terminates the original offer[1]. Once an offer has been accepted, both parties are bound.

It is sometimes said that silence cannot amount to acceptance[2]; however, it seems that the better view is that there is no such absolute rule. Normally silence will not be an unequivocal indication of acceptance; however, in an appropriate case, silence may be held to amount to acceptance[3]. Even if an offeree's silence does not amount to acceptance, it may create an estoppel which prevents the offeree denying that the offer has been accepted[4].

Generally, acceptance must be communicated to the offeror, and will not be effective until the offeror receives notification of acceptance. However, an offeror can waive the need for communication of acceptance, so that, since acceptance can be by conduct, a seller may accept an offer to buy goods by despatching goods in response to the customer's order. Similarly, if the buyer orders goods which are delivered together with a statement of the seller's terms of contract, the buyer may be taken to have accepted the terms by keeping the goods.

A posted acceptance, if correctly addressed and stamped, is generally effective as soon as posted[5], provided it was reasonable in the circumstances to use the post as a means of acceptance. This is a rule of convenience, to bring an end to communication. However, it is exceptional, and the general rule that notification of acceptance must reach the offeror is applied to other forms of acceptance, such as telephone and telex, where communication is instantaneous[6]. Where devices such as telex, fax or computer are used for the delivery of acceptances, problems may arise in deciding exactly when the message is 'received': a message may be received on the offeror's machine some time before it comes to his attention. In such a case it seems that the decision when the message is received will depend on an allocation of risk in accordance with such factors as normal business practice, the expectations of the parties and the circumstances of the case[7].

The application of these rules to acceptance sent by e-mail is uncertain. On the one hand, e-mail is instantaneously transmitted; on the other, it is not necessarily immediately read by the offeror. Moreover, it is generally sent by means of an intermediary. It may therefore be thought to share some characteristics with the post. It is submitted that there can be no single rule as to when an e-mail acceptance is effective. The closest analogy is with the fax, so that the decision as to when and where an e-mail acceptance is effective must depend on all the circumstances of the case.

1   *Hyde v Wrench* (1840) 3 Beav 334; contrast the position under the Vienna Convention on Contracts for the International Sale of Goods, under which a response which does not *materially* alter the terms of the offer is effective as an acceptance: see 33.3. See also the UNIDROIT Principles of International Commercial Contracts, art 2.11.
2   Relying on *Felthouse v Bindley* (1863) 1 New Rep 401.
3   See Miller (1972) 35 MLR 489; *The Leonidas D* [1985] 2 All ER 796, [1985] 1 WLR 925, CA; *The Golden Bear* [1987] 1 Lloyd's Rep 330.
4   For an analogous situation see *Spiro v Lintern* [1973] 3 All ER 319, [1973] 1 WLR 1002.
5   *Adams v Lindsell* (1818) 1 B & Ald 681.
6   See *Entores v Miles Far East Corpn* [1955] 2 QB 327, [1955] 2 All ER 493, CA.
7   Per Lord Wilberforce in *Brinkibon Ltd v Stahag Stahl GmbH* [1983] 2 AC 34 at 42.

2.3.3   *Completeness and certainty*

Since the acceptance must agree to all the terms of the offer, it follows that the offer must contain all the terms of the contract. The terms must be clear, complete and certain. If a statement contains terms which are unclear or ambiguous, it is unlikely to be regarded as an offer[1]. Similarly, failure to agree on essential terms may mean that the agreement does not amount to a contract.

If the requirement of certainty were rigidly applied, it might prevent many business agreements being regarded as contracts. Businessmen do not share the lawyer's desire for certainty and precision and may deliberately avoid using precise terms, either as a result of familiarity, trust and knowledge of trade custom and practice, or in order to avoid disagreement. The courts recognise this:

> 'When two businessmen wish to conclude a bargain but find that on some particular aspect of it they cannot agree, I believe that it is not uncommon for them to adopt language of deliberate equivocation, so that the contract may be signed and their main objective achieved. No doubt they console themselves with the thought that all will go well and that the term in question will never come into operation or encounter scrutiny'[2].

In general, the courts will therefore tolerate a degree of imprecision in commercial agreements and seek to enforce them, so that 'the dealings of men may so far as possible be treated as effective, and that the law may not incur the reproach of being the destroyer of bargains'[3]. Even a failure to agree on important matters will not prevent a contract coming into being if 'the parties' objective intentions as expressed to each other were to enter into a mutually binding contract'[4]. Thus failure to agree on a price will not necessarily prevent a contract being formed, if the parties have agreed the other essential terms of their agreement, since if an agreement is silent as to the price payable, it will normally be implied that a reasonable price should be paid[5]. Similarly, failure to agree other terms can be made good by the court implying the missing terms, if in all the circumstances it appears that the parties intended to enter into a binding agreement:

> 'It is for the parties to decide whether they wish to be bound and, if so, by what terms, whether important or unimportant . . . Of course, the more important the term is, the less likely it is that the parties will have left it for future decision. But there is no legal obstacle which stands in the way of the parties agreeing to be bound now while deferring important matters to be agreed later'[6].

However, an agreement which expressly recognises that important terms are to be agreed in the future may be regarded as insufficiently certain to amount to a contract. Thus an agreement to sell goods at 'prices to be agreed' may not amount to a contract, since it makes clear that a vital term remains to be agreed[7] and, by reserving the matter of the price to the parties, it excludes the implied term that a reasonable price should be paid. Generally, an 'agreement to agree' cannot be enforced as a contract. Nor can an 'agreement to negotiate'[8]. In *Walford v Miles*[9] the House of Lords held that an agreement to negotiate in good faith could not be contractually enforceable 'because it lacks the necessary certainty . . . The concept of a duty to carry on negotiations in good faith is inherently repugnant to the adversarial position of the parties when involved in negotiations'[10]. However, the House held that a lock-out agreement, by which one negotiating party promises the other for a fixed period not to negotiate with anyone else, is enforceable provided it is supported by consideration moving from the promisee[11].

Where a commercial agreement is incomplete or unclear, the court will strive to enforce it by reference to any previous dealings between the parties, or trade customs, especially where the parties have acted on the agreement and assumed it to be binding[12].

1 *G Scammell & Nephew Ltd v Ouston* [1941] AC 251.
2 Per Staughton J in *Chemco Leasing SpA v Rediffusion plc* (1985) unreported, quoted by Hirst J in *Kleinwort Benson Ltd v Malaysia Mining Corpn* [1988] 1 All ER 714 at 720.
3 Per Lord Tomlin in *Hillas v Arcos* [1932] All ER Rep 494 at 499.
4 *Pagnan SpA v Feed Products Ltd* [1987] 2 Lloyds Rep 601 at 610 per Bingham J.
5 See Sale of Goods Act 1979, s 8, below 8.1.3.1; Supply of Goods and Services Act 1982, s 15, below 19.3. Compare the UN Vienna Convention on Contracts for the International Sale of Goods, under which a proposal is not sufficiently definite to constitute an offer unless, inter alia, it 'expressly or implicitly fixes or makes provision for determining the . . . price' (art 14). See 33.3.
6 *Pagnan SpA v Feed Products Ltd* [1987] 2 Lloyds Rep 601 at 619 per Lloyd LJ.
7 *May and Butcher v R* [1934] 2 KB 17n.
8 *Courtney & Fairbairn Ltd v Tolaini Bros (Hotels) Ltd* [1975] 1 All ER 716.
9 [1992] 2 AC 128, [1992] 1 All ER 453; see Neill (1992) 107 LQR 405; Brown [1992] JBL 353.
10 Per Lord Ackner at [1992] 2 AC 128 at 138, [1992] 1 All ER 453 at 460. Compare the UNIDROIT Principles of International Commercial Contracts under which parties are free to negotiate and not liable for failure to reach an agreement, but a party who breaks off negotiations in bad faith is liable for losses caused to the other party (art 2.15). Lord Steyn has indicated that the question of a duty to negotiate in good faith might be reconsidered by the House of Lords: see (1997) 113 LQR 433 at 439.
11 [1992] 2 AC 128 at 138, [1992] 1 All ER 453 at 460; see also *Pitt v PHH Asset Management Ltd* [1993] 4 All ER 961.
12 See *Foley v Classique Coaches Ltd* [1934] 2 KB 1.

2.3.4 *Negotiations and the battle of forms*

A contract may be preceded by extensive negotiations, during which each party puts
forward terms in an effort to reach agreement. Those negotiations will be analysed
as a series of offers and counter-offers so that problems may occur if the parties fail
to reach agreement. In *British Steel Corpn v Cleveland Bridge and Engineering Co
Ltd*[1] the parties were negotiating towards a contract for the manufacture and supply
of steel nodes. The intending buyers requested the suppliers to commence manufacture
on the basis of a 'letter of intent' whilst negotiations continued, and all but one of the
steel nodes was eventually delivered. However, the communications between the
parties made clear that they had not yet agreed on all of the terms, or even a price. It
was held that there was no contract, although the customer was required to pay on a
quantum meruit basis for the nodes actually delivered.

In contrast, in *Trentham v Archital Luxfer Ltd*[2] the parties were seeking to negotiate
a building sub-contract. According to Steyn LJ, 'There was no orderly negotiation
of terms. Rather, the picture is one of the parties, jockeying for advantage, inching
towards finalisation of the transaction'[3]. No formal sub-contract was concluded,
although the work was done and paid for. However, when the main contractors
sued them for breach of contract, the sub-contractors argued that there was no
binding contract. Having reviewed all of the negotiations and the actions of the
parties, the Court of Appeal concluded that the correct inference was that the parties
had reached agreement. However, Steyn LJ added that he would be prepared to
find that a contract had come into being during performance 'even if it cannot be
precisely analysed in terms of offer and acceptance'[4]. Moreover, if in such a situation
the contract is not finalised until after some of the work has been carried out, it
may nevertheless retrospectively govern the work already completed[5].

Similar difficulties may arise where two contracting parties both try to rely on
their own terms: for instance, the buyer may order goods on his terms of purchase,
and the seller may acknowledge the order on his own standard terms of sale. The
approach of the English courts seems to be to analyse such negotiations in terms of
offer and counter-offer. In *Butler Machine Tool Co Ltd v Ex-Cell-O Corpn*[6] the
plaintiffs quoted for the manufacture and supply of a machine tool on a form which
incorporated their own standard terms. The defendants responded with an order
for the machine on a form which incorporated their own terms. The defendants'
form included a tear-off slip which stated 'we accept your order on the terms and
conditions stated therein'. The plaintiffs signed and returned that slip, together
with a letter which confirmed the order in accordance with the terms of the plaintiffs'
original quotation. It was held that there was a contract on the defendant buyers'
terms: the defendants' order was a counter-offer, which the plaintiff sellers accepted
by returning the tear-off slip. The plaintiffs' letter was held to refer only to the
price in the original quotation. The plaintiffs' terms included a provision which
made clear that they would only contract on their own terms; however, that term
had been rejected by the defendants' counter-offer, so that the plaintiffs had waived
it when they returned the tear-off slip.

If the traditional offer/counter-offer analysis is adopted, the battle of forms will
normally be won by the person who fires the 'last shot'. Often the seller will be
best placed to do so: for instance, by delivering goods with a delivery note containing
his standard terms, which the buyer may be deemed to accept by keeping the goods[7].
However, if both parties make clear from the start that they will only contract on
their own terms, it may be that no act, such as despatching or retaining goods, can
be regarded as acceptance of the other side's terms. In such a case it would seem

that a court would be bound to hold that there is no contract at all, or that there is a contract containing no express terms. In the *Butler* case, Lord Denning MR suggested an alternative approach which would avoid such drastic results: the court should construe a contract from the whole of the negotiations and communications between the parties. If such an approach is adopted, the court could find a contract containing such terms from each party's standard form as are not contradicted by any terms in the other party's form[8].

It is clear that in a case such as *Butler* the finding of agreement is wholly artificial, resulting from the objective approach of the law. The parties never were in agreement as to the terms of their contract, and the sellers never intended to accept the buyers' terms. However, there is evidence that the business world is less troubled than the lawyer by the theoretical difficulties created by the battle of forms. In 1974, Beale and Dugdale found that:

> '. . . there was considerable awareness of the fact that in many cases an exchange of conditions would not necessarily lead to an enforceable contract, and in some that the last set of conditions might prevail . . . But most firms seemed unconcerned about the failure to make a contract . . . Legal enforceability seemed secondary to reaching a common understanding'[9].

1   [1984] 1 All ER 504.
2   [1993] 1 Lloyd's Rep 25.
3   [1993] 1 Lloyd's Rep 25 at 26.
4   [1993] 1 Lloyd's Rep 25 at 29.
5   [1993] 1 Lloyd's Rep 25 at 30; see also *Trollope & Colls Ltd v Atomic Power Construction Ltd* [1963] 1 WLR 333.
6   [1979] 1 All ER 965, [1979] 1 WLR 401, CA; see also *British Road Services Ltd v Arthur Crutchley & Co Ltd* [1968] 1 All ER 811 and *Sauter Automation v Goodman* (1986) 34 BLR 81.
7   Although many buyers have adopted the practice of stamping delivery notes 'accepted subject to our terms' in order to avoid this result.
8   Under the UN Vienna Convention for Contracts for the International Sale of Goods a response to an offer which purports to be an acceptance but contains additional or different terms which do not materially alter the terms of the offer is an acceptance unless without delay the offeror objects to the variations (art 19(2)). See similarly the UNDIROIT *Principles*, art 2.22.
9   'Contracts between Businessmen: Planning and the use of Contractual remedies' (1975) 2 BJ Law and Society (1975) 45 at 50.

2.3.5   *Intention to create legal relations*

It is sometimes said that in order to create a legally binding contract, an agreement must be intended to create legal relations. Although it is sometimes doubted whether there is a separate requirement of such intention in the common law, the better view seems to be that an agreement which satisfies the other criteria for creation of a contract, by consisting of offer and acceptance, supported by consideration, may nevertheless be held not to create a contract if not intended to do so. However, it is normally presumed that commercial and business agreements, in contrast to social or domestic arrangements, are intended to create legal relations. Even so, it is clear that the parties to a commercial agreement may make clear, expressly or impliedly, that their agreement is not intended to be legally enforceable. Thus a letter of intent, as used in the *British Steel* case, will be presumed not to create legal relations, since it clearly indicates the intention of the parties to continue negotiations towards a finalised agreement.

In *Kleinwort Benson Ltd v Malaysia Mining Corpn*[1] the court had to consider whether a letter of comfort gave rise to a legally enforceable obligation. The plaintiff bank agreed to advance money to a subsidiary of the defendant company which was involved in tin trading on the London Metal Exchange. The defendants were asked to give a guarantee of the subsidiary's liabilities under the loan, but refused to do so. However, they did provide the plaintiffs with a letter of comfort which provided that 'it is our policy to ensure that the business of [the subsidiary] is at all times in a position to meet its liabilities to you'. When the tin market collapsed the subsidiary went into insolvent liquidation. The bank sought to recover the outstanding debt from the defendants, relying on the comfort letter. Hirst J held that, as the letter was part of a commercial agreement, the general presumption that commercial agreements are intended to create legal obligations applied, so that the letter created a binding contract. The decision caused some consternation in commercial circles, where letters of comfort are commonly used where parties wish to avoid creating legal obligations. The defendants appealed and the Court of Appeal reversed the decision[2]. The words in question amounted to no more than a statement of the defendants' general policy; they could not be construed as a promise not to change that policy, and therefore could not create a legal obligation. The court emphasised that the question whether an agreement gives rise to legal relations will depend on the facts of the individual case: in this case it was relevant that the parties were of equal bargaining power, that the defendants had expressly declined to give a legally binding guarantee, and that the plaintiffs had, apparently, agreed to accept a letter of comfort instead, on the basis that the rate of interest on the loan would be higher than would have been charged had the defendants provided a guarantee.

The Court of Appeal did not doubt the proposition that, as a general rule, commercial agreements will be presumed to create legal relations. However, the case illustrates that the facts may indicate that no legal relationship is intended. It is also clear that the parties can expressly agree that even a commercial agreement shall not be legally enforceable. In *Rose and Frank Co v J R Crompton Bros*[3] the parties entered into an agreement for the defendants to supply goods manufactured by them to the plaintiffs for a period of six months. The defendants terminated the agreement without notice and the plaintiffs sued for breach of contract. The agreement contained a clause which provided that the agreement was not intended to be legally binding or to be enforced in the courts, but was intended to be binding only in honour. It was held that the agreement was not legally binding. Scrutton LJ said:

'I can see no reason why, even in business matters, the parties should not intend to rely on each other's good faith and honour and to exclude all idea of settling disputes by any outside intervention with the accompanying necessity of expressing themselves so clearly that outsiders have no difficulty in understanding what they mean. If they clearly express such an intention I can see no reason in public policy why effect should not be given to their intention'[4].

1 [1988] 1 All ER 714, [1988] 1 WLR 799 (Hirst J); *revsd* [1989] 1 All ER 785, [1989] 1 WLR 379, CA.
2 [1989] 1 All ER 785, [1989] 1 WLR 379, CA. Cf *Re Atlantic Computers Ltd* [1995] BCC 696.
3 [1925] AC 445, [1924] All ER Rep 245, HL.
4 [1923] 2 KB 261 at 288, [1924] All ER Rep 245 at 249–250.

2.3.6   *Formality*

It is normally said that, as a general rule, English law does not require contracts to be made in any particular form. Provided that there is a promise, intended to be legally binding and supported by consideration, and that the requirements of offer and acceptance are satisfied, a valid contract can be made at common law by informal writing or orally, or may even be inferred from conduct, regardless of the value of its subject matter. Writing may be useful for evidential purposes, and the use of a deed may enable a promise to be enforced even though not supported by consideration, but the use of writing and deeds is generally optional.

To the extent that there is no single requirement that contracts generally be in any particular form, this is true. However, the general rule is qualified by a number of statutory rules requiring particular contracts to comply with particular formal requirements. Thus, for instance, contracts for the sale or disposition of an interest in land must be made in writing, signed by both parties[1]. Contracts of guarantee must be evidenced by a signed, written memorandum[2]. Certain contracts of insurance must be in writing[3]. A bill of exchange must be in writing and signed[4]. Consumer credit agreements must comply with detailed formal requirements under the Consumer Credit Act 1974[5]. Certain contracts for the sale or supply of goods or services to consumers are now subject to formal requirements[6].

In some cases written evidence of a contract is required in order to facilitate proof and guard against fraud. In others, writing is required in the interests of 'consumer protection', to give notice of the fact that a legal undertaking has been given and provide a record of the terms of the contract. The consequences of non-compliance with a particular formal requirement vary. In some cases the contract may be wholly void[7] or ineffective[8]. In others, the contract may be unenforceable, either at all[9] or without the permission of the court[10], or failure to comply with the relevant formal requirements may mean that a promise does not have the effects which it otherwise would have[11].

The general 'no formality' rule therefore holds good only to the extent that there is no single formal requirement applicable to contracts generally. It therefore remains possible to create a valid contract not caught by any of the special statutory regimes without complying with any particular formalities. In particular, commercial contracts for the supply of goods and services can normally be created without any formality.

---

1   Law of Property (Miscellaneous Provisions) Act 1989.
2   Statute of Frauds, 1677, s 4: see 23.1.3.
3   Marine Insurance Act 1906, s 22: see 35.2.
4   Bills of Exchange Act 1882, s 3: see 28.2.
5   See 26.1.
6   Consumer Protection (Cancellation of Contracts Concluded Away From Business Premises) Regulations 1987, SI 1987/21117; see 8.1. See also the Consumer Protection (Distance Selling) Regulations 2000, SI 2000/2334.
7   Eg under the Bills of Sale Act 1882. See 22.0.3.
8   Law of Property (Miscellaneous Provisions) Act 1989, s 2.
9   As in the case of contracts of guarantee under the Statute of Frauds. See 22.1.1.3. Under the Marine Insurance Act 1906, ss 21–24, a policy of marine insurance is inadmissible in evidence unless contained in a written document signed by the insurer but strictly speaking the policy is not the contract.
10   Eg Consumer Credit Act 1974, ss 65 and 127. The court's permission may be subject to conditions: see below 26.7.
11   Eg a bill of exchange must be in the form stipulated by s 1 of the Bills of Exchange Act 1882. If not, it cannot be a bill of exchange. Similarly, a promissory note must be in the form stipulated in

s 83 of the Act. The contractual effects of a bill or note may be simulated by informal promises not in the statutory form but such informal promises will not have the special legal attributes of a bill of exchange or promissory note. See 28.2.

2.3.7 *Rights of withdrawal and cancellation*

In a number of situations the common law rules on contract formation are further modified by statutory provisions giving one of the contracting parties a right to withdraw from, or cancel, the agreement within a short period after its conclusion. In these cases there may be a binding contract at common law, but if the right of withdrawal is exercised, the parties are restored to their pre-contract positions. Such rights are normally given as a form of consumer protection, often to protect consumers against high-pressure sales techniques. Thus, for instance, a consumer who enters into a consumer credit agreement other than at the business premises of the creditor or certain related persons, after oral representations have been made to him, has a statutory right to cancel the agreement[1]. Similarly, a consumer is given the right in certain circumstances to cancel a contract made with a trader during an unsolicited visit by the trader to the consumer's home or place of work, or otherwise away from the business premises of the trader[2], and a similar right to cancel is given in the case of contracts for financial services[3].

Consumers are given similar cancellation rights in relation to distance contracts under the Consumer Protection (Distance Selling) Regulations 2000[4], implementing the EC's Directive on the protection of consumers in respect of distance contracts[5]. The regulations apply to 'any contract concerning goods or services concluded between a supplier and a consumer under an organised distance sales or service provision scheme run by the supplier who, for the purposes of the contract, makes exclusive use of one or more means of distance communication up to and including the moment at which the contract is concluded'[6]. They require consumers to be provided with certain information – including, in effect, all the main terms of the contract – prior to entering into a contract[7], and require that information to be confirmed in some 'durable medium' after the contract is made[8].

The regulations give the consumer a right to cancel a distance contract within a short period after its conclusion[9]. The effect of non-compliance with the requirements for the provision of information is to extend the period during which the consumer may exercise the cancellation right. The regulations thus further qualify the general rule that no formality is required for the creation of a valid contract and that a concluded agreement is final. Significantly the regulations require the information to be provided 'with due regard . . . to the principles of good faith in commercial transactions'[10]. They therefore mark yet another incursion of good faith into English law.

1 Consumer Credit Act 1974, s 67.
2 Consumer Protection (Cancellation of Contracts Concluded Away From Business Premises) Regulations 1987, SI 1987/21117.
3 Financial Services (Cancellation) Rules 1989.
4 SI 2000/2334.
5 Directive 97/7/EC OJ L 144/19. The directive was to have been implemented by 4 June 2000. See generally Bradgate (1997) 4 Web JCLI.
6 Regulation 3(1). Certain categories of contract are excluded: see reg 5(1).
7 Regulation 7.
8 Regulation 8.
9 Regulations 10–18.
10 Regulation 7(2).

2.4   Defects in formation

Although parties may appear to be in agreement, their negotiations may have been flawed so that one later alleges that he agreed as a result of being misled, under pressure or as a result of a misunderstanding, so that he should be released from the agreement. Although there are several doctrines – mistake, misrepresentation, duress and undue influence among them – which may allow a person to be released from a contract in such a case, they are very narrowly applied, and parties are generally held to their bargains. One of the characteristics of a market is that persons with superior information or bargaining power should be free to exploit it, thus encouraging a process of economic Darwinism by which the strong prosper, and market participants are encouraged to develop their own information-gathering systems. Inevitably, there are limits to this principle: the use of information obtained in certain ways, such as inside information relating to company shares, or of certain types of pressure, may be frowned upon. The role of the law is therefore to decide which advantages are legitimate, and which are illegitimate.

A distinction must be drawn between those negotiation defects which make a contract void and those which only make it voidable. Where a contract is void, it is of no legal effect at all. A void contract is therefore ineffective to transfer property so that property transferred under such a contract can be recovered, even if it has come into the hands of a third party. In contrast, a voidable contract may be set aside, or rescinded, at the instigation of one of the parties, but until it is set aside it is valid and effective in law. Thus a transfer of property under a voidable contract passes title to the transferee, subject to the transferor's right to recover the property if the contract is rescinded. If a third party acquires rights in the property after the transfer and before rescission, those rights will be binding on the original transferor[1]. If the contract is rescinded, both parties must be restored, so far as possible, to their original positions. The right to rescind may therefore be lost if such restoration is not possible.

1   See 17.4.1 below.

2.4.1   *Mistake*

A person may consider a wide range of factors when deciding to enter into a contract: his ability to perform the contract, the nature of the goods or services contracted for, their price, quality, suitability for his needs, his financial circumstances, the present and likely future economic situation and so on. If the law generally allowed a party who made a mistake in deciding to enter into a contract to be released from the contract on that ground, the certainty of contractual obligations would be undermined. The law therefore recognises a very narrow category of mistakes which may affect the validity of contracts. The effect of a mistake is to make the contract void at common law, although equity may recognise a wider category of mistakes as making a contract voidable.

'Mistake' is rarely pleaded: often, where one party is mistaken, the mistake will have been induced by the other. In that case, it may be preferable to argue that there is a misrepresentation or breach of term, either of which may give rise to a right to damages, rather than a mistake which merely makes the contract void. Even those cases where there is held to be a mistake may often be explicable on other grounds[1].

Generally, the law maintains the objective approach in the face of claims of mistake: provided that the parties, viewed objectively, appear to have agreed to the terms of their contract, they will be held to have agreed, and to be bound by them. Thus if one party agrees to a contract on the basis of a mistake about his ability to perform the contract, the surrounding circumstances, or even the nature or quality of the subject matter[2], he will nevertheless be held to the contract, and it will make no difference that the other party was aware of his mistake[3]. There is generally no duty on a contracting party to disclose facts in his knowledge: the rule is 'caveat emptor': a contracting party is expected to look out for his own interests; and if all contracting parties develop the skills necessary to enable them to do so, society as a whole will benefit. The position is different if the mistake is induced by the deliberate or negligent behaviour of the other contracting party[4]: it would then be unreasonable to hold the mistaken party to his apparent intention. Of course, a contractor may well not insist on his strict legal rights and may be happy to allow the other to escape the contract on the grounds of mistake. Many retailers adopt a policy of exchanging consumer goods which are not defective, merely because the customer has changed his mind, the goods do not fit or are the wrong colour.

The objective approach is abandoned where the terms to which a person apparently agrees are not the terms he intended to agree to, so that the terms of the contract do not reflect his real intention, and that mistake is known (or ought to be known) to the other party, so that, in effect, there is a mistake as to the terms of the contract[5]. The justification for holding a person bound by their apparent intention is that the other party must rely on the appearance, but it would be unreasonable to allow one contracting party to hold another to a contract which he knew did not represent the other's true intentions.

Particular problems arise where A contracts with B, mistakenly believing him to be C. The crucial question in such a case is whether A intended to contract with B or with C. Where the parties are not dealing face to face, it may be possible to establish that A only intended to contract with C; if so, there is no contract between A and B[6]. However, if A does intend to contract with B, a mistake merely about B's attributes – for instance his creditworthiness – will have no effect on the contract[7]. Where the parties deal face to face, the objective interpretation of the situation will normally be that A intends to deal with the person physically before him[8]. In such a situation, B is normally responsible for A's mistake, having fraudulently misled him, and their contract will be voidable on the grounds of misrepresentation. However, if B has acquired property from A under the contract and transferred it to a third party, A will only be able to recover the property from the third party if he can establish that his contract with B was void for mistake. The real question then is: who should bear the loss caused by B's fraud? This is a recurring problem in commercial law; it is examined in more detail below[9].

In very rare cases the parties may be so at cross-purposes that it is impossible objectively to identify any agreed intention. In that case there is no contract[10].

Where the parties are in agreement, one may later allege that the agreement is vitiated because of some shared mistake. For instance, they may have contracted to buy and sell a painting which both believe to be a genuine Constable, but which turns out to be a copy. Such 'common mistakes' will only affect the parties' agreement if, on the proper construction of the contract, neither of them has expressly or impliedly agreed to take the risk. Thus if the court finds that B has agreed to buy the painting whatever its provenance, and take the risk that it is genuine, the mistake is irrelevant to the rights and duties of the parties. Similarly, if S has expressly or impliedly warranted that the painting is genuine, S will be in breach of contract if the painting is actually a fake. The relative expertise of the parties is likely to be an important factor in deciding if one has impliedly undertaken the risk. Thus in *McRae v Commonwealth Disposals Commission*[11], where the Commission contracted to sell to the plaintiffs a named wreck, said to be located on a named reef, the Commission was held to have impliedly promised that there was such a wreck; it was therefore liable to the plaintiff when it was discovered that there was no wreck and no reef.

It seems that the category of mistakes which will make a contract void on this basis is very small. If the subject matter of the contract does not exist, or if the contract cannot be performed, it seems that there will be a fundamental mistake which makes the contract void. In *Bell v Lever Bros*[12] Lord Atkin said that the contract will also be void for a 'mistake as to the existence of some quality which makes the thing without the quality essentially different from the thing as it is believed to be'[13]. In that case, the plaintiffs paid the defendant £30,000 compensation on termination of his contract; the parties were unaware that, as a result of previous breaches of contract by the plaintiff, the contract could have been terminated without compensation. The mistake was held not to be fundamental, and that has led to doubts as to whether a mistake as to the quality of the subject matter of the contract can ever be fundamental. However, in *Associated Japanese Bank (International) Ltd v Crédit du Nord SA*[14] the defendants guaranteed the obligations of X to the plaintiffs under an agreement by which X purported to sell four machines to the plaintiffs and then lease them back. It transpired that the machines never existed, and it was held that the mistake as to the existence of the machines made the guarantee void. Steyn J held that a contract will be void where a common mistake renders the subject matter of the contract essentially different from what it was believed to be. This is similar to the test for frustration of a contract.

A further line of authority[15] suggests that mistakes which would not make a contract void at common law may nevertheless make it voidable in equity. However, those cases are of doubtful authority, and seem to conflict with the more general principle of caveat emptor.

1   See eg Smith (1994) 110 LQR 400, who argues that there is no need for a separate doctrine of 'mistake'.
2   As in *Tamplin v James* (1879) 15 Ch D 215.
3   *Smith v Hughes* (1871) LR 6 QB 597.
4   *Scriven Bros v Hindley & Co* [1913] 3 KB 564, where it seems that the facts might be regarded as involving an innocent misrepresentation.
5   *Hartog v Colin and Shields* [1939] 3 All ER 566.
6   As in *Cundy v Lindsay* (1878) 3 App Cas 459, HL.
7   *King's Norton Metal Co Ltd v Edridge, Merrett & Co Ltd* (1897) 14 TLR 98, CA.
8   *Phillips v Brooks* [1919] 2 KB 243; *Lewis v Averay* [1972] 1 QB 198, [1971] 3 All ER 907, CA; cf *Ingram v Little* [1961] 1 QB 31, [1960] 3 All ER 332, CA.
9   See 17.4.1.
10 *Raffles v Wichelhaus* (1864) 2 H & C 906.
11 (1950) 84 CLR 377.
12 [1932] AC 161, HL.
13 [1932] AC 161 at 218.
14 [1988] 3 All ER 902, [1989] 1 WLR 255.
15 *Solle v Butcher* [1950] 1 KB 671, [1949] 2 All ER 1107, CA; *Grist v Bailey* [1967] Ch 532, [1966] 2 All ER 875; *Magee v Pennine Insurance Co Ltd* [1969] 2 QB 507 [1969] 2 All ER 891, CA.

2.4.2 *Misrepresentation*

A person who makes a mistake about the subject matter of a contract often does so as a result of being misled by the other contracting party. In such a case the mistaken party intends to enter into the contract, but it would be unfair to hold him to the bargain and to allow the other party to profit from his own error or dishonesty. The courts of equity therefore recognised that a person who was induced to enter into a contract as a result of a misrepresentation made by the other party was entitled to have the contract set aside, or rescinded. Damages were also available at common law where the misrepresentation was fraudulent, and are now available where the misrepresentation was made negligently[1], but rescission of the contract remains the primary remedy for misrepresentation.

A representation is a statement made during negotiations leading to the formation of the contract. However, only a limited class of statements will make a contract voidable if they prove false. Some statements are clearly not intended to have any legal effect: such statements, such as those typically made in advertising campaigns, may make extravagant claims for a product, which could not reasonably be taken seriously. Historically, such 'sales talk' claims have been known as 'mere puffs'. However, it should be borne in mind that although such statements may have no effect on the validity of any subsequent contract and create no civil liability, consumer protection legislation makes it a criminal offence to apply a false trade description to goods[2], and that advertising is also subject to a measure of self-regulation[3].

In order to make a contract voidable, a misrepresentation must be a false statement of fact which induces the representee to enter into the contract. The requirement that the statement be one of fact excludes statements of intention (although a statement of future intention may give rise to liability if it is a term of the contract[4]), opinion and law. However, these distinctions are not clear cut. A person who states his future intention impliedly states that he actually holds that intention[5]. Similarly, a person who states his opinion impliedly states that he actually holds that opinion, and that he knows of facts which reasonably support it, especially if he has special knowledge or expertise so that the other party is likely to rely on the statement[6]. Thus if a person does not hold the intention or opinion stated, he is guilty of a misrepresentation of fact.

A representation may be made by words or conduct, for instance by deliberately concealing a defect in goods[7], but since there is generally no duty of disclosure between parties negotiating a contract, silence normally does not amount to a misrepresentation. A duty to speak does arise, however, in certain limited situations: for instance, where a person makes a statement which is strictly true but which is incomplete and therefore misleading[8]; or where a person makes a statement which is true when made, but which becomes false due to a later change in circumstances: there will then be a duty to correct the misleading impression created by the earlier statement[9].

There is a duty of disclosure where the contract is regarded as one of the utmost good faith. The best-known example of such a contract is the contract of insurance, where the insured is required to disclose to the insurer all material facts; failure to do so makes the contract voidable at the instance of the insurer[10]. In fact the duty is a mutual one[11], but it impinges more heavily on the insured than on the insurer. Traditionally, this duty has been justified on the grounds that the facts relevant to the assessment of risk in insurance are known only to the insured, but the same might be said of many other contracts: for instance, the seller of goods is likely to know much more about the goods than the buyer. Moreover, the duty of disclosure often works unfairly to the prejudice of the insured and many commentators have criticised its continued existence. Insurance companies are generally in a position to protect their interests by asking for relevant information, rather than by requiring the insured to disclose facts which may not appear to him to be important[12].

A duty of disclosure may also arise in a particular case if there is a fiduciary relationship between the parties. Thus if an agent contracts with his principal, the agent must make full disclosure of all material facts[13].

A representation will only affect a contract if it is material and if it actually induces the representee to enter into the contract. Thus it must be a statement which would influence the judgment of a reasonable person to enter into the contract, and it must have been relied on by the representee. If the representee does rely on the representation, it is irrelevant that he had the opportunity to check it and failed to do so[14], or that he also had other inducements to enter the contract[15]. However, if he does check the validity of the representation, the representee cannot then claim to have relied on it, even if he fails to discover that it was false[16].

1   Under s 2(1) of the Misrepresentation Act 1967 or under the doctrine of *Hedley Byrne & Co Ltd v Heller & Partners Ltd* [1964] AC 465, [1963] 2 All ER 575, HL.
2   Trade Descriptions Act 1968, s 1.
3   By the Advertising Standards Authority.
4   See 2.5.2.
5   *Edgington v Fitzmaurice* (1885) 29 Ch D 459, CA.
6   *Smith v Land and House Property Corpn* (1884) 28 Ch D 7, CA; *Esso Petroleum Co v Mardon* [1976] QB 801; contrast *Bisset v Wilkinson* [1927] AC 177, PC, where the representor had no special knowledge and the representee knew that.
7   *Horsfall v Thomas* (1862) 1 H & C 90.
8   *Dimmock v Hallett* (1866) 2 Ch App 21.
9   *With v O'Flanagan* [1936] Ch 575, [1936] 1 All ER 727, CA.
10   See 35.3.
11   *Banque Financière de la Cite SA v Westgate Insurance Co Ltd* [1990] 1 QB 665, [1989] 2 All ER 952, CA affd [1991] 2 AC 249, [1990] 2 All ER 947, HL; see 35.3.3.
12   See 35.3.2.
13   A more general duty of disclosure might be imposed if English law were to accept a general duty of good faith between contractors.
14   *Redgrave v Hurd* (1881) 20 Ch D 1, CA.
15   *Edgington v Fitzmaurice* (1885) 29 Ch D 459, CA.
16   *Attwood v Small* (1838) 6 Cl & Fin 232, HL.

2.4.2.1   *Remedies for misrepresentation*

Some representations may also become terms of the contract[1]: if such representations prove false, the representee may be able to exercise remedies for breach of contract. However, when the conditions outlined above are fulfilled, remedies for misrepresentation may also be available[2].

Generally, a person who enters a contract as a result of a misrepresentation has the option of rescinding the contract. However, rescission of a contract is a drastic step and since the right to rescind is equitable, it may be barred where rescission would be inequitable. The right may therefore be lost if innocent third parties have acquired rights pursuant to the contract which would be prejudiced by its rescission. Similarly, rescission will be barred if it is impossible to restore the parties to their original position, for instance, because a buyer of goods has consumed them; however, accidental deterioration or damage, or deterioration caused by the defect the subject of the misrepresentation will not bar rescission. The right is also lost if the innocent party affirms the contract after discovering the misrepresentation[3]; or, in cases of non-fraudulent misrepresentation, by lapse of time. In this last case the right may be lost even before the misrepresentation is discovered[4]. Even so, rescission might be available for quite trivial misrepresentations. The right is therefore further restricted by s 2(2) of the Misrepresentation Act 1967, which allows a court to award damages in lieu of misrepresentation in cases where the misrepresentation was not fraudulent[5].

Rescission aims to restore the contracting parties to their original position. However, a person who enters a contract as a result of a misrepresentation may suffer other, additional losses. Damages have always been available where the representee proves that the representor acted fraudulently, that is to say, either knowing the representation to be false, or being reckless as to whether it was true or not[6]. However, since fraud is notoriously difficult to prove, many victims of misrepresentation would suffer losses which would be uncompensated at common law, unless it could be shown that the statement in question had become a term of the contract[7]. The position is ameliorated by s 2(1) of the Misrepresentation Act 1967, which allows the court to award damages to the victim of a non-fraudulent misrepresentation unless the representor can prove that 'he had reasonable grounds to believe and did believe up to the time that the contract was made that the facts represented were true'. The result is that damages are available where the representor acted negligently. Damages may also be available in the general law of negligence[8], but the representee will normally prefer to rely on the statutory right, since the statute throws the burden onto the representor to prove that he was not negligent, whereas in a common law negligence action the burden would be on the representee to prove negligence. Moreover, damages under the statute will generally be more generous than damages for common law negligence.

Damages under the 1967 Act and at common law are assessed according to the rules applicable to damages in tort, so that the aim is to put the plaintiff in the same position as if the statement had not been made: ie as if no contract had been made. Normally, they are assessed as at the date of the contract, so that where a person buys something as a result of a misrepresentation, damages are prima facie the difference between the contract price and the actual value of the thing purchased at the date of the contract. However, this is not an absolute rule. In *Naughton v O'Callaghan*[9] N purchased a racehorse as a result of a misrepresentation about its pedigree. By the time the misrepresentation was discovered, the value of the horse had declined considerably as a result of its lack of success on the race course. It was held that damages could be assessed as at the later date so that the plaintiff recovered the loss caused by the fall in the horse's value. This approach was confirmed by the House of Lords in *Smith New Court Securities Ltd v Scrimgeour Vickers (Asset Management) Ltd*[10]. P was induced by a fraudulent misrepresentation to buy shares in a company. Subsequently, the value of the company's shares fell sharply when it was discovered that the company had been the victim of a separate fraud committed by a third party and unconnected with the misrepresentation. The House of Lords held that P was entitled to the difference between the contract price and the value of the shares after discovery of the second fraud, even though that was not known to the market at the time of the transaction. The Court of Appeal had held that damages should be assessed by reference to the market value of the shares at the date of the sale, which was substantially higher[11]. No doubt this was in part because they were concerned that D should not be liable for losses caused by a general fall in the market for shares. The House of Lords rejected this approach. The victim of fraud is entitled to be compensated for all losses he suffers as a result of the fraud. Normally in a case such as this, that loss will be the difference between the contract price and the market value for the asset purchased, be it goods or shares[12], at the date of the contract, but where the effect of the fraud continues so as to induce the victim to retain the asset or to lock him into the transaction by making it difficult to dispose of the asset, damages may be assessed by reference to a later date.

A claim for damages for common law negligent misstatement is governed by the ordinary rules of remoteness applicable to damages for negligence. However, damages for fraud are not limited by remoteness, so that a plaintiff who proves fraud is entitled to be compensated for all losses caused by the misrepresentation, whether or not they were foreseeable[13], and it has been held that the same rule applies to damages awarded under s 2(1) of the 1967 Act[14]. Moreover, although in an action for misrepresentation the plaintiff cannot recover damages in respect of profits he would have made had the misrepresentation been true, he may recover damages in respect of profits he would have made had the misrepresentation not been made. Thus if a plaintiff who makes a contract as a result of a misrepresentation can show that, had the misrepresentation not been made he would have made an alternative contract which would have been profitable, he may recover damages in respect of the profits he would thus have made[15].

Damages awarded under s 2(1) of the 1967 Act and at common law may be reduced to take account of any contributory negligence of the plaintiff which contributed to his loss[16].

The basis of assessment of damages awarded in lieu of rescission under s 2(2) of the 1967 Act is not clearly settled but it seems clear that they should be less than damages under s 2(1)[17] and would ordinarily be assessed as at the date of the contract and take no account of subsequent falls in value[18].

Contracts commonly include terms which seek to limit or exclude liability for misrepresentation. Such terms are only effective if they satisfy the test of reasonableness[19].

1 See 2.5.
2 Misrepresentation Act 1967, s 1.
3 *Long v Lloyd* [1958] 2 All ER 402, [1958] 1 WLR 753, CA.
4 *Leaf v International Galleries* [1950] 2 KB 86, [1950] 1 All ER 693, CA.
5 On a literal reading of s 2(2) the court can only award damages on this basis where the right to rescind would otherwise be available, but in *Thos Witter Ltd v TBP Industries Ltd* [1996] 2 All ER 573 Jacob J held that the court may award damages under s 2(2) even if the right to rescind has been lost, for instance due to passage of time or because restitution is impossible: see Beale (1995) 111 LQR 385.
6 *Peek v Derry* (1887) 37 Ch D 541, CA.
7 See 2.5.1.
8 *Hedley Byrne & Co Ltd v Heller & Partners Ltd* [1964] AC 465, [1963] 2 All ER 575, HL: see *Esso Petroleum Co v Mardon* [1976] QB 801, [1976] 2 All ER 5, CA.
9 [1990] 3 All ER 191.
10 [1997] AC 254, [1996] 4 All ER 769.
11 [1994] 4 All ER 225.
12 Their Lordships rejected the suggestion that the rule applicable to shares is different from that applicable to goods.
13 *Doyle v Olby (Ironmongers) Ltd* [1969] 2 QB 158.
14 *Royscott Trust Ltd v Rogerson* [1991] 3 All ER 294. The House of Lords in *Scrimgeour Vickers* expressly declined to comment on the correctness of this decision.
15 *East v Maurer* [1991] 2 All ER 733, approved by the House of Lords in *Scrimgeour Vickers*.
16 *Gran Gelato Ltd v Richcliff Group Ltd* [1992] 1 All ER 865.
17 *Thos Witter Ltd v TBP Industries Ltd* [1996] 2 All ER 573 per Jacob J.
18 See *William Sindall plc v Cambridgeshire County Council* [1994] 3 All ER 932; Beale (1995) 111 LQR 60.
19 Misrepresentation Act 1967, s 3.

2.4.3 Duress and undue influence

Many factors may influence a person's decision to enter into a contract, including commercial, economic and social pressures. For instance, a company may have to buy a new machine to fulfil a contract with a customer; there may be only one manufacturer able to supply the required machine. Modern advertising and sales techniques may place strong pressures on consumers to buy products or services. Advertising may emphasise that buying a new car or video will allow a consumer to maintain social status, or to build, or reinforce, an image or lifestyle. Alternatively, advertising may play on concern for others: for instance, a consumer may be urged that a new car or a fire alarm is necessary because it offers safety to members of the consumer's family. The emphasis on freedom of contract and values of the market means that most of those pressures have traditionally been disregarded by the law. In recent years, as part of the general trend in favour of protecting consumers, legislation has been introduced to protect consumers against some high-pressure sales techniques: for instance, a person may not have to pay for unsolicited goods or services[1] and, where a person enters into certain credit[2] and other contracts[3] away from business premises, he is allowed a cooling-off period during which the agreement is cancellable.

The law has, however, long recognised that some forms of pressure are unacceptable and several doctrines have been developed to control contracts made as a result of illegitimate pressure. In recent years the courts have shown an increased willingness to use these doctrines and, in particular, the doctrines of duress and undue influence, to intervene even in commercial contracts. Traditionally, intervention in such cases has been justified on the basis that a person who enters into a contract as a result of duress or undue influence does not genuinely consent to the contract, but this justification is not satisfactory. The crucial question for a court in a case in which duress or undue influence is alleged is to decide whether or not the pressure exerted on a contracting party was legally acceptable.

The common law recognised that certain types of threat could lead to a person acting in a way which could be considered involuntary. Since freedom of contract emphasised free choice, the law therefore recognised that a consent to a contract obtained by duress was not a fully effective consent, and allowed a person who entered into a contract as the result of duress to have it set aside. The crucial question is to decide what sort of threats will be recognised as amounting to 'duress'. Threats to a person's life or person have long been regarded as constituting duress[4], and more recently it has been accepted that threats to property could also amount to duress. In recent years the courts have recognised the concept of 'economic duress', which is particularly significant in a commercial context, especially where one of the parties to an existing contract threatens to break it in order to force the other party to agree to new terms: for instance, by demanding an increase in the price[5]. Even a threat to perform a lawful act might amount to duress, at least if accompanied by a demand for money. However, a threat to perform a lawful act in pursuit of a claim bona fide believed to be valid will not ordinarily amount to duress in the context of arm's length commercial dealings[6]. Similarly, mere economic pressure, or the use of a superior bargaining position, will not ordinarily amount to economic duress[7], so that a threat not to enter into a contract unless certain terms are accepted will not normally be duress[8].

The cases define duress as a 'coercion of will which vitiates consent'[9]. In *Pao On v Lau Yiu Long* the Privy Council recognised that economic duress could vitiate a contract, but held that, on the facts of that case, where the plaintiffs had threatened to break an existing contract with a third party unless the defendants entered into a contract of guarantee, there was no duress because the defendants had considered the situation and decided to give the guarantee because they felt it unlikely that they would be called upon to make payment under it. Thus where the threat is to break an existing contract, the court will take into account whether or not the party asserting duress protested and the effectiveness of any alternative course of action available, such as suing to enforce the original contract.

Where duress is found to exist, its effect is to make a contract voidable, rather than void[10]. Thus the victim of duress may rescind the contract, but may lose that right, for instance by affirming the contract or by delaying before seeking rescission. In *The Atlantic Baron*[11] the plaintiffs lost the right to rescind by waiting eight months before commencing proceedings to recover a payment made as a result of an agreement made under duress.

A contract can also be set aside on the basis of the equitable doctrine of undue influence if it is shown to have resulted from one party exercising a dominating influence over the other. Normally, the party complaining of undue influence must actually show that the other exercised a dominating influence but certain relationships – including those between solicitor and client, trustee and beneficiary and agent and principal – give rise to a presumption of undue influence as a matter of law. Most commercial relationships do not give rise to such a presumption, but a presumption may arise on the facts of a particular case if it is shown that a special relationship of trust and confidence existed between the parties. Thus, although the relationship between banker and customer does not give rise to a presumption of undue influence[12], a special relationship may arise in a particular case if the customer relies on the banker for advice to such an extent that the banker comes to have a dominating influence[13]. Where there is a presumption of undue influence, whether as a matter of law or on the facts of a particular case, a party seeking to have a contract set aside on the grounds of undue influence must show that the terms of the contract were unfair or manifestly disadvantageous to him[14]; but, if he does so, the contract will be set aside unless the other party can establish that the complainant entered the contract as a result of the 'free exercise of his independent will'[15], for instance by showing that the complainant received competent and independent advice before entering the transaction.

A contract between A and B may also be set aside on the basis of undue influence exerted over B by C where C is appointed to act as A's agent, for instance, to get B to sign a contract, or where A has actual or constructive notice of B's conduct[16].

The doctrines of duress and undue influence can be seen as amongst those by which English law seeks to promote good faith between contractors. The courts have, however, always been anxious to restrict the grounds of intervention in contracts to avoid undermining the certainty that contractual obligations can be enforced. Thus the courts will not intervene in a contract simply because its terms are unfair, or the price is extortionate. The position is now modified by statute, which gives courts extensive powers to intervene, particularly in consumer contracts, to relieve the weaker party from unfair terms[17]. On the other hand, there are other longstanding powers to intervene in other, restricted cases: for instance, the courts may grant relief to prevent unfair advantage being taken of 'poor or ignorant' persons. In *Lloyds Bank Ltd v Bundy* Lord Denning suggested that the courts had a general power of intervention wherever there is 'inequality of bargaining power'. However, the House of Lords has rejected such a broad principle as too uncertain[18].

---

1   Unsolicited Goods and Services Act 1971; Consumer Protection (Distance Selling) Regulation 2000, SI 2000/2334.

2 Consumer Credit Act 1974, below 26.2.3.
3 Consumer Protection (Cancellation of Contracts Concluded Away from Business Premises) Regulations 1987, SI 1987/2117, implementing Directive 85/557 EC.
4 See also *Williams v Bayley* (1866) LR 1 HL 200, where a threat to institute criminal proceedings against the promisor's son was held to amount to duress.
5 *North Ocean Shipping Co Ltd v Hyundai Construction Co, The Atlantic Baron* [1979] QB 705, [1978] 3 All ER 1170; *Atlas Express Ltd v Kafco (Importers and Distributors) Ltd* [1989] QB 833, [1989] 1 All ER 641.
6 *CTN Cash and Carry Ltd v Gallaher Ltd* [1994] 4 All ER 714.
7 *Pao On v Lau Yiu Long* [1980] AC 614, [1979] 3 All ER 65, PC.
8 Goff and Jones, *The Law of Restitution* (5th edn, 1998) p 342.
9 Per Lord Wilberforce in *Pao On v Lau Yiu Long* [1980] AC 614 at 653, [1979] 3 All ER 65 at 78.
10 There are comments to the contrary in *Barton v Armstrong* [1976] AC 104, [1975] 2 All ER 465, PC, but they are contrary to most authority and are thought to be wrong.
11 *North Ocean Shipping Co Ltd v Hyundai Construction Co* [1979] QB 705, [1978] 3 All ER 1170.
12 *National Westminster Bank plc v Morgan* [1985] AC 686, [1985] 1 All ER 821, HL.
13 *Lloyds Bank Ltd v Bundy* [1975] QB 326, [1974] 3 All ER 757, CA; see ch 29.
14 *CIBC Mortgages plc v Pitt* [1994] 1 AC 200, [1993] 4 All ER 433. The disadvantage must be 'manifest' – ie: apparent – but need not be great: *Barclays Bank plc v Coleman* [2000] 1 All ER 385.
15 *Inche Noriah v Shaik Allie bin Omar* [1929] AC 127 at 136, PC.
16 *Barclays Bank plc v O'Brien* [1994] 1 AC 180, [1993] 4 All ER 417. There is now a significant body of case law applying this principle: see 23.1.2.2.
17 For instance, under the Unfair Contract Terms Act 1977, below 2.6.4, and the Unfair Terms in Consumer Contracts Regulations 1999, SI 1999/2083, below 2.6.5. See also the power to intervene in extortionate credit bargains under the Consumer Credit Act 1974, ss 137–40, below 26.7.1.
18 Per Lord Scarman in *National Westminster Bank plc v Morgan* [1985] AC 686 at 708 [1985] 1 All ER 821 at 830; see also *Pao On v Lau Yiu Long* [1980] AC 614 at 634, [1979] 3 All ER 65 at 78.

2.5 The terms of the contract

The obligations undertaken by the parties to a contract are defined by the terms of the contract. In order to decide what those obligations are it is therefore necessary to decide what the terms of the contract are. That task may be easier where the parties have recorded their agreement in writing. However, although it may be preferable for a contract to be expressed in writing, in order to provide concrete evidence of the terms and minimise the scope for dispute as to what was agreed, there is generally no legal requirement that contracts be in written form[1], and a great many commercial agreements may be – and often are – made informally, orally, over dinner, at trade fairs, by telephone, fax, telex or computer.

Even where the contract is embodied in a written agreement, there may still be a dispute over its terms: one party may allege that the document does not accurately record the agreed terms, or that additional terms must be implied. It may therefore be necessary to examine everything written or said by the parties during negotiations, and the surrounding circumstances, in order to decide what the terms of the contract were.

1 See 2.3.6.

2.5.1 *The classification of statements: representations and terms*

Many statements may be made by the parties, either orally or in writing, during the course of negotiations leading to the conclusion of a contract. A seller may extol the virtues of his product in general terms in advertising literature or in response to an enquiry from a prospective customer. The customer may pose specific questions in order to ascertain that the product will satisfy his requirements. In the event of a dispute arising, it may be necessary to examine all the statements made by the parties in order to decide their legal effect, if any.

In general, such statements can be divided into three groups. Their classification depends on the intention of the parties, as objectively ascertained by the court. Some statements are regarded as intended to have no legal effect, and can be regarded simply as sales talk or 'puffs'. For instance, the seller of a used car might describe it as 'a superb bargain; it will run forever'. No one expects a car to 'run forever', and such a statement almost certainly has no legal effect. Many of the claims made for products in advertising, especially those which are humorous or light-hearted or which can be regarded as subjective value judgments, probably fall into this category.

Other statements may be classified either as representations or as terms of the contract, or as both. Statements of either type have legal effects and give rise to legal liability if false. A person will also be liable for false statements made by his agent[1] and where goods are acquired on credit, the credit supplier may be liable for false statements made during negotiations by the supplier of the goods[2].

The distinction between the representations and terms may be important if the statement proves false and the victim of the false statement seeks legal redress for misrepresentation or for breach of contract. A misrepresentation is an untrue statement of past or present fact which induces the hearer to enter into a contract in reliance on the statement, whereas a term is part of the contractual promise. A statement of future intention may be promissory, and thus become a term of the contract, but will not normally be a representation. A statement of fact made during negotiations may be a representation; it will also be a term, if the representor promises that it is true[3]. Whether a statement becomes a term of the contract depends on the intention of the parties, and since the court's view of the parties' intention will depend on the facts of each case, it may often be difficult to classify a particular statement with certainty. Many of the cases concerned with the classification of statements are difficult to reconcile. However, the courts do follow certain guidelines when classifying statements. Thus a statement made at a crucial stage of the negotiations is more likely to be classified as a term; in particular, a statement made close to the time of conclusion of the contract is more likely to be a term than one made some time before the contract[4]. A statement which is particularly important to the hearer is more likely to be a term[5]; and a statement made by a party who can reasonably be expected to have greater expertise than the other is more likely to be regarded as a term than a statement made by the less knowledgeable party[6].

On the other hand, if the parties have reduced their agreement to a full written contract, it may be difficult to persuade the court that a statement not included in the document was intended to be a part of the contract. This is the so-called 'parol evidence' rule. Over the years the courts have developed a number of devices to evade the rule: thus, for instance, it may be found that an oral statement constitutes a collateral contract, parallel to the formal written one[7] or that it was intended that the contract should be partly written and partly oral[8]. It is now clear that there is no absolute rule that the existence of a full written contract precludes a finding that other terms were intended to form part of the contract[9]. The 'rule' is based on the presumed intention of the parties, and can be rebutted by clear evidence that the written document was not intended to be the whole of the parties' agreement.

The classification of statements as misrepresentations or terms is no longer so important as it once was. Liability for breach of contract is strict, so that a party may claim damages for breach of term even though the other party made the statement wholly innocently, believing it to be true; but prior to 1967, damages were only available for misrepresentation if the plaintiff could prove that the false statement was made fraudulently[10]. There was therefore a strong incentive to classify statements as terms, especially where the right to rescind the contract for misrepresentation might have been lost. Since the Misrepresentation Act 1967, the victim of a misrepresentation may now claim damages in any case. However, the maker of the statement may still escape liability for damages for misrepresentation if he can show that the statement was made without negligence[11]. In addition, the remedies available for breach of contract differ from those for misrepresentation. A breach of contract gives the innocent party a right to damages and, in some cases, a right to withhold performance of his obligations and even to terminate the contract for the future. The victim of a misrepresentation may rescind the contract and/or claim damages. Rescission and termination are apparently similar and, indeed, the term 'rescission' is sometimes used to refer to termination of a contract for breach. The two concepts differ, however. Termination of a contract operates prospectively, releasing parties from their future, unperformed obligations under the contract. In contrast, rescission for misrepresentation or other formation defect operates retrospectively and seeks to restore the parties to their pre-contract positions[12]. There are other remedial differences. Damages for misrepresentation are assessed differently from those for breach of contract; and the right to terminate for breach may be lost more quickly than the right to rescind for misrepresentation.

The availability of two different groups of remedies for victims of false statements makes the law unnecessarily complicated. The position is further confused by the fact that the same statement can be both a representation and a term of the contract[13], giving the victim a choice of remedies; and, in a sale of goods case, an express statement may also be regarded as forming part of the contractual description of the goods[14].

1 See 5.4.
2 Under s 56 or s 75 of the Consumer Credit Act 1974: see 26.4.
3 In such a case the representee may pursue remedies for misrepresentation or for breach of contract: see Misrepresentation Act 1967, s 1(a).
4 See *Routledge v McKay* [1954] 1 All ER 855, [1954] 1 WLR 615, CA; contrast *Schawel v Reade* [1913] 2 IR 81.
5 *Bannerman v White* (1861) 10 CBNS 844.
6 Contrast *Dick Bentley Productions Ltd v Harold Smith (Motors) Ltd* [1965] 2 All ER 65, [1965] 1 WLR 623, CA with *Oscar Chess v Williams* [1957] 1 All ER 325, [1957] 1 WLR 370, CA.
7 See eg *City and Westminster Properties (1934) Ltd v Mudd* [1959] Ch 129, [1958] 2 All ER 733.
8 See *J Evans & Son (Portsmouth) Ltd v Andrea Merzario Ltd* [1976] 2 All ER 930, [1976], 1 WLR 1078.
9 Law Commission 154 'The Parol Evidence Rule' (1986).
10 Unless the plaintiff could frame an action in negligence under the authority of *Hedley Byrne & Co Ltd v Heller & Partners Ltd* [1964] AC 465, [1963] 2 All ER 575, HL.
11 See 2.4.2.
12 This distinction is somewhat blurred in relation to contracts for the sale of goods under which a buyer may withhold performance, or terminate the contract, after goods are delivered by rejecting them and recovering the price, if paid: see ch 12.
13 Misrepresentation Act 1967, s 1.
14 See 11.1.

2.5.2 Incorporation of express terms

The terms of the contract may be derived from a range of sources, including advertisements, oral statements, letters, notices, standard terms printed on order forms, catalogues and so on. None of those statements can become a term of the contract unless introduced no later than the time the contract is concluded: any statement made after that time will be unsupported by consideration, unless there is a valid variation of the contract[1]. In view of the rules relating to offer and acceptance, the terms of the contract must therefore be contained in the effective final offer, although terms introduced earlier during negotiations may impliedly be included in that offer.

It is well established that a person who signs a document containing contract terms is bound by those terms, even though he may not have read or understood them[2] and even though he could not read them[3]. The rule is justified by the objective approach to contract: a person who signs a contract objectively appears to be assenting to its terms. However, the rule operates harshly against the interests of individuals, particularly consumers, and it is hard to justify its application in cases where the other party knows that the document has not been read. There have therefore been some attempts to limit the rule: for instance by holding that if a person misrepresents the effect of a term, he will be bound by the representation and the term will be given the meaning he ascribed to it[4].

Often, terms are set out in unsigned documents, such as order forms, acknowledgments, delivery notes, catalogues, tickets etc. Terms from such documents will become part of the contract provided that the document is the type of document which might be expected to contain contract terms[5] and the person receiving the document has been given reasonable notice of the terms. If the recipient of the document knows that it contains printing or writing, he will be bound by the terms, regardless of his actual knowledge of them, provided that the person putting the document forward has taken reasonable steps to bring the terms to his notice. What is reasonable will depend on all the facts of the individual case, but the test is generally objective, so that provided sufficient has been done to bring the terms to the attention of persons generally, no account is taken of any personal disability of the individual contracting party: for instance, it is irrelevant that the recipient of the document is illiterate, blind, or unable to read the language in which the terms are written. However, again there are signs that this rule may be relaxed: for instance, the person putting forward the terms may have to take extra steps if he knows that the other party cannot read them, for example by translating them for a person unable to understand the language[6].

Generally, the person putting forward a contract document is required to give the other party reasonable notice of the terms as a whole. However, if any of the terms is unusual or particularly onerous, special notice of that term may have to be given, for instance, by highlighting it or, as Lord Denning once put it, by having it 'printed in red ink . . . with a red hand pointing to it'[7]. Failure to give special notice to such a term will mean that the term in question will not be incorporated into the contract, even though other terms in the same document may be[8]. The 'red hand' test was developed in cases concerned with exclusion clauses, but it is now clear that it applies generally to clauses of any type[9]. It seems that in deciding whether the clause is 'unusual' or 'particularly onerous' so as to require special notice, the term will be compared with terms used by other businesses in the same line; a term of a common type may nevertheless be 'unusual' or 'particularly onerous' if it is harsher or more extensive than the terms used by such businesses. In effect, the special notice requirement operates as a common law test of reasonableness: 'the more *unreasonable* a clause is, the greater the notice which must be given of it[10]'. It is one of the techniques by which English law seeks to promote and protect good faith in contractual dealings[11].

1 *Roscorla v Thomas* (1842) 3 QB 234; *Olley v Marlborough Court Hotel* [1949] 1 KB 532, [1949] 1 All ER 127, CA.
2 *L'Estrange v Graucob* [1934] 2 KB 394.
3 But see *Geier v Kujawa Weston and Warne Bros (Transport) Ltd* [1970] 1 Lloyd's Rep 364; *H Glynn (Covent Garden) Ltd v Wittleder* [1959] 2 Lloyd's Rep 409, below.
4 *Curtis v Chemical Cleaning and Dying Co* [1951] 1 KB 805, [1951] 1 All ER 631, CA; *Harvey v Ventilatoren Fabrik Oelde GmbH* [1988] BTLR 138. See also *Tilden Rent-A-Car Co v Clendenning* (1978) 83 DLR (3d) 400.
5 *Chapelton v Barry UDC* [1940] 1 KB 532.
6 *Geier v Kujawa Weston and Warne Bros (Transport) Ltd* [1970] 1 Lloyd's Rep 364; *H Glynn (Covent Garden) Ltd v Wittleder* [1959] 2 Lloyd's Rep 409, where a partial translation was held misleading. Contrast *Barclays Bank plc v Schwartz* [1995] CLY 2492.
7 In *J Spurling Ltd v Bradshaw* [1956] 2 All ER 121 at 125, CA.
8 The rule may apply even to terms in a signed document: see the Canadian case of *Tilden Rent-A-Car Co v Clendenning* (1978) 83 DLR (3d) 400.
9 *Interfoto Picture Library Ltd v Stiletto Visual Programmes Ltd* [1989] QB 433, [1988] 1 All ER 348, CA.
10 *J Spurling Ltd v Bradshaw* [1956] 2 All ER 121 at 125 per Denning LJ. See *AEG (UK) Ltd v Logic Resource Ltd* [1996] CLC 265; Bradgate (1997) 60 MLR 582.
11 See per Brooke LJ in *Lacey's Footwear (Wholesale) Ltd v Bowler International Freight Ltd* [1997] 2 Lloyd's Rep 369 at 385.

2.5.3 Standard terms

The expansion of commercial activity which followed the Industrial Revolution led to new methods of doing business. Businesses would now be making many contracts for the supply of similar goods and services. It quickly became apparent that it would be impractical to negotiate a new contract to cover each individual transaction, and in an age of mass production and supply of goods and services, the attractions of a mass produced contract were obvious. Thus in recent years there has been great growth in the use of standard terms of business, both by suppliers and purchasers of goods and services. Many important commercial contracts are made on standard forms prepared by trade organisations and professional bodies to govern all transactions of a particular type: for instance, standard form contracts are commonly used in the commodity trades, for ship and aircraft charters, and for construction and engineering contracts. In addition, individual businesses, including buyers and sellers of goods and services, banks and insurers, have their own standard terms which they seek to use for all their contracts.

Standard terms offer several advantages to the business community. As we have noted, a business may use contract terms to plan its business relationships, allocate risks arising from the contract, and arrange insurance etc on the basis of that allocation. Standard terms are often extensive, covering a wide range of eventualities. By using the same terms for all its contracts, the business is able to plan more easily. Moreover, the use of standard terms reduces the costs and time spent in negotiations, reducing transaction costs and therefore allowing the business to reduce prices to its customers. Contract arrangement can be delegated to relatively junior employees without giving them authority to bargain and possibly commit the business to contracts on unfavourable terms. The advent of the word processor allows the process to become more sophisticated: standard terms can now be modified to meet the needs of individual transactions. In addition, the meaning of individual terms within a standard form may have been considered in previous litigation and thus be clarified by precedent[1].

However, standard terms have their drawbacks, even for the businesses using them. They may encourage complacency, particularly in contract formation, and will be wholly ineffective unless validly incorporated into the contract. Since businesses now increasingly use standard terms both to supply goods and services and to buy them, there is a danger that the use of standard terms may encourage a battle of forms, with the difficulties we have considered above[2].

Even more significantly, the use of standard terms further undermines the fiction of 'freedom of contract', especially where they are used, as is often the case, to govern contracts with consumers. In such cases, 'the freedom [is] all on the side of the big concern which ha[s] the use of the printing press. No freedom for the little man who [takes] the ticket or order form or invoice'[3].

> 'The overwhelming proportion of standard forms are not . . . under any reasonable test, the agreement of the consumer or business recipient to whom they are delivered. Indeed, in the usual case, the consumer never reads the form, or reads it only after he has become bound by its terms. Even the fastidious few who take the time to read the standard form may be helpless to vary it'[4].

On the other hand, even consumers may benefit from the use of standard forms: the reduction in transaction costs which they produce are likely to be passed on, in a competitive market, to the customer in the form of reduced prices. In addition, the standard form may be a vehicle for informing consumers of their rights and how to proceed if difficulties arise: indeed, some statutes prescribe the content of standard terms for use in consumer contracts to allow them to be used in this way[5]. There is nothing inherently objectionable about standard form contracts, provided that they are subjected to adequate control by the courts. In the past the courts developed various devices to control the use of exclusion clauses, seen as the most objectionable of the terms likely to be imposed via standard form contracts, and recent decisions have indicated that those devices are available for the control of other classes of term[6]. The common law adherence to the doctrine of freedom of contract, the preference for certainty over fairness and the emphasis on objectivity in interpreting contractual behaviour leaves the English courts inadequately equipped to control standard forms. Although there have recently been indications that the courts may be more willing to adopt a more interventionist role, for instance through the development of doctrines such as economic duress, the rejection of general concepts such as inequality of bargaining power or a duty to negotiate in good faith means that intervention tends to be on an ad hoc basis. Similarly, statutory control in the UK has hitherto been ad hoc, dealing either with particular types of term, such as exclusion clauses[7] or types of contract[8]. Other methods of control are possible: for instance, the United States Uniform Commercial Code allows the court a wide range of powers if it finds the contract, or any clause, to have been unconscionable when the contract was made[9], whilst other jurisdictions favour centralised control, for instance prior approval of standard terms, or centralised action against terms perceived to be unfair. The Unfair Terms in Consumer Contracts Regulations[10] therefore mark a significant new departure for the UK. In effect, they render ineffective any standard term in a contract between a business and a consumer if the term is 'unfair'[11]. Moreover, recognising the difficulty for individual consumers in taking action against unfair terms, they allow the Director General of Fair Trading and other 'qualifying bodies', including regulatory officers and the Consumers' Association, to seek injunctions against the use of unfair terms[12].

---

1   For a discussion of the role of the Commercial Court in interpreting standard form contracts, see Goff [1984] LMCLQ 382.

2 See 2.3.4.
3 Lord Denning in *George Mitchell (Chesterhall) Ltd v Finney Lock Seeds Ltd* [1983] QB 284 at 297.
4 Slawson, 'Standard Form Contracts and Democratic Control of Lawmaking Power' (1971) 84 Harv LR 529.
5 Eg the Consumer Credit Act 1974, see 26.1.2.
6 See *Interfoto Picture Library Ltd v Stilletto Visual Programmes Ltd* [1989] QB 433, [1988] 1 All ER 348, CA, above 2.5.2.
7 Under the Unfair Contract Terms Act 1977.
8 Such as the Consumer Credit Act 1974.
9 Uniform Commercial Code, s 2–302.
10 SI 1999/2083, replacing the Unfair Terms in Consumer Contracts Regulations 1994, SI 1994/3159 and implementing the EC Directive on Unfair Terms in Consumer Contracts (93/13/EEC); see below 2.6.5.
11 Regulation 5.
12 Regulation 8.

2.5.4 Implied terms

Even where a contract is governed by express terms, whether contained in a full written contract or in a standard form, it is unlikely that the parties will be able to foresee in advance all the situations which may arise in performance of the contract. If such a situation gives rise to a dispute, the parties may attempt to deal with it informally by negotiation, but if negotiation fails to produce a solution, it must be dealt with by the court, either by implying terms into the contract, or by means of the doctrine of frustration. In recent years the courts have abandoned the fiction that when they find a contract to be frustrated they are giving effect to the intention of the parties. However, when the court is invited to imply terms into the contract, it will still claim to be giving effect to the intentions of the parties. As a result, terms can only be implied into contracts in certain restricted circumstances.

When parties have regularly done business together on the same terms, the court will be prepared to assume that a transaction was intended to be on those terms, even though they may not have been expressly incorporated into the particular contract. However, terms will only be implied on this basis where there have been sufficient dealings between the parties to constitute a consistent course of dealing[1]. The existence of such a course of dealing may therefore cure a failure to incorporate terms on a particular occasion due to a breakdown in contract formation procedures.

Where the parties deal in the context of a particular trade or market, they may be taken to have contracted on the basis of the customs and practices of that trade or market. Such customs may be given legal effect as implied terms provided that they are clear and certain and are not inconsistent with the express terms of the contract[2].

The court may be prepared to imply a term into an individual contract where, on the facts of the particular case, the term is necessary to give 'business efficacy' to the contract and to make the contract work in the way it must have been intended[3], or where the term is one which the court feels that the parties must have intended. The test is often expressed by reference to the intervention of an officious bystander: the term will be implied if, had the bystander suggested it at the time the contract was being negotiated, the parties would have 'testily suppress[ed] him with a common "Oh, of course" '[4]. The application of these tests is not entirely clear: sometimes they appear to be different tests[5], but some cases suggest that they are the same.

Terms may also be implied as a matter of law into all contracts of a particular class or type; such terms are said to be implied 'in law'. The courts have denied that a term can be implied in law merely because its implication would be reasonable and insist that such terms can only be implied if they are 'necessary'[6]. On the other hand, it has been said that the test for implication is based on 'wider considerations' than business efficacy[7]. It seems that this means that, in deciding whether to imply such a term, the court will consider broader issues of policy involving the particular category of contracts in question, rather than merely the circumstances of the particular contract in question[8]. A term can therefore only be implied on this basis if the contract in question belongs to a definable category[9]. A decision to imply a term on this basis means that the term will be implied into all contracts of that type unless excluded or contradicted by the express terms of a particular contract. Effectively, the implied term in question becomes a legal incident of the type of contract. Several common forms of contract have developed bodies of terms which are implied in this way. The best example of such terms in commercial contracts is the body of terms concerning such matters as quality and fitness for purpose implied into contracts for the sale of goods. Those terms originated in the recognition of commercial custom and expectation and became so frequently implied as to become common law incidents of sale contracts, but are now implied on a statutory basis under the Sale of Goods Act 1979.

Terms may also be implied into contracts by statute. Statutory implied terms are particularly important in commercial supply contracts[10], and in certain circumstances the law prohibits their exclusion or modification. Such terms are largely divorced from the intentions of the parties, and are effectively legal duties, prescribed by statute.

1   *McCutcheon v David MacBrayne Ltd* [1964] 1 All ER 430, [1964] 1 WLR 125, HL.
2   *Les Affréteurs Réunis Societe Anonyme v Leopold Walford (London) Ltd* [1919] AC 801; *London Export Corpn Ltd v Jubilee Coffee Roasting Co Ltd* [1958] 2 All ER 411, [1958] 1 WLR 661, CA.
3   *The Moorcock* (1889) 14 PD 64.
4   *Shirlaw v Southern Foundries (1926) Ltd* [1939] 2 KB 206 at 227, CA.
5   See eg *Ashmore v Corpn of Lloyds (No 2)* [1992] 2 Lloyd's Rep 620.
6   See *Liverpool City Council v Irwin* [1977] AC 239, [1976] 2 All ER 39, HL.
7   *Scally v Southern Health and Social Services Board* [1992] 1 AC 294 at 307, [1991] 4 All ER 563 at 571 per Lord Bridge.
8   See Phang, 'Implied Terms in English Law – Some Recent Developments' [1993] JBL 242.
9   *Scally v Southern Health and Social Services Board*, above, although in this case the 'category' was very narrowly defined.
10 See ch 11.

2.5.5   *Interpretation of contracts*

The obligations of contractors are defined by the terms of the contract. It is not enough, however, to identify the terms, express and implied, of the contract. Often the real question is: what do the terms mean? Lord Goff, one of the most eminent commercial judges of recent years, has written that:

'In point of fact, if not the meat and drink, then at least the staple diet, of the Commercial Court can be summed up in one word – "Construction". Commercial lawyers – solicitors, barristers and judges – spend a very substantial part of their time interpreting contracts'[1].

The role of the court when interpreting (or construing) a contract is to decide what it means. Strictly speaking, this is separate from the tasks of (a) identifying what the terms of the contract are and (b) determining their legal effect. In fact it is often difficult to separate the three. Terms are implied only where the contract makes no express provision for a situation, and one cannot decide whether express provision is made until one has determined what the express terms mean; and the legal effect of words must depend on their meaning.

It is almost trite to say that the objective of a court interpreting a contract is to determine the intentions of the contracting parties. It is equally almost trite to say that the parties' intention is assessed objectively. 'The methodology is not to probe the real intentions of the parties but to ascertain the contextual meaning of the relevant contractual language. Intention is determined by reference to expressed rather than actual intention'[2]. In other words, the parties' intention is to be determined from the words used in their context. It has recently been said, however, that 'a fundamental change . . . has overtaken this branch of the law'[3]. The courts have shown a new willingness to look beyond the literal meaning of words used in a contract, and even beyond the words of the contract itself, in order to determine the intentions of the parties. The result has been 'to assimilate the way in which [contracts] are interpreted by judges to the common sense principles by which any serious utterance would be interpreted in ordinary life'[4]. It is tempting to draw a parallel with the increased willingness of the courts to adopt a purposive approach to the interpretation of statutes[5], and the 'new' approach to contract interpretation has variously been referred to as 'purposive' or 'contextual', but the preference now seems to be to speak of 'commercial'[6] or 'common sense'[7] interpretation.

The new approach is said to have its origins in the decisions of the House of Lords in *Prenn v Simmonds*[8] and *Schuler v Wickman Machine Tool Sales Ltd*[9], and, especially, in the speeches in those cases of Lords Wilberforce and Reid respectively[10]. Its objective is to interpret the contract in a common sense way so as to give effect to the parties' commercial purpose. In essence it requires the court to interpret the words of the contract in the light of their contractual and commercial context. The principles of the 'new' approach were set out by Lord Hoffmann in *Investors Compensation Scheme Ltd v West Bromwich Building Society* in a passage which seems now to be cited almost routinely in disputes about the interpretation of contracts.

'1. Interpretation is the ascertainment of the meaning which the document would convey to a reasonable person having all the background knowledge which would reasonably have been available to the parties in the situation in which they were at the time of the contract.

2. . . . [S]ubject to the restriction that it should have been reasonably available to the parties . . . [the background] includes absolutely anything which would have affected the way in which the language of the document would have been understood by a reasonable man . . .

3. The law excludes from the admissible background the previous negotiations of the parties and their declarations of subjective intent . . .

4. The meaning which a document (or any other utterance) would convey to a reasonable man is not the same thing as the meaning of its words . . . the meaning of the document is what the parties using those words against the relevant background would reasonably have been understood to mean . . .

5. The "rule" that words should be given their 'natural and ordinary meaning' reflects the common sense proposition that we do not easily accept that people have made linguistic mistakes, particularly in formal documents.

On the other hand, if one would nevertheless conclude from the background that something must have gone wrong with the language, the law does not require judges to attribute to the parties an intention which they plainly could not have had'[11].

The starting point is still that the words of the contract are given their ordinary, literal meaning, except where the context indicates that the words have a special technical meaning. However, it is recognised that words often take their meaning from the context in which they are used. This means, first, that the words of a particular term or clause must be set in the context of the contract as a whole: 'The words must be set in the landscape of the instrument as a whole'[12]. Then the contract must be construed against its factual context, or 'matrix of facts', as Lord Wilberforce put it[13]. As indicated in the extract from Lord Hoffmann's speech in the *Investors Compensation Scheme* case quoted above, this can include 'absolutely anything', subject only to the caveat that it must have been available to the parties at the time the contract was made so that it could have influenced the way they expressed themselves[14]. Thus the words of a contract may be judged against the background of previous dealings between the parties and of practices and customs in the particular trade or market. Evidence of the parties' prior negotiations is excluded, because, almost by definition, that does not indicate their final intention, as is evidence of each party's subjective intention and of the parties' subsequent conduct. However, none of these exclusions is absolute. Lord Hoffmann in *Investors Compensation Scheme*, referring to the exclusion of evidence of prior negotiations and subjective intention, observed that 'the boundaries of this exception are in some respects unclear'[15]. What is clear is that the court can take account of the parties' objective or purpose, and the contract will be interpreted so as to further rather than frustrate that purpose. Finally:

'The fact that a particular construction leads to a very unreasonable result must be a relevant consideration. The more unreasonable the result the more unlikely it is that the parties can have intended it, and if they do intend it the more necessary it is that they shall make that intention abundantly clear'[16].

To put it another way, there is a presumption that the parties are reasonable people and that they intend to make a reasonable contract. They can make an unreasonable contract if they wish to do so, but they will need to use clear words to convince the court that that is their intention. The court will seek a construction which makes 'business common sense'. '[I]f detailed semantic and syntactical analysis of words in a commercial contract is going to lead to a conclusion that flouts business common sense, it must be made to yield to business common sense'[17].

The result, as Lord Hoffmann has explained[18], is that words in legal documents are interpreted in much the same way that words are interpreted in ordinary language in everyday life. The approach is applied not only to contracts but to commercial documents generally. Thus, for instance, in *Mannai v Eagle Star* it was applied to interpret a notice to quit served under a lease. The tenant had mistakenly entered the wrong date in the notice, but it was otherwise clear what was intended, and sufficient notice was given to comply with the lease. The majority of the House of Lords refused to hold the notice invalid for what was a technical error.

There are, however, limits. The court 'must not try to divine the intention of the contract by speculating about the real intention of the parties'[19]. Similarly, Lord Mustill, in *Charter Reinsurance v Fagan,* said:

'There comes a point at which the court should remind itself that the task is to discover what the parties meant from what they have said, and that to force upon the words a meaning which they cannot fairly bear is to substitute for the bargains actually made one which the court believes could better have been made. That is an illegitimate role for a court. Particularly in the field of commerce, where the parties need to know what they must do and what they can insist on not doing. It is essential for them to be confident that they can rely on the court to enforce their contract according to its terms'[20].

Where the contractual language is clear, the court must apply it. Moreover, the 'commercial common sense' approach is not applicable in all cases. Lord Hoffmann recognised that –

'there are documents in which the need for certainty is paramount and [in relation to] which admissible background is restricted to avoid the possibility that the same background may have different meanings for different people according to their knowledge of the background'[21].

He cited documentary letters of credit[22] as an example. Similarly, where the meaning of a term in a standard form contract has been settled by precedent, the court will not easily reinterpret the term in the light of the circumstances of a particular case, the need for commercial certainty outweighing the interests of 'commercial common sense'[23].

'Commercial construction' has its critics. The identification of the purpose in order to interpret the contract may be said to be a circular process. One might as easily talk of identifying the purpose from the language used. The vagueness of the concept of the 'factual matrix' may be said to create uncertainty and increase the costs of litigation by encouraging litigants to explore the background to a transaction in the hope of finding evidence supporting their preferred interpretation of the contract. Sir Christopher Staughton, formerly a Lord Justice of Appeal of great commercial experience, commented on Lord Hoffmann's formulation in *Investors' Compensation Scheme*: 'It is hard to imagine a ruling more calculated to perpetuate the vast cost of commercial litigation[24].' Above all, the test may be said to be unpredictable. Judges who might all be considered to be commercially minded advocates of purposive, or common sense, interpretation are found in disagreement about what is the commercially sensible interpretation of a particular contract[25]. These criticisms notwithstanding, it is probably fair to say that 'a commercial construction is more likely to give effect to the intention of the parties. Words are . . . interpreted in the way in which a reasonable commercial person would construe them'[26]. In other words, one might say, such an approach is more likely than a strictly literal approach to give effect to the (legitimate) expectations of the parties.

1   Commercial Contracts and the Commercial Court [1984] LMCLQ 382 at 385; see also Staughton [1999] CLJ 303.
2   Per Lord Steyn in *Deutsche Genossenschaftsbank v Burnhope* [1995] 4 All ER 717 at 724.
3   Per Lord Hoffmann in *Investors Compensation Scheme Ltd v West Bromwich Building Society* [1998] 1 All ER 98 at 114.
4   [1998] 1 All ER 98 at 114.
5   See the comments of Lord Steyn in *Deutsche Genossenschaftsbank v Burnhope* [1995] 4 All ER 717 at 726, although Lord Steyn has also warned against pursuing the analogy too far: see *Mannai Investment Co Ltd v Eagle Star Life Assurance Co Ltd* [1997] 3 All ER 352 at 371–372.
6   Per Lord Steyn in *Mannai Investment Co Ltd v Eagle Star Life Assurance Co Ltd* [1997] 3 All ER 352 at 371–372.

7   Per Lord Diplock in *Antaios Cia Naviera SA v Salen Rederierna AB, The Antaios* [1985] AC 191 at 201.
8   [1971] 3 All ER 237.
9   [1974] AC 235, [1973] 2 All ER 39.
10   Its origins may be said to be much older: see eg the comments of Lord Blackburn in *River Wear Comrs v Adamson* (1877) 2 App Cas 743 at 763.
11   [1998] 1 All ER 98 at 114.
12   Per Lord Mustill in *Charter Reinsurance Co Ltd v Fagan* [1997] AC 313 at 384, [1996] 3 All ER 46 at 51.
13   *Prenn v Simonds* [1971] 3 All ER 237 at 239.
14   Not everyone agrees that the 'matrix' is as wide as this: see Staughton [1999] CLJ 303 at 307. In *Zoan v Rouamba* [2000] 2 All ER 620 the Court of Appeal refused to attribute to a consumer hiring a car knowledge that the agreement might be regulated by consumer credit legislation and knowledge of the provisions of that legislation. That information was therefore not part of the relevant 'matrix'. That information was 'available' but could not reasonably be expected to have been in the hirer's mind.
15   [1998] 1 All ER 98 at 115.
16   Lord Reid in *Schuler v Wickman Machine Tool Sales Ltd* [1974] AC 235 at 251, [1973] 2 All ER 39 at 45.
17   Lord Diplock in *Antaios Cia Naviera SA v Salen Rederierna AB, The Antaios* [1985] AC 191 at 201; see also *Miramar Maritime Corpn v Holborn Oil Trading Ltd* [1984] AC 676.
18   See his example in *Mannai Investment Co Ltd v Eagle Star Life Assurance Co Ltd* [1997] 3 All ER 352 at 375.
19   Lord Steyn in *Deutsche Genossenschaftsbank v Burnhope* [1995] 4 All ER 717 at 724.
20   [1996] 3 All ER 46 at 51.
21   *Mannai Investment Co Ltd v Eagle Star Life Assurance Co Ltd* [1997] 3 All ER 352 at 381.
22   See ch 34.
23   One might equally say that the settled meaning is a key part of the 'matrix of fact'.
24   [1999] CLJ 303 at 307.
25   See McMeel [1998] LMCLQ 382.
26   Lord Steyn in *Mannai Investment Co Ltd v Eagle Star Life Assurance Co Ltd* [1997] 3 All ER 352 at 372.

2.5.6   *The classification of terms*

The classification of a statement as a term of the contract is not conclusive of its legal effect. In order to decide what rights are available to the victim of a breach of contract, it is necessary to classify the term broken. In the modern law of contract, four categories of terms are recognised: warranties, conditions, innominate terms and fundamental terms. However, the Sale of Goods Act 1893[1] referred only to conditions and warranties, and, until relatively recently, it was assumed that all terms must be either conditions or warranties. Relying on the definitions in the Sale of Goods Act, the general law of contract[2] defined a condition as an important term, breach of which gives the innocent party the option to terminate the contract, or to affirm the contract, and, in either case, to claim damages. A warranty was a minor term: breach would never entitle the innocent party to terminate the contract but would only allow him to claim damages.

Two developments in the 1950s and 1960s challenged this rigid classification. In a series of cases the courts recognised the existence of fundamental terms: terms so important that any breach would amount to a total non-performance of the contract. Thus there was a breach of a fundamental term where a seller delivered goods of a wholly different kind from those required by the contract[3], or where the seller of a car delivered a vehicle whose engine was totally burned out and which was therefore incapable of independent propulsion[4]. The fundamental term was 'invented' by the courts as a means of controlling exclusion clauses, and in a series of cases it was held that an exclusion clause could never excuse liability for breach of a fundamental term. It is now clear that there is no general rule of law that an exclusion clause cannot cover breach of a fundamental term[5], although a court will generally be reluctant to construe an exclusion clause as covering breach of a fundamental term unless it does so in very clear and unambiguous terms. Exclusion clauses are now controlled by the Unfair Contract Terms Act 1977, but it seems that certain terms may still be regarded as 'fundamental'[6].

The second development involved recognition that the rigid division into conditions and warranties was capable of producing injustice. If a term was classified as a 'condition', any breach, even if its consequences were trivial, would entitle the innocent party to terminate the contract. In *Hong Kong Fir Shipping Co Ltd v Kawasaki Kisen Kaisha*[7] the Court of Appeal recognised an intermediate category of innominate terms. Remedies for breach of such terms would depend on the seriousness of the consequences of the breach. However, it is clear that despite the development of the innominate term, some terms will always be classified in advance as conditions. First, a term will be recognised as a condition if it has already been classified as such either by statute or by precedent; thus, for instance, the implied terms relating to goods in the Sale of Goods Act are all classified by the Act, most as conditions[8]. A term will also be classified as a condition, so that any breach will give rise to a right to terminate the contract, if, on the proper construction of the contract, it appears that that was the intention of the parties. Thus, for example, terms fixing time limits for performance in commercial contracts are generally regarded as conditions[9]. The flexibility of the innominate term allows the court to tailor the remedy to suit the seriousness of the breach. However, flexibility in contract law is generally achieved at the cost of certainty, so that where it is important that the innocent party should know his rights immediately in the event of a breach of contract, a term may be classified in advance as a warranty or condition.

The parties to a contract may attempt to define their rights by expressly classifying its terms. However, whilst the court must give effect to their intentions if the parties have defined the consequences of a breach, for instance by providing that a breach will give the innocent party the right to terminate the contract, the court will not necessarily be bound by the label attached to a term, so that even though a term is described as a 'condition' the court may hold that the parties did not intend that any breach of that term should entitle the innocent party to terminate the contract. The fact that classification of a term as a 'condition' would produce unreasonable results may weigh heavily against the its being so classified[10].

1   The same terminology is used in the 1979 Act: see 9.2.3.
2   Different terminology is used in some cases: for instance, in contracts of insurance: see 35.4.
3   Eg peas instead of beans: see *Chanter v Hopkins* (1838) 4 M&W 399.
4   *Karsales (Harrow) Ltd v Wallis* [1956] 2 All ER 866, [1956] 1 WLR 936, CA.
5   *Photo Productions Ltd v Securicor Transport Ltd* [1980] AC 827, [1980] 1 All ER 556, HL; UCTA, s 9. For an example see *Glebe Island Terminals Pty Ltd v Continental Seagram Pty Ltd* [1994] 1 Lloyd's Rep 213.
6   See *George Mitchell (Chesterhall) Ltd v Finney Lock Seeds Ltd* [1983] 2 AC 803, [1983] 2 All ER 737, HL.
7   [1962] 2 QB 26, [1962] 1 All ER 474, CA.
8   Sale of Goods Act 1979, ss 12(5A), 13(1A), 14(6) and 15(3) as amended. The classification does not apply in Scotland. Although most of the terms are conditions, the right of a non-consumer buyer to reject the goods and terminate the contract is restricted where the breach is slight: Sale of Goods Act 1979, s 15A. See 9.2.3; 12.2.
9   See eg *Bunge Corpn v Tradax Export SA* [1981] 2 All ER 513, [1981] 1 WLR 711; below 10.2.1.
10 *Schuler AG v Wickman Machine Tool Sales Ltd* [1974] AC 235, [1973] 2 All ER 39, HL.

2.6 Exclusion clauses

Amongst the most important of the express terms likely to be found in a commercial contract will be those which seek to exclude or restrict the liability of one or other of the parties for breach of contract. Such clauses are particularly common in standard terms. Between parties of equal bargaining power they may be perfectly acceptable, allowing the parties to allocate risks and plan their relationship. However, they are open to abuse when imposed by a party with stronger bargaining power on another with weaker bargaining power, particularly in consumer contracts. The potential for abuse was recognised by the common law, and the judges developed a number of ways of controlling exclusion and limitation clauses, in particular by applying stringent rules requiring the terms to be effectively incorporated into the contract, and by construing such clauses in a restrictive, sometimes artificial, way. The judicial techniques of control ultimately, however, proved inadequate, in particular because they concentrated on procedural, rather than substantive, considerations. Provided a clause was sufficiently clearly drafted and was effectively incorporated into the contract, the courts had no power at common law to strike it down. Moreover, the contortions necessary to control exclusions by these techniques often resulted in the law becoming distorted. The powers of the courts have therefore been supplemented by statutory powers, in the Unfair Contract Terms Act 1977 and the Unfair Terms in Consumer Contracts Regulations 1999, which do allow the court to attack such clauses directly and consider their substantive fairness. However, despite the extensive statutory powers to strike down exclusions and similar clauses now available to the courts the common law rules remain important.

2.6.1 *Incorporation*

In order to be effective, a contractual exclusion must be validly incorporated into the contract in question. The rules concerning the incorporation of contract terms generally, which were examined above[1], were largely developed in cases concerned with the effectiveness of exclusion and limitation clauses. However, despite innovatory developments such as the 'red hand' principle, the effectiveness of this technique is limited by the objective approach to consent: in particular, since a person who signs a contract is bound by all its terms, regardless of whether or not he has read and understood them[2], an exclusion clause in a signed document will almost always be incorporated[3].

1 See 2.5.2.
2 *L'Estrange v Graucob* [1934] 2 KB 394.
3 See 2.5.2.

2.6.2 *Construction*

The general rules of contract construction apply to exclusion clauses as to any other term. However, in order to restrict the effectiveness of exclusion clauses, the courts adopted a strict approach, construing exclusion and similar clauses *contra proferentem*, meaning that any ambiguities in the clause would be construed contrary to the interests of the party seeking to rely on it. In practice, this approach often resulted in the court straining to find ambiguity in order to restrict a clause.

Contractual liabilities are often strict, but a party may also be subject to negligence liabilities. For instance, a manufacturer of goods who sells direct to customers is potentially strictly liable on the contract of sale and in negligence for any failure to take care in the process of manufacture. The courts took the view that clear and unambiguous words were required to exclude liability for negligence. In particular, where a party was potentially liable on both strict and negligence bases, the court would construe a clause excluding or limiting liability as applying only to the strict liability unless it clearly referred to negligence[1]. Where a party could only incur liability in negligence, a clause should generally be construed as covering that liability, but this is not an absolute rule[2]. In *Hollier v Rambler Motors (AMC) Ltd*[3] a car left with a garage for repair was badly damaged in a fire and the car owner sued the garage. The garage's standard terms provided that 'the company is not responsible for damage caused by fire'. The garage could only be liable if it was found to be negligent; nevertheless, the court found that the clause did not cover damage caused by a negligent fire: in effect, it was interpreted as no more than a warning that the garage would only be liable if it was shown to be negligent[4].

In a similar way, clauses were construed so that an exclusion of 'warranties' would not exclude conditions[5], such as those in the Sale of Goods Act 1979 and an exclusion of liability for breach of implied terms would not exclude liability for breach of express terms[6].

As part of the attack on exclusion clauses, the courts developed the doctrine of fundamental breach[7] and in a line of cases the courts, especially the Court of Appeal under Lord Denning, held that where a party was guilty of a fundamental breach, so that effectively he had wholly failed to perform the contract, he could not rely on a clause excluding liability for breach[8]. In 1967 the House of Lords ruled that there was no absolute rule of law that a person guilty of a fundamental breach could not rely on an exclusion clause; the question depended on the proper construction of the clause: if it was clearly worded so as to cover the breach in question, it would be effective to protect the party in breach[9]. However, in later cases the Court of Appeal appeared to revert to its former position and it was not until the House of Lords' decision in *Photo Production Ltd v Securicor Transport Ltd*[10] that it was finally settled that a clearly worded exclusion clause can cover even a fundamental breach. The position is now effectively confirmed by statute[11]. However, it is likely that the courts will generally still be reluctant to hold that a clause excludes liability for a fundamental breach unless it is clearly worded[12].

The weaknesses of judicial control of contract terms are illustrated by the approach to the interpretation of exclusion clauses. The approach disguises the true reason for intervention: in the case of the fundamental breach doctrine the rationale of the doctrine became so lost that the doctrine became 'confused and aimless'[13]. Moreover, the approach was ultimately unable to control exclusions: provided the draftsman of a clause worded it clearly and widely enough, there was no scope for the court to cut it down.

The Unfair Contract Terms Act now allows the courts to attack exclusion clauses directly, by holding them to be unreasonable and therefore ineffective. In some of the most objectionable cases where exclusions might be used, the Act makes them wholly ineffective. There should therefore be less need for the courts to adopt strained interpretations of clauses in order to control them. On the other hand, the judicial techniques remain available. A party wishing to challenge the effectiveness of an exclusion, especially one not made wholly ineffective by the Unfair Contract Terms Act, can be expected to put forward every argument available, including that the clause was not incorporated into the contract and that it does not cover the breach in question.

1   See *White v John Warrwick & Co Ltd* [1953] 2 All ER 1021, [1953] 1 WLR 1285, CA.
2   *Alderslade v Hendon Laundry Ltd* [1945] KB 189, [1945] 1 All ER 244, CA.
3   [1972] 2 QB 71, [1972] 1 All ER 399, CA.
4   Strictly this ruling was obiter, as the clause was found not to have been incorporated into the contract.
5   *Baldry v Marshall* [1925] 1 KB 260, CA.
6   *Andrews Bros Ltd v Singer & Co Ltd* [1934] 1 KB 17, CA.
7   See 2.5.5.
8   See eg *Karsales (Harrow) Ltd v Wallis* [1956] 2 All ER 866, [1956] 1 WLR 936, CA.
9   *Suisse Atlantique Société d'Armement Maritime SA v Rotterdamsche Kolen Centrale NV* [1967] 1 AC 361, [1966] 2 All ER 61, HL.
10 [1980] AC 827, [1980] 1 All ER 556, HL.
11 Unfair Contract Terms Act 1977, s 9; see *Edmund Murray v BSP International Foundations Ltd* (1992) 33 Con LR 1. A variant of the fundamental breach rule applies in the form of the deviation doctrine in relation to contracts for carriage of goods by sea under which any deviation by the carrier from the agreed route deprives him of the protection of exclusions and limitations in the contract. A similar rule applies to contracts of bailment.
12 But see *Glebe Island Terminals Pty Ltd v Continental Seagram Pty Ltd* [1994] 1 Lloyds Rep 213, where a clause expressly stated to apply in a case of fundamental breach was upheld.
13 Trebilcock and Dewees, 'Judicial Control of Standard Form Contracts' in Burrows and Veljanowski (eds) *The Economic Approach to Law* (1981) pp 97–98.

2.6.3   *Statutory control*

One of the weaknesses of the common law techniques used for the control of exclusion clauses, exemplified by the fundamental breach doctrine, was their inability to distinguish between commercial contracts, in which exclusions might be perfectly acceptable as a means of allocating risks, and consumer contracts. As Lord Diplock observed:

> 'In commercial contracts negotiated between businessmen capable of looking after their own interests and deciding how risks inherent in the performance of various kinds of contract can most economically be borne (generally by insurance) it is, in my view, wrong to place a strained construction on words in an exclusion clause which are clear and fairly susceptible of one meaning only'[1].

The statutory controls on exclusion clauses in the Unfair Contract Terms Act 1977 and the Unfair Terms in Consumer Contracts Regulations 1999 do make such a distinction. In general terms, the 1977 Act provides greater protection to consumers than to business contractors, whilst the regulations only protect consumers dealing in their private capacity with businesses.

The regulations replace earlier regulations made in 1994 which were introduced to comply with an EC directive[2]. Ideally, the opportunity should have been taken to consolidate the new rules with those already contained in the 1977 Act. However, the directive had to be implemented in a relatively short time and, due to pressure on parliamentary time, the British government felt unable to undertake such a consolidation at the time of initial implementation in 1994. Unfortunately, the opportunity to rectify this mistake was not taken in 1999. As a result there are two separate but overlapping statutory regimes applicable to exclusion and similar clauses in contracts and, although the controls under the two regimes are broadly similar in many respects, there are subtle but important differences between them. Moreover, the common law remains relevant. When considering the effectiveness of an exclusion in future it will therefore be necessary to consider the common law rules, the effect of the 1977 Act and that of the 1999 regulations.

1 *Photo Productions Ltd v Securicor Transport Ltd* [1980] 1 All ER 556 at 568.
2 Directive 93/13/EEC.

2.6.4 *The Unfair Contract Terms Act*[1]

The Unfair Contract Terms Act 1977 creates a two-tier system for the regulation of exclusions, providing greater protection for consumers and those who are required to contract on another party's standard terms, than for businesses who may be better placed to guard their own interests. In addition, the Act only applies to exclusions of 'business liability', defined as liability for breach of an obligation or duty arising from anything done or to be done in the course of a business or from the occupation of business premises[2].

Certain types of contract are excluded from the Act's control[3]. These include: contracts of insurance and 'any contract so far as it relates to' the creation, transfer or termination of interests in land[4]; the creation, transfer or termination of intellectual property rights; the formation, dissolution or constitution of companies; and the creation and transfer of securities[5]. Such contracts are all regulated by other legislation. In addition, international supply contracts are excluded[6]: parties involved in international trade can probably protect their own interests, and the uncertainty created by the court's power to review exclusion clauses under the Act might undermine the international trading community's confidence in English law if the Act applied to such contracts.

1 The 1977 Act is not the only statutory control on exclusion clauses, but it is by far the most important, particularly in relation to commercial contracts.
2 Section 1(3). 'Business' includes the activities of professions, government departments, local and public authorities (s 14).
3 Schedule 1, para 1.
4 See *Electricity Supply Nominees Ltd v IAF Group plc* [1993] 3 All ER 372.
5 See *Micklefield v SAC Technology Ltd* [1991] 1 All ER 275.
6 Section 26.

2.6.4.1 *What types of terms are regulated?*

Despite its title, the 1977 Act does not apply a general test of fairness to contract terms. Its main purpose is to control contract terms and notices which seek to exclude liability. The main controls are contained in ss 2, 3, 5, 6 and 7. Section 2 applies to contract terms and notices which exclude or restrict liability for loss caused by negligence. Negligence includes not merely liability arising from a common law duty of care, such as that in tort, but also to liability arising from breach of a contractual duty to exercise reasonable care, such as that implied into contracts for services[1] and to liability for breach of the common duty of care imposed on occupiers of premises[2]. The effectiveness of the term depends on the nature of the loss suffered. Liability for personal injury or death caused by negligence cannot be excluded or restricted; liability for other types of loss can be excluded if the exclusion satisfies the requirement of reasonableness.

Sections 6 and 7 regulate contract terms which exclude (etc) liability for breach of the implied terms relating to the goods in supply contracts[3]. In general, the implied terms relating to title and the supplier's right to transfer ownership of the goods can never be excluded; exclusion of liability in respect of the other terms concerned with the goods themselves depends on the status of the buyer. If the buyer 'deals as a consumer', liability for breach of those terms cannot be excluded; where the buyer does not deal as a consumer, liability can be excluded provided the exclusion satisfies the requirement of reasonableness.

Section 3 provides that where a person makes a contract on his own standard terms of business, or with a consumer, he cannot by reference to any term in the contract exclude or restrict his liability for breach of contract or '(b) claim to be entitled (i) to render a contractual performance substantially different from that which was reasonably expected of him or (ii) in respect of the whole or any part of his contractual obligation, to render no performance at all' unless the clause is a fair and reasonable one to have been included in the contract. Section 3 may overlap with the other sections of the Act. It may, however, apply to a wide range of terms not covered by other provisions of the Act. Section 3(b) is particularly important. If given a wide reading it extends the reach of the 1977 Act to many of the types of term commonly found in standard form contracts such as clauses excluding liability for late delivery, or allowing a seller to deliver a greater or lesser quantity of goods than provided for in the contract. Similarly, force majeure clauses, which excuse a party from liability where he is unable to perform due to circumstances outside his control, or which extend the time for performance in such a case, are probably subject to s 3[4].

The key question in determining the ambit of s 3 is how is the 'contractual performance' reasonably expected of a contractor to be defined. Is the disputed term to be taken into account in defining that expectation? To take an example: if, say, a contract for the sale of goods quotes a delivery date and then provides that the seller may vary the delivery date, can the buyer 'reasonably expect' delivery on the quoted date, or can it be argued that, in view of the provision permitting variation, he cannot reasonably expect delivery then? In *Zockoll Group Ltd v Mercury Communications Ltd*[5] the Court of Appeal held that the court should first define the contractual performance reasonably expected without reference to the contract terms under challenge –

> 'for if it were held that [a contractor] could only reasonably expect such performance as it was strictly entitled to under the contract, there could never be a discrepancy between its reasonable expectations and [the other party's claim], and any term, if duly incorporated, would stand, however unfair it might be, so long as it was clear and unambiguous. This would frustrate the purpose of the legislation'[6].

This considerably widens the scope of the section. It must be borne in mind, however, that the section only applies where the term in question permits a contractor to render a contractual performance which is substantially different from that reasonably expected. It therefore remains open to the court to hold a term valid on the grounds either that the variation permitted is not substantial, or that the clause is reasonable.

Section 5 of the Act applies to exclusion clauses in manufacturers' guarantees, and provides that a term or notice in such a guarantee cannot exclude or restrict liability for any kind of loss or damage caused by goods of a type ordinarily supplied for private use or consumption which prove defective whilst in consumer use as a result of negligence in manufacture or distribution[7]. In some cases s 5 may overlap with s 2; however, where s 5 applies it will generally offer consumers greater protection than s 2, since s 5 prohibits exclusion of liability for any kind of loss.

The Act does not apply only to terms worded as exclusions of liability. Section 13 extends its scope to other types of contract term. Thus the Act applies to terms which:

(a) make a liability or its enforcement subject to restrictive or onerous conditions, such as terms requiring claims to be notified within a specified time;

(b) exclude or restrict any right or remedy, or subject a person to any prejudice in consequence of pursuing a remedy: for instance, a term providing that damages shall be limited to a specified maximum amount, or, in a sale of goods contract, providing that the seller will give no refunds; or

(c) exclude or restrict rules of evidence or procedure: for instance, by providing that a signature on a delivery note shall be conclusive evidence that goods were delivered in satisfactory condition, or that a bank's record of transactions shall be conclusive[8].

In addition, the courts have shown a tendency to interpret the Act purposively so as to prevent its evasion. Thus it has been held that a term requiring a buyer of goods and services to pay for them in full without set-off or deduction was subject to the Act where the buyer wished to make a set-off in respect of a claim for breach of contract by the supplier[9]. The effect of the clause was to exclude the buyers' *right* to set off their claim against sums due to the suppliers, to exclude the *remedy*, otherwise available, of enforcing their claim by means of a set-off and to exclude the procedural rules as to set-off[10]. This is an important decision: such clauses are common in commercial contracts. Their purpose is to require the buyer of goods or services to pay for them in full and pursue any claim he may have against the supplier in separate proceedings, thus giving the supplier the practical advantage in any negotiations of having received payment.

Clauses which purport to exclude the creation of a legal duty are in some cases covered by the Act: for instance, a clause providing that the terms implied by ss 12–15 of the Sale of Goods Act 1979 are excluded from the contract, would be caught by the Act. In *Harris v Wyre Forest District Council*[11] the House of Lords considered a disclaimer on a surveyors' report which indicated that the surveyors accepted no responsibility for its accuracy. Prior to the Act it had been held that such disclaimers could be effective to prevent a duty of care in negligence arising at all[12]. However, in this case the House of Lords held that the disclaimer was subject to the Act and, on the facts of the case, was unreasonable; the surveyors were therefore held liable.

The Act also seeks to prevent contractors evading its controls by using a secondary contract to impose restrictions on liability which would have been invalidated by the Act if contained in the primary contract. It provides that:

'A person is not bound by any contract term prejudicing or taking away rights of his which arise under, or in connection with the performance of, another contract, so far as those rights extend to the enforcement of another's liability which this Part of this Act prevents that other from excluding or restricting'[13].

This is a difficult provision to apply because its language is inconsistent with that of the rest of the Act[14]. In the only reported decision on the section it was held that it did not apply to agreements compromising existing contractual disputes and, moreover, that it would only apply to a tri-partite situation where the parties to the primary and secondary contracts are different[15]. Thus, for instance, a term in a manufacturer's guarantee of goods which sought to prevent a consumer buyer suing the retailer if the goods proved defective would be caught by the section. The language of the section seems equally applicable to cases where the parties to both contracts are the same, as, for instance, where a consumer who buys goods from a supplier enters into a second contract with the supplier for servicing of the goods and the second contract contains a term restricting the consumer's right to sue for breach of the main, supply contract. Arguably, the exclusion would, in any case, be subject to the Act without reference to s 10[16]; certainly it is to be hoped that a court would not allow the Act to be evaded by a secondary contract in such a case.

Certain types of indemnity clause are also regulated by the Act: a person dealing as consumer cannot be required to indemnify the other party to the contract against liability, whether to the consumer or any other person, for negligence or breach of contract, unless the indemnity clause is reasonable[17]. As against a person dealing other than as a consumer, an indemnity may fall outside the Act. A term in a contract between A and B which requires B to indemnify A against liability to C is not caught by the Act[18]; however, if the clause operates to require B to indemnify A against liability to B himself, the clause has the same effect as an exclusion of liability and is subject to the reasonableness test[19].

The Act does not apply to arbitration clauses[20] but such clauses are subject to control under the Arbitration Act 1996 and Unfair Terms in Consumer Contracts Regulations 1999[21].

---

1   Supply of Goods and Services Act 1982, s 13; below 19.1.
2   Under the Occupiers' Liability Act 1957.
3   Sale of Goods Act 1979, ss 12–15; Supply of Goods and Services Act 1982, ss 2–5 and 7–10; Supply of Goods (Implied Terms) Act 1973, ss 8–11; below ch 11.
4   Force majeure clauses are probably more likely to be held to be reasonable than simple exclusions of liability.
5   [1998] EMLR 385.
6   Per Lord Bingham MR at 395.
7   See 13.1; 13.2.1.
8   See s 13.
9   *Stewart Gill v Horatio Myer Ltd* [1992] QB 600, [1992] 2 All ER 257; see also *Fastframe Ltd v Lohinski* (3 March 1993, unreported) noted (1994) 57 MLR 960. See also *Connaught Restaurants Ltd v Indoor Leisure* [1994] 4 All ER 834; *BOC Group v Centeon LLC* [1999] 1 All ER (Comm) 970. A clause excluding rights of set-off will not necessarily be unreasonable: see eg *Schenkers Ltd v Overland Shoes Ltd* [1998] 1 Lloyd's Rep 498; *WRM Group Ltd v Wood* [1998] CLC 189.
10 Per Lord Donaldson MR at 260.
11 [1990] 1 AC 831, [1989] 2 All ER 514.
12 *Hedley Byrne & Co Ltd v Heller & Partners Ltd* [1964] AC 465.
13 Section 10.
14 See Treitel, *The Law of Contract* (10th edn, 1999) p 239.
15 *Tudor Grange Holdings Ltd v Citibank NA* [1992] Ch 53, [1991] 4 All ER 1; see Brown (1992) 108 LQR 223.
16 Per Browne-Wilkinson V-C, [1991] 4 All ER 1 at 13.
17 Section 4.
18 *Thompson v T Lohan (Plant Hire) Ltd* [1987] 2 All ER 631.
19 *Phillips Products Ltd v Hyland* [1987] 2 All ER 620, [1987] 1 WLR 659n, CA.
20 Section 13(2).
21 Arbitration Act 1996, ss 89–91: below 36.2.3.7.

2.6.4.2 *Dealing as a consumer*

As we have noted, one of the crucial distinctions drawn by the Unfair Contract Terms Act is between persons who deal as consumers and others.

A person deals as a consumer if three conditions are satisfied:

(a) he neither makes, nor holds himself out as making, the contract in the course of a business;
(b) the other party does make the contract in the course of a business; and
(c) where the contract involves the supply of goods, the goods are of a type ordinarily supplied for private use or consumption[1].

A buyer in a sale by auction or by competitive tender is deemed not to deal as a consumer. In other cases the burden of proof is placed upon the person seeking to rely on the exclusion clause to show that the other party did not deal as a consumer.

The key to consumer status is 'dealing in the course of a business'. It should be noted that the emphasis is not on the contractor's general status but on its status in the particular contract[2]. In *R&B Customs Brokers Ltd v UDT Finance Ltd*[3] the plaintiff was a small company operating the business of shipping brokers. It was owned and managed by a husband and wife and ran a car for their business and private use. The company contracted to buy a second-hand Colt Shogun motor car from the defendant finance company under a conditional sale agreement. The car proved defective and the plaintiff sought to reject it. A clause in the contract excluded the implied conditions that the car should be of merchantable quality and fit for the buyer's purpose[4], but provided that it should not apply where the buyer dealt as a consumer within the definition of the 1977 Act; it would, in any case, have been ineffective against such a person under the Act by virtue of s 6. The defendant argued that the plaintiff was not dealing as a consumer, since the car was bought in the course of the plaintiff company's business. In one sense this was clearly correct, otherwise the purchase would have been ultra vires the company. However, the Court of Appeal held that the plaintiff company was dealing as a consumer, and not in the course of a business. Following decisions on the meaning of 'in the course of a business' in cases under the Trade Descriptions Act[5], it held that a contract would only be made 'in the course of a business' if it was an integral part of the business, or if there was a degree of regularity of similar transactions. A one-off purchase with a view to resale in the course of trade could be in the course of business, but on the facts of the case, where the plaintiff had bought only two or three cars on similar terms, the purchase of a car was not 'integral' and there was insufficient regularity.

The result is surprising, and the decision seems to have some unfortunate consequences. The emphasis on 'regularity' of similar transactions introduces an element of uncertainty into this area of the Act; this is particularly undesirable, since it is a criminal offence to display a notice or contract term rendered ineffective as against a person dealing as a consumer by s 6 of the 1977 Act[6]. Moreover, the decision appears to open a gap between the protection offered to consumers by s 5 and the other sections of the 1977 Act. Under s 5, a clause in a guarantee is ineffective if the goods prove defective whilst in 'consumer use', defined as meaning use other than exclusively for the purposes of a business: thus if the car in *R&B* had been used only for the purposes of the company, it would not have been in 'consumer use' for the purposes of s 5, but the company would still have bought as a 'consumer' for the purposes of s 6 and s 3.

The decision could also cause problems if a company such as the plaintiff in *R&B* resold the car. Presumably, the company would not be acting in the course of a business then, so that anyone buying the car could not be regarded as 'dealing as a consumer'. In any case, since the 1977 Act only applies to exclusions of 'business liability' it would have no impact on any exclusion or limitation clause included in the contract of sale.

It would seem preferable in a case such as *R&B* to regard the company as buying in the course of a business and then consider the reasonableness of the clause, taking into account the company's lack of expertise and bargaining power. Dillon LJ, obiter, thought that in that case the clause would have been reasonable, stressing that the defendant finance company had never seen the car. It is submitted, however, that this need not necessarily be the case and in subsequent cases the courts have held similar exclusions by finance companies to be unreasonable[7].

As noted above, the court in *R&B* based its decision on decisions interpreting the phrase 'in the course of a business' in other legislation. The same phrase also appears in s 14 of the Sale of Goods Act 1979, under which the implied terms requiring the goods supplied to be of satisfactory quality and fit for their purpose only apply where the seller sells in the course of a business[8]. In *Stevenson v Rogers*[9] a fisherman sold a trawler. It was argued, on the basis of *R&B* and similar cases, that the sale was not in the course of a business so that the implied quality term did not apply. The Court of Appeal rejected that argument and, distinguishing *R&B* and the cases it followed, held that there is no requirement of regularity for a sale to be in the course of a business under the Sale of Goods Act. The court concluded that a sale is 'in the course of a business' under that Act whenever it is otherwise than a purely private transaction.

The court in *Stevenson* based its decision on the legislative history of the Sale of Goods Act provisions. Strictly speaking, therefore, *R&B* remains good law on the interpretation of 'in the course of a business' in the 1977 Act. It is questionable, however, whether *R&B* can stand with *Stevenson*. There is much to be said for treating the Sale of Goods Act and Unfair Contract Terms Act, which, amongst other things regulates attempts to exclude the Sale of Goods Act implied terms, as a single legislative code. Indeed, the phrase 'in the course of a business', which now appears in s 14 of the Sale of Goods Act, first appeared in the Supply of Goods (Implied Terms) Act 1973, which also introduced restrictions on exclusion of the implied terms, the predecessor of the controls which now appear in s 6 of the 1977 Act. Both provisions had their origins in the same Law Commission report[10]. In any event, so long as both decisions remain good law, difficult questions may arise. The question in *R&B* was whether the buyer acted in the course of a business under the 1977 Act, in *Stevenson* whether the seller did so under the 1979 Act. However, the seller's status is also relevant under the 1977 Act, and the buyer's is relevant for certain purposes under the 1979 Act. It is not clear which test is to be applied to determine the seller's status under the 1977 Act or the buyer's under the 1979.

It therefore seems likely that in due course either *R&B* or *Stevenson* will have to be reconsidered, and it is submitted that it is *R&B* which should go. Whilst on its particular facts it widened the scope of consumer protection, application of its reasoning in other contexts would have the opposite effect. Adoption of the *Stevenson* test would also have the beneficial effect of narrowing the gap between the scope of the 1977 Act and the Unfair Terms in Consumer Contracts Regulations, under which the buyer in *R&B* could never be a consumer[11]. One beneficial effect of the *R&B* decision should, however, be noted. The extended meaning of 'consumer' widens the ambit of s 3 of the 1977 Act. That section, it will be recalled, protects a person who deals either as a consumer or on the other party's written standard terms of business. Suppose that a small business, A, deals with a larger one, B. B instructs its solicitors to prepare a contract which it presents to A on a 'take it or leave it' basis. The terms of the contract may – indeed very probably will – favour B, maybe unfairly so, but the contract cannot be said to be on B's written standard terms of business. The effect of *R&B* is that in some circumstances it may be possible to regard A as dealing as a consumer, and therefore invoke the reasonableness test in the Unfair Contract Terms Act, s 3 so as to give A a measure of protection.

For the present, *R&B* remains good law. Its effect is somewhat limited by the third limb of the definition of 'consumer', which requires that in a contract for the supply of goods, the goods should be of a kind ordinarily supplied for private use or consumption. However, businesses may buy many items which are also commonly supplied for private use, such as motor cars, office furniture, and stationery. On the other hand, problems may arise at the other end of the scale where an individual buys goods for private use. The courts must take account of changing fashions and patterns of social behaviour. Many 'business' items are increasingly bought for private use: for instance, industrial shelving and the like were fashionable as furniture a few years ago; similarly, office and DIY equipment which in the past might have been bought only by businesses is now commonly bought by individuals for private use.

1 Section 12.
2 The Court of Appeal appears to have overlooked this in *St Albans City and District Council v International Computers Ltd* [1996] 4 All ER 481, where it concluded that since the plaintiff was a local authority it could not be a consumer. The court failed to consider whether the authority was dealing as a consumer in the particular transaction. In view of the comments below, this may have produced the right decision.
3 [1988] 1 All ER 847, [1988] 1 WLR 321, CA. See also *Rasbora Ltd v JCL Marine Ltd* [1977] 1 Lloyd's Rep 645 and *Peter Symons & Co v Cook* (1981) 131 NLJ 758.
4 Under ss 14(2) and (3) of the Sale of Goods Act 1979; below 11.2; 11.3. The first term now requires goods to be of satisfactory quality.
5 *Davies v Sumner* [1984] 3 All ER 831, [1984] 1 WLR 1301; *Havering London Borough v Stevenson* [1970] 3 All ER 609.
6 Consumer Transactions (Restriction On Statements) Order 1976, SI 1976/1813.
7 *Lease Management Services Ltd v Purnell Secretarial Services Ltd* [1994] CCLR 127; *Sovereign Finance Ltd v Silver Crest Furniture* [1997] CCLR 76.
8 See 11.2.1.
9 [1999] 1 All ER 613; see de Lacey (1999) 62 MLR 776; MacDonald (1999), 3 Web JCL 1.
10 *Exclusion Clauses in Contracts (Amendments to the Sale of Goods Act 1893)* Law Com 24, which in turn drew on the report of the Moloney Committee on Consumer Protection (Cmnd 1787).
11 Below 2.6.5.1.

2.6.4.3 *Written standard terms*

Section 3 of the 1977 Act applies in favour of a person who in making a contract deals as a consumer or on the other party's 'written standard terms' of business. The section was clearly intended to help guard against the abuses of standard form contracts. However, the Act deliberately avoids defining 'written standard terms of business': the Law Commission had advised that any attempt at a definition might enable businesses to avoid the definition[1].

The better view seems to be that the expression should be given a wide interpretation to include both terms prepared by or for an individual business and those prepared for a particular trade by or under the auspices of a trade association or similar body, provided that those terms are regularly used by the contractor seeking to rely on them[2].

The section does not require that the contract in question be made in writing, but only that it be made on one party's written standard terms. It would seem, therefore, that it would apply where terms are incorporated into an oral contract by reference, or on the basis of a course of dealing, provided only that the terms are written down somewhere. The equivalent provision which applies in Scotland was considered by the court in *McCrone v Boots Farm Sales Ltd*[3]. The relevant section refers to 'standard form contract', which Lord Dunpark said includes 'any contract whether wholly written or partly oral which includes a set of fixed terms or conditions which the proposer applies, without material alteration, to contracts of the kind in question'[4]. Expressions such as 'standard form contract' and 'written standard terms' are often used more or less interchangeably and it may be that the two expressions are intended to have the same meaning. In *McCrone* it was held that the Scottish provision applied where the contract was on the defendants' standard terms which had been incorporated into the contract by a course of dealing; if anything, it would seem easier to reach the same result under the English provision with its reference to 'written standard terms'.

A standard form may be used as the basis for a contract in a number of ways. In the simplest case, one party puts forward its standard terms and the other accepts them, voluntarily, inadvertently or through economic necessity. In other cases, one party may put forward its standard terms as a basis for negotiation. A further possibility is that the party putting forward the standard terms himself amends them to suit the particular transaction: for instance, by including a special exclusion clause. Do such arrangements fall within the scope of s 3? The extensive use of word processors facilitates such variation. In fact, even contracts on standard terms will often contain some terms which are specifically agreed – for example, terms dealing with matters such as delivery dates, price etc. It seems clear that inclusion of express terms to cover such matters cannot be sufficient to take a contract outside the ambit of s 3 if it is concluded using a set of otherwise standard, pre-printed terms. In so far as Lord Dunpark's comments in *McCrone* go to the question whether the terms were standard, they appear to be equally applicable to s 3. More recent English authority suggested that where the parties use a set of standard terms as a basis for negotiation and make alterations to suit the particular case, the resulting contract may fall outside the ambit of s 3[5]. In *Salvage Association v CAP Financial Services Ltd*[6] the judge suggested that the following factors should be considered in order to decide if terms were one party's 'standard' terms:

(a) the degree of consideration given to them by the other party;
(b) the degree to which the terms were imposed;
(c) the relative bargaining strength of the parties;
(d) the willingness of the proponent of the terms to negotiate;
(e) the extent and nature of the alterations; and
(f) the extent and duration of the negotiations.

This is, however, not especially helpful. With the exception of (e), these all seem to be matters which would go to the reasonableness of the inclusion of the term. In *St Albans City and DC v International Computers Ltd*[7] the parties contracted for the supply of a computer system. The defendants put forward their standard terms as a basis for negotiation but, as the trial judge found, the terms 'remained effectively untouched by the negotiations'. The Court of Appeal held that the fact that there had been negotiations did not prevent the contract being on the defendants' written standard terms if the result of the negotiations was that those terms were incorporated, largely unamended. As the court emphasised, the crucial question is whether the party challenging the terms 'deals' – ie contracts – on the other's written standard terms. This seems correct in principle. The willingness of the party putting forward the terms to negotiate should be considered in relation to reasonableness. However, *St Albans* leaves unanswered the more difficult question whether the contract would have been held to be on the defendants' written standard terms if the terms had been amended as a result of the negotiations. It seems that this must be a matter of degree.

1   Law Commission report on Exemption Clauses, Law Comm no 69, para 157.
2   *British Fermentation Products Ltd v Compair Reavell Ltd* [1999] 2 All ER (Comm) 389.
3   1981 SLT 103.
4   1981 SLT at 105.
5   *Flamar Interocean Ltd v Denmac Ltd, The Flamar Pride* [1990] 1 Lloyd's Rep 434.
6   (9 July 1993, unreported).
7   [1996] 4 All ER 481; affg [1985] FSR 686; see (1995) 58 MLR 585.

2.6.4.4 *Reasonableness*

Although the Act invalidates certain exclusion clauses, many are subjected to a test of reasonableness: such exclusions will be effective if they satisfy the 'reasonableness test'. The Act provides some guidance as to how reasonableness is to be assessed, which applies not only to clauses caught by the 1977 Act but also to clauses excluding liability for misrepresentation, which are subjected to a reasonableness test under s 3 of the Misrepresentation Act 1967[1].

A person who asserts that a clause is reasonable must prove that it is[2]. In relation to notices which have no contractual effect, the question is whether it is fair and reasonable to allow reliance on the notice having regard to all the circumstances at the time that liability arose, or would have arisen if not for the notice. However, in relation to contract terms, the question is whether the term was a fair and reasonable one to have included in the contract, having regard to circumstances which were, or ought reasonably to have been, known to the parties at the time the contract was made[3]. In the important case of *Stewart Gill Ltd v Horatio Myer Ltd*[4] the Court of Appeal emphasised that the assessment of reasonableness must be made as at the time the contract was made: the question is whether the term itself, not reliance on it, is reasonable. The court must therefore evaluate the clause as a whole; it cannot 'sever' unreasonable parts of a clause so as to leave the remainder enforceable. 'The issue is whether "the term [the whole term and nothing but the term] is a fair and reasonable one to be included" '[5]. Thus where a clause was capable of unreasonable application it failed the reasonableness test and could not be relied on[6].

Where liability is restricted by reference to a sum of money, the reasonableness of that restriction must be considered. Regard is to be had (i) to the resources available to the party relying on the term for the purposes of meeting the potential liability and (ii) how far it was open to him to protect himself by insurance[7]. As a general rule, clauses which limit liability are more likely to be considered reasonable than those which wholly exclude liability. Evidence of the availability to the party in breach of insurance cover against liability will be highly relevant to the reasonableness of the limitation. For instance, in *Salvage Association v CAP*[8] a clause limiting liability to £25,000 was held unreasonable when the party relying on the clause had indemnity insurance of £5,000,000.

Schedule 2 to the 1977 Act contains further guidelines. Strictly, they are only required to be used in assessing reasonableness under ss 6 and 7 of the Act, ie in relation to clauses excluding liability for breach of the implied terms in supply contracts. However, the courts are likely to consider the guidelines in other cases[9]. They include the following factors:

(a) The relative strengths of the parties' bargaining positions, taking into account alternative means by which the customer's requirements might be met.
(b) Whether the customer received any inducement to agree the term, or in accepting it had an opportunity of entering into a similar contract with any other person without accepting a similar term. In *Woodman v Photo Trade Processing*[10] a county court judge held a clause in a contract for the processing of a roll of photographic film unreasonable. The clause provided that, in the event of loss, the developer's liability should be limited to the cost of replacement of the unprocessed film; the customer was claiming damages because the film contained pictures of a family wedding. The court was influenced by the fact that the customer had little choice: few film processors accepted greater liability than the defendants. The industry code of practice urged processors to offer a two-tier service whereby the processor would accept greater liability on payment of an increased price.
(c) Whether the customer knew or ought reasonably to have known of the existence and extent of the term. The mere fact that the supplier has taken reasonable steps to bring the term to the customer's notice and thus satisfied the common law requirements for incorporation of the term into the contract does not mean that the customer 'ought reasonably' to know its existence and extent. The common law applies an objective test of consent[11]. The Act here looks to the reality of that consent. Thus terms in small print, or in difficult language, may be less likely to be held reasonable. In *The Zinnia*[12] Staughton J was tempted to hold exclusions unreasonable because 'first they are in such small print that one can barely read them; secondly, the draftsmanship is so convoluted and prolix that one almost needs an LLB to understand them'[13]. Similarly, although a clause in a signed document may be incorporated into the contract despite the customer not having read the document, if the other party knows that fact, the term may be considered unreasonable.
(d) Where the term excludes or restricts liability unless some condition is complied with, whether it was reasonable at the time of the contract to expect that compliance with that condition would be practicable. In *RW Green v Cade Bros Farms*[14] a clause in a contract for the sale of seed potatoes required the buyer to notify the seller of complaints within three or seven days of delivery. It was held that the clause was unreasonable: many defects would not be apparent until the crop had been harvested.
(e) Whether the goods were manufactured, processed or adapted to the special order of the customer.

In cases involving consumers, it seems likely that the courts will apply the reasonableness test stringently. In *Lally v Bird*[15] a clause in a removal contract which limited liability to a specified amount per item was held unreasonable. In commercial contracts between parties of equal bargaining power, the courts might be expected to uphold exclusions and allow risks to be allocated between the parties, and, indeed, such an approach appeared to be approved by the decision in *Photo Productions Ltd v Securicor*. In *W Green v Cade Bros Farms* the contract also contained a clause limiting damages to the contract price: this was held reasonable. However, in the leading case of *George Mitchell (Chesterhall) Ltd v Finney Lock Seeds Ltd*[16] a different approach is apparent. A seed supplier contracted to supply Dutch winter cabbage seed under a contract which limited the seller's liability to the contract price. The seed turned out to be a wholly different and inferior type, and the crop had to be ploughed in, resulting in a considerable loss of profit for the plaintiff. The House of Lords, overruling the Court of Appeal, held that the clause did cover the breach; however, it would be unreasonable to allow reliance on it. The buyers were found to be aware of the term and, although the term had not been negotiated, but had been drafted by the seed supplier's trade association, the National Farmers' Union had not objected to it. The crucial factors in deciding that the clause was unreasonable were that: (a) the breach had been the result of negligence by the sellers; (b) it was possible for seed suppliers to insure against such claims; and (c) when similar claims had arisen in the past the sellers had adopted a practice of settling the claims without seeking to rely on the clause[17]. This approach –

'surprises and disturbs some academics, [but] it surely will horrify commercial contractors . . . It undermines one of the law of contract's supposedly primary functions, namely the facilitation of the planning of transactions and business relationships'[18].

1 See 2.4.2.
2 Section 11(5).
3 Section 11(1). This was the test favoured by the Scottish Law Commission. The English Law Commission advocated a test which would judge whether it was reasonable to allow reliance on the clause.
4 [1992] QB 600, [1992] 2 All ER 257.
5 Per Lord Donaldson MR [1992] 2 All ER 257 at 261.
6 See *Thos Witter Ltd v TBP Industries Ltd* [1996] 2 All ER 573 where a clause excluding liability for misrepresentation was held unreasonable because it purported to exclude liability for fraudulent misrepresentation.
7 Section 11(4).
8 (9 July 1993, unreported). See also *St Albans City and District Council v International Computers Ltd* [1995] FSR 686, (1995) 58 MLR 585.
9 See eg *Gill v Myer* [1992] QB 600, [1992] 2 All ER 257; *Flamar Interocean Ltd v Denmac Ltd, The Flamar Pride* [1990] 1 Lloyd's Rep 434.
10 (17 May 1981, unreported), cited in (1981) 131 NLJ 935.
11 *AEG (UK) Ltd v Logic Resource Ltd* [1996] CLC 265; Bradgate (1997) 60 MLR 582.
12 [1984] 2 Lloyd's Rep 211.
13 [1984] 2 Lloyd's Rep 211 at 222.
14 [1978] 1 Lloyd's Rep 602; see also *Rees-Hough Ltd v Redland Reinforced Plastics* (1984) 1 Const LJ 67.
15 (23 May 1980, unreported).
16 [1983] 2 AC 803, [1983] 2 All ER 737.
17 Contrast *Schenkers Ltd v Overland Shoes Ltd* [1998] 1 Lloyd's Rep 498, where a similar practice of settling claims without relying on an exclusion clause was held to be part of the 'give and take conducive to good business' and did not preclude reliance on the clause in the particular case.
18 Adams and Brownsword, 'The Unfair Contract Terms Act: A Decade of Discretion' (1988) 104 LQR 94 at 118.

2.6.5   *The Unfair Terms in Consumer Contracts Regulations 1994*

The Unfair Terms in Consumer Contracts Regulations 1999[1] came into force on 1 October 1999 and apply to contracts made after that date. The regulations are intended to implement the 1993 EC Directive on 'Unfair Terms in Consumer Contracts'[2]. The directive was introduced under art 100A of the Treaty of Rome, in order to assimilate the laws of member states on the protection of consumers and thus encourage consumers to take advantage of the single market, whilst maintaining a high level of consumer protection[3].

Member states were required to implement the directive by 31 December 1994. Initially, it was implemented in the UK by the Unfair Terms in Consumer Contracts Regulations 1994[4], made under s 2(2) of the European Communities Act 1972. On the whole, the 1994 regulations followed the text of the directive almost verbatim. There were, however, some small, but significant, differences between the wording of the two instruments and in some respects, as a result, the 1994 regulations did not properly implement the directive. The 1999 regulations are intended to reflect more accurately the text of the directive. Whilst this minimises any risk of the UK being found to have failed properly to implement the directive, it is in some respects regrettable because there are areas in which the directive is unclear and clarification would have been helpful. Such clarification will now be a matter for the courts.

Of course, in the UK the Unfair Contract Terms Act 1977 already provided consumers with protection against some types of unfair contract term prior to 1994. It would have been better if the directive had been implemented by amending the 1977 Act. Instead, the 1994 regulations left the 1977 Act in place unamended[5]. The result is two overlapping, but different, sets of controls over unfair terms, creating 'a situation of nightmarish complexity in an area . . . where simple and "user friendly" rules should be the order of the day'[6]. The original motive was no doubt the need to implement the directive within a relatively short time. It is regrettable, however, that the opportunity was not taken to consolidate the two regimes when the regulations were replaced in 1999.

The fact that the 1977 Act remains in force is significant because the directive prescribes a minimum level of protection for consumers but permits member states to provide higher levels of consumer protection[7] and, although, arguably, the regulations apply to a wider range of terms than the Act, the Act offers wider protection in other respects: for instance because its definition of 'consumer' is wider than that in the regulations and because the regulations only apply to standard term contracts.

As noted above, the wording of the 1999 regulations follows very closely that of the directive. There are, nevertheless, some small differences between the two. It is clear that any court applying the regulations will endeavour to interpret them in accordance with and so as to give effect to the directive[8], and the regulations must therefore be construed in the light of the directive[9].

1   SI 1999/2083.
2   Directive 93/13/EEC (OJ L 95 21/4/93). For a description of the background to the directive see Duffy [1993] JBL 67.
3   See the Commission's explanatory memorandum to the directive.
4   SI 1994/3159; see generally Howells and Brownsword [1995] JBL 243. The regulations were made on 8 December 1994, but did not come into force until 1 July 1995. The reason for the delay seems to have been a desire to provide a transitional period during which businesses could adjust their contracts to conform to the regulations. Strictly, therefore, there was a failure properly to implement the directive.
5   Other member states also had existing legislation. The directive is closely based on the existing German law.

6 See Reynolds (1994) 110 LQR 1.
7 Article 8.
8 *Litster v Forth Dry Dock and Engineering Ltd* [1990] 1 AC 546.
9 The directive itself cannot be relied on in litigation before a UK court except against those contractors who may be regarded as subject to the authority or control of the state. In so far as the regulations fail properly to implement the directive, a consumer who suffers loss as a result of the failure may be able to bring a claim for damages against the UK government under the principle of *Francovich and Bonifaci v Italy* [1992] IRLR 84.

2.6.5.1 *Scope of the regulations*

The regulations apply to any contract concluded between a 'seller or supplier' and 'consumer' as defined, subject to certain exclusions.

'Consumer' is defined for the purposes of the regulations as 'a natural person who, in contracts covered by these Regulations, is acting for purposes which are outside his trade, business or profession'[1]. This is a narrower definition than that in the 1977 Act[2], since it clearly excludes corporations: thus the buyer in *R & B Customs Brokers*[3] would not be a 'consumer' for the purposes of the regulations. The status of partnerships is unclear: it seems that in civil law jurisdictions they would not be regarded as 'natural persons' but a common law interpretation of the expression would include partnerships and, since there is no reason why the regulations should not give greater protection than the directive, partnerships could be protected by the regulations. However, the expression 'purposes which are outside his . . . business' is wider than the equivalent requirement in the Unfair Contract Terms Act that a purchase not be 'in the course of a business'[4] and will probably take most partnership contracts outside the regulations. It is not clear if the Regulations apply where a contract is made partly for private and partly for business purposes, or where a natural person purports to be acting for business purposes, as, for example, where a business proprietor buys goods for private use using a cheque drawn on a business account.

'Seller or supplier' for the purposes of the regulations means 'any natural or legal person who, in contracts covered by these Regulations, is acting for purposes relating to his trade, business or profession, whether publicly owned or privately owned'[5]. This is considerably changed from the definition in the 1994 regulations, which defined 'seller' as 'a person who sells goods'[6] and thus created the impression that the regulations only applied to contracts for the supply of goods or services to a consumer. Such a restriction was not justified by the text of the directive[7], but led to considerable discussion about such issues as whether the regulations could apply to contracts for the sale of land. Such issues should now be put beyond doubt. In effect, 'seller or supplier' is shorthand for 'business contractor' or, perhaps, 'trader'.

Again, there is a difference between the regulations and the 1977 Act. The Act only applies where the supplier makes the contract in question '*in the course of* a business'[8]. Suppose, therefore, that a business sells off one of its old vehicles or a piece of equipment. It will be a 'seller' for the purposes of the regulations. The application of the 1977 Act will depend on the interpretation of 'in the course of a business'. If that phrase is interpreted as in *R&B Customs Brokers Ltd v UDT Finance Ltd*[9], the sale will not be 'in the course of a business' and the 1977 Act will therefore not apply. If, however, 'in the course of a business' is interpreted as in *Stevenson v Rogers*[10], any transaction other than a purely private one is 'in the course of a business' and the sale will be subject to both the regulations and the 1977 Act.

The regulations do not apply to:

'contractual terms which reflect —
(a) mandatory statutory or regulatory provisions (including such provisions under the law of any Member State or in Community legislation having effect in the United Kingdom without further enactment); or
(b) the provisions or principles of international conventions to which the Member States of the Community are party'[11].

This last exclusion is a little obscure but it seems that the intention is that terms prescribed by law should not be considered unfair. The recitals to the directive also state that contracts relating to employment, succession rights, rights under family law and contracts relating to the incorporation and management of companies or partnership agreements are also to be excluded from the directive, but there is no provision to this effect in the text of the directive. The 1994 regulations expressly excluded such contracts from their scope. There is no such exclusion in the 1999 regulations. It is submitted, however, that the regulations should be interpreted in the light of the directive, including the recitals, and that such contracts are intended to be outside the scope of the regulations on the grounds that they are not 'consumer contracts'. On the other hand, it should be noted that, unlike the 1977 Act, the regulations do not exclude contracts of insurance or contracts relating to interests in land[12].

1   Regulation 3(1). The 1994 regulations referred to 'a natural person who, in making a contract to which these Regulations apply, is acting for purposes which are outside his business'. The text of the 1999 regulations is identical to that of the directive. It is submitted, however, that in so far as it creates the impression that a person's status as consumer or otherwise depends on his status in contracts generally, rather than in relation to the particular contract in question, it is misleading and the 1994 wording was to be preferred.
2   Unfair Contract Terms Act, s 12; see 2.6.4.2.
3   [1988] 1 All ER 847, [1988] 1 WLR 321, CA.
4   Unfair Contract Terms Act 1977, s 12.
5   Regulation 3(1).
6   SI 1994/3159, reg 2(1).
7   See art 2(c).
8   Unfair Contract Terms Act 1977, s 12(1).
9   [1988] 1 All ER 847, [1988] 1 WLR 321, CA see above 2.6.4.2.
10 [1999] 1 All ER 613.
11 Regulation 4(2).
12 It was argued that such contracts were excluded from the 1994 regulations because of the reference to 'goods' in the definition of 'seller': see Bright and Bright (1995) 111 LQR 658; cf Dean (1993) 56 MLR 581. In view of the corrected definition of seller in the 1999 regulations it seems clear that such contracts are now subject to the Regulations.

2.6.5.2   *Unfair terms*

The regulations seek to control terms in contracts between sellers or suppliers and consumers in two ways. The main substantive control is in reg 8, which provides that 'An unfair term in a contract concluded with a consumer by a seller or supplier shall not be binding on the consumer'. In effect, therefore, an unfair term is 'voidable' at the option of the consumer. The regulations provide, however, that where a term is unfair the remainder of the contract remains valid and binding on the parties if it is capable of continuing in existence without the unfair term[1]. 'Unfair terms' are defined as 'the terms referred to in regulation 5'[2] and reg 5 provides that:

'(1) A contractual term which has not been individually negotiated shall be regarded as unfair if, contrary to the requirement of good faith, it causes a significant imbalance in the parties' rights and obligations arising under the contract, to the detriment of the consumer.

(2) A term shall always be regarded as not having been individually negotiated where it has been drafted in advance and the consumer has therefore not been able to influence the substance of the term.'

Regulation 5(1) therefore sets out a test of fairness applicable to terms which have not been 'individually negotiated', as defined in reg 5(2). It is clear that no other terms can be regarded as unfair under the regulations, and the directive is to the same effect. As a result, neither is applicable to negotiated terms and to that extent the regulations are therefore much narrower in scope than is the 1977 Act, which is capable of applying both to negotiated and non-negotiated terms in consumer contracts. There is, however, no requirement that the contract as a whole be on standard terms; the regulations apply to individual terms and it is expressly provided that the fact that an individual term has not been individually negotiated shall not prevent the application of the regulations to the remainder of the contract if an overall assessment of it indicates that it is a pre-formulated standard contract.[3] The difficulties which arise under s 3 of the 1977 Act, where a standard form is used as a basis for negotiation leading to variation of some of its terms, therefore does not arise under the regulations[4]. The burden of proof that a term was individually negotiated is on the seller or supplier[5].

The test of fairness under reg 5 appears to involve consideration of two elements: the term must create a significant imbalance in the rights and obligations of the parties under the contract, to the detriment of the consumer, and the creation of that imbalance must be contrary to the requirement of good faith. Regulation 6 provides further guidance on the assessment of 'fairness'. That assessment should take account of the nature of the goods or services in question, all the circumstances attending the conclusion of the contract, and all the other terms of the contract or any other contract on which it is dependent[6]. Regulation 6 continues:

'(2) In so far as it is in plain and intelligible language, the assessment of the fairness of a term shall not relate to —
(a) to the definition of the main subject matter of the contract; or
(b) to the adequacy of the price or remuneration, as against the goods or services supplied in exchange.'

This provision may be difficult to apply: for instance, in a contract of sale, the seller's basic obligation is to deliver the goods[7] and most of the express and implied terms of the contract, including the terms implied by the Sale of Goods Act[8], qualify or define that duty. To exclude terms relating to delivery and the quality of the goods supplied under the contract from the test of fairness would emasculate the regulations[9]. It is submitted, therefore, that the provision should be construed narrowly. The intention, as confirmed by the language of the corresponding provision in the directive, is to prevent a court being called on to evaluate the fairness of the bargain itself, by questioning the adequacy of the consideration. In the only reported English decision on the regulations in the higher courts, *Director General of Fair Trading v First National Bank plc*[10], the Court of Appeal held that a term in a consumer credit agreement which provided that, in the event of default by the consumer, interest should continue to be payable on any outstanding sums at the contract rate and that interest on the debt would continue to run after any judgment, was unfair. It was argued that, since the term in question related to the payment of interest under a loan agreement, it related to the consideration in return for which the loan was provided, and was therefore exempt from the test of fairness. The Court of Appeal rejected that argument. The term did not 'define the main subject matter' of the agreement and, since it related to default interest, it did not concern the adequacy of the price or remuneration.

It should be noted that, in any case, the exclusion of the 'core terms' is not total. First, it only applies in so far as the term in question is expressed in plain and intelligible language. Second, it seems clear that the price and other core terms can be taken into account when assessing the fairness of individual terms covered by the regulations[11]. It may therefore be impossible for the court to avoid indirectly assessing the fairness of the overall bargain. A term which would be unfair in a contract at a higher price may be fair if the price is lower.

Finally, the Schedule to the regulations contains an 'indicative and non-exhaustive list' of terms which 'may' be considered unfair[12]. Earlier drafts of the directive contained a list of terms which were absolutely proscribed, but in the final version this was watered down to its present status. The list therefore provides guidance as to the sorts of terms which may be covered by the regulations, but a term of the type included in the list may be considered fair in a particular context, just as terms not included in the list might be considered unfair. It seems, however, that there will generally be a presumption that a term of a type included in the indicative list is unfair, and a party seeking to rely on such a term will have to justify it.

In most cases the key elements in the assessment of fairness are likely to be 'good faith' and its relationship with the requirement of 'significant imbalance'. As we have seen, a general requirement of 'good faith' is largely new to English contract law. There is little guidance as to its meaning in the regulations. In civil law systems, however, where a similar requirement is well established, 'good faith' requires openness and transparency in the dealings between the parties. The recitals to the directive expressly state that:

> 'in making the assessment of good faith, particular regard shall be had to the strength of the bargaining position of the parties, whether the consumer had an inducement to agree to the term and whether the goods or services were sold or supplied to the special order of the consumer'

and continue 'the requirement of good faith may be satisfied by the seller or supplier where he deals fairly and equitably with the other party whose legitimate interests he takes into account'[13]. This seems to suggest that the evaluation of good faith is concerned, at least in part, with the procedure by which a term is introduced into the contract. A term which creates a significant imbalance is not necessarily unfair, provided that it is introduced into the contract fairly and openly. The Court of Appeal seems to have taken this line in the *First National Bank* case. Holding that the interest term in question was unfair, the court emphasised the imbalance of bargaining power and that the term would create 'unfair surprise and so does not satisfy the requirement of good faith':

> 'A term to which the consumer's attention is not specifically drawn but which may operate in a way which the consumer might not reasonably expect and to his disadvantage may offend the requirement of good faith. Terms must be reasonably transparent and should not operate to defeat the reasonable

expectations of the consumer. The consumer in choosing whether to enter into a contract should be put in a position where he can make an informed choice'[14].

On the other hand, the test of good faith cannot be entirely procedural. Some terms would be so substantively unfair that they could never be regarded as fair, no matter how clearly drawn to the consumer's attention. An example might be a term purporting to exclude liability for personal injury or death caused by the supplier's negligence. The better view, therefore, is that good faith is concerned with both the substantive fairness of the term and the procedure by which it is introduced, and to that extent there is an overlap between the requirements of 'good faith' and 'significant imbalance'. This seems to have been the view of the Court of Appeal in the *First National Bank* case[15].

1 Regulation 8(2).
2 Regulation 3(1).
3 Regulation 5(3).
4 See 2.6.4.3.
5 Regulation 5(4).
6 Regulation 4(2).
7 See ch 10.
8 See ch 11.
9 Unless such terms are brought within the scope of the regulations by not being expressed in clear and intelligible language.
10 [2000] 2 All ER 759. See also *Falco Finance Ltd v Gough* [1999] CCLR 208; Bright (1999) 115 LQR 360; *Kindlance Ltd v Murphy* (1997) unreported.
11 This appears more clearly from the text of the directive (art 4.2) and is expressly confirmed by the recitals thereto. On the legal effect of recitals to a directive, see Beyleveld [2000] IPQ 1. The 1994 regulations were clearer on this point than are the 1999 regulations.
12 Schedule 3.
13 The first three factors in the list are very similar to the factors to be considered under the Unfair Contract Terms Act 1977 in making an assessment of reasonableness (see above 2.6.4.4). The 1994 regulations included a Schedule listing these as factors to be considered in making the assessment of good faith. The Schedule was not, however, justified by the text of the directive and has therefore been omitted from the 1999 regulations.
14 [2000] 2 All ER 759 at 769.
15 Approving the views of Professor Beale in *Legislative Control of Fairness: The Directive on Unfair Terms in Consumer Contracts*' in Beatson and Friedmann (eds) *Good Faith and Fault in Contract Law* (1995) p 245: see [2000] 2 All ER 759 at 769.

2.6.5.3 Plain language

In addition to the test of fairness, the regulations impose on the seller or supplier a general duty to ensure that any written term of a contract is expressed in plain and intelligible language[1] and provide that if there is doubt about the meaning of a written term, 'the interpretation which is most favourable to the consumer shall prevail'[2].

These provisions raise a number of difficulties. It should be noted that they apply to all written terms, and not merely to 'standard' terms. It is not clear whether the test of clarity and intelligibility is subjective or objective, nor whether clear but non-colloquial legal technical language is acceptable. No sanction is provided in the regulations or directive for breach of the duty to express terms clearly, although it seems clear that lack of intelligibility will be relevant to fairness, just as lack of clarity of expression has been held relevant when assessing reasonableness under the 1977 Act[3]. The requirement for ambiguous terms to be given the interpretation most favourable to the consumer has been said to confirm the common law rule of contra proferentem construction. It is, however, open to a different interpretation. Suppose that a contract contains an ambiguous term which may be interpreted narrowly or widely, and that the wide interpretation, but not the narrow interpretation, would be considered unfair. At common law, contra proferentem construction would lead to the term being given the narrow interpretation. That, however, will leave the consumer bound by the term. The wide interpretation will lead to its being found to be unfair under the regulations and therefore not binding on the consumer. It may therefore be argued that the regulations require the term to be given the wide, unfair interpretation in such a case[4].

1   Regulation 7(1).
2   Regulation 7(2).
3   See *The Zinnia* [1984] 2 Lloyd's Rep 211.
4   See Furmston (ed) *Butterworths Law of Contract* (1999) p 542.

2.6.5.4   *Enforcement*

Individual consumers may rely on the regulations to challenge unfair terms in contracts to which they are a party. If a term is found to be unfair, the term is not binding on the consumer[1], but the remainder of the contract remains in force if it is capable of continuing in existence without the term[2].

In many cases consumers may be ignorant of their rights or lack the resources or inclination to enforce them by litigation. The directive therefore requires member states to 'ensure that in the interests of consumers and of competitors, adequate and effective means exist to prevent the continued use of unfair terms', including by giving rights of enforcement to 'persons or organisations having a legitimate interest under national law in protecting consumers'[3]. The 1994 regulations purported to implement this provision by providing for the Director General of Fair Trading (DGFT) to take action, including by seeking an injunction, against anyone using or recommending the use of an unfair term[4]. It was argued, however, that this did not go far enough, and that the directive required similar powers to be given to other organisations representative of consumer interests, such as the Consumers' Association, and following commencement by the Association of proceedings against the UK government for judicial review[5], on the grounds that, by restricting the power to take action against unfair terms to the DGFT, the government had failed properly to implement the directive, the government agreed to extend the power of enforcement to other organisations. The 1999 regulations therefore now provide for action to restrain the use of unfair terms to be taken by the DGFT or by any 'qualifying body' as listed in Sch 1. 'Qualifying bodies' include regulatory officers responsible for particular sectors, such as the Data Protection Registrar and the Director General of Telecommunications, and also the Consumers' Association.

The DGFT may only take action under the regulations on the basis of a complaint, but complaints may be made by anyone including individual consumers, local trading standards or other officers, consumer organisations or even by one business against another. Where a complaint is made, the DGFT has a duty to consider it, unless he considers it frivolous or vexatious, or a qualifying body notifies him that it agrees to consider it. He must give reasons for his decision to apply or not to apply for an injunction, but may, if he considers it appropriate, accept an undertaking in lieu of an injunction. Qualifying bodies have similar powers to the DGFT.

A special Unfair Contract Terms Unit has been established within the Office of Fair Trading (OFT) to enforce the regulations. By the end of June 1999 the unit had received 4,140 complaints under the regulations[6]. The DGFT is empowered to arrange for the dissemination of information and advice to the public and all persons likely to be affected by the regulations[7]. To this end, the OFT has published a series of Bulletins giving details of the Unfair Terms Unit's activities, and guidance as to its approach to the regulations and the types of terms it considers unfair, including details of the terms against which it has taken action and the businesses using them. The Bulletins are an important source of information as to the practice of the OFT in implementing the regulations. It seems that where it receives a complaint about a term which it considers to be unfair, it will normally seek first to negotiate a change to the term before seeking an injunction or undertaking. To date it has had only had to resort to formal court proceedings in the one case[8].

1   Regulation 5(1).
2   Regulation 5(2). The ECJ has held that a court has jurisdiction to consider the fairness of a term in a case before the court of its own motion, even if the term is not challenged by the consumer: Cases C-240/98 to C-244/98.
3   Article 7.
4   Regulation 8.
5   The association was granted leave for a review: *R v Secretary of State for Trade and Industry, ex p Consumers' Association* (28 February 1996, unreported).
6   Unfair Contract Terms Bulletin No 8 (OFT, December 1999).
7   Regulation 15.
8   *Director General of Fair Trading v First National Bank* [2000] 1 All ER 240, above 2.6.5.2.

2.6.5.5   *Evaluation*

It is not clear that the regulations offer individual consumers a great deal more protection than was already provided by the Unfair Contract Terms Act 1977 and various common law rules. The test of fairness in the regulations is in many respects similar to the test of reasonableness under the Act and most of the terms included in the 'indicative list' of potentially unfair terms in the regulations would probably be covered by the Act, in light of the way in which it has been interpreted by the courts[1]. Indeed, since the Act totally invalidates certain types of contract term, in many cases it will offer greater protection than do the regulations.

The regulations are, however, important. Notwithstanding the wide range of powers available to the courts at common law and under statute to control unfair terms and exclusion clauses, many unfair terms remained in widespread use. The most significant aspect of the regulations is undoubtedly the power given by the regulations to the DGFT and to other qualifying bodies to take action to prevent the continued use of unfair terms. It is significant that, during the first five years after introduction of the 1994 regulations, many of the terms referred to the OFT would have been invalid under the Unfair Contract Terms Act or under common law rules, but remained in use, no doubt because in many cases individual consumers were ignorant of or unwilling to invoke the law. Vigorous use of the new enforcement powers is likely to lead to a considerable reduction in the use of unfair standard terms in consumer contracts and perhaps, over time, to a change in contracting culture.

The regulations may, however, have even wider effect. They are a significant step in the 'Europeanisation' of English contract law. They have forced English lawyers to confront and think about the concept of 'good faith'. It seems unlikely that the new attitudes can be permanently confined to the consumer contracts arena[2].

1   See 2.6.4.
2   See the comments of Brooke LJ in *Lacey's Footwear Ltd v Bowler International Freight Ltd*
    [1997] 2 Lloyd's Rep 369 at 385.

2.7   Privity of contract

It was the view of the 'classical' English law of contract that no one can sue or be
sued on a contract unless he is a party to it, even if it expressly purports to bind or
to confer a benefit on him. In 1915 Viscount Haldane LC described it as a
fundamental principle of English law[1]. Thus, for instance, if A buys goods from B
and gives them as a gift to C, at common law C has no contractual remedy against
A if the goods prove defective. C may be able to sue in tort for damages for personal
injuries or property damage[2], but will generally have no remedy in respect of defects
in the goods themselves.

This principle of 'privity of contract' has generally been seen as closely connected
to the doctrine of consideration. It has probably caused more difficulty in relation
to commercial operations than any other, and the courts have often been forced
into convoluted and fictional reasoning in order to evade it. The problem is
compounded by a second rule that a party to the contract can normally recover
damages only in respect of the losses he suffers[3]. Thus, in the example given, A, as
a party to the original contract, is entitled to enforce it. However, in many cases,
including the example given, A will probably have suffered no, – or only minimal
– loss.

Many commercial arrangements actually give rise to multi-partite relationships.
Suppose, for instance, that a person buys a new car from a garage with the aid of a
loan from a finance company, arranged by the garage, and gets the benefit of a
manufacturer's guarantee. The contractual relationships created by the transaction
can be represented by the following diagram:

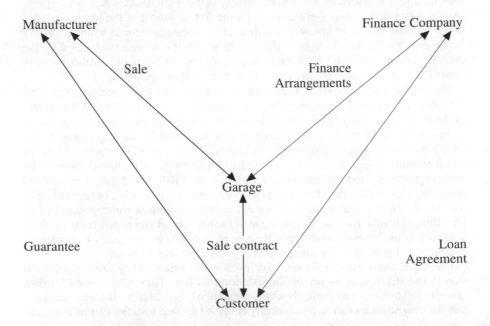

The law treats the customer as entering into three separate bilateral contracts; in addition, there will be contracts between the garage and the manufacturer for the supply of the car, and between the garage and the finance company for the loan arrangements and, at least at common law, the parties to each contract will be unaffected by the relationships created by the others. (The position is modified in this particular case by the Consumer Credit Act 1974[4].)

Similarly, in contracts for the construction of buildings or complex machinery, or for the carriage and storage of goods, the parties may anticipate that sub-contractors, agents and employees will actually perform some, or all, of the duties under the contract; yet such persons will be strangers to the contract and unable to take any benefit or be subject to any obligation under it.

In order to avoid the inconvenience of the privity doctrine, a number of exceptions to it were developed by statute and at common law. The doctrine is now further qualified by the Contracts (Rights of Third Parties) Act 1999.

1   *Dunlop Pneumatic Tyre Co Ltd v Selfridge & Co Ltd* [1915] AC 847 at 853. It is in fact doubted whether the rule was so well established prior to *Dunlop v Selfridge*. The rule is generally traced back to *Tweddle v Atkinson* (1861) 1 B & S 393, although that case could equally be explained on the basis of the rule that 'consideration must move from the promisee'. It has therefore been said that 'the genesis of the privity rule is suspect': per Steyn LJ in *Darlington Borough Council v Wiltshier Northern Ltd* [1995] 3 All ER 895 at 904.
2   Under the principle of *Donoghue v Stevenson* [1932] AC 562 or under the Consumer Protection Act 1987: see 13.1.
3   *Woodar Investment Development Ltd v Wimpey Construction UK Ltd* [1980] 1 All ER 571, [1980] 1 WLR 277, HL. The existence of the rule has been doubted: see, eg, per Lord Goff in *Panatown Ltd v Alfred McAlpine Construction Ltd* [2000] 4 All ER 97 at 114–115.
4   See 26.4.

2.7.1   *Common law exceptions to the privity rule*

Some of the problems of privity may be evaded by allowing a person affected by negligent performance of a contract to which he is not party to sue in negligence. For instance, if A has a contract with B, which is performed by a sub contractor, C, A may sue C in the tort of negligence if he suffers damage as a result of C's negligent performance. However, a negligence action will generally not be available where A's losses are purely economic[1]. Moreover, allowing A to sue creates its own problems: B may have excluded or limited his liability to A in their contract; similarly, the contract between B and C may contain exclusions. If A sues C direct, neither set of exclusions will protect C at common law, since there is no privity between A and C[2]. Thus A may evade a perfectly reasonable allocation of risks and gain an unfair advantage, since the price of his contract with B may have been fixed on the basis that A was assuming the risk in question, whilst C may have arranged his affairs on the basis of the terms of his contract with B, and therefore not be insured against the liability in question. The problem is particularly acute if, as is often the case, C is B's employee on whom B relies to perform his contract[3]. In order to avoid such an outcome, the court may be forced to find an agency[4], or implied contract[5], often distorting the concepts of offer, acceptance and consideration.

The inconvenience of the privity rule has led to the development of a number of exceptions. Some of these are well established. A person may employ an agent to make contracts on his behalf: in most cases the agent will play no part in performance of the contract which will be fully enforceable by and against the principal[6]. Alternatively, contractual rights, but not obligations, may be assigned[7]. Thus, in theory, where A buys goods as a gift for B, A could assign to B the right to enforce the sale contract[8]. However, to be fully effective an assignment must be in writing and notice be given to the party against whom the right assigned is to be asserted and defences available against the assignor can be raised against the assignee; thus if the original contract prohibits its assignment, any purported assignment will be ineffective[9]. In many cases assignment will be impractical and unrealistic[10]. Alternatively, a contract between A and B can be novated so as to replace it by a contract between B and C. However, novation requires the agreement of A, B and C. Again, it will be impractical in many cases.

Many other devices, including trusts[11], implied agency and collateral contracts[12], have been employed by the courts in order to evade the effects of the privity doctrine.

In some cases it may be possible for the party to the contract to enforce it on behalf of another. If A and B make a contract for the benefit of C, A may be able to obtain an order for specific performance against B, requiring him to provide C with the intended benefit[13]. However, specific performance is a discretionary remedy and it will often not be available in a commercial context; in many cases it would be inappropriate. A number of cases have recognised that, exceptionally, A may be able to enforce the contract and recover damages in respect of losses suffered by C. A special exception to the general rule has therefore been recognised in a number of consumer contexts – for instance, where one member of a family books a family holiday[14]. A further long-established exception applied in the context of contracts for the carriage of goods by sea, whereby if A contracted with B for the carriage of A's goods and then sold the goods to C, and the goods were then damaged, A could sue B and recover substantial damages on behalf of C[15]. It was thought that this principle was limited to contracts concerning goods where both contracting parties contemplated that the goods would be sold. In *Linden Gardens Trust Ltd v Lenesta Sludge Disposals Ltd*[16], however, the House of Lords suggested that the exception might be wider than previously thought. In that case the plaintiffs had entered into a building contract for the development of a site, but before the construction work was completed they disposed of their whole interest in the site. A purported assignment to the transferees of the right to sue for breaches of the building contract was held ineffective but the majority of the House of Lords held that the plaintiffs could nevertheless recover full damages for the difference in value between the service contracted for and that actually provided. At the time the contract was made, the parties knew that the property was to be occupied, and perhaps even owned, by third parties who would suffer damage as a result of any breach of contract by the developers, and, moreover, that such third parties would acquire no rights of suit of their own. The parties were therefore treated as having entered into the contract on the basis that the plaintiffs could enforce it for the benefit of the third parties who suffered from defective performance. Were the law otherwise, 'the claim for damages would disappear into some legal black hole, so that the wrongdoer escaped scot-free'[17].

The exception recognised in *Linden Gardens* was extended in *Darlington Borough Council v Wiltshier Northern Ltd*[18] in which A contracted with B for B to do work on property owned by C. The Court of Appeal held that A could recover damages for the breach, despite the fact that A had never had any interest in the property affected by the breach. In *Panatown Ltd v Alfred McAlpine Construction Ltd*[19], however, the majority of the House of Lords held that the exception would not apply where the contracting parties, A and B, intended that the third party, C should have his own right of action against B for defective performance, since there would then be no risk of a breach of contract going uncompensated.

The scope of the exception recognised in these cases is unclear. In particular, whilst the *ratio* of the decision of the majority of the House of Lords in *Linden Gardens* was that A recovers damages in respect of losses suffered by C, Lord Griffiths, decided the case on the broader principle that in such a case A recovers damages in respect of his own expectation interest under his contract with B, and this broader principle was approved and adopted by Lord Goff and Lord Millett, the dissenting minority, in *Panatown*. It is not clear if a claim by A on this basis is excluded where C has a separate claim in respect of his loss[20]. Further development of the law in this area therefore seems likely. Whichever rationale is adopted, it seems that the exception recognised in these cases is not limited to carriage or construction contracts but is capable of applying generally, including to contracts for services and for the sale of goods. However, its significance is now somewhat reduced by the passing of the Contracts (Rights of Third Parties) Act 1999.

1   See *Murphy v Brentwood District Council* [1991] 1 AC 398, [1990] 2 All ER 269, HL; *Simaan General Contracting Co Ltd v Pilkington Glass Ltd (No 2)* [1988] QB 758, [1988] 1 All ER 791, CA; *Muirhead v Industrial Tank Specialities Ltd* [1986] QB 507, [1985] 3 All ER 705, CA.
2   *Scruttons v Midland Silicones Ltd* [1962] AC 446, [1962] 1 All ER 1, HL.
3   See *London Drugs v Kuehne & Nagel* (1992) 97 DLR (4th) 261, noted (1993) 56 MLR 722, [1994] LMCLQ 22.
4   *New Zealand Shipping Co Ltd v A M Satterthwaite & Co Ltd* [1975] AC 154, [1974] 1 All ER 1015, PC, below 32.4.3.
5   *Pyrene Co v Scindia Navigation Co* [1954] 2 QB 402, [1954] 2 All ER 158, below 33.1.0.
6   See Pt II.
7   See 27.3.
8   From time to time consumer advisers have recommended that gifts should be accompanied by such an assignment.
9   *Linden Gardens Trust Ltd v Lenesta Sludge Disposals Ltd* [1994] 1 AC 85, [1993] 3 All ER 417.
10 As recognised by the Law Commissions in their Report 196, Scot Law Com 130, *Rights of Suit in Respect of Goods Carried by Sea* (1991).
11 See *Re Flavell* (1883) 25 Ch D 89, CA.
12 *Shanklin Pier Ltd v Detel Products Ltd* [1951] 2 KB 854, [1951] 2 All ER 471.
13 *Beswick v Beswick* [1968] AC 58, [1967] 2 All ER 1197, HL.
14 See *Jackson v Horizon Holidays Ltd* [1975] 3 All ER 92, [1975] 1 WLR 1468, CA, as explained in *Woodar Investment Development Ltd v Wimpey Construction UK Ltd* [1980] 1 All ER 571, [1980] 1 WLR 277, HL.
15 *Dunlop v Lambert* (1839) 6 Cl & Fin 600; *The Albazero, Albacruz (cargo owners) v Albazero (owners)* [1977] AC 774, [1976] 3 All ER 129; see 32.6.4.
16 [1994] 1 AC 85, [1993] 3 All ER 417.
17 Per Lord Keith in *GUS Property Management Ltd v Littlewoods Mail Order Stores Ltd* (1982) SC (HL) 157 at 177.
18 [1995] 3 All ER 895, CA.
19 [2000] 4 All ER 97.
20 Contrast the views of Lord Goff and Lord Millett in *Panatown* with those of Lord Jauncey and Lord Browne-Wilkinson.

2.7.2 Statutory reform of the privity doctrine

By the 1990s there was widespread recognition that the privity doctrine was, at the very least, commercially inconvenient. In a series of cases senior members of the judiciary criticised it and indicated that it might be reformed should a suitable case arise[1]. Indeed, that step had already been taken in some Commonwealth jurisdictions[2].

In addition to the common law exceptions to the rule mentioned above, a number of specific exceptions or modifications to the rule had already been created by statute in particular commercial contexts[3]. In 1996, however, the Law Commissions proposed a more general reform of the rule to allow a third party to enforce a contract term where the parties to the contract intended that the term should be (a) for his benefit and (b) legally enforceable by him[4]. The Commissions' proposals were implemented by the Contracts (Rights of Third Parties) Act 1999, which is closely based on the draft Bill appended to the Commissions' report. The Act came into force on 11 November 1999 and applies to contracts made on or after 11 May 2000. It effects only limited reform to the privity doctrine. It allows a third party to take the benefit of a contract term intended to be for his benefit. It leaves untouched the other half of the privity rule, that a contract cannot be enforced against a person not party to it[5]. Certain types of contract are expressly excluded, including those already covered by separate statutory rules. The most important in the commercial context are negotiable instruments[6] and contracts for the carriage of goods[7]. The existing common law and statutory exceptions to the rule are left intact and the Law Commissions expressly stated that their proposals were not intended to exclude the possibility of further judicial reform of the doctrine.

The basic principle of the Act is set out in s 1(1). It permits a third party (T) to enforce a term of a contract made between A and B where either:

'(a) the contract expressly provides that he may; or
(b) the term purports to confer a benefit on him, unless it appears on a proper construction of the contract that the parties did not intend him to be able to enforce the term'[8].

T must be identified in the contract by name, as a member of a class or by description, but there is no requirement that T be in existence at the time the contract is made[9]. The Act enables T not only to enforce 'positive' rights, such as a right to payment of money, but also to take the benefit of exclusion and limitation clauses in a contract. Thus, if T is sued by A or B, T is entitled to rely on an exclusion or limitation clause in the contract between A and B if either of the requirements in s 1 is satisfied.

T's claim to enforce positive rights under the contract is treated as one in contract for the purposes of the rules governing remedies and limitation[10]. Any damages are therefore assessed in accordance with the rules applicable to contractual claims for damages[11]. T is not, however, a party to the contract. He may enforce the contract but is not bound by it, except in so far as his right to enforce the contract is subject to and in accordance with the other terms of the contract[12], so that if T enforces against A, A can rely on any defence or set-off which would have been available against a claim by B, the other contracting party[13]. T's right to enforce the contract is without prejudice to the rights of A and B to enforce it against each other, including any rule allowing a promisee to recover damages for his own, or for T's loss. Any damages awarded to T will, however, take account of any sum recovered by the promisee in respect of T's loss[14].

One of the obstacles to granting a third party rights to enforce a contract to which he is not party is that it may impinge on the freedom of the contracting parties to vary or discharge their contract by agreement. The Act therefore provides that, in general, the parties remain free to vary the contract in accordance with general principles. However, the parties lose the right to vary the contract so as to affect T's rights without T's consent if either (a) T communicates to the promisor his acceptance of the promise by words or conduct or (b) T relies on the promise and either (i) the promisor is aware of his reliance or (ii) the promisor can reasonably be expected to have foreseen that T would rely on the promise[15]. In accordance with the general principle of party autonomy it is possible for the contracting parties to modify these rules by the terms of the contract.

As explained above, T's right under the Act to enforce a term in a contract between A and B is subject to any defences which could be raised by the promisor in an action by the contractual promisee. Thus, if T brings a claim against A, relying on the 1999 Act, A may seek to set up exclusion clauses in the contract to rebut T's claim. Such clauses are normally subject to statutory control[16]. However, the statutory controls will generally not apply to a claim by T under the 1999 Act. The Unfair Terms in Consumer Contracts Regulations 1999 only apply to terms in a contract between a consumer and seller or supplier. They therefore do not apply in relation to a claim by T since there is no contract between A and T. Sections 3, 6 and 7 of the Unfair Contract Terms Act 1977 (UCTA) cannot apply to T's claim for the same reason. The restrictions in UCTA, s 2 could, in principle apply. However, the 1999 Act expressly provides that T may not rely on s 2(2) of the 1977 Act to challenge an exclusion or limitation clause relied on by A[17]. The reason for this is that the contracting parties remain free under the Act to exclude or limit T's right to enforce the contract and it would be difficult to differentiate between a clause restricting T's right to enforce and one restricting A's liability to T for breach of duty. UCTA, s 2(2) controls terms and notices which purport to exclude liability for loss other than personal injury or death caused by negligence. T may rely on UCTA, s 2(1) which renders ineffective terms and notices which purport to exclude liability for personal injury or death caused by negligence. T would have a right to claim for any such injury without relying on the 1999 Act and any term in the contract between A and B would be ineffective against such a claim.

The 1999 Act is an important piece of legislation which, it has been said, removes a significant blot on the landscape of English commercial law[18]. It brings English law into line with that of several other jurisdictions. It remains to be seen, however, what practical impact it will have. Its application was delayed in order to allow certain standard form contracts, including those in the construction and engineering industries, to be redrafted to take account of its provisions. Where a contract specifically provides for it to be enforceable, or not to be enforceable, by a third party, there should be little difficulty. Where, however, the contract contains no express provision, it will be necessary to consider whether the contracting parties intended to confer a benefit on the third party, and intended the third party to be able to enforce the contract. That may lead to difficult questions of interpretation.

---

1 See per Lord Scarman in *Woodar Investment Development Ltd v Wimpey Construction UK Ltd* [1980] 1 All ER 571 at 591, [1980] 1 WLR 277 at 300–301; Steyn LJ in *Darlington Borough Council v Wiltshier Northern Ltd* [1995] 3 All ER 895 at 903–904; Lord Goff in *The Pioneer Container: KH Enterprise (cargo owners) v Pioneer (owners)* [1994] 2 AC 324 at 335, [1994] 2 All ER 250 at 255–256. See also Lord Steyn (1997) 113 LQR 433 at 437. There was academic criticism too: see eg Adams and Brownsword (1993) 56 MLR 722.

2 See *Trident General Insurance Co Ltd v McNiece Bros Pty Ltd* (1988) 80 ALR 574, where a seven member High Court of Australia found a variety of different ways to avoid the rule: two members of the court were prepared to modify privity of contract directly; see 35.1.5. See also the majority judgments in the Supreme Court of Canada in *London Drugs v Kuehne & Nagel* (1992) 97 DLR (4th) 261.

3 Eg Consumer Credit Act 1974, s 56, below 26.4; Carriage of Goods by Sea Act 1992, below 32.6.5.

4 Law Commission 242 (Cmnd 3329) *Privity of Contract: Contracts for the Benefit of Third Parties*, (July 1996). See Adams, Beyleveld and Brownsword (1997) 60 MLR 238. See also Law Commission Consultation Paper 121 *Privity of Contract: Contracts for the Benefit of Third Parties* (1991).

5 A special rule applies to arbitration clauses (s 8). See 32.6.3.2.

6 Section 6(1).

7 Section 6(5).

8 Section 1(2).

9 Section 1(3).

10 Section 7(3).

11   Section 1(5).
12   Section 1(4). This includes terms requiring disputes to be referred to arbitration (s 8): see 32.6.3.2.
13   Section 3.
14   Section 5.
15   Section 2(2). The court may dispense with T's consent in certain circumstances.
16   See 2.6.4, 2.6.5.
17   Section 7(2).
18   Dean [2000] JBL 143.

2.8   Variation of contracts

Although the parties may initially be perfectly happy with their bargain, circumstances may lead them to want to vary its terms. One of them may discover that he made a mistake – for instance, by fixing the price too low – or circumstances may change unexpectedly, rendering continued performance impossible, difficult or uneconomic. The problem may be particularly acute in a long-term contract involving a continuing relationship, such as a requirements or construction contract, or an agency, distribution or franchise arrangement. It may be that the error, or change in circumstances, is so fundamental that the contract is affected by mistake, or becomes frustrated. The original contract can then be forgotten: it is either void for mistake, or discharged by frustration, and the parties can make a new one. However, the legal doctrines of mistake and frustration are very narrow; they will rarely apply where an error or change in circumstances makes the contract uneconomic[1].

In many cases the parties may simply agree a variation and proceed with the contract as varied: there may be sound commercial reasons for accepting a variation, even though it benefits the other party, for instance, in order to preserve goodwill, win future contracts, or to avoid causing financial difficulties, and even insolvency, to the other party and thus ensure performance. However, if one party, having agreed to the variation, seeks to go back on it and deny its validity, a court may have to decide if the variation was legally binding.

Some contracts contain terms which expressly permit variation, either by mutual consent, or unilaterally. For example, price variation clauses are commonly found in supply contracts, especially where the supplier is also manufacturing the goods and there is a risk of increases in raw material or labour costs. Similarly, credit agreements normally contain provisions allowing the creditor to alter the interest rate, and even other terms of the contract. Such provisions may be regulated by statute[2] and may be unfair in a contract governed by the Unfair Terms in Consumer Contracts Regulations 1999 but are perfectly valid at common law[3]. Where a contract is varied in accordance with such a term, the variation is legally binding because all that is varied is the performance, not the terms, of the contract.

Where there is no term permitting variation, the position is more difficult. The parties can then only vary their obligations by varying the terms of their existing contract, or by terminating the contract and entering into a new one, on the revised terms. A contract can be varied, or terminated, by consent, but the law requires the agreement to vary or terminate to be a valid contract in its own right: in other words, the parties must freely agree to the variation/termination, and there must be consideration for the agreement to vary/terminate.

1   See *Leaf v International Galleries* [1950] 2 KB 86, [1950] 1 All ER 693, CA (mistake), above
    2.4.1; *Davis Contractors Ltd v Fareham UDC* [1956] AC 696, [1956] 2 All ER 145, HL (frustration),
    below 2.9.4.

2   Eg the Consumer Credit Act 1974 and Consumer Credit (Agreements) Regulations 1983.
3   *Lombard Tricity Finance Ltd v Paton* [1989] 1 All ER 918 at 923, CA.

2.8.1   Consideration and variation

Where parties are committed to a contractual relationship, each effectively has monopoly power over the other. For instance, if A agrees with B to carry B's goods to a customer, once the goods have been collected by A, B is at A's mercy. If A now demands an increased payment for performing the contract, B may have no choice but to agree, or risk being in breach of contract with his customer. Similarly, if X and Y agree that Y should build a complex piece of machinery for X's business and, after the agreement has been made, Y demands an increase in the price, X may have no choice but to agree, in order to avoid the delays which would be involved in negotiating a new contract from scratch with another manufacturer. The law must therefore guard against such abuses, and traditionally it has used the doctrine of consideration to do so. Thus there will be consideration for a variation if both parties undertake extra, or changed duties[1]; or if a variation is capable of benefiting either party, as, for instance, where the parties agree to change the currency or method of payment. In the case of an agreed termination, there will be valid consideration provided both parties still have obligations to perform under the original contract, for in that case each party gives up something by agreeing to the termination.

Suppose, however, the parties agree a variation where only one party accepts a changed obligation, or only one can benefit from the changed terms, as where A and B make a contract and subsequently agree that A will pay extra for B's performance. According to the classical doctrine of consideration, there is no consideration for A's promise. It is well established that a party who simply performs his existing duties under a contract provides no consideration for a promise by the other to perform extra duties[2]. Similarly, if a creditor agrees to accept part payment of a debt in full settlement, the creditor may retract the agreement and claim the balance, because the debtor provides no consideration for it simply by paying part of the existing debt[3].

This approach has often been criticised. The agreement to vary the contract, or accept part payment, may be perfectly voluntary and, indeed, commercially sensible. For example, if the debtor's solvency is in doubt, an agreement to accept part of the debt may be commercially better for the creditor than insisting on full payment and receiving nothing as a result. The courts have therefore been adept at discovering consideration in even trivial variations of contract duties[4]; for instance, a change in the place, or mode[5], of payment of a debt can provide consideration for an agreement to accept part payment, and recently there has been an increased willingness to discover consideration for the variation in this way, leaving the validity of the agreement to be assessed by reference to the developing doctrines of duress and undue influence. In *Williams v Roffey Bros and Nicholls (Contractors) Ltd*[6] the Court of Appeal held that an agreement by a building sub-contractor to perform existing duties under a contract was good consideration for a promise by the main contractor to pay an increased price, so that the main contractor's promise was binding provided that it was not obtained by duress. The performance of the existing contract provided a practical commercial benefit to the main contractor: the sub-contractor was on the verge of insolvency, and performance of its existing duties helped the main contractor avoid financial penalties for delayed completion of its contract. This development has introduced greater flexibility into the law: a finding of 'no consideration' is unable to distinguish between consent voluntarily given and consent obtained by extortion. Of course, the price of flexibility is uncertainty: the new doctrines are still developing and their scope is therefore unclear. It has been held, for instance, that the 'practical benefit' principle recognised in *Williams v Roffey* does not apply to the situation of part payment of a debt[7]. More importantly, the new doctrines of practical benefit and duress require examination of the facts of each case in order to decide if the variation is valid.

1   *The Atlantic Baron* [1979] QB 705, [1978] 3 All ER 1170.
2   *Stilk v Myrick* (1809) 2 Camp 317.
3   *Pinnels' Case* (1602) 5 Co Rep 117a; *Foakes v Beer* (1884) 9 App Cas 605, HL.
4   See eg *The Atlantic Baron* [1979] QB 705, [1978] 3 All ER 1170; *Pao On v Lau Yiu Long* [1980] AC 614, [1979] 3 All ER 65, PC.
5   It is now settled that payment by cheque is to be treated as equivalent to payment in cash, so that an agreement to pay by a cheque is no consideration for a promise to accept part payment: *D & C Builders Ltd v Rees* [1966] 2 QB 617, [1965] 3 All ER 837, CA.
6   [1991] 1 QB 1, [1990] 1 All ER 512.
7   *Re Selectmove Ltd* [1995] 2 All ER 531; (1994) 110 LQR 353. See also *Re C (a debtor)* (11 May 1994, unreported), CA.

2.8.2   *Estoppel and waiver*

Even if there is no consideration for a promise to vary a contract, the promise may still be binding on the promisor as a result of the doctrines of waiver and 'promissory estoppel'. It was recognised at common law that if a party to a contract either agreed not to insist on his strict contractual rights, or represented to the other contract party that he would not insist on strict performance, or would not enforce it according to its terms, he might be held to have waived his right to strict performance. A waiver of a past breach would be irrevocable; but in other cases a waiver might be withdrawn on giving reasonable notice. For instance, in *Charles Rickards Ltd v Oppenhaim*[1] B agreed to buy a car body. When it was not delivered on time he continued to press for delivery, but finally lost patience and, in June 1948, three months after the original delivery date, gave notice that if it was not ready in four weeks he would not take it. The body was not delivered by that time limit, and when it was ready (in October) B refused delivery. It was held that B had waived the original delivery date, but had given reasonable notice of his intention to insist on delivery, and so was entitled to refuse delivery when his four-week deadline was not satisfied.

A similar doctrine was developed in equity, whereby if one party to a contract expressly or impliedly promised to the other that he would not insist on his strict contractual rights, he would not be allowed to retract that promise and insist on those rights if the promise had been acted on by the other party[2]. The doctrine is generally called either 'promissory' or 'equitable' estoppel, and although this is sometimes regarded as a misnomer, it is a convenient label. It was extended by Lord Denning, who (as Denning J) applied it for the first time to cases of part payment of debts in *Central London Property Trust Ltd v High Trees House Ltd*[3]. The exact ambit of the doctrine is not clear. However, it seems that the following requirements must be satisfied before a promise can be enforced on this basis:

(a)   the promisor must have made an unambiguous representation, expressly or impliedly, that he will not insist on strict performance of an existing contract;
(b)   the promisee must have relied on that promise; it is not clear if he must have acted to his 'detriment', but the better view is that there is no such requirement[4]; and
(c)   it must be inequitable to allow the promisor to revoke the promise[5].

Where the doctrine applies, its effect is normally to suspend, rather than extinguish, contractual rights. Thus the promisor can return to the original contract and enforce it upon giving reasonable notice to the promisee[6], although the promise may wholly extinguish the original rights if it is impossible to restore the parties to their original position[7]. In that case, a variation of a contract on the basis of promissory estoppel may have much the same effect as one supported by consideration. However, there is the crucial difference that promissory estoppel operates as 'a shield, not a sword': it creates no new rights of action in the promisee[8].

The doctrines of waiver and 'promissory estoppel' are clearly closely related. Strictly, they differ, in that waiver is concerned with the promisor's knowledge whereas 'promissory estoppel' focuses on the promisee's reaction. However, many cases treat the two doctrines as interchangeable[9]. Both may be regarded as ways in which English contract law seeks to give effect to the legitimate expectations of contractors and thus, in effect, protect 'good faith', although the existence of a broader principle of fair dealing 'negativing any liberty to blow hot and cold in commercial conduct'[10] has been expressly rejected[11].

1 [1950] 1 KB 616, [1950] 1 All ER 520, CA; see 10.2.1.
2 *Hughes v Metropolitan Rly Co* (1877) 2 App Cas 439, HL.
3 [1947] KB 130.
4 See *W J Alan & Co v El Nasr Export and Import Co* [1972] 2 QB 189, [1972] 2 All ER 127, CA; *The Post Chaser* [1981] 2 Lloyd's Rep 695.
5 *The Post Chaser* [1981] 2 Lloyd's Rep 695; *D & C Builders Ltd v Rees* [1966] 2 QB 617, [1965] 3 All ER 837, CA; *Re Selectmove Ltd* [1995] 2 All ER 531; (1994) 110 LQR 353.
6 *Tool Metal Manufacturing Co Ltd v Tungsten Electric Co Ltd* [1955] 2 All ER 657, [1955] 1 WLR 761, HL; the meaning of 'suspension' is unclear where the obligation in question is of a continuing, periodic, nature, such as an obligation to pay rent: see the *High Trees* case itself.
7 *Birmingham and District Land Co v London and North Western Rly Co* (1888) 40 Ch D 268, CA.
8 *Combe v Combe* [1951] 2 KB 215, [1951] 1 All ER 767, CA. There are signs that this restriction may be eased. The High Court of Australia allowed a claim to be based on estoppel in *Walton's Stores (Interstate) Ltd v Maher* (1988) 164 CLR 387. In *Williams v Roffey Bros and Nicholls (Contractors) Ltd* [1991] 1 QB 1, [1990] 1 All ER 512 both Glidewell LJ (at 13, 520) and Russell LJ (at 17, 523) indicated that they would have been prepared to consider an argument based on estoppel.
9 Eg Lord Denning in *Charles Rickards Ltd v Oppenhaim* [1950] 1 KB 616, [1950] 1 All ER 420, CA; *W J Alan & Co v El Nasr Export and Import Co* [1972] 2 QB 189; *Woodhouse AC Israel Cocoa Ltd v Nigerian Produce Marketing Co Ltd* [1972] AC 741, [1972] 2 All ER 271, HL.
10 *Panchaud Frères SA v Etablissements General Grain Co* [1970] 1 Lloyd's Rep 53 at 59, CA, per Winn LJ.
11 *Glencore Grain Rotterdam BV v Lebanese Organisation for International Commerce* [1997] 4 All ER 514.

2.9 Discharge

When a contract is discharged it is terminated and both parties are released from their obligations under it, although in some cases the parties may be subject to secondary obligations, possibly as a result of the discharge, to make restitution or pay compensation. Disputes arise where one party demands performance from the other who claims to have discharged, or to have been discharged from, his obligation to perform. The crucial question, therefore, is not whether the contract is discharged, but whether an individual party is discharged, from the contract as a whole, or from a particular obligation under it. Contractual obligations can be discharged by agreement, performance, breach or frustration.

2.9.1   *Discharge by agreement*

Since contractual obligations are created by agreement, they can be discharged by agreement. In order to be binding, such an agreement must satisfy the requirements for the creation of a valid contract; crucially, the party to be bound must supply consideration for the agreement to release him from his obligations. Where the parties agree to terminate the contract as a whole at a time when both still have obligations to perform, there is no difficulty: each party's promise to discharge the other is consideration for the other's counter-promise. Where only one party is discharged, that party must supply some other consideration. The problems raised are identical to those discussed above in relation to variation, and the principles discussed there apply.

2.9.2   *Discharge by performance*

When both parties have fully performed their obligations under the contract, it is discharged, although if one party's performance is defective in any way, he may come under an obligation to pay damages. However, disputes arise where one party claims to have performed and demands performance from the other. Normally, the performance demanded is payment for goods or services supplied and many of the cases have concerned contracts for building work and similar services. Suppose that A agrees to do work for B in return for a lump sum payment payable on completion of the work. A's entitlement to payment depends on two questions, the answers to which depend on the construction of the contract. First, is B's obligation to pay dependent on A's to do the work? If so, A's obligation can be said to be a condition of B's: it will be a condition precedent if it is intended that A should perform before B does so. In other cases, where it is intended that both parties should be willing to perform at the same time, their obligations may be concurrent conditions, each dependent on the other[1]. Second, if B's obligation is dependent on A's performance, is A's obligation to perform entire or severable? Construing an obligation as entire means that it must be fully performed in accordance with all its qualifying terms before it is discharged. Thus if A's obligation is construed as both a condition precedent to B's obligation to pay and entire, A will only be entitled to demand payment if he has fully performed his obligations. If for any reason A has performed only part of his work, he will generally be entitled to no payment[2].

In certain exceptional cases a party may claim payment for partial performance of an entire obligation. If B freely accepts A's partial performance, B must pay a reasonable sum. In such a case A's claim is restitutionary rather than being based on the contract[3]. The courts apply the test restrictively: in *Sumpter v Hedges*[4] where a builder left the contract work half finished when he became insolvent, the court held that the landowner had not freely accepted the partially completed work: it was on his land and he had no choice but to accept it[5].

Some cases suggest that a party who 'substantially' performs an entire obligation is entitled to be paid under the contract. In *Hoenig v Isaacs*[6] P contracted to decorate and furnish D's flat for £750. P completed the work but there were defects in the furnishing, which would cost £55 to correct. It was held that P was entitled to claim the contract price less the cost of the defects. The difficulty is to know what is 'substantial performance': in *Bolton v Mahadeva* the contract price for installation of central heating was £560; there were defects in the work which cost £170 to correct, and the builder recovered nothing. It has been suggested that cases like

Hoenig v Isaacs can be explained on the basis that P had completely performed his obligation to do the contract work, but was in breach of the separate obligation that the work be carried out with reasonable skill and care, which is classified as an innominate term[7]. Since the breach was not serious, it did not entitle D to terminate the contract, but did entitle D to claim damages in respect of the defects[8]. However, the distinction which this approach requires to be drawn between incomplete and complete but defective performance may be difficult to draw.

A party may also be entitled to be paid for partial performance of an entire obligation if the other party wrongfully prevents him completing performance. In such a case the innocent party may claim damages and choose between claiming compensation in respect of the profit he would have made by completing the work, or a quantum meruit for the value of the work done[9].

The various exceptions to the rule that complete performance of an entire obligation is needed to discharge the obligation are largely mitigated by the available exceptions[10]. In particular, the parties to a contract can avoid the rule by making obligations severable, so that payment is due as each severable part is performed. This is commonly done in contracts for large projects, such as major construction, shipbuilding and engineering contracts, where the contract calls for 'stage payments' to be made as each stage of the work is completed. However, the rule is still capable of applying and may produce unfair results: small-scale building and similar contracts are unlikely to provide for stage payments and, in a situation such as that in *Sumpter v Hedges*, the landowner appears to receive a benefit at the expense of the builder. In 1983 the Law Commission therefore recommended that the law be changed to require a party who received a net benefit as a result of the partial performance of an entire contract to pay for that benefit[11]. However, that recommendation is unlikely to be implemented; one member of the Commission dissented pointing out that the existing rule provided a measure of protection for householders and similar persons who contract with builders for small construction works: 'Experience has shown that it is all too common for such builders not to complete one job of work before moving on to the next'[12]. At least the present rule gives the householder the lever of refusing to pay for the uncompleted work.

1 An example is provided by Sale of Goods Act 1979, s 28, which makes the seller's duty to deliver the goods and the buyer's to accept them and pay the price concurrent conditions: see 9.1.
2 *Cutter v Powell* (1795) 6 Term Rep 320; *Sumpter v Hedges* [1898] 1 QB 673, CA.
3 Older cases speak of the circumstances justifying the implication of a new contract to pay for the part performance, but restitutionary claims were often explained on the basis of implied contract.
4 [1898] 1 QB 673; see also *Bolton v Mahadeva* [1972] 2 All ER 1322, CA.
5 Sale of Goods Act 1979, s 30(1), below 10.3.
6 [1952] 2 All ER 176, CA.
7 Treitel, *Law of Contract* (10th edn, 1999) p 730.
8 See below 19.1.
9 *Planché v Colburn* (1831) 8 Bing 14.
10 See also Apportionment Act 1870 which abrogates the rule in relation to periodic payments such as salaries.
11 Law Commission 121 *Pecuniary Restitution for Breach of Contract* (1983).
12 Brian Davenport QC, note of dissent to Law Commission 121 *Pecuniary Restitution for Breach of Contract* (1983).

2.9.3 *Discharge by breach*

A breach of contract does not discharge the contract, or either party. However, a breach may entitle the innocent party to terminate the contract, and thus treat himself as discharged from any outstanding obligations thereunder[1]. Whether the breach has this effect depends on the nature of the term broken and, in some cases, on the effect of the breach. The innocent party has the right to terminate the contract:

(a) where the term broken is a condition[2];
(b) where an intermediate stipulation[3] is broken and the breach deprives the innocent party of 'substantially the whole benefit which it was intended that he should receive'; or
(c) if the other party repudiates the contract, by indicating that he no longer intends to be bound by it: for instance by making clear that he will not perform or will only perform in a way which is inconsistent with the contract[4].

Generally, a party who refuses to perform his obligations under the contract when they fall due himself repudiates the contract, unless his refusal is justified by some prior breach by the other party. However, a party may justify a repudiation by reference to any prior breach even if he was not aware of it at the time of his refusal to perform[5]. Moreover, a party who seeks to justify a repudiation on one ground may generally subsequently justify it on a different ground, provided that it existed at the time of the refusal[6]. A party who honestly, but mistakenly, believes that he is entitled to refuse to perform may be held not to have repudiated[7].

Repudiation may occur before the time for, or during, performance. There is authority that where the contract allows a period of time for performance it cannot be said that a condition or intermediate stipulation is broken until the time for its performance has expired; in that case a party who has rendered a defective performance may be able to 'cure' it, provided he can do so before expiry of the time for performance[8]. It is clear, however, that 'cure' is impossible where the breach is incapable of remedy, for instance where the term broken consists of a promise as to an existing state of facts which must either be true or false when made, or failure to perform at the right time where time is of the essence[9]. In addition, there will be no right of cure where the initial performance is so defective as to amount to a repudiation of the contract.

A breach of contract, whatever its nature, does not oblige the innocent party to terminate, but gives him the option to do so. If, with full knowledge[10] of the breach, he chooses to go on with the contract, he is said to affirm the contract. The right to terminate the contract for that breach is then lost, although the innocent party may still claim damages, and further breaches may give rise to fresh rights to terminate. Both parties remain liable to perform the contract[11]. If the innocent party does choose to terminate, both parties are released from their primary obligations under the contract and no further performance is due. However, obligations due to be performed prior to termination remain binding, and damages are payable in respect of breaches of contract, by either party, which occurred prior to termination. Damages are also payable in respect of any losses caused by the breach which gives rise to the right to terminate. It is now settled that termination does not prevent the party in breach relying on any exclusion clauses in the contract[12].

A party who repudiates before the time for performance by indicating that he will not perform is said to commit an anticipatory breach, which gives the innocent party the option either to accept the anticipatory breach as terminating the contract immediately, or to keep the contract alive and press for performance at the due time. Acceptance of the breach needs no special form. He may accept the breach by any conduct which clearly demonstrates that he treats the contract as at an end and which comes to the attention of the party in breach, including, in an appropriate case, by failing to perform his own obligations[13]. If he does opt to terminate the contract, both parties are released from their further obligations under the contract and he may claim damages for breach of contract immediately[14]. If he keeps the contract alive but no actual performance is made, the innocent party has a further right to terminate for the actual breach. However, non-acceptance of an anticipatory breach involves a measure of risk: the contract remains fully in force for the benefit of both parties, so that if before the time for actual performance the contract is frustrated[15] or the 'innocent party' commits a breach justifying the other in terminating[16], the innocent party will be unable to claim damages in respect of the anticipatory breach or the eventual failure to perform.

1   See generally Bradgate, 'Termination for Breach' in Birds, Bradgate and Villiers (eds)*Termination of Contracts*.
2   See above 2.5.6.
3   See above 2.5.6.
4   See eg *Torvald Klaveness A/S v Arni Maritime Corpn* [1994] 4 All ER 998, [1994] 1 WLR 1465, HL.
5   *Boston Deep Sea Fishing and Ice Co v Ansell* (1888) 39 Ch D 339.
6   *Glencore Grain Rotterdam BV v Lebanese Organisation for International Commerce* [1997] 4 All ER 514.
7   *Woodar Development Ltd v Wimpey Construction UK Ltd* [1980] 1 All ER 571, [1980] 1 WLR 277; *Vaswani v Italian Motors (Sales and Service) Ltd* [1996] 1 WLR 270, PC.
8   See eg *Motor Oil Hellas (Corinth) Refineries SA v Shipping Corpn of India, The Kanchenjunga* [1990] 1 Lloyd's Rep 391 at 399 per Lord Goff; see Beale, *Remedies for Breach of Contract* (1990) p 91; Apps [1994] LMCLQ 525.
9   See *Union Eagle Ltd v Golden Achievement Ltd* [1997] 2 All ER 215, PC.
10   But in the case of sale contracts the general rule is modified: see Sale of Goods Act 1979, ss 34–35, below 12.1.3.
11   See *Fercometal SARL v MSC Mediterranean Shipping Co SA* [1989] AC 788, [1988] 2 All ER 742, discussed below at 9.1.
12   *Photo-Productions Ltd v Securicor Transport Ltd* [1980] AC 827, [1980] 1 All ER 556, HL.
13   *Vitol SA v Norelf Ltd, The Santa Clara* [1996] AC 800, [1996] 4 All ER 193; see Hedley [1996] CLJ 430.
14   *Hochester v de la Tour* (1853) 2 E & B 678.
15   *Avery v Bowden* (1855) 5 E & B 714.
16   *Fercometal SARL v MSC Mediterranean Shipping Co SA* [1989] AC 788, [1988] 2 All ER 742.

2.9.4   *Discharge by frustration*

Even the most sophisticated contract cannot anticipate and provide for all eventualities. Particularly where a contract is to be performed over a long period, events may arise which make performance impossible, illegal, difficult, or more expensive than anticipated, and therefore unprofitable. The parties may often provide for some such eventualities by including appropriate terms in the contract, such as price variation clauses to cover cost increases or force majeure clauses to relieve a party, or allow an extension of time for performance, where performance is prevented or hindered by events such as storms, strikes or embargoes. However, if an event not provided for by the contract occurs, it will be necessary to decide what effect that event has on the parties' obligations under the contract. If an unforeseeable event makes performance of the contract impossible, illegal, or radically different from what the parties anticipated, the contract will be frustrated: both parties will then be discharged from their obligations.

Because frustration has a drastic impact on the obligations of the parties, the courts have tended to apply the doctrine restrictively. Thus a contract may be frustrated by events which make performance impossible, such as the destruction or non-availability of the contract subject matter[1], or death or incapacity of one of the parties to a contract requiring personal performance[2]; or by supervening illegality, such as a trade embargo imposed after the contract is made. In addition, a contract may be frustrated by an event which frustrates the common adventure of the parties so that performance in the changed circumstances would be radically different from what was anticipated[3]. However, the contract will not be frustrated by an event which merely makes performance more difficult, or more expensive than anticipated[4], so that, for instance, a cif[5] contract for the sale of goods was not frustrated when the Suez Canal was closed. The effect of the closure was to require the seller, who had anticipated that the goods would be carried via the canal, to pay considerably more than he had anticipated to ship the goods, because he had to arrange for them to be carried via the Cape of Good Hope[6].

A contract will not be frustrated by an event which the parties foresaw, or which was foreseeable as likely. The explanation for this is that, as we have seen, contracts are used as a means to allocate risks. A contract can only be frustrated where it has not, expressly or impliedly, allocated the risk of the event in question to one of the parties. Commercial contracts often make express provision for many risks which might interfere with performance in order to avoid the uncertainties of the doctrine of frustration. For instance, force majeure clauses may allow an extension of time for performance, or even provide for the parties to be released from their obligations, where performance is delayed, hindered or made impossible by circumstances outside their control, such as bad weather. Alternatively, a party may be held to have impliedly accepted a risk if, for instance, he has contracted to achieve a particular result, as, for instance, where a cif shipper contracts, for a stated price, to arrange shipment to a stated destination[7], or if he is to be paid a price considerably higher than would be normal for such a contract[8]. Where a contract is of a speculative nature it is unlikely to be frustrated: the essence of such a contract is the taking of a risk:

> 'No-one can tell how long a spell of commercial depression may last; no suspense can be more harassing than the vagaries of foreign exchanges, but contracts are made for the purpose of fixing such risks in advance, and their occurrence only makes it more necessary to uphold a contract and not to make them a ground for discharging it'[9].

A party cannot rely on 'self-induced frustration' to excuse him from performance. If one of the parties is responsible for an event which makes performance impossible, that party will be in breach of contract. It seems that only events outside the control of the party alleging frustration will frustrate the contract, so that a negligent act or omission which makes performance impossible will be regarded as 'self-induced frustration'[10]. Similarly, frustration will be self-induced if some act of the party alleging frustration intervenes and breaks the chain of causation between the allegedly frustrating event and its impact on the contract: for instance, if a party's sources of supply partially fail and he decides to allocate the available supplies to one contract rather than to another[11].

Where a contract is frustrated, the contract is automatically discharged, so that the parties are relieved from performance of future obligations. However, obligations which had already fallen due for performance remain due, and the parties are liable for any breaches which occurred prior to frustration. At common law losses caused by the frustration lay where they fell. The position is now governed by the Law Reform (Frustrated Contracts) Act 1943, which gives the court a discretion to apportion losses caused by frustration. Unfortunately, its drafting is far from clear, and to date there are only two reported decisions on its interpretation. It seems that both businesses and lawyers prefer to deal with problems caused by frustration by negotiation.

The Act applies to all contracts except: (a) charterparties other than time charters or charterparties by demise; (b) contracts of insurance; (c) contracts for the sale of specific goods frustrated by the goods' perishing[12]. Where the Act applies, it provides that:

(a) all moneys paid prior to frustration are refundable and sums payable but not paid cease to be payable, subject to the court's discretion to allow the payee to retain some or all of the payment if he has incurred expenses in performing his side of the contract, if the court deems it just to do so in all the circumstances[13]; and

(b) if prior to frustration one party has received a 'valuable benefit' from the other, the court has a discretion to order him to pay the other 'such sum as it considers just', not exceeding the value of the benefit[14]; it seems that the effects of the frustrating event are to be taken into account in deciding if there is a valuable benefit[15].

1 *Taylor v Caldwell* (1863) 3 B & S 826.
2 *Poussard v Spiers and Pond* (1876) 1 QBD 410.
3 *Krell v Henry* [1903] 2 KB 740.
4 *Davis Contractors Ltd v Fareham UDC* [1956] AC 696, [1956] 2 All ER 145, HL.
5 Cost-insurance-freight. Under such a contract the seller arranges carriage of the goods to their destination, and insurance, at a fixed price. See 33.2.
6 *Tsakiroglou & Co Ltd v Noblee Thorl GmbH* [1962] AC 93, [1961] 2 All ER 179, HL.
7 See 33.2.
8 Eg *Krell v Henry* [1903] 2 KB 740; *W J Tatem Ltd v Gamboa* [1939] 1 KB 132, [1938] 3 All ER 135.
9 Lord Sumner in *Larrinaga v Société Franco-Américaine des Phosphates de Médulla* (1923) 92 LJKB 455 at 464.
10 *The Super Servant Two* [1989] 1 Lloyd's Rep 148; affd [1990] 1 Lloyd's Rep 1, CA.
11 *Maritime National Fish Ltd v Ocean Trawlers Ltd* [1935] AC 524; *The Super Servant Two* [1989] 1 Lloyd's Rep 148; affd [1990] 1 Lloyd's Rep 1.
12 Section 7 of the Sale of Goods Act 1979 applies: see 16.2.5.
13 Section 1(2); see *Gamerco SA v ICM (Fair Warning) Agency Ltd* [1995] 1 WLR 1226.
14 Section 1(3).
15 *BP Exploration Co (Libya) Ltd v Hunt (No 2)* [1982] 1 All ER 925.

2.10   Remedies

Where a party fails, without lawful excuse, to perform his contractual obligations, he will be in breach of contract. The law offers the innocent party a range of sanctions which may be invoked in response to such a breach. However, although contracts are often defined as 'legally enforceable agreements', the primary legal remedy for a breach of contract is an order that the contract breaker pay monetary compensation. Although the courts have power to order contractual obligations to be performed, that power is rarely exercised, especially in relation to commercial contracts.

Although the action for unliquidated damages is the law's basic remedy for breach of contract, commercial people tend to prefer to avoid litigation and the courts if at all possible. Court proceedings may be slow, unpredictable, expensive and attended by publicity. Moreover, where the breach is not so serious as to destroy the trading relationship between the parties, protracted litigation may generate ill-feeling and slow the healing of the relationship. Where possible, therefore, the innocent party will prefer a remedy which can be exercised without the court's assistance. If court proceedings are necessary, a remedy which is quick and procedurally simple to obtain will be preferable. Contracts are therefore often arranged so as to enable parties to exercise self-help remedies or to seek procedurally simple remedies such as an action for a liquidated amount in preference to a fully fledged action for unliquidated damages.

2.10.1 *Self-help remedies*

The great advantage of self-help remedies for breach of contract is that they can be exercised without the assistance of the court. The onus is thrown onto the party in breach to take proceedings to challenge action taken by way of self-help, shifting the balance of bargaining power. The simplest of such remedies is for the innocent party to refuse to perform his own obligations altogether. Thus, as we have seen, a party can withhold performance of his own obligations until the other has completed performance of an entire obligation whose performance is a condition precedent to his own liability[1]; and if the other commits a repudiatory breach, a breach of condition or a serious breach of an innominate term the innocent party may choose to bring the contract to an end and thus refuse performance of any outstanding obligations[2]. Careful drafting of the contract can maximise the power to exercise such remedies, by defining terms as conditions, or by expressly providing for a right to withhold performance and/or terminate the contract.

Generally, the right to withhold performance is only effective where the innocent party has not yet performed his obligations. If the innocent party has already performed his obligations, for instance by paying in advance, termination of the contract will achieve nothing alone: the innocent party will still need the assistance of the court to recover the money paid.

The contract will often bolster the right to withhold performance by providing for some form of security to be given to guard against breach. For instance, the contract may require one party to give the other security, such as a charge, over property; in the event of default, the innocent party can then enforce the security. Contracts for the supply of goods may protect the supplier against the customer's non-performance by allowing him to retain title to the goods under a retention of title[3] or hire purchase arrangement[4]; the contract will normally contain an express indication of the circumstances in which the seller can enforce his security. The potency of such self-help remedies is confirmed by the fact that in consumer contracts it has been thought necessary to provide for some limitation on their exercise[5].

The contract may require advance payments, such as deposits or instalments, and provide for them to be retained in the event of default. Advance payments can be recovered where the contract is terminated and there is a total failure of consideration for which they were paid[6], but where part of the work required by the contract has been performed, there will not be a total failure[7] and if the payment is properly categorised as a deposit, even under a sale contract, it is not recoverable if the contract is terminated: a deposit is paid as a security for the payer's performance so that even if the contract is not performed, there is no failure of the consideration for which the deposit was paid. A true deposit is not subject to the rule against penalties[8], although if the amount paid as a 'deposit' is unreasonable, the court may infer that it was not paid as security for performance, in which case no part of it may be retained[9]. Again, however, there are statutory limitations on the forfeiture of deposits and part payments under certain consumer contracts[10]. In addition, the court has a general equitable power to grant relief from forfeiture, and although the position is far from clear, there is some support for the view that this power may be exercised to grant relief from the retention of instalment payments made pursuant to a commercial contract[11]; however, it is clear that the power will rarely be exercised under a commercial contract.

> 'Equitable relief of this kind is really inconsistent with the principle that in commercial transactions parties must, so far as possible, be able to know where they stand, or at least to obtain helpful advice from their lawyers on the basis of which they can act with a reasonable degree of confidence'[12].

A further alternative is for the contract to provide for one or both parties to offer security in the form of a guarantee from a trusted third party, such as a bank; in the event of default by one party, the other can then obtain recompense by enforcing the guarantee. Such arrangements are particularly common in commercial contracts. In theory, such provisions do not provide for self-help: if the guarantor fails to honour the guarantee, court proceedings must be used to enforce it. However, in practice it is very rare for such guarantors (as opposed to individuals giving personal guarantees) to dispute liability[13].

1   Above 2.9.3.
2   Above 2.5.6.
3   Below 18.4.
4   Below 8.2.1.
5   Consumer Credit Act 1974, ss 90–92, below 26.6.5.
6   *Dies v British and International Mining and Finance Corpn Ltd* [1939] 1 KB 724.
7   *Hyundai Heavy Industries Co Ltd v Papadopoulous* [1980] 2 All ER 29, [1980] 1 WLR 1129; *Stocznia Gdanska SA v Latvian Shipping Co* [1998] 1 All ER 883, HL.
8   Below 2.10.2.
9   *Workers Trust and Merchant Bank Ltd v Dojap Investments Ltd* [1993] AC 573, [1993] 2 All ER 370.
10 Consumer Credit Act 1974, s 132(1), below 26.6.7.
11 *Stockloser v Johnson* [1954] 1 QB 476, [1954] 1 All ER 630, CA; *The Afovos* [1980] 2 Lloyd's Rep 469; *Shiloh Spinners Ltd v Harding* [1973] AC 691 at 726, HL; contra *The Scaptrade* [1983] 2 AC 694, [1983] 2 All ER 763, HL.
12 Lord Goff, 'Commercial Contracts and the Commercial Court' [1984] LMCLQ 382 at 392.
13 See ch 23 and the discussion of performance bonds, below 34.3.

2.10.2   *Judicial remedies*

A party who cannot obtain satisfaction by self-help remedies may have to seek the assistance of the court. The normal remedy is an award of damages, quantified by the court. However, other remedies are available. The court has an equitable discretion to order specific performance of the contract, but specific performance will not normally be ordered where damages would be a sufficient remedy, nor in respect of a contract requiring personal performance or constant supervision[1]. It is therefore rarely available for the breach of a commercial contract. Similarly, an injunction may be available in certain circumstances, particularly to prevent breach of a negative stipulation such as a restrictive covenant in a contract for the sale of land, or a non-competition clause on the sale of a business or in a contract of employment or agency, but a mandatory injunction to perform a contract will not be available where specific performance would not be ordered[2].

1   See *Co-operative Insurance Society Ltd v Argyll Stores (Holdings) Ltd* [1998] AC 1, [1997] 3 All ER 297; McMeel (1998) 114 LQR 43; Phang (1998) 61 MLR 421.
2   See *Sky Petroleum Ltd v VIP Petroleum Ltd* [1974] 1 All ER 954.

2.10.2.1   *Liquidated claims*

In order to avoid the uncertainty, and possible delay, involved in the court assessing damages, a contract may contain provisions allowing a party to bring a liquidated claim in the event of default by the other. The advantages of a liquidated claim are that the amount recoverable is ascertainable in advance and, in addition, the procedure for its recovery is simpler than that for an unliquidated sum. In particular, where a claim is for a liquidated sum, it is possible in certain circumstances to obtain final judgment at an early stage of the proceedings. In the case of an unliquidated claim, summary judgment is possible, but it will be for damages to be assessed by the court at a later date[1].

(a)   Debt

A contractor who has performed his obligations may be able to claim the contract price as a debt rather than damages. Special rules govern the availability of the claim for the price under sale of goods contracts[2]; in other cases, the ability to claim the price for goods, work or services depends on the construction of the contract. If the obligation to do the work etc is entire and its performance is a condition precedent to the customer's obligation to pay, the price is only payable on completion of the work[3]. In *White and Carter Councils Ltd v McGregor*[4] the House of Lords held that where the defendant had repudiated the contract at an early stage, before the plaintiffs had begun to perform, the plaintiffs were nevertheless entitled to go on and complete performance of their obligations and then claim the contract price. The result is sometimes criticised on the grounds that the plaintiffs should have been required to mitigate their loss[5] and that allowing the plaintiffs to render an unwanted performance was economically wasteful, as it benefited no one. However, the principle of *White and Carter* will rarely be applied. It is limited to cases where one party can perform without the co-operation of the other: it will therefore be inapplicable in many cases. Lord Reid also suggested that it may be further limited so that it will not apply if it can be shown that the person performing the contract has no legitimate interest in performing it, other than claiming damages[6].

(b)   Interest

Interest may be payable on sums due under a commercial contract. Prior to 1998 the court had jurisdiction to award interest on sums (other than damages) paid late under a contract (a) if the contract provided for payment of interest or (b) under statute, but only if proceedings were commenced before payment[7]. A creditor therefore had no legal right to interest if his debtor paid late but before the commencement of proceedings, unless the contract provided for interest to be payable. This was considered to be adverse to the interests especially of small businesses, which often lacked the bargaining power to insist on the inclusion in their contracts of a provision for payment of interest, especially when contracting with larger businesses.

These powers are now supplemented by the Late Payment of Commercial Debts (Interest) Act 1998 which implies a term into contracts for the supply of goods or services where both parties act in the course of business that debts created by the contract carry simple (not compound) interest[8]. Any term which purports to exclude or vary the statutory right is void unless it provides a substantial remedy for late payment[9]. A remedy is not 'substantial' if it would be insufficient to deter late payment, or to compensate the supplier for late payment, or it would not be 'fair and reasonable' to allow it to exclude the statutory right[10].

The Act is intended to improve the position (especially) of small businesses in dealings with their customers. It will allow such a business to claim interest, as a legal debt, if the customer is late paying sums due under the contract, even if payment is made before commencement of court proceedings. However, many of the Act's provisions may prove to be uncertain in their application and it is not especially cynical to suspect that if a business lacks the bargaining power to insist on the inclusion in its contracts of a term for payment of interest, it may be commercially difficult for it to enforce the statutory right to interest under the Act.

(c) Negotiable instruments
The advantages of a liquidated claim can be obtained by the contract providing for payment to be made by cheque or bill of exchange, since such instruments give rise to a legal obligation to honour the instrument, which can be enforced separately from the underlying contract[11].

(d) Liquidated damages
The buyer of goods or services does not have the option of bringing a claim in debt or requiring payment by cheque[12], but the contract may contain provisions fixing the amount of damages payable in the event of breach. Such clauses may be attractive to both parties: they offer the victim of the breach the advantages of a liquidated claim and, since they define the amount of damages payable, they allow the contract breaker to anticipate his potential liability and make it easier to obtain insurance against it. However, such a provision will only be enforceable if the amount payable as liquidated damages is 'a genuine pre-estimate' of the loss likely to be caused by a breach of contract, rather than being intended as a fine, or penalty for breach, or to operate 'in terrorem'[13]. Damages for breach of contract are intended to compensate the innocent party rather than to punish the contract breaker, and the courts will not allow this basic principle to be evaded by an express term fixing the amount of damages payable. This does not mean that a clause will necessarily be regarded as an unenforceable penalty merely because it is difficult to pre-estimate the damages likely to be caused by a breach: on the contrary, that is just the sort of situation where a liquidated damages clause might be most useful. However, the sum payable must not be extravagant or disproportionately greater than any loss which could conceivably flow from the breach. Where a clause makes one sum payable in the event of any of a series of breaches of differing degrees of seriousness, the clause may be regarded as a penalty[14]; thus, for instance, a clause fixing damages for late delivery of goods should provide for the sum payable to vary according to the length of the delay.

A requirement for payment of a deposit is generally not regarded as a penalty. However, if the amount payable as a 'deposit' is unreasonable, the court may regard it as paid not by way of security for performance but 'in terrorem', as a penalty, and order its repayment[15]. A clause requiring the transfer of property in the event of a breach of contract may also be regarded as a penalty if the value of the property is disproportionate to the consequences of the breach[16].

1   See 36.1.2.
2   See 18.2.1.
3   Above 2.9.2.
4   [1962] AC 413, [1961] 3 All ER 1178.
5   But see Treitel, *The Law of Contracts* (10th edn, 1999) p 948.
6   [1962] AC 413 at 431; see *Attica Sea Carriers Corpn v Ferrostaal Poseidon Bulk Reederei GmbH* [1976] 1 Lloyd's Rep 250, CA.
7   Supreme Court Act 1981, s 35A; County Courts Act 1984, s 69.
8   Section 1. The rate of interest is to be fixed by the Secretary of State. It has been fixed, initially, at the apparently generous rate of 8% per annum: Late Payment of Commercial Debts (Rate of Interest) Orders 1998, SI 1998/2480, SI 2765. The Act is to be brought into force in stages by statutory instrument. At present it applies in favour of small business suppliers (with not more than 50 employees) in contracts with large business customers or UK public authorities. It is expected to be applied to all business contracts by 2002.
9   Section 8.
10 Section 9.
11 See below 28.1.1.
12 Although he may require the supplier to provide a performance bond for a liquidated amount: see below 34.3.
13 *Dunlop Pneumatic Tyre Co Ltd v New Garage and Motor Co Ltd* [1915] AC 79, HL.
14 In a contract with a consumer such a clause will also be subject to the Unfair Terms in Consumer Contracts Regulations 1999: see 2.6.5.
15 *Workers Trust and Merchant Bank Ltd v Dojap Investments Ltd* [1993] AC 573, [1993] 2 All ER 370.
16 *Jobson v Johnson* [1989] 1 All ER 621, [1989] 1 WLR 1026, CA.

2.10.3   *Unliquidated damages*

Damages for breach of contract are intended to compensate the innocent party for losses suffered as a result of the breach, so that if the innocent party suffers no loss, no, or only minimal, damages are payable. However, damages are not limited simply to out of pocket losses, but normally seek to compensate the innocent party for his lost expectations by seeking to put him, so far as an award of damages can do so, in the position he would have been in had the contract been performed[1]. So, for instance, damages for breach of a commercial contract would normally include the profit the plaintiff would have made had the contract been performed.

The contract breaker may be able to make a profit by breaking his contract. For example, a seller of goods may break his contract with his buyer and then sell the goods at more than the current market price to another buyer, or use them more profitably himself; or a supplier of services may contract to provide a particular level of service and be paid accordingly, but then provide a lower level of service which nevertheless causes no loss to his customer[2]. As a general rule, the compensatory principle means that, subject to compensating his victim for his losses, the contract breaker is entitled in such a case to keep his profit[3]. In 1997 the Law Commission considered whether the law should be changed to allow the victim in such cases to make a claim for restitutionary damages so as to prevent the contract breaker making a profit. It concluded that any development in the law should be left to the courts[4]. In *A-G v Blake*[5] Lord Woolf MR indicated, obiter, that the courts might make just such a development. He observed that 'if the law of contract is unable to award restitutionary damages for breach of contract, then the law of contract is seriously defective'. An award of restitutionary damages would only be made in an exceptional case, and Lord Woolf indicated that it might be limited to cases (a) where the defendant contracts to provide a service and makes a profit by providing a lower level of service (so that in effect the claimant is over charged) or (b) where the defendant in breach of contract does the very thing he contracted not to do. When the case came before the House of Lords, however, their Lordships expressly declined to make any such development, observing that the categories proposed by Lord Woolf were uncertain in their scope[6]. Their Lordships recognised that the court has jurisdiction in an exceptional case to make an order for an account of profits against a defendant who profits from a breach of contract. They held however that such an order would only be made where the claimant has a 'legitimate interest' in preventing the defendant's profit making activity. Such an order was justified in the present case where the defendant (a former member of the intelligence services) was in breach of a contractual duty of confidentiality, similar in nature to a fiduciary duty. Their Lordships indicated that such an order would rarely if ever be appropriate in cases involving ordinary commercial contracts.

As an alternative to claiming expectation losses, a party who has incurred expenditure in reliance on a contract can claim damages to compensate for that wasted expenditure. Damages then cover the innocent party's reliance loss rather than expectation loss[7]. Reliance losses can include expenditure wasted in actually performing the contract and, in some cases, expenditure incurred prior to the contract in anticipation of it[8]. However, a plaintiff cannot claim both reliance and expectation losses where that would compensate him twice in respect of the same loss. Thus a person who has contracted to buy goods which are not delivered cannot claim both the gross profit he would have made on the contract and the costs of arranging to collect the goods, since he would have incurred those costs in order to earn the profits. It seems that the plaintiff may choose whether to claim expectation or reliance losses, but a claim for reliance losses cannot put the plaintiff in a better position than if the contract had been performed; thus if he has made a bad bargain, so that his reliance losses exceed the value of the profit he would have made if the contract had been performed, the court will not allow him to claim the full reliance losses. It is for the defendant to prove that the reliance losses exceed the expected profits from the contract[9]. In practice, therefore, the plaintiff will claim reliance losses where it is impossible to prove what profits would have been earned had the contract been performed.

Damages may be awarded in contract in respect of economic losses, damage to property and personal injuries. Generally, damages are not available for emotional distress, or for anguish and vexation[10], except in special cases where the object of the contract is to provide enjoyment or peace of mind[11]; such damages may therefore be available for breach of consumer contracts[12], but not of commercial contracts.

Clearly some limit must be placed on the scope of the losses which may be compensated by an award of damages for a breach of contract 'because it were infinite for the law to judge the cause of causes or the consequence of consequences'[13]. Damages for breach of contract are limited by three principles: first, the plaintiff must prove that the losses in respect of which he claims were caused by the breach of contract in question; second, the losses in question must not be too remote in law from the breach; and third, the plaintiff must take reasonable steps to mitigate his loss.

1 *Robinson v Harman* (1848) 1 Exch 850.
2 See *White Arrow Express Ltd v Lamey's Distribution Ltd* [1995] NLJR 1504, CA; see Beale (1996) 112 LQR 203.
3 *Surrey County Council v Bredero Homes Ltd* [1993] 3 All ER 705; see Birks (1993) 109 LQR 518; Burrows [1993] LMCLQ 453.
4 Law Commission 247 *Aggravated, Exemplary and Restitutionary Damages* (1997).
5 [1998] Ch 439, [1998] 1 All ER 833.

6   [2000] 4 All ER 385.
7   See Fuller and Perdue, 'The Reliance Interest in Contract Damages' (1936–37) 46 Yale LJ 52, 573 for a full discussion of the problems of reliance damages.
8   *Anglia Television Ltd v Reed* [1972] 1 QB 60, [1971] 3 All ER 690, CA.
9   *CCC Films (London) Ltd v Impact Quadrant Films Ltd* [1985] QB 16, [1984] 3 All ER 298.
10 *Addis v Gramophone Co Ltd* [1909] AC 488; *Bliss v South East Thames Regional Health Authority* [1987] ICR 700, CA; *Hayes v James & Charles Dodd* [1990] 2 All ER 815, CA; *Watts v Morrow* [1991] 4 All ER 937.
11 *Jarvis v Swans Tours* [1973] QB 233, [1973] 1 All ER 71, CA; *Jackson v Horizon Holidays Ltd* [1975] 3 All ER 92, [1975] 1 WLR 1468 (package holidays); *Heywood v Wellers* [1976] QB 446, [1976] 1 All ER 300, CA (solicitor instructed to obtain injunction preventing harassment).
12 See *Ruxley Electronics and Construction Ltd v Forsyth* [1996] AC 344, [1995] 3 All ER 268.
13 Per Lord Wright in *Liesbosch Dredger (Owners) v SS Edison (Owners)* [1933] AC 449 at 460, HL.

2.10.3.1   *Causation*

The plaintiff can only recover damages in respect of losses which he can prove were caused by the breach of contract complained of. The contract breaker is not liable for losses caused by some supervening act, whether of a third party or of the plaintiff, unless the supervening act was reasonably foreseeable as liable to result from the breach, ie it is not too remote[1]. If a supervening act does break the chain of causation, the plaintiff can recover damages from the contract breaker in respect of any losses he suffered before the supervening act but not in respect of subsequent losses, nor for hypothetical losses he would have incurred as a result of the original breach if the supervening act had not occurred[2].

Contributory negligence by the plaintiff which does not break the chain of causation will reduce the damages recoverable from the defendant where the breach of contract consists of a failure to take reasonable care which would also give rise to liability in tort[3]. Contributory negligence is no defence to a claim for damages for breach of a strict contractual duty[4]. It is not clear if it provides a defence to a claim for breach of a contractual duty to take reasonable care where there is no concurrent tortious liability.

1   See 2.10.3.2.
2   *Beoco Ltd v Alfa Laval Co Ltd* [1995] QB 137, [1994] 1 All ER 464.
3   *Forsikringsaktieselskapet Vesta v Butcher* [1986] 2 All ER 488; affd [1989] AC 852, [1988] 2 All ER 43.
4   *Barclays Bank plc v Fairclough Building Ltd* [1995] QB 214, [1995] 1 All ER 289.

2.10.3.2   *Remoteness*

The rules of remoteness of damage in contract cases are derived from the famous case of *Hadley v Baxendale*[1]. The defendant is liable for those losses which he foresaw, or could have foreseen, at the time the contract was made as being not unlikely[2] to result from the breach of contract. Losses will be regarded as foreseeable, according to *Hadley v Baxendale,* in two situations:

(a) if they arise naturally, in the ordinary course of events, from the breach; or
(b) if they could reasonably be supposed to have been in the contemplation of the parties, when they made the contract, as the probable result of it.

The first limb of the rule covers losses which any person would foresee as the natural consequence of a breach of contract; the second limb covers losses which result from circumstances special to the particular case: in that case, the defendant is only liable for those losses if he was aware of the special circumstances. The operation of the rule is illustrated by the case of *Victoria Laundry (Windsor) Ltd v Newman Industries Ltd*[3], where the defendants contracted to manufacture and supply a boiler to the plaintiffs, but delivered late. The defendants knew that the plaintiffs operated a laundry and that they intended to put the boiler into immediate use in their business; they did not know that the plaintiffs intended to use the boiler in performing a lucrative dyeing contract; the defendants were therefore liable for the ordinary profits the plaintiffs would have made from the ordinary use of the boiler, but not for the additional profits they would have made from the special contract. The rationale for the rule is that the defendant should not be held liable for losses which he could not foresee: if one party knows of special circumstances which give rise to special risks, and wants the other party to bear those risks, he should disclose them. The other party may then protect himself, for instance, by including an appropriate exclusion in the contract, increasing the price or arranging insurance against the risk.

However, all that the rule requires is that the type of damage sustained should be foreseeable. Provided that the type of damage was foreseeable, the defendant is liable for all damage of that type, even though it may be far greater in extent than what was expected[4]. This may lead to difficult questions of classification of types of loss. In *Parsons (Livestock) Ltd v Uttley Ingham & Co Ltd* the plaintiff's pigs were killed by a rare disease caused by the defendant's breach of contract. It was foreseeable that the breach might cause the pigs to become ill, but neither the particular disease nor the death of the pigs was foreseeable. However, the majority of the Court of Appeal held that the damage was of the same kind as that which was foreseeable, and so was recoverable. In contrast, in *Victoria Laundry* the Court of Appeal distinguished between different kinds of lost profits[5].

1   (1854) 23 LJ Ex 179.
2   See *The Heron II* [1969] 1 AC 350, [1967] 3 All ER 686, HL.
3   [1949] 2 KB 528, [1949] 1 All ER 997, CA.
4   *Parsons (Livestock) Ltd v Uttley Ingham & Co Ltd* [1978] QB 791, [1978] 1 All ER 525, CA.
5   It may be that a different approach is taken to claims for economic loss and claims for physical damage; however, that is not the basis on which the majority decided *Parsons*. Lord Denning did draw such a distinction, but did not take the 'type of loss' point.

2.10.3.3   *Mitigation*

Even where damages are of a foreseeable type, the plaintiff may not recover the full amount of his loss. Once he becomes aware of a breach of contract he must take reasonable steps to mitigate his loss. If the plaintiff fails to take reasonable steps in mitigation, he will recover no damages in respect of losses which he could have avoided[1]. The requirement to mitigate may require the plaintiff to buy replacement goods[2] or even accept an offer of alternative performance from the defendant[3], but will generally not require the plaintiff to go to excessive lengths, such as embarking on hazardous litigation, or risking his reputation[4]. In contrast, if the plaintiff acts reasonably, he will recover for all his losses, even if his actions increase the loss[5].

If the plaintiff accepts an anticipatory breach and terminates the contract, his obligation to mitigate his damages arises at once[6]. However, if he chooses to affirm the contract, the obligation to mitigate does not arise until actual performance is refused[7].

1   *British Westinghouse Electric v Underground Electric Railways Co of London Ltd* [1912] AC 673, HL.

2   See 12.3.1 below for the rule in sale of goods cases.
3   *Payzu v Saunders* [1919] 2 KB 581; *The Solholt* [1983] 1 Lloyd's Rep 605, CA.
4   *Pilkington v Wood* [1953] Ch 770; *James Finlay & Co Ltd v Kwik Hoo Tong* [1929] 1 KB 400, CA.
5   *Banco de Portugal v Waterlow and Sons Ltd* [1932] AC 452, HL.
6   *Kaines (UK) Ltd v Osterriechische Warrenhandelsgesellschaft* [1993] 2 Lloyd's Rep 1.
7   *Gebrüder Metelmann GmbH & Co KG v NBR (London) Ltd* [1984] 1 Lloyd's Rep 614.

2.10.3.4   *Quantification of loss*

The plaintiff's loss may be quantified either by reference to the difference in value
between the performance contracted for and that actually rendered or by reference
to the cost of remedying the defective performance in order to bring it up to the
expected standard. In many cases damages will be the same whichever measure is
adopted. However, in some cases the 'cost of cure' may exceed the difference in
value. In *Ruxley Electronics and Construction Ltd v Forsyth*[1] a householder engaged
builders to build a swimming pool at his property and specified that it should have
maximum depth of 7ft 6in to make it safe for diving. The pool actually built was
only 6ft 9in deep at its deepest. It was found as fact that the difference in depth did
not make the pool unsafe or materially affect its value, but the defective performance
could only be cured by replacing the pool at a cost of £21,560. The majority of the
Court of Appeal held that the householder was nevertheless entitled to recover the
cost of cure and it was irrelevant whether he actually intended to do the repairs or
that it would be unreasonable to do so. That decision was unanimously overturned
by the House of Lords[2], which held that the court will not award the plaintiff the
cost of cure where such an award would be disproportionate to the benefit it would
provide to the plaintiff. Moreover, in deciding whether it would be reasonable to
award the cost of cure, it was relevant for the court to consider whether the plaintiff
actually intended to carry out repairs. On the facts of the case it would be
unreasonable to award the cost of cure, but the court could award the plaintiff
damages for loss of amenity resulting from the breach of contract.

1   [1994] 1 WLR 650; see Beale (1995) 111 LQR 54.
2   [1996] AC 344, [1995] 3 All ER 268.

2.10.3.5   *Limitations of damages*

A contract may contain terms which purport to limit the damages recoverable in
the event of breach, either by reference to a sum of money, or to particular types of
loss. Such clauses are subject to the rules governing the effectiveness of exclusion
clauses, both at common law and under statute[1].

A common formula used to limit liability in commercial contracts is to exclude
liability for 'indirect or consequential loss'. It is often thought that this excludes
liability for economic losses such as lost profits incurred as a result of a breach of
contract. The courts have, however, given it a more restricted meaning and interpret
'consequential loss' as loss which does *not* arise directly and naturally as a result
of the breach of contract, and which is therefore recoverable, if at all, only under
the second limb of the rule in *Hadley v Baxendale*. Exclusion of liability for
'consequential loss' therefore does not necessarily exclude liability for loss of
profits[2]. For instance, the lost profits recovered in *Victoria Laundry* were not
'consequential losses' in this sense.

1 See 2.6.
2 *Croudace Construction Ltd v Cawoods Concrete Products Ltd* [1978] 2 Lloyd's Rep 55); *British Sugar v NEI Power International* (1997) 87 BLR 42; *Deepak Fertiliser & Petrochemical v Davy McKee* [1999] 1 All ER (Comm) 69; *Hotel Services Ltd v Hilton International Hotels (UK) Ltd* [2000] 1 All ER (Comm) 750.

2.10.4 *Restitutionary claims*

A claim for damages may include a claim for restitution of money paid to the defendant: for instance, a buyer who pays in advance for goods which are not delivered may claim their full value at the date they should have been delivered. The damages will therefore include the sum paid by the plaintiff and the profit he would have made. However, the plaintiff cannot claim refund of the price and the full value of the goods, because that would give him double compensation.

In other cases a person may be able to recover money paid by way of a restitutionary claim where a claim for damages is not available. Such claims are sometimes referred to as 'quasi-contractual'; they are not limited to a contractual context, but may be particularly important where money has been paid but there is no valid contract between the parties. Thus a restitutionary claim may be made for:

(a) a quantum meruit where goods or services are supplied but there is no contract between the parties, for instance because the contract is void[1], or where goods or services were supplied in anticipation of a contract which never materialised[2];

(b) recovery of money paid under a void[3] (but not, normally, an illegal[4]) contract; or

(c) money paid under a contract where there is a total failure of consideration[5] so that the plaintiff receives none of the benefit he contracted for; the doctrine of total failure is somewhat artificial and may disregard actual benefits if, on a proper construction of the contract, they were not part of the contractual consideration for the payment[6].

1 *Craven-Ellis v Canons Ltd* [1936] 2 KB 403, [1936] 2 All ER 1066, CA.
2 *British Steel Corpn v Cleveland Bridge and Engineering Co Ltd* [1984] 1 All ER 504.
3 *Strickland v Turner (Executrix of Lane)* (1852) 7 Exch 208; *Westdeutsche Landesbank Girozentrale v Islington London Borough Council* [1996] AC 669, [1996] 3 All ER 961.
4 *Kingsley v Stirling Industrial Securities Ltd* [1967] 2 QB 747, [1966] 2 All ER 414, CA.
5 *Dies v British and International Mining and Finance Corpn Ltd* [1939] 1 KB 724; cf *Hyundai Heavy Industries Co Ltd v Papadopoulous* [1980] 2 All ER 29, [1980] 1 WLR 1129; *Stocznia Gdanska SA v Latvian Shipping Co* [1998] 1 All ER 883, HL.
6 See *Rowland v Divall* [1923] 2 KB 500, CA, below 14.1.1; *Rover International Ltd v Canon Film Sales Ltd (No 3)* [1989] 3 All ER 423.

Part II

Arranging the transaction: the law of agency

Chapter 3

Agency

3.0   The nature of agency and the role of agents

Agents play a vital role in commercial activity. 'Commerce would literally grind to a halt if businessmen and merchants could not employ the services of factors, brokers, forwarding agents, estate agents, auctioneers and the like and were expected to do everything themselves'[1]. The primary role of the agent in commerce is to negotiate and conclude contracts on behalf of someone else: the principal. The agent may possess special skill or expertise, or have special knowledge of a particular market, area or commodity; the principal may need someone 'on the spot' to negotiate the contract, particularly in an international context; or the principal may simply be too busy to make every contract personally. Agents 'are to be found in all advanced societies and . . . [their] activities are an inevitable feature of a developed economy'[2].

This concept of the agent as 'middleman' is familiar in everyday life: travel agents, estate agents and insurance brokers all take part in the negotiation of what might be termed 'consumer' transactions[3]. The doctrine of privity of contract normally prevents a person acquiring rights under a contract unless he is a party to it but, by a long established exception to that rule, where the contract is concluded by an agent on behalf of a principal, the agent's acts are treated as if they were the acts of the principal. Thus the principal steps into the shoes of the agent and becomes a party to the contract through the agent.

Whilst the primary role of agents in commerce is the negotiation and conclusion of contracts, 'agency' is a flexible concept. As we will see, it is used outside the context of commercial law. Moreover, within that context, agency concepts may be, and often are, invoked in order to produce commercially desirable results whilst distorting the law as little as possible[4]. '[A]gency is a purely legal concept employed by the courts as and when it is necessary to explain and resolve the problems created by certain fact situations'[5]. Some of the situations in which this type of reasoning has been used in the past will now be covered by the Contracts (Rights of Third Parties) Act 1999 and it may be that the relaxation of the privity doctrine effected by that Act will reduce the need to invoke agency concepts in this way in future. In situations which fall outside that Act, however, agency concepts will continue to play a vital role in commercial law.

1   Markesinis and Munday, *An Outline of the Law of Agency* (4th edn, 1998) p 4.
2   Ibid.

3   Special rules apply to all three: see below 3.2.2.
4   See eg *New Zealand Shipping Co Ltd v A M Satterthwaite & Co Ltd* [1975] AC 154, [1974]
    1 All ER 1015, PC, below 32.7; *Aluminium Industrie Vaassen BV v Romalpa Aluminium Ltd*
    [1976] 2 All ER 552, [1976] 1 WLR 676, below 18.4.1, 18.4.5; *First Sport Ltd v Barclays Bank plc*
    [1993] 3 All ER 789, [1993] 1 WLR 1229, and for an example from outside the commercial
    sphere, see *Ormrod v Crosville Motor Services* [1953] 2 All ER 753, [1953] 1 WLR 1120, CA.
5   Fridman, 'Establishing Agency' (1968) 84 LQR 224 at 231.

3.1   The definition of agency

It is notoriously difficult to produce a definition of 'agency' which adequately
covers all legal uses of the concept, and it is doubtful if it is worthwhile to try to do
so; as we have noted, agency is a flexible concept. However, a working definition
of 'agent' might be 'a person who is recognised by the law as having power to
affect the legal rights, liabilities and relationships of another person ("the
principal")'.

One defect of this and similar definitions[1] is that it focuses on the relationship
between the principal and the outside world, as that relationship is affected by the
actions of the agent, to the exclusion of the relationship between principal and
agent. As we shall see, that relationship is a special one, of a fiduciary nature, and
that gives rise to important rights and obligations between principal and agent.
Some authors therefore prefer to focus on that relationship[2] and define agency as
the relationship which arises from the consent of principal and agent to act in those
capacities.

Over the years the jurisprudential basis of agency has been the subject of much
academic debate[3]. Most authors now agree that the essence of agency is the agent's
power to affect the position of the principal, rather than the agent's 'authority'. In
the paradigm case of agency the source of the agent's power is the agency
relationship created by the consent of the parties. Where the principal consents to
the agent having such power we may say that the agent has the principal's authority
to act in that capacity. As we shall see, however, an agent has power to affect the
principal's position in a number of situations where his actions are not authorised
by the principal, and even where his actions have been expressly prohibited. To
speak of the agent having 'authority' in such cases is thus misleading, and it would
be better to think in terms of the power the agent has to affect the principal's legal
position. If agency is defined in terms of 'consent' or 'authority', those cases must
be explained as cases of 'deemed' consent or authority.

However, whilst a definition which emphasises the 'external' relationship of
the principal and the outside world may be preferable as explaining those difficult
cases where the principal does not in fact consent to the agent's actions, in the
great majority of cases of agency, especially in the commercial context, the
principal does in fact consent to the agent's actions, the agent does act in
accordance with his authority and no difficulty arises. Moreover, it must be borne
in mind that in the law of contract consent is normally assessed objectively, so
that a person is deemed to consent to that to which he objectively appears to
consent. Thus although 'the relationship of principal and agent can only be
established by the consent of the principal and the agent . . . they will be held to
have consented if they have agreed to what amounts in law to such a relationship,
even if they do not recognise it themselves and even if they have professed to
disclaim it'[4]. Where the relationship of principal and agent is thus established by
consent, the agent's power to act for the principal derives from that consent.

Even adopting an objective test of consent, however, there are still cases where one person is deemed by law to have power to bind another as his agent without that other's consent and, in some cases, without there being any relationship of principal and agent between them. Such cases must be explained solely on the basis of the agent's power which arises as a matter of law rather than on the basis of consent[5].

The agent was described earlier as having power to affect 'the legal rights, liabilities and relationships' of the principal. As we have seen, the primary function of agents in commerce is to make contracts on behalf of their principals. However, an agent may also affect the principal's legal position in other ways. An agent may dispose of the principal's property so as to transfer ownership to a third party; or acquire property on the principal's behalf. Statements made by the agent may bind the principal, both in a contractual context and otherwise. If an agent exerts undue influence on the other contracting party during negotiations, or in obtaining that party's signature to a document, the principal will be bound by the agent's actions and may be unable to enforce the contract[6]. The actions of an agent may make the principal criminally liable, especially for offences concerned with the 'sale' or 'supply' of goods[7].

In so far as an agent has power to affect the legal position of his principal, agency may appear to be connected to the doctrine of vicarious liability in tort whereby an employer is legally responsible for the torts of employees acting in the course of their employment. However, the two doctrines are distinct. Vicarious liability gives rise only to liabilities, whereas an agent may create rights or liabilities for his principal; an employer is vicariously liable only for the torts of 'employees' or 'servants', not for independent contractors, whereas an agent may be an employee but is often an independent contractor; and vicarious liability is imposed only where the employee is acting 'in the course of employment', whilst a principal is bound by the actions of his agent provided they are within the scope of the agent's power derived from his 'authority', actual, apparent or deemed. However, the two concepts are similar in certain situations, particularly where an employer is held liable for deliberate acts of an employee, including fraudulent statements. An employer is vicariously liable for fraudulent acts of an employee where he has put the employee in a position to commit the fraud and has held out the employee as acting on his behalf or in the course of his business: as we shall see, this is essentially the same test as that used to define 'apparent authority': in other words, the employer is only vicariously liable for an employee's frauds where he has given the employee actual or (more commonly) apparent authority to commit the fraud[8].

1 See Markesinis and Munday, *An Outline of the Law of Agency* (4th edn, 1998) ch 1; *Fridman Law of Agency* (7th edn, 1996) p 10.
2 See *Bowstead on Agency* (16th edn, 1996) art 1.
3 See *Bowstead*, art 1 and accompanying commentary; *Fridman*, ch 1; Markesinis and Munday, ch 1; Seavey, 'The Rationale of Agency' (1920) Yale LJ 859; Dowrick, 'The Relationship of Principal and Agent' (1954) 17 MLR 24.
4 Per Lord Pearson in *Garnac Grain Co Inc v Faure & Fairclough and Bunge Corpn* [1968] AC 1130n at 1137, [1967] 2 All ER 353 at 358.
5 For an extended discussion of the relationship between the 'consent' and 'power-liability' theories of agency, see McMeel (2000) 116 LQR 387.
6 *Avon Finance Ltd v Bridger* [1985] 2 All ER 281, CA; *Kingsnorth Trust Ltd v Bell* [1986] 1 All ER 423, [1986] 1 WLR 119, CA.
7 See eg *Gardener v Ackeroyd* [1952] 2 QB 743, [1952] 2 All ER 306.
8 *Lloyd v Grace Smith & Co* [1912] AC 716; *Armagas Ltd v Mundogas SA, The Ocean Frost* [1986] AC 717, [1986] 2 All ER 385, below 4.2.3.

3.2   Who is an agent?

For most practical purposes it is more important to be able to recognise an agent, or an agency situation, than to be able to define 'agency'. When will the law recognise a person as having power to act on behalf of another and affect that other's legal rights and liabilities? Although agency is a common commercial phenomenon, it is not always easy to recognise an agent. This is partly because of the flexibility of agency and the willingness of the courts to use agency concepts in an imaginative and often innovatory way; but it is also due to terminological difficulties. An agent may not be called an agent: for instance, 'brokers' and 'factors' are agents. Conversely, some of those engaged in commercial activity who are called 'agents' or 'representatives' are not agents in law at all, whilst others have only very limited powers.

3.2.1   *Agents in fact but not in name*

The following are agents in law, at least for some purposes, even though they do not bear the title 'agent'.

(a)   Company directors and other officers
A company is a legal person, but as an artificial person it must act through human agents. Authority to act on behalf of and in the name of the company is vested primarily in the board of directors as a whole: they therefore act as the company's agents. In general, the board must act collectively; however, a company's articles of association will generally contain power for the board to delegate part or all of its functions to individual members of the board[1], and it is common for one or more executive directors to be appointed, with authority to manage the day to day activities of the company. Those directors are then agents, exercising powers delegated to them by the board as a whole[2]. Powers of management may also be delegated to other officers of the company, such as the company secretary[3].

(b)   Partners
A partnership has no separate legal identity from its members. By statute, every partner in a firm is an agent of the firm and all the other partners for the purpose of the business of the firm, and every partner who does an act for carrying on in the usual way business of the kind carried on by the firm binds the firm and the other partners[4]. Other agency principles are applied to partnerships: for instance, an outsider cannot hold one member of a partnership liable on a contract made by another partner if he either knew the partner had no authority to make the contract, or did not believe he was a partner[5]. A person who is not a partner but allows himself to be held out as if he were, may be liable as a partner to any person who relies on such holding out and extends credit to the firm[6]; this is akin to the liability of a principal on the basis of apparent authority[7].

(c)   Employees
Employment law draws a distinction between employees, or 'servants', who work under contracts of service, and independent contractors working under contracts for services. An employer is only vicariously liable for the torts of employees. A

person working as an independent contractor may be an agent of the employer; indeed, he often will be an agent, having authority to bind the employer in accordance with the contract between them. However, an employee may also be an agent of the employer: for instance, a shop assistant is an agent of the shop's owner for the purposes of making contracts of sale with customers and will probably also have authority to make statements about the goods sold, binding on the employer. The power of the shop assistant to bind the shop owner derives from the assistant's status as an agent, not from the status of employee.

(d) Hire purchase and credit transactions

Where goods are bought on hire purchase or credit terms, it is often the case that the buyer actually contracts with a finance company. However, the buyer's only contact is likely to be with a dealer. The dealer will transfer the goods to the finance company and arrange the credit; in most cases the dealer will present the buyer with the necessary forms for completion and signature; the goods will probably be collected from the dealer's premises. To all outward appearances the buyer may appear to contract with the dealer. The position is represented diagrammatically below:

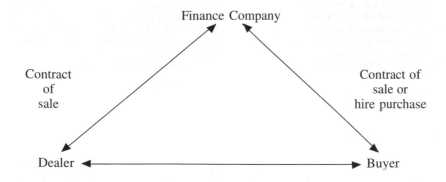

Negotiations and arrangements

In this situation 'the mercantile reality . . . has become well known . . . the identity or even existence of the finance company is a matter [to customers] of indifference; they look to the dealer, or his representative, as the person who fixes the payment terms and makes all the necessary arrangements[8]'. For these reasons it has been suggested that in such cases the dealer should be treated at common law as the agent of the finance company for purposes connected with the transaction, but the comments just quoted were made in a dissenting judgment. The decision of the majority of the House of Lords was that the dealer was not normally the agent of the supplier at common law. It may, nevertheless, be possible to find an agency in special circumstances; thus where a finance company used forms and a trading name which made it appear to be part of the same corporate group as the supplier, it was held to be estopped from denying the authority of the supplier to make statements on its behalf as to the goods[9]. Where the transaction is a regulated agreement under the Consumer Credit Act 1974, the Act deems the dealer the agent of the finance company for purposes connected with the transaction, so that the finance company will be bound by statements made by the dealer about the credit or about the goods[10].

(e) Professionals

Professionals acting on behalf of clients may be the agents of those clients for limited purposes. Thus a solicitor conducting litigation on behalf of a client is the client's agent and may have authority to make a settlement of the case binding on the client[11]. Similarly, an accountant who negotiates with the Inland Revenue on behalf of a client is the client's agent, and the accountant's statements or agreements may bind the client according to agency principles.

1 See eg Companies Act 1985, Table A, arts 71–72.
2 See *Freeman and Lockyer v Buckhurst Park Properties (Mangal) Ltd* [1964] 2 QB 480, [1964] 1 All ER 630, CA.
3 See *Panorama Developments (Guildford) Ltd v Fidelis Furnishing Fabrics Ltd* [1971] 2 QB 711, [1971] 3 All ER 16, CA.
4 Partnership Act 1890, s 5.
5 Partnership Act 1890, s 3.
6 Partnership Act 1890, s 14.
7 See below 4.3.
8 Per Lord Wilberforce (dissenting) in *Branwhite v Worcester Works Finance Ltd* [1969] 1 AC 552, [1968] 3 All ER 104, HL; see *J D Williams & Co v McCauley Parsons & Jones* [1994] CCLR 78.
9 *Lease Management Services Ltd v Purnell Secretarial Services Ltd* [1994] CCLR 127; see also *Woodchester Leasing Ltd v Clayton* [1994] CCLR 87 (supplier found to be agent of finance company when negotiating tri-partite leasing contract); see 26.4.
10 Consumer Credit Act 1974, s 56. See *Forthright Finance Ltd v Ingate* [1997] 4 All ER 99; see 26.4.0.
11 *Waugh v H B Clifford and Sons Ltd* [1982] Ch 374, [1982] 1 All ER 1095, CA.

3.2.2 Difficult cases

Words such as 'agent' and 'representative' are frequently used in business to describe persons who are not agents in law at all. Thus a car dealer may be described as 'sole agent' for a particular manufacturer. The dealer is not the agent of the manufacturer in law, and the expression 'sole agent' means 'sole distributor'. If the dealer were an agent, customers would be in direct contractual relations with the manufacturer; the 'agent' would not be entitled to make a profit from sales, but would receive a commission and have to account to the manufacturer for profits. Since the dealer is not an agent, he is liable to the customer on the contract of sale, but is entitled to fix resale prices and keep any profits he makes. Moreover, a contract of agency may be more likely to be construed as permitting the principal to sell in competition with the agent than would a distributorship agreement[1]. Similarly, 'advertising agents' do not act as agents when they place advertisements on behalf of clients: the agency is liable for the price of the advertising and will seek reimbursement from its client along with payment of its fees.

Other persons described as agents may indeed be agents in law, but have only very limited power to affect their principals' positions. Insurance brokers or agents are agents in law, but the normal rules of agency law are sometimes modified in their application[2], so that, for instance, an agent working for the insurer may be deemed to be the agent of the insured for certain limited purposes. Estate agents acting for prospective vendors of property are agents in law of the vendors but they have only very limited authority. For instance, they have no authority to enter into a contract of sale on behalf of the vendor unless they are expressly authorised to do so[3].

Problems may arise where persons described as 'agents' act in sale transactions; for instance, if the 'agent' sells in breach of his instructions, it may be vital to decide if he is in reality an agent (see Fig 2 below), or has agreed to buy and resell on his own account (see Fig 3). If he is an agent, the third party is likely to get a good title to the goods[4]. On the other hand, if the 'agent' resells goods to his principal, his capacity may affect the extent to which he is liable for defects in the goods. If he is an agent, his primary duty is to execute his instructions with reasonable care; but if he is held to be buying and reselling the goods on his own account, he is strictly liable for defects in the goods as a seller[5]. The question may also become important if the 'agent' becomes insolvent: in that case money received by the agent in respect of sales of the principal's property will belong to the principal. But if the 'agent' is not a true agent in law, the 'principal' will only be entitled to claim as an unpaid seller in the 'agent's' insolvency[6]. It may be difficult to decide in a particular case whether the 'agent' is acting as an agent in law, or is buying and reselling on his own account; all the circumstances of the case may have to be examined[7]. A particularly important factor is likely to be whether the agent is free to fix the price at which he resells and makes a profit, which suggests that he acts on his own behalf. However, it is hard to escape the conclusion that where third party rights in the goods are in issue the courts are likely to favour the interpretation of the situation which best protects the third party.

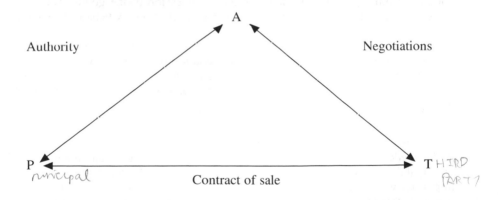

Fig 2: A acts as agent

Fig 3: A buys and resells

1   See *W T Lamb & Sons v Goring Brick Co Ltd* [1932] 1 KB 710, CA, below 3.2.4.
2   See below 35.5.
3   *Hamer v Sharp* (1874) LR 19 Eq 108.
4   Under the Factors Act 1889; see *Weiner v Harris* [1910] 1 KB 285, CA; below 17.1.1.

5   Under the Sale of Goods Act 1979, ss 13–15; below ch 11.
6   For example, see *Re Nevill, ex p White* (1871) LR 6 Ch App 397; cf *Triffit Nurseries v Salads Etcetera Ltd* [1999] 1 All ER (Comm) 110.
7   See *Welsh Development Agency v Export Finance Co Ltd* [1992] BCC 270.

3.2.3   *Agency relationships in commerce*

Although the primary role of agents in commerce is to negotiate and/or enter into contracts on behalf of their principals, a number of different classes of agent are identified both in practice and in the case law.

(a)   General and special agents
The distinction between general and special agents depends on the nature of the authority given by the principal to the agent. A general agent has general authority to act for the principal in a particular trade or class of transactions; a special agent is authorised only to act in one particular transaction. The distinction is no longer so significant as it once was.

(b)   Factors and brokers
Factors (or 'mercantile agents') are agents whose business is to dispose of goods on behalf of their principals and who are given possession of the goods for that purpose. In contrast, a broker negotiates contracts for the sale and purchase of goods and other property but does not have possession of the goods. Thus if I leave my car with a garage to display the car and sell it on my behalf, the garage proprietor is a factor.
   The terms 'factor' and 'broker' are not always used in modern practice, and the label given to any particular relationship is of course not determinative of its effect, but the distinction between factors and brokers remains important, as the law gives factors extensive powers to dispose of their principals' property in order to protect third parties who deal with them[1].

(c)   Del credere agents
A del credere agent negotiates contracts for a principal and guarantees to the principal that the third party will pay any sums due under the contract; this may be important where the third party is not known to the principal. The del credere agent charges the principal an extra commission for providing the guarantee.

(d)   Commercial agents
A special category of 'commercial agents' is now recognised in UK law as a result of the Council Directive (Commercial Agents) Regulations 1993[2] which implement an EC Directive[3]. A 'commercial agent' is defined as:

> 'a self-employed intermediary who has continuing authority to negotiate the sale or purchase of goods on behalf of another person ("the principal") or to negotiate and conclude the sale of purchase of goods on behalf of and in the name of the principal'[4].

Prior to 1993 commercial agents were not recognised as a separate category in English law, and the concept of commercial agency has been described as 'alien' to English law[5]. The concept of commercial agency was, however, familiar in many civil law jurisdictions.

The essence of commercial agency is that the agent has 'continuing authority to negotiate' contracts on behalf of its principal. It has therefore been held that the regulations do not apply to an intermediary who buys or sells goods in his own name as principal on his own behalf[6], nor to a person who acts as an agent and concludes contracts on behalf of a principal with customers who contract on a 'self-service' basis so that the agent had no negotiating function[7].

The main impact of the regulations is on the relationship between principal and agent. Commercial agents as defined are given extensive rights against their principals, in particular on termination of the agency relationship. The regulations are therefore considered in detail in Chapter 6.

(e)   Commission agents

A commission agent acts to buy or sell property on behalf of a principal, but is not authorised to create privity of contract with the third party with whom he deals. Thus, vis-à-vis the third party, the agent contracts as principal; but as against his principal, the agent is an agent and owes the duties owed by an agent to his principal (see Fig 4). The result is that the agent is liable to the third party for the price, if he purchases goods, or for the quality of the goods if he sells. However, as against his principal, the agent is not answerable for the quality of the goods: as an agent he is required only to take reasonable care in the performance of his duties.

P ◄—————————————► A ◄—————————————► T
            Agency   Sale Contract

Fig 4: Commission agency

This arrangement is effectively a halfway house between the two situations discussed above[8], where the agent is either a true agent, authorised to create privity between principal and third party, or buys and resells on his own behalf. It is common in civil law systems, but is less widely used in common law systems. The common law developed the doctrine of undisclosed agency which enables a principal to sue, and be sued, on a contract made on his behalf even where he has instructed the agent not to reveal the fact of the agency[9]. However, commission agency was recognised by the common law at one time[10]; and it remains possible to create an agency under which the agent is authorised to contract in his own name, so that he alone can enforce, and is liable on, the contracts he makes, but is remunerated as an agent by commission[11].

(f)   Confirming houses

Confirming houses play an important role in international trade. They normally act on behalf of an overseas client who wishes to import goods, thus providing local knowledge. A confirming house may act in different ways according to its instructions from its client. At the simplest it may buy goods in the domestic market and resell them to its client overseas: it then enters into two contracts of sale. Alternatively, it may act simply as an agent, negotiating a purchase on behalf of its client and revealing its capacity as agent; there is then one contract of sale, between domestic supplier and overseas buyer. However, the domestic seller may be unhappy about dealing solely with an overseas customer whose reputation and credit standing may be unknown. In this situation the confirming house may make the contract to purchase the goods as agent on behalf of its overseas principal but enter into a separate contract with the supplier to 'confirm', or guarantee, that the buyer will perform its obligations under the sale contract (Fig 5).

Fig 5: Agent confirms principal's obligations

The confirming house's obligation to pay is independent of that of the overseas customer; the domestic seller thus has the security of being able to claim the price direct from the confirming house which is both within the jurisdiction of domestic courts and known to be creditworthy.

1 Factors Act 1889; see below 17.1.
2 Commercial Agents (Council Directive) Regulations 1993, SI 1993/3053, as amended by SI 1993/3173, SI 1998/2868.
3 Directive 86/653/EEC.
4 Regulation 2(1).
5 Per Peter Gibson LJ in *AMB Imballaggi Plastici SRL v Pacflex Ltd* [1999] 2 All ER (Comm) 249 at 255.
6 *AMB Imballaggi Plastici SRL v Pacflex Ltd* [1999] 2 All ER (Comm) 249.
7 *Garry Parkes v Esso Petroleum Co Ltd* [1999] Tr Law 232; see 6.0.1.1.
8 See 3.2.2.
9 See below 5.3.
10 See *Ireland v Livingstone* (1872) LR 5 HL 395.
11 See *Triffits Nurseries v Salads Etcetera Ltd* [1999] 1 All ER (Comm) 110. The Court of Appeal appears to have recognised the possibility of such an arrangement in the *Romalpa* case: *Aluminium Industrie Vaassen BV v Romalpa Aluminium Ltd* [1976] 2 All ER 552, [1976] 1 WLR 676; see below 18.4.5.

3.2.4 *Commercial marketing arrangements*

A business may well use agents as a means of marketing its products or services. However, in view of what has been said above, it will be apparent that agency is only one of the possible arrangements which may be used. In any particular case it may be necessary to examine the arrangement closely in order to decide if it does amount in law to an agency. There are a number of other possible relationships which may be used.

None of the terms below is a term of art. In almost every case there will be a detailed contract between the parties, upon which their relationship will depend. That contract may impose upon the parties duties very similar to those which apply between principal and agent, such as, for example, duties of confidentiality.

(a) Distributorship

A business, normally a manufacturer, may enter into contracts of distributorship with one or more dealers. As noted earlier[1], distributors may be referred to as 'agents' but there are important differences between distributorship and true agency. Most importantly, a distributor sells goods in his own name and thus has no authority to create privity between the manufacturer and the customers with whom the distributor deals. Unlike a commission agent, who also has no authority to create privity between his principal and the parties with whom he deals, a distributor is not entitled to the rights, nor subject to the duties, of an agent. Instead, the relationship between manufacturer and distributor will largely depend on the terms of the distributorship agreement.

Under a typical distributorship contract the manufacturer will agree to supply the dealer with products, and possibly with other back-up supplies and services, from time to time, and may well agree not to appoint any other distributor for its products in the dealer's area. The manufacturer's right to sell its products direct, in competition with the distributor, will depend on the construction of the agreement. If the dealer is appointed 'sole distributor' the manufacturer may be entitled to compete with the dealer, but if the distributorship is 'exclusive' it will be a breach of contract for the manufacturer to compete. In *Lamb v Goring Brick*[2] a manufacturer appointed a dealer as its 'sole selling agent' for its products. This was properly construed as a distributorship rather than an agency and it was held that the wording of the contract excluded the manufacturer's right to sell its products direct to the public. In return, the distributor will normally agree to develop the market for the manufacturer's products, and, possibly, not to sell competing products. As regards products supplied by the manufacturer, the relationship will be that of seller and buyer, a separate contract of sale being formed each time the distributor orders goods. The distributor will be responsible as seller for the products it resells to customers.

Distributorship offers the manufacturer some advantages over true agency. First, since the manufacturer is not in privity with the ultimate purchasers of its products, it incurs no contractual product liability to them[3], and it may be able to exclude or restrict its contractual liability to the distributor[4]. However, it may still be liable to ultimate customers in tort[5]; moreover, it seems that a principal may effectively restrict its liability by requiring an agent to act without disclosing the agency and excluding the agent's authority to sell defective products[6]. Second, the manufacturer need only look to its distributor for payment for products supplied, whereas under an agency the agent is normally merely a channel to arrange the contract and, possibly, collect payment so that the principal is concerned with the solvency of the ultimate customers. However, under a del credere agency the agent guarantees payment. Moreover, where an agent receives payment on behalf of his principal, the money may belong to the principal in equity, enabling the principal to make a priority claim to it if the agent becomes insolvent[7]. Third, as a result of the rights now given to commercial agents[8] it may be easier to terminate a distributorship than an agency without incurring legal liability.

Conversely, a principal will have more control over an agent, and over the terms of the contracts made by the agent, than over a distributor because the agent contracts on the principal's behalf. Distributorship contracts are subject to restrictions under domestic and European competition law. Article 81 of the Treaty of Rome prohibits agreements whose object or effect is the prevention, restriction or distortion of competition within the common market and renders such agreements void unless notified to the EC Commission and cleared. In principle certain types of distributorship agreement contravene art 81[9]. However, agreements which are considered not to be anti-competitive may be granted exemption from art 81. Vertical agreements, between organisations at different levels in the supply chain, are generally considered not to be anti-competitive and in 1999 the European Commission issued a block exemption covering certain categories of vertical agreements[10]. Distributorship agreements are protected by the block exemption provided that they do not contain certain prohibited terms. In contrast a Commission Notice accompanying the block exemption indicates that true agency agreements will be regarded as exempt provided that the agent undertakes no 'financial risk'[11].

(b)   Franchising
Franchising has become increasingly common in recent years. An entrepreneur with a product or service to market may, instead of selling direct to the public, authorise other businesses to supply the product or service. In general, franchisees accept more restrictions than distributors; in return, and for payment of a franchise fee, they are given the right not only to supply the product or service but also to use the trade name, style or logo of the franchisor, and may thus benefit from the goodwill built up by the franchisor. Each franchisee is a separate business, but the outward appearance is of a uniform organisation. The franchisor normally agrees to supply the franchisee with goods to sell, as well as with other support; their relationship in respect of such goods is therefore that of seller and buyer, and the franchisee deals with the public as seller. Franchise agreements are prima facie subject to art 81 of the Treaty of Rome, but, like distributorship agreements, may be protected by the block exemption for certain categories of vertical agreement[12].

(c)   Licensing
Similarly, a manufacturer may grant another business a licence to sell or even to manufacture its products. The manufacture of 'copied' products without such a licence would normally breach the manufacturer's intellectual property rights. Again, licensing arrangements may infringe art 81 of the Treaty of Rome but there is a block exemption for patent licences[13].

(d)   Subsidiaries
An alternative course is for a business to establish a network of subsidiaries to market its products and/or services. This course is often taken by companies, which market products through a network of trading subsidiaries. Each subsidiary company will have a separate legal personality from the holding company or proprietor. The subsidiary may act as agent for the holding company or proprietor, but it is more common for the relationship between them to be that of seller and buyer, leaving the subsidiary to act as seller vis-à-vis its customers.

1   See 3.2.2.
2   *W T Lamb & Sons v Goring Brick Co Ltd* [1932] 1 KB 710, CA.
3   Under the implied terms in the Sale of Goods Act 1979, ss 13–15: see ch 11.
4   Subject to the provisions of the Unfair Contract Terms Act 1977: see 2.6.4.

5 Either in negligence or under the Consumer Protection Act 1987: see ch 13.
6 See *Welsh Development Agency Ltd v Export Finance Co* [1992] BCC 270; see 22.0.4.2.
7 See 6.2.1.8.
8 Under the Commercial Agents (Council Directive) Regulations 1993, SI 1993/3053, as amended by SI 1993/3173, SI 1998/2868, implementing the EC Commercial Agents Directive (86/653/EEC): see ch 6.
9 Distributorship agreements may also, in principle, contravene the ch 1 prohibition in the Competition Act 1998. However, the Office of Fair Trading, which has primary responsibility for enforcing the Act, has indicated that it considers that vertical agreements, between organisations at different levels in the supply chain, are in principle not anti-competitive. In any case, a distributorship agreement which is entitled to the protection of an individual or block exemption under EC competition law is also exempt from the domestic prohibition.
10 Regulation 790/99, 1999 OJ 336/21.
11 Commission Notice, Guidelines on Vertical Restraints (1999 OJ 336/21) Chap 2 Section II, replacing a Commission Notice of 1962 to similar effect. An agent may be held to take a 'risk' and fall outside the notice if (for instance) he maintains a stock of goods at his own risk or cost, or takes responsibility for customers' non-performance.
12 Regulation 790/99, above, note 10. A franchise agreement may also, in principle, contravene the ch 1 Prohibition in the Competition Act 1998. However, most agreements will be protected in the same way as distributorship agreements: see above, note 9.
13 Regulation 2394/84.

3.3 Harmonisation of agency law

Most developed legal systems recognise the concept of agency and in most areas, there is a marked similarity between the rules of different legal systems. In recent years there have been attempts to harmonise national laws on agency as part of the general trend towards harmonisation of laws applying to international commercial activity.

A Convention on Agency in the International Sale of Goods, drafted under the auspices of UNIDROIT, was adopted at Geneva in 1983. Intended to complement the Vienna Convention on International Sales Law[1], the Convention applies where the agent has his place of business in a contracting state, or where the rules of private international law lead to the application of the law of a member state[2]. It has not yet been ratified by the UK government.

The Convention does not create a complete code governing all aspects of agency. It applies only to agency in contracts for the international sale of goods, and only to cases where the agent has authority to conclude a contract. The activities of agents with authority only to negotiate contracts are outside its scope, as are those of company directors and officers. Moreover, the Convention is concerned only with the external aspects of agency, that is with the relations of principal and agent with third parties with whom the agent deals; it does not regulate the relationship between principal and agent.

Many provisions of the Convention are broadly similar to those of English law. The one major area of difficulty encountered in drafting the Convention was in dealing with the situation where an agent deals with a third party without revealing that he acts as agent. Common law systems recognise the right of an undisclosed principal to intervene in and enforce such contracts made on his behalf; civil law systems have no such rule, but do recognise the concept of commission agency, whereby an agent acts as principal vis-à-vis third parties with whom he contracts, but owes the duties of agent to his principal. The status of commission agency in common law systems is unclear. The Convention seeks to strike a compromise between these two concepts by producing a hybrid, which gives principal and third party greater rights against each other than they would enjoy under the concept of commission agency, but less than they would have under the doctrine of undisclosed agency[3].

Mention has already been made of the 1986 EC Directive on Commercial Agency[4], which seeks to harmonise aspects of agency law in the European Community. The directive was introduced because the legal systems of some member states of the Community gave extensive rights to commercial agents, creating a possible barrier to the proper functioning of the single market. Unlike the Geneva Convention, the directive is concerned only with the internal relationship between principal and agent. Its effects are considered in Chapter 6.

1   See 31.4.1.
2   Article 2(1).
3   See 5.3.
4   86/653/EEC; see above 3.2.3.

3.4   The relationships created by agency

Having considered some of the different categories of agency relationship, we can now return to the normal case where the agent (A) is instructed to make a contract with a third party (T) on behalf of a principal (P). If A carries out P's instructions, privity of contract will be created between P and T; however, in certain situations the normal rule breaks down and A may incur liability to T, even outside the special situations discussed above. There are thus three relationships to be considered: between P and A, between P and T, and between A and T. The key to all these relationships is the authority given by P to A. P is bound to T by acts which he has authorised or appears to have authorised. As between P and A, A's entitlement to remuneration will depend on performance of his authority[1] and if he acts in breach of his authority, he will be liable to P[2]. As between A and T, A may incur personal liability if he claims authority he does not have[3].

1   See 6.1.1.1.
2   See 6.2.1.1.
3   See 5.2.

Chapter 4

The Authority of the Agent

4.0 Power and authority

We have seen that an agent is a person who has power to act on behalf of another person, the principal, and affect the principal's legal position. The (external) relationship between P and T therefore depends on the scope of A's power. However, the (internal) agency relationship between P and A depends on consent. The law recognises that A has power to act on P's behalf when P has consented to A having such power, and in such a case A is said to have 'authority' to act on P's behalf. However, A may also have power, in law, to act on P's behalf even though P has not expressly consented to A's having such power. In fact the law recognises A as having power to bind P in four situations:

(a) where P gives prior consent to A's actions: A has 'actual authority';
(b) where A acts without prior authority but P gives retrospective consent by ratification;
(c) where A acts without P's consent, but the law deems P to have consented, as in 'agency of necessity'[1]; and
(d) where A acts without P's consent but P is estopped from denying A's authority: A is said to have 'apparent' authority.

P consents to A's actions in situations (a) and (b); in (c), P does not consent but is deemed to do so. In (d), A has power to bind P without P's consent. This will happen where A appears to have greater 'authority' than he actually has: for instance, where P imposes a limit on A's authority, or where A's authority has been terminated.

In the modern law of agency the distinction between 'actual' and 'apparent' authority is fundamental. The distinction was explained by Diplock LJ in *Freeman and Lockyer v Buckhurst Park Properties (Mangal) Ltd*[2]:

> 'An actual authority is a legal relationship between principal and agent created by a consensual agreement to which they alone are parties. To this agreement the [third party] is a stranger; he may be totally ignorant of the existence of any authority on the part of the agent. Nevertheless, if the agent does enter into a contract pursuant to the actual authority it does create contractual rights and liabilities between the principal and [third party]. An "apparent" authority, on the other hand, is a legal relationship between the principal and [third party] created by a representation made by the principal to the [third party], intended to be and in fact acted on by the [third party],

that the agent has authority . . . To the relationship so created the agent is a stranger'.

In the ordinary course of events the third party relies not on the agent's actual authority, but on his apparent authority. Where A has only apparent authority he acts without P's consent but nevertheless has power to bind P, and the relationship between P and T depends solely on A's power to bind P. On the other hand, the relationship between P and A depends on P's consent to A's actions. Thus, as between P and A, actual authority is paramount. If A acts without actual authority he acts without P's consent and, regardless of his power to affect P's *external* relationship, may incur liability for acting in breach of the terms of their *internal* relationship.

1   See 4.5.
2   *Freeman and Lockyer v Buckhurst Park Properties (Mangal) Ltd* [1964] 2 QB 480, CA at 504.

4.1   The types of authority

One of the great difficulties of the law of agency is that terminology is not used consistently by judges or textbook writers. It may therefore help if we define our terminology before going on to examine the different ways in which an agent may be authorised.

We have already seen the distinction between 'actual' and 'apparent' authority, which is now commonly accepted since the landmark decision of the Court of Appeal in *Freeman and Lockyer*. Actual authority may be 'express' or 'implied'; and authority may be implied in a number of situations[1]. The cases and textbooks also speak of 'usual' and 'customary' authority. Sometimes these appear to be a type of implied (actual) authority, sometimes a form of apparent authority[2]. It is probably better to regard 'usual' and 'customary' authority not as separate heads of authority but as ways of defining the scope of the agent's actual or apparent authority. The following examples illustrate this.

(a)   A is appointed to be managing director of a company (P). His authority is not expressly defined; he therefore impliedly has all the authority which it is usual for a managing director to have (actual implied authority).

(b)   A is appointed to be managing director of a company (P). His authority is expressly limited so that he cannot enter into contracts worth more than £50,000 without the approval of the full board of directors. His actual authority is subject to the express limitation; but if he makes a contract with T, who is unaware of the limitation, his apparent authority will be unlimited and he will appear to have such authority as a managing director usually has (apparent authority).

(c)   A is not expressly appointed managing director, but is allowed by the company (P) to act as if he had been appointed. If he deals with T, who is unaware of the true position, he will have apparent authority as if he were managing director. His authority is *apparent* because he was not actually appointed to the position of managing director. The scope of that authority will be determined by what is usual for a managing director[3]. Alternatively, a court might interpret the situation as one where A has been impliedly appointed to the post of managing director; his authority will then be implied actual authority, but its scope will be what is usual for a managing director[4].

As this last example illustrates, a further difficulty is that the same situation may be interpreted in more than one way. The example is based on the facts of *Hely-Hutchinson v Brayhead Ltd*. A, who had been allowed to act as if he were a managing director, although he had never been expressly appointed to that position, concluded a contract on behalf of the company with T. When T sought to enforce the contract, the company denied that A had authority to act on its behalf. Roskill J held that the company was bound on the basis that it had held A out as managing director, and so he had apparent authority as if he occupied that position. The Court of Appeal upheld the decision, but on the grounds that, by allowing A to act in this way, the company had given him implied actual authority to act as managing director. Of course, the company was bound to T in either case; but as between P and A the difference between the two interpretations would be crucial, for if A had only apparent authority, he would be liable to P for acting without P's consent.

The expression 'usual authority' is also sometimes used to describe a separate type of authority to explain a group of anomalous cases which do not fit happily into the categories of 'actual' and 'apparent' authority[5]. However, the expression 'usual authority' will be used in the following discussion to define the scope of the agent's authority.

1   See 4.1.2.
2   See per Steyn LJ in *First Energy (UK) Ltd v Hungarian International Bank Ltd* [1993] 2 Lloyd's Rep 194 at 201.
3   *Freeman and Lockyer v Buckhurst Park Properties (Mangal) Ltd* [1964] 2 QB 480 at 504, CA.
4   *Hely-Hutchinson v Brayhead Ltd* [1968] 1 QB 549, [1967] 3 All ER 98, CA.
5   See below 4.4 and see Stone [1993] JBL 325, arguing that the law should recognise a separate category of usual authority.

4.1.1   *Express actual authority*

We have seen that 'actual authority' is that authority which P consents to A exercising on his behalf; it therefore derives from the agreement between P and A. It is important to note that although the relationship between P and A must be consensual, there is no need for it to be contractual. Often, particularly in a commercial context, there will be a contract between P and A. In that case, A is entitled to be paid for his services, and will be liable for breach of contract if he fails to perform his contractual duties[1]. However, there is no reason why A should not agree to act gratuitously. All that is necessary to give rise to the relationship of principal and agent is that they should agree to enter that relationship.

As a general rule no formalities are required for the appointment of an agent. The agreement between P and A may therefore be express or implied, and, if express, may be made orally, in writing or by deed. However, where the agreement is governed by the Commercial Agents (Council Directive) Regulations 1993, each party is entitled to demand of the other a written statement of the terms of the agency agreement[2] and an agent appointed to execute a deed must be appointed by a deed known as a 'power of attorney'[3], although a deed is not required to authorise an agent to deliver a deed[4]. Similarly, anyone can act as an agent. An adult principal may appoint a minor to act on his behalf and, because the agent's actions are deemed to be those of the principal, contracts made by the minor agent will be fully binding on the adult principal. However, the agency contract between P and A may not be binding on A because of A's minority.

Where the agent is expressly appointed the scope of his authority depends on the construction of the agreement and, in the case of an oral appointment, proof of what was said. As part of the process of construction, the court may imply terms into the agreement. Thus A's express actual authority may be expanded by any implied authority.

There is no reason why the agent should not be given wide authority to act as he thinks fit[5]. In general, if the words of appointment used are ambiguous, the court will construe them in the way which is most favourable to the agent[6], although an agent faced with ambiguous instructions will normally be expected to seek clarification from his principal, especially in light of the speed and ease of modern communications. Where the authority is conferred by deed, its provisions are likely to be construed more strictly[7], in accordance with the general rule applied to the construction of deeds.

1   See 6.1.1.1 and 6.2.1.1.
2   Commercial Agents (Council Directive) Regulations 1993, reg 11; see below 6.0.1.
3   *Berkeley v Hardy* (1826) 5 B & C 355.
4   By the Law of Property (Miscellaneous Provisions) Act 1989, s 1(1)(c).
5   *Henderson v Merrett* [1995] 2 AC 145, [1994] 3 All ER 506.
6   *Ireland v Livingstone* (1872) LR 5 HL 395.
7   See *Midland Bank Ltd v Reckitt* [1933] AC 1.

4.1.2   *Implied actual authority*

An agent's action is impliedly authorised where, although it is not sanctioned by any express agreement between P and A, P is nevertheless taken to have given implied consent to the action or transaction in question. It is important to appreciate that implied authority is a species of actual authority, for that affects the rights of P and A inter se.

Implied authority may arise in a number of ways. In the most extreme case, A's appointment is wholly implicit. Thus in *Hely-Hutchinson v Brayhead Ltd*[1] where the directors of a company allowed the company chairman to act as if he were managing director, the Court of Appeal held that although he had never been expressly appointed to that position, he had implied actual authority to act as managing director.

> 'The relationship of principal and agent can only be established by the consent of the principal and the agent. They will be taken to have consented if they have agreed to what amounts in law to such a relationship, even if they do not recognise it themselves and even if they have professed to disclaim it'[2].

More commonly, an agent who is expressly appointed may have his authority defined or expanded by implication. Terms may be implied into an agency agreement in the same way that terms are implied into any contract. Thus an agent who is given express authority to carry out a task may have additional, incidental authority to do those acts reasonably incidental to and necessary to enable him to carry out his authorised task. Such implication depends on construction of the agent's express authority. Thus, for instance, where an agent was given express authority 'to sell' the principal's property, he had implied incidental authority to sign a written memorandum of the contract, as was then required[3]. In contrast, an agent instructed to 'find a purchaser' had no authority to sign a written memorandum[4].

An agent's express authority may also be impliedly expanded by usual or customary authority. If P appoints A, expressly or impliedly, to a position or to perform a task, A will impliedly have all the authority which an agent in that position or performing that task usually has, unless that authority is excluded or limited, either expressly by the terms of the appointment, or impliedly by the circumstances. However, whilst such an express limitation may prevent A having actual authority to perform tasks such an agent would usually perform, he may still appear to third parties to have the full authority which an agent in his position would have. Third parties may therefore be able to rely on A's apparent authority, unless they know of the express limitation[5].

The implication of usual authority may be very important. When agents are appointed it is often the case that their authority is not spelled out in detail, particularly where the agent is appointed to perform an everyday function. The courts have therefore had to consider the usual authority of several classes of agent. Thus it has been held that a company secretary usually has authority to make contracts concerned with the day-to-day running of the company or 'the administrative side of the company's affairs' such as hiring cars, hiring staff and so on[6]. In contrast, a company secretary would not normally have authority to enter into large-scale commercial contracts on behalf of the company, but an executive or managing director would normally have such authority, so that transactions such as engaging the services of professional advisers[7] or committing the company to a guarantee[8] would be within the scope of the usual authority of a managing director. A ship's master does not have usual authority to sign a bill of lading for goods not loaded[9].

A decision whether a particular transaction is within the scope of the usual authority of a class of agent must reflect commercial practice and the ordinary business expectations of practitioners of the particular trade or profession, and where there is a dispute about the scope of the usual authority of a particular class of agent, the court must hear expert evidence as to the practice of the particular trade or profession. Thus in a case concerned with the authority of a solicitor to give undertakings so as to bind his firm, the court heard expert evidence from senior solicitors including a former President of the Law Society[10]. It was held that employed solicitors do have usual authority from their employers to give undertakings to pay money out of funds in their control, provided the undertaking is given in connection with an underlying transaction. Similarly, it has been held that a solicitor conducting litigation usually has the authority of the client to compromise the action[11].

A number of cases have considered the extent of the usual authority of estate agents. They usually have authority to make statements describing the property, so that the principal will be liable for misrepresentation if such statements prove false (subject to any exclusion of liability for such statements), but not to make statements about the permitted user of the premises for planning purposes[12]. The estate agent has no general authority to sign a written memorandum of a contract for sale of the property, nor to sign a contract, although such authority could be expressly or impliedly conferred in a particular case. It has also been held that an estate agent does not usually have authority to take a pre-contract deposit from the intending purchaser, so that if such a deposit is taken, the agent, but not the vendor, is liable for the refund of the deposit[13]. If such a deposit is taken it is held on behalf of the purchaser and is refundable on demand[14].

The agent's actual authority may be similarly extended by 'customary authority', another head of implied authority, very similar to usual authority. 'If there is, in a particular place, an established usage of dealing and making contracts, a person who is employed to deal or make a contract there has an implied authority to act in the usual way'[15]. Authority will be implied on the basis of custom in the same way that terms may be implied into contracts generally on the basis of custom. The party seeking to rely on the custom must establish that it is certain, notorious and reasonable: if so, the principal who appoints an agent to work in that market is assumed to have known of the custom and, by failing to exclude it, to have impliedly consented to the agent acting in accordance with it. Thus where an agent sold a quantity of manure on behalf of a principal and warranted the quality of the manure to the buyer, the principal was bound by the warranty even though he had not expressly authorised it: it was the custom for agents in the trade to give such warranties[16]. On the other hand, an alleged custom which conflicts with the normal incidents of agency may be held unreasonable and so not bind the principal. A custom purporting to allow the agent to buy goods in his own name and resell to the principal at a profit has been held unreasonable, as contradicting the fiduciary duty of the agent, and so did not bind the principal who was unaware of it[17]. If the principal had known of the custom he would have been bound by it even though it was unreasonable.

1 [1968] 1 QB 549, [1967] 3 All ER 98, CA.
2 Per Lord Pearson in *Garnac Grain Co Inc v H M F Faure and Fairclough Ltd* [1968] AC 1130n at 1137, [1967] 2 All ER 353 at 358, HL.
3 *Rosenbaum v Belson* [1900] 2 Ch 267.
4 *Hamer v Sharp* (1874) LR 19 Eq 108.
5 See below 4.2 and 4.4.
6 *Panorama Developments (Guildford) Ltd v Fidelis Furnishing Fabrics Ltd* [1971] 2 QB 711, [1971] 3 All ER 16, CA.
7 *Freeman and Lockyer v Buckhurst Park Properties (Mangal) Ltd* [1964] 2 QB 480 at 504, CA.
8 *Hely-Hutchinson v Brayhead Ltd* [1968] 1 QB 549, [1967] 3 All ER 98, CA.
9 *Grant v Norway* (1851) 10 CB 665. The case is difficult: a principal is normally liable for fraudulent statements made by an agent acting in the course of his actual or apparent authority, and the master generally has authority to sign bills of lading. The effect of the decision is now reversed by s 4 of the Carriage of Goods by Sea Act 1992: see 32.3.2.
10 *United Bank of Kuwait v Hammoud; City Trust Ltd v Levy* [1988] 3 All ER 418, [1988] 1 WLR 1051, CA.
11 *Waugh v H B Clifford & Sons* [1982] 1 Ch 374, [1982] 1 All ER 1095, CA.
12 *Hill v Harris* [1965] 2 QB 601, [1965] 2 All ER 358, CA.
13 *Sorrell v Finch* [1977] AC 728, [1976] 2 All ER 371, HL.
14 Estate Agents Act 1979, s 13.
15 Parke B in *Bayliffe v Butterworth* (1847) 1 Exch 425.
16 *Dingle v Hare* (1859) 7 CBNS 145.
17 *Robinson v Mollett* (1875) LR 7 HL 802.

4.2   Apparent authority

A principal is bound by the authorised acts of his agent because he has consented to them and to be bound. A person may also be bound by acts done by another on his behalf without his consent, or even in breach of an express prohibition, if his words or actions give the impression that he has authorised them. Such cases are described as cases of apparent (or ostensible) agency or authority. However, as we noted earlier, this is potentially misleading: the agency relationship, and the concept of authority, is concerned with the relationship between principal and agent. In cases of 'apparent authority' there may be no such relationship at all, or the agent may be acting outside it; the true position is that the 'agent' has power in law to bind the 'principal' without the latter's consent, and the source of that power is an estoppel created by the conduct of the 'principal'. As Diplock LJ explained in *Freeman and Lockyer v Buckhurst Park Properties (Mangal) Ltd*[1]:

'An "apparent" authority . . . is a legal relationship between the principal and [third party] created by a representation made by the principal to the [third party], intended to be and in fact acted on by the [third party], that the agent has authority . . . To the relationship so created the agent is a stranger'.

For this reason it may be strictly inaccurate to speak of 'principal' and 'agent' in cases of apparent authority. However, it is convenient to describe the parties in that way and it is therefore proposed to use those terms.

'Apparent authority' is therefore the authority which a person appears to have to act on behalf of another. In many cases an agent's actual and apparent authority will coincide. However, 'apparent authority' may exceed or expand on actual authority, or even exist independently of it. Thus A has apparent authority in the following situations:

(a) A is appointed to act as P's agent in a capacity which would ordinarily carry 'usual authority': for instance, to act as managing director of P. However, P places an express limitation on A's actual authority, preventing him entering into contracts involving sums in excess of £1,000 without the approval of the Board of Directors. A orders goods worth £5,000 from T, who is unaware of the limitation on A's authority. A has apparent authority to order the goods and P is bound[2].
(b) A is appointed to act as P's agent, but his agency is terminated. He continues to act and enters into a contract with T who is unaware of the termination. P is bound[3].
(c) A is never appointed P's agent, but P allows him to act as if he were, or leads T to believe that A is his agent. P will be bound to T in transactions entered into by A on his behalf within the scope of his apparent agency[4].

As we have seen, the scope of A's apparent authority will often be defined by what is usual for an agent occupying the position he holds, or appears to hold[5].

1 [1964] 2 QB 480 at 504, CA.
2 Some commentators would treat these as cases of a separate type of 'usual' authority: see eg Stone [1993] JBL 325; below 4.4.
3 See *Summers v Solomon* (1857) 7 E & B 879; *Drew v Nunn* (1879) 4 QBD 661, CA.
4 *Freeman and Lockyer v Buckhurst Park Properties (Mangal) Ltd* [1994] 2 QB 480, CA.
5 Above, 4.1.

4.2.1 *The basis of apparent authority*

It was recognised in *Rama Corpn v Proved Tin and General Investment Ltd*[1] and confirmed by the Court of Appeal in *Freeman and Lockyer v Buckhurst Park Properties (Mangal) Ltd* [2] that the basis of the doctrine of 'apparent authority' is estoppel. In *Freeman and Lockyer* the defendant company had power under its constitution to appoint a managing director. That power had never been exercised, but A acted as if he had been appointed to the post, handling the day-to-day affairs of the company. The other directors knew of A's actions and did nothing to prevent them. A instructed the plaintiffs, a firm of architects, in connection with a property development scheme on behalf of the company, but the company later refused to pay the plaintiffs' fees, and they therefore sued the company. The Court of Appeal held the defendant company liable. By knowingly acquiescing in A's conduct, the directors, on behalf of the company, had represented that he was authorised to act as managing director. The plaintiffs had relied on that representation and the defendants were now estopped from denying it.

From the decisions in *Rama Corpn* and *Freeman and Lockyer* it is possible to identify the factors which must be present to give rise to such an estoppel and create apparent authority. There must be:

(1) a representation that A has authority; which must
(2) be made by the alleged principal or someone acting on his behalf; and
(3) be relied upon by the third party alleging apparent authority.

There is no doubt that there are some difficulties in treating estoppel as the basis of apparent authority[3]. It has been said that:

> 'The development of the doctrine [of "apparent authority"] has been based in part upon the principle that where the court has to decide which of two innocent parties is to suffer from the wrongdoing of a third party the court will incline towards placing the burden upon the party who was responsible for putting the wrongdoer in the position in which he could commit the wrong'[4].

and, although this cannot be an absolute rule[5], the courts are generally anxious to give effect to reasonable commercial expectations. In order to do so it may sometimes be necessary to 'stretch' the elements of estoppel, and, in particular, the concept of 'representation', in order to accommodate cases within the doctrine of apparent authority. However, despite these difficulties it is now generally accepted that estoppel is the basis of apparent authority[6] and we must therefore examine each of the above three requirements in turn.

1   [1952] 2 QB 147, [1952] 1 All ER 554.
2   [1964] 2 QB 480, [1964] 1 All ER 680, CA.
3   See *Bowstead on Agency* (16th edn 1996) para 8-029.
4   Per Neill LJ in *Gurtner v Beaton* [1993] 2 Lloyd's Rep 369 at 379.
5   See Robert Goff LJ in *Armagas Ltd v Mundogas SA* [1985] 3 All ER 795 at 806.
6   Per Neill LJ in *Gurtner v Beaton* [1993] 2 Lloyd's Rep 369 at 379.

4.2.2   *A representation*

The representation must be that the agent has authority to enter into the transaction in question. The representation may be either that the agent has general authority to enter into a class of transactions, as, for instance, where the agent is appointed (or held out as if he were appointed) to a position carrying 'usual' authority; or that the agent has specific authority to enter into a particular transaction. A representation of general authority may also be made where the principal allows the agent to enter into a course of dealing with a particular third party[1].

The representation must be one of fact, as opposed to law: thus a representation as to the contents of a power of attorney would create apparent authority, but a representation as to the meaning of its terms would not.

The representation may be made by words or by conduct. Often the representation will consist of appointing the agent to a position; in *Freeman and Lockyer* the representation was made tacitly, by acquiescing in the conduct of the agent[2]. If the representation is made negligently, it seems that it will only bind the principal if a duty of care is owed to the representee. There is no decisive authority exactly on the point, but cases concerned with estoppel in related areas suggest that this is the case[3]. Such a duty of care will probably be imposed where representor and representee are in an existing contractual or fiduciary relationship and in other cases in accordance with the principles of the law of negligence. Recent developments in the general law of negligence suggest that such a duty will only be imposed where there is a voluntary assumption of responsibility by the representor towards the representee[4]. The courts may be willing to recognise such an assumption of responsibility towards one individual or a defined and limited class of persons, but are unlikely to do so where the duty would be owed to an indeterminate class of potential claimants. Therefore, if a negligent statement is made to the world in general, it will only give rise to a duty of care in favour of a particular contractor who relies on it if it was foreseeable that it would be communicated to him as an individual or as a member of a particular class[5].

Generally, some positive representation is required. An estoppel by silence can only arise where there is a duty on the party against whom the estoppel is asserted to speak[6]. Such a duty will arise where, during dealings between two parties, one becomes aware that the other is mistaken as to their respective rights and liabilities and a reasonable person would expect him, acting honestly and responsibly, to bring the true facts to the attention of the other party[7].

1 See *Armagas Ltd v Mundogas SA, The Ocean Frost* [1986] AC 717 at 777, [1986] 2 All ER 385 at 390, HL, per Lord Keith.
2 Brown [1995] JBL 360 makes the point that to regard the appointment of an agent to a position as constituting a representation stretches the concept of representation, and that it would generally be more accurate to regard the representation as consisting of the principal's acquiescence in the agent's actions.
3 See *Moorgate Mercantile Ltd v Twitchings* [1977] AC 890, [1976] 2 All ER 641, HL; *Mercantile Credit Ltd v Hamblin* [1965] 2 QB 242, [1964] 3 All ER 592, CA.
4 *Henderson v Merrett Syndicates Ltd* [1995] 2 AC 145, [1994] 3 All ER 506; *White v Jones* [1995] 2 AC 207, [1995] 1 All ER 691; *Williams v Natural Life Health Foods Ltd* [1998] 2 All ER 577.
5 See *Caparo Industries plc v Dickman* [1990] 2 AC 605, [1990] 1 All ER 568, HL.
6 *The Tatra* [1990] 2 Lloyd's Rep 51.
7 *The Henrik Sif* [1982] 1 Lloyd's Rep 456 at 465.

4.2.3 *The representation must be made by P or someone on his behalf*

In general, the representation will only be binding on the alleged principal if it is made by him, or by someone authorised by him to make such representations. Where the principal is a company, representations about the authority of individual agents will normally be made by the board of directors as a whole, who have actual authority to conduct the day-to-day business of the company.

There are dicta in *Freeman and Lockyer* that where the representation is made by an agent of the principal, the agent must have actual authority to make the representation. However, there seems no reason why this should be the case. If P's actions or words give A1 apparent authority to make statements about the authority of his colleagues, P should be bound by A1's statements, including if A1 (wrongly) represents to T that A2 has authority to enter into a contract on P's behalf. Thus, in *Freeman and Lockyer*, if the apparent managing director had purported to appoint X as manager of the business, there seems no reason in principle why the company would not have been bound by X's actions, provided they fell within the scope of the authority of his apparent office.

Generally, apparent authority will not arise from the agent's own statements as to his own authority. In *Freeman and Lockyer* the operative representation was the knowing acquiescence of the board of directors in the conduct of the purported managing director. In contrast, in *The Rhodian River and the Rhodian Sailor*[1], where an agent claimed authority on behalf of a company, the company was not bound because the board of directors did not know of the representation. The position was confirmed by the decision of the House of Lords in *Armagas Ltd v Mundogas SA*[2]. T owned a ship and wished to charter it to P for three years. T dealt with P's employee, A, who, as T knew, generally had no authority to enter into such a transaction. However, A fraudulently claimed to have been given specific authority to enter into the particular charter and agreed a three year charter on behalf of P. T argued that P was bound by the charter, on the basis that A had apparent authority to claim to have received actual authority to make the contract. The claim failed. The House of Lords observed that, since T knew A generally had no actual authority to make a contract such as that in question, they could not reasonably believe that he was authorised to claim specific authority on a one off basis. It was argued in the alternative that P was vicariously liable for A's fraud as his employer. This argument also failed, the House holding that the employer would only be vicariously liable for an employee's frauds where the employee had actual or apparent authority to act as he did.

However, there is no absolute rule to mean that a representation by A as to his own authority can never bind P. In *The Raffaella*[3] Browne-Wilkinson LJ observed, obiter, that since P may give an agent, A1, actual or apparent authority to make statements about the authority of a fellow agent, A2, there is no reason in principle why P should not be able to give A1 actual or apparent authority to make statements about his own authority. The issue will generally only arise where it is claimed that A had apparent authority to claim to be authorised to act in a particular way, since it is hardly credible that P can have given A actual authority to *claim* to be authorised to do something which P has not given A actual authority to *do*. In *City Trust Ltd v Levy*[4] the Court of Appeal had to decide if a firm of solicitors was bound by an undertaking given on its behalf by an assistant solicitor. It was found as fact that it was usual for solicitors to give such undertakings only in the context of an underlying transaction on behalf of a client. The third party believed that there was such a transaction because the solicitor falsely said that there was. The court decided that the solicitor had authority to say that there was an underlying transaction and the firm was therefore bound by the undertaking. The assistant's authority to give the undertaking therefore derived from his own statement that there was an underlying transaction, which was binding on the firm because it was usual for solicitors to make such statements. However, the firm clearly did not give the assistant actual authority *falsely* to say that there was a transaction when there was none; his authority to make the representation that there was an underlying transaction could therefore only be apparent.

In *First Energy Ltd v Hungarian International Bank Ltd*[5] the plaintiffs approached the defendant bank for credit facilities. They dealt throughout with A, the manager of the defendants' Manchester office. A sent the plaintiffs a letter which was construed as an offer of a credit facility. The plaintiffs knew that A had no authority to grant a credit facility and that the decision to grant a facility was a matter for the defendants' head office; however, the Court of Appeal held that, by virtue of his position, A had apparent authority to communicate decisions of head office and held that the bank was therefore bound by A's letter which indicated that the bank's head office had approved the grant of the required facility. The court distinguished *Armagas* on the basis that the decision in that case was that the agent had no apparent authority to claim that he had been specifically authorised to enter into the charterparty, whereas here the agent had a general apparent authority by virtue of his position to make representations and to communicate decisions of head office.

The decision in *First Energy* may be said to be difficult to reconcile with orthodox agency doctrine. The distinction between A's statement in *Armagas* that 'P has authorised me to make this offer' and A's statement in *First Energy* that 'P has authorised me to say that he makes this offer' is a fine one. It is submitted, however, that the decision in *First Energy* is correct in its result and is to be welcomed. As all three members of the Court of Appeal emphasised, the plaintiffs had behaved reasonably in relying on A's letter and a decision that the plaintiffs could not rely on it would require them to check his statements with the bank's head office which would 'defeat the reasonable expectations of the parties'[6] and 'defeat the apparent object of appointing a senior manager in charge of the office in Manchester so that local businessmen could deal with him there'[7]. The real question in cases such as this is whether P or T should bear the risk of the agent's mistake or fraud, and that question must be answered bearing in mind the particular commercial matrix in which the agent operates[8].

Nevertheless, cases in which an agent has apparent authority as a result of his own statements are likely to be relatively rare[9]. They may be limited to cases where (a) the agent has authority to act provided certain underlying circumstances exist, in which the third party is entitled to rely on the agent's own statement that the necessary circumstances exist (as in *City Trust v Levy*), or (b) the agent occupies a relatively senior position which gives wide usual authority to make representations. In any case, it must ultimately be possible to find some representation by the principal which provides the basis for the agent's apparent authority. In both *City Trust* and *First Energy* the representation consisted of appointing A to a position in which it was usual for him to make statements, including ones about his own authority.

This does not mean that outside these cases A's claims to authority have no effect. Where T enters into a contract in reliance on A's claim to be authorised by P, T may sue A for breach of warranty of authority if he proves not to be authorised[10].

1 [1984] 1 Lloyd's Rep 373.
2 *Armagas Ltd v Mundogas SA, The Ocean Frost* [1986] AC 717, [1986] 2 All ER 385, HL.
3 *Egyptian International Foreign Trade Co v Soplex Wholesale Supplies and P S Refson and Co Ltd* [1985] 2 Lloyd's Rep 36, CA; see Reynolds, [1985] JBL 140.
4 [1988] 3 All ER 418.
5 [1993] 2 Lloyds Rep 194; see Reynolds [1994] JBL 144.
6 Per Steyn LJ at 204.
7 Per Evans LJ at 207.
8 See Brown [1995] JBL 360.
9 See *Suncorp Insurance and Finance Ltd v Milano Assicurazioni SpA* [1993] 2 Lloyd's Rep 225 at 234 per Waller J.
10 See 5.2.

4.2.4   *The third party must rely on the representation*

Since apparent authority is based on estoppel, P is only bound if T relies on his representation that A had authority to act on his behalf. Obviously, therefore, T must know of the representation: constructive notice is insufficient so that a statement in the articles of a company that it has power to appoint a managing director will not give rise to an estoppel as against a third party who has not read the articles[1]. Further, apparent authority will only arise if the representation leads T to believe A is agent for P: there can be no question of apparent authority if T believes A is acting on his own behalf, although P may be bound to T on some other basis[2].

T cannot claim to rely on any representation that A has authority if he knows that A does not actually possess such authority. The position is less clear where the circumstances are suspicious so that T ought to be aware of A's lack of authority. In *Overbrooke Estates Ltd v Glencombe Properties Ltd*[3] T bought property at an auction in reliance on a statement by the auctioneer which proved false. T alleged that P was liable for the statement on the basis of apparent authority, but failed: the auction particulars contained a notice that the auctioneer had no authority to make such statements so T could not claim to rely on any representation that he had such authority.

In *Overbrooke* P had taken reasonable steps to bring the limitation of A's authority to T's attention. Generally, where an agent is acting within the scope of the usual authority of an agent in his position, T is not required to check his authority: to require T constantly to make enquiries of P would be inconvenient and time-consuming for T and P, and it has been said that such enquiries would be 'officious'[4]; but where A is acting in a way which would not be usual for an agent in his position, T may be put on notice and required to check on his authority[5].

T will normally rely on the representation of A's authority by entering into a contract with P on the strength of it. It is sometimes suggested that there is a further requirement, that T should act to his detriment in reliance on the representation, but that seems unnecessary[6].

1   *Rama Corpn v Proved Tin and General Investments Ltd* [1952] 2 QB 147, [1952] 1 All ER 554.
2   See *Watteau v Fenwick* [1893] 1 QB 346, below 4.4.
3   [1974] 3 All ER 511, [1974] 1 WLR 1335.
4   *Waugh v H B Clifford & Sons* [1982] Ch 374, [1982] 1 All ER 1095, CA.
5   *British Bank of Middle East v Sun Life Assurance Ltd* [1983] 2 Lloyd's Rep 9, HL; see Collier (1984) 43 CLJ 26.
6   See *The Tatra* [1990] 2 Lloyd's Rep 51.

4.3   Estoppel arising after the event

In most cases of apparent authority, the 'principal' makes a representation that the 'agent' has authority which the third party relies upon by entering into a contract. However, the 'principal' may also be estopped from denying the 'agent's' conduct by his behaviour after the contract has been made. In *Spiro v Lintern*[1] the defendant instructed his wife to place his house in the hands of estate agents. He did not authorise her to sign a contract of sale, but she instructed the estate agents to do so. The defendant, with full knowledge of the contract entered into in his name, made no objection whilst the plaintiffs, the intending purchasers, made arrangements for alterations to the property, including allowing them to visit and measure up for those alterations. However, he then refused to complete the sale, raising for the first time his wife's, and the estate agents', lack of authority. He was held to be bound. By failing to correct the plaintiffs' mistaken belief that he had authorised the contract he had made a representation that he had given his wife the requisite authority and that there was a binding contract. Since the plaintiffs had relied on that representation and acted to their detriment by incurring expenses related to the expected purchase, the defendant was estopped from asserting his wife's lack of authority.

1   [1973] 3 All ER 319, [1973] 1 WLR 1002, CA.

4.4   *Watteau v Fenwick*: a separate category of 'usual authority'?

The explanation of apparent authority by Diplock LJ in *Freeman and Lockyer* has clarified the law in many ways. However, difficulty is caused by a small group of cases dating mainly from the nineteenth century, which do not fit easily into the framework of actual and apparent authority as now understood. The leading case is *Watteau v Fenwick*[1]. P appointed A to manage a public house, but forbade him to buy anything other than mineral water and bottled beer. A had previously owned the public house and his name continued to appear over the door. A ordered a quantity of cigars from T, who believed that A was the owner of the premises. When T discovered the truth he claimed the price from P and P was held liable.

At first this appears to be a case of 'apparent authority': the contract made by A was within the scope of the usual authority of an agent in his position, and T was unaware of the limitation. However, an essential requirement of 'apparent authority' is that T should believe that A is an agent for P; here T believed that A was the proprietor of the business and he was unaware of P's existence. Equally clearly, A had no actual authority to make the contract.

Despite the fact that the judgment in the case takes up only one and a half pages in the law reports, it has provoked considerable academic debate in an attempt to identify its rationale. Some of the language used in the case is the language of 'apparent authority' but, as noted above, it is not 'apparent authority' as it is now understood. Some writers have suggested that the case is evidence of a separate category of 'usual authority'[2], relying on the words of Wills J:

> 'once it is established that the defendant was the real principal, the ordinary doctrine as to principal and agent applies – that the principal is liable for all acts of the agent which are within the authority usually confided to an agent of that character, notwithstanding limitations, as between the principal and agent, put upon that authority'[3].

Such a separate category of 'usual authority' could be used to explain cases currently categorised as cases of apparent authority, where the principal's representation consists of appointing A to a position, avoiding the need to 'stretch' the concept of 'representation'[4], as well as cases such as *Watteau v Fenwick,* which do not fit into the actual/apparent authority dichotomy. However, it is not clear what practical benefit recognition of a separate category would provide, since it would still be necessary to decide what was the 'usual authority' of an agent in any particular case. Moreover, it is not clear why the principal should be held bound by the agent's actions in a case such as *Watteau v Fenwick* where T never thought he was dealing with an agent.

Other writers have suggested that *Watteau v Fenwick* can be explained on the basis of 'apparent ownership': P allowed A to appear to be the owner of the business, and should therefore be liable on contracts which an owner could make. Some support for this approach appears in the judgment in a similar, earlier case[5], where Shee J said:

> '[the] natural inference where a person allows an agent to carry on a particular business as an ostensible principal [is] that he clothes him with every authority incidental to a principal in the business'[6].

However, the doctrine of 'apparent ownership' is normally concerned with cases where the agent has disposed of property belonging to the principal[7]. Alternatively, it has been suggested that the basis of the decision is something akin to vicarious liability[8], whilst the American Law Institute's Second Restatement of the Law of Agency speaks of a broad category of 'inherent agency power', which would cover cases like *Watteau v Fenwick* and other cases where an 'agent' has power to bind his 'principal' without having actual or apparent authority, but this fails to explain *why* P should be held liable for A's unauthorised actions on such facts.

Perhaps the theoretical basis of the decision is less important than its effect. Here too opinions are divided. It might seem fair that the principal, who would take the benefit of contracts made by the manager, should also be bound by them. However, on the facts of *Watteau v Fenwick*, the owner could not have enforced the contract against the third party: he had not given prior authority, and an undisclosed principal cannot ratify a contract[9]. None of the theoretical explanations for the decision convincingly explains why the principal should be held liable on an unauthorised contract in favour of a third party who did not realise that he was dealing with an agent, unless it is possibly on the basis that the principal having appointed the agent should take responsibility for his actions[10].

The problem raised by *Watteau v Fenwick* does not appear to have been raised in many other cases. In Canada it has not been followed in cases in Ontario[11] and Alberta[12] and was recently overruled in British Columbia[13], and in a recent English case the judge described it as 'a somewhat puzzling case' and doubted if it was correct[14]. What is clear is that T cannot rely on *Watteau v Fenwick* if he knows of the limit placed on A's authority, or if he should know of it[15], and if the facts show that A contracted for his own benefit, A will be personally liable to the exclusion of P[16].

1   [1893] 1 QB 346.
2   See Fridman, *Law of Agency* (7th edn, 1996) p 70; Powell, *Law of Agency* (2nd edn, 1961) p 75.
3   [1893] 1 QB 346 at 348.
4   Such as *City Trust Ltd v Levy* [1988] 3 All ER 418 and *First Energy Ltd v Hungarian International Bank Ltd* [1993] 2 Lloyd's Rep 194, above 4.2.3; see Stone [1993] JBL 325. Note that 'usual authority' is here used in a different sense from the way in which it was used earlier: see 4.1.2.
5   *Edmunds v Bushell and Jones* (1865) LR 1 QB 97.
6   (1865) LR QB 97 at 100.
7   See 17.2.
8   Treitel, *Law of Contract* (10th edn, 1999) p 663.
9   See 4.7.
10 Tettenborn (1998) 57 CLJ suggests that *Watteau* can be explained on the basis that P was estopped from denying that A was the proprietor of the business. It is difficult, however, to see why this should enable T to enforce a contract against P.
11 *McLaughlin v Gentles* (1919) 51 DLR 383.
12 *Massey-Harris Co Ltd v Bond* [1930] 2 DLR 57.
13 *Sign-O-Lite Plastics Ltd v Metropolitan Life Insurance Co* (1990) 73 DLR (4th) 541; Fridman (1991) 70 Can Bar Rev 329.

14 *The Rhodian River and The Rhodian Sailor* [1984] 1 Lloyd's Rep 373, Bingham J at p 378.
15 *Daun v Simmins* (1879) 41 LT 783, CA.
16 *Kinahan v Parry* [1911] 1 KB 459 (where *Watteau v Fenwick* had been followed at first instance); and see *A-G's Reference (No 1 of 1985)* [1986] 2 All ER 219 at 225, CA.

4.5   Agency of necessity

In certain circumstances a person who acts in an emergency to preserve the property or interests of another may be treated as an agent of necessity, with the result that his actions will be deemed to be authorised even if no actual authority had been given. As in cases of apparent authority, agency of necessity can arise regardless of the absence of consent by the principal. However, unlike cases of apparent authority, agency of necessity can give the agent rights against the principal. Indeed, some cases of agency of necessity, where there is a pre-existing relationship between principal and agent, might be explained on the basis of implied authority; but the better view is that agency of necessity arises by operation of law.

Agency of necessity covers two types of situation. In the first, the agent of necessity creates privity of contract between the 'principal' and a third party, for example by arranging for the third party to store goods belonging to the principal. In the second class of case, the agent relies on the necessity either to provide him with a defence to a claim by the 'principal' for wrongful interference with his property, or as the basis for a claim to be reimbursed expenses incurred in preserving the principal's property[1]. It has been suggested that the term 'agency of necessity' should be restricted to the first class of case and that an agent of necessity's restitutionary claim should be regarded as forming part of the law of restitution[2].

In the first type of case, the effect of the emergency may be either to create authority where there was no pre-existing relationship between principal and agent, or to expand the authority of an existing agent. In the second type of case, however, it seems that there must be some pre-existing relationship: they need not be principal and agent, but it seems that if a person acts, even in an emergency, to preserve the property of a total stranger, he has no claim for reimbursement in English law[3].

Agency of necessity is founded on cases concerned with the carriage of goods by sea, and it is well established that a ship's master has wide powers to take such action in relation to his ship or its cargo in an emergency as he deems appropriate to preserve either: for instance, he may sell or pledge cargo to raise capital for repairs[4], incur expenses on behalf of cargo owners to preserve the cargo[5], or even jettison cargo to preserve the ship[6]. It may also apply in other situations, and has been applied to cases of carriage by land[7] and even storage of goods[8]. However, it will be rare that such cases will give rise to the kind of circumstances which create agency of necessity, except, perhaps, in cases of perishable goods or livestock.

An agency of necessity will only arise in extreme circumstances. There must be 'an actual and definite commercial necessity' for the agent's actions[9]. The agent must show that four requirements are satisfied.

(a) There must have been an emergency.
(b) As a result it must have been practically impossible to obtain instructions from the principal.
(c) The agent must have acted bona fide in the principal's interests, rather than his own[10].
(d) The agent must have acted reasonably in all the circumstances.

Given modern methods of communication, it will probably be rare that an agent can establish the second requirement today[11].

1   Similar rights are given to a person who accepts a bill of exchange for the honour of the drawer: Bills of Exchange Act 1882, ss 65–69.
2   *The Winson* [1982] AC 939, [1981] 3 All ER 688, HL; contrast Treitel, *The Law of Contract* (10th edn, 1999) p 667.
3   See Goff and Jones, *Law of Restitution* (5th edn, 1998) p 461 ff.
4   *Gunn v Roberts* (1874) LR 9 CP 331.
5   *Notara v Henderson* (1872) LR 7 QB 225.
6   *The Gratitudine* (1801) 3 Ch Rob 240.
7   *Great Northern Rly Co v Swaffield* (1874) LR 9 Exch 132.
8   *Sachs v Miklos* [1948] 2 KB 23; although on the facts the requirements for an agency of necessity were not made out.
9   *Springer v Great Western Rly Co* [1921] 1 KB 257 at 267.
10 *Prager v Blatspiel, Stamp & Heacock Ltd* [1924] 1 KB 566.
11 See *The Choko Star* [1989] 2 Lloyd's Rep 42, where the requirements for agency of necessity were not established and it was held that a ship's master has no implied authority to enter into salvage arrangements binding on cargo owners: see Brown (1992) 55 MLR 414; Reynolds [1990] JBL 505; Munday [1990] LMCLQ 1. See also *Surrey Breakdown Ltd v Knight* [1999] RTR 84.

4.6   Agency arising from cohabitation

It is sometimes said that a wife has authority to pledge her husband's credit for necessaries. However, this is inaccurate in two regards. First, the rule does not apply only to husband and wife, but to all cohabiting couples. Second, the fact of cohabitation does not give rise to authority, but to a rebuttable presumption 'that the husband really did give his wife such authority'[1]. The presumption is rebutted by the husband showing that his wife is adequately supplied with necessaries, or that he has provided his wife with an adequate allowance; or that he has forbidden his wife to pledge his credit, which suggests that this should perhaps be regarded as a case of implied authority[2].

Of course, there is no reason why actual or apparent authority should not arise between husband and wife on ordinary principles, and, given modern social conditions, the presumption of agency from cohabitation seems wholly anachronistic.

1   *Debenham v Mellon* (1880) 6 App Cas 24 at 36, per Lord Blackburn.
2   See Treitel, *The Law of Contract* (10th edn, 1999) p 657.

4.7   Ratification

We have seen that P is bound by A's actions when, at the time of those actions, A has actual or apparent authority from P, but that in the absence of apparent authority A's own claim to authority has no effect on P's position, although A may be liable to any third party he deals with for breach of his implied warranty of authority[1]. However, P may adopt acts done in his name without his authority by ratifying those acts. If P does choose to ratify unauthorised acts, the result is as if A had always been authorised: if a contract has been made with T, there is privity between P and T, and A can claim the rights of an agent vis-à-vis P. This doctrine of 'relation back' can have surprising effects, and because of the serious effect on the rights and liabilities of third parties, ratification is only possible if certain requirements are satisfied.

1   See 5.2.

4.7.1 *Requirements for effective ratification*

P can only ratify acts which were done in his name: A must have purported to have authority, and not have acted in his own name. As we will see, an undisclosed principal can enforce a contract made with his authority[1], but an undisclosed principal can never ratify a contract. Thus in *Watteau v Fenwick*[2] the owner of the public house could not have enforced the contract made by the manager. The rule is illustrated by the House of Lords' decision in *Keighley Maxsted & Co v Durant*[3], where P authorised A to buy wheat on their joint behalf. P limited A's authority by stipulating a limit to the price he was prepared to pay. In breach of that restriction A bought at a higher price, but in his sole name. P purported to ratify the contract, but later refused to take the wheat and T sued P for breach of contract. T's claim failed on the grounds that P's purported ratification was ineffective: A had not claimed to have P's authority. '[C]ivil obligations are not to be created by, or founded upon, undisclosed intentions'[4].

The result appears anomalous: P had purported to ratify, but was now allowed to withdraw his approval. Moreover, it appears that the reason for refusing to allow the undisclosed principal to ratify is to prevent a total stranger seeking to adopt or intervene in a contract by ratifying it. In this case P was not a total stranger: A was an agent exceeding his authority. However, the distinction between an agent exceeding his authority and one with no authority at all may be difficult to draw. In any case, the result of *Keighley Maxsted* accorded with T's expectations: he thought that he was dealing only with A, was prepared to do so, and so appears to have suffered no hardship.

The corollary of this rule is that, provided A did purport to act for P, P can ratify even though A's real intention was to contract for his own benefit[5].

The decision in *Spiro v Lintern*[6] suggests a way in which the restriction in *Keighley Maxsted* may be modified in favour of the third party. In that case P was an undisclosed principal, so that his conduct could not be construed as ratification, but his apparent consent to the acts done by A estopped him from denying A's authority. However, T can only rely on this reasoning where all the requirements for estoppel are satisfied: in particular, he must have done some act in reliance on P's representation. Ex hypothesi he cannot claim to have entered into a contract, since the contract has already been concluded.

In general, a principal is disclosed provided A indicates that he is an agent without disclosing the identity of his principal. However, in the present context it seems that it is not enough for A simply to declare that he acts as an agent; the particular principal on behalf of whom he acts must be ascertainable at the time of A's actions[7]. This means that there must be sufficient information given to T to enable him to identify P. The rule has been criticised[8] but still represents the law and may cause difficulties where contracts are to be performed by sub-contractors and the sub-contractors seek to take advantage of exclusion clauses in the main contract, or of insurance taken out by the main contractor. Thus in *Southern Water Authority v Carey*[9] the main contractor on a construction project entered into a contract including exclusions of liability which purported to benefit its sub-contractors, amongst others, and provided that the main contractor entered into the contract for the benefit of itself and any sub-contractors. However, when the employer under the contract sued one of the sub-contractors, it was held that they could not claim the benefit of the exclusion clause because, inter alia, they had not authorised the contract and could not ratify because at the time the contract was made they were not ascertainable to the employer, even though the main contractor had them in mind as possible sub-contractors. However, provided P is ascertainable, he need not be named.

155

The second requirement is that P must have been in existence at the time of A's actions on his behalf. In the past this has caused difficulties for promoters of new companies. It may be commercially necessary to enter into contracts before the company is actually incorporated. However, such contracts can neither bind nor benefit the company, and the company cannot ratify them after incorporation[10]. The agent who contracts on behalf of a non-existent principal may be personally liable on the contract if that is its true construction[11]. In the case of companies the position is now governed by statute and the promoters who make the contract are personally liable on it, subject to any contrary agreement[12]. It has been suggested that the promoters cannot escape personal liability by simply contracting 'as agent' for the intended company, and that the contract must unequivocally state that their personal liability is excluded[13]. The problem can be avoided by all parties agreeing to a novation of the contract, substituting the company for the promoters.

The third requirement is that P can only ratify a contract if he was competent to make it at the time of the agent's actions and at the time of ratification. Thus a minor cannot effectively ratify a contract after attaining majority if the contract would not have bound him during minority, and a company cannot ratify contracts which are ultra vires under its constitution.

It is sometimes said that P can ratify a voidable act but not a void act. Thus a company cannot ratify an act ultra vires its constitution. However, that rule can be explained on the basis of the company's lack of capacity. Clearly voidable acts can be ratified: whenever an agent claims authority he does not have, any resulting contract will be voidable for misrepresentation. The distinction between void and voidable acts comes from the case of *Brook v Hook*[14], where A forged P's signature on a promissory note. P purported to 'ratify' the signature (to avoid the scandal of litigation against A) but failed to honour the note. It was held that his ratification was ineffective because the signature, as a forgery, was a nullity and could not be ratified.

The distinction between 'void' and 'voidable' acts may be difficult to draw – for instance, P can ratify litigation commenced in his name without authority[15] – and has been criticised. The rule that a forgery cannot be ratified could be explained instead on the basis that the forger does not claim to have P's authority, but in fact claims to be P; indeed, this explanation appears in *Brook v Hook*[16]. A distinction may therefore have to be drawn between cases where A forges P's signature by claiming to be P, or that P has signed, and cases where A claims to have authority to sign on P's behalf, where A's signature can be ratified[17]. Other cases may be explained on the basis that P cannot effectively ratify an act which the law forbids him to do[18]. Nevertheless, the distinction between 'void' acts, which cannot be ratified, and 'voidable' acts, which can, was reaffirmed in the most recent case on the subject in which it was held that a writ issued without authority could be ratified[19].

1   See 5.3.
2   [1893] 1 QB 346, above 4.4.
3   [1901] AC 240.
4   [1901] AC 240 at 247, per Lord MacNaghten.
5   *Re Tiedemann and Ledermann Frères* [1899] 2 QB 66.
6   [1973] 3 All ER 319, [1973] 1 WLR 1002, CA, above 4.3.
7   *Watson v Swann* (1862) 11 CBNS 756; this was a case concerned with insurance, but there may be an exception to the general rule in cases of marine insurance where policies are commonly taken out for an unidentified future class who may acquire an interest in the goods insured. However, such policies are in general assignable in any case.
8   See *Bowstead on Agency* (16th edn, 1996) para 2-063.

9 [1985] 2 All ER 1077. See also *Trident General Insurance Co Ltd v McNiece Bros Pty Ltd* (1987) 8 NSWLR 270, [1987] JBL 378; affd (1988) 80 ALR 574. It is sufficient if P is identifiable as a member of a class covered by the contract: *National Oilwell (UK) Ltd v Davy Offshore Ltd* [1993] 2 Lloyd's Rep 582.

10 *Kelner v Baxter* (1866) LR 2 CP 174.

11 Contrast *Kelner v Baxter* with *Newborne v Sensolid (GB) Ltd* [1954] 1 QB 45, [1953] 1 All ER 708, CA.

12 Companies Act 1985, s 36C. The provision does not apply if, objectively, the intention of the parties is to contract with an existing company which is wrongly named in the contract: *Oshkosh B'Gosh Inc v Dan Marbel Inc Ltd* (1988) 4 BCC 795.

13 *Phonogram Ltd v Lane* [1982] QB 938, [1981] 3 All ER 182, CA, per Lord Denning MR.

14 (1871) LR 6 Exch 89.

15 *Danish Mercantile Ltd v Beaumont* [1951] Ch 680, [1951] 1 All ER 925, CA; *Presentaciones Musicales SA v Secunda* [1994] Ch 271, [1994] 2 All ER 737, CA.

16 (1871) LR 6 Exch 89 at 100.

17 A person may also be estopped from setting up a forgery in certain cases: see *Greenwood v Martins Bank* [1933] AC 51, HL, below 28.4.3.

18 *Bedford Insurance Co Ltd v Instituto des Resseguros do Brasil* [1985] QB 966, [1984] 3 All ER 766.

19 *Presentaciones Musicales SA v Secunda* [1994] Ch 271, [1994] 2 All ER 737, CA.

4.7.2 The effect of ratification

If the above requirements are fulfilled and P does in fact ratify a contract made in his name, the effect is as if A had been authorised at the time of his actions. Thus where A has made a contract with T on P's behalf, privity exists between P and T, whilst as between P and A the relationship of principal and agent exists: A is not liable for exceeding his authority and may be entitled to the rights of an agent[1]. T has no claim against A for breach of warranty of authority.

The retroactive effect of ratification can produce anomalous results. It was held in *Bolton & Partners v Lambert*[2] that if T makes an offer to A which A accepts on P's behalf and P then ratifies the contract, T is bound, even if he purports to withdraw the offer from the contract before the ratification. This may seem harsh: P may choose whether or not to ratify, but if P does ratify, T is bound. *Bolton v Lambert* is arguably inconsistent with an earlier case, *Kidderminster Corpn v Hardwick*[3], which suggests that T cannot be sued for breaches of contract which occur before ratification and which was not cited in *Bolton v Lambert*, and in *Fleming v Bank of New Zealand*[4] the Privy Council doubted *Bolton v Lambert* and expressly reserved the right to reconsider it at a future date. However, the principle of *Bolton v Lambert*, that ratification has retroactive effect, was reaffirmed by the Court of Appeal in the recent case of *Presentaciones Musicales SA v Secunda*[5].

The principle may be less harsh than at first appears: if P does ratify, there is a contract between T and P, as T always believed there to be; if not, T has an action against A for breach of warranty of authority. Furthermore, the rule is subject to a number of restrictions to prevent injustice to third parties. Unfortunately the scope and rationale of the exceptions are difficult to discern.

(a) The rule does not apply if A makes his lack of authority known to T and expressly contracts 'subject to ratification'[6]: in that case, A's 'acceptance' has no legal effect and P's ratification amounts to acceptance of Ts offer, which can therefore be withdrawn prior to ratification. (The Geneva Convention on Agency in International Sales of Goods would seem to reverse the common law position: if T is unaware of A's lack of authority at the time of contracting, he may, at any time before ratification, refuse to be bound by any ratification;

but if T is aware of A's lack of authority, he may not refuse to be bound by a subsequent ratification[7].)

(b) The rule in *Bolton v Lambert* does not apply if, before ratification, T and A agree to rescind their agreement[8].

(c) It may be that the rule does not permit P to sue for damages in respect of breaches which occurred before ratification[9].

(d) It is said that where a time limit is prescribed for the doing of an act, P may not ratify outside that time limit if that would prejudice T[10]. The extent of this exception is unclear. Most of the cases concerned with it involve property rights and can be explained on a narrower basis that 'an estate once vested cannot be divested'[11]. Thus in *Bird v Brown*[12], A, without authority, gave notice on behalf of P to stop goods in transit under the Sale of Goods Act[13]. P purported to ratify, but by then the goods had reached T. P's ratification was ineffective. In *Presentaciones Musicales SA v Secunda* a writ claiming damages for breach of copyright was issued without authority of the plaintiff. Subsequently, the plaintiff purported to ratify the writ but by that time the limitation period on some of the claims had expired. The Court of Appeal nevertheless held that the ratification was effective. The reasoning of the majority seems to have been that in cases where ratification outside a time limit was prohibited the agent's initial act was void without ratification. Roch LJ explained the cases on the narrower basis that ratification outside a prescribed time limit is ineffective where it would deprive T of vested property rights. The reasoning of the majority, perpetuating the distinction between voidable (ratifiable) and void (non-ratifiable) acts is difficult to follow. Dillon LJ seemed to recognise this, observing that:

> 'On the one hand it is well established that that ratification is retrospective; on the other hand there are authorities decided over a long period which show that in certain circumstances "ratification" may come too late to be effective. What the logic of the dividing line between the two should be is not easy to discern'[14].

The result in *Secunda* can perhaps be explained on the grounds that the third party, the defendant to the action, was in no way prejudiced by ratification.

(e) It is said that ratification will be ineffective if P could not validly have done the act ratified at the time of ratification. Thus it has been held that a contract of insurance cannot be ratified after occurrence of the loss insured against[15]. However, contracts of marine insurance are an exception to the general rule and can be ratified after loss of the insured goods[16] and it has been suggested that the general rule itself should be relaxed[17]. It is not clear that this is a separate exception from the previous one.

(f) Ratification will only be effective to bind T if it takes place within a reasonable time[18]. The explanation for this exception seems to be that ratification beyond a reasonable time would unfairly prejudice T, so that the lapse of time would operate rather like a form of estoppel against P. What is a reasonable time will be a question of fact in each case. There are dicta in *Metropolitan Asylums Board v Kingham* that P can never ratify a contract after the time for performance has arrived. However, in *Bedford Insurance Co Ltd v Instituto des Resseguros do Brasil*[19] Parker J doubted that there is any such general rule, and it seems that the better view is that P can ratify after the time for performance, but not so as to prejudice T.

(g) Ratification will also be ineffective where third parties have acquired property rights which would be adversely affected by ratification.

In so far as there does seem to be any underlying rationale to the various exceptions, it may be simply that ratification will not be permitted to have retroactive effect where that would unfairly prejudice T or third party property rights. However, the area would benefit from reconsideration and rationalisation.

1 See ch 6.
2 (1889) 41 Ch D 295.
3 (1873) LR 9 Exch 13. The case could perhaps be distinguished on the basis that the original acceptance in *Hardwick* was ineffective.
4 [1900] AC 577. *Bolton v Lambert* has also been criticised in other Commonwealth jurisdictions.
5 [1994] Ch 271, [1994] 2 All ER 737, CA; see Brown (1994) 110 LQR 531.
6 *Watson v Davies* [1931] 1 Ch 455; *Warehousing and Forwarding Co of E Africa Ltd v Jafferali & Sons Ltd* [1964] AC 1, [1963] 3 All ER 571, PC.
7 Article 15(1)–(2).
8 *Walter v James* (1871) LR 6 Exch 124.
9 A possible explanation of *Kidderminster Corpn v Hardwick* (1873) LR 9 Exch 13.
10 *Dibbins v Dibbins* [1896] 2 Ch 348.
11 Per Cotton LJ in *Bolton & Partners v Lambert* at 307.
12 (1850) 4 Exch 786.
13 Section 44; see 18.3.2.
14 [1994] Ch 271 at 280, [1994] 2 All ER 737 at 746.
15 *Grover and Grover Ltd v Matthews* [1910] 2 KB 401.
16 Marine Insurance Act 1906, s 6.
17 Per Colman J in *National Oilwell (UK) Ltd v Davy Offshore Ltd* [1993] 2 Lloyd's Rep 582 at 607.
18 *Metropolitan Asylums Board v Kingham* (1890) 6 TLR 217.
19 [1985] QB 966, [1984] 3 All ER 766.

4.7.3 *Method of ratification*

P may expressly ratify A's actions, but it seems that he may also impliedly ratify by any act which unequivocally shows an intention to ratify, for instance, by commencing legal proceedings to enforce the contract[1]; but where P repossessed his property he did not impliedly authorise a contract for its repair entered into without authority[2]: his actions were not unequivocal. There seems no reason in principle why inactivity could not amount to ratification, but mere inactivity is rarely unequivocal: a similar problem occurs in relation to the question whether silence can amount to acceptance in contract generally. A principal who passively concurs in acts done on his behalf may also be bound by them on the basis of estoppel as in *Spiro v Lintern*. P will not be taken to have ratified unless he had a real choice whether or not to do so, and had full knowledge of all the circumstances[3].

1 *Bedford Insurance Co Ltd v Instituto des Resseguros do Brasil* [1985] QB 966, [1984] 3 All ER 766.
2 *Forman & Co Pty Ltd v The Liddlesdale* [1900] AC 190.
3 *The Bonita; The Charlotte* (1861) 1 Lush 252.

4.7.4 *Ratification and the Contracts (Rights of Third Parties) Act 1999*

Ratification allows P to take the benefit of a contract made in his name but without his prior authority. It is now possible for a person to enforce a contract made for his benefit under the Contracts (Rights of Third Parties) Act 1999[1]. There are, however, important differences between the right under the 1999 Act and that created by ratification. In particular, where P ratifies an unauthorised contract he becomes a party to it as if it had been authorised when made. He thus not only acquires the right to enforce it but also becomes liable on it as a party. In contrast, under the 1999 Act the beneficiary becomes entitled to enforce, but not liable under, the contract. It is submitted, however, that where ratification is possible the 1999 Act will generally not apply. The Act only applies where a contract is made between two parties and purports to confer a benefit on a third[2]. Where A contracts with T claiming to act as agent for P, there is no contract between A and T. There is an assumed contract between P and T, but it is submitted that this situation falls outside the 1999 Act. Where A contracts with T purporting to act for himself and as agent for P it may be argued that the situation falls within the 1999 Act. However, P acquires no benefit under the Act if on its proper construction it appears that the parties did not intend him to have an enforceable benefit[3]. It is submitted that in this situation the fact that A purports to have P's authority indicates that the parties intend P to take the benefit of the contract as a party to it, not as a beneficiary, so that the Act does not apply.

1   See 2.7.2.
2   Section 1(1).
3   Section 1(2).

Chapter 5

Relations with Third Parties

5.0 Disclosed and undisclosed agency

We have seen that the essence of agency is the agent's power to affect the principal's legal position vis-à-vis third parties, and that agency principles may apply in many areas of law. However, agency in commercial law is primarily concerned with the role of agents in making contracts on behalf of others, and it is on that aspect of the agent's role that we concentrate here.

   The general rule is that where an agent makes a contract on behalf of his principal, 'the contract is that of the principal, not that of the agent, and prima facie at common law the only person who can sue is the principal and the only person who can be sued is the principal'[1]. Having performed his task by bringing about a contract, the agent drops out of the picture, subject to any outstanding matters between agent and principal. This general rule applies where the agent's contract was authorised, either in advance, or after the fact by ratification; the position may be different where the agent has apparent but not actual authority. However, the general rule is modified in some situations. In particular, the rights and liabilities of principal and agent against third parties may differ according to whether the agency is disclosed or undisclosed. Agency is disclosed where the agent reveals that he is acting as an agent; it is sufficient that the fact of agency is revealed, and there is no need for the principal to be named. In contrast, the agency is undisclosed where the agent does not reveal the fact of agency at all and purports to be acting on his own behalf.

1   Per Wright J in *Montgomerie v United Kingdom Mutual Steamship Association* [1891] 1 QB 370 at 371.

5.1 Disclosed agency

Where an agent makes a contract disclosing the fact of the agency, the normal rule is that the principal can sue and be sued on the contract provided he has actually authorised or ratified it. Where the agent acts outside his actual authority but has apparent authority, the principal is liable on the contract but cannot enforce on the basis of apparent authority alone; however, as a disclosed principal he should be able to ratify provided the conditions set out earlier[1] are fulfilled. Where the agent does not have actual authority, in the absence of ratification, the agent is liable to the third party for breach of warranty of authority[2].

Problems may arise where money is paid to the agent under the contract, as, for instance, where A, acting on behalf of P, sells property to T, and T pays A. If A becomes insolvent, or misappropriates the money, it becomes important to know whether payment to A is effective as settlement under the contract. In cases of payment by T the answer depends entirely on A's authority: payment to A will discharge T if A had actual or apparent authority to receive payment; authority to sell property does not per se give an agent implied authority to receive payment[3]. T will only be discharged if the payment is made in a manner which A is authorised to accept: for instance, if A is authorised to accept cash, T's liability to P will not be discharged by a bill of exchange. Further, since the effect of agency is to create a contract between P and T, T may not set off sums due from A personally against sums due under the contract with P. Surprisingly, in the converse situation, where A buys property from T on P's behalf, payment by P to A may also operate to discharge P's liability. This will only be the case where T, by words or conduct, leads P to believe that A has settled the debt (so that A is entitled to an indemnity from P), for instance by giving A a receipt, or taking security from A[4]. The proper basis of this rule seems to be that in such cases T is estopped from asserting that A has not paid[5].

Where A transfers property to T, T acquires property rights provided that A had actual or apparent authority, or his actions were ratified. However, T may acquire property even outside those situations as a result of rules designed to protect third party transferees of property. Thus mercantile agents have wide powers to make effective dispositions of goods placed in their possession for a purpose connected with sale[6] and an owner of goods will be bound by any disposition of those goods under the doctrine of 'apparent ownership'. This applies where the true owner of property allows another person to appear to be the owner: he is then estopped from denying that person's right to deal with the property and is therefore bound by any dealing with the property, regardless of actual or apparent authority. Although the rule is of general application, many of the cases concern dealings with goods and we examine it in the context of sale of goods[7]. In general, a person will not be estopped on the basis of 'apparent ownership' merely because he allows someone else to have possession of his property; something more is required to give the possessor the 'indicia of ownership'.

Where A is instructed to acquire goods on P's behalf and P is a disclosed principal, the transfer of property will normally be direct from T to P, provided T intends to deal with P.

1   See 4.7.1.
2   See 5.2.
3   *Pole v Leask* (1860) 28 Beav 562.
4   *Wyatt v Marquis of Hertford* (1802) 3 East 147.
5   *Irvine v Watson* (1880) 5 QBD 414, CA. On the facts of the case T was not estopped.
6   Factors Act 1889; see 17.1.
7   See 17.2.

5.1.1   *Exceptional cases*

Despite the general rule, in some cases the position is modified with the result that A may be able to enforce or be held liable on the contract, either together with or to the exclusion of P.

(a)   Foreign principals

At one time there was a general rule that where an agent made a contract on behalf of a foreign principal, only the agent acquired rights or liabilities under the contract. The rule was explained by reference to commercial practice, on the grounds that:

> 'the foreign constituent has not authorised the merchant to pledge his credit to the contract, to establish privity between him and the home supplier, . . . [and] the home supplier, knowing that to be the usage . . . does not trust the foreigner and so does not make the foreigner responsible to him, and does not make himself responsible to the foreigner'[1].

However, in 1968 the Court of Appeal recognised that 'commercial usages are far from immutable'[2] and ruled that there is no longer a general rule to this effect. In any case involving a contract made on behalf of a foreign principal the court must now consider all the facts to decide whether the contract has created privity between T and P; the foreign nationality of P will be only one factor to be taken into account. Of course, an agent instructed to act on behalf of a foreign principal may well be asked to confirm the contract[3].

(b)   Agent a party to the contract

Despite the general rule, A will become a party to the contract with T if, on its proper construction, it appears that that was the intention of the parties. The contract may expressly state that A is a party; for instance, A may contract on behalf of himself and P, so that they are jointly liable on the contract and may both enforce it. However, A may become a party to a contract even in the absence of such express statement. The agent's liability will depend on the construction of the individual contract, and so each case will depend on its own facts[4] but, as a general rule, if an agent signs a contract in his own name, he will be held personally liable on it. In order to escape liability the contract must make clear that the agent signs only in a representative capacity. Merely using words such as 'director', 'agent' or 'broker' after a signature will be insufficient. Thus where a civil engineer signed a contract on behalf of a client using his own name, adding the words 'chartered civil engineer', he was nevertheless held liable on the contract, as the words could be read merely as describing his occupation rather than the capacity in which he signed[5]. This may be so even where the body of the contract makes clear that the signatory is acting as agent for someone else[6]. In order to avoid liability, the agent should make clear that he signs in a representative capacity: for example by signing 'A, agent for P'.

If on the proper construction of the contract the agent is liable on it he may also be able to enforce it, according to its construction. However, although he may be liable without being entitled to enforce, he cannot enforce a contract on which he is not liable.

(c)   Deeds

If an agent personally executes a deed, he is liable on it and able to enforce it to the exclusion of his principal, except where the deed is executed pursuant to a power of attorney[7].

(d)   Bills of exchange

Similarly, an agent who signs a bill of exchange, including a cheque, may become personally liable on it. A person can only be held liable on a bill of exchange if his name appears on it[8], but a person who signs a bill will be personally liable on it unless the signature makes clear that it is signed only in a representative capacity; merely adding words such as 'agent' or 'director' is insufficient to avoid personal liability[9] and where it is unclear whether a signature should be regarded as that of the principal or the agent, the 'construction most favourable to the validity of the instrument' will be preferred[10].

(e)   Custom

An agent may also incur personal liability on a contract if there is a trade custom to that effect. Although there is no need for an agent to identify his principal in order to make the principal 'disclosed', in many trades there is a custom that if the principal is not named, the agent is personally liable[11].

(f)   Agent the real principal

As noted above, an agent may become a party to the contract directly, as where he contracts for himself and a principal jointly. In that case the agent can both enforce and be held liable on the contract. There is also a small body of authority that a person who makes a contract as an agent but actually for his own benefit may be liable on and even enforce the contract. The agent's liability causes few problems. Where the named principal exists, an agent acting for his own benefit would be liable in any case for breach of his warranty of authority; an agent who professes to act for a non-existent or fictitious principal can be liable on the contract if the proper construction is that the agent undertook personal liability. However, allowing the agent to reveal himself as the true principal and enforce the contract runs counter to the expectations of the other contracting party and is less easy to justify.

   Three situations may arise:

   (i)   A acts for a non-existent or fictitious principal;
   (ii)   A purports to act for an identified principal;
   (iii) A purports to act as agent but without identifying a principal.

Most of the cases in the first category are concerned with contracts made on behalf of companies to be incorporated at a future date. Whether or not A is a party to the contract is a question of construction at common law but is now governed by statute in the case of companies' pre-incorporation contracts[12].

   In the second case, A will be liable for breach of warranty of authority if he does not have the authority of his named principal. However, there are cases to the effect that A may be sued directly on the contract, and in some cases this may be preferable for the third party. There is also authority that A may actually enforce the contract[13], but not where 'the skill or solvency of the person who is named as principal may reasonably be considered as a material ingredient in the contract'[14] or where A's enforcement would otherwise prejudice the third party. Prejudice may, however, be difficult to prove[15]. Where the identity of the other party to the contract is material, the third party may be able to avoid the contract on the grounds of misrepresentation, or it may be void for mistake.

In the third group of cases it would be possible to hold A liable for breach of a collateral contract that there is a principal, but again there is authority that instead A may be held directly liable on the contract[16]. There is also authority that A may enforce the contract as the true principal[17], except, possibly, where the other party would not have agreed to contract with A personally.

(g) Collateral contracts

In some cases an agent who brings about a contract between his principal and a third party may enter into a separate, collateral contract with the third party. In such a case the agent may incur liabilities and be entitled to sue under the collateral contract. The agent's rights and liabilities are therefore separate from those of the principal. The agent's warranty of authority is a collateral contract, although of a different type. The best example of the sort of collateral contract under consideration here occurs where goods are sold by an auctioneer. Even though the identity of the principal vendor may be disclosed, the auctioneer enters into a collateral contract with the highest bidder under which the auctioneer warrants that he has authority to sell and that he knows of no defects in the principal's title, and which allows him to sue the bidder for the price. Older cases explain this contract as arising from the auctioneer's lien over the goods which gives him a special property in them, but the better view is that the rights and liabilities arise under a collateral contract.

(h) Merger and election

Where agent and principal are both liable on the main contract (except where they are jointly liable as joint contractors), the third party may be prevented from suing one if he has elected to hold the other liable. The third party's rights are only limited in this way if he has made an irrevocable and unequivocal election to pursue only one of the potential defendants. The same rule applies in cases of undisclosed principals and is examined in that context[18].

1 Blackburn J in *Elbinger AG für Fabrication von Eisenbahn Material v Claye* (1873) LR 8 QB 313.
2 Diplock LJ in *Teheran-Europe Co Ltd v S T Belton (Tractors) Ltd* [1968] 2 QB 545, [1968] 2 All ER 886, CA.
3 See 3.2.3.
4 See *Chitty on Contracts* (28th edn, 1999) para 31-078; *Bowstead on Agency* (16th edn, 1996) para 9-034.
5 *Sika Contracts Ltd v B L Gill & Closegate Properties Ltd* (1978) 9 BLR 11. See *Punjab National Bank v de Boinville* [1992] 3 All ER 104, where a policy of insurance arranged by a bank for a customer described the assured as '[the bank] a/c [the customer]' and it was held that the bank was the assured. The expression 'a/c' merely meant 're', indicating to which customer the policy related. Cf *Gadd v Houghton* (1876) 1 Ex D 357.
6 *Tudor Marine Ltd v Tradax Export SA, The Virgo* [1976] 2 Lloyd's Rep 135, CA.
7 Powers of Attorney Act 1971, s 7.
8 Bills of Exchange Act 1882, s 23.
9 Bills of Exchange Act 1882, s 26(1).
10 Bills of Exchange Act 1882, s 26(2); see *Elliott v Bax-Ironside* [1925] 2 KB 301, below 25.2.
11 See eg *Thornton v Fehr* (1935) 51 Ll L Rep 330 (tallow trade); see *Bowstead on Agency* (16th edn, 1996) para 9-039.
12 Companies Act 1985, s 36, above 4.7.1.
13 *Rayner v Grote* (1846) 15 M & W 359; *Gewa Chartering BV v Remco Shipping Lines Ltd, The Remco* [1984] 2 Lloyd's Rep 205; contra *Bickerton v Burrell* (1816) 5 M & S 383.
14 Per Alderson B in *Rayner v Grote* (1846) 15 M & W 359 at 365.
15 See *Harper & Co v Vigers Bros* [1909] 2 KB 549.

16   *Hersom v Bernett* [1955] 1 QB 98, [1954] 3 All ER 370.
17   *Schmaltz v Avery* (1851) 16 QB 655.
18   Below 5.3.4.

5.2   Warranty of authority

We have seen that an agent's claim to have authority to enter into a transaction
normally does not give the agent apparent authority[1]: apparent authority depends
on a statement by the principal. However, often the person who deals with an
agent will have no direct contact with the agent's principal, and to require such a
person to contact the principal to seek verification of the agent's authority would
often be impractical and would destroy much of the commercial convenience of
agency arrangements[2]. As a matter of commercial convenience, therefore, a person
dealing with an agent must be able to rely on the agent's assertion of authority.
This problem has been resolved by allowing the person who deals with an agent
on the strength of the latter's claim to authority to hold the agent liable if that
claim proves false. Where the agent claims authority which he knows he does not
possess, he may be held liable in the tort of deceit, but fraud is notoriously difficult
to prove and would rarely give a right to recovery against the agent. If the agent
acts negligently in claiming authority, there seems no reason why he should not be
held liable in negligence on the basis of *Hedley Byrne & Co Ltd v Heller & Partners*[3].
However, such liability would depend on the third party proving that the agent
acted negligently and that he had suffered loss in reliance on the agent's claim.

   In fact the third party generally does not have to prove negligence or fraud because
it is now established that the agent who falsely claims authority may be held liable
for breach of warranty of authority, in which case liability is strict and its basis is
contractual. After some doubt it was settled in *Collen v Wright*[4] that where an
agent enters into a transaction purporting to act for a principal, the agent impliedly
warrants that he has the principal's authority to enter the transaction in question,
and if, in fact, he proves not to have such authority, is liable to the third party for
breach of that warranty. At the time the tort of negligence was not developed and,
in particular, liability in negligence for false statements causing economic loss
was not recognised. As a result, the agent's liability was based on an implied
contract. The contract is unilateral: the agent impliedly promises that he will warrant
that he has authority if the third party enters into the contract with the alleged
principal. By entering into the main contract with the principal in reliance on the
agent's assertion of authority, the third party accepts the offer and provides
consideration for the agent's promise, giving rise to a collateral contract between
himself and the agent.

   Typically, the agent gives a warranty of his own authority to the third party who,
on the strength of it, contracts with the agent's principal. In certain situations,
however, the liability created by warranty of authority may be extended. Thus an
agent, A1, may be held liable for warranting the authority of a fellow agent, A2[5].
In addition, the protection of the agent's warranty may extend to any third party to
whom it is addressed and who acts in reliance on it. Thus where a house was
owned by a husband and wife, a solicitor instructed to sell it impliedly warranted
that he had the authority of both husband and wife and that warranty was given not
only to the purchaser of the property but also to the building society which advanced
funds on the security of a mortgage of the property to finance the purchase[6]. The
solicitor was therefore liable to the building society when it was discovered that he

did not in fact have the authority of the wife. The third party in such a case provides consideration for the agent's warranty by acting in reliance on it. In most cases the offer of the warranty will be addressed to a limited class of offerees. It has been held that a person who signs a bill of lading falsely declaring goods to have been shipped is liable for breach of warranty and may be sued by any assignee of the bill of lading[7], but this rule probably only applies to warranties arising from the signature of documents such as bills of lading and bills of exchange which are transferable, and not to warranties generally.

The contractual nature of the agent's liability has two important consequences. First, the agent is strictly liable if the warranty proves false. This is well illustrated by *Yonge v Toynbee*[8], where solicitors were instructed by a client to defend legal proceedings. Unknown to them, their client became insane, so that their authority to act for him was terminated. In ignorance of his insanity they continued to act. When the truth was discovered, they were held liable for breach of their warranty of authority and ordered to pay the costs of the other litigant.

The strict nature of the liability imposes a heavy burden on the agent, who may be liable even though he honestly and reasonably believed he had authority. However, the harshness of the rule is mitigated by a number of limitations.

(a) If A is unsure of his position he may warn T that he does not, or may not, have authority. If T nevertheless contracts with him on that basis, T cannot complain if in fact A does not have authority[9].

(b) If A acts without authority but P ratifies his actions, A's lack of authority is retroactively cured and he is treated as if he had always been authorised.

(c) A's authority may be terminated automatically if P becomes bankrupt. However, A is not liable to T where his authority has been terminated in this way provided he acts in good faith and without notice of the bankruptcy[10].

(d) If A is the donee of a power of attorney, he is not liable for acts done after revocation of that power provided he acts without knowledge of the revocation[11].

(e) If A has no actual authority but has apparent authority, the position is unclear. Despite statements to the contrary, it seems that there is at least a technical breach of the warranty but, since T can enforce the contract against P on the basis of apparent authority, he will suffer no loss due to the breach and so should be unable to recover more than nominal damages. There may be some doubt as to whether a court would allow A to raise the defence of apparent authority so as to require T to embark on potentially hazardous litigation against P; however, in practice, T will sue P on the main contract and join in A as a second defendant when P denies authority. Thus the two questions will be dealt with together.

The second consequence of the contractual nature of the agent's liability is that, where the warranty is false, T may claim from A damages assessed on the contractual basis – ie to put him in the position he would have been in had the warranty proved true. Generally, this will be the amount he could have recovered from P in an action to enforce the main contract. In *Suleman v Shahsavari*[12] A signed a contract for the sale of a house without P's authority. When P refused to complete the transaction and denied authority, T brought proceedings against P and A to establish the true position. By the time judgment was given, the value of the property had risen considerably. It was held that since, if the contract had been authorised, T would have been entitled to damages assessed at the date of judgment[13], damages for breach of warranty should also be assessed at that date. However, where the amount recoverable from P would have been limited in some way, the damages available for breach of warranty will be similarly limited. Thus if P has become insolvent, T will only be able to recover from A such sum as he would have been able to recover in P's insolvency; in such a case an action in tort, where damages will aim to put T in the same position as if A's statement had not been made, might be preferable for T.

1 Above 4.2.3.
2 See the comments of Steyn and Evans LJJ in *First Energy Ltd v Hungarian International Bank Ltd* [1993] 2 Lloyd's Rep 194 at 204, 207, above 4.2.3.
3 [1964] AC 465, [1963] 2 All ER 575, HL.
4 (1857) 8 E & B 647.
5 *Chapleo v Brunswick Permanent Building Society* (1881) 6 QBD 696.
6 *Penn v Bristol and West Building Society* [1997] 3 All ER 470, [1997] 1 WLR 1356; see Reynolds [1998] JBL 151.
7 *Rasnoimport V O v Guthrie & Co Ltd* [1966] 1 Lloyd's Rep 1. The decision in this case is now of less significance as a result of the passing of the Carriage of Goods by Sea Act 1992, s 4. See 32.3.2.
8 [1910] 1 KB 215, CA; and see *Babury Ltd v London Industrial plc* [1989] NLJR 1596, where solicitors were similarly held liable even though they had been deceived into acting for a defunct company.
9 *Halbot v Lens* [1901] 1 Ch 344.
10 Insolvency Act 1986, s 342.
11 Powers of Attorney Act 1971, s 5(1).
12 [1989] 2 All ER 460, [1988] 1 WLR 1181.
13 According to *Johnson v Agnew* [1980] AC 367.

5.3 Undisclosed agency

We have seen that there is generally no need for an agent to identify his principal. An agent may also act without disclosing the fact that he is acting on behalf of another person so that the agency is wholly undisclosed. Perhaps surprisingly, provided that the agent has actual authority for his actions, undisclosed agency may give rise to a contract which may be enforced by principal and third party against each other. Where the contract is one of sale, the situation must be analysed closely to ensure that the agent is acting as an agent, rather than buying in his own name and reselling to the third party or to the 'principal'.

Undisclosed agency is concerned almost exclusively with cases where the agent's actions have the prior sanction of actual authority. An undisclosed principal may sometimes be held liable for unauthorised acts on the basis of *Watteau v Fenwick*[1] but, subject to that, there can be no question of apparent authority in a case of undisclosed agency, because apparent authority arises where T deals with A on the strength of a representation from P and in the belief that A is P's authorised agent. Nor, as we have seen, can an undisclosed principal ratify acts done without his authority[2].

The undisclosed agency doctrine may appear harsh: its effect is that T may deal with A, in ignorance of any other person being interested in the contract, and then find that P may intervene and enforce the contract. The rule has been described as anomalous and 'inconsistent with elementary doctrines of the law of contract'[3] such as the doctrine of privity[4], and it has no equivalent in civil law doctrines. However, the doctrine is justified on the grounds of commercial convenience:

'Middlemen, through whom contracts are made, are common and useful in business transactions and in the great mass of contracts it is a matter of indifference to either party whether there is an undisclosed principal or not. If he exists, it is to say the least, extremely convenient that he should be able to sue and be sued as a principal, and he is only allowed to do so upon terms which exclude injustice'[5].

As this statement indicates, the doctrine is hedged with restrictions to protect the position of the third party. The third party is entitled to enforce the contract against the agent and, even though the undisclosed principal may intervene, he may do so only on the same terms on which the contract could have been enforced by the agent and, in some cases, is entirely prohibited from intervening on the contract.

It seems that the rule allowing the undisclosed principal to intervene in contracts made on his behalf developed during the eighteenth century[6]. It originated in cases involving factors, who sold property on behalf of their principals. Since the factor had possession of the property, a person dealing with a factor was not greatly concerned with the principal's identity. Problems arose where, as became increasingly common in the eighteenth century, the factor became insolvent. If the third party paid the factor, the money would go to the factor's estate and the principal would be left with a claim for a dividend in the insolvency. However, it was felt unjust that the third party should have the benefit of the goods and the principal only a claim in the insolvency. It was recognised that the factor held the principal's goods for the principal, and should therefore hold the proceeds of sale on the same terms[7]. In the earliest cases the principal was thus allowed to intervene in executed contracts in order to claim the price direct from the third party buyer. From there it became possible for the undisclosed principal to enforce wholly executory contracts, particularly as contracts came increasingly to be concluded by brokers who, unlike factors, did not have possession of their principals' goods. The natural corollary was, of course, that the undisclosed principal should be liable on executory contracts and that was established by 1784[8]. Although doubts about the wisdom of the doctrine were expressed, by 1872 Blackburn J said that 'doubts of this kind come now too late'[9]. As Diplock LJ observed[10], the undisclosed principal doctrine avoids circuity of actions: if the principal could not intervene directly he could only enforce the contract by requiring the agent to lend his name to an action; and the third party would enforce against the agent leaving him to claim indemnity from the principal.

Unfortunately, much of the law concerned with the effects of undisclosed agency is unclear. Many of the cases are old, and it seems that, in some, difficulty arises from the failure of the courts to recognise that undisclosed agency is very different from disclosed agency. Whereas the effect of disclosed agency is to create privity between principal and third party from the outset, it seems that the true basis of the undisclosed agency doctrine is that the contract is initially made between agent and third party, but that rights and liabilities are transferred to the principal, rather as if they were automatically assigned by operation of law[11], although as the Privy Council recently observed, the analogy with assignment should not be pursued too far[12].

1   [1893] 1 QB 346, above 4.4.
2   Above 4.7.1.
3   *Pollock* (1887) 3 LQR 358, 359.
4   An undisclosed principal may be entitled to intervene on an authorised contract in circumstances where he could not take the benefit of the contract under the Contracts (Rights of Third Parties) Act 1999, since under that Act a third party beneficiary can only enforce a contract, inter alia, if he is identifiable as an individual or member of a class. See 2.7.2.
5   Per Lord Lindley in *Keighley Maxsted & Co v Durant* [1901] AC 240 at 261, HL.

6   The historical development of the undisclosed principal doctrine is more fully discussed in Stoljar, *The Law of Agency* (1961) pp 204–210 and Goodhart and Hamson, 'The Undisclosed Principal in Contract' (1932) 4 CLJ 320.
7   *Garrat v Cullum* (1709) Bull NP 42.
8   *Nelson v Powell* (1784) 3 Doug KB 410.
9   *Armstrong v Stokes* (1872) LR 7 QB 598 at 604.
10 In *Freeman and Lockyer v Buckhurst Park Properties (Mangal) Ltd* [1964] 2 QB 480, [1964] 1 All ER 630 at 644, CA.
11 Goodhart and Hamson, 'The Undisclosed Principal in Contract' (1932) 4 CLJ 320.
12 *Siu Yin Kwan v Eastern Insurance Ltd, The Osprey* [1994] 2 AC 199, [1994] 1 All ER 213.

5.3.1   *Rights of action*

Since in cases of undisclosed agency the contract is initially made between agent and third party, it follows that the third party can enforce the contract against the agent, and, provided the principal has not intervened, the agent can enforce against the third party. This merely accords with the third party's expectations. In addition, if the principal's identity is discovered, the third party can enforce the contract against him and the principal is generally allowed to intervene and enforce the contract on his own behalf.

The third party therefore has a choice of targets against whom he may enforce the contract. There is some authority that the rights of a third party are limited by the doctrines of merger and election. The doctrine of merger used to apply to cases where two or more people were jointly liable on the same obligation. Since there is only one obligation, a judgment against one bars proceedings against the other, because two sets of proceedings cannot be taken on the same obligation. Although the rule has been abolished for joint contractors[1], it has been applied in cases of undisclosed agency (and in cases of disclosed agency where the agent is liable on the contract) on the basis that principal and agent are alternately liable on one obligation. It also seems that the third party's rights are further limited by the doctrine of election so that if, with full knowledge of the facts, including the existence of the principal, he chooses to hold principal or agent exclusively liable on the contract, he is bound by his election and cannot then pursue the other. However, although there is authority that such an election is binding, it is not clear what acts, short of suing to judgment, will amount to an election. The election must be an unequivocal indication of an intention to hold only principal or agent liable. In *Clarkson Booker Ltd v Andjel*[2] it was held that issuing a writ against the principal did not amount to an election so as to bar the commencement of an action against the agent when the principal became insolvent. The third party had not obtained judgment against the principal, and, before commencing any proceedings, had sent letters before action to both parties.

The third party's rights of action may also be limited if his conduct is such as to raise an estoppel.

1   Civil Liability (Contribution) Act 1978, s 3.
2   [1964] 2 QB 775, [1964] 3 All ER 260, CA.

5.3.2   *Cases where the undisclosed principal is excluded*

Although there is a general right for the undisclosed principal to intervene on and enforce the contract made on his behalf, that right is hedged about with restrictions to protect the third party. In several cases the principal is excluded altogether. The circumstances in which the principal is excluded were recently reconsidered by the Privy Council in *Siu Yin Kwan v Eastern Insurance Ltd*[1] but some of the case law in this area remains problematic. The following propositions may be advanced.

(a) The undisclosed principal can only intervene if he was in existence and had capacity to make the contract in question at the time it was made.

(b) The undisclosed principal can only intervene if he had given actual authority for the making of the contract prior to its conclusion[2].

(c) The undisclosed principal cannot intervene if there is an express or implied term of the contract to that effect. The difficulty is to know when the terms of the contract will be taken impliedly to exclude the principal. In *Humble v Hunter*[3] an agent concluded a charterparty on behalf of an undisclosed principal. The contract described the agent as 'owner of the good ship Ann'. It was held that the wording of the contract excluded the principal who therefore could not enforce it. One explanation of the case is that the principal could not bring parol evidence to contradict the terms of the contract. However, a better explanation seems to be that the words of the contract implied that there was no one other than the agent interested in the contract, so that the principal was impliedly excluded. *Humble v Hunter* was distinguished in a later case where the agent signed a charterparty as 'charterer'[4] and it was suggested that the principal will only be excluded where the agent is described in the contract by words indicating property rights rather than merely identifying the agent as a contracting party. Subsequently, it has been held that the principal was not excluded where the agent was described as 'landlord'[5] or 'tenant'[6], although in one case the principal was excluded when a charterparty described the agent as 'disponent owner'[7]. In *Siu Yin Kwan v Eastern Insurance Ltd*[8] a policy of compulsory workmen's insurance to cover the crew of a ship was taken out on behalf of the ship's owners by the agents who managed the vessel on their behalf and it was found as fact that this was an undisclosed agency. The Privy Council held that the fact that the agent was named in the policy as 'the insured' was insufficient to exclude the intervention of the principal and indicated that the court should be slow to find that the principal is impliedly excluded in a commercial contract. *Humble v Hunter* can therefore perhaps be regarded as an exceptional case.

(d) The undisclosed principal may be prevented from intervening where the third party had special reasons for contracting with the agent or for not contracting with the principal. It seems that this should be regarded merely as a specific example of the rule that the principal cannot intervene where he is excluded by the express or implied terms of the contract. It is clear that P cannot intervene on a contract which requires personal performance: for instance, on a contract of employment or a contract to act as 'agent' for an artist or performer. However, in commercial contracts it will generally be assumed that T is willing to contract with anyone unless he expressly or impliedly indicates otherwise. Beyond this, the position is unclear. In *Siu Yin Kwan v Eastern Insurance Ltd* it was argued that, because a contract of insurance cannot be assigned[9], it was so personal as to exclude the intervention of the undisclosed principal. The Privy Council rejected that argument: although a contract of insurance cannot be assigned, the analogy between the undisclosed principal doctrine and assignment is incomplete, and the contract was not so personal as to preclude the principal's intervention[10]. Nevertheless, the circumstances surrounding the contract may indicate either that T impliedly wished to contract with A and no one else, or that T would not contract with P. In one case T contracted to buy goods from A because A owed him money from previous deals, intending to set off A's debt against sums due from him under the contract. It was held that P could not intervene[11]. However, it is difficult to see why this should be. If P had intervened, there is authority for the view that he would have done so subject to the set-off. Similarly, where A underwrote a share issue for an undisclosed P, it was held that P could not intervene on the grounds that a company has an interest in the identity of its shareholders[12]. However, this is also a difficult case: the members of the court offered at least three reasons for their decision.

In general, P can intervene and enforce a contract made by A, even though he knows that T would not have contracted with him[13]; there is no positive obligation on the agent to disclose the principal's identity. However, if A positively misrepresents the position, for instance by asserting that he is the true principal, or by denying P's interest if asked, P cannot intervene[14] because T will then be entitled to have the contract set aside for misrepresentation. Some difficulty is caused by the case of *Said v Butt*[15], in which it was said that P cannot intervene if 'the personal element is strikingly present' in the contract. In that case P was a theatre critic who had been banned from a particular theatre after a bad review. He wanted to obtain a ticket for the first night of a new play, but knew the theatre manager would not let him have one, and so employed an agent to obtain one for him. When he arrived at the theatre he was refused admission, and he then sued for breach of contract. It was held that he could not enforce the contract because of the 'personal element'. However, the case is generally regarded as unsatisfactory. The strong personal element must depend on more than the opposition to the principal. It is not uncommon for people to resell tickets for plays and concerts, and theatres do not normally object (provided there is no element of profiteering or touting). Perhaps it could be said that a first night performance is special: audiences are often invited. Personal dislike of the undisclosed principal should not normally prevent him intervening to enforce an ordinary commercial contract.

If cases (c) and (d) above are both regarded as examples of situations where the principal's intervention is precluded by the express or implied terms of the contract, the principal's right to intervene will generally depend on the construction of the contract and will involve consideration of its terms in the light of surrounding circumstances.

There is no authority on the question whether any of the above restrictions prevent the third party suing the principal. The analogy with assignment is no help because the burden of a contract is not normally assignable. A party to a contract can waive a term inserted solely for his benefit, and so it may be that the principal cannot raise those defences if on the proper construction of the particular contract the term excluding the principal was inserted (or implied) solely for the benefit of the third party.

1 *Siu Yin Kwan v Eastern Insurance Ltd, The Osprey* [1994] 2 AC 199, [1994] 1 All ER 213; see Halladay [1994] LMCLQ 174; Reynolds [1994] JBL 260.
2 *Keighley Maxsted & Co v Durant* [1901] AC 240, HL.
3 (1848) 12 QB 310.
4 *Fred Drughorn Ltd v Rederiaktiebolaget Trans-Atlantic* [1919] AC 203, HL.
5 *Epps v Rothnie* [1945] KB 562, [1946] 1 All ER 146, CA.
6 *Danziger v Thompson* [1944] KB 654, [1944] 2 All ER 151.

7 *The Astyanax* [1985] 2 Lloyd's Rep 109, CA.
8 [1994] 2 AC 199, [1994] 1 All ER 213.
9 *Peters v General Accident Fire and Life Assurance Corpn Ltd* [1937] 4 All ER 628.
10 Recognising the right of the undisclosed principal to intervene in a contract of insurance causes some difficulty, not least because of the doctrine of utmost good faith which applies to contracts of insurance: see below ch 35 and see Birds [1994] JBL 374.
11 *Greer v Downs Supply Co* [1927] 2 KB 28, CA.
12 *Collins v Associated Greyhound Racecourses Ltd* [1930] 1 Ch 1, CA.
13 *Dyster v Randall & Sons* [1926] Ch 932.
14 *Archer v Stone* (1898) 78 LT 34.
15 [1920] 3 KB 497.

5.3.3   T may raise defences available against A

If the undisclosed principal does intervene to enforce the contract, he generally does so on the same terms on which the agent could have enforced the contract, so that he is bound by any variation agreed between agent and third party before his position is revealed, and the third party can raise any defence he could raise in an action by the agent, in the same way that an assignee of the benefit of a contract takes and enforces it 'subject to equities'. However, some cases suggest that T's right to raise against P defences available against A depends on estoppel, so that the right arises where P has led T to believe that A was contracting on his own behalf.

Set-off may offer a partial defence to a claim for a sum of money. If X sues Y, in certain circumstances Y can 'set off' against the sum due to X sums due to him from X, so reducing (or even extinguishing) the debt. In cases of undisclosed agency, if T is sued by P, he should be able to claim a right of set-off if he would have been able to exercise one against the agent. However, in *Cooke & Sons v Eshelby*[1] the House of Lords refused to allow T to raise a set-off in such a situation and held that a set off of debts due from A is only available against P on the basis of estoppel where P allows A to appear to be the true principal and T relies on that representation in contracting with A. On the facts there was no such estoppel: A was a broker who sometimes acted as an agent and sometimes for his own benefit. T had dealt with him in the past and was owed money by him, but the evidence was that T knew that A sometimes acted as an agent and gave no thought to his capacity on this particular occasion.

Similarly, settlement offers a complete defence by extinguishing the debt. In cases of undisclosed agency it will be natural for T to settle with A and settlement will provide a complete defence to a claim by P. However, it has been held that the defence of settlement also depends on estoppel so that T is only discharged where P's conduct leads him to believe that A is acting as principal[2].

In most cases this approach will still allow T to raise against P any defence he would have against A, including a personal right such as set-off. However, some defences may not be available against P where the requirements for estoppel are not made out. For instance, if P instructs A to conceal his involvement in the contract, his conduct may raise an estoppel; but if A conceals the agency on his own initiative, P may not be estopped. Similarly, as *Cooke v Eshelby* illustrates, T can only rely on estoppel if he relied on P's statement; if he gives no thought to the situation he may find it difficult to raise the defence. In cases of undisclosed agency it might be preferable, and fairer, to allow T to raise against P any defences he could raise against A, provided those defences arose before he became aware of P's interest in the contract[3].

The undisclosed principal doctrine caused particular problems for the attempt to harmonise agency laws in the Geneva Convention. Article 13 of the Convention allows a principal to intervene on the contract subject to any defences available to the third party in an action by the agent, and allows the third party to enforce the contract against the principal subject to defences available to the agent and subject to defences available to the principal in a claim by the agent.

1   (1887) 12 App Cas 271.
2   *Coates v Lewes* (1808) 1 Camp 444.
3   See Reynolds, 'Practical Problems of the Undisclosed Principal Doctrine' (1983) 36 CLP 119.

5.3.4   *Settlement with the agent*

Just as in the case of disclosed agency, questions may arise as to the effect of payments made to the agent, especially where the agent becomes insolvent or misappropriates the money. It was suggested above that, generally, payments made by T to A before T becomes aware of P's interest in the contract should operate to discharge T's liability to P. Once T becomes aware of P's interest in the contract, payment to A will only be effective if A had some authority to receive payment.

Where money is due from P, he may wish to pay through A in order to preserve his anonymity. It was held in *Heald v Kenworthy*[1] that a payment by P to A only operated to discharge P's liability under a contract where T's conduct had led P to settle with A: for instance, by giving A a receipt showing the debt as paid. This is the same rule which applies in cases of disclosed agency. However, in *Armstrong v Stokes*[2] it was held that if P has paid A, T cannot claim payment from P if that would unfairly prejudice P: the alternative would produce 'intolerable hardship' for P. This is a much less stringent requirement than that in *Heald v Kenworthy*, and in *Irvine v Watson*[3] the Court of Appeal preferred *Heald*. However, *Irvine* was a case of disclosed agency and it is difficult to see how the rules of estoppel can be applied to cases of undisclosed agency.

1   (1855) 10 Exch 739.
2   (1872) LR 7 QB 598.
3   (1880) 5 QBD 414.

5.3.5   *Transfer of property*

Where an undisclosed principal uses an agent to sell, or dispose of, property on his behalf, he is obviously bound by any transaction within the scope of the agent's actual authority. Equally, in cases of undisclosed agency there can be no question of 'apparent authority'. However, P may still be bound by unauthorised dealings with his property by the doctrine of apparent ownership, if his conduct is such as to make A appear to be the owner of the property. In addition, if A is a factor and has P's goods in his possession, P may be bound by dealings with those goods under the provisions of the Factors Act 1889[1].

Where an undisclosed principal instructs an agent to buy goods on his behalf, difficulties may arise if the agent becomes insolvent. Since T believes that he is contracting with A, he will intend title to pass to A, who will therefore become owner of the goods. However, if A intends to buy for P, and does some act appropriating the goods to his contract with P, such as indorsing a bill of lading in his favour, title will pass immediately to P. Alternatively, if P has put A in funds to make the purchase, P may acquire an equitable interest in the goods; but in the absence of an equitable interest, if A buys and intends to keep the goods for himself,

P will acquire no interest in the goods, and his only right will be to sue A for breach of his duty as agent. If A is insolvent, that right may be worthless[2].

1   See 17.1.1.
2   See Goode, *Proprietary Rights and Insolvency in Sale Transactions* (2nd edn, 1989) ch 3.

5.4   Liability for misstatements

Where A is employed to negotiate or enter into a contract on behalf of P, the question arises as to what is the effect of statements made by A during negotiations which do not form part of the contract. In the general law of contract, false statements made during negotiations may be categorised as misrepresentations and allow the representee to claim damages and/or have the resulting contract set aside, depending on the state of mind of the representor. Where the contract is negotiated by an agent the position is complicated by questions of the agent's authority and the fact that the states of mind of both principal and agent may have to be considered.

If A makes a false representation he may be personally liable to the representee, either in the tort of deceit, if he can be shown to have known his statement to be false, or to have been reckless as to its truth or falsity, or in negligence on the basis of *Hedley Byrne & Co Ltd v Heller & Partners*[1] if negligence can be proved. In order to establish negligence on this basis, it must be shown that there was an assumption of responsibility by A such as to create a special relationship between himself and T and thus give rise to the requisite duty of care[2].

P may also be liable in tort for A's misstatements. He will be liable, even if he is ignorant of the statement, if it is made while A is acting within the scope of his actual or apparent authority[3]. P will also be liable where A acts innocently, believing his statement to be true, if P knows or ought to know that the statement is false, and knows that the statement is made: in this case P is liable for his own fault, A being regarded merely as P's mouthpiece. However, if A innocently makes a false statement without P's knowledge, P is not liable in tort at all, even though he may know the true state of affairs and would have known the statement to be false.

Any misrepresentation, even if wholly innocent, may also give the representee a right to rescind any contract made in reliance on it. Thus if A makes a representation to T which induces T to contract with P, T may rescind the contract provided A was acting within the scope of his actual or apparent authority, and subject to the normal restrictions on rescission.

Damages may also be available to T under the Misrepresentation Act 1967, s 2[4]. However, damages under the Act may only be awarded against a party to a contract, so that T can generally only obtain damages under the Act from P, unless A is also a party to the contract[5].

1   [1964] AC 465, [1963] 2 All ER 575, HL.
2   *Williams v Natural Life Health Foods Ltd* [1998] 2 All ER 577, where it was held that the managing director of a company conducting negotiations on behalf of the company for the grant of a franchise to the plaintiffs owed no duty of care to the plaintiffs for his statements. It seems likely that, in the absence of special facts, the court will generally be reluctant to find a duty of care in such a case where the agent is a director or employee of a company or other business. Cf *Fairline Shipping Corpn v Adamson* [1975] QB 180, [1974] 2 All ER 967, where such a duty was established.
3   *Lloyd v Grace, Smith & Co* [1912] AC 716, HL; *Armagas Ltd v Mundogas SA, The Ocean Frost* [1986] AC 717, [1986] 2 All ER 385.
4   See 2.4.2.1.
5   *Resolute Maritime Inc v Nippon Kaiji Kyolai, The Skopas* [1983] 2 All ER 1, [1983] 1 WLR 857.

Chapter 6

Principal and Agent

6.0 Consent and contract

The relationship of principal and agent can only be created by the consent of the parties: the agent must agree to act for the principal, and the principal must agree to the agent so acting. The principal's consent gives the agent his authority. The principal may give his consent after the agent has acted, by ratifying acts done by the agent without prior authority. Where the agent's only authority is apparent, he has power to affect the principal's position and the principal may thus be bound by the agent's actions, but there is no relationship of principal and agent between them because the principal does not consent to the agent's actions.

Principal and agent have certain rights against each other which spring from their relationship. That relationship may be contractual: it will be so where the principal agrees, expressly or impliedly, to pay the agent for his services, and that will generally be the case in relation to agents acting in a commercial context. If there is a contract it may be express or implied, oral or written, or contained in a power of attorney, and the terms of that contract will be the primary source of the mutual rights and obligations of the parties. However, many of the rights and liabilities of principal and agent do not depend on any contract between them but are imposed by law because of the relationship of principal and agent. That relationship is recognised as a fiduciary one, and the agent therefore owes to the principal fiduciary duties of loyalty, similar to those imposed on other fiduciaries, which arise as a matter of law and are imposed on gratuitous as well as contractual agents. Similarly, the agent enjoys certain rights even where he has no contractual right to payment[1]. In addition, commercial agents involved in the sale and purchase of goods may enjoy extensive rights under the Commercial Agents (Council Directive) Regulations 1993[2], which cannot be abrogated by the contract.

Where there is a contract between principal and agent, many of the rights and duties of the parties will take effect as implied terms in that contract; and the contract may vary some of those rights and duties. A contract of agency is governed by the general law of contract and is subject to the same rules as other contracts. Terms may be implied into a contract of agency to give effect to the intentions of the parties in order to give business efficacy to the contract. However, unlike other types of contract, such as contracts of employment and contracts between landlords and tenants, there are relatively few implied terms recognised as general incidents of agency contracts.

A contract of agency may be unilateral or bilateral. The contract will be bilateral where the agent undertakes, expressly or impliedly, to perform some particular act: for instance, to use best endeavours to bring about a result. The contract may, however, be unilateral, where the agent promises to do nothing, but the principal promises to pay the agent if the desired result is brought about. It seems that estate agency contracts are unilateral in this way: the agent does not contract to do anything, but if the agent brings about a sale the principal is obliged to pay the agreed commission[3].

1   See generally Dowrick, 'The Relationship of Principal and Agent' (1954) 17 MLR 24.
2   SI 1993/3053, implementing Council Directive 86/653/EEC.
3   *Luxor (Eastbourne) Ltd v Cooper* [1941] AC 108, [1941] 1 All ER 33, HL.

6.0.1   *The Commercial Agents (Council Directive) Regulations 1993*[1]

The Commercial Agents (Council Directive) Regulations 1993 came into force on 1 January 1994. Broadly speaking, they give commercial agents, as defined, extensive rights against their principals, considerably greater than such agents would have enjoyed at common law. The regulations were made to implement an EC directive of 1986[2]. The laws of many member states of the European Community already gave extensive rights to commercial agents and it was thought that, without harmonisation, discrepancies between national laws might act as an obstacle to completion of the internal market[3]. The directive was to be implemented by 1 January 1990; however, the UK, the Republic of Ireland and Italy[4] were given extra time to implement it, because those states had to make 'a particular effort to adapt their regulations'[5]. In the case of the UK and Ireland this was primarily because there was no existing legal regulation of the relationship between commercial agents and their principals; indeed, it was argued that 'commercial agents' were not recognised as a distinct category by UK law[6].

The regulations create both rights and obligations for both parties to the agency agreement. In general, they require both principal and agent to 'act dutifully and in good faith' towards each other[7], and thus represent another example of the infiltration of civil law concepts of 'good faith' into UK commercial law. However, their impact on agents' rights is greater than on their duties. The common law traditionally regarded agents involved in the marketing of goods as independent businesses and, in so far as either party to the agency relationship required protection from the other, took the view that the agent had a stronger position than the principal and that the principal therefore needed to be protected by the imposition on the agent of fiduciary duties. In contrast, the approach of many civil law countries, reflected in the attitude of the European Community, is to regard the agent as integrated to a large degree in the business of the principal[8]. This is the approach taken by the directive and, therefore, by the regulations. To a large extent they equate the position of self-employed commercial agents to that of employees, granting the agent extensive rights to commission and protection against dismissal.

The wording of the regulations largely mirrors that of the directive. This is perhaps unfortunate, for many of the expressions used are unfamiliar to a common lawyer and there is thus uncertainty about the meaning or application of some of the provisions.

There is now a small, but significant, body of case law applying the regulations. In several of the cases the courts have been critical of the wording of the UK regulations[9]. On the whole, however, the courts have adopted a purposive approach, interpreting the regulations so as to further the perceived objectives of the underlying directive, ie (a) harmonising the laws of member states and (b) protecting the interests of commercial agents[10]. As Staughton LJ has put it, 'the second objective . . . appears to be a motive of social policy, that commercial agents are a down-trodden race, and need and should be afforded protection against their principals'[11]. The directive was heavily influenced by the laws of Germany and France, and the courts have indicated that, when applying its provisions, it is appropriate for them to draw guidance as to their meaning and application by considering the established practice in those countries[12].

1   See generally Reynolds [1994] JBL 265; Scholes and Blane (1993) PLC 31.
2   Council Directive 86/653/EEC.
3   Preamble to the directive.
4   In the case of the UK and Ireland until 1 January 1994; in the case of Italy until 1 January 1993: art 22(3) of the directive.
5   Preamble to the directive.
6   Law Commission Report no 84 (1977) p 6. The Law Commission (ibid p 32) commenting on the original proposal for the directive suggested that it 'in many respects offends against the basic principles of the English law of agency'. The editor of *Bowstead & Reynolds on Agency* describes this comment as 'rather hysterical': *Bowstead & Reynolds on Agency* (16th edn, 1996) para 11-001.
7   Regulations 3(1), 4(1).
8   See the Commission Notice of 24 December 1962; OJ 1962 139 2921, above 3.2.4.
9   See eg *AMB Imballaggi Plastici SRL v Pacflex Ltd* [1999] 2 All ER (Comm) 249; *Moore v Piretta PTA Ltd* [1999] 1 All ER 174; *King v T Tunnock Ltd* [2000] IRLR 569, Ct of Sess.
10 See *Barbara Bellone v Yokohama SpA* [1998] ECR 1-2191.
11 *Page v Combined Shipping and Trading Co Ltd* [1997] 3 All ER 656 at 660.
12 See eg *Moore v Piretta PTA Ltd*; *Roy v M R Pearlman* [1999] CLR 36, *King v Tunnock*.

6.0.1.1   *Scope of the regulations*

The regulations only came into force on 1 January 1994 but they apply retrospectively to agency agreements already in force at that date[1]. They do not apply to all agency agreements but only to the relationship between 'commercial agents', as defined, and their principals. A commercial agent is:

> 'A self-employed intermediary who has continuing authority to negotiate the sale or purchase of goods on behalf of another person ("the principal") or to negotiate and conclude the sale or purchase of goods on behalf of and in the name of the principal'[2].

This definition is not straightforward and has already given rise to a number of questions. It is clear that, in order to be protected by the regulations, an agent must be an agent in law, acting 'on behalf of' a principal, so that the regulations will not protect a person who buys and resells goods in his own name[3]. The agent must be 'self-employed'. Thus employees (who enjoy considerable protection under other laws) are not protected by the regulations. However, the reference to a 'self-employed intermediary' does not require that the agent be a natural person. It has been held that 'self-employed' should be interpreted as requiring the agent to be an 'independent contractor'. Thus a limited company can be a commercial agent protected by the regulations[4].

The agent must have 'continuing authority' to negotiate, or to negotiate and conclude, contracts on behalf of another person. In *Parkes v Esso Petroleum Co Ltd* the plaintiff was the licensee of a tied, self-service petrol station. The licence described him as an 'agent' for the purposes of selling motor fuel on behalf of the petrol company, and provided for him to receive a commission on sales. He claimed to be a commercial agent protected by the regulations. At first instance, Sir Richard Scott V-C[5] held that he was not a commercial agent because fuel sales were not 'negotiated' giving that word 'its ordinary English meaning'. The price at, and terms on, which fuel was sold were fixed by the petrol company. The Court of Appeal upheld the decision, but on slightly different grounds[6]. The court recognised that there could be 'negotiations' without there necessarily being any haggling over price[7] but emphasised that the petrol sales in question were concluded on a self-service basis. The regulations exclude from their protection agents whose activities as a commercial agent 'are to be considered secondary' (see below), and the Schedule to the regulations contains provisions intended to determine when an agent's activities are 'secondary'. Referring to those provisions, the court concluded that a distinction should be drawn between 'negotiated' contracts and those concluded as a result of customer self-service[8] and concluded that, on the facts, the claimant did not 'negotiate' contracts.

It is submitted that the reasoning of the Court of Appeal is to be preferred. The implication of the Vice-Chancellor's approach would be that whenever the principal stipulates in advance the terms on which he is prepared to sell, his agent will be unprotected by the regulations. This would exclude a great many agencies from the scope of the regulations. Nevertheless, it is submitted that, although the result may be correct, the reasoning of the Court of Appeal is still not entirely convincing. The essence of commercial agency is that the agent's activities contribute to the creation of goodwill for the principal's business, and that transactions are concluded as a result of the agent's efforts[9]. A better explanation for the decision would therefore be that the agent in *Parkes* was not employed to develop the goodwill of the principal's business. Alternatively the same result might have been reached by finding that, on the wording of the UK regulations, the commercial agency activities of the plaintiff in *Parkes* might have been considered secondary.

The regulations only apply to agents involved in the sale or purchase of goods. Agents concerned solely with the marketing of services are therefore unprotected. Where the agent is concerned with the sale or purchase of goods *and* services it seems that protection will depend on which is the more important element of the agency[10]. Agents authorised to act only in single transactions clearly lack 'continuing authority', and are therefore excluded, and it may be that the same is true for an agent appointed to act in a fixed number of transactions[11], rather than for a fixed period. The regulations do apply both to agents who simply introduce potential contract partners and to those who negotiate the terms of contracts; however, in this latter case, the regulations only apply where the contract is made in the name of the principal. This limitation in the directive is presumably intended to exclude commission agents, who may properly be regarded as being in business on their own account. In England it would seem to exclude agents who act for undisclosed and, possibly, even unnamed principals. This exclusion is probably justified, since a main rationale for protecting 'commercial agents' is that their activities benefit the principal by building goodwill for the principal's business. This is obviously not the case if the principal's identity is not disclosed.

The activities of a number of other classes of agents are also excluded from the regulations. Thus company officers acting for their companies, partners acting on behalf of partnerships and insolvency practitioners are not commercial agents[12], and the activities of unpaid agents, agents acting on commodity exchanges and Crown agents are excluded[13]. The regulations also exclude agents whose activities as commercial agents may be regarded as 'secondary'[14]. The Schedule to the regulations contains guidelines to indicate whether the activities of an agent may be regarded as 'secondary'[15] but the relevant provisions are complex and awkwardly drafted. Paragraph 1 provides that 'the activities of a person as a commercial agent are to be considered secondary where it may reasonably be taken that the primary purpose of the arrangement with his principal is other than as set out in paragraph 2'. An arrangement falls within para 2 if:

'(a) the business of the principal is the sale or purchase of goods of a particular kind; and
(b) the goods are such that:
    (i) transactions are normally individually negotiated and concluded on a commercial basis; and
    (ii) procuring a transaction on one occasion is likely to lead to further transactions in those goods with [the same] customer . . . or to transactions in those goods with other customers in the same geographical area or among the same group of customers
    and that accordingly it is in the commercial interests of the principal in developing the market in those goods to appoint a representative to such customers with a view to the representative devoting effort, skill and expenditure from his own resources to that end.'

Paragraph 3 then lists a number of factors which are indicators that the arrangement falls within para 2 (so that activities under it are not 'secondary') and para 4 lists a number of factors which indicate that the arrangement falls outside para 2 (so that activities under it are 'secondary'), including that promotional material is supplied direct to customers and that customers normally select goods for themselves and simply place orders through agents.

Finally, para 5 of the Schedule provides that the activities of consumer credit agents and mail order catalogue agents for consumer goods are generally to be regarded as 'secondary'.

Pausing briefly, it is submitted that the result in *Parkes v Esso* might have been reached on the basis that, applying the test contained in the Regulations, the agency activities in that case were 'secondary'. Procuring a sale of petrol on one occasion is not 'likely to lead to further transactions in those goods with the same customer' or other customers in the same area or group, and such transactions therefore fall outside para 2. In contrast, where an agent is appointed to sell (say) double glazing, his activities ought not to be regarded as secondary on this basis. Although a contract with an individual customer may not lead to 'repeat orders' from that customer, it often will lead to orders from other customers in the same area[16].

It is questionable whether the provisions of the Schedule properly implement the directive. The directive leaves the definition of 'secondary activities' to national law, but it seems that the intention is that an agent should be excluded if his agency activities are 'secondary' in comparison to his other activities – ie a minor part of his business[17]. The UK regulations seem to have a slightly different emphasis and look to the significance of agency activities in the agent's relations with his principal. Indeed, many of the factors listed in the Schedule would seem to go to the question whether the agent is a commercial agent at all. In *Imballaggi v Pacflex* the Court of Appeal commented critically on the drafting of the Schedule and called for it to be clarified[18].

One objective of the directive was to ensure that commercial agents were granted equal protection throughout the EU. Unfortunately, the regulations contain provisions restricting their territorial scope, which give rise to a number of difficulties and which may result in there being odd gaps in the protection of agents. As originally drafted, the regulations only applied (a) in relation to the agent's acts in Great Britain, and (b) provided that the parties had not chosen to apply the law of another EC member state[19]. A loophole was thus created whereby if the parties chose English law to apply to a contract where the agent acted outside Great Britain, the agent could be unprotected[20]. An agent acting within Great Britain might also be unprotected if the parties chose to subject their contract to the law of another member state which had a similar territorial restriction. Following criticism by the European Commission, the regulations were amended in 1998[21]. However, the amended regulations only partially resolve the difficulty. They apply (a) where the contract is governed by the law of any part of the United Kingdom, to the agent's activities in Great Britain and (b) where the agent acts in another member state and the parties have chosen to have their contract governed by the law of England and Wales or Scotland, provided that the law of that member state permits such a choice. The regulations also provide that where the agent's activities are in Great Britain and the contract provides for it to be governed by the law of another member state, the court shall apply the law of that member state. However, this may still leave the agent unprotected if the law of the relevant member state is limited to activities of agents within its territory. A simpler solution would have been to provide that the regulations should apply regardless of the place of the agent's activities, whenever the agency contract is governed by the law of part of Great Britain[22].

Although the regulations give significant rights to commercial agents, they do not prescribe the whole content of commercial agency agreements. In particular, the duties imposed on agents by the general common law and equity continue to apply. Moreover, many important agency arrangements are not covered by the regulations. It will therefore be necessary to consider the rights and duties of agents both at common law and under the regulations.

1 Regulation 23.
2 Regulation 2(1).
3 *AMB Imballaggi Plastici SRL v Pacflex Ltd* (1998) Tr LR 557; affd [1999] 2 All ER (Comm) 249.
4 *AMB Imballaggi Plastici SRL v Pacflex Ltd* (1998) Tr LR 557; affd [1999] 2 All ER (Comm) 249.
5 *Gary Parkes v Esso Petroleum Co Ltd* [1998] Eu LR 550.
6 (1999) Tr LR 232.
7 (1999) Tr LR 232 at 238, per Morritt LJ.
8 Paragraph 4(c).
9 See *Tamarind International Ltd v Eastern Natural Gas (Retail) Ltd* [2000] 26 LS Gaz R 35.
10 It has been held that the regulations apply to agents negotiating the sale of gas and electricity: *Tamarind International Ltd v Eastern Natural Gas (Retail) Ltd* [2000] 26 LS Gaz R 35. Difficult questions may arise in relation to agents concerned with the marketing of computer software. It is not clear whether software is properly regarded as 'goods' in English law. See 8.2.2.1. It is submitted that, applying a purposive approach to the regulations such agents should be protected.
11 See the DTI's Guidance Notes to the Regulations, published in September 1994.
12 Regulation 2(1).
13 Regulation 2(2).
14 Regulation 2(3).
15 The exclusion is permitted but not mandatory under the directive. There is therefore no equivalent to the Schedule in the directive.
16 But see *Hunter v Zenith Windows* (13 June 1997, unreported), where the court reached the opposite conclusion.
17 Article 2.2.
18 Waller LJ said that he was 'quite bewildered as to what is the proper construction' of the Schedule and Peter Gibson LJ described it as 'unhappily worded': see [1999] 2 All ER (Comm) 249 at 253, 256. See also *Tamarind International Ltd v Eastern Natural Gas (Retail) Ltd* [2000] 26 LS Gaz R 35 per Morison J.

19 Regulation 1.
20 Unless the agent acts in another Community state where the corresponding law applies as a mandatory rule.
21 Commercial Agents (Council Directive) Amendment Regulations 1998, SI 1998/2868.
22 The question whether the regulations properly implement the directive has been referred to the ECJ: *Pace Airline Services Ltd v Eurotrans Luftfahrtagentur GmbH* (2000, unreported). The agent also seems to be unprotected if the parties choose the law of a non-EU member state, unless it can be argued that the Directive, or some of its provisions, are to be regarded as 'mandatory rules of law' for the purposes of the Hague Convention 1977 and the Rome Convention 1980 on the law applicable to contractual obligations. This question was referred to the ECJ by the Court of Appeal in *Ingmar GB Ltd v Eaton Leonard Technologies Inc* [1999] Eu LR 88, where an English agent acted as UK representative for a Californian principal under a contract governed by Californian law.

6.1   Rights of the agent

The agency relationship is recognised as a fiduciary one. As a result, a number of duties are cast on the agent by the general law. In contrast, the general common law gave the agent relatively few rights. It may be that, in some cases, the principal could owe reciprocal fiduciary duties to his agent, in the same way that it has been tentatively recognised that an insurer may owe a duty of good faith to an insured, corresponding to the insured's duty[1]. However, such duties are not generally recognised at present and the agent's rights must therefore generally depend on the contract, if any, between him and the principal. Commercial agents protected by the 1993 regulations enjoy significantly greater rights.

1   See *Banque Financière de la Cité v Westgate Insurance Co Ltd* [1990] 1 QB 665, [1989] 2 All ER 952, CA; affd [1991] 2 AC 249, [1990] 2 All ER 947, HL; see 35.3.3.

6.1.1   *Agent's rights at common law*

Apart from any particular rights conferred on the agent by the contract of agency, the common law recognises three general rights to remuneration, indemnity and a lien.

6.1.1.1   *Remuneration*

An agent is only entitled to remuneration if that has been agreed with the principal. However, even if there is no express agreement that the agent should be paid for his services, the court may imply a term giving him a right to remuneration. Such a right will probably be implied where the agent is acting in the course of a profession or business, and will be more readily implied where the agent has performed his services. It will be rare that an agent acting in a commercial context will agree to act gratuitously.

A right to payment will be implied on the same basis on which terms are generally implied into contracts. Thus no term can be implied where that would contradict the express terms of the contract. Where a right to payment is implied, the agent will be entitled to receive a reasonable sum for his services, assessed on a quantum meruit basis[1], but if the agency agreement provides for the agent to be paid a sum to be fixed at the principal's discretion, the court cannot imply a right to be paid a reasonable sum: to do so would usurp the principal's rights under the contract and would substitute the court's discretion for the agreed term[2].

The agent is only entitled to receive remuneration in accordance with the terms of the agency contract. The contract may entitle the agent to receive a retainer. Alternatively, the agent may be employed to achieve a specified task, for instance, to sell a particular item of property. In that case the agent only becomes entitled to remuneration when the specified event occurs. Moreover, in such a case the agent is only entitled to remuneration if he has been the 'effective cause' of the event he was employed to bring about, unless the contract provides otherwise. Although there are a number of cases in which the question whether the agent has been the 'effective cause' of an event has been considered, there is no judicial definition of 'effective cause', and it will be a question of fact in each case whether the agent has earned his commission[3]. In *Coles v Enoch*[4] A was employed to find a tenant for P's property. While he was describing the premises to an interested party, T overheard him and enquired about the premises. A gave T only a general description of their location, but T found the premises himself and made an offer direct to P which P accepted. A's claim for commission failed as he had not been the direct cause of T taking a lease of the premises. In general, it seems that the agent will lose his right to commission if some event breaks the chain of causation between his actions and the event on which payment of commission depends. In *Coles v Enoch* the agent's withholding of the full address broke that chain[5].

In a number of cases the question has arisen whether the principal may prevent the agent earning the agreed commission. The agent may be able to claim damages if there is an express or implied term of the contract that the principal may not prevent or hinder him earning his commission, but it seems that the courts will generally be reluctant to imply such a term, particularly where its effect would be to restrict the principal's right to deal with his property, or where the contract is unilateral[6]. Thus in *Rhodes v Forwood*[7] an agent failed in a claim for damages where the principal closed down his business before the expiry of the term of the agency contract[8].

In the leading case of *Luxor (Eastbourne) Ltd v Cooper*[9] estate agents were instructed to sell two cinemas. Commission of £10,000 was payable on a sale and the agents introduced a buyer, but the owners decided not to proceed. The agents claimed damages for breach of an implied term that the owners should not refuse to sell to a buyer introduced by the agents. The House of Lords refused to imply such a term. A term can only be implied in order to give business efficacy to the contract; here no such term was necessary. The House seems to have been influenced by the scale of the commission payable on a sale: 'A sum of £10,000 (the equivalent of the remuneration of a year's work by the Lord Chancellor) for work done in a period of eight or nine days is no mean reward and is one well worth a risk'[10]. The agents were therefore held to have assumed the risk that the sale would not be completed.

However, a term was implied in the more recent case of *Alpha Trading Ltd v Dunnshaw-Patten*[11]. The agents there were employed to arrange a contract for the sale of a quantity of cement. A contract was concluded and the principals deliberately broke it in order to take advantage of a rising market. The Court of Appeal felt that this was a risk which the agents had not agreed to bear. The implication of a term was commercially necessary to prevent the principal 'playing a dirty trick on the agent'. Without such a term, the court felt, commercial agency arrangements would be unworkable. The court distinguished the earlier case of *French & Co v Leeston Shipping Co Ltd*[12], where the House of Lords had refused to imply a term which would have prevented a ship-owner selling the ship during a charterparty: such a term would have restricted the principal's right to deal freely with its property.

Where a person is appointed 'sole agent', he is entitled to be paid even if a sale is effected by another agent[13]; payment is by way of damages for breach of the term that he should be 'sole agent', which prevents him earning commission. However, such a term is not broken if the principal sells in person; but if the agent is described as having 'sole right to sell' the principal will commit a breach even if he sells in person[14].

Where the agent is entitled to commission on accomplishing a task, a question may arise as to the stage at which the commission is earned. This will depend on the construction of the particular contract, and there is an extensive body of case law concerned especially with estate agency contracts which is beyond the scope of this book[15]. In the absence of express words to the contrary, no commission is payable until a sale is completed.

The agent is only entitled to remuneration if he acts within the scope of his authority. If he acts outside his authority, or without authority, for instance by selling property at a lower price than instructed, he is not entitled to commission, even though the principal may be bound by the transaction. It also seems that an agent who has performed his authorised task will nevertheless lose his right to commission if he commits a serious breach of any of his duties as agent.

1   *Way v Latilla* [1937] 3 All ER 759, HL. The failure to agree remuneration in a commercial context may indicate that the parties have not reached a concluded contract. In that case if the agent has nevertheless performed his duties he may be entitled to be paid a reasonable sum on a restitutionary basis.
2   *Kofi Sunkersette Obu v Strauss & Co Ltd* [1951] AC 243, PC; *Re Richmond Gate Property Co Ltd* [1964] 3 All ER 936, [1965] 1 WLR 335.
3   Difficult questions may arise where there is a chain of agents and sub-agents, all of whom may legitimately claim to be 'the effective cause' of a transaction: see *Harding Maughan Hambly Ltd v Cie Européenne de Courtage D'assurances et de Réassurances SA* [2000] 1 All ER (Comm) 225.
4   [1939] 3 All ER 327, CA.
5   See also *Toulmin v Millar* (1887) 12 App Cas 746, 58 LT 96, HL.
6   It may be that where the agency contract is a unilateral contract it is more correct to speak of the court implying a collateral *contract* rather than implying a *term*: see *Bowstead and Reynolds on Agency* (16th edn, 1996) para 7-035.
7   (1876) 1 App Cas 256.
8   The agent's claim for damages succeeded in *Turner v Goldsmith* [1891] 1 QB 544, where only part of the business was closed down.
9   [1941] AC 108.
10 [1941] AC 108 at 120.
11 [1981] QB 290, [1981] 1 All ER 482.
12 [1922] 1 AC 451, HL.
13 *Bentall, Horsley and Baldry v Vicary* [1931] 1 KB 253. Cf *Lamb (WT) & Sons v Goring Brick Co* [1932] 1 KB 710 (distributorship contract).
14 *Brodie Marshall & Co v Sharer* [1988] 19 EG 129. Most of the cases on this point concern estate agents.
15 See Markesinis and Munday, *An Outline of the Law of Agency* (4th edn, 1998) pp 125 ff.

6.1.1.2   *Indemnity*

All agents, whether acting under a contract of agency or not, are entitled to be reimbursed expenses and indemnified against expenses incurred in the course of performing their duties. Where the agency is contractual the indemnity will be an implied (or express) term of the contract; where there is no contract, the agent will still be entitled to an indemnity, but the basis will be restitutionary. As a result, a non-contractual agent is only entitled to be indemnified against expenditure necessarily incurred on the principal's behalf, and cannot claim reimbursement for payments the principal would not have been obliged to make[1]. In general, the indemnity only covers expenses and liabilities incurred whilst the agent is acting within the scope of his actual authority; but an unauthorised agent is entitled to an indemnity if his actions are ratified, and an agent of necessity may also claim indemnity where the requirements for agency of necessity are fulfilled.

Where the agency is contractual, the contract may extend or restrict the agent's right to indemnity. Alternatively, the agent's right to indemnity may be restricted by customary implied term. Thus, for instance, in the absence of an express right in the agency contract, an estate agent is not entitled to reimbursement of any advertising costs[2]; and del credere agents who agree to guarantee to their principals that third parties with whom they contract will perform their contracts are clearly not entitled to indemnity against any payment made on that basis.

The right to indemnity covers all expenses and liabilities necessarily incurred by the agent whilst acting within his actual authority, including contractual and tortious liabilities, but does not cover any liabilities incurred due to the agent's own fault, nor any liabilities in respect of acts which the agent knew to be unlawful or illegal[3]. So, for instance, an auctioneer who sold goods on P's instructions, ignorant of the fact that P had no right to dispose of them, was entitled to an indemnity against liability to the true owner[4].

In certain circumstances the indemnity may extend to cover payments made by the agent even though there was no legal obligation to pay. In one case a firm of London solicitors acted as agents for a provincial firm and instructed counsel on behalf of their principals. Contrary to their principals' instructions, they paid counsel's fees. A barrister may not sue for his fees. However, it was held that the agents were entitled to be reimbursed the fees paid to counsel: there was strong moral and professional pressure to pay, even though there was no enforceable legal obligation[5]. In this case the indemnity was contractual; a restitutionary indemnity might not cover such expenditure.

1   See generally Goff and Jones, *The Law of Restitution* (5th edn, 1998) chs 14 and 15.
2   *Morris v Cleasby* (1816) 4 M & S 566.
3   *Re Parker* (1882) 21 Ch D 408, CA.
4   *Adamson v Jarvis* (1827) 4 Bing 66.
5   *Rhodes v Fielder, Jones and Harrison* (1919) 89 LJKB 15.

6.1.1.3   *Lien*

In order to protect his rights to remuneration or indemnity, an agent may be entitled to a lien over property belonging to the principal which is in his possession. A lien is a right to retain property by way of security until some debt is paid[1]. The law recognises two types of lien: the general lien and the particular lien. A person entitled to a general lien is entitled to retain any property belonging to the debtor until the debt is discharged; a particular lien only entitles the beneficiary to retain an item of property until debts relating to that property or a related transaction are discharged. The law is reluctant to recognise rights to general liens and most agents are entitled only to a particular lien, but bankers, factors, solicitors and stockbrokers are amongst the agents entitled to a general lien. A commission agent, who buys on behalf of a principal but does not create privity between the principal and the seller, is entitled to a lien over the goods purchased by virtue of the Sale of Goods Act 1979, s 38(2).

The agent may exercise a lien over property belonging to his principal which comes into his possession in his capacity as agent by lawful means so long as it remains in his lawful possession. Generally, the right to a lien depends on possession so that it is lost if the agent voluntarily parts with the property. However, constructive possession will suffice, so that the agent may exercise a lien over goods covered by a bill of lading in his possession, or goods held by a bailee if the bailee attorns to the agent[2]. The lien is not lost if the principal recovers the goods by a trick, and if the agent releases the goods subject to an agreement that they are held for his benefit, the lien is preserved. This commonly happens when banks acting in documentary credit operations release goods to their clients under a trust receipt[3]. The agent will also lose his lien if his conduct indicates an intention to waive it[4], and it may be excluded by an express term in an agency contract[5].

If the agent is entitled to a lien he takes the property subject to any existing interests in it, but the lien is good against the principal and all persons claiming an interest in the property through the principal. The lien gives an immediate right to possession, so that the agent can sue the principal, or anyone else, for wrongfully removing the property, and the right to possession will allow the agent to sue a third party for negligent damage to the property[6].

1   See generally 22.1.2.
2   *Bryans v Nix* (1839) 4 M & W 775.
3   See 34.2.7.
4   *Weeks v Goode* (1859) 6 CBNS 367.
5   *Re Bowes* (1886) 33 Ch D 586.
6   *The Aliakmon* [1986] AC 785, [1986] 2 All ER 145, HL.

6.1.2   *Agent's rights under the Commercial Agents (Council Directive) Regulations 1993*

Where the regulations apply they modify the agent's right to commission and give him certain other rights including, in particular, rights to be supplied with information.

6.1.2.1   *Good faith*

The regulations require the principal in his dealings with the agent to act 'dutifully and in good faith'[1]. The content of this duty will have to be developed by case law, but it seems that it will involve a general duty to co-operate with the agent. The regulations state that it requires 'in particular' that the principal provide the agent with 'the necessary documentation relating to the goods concerned' and obtain for the agent 'the information necessary for the performance of the agency contract'[2]. This requires the principal to supply the agent with information relating to his business, and to transactions, which principals might otherwise regard as confidential. For instance, the principal must notify the agent within a reasonable time if he anticipates that the volume of transactions will be significantly lower than the agent could normally have expected[3] and notify the agent within a reasonable time of his acceptance, refusal or non-performance of any transaction introduced by the agent[4].

The parties cannot derogate from the duty of good faith[5].

1   Regulation 4.
2   Regulation 4(2).
3   Regulation 4(2).
4   Regulation 4(3).
5   Regulation 5.

6.1.2.2   *Remuneration*

In the absence of agreement as to the agent's remuneration, the agent is entitled to whatever remuneration is customary for agents dealing in the goods the subject of his agency in the place in which he carries on his activities and, in the absence of any custom, to reasonable remuneration 'taking into account all aspects of the transaction'[1]. This seems to add little to the common law rules.

Further, detailed, provisions apply where the agent is remunerated wholly or partly by commission, defined as 'any part of the remuneration of a commercial agent which varies with the number or value of business transactions'[2]. The agent is entitled to receive commission on transactions concluded during the period of the agency 'as a result of his action'[3]. This is effectively the same as the common law rule. However, the agent is also entitled to commission on 'repeat orders' from third parties he has introduced as customers 'for transactions of the same kind'[4]. It is not clear whether an agent is entitled to commission on repeat orders at common law. Such entitlement normally depends on the construction of the agency agreement. In addition, an agent who has exclusive rights to a specific area or group of customers is entitled under the regulations to commission on any transaction entered into with a customer from that group or area during the agency[5]. At common law an agent with exclusive rights would be entitled to damages for breach of contract in such a case; the measure of damages would prima facie be the amount of commission lost[6]. Whether the agent does have such exclusive rights will depend on the construction of the agreement. Further provisions entitle the agent to commission on transactions entered into after termination of the agency; these are considered below[7].

We have seen that, at common law, difficult questions of construction may arise where there is a dispute as to whether commission has become due to the agent or where the principal seeks to deny payment of commission following a breach of the contract with the third party. The regulations fix the point at which commission becomes due to the agent. The parties cannot derogate from these provisions to the prejudice of the agent. They are free to agree that commission becomes due when:

'(a) the principal has executed the transaction;
(b) the principal should, according to his agreement with the third party, have executed the transaction; or
(c) the third party has executed the transaction[8]'

but commission becomes due at the latest 'when the third party has executed his part of the transaction or should have done so if the principal had executed his part . . . as he should have'[9]. It seems clear that 'execute' here means 'perform'. Thus the principal cannot deprive the agent of commission by defaulting on his contract with the third party. However, no commission is payable where the contract between principal and third party is not performed 'due to a reason for which the principal is not to blame'[10]. Any commission already paid in such a case is refundable. This is a difficult provision. 'Blame', in the sense of 'fault', is not normally relevant to liability for breach of contract in English law. A contract may be terminated without 'fault' on the principal's part in a number of ways. It seems clear that the principal should not be liable for commission where the contract with the third party is frustrated. What, however, if the contract is lawfully terminated by the principal due to the third party's breach, or in circumstances permitted by the contract with the third party but not amounting to breach? It seems that, although in such cases he is responsible for termination, and therefore for non-performance, the principal could be said not to be to 'blame' so that no commission would be payable. It might also be argued that the principal is 'not to blame' where non-performance results from circumstances which amount to a breach by the principal but without fault on his part; however, it seems more likely that the intention is that commission is payable wherever non-performance is a result of the principal's breach[11].

Further provisions fix the date when commission due to the agent should be paid[12], require the principal to provide the agent with a statement of commission due and allow the agent to demand information and have access to the principal's books to check the amount[13].

1   Regulation 6(1).
2   Regulation 2(1).
3   Regulation 7(1)(a).
4   Regulation 7(1)(b).
5   Regulation 7(2).
6   See above 6.1.1.1.
7   See 6.3.2.2.
8   Regulation 10(1).
9   Regulation 10(2).
10 Regulation 11.
11 Other language texts of the directive use expressions which indicate that commission is not payable when the contract is not performed for reasons which are not 'attributable' to the principal: see *Bowstead and Reynolds on Agency* (16th edn, 1996) para 11-031.
12 Regulation 10(3).
13 Regulation 12.

6.2   Duties of the agent

Any contract between principal and agent may expressly or impliedly impose specific duties on the agent. However, even in the absence of a contract, the agent will be subject as a matter of law to a number of duties which arise either under the general law or under the 1993 regulations, where they apply. Many professionals, including solicitors, estate agents and agents operating in the financial services industry are also required to comply with codes of conduct promulgated by professional and/or self-regulatory bodies. The duties imposed on all agents by the general law overlap to a considerable extent with the duties imposed on commercial agents by the 1993 regulations on the one hand, and some of the self-regulatory rules applicable to professionals on the other; however, the precise relationship between them is often unclear.

6.2.1   *Duties under the general law*

An agent is subject to a number of duties imposed by the general law as legal incidents of the agency relationship. Where the agency is contractual, some of the duties may take effect as implied terms in the contract, or be modified by its express terms. However, certain duties are imposed on the agent automatically; in particular:

> 'The position of principal and agent gives rise to particular and onerous duties on the part of the agent, and the high standard required from him springs from the fiduciary relationship between his employer and himself. His position is confidential. It readily lends itself to abuse. A strict and salutary rule is required to meet the special situation. The rules of English law as they now exist spring from the strictness originally required by Courts of Equity in cases where the fiduciary relationship exists'[1].

Although the fiduciary duties imposed on agents arise in equity it seems that their scope may be determined by reference to the terms of any underlying contract between principal and agent[2] and the surrounding circumstances.

1 McCardie J in *Armstrong v Jackson* [1917] 2 KB 822 at 826.
2 See *Kelly v Cooper* [1993] AC 205; *Henderson v Merrett Syndicates Ltd* [1995] 2 AC 145 at 206, [1994] 3 All ER 506 at 543-4 per Lord Browne-Wilkinson.

6.2.1.1 *The duty to obey instructions*

An agent is under a general duty to obey the instructions of his principal. However, a distinction must be drawn between contractual and gratuitous agency. An agent acting under a contract is contractually obliged to perform the duties undertaken under that contract and is liable for breach of contract if he fails to perform[1]; of course, where the contract is unilateral, it may be that the agent has not undertaken to do anything. However, if the agency is non-contractual, the agent is generally under no duty to act, so that he cannot be liable if he simply does nothing, unless his failure to act gives rise to liability in tort. There is generally no liability in tort for negligent omissions, but it has been suggested that liability might arise in certain situations. For instance, suppose that A agrees to insure property on P's behalf, but then decides not to do so. If he fails to inform P and P, believing that A has arranged insurance, also fails to insure, can A be held liable to P in negligence if the property is damaged or destroyed? P's loss is purely economic. It appears that liability may be imposed on the basis of *Hedley Byrne & Co Ltd v Heller & Partners Ltd*[2] for loss caused by a failure to warn, where the defendant has voluntarily assumed a responsibility to warn, and that such an assumption may be found in cases where there is a particularly close relationship between defendant and plaintiff[3]. The relationship between principal and agent is especially close, and it would not be difficult to interpret the situation as one where the agent had voluntarily assumed a responsibility to warn the principal if he failed to effect the insurance. However, the point remains undecided[4].

A contractual agent is under a duty to obey the instructions of his principal given during the course of the agency as to the performance of his tasks, although a professional agent may be under a duty to warn the principal of any risks or dangers inherent in those instructions. However, an agent is not obliged to obey instructions which require him to act illegally, and the duty of a professional agent to obey instructions may also be limited by rules of professional conduct.

If the agent's instructions are ambiguous, he will not be liable if he acts on a reasonable interpretation of them[5]. However, there will probably be a duty to seek clarification of the instructions[6].

The duty of obedience means that the agent must not exceed his authority. This applies equally to contractual and gratuitous agency.

1   *Turpin v Bilton* (1843) 5 Man & G 455.
2   [1964] AC 465, [1963] 2 All ER 575, HL. Liability under the *Hedley Byrne* principle is now regarded as depending on a 'voluntary assumption of responsibility': see *White v Jones* [1995] 2 AC 207; *Henderson v Merrett Syndicates Ltd* [1995] 2 AC 145, [1994] 3 All ER 506; *Williams v Natural Life Health Foods Ltd* [1998] 2 All ER 577.
3   *Banque Financière de la Cité SA v Westgate Insurance Co Ltd* [1989] 2 All ER 952, CA (no duty was found on the facts). See also *Reid v Rush & Tompkins Group plc* [1989] 3 All ER 228, [1990] 1 WLR 212, CA (no duty between employer and employee); *Van Oppen v Clerk to the Bedford Charity Trustees* [1989] 3 All ER 389, [1990] 1 WLR 235, CA (no duty owed by school to pupil).
4   See *General Accident Fire and Life Insurance Corpn v Tanter* [1984] 1 Lloyd's Rep 58 for an example of liability in an analogous situation. See *Bowstead and Reynolds on Agency* (16th edn, 1996) para 6-027; contrast Fridman, *The Law of Agency* (7th edn, 1996) p 156-157; Markesinis and Munday, *An Outline of the Law of Agency* (4th edn, 1998) p 95.
5   *Ireland v Livingstone* (1872) LR 5 HL 395.
6   *Woodhouse AC Israel Cocoa Ltd. SA v Nigerian Produce Marketing Co Ltd* [1972] AC 741 at 772 per Lord Salmon; *European Asian Bank AG v Punjab and Sind Bank* [1983] 2 All ER 508 at 517 per Robert Goff LJ.

6.2.1.2   *The agent must exercise reasonable care*

All agents owe a duty of care to their principals which requires them to exercise reasonable care in the execution of their authority. Where the agency is non-contractual, this duty of care arises only in tort. However, where the agency is contractual, a term will normally be implied into the contract requiring the agent to act with reasonable skill and care. Such a term is implied by statute where the agent performs a service and acts in the course of a business[1] but a similar term is implied at common law. A contractual agent is therefore subject to concurrent duties in contract and tort[2], unless either is modified or excluded by the express terms of the contract, and the principal may choose to sue in contract or tort in order to benefit from the procedural advantages of either form of action[3]. It is not clear whether there is a separate, third duty of care imposed as a result of the agent's fiduciary position[4].

The agent's contractual and tortious duties of care may be limited or excluded by a term in a contract of agency. However, clear words are needed to exclude liability for negligence. In *Henderson v Merrett Syndicates Ltd*[5] the contracts between names at Lloyd's and the agents who managed underwriting business on their behalf contained a term giving the agents 'absolute discretion' in respect of underwriting business. It was argued that this excluded both contractual and tortious duties of care. However, the House of Lords held that it merely defined the agents' authority but did not exclude their duties to act with reasonable care in exercising that authority. Any term which does purport to exclude either the duty of care or to exclude or limit liability for its breach is in any case subject to the Unfair Contract Terms Act 1977[6].

The standard of care required is what is reasonable in all the circumstances of the case. This will vary according to the facts of the particular case. For instance, if an agent holds himself out as a member of a profession, he will be expected to show the standard of skill and care reasonably to be expected of a reasonably competent member of that profession. Older cases suggested that a lower standard was expected of a gratuitous agent, who was only expected to show the same degree of care as he would show in the management of his own affairs[7]. However, this approach was inconsistent with the modern development of the general law of negligence and it is now settled that even a gratuitous agent owes a duty to his principal to act with reasonable skill and care. The issue came before the Court of Appeal in *Chaudhry v Prabhakar*[8]. P, who had recently passed her driving test, wished to buy a car, and, being inexperienced, asked A, a friend, to find her a suitable car, specifying that it must be one which had not been in an accident. A, who was not a mechanic and acted purely gratuitously, found and recommended a one-year-old Volkswagen Golf which was being sold by a firm of panel-beaters and paint sprayers. P bought the car and only later found it had been badly damaged in an accident. She sued A, who sought to rely on the old cases as to the standard of care required of a gratuitous agent. The Court of Appeal held that the standard required of any agent is such as is reasonable in all the circumstances. In deciding what care is reasonable, the court would take into account the fact that the agent was paid or unpaid, the degree of skill possessed or claimed by the agent, and the degree of reliance placed on the agent by the principal. On the facts of this case A had failed to exercise reasonable skill and was liable to P.

1   Supply of Goods and Services Act 1982, s 13.
2   See *Iron Trade Mutual Insurance Co Ltd v J K Buckenham Ltd* [1990] 1 All ER 808; *Henderson v Merrett Syndicates Ltd* [1995] 2 AC 145, [1994] 3 All ER 506.
3   *Henderson v Merrett Syndicates Ltd* [1995] 2 AC 145, [1994] 3 All ER 506; *Midland Bank Trust Co Ltd v Hett Stubbs & Kemp* [1979] Ch 384, [1978] 3 All ER 571, see 19.1.1.
4   The point was left undecided by the majority in *Henderson v Merrett*, but Lord Browne-Wilkinson ([1995] 2 AC 145 at 205, [1994] 3 All ER 506 at 543-554 expressed the view that there was no separate fiduciary duty of care.
5   [1995] 2 AC 145, [1994] 3 All ER 506.
6   Section 2. See 2.6.4.1; 19.1.2.
7   *Shiells and Thorne v Blackburne* (1789) 1 Hy Bl 159; *Giblin v McMullen* (1868) LR 2 PC 317.
8   [1988] 3 All ER 718, [1989] 1 WLR 29.

6.2.1.3 *Personal performance*

A principal chooses an agent to carry out some task on his behalf. The personal characteristics of the agent may well be a reason for his being chosen; furthermore, in every case the principal places trust in the agent: 'confidence in the particular person employed is at the root of agency'[1]. The agency relationship is therefore a personal one and the law requires that the agent perform personally so that, as a general rule, the agent may not delegate performance of his duties to someone else. This is often expressed in the Latin maxim *delegatus non potest delegare*. However, a more accurate statement of the law would be that an agent is not permitted to delegate performance of his duties unless delegation is authorised by the principal.

In fact delegation is quite common. In particular, in corporate business structures, where authority to act on behalf of the company is vested in the board of directors, the directors will generally have authority to appoint sub-agents, such as senior executives, who in turn will generally have authority to appoint sub-sub-agents as employees of the business with some agency function. As a result, a long chain of representation may be built up. To take a simple example, a check-out operator working in a supermarket may be regarded as an agent of the company when concluding contracts with customers. He or she will probably be appointed by the branch manager, who in turn will be an agent of the company appointed by an area manager. The area manager will be an agent of the company appointed by a more senior employee, say the retail sales director, who will, in turn, be an agent appointed, let us say for the sake of argument, by the board of directors who themselves are agents of the principal, the company.

In the example just given, there is little difficulty in concluding that: (a) each act of delegation was authorised; (b) each agent in the chain is an agent of the company; and (c) the company is therefore bound by the acts of each agent in the chain insofar as they are covered by actual or apparent authority. In other situations the analysis may be less straightforward and in cases of delegation it will be necessary to consider (i) the consequences of delegation for the relationship between principal and agent, (ii) whether the principal is bound by the actions of the sub-agent and, (iii) what, if any, relationship is created between the principal and sub-agent. The answers to these questions will depend on whether the agent's delegation was authorised. Delegation will be a breach of the agent's duty to his principal unless covered by actual authority. Moreover, unless the agent had actual or apparent authority to delegate, the principal will not be bound by the acts of the sub-agent.

As usual, as between principal and agent, actual authority is paramount. The principal may authorise delegation expressly or impliedly; and authority may be implied on the basis of necessity on the facts of a particular case, as a result of the conduct of the parties, the nature of the transaction to be carried out, or on the basis of a custom in a particular trade. Thus, for instance, it is customary for provincial solicitors to appoint London agents to represent them in High Court litigation in London[2]. An agent also generally has authority to delegate the performance of purely ministerial acts which require no exercise of discretion, such as the service of notices to quit[3]. Where a company is appointed agent, it must act through human agents and so may delegate performance to its employees.

A much more difficult question, even where delegation is authorised, is: what relationship is created between principal and sub-agent? To put it another way, if P appoints A to act as his agent and A, with authority, delegates performance of some or all of his tasks to S, is S the agent of P, or the agent of A, or the agent of both P and A? The answer to this question will be crucial for determining the rights and liabilities of the parties against each other. Once again, the answer depends on the authority given to A. In the supermarket example given above the answer is straightforward. Each agent has authority to appoint sub-agents who become agents of the company for certain purposes so that the final sub-agent in the chain, the check-out operator, is an agent of the company for certain limited purposes. In other situations the answer may be much less straightforward. The question has arisen in a series of recent cases concerned with the operation of the Lloyd's insurance market, where it is normal for agents to act through sub-agents for certain purposes[4]. The key question is whether A is authorised to create privity between P and S. It does not follow that because P has authorised A to appoint a sub-agent, S, with power to create privity between P and third parties with whom S deals, that P has also authorised A to create privity between P and S[5]. In *de Bussche v Alt* [6] P employed A to sell a ship in India, China or Japan. A had no offices in Japan and, being unable to sell the ship, obtained P's authority to appoint S, who did have a presence in Japan, to sell the ship. The Court of Appeal held that the delegation was authorised and that it had the effect of creating privity between P and S with the result that S owed the duties of an agent to P.

Certain dicta of Thesiger LJ in *de Bussche v Alt* [7] appear to suggest that wherever delegation is authorised the agent creates privity of contract between principal and sub-agent. However, it was found in *de Bussche* that A was given express authority to create privity between P and S. Subsequent cases indicate that *de Bussche* should be regarded as an exceptional case, dependent on its special facts, and that in the absence of clear evidence, the courts will generally be slow to find that A was authorised to create privity between P and S. The more common interpretation will be that A is authorised to appoint an agent to act on A's behalf[8]. There will then be no privity of contract between P and S, nor will there be a principal-agent relationship between them. Instead, A will remain liable as agent, including for the acts of S, his agent and will be liable to account to P for money received by S[9]. S will not be entitled to the rights of an agent against P, and will look to A for payment. Thus in *Prentis Donegan & Partners Ltd v Leeds & Leeds Co Inc*[10] P, shipowners, instructed A, a firm of New York insurance brokers, to obtain a quotation for renewal of insurance. A in turn instructed S, a firm of Lloyd's brokers, to obtain a quotation and, in due course, instructed S to obtain cover. Rix J held that although delegation was authorised, A had no authority to create privity between P and S, with the result that A was liable to pay S commission. It made no difference that S was a Lloyd's broker and only a Lloyd's broker could do business at Lloyd's, so that P and A must have known that delegation would be necessary. Rix J emphasised that privity between P and S would arise only in an exceptional case and that:

> 'There are good commercial reasons for such a rule. It emphasises the importance of the contractual chain. It is natural for each agent in the chain to give credit to the party known to him, rather than to someone perhaps unknown. It reflects an agent's general desire to keep his client to himself. It reflects the professional or semi-professional relationships of agents and sub-agents'[11].

The absence of a direct agency relationship between S and P does not mean that S owes no duties to P. S may still owe a duty of care to P in tort in accordance with general principles of the law of negligence. Thus in *Henderson v Merrett Syndicates Ltd*[12] Lloyd's 'names' sued the agents who managed the syndicates of which the names were members. In some cases the names were represented by 'members' agents' who placed business, on behalf of the names, with syndicates managed by separate 'managing agents'. The terms of the relevant contracts made it clear that the managing agents were the agents of the members' agents who appointed them. There was thus no direct relationship between the names and the managing agents. Nevertheless, it was held that the managing agents performed a professional service on behalf of the names who, to their knowledge, relied on them to exercise skill and care, and that they therefore owed a duty of care to the names in accordance with the principle in *Hedley Byrne & Co Ltd v Heller & Partners Ltd*[13]. This is striking because the names' losses in this case were purely economic. However, the House of Lords emphasised that there is no absolute rule that a sub-agent will always owe a duty of care to the principal[14]. It may be easier to find a duty of care where the sub-agent's activities cause injury to P or damage to his property.

In addition, even if there is no direct agency relationship between P and S, it may still be that S owes fiduciary duties to P so that, for instance, S will be liable to account to P if he makes a secret profit from his position[15]. Moreover, as Rix J recognised in *Prentis Donegan v Leeds & Leeds*, even if privity is established between P and S, that does not exclude the possibility that there may also be a contractual relationship between A and S[16].

One final point remains to be considered. Even if an authorised delegation by A to S does not create privity between P and S, the contract between A and S would appear to be one whose object is to confer a benefit on P. It may therefore be arguable that P can enforce performance of S's undertaking by virtue of the Contracts (Rights of Third Parties) Act 1999. However, where the contract does not expressly provide that it is to be enforceable by a third party beneficiary, the beneficiary is not entitled to enforce 'if on a proper construction of the contract it appears that the [contracting] parties did not intend the term to be enforceable by the third party'[17]. The Law Commission took the view that, applying this test, a third party beneficiary would not be entitled to enforce a contract term where the contracting parties had deliberately arranged their relationships by means of a chain of contracts, where direct enforcement would subvert that chain[18]. This appears to be much the same reasoning used by Rix J in *Prentis Donegan v Leeds & Leeds* in the passage quoted above, suggesting that, in the absence of special circumstances, the position will continue to be that even in cases of authorised delegation there is no direct contractual relationship between principal and sub-agent.

1 Thesiger LJ in *de Bussche v Alt* (1878) 8 Ch D 286 at 310, CA.
2 *Solley v Wood* (1852) 16 Beav 370.
3 *Allam & Co v Europa Poster Services Ltd* [1968] 1 All ER 826, [1968] 1 WLR 638.
4 See *Henderson v Merrett Syndicates Ltd* [1995] 2 AC 145, [1994] 3 All ER 506; *Aiken v Stewart Wrightson Members' Agency Ltd* [1995] 3 All ER 449; *Velos Group Ltd v Harbour Insurance Services Ltd* [1997] 2 Lloyd's Rep 461; *Prentis Donegan & Partners Ltd v Leeds & Leeds Co Inc* [1998] 2 Lloyd's Rep 326; *Pangood Ltd v Barclay Brown & Co Ltd* [1999] 1 All ER (Comm) 460.
5 See per Bramwell LJ in *New Zealand and Australian Land Co Ltd v Watson* (1881) 7 QBD 374 at 381–382.
6 *de Bussche v Alt* (1878) 8 Ch D 286.
7 (1878) 8 Ch D 286 at 310–311.
8 *Calico Printers' Association v Barclays Bank Ltd* (1931) 145 LT 51, CA.
9 *Lockwood v Abdy* (1845) 14 Sim 437.
10 [1998] 2 Lloyd's Rep 326. Cf *Velos Group Ltd v Harbour Insurance Services Ltd* [1997] 2 Lloyd's Rep 461, described by Rix J in *Prentis* as involving 'special facts'.
11 [1998] 2 Lloyd's Rep 326 at 334. Compare the views of Matthew LJ in *Powell & Thomas v Evan Jones & Co* [1905] 1 KB 11 at 22.
12 [1995] 2 AC 145, [1994] 3 All ER 506.
13 [1964] AC 465.
14 Contrast *Balsamo v Medici* [1984] 2 All ER 304, [1984] 1 WLR 951, where it was held that a sub-agent was not liable in negligence for economic loss caused to the ultimate principal; see Whittaker (1985) MLR 86.
15 *Powell & Thomas v Evan Jones & Co* [1905] 1 KB 11. See Tettenborn (1999) 115 LQR 655.
16 [1998] 2 Lloyd's Rep 326 at 334.
17 Section 1(2).
18 Law Com no 242 *Privity of Contract: Contracts for the benefit of Third Parties* (Cm 3329, July 1996) para 7.18. The Commission's comments referred specifically construction contracts.

6.2.1.4 *The agent's fiduciary duties*

The relationship between principal and agent has traditionally been regarded as being a fiduciary one, under which the agent owes to his principal fiduciary duties, similar to those owed by a trustee to the beneficiaries of the trust. The concepts of fiduciary relationships and fiduciary duties were developed by the courts of equity and originally applied to trustees. They were subsequently extended, and similar duties were applied to other, analogous relationships including those involving agents and company directors. In the past there has been a tendency to treat all fiduciaries of all types as being subject to similar duties. In light of recent case law, however, it seems that this approach may have to be reconsidered. The duties of a fiduciary may depend on the circumstances of the individual case[1].

In particular, it is now recognised that the imposition of fiduciary duties may not always be appropriate where the parties are in a commercial relationship[2].

In general, fiduciary duties of loyalty are imposed wherever the relationship between X and Y is such that X has a legitimate expectation that Y will act in X's interests and not use his position in a way which is adverse to X's interests[3]. This was explained by Millett LJ in *Bristol and South West Building Society v Mothew* in a passage subsequently approved by the Privy Council[4]:

> 'A fiduciary is someone who has undertaken to act for or on behalf of another in a particular matter in circumstances which give rise to a relationship of trust and confidence. The distinguishing obligation of a fiduciary is the obligation of loyalty. The principal is entitled to the single-minded loyalty of his fiduciary. This core liability has several facets. A fiduciary must act in good faith; he must not make a profit out of his trust; he must not place himself in a position where his duty and his interest may conflict; he may not act for his own benefit or the benefit of a third person without the informed consent of his principal. This is not intended to be an exhaustive list, but it is sufficient to indicate the nature of fiduciary obligations. They are the defining characteristics of the fiduciary'[5].

Fiduciary duties arise independently of any contract. They are imposed on the fiduciary as a matter of law by virtue of the position he holds. Traditionally, they have been applied strictly – partly, at least, as a deterrent, to prevent fiduciaries being tempted to seek to profit from their position[6].

The same approach has tended to be applied to agents. An agent is entrusted by his principal with considerable power to affect his principal's legal position and has therefore been regarded as owing his principal fiduciary duties of loyalty. These duties are imposed on the agent as an incident of his position as a matter of law: 'the matter is too important to be left to the agreement of the parties'[7]. According to Lord Cottenham, in 1848, the agent was regarded as occupying a position 'quasi a trustee for [the] particular transaction in which he is engaged'[8] and, indeed, many of the rules concerning the duties of the agent as fiduciary have been developed in cases concerned with other fiduciaries, such as trustees and company directors. The duties have therefore been applied strictly so that an agent may be liable for breach of duty even though he acted in good faith and produced a benefit for his principal[9].

However, 'the law concerning an agent as fiduciary . . . has developed considerably since the time of Lord Cottenham'[10]. Some of the older cases should perhaps now be treated with caution, as imposing liabilities stricter than may be necessary in some cases of principal and agent. Agency itself is a broad and flexible concept, and it may well be that the circumstances of individual cases justify the imposition of obligations of differing degrees of strictness, according to the particular relationship between the parties. Thus it seems that the fiduciary duties imposed on an agent may be less stringent where the agency is primarily a commercial relationship[11]. It has been said that not all agents are fiduciaries[12], and that even where an agent is a fiduciary the scope and extent of the duties owed by the agent to the principal may be defined or modified by any contract between the parties: 'agency is a contract made between principal and agent; . . . like every other contract, the rights and duties of the principal and agent are dependent upon the terms of the agreement between them, whether express or implied'[13]. It must also be emphasised that, even where the agency is fiduciary, it does not follow that all of the agent's duties are fiduciary duties, and the agent may be subject to duties which arise in contract and/or tort[14].

It therefore now seems that there may be considerably more flexibility in the application of fiduciary duties to agents than was thought in the past. Conversely, fiduciary duties may be imposed in the context of relationships other than agency in an appropriate case. Distribution and franchising agreements do not ordinarily give rise to fiduciary relationships but may expressly impose similar duties on persons who are not agents or fiduciaries in the strict legal sense. Finally, it should be noted that an agent may continue to owe certain fiduciary duties to his former principal even after termination of the agency relationship[15].

Notwithstanding what has been said above, as a general rule an agent will owe certain, fairly well defined, duties of loyalty to his principal, as indicated in the statement of Millett LJ quoted above. Different writers classify the agent's duties in different ways but we will examine the agent's duties under four headings:

  (i)   the duty to avoid conflicts of interest;
 (ii)   the duty not to make a secret profit;
(iii)   the duty not to take a bribe; and
(iv)   the duty to account.

These are not water-tight classifications: the first three headings overlap to a considerable degree and some cases may be regarded as falling under more than one heading. Thus, for instance, the duty not to make a secret profit may be seen as an aspect of the more general duty to avoid conflicts of interest, whilst a bribe is merely a particular form of secret profit.

There is further flexibility in the remedies which may be awarded in the event of a breach of the agent's duties. Where the agent is in breach of his duty the principal may have a choice of a wide range of remedies – proprietary or personal, at common law or in equity. Thus, in particular cases, it may be possible to obtain damages in tort or for breach of contract; an account of profits; rescission of a contract; an injunction; a charge over property; an order for transfer of property; a declaration that property is held on constructive trust; or other orders. The availability of a range of remedies offers flexibility, which may well be desirable given the wide range of fiduciary relationships which may exist, both in general and within the scope of agency, and the range of possible situations which may amount to a breach of duty. However, flexibility in the law is always achieved at the cost of certainty, and in a commercial context such uncertainty is never satisfactory.

One particular question which has not been satisfactorily answered is particularly important in the context of commercial relationships. In some situations it is not clear whether the principal's remedy is personal or proprietary. There are references in the cases to agents and other fiduciaries holding property 'on constructive trust' for the principal or other plaintiff, whereas in others the agent is required personally to account for property. The question whether the remedy is proprietary becomes crucial if the agent has become insolvent, for then a proprietary remedy will give the principal priority over other creditors in the insolvency, whereas a purely personal remedy will place his claim on the same footing as those of other creditors, and it can be argued that the nature of the remedy ought therefore to take account of the policy question whether the principal should gain priority over other creditors. To date, English courts have been reluctant to develop a remedial constructive trust, which might be applied flexibly, taking account of such factors. It does seem, however, that the availability of a proprietary remedy may depend on the facts of the case. The courts may be reluctant to impose a trust on the agent where that would be incompatible with the commercial relationship between the parties, whereas it may be easier to establish that property is held on trust when it is transferred to the agent by the principal or a third party to be used for a particular specified purpose. In general, however, it seems that where the agent is guilty of breach of fiduciary duty, the principal is entitled to a proprietary remedy.

1 See especially per Lord Browne-Wilkinson in *Kelly v Cooper* [1993] AC 205 at 214; *Henderson v Merrett Syndicates*[1995] 2 AC 145 at 206, [1994] 3 All ER 506 at 543.
2 See Millett (1998) 114 LQR 214 at 215.
3 See Millett (1998) 114 LQR 214; *Arklow Developments v Maclean* [2000] 1 WLR 594.
4 *Arklow Developments v Maclean* [2000] 1 WLR 594.
5 [1996] 4 All ER 698 at 711-712. See Finn, *Fiduciary Obligations* (1977).
6 See eg *Boardman v Phipps* [1967] 2 AC 46, [1966] 3 All ER 721, HL.
7 *Bowstead and Reynolds on Agency* (16th edn, 1996) para 6-034.
8 Per Lord Cottenham in *Foley v Hill* (1848) 2 HL Cas 28 at 36.
9 As in *Boardman v Phipps* [1967] 2 AC 46, [1966] 3 All ER 721, HL.
10 Per Longmore J in *Triffit Nurseries v Salads Etc Ltd* [1999] 1 All ER (Comm) 110 at 116.
11 See eg *Kelly v Cooper* [1993] AC 205, *Neste Oy v Lloyds Bank plc* [1983] 2 Lloyd's Rep 658; *Kingscroft Insurance Co Ltd v H S Weavers (Underwriting) Agencies Ltd* [1993] 1 Lloyd's Rep 187, below 6.2.1.8.
12 Whether the agent is a fiduciary will depend on what he is authorised to do. See Dowrick (1954) 17 MLR 24. See also the retention of title cases such as *Clough Mill Ltd v Martin* [1984] 3 All ER 982, [1985] 1 WLR 111, below 18.4.
13 Per Lord Browne-Wilkinson in *Kelly v Cooper* [1993] AC 205 at 213. Certain of his Lordship's comments in *Kelly* suggest that where there is a contractual relationship between principal and agent the contract is the source of the agent's duties. However, in *Henderson v Merrett Syndicates* [1995] 2 AC 145, [1994] 3 All ER 506 his Lordship made clear that the agent's fiduciary duties arise independently of, but are capable of being modified by, the express and implied terms of the contract and the surrounding circumstances.
14 See *Henderson v Merrett Syndicates* [1995] 2 AC 145 at 205, [1994] 3 All ER 506 at 543; *Bristol and South West Building Society v Mothew* [1996] 4 All ER 698 at 710.
15 See *Yasuda Fire and Marine Insurance Co of Europe Ltd v Orion Marine Insurance Underwriting Agency Ltd* [1995] 3 All ER 211, below 6.2.1.8 (duty to provide accounts); *A-G v Blake* [1998] 1 All ER 833, below 6.2.1.6 (duty of confidentiality).

6.2.1.5 *No conflict of interest*

'It is a rule of universal application, that no one, having [fiduciary] duties to discharge, shall be allowed to enter into engagements in which he has, or can have, a personal interest conflicting, or which possibly may conflict, with the interests of those whom he is bound to protect'[1].

This rule is 'inflexible' and is 'applied inexorably' and it can be seen as the basis of the agent's other fiduciary duties, which are really only particular applications of this general rule. A breach may arise even if there is in fact no conflict: it is enough that there is the possibility of conflict. The law requires the agent to avoid temptation.

Two particularly important aspects of this rule occur in a commercial context where the agent is instructed to buy or sell property on behalf of the principal. There will be a breach if an agent instructed to buy sells his own property to the principal[2], or if an agent instructed to sell buys the principal's property[3]. In such a case there is clear potential for conflict, since a seller's interest is to get the best possible price, whilst a buyer's is to pay as little as possible. It is irrelevant that the agent in fact acted fairly and paid a fair price: he will be in breach of duty unless there is full disclosure to the principal of all relevant facts, and the principal consents to the transaction. The duty may continue even after the termination of the agency if the confidential relationship created by the agency continues, or if it gives the agent a special position of dominance over the principal and the transaction is connected to that relationship[4].

The agent may not evade the rule by dealing with the principal through a third party. In *McPherson v Watt*[5] an agent was instructed to sell property. He arranged for his brother to buy it for him. When the facts were discovered, the principal refused to complete and the court refused to order specific performance on the grounds of the agent's breach of duty. An agent will normally be unable to rely on an alleged custom sanctioning such deals, because the custom itself would be repugnant to the fiduciary nature of agency and so not be recognised by the court[6].

Where the agent deals with the principal in breach of this duty, the principal may rescind the contract. Although delay will normally bar rescission, in this case time does not run against the principal until the breach is discovered, so that in *Oliver v Court*[7] the principal was able to rescind thirteen years after the transaction. Alternatively, the principal may affirm the contract. In that case, where A has bought property from P, A must account for any profit made on the deal, for instance, where A has resold the property, on the basis that that profit should have gone to P. If A has sold property to P, P's remedy depends on whether A already owned the property, or bought it specifically to sell to P. In the latter case, A must account for any profit. However, where the property is not bought specifically for resale, P may not seek an account but may claim damages for any loss he has suffered[8].

The relationship between principal and agent may also give rise to a presumption of undue influence, so that if P makes a gift to A, the gift may be set aside unless A can show that no undue influence was exercised.

A slightly different question arises where an agent acts for two principals whose interests conflict. This problem, which is increasingly common, was considered by the Privy Council in *Kelly v Cooper*[9]. P and X, owners of two adjacent properties, instructed the same estate agent, A, to sell them. A showed both properties to a potential buyer, T, who agreed to buy X's property. T then made an offer to P to buy his property. P was unaware that T had already agreed to buy X's property and accepted the offer. When he discovered that T had already bought the adjacent property, P argued that had he known of that fact he would have been able to negotiate a higher price for the sale of his property since it was clear that T wanted to buy both. P therefore argued that A was in breach of duty (a) in failing to disclose to him the fact that T had already agreed to buy X's property, and (b) in putting himself in a position where his duties to his two principals, P and X, could conflict, and claimed damages for the loss of the chance to negotiate a higher price. Clearly, A was in a difficult position since disclosing to P T's purchase of X's property would have been a breach of A's duties to X. The Privy Council held that where an agent acts in pursuance of a contract the scope of the agent's fiduciary duties is determined by the terms of the contract. Since it was well known that estate agents might act for more than one principal the agency contract here contained an implied term that the agent would be permitted to act for more than one principal, whose interests might compete, and to keep confidential information received whilst acting for other principals[10]. On the facts the contract could not include an implied term precluding the agent's power to act for other principals.

Kelly v Cooper is an important decision because such situations are common, and are not restricted to estate agency. Such situations of conflict between the interests of different client-principals are likely to become increasingly common as professional firms become larger. For instance, it is well known that large accountancy firms may carry out audit work for clients who are in competition with one another. Since this is common knowledge it will readily be inferred that clients consent to them doing so, provided only that they keep confidential information received from each client in the course of their activities[11]. Similar problems arise in the financial services industry, where an agent such as a stockbroker will often act for more than one principal, as the Privy Council expressly recognised. It may be argued that the decision in *Kelly* recognises the commercial reality of the situation[12]; however, it comes close to denying the fiduciary nature of the agency relationship. The result could perhaps be explained on the basis that the claim for damages did depend on the terms of the contract, rather than the agent's fiduciary duties; the result might have been different had the agent made a profit, for which he could be required to account, by virtue of any breach of duty. However, here the agent's profit was the commission he received and the Privy Council held that the agent would only be denied his commission if he acted dishonestly or in bad faith[13].

As just noted, the problem which arose in *Kelly v Cooper* is likely to be a common one in the financial services industry. The reorganisation of that industry in the so-called 'Big Bang' in the 1980s created considerable potential for conflicts of interest. Prior to Big Bang, stockbroking firms acted either as 'brokers' who acted to buy and sell shares for principals, or as 'jobbers', who held shares on their own account. Following Big Bang, it became possible for a single firm to combine both functions. In order to minimise the potential for conflicts of interest thus created, the Financial Services Act 1986 required different functions to be performed by separate departments within firms, the departments to be kept separate by so-called 'Chinese walls' – information barriers designed to avoid the transfer of sensitive information between them – and firms to appoint compliance officers to ensure compliance and avoid other conflicts. In many respects, such statutory requirements are less stringent than those imposed by the common law, and it is not clear if a person complying with the statutory requirements could nevertheless be held to be in breach of duty at common law. For instance, if a client instructs a firm performing both broking and jobbing functions to buy shares on his behalf, the firm's broking division might purchase them from the jobbing division. Such a transaction would be permitted by the legislation, but would involve a conflict of interest at common law[14].

This problem is not confined to the financial services sector: many professional organisations require their members to comply with rules of conduct which may reflect but not precisely correspond to the rule against conflict of interest. In a 1992 consultation paper the Law Commission therefore recommended a change in the law to enable a court considering a claim for breach of fiduciary duty in such a context to consider any relevant regulatory rules and the efforts made by the fiduciary to comply with them in determining the scope of the relevant fiduciary duty[15]. In its final report[16] the Commission recommended legislation which would protect a fiduciary from liability where it failed to provide information to a client or was unaware of a potential conflict of interest as a result of a Chinese wall maintained in order to comply with regulatory rules. However, this recommendation has not been implemented.

The Financial Services Act will be repealed by the Financial Services and Markets Act 2000, which, when implemented, will establish a new regulatory regime for financial services. The Act establishes a new Financial Services Agency, which has power to make rules and issue statements of principle, stating in general terms the behaviour required of persons carrying on financial services business, and codes of practice elaborating the statements of principle by providing examples of conduct permitted and prohibited by the statements. The agency has power to take action against persons who fail to act in accordance with any relevant statements of principle, as elaborated by the relevant code. A person who suffers loss as a result of a breach by an authorised person of an FSA rule may have a right to claim damages for such loss[17]. A failure to comply with a statement of principle will not of itself permit a customer to take action against any person[18]. It seems, however, that the Act's provisions are without prejudice to any other civil rights which the customer may have[19]. It therefore does not appear to address the question considered here, whether compliance with relevant statements of principle and codes of practice can provide a defence to a claim for breach of fiduciary duty. Generally, in cases arising out of the provision of professional or financial services, there will be a contract between the parties. Since it is now accepted that fiduciary duties can be modified by any relevant contract terms, it may be that, if the relevant contract expressly or impliedly requires compliance with relevant statements of principle and codes of practice, a court would conclude that the fiduciary duties owed are defined by the statement/code as reflected in the terms of the contract.

1 Lord Cranworth LC in *Aberdeen Rly Co v Blaikie Bros* (1854) 1 Macq 461 at 471, HL.
2 *Lucifero v Castell* (1887) 3 TLR 371; *Kimber v Barber* (1872) 8 Ch App 56, CA; *Armstrong v Jackson* [1917] 2 KB 822.
3 *de Bussche v Alt* (1878) 8 Ch D 286.
4 *McMaster v Byrne* [1952] 1 All ER 1362, PC.
5 (1877) 3 App Cas 254.
6 *Robinson v Mollett* (1875) LR 7 HL 802.
7 (1820) 8 Price 127.
8 *Burland v Earle* [1902] AC 83.
9 [1993] AC 205; see Brown (1993) 109 LQR 206; Reynolds [1994] JBL 147; see also *Clark Boyce v Mouat* [1994] 1 AC 428, [1993] 4 All ER 268.
10 Strictly, since estate agency is a unilateral contract, the Privy Council should have found an implied collateral contract: see above 6.1.1.
11 See *Prince Jefri Bolkiah v KPMG* [1999] 1 All ER 517 at 526.
12 See Nolan (1994) 53 CLJ 34.
13 See *Hippisley v Knee Bros* [1905] 1 KB 1, below 6.2.1.6.
14 The effectiveness of such arrangements was considered by the House of Lords in *Prince Jefri Bolkiah v KPMG* [1999] 1 All ER 517. Their Lordships seem to have accepted that an institutional Chinese wall may be sufficient at common law to prevent the risk of the transfer of confidential information between departments and thus prevent a conflict of interest arising, but found that on the facts of that case the erection of an ad hoc Chinese wall was insufficient to negate the risk of confidential information being abused: see 6.2.1.6.
15 Fiduciary Duties and Regulatory Rules, LCCP No 124 (1992).
16 Law Comm 236 *Fiduciary Duties and Regulatory Rules* (1995) para 16.7.
17 Section 150.
18 Section 64(8).
19 See Explanatory notes to the Act, para 145.

6.2.1.6 *The agent must not make a secret profit*

It is 'a broad principle of equity . . . that trustees or agents shall not retain a profit made in the course of or by means of their office'[1]. The rule is strictly applied. It applies even to unpaid agents[2]. It is irrelevant that the agent acted in complete good faith, that the principal suffered no loss, that the agent made a profit which the principal could not have made, or that the principal actually benefited from the agent's actions. 'The liability arises from the mere fact of a profit having, in the stated circumstances, been made'[3]. The stringency of the rule is illustrated by *Boardman v Phipps*[4], where two representatives (described as 'self-appointed agents') of a trust fund entered into negotiations, with the concurrence of the trustees, with a company in which the trust held shares. Using information acquired during those negotiations, and at considerable expense, they eventually acquired the majority of the shares in the company. The trust fund made a considerable profit on its shares as a result of their efforts; it had already turned down the suggestion that it should acquire the shares itself. Nevertheless, the representatives were held to be in breach of duty, and were required to hand over their profits to the trust fund. The duty may be breached where the agent uses the principal's property in order to make a profit. For instance, if P gives A money to spend on his behalf, and A invests it and receives interest, the interest is P's property[5]. Similarly, there is a breach if A uses confidential information which he acquires in the course of his agency duties in order to make a profit for himself[6]. Some decisions seem to regard such confidential information as property belonging to the principal, although it is not clear if this is correct. In *Boardman v Phipps* the members of the House of Lords disagreed on this point, and the better view now is that confidential information is not property. Nor is it clear if the duty not to use confidential information should be regarded as an incident of agency or as arising separately. A similar duty is imposed on other persons who acquire information in confidence, and the better explanation seems to be that the imparting of information in confidence itself gives rise to a fiduciary duty of loyalty on the confidee not to use the information for his own benefit. If the confidee does use the information he is treated as using it properly, for the benefit of the confider[7]. However, a duty to respect confidentiality will only be imposed where (a) the information has the 'necessary quality of confidence'[8] and (b) the information is imparted in circumstances importing an obligation of confidence[9]. Where the recipient of the information is an agent, the very existence of the agency relationship will satisfy the second requirement so that, provided that the information is itself of a confidential nature, the duty to respect the confidence will be imposed. The agent must therefore treat as confidential information relating to his principal received during the course of his agency even if it is not imparted in circumstances which would otherwise give rise to a duty of confidence.

It is clear that the duty to respect the confidentiality of information received during agency can continue beyond the termination of the agency[10]. Thus where an agent has acquired confidential information relating to his principal he may not subsequently use that information for his own benefit or for the benefit of other clients[11]. However, the duty only restricts the use of information which is properly regarded as confidential, and not in the 'public domain'. In an employment case, it was held that employees could not be prevented from using for their own benefit information which was readily available from public sources such as maps and telephone directories[12]. The duty ceases if information which was originally confidential comes into the public domain[13].

It seems that the agent's duty not to make a secret profit is not limited to cases where the profit is made by use of the principal's property or confidential information. The agent will be in breach if he makes a secret profit out of his position, even though no property or information is used. In *Hippisley v Knee Bros*[14], A was instructed to sell property for P. A placed advertisements on P's behalf, and received a discount on the price, but charged P with the full cost. A was in breach of duty in keeping the discounts[15].

An agent who makes a profit will be in breach of duty unless all the circumstances are revealed to the principal, and the principal consents to the agent retaining the profit. Where the agent breaches the duty, the principal may require him to account for the profit. The duty to account is personal. Where the profit is made by using the principal's property, it seems that the principal's rights are proprietary, so that the agent must hold the profit on constructive trust for the principal. The position in relation to profits made with information, or from use of position, is less clear. In *Boardman v Phipps* it was held that the agents held their profits on constructive trust[16]. The principal may also obtain an injunction to restrain his agent making further use of confidential information. However, the agent's duties arise in equity, and equity is sufficiently flexible to distinguish between agents acting fraudulently and those acting in good faith. In *Hippisley v Knee Bros* the court found that the agent had acted in good faith and so, although he was in breach of duty, he was allowed to keep his commission on the transaction. Similarly, in *Boardman v Phipps*, the agents were allowed some payment for their expenditure[17].

1   Wilberforce J in *Phipps v Boardman* [1964] 1 WLR 993 at 1010.
2   *Turnbull v Garden* (1869) 38 LJ Ch 331.
3   Lord Russell in *Regal (Hastings) Ltd v Gulliver* [1942] 1 All ER 378 at 386, HL.
4   [1967] 2 AC 46, [1966] 3 All ER 721, HL.
5   Special rules of conduct apply to solicitors and allow them to keep the interest made on clients' money in certain circumstances.
6   *Peter Pan Manufacturing Corpn v Corsets Silhouette Ltd* [1963] 3 All ER 402, [1964] 1 WLR 96.
7   Millett (1998) 114 LQR 214; *Arklow Investments Ltd v Maclean* [2000] 1 WLR 594.
8   Per Lord Greene MR in *Saltman v Campbell* (1948) 65 RPC 203 at 215.
9   Per Megarry J in *Coco v Clark* [1969] RPC 41 at 47.
10 *Industrial Development Consultants Ltd v Cooley* [1972] 1 WLR 443; *A-G v Blake* [1998] 1 All ER 833; *Prince Jefri Bolkiah v KPMG* [1999] 1 All ER 517.
11 In the case of agents such as solicitors and accountants involved in litigation the duty is particularly stringent and the court will grant an injunction to prevent them acting for a client with a contrary interest to the former client unless satisfied on clear and convincing evidence that there is no risk of the disclosure of confidential information to the detriment of the former client: see *Prince Jefri Bolkiah v KPMG* [1999] 1 All ER 517.
12 *Faccenda Chicken Ltd v Fowler* [1985] 1 All ER 724; affd [1987] Ch 117, [1986] 1 All ER 617.
13 *A-G v Blake* [1998] 1 All ER 833.
14 [1905] 1 KB 1.
15 See also *Stewart Chartering Ltd v Owners of the Ship Peppy* [1997] 2 Lloyd's Rep 722.
16 The decision is criticised in Goff and Jones, *The Law of Restitution* (5th edn, 1998) p 736.
17 See also *Kelly v Cooper* [1993] AC 205; *Stewart Chartering Ltd v Owners of the Ship Peppy* [1997] 2 Lloyd's Rep 722. Contrast *Guinness plc v Saunders* [1990] 2 AC 663; *Estate Realties Ltd v Wignall (No 2)* [1992] 2 NZLR 615.

6.2.1.7   *The agent must not take a bribe*

A bribe is a particular form of secret profit: 'a commission or other inducement which is given by a third party to an agent as such, and which is secret from his principal'[1]. In this context, 'bribe' may not necessarily indicate corruption. Where A deals with T on P's behalf, a bribe is any payment made by T to A, where T knows that A is P's agent and the payment is kept secret from P[2]. The law takes a particularly dim view of such payments: 'Bribery is an evil practice which threatens the foundations of any civilised society'[3] and therefore gives P a wide range of rights against both T and A:

(a) P may dismiss A without notice.
(b) P may refuse to pay any commission due to A, or recover commission paid before discovering the bribe.
(c) P may rescind the contract with T.

(d) P may claim damages in the tort of deceit for any loss caused by the bribe. T and A are jointly and severally liable for such damages.

(e) P may claim the amount of the bribe as money had and received from either T or A[4].

In *Lister v Stubbs* it was held that the principal's claim to recover the amount of the bribe was a purely personal, not a proprietary claim, so that the bribe was not held on trust[5]. As noted above, an agent who makes a secret profit from his position or by using his principal's property generally holds the profit on constructive trust for his principal. The rule in *Lister* was therefore often criticised as allowing the agent to retain any profits made with the bribe and thus treating a dishonest agent more leniently than an honest one[6] and in *A-G for Hong Kong v Reid*[7] the Privy Council, having reconsidered the position, held that *Lister* was wrongly decided and should no longer be followed. Instead, it should be recognised that the agent holds the amount of any bribe paid to him on constructive trust for the principal so that the principal is entitled to claim the proceeds of the bribe and any profits made with it. The constructive trust arises automatically, by operation of law, as soon as the bribe is received by the agent. This approach was justified on the grounds that the agent should not be entitled to profit from his position, the bribe was money which should have been paid to the principal immediately on its receipt and, since equity looks on as done that which ought to be done, the bribe should therefore be regarded as the principal's property in equity from the time of its receipt. However, whilst the decision in *Reid* may be applauded as providing a powerful remedy against corruption, the reasoning in the case is open to question[8]. Moreover, one effect of the decision is that where the agent is insolvent the principal's claim to the proceeds of the bribe will take priority over those of other creditors. According to the Privy Council, the agent's creditors can be in no better position than the agent. However, this fails to address the difficult policy question who should have priority in such a case[9]. It has been suggested that the result could be avoided: a personal duty to account could extend to the proceeds of the bribe[10] leaving a constructive trust to be imposed by the court as a remedy when it is just to do so[11]. Since *Reid* is a decision of the Privy Council, the matter cannot be taken as finally settled and further explanation of the law may be required.

Where the principal makes a restitutionary claim for the amount of the bribe, there is no need to prove it caused him any loss. Where the agent who is bribed buys property on behalf of the principal, it is presumed that the price charged to the principal is increased by the amount of the bribe[12]; where the agent sells the principal's property, the bribe can be regarded as money which ought to have been paid to the principal as part of the price[13]. In contrast, a claim for damages in deceit depends on P proving that he has suffered a loss as a result of the bribe. In *Salford Corpn v Lever*[14] the Court of Appeal held that the principal of a bribed agent could claim damages and the amount of the bribe. However, in *Mahesan v Malaysian Government Officers' Co-operative Housing Society Ltd*[15] the Privy Council doubted *Lever* and held that the principal must elect between the two remedies. Whilst double recovery might have the desirable effect of discouraging corruption, it would allow the principal a windfall profit. However, it is clear that the other remedies are cumulative: P may therefore, for instance, rescind the contract with T and keep the amount of the bribe[16].

In addition, the payment of a bribe may give rise to criminal liability. If it can be shown that the bribe was paid or received with a corrupt motive, the briber or agent will be guilty of an offence under the Prevention of Corruption Act 1916[17].

1   Per Leggatt J in *Anangel Atlas Compania Naviera SA v Ishikawajima-Harima Heavy Industries Ltd* [1990] 1 Lloyd's Rep 167 at 171.
2   *Industries and General Mortgage Co Ltd v Lewis* [1949] 2 All ER 573.
3   Per Lord Templeman in *A-G for Hong Kong v Reid* [1994] 1 AC 324 at 330; [1994] 1 All ER 1 at 5.
4   See *Arab Monetary Fund v Hashim* [1993] 1 Lloyd's Rep 543 at 564.
5   *Lister & Co v Stubbs* (1890) 45 Ch D 1, CA; and see *A-G's Reference (No 1 of 1985)* [1986] QB 491, [1986] 2 All ER 219.
6   See Goff and Jones, *The Law of Restitution* (5th edn, 1998) p 740ff; Sir Peter Millett, 'Bribes and Secret Commissions' [1993] RLR 7. Contrast Goode, 'Property and Unjust Enrichment' in Burrows, *Essays on the Law of Restitution* (1991) p 215; 'Recovery of a Director's Improper Gains' in McKendrick, *Commercial Aspects of Trusts and Fiduciary Obligations* (1992) p 137.
7   [1994] 1 AC 324, [1994] 1 All ER 1.
8   See Pearce [1994] LMCLQ 189; Oakley (1994) 53 CLJ 31.
9   See Allen (1995) 58 MLR 87.
10 Goode, 'Ownership and Obligation in Commercial Transactions' (1987) 103 LQR 433 at 441–445; Birks, *An Introduction to the Law of Restitution* (1985) p 387.
11 Allen (1995) 58 MLR 87.
12 *Industries and General Mortgage Co Ltd v Lewis* [1949] 2 All ER 573.
13 But the principal is not obliged to treat it as part of the price: *Logicrose Ltd v Southend Utd Football Club Ltd* [1988] 1 WLR 1256.
14 [1891] 1 QB 168.
15 [1979] AC 374, [1978] 2 All ER 405; see Tettenborn (1978) 94 LQR 344.
16 *Logicrose Ltd v Southend Utd Football Club Ltd* [1988] 1 WLR 1256.
17 Section 1.

6.2.1.8   *The duty to account*

As a fiduciary an agent has a duty to account to his principal for all property of the principal in his possession, whether received from the principal or from a third party for the principal's account.

The duty to account is a personal one. An agent is not normally a trustee of the principal's property. This will be important if the agent should become insolvent having received property from his principal or for the principal's account. In such a case the principal may try to establish that the agent holds the property in question on trust for him in order to secure priority over other creditors of the agent. The existence of a trust will depend on the intention of the parties. In assessing the parties' intentions the court will take account of the terms of any agreement between them and all the circumstances of the case, and in a commercial context, especially where the agent is appointed to act on a continuing basis over a period of time, the facts may show that the parties anticipated that the agent should be free to use money received in his own business and account to the principal from time to time as a debtor[1]. So no trust was created where the parties' agreement expressly disclaimed any intention to create a trust[2]. Similarly, where an agent sold goods on behalf of several principals on terms which permitted it to mix their goods prior to sale so that it was impossible to connect any particular sale with any particular principal, the agent received payments for the goods on its own account, not as trustee for its principals, with whom it had merely a debtor-creditor relationship[3].

In recent years it has become common for goods to be sold on terms under which they remain the seller's property until paid for. The aim of such terms is to protect the seller against the buyer becoming insolvent without paying for goods delivered. If the goods are resold, the seller may try to claim the proceeds of sale and in order to try and establish such a claim, many contracts seek to make the buyer the seller's 'agent'. However, it is clear that in many cases a requirement to act as a fiduciary would stultify the real commercial intentions of the parties and a court may well look to the commercial reality in such a case[4] and infer that the true intention of the parties was that the buyer/agent would not hold money as a fiduciary, but should be merely a debtor of the principal/seller.

The fact that the agent is entitled to mix property received for his principal with his own will be evidence that the parties did not intend to create a trust. Conversely, if the agent does hold property on trust for his principal, he will be required to keep it separate from his own. If he mixes his own property with that of his principal, the principal is entitled to the whole of the mixed fund, unless the agent can identify any part of it as his own property[5]. Moreover, if the agent disposes of the principal's property, the principal may be able to trace his property into and claim any identifiable replacement item which represents it.

An agent who holds or receives money on behalf of his principal must pay it over to the principal on demand, even if it is claimed by some third party, unless he knows that the third party's claim is well founded[6]. An agent is estopped from claiming that a third party has a better right than his principal to money which he holds as agent for his principal.

As part of the duty to account, the agent must keep full and accurate records of all transactions entered into for the principal's benefit, and make them available for inspection by his principal. If he fails to do so, a court may feel 'compelled to . . . presume everything most unfavourable to him'[7]. This duty:

> 'arises by reason of the fact that the agent has been entrusted with the authority to bind the principal to transactions with third parties and the principal is entitled to know what his personal contractual rights and duties are in relation to those third parties as well as what he is entitled to receive by way of payment from the agent. He is entitled to be provided with those records because they have been created for preserving information as to the very transactions which the agent was authorised by him to enter into. Being the participant in the transactions, the principal is entitled to the records of them'[8].

The duty arises independently of any contract between principal and agent. If there is such a contract, it may modify the duty, but clear words are needed. Moreover, since the duty arises independently of contract it may, in the absence of any contrary stipulation in the contract, survive termination of both the agency and any contract between principal and agent so that the principal may continue to be entitled to inspect the agent's records even after such termination[9]. On termination of the agency, the agent must also deliver up to the principal all books, accounts, documents and papers given to him by the principal, or prepared for use in the course of the agency relationship, unless he is entitled to exercise a lien over them.

If the agent is instructed to purchase land on behalf of the principal, and does so in his own name, he holds the property on trust for the principal.

1 See *Neste Oy v Lloyds Bank plc* [1983] 2 Lloyd's Rep 658; *Kingscroft Insurance Co Ltd v H S Weavers (Underwriting) Agencies Ltd* [1993] 1 Lloyd's Rep 187 at 191; *Triffit Nurseries v Salads Etc Ltd* [2000] 1 All ER (Comm) 737.
2 *Re Japan Leasing (Europe) plc* [1999] BPIR 911.
3 *Triffit Nurseries v Salads Etc Ltd* [2000] 1 All ER (Comm) 737.
4 See below, 18.4.5.
5 *Lupton v White* (1808) 15 Ves 432.
6 Per Edmund Davies LJ in *Carl-Zeiss Stiftung v Herbert Smith & Co (No 2)* [1969] 2 All ER 367 at 384.
7 Romilly MR in *Gray v Haig* (1855) 20 Beav 219.
8 Per Colman J in *Yasuda Fire and Marine Insurance Company of Europe Ltd v Orion Marine Insurance Underwriting Agency Ltd* [1995] 3 All ER 211 at 219.

9   Yasuda Fire and Marine Insurance Company of Europe Ltd v Orion Marine Insurance Underwriting Agency Ltd [1995] 3 All ER 211 at 219.

6.2.2   Agent's duties under the Commercial Agents (Council Directive) Regulations 1993

The 1993 regulations impose a general duty on commercial agents to look after the interests of their principals and act dutifully and in good faith[1]. In particular, they require the agent to 'make proper efforts' to negotiate or conclude, as appropriate, transactions he is instructed to handle, to communicate to the principal 'all the necessary information available to him' and to comply with the principal's reasonable instructions[2]. This seems to add little, if anything, to the duties imposed on an agent by the fiduciary nature of the agency. However, the decision in *Kelly v Cooper*[3] seems to permit contractual restriction of the agent's fiduciary duties at common law. In contrast, where the regulations apply the parties may not derogate from these duties[4]. Nevertheless, the terms of the agency agreement will obviously be relevant in determining the precise requirements of the duties imposed by the regulations, such as the meaning of 'proper efforts' or 'necessary information'.

1   Regulation 3(1).
2   Regulation 3(2).
3   [1993] AC 205, above 6.2.1.5.
4   Regulation 5.

6.3   Termination of agency

Since the relationship between principal and agent depends on consent, withdrawal of consent by either party will terminate the relationship and, with it, the agent's actual authority to bind the principal. In certain circumstances the agent's authority may also be terminated automatically by operation of law. However, termination of the relationship may give rise to secondary liabilities or obligations. Furthermore, the agent may still have power to affect the principal's position vis-à-vis third parties even after termination of his actual authority. In certain situations the right to terminate the relationship is itself restricted. We must therefore consider the ways in which the relationship may be terminated, and the effects of termination on both the relationship between principal and agent and on their relationships with third parties.

6.3.1   Termination of the relationship between principal and agent

At common law an agency may be terminated by mutual consent, by operation of law or by the unilateral act of either party. However, certain agencies are irrevocable at common law.

6.3.1.1   Termination by the parties

In any case of agency the parties may agree to terminate the relationship at any time. Such agreement is effective to terminate the agent's authority and, if the agency is contractual, will discharge the contract by agreement so that there can be no question of liability for breach of contract. Where the agent is appointed for a fixed period of time, or to perform a specified task – for example, to sell a named ship, or to make arrangements for the loading of a consignment of goods for export – the relationship, and the agent's authority, are determined at the expiry of the stated period or on completion of the allotted task. If the agency is contractual, the agent will be entitled to commission in accordance with the terms of the contract.

The position is more difficult where one party seeks to terminate the relationship unilaterally. A distinction must be drawn between the effect of such termination on the agency and the effect on any contract between the parties. It is clear that the principal may revoke, or the agent renounce, the agent's authority at any time and such revocation/renunciation will be effective to terminate the agent's authority and the agency relationship, even if it is in breach of contract. The effect on the contract will depend on general contractual principles. It may, therefore, result in liability for breach of contract, at common law. Termination by the principal may also result in liability to pay the agent compensation or indemnity under the Commercial Agents (Council Directive) Regulations 1993. Where the agent is an employee, unilateral termination by the employer may also give rise to a claim for compensation for unfair dismissal or for a redundancy payment.

Where A is appointed for a fixed term, eg 'to sell P's products in the UK for six years', termination by either party before expiry of the term will be a repudiatory breach of the contract, unless justified by a prior breach by the other party[1]. Where A is appointed for an indefinite term, the right to terminate depends on the terms of the contract. If the contract provides for termination by notice, either party may terminate by giving notice in accordance with the contract. In the absence of an express provision for termination by notice, the court may imply a term allowing the contract to be terminated by reasonable notice. What is reasonable will depend on the facts of the individual case. In *Martin Baker Aircraft Co Ltd v Canadian Flight Equipment Ltd*[2]. A agreed to act as sole agent for the sale of P's products, to be paid by commission. In return he agreed to spend time and money promoting P's products and not to sell competing products. It was held that the contract was terminable on 12 months' notice.

Where the Commercial Agents (Council Directive) Regulations 1993 apply, they stipulate minimum periods of notice which must be given to terminate the agency. At least one month's notice is required during the first year, two months' notice in the second and three months' thereafter[3]. The agreement may provide for longer notice provided that the length of notice to be given by the agent may not exceed that to be given to him. Presumably, where the contract does not expressly fix a notice period a court could still find an implied term requiring reasonable notice, exceeding the minimum periods prescribed by the regulations. Termination by either party without giving the notice required by the contract will be a repudiatory breach of contract at common law, unless justified by a prior breach of contract by the other party.

The general rule at common law is that repudiation of a contract by one party has no effect unless accepted by the other.

> '. . . repudiation by one party standing alone does not terminate the contract. It takes two to end it, by repudiation, on the one side, and acceptance of the repudiation, on the other'[4].

There are dicta which suggest that contracts of employment, and other contracts for personal services, such as contracts of agency, are an exception to this general rule, so that summary dismissal of an agent by his principal automatically ends the agency contract without the need for acceptance by the agent[5]. However, the better view now is that there is no such exception and that the normal contract rule applies to contracts of employment[6] and agency[7], with the result that a repudiation of the contract by one party will only end the contract, as a matter of law, if accepted by the other. Suppose, therefore, that P appoints A to act as his agent for a period of three years but then purports to dismiss him after six months. Unless A has been guilty of a repudiatory breach of contract justifying his dismissal, P's act amounts to a repudiation of contract. As a matter of law A may choose whether or not to accept the repudiation. If he does so, the contract is terminated. If not, it remains in force and binding on both parties. However, it has been recognised that a dismissed employee will generally have no practical alternative but to accept his employer's repudiation, and it is submitted that the same will generally be true of an agent dismissed in breach of contract. He will generally be unable to perform his contract without P's co-operation. The court will generally not order specific performance of a contract for personal services, such as agency. Moreover, since dismissal terminates A's authority to act for P, if he continues to act he will be in breach of his warranty of authority. His only claim against P will therefore be one for damages for breach of contract, in which he will be required to mitigate his loss. If A seeks an alternative agency in order to mitigate, he will generally have to terminate his agency with P, since to take another agency will often be a breach of his fiduciary duty to P and/or to his new principal. The net result, therefore, will be that A is generally advised to accept P's repudiation and thus put an end to the contract. It is worth noting, however, that where P dismisses A in breach of contract, as a matter of common law, it is A who terminates the contract by accepting P's repudiation. Similarly, if A resigns in breach of contract, P terminates by accepting his resignation.

Where the contract is covered by the 1993 Commercial Agents Regulation the regulations[8], and directive[9], provide that the parties may not agree on shorter periods of notice than those prescribed. It might be argued that, since the objective of the regulations and directive is the protection of the agent, dismissal with less than the required minimum period of notice should be ineffective. If accepted, this would mean that where the principal gives less than the minimum period of notice the agency would continue in force at least for that period and the agent would therefore be entitled to commission for that period. However, that argument was rejected in the Scottish case of *Roy v MR Pearlman*[10]. The contract in that case provided for either party to terminate by giving six months' notice. P purported to terminate the contract summarily. It was held that, on the facts of the case, A had accepted P's repudiation, bringing the contract to an end. Neither the regulations nor the directive prescribe any remedy for failure to give the required minimum notice and Lord Hamilton, the Lord Ordinary, concluded that the consequences of failure to give proper notice depended on domestic law. Failure to give the notice required therefore gave rise to a claim for damages for breach of contract but, since A had accepted the repudiation, the contract was terminated. This appears to be correct. The minimum periods prescribed also apply to the notice to be given *by* the agent. It would be surprising if the agent could purport to resign without proper notice but then argue that his resignation was ineffective and claim commission for the period of notice he should have given.

Where an agent is appointed on a commission basis to perform a single task, the contract may be interpreted as a unilateral one. In that case the principal may be entitled to withdraw the offer of commission and terminate the agency at any stage before the agent has performed the specified task. This is the normal interpretation of estate agency contracts, in the absence of express provisions to the contrary[11]. However, in certain cases a term, or a collateral contract, may be implied to restrict the principal's freedom to revoke the offer[12]. If the contract is unilateral, the agent is under no commitment to act and can withdraw at any stage.

Where one party makes it impossible for himself to perform his contract he will normally be treated as repudiating the contract. This gives rise to difficult questions where P ceases business, wholly or in part, before expiry of the agency, or without giving notice to terminate it. Such cessation will amount to a repudiation of the contract unless permitted by the agency agreement. Each case will therefore depend on the proper construction of the agency agreement. In *Rhodes v Forwood*[13] P owned a colliery and appointed A to act as agent to sell coal from the colliery in Liverpool for seven years or so long as A carried on business in Liverpool. After four years P sold the colliery and A's authority therefore terminated. A claimed damages for breach of contract but failed. The court refused to imply a term that P would stay in business for the full period of the agreement. In general, the courts are reluctant to imply terms into agency agreements which would restrict a principal's freedom to deal as he pleases with his property. In contrast, in *Turner v Goldsmith*[14] P appointed A for five years to sell shirts or other goods manufactured or sold by P. P's shirt factory burned down and P terminated the agency. A's claim for damages for breach of contract succeeded: P could manufacture other goods, or could send A shirts manufactured by someone else.

1 It is not necessary that the party terminating the contract should be aware of the breach at the time of termination: *Boston Deep Sea Fishing and Ice Co v Ansell* (1888) 39 Ch D 339, CA.
2 [1955] 2 QB 556, [1955] 2 All ER 722.
3 Regulation 15.
4 Viscount Simon LC in *Heyman v Darwins Ltd* [1942] AC 356 at 361, [1942] 1 All ER 337 at 341. See generally 2.9.3.
5 See eg *Vine v National Dock Labour Board* [1957] AC 488, [1956] 3 All ER 939; *Denmark Productions Ltd v Boscobel Productions Ltd* [1969] 1 QB 699, [1968] 3 All ER 513.
6 *Decro-Wall International SA v Practitioners in Marketing Ltd* [1971] 2 All ER 216, [1971] 1 WLR 361; *Marshall (Thomas) (Exports) Ltd v Guinle* [1979] Ch 227, [1978] 3 All ER 193; *Gunton v Richmond-upon-Thames London Borough Council* [1981] Ch 448, [1980] 3 All ER 577. The point is not definitely settled: see the dissenting view of Shaw LJ in *Gunton v Richmond-upon-Thames London Borough Council* and see *Boyo v Lambeth London BC* [1994] ICR 727.
7 *Atlantic Underwriting Agencies Ltd v Compagnia di Assicurazione di Milano SpA* [1979] 2 Lloyd's Rep 240.
8 Regulation 15(2).
9 Article 15.2.
10 [1999] CLR 36.
11 See 6.1.1.1.
12 See *Alpha Trading Ltd v Dunnshaw-Patten* [1981] QB 290, [1981] 1 All ER 482, CA, above 6.1.1.1.
13 (1876) 1 App Cas 256, HL.
14 [1891] 1 QB 544, CA.

6.3.1.2 *Termination by operation of law*

Certain events terminate an agent's authority automatically. In general they will also operate to terminate any contract of agency.

1. *Frustration.* An agency agreement may be frustrated in any of the ways in which contracts generally may be frustrated. Thus if the performance of the agency becomes illegal or impossible, the agency is frustrated, and both the agent's authority and the contract of agency will be terminated.

2. *Death.* The death of either party will terminate the agency and any contract between them. If the principal dies, the agent does not even have apparent authority to bind the principal's estate; and the same rule applies if the principal is a company which is wound up.
3. *Insanity.* If either party becomes insane, the relationship is terminated. However, there is now provision for an agent to be appointed under an enduring power of attorney which may remain effective despite the insanity of the principal[1].
4. *Bankruptcy.* Bankruptcy of the principal determines his capacity to deal with any property affected by the bankruptcy and so terminates the authority of any agent to deal with such property. The appointment of a provisional liquidator of a company has been held to determine the authority of agents appointed by the directors to act for the company on the grounds that it determines the authority of the directors to act on behalf of the company[2]. In contrast, a cessation of business by the principal does not of itself bring the agency to an end, although it may amount to a repudiation of the agency if it makes it impossible for the principal to perform[3]. The bankruptcy of the agent will also terminate the agency if it makes him unfit to continue to act.

1   Enduring Powers of Attorney Act 1985: see Fridman, *Law of Agency* (7th edn, 1996) pp 408-410.
2   *Pacific and General Insurance Co Ltd v Hazell* [1997] BCC 400.
3   *Triffit Nurseries v Salads Etc Ltd* [1999] 1 All ER (Comm) 110; affd [2000] 1 All ER (Comm) 737.

6.3.1.3 *Irrevocable agencies*[1]

Although at common law unilateral revocation of authority by the principal is effective to terminate A's authority, in two situations the agent's authority may be irrevocable. In these cases A's authority cannot be revoked by unilateral act of P or by P's insanity, death or bankruptcy.

First, the agent's authority is irrevocable where the agent has authority coupled with an interest, as for instance where P owes A money, and appoints A to act as his agent to sell property and realise funds to pay the debt. However, this rule only applies where A had an interest at the time the authority was granted: an interest which arises after the grant of authority does not make the authority irrevocable.

Secondly, if a power of attorney is expressed to be irrevocable and is given to secure a proprietary interest of, or some obligation owed to, the donee, it may not be revoked without the consent of the donee[2].

1   See Reynolds in Cranston (ed), *Making Commercial Law: Essays in Honour of Roy Goode* (1997).
2   Powers of Attorney Act 1971, s 4.

6.3.2 *Rights of the parties on termination*

On termination of the agency relationship it may be necessary to consider the rights of principal and agent against each other. At common law their rights depend on the construction of the contract and application of general rules of contract law. A commercial agent is entitled to considerably enhanced rights under the Commercial Agents (Council Directive) Regulations 1993.

6.3.2.1 *Rights at common law*

Termination of agency does not affect accrued rights and obligations. Thus the agent is entitled to be paid any commission earned prior to termination; this may include commission on transactions negotiated before but entered into after termination of the agency.

In cases of contractual agency, renunciation of authority by the agent, or revocation by the principal, in breach of contract will be a repudiation of the contract, unless justified by a prior repudiation by the other party. The party in breach will then be liable for damages. Where P dismisses A in breach of contract, A may claim damages representing the commission he would have earned had the contract been performed, for instance by P giving proper notice. Repudiation will only terminate the contract of agency if accepted by the other party. However, since the agency contract is personal, the court will normally not order specific performance, nor grant an injunction which would force the parties to continue their relationship[1], and although there are signs in recent cases concerned with contracts of employment that this rule is less strictly applied than formerly, in most cases the only practical course open to a dismissed agent will be to claim damages[2].

1 *Warren v Mendy* [1989] 3 All ER 103, [1989] 1 WLR 853, CA.
2 See above 6.3.1.1.

6.3.2.2 *Rights under the Commercial Agents (Council Directive) Regulations 1993*

Where the 1993 Regulations apply, the agent is in certain circumstances entitled to commission on transactions entered into after termination of the agency[1]. Where an agency is terminated and a new agent appointed, this could result in commission being payable to two agents; however, the regulations provide for commission to be payable to the first agent in preference to the second 'unless it is equitable because of the circumstances for the commission to be shared' between the agents[2].

At common law an agent will be entitled to damages if the agency is terminated as a result of a breach by the principal, including where the principal repudiates the contract by dismissing the agent in breach of contract and the agent accepts that repudiation. The regulations introduced a system of 'no-fault' compensation under which, in the event of termination of the agency, the agent is entitled to receive a payment in compensation for loss of his agency regardless of whether the principal is in breach of contract. The Commercial Agents Directive[3] requires that on termination of an agency contract the agent should be entitled to either an 'indemnity' or 'compensation'. The payment referred to as 'indemnity' is based on German law. 'Compensation' is based on French law. Although the systems differ somewhat in their application, they share a common basis in that both recognise that the agent has a quasi-property interest in his agency, for loss of which he should be compensated on its termination.

The intention was undoubtedly that member states, when implementing the directive, should opt for either 'indemnity' or 'compensation'. We may note, in passing, that by providing this choice the directive undermines its own objective of harmonisation[4]. In fact, most member states have opted for the 'indemnity' system. The UK regulations, however, provide for both and effectively leave the choice to the parties. Regulation 17 provides for the agent to be paid compensation unless the contract expressly provides for payment of an indemnity[5].

The choice of 'indemnity' and 'compensation' as names for the two systems is perhaps misleading. Both differ significantly from common law damages, and may be payable where damages would not be. First, it is expressly stated that both indemnity and compensation are payable where the agency is terminated by the agent's death[6]. Regulation 18 then states that neither indemnity nor compensation is to be payable (i) where the contract is terminated by the principal because of default by the agent which would justify immediate termination, (ii) in any case where the agent terminates the agreement, unless termination is justified by 'circumstances attributable to the principal' or where on grounds of age, infirmity or illness the agent cannot reasonably be required to continue his activities, or (iii) where, with the principal's consent, the agent assigns his rights and obligations under the contract[7]. It is expressly stated[8] that nothing in the regulations or directive affects any rule of domestic law which provides for immediate termination of an agency contract because of the failure of either party to perform his obligations thereunder. It follows, therefore, that the right of either party to end the contract without notice in response to a repudiation by the other depends on ordinary common law principles. Thus if P dismisses A on grounds of a serious or repudiatory breach by A, no compensation or indemnity is payable. Conversely, if A resigns, he loses his right to compensation or indemnity unless his resignation is justified on one of the grounds listed in reg 18. The reference to 'circumstances attributable to the principal' would include cases where the agent resigns due to the principal's repudiatory breach of contract, in which case damages would be payable at common law, but it could be interpreted as extending more widely to circumstances not amounting to repudiatory breach and this seems more likely since there is no requirement for the resignation to be in circumstances where 'immediate termination' would be 'justified'. It should be noted that, unlike common law damages, compensation or indemnity may be payable where the contract is terminated by the principal giving proper notice, unless the principal would have been justified in dismissing without notice because of the agent's breach.

It is not clear if payment is due where the contract is for a fixed term which expires. On the one hand, payment is due where the contract is 'terminated' and both the regulations and directive seem to differentiate between 'expiry' and 'termination'. It would be surprising if compensation or indemnity were payable where a fixed term contract expires but is renewed. On the other hand, if no payment is due on expiry, a principal might avoid liability to pay compensation or indemnity by entering into a series of short, fixed term contracts and, in the event of wishing to dismiss the agent, allowing the contract to expire without renewal[9]. The better view would therefore seem to be that payment is due where a fixed term contract expires without renewal. In *Moore v Piretta PTA Ltd*[10] it was held that the reference to 'termination of the agency contract' in reg 17(1) should be read as 'termination of the agency *relationship*', which would mean that no compensation would be payable where a fixed term expires but is renewed so that the relationship continues.

The parties may not derogate from the indemnity and compensation provisions to the detriment of the agent before the contract expires[11]. There is nothing to prevent them doing so after termination of the contract, so that agreements to settle claims for compensation or indemnity will be valid. However, the agent will lose his right to compensation or indemnity under the regulations unless he notifies the principal of his intention to pursue a claim within a year of termination of the agency[12].

Where the agency contract provides for payment of an indemnity, the regulations provide that the agent shall be entitled to an indemnity 'if and to the extent that –

'(a) he has brought the principal new customers or has significantly increased the volume of business with existing customers and the principal continues to derive substantial benefits from the business with such customers; and
(b) the payment of this indemnity is equitable having regard to all the circumstances, and, in particular, the commission lost by the . . . agent on . . . business . . . with such customers'[13].

The maximum amount of any indemnity payable is an amount equivalent to one year's commission based on the agent's average commission over the last five years[14]. The application of these provisions was considered in *Moore v Piretta*. The judge, having considered the operation of the rules of German law on which the directive was based, concluded that calculation of the indemnity involved a three stage process. It should be noted that no payment is due at all unless the agent has brought in new business. The first stage is therefore to calculate the value to the principal of the business from customers introduced by the agent during the agency. The judge held that he was entitled to take into account business introduced by the agent during the whole period of the agency relationship, and not merely under the contract which had been terminated. That sum was then to be reduced by such sum as was equitable in all the circumstances of the case. On this basis the judge took into account the net amount of commission the agent would have earned, after deduction of the expenses of earning it, and made a deduction on account of accelerated receipt. He held, however, that there is no duty on the agent to mitigate his loss when claiming indemnity. No account is taken of any earnings of the agent from any new position. The third and final stage is to apply the one year maximum. On the facts of *Moore* the amount payable was in excess of £64,000.

The principal in *Moore* had terminated the contract by giving notice and was therefore not in breach of contract. However, if the principal is in breach a greater sum may be recoverable. Regulation 17(5) expressly provides that payment of an indemnity shall not prevent the agent claiming damages. Since indemnity and damages compensate different types of loss, there is no overlap between the two, so that where the agent is dismissed without notice he may claim for both damages and indemnity.

Where the contract does not expressly provide for payment of an indemnity the regulations provide that the agent is to be entitled to compensation for 'the damage he suffers as a result of termination', and state that he is deemed to suffer such damage 'particularly' where termination takes place in circumstances which either:

'(i) deprive him of commission 'which proper performance of the agency contract would have procured for him', while providing the principal with substantial benefits linked to the agent's activities; or
(ii) prevent the agent recouping the costs and expenses incurred in performing his duties'[15].

The use of 'compensation' and 'damage' may suggest that this is similar to common law damages. This is misleading. The concept of 'compensation' in the directive is based on a French law concept which is quite unlike damages for breach of contract. The courts have now considered the compensation provisions in several cases and, on the whole, have recognised their origins. In *Page v Combined Shipping & Trading Co Ltd*[16] the parties had entered into a four-year contract the terms of which effectively allowed P to control the amount of business handled by A and therefore the amount of commission A would earn. After six months P closed down part of its business and A terminated the contract and claimed compensation. P argued that since the contract allowed it to control the amount of commission A could earn, A had not been deprived of commission which 'proper performance' of the contract would have produced. The Court of Appeal rejected this interpretation. Taking account of the directive's objective of protecting agents, and the different language texts of the directive, they concluded that 'proper' should be read as indicating 'normal', or the type of performance the parties might have expected. Significantly, Millett LJ also referred to the principal's obligation under the regulations to act in good faith as a factor relevant to the construction of what would be 'proper performance' of the contract.

Neither the regulations nor the directive offer any guidance as to how compensation is to be calculated. However, guidance is provided by the practice of the French courts. French law treats the agency as being a 'quasi partnership' for the common interest of principal and agent[17]. Both benefit from their joint efforts, so that on termination the agent, who ceases to benefit from the trade connection he has established, is entitled to be compensated for the loss of his share of the business. In effect, he is paid a sum as if for the purchase of his share. There is therefore no need for the agent to prove loss, and no duty to mitigate his loss. The practice of the French courts is, apparently, to award a sum equal to two years' average commission. In *King v Tunnock Ltd*[18] a long established agency was terminated when P decided to close the relevant part of its business. P therefore derived no benefit from A's past efforts after termination of the agency. It was held, however, that this had no effect on the compensation payable. The circumstances listed in reg 17 when damage is 'particularly' deemed to occur were not exclusive so that it was not fatal to A's claim that P would not continue to enjoy 'substantial benefits' from A's activities. The court therefore awarded the agent a sum equal to two years' commission[19].

The relationship between compensation and common law damages is not dealt with in the regulations. It is submitted, however, that compensation, like indemnity, represents a payment for loss of the agent's interest so that there is no overlap between the two. Thus where A is dismissed in breach of contract both damages and compensation may be recoverable: damages to compensate A for the commission he would have earned had the contract been performed and compensation for the loss of his interest in the agency[20]. In *Duffen v FRABo Spa*[21] the contract provided for A to be paid £100,000 on termination of the contract. The Court of Appeal held this unenforceable as a penalty but held that A was nevertheless entitled to bring a claim for compensation under the regulations. This seems to be based on a misunderstanding of the regulations. Although the parties may not derogate from the rights to compensation or indemnity to the detriment of the agent, there would seem to be nothing to prevent them varying the statutory rules to the agent's benefit by agreeing that a greater sum should be payable by way of indemnity or compensation than would be payable under the regulations, and since neither indemnity nor compensation represents damages for breach of contract the rule against penalties should have no impact on such a provision.

1   Regulation 8.
2   Regulation 9.

3   86/653/EEC, art 17.
4   The operation of the compensation/indemnity provisions was reviewed by the Commission in a
    1996 report: Com (96) 364.
5   Regulation 17(2).
6   Regulation 17(8).
7   Regulation 18.
8   Regulation 16, art 16.
9   See *Bowstead and Reynolds on Agency* (16th edn, 1996) para 11-040.
10 [1999] 1 All ER 174.
11 Regulation 19.
12 Regulation 17(9). Notification need not be in any particular form, so long as it clearly indicates
    the agent's intention to pursue a claim under the regulations: *Hackett v Advanced Medical Computer
    Systems Ltd* [1999] CLC 160.
13 Regulation 17(3).
14 Regulation 17(4).
15 Regulation 17(7).
16 [1997] 3 All ER 656.
17 See Saintier [1997] JBL 77; (1999) 20 Co Law 149.
18 [2000] IRLR 569.
19 In *Duffen v FRABo SpA (No 2)* [2000] 1 Lloyd's Rep 180, Judge Hallgarten refused to follow the
    French practice and awarded the agent no compensation. On the facts the agent had brought
    the principal no new business. The agent was entitled to substantial sums under the terms of the
    agency agreement which enabled him to recoup his costs and expenses connected with the agency.
20 See *King v Tunnock* [2000] IRLR 569.
21 (1998) 17 Tr LR 460.

6.3.2.3   *Restraint of trade*

A principal may wish to restrain the activities of his former agent after termination
of the agency, for instance, to prevent him using information or customer contacts
acquired during the agency to compete with the principal. At common law any
clause in the agency contract which seeks to restrict the agent's activities after
termination would be valid only if it could be shown not to be an unreasonable
restraint of trade. In particular it would be invalid unless reasonable in duration
and extent. Where the 1993 regulations apply they impose similar restrictions but
provide that in any case a restraint shall be valid for no more than two years after
termination[1].

1   Regulation 20.

6.3.3   *Effect of termination on relations with third parties*

Even where the agency is terminated, the agent may continue to have power to
bind the principal. First, where the agency is irrevocable, any purported revocation
of authority will be ineffective[1]. Secondly, an agent may continue to have apparent
authority even though his actual authority has been terminated, if the principal
holds out the agent as continuing to have authority. Where the principal has
previously held out the agent as having authority, for instance, to enter into a class
of transactions, or to act for a specified period, the agent may continue to have
apparent authority on the strength of that representation, until the principal brings
the termination of authority to the notice of third parties dealing with the agent[2]. The
same result may follow where A's authority is terminated automatically. In *Drew
v Nunn*[3] P became insane but A, his wife, continued to act in his name. When P

recovered, he disclaimed liability for acts done by A during his incapacity, but it was held that A had apparent authority and P was bound. However, where A's actual authority is terminated by P's death or bankruptcy, A also ceases to have apparent authority.

Where A is appointed by power of attorney, a transaction executed in pursuance of the power of attorney is valid, notwithstanding revocation of the power, in favour of a person who did not know of the revocation[4].

If A continues to act after termination of authority, he may incur personal liability for breach of the implied warranty of authority. There is an obvious potential risk for an agent whose authority may be determined automatically without his knowledge. In *Yonge v Toynbee*[5] solicitors acted for P in litigation. Unknown to them, P became mentally incapacitated so that their authority was terminated. However, they continued the litigation and were held liable for breach of their warranty of authority and were ordered personally to pay costs to the other litigant. This seems odd, because P could have been held liable for the actions taken on his behalf on the basis of *Drew v Nunn* so that any damages for breach of the warranty should have been nominal[6]. It may be that the case is limited to cases of solicitors conducting litigation, where the court has an inherent jurisdiction to order payment of costs. If it applies more generally, it would seem that it allows T to choose whether to sue P or A.

1   Above 6.3.1.3.
2   See *Summers v Solomon* (1857) 7 E & B 879; see also *Rockland Industries Inc v Amerada Minerals Corpn of Canada Ltd* (1980) 108 DLR (3d) 513, where A's authority was not terminated but limited.
3   (1879) 4 QBD 661, CA.
4   Powers of Attorney Act 1971, s 5.
5   [1910] 1 KB 215, CA.
6   See 4.2.

Part III

The sale and supply of goods

Chapter 7

Background to the Sale of Goods Act

7.0   Introduction

'Commerce' is concerned with buying and selling, and the law of sale of goods is
the central topic in commercial law. Of course, services can be bought and sold,
and in recent years the sale and supply of services has assumed an increasing
economic importance. However, the sale of goods remains of vital importance to
the national economy, to manufacturing industry, and to individual consumers.
Every day an immense number of sales take place, ranging from bulk sales of
commodities through sales of manufactured products down to sales of everyday
consumer items. All these transactions – although they may vary in scale, be for
different types of goods and be between parties of different status – are governed
by the same set of legal rules, contained primarily in the Sale of Goods Act 1979,
as amended. Although there is now a legal code governing other contracts for the
supply of goods and services, it is less complete and less developed than that which
relates to the sale of goods.

7.1   History of sales law

The modern law of sale is largely contained in the Sale of Goods Act 1979. However,
in order to understand the present law it is necessary to bear in mind its historical
development, for that may not only throw a light on the possible interpretation of the
Act, but may also offer an insight into the reasons for decisions made in the past.
   Most of the legal principles applicable to contracts of sale were developed at
common law, particularly during the eighteenth and nineteenth centuries. This was
the classic era of the development of contract law, when the prevailing economic
philosophy was 'laissez-faire'; the principles, developed in disputes between
merchants, were therefore intended to reflect the practices and expectations of the
mercantile community rather than to represent judicial intervention.
   By the late nineteenth century an extensive body of rules concerned with the rights
and duties of buyers and sellers had developed, and the law of sale was therefore
included (at the instigation of the commercial community who were concerned that
the law was inaccessible) in the partial codification of commercial law which took
place at that time. Sir Mackenzie Chalmers, who had prepared the Bills of Exchange
Act 1882, drafted the Sale of Goods Bill which was presented to Parliament in 1889.
However, the Bill did not complete its passage at the first attempt, and did not finally

become law until 1894. The Bill was intended on the whole to codify the existing common law, but, as a result of both drafting details and amendments made in Parliament, it seems that in places the Act modified the previous law.

The 1893 Act remained in force until 1979. During that time some minor amendments were made, two of which were particularly significant. The 1893 Act required contracts for the sale of goods of ten pounds value or more to be evidenced in writing and, in default, made such contracts unenforceable[1]. As inflation eroded the value of money, that rule became increasingly restrictive, and it was repealed in 1954[2]. A further set of amendments was made in 1973 by the Supply of Goods (Implied Terms) Act 1973, which restricted the extent to which the seller could exclude liability for breach of the implied terms relating to the goods[3] and introduced a new definition of 'merchantable quality'.

In 1979 a new Sale of Goods Act was passed. However, that Act made few changes to the existing law: its main function was to consolidate the 1893 Act and the amendments made to it by subsequent legislation. As a result, much of the law contained in the 1979 Act derived from the 1893 Act, which in turn was based on the previous common law and derived from mercantile practices of the eighteenth and nineteenth centuries. Many of the rules in the Act therefore seem increasingly inappropriate to modern social and economic conditions. Since the common law rules on which the Sale of Goods Act is based were developed in cases concerned with disputes between merchants, many of them seem poorly suited for application to consumer contracts. Moreover, as Professor Bridge has observed[4], the mercantile contracts with which the eighteenth and nineteenth century cases were concerned were very different from modern commercial contracts:

> 'It is very much merchants' law, but merchants' law of a particular type. It does not deal with massive shipments or supertankers or with the sale of complex, manufactured machinery. It is heavily concentrated in the area of relatively small-scale transactions involving raw materials soon to be used in the manufacturing process'[5].

Partly in recognition of this, the 1979 Act was amended three times in 1994 and 1995[6] to alter rules seen as anachronistic or obsolete and make the law more appropriate to modern consumer and commercial transactions, and further reforms to sales law have been proposed[7].

Even before the 1994 and 1995 amendments, the Sale of Goods Act 1979 did not contain a complete sales code. The twentienth century saw a significant growth in the volume of consumer participation in commercial activity and, particularly since the 1960s, a large body of legislation has been passed to protect consumers and correct inequalities in bargaining power. The SoG(IT)A 1973 restricted the seller's ability to exclude liability for breach of the implied terms relating to the goods in a sale of goods contract. Those restrictions are now contained in the Unfair Contract Terms Act 1977, which is therefore an important part of the law of sale of goods and is now supplemented by the overlapping restrictions contained in the Unfair Terms in Consumer Contracts Regulations 1999. A significant body of other consumer protection legislation, including the Consumer Credit Act 1974 (where goods are sold on credit)[8], the Consumer Protection Act 1987[9] (in the context of manufacturers' and vendors' liability for unsafe products), and trade descriptions legislation[10] may also affect the rights and duties of parties to sale contracts and exert an influence on the terms included in the contract[11]. The trend of protecting consumers continues and is an important objective of the European Community[12].

At the time of writing, a directive on distances sales has recently been implemented[13] and one on consumer guarantees[14] is awaiting implementation. Consumer and commercial sales law therefore seem likely to follow increasingly divergent paths.

Outside the consumer context, legislation intended to promote competition, including the Competition Act 1998 and arts 81 and 82 of the Treaty of Rome[15], may also be relevant, whilst there is a further supplementary body of law concerned with international sales, including the Carriage of Goods by Sea Acts of 1971 and 1992[16]. Finally, the rights and duties of parties to sale contracts may also be affected by other, apparently unconnected, legislation, such as the Factors Act 1889 (whose provisions must be read alongside those of ss 21–25 of the 1979 Act), the Torts (Interference with Goods) Act 1977, the Bills of Sale Acts 1878–82 and the Companies Act 1985.

Even more importantly, sales of goods are effected by contracts and it is expressly provided that 'the rules of the common law, including the law merchant' apply to contracts for the sale of goods, except in so far as they are modified by the Sale of Goods Act[17]. Many of those rules, including those relating to mistake and frustration, damages and the classification of terms, are modified, but much of the general law of contract remains relevant, including the rules relating to contract formation, misrepresentation, express terms and privity of contract. Although the Act refers to the rules of 'the common law', it seems clear that this should now be interpreted to mean 'judge-made law' and thus include the rules of equity; certainly there is no doubt that rules developed by equity are applied to sale contracts.

Finally, and perhaps most significantly, it should be borne in mind that many of the rules set out in the Sale of Goods Act are capable of being modified or excluded by the parties, especially in a commercial context. Many commercial sales, and particularly large-scale commodity transactions, are effected on standard term contracts which contain a detailed set of rules to govern the particular transaction. Where such standard forms are used, the Sale of Goods Act may do no more than provide a backdrop against which the contract is drafted and interpreted, the rights and obligations of the parties being primarily dependent on the terms of the contract.

1 Sale of Goods Act 1893, s 4.
2 By the Law Reform (Enforcement of Contracts) Act 1954.
3 Sale of Goods Act 1893, ss 12–15; see chs 11 and 14.
4 'The evolution of modern sales law' [1991] LMCLQ 52.
5 [1991] LMCLQ 52 at 53.
6 Sale and Supply of Goods Act 1994; see chs 11 and 12; Sale of Goods Amendment Act 1994; see 17.5; Sale of Goods (Amendment) Act 1995.
7 DTI, *Transfer of Title: ss 21–26 of the Sale of Goods Act 1979: A Consultation Document* (1994).
8 See chs 24–26.
9 See ch 13.
10 Trade Descriptions Act 1968, Consumer Protection Act 1987, Pt III.
11 This is not intended to be an exhaustive list; much other consumer protection legislation may directly or indirectly relate to contracts of sale.
12 Article 129a, introduced into the Treaty of Rome by the Maastricht Treaty, expressly authorises Community action to achieve a high level of consumer protection.
13 Directive 1997/7/EC on the protection of consumers in respect of distance contracts, implemented by the Consumer Protection (Distance Selling) Regulations 2000, SI 2000/2334: see 2.3.7.
14 Directive 1999/44/EC on certain aspects of the sale of consumer goods and associated guarantees (1999) OJ L 171/12 7.7.99. See 11.8, 12.5.
15 As amended by the Treaty of Amsterdam. The provisions were originally arts 85 and 86.
16 See Pt V.
17 Sale of Goods Act 1979, s 62(2); see also s 54 relating to remedies, below 12.0.

7.2   Problems in the Sale of Goods Act

The Sale of Goods Act is superficially simple. Some of its provisions, particularly those relating to the quality of goods supplied under the contract, are well known. However, the appearance of simplicity is misleading and disguises a number of problems. Many of the difficulties derive from the fact that the 1979 Act is closely based on the original Act of 1893. Although the 1979 Act consolidated a number of amendments which had been made to the original Act between its passing and 1979, as already noted, the 1979 Act is not a complete code, so that much of the law relevant to sale of goods transactions must be found outside the Act, either in the common law or in other statutes as mentioned above, in particular in the mass of modern consumer protection legislation. Moreover, the 1979 Act itself has now been amended three times in 1994 and 1995. Furthermore, as sale is a contract, it is generally open to the parties to the contract to vary or add to the provisions of the contract by express stipulation, although the freedom to modify some of the terms is now subject to statutory control[1].

Since the Act is based on the 1893 Act, which in turn was based on the pre-existing common law, many of the issues which had not been considered by the courts prior to the 1893 Act are not covered by the statute[2].

Some difficulties are also caused by what is included in the Act. Some terms are undefined: for instance, there is no definition of 'condition', although 'warranty' is defined. Some of the language used is archaic and may be difficult to apply to the conditions of modern commerce[3]. Many of the rules are 'open textured' and flexible, their application to particular facts being a matter of interpretation. However, it has been suggested that the incomplete nature of the code laid down by the 1893 and 1979 Acts may have contributed to their longevity, by providing a measure of flexibility, enabling the law to respond to and accommodate changes in mercantile practice[4].

1   Under the Unfair Contract Terms Act 1977, see 2.6.3.
2   See eg *Sainsbury Ltd v Street* [1972] 3 All ER 1127, [1972] 1 WLR 834, below 16.2.1.
3   Perhaps the best known example of 'archaic' language, the requirement that goods should be of 'merchantable quality', was removed by the Sale and Supply of Goods Act 1994, which replaced it with a requirement that goods should be of 'satisfactory' quality: see 11.2.
4   See Law Commission 160, *Sale and Supply of Goods* para 1.9. For an example of a modern development, see the consideration of the effect of 'payment' by credit card in *Re Charge Card Services Ltd* [1989] Ch 497, [1988] 3 All ER 702, below 8.1.3.

7.3   Interpretation of the Sale of Goods Act

The 1979 Act was a consolidating Act, based on the 1893 Act, which was itself at least partly a codification of the existing common law. The correct approach to the interpretation of a codifying, or consolidating, statute is 'in the first instance to examine the language of the statute and to ask what is its natural meaning', rather than to 'start with inquiring how the law previously stood and then assuming that it was probably intended to leave it unaltered, to see if the words of the enactment will bear an interpretation in conformity with this view'[1]. In other words, decisions of courts in cases prior to the Act in question should only be examined for guidance in cases where the language of the Act is unclear or ambiguous; the purpose of a codifying or consolidating statute is to remove the need to consult prior case law. However, although this approach is well established, it is often ignored, and cases on the 1893 Act, or even from before 1893, are examined for guidance as to the meaning of the Act. In a 1987 case the Court of Appeal had to consider the meaning of 'merchantable quality' in the light of a statutory definition inserted in 1973, which required goods to be reasonably fit for the 'purpose or purposes for which such goods are ordinarily supplied'. Cases decided prior to 1973 had established that 'multi-purpose' goods would be merchantable provided they were fit for at least one of their ordinary purposes. The Court of Appeal considered those cases in detail and decided that, notwithstanding the apparently clear words of the new statutory definition, it had made no difference to the law laid down by the cases on the 1893 Act[2].

1   Per Lord Herschell in *Bank of England v Vagliano Bros* [1891] AC 107 at 144.
2   *Aswan Engineering Establishment Co v Lupdine Ltd* [1987] 1 All ER 135, [1987] 1 WLR 1; see 11.2.4.1. There is as yet little case law applying the most recent amendments to the 1979 Act. In the one reported decision on the new requirement that goods be of 'satisfactory quality', *Thain v Anniesland Trade Centre* 1997 SLT 102, Sh Ct, a number of cases decided under the old law and concerned with the meaning of 'merchantable quality' were cited to the court, but the court found them not to be 'of much assistance'.

7.4   The future of sales law

The sale of goods is an everyday transaction. The law of sale therefore directly affects the interests of traders, whether as buyers and sellers, and consumers. The law should be accessible, clear and comprehensible to those it affects. Indeed, that was the motive for the original codification of the law of sale in Chalmers' 1893 Sale of Goods Act. The modern law no longer satisfies those criteria of accessibility, clarity and comprehensibility, if it ever did. It is true, of course, that the law never was completely codified and may of its provisions were technical. Today, however, the law is no longer even readily accessible. The 1979 Act – which itself was intended to simplify the law by consolidating it – must be read subject to the amending Acts of 1994 and 1995 and a mass of other satellite legislation dealing with such topics as exclusion clauses and consumer protection as well as more peripheral topics. In the near future the situation is likely to get worse, especially as EU-inspired consumer protection measures are implemented, often by secondary legislation.

It is a striking feature of English sales law that no formal distinction is drawn between consumer and commercial sales. Nor, for that matter, is any formal distinction made between domestic and international sales. Apart from a handful of special provisions[1], the same rules apply to international sales as to domestic ones. This is not to say that no distinction is made between consumer and business, or domestic and international, sales. There are individual provisions of the Sale of Goods Act, for instance, which only apply to consumer or non-consumer sales[2], but the distinctions are drawn individually, on an ad hoc basis. It is clear, however, that the same rules are not always appropriate to different types of transaction. To take an example, the 1995 reforms to the rules on passing of property were introduced primarily to meet the needs of the international commodity trades. Problems similar to those addressed by the reforms also affect consumers, but the Act does little to protect consumers and was not intended to do so[3]. Conversely, the 1994 reform which replaced the requirement that goods be of 'merchantable quality' with one that they be of 'satisfactory quality' was driven primarily by concern for the perceived needs of consumers.

Chalmers' 1893 codification of sales law has proved remarkably resilient. Much of it remains in force today, but it is now over 100 years old. As new elements are grafted onto the Sale of Goods Act, the coherence of Chalmers' original legislation is increasingly eroded. Consumer and commercial sales law are growing apart, but in a haphazard fashion. It must be open to question how long the UK can maintain a unitary sales law applicable to all classes of transaction[4]. In 1987 the Law Commission rejected the idea of a wholesale review of sales law and yet, at the dawn of the twenty-first century, the law is, at the very least, in need of consolidation. The UK government has indicated an intention to ratify the Vienna Convention on Contracts for the International Sale of Goods. If so, the UK will at least have a separate code for international sales. Some commentators have argued, however, that many of the Convention's provisions are more suited to modern commercial sales than are those of existing domestic law, and that it could therefore provide a model for a more general reform of commercial sales law. It is to be hoped that, if the UK government does eventually ratify the Convention, the opportunity will be taken to review sales law generally.

1   The most important is s 26 of the Unfair Contract Terms Act 1977, excluding 'international supply contracts' from the Act's control: see 33.0. Although the Uniform Laws on International Sales Act 1967 applies specifically to international sales contracts, the Act is largely a dead letter with no practical relevance: see 33.0.
2   The most important is the modification of the buyer's right to reject goods for breach of condition in s 15A of the 1979 Act, which only applies where the buyer does not deal as a consumer.
3   See 15.5.2.5.
4   One solution would be to pass a separate Consumer Sales Act: see *Benjamin's Sale of Goods* (5th edn, 1997) para 11-057.

Chapter 8

The Contract of Sale and the Classification of Transactions

8.0 Introduction

Ownership and/or possession of goods may be transferred pursuant to a wide range of different contractual arrangements with different characteristics. Different arrangements may offer the parties a range of advantages and their popularity may vary from time to time according to changes in such factors as commercial practice, economic circumstances, statutory regulation, fiscal policy and consumer preferences. The Sale of Goods Act 1979 (SoGA) only applies to contracts for the sale of goods, as defined in the Act, and although for some purposes the law applying to other supply contracts is closely assimilated to that applying to contracts for the sale of goods, a number of important differences remain. It is therefore important to understand the differences between the different types of supply contract. Those differences can best be understood by analysing the statutory definition of a contract of sale in the 1979 Act[1], for a contract which does not satisfy all the elements of that definition is not governed by the 1979 Act.

The wide range of arrangements pursuant to which goods may be supplied provides another example of the ingenuity of commerce. However, it must be said that in many cases the distinctions between different classes of contract are unclear or technical; it must be open to question whether it is desirable that the rights of the parties to a contract should depend on distinctions which may not be fully understood by the parties and which in some cases are unclear or artificial.

1   Section 2(1).

8.1 The contract of sale

Section 2(1) of the 1979 Act provides that:

> 'A contract of sale of goods is a contract by which the seller transfers or agrees to transfer the property in goods to the buyer for a money consideration called the price'.

The Act therefore applies only where goods are supplied pursuant to a contract. The formation of the contract is governed by the general law of contract and all the elements required for the formation of a valid contract – offer, acceptance, consideration and intention to create legal relations – must be present. Thus gifts are not regulated by the Act, since there is no contract between donor and donee. Where 'free gifts' are offered by a retailer or manufacturer as part of a sales promotion there may be a contract, but the contract will generally not be one of sale[1]. In *Esso Petroleum Ltd v Customs and Excise Comrs*[2] a petrol company offered free 'coins' to drivers who bought four gallons of their petrol, as a sales promotion. Each coin bore the likeness of a member of the 1970 England football World Cup squad, and motorists (or their children) were encouraged to collect the full set of coins. The House of Lords had to decide if the coins were supplied for retail sale, in order to decide if the company was liable to purchase tax on their value. Two members of the House felt that there was no contract at all because there was no intention to create legal relations: garages had a powerful incentive to supply coins, in order to maintain goodwill, but there was no legal obligation to do so.

The fact that goods are supplied in return for payment does not necessarily mean that the supply is contractual. A contract is a voluntary arrangement: there will only be a contract where the parties intend to contract. Thus where goods are supplied pursuant to a statutory scheme, as where drugs are supplied by a pharmacist to an NHS patient, there is no contract and therefore no sale[3]. This is particularly important in relation to supplies of gas and water by privatised utility companies. Although the customer pays for the goods supplied, the terms of the supply are generally strictly controlled by statute. In *NORWEB v Dixon*[4] the Divisional Court held that the relationship between an electricity supply company and a domestic customer was not contractual. The company had a statutory duty to supply the customer provided that certain conditions were satisfied and the terms of the supply and the payment tariff were fixed by statute and this element of compulsion 'both as to the creation of the relationship and as to the fixing of its terms' was inconsistent with a contractual relationship[5].

In general, no formalities are required for the creation of a contract of sale. The contract may be written, oral, or even inferred from the conduct of the parties. Thus if a seller despatches goods in response to an order, he accepts an offer from the buyer and a contract is formed. Similarly, if a buyer keeps and uses goods sent to him in response to his request, he may be treated as accepting the goods on the terms of any delivery note sent with them. However, certain formalities are prescribed by statute in order to protect consumers against high pressure sales techniques. If goods or services are supplied to a person without his prior request, he may be entitled in certain circumstances to treat them as a gift[6] and where a business makes a contract with a consumer to supply goods or services and the contract is made away from the business premises of the supplier, the consumer has a right to cancel the contract within seven days, and the contract must contain a written notice of that right[7].

Consumers are now given similar protection in relation to contracts for the supply of goods made at a distance by regulations implementing the EC's directive on the protection of consumers in respect of distance contracts[8]. The regulations apply to contracts made by any method of distance communication and therefore cover contracts made by telephone and over the Internet as well as those made by traditional mail order. As explained in Chapter 2, the regulations require that the consumer be provided with certain information prior to entering into a contract, and that that information is to be confirmed in some 'durable medium' after the contract is made, and give the consumer a right to cancel a distance contract within seven days of receipt of the goods[9].

Where goods are sold by auction, each bidder makes an offer to buy; each new bid cancels any prior offer, and the highest bid is accepted, and the contract is concluded, when the auctioneer's hammer falls[10].

Problems may arise where the parties fail to agree on terms, perhaps as a result of a 'battle of forms'[11]. In that case there may be no effective offer and acceptance, and thus no contract. In *British Steel Corpn v Cleveland Bridge and Engineering Co Ltd*[12] CBE entered into negotiations to buy steel nodes from BSC for use in a construction project. The parties were unable to agree on all the terms of the contract, but CBE needed the nodes urgently and therefore asked BSC to commence manufacture and delivery immediately, pursuant to a letter of intent. When all but one of the nodes had been delivered negotiations had still not been finalised[13]. BSC therefore retained the last node to strengthen their bargaining position, and it became trapped as a result of a strike. When it was delivered, BSC claimed for the price of the nodes and CBE counterclaimed damages for late delivery. It was held that there was no contract at all; CBE were therefore not entitled to damages. However, BSC were entitled to claim a reasonable price for the nodes delivered, on a quantum meruit basis. On this analysis, CBE would have had no claim if the nodes had proved defective, unless they could claim in negligence.

Provided there is a valid contract, the contract may be absolute or subject to a condition precedent or subsequent[14]. For instance, a buyer may agree to buy a machine provided it meets certain performance standards: there is then a binding contract of sale, subject to a condition precedent. Similarly, the buyer may agree to buy a cargo of a commodity such as grain or soya, provided an independent expert gives a certificate of quality. Alternatively, the contract may be subject to a condition subsequent, so that although a binding contract comes into force immediately, it will terminate if the condition is fulfilled; for instance, the seller may agree to take back goods and provide a refund if the buyer is not fully satisfied with them.

1 See 8.1.3.
2 [1976] 1 All ER 117, [1976] 1 WLR 1, HL.
3 *Pfizer v Ministry of Health* [1965] AC 512. See also *Appleby v Sleep* [1968] 2 All ER 265.
4 [1995] 3 All ER 952, [1995] 1 WLR 636.
5 [1995] 3 All ER 952 at 959, [1995] 1 WLR 636 at 643, per Dyson J. The relevant statutory scheme did provide for electricity companies to enter into 'special arrangements' on negotiated terms with individual customers. Such arrangements would be contractual. Note that electricity probably would not be 'goods' in any case.
6 Consumer Protection (Distance Selling) Regulations 2000, SI 2000/2334.
7 Under the Consumer Protection (Cancellation of Contracts Concluded Away from Business Premises) Regulations 1987, SI 1987/2117.
8 Consumer Protection (Distance Selling) Regulations 2000, SI 2000/2334, implementing directive 97/7/EC (OJ 1997 L 144/19). The directive should have been implemented by 4 June 2000. See generally Bradgate (1997) 4 Web JCLI.
9 Regulations 14-18. If the required information is not provided before the goods are supplied, the cancellation period ends seven days after receipt of the information or three months after the date of receipt of the goods, whichever is later. Whereas the right of cancellation in relation to 'doorstep' contracts is intended to protect the consumer against high pressure sales techniques, the rationale for the consumer's right of cancellation in this context is to allow him to examine and evaluate the goods before being committed to buy them.
10 SoGA, s 57(2).
11 See 2.3.4.
12 [1984] 1 All ER 504.
13 If terms had been agreed, they could have been given retroactive effect and govern those deliveries already made: *Trollope & Colls Ltd v Atomic Power Constructions* [1962] 3 All ER 1035.
14 SoGA, s 2(3).

8.1.1   *Seller and buyer*

There must be a seller and a buyer, who must have full capacity to enter into the particular contract. Clearly, seller and buyer must be different people; however, there may be a valid contract of sale between one part owner of goods and another[1]: thus if A and B are partners, A can contract to buy his firm's car from the partnership.

More importantly, the parties must be committed to sell and buy. This requirement distinguishes a contract of sale from a contract of hire purchase. The legal analysis of a hire purchase contract is of a bailment, or hire, with an option to purchase the goods at the end of the hire period; thus the parties are not committed to sell and buy until the hirer exercises the option at the end of the term. It may often be difficult to distinguish a hire purchase contract from a contract of conditional sale[2], where the seller supplies goods to the buyer on terms which allow the buyer to pay by instalments and provide that no property is to pass to the buyer until all the instalments are paid. For many purposes, the two types of transaction are treated alike; however, strictly speaking, a conditional sale is a sale contract from the outset, and is governed by the 1979 Act, whereas a hire purchase contract is not.

Goods are often delivered on 'sale or return' terms, for instance where the buyer intends to resell the goods, but is unsure of the quantity he can resell. The buyer is free to buy the goods or return them to the seller, although in certain circumstances, notably if he resells them, he will be deemed to have bought them[3]. Under such an arrangement, the buyer is in possession of the goods as a bailee with an option to purchase; there is therefore no contract of sale unless and until the buyer opts to purchase the goods[4].

Where agents are employed to buy or sell goods it may be important to decide if they are agents in law, or if they are buying and selling on their own account[5]. It may be particularly difficult to distinguish between an agency and a sale or return arrangement. The court may have to examine all the terms of the arrangement to decide if they are consistent with sale or agency. The language used will not be conclusive. The word 'agent' is often used to describe persons who are not agents in law. In *Weiner v Harris*[6] a manufacturer delivered jewellery to a dealer 'on sale for cash only or return', so that it remained the manufacturer's property until sold or paid for. The contract required the dealer to keep the jewellery separate from his own property and provided that he was to receive half the profit from any resale; on resale he was to pay the cost price and the other half of the profit to the manufacturer. It was held that the dealer was the manufacturer's agent, with the result that a person who bought jewellery from the dealer obtained a good title to it even though the dealer failed to pay the manufacturer.

Where goods are sold subject to a retention of title clause, the relationship of seller and buyer may have some of the characteristics of agency super-added. There is a contract of sale, but the buyer may be treated as the seller's agent for some purposes so that he may be required to account as an agent for proceeds made by reselling the goods[7].

1   SoGA, s 2(2). It is now confirmed that a sale of a share in goods is a sale of goods: SoGA, s 61, as amended by Sale of Goods (Amendment) Act 1995.
2   A conditional sale should not be confused with a conditional contract, as described above, 8.1.
3   SoGA, s 18, r 4, below 15.3.4.
4   *Atari Corpn (UK) Ltd v Electronics Boutique Stores (UK) Ltd* [1998] 1 All ER 1010; see 15.3.4.
5   See 3.2.2. The agent may be a commission agent, acting as an agent vis-à-vis his principal but selling as a principal vis-à-vis customers: see *Triffit Nurseries v Salads Etcetera Ltd* [1999] 1 All ER (Comm) 110.

6   [1910] 1 KB 285.
7   *Aluminium Industrie Vaassen BV v Romalpa Aluminium Ltd* [1976] 2 All ER 552, [1976] 1 WLR 676; see 18.4.1.

8.1.2   *The contract must be for the transfer of property*

The seller must transfer or agree to transfer to the buyer the property in the goods; if not, the contract is not one of sale. According to s 61(1) of the Act, 'property means the general property in the goods, not merely a special property'. The better view is that 'property' therefore means the absolute legal interest, or 'ownership'[1]. The transfer of ownership from seller to buyer is therefore the essence of a sale. If the contract is for the transfer of some lesser interest, then it is not a contract of sale.

The Act makes a distinction between the concepts of 'property' and 'title'. The seller's 'title' to the goods is his claim to the absolute property interest in them. The seller can only transfer such title to the goods as he himself has (although the buyer may in certain circumstances obtain a better title than the seller had[2]). SoGA, s 12 makes it an implied condition of the contract that the seller has 'the right to sell' the goods – in effect, that the seller should have and transfer to the buyer the best title to the absolute interest in the goods sold. In *Rowland v Divall*[3] Atkin LJ went so far as to say that in such a case if the seller had no right to sell the goods, no property would be transferred and the contract would therefore not be one of sale because 'the whole object of a sale is to transfer property'[4]. It is generally thought, however, that Atkin LJ was mistaken. The requirement in s 2 is that the contract be for the transfer of property – ie for the transfer of the seller's title to the absolute interest. Provided that the contract as made is for the transfer of that interest, and not for some lesser interest, the contract is one of sale. If the seller's title to that interest is less than perfect the contract is still one of sale but the seller will be in breach of the implied term in s 12.

Essentially, therefore, the requirement that a contract of sale be for the transfer of the general property in goods distinguishes sale contracts from other arrangements under which only a special property, or limited interest, is transferred. A contract involving the transfer of a special property in goods will normally be for the transfer of possession and will therefore be a form of bailment. A wide range of different transactions is included within the general term 'bailment'[5], but one common feature they share is that O, the owner of goods, transfers possession of the goods to B, the bailee; O remains owner of the goods and B is under a legal obligation to return the same goods to O. Thus, as a general rule, if B is intended never to return the same goods, the contract is not one of bailment. In *South Australian Insurance Co v Randell*[6] farmers deposited grain with B under a contract which required B on demand either to return to the farmers the same quantity of grain of equivalent quality to that deposited, or to pay its cash value. The grain deposited with B was stored in B's warehouse where it was mixed with other grain so as to be indistinguishable. It was held that the intention of the parties was that grain deposited with B should become B's property, in the same way that money deposited with a bank becomes the property of the bank. However, this is not an absolute rule. The contract between O and B may qualify B's obligation and the analysis of their relationship therefore involves a search for their intentions. In *Mercer v Craven*[7] several farmers deposited grain with a company for storage on terms which permitted the company to make sales from the bulk but provided that the stored grain should at all times remain the property of the depositors. The House of Lords held that the mere fact that goods belonging to more than one owner are mixed does not destroy the owners' property rights in those goods and that on the facts here the intention was that the relationship was one of bailment, notwithstanding the fact that the parties must have appreciated that the depositors would not recover the actual same grain deposited.

Although the distinction between sale and bailment is generally clear, elements of bailment may be superimposed onto a sale contract. The Act recognises two different types of contract of sale. Where property passes at the time of the contract, the contract is called 'a sale'[8]: contract and conveyance are simultaneous. Where property is to pass at some time in the future, after the contract, or only subject to some condition being fulfilled, the contract is called an 'agreement to sell', which becomes a sale at the date fixed, or when the condition is fulfilled[9]. The most common condition imposed on the passing of property is that it will not pass until the buyer has paid the price of the goods to the seller. Such an agreement is a 'conditional sale'. The buyer may be allowed to pay by instalments, particularly in a consumer context, in which case the contract will be regulated by the Consumer Credit Act 1974, and the arrangement closely resembles hire purchase; alternatively, the buyer may be expected to pay the price in one lump sum, at the expiry of a credit period. In either case, although the contract is one of sale, the buyer holds the goods as bailee pending payment, and it has been recognised that this may be so even where the contract anticipates that the buyer will use, consume or resell the goods before paying for them, so that the seller never expects them to be returned[10].

1   See Battersby and Preston (1972) 35 MLR 269; cf Ho [1997] CLJ 571.
2   SoGA, ss 21–25: see ch 17.
3   [1923] 2 KB 500, CA; below 14.1.1.
4   [1923] 2 KB 500 at 507.
5   See below 8.2.4.
6   (1869) LR 3 PC 101.
7   [1994] CLC 328, HL; see Smith (1995) 111 LQR10; cf *Coleman v Harvey* [1989] 1 NZLR 723.
8   SoGA, s 2(4).
9   SoGA, s 2(5)–(6).
10   *Aluminium Industrie Vaasen BV v Romalpa Aluminium Ltd* [1976] 2 All ER 552, [1976] 1 WLR 676; see 18.4.1.

8.1.3   *Money consideration*

The contract will only be one of sale if the property in the goods is transferred to the buyer in exchange for a money consideration. 'Money' is not defined in the SoGA, but 'goods' is defined as excluding 'money'[1]. Money has been defined as 'chattels issued by the authority of the law and denominated with reference to a unit of account and meant to serve as a universal means of exchange in the state of issue'[2]. The classification of notes and coins as 'money' may depend on the intentions of the parties: notes and coins may also be goods, where they are kept as curios or artefacts[3]: thus, for instance, the coins in a numismatist's coin collection would be goods, not money.

Where goods are transferred for a consideration other than money, the transaction is one of barter, or exchange, rather than sale. In *Esso Petroleum Ltd v Customs and Excise Comrs*[4] coins featuring images of members of the 1970 England World Cup Squad were given as free gifts to motorists who bought four gallons of Esso petrol. Four members of the House of Lords held that if there was a contract entitling the motorist to a coin, the consideration provided by the motorist was entering into the main contract to buy petrol; any contract relating to the free coin was therefore not one of sale.

However, although the Act requires the consideration to be money, the consideration may be satisfied in some other way. For instance, if S and B have mutual dealings, they may agree that their respective debts be set off against each other, so that no cash, or only a cash balance changes hands. Provided the goods are given a money value, the contract is still one of sale, even though the consideration is actually satisfied by the buyer transferring property to or performing some service for the seller. In *Aldridge v Johnson*[5] D agreed to transfer 100 quarters of barley to P for £1 1s 3d per quarter, in exchange for P's transfer of 32 bullocks, valued at £6 each, plus £23 in cash. It was assumed that the transaction was one of sale; the crucial factor appears to have been that both barley and bullocks had been valued in money terms.

In such cases the decisive factor appears to be the intention of the parties as to what should be the consideration for the transfer of the property in the goods. In line with the general contract rule, intention is assessed objectively, and the fact that the goods have been valued in cash terms is a strong indicator that the parties intended that the consideration should be a money payment. In an Irish case[6], a dealer agreed to supply a motorist with a new car in exchange for the motorist's old car plus £250 in cash. Neither car was given a cash value, and it was held that the contract was one of barter rather than sale but 'if the transaction had been that the new car was to be a particular price but that in lieu of that price the vendor would take the existing car and cash for the balance, the contract would have been a contract for sale'[7].

On this view, when goods are bought on a part exchange basis, it will generally be correct to regard the supply of the new goods as a sale. However, other analyses are possible, and it should be remembered that in a part exchange transaction there are two transfers of goods. Suppose that B acquires a new car and part exchanges his old car. The transaction could be regarded as two sales, with a mutual set-off of the sums due, leaving a cash balance to be paid; or as a sale of the new car, with the old car being transferred to the seller for the partial release of the debt; or the arrangement could be regarded as one contract of barter. The simplest analysis is the first, and where the part exchange vehicle is valued by the seller, as is normally the case, it should be preferred[8].

Where goods or services are paid for by credit card, the cardholder's signature on the sales voucher operates to give the supplier a right to claim a money payment from the card company, and the buyer is not liable for the price if the card company fails to pay[9]. It could therefore be argued that where goods are 'purchased' with a credit card, the consideration for which they are transferred is not money, but the transfer of the right to claim payment from the card company, so that the transaction is not a sale[10]. However, this would produce anomalous results, and it seems better to analyse the transaction as a sale: the goods are sold for a money price, but the seller agrees to the buyer satisfying that obligation by giving him the right to claim payment from the card company[11].

1   SoGA, s 61(1).
2   Mann, *The Legal Aspect of Money* (5th edn, 1992) p 8.
3   *Moss v Hancock* [1899] 2 QB 111.
4   [1976] 1 All ER 117, [1976] 1 WLR 1, HL.

5 (1857) 7 E & B 885; see also *GJ Dawson (Clapham) Ltd v H & G Dutfield* [1936] 2 All ER 232;
   Bull v Parker (1842) 2 Dowl NS 345.
6 *Flynn v Mackin and Mahon* [1974] IR 101.
7 At 111.
8 In *Connell Estate Agents v Begej* [1993] 2 EGLR 35 at 38 Hirst LJ observed that 'I would have
   thought that in the 1990s a part exchange transaction would be regarded in everyday language as
   a sale'. Part exchange transactions may often be more complex, multi-partite arrangements.
   For instance, where a consumer buys a new car on credit the car may be supplied by a garage
   which, as a matter of law, sells the car to a credit company which in turn supplies it to the
   consumer. The garage may agree to take the consumer's old car 'in part exchange'. The reality in
   such a case is that the consumer sells the old car to the garage which applies the trade-in price, on
   the consumer's behalf, in full or partial satisfaction of the deposit payable to the credit company
   under the credit contract. In *Forthright Finance Ltd v Ingate* [1997] 4 All ER 99 the Court of
   Appeal held that such an arrangement amounts to a single transaction for the purposes of the
   Consumer Credit Act, but seems to have accepted that there were two contracts of sale.
9 *Re Charge Card Services Ltd* [1989] Ch 497, [1988] 3 All ER 702, CA.
10 See Tiplady [1989] LMCLQ 22.
11 See *Davies v Customs and Excise Comrs* [1975] 1 All ER 309, [1975] 1 WLR 204; but contrast
   Read v Hutchinson (1813) 3 Camp 352.

8.1.3.1   *Fixing the price*

The amount of the consideration to be paid by the buyer will normally be
expressly agreed by the parties, but if no price is agreed, s 8 of the Act provides
that the buyer must pay a reasonable price. However, this provision can only
apply if the parties have entered into a contract, and the failure to agree on a price
may well be evidence that the parties have not yet reached a binding agreement.
In *May and Butcher Ltd v R*[1] the parties agreed that S should supply goods to B at
'prices to be agreed upon from time to time'. It was held that the parties had not
yet reached a concluded contract; the agreement indicated that the price was to be
agreed by the parties, so that there was no scope for the court to fix the price
under s 8: to do so would have been to usurp the rights of the parties. In contrast
in *Foley v Classique Coaches Ltd*[2] an agreement which provided for S to supply
petrol to B at 'prices to be agreed' was enforced. The agreement formed part of a
larger agreement, under which B had acquired land for its coach business from
S, a garage owner. Moreover, petrol had been supplied under the agreement
without difficulty for three years, and the agreement contained an arbitration
clause. The court felt that if the parties failed to agree, the question of the proper
price to be paid for petrol could be referred to arbitration.

In most cases, the court will strive to interpret an agreement between businesses
as a contract, particularly where it has been acted on, as in *Foley*, and so prevent it
being frustrated. Where goods have been delivered at the buyer's request, the court
will normally find an implied promise to pay a reasonable price[3]; alternatively, if
B asks S to deliver goods and uses them, B may be required to pay a quantum
meruit even if there is no contract[4].

The parties may agree that the price is to be fixed by a third party, such as a
named valuer. If the nominated person fails to fix a price, there is no scope for the
operation of s 8 and the contract is avoided[5]. However, where the parties have
agreed to allow a third party to fix the price, neither party will be allowed to frustrate
the contract by preventing the valuation being made. If either party does prevent
the third party making the valuation, he may be sued by the other party to the sale
contract[6], and the court may grant an injunction to prevent one party obstructing
the agreed price fixing mechanism[7].

Where no valuer is named, but the contract is for a sale 'at valuation', the court may treat that as an agreement to pay a reasonable price. In *Sudbrook Trading Estate v Eggleton*[8] a landlord granted a tenant an option to purchase land at a price to be fixed by two valuers, one to be appointed by each party. The landlord refused to appoint a valuer and the House of Lords held that the contract was essentially one for a sale at a reasonable price. The court could not force the landlord to appoint a valuer, but if the machinery agreed by the parties for the fixing of the price broke down, the court could substitute other machinery, by hearing expert evidence as to a fair valuation for the property.

1   [1934] 2 KB 17n, HL.
2   [1934] 2 KB 1, CA.
3   *Mack and Edwards (Sales) Ltd v McPhail Bros* (1968) 112 Sol Jo 211, CA.
4   *British Steel Corpn v Cleveland Bridge and Engineering Co Ltd* [1984] 1 All ER 504.
5   SoGA 1979, s 9(1).
6   SoGA 1979, s 9(2).
7   *Essoldo v Ladbroke Group* [1976] CLY 337.
8   [1983] 1 AC 444.

8.1.4   *Goods*

According to SoGA s 61(1):

> 'goods includes all personal chattels other than things in action and money, and in Scotland, all corporeal moveables except money; and in particular, "goods" includes emblements, industrial growing crops and things attached to or forming part of the land which are agreed to be severed before sale or under the contract of sale'.

A contract to sell freehold or leasehold land is therefore not a contract for the sale of goods. However, crops and structures amounting to fixtures, may be sold as goods, provided they are to be severed before the sale or under the contract. The Act specifically refers to two categories of crops: 'emblements' are annual crops grown by agricultural labour, as opposed to naturally occurring crops or plants; similarly, 'industrial growing crops' are cultivated, as opposed to natural crops, but are not expected to mature in one year. Naturally growing crops are included, with structures and other fixtures, in the expression 'things attached to or forming part of the land'. Thus a contract for the sale of 'pick your own' fruit would be a contract for the sale of goods (emblements), as would a contract for the sale of a Christmas tree to be cut by the buyer or seller (industrial growing crops). Indeed, it seems that the sale of any growing thing or fixture, separate from the land itself, will normally be a sale, since it must always be intended that the crop or fixture will be severed before sale or under the contract. However, it may be necessary to distinguish between a contract to sell a defined fixture or item and a sale of a part of the land. Thus a contract giving the 'buyer' a right to extract minerals from land ought to be regarded as a contract for the sale of an interest in the land, rather than as a sale of goods, even though the buyer must extract the minerals under the contract. In *Morgan v Russell*[1] D was the tenant of a plot of land and contracted to allow P to enter onto the land and remove slag and cinders which lay on the land but not in defined heaps. D's landlord prevented P entering the land, and P sued for damages for breach. It was held that the contract was not a sale of goods but a sale of an interest in land, similar to a mining lease or profit. However, the case does not seem to establish a general rule that a sale of minerals to be extracted can never be a sale of goods[2]. One factor which influenced the decision of the court was that the contract did not fix the quantity to be removed, and allowed P to take as much as he pleased. It is also worth noting that D's breach resulted from a defect in his title to the land. In an action for breach of contract for sale of an interest in land, P's damages would have been limited by the rule in *Bain v Fothergill*[3]; treating the contract as one of sale of goods would have allowed P to evade that restriction.

A contract for the sale of money is not a sale of goods, but a contract to sell a note or coin as a curio, as opposed to an item of currency, would be a sale of goods[4]. Where money is sold as a commodity in foreign exchange markets, the status of the transaction is unclear.

'Things in action' are items of intangible property such as debts, shares and intellectual property rights. The rights to such property cannot be claimed by taking physical possession of goods (even though the property right may be evidenced in a document or other physical form) but must be asserted by legal action. Contracts for the sale of such items are not contracts for the sale of goods, although the physical document in which a right is evidenced, such as an antique share certificate, could be sold as goods.

As noted earlier, the Act recognises that there may be a contract of sale by one part owner to another, to which the Act applies, and it is now expressly provided that such a transaction is a sale of goods[5].

It is submitted that, in general, 'goods' must be tangible items. Thus electricity is not 'goods'[6]. This approach has been applied to computer software, it being suggested that a contract for the supply of a software program as such is not one for the sale of goods, but that the position is different if the software is supplied via some physical medium such as a diskette[7]. The treatment of computer software raises difficult issues and it is considered further below[8].

Another difficult question with serious modern implications is whether parts of the human body or body products can be regarded as 'goods'. In an American case it was held that a private patient who received a blood transfusion with contaminated blood could not hold the hospital strictly liable for the condition of the blood: the contract was essentially one for services[9]. However, it is clear that body parts or products can be supplied independently of any supply of services, as where blood or organs are supplied from a 'bank', and therefore there may be cases where they may be regarded as 'goods'[10].

Despite these doubts, it is clear that the definition of 'goods' includes a wide range of items. Thus a contract for the sale of a ship[11] or aircraft is as much a sale of goods as a contract for the sale of a tin of beans, a horse or a car.

1   [1909] 1 KB 357.
2   Walton J expressly disclaimed any intention to lay down such a general rule.
3   (1874) LR 7 HL 158.
4   *Moss v Hancock* [1899] 2 QB 111.
5   Section 2(2).
6   It has nevertheless been held that a contract for the supply of electricity would include an implied term at common law that the electricity should be reasonably fit for the buyer's purpose: *Bentley Bros v Metcalfe & Co* [1906] 2 KB 548.
7   *St Albans City Council v International Computers Ltd* [1996] 4 All ER 481 at 493, per Sir Iain Glidewell LJ.
8   Similar problems arise in relation to product liability, where the question is whether software is a 'product' for the purposes of the Consumer Protection Act 1987 and the EC Product Liability Directive: see Whittaker (1989) 105 LQR 125.

9 *Perlmutter v Beth David Hospital* 123 NE 2d 792 (1955); contrast *Belle Bonfils Memorial Blood Bank v Hansen* 579 P 2d 1158 (1978): supply of blood by blood bank was a sale.
10 Trade in human organs is prohibited in the UK by the Human Organ Transplants Act 1989.
11 *Behnke v Bede Shipping Co Ltd* [1927] 1 KB 649.

8.1.4.1   *The classification of goods*

SoGA 1979 classifies goods in two ways. Section 5 of the Act distinguishes between 'existing' and 'future' goods. 'Existing goods' are goods owned or possessed by the seller at the time of the contract of sale. 'Future goods' are goods which are to be manufactured or acquired by the seller after the making of the contract[1]. Thus if a manufacturer agrees to build and supply a piece of machinery to a customer, if the contract is a sale of goods, it is a sale of future goods[2]. Similarly, if an antique dealer mentions to a customer that he intends to acquire a particular piece and the customer agrees to buy it, the contract is for the sale of future goods. Obviously, when goods are not in existence, or have yet to be acquired by the seller at the time the contract is made, the parties cannot intend property in those goods to pass at the time the contract is made. A sale of future goods therefore operates as an agreement to sell[3].

The Act also provides that there may be a contract for the sale of goods whose acquisition by the seller depends on a contingency[4]. Thus if a farmer contracts to sell 275 tons of barley to be grown on a specified field in the following year, the contract is subject to the contingency that the specified field produces at least 275 tons[5]. In such a case, if the contingency fails, the contract may lapse, either wholly or in part. However, the terms of the contract must be construed carefully in order to decide what exactly has been agreed. The parties may have entered into a speculative bargain under which the buyer agrees to buy whatever crop is actually produced on the field: such a contract is a sale of a 'spes' or chance: the buyer agrees to take the risk of crop failure and must pay the contract price no matter how much is produced.

The second distinction, which is of rather more practical importance, is that between 'specific' and 'unascertained' goods, which cuts across the distinction between existing and future goods, and which is particularly important in the context of the rules relating to the passing of property and risk[6]. Goods are specific if they are 'identified and agreed upon at the time [the] contract is made'[7]; thus a contract to sell a particular secondhand car is a contract to sell specific goods. 'Unascertained goods' are not defined by the Act, but it is clear that any goods which are not specific are unascertained. Thus wherever goods are sold purely by a generic description, they are unascertained: for instance, a contract to sell '1,000 gallons of oil' or 'a new Ford Focus' would be a contract to sell unascertained goods. The contract may be for wholly unascertained goods, as in the two examples given, or be for unascertained goods to come from a particular, identified source. Thus, for instance, if S contracts to sell 1,000 gallons of oil from a named tanker, carrying 5,000 gallons, the contract is for unascertained goods, even though the source is identified and agreed, and the seller cannot supply goods from some other source. Professor Goode refers to such goods as 'quasi specific'[8]; that expression is not used in the Act, but is a useful label. Although such goods are unascertained, there are important differences between the rules applying to them and those which apply to wholly unascertained goods. In particular, the Sale of Goods (Amendment) Act 1995 introduced special rules to govern the passing of property in unascertained goods to be supplied from an identified bulk source[9].

Where a contract is made for the sale of unascertained goods, the goods to be used for the contract must be identified before any property can pass to the buyer. The goods are then ascertained. The classification of goods as 'specific' or 'unascertained' is fixed at the time the contract is made: 'unascertained goods' may become ascertained, but will never become specific.

It is clear that existing goods may be specific or unascertained. It is argued by some authors that future goods can never be specific[10] but the better view would seem to be that future goods can be specific for some, but not other, purposes[11]. Thus, for instance, in the example of the antique dealer given above, the goods should be regarded as specific at least for some purposes[12].

As noted above, a sale of a share in goods is a sale of goods and the Act now expressly provides that a contract for the sale of a share in specific goods – for instance, a sale of a half share in a named race horse – is to be treated as a sale of specific goods[13].

1   Although the Act does not expressly so provide, a contract for the sale of crops to be grown by the seller must also be a sale of future goods since crops to be grown cannot be existing goods.
2   As to whether or not it is a sale, see 8.2.2.
3   SoGA, s 5(3).
4   SoGA, s 5(2).
5   *Sainsbury Ltd v Street* [1972] 3 All ER 1127, [1972] 1 WLR 834; see below 16.2.1.
6   See chs 15 and 16.
7   SoGA, s 61(1).
8   Goode, *Commercial Law* (2nd edn, 1995) p 218. Such contracts are also referred to as sales of goods '*ex bulk*'.
9   See 15.5.
10   See Chalmers, *The Sale of Goods Act 1893* (18th edn, 1981) p 271; Atiyah, *Sale of Goods* (10th edn, 2000) p 72.
11   See *Benjamin's Sale of Goods* (5th edn, 1997) para 1-113; Goode, *Commercial Law* (2nd edn, 1995) p 231-232. Thus property in future goods can never pass under s 18, r 1 at the time the contract is made: see 15.2.1.1.
12   For instance, the application of the rules relating to mistake and frustration in ss 6 and 7 of the Act: see 16.2.
13   SoGA, s 61, as amended by Sale of Goods (Amendment) Act 1995, s 2(c): see Law Com 215 *Sale of goods forming part of bulk* (1993) paras 2.6, 5.4.

8.2   The classification of transactions

Where goods are transferred pursuant to an arrangement which does not satisfy the requirements of SoGA, s 2, the arrangement is not a contract for the sale of goods, and the provisions of SoGA will not apply. Distinguishing between sale and other, similar transactions may often involve the drawing of fine distinctions, and many arrangements may be susceptible of more than one interpretation. The law in this area often pays more attention to form than to substance.

In the past the distinctions may have been more important than they are today. Under the Sale of Goods Act 1893, s 4, contracts for sale of goods of the value of £10 or more were required to be evidenced by a note or memorandum in writing; if not, the contract was unenforceable unless the buyer accepted and actually received some part of the goods. This requirement did not apply to other, similar transactions, and thus it was often important to decide if a contract was one of sale, required to be evidenced in writing, or one for some other type of supply. With the erosion of the value of money by inflation, this requirement became excessively burdensome and s 4 was repealed in 1954[1]. The historical background should be borne in mind when considering cases decided prior to 1954; the potentially disastrous effects of construing a contract as one of sale may have influenced many of the borderline decisions.

In contrast, a powerful incentive for interpreting a contract as one of sale was the desire to grant the purchaser of the goods the protection of the implied terms relating to the quality, etc, of the goods contained in SoGA[2]. However, it was recognised at common law that it was anomalous that the buyer's rights should depend on fine classifications and the courts therefore indicated that they were prepared to imply into other supply contracts terms similar to those implied by SoGA[3]. Now such terms are implied by statute into all contracts of supply: contracts of hire purchase are regulated by the Supply of Goods (Implied Terms) Act 1973 (SoG(IT)A), whilst other contracts under which the property in goods is transferred, other than excepted contracts, are governed by the Supply of Goods and Services Act 1982 (SGSA). 'Excepted contracts' are (i) those covered by other legislation: sale, hire purchase and the provision of goods in exchange for trading stamps; (ii) contracts contained in deeds under which goods are transferred for no consideration; and (iii) contracts where property in goods is transferred by way of mortgage, pledge, charge or other security[4]. The 1982 Act therefore applies to a wide range of contracts, including hire, barter, exchange and work and materials. Different forms of contract under which goods are supplied on credit terms are all also regulated by the Consumer Credit Act 1974.

Nevertheless, there are still important distinctions between the different classes of supply contract. The 1973 and 1982 Acts, although implying terms about the goods supplied similar to those implied by the 1979 Act, do not contain such complete codes as the 1979 Act: for instance, the 1979 Act contains a detailed code concerned with the passing of property, not reproduced in the other statutes; and special rules replace the general contract rules relating to mistake and frustration in contracts of sale. It may be that, as the provisions of the 1979 Act are based on the rules of common law existing prior to 1893, similar provisions could be applied to other supply contracts at common law. However, it is clear that some rules apply uniquely to sale contracts. For instance, the buyer under a sale contract loses the right to reject the goods and terminate the contract if he accepts the goods, but the rules relating to acceptance apply only to sale contracts and are generally less favourable to the buyer than the rules which apply to other supply contracts. It may seem anomalous, and even unfair, that the buyer's rights should depend on distinctions which may be incomprehensible to most ordinary buyers and sellers, but in its 1987 Report on Sale and Supply of Goods, the Law Commission recommended that there was no need to abolish the distinction[5]. The supplier's ability to exclude or limit liability for breach of contract may also depend on the classification of the contract. We must therefore now consider how different transactions are classified.

1   By the Law Reform (Enforcement of Contracts) Act 1954, s 2.
2   Now contained in SoGA ss 13–15; see ch 11.
3   See *Young & Marten Ltd v McManus & Childs Ltd* [1969] 1 AC 454, [1968] 2 All ER 1169, HL.
4   SGSA 1982, s 1.
5   Law Commission 160 *Sale and Supply of Goods* (1987) paras 5.6–5.9, 5.44.

8.2.1   *Hire purchase and conditional sale*

As we have seen, the legal form of a hire purchase agreement is of a hiring, or bailment, of goods, by their owner (bailor) to the hirer (bailee), with the hirer being granted an option to purchase the goods at the end of the hire period. However, in reality this arrangement is almost wholly fictional. Certainly the hirer is not bound to exercise the option and complete the purchase of the goods, but the payments required of the hirer are normally greatly in excess of the sums which would be required under an ordinary hire or rental agreement. The truth is that the objective of hire purchase is the supply of goods on credit terms, coupled with security for the supplier. Since the goods do not become the hirer's property until all the instalments, including the option payment, are paid, if the hirer defaults the seller can repossess the goods (although the right to repossess may be restricted by statute[1]).

Goods may also be supplied on credit under a conditional sale agreement or under a simple credit sale. Under a conditional sale, the parties are committed to buy and sell at the outset, but the seller retains the property in the goods until the buyer pays the whole of the price (often by instalments, and inclusive of interest) as security. In contrast, under a credit sale, although the buyer is given credit, property in the goods passes to the buyer immediately, either at the time the contract is made or on delivery. Both conditional sale and credit sale contracts are sales from the outset and are therefore governed by SoGA.

In truth, a hire purchase agreement is closely analogous to a conditional sale agreement; indeed, consumers may find the three arrangements difficult to distinguish and refer to all three as 'hp' if payment is by instalments. For this reason, the different forms of transaction are now assimilated for several purposes. All three forms of contract are regulated by the Consumer Credit Act 1974, and some of the provisions of SoGA are modified when applied to consumer conditional sale agreements[2]. Nevertheless, the theoretical distinction remains, and, in the context of non-consumer transactions, the distinction may be crucial.

Both hire purchase and conditional sale offer the supplier protection against default or insolvency of the buyer or hirer. In each case, the supplier is secured by the retention of ownership. This was established in *McEntire v Crossley Bros*[3]. Under the Bills of Sale Acts 1878 and 1882 a document recording the transfer of ownership of goods without the transfer of possession is void against a trustee in bankruptcy or an execution creditor unless certain formalities are complied with and the agreement registered, and an agreement transferring ownership of goods as security for the payment of money is void even as between the parties to the agreement unless it complies with the statutory requirements and is registered[4]. The objective of the statutes is to prevent a person giving concealed security, by transferring property to creditors whilst retaining possession. In *McEntire v Crossley Bros* the House of Lords held that the Acts did not apply to a conditional sale agreement: the Acts only applied where the owner of goods transferred or granted a security interest over his own property; in a conditional sale agreement, the supplier retains property in order to secure himself; the debtor has no property over which to grant security. Obviously, the same reasoning applies to a hire purchase agreement.

Historically, hire purchase was developed because it offered the supplier protection against a wrongful disposition of the goods. Under the Factors Act 1889[5] a person who has 'bought or agreed to buy' goods may, in certain circumstances, dispose of them to a third party so as to pass a good title to the third party, even though the goods are still owned by the seller[6]. Thus a person who supplied goods under a conditional sale agreement could find his rights destroyed if the buyer resold the goods to an innocent third party[7]. However, in a landmark decision in 1895[8] the House of Lords held that a hirer under a hire purchase agreement is not a person who has agreed to buy goods; thus a wrongful disposition by the hirer would not affect the owner's rights. Hire purchase thus offered the supplier greater security than conditional sale. This distinction is no longer so important as it was. Where a conditional sale agreement is a consumer credit agreement within the meaning of the Consumer Credit Act 1974, it is treated for this purpose as if it were a hire purchase agreement[9]. In the consumer context, therefore, a conditional sale agreement now offers the supplier much the same protection, as hire purchase. Where, however, a conditional sale agreement is not a consumer credit agreement for the purposes of the 1974 Act, the distinction between conditional sale and hire purchase remains significant. The fine nature of that distinction is indicated by the recent decision in *Forthright Finance Ltd v Carlyle Finance Ltd*[10]. O, a finance company, delivered a car to a car dealer under an agreement which was described as a 'hire purchase agreement'. The agreement used the language of hire purchase, referring to the parties as 'owner' and 'hirer', and provided for the dealer to hold the car as bailee with an option to purchase, but then provided that the option would be deemed to have been exercised and that property in the car would to pass to the dealer when all the instalments had been paid unless the dealer expressly indicated otherwise. Before property passed the dealer sold the car to a third party. O sought to recover the car arguing that the agreement was one of hire purchase and that therefore the dealer was not a person who had 'bought or agreed to buy' the car and was unable to pass a good title. The Court of Appeal held that the agreement was in reality a conditional sale. It had all the characteristics of a conditional sale. The inclusion of the 'option' was regarded as artificial. It was most unlikely that the dealer, having paid all of the instalments, would exercise the option not to acquire the car.

The assimilation of the rules applicable to consumer hire purchase and conditional sale agreements has contributed to a decline in the use of hire purchase. At the same time, both types of agreement have been subject to increased legislative regulation both to protect consumers and, from time to time, through controls such as minimum deposit requirements, to regulate demand in the economy.

1   Consumer Credit Act 1974, s 90; see 26.6.4.
2   See SoGA, s 25(2), below 17.4.2; SoGITA, s 14(1), below 12.2.4.
3   [1895] AC 457.
4   See 22.0.3.1.
5   Section 9; a similar rule is contained in SoGA, s 25.
6   See 17.4.2.
7   *Lee v Butler* [1893] 2 QB 318, CA.
8   *Helby v Matthews* [1895] AC 471, HA.
9   SoGA, s 25(2).
10   [1997] 4 All ER 90, CA.

8.2.2   *Work and materials*

The distinction between contracts of sale and contracts for work and materials has always been a particularly difficult one. Whereas the object of a contract of sale is the transfer of property in goods to the buyer, the object of a contract of work and materials is the performance of a service for the customer, involving the transfer of property in goods in the performance of that service. Where no goods are transferred, the contract is purely one for services.

The distinction was of particular importance prior to 1954, when contracts for the sale of goods of the value of £10 or more were required to be evidenced in writing. However, even after the repeal of that requirement, the distinction continues to be important in some situations. A contract of sale contains implied terms which in certain circumstances require the goods delivered by the seller to comply with their description, be of satisfactory quality and fit for the buyer's purpose[1]. In 1969[2] the House of Lords recognised that it was illogical that the buyer's rights should depend on fine and technical distinctions between similar contracts and ruled that similar terms would be implied into a contract for work and materials at common law. The position is now regulated by SGSA 1982, which implies into a contract for work and materials terms similar to those implied into sale contracts by SoGA[3] and a further term requiring the work performed under the contract to be carried out with reasonable skill and care[4]. However, where the contract requires the seller to supply work and materials to produce a finished product, it may still be important to decide whether the contract is a sale of the finished product or a contract for work and materials. Liability for breach of the implied terms relating to goods is strict under both statutes, but if the buyer's complaint relates to the finished item rather than an individual component, the seller will be strictly liable if the contract is one of sale; whereas if the contract is for work and materials, the seller will only be liable if the buyer can prove he was negligent. In addition, where the buyer is a consumer, it is impossible for the seller to exclude or limit his liability for breach of the implied terms relating to goods[5]; but the duty of care in relation to services may be excluded provided the exclusion satisfies the test of reasonableness[6]. Classification of the contract may also affect the buyer's right to reject the goods and terminate the contract[7], and the timing of the passing of property[8].

At different times, different tests have been proposed to distinguish between the two types of contract. However, it is probably important to bear in mind that several different types of transaction may be regarded as contracts for work and materials. In particular, it may be important to distinguish between the situation where the 'seller' supplies work and labour to perform a service on the 'buyer's' property, such as a contract to service a car, and the situation where the 'seller' supplies work and materials to produce a finished product, such as a contract to build a machine or to paint a portrait.

In any given situation, four interpretations may be possible.

1.   There may be one contract of sale, or for services, with labour, or goods, being supplied as an ancillary element. Such an interpretation will only be likely where one element is far more significant than the other.
2.   The contract may simply be one for work and materials regulated by the 1982 Act.
3.   It may be that there are two separate contracts governing the work and materials respectively.
4.   Where the 'seller' is to produce a finished product, the contract may be one for sale of the finished product.

The EC Directive on Consumer Guarantees[9] deals with this point explicitly and provides that 'contracts for the supply of consumer goods to be manufactured or produced shall . . . be deemed contracts of sale for the purpose of this Directive'[10]. The classification of the contract for the purposes of the Sale of Goods Act, however, depends on the intention of the parties as indicated by the terms of the contract, their behaviour and the surrounding circumstances, such as the way in which the work and materials were invoiced to the 'buyer'. In most cases where the 'buyer' supplies materials for the 'seller' to work on, the correct interpretation will be that the contract is one purely for services[11]. Where the 'seller' supplies goods and services, the courts have, in the past, applied a 'substance of the contract' test, and thus ruled that contracts to supply a meal in a restaurant[12] and to manufacture a ship's propeller (to a design supplied by the buyer)[13] were contracts of sale, whereas contracts to repair a car[14], apply a hair dye[15] and for a vet to supply and administer medicine to an animal[16] were contracts for work and materials. The natural interpretation of most of these arrangements would now be that they should be governed by the 1982 Act.

Where the contract is for the production and supply of a finished article, the courts have suggested two different tests. In *Clay v Yates*[17] a contract for a printer to print a book, the printer supplying the paper, was interpreted as one for work and materials, applying the 'substance of the contract' test. In contrast, in *Lee v Griffin*[18] the court ruled that wherever the contract results in the production of a finished product which is transferred under the contract, the contract is a sale and therefore held that a contract for a dentist to make and supply false teeth was a sale of the finished product. However, in *Robinson v Graves*[19] the Court of Appeal reverted to the 'substance of the contract' test. As Greer LJ observed:

> 'If you find . . . that the substance of the contract was the production of something to be sold . . . then it is a sale of goods. But if the substance of the contract, on the other hand, is that skill and labour have to be used for the production of the article and that it is only ancillary to that that there will pass . . . some materials, the substance of the contract is the skill and experience'[20].

The court therefore held that a contract for a painter to paint a portrait was one for work and materials. However, the reference to materials passing ancillary to the exercise of skill suggests that the court was thinking in terms of the painter selling the canvas and paint used in the portrait, rather than of the possibility of the sale of the finished painting. Indeed, the case should not be taken as laying down an absolute rule, since the court recognised that a contract for a sculptor to produce a statue might be construed as a sale of the finished statue. The effect of the decision in *Robinson v Graves* was to prevent the buyer repudiating the contract and sheltering behind s 4 of the Sales of Goods Act 1893. A different approach might be adopted where a buyer complains of a defect in the finished goods[21], and it is submitted that the approach of the EC Directive, treating contracts for the manufacture and supply of a finished item as contracts of sale, has much to commend it, at least in a consumer context. Indeed, in Australia the Supreme Court of Victoria has described *Robinson v Graves* as a 'hard case' and expressly rejected its test as 'illogical and unsatisfactory', 'wrong in principle' and 'too erratic' to be useful[22].

In recent years the courts have been prepared to be more flexible in their approach. In *Hyundai Heavy Industries Ltd v Papadopoulos*[23] the House of Lords held that a contract to build and supply a ship was a contract of sale; however, it was not a pure sale, and had some of the characteristics of a building contract. Similarly, where a contract for work and materials results in the production of a finished item terms relating to the quality and fitness of the finished item may be implied at common law[24].

1   SoGA, ss 13–15, below ch 11.
2   *Young & Marten Ltd v McManus Childs Ltd* [1969] 1 AC 454, [1969] 2 All ER 1169, HL.
3   SGSA 1982, ss 3–5.
4   SGSA 1982, s 13.
5   UCTA 1977, ss 6–7.

6 UCTA 1977, s 2.
7 See 12.2.4.
8 See ch 15.
9 Directive 1999/44/EC of the European Parliament and of the Council of 25 May 1999 on certain aspects of the sale of consumer goods and associated guarantees (1999) OJ L 171/12 7.7.99.
10 Article 1(4).
11 But see *Dixon v London Small Arms Co* (1876) 1 App Cas 632, where such an arrangement was interpreted as a sale of components by B to S, with a sale back of the finished product. See also *Truk (UK) Ltd v Tokmakidis GmbH* [2000] 1 Lloyd's Rep 543: contract of sale.
12 *Lockett v A & M Charles Ltd* [1938] 4 All ER 170.
13 *Cammell Laird & Co Ltd v Manganese Bronze and Brass Co Ltd* [1934] AC 402, HL.
14 *G H Myers & Co v Brent Cross Service Co* [1934] 1 KB 46.
15 *Watson v Buckley, Osborne, Garrett & Co Ltd* [1940] 1 All ER 174.
16 *Dodd and Dodd v Wilson & McWilliam* [1946] 2 All ER 691.
17 (1856) 1 H & N 73.
18 (1861) 1 B & S 272.
19 [1935] 1 KB 579, CA.
20 At 587.
21 Alternatively, the court could imply terms into a contract for work and materials requiring the finished product to be of satisfactory quality, fit for the buyer's purpose etc: SGSA, s 16(3): see 19.1.
22 *Deta Nominees v Viscount Plastic Products Ltd* [1979] VR 167. See also *Marcel Furriers v Tapper* [1953] 1 WLR 49; *R v Wood Green Profiteering Committee, ex p Boots Cash Chemists (Southern) Ltd* (1920) 89 LJKB 55.
23 [1980] 2 All ER 29, [1980] 1 WLR 1129, HL; see *Stocznia Gdanska SA v Latvian Shipping Co* [1998] 1 All ER 883.
24 *IBA v EMI Electronics and BICC Construction Ltd* (1980) 14 BLR 9.

8.2.2.1 Computer software

The classification of contracts for the supply of computer software has provoked much debate[1]. The issue has now arisen in several decided cases but has not yet been conclusively settled. The question may arise in several different contexts and it may well be that individual contracts may be classified differently according to the particular circumstances of the case. Even if software is capable of being 'goods', the particular contract under which software is supplied may not be a contract for the sale of goods.

Software is supplied in many different ways. Many everyday items, such as motor cars, video recorders, burglar alarms and so on, include systems which depend on computer programs. In many cases this will be in the form of an embedded program. It seems clear that the fact that an item incorporates and depends for its operation on such software does not affect the classification of the item as goods, so that if I buy a new car the contract is still one for the sale of goods even if the car has a computerised engine management system.

It has been held that computer hardware is goods[2] and a contract for the sale of computer hardware should therefore be a contract for the sale of goods, notwithstanding that the computer incorporates some embedded software. Slightly more difficult is the case of a contract for the supply of hardware and (separate) software together, as a package. It has been held in Australia that a contract for the supply of a computer system comprising hardware and software was a contract for the sale of goods[3], and that was accepted as correct, albeit obiter, by Sir Iain Glidewell in the leading English case of *St Albans City and District Council v International Computers Ltd*[4].

Most debate has centred on the status of contracts for the supply of software alone. Two factors have been regarded as significant: first, whether the software in question is a mass produced or 'off-the-shelf' package or a 'bespoke' program produced for a particular customer/client; and, second, whether the program is supplied on a physical medium, such as a floppy diskette. In the *St Albans* case Sir Iain Glidewell considered the status of a contract for the supply of software and concluded that the classification of the contract would depend in part on the manner in which the software is supplied. He concluded that 'goods' must be a tangible item and that the software program itself is not, as such, 'goods'. However, he took the view that where the program is supplied on some physical medium, such as a diskette or CD-ROM, the medium is 'goods', and that 'defects' in the program would therefore make the diskette or CD-ROM unsatisfactory. On the facts of the case the program had been supplied by being installed by the defendants directly onto the plaintiffs' computer system so that there was no sale. Similarly, there would therefore be no sale of goods where a program is simply downloaded from the Internet.

According to this approach, therefore, the classification of the contract will depend on whether the program is supplied via a physical medium. This may result in fine distinctions with two contracts for the supply of the same program being classified differently. A more attractive analysis is that offered by Lord Penrose, the Lord Ordinary, in the Scots case of *Beta Computers (Europe) Ltd v Adobe Systems Ltd*[5]. He took the view that a contract for the supply of software should not be regarded as a sale but as a contract *sui generis*, having some of the characteristics of a sale and some of a licence. It is submitted that, conceptually, this is more satisfying. The user of a software program will normally require a licence to use it lawfully, and the essence of the supply of software is the grant of such a licence.

To some extent the attempt to classify software contracts in the abstract is meaningless. The question of classification is most likely to arise where the software proves defective and the end user seeks to rely on the statutory implied terms relating to the quality etc of the goods implied into contracts for the sale of goods by the Sale of Goods Act[6]. The classification of software as goods or otherwise will not necessarily determine this issue either way. Even if software is capable of being 'goods', the contract under which it is supplied is not necessarily a sale, whilst even if software is not goods, or the contract is not a sale, the contract may still contain implied terms about the quality etc of the software. It has been suggested that a distinction should be drawn between contracts for the supply of standard, off the shelf software, which could be classified as contracts of sale, and contracts for the production of 'bespoke' programs for individual clients, which should be regarded as contracts for professional services, or for work and materials[7], on the basis that applying the 'substance of the contract' test from *Robinson v Graves*, the essence of the contract is the supplier's professional skill. However, this too may be simplistic. There may be intermediate positions between the two extremes where a contractor supplies a more or less standard package but adapts it for an individual client. Moreover, as already noted, the *Robinson v Graves* test has been criticised. And even if a contract for bespoke software is one for professional services, it does not follow that a contract for 'off-the-shelf' software is a sale of goods. Even the buyer of an off-the-shelf program needs a licence from the software copyright holder.

The real issues for consideration in software cases are likely to be (a) whether it is right to impose strict liability for defective software and (b) if so, on whom? Treating software as goods means that strict liability under the statutory implied terms is imposed on the contractual supplier. Sir Ian Glidewell was clearly correct in the *St Albans* case to conclude that where a program is supplied on a diskette the diskette is goods. But should defects in the intellectual content of the program itself make the diskette unsatisfactory so that the supplier is strictly liable for losses caused by 'defects'? A distinction can be drawn between the intellectual content of the program and the physical medium on which it is supplied. The intellectual content of the program is not 'sold'. This issue is not confined to software. Similar issues could arise in relation to books. Sir Iain Glidewell recognised this and suggested that if a car maintenance manual contains inaccurate instructions that would make the manual unsatisfactory and/or unfit for its purpose[8].

In fact, it is submitted that in relation to this issue classification of software as goods or otherwise need not be decisive. Even if a contract for the supply of software is not one for the sale of goods it might be possible to imply into the contract terms as to the quality and fitness for purpose of the software at common law. In the *St Albans* case Sir Iain Glidewell thought that terms would be implied on this basis where software is supplied without a physical medium[9]. So where a standard, off-the-shelf, program is supplied, whether via a physical medium or otherwise, the contract may include similar implied terms. Similar terms could be implied at common law into a contract for the production and supply of a 'bespoke' program. Secondly, it should be remembered that there will normally be a licence between the software producer and the end user[10]. It might be possible in an appropriate case to imply terms as to the quality, fitness for purpose and so on of software into that contract.

It may therefore be that the classification of software contracts as sales of goods or otherwise will not be decisive as to the rights and liabilities of the parties. It should be borne in mind, however, that the statutory implied terms as to quality etc in the Sale of Goods Act arise automatically and their exclusion is strictly controlled by the Unfair Contract Terms Act[11]. Careful wording of the appropriate contract may prevent implication of a term into a contract at common law, since such a term cannot be implied if it would contradict the express terms of the contract.

1   Similar problems arise in relation to product liability, where the question is whether software is a 'product' for the purposes of the Consumer Protection Act 1987 and the EC Product Liability Directive 1985/374, dated 25 July 1985: see generally Whittaker (1989) 105 LQR 125.

2   *Amstrad plc v Seagate Technology Inc* (1997) 86 BLR 34.

3   *Toby Constructions Products Pty Ltd v Computa Bar (Sales) Pty Ltd* [1983] 2 NSWLR 48.

4   [1996] 4 All ER 481. The question was not considered by the other members of the Court of Appeal. Scott Baker J at first instance had held that the contract in question was one for the sale of goods: see [1995] FSR 686. The status of software was left unresolved in the earlier case of *Eurodynamics Ltd v General Automation Ltd* (6 September 1988, unreported), QBD.

5   1996 SLT 604. See Adams (1997) Edinburgh Law Rev 386.

6   SoGA, ss 13–15: see ch 11. This was not the issue in *Beta Computers (Europe) Ltd v Adobe Systems Ltd* 1996 SLT 604. Application of the implied terms to software may be problematic: see Bradgate (1999) 2 J Information Law and Technology <http://www.law.warwick.ac.uk/jilt/99-2/bradgate.html>.

7   See *Salvage Association v CAP Financial Services Ltd* (9 July 1993, unreported).

8   [1996] 4 All ER 481 at 493. In the American case of *Cardozo v True* 342 So 2d 1053 (1977) it was held that booksellers who sold a cookery book were not liable for errors in its contents, drawing the distinction suggested above between the physical book and its intellectual content. Contrast *Winter v G P Puttnam & Sons* F 2d 1033 (9th Circ 1991), where it was suggested that information in software might be a product.

9   [1996] 4 All ER 481 at 494.

10 Software packages sold 'off-the-shelf' normally contain so-called 'shrink-wrap' licences which constitute an offer by the copyright holder to grant the user a licence to use the program on certain terms. The user accepts the offer by opening the package. Where software is supplied 'on-line' the practice has developed of requiring the customer to agree to a similar 'click-wrap' licence.

11 UCTA, s 6: see 11.5.

8.2.3 Contracts of exchange and barter

Although goods and services are normally supplied in exchange for money payments, contracts where the consideration is not money but is by the provision of other goods or services are not uncommon and, in times of high inflation and unpredictable foreign exchange rates, goods provide a reliable form of payment. As an eminent Scots lawyer put it, 'Even if the currency may suffer unwelcome and involuntary dilution in value at the present time, a Scotsman may hope that whisky will not suffer likewise'[1].

As explained earlier, part exchange contracts may be analysed as contracts of barter. Goods may be transferred under barter agreements even in large-scale international dealings, under countertrade arrangements. Many countries, particularly those with developing economies, insist that exporters wishing to supply goods or services to them must enter into reciprocal arrangements to acquire their goods as a condition of entering into the export sale contract. Such arrangements allow less developed countries, often short of hard currency, to use their own products in order to acquire imported goods and services. Oil-exporting countries often use oil in this way. Countertrade is unpopular with the governments of developed economies: it is 'potentially distortive and disruptive to the growth of trade as it replaces the pressures of competition and market forces with reciprocity, protection and price setting'[2]. Countertrade arrangements are also hazardous for exporters, who may find themselves burdened with goods which are difficult to resell. However, an exporter may often have to accept a countertrade arrangement in order to do business in certain export markets. Often, such arrangements may be analysed as mutual, dependent sales, with the prices due under the contracts being set off one against the other. However, in some cases the correct analysis may be that there is one contract of barter.

In a consumer context, goods are often supplied as part of marketing promotions in exchange for vouchers or coupons. The vouchers may be accepted by the seller either as part of the consideration for goods, entitling the consumer to a reduction in the price, or as the whole consideration, allowing the consumer to acquire extra goods without any money payment. Alternatively, consumers may be offered 'free gifts', either on purchasing goods or services, or on doing some further act, such as sending labels or tokens to the manufacturer of goods.

Such transactions could be interpreted in several different ways, depending on the circumstances. Where goods are on general sale, and the consumer can choose to 'buy' with cash, or with vouchers having a 'cash value', the transaction is probably a sale. A transaction where a consumer is given a 'gift' on purchasing goods could be regarded as a sale of the goods and the 'gift' together, as a sale of the goods with a genuine gift, or as a sale of the goods together with a contract to supply the 'gift' in exchange for contracting to buy the goods[3]. Under the third analysis, the 'gift' is supplied under a contract of barter. Where the consumer has to send vouchers, tokens or labels, either alone or with cash, in order to obtain a 'gift', the vouchers etc may be regarded as part or all of the consideration[4], so that the 'gift' is supplied under a contract of barter.

In all these cases it may be very difficult to draw a clear distinction between contracts of barter and contracts of sale. The deciding factor in any particular case is the intention of the parties, which will be found by an examination of all the circumstances of the case. The fact that the consideration supplied by each party is given a monetary value may well be a significant factor allowing the contract to be classified as a sale[5]. However, the classification will have less impact on the rights of the buyer than in the case of contracts for work and materials. In contracts of both sale and barter, statutory implied terms require the goods to comply with their description, be of satisfactory quality and fit for the buyer's purpose.

A different form of sales promotion, popular in the 1960s, involved the use of trading stamps. Retailers entered into arrangements with trading stamp companies, under which the retailers were allowed to supply stamps to consumers who bought goods or services from them, the number of stamps supplied depending on the value of the purchase. The consumer was allowed to redeem the stamps for goods with the trading stamp company. It is not clear if the supply of goods in exchange for stamps should be regarded as a sale or as a contract of barter. Such arrangements are open to abuse, and they are therefore strictly regulated by statute[6] which, inter alia, requires stamps to be marked with their cash value, requires the consumer to be allowed to redeem stamps for cash, and implies into the contract for the supply of goods in exchange for stamps, terms relating to the goods similar to those contained in SoGA. Such arrangements declined in popularity during the latter part of the 1970s and the 1980s, although there has been something of a revival in recent years[7]. In some jurisdictions they are subject to even stronger regulation than in the UK[8].

1   T B Smith (1974) 47 Tulane LR 1029 at 1042. This Englishman respectfully concurs.
2   *Countertrade: some guidance for exporters*, brochure issued by the Department of Trade and Industry (1985).
3   See *Esso Petroleum Ltd v Customs and Excise Comrs* [1976] 1 All ER 117, [1976] 1 WLR 1, CA; above 8.1.3.
4   *Chappell & Co Ltd v Nestlé & Co Ltd* [1960] AC 87, [1959] 2 All ER 701, HL.
5   See above 8.1.3.
6   Trading Stamps Act 1964.
7   An analogy could perhaps be drawn with the modern loyalty 'points' schemes operated by some retailers, credit card issuers etc, under which consumers are awarded points for purchases made within the scheme, depending on the value of the purchase. Points are normally redeemable in exchange for goods or services. Where points are given a cash value and are redeemable for cash it may be possible to view a supply of goods for points as a sale. Where, however, the points have no cash value and goods are supplied solely in exchange for points the transaction would appear to be more in the nature of a barter.
8   See Cranston, *Consumers and the Law* (2nd edn, 1984) p 342.

8.2.4   *Hire and bailment*[1]

The term 'bailment' takes in a wide range of different arrangements, including the following:

*   contracts for the hire of goods, such as rental and leasing contracts;
*   contracts for work and labour, as for instance where the owner of a car leaves it at a garage for repair;
*   contracts for custody for reward, where the owner of goods leaves them with someone, such as a warehouseman, for safekeeping; and
*   contracts of pledge, where the owner of goods deposits them with a bailee as security for a loan.

In addition, bailments may arise in the course of other commercial operations; like agency, bailment is a flexible concept, which may be invoked by the courts in a wide range of circumstances[2]. In particular, bailments may arise within sale transactions. Thus where a seller supplies goods under a conditional sale agreement, including where goods are sold subject to a retention of title[3], the buyer will hold the goods as bailee until property passes. Similarly, where goods are supplied on sale or return terms, the goods are bailed until the 'buyer' agrees to buy them or returns them[4]. Alternatively, where the seller remains in possession of the goods after title has passed to the buyer, the seller will hold goods as bailee for the buyer[5]. As we have seen[6], a contract of hire purchase is, strictly speaking, a contract of bailment coupled with an option for the bailee to buy.

Not all of these arrangements involve the supply of goods. In general, however, bailments in a commercial context involve the supply of goods or of services, and it will be convenient to outline the common features of bailments here.

Bailments may be voluntary or involuntary. An involuntary bailment will arise where a person finds another person's goods in his possession or on his premises without his consent. A voluntary bailment may become involuntary, as, for instance, where a bailor fails to collect his goods on termination of the bailment: however, a bailee in such a position may have a statutory right to sell the uncollected goods under the Torts (Interference with Goods) Act 1977[7], provided certain conditions are fulfilled.

Voluntary bailments may be gratuitous or for reward. Where a bailment is contractual, the transaction may involve the bailor supplying goods to the bailee, as under a hire or hire purchase contract; or the bailee may supply services to the bailor, as under a contract for work and materials or a warehousing contract. Where the bailment is contractual, the contract may contain terms defining the obligations of the parties, including, for instance, defining the duration of the bailment. However, even where a bailment is not contractual it may be a bailment on terms defining the scope of the bailee's liability for the goods.

The common feature of all these arrangements is that the bailor transfers possession of the goods to the bailee; ownership remains in the bailor. In certain situations the bailor may have 'constructive possession' of goods which are in the actual possession of the bailee. It seems that this will be the case where the bailee holds the goods to the bailor's order, as under a warehousing contract. In contrast, where the bailee holds for his own interest, as under a contract of hire, it is better to regard the bailee as having exclusive possession:

'Any person is to be regarded as a bailee who otherwise than as a servant either receives possession of a thing from another or consents to receive or hold possession of a thing for another upon an undertaking with the other person either to keep and return or to deliver to him the specific thing or to (convey and apply) the specific thing according to the directions antecedent or future of the other person'[8].

---

1   See generally Palmer, *Bailment* (2nd edn, 1991); Bell in Palmer and McKendrick (eds), *Interests in Goods* (2nd edn, 1998).
2   See per Robert Goff LJ in *Clough Mill Ltd v Martin* [1984] 3 All ER 982 at 987, [1985] 1 WLR 111 at 116, CA.
3   See *Aluminium Industrie Vaassen BV v Romalpa Aluminium Ltd* [1976] 2 All ER 552, [1976] 1 WLR 676, CA; below 18.4.1.
4   See 15.2.2.
5   See 16.1.3.
6   See 8.2.1.
7   Sections 12–13.
8   Pollock and Wright, *Possession in the Common Law* (1866) p 163.

8.2.4.1   *Common features of bailments*

The bailee's right to possession of the goods gives sufficient legal interest in the goods to enable him to bring proceedings against any third party who wrongfully interferes with them, or against a third party who negligently damages them[1]. Moreover, the bailee has sufficient interest in the goods to insure them against loss or damage[2]; the bailee may insure the goods for their full value but if he makes a claim under the policy, he may retain only such amount as will cover his own interest and hold the balance as trustee for the bailor[3].

In general, bailment depends on consent; the bailee's right to possession can therefore be determined by the bailor withdrawing consent and demanding the return of the goods. A failure to return the goods at the end of the bailment is a conversion by the bailee. However, where the bailment is contractual, the terms of the contract may restrict the bailor's right to terminate the bailment. Moreover, the bailor's right to demand the return of the goods may be restricted by law. Thus certain contracts of hire are regulated by the Consumer Credit Act 1974, which restricts the right of the bailor[4] and extends the right of the bailee[5] to terminate the hiring and a person who performs work on a chattel under a contract of work and materials, such as a garage repairing a car, is entitled to a lien over the chattel in question to secure payment of any sums due to him in respect of the work done, and may therefore be able to resist a demand for its return[6]. If the bailee intentionally does in relation to the goods any act inconsistent with the bailor's ownership, such as selling, pledging or offering the goods for sale, he is guilty of conversion and the bailment is automatically terminated. However, again the position is modified by statute; in particular, where a bailor is in breach of an obligation to retake delivery of goods, the bailee has a statutory right to dispose of the goods in certain circumstances[7]. In addition, a bailee may escape liability where he deals with the bailor's goods in circumstances which make him an agent of necessity[8].

A person in possession of goods may become a bailee of them for another by acknowledging that he holds the goods on behalf of that person. Such acknowledgment is known as an 'attornment'; thus a seller in possession of goods may attorn in favour of the buyer. Alternatively, attornment may take place in the context of an existing bailment, for instance where goods are held in a warehouse on behalf of their owner. If the owner wishes to dispose of the goods, he may instruct the warehouseman to attorn in favour of the buyer, and if the warehouseman does so, he becomes bailee of the goods for the buyer.

The bailee may be placed in a difficult position where a third party claims the goods: failure to return the goods to the bailor on demand would be a conversion, but retention of the goods, or delivering them to the bailor, would expose the bailee to liability in conversion as against the third party, if his claim proves to be valid. At common law the bailee was not entitled to set up the third party's right to the goods, or jus tertii, in defence to a claim for the goods by the bailor. However, the position is again modified by statute: the bailee is now entitled to set up the jus tertii and there are provisions designed to protect the bailee against double liability in such cases[9].

A bailee will often be selected, like an agent, for personal reasons. A bailee will therefore be liable in conversion if he sub-bails goods entrusted to his possession. A sub-bailment may be expressly or impliedly authorised by the owner; in that case, the relationship of bailor and bailee may arise between the owner and the sub-bailee, so that the latter will owe the duties of a bailee to the owner. However, even where the sub-bailment was not authorised, the sub-bailee may be liable in negligence for any loss of or damage to the goods in his possession. A sub-bailment may often arise in commercial operations: for instance, where a warehouse keeper entrusts the goods to another warehouse for storage, or where a carrier sub-contracts part or all of the carriage of goods. In such a case, the sub-bailee may often seek to rely on contract terms excluding or limiting his liability for loss of or damage to the goods, and the question may arise whether such terms are binding on the bailor. Clearly, the bailor will be bound where he gives the bailee authority to act as his agent and conclude a contract of bailment between him and the 'sub-bailee'. However, even where the original bailee is not authorised to act as agent in this way, so that there is no privity between the bailor and the sub-bailee, the bailor will be bound by the terms of the sub-bailment if he has expressly or impliedly consented to the bailee entering into a sub-bailment containing such terms and the sub-bailee has sufficient notice that someone is interested in the goods other than the bailee who entrusts them to him[10]. The result will be that the bailor will be bound by the sub-bailee's terms and the sub-bailee will owe the bailor the duties of a bailee, as qualified by his terms, even though there is no contract between them.

In general, a bailee owes the bailor a duty to take care of the goods in his possession. The standard of care required of the bailee will depend on all the circumstances of the case. Usually, it seems that an involuntary bailee is only liable for gross negligence or deliberate damage to the goods. However, a voluntary bailee, whether acting for reward or gratuitously, owes a duty to take reasonable care of the goods. The fact that the bailee is paid for his services may increase the standard of care required to discharge the duty. In the event that the goods are lost or damaged whilst in the bailee's possession, the onus is on the bailee to prove that he took reasonable care of the goods. If a bailee deviates from the terms of the bailment, he becomes liable as an insurer of the goods, and is liable even for wholly accidental loss or damage. Thus if a warehouseman agrees to store goods in one warehouse, and then moves them, without authority, to another, he is liable for any loss or damage, even though he takes all reasonable care to avoid it, unless he can show that the loss would have occurred even had the goods been stored as agreed[11]. A bailee is liable for loss or damage caused by the negligence of his employees or independent agents[12]; and he will also be liable for dishonest or fraudulent acts of his employees[13].

1 *The Winkfield* [1902] P 42, CA; *Leigh and Sillivan Ltd v Aliakmon Shipping Co Ltd* [1986] AC 785, [1986] 2 All ER 145, HL.
2 See 35.1.3.
3 *Hepburn v A Tomlinson (Hauliers) Ltd* [1966] AC 451, [1966] 1 All ER 418, HL; see 35.1.5.
4 Consumer Credit Act 1974, ss 76, 86–92 and 98; see 26.6.7.
5 CCA, ss 69–72, 101; see 26.6.2.
6 See 22.1.2.
7 Torts (Interference with Goods) Act 1977, ss 12–13.
8 Above 4.5.
9 Torts (Interference with Goods) Act 1977, ss 7–8.
10 *Morris v C W Martin* [1966] 1 QB 716, [1965] 2 All ER 725, CA; *Singer Co (UK) Ltd v Tees and Hartlepool Port Authority* [1988] 2 Lloyd's Rep 164; [1988] JBL 255; *KH Enterprise (cargo owners) v Pioneer Container (owners), The Pioneer Container* [1994] 2 AC 324, [1994] 2 All ER 250, PC; see 32.7.
11 *Lilley v Doubleday* (1881) 7 QBD 510. This is effectively a variant of the 'fundamental breach' rule: see 2.6.2.
12 *British Road Services Ltd v Arthur V Crutchley & Co Ltd* [1968] 1 All ER 811, CA.
13 *Morris v C W Martin* [1966] 1 QB 716.

8.2.4.2   *Contracts of hire*

A contract for the hire of goods is a bailment, and is therefore subject to the common law rules outlined above. Contracts of hire may take a number of different forms, including contract hire, rental, operating lease and finance lease. The common feature of all these arrangements is that, although they involve the supply of goods, only possession, rather than ownership, is transferred. It should be noted that the use of goods may be 'lent' pursuant to contracts under which possession and control of the goods remains with the lender. This will normally be the case where a piece of machinery, such as a crane, is hired together with an operator for a particular job. In such a case, the owner remains in possession and control of the goods, and the correct analysis of such a contract is that it is a contract for services, rather than one of hire. Where a ship is chartered, complete with crew, under a voyage or time charterparty the contract does not involve a hiring of the ship; in contrast, where a ship is leased, with or without crew, under a demise charterparty, there is a contract for the hire of the ship. Similar arrangements may be made in respect of aircraft.

Hiring, rather than selling, goods may offer a number of commercial advantages. As long ago as 1798 it was recognised that 'whatsoever may be granted or parted with for ever, may be granted or parted with for a time, and therefore not only lands and houses have been let for years, but also goods and chattels'[1].

Hiring may be particularly attractive at times of rapid technological change, when there may be uncertainty about the reliability or economic life of equipment. Thus, for instance, in the early days of television – and, more recently, video recorders – many consumers chose to rent equipment until technology became standardised, more reliable and cheaper. Under such rental agreements, the owner generally remains responsible for maintenance and repair, freeing the hirer from some of the responsibilities and risks of ownership. Another attraction of hire contracts at one time was that they escaped many of the statutory controls designed to protect consumers. Legislation to regulate hire purchase contracts and protect consumers was first introduced in 1938; in subsequent years, further legislation followed, and provisions requiring minimum deposits and imposing credit controls were introduced. In 1971 the Crowther Committee observed that the –

'wide extent of television rental is a phenomenon unique to this country, in other countries people buy their television sets by one means of finance or another. It is difficult not to connect this with the fact that, in the early days of statutory control of the terms of hire purchase lending in this country, rental was exempt, and it was therefore possible to obtain a television set on weekly or monthly payments without the necessity of putting down a substantial deposit'[2].

It is now recognised that the practical effect of a hire agreement may be virtually identical to that of a contract for the supply of goods on credit terms, such as hire purchase or conditional sale. The Consumer Credit Act 1974 therefore subjects consumer hire agreements to controls similar to those applicable to consumer credit agreements[3] and the Supply of Goods and Services Act 1982 implies certain terms into all contracts of hire similar to those implied into contracts of sale and other supply contracts, including that the goods hired should comply with description, and be of satisfactory quality and fit for their purpose[4].

Although the 1982 Act applies to all forms of hire contract, for commercial purposes contracts of hire can be divided into three broad categories – lease, rental and contract hire – each having its own particular commercial characteristics.

1   Bacon, *A treatise on leases and terms for years* (1798) p 7.
2   Report of the Committee on Consumer Credit (Cmnd 4596) (1971) para 1.1.2.
3   See 25.1.
4   SGSA, ss 6–10.

8.2.4.3   *Leases*

A lease may be described as a contract between a lessor and lessee for the hire of a specific asset selected from a manufacturer or vendor of such assets. The lessor is not necessarily the manufacturer or vendor: he may purchase the asset for the purpose of leasing it to the lessee. The lessor is owner of the asset, and retains ownership. The lessee has the right to possess and use the asset over the period of the lease on payment of the rentals specified in the contract.

Leasing of business equipment first became common in the nineteenth century when companies were established to lease rolling stock to the new railway companies; in recent years it has become increasingly popular, sophisticated and international. In the early 1960s financial institutions, having previously concentrated on consumer transactions, began to turn their attention to industrial financing. The growing use of increasingly expensive technology, which was likely to become obsolete more quickly than had been the case with more traditional plant and machinery, coupled with high inflation and government policies in relation to investment incentives in the 1970s, encouraged the growth of leasing. As a result, leasing is now seen as an attractive alternative to purchasing a wide range of assets, from small items such as office equipment, to such items as aircraft and drilling rigs. 'The huge growth in finance leasing illustrates how little importance is attached by the businessman to the legal concept of ownership. To him what matters is the substance, not the form'[1].

Commercial chattel leases can be divided into two broad categories: finance leases and operating leases.

A finance lease normally involves the lease of an asset to a commercial customer under an agreement which is non-cancellable, or only cancellable on payment of a financial penalty, for the major part of the asset's economic life. The rental payments are fixed at a level to allow the lessor to recover all, or a major part, of the capital cost of the asset, together with his own costs and a profit. The lessee is normally responsible for maintenance, repairs and insurance and will often have the option of continuing the lease at a reduced rental, at the end of the contract period; he will not, however, have the option of purchasing the equipment, as that would convert the agreement into hire purchase.

The equipment to be leased is normally selected by the lessee; often it is manufactured to his specification. The lessor will have little or no part in choosing the goods, the supplier or the manufacturer. Essentially, the lessor supplies the lessee with financial assistance to acquire the asset; the leasing arrangement provides the lessor with security against the lessee's default.

'A transaction which is in form a lease may achieve much the same result as an outright sale, as where the lease is for the full working life of the equipment at rentals totalling a sum equivalent to what would be charged for a sale on credit. Such a transaction is regarded by the business world as a financing transaction, not as a lease in the sense of a conventional hiring'[2].

The legal analysis of the arrangement disguises this reality. In law, the supplier contracts to supply the goods to the lessor, who in turn supplies them to the lessee. Thus if the goods are defective or unsatisfactory, the lessee's right of redress is against the lessor[3] who, in turn, has a right of redress against the supplier. The lessor may, and normally will, seek to exclude liability for the condition and suitability of the equipment by express terms in the lease. However, such exclusion will only be effective to the extent it is judged to be reasonable[4]. If the lessee does succeed in claiming damages from the lessor, the lessor will be able to recover his losses from the supplier, subject to any exclusion clauses in the supply contract.

Liability for defects can therefore be passed back to the supplier/manufacturer, but only by a circuitous route. The doctrine of privity will generally prevent the lessee bringing a direct action against the supplier. There are ways in which the privity problem might be evaded, but their effectiveness is uncertain. If the lessee is identified in the contract between supplier and lessor it may be possible to construe that contract as one to confer a benefit on the lessee so as to allow the lessee to rely on the Contracts (Rights of Third Parties) Act 1999. The lessee will gain enforceable rights under the Act if the supplier-lessor contract expressly provides that he is to be entitled to enforce. In the absence of such a provision, the lessee's rights will depend on the proper construction of the contract. It is therefore not clear if the Act would apply in this situation. The Law Commission took the view that in the absence of an express provision a contract would not be interpreted as conferring a right of action on the beneficiary where the contracting parties had deliberately arranged their relationships by means of a chain of contracts and direct enforcement would subvert that chain[5]. Alternatively, the lessor could, subject to the terms of the supply contract, assign to the lessee any rights of action he may have under the supply contract. The lessor's losses will probably be minimal, since it will normally be a term of the lease that the lessee continues to pay rental despite any defects or complaints about the goods[6], although it might be possible to rely on the principle that allows a contractor to recover damages for losses suffered by third parties where that is the intention of the parties[7]. It may be that the relationship between supplier and lessee is close enough to give rise to a duty of care in negligence[8] or that it could give rise to a collateral contract[9]; or that the lessor could be the actual or apparent agent of the supplier[10]. Subject to these possibilities, liability for the condition of the goods will fall, primarily, on the lessor. In addition, where the lessor imports the goods from an overseas supplier, he may incur liability under the Consumer Protection Act 1987 as the importer into the European Community[11].

A convention on international finance leasing, adopted by Unidroit in 1988, attempts to deal with this problem more directly. The convention applies only to tripartite finance leases, where lessor and lessee have their places of business in different countries[12]. Consumer transactions are outside its scope. Under the convention, the lessor would be liable for the goods only to the extent that the lessee relied on him, or that he was involved in the selection of the supplier[13]. Instead, the supplier would be directly liable to the lessee and would owe the lessee the same duties as he would otherwise owe the lessor under the contract of supply[14].

The analysis of the finance lease as a contract of hire also means that the transaction falls outside the schemes of registration and formalities designed to ensure publicity for securities over moveable property and to decide priorities between competing claims[15]. Hire purchase and conditional sale agreements and sales subject to retention of title also avoid registration. In 1974 the Crowther Committee recommended that there should be a Lending and Security Act, governing all forms of security arrangement, and similar proposals were made in a Report for the DTI by Professor Diamond in 1989[16] but nothing has come of them.

In contrast, an operating lease is generally for a short period and the agreement is terminable on short notice without penalty. The lessor contemplates that the asset will be let under a series of successive leases to different lessees. The lessor is normally responsible for repairs, maintenance and insurance and will ultimately dispose of the asset. The lessor thus assumes the risk of obsolescence, and the rentals take that risk into account. The lessor is liable to the lessee for any defects in the goods leased, but the analysis of the operating lease as a contract of supply is more realistic than in the case of a finance lease. The operating lease is particularly attractive to businesses wishing to acquire computing or similar equipment, especially for a short period.

1 Goode, *Commercial Law* (2nd edn, 1995) p 778.
2 Report of the Committee on Consumer Credit (Cmnd 4596) (1971) para 5.2.7.
3 Under SGSA 1982, ss 6–10; see ch 11.
4 Under the Unfair Contract Terms Act 1977, s 7; see 2.6.4.1.
5 *Privity of Contract: Contracts for the benefit of Third Parties* (Law Com No 242) (Cm 3329, July 1996) para 7.18. The Commission's comments referred specifically to construction contracts. See 2.7.2.
6 Such a provision would be subject to a test of reasonableness under the Unfair Contract Terms Act, s 7; see 2.6.4.1. There is no absolute rule that it is reasonable for a finance company to exclude liability for defects in goods which it supplies under a lease or hire contract: see *Lease Management Services Ltd v Purnell Secretarial Services Ltd* [1994] CCLR 127; *Danka Rentals Ltd v Xi Software* (1998) 17 Tr LR 74; *Sovereign Finance v Silver Crest Furniture* [1997] CCLR 76.
7 *Linden Gardens Trust Ltd v Lenesta Sludge Disposals Ltd* [1993] 3 All ER 417; *Darlington Borough Council v Wiltshier Northern Ltd* [1995] 3 All ER 895, CA; *Alfred McAlpine Construction Ltd v Panatown Ltd* [2000] 4 All ER 97, HL; see 2.7.1.
8 As in *Junior Books Ltd v Veitchi Co Ltd* [1983] 1 AC 520, [1982] 3 All ER 201, HL.
9 As in *Shanklin Pier Ltd v Detel Products Ltd* [1951] 2 KB 854, [1951] 2 All ER 471.
10 See eg *Purnell Secretarial Services Ltd v Lease Management Services Ltd* [1994] CCLR 127; *Woodchester Leasing Ltd v Clayton* [1994] CCLR 87; see generally ch 4.
11 Consumer Protection Act 1987, s 2(2)(c); see 13.1.4. The lessor is not liable as a supplier: Consumer Protection Act, s 46(2).
12 Article 1.
13 Article 8.
14 Article 10.
15 Eg the Bills of Sale Acts 1878 and 1882; Companies Act 1985, s 395; see 22.0.3.
16 In DTI, *A Review of Security Interests in Property* (1989); see 18.4.7; 22.3.

8.2.4.4 Contract hire

The term 'contract hire' normally describes a contract for the letting of motor vehicles for a period of between 12 and 36 months. Vehicles are often supplied to businesses on a fleet basis. A finance house may be involved, in the same way as under a finance lease, acquiring the goods from a dealer for rent to the customer business. Since the contract is one of hire, the owner will be liable for defects in the goods under the Supply of Goods and Services Act 1982. At the end of the hire period the goods will normally have a reasonable residual value, and the contract of supply may include a term by which the supplier agrees to repurchase the goods from the financier. The agreement may impose responsibility for maintenance on the owner, in which case the cost will be built into the hire charge, or on the hirer.

8.2.4.5   *Rental*

A 'rental agreement' is usually a periodic contract, terminable by short notice, to hire consumer goods such as a television or video recorder, or a contract for the short-term hire of articles such as a motor car or DIY equipment. The owner may be a dealer in goods of the type hired, or a specialist rental company. In either case, the owner acquires goods for the specific purpose of renting them to its rental customers. The owner will be responsible for the costs of maintenance, making the arrangement attractive and convenient to consumers. The owner will also be responsible for defects in the goods under SGSA 1982.

8.2.4.6   *Hire or acquire?*

A wide variety of arrangements is available to finance the acquisition or use of goods. The decision whether to enter into a contract, such as sale or hire purchase, which will ultimately result in the transfer of ownership, or a contract of hire which transfers possession and use without ownership, is a complex one, affected by social and economic considerations, and, for businesses, by tax and fiscal considerations. The nature of the goods and of the business, the speed of technological change, the financial state of the business and its existing commitments will all be relevant.

Leasing may offer more flexibility than outright purchase, and it may be possible to arrange short-term hiring more quickly than a sale or hire purchase contract. In addition, unlike some conditional sale and hire purchase agreements, a lease may not require a deposit, so that a lease may offer the hirer cash flow advantages. However, the continuing hire charges may be a substantial burden.

One reason for the increased popularity of leasing arrangements with businesses was that liabilities under such contracts did not have to be disclosed in the business's balance sheet. This could lead to potential lenders and creditors overestimating the creditworthiness of a business with substantial leasing commitments, and the problem was exacerbated by the fact that the owner was not required to register the transaction in any way. In 1974, Court Line Ltd collapsed. The subsequent investigation by Department of Trade Inspectors revealed that the company's annual accounts had not revealed that the company had leasing obligations of £38m in respect of aircraft; there was no requirement to make such disclosure, either in law, or under the relevant accounting standards[1]. In recent years, however, as a result, no doubt, of the increased incidence of insolvency in the early 1980s, lenders have become much more aware of leasing obligations and more adept at identifying them.

Against the advantages of hiring are the possible benefits of ownership. A business which purchases plant or machinery is entitled to claim allowances, based on the cost of the asset, in calculating its liability to income tax[2]. Where goods are leased, those allowances are claimed by the lessor, not the lessee; the rental charge may therefore be reduced accordingly. Under a lease, the goods leased are effectively used as security for cost of use of those goods. A business may use its own assets as security for borrowing for other purposes; and when the asset is no longer required, it can be sold, liberating any residual value as capital.

1   Department of Trade Inspectors' Report into the affairs of Court Line Ltd (1978) HMSO.
2   A writing down allowance of 25% of the cost of the asset is available in the first year; 25% of the residual value may be claimed in each subsequent year: Capital Allowances Act 1990, s 24.

8.2.5 *Mortgages and charges*

Goods, like land and other property, may be used as security in order to obtain credit. The owner may pledge goods, as where goods are deposited with a pawnbroker as security for a cash advance. Such a transaction involves a bailment of the goods. The drawback of a pledge is that possession of the goods must be transferred to the lender, so that the owner is unable to use the goods. If the owner wishes to raise money on the security of goods which he needs to use in the course of his business, he must create a security interest which does not give the lender possession of the goods, such as a mortgage or a charge. Non-possessory securities pose a serious hazard for other potential creditors, because they allow the borrower to appear to be more creditworthy than he really is: assets which he possesses, and appears to own, may in fact be subject to a security interest and therefore not be available for other creditors if the borrower becomes insolvent. Many non-possessory securities are therefore required by legislation to be registered in order to give notice of their existence to third parties and, in default of registration, they may be wholly void or unenforceable against certain classes of creditor. The Bills of Sale Acts 1878 and 1882 apply to any agreement contained or evidenced in a document under which an owner of goods transfers their ownership to a creditor by way of security, whilst remaining in possession of them, or grants the lender a charge over them, and require such agreements to be in a prescribed form and to be registered. If the bill is not registered, the security it creates is unenforceable and if the bill is not in the prescribed form, the whole agreement is void[1]. Similar agreements made by companies must be registered as charges at the Companies Registry and, in default of registration, are unenforceable against a liquidator or creditor of the company[2].

These statutory requirements are often onerous and inconvenient and the commercial world has therefore gone to great lengths to devise new security arrangements to avoid them and to overcome the priority problems involved in registering bills of sale and charges. Many of these arrangements involve a transfer by way of sale, with the seller remaining in possession of the goods. How are such transactions to be treated?

Section 62(4) of the SoGA provides that:

> 'The provisions of this Act about contracts of sale do not apply to a transaction in the form of a contract of sale which is intended to operate by way of mortgage, pledge, charge or other security'.

A sale is distinguished from a pledge by the fact that a pledge involves a transfer of possession but not of ownership[3]. A charge involves the transfer of neither possession nor ownership[4].

However, it may be very difficult to distinguish a sale from other types of transaction intended to grant a non-possessory security. A mortgage of goods involves the transfer of their ownership to the creditor subject to the transferor's 'equity of redemption' which entitles him to recover ownership by repaying the secured debt[5]. Moreover, a genuine sale may be used as part of a composite financing arrangement. For instance, there may be little practical difference between a mortgage and a sale subject to a contractual right to repurchase. Alternatively, the owner of goods may use them as security for an advance by entering into a sale and lease-back arrangement under which the owner of goods transfers them to a finance company in return for a cash payment, and then reacquires them under a lease or hire purchase arrangement. A substantial body of highly technical case law has grown up concerned with the classification of transactions and, especially, with the application of the Bills of Sale Acts[6]. The job of the court in these cases is to identify the intention of the parties, and it has been stressed that the court should have regard to the substance rather than the form of the relevant transaction[7]. However, although in some cases the courts have emphasised a purposive approach to the legislation, they have also recognised that the parties may intend to grant security and to do so wholly or partly by means of a sale of goods. Thus, on the whole, the courts have tended to uphold the validity of such transactions even when it means that they evade the statutory controls on non-possessory securities.

The law in this area is widely, if not universally, considered unsatisfactory. Each of these different transactions is intended to serve the same purpose: to provide security to a person providing credit to a business, in order to protect the creditor against the debtor becoming insolvent. Transactions with like purpose and commercial effect should be treated alike, and proposals for a comprehensive system requiring registration of all non-possessory security devices were made in 1971[8] and again in 1989[9]. However, neither set of proposals has been implemented and it seems unlikely that there will be legislative reform in the foreseeable future.

1   Bills of Sale Act 1878, ss 8–10; Bills of Sale (Amendment) Act 1882; see 22.0.3.1.
2   Companies Act 1985, Pt XII; see 22.0.3.2.
3   See 22.1.
4   See 22.2.1.
5   See 22.2.1.
6   See 22.0.3.1.
7   See *Welsh Development Agency Ltd v Export Finance Co Ltd* [1992] BCLC 148.
8   Report of the Crowther Committee on Consumer Credit (Cmnd 4596, 1971).
9   Diamond, *A Review of Security Interests in Property* (1989).

Chapter 9

Duties of the Parties

9.0 Delivery, acceptance and payment

The essential duties of the parties to a contract of sale are defined by s 27 of the Sale of Goods Act 1979 which provides that:

'It is the duty of the seller to deliver the goods, and of the buyer to accept and pay for them, in accordance with the terms of the contract'.

These duties are fundamental, so that a failure by the seller to deliver, or by the buyer to accept and pay, constitutes a total failure to perform the contract.

Section 27 is not a complete statement of the parties' duties. In particular, it makes no mention of the seller's duty to transfer property in the goods[1]. As we have seen[2], a contract for the sale of goods must be a contract by which the seller transfers or agrees to transfer the property in the goods. The seller must therefore be under a duty to transfer to the buyer 'the property' in the goods – which, as we have seen, means that he must transfer such title as he has to the general property interest in the goods. That duty is of the essence of a contract of sale. If the seller fails to transfer to the buyer property in the goods he will be in fundamental breach of contract. Section 27, however, makes no mention of that duty. It is a condition of the contract that the seller has a right to sell the goods[3], so that if the seller delivers goods which he has no right to sell, he has not delivered 'in accordance with the terms of the contract'. However, that is a separate matter from the seller's duty to transfer property which arises from the very nature of a sale contract.

1   Nor does it mention the buyer's duty to take delivery of the goods: see 18.0.2.
2   See 8.1.2.
3   SoGA, s 12; see ch 14.

9.1 The duties are concurrent

Section 28 explains the relationship between the duties of seller and buyer under s 27. It provides that delivery and payment are 'concurrent conditions, that is to say the seller must be ready and willing to give possession of the goods to the buyer in exchange for the price and the buyer must be ready and willing to pay the price in exchange for possession of the goods'. Put another way, each party's duty to perform is conditional on the readiness and willingness of the other to perform. Thus, unless otherwise agreed, the normal rule is 'cash on delivery'. However, commercial agreements normally provide for the goods to be delivered on credit terms so that payment is due after delivery.

Problems arise if, before the time for performance, one party makes clear to the other that he will not perform the contract: for instance, the buyer may indicate that he no longer wants the goods and that he will not accept them, or the seller may indicate that he will be unable to deliver at the time or place agreed in the contract. There is then an anticipatory breach of contract. The normal rule in such a case is that the innocent party may choose either to treat the contract as immediately terminated, and claim damages, or to ignore the breach and keep the contract alive. If the innocent party chooses the latter course, the contract remains fully in force: both parties remain committed to perform their obligations under it at the time for performance, and the anticipatory breach is forgotten, so that if before the time for actual performance an event occurs which would frustrate the contract, both parties are released from their obligations and the innocent party has no right to claim damages in respect of the anticipatory breach[1]. In the past, doubt was cast on this interpretation by the decision in *Braithwaite v Foreign Hardwood Co*[2], which seemed to suggest that the innocent party could elect to ignore an anticipatory breach and keep the contract alive, and yet claim damages for breach by the other party even though he would not have been able to perform his own obligations when the time for actual performance arrived. However, the facts of *Braithwaite* are not clear, and the position was clarified by the decision of the House of Lords in *The Simona*[3], which makes clear that the innocent party has a choice either to accept an anticipatory breach, in which case the contract is discharged and he is absolved from his own duty to perform, or to affirm the contract, in which case it remains fully in force and both parties must remain willing and able to perform at the time for actual performance.

> 'There is no third choice, as a sort of via media, to affirm the contract and yet be absolved from tendering further performance unless and until [the other party] gives reasonable notice that he is once again able and willing to perform'[4].

Suppose, therefore, that, before the time for performance of a sale contract, the buyer indicates that he will not accept the goods[5].

1. The seller may accept the breach and treat the contract as repudiated by any words or conduct which clearly show that he treats the contract as at an end[6], including, possibly, by simply failing to perform his own obligations under the contract[7] or by selling the goods to a third party[8]. He is released from performance of future duties under the contract[9] and is entitled to claim damages. It is no defence for the buyer to claim that had the contract remained in force, the seller would have been unable to perform his own duties[10], although the damages recoverable by the seller may be reduced if, for instance, it is shown that had the goods been delivered, they would have been defective. The seller remains liable in damages for any breach committed before the buyer's breach; and if the buyer can show that the seller committed a prior repudiatory breach, the buyer will be able to justify his own refusal to perform, and thus avoid liability altogether.

2. Alternatively, the seller may elect to keep the contract alive. If the buyer fails to perform at the date fixed for performance, the seller may then treat the contract as discharged by that actual breach, and claim damages. However, the seller will lose the right to claim if, at the time for actual performance, he is unable to deliver goods in accordance with the terms of the contract[11]. The only exception will be if the buyer's conduct leads the seller to put it out of his power to perform. For instance, there may be repeated communications between the parties; if the buyer maintains that he will not accept the goods, the seller may reasonably conclude that there is no point delivering, and sell the goods elsewhere. Such a situation could also be interpreted as one where the buyer continued in anticipatory breach and the seller, having initially affirmed the contract, finally treats it as discharged.

These rules mean that in order to decide a dispute, detailed examination of the facts may be required in order to answer the questions 'Who committed the first breach?', 'Was it repudiatory?', and 'Was the repudiation accepted?' It should be borne in mind that a party who terminates a contract for a bad reason may justify his action by reference to a valid reason for termination provided that reason existed at the time of termination[12]. Thus, for example, if the buyer indicates that he will not accept the goods, having decided that he can do without them, he may justify his conduct if he later discovers that the seller had already committed a repudiatory breach. Such cases will be rare in simple contracts of sale, where the seller's obligations to perform do not arise until the time for delivery.

1 *Avery v Bowden* (1855) 5 E & B 714; see 2.9.3.
2 [1905] 2 KB 543, CA.
3 *Fercometal SARL v Mediterranean Shipping Co SA, The Simona* [1989] AC 788, [1988] 2 All ER 742.
4 Per Lord Ackner [1989] 2 AC 788 at 805, [1988] 2 All ER 742 at 751–752.
5 The results are the same, but the roles are reversed, if it is the seller who commits the anticipatory breach.
6 *Vitol SA v Norelf Ltd, The Santa Clara* [1996] AC 800, [1996] 3 All ER 193.
7 [1996] AC 800, [1996] 3 All ER 193.
8 [1996] AC 800, [1996] 3 All ER 193; see also the explanation of *Braithwaite* offered by Lord Ackner in *The Simona* [1989] 2 AC 788 at 801–805, [1988] 2 All ER 742 at 748–751.
9 See *Berger & Co Inc v Gill & Duffus SA* [1984] AC 382; see 33.2.8.
10 *British and Benningtons Ltd v North Western Cachar Tea Co* [1923] AC 48, HL.
11 *The Simona* [1989] 2 AC 788, [1988] 2 All ER 742.
12 *Boston Deep Sea Fishing and Ice Co v Ansell* (1888) 39 Ch D 339; *Glencore Grain Rotterdam BV v Lebanese Organisation for International Commerce* [1997] 4 All ER 514. See 2.9.3.

9.2 The terms of the contract

The duties of the parties according to s 27 are to deliver and accept and pay 'in accordance with the terms of the contract'. Thus the buyer is not obliged to accept a tender of delivery which is not in accordance with those terms of the contract which qualify the duty to deliver, for example because it is at the wrong time or place, or because the goods do not comply with the contract, or the wrong quantity is tendered. At face value this would suggest that the buyer is entitled to withhold performance of his obligations if the seller's performance is in breach of any of the terms of the contract. It is clear, however, that this is not the case and the buyer can only withhold performance where the seller's breach amounts to a breach of condition.

If the buyer does reject a delivery as not conforming to the terms of the contract, then, provided that the time for performance has not expired, the seller may be able to make a second tender and cure his defective performance[1], unless his breach is repudiatory and the buyer accepts it as discharging the contract. Similarly, the seller may withhold delivery unless the buyer is ready and willing to accept and pay exactly in accordance with the terms of the contract[2]. Therefore, in order to decide if either party has tendered an acceptable performance, obliging the other to perform, it will be necessary to examine all the terms of the contract.

1   *Borrowman Phillips & Co v Free and Hollis* (1878) 4 QBD 500, CA; see 12.1.3.1.
2   The seller's right to withhold performance, like the buyer's, is only available where the term broken is a condition. However, if the buyer fails to pay at the due time the seller may withhold delivery regardless of the nature of the breach by virtue of his right of lien under SoGA, s 41: see 18.3.1.

9.2.1   *Express and implied terms*

Certain terms are implied into contracts of sale by SoGA[1]. Some, such as the buyer's implied obligation to pay a reasonable price[2], apply only if there is no express term dealing with the same point. In contrast, the implied terms concerned with title and the seller's right to sell the goods[3] apply to all contracts of sale and can never be excluded[4]. Perhaps the most important, and best-known, implied terms are those concerned with the condition of the goods in ss 13–15. The exclusion, limitation or modification of those terms is restricted by the Unfair Contract Terms Act 1977[5]: it is totally prohibited in cases where the buyer deals as a consumer, whilst in other contracts it is permitted only so far as reasonable.

For reasons which are discussed later, there is a tendency to concentrate on the statutory implied terms, particularly those concerned with the physical condition of the goods, when considering problems arising from sale transactions. However, it should be borne in mind that a contract of sale, like any other contract, will normally include express terms in addition to the statutory implied terms. Thus the price, if nothing else, will normally be the subject of an express term. It is true that some simple consumer contracts may contain few other terms, but, as a general rule, most commercial contracts will also contain express terms dealing with such matters as delivery dates and methods, the quantity to be delivered, and so on. Often there will be a detailed document setting out contract terms covering a range of other matters. Many businesses supply, or purchase, goods on standard terms of business[6], which will contain express provisions dealing with matters such as the amount of the price, the time and method of payment, the passing of ownership and risk, the extent of the supplier's liability for the goods and the consequences of force majeure events which hinder, delay or prevent performance. In some cases, especially for long-term supply contracts or contracts for the supply of large and expensive items, a full written contract may be prepared for the particular transaction containing terms covering almost every aspect of it. In such a case the statutory implied terms may remain relevant, but provided its terms are reasonable, the express terms of the contract may totally supplant them.

Furthermore, terms may be implied into an individual sale or supply contract just as they can be implied into any other contract at common law[7], for instance where it is necessary to imply a term to give business efficacy to the contract. In deciding the extent and nature of the seller's duty to deliver and the buyer's duty to accept and pay, all the terms of the contract must be examined.

1   Terms may also be implied by other legislation: for example the contract may contain an implied term that the buyer will pay interest on the price in the event of late payment by virtue of the Late Payment of Commercial Debts (Interest) Act 1998: see 18.0.1.1.
2   SoGA, s 8; see 8.1.3.1.
3   SoGA, s 12; see ch 14.
4   UCTA, s 6(1); a similar prohibition applies in relation to the equivalent terms in other supply contracts: UCTA, s 7(3A): see 2.6.4.1.
5   UCTA, s 6(2)–(3) (sale and hire purchase); UCTA, s 7(1)–(3) (other supply contracts).
6   See 2.5.3.
7   See 2.5.4.

9.2.2   Terms and representations

Just as in other contracts, many statements may be made during negotiations leading to a sale, including those made orally and in advertising, catalogues, brochures and so on. Such statements may become terms of the contract; in addition, they may give rise to liability for misrepresentation[1] and be relevant in fixing the standard expected of the goods to comply with the statutory implied terms relating to the goods[2], so that, if such a statement proves false, the buyer may be able to claim remedies on three different grounds. Indeed, where a person buys goods as a result of a false statement made during negotiations, it is not uncommon to see the case pleaded in the alternative as one of (a) breach of the implied term that the goods should correspond with their description, (b) breach of an express term, and (c) misrepresentation.

1   See 2.5.1.
2   Under SoGA, ss 13–15; see ch 11.

9.2.3   The classification of terms

The modern law of contract recognises four categories of terms: warranties, conditions, innominate terms and fundamental terms[1]. However, SoGA refers only to conditions and warranties, and classifies the implied terms relating to the goods into one or other of those categories[2].
    According to the Act, a warranty is:

> 'an agreement with reference to goods which are the subject of a contract of sale, but collateral to the main purpose of such a contract, the breach of which gives rise to a claim for damages but not to a right to reject the goods and treat the contract as repudiated[3]'.

'Condition' is not expressly defined in the Act, but it seems that implicitly, in this context[4], it indicates a more important term, breach of which does give right to reject the goods and treat the contract as repudiated[5].
    It seems that the division of terms into conditions and warranties was intended to reflect the existing common law, but in fact failed to do so[6]. Nevertheless, the rigid division into conditions and warranties was adopted into the general law of contract and for over half a century all contract terms were classified as either conditions or warranties. However, this simple dichotomy was eroded by two developments in the second half of the twentieth century. First, in a series of cases concerned with exclusion clauses, the courts recognised a category of fundamental

terms – terms so important that any breach would amount to a total non-performance of the contract[7]. Many of the cases in which fundamental terms were first recognised involved contracts for the sale of goods[8]; it is therefore clear that terms of sale contracts may be regarded as 'fundamental'. However, the distinction between a breach of fundamental term and a simple breach of condition may be difficult to draw[9]; in particular, it may be difficult to decide if the seller has simply delivered goods not complying with the contract description[10] or has delivered goods wholly different from those required by the contract[11].

Secondly, in *Hong Kong Fir Shipping Co Ltd v Kawasaki Kisen Kaisha*[12] the Court of Appeal recognised the category of innominate terms, intermediate between conditions and warranties. The remedy for breach of such terms would depend on the seriousness of the consequences of the breach. *Hong Kong Fir* was not a sale of goods case, but in *The Hansa Nord*[13] the Court of Appeal held that terms in sale contracts could be classified as innominate. In that case a contract for the sale of citrus pulp pellets contained an express term requiring that the goods be shipped 'in good condition'. Some of the pellets were not in good condition when loaded and, when the market price fell, the buyer refused to accept the pellets in order to escape the contract and buy at a cheaper price. The seller was forced to resell the pellets in the market and they were ultimately bought by the original buyer, who used them for making cattle food, as originally intended. The seller claimed damages for non-acceptance; the buyer claimed to be entitled to reject on the grounds either that the goods were unmerchantable, in breach of an implied condition[14], or that the seller was in breach of the express term that the goods be loaded in 'good condition'. The court held, first, that the goods were merchantable despite the defect; and, secondly, that, although there was a breach of the express term, that term was not a condition but was innominate and, since the breach was not serious, the buyer was not entitled to reject.

It is therefore clear that express terms in sale contracts may be classified as 'innominate'. However, the condition/warranty distinction remains important. The terms implied into sale contracts by SoGA are classified by the Act as conditions or warranties[15]. In addition, it is clear that, in order to promote certainty in commercial contracts, some express terms will be classified as conditions, so that any breach gives a right to terminate. Thus, for instance, stipulations about time in commercial contracts are normally regarded as conditions[16].

---

1   See 2.5.5.
2   See ch 11.
3   SoGA, s 61.
4   'Condition' is used in at least two senses in the Act: see Stoljar (1952) 15 MLR 421; (1953) 16 MLR 174; Bradgate and White, 'Rejection and termination in contracts for the sale of goods' in Birds, Bradgate and Villiers (eds), *Termination of Contracts* (1995).
5   See s 11(3), and below 12.1.
6   See Goode, *Commercial Law* (2nd edn, 1995) pp 290–294; Stoljar (1952) 15 MLR 421; (1953) 16 MLR 174.
7   See 2.5.5.
8   See eg *Karsales (Harrow) Ltd v Wallis* [1956] 2 All ER 866, [1956] 1 WLR 936, CA.
9   In *Hong Kong Fir Shipping Co Ltd v Kawasaki Kisen Kaisha* [1962] 2 QB 26 at 45 Lord Diplock seems to have regarded 'fundamental term' and 'condition' as synonymous.
10 In breach of the condition implied by SoGA, s 13; see 11.1.
11 Eg peas instead of beans: see *Chanter v Hopkins* (1838) 4 M & W 399.
12 [1962] 2 QB 26, [1962] 1 All ER 474.
13 *Cehave NV v Bremer Handelsgesellschaft GmbH* [1976] QB 44, [1975] 3 All ER 739.
14 Under SoGA, s 14(2); see 11.2.
15 In non-consumer cases the status of the implied terms in ss 13–15 as conditions is qualified by restrictions on the buyer's right to reject for their breach: see 12.2.
16 *Bunge Corpn v Tradax Export SA* [1981] 2 All ER 513, [1981] 1 WLR 711, HL; see 10.2.

9.3   Exclusion clauses

Amongst the most important of the express terms likely to be found in a contract of sale will be those which seek to exclude or restrict the liability of one or other of the parties for breach of contract. Such clauses are particularly extensively used in standard terms. They will be subject to both the common law rules developed to control exclusion clauses and to statutory control under the Unfair Contract Terms Act 1977[1], and, where they appear in a standard form contract with a consumer, under the Unfair Terms in Consumer Contracts Regulations 1999[2]. In particular, clauses which seek to exclude the statutory implied terms relating to the goods[3], or to exclude or limit liability for breach of those terms, will be subject to s 6 of the 1977 Act, and many of the other terms commonly included in standard terms of trading, such as clauses excluding liability for late delivery, or allowing the seller to deliver a greater or lesser quantity of goods than provided for in the contract, or force majeure clauses, which excuse a party from liability where he is unable to perform due to circumstances outside his control, or which extend the time for performance in such a case, are probably subject to s 3[4]. Therefore, as against a consumer or a person dealing on the seller's standard terms of business, such clauses will be effective only if reasonable.

1   See 2.6.4.
2   See 2.6.5.
3   Implied by SoGA, ss 12–15; see ch 11.
4   See 2.6.4.1. Force majeure clauses are probably more likely to be held to be reasonable than simple exclusions of liability.

Chapter 10

Delivery

10.0 The importance of delivery

According to s 27 of the Sale of Goods Act 1979, the seller's basic obligation is to deliver the goods in accordance with the terms of the contract. The law attaches great significance to the passing of property from seller to buyer, and, as has been suggested, the seller's duty to transfer property in the goods can be seen as a fundamental obligation. However, for practical purposes the buyer's immediate concern is often to get physical possession of the goods for use or resale. Moreover, legal significance is attached to delivery and the transfer of possession: once the seller has tendered delivery he is entitled to demand payment[1] and the buyer is obliged to accept the goods, failing which the seller may sue for damages for non-acceptance; in contrast, should the seller fail to deliver, the buyer can claim damages for non-delivery. The point of delivery will normally be the point at which the goods' conformity with the contract must be judged[2]. In addition, delivery terminates the seller's possession of the goods and therefore terminates his lien over the goods[3]. However, the passing of possession, by means of delivery, and the passing of property need not necessarily be connected[4].

The seller's obligation is to deliver 'the goods in accordance with the terms of the contract'. Thus where the contract is for specific goods, the seller must deliver the specific goods agreed to be sold; where the contract is for unascertained goods, the seller must deliver goods which correspond with the contract description. In either case, the goods must comply with all of the terms of the contract: they must be goods of the right quality and description, which the seller has a right to sell, and the seller must deliver the right quantity in the right place at the right time.

If the seller wholly fails or refuses to deliver, he is in breach of contract. The buyer may then claim damages for non-delivery[5] or, where the price has been paid in advance, reclaim the sum paid by means of a restitutionary claim. In some cases, for instance where the contract is for specific goods which are unique, the buyer may be able to claim specific performance of the contract, but generally, especially in commercial cases, damages will be a sufficient remedy and specific performance will not be available. If the seller delivers but not in accordance with the contract he will be in breach. In certain circumstances the buyer may be able to reject the delivery, in which case the position is as if the seller had not delivered. Moreover, where the breach is of a condition the buyer may reject the delivery and treat the contract as repudiated[6].

1   Although he may not be entitled to sue for the price: see 18.2.1.
2   *Viskase Ltd v Paul Kiefel GmbH* [1999] 1 All ER (Comm) 641. The better view is that conformity should be judged at the time when risk passes from seller to buyer, but that will normally be at the point of delivery: see 11.2.5.
3   See 18.3.1.
4   See ch 15.
5   See 12.3.1.
6   See 9.2.3. and ch 12.

10.1   The meaning of delivery

In law 'delivery' has a meaning very different from its colloquial meaning. Whereas the ordinary meaning of 'delivery' involves the physical transport of goods from A to B, in law delivery means simply the 'voluntary transfer of possession from one person to another'[1]. In many cases, delivery merely involves the seller allowing the buyer to collect the goods, which may be very much contrary to the expectations of consumer buyers. However, the contract may contain an express or implied term requiring the seller to undertake the physical delivery of the goods to the buyer's premises, and such a term may be readily implied, especially where the goods are bulky and the buyer is a consumer[2].

1   SoGA, s 61.
2   See Cranston, *Consumers and the Law* (2nd edn, 1984) p 171.

10.1.1   *Effecting delivery*

In the ordinary case, delivery is effected by the seller transferring physical possession of the goods. However, in many business transactions that may be impracticable: for instance, the goods may be stored in a warehouse or be on board a ship, or be in bulk. Thus, as an alternative to actual delivery of the goods, the seller may fulfil his obligation to deliver by making symbolic or constructive delivery. The seller may deliver the goods by delivering a document of title covering the goods. The most important document of title in commercial use is the bill of lading, used where goods are carried by sea[1], although certain warehouse warrants are treated as documents of title by statute[2] and a wider range of documents may be classified as documents of title for certain other purposes[3]. The seller may symbolically deliver the goods by handing over a means of taking control of them: for instance, under a contract for sale of the whole of a quantity of goods in a warehouse the seller could deliver by handing over the keys to the warehouse. Where the goods are in the possession of a bailee, they may be delivered by the bailee 'attorning' to the buyer, confirming that the goods are held on behalf of the buyer, and there is no delivery until such attornment[4]. In some cases the seller may remain in possession of the goods after the contract, but the circumstances indicate that he does so as bailee for the buyer: for instance, pending collection. In that case the seller may be a bailee on behalf of the buyer, and the buyer will have possession[5]. In *Four Point Garage v Carter*[6] S agreed to sell a car to B and, at B's request, delivered the car direct to X, to whom B had sold the car. It was held that in making delivery to X, S was acting as B's agent and that B was therefore in constructive possession of the car even though he never had physical possession.

1 See 32.1.
2 See eg Port of London Act 1968, s 146(4); see 32.1.
3 Under the Factors Act 1889, s 1(4); see 17.1.1.2.
4 SoGA, s 29(3).
5 This is normally regarded as a type of 'constructive' possession, although it could also be regarded as a type of 'actual possession'. The meaning of 'possession' in the context of bailment is far from clear: see Crossley Vaines, *Personal Property* (5th edn, 1973) pp 47–55; Bell, *Modern Law of Personal Property in England and Ireland* (1989) p 53.
6 [1985] 3 All ER 12; see 17.4.2.

10.1.2 The place of delivery

Unless the contract makes contrary provision, the place of delivery is the seller's place of business, or, if he has none, his home, or, where the contract is for the sale of specific goods which are in some other place at the time of the contract, the place where the goods are situated[1]. In many cases the contract will contain an express term fixing the place of delivery: for instance, under an 'ex works' contract the place of delivery is the seller's place of business; under an f o b contract, the place of delivery is at the ship's rail when goods are loaded[2].

Often the seller will undertake to physically 'deliver' the goods to the buyer's premises. In that case it is important to construe the contract and decide where is the contractual place of delivery. If the place of delivery is the seller's premises, the seller fulfils his obligation by delivering the goods to a carrier for transport to the buyer. Thus, for example, if the buyer asks the seller to 'send' or 'despatch' the goods, the seller fulfils his obligations by delivering the goods to the carrier, and the carrier is deemed to be the buyer's agent[3]. Delivery of the goods to the carrier in such a case may also result in property and the risk of loss of the goods passing to the buyer[4], and in the seller losing his lien over the goods[5]. On the other hand, if the place of delivery is the buyer's premises, the carrier is the seller's agent and the seller does not fulfil his obligation to deliver until the goods reach the buyer's premises; however, he fulfils his obligation to deliver by handing the goods to a person at the buyer's premises who appears to have authority to receive them, and provided he is not negligent, is not liable if the goods are misappropriated and never reach the buyer[6]. The seller will often require the person receiving the goods to sign a form acknowledging delivery.

1 SoGA, s 29(2).
2 'f o b' means 'free on board'. See 33.1.3.
3 SoGA, s 32(1).
4 See 15.2.3.2.
5 See 18.3.1.
6 *Galbraith & Grant Ltd v Block* [1922] 2 KB 155.

10.2 The time for delivery

Just as the contract will normally fix the place of delivery, it will normally fix the time for delivery. Often the contract may provide for the giving of notices: for instance, for the seller who manufactures goods to give the buyer notice that they are ready for collection. If the contract is silent, the Act provides that a tender of or demand for delivery is only effective if made at a reasonable hour[1] and that if the seller is required to send the goods to the buyer he must do so within a reasonable time[2]. In any case, if no time for delivery is fixed, it will normally be implied that delivery should take place within a reasonable time. What is reasonable will depend on the facts of the case, including the nature of the goods and the volatility of prices in the particular market.

1   Section 29(5).
2   Section 29(3).

10.2.1   *Late delivery*

If delivery is late, the buyer is entitled to damages. However, if the term fixing the time for delivery is properly classified as a condition, he may also be entitled to refuse delivery and terminate the contract. In such cases time for delivery is said to be 'of the essence'. The Act provides that whether any stipulation as to time is of the essence depends on the construction of the contract[1]; it therefore depends on the intention of the parties and the contract may expressly provide that the time for delivery is (or is not) of the essence.

Where time is of the essence the result is that if delivery is late the buyer is entitled to terminate the contract at once, even though the delay is only slight. However, time can only be of the essence where the date for delivery can be fixed with certainty in accordance with the terms of the contract[2].

Where time is not of the essence, late delivery will be a breach of contract but not a breach of condition entitling the buyer immediately to terminate the contract. Whether the buyer is entitled to terminate will, in accordance with general principles of contract law, depend on the seriousness of the breach – ie the length of the delay. To avoid the uncertainty this involves the buyer may, once the delivery date has passed, fix a new date for delivery and, provided he gives the seller reasonable notice, make time of the essence of the new date.

Where the contract does not fix a delivery date but requires delivery within a reasonable time, time cannot initially be of the essence, although in such a case the buyer may be able to serve reasonable notice fixing a delivery date and making time of the essence[3].

Even if the contract does not expressly make time of the essence, it may be held that on its proper construction it does so impliedly. It has been said that '[i]n ordinary commercial contracts for the sale of goods the rule clearly is that time is prima facie of the essence with respect to delivery'[4] and it has been confirmed by the House of Lords that this general rule survives, even though many other express terms may be classified as innominate terms[5]. It is not clear, however, how widely this presumption applies. Treating the time for delivery as essential has potentially harsh consequences: it may allow an unscrupulous buyer to escape a bad bargain, for instance where the market falls. Moreover, it seems unfair because unless the contract otherwise provides, the time for payment is generally not of the essence[6].

The rule is justified by the need for certainty. The buyer may have contracted to resell the goods: if they are not delivered on time, the buyer may need to know immediately whether he is entitled to go out into the market and buy alternative goods, in order to avoid being in breach of his own contract. In contrast, the consequences of late payment for the seller may be costly, but can normally be compensated by an award of interest, either under statute[7] or quite commonly under the express terms of the contract.

The buyer's dilemma is particularly acute in large-scale 'string' transactions where the same goods may be resold several times. In *Bunge Corpn v Tradax SA*[8] the contract required the buyer to give the seller notice of readiness. As Lord Wilberforce explained:

'It is clearly essential that both buyer and seller (who may change roles in the next series of contracts, or even in the same series of contracts) should know precisely what their obligations are, most especially because the ability of the seller to fulfil his obligation may well be totally dependent on punctual performance by the buyer'[9].

The rule is therefore appropriate in large-scale commercial contracts, particularly those which take place in a market context such as contracts for commodities. It may be, therefore, that the presumption that the time for delivery is essential should be restricted to such contracts. Significantly, in *Bunge* Lord Wilberforce referred to time being of the essence in 'mercantile contracts'[10]. The presumption may therefore not apply to all commercial contracts. It seems most unlikely that it will apply as a matter of course to consumer contracts. It remains possible, however, that on the facts of a particular case, in light of all the circumstances including the nature of the goods, time may impliedly be essential even in a non-mercantile contract.

Where the contract is on the seller's terms, it will normally seek to prevent the buyer terminating for delay in delivery, for example by expressly stating that time is not of the essence or by providing for delivery 'on or about' a certain date. Even if time is of the essence, the buyer will often prefer to accept late delivery rather than terminate the contract, for instance, in order to preserve a good trading relationship, because the terms are better than could be obtained elsewhere, or, where the goods are manufactured to order, because terminating the contract and placing an order elsewhere would involve a greater delay[11]. Alternatively, the buyer may accept late delivery as part of a negotiated settlement: for instance, in return for a reduction in the price. Moreover, the buyer will generally be under a duty to mitigate damages, and if the buyer unreasonably refuses to accept late delivery, his damages for non-delivery may be restricted by his failure to mitigate[12].

If the buyer does not terminate the contract in response to a delay in delivery, but acts so as to lead the seller to believe that he intends to continue to perform the contract, for instance by continuing to press for delivery, he may be held to have waived the right to do so, or to be estopped from relying on the original delivery date[13]. In *Hartley v Hymans*[14] a contract for the sale of cotton yarn called for deliveries to commence in September and be completed by 15 November. No deliveries were made until 26 October, and deliveries had not been completed by 13 March in the following year. Throughout this period B had continued to press for delivery but on 13 March, without warning, B wrote terminating the contract on grounds of delay. It was held that B was in breach by terminating: by pressing for delivery, he had waived the original requirement for prompt delivery. However, as in other cases of waiver or estoppel, the buyer may reassert his original rights by giving reasonable notice. In *Charles Rickards v Oppenhaim*[15] a contract called for S to build and supply a Rolls Royce chassis by 20 March 1948, time to be of the essence. The chassis was not delivered on time and B continued to press for delivery until 29 June when he gave notice that he would not accept it unless it was delivered within four weeks. In fact the chassis was delivered in

October, and B refused to accept it. The Court of Appeal held that, although he had waived (or was estopped from relying on) the original requirement that the delivery date was of the essence, he was entitled to fix a new date, and make time of the essence again by giving reasonable notice. This he had done. He was therefore entitled to reject the chassis.

1   Section 10(2).
2   See *Cie Commerciale Sucres et Denrées v C Czarnikow Ltd, The Naxos* [1990] 3 All ER 641, HL.
3   *British and Commonwealth Holdings plc v Quadrex Holdings Inc* [1989] 3 All ER 492, CA.
4   Per McCardie J in *Hartley v Hymans* [1920] 3 KB 475 at 484.
5   *Bunge Corpn v Tradax SA* [1981] 2 All ER 513, [1981] 1 WLR 711, HL; *Cie Commerciale Sucres et Denrées v C Czarnikow Ltd, The Naxos* [1990] 3 All ER 641.
6   Section 10(1).
7   Interest may be payable on sums paid late either under the Late Payment of Commercial Debts (Interest) Act 1998 or, where the seller brings proceedings for the price, under the Supreme Court Act 1981, s 35A.
8   [1981] 2 All ER 513, [1981] 1 WLR 711.
9   [1981] 1 WLR 711 at 716.
10 [1981] 1 WLR 711 at 716.
11 See Beale and Dugdale, 'Contracts between businessmen: planning and the use of contractual remedies' (1975) 2 BJLS 45.
12 *Sotiros Shipping Inc and Aeco Maritime SA v Sameiet Solholt, The Solholt* [1983] 1 Lloyd's Rep 605, CA.
13 For a discussion of waiver and estoppel, see 2.8.2.
14 [1920] 3 KB 475.
15 *Charles Rickards Ltd v Oppenhaim* [1950] 1 KB 616, [1950] 1 All ER 420.

10.3   How much to deliver?

The contract will normally expressly fix the quantity of goods to be delivered and failure to agree on the quantity will generally mean that there is no concluded contract. Section 30 of the Act contains a detailed set of rules defining the buyer's rights where the seller delivers more or less than the agreed quantity of goods[1]. Essentially, it requires the seller to deliver precisely the quantity of goods required by the contract and allows the buyer to reject the whole delivery if there is any variation, other than a minimal one, from the contract quantity. However, the buyer is not obliged to reject a delivery of the wrong quantity and his right to reject is subject to three limitations.

The rules in s 30 are as follows:

(a) The buyer is not obliged to accept delivery by instalments, unless the contract provides for delivery by instalments[2].
(b) If the seller delivers less than the contract quantity, the buyer may reject the whole delivery or keep the goods delivered and pay for them at the contract rate[3]; the seller cannot make good the shortfall in a later delivery, because that would amount to delivery by instalments.
(c) If the seller delivers more than the contract quantity, the buyer may: (i) reject the whole delivery; (ii) keep the contract quantity and reject the excess[4]; or (iii) keep the whole quantity paying for the excess at the contract rate[5]. Presumably, this third option will only be available when the circumstances are such that the buyer is entitled to treat the seller as making an offer to sell the excess; the buyer will therefore not be entitled to accept the excess at the contract rate where he knows that the seller is mistaken and does not intend such an offer[6].

It should be noted that s 30 does not make it a condition that the seller delivers the correct quantity. Delivery of the wrong quantity may therefore entitle the buyer to reject the delivery but not to treat the contract as repudiated. The effect of rejection is to put the parties in the same position as if the seller had not delivered. Where the time for delivery has not expired, it will therefore be possible for the seller to retender the correct quantity. However, it is normally for the seller to collect rejected goods so that rejection will often be inconvenient for the seller and in many cases there will be insufficient time for the seller to make a second tender.

Clearly, commercial buyers do not normally seek to reject on the grounds of slight variations in the quantity of goods delivered, and any variation is normally dealt with by an adjustment in the price. Normally, the contract will contain express provisions providing for tolerances in the quantity to be delivered, such as 'plus or minus 5%', although such a provision is probably subject to the reasonableness test under s 3 of the Unfair Contract Terms Act where that section applies. Even in the absence of such a provision, it is well established that a de minimis variation from the contract quantity will not allow the buyer to reject the delivery. In *Shipton Anderson & Co v Weil Bros*[7] the contract called for a delivery of not more than 4,950 tons of wheat; the seller delivered an extra 55 pounds in weight, an excess of 0.0005%, worth four shillings[8] in a contract worth £40,000. Lush J held that the variation was so slight that the buyer was not entitled to reject; he was not being asked to pay for the excess and 'No businessman would regard it as in any way affecting the substance of the contract'.

However, the de minimis exception is likely to be very narrowly construed, as indicated by decisions on other provisions of the Act[9]. In 1987 the Law Commission expressed concern that the strict rules in s 30 could be used by an unscrupulous buyer to reject goods, and thus escape from a bad bargain, on the grounds of even a minute variation from the contract quantity[10]. The 1979 Act was therefore amended as the Commission recommended by the Sale and Supply of Goods Act 1994 and now provides that a buyer who does not deal as a consumer may not reject the whole quantity delivered where the excess or shortfall is so slight that it would be unreasonable for him to do so[11]. It is for the seller to prove that the excess or shortfall is so slight that rejection of the whole would be unreasonable[12] but presumably this exception will be more favourable to the seller than the common law de minimis exception. The rights of a buyer who 'deals as a consumer' remain unaffected. The definition of 'dealing as a consumer' for this purpose is the same as that in the Unfair Contract Terms Act 1977[13].

---

1 There are no equivalent provisions applicable to other supply contracts.
2 Section 31(1). Where the contract does allow instalment deliveries it will be necessary to decide if the delivery obligation is entire or severable: see 12.2.3.
3 Section 30(1).
4 Section 30(2).
5 Section 30(3).
6 See Atiyah, *Sale of Goods* (10th edn, 2000) p 132; Law Comm 160, para 6.23.
7 [1912] 1 KB 574.
8 Equivalent to 20p.
9 See 11.1.
10 Law Commission Report 160, paras 6.17–6.23.
11 SoGA, s 30(2A).
12 SoGA, s 30(2B).
13 SoGA, s 61(5A); see 2.6.4.2.

Chapter 11

The Condition of the Goods and Statutory Implied Terms

11.0 Introduction

As we have seen, the seller must not only deliver the goods but the goods delivered must conform to the terms of the contract: if not, the seller is in breach and the buyer is entitled to damages. Moreover, if the term broken is a condition, the buyer may be entitled to reject the goods and terminate the contract.

All contracts for the supply of goods now contain terms, implied by statute, which require the goods delivered to be of a certain standard and quality. In the SoGA 1979 (as amended by the Sale and Supply of Goods Act 1994) the implied terms are set out in ss 12–15[1], and require:

(a) that the seller should have a right to sell the goods, that the goods should be free from encumbrances and that the buyer should enjoy quiet possession of them (s 12);
(b) that where the goods are sold by description, they should correspond with that description (s 13);
(c) that the goods should be of satisfactory quality (s 14(2));
(d) that the goods should be fit for the buyer's purpose where he makes that known to the seller (s 14(3)); and
(e) that where goods are sold by sample, the goods should correspond with the sample (s 15).

Although the contract may contain other terms, either express or implied at common law, relating to the goods delivered, in practice the statutory implied terms are the most important source of contractual redress for the buyer if the goods are defective in any way. There are three reasons for their importance. First, the implied terms arise automatically, by operation of law, and are thus relatively easy to prove: for instance, in order to rely upon the implied term that the goods must be of satisfactory quality, the buyer need only prove that the seller sold the goods in the course of a business. There is thus only limited scope for disputes of fact over what was said. Secondly, the implied terms are classified by the Act as either conditions or warranties, so that the buyer's rights are clearly defined. In fact, all but two of the implied terms, those relating to freedom from encumbrances and quiet enjoyment in s 12, are classified as conditions. As a result, if the seller delivers goods which do not conform to the requirements of the terms in ss 13–15 the buyer is entitled to reject the goods and terminate the contract. The buyer may choose instead to accept the goods and simply claim damages in respect of the breach[2], and in certain circumstances the right to reject may be lost unintentionally, if the buyer is taken to have accepted the goods[3]. In addition, a non-consumer buyer may not reject the goods if the seller's breach is so slight that rejection would be unreasonable. In many cases, however, the buyer's remedies in the event of breach are clear and where the buyer has not paid for the goods he may place himself in a strong bargaining position by rejecting the goods and withholding the price. Thirdly, the exclusion or limitation of the implied terms, or of liability or remedies for their breach, is regulated by the Unfair Contract Terms Act 1977. In particular, the implied terms can never be excluded as against a buyer dealing as a consumer[4]. As a result the implied terms have come to be regarded as the central pillar of the contractual protection of consumers. However, it should be emphasised at the outset that, in the absence of contractual restrictions, the implied terms apply equally in favour of consumer and commercial buyers. In practice, in contracts with non-consumers, the implied terms often are restricted or excluded, and are often replaced by express warranties.

The implied terms in ss 13–15 relating to the goods themselves interrelate and, to some degree, overlap each other; the implied terms in s 12 concerned with title are somewhat different and have been approached differently by the courts. We will therefore postpone examination of the terms in s12 until later[5] and concentrate here on the terms relating to the goods themselves. However, before doing so we must briefly consider the historical development of the terms, which may assist an understanding of the current position.

1   The equivalent terms in other supply contracts are contained in SoG(IT)A 1973, ss 8–11 (hire purchase); SGSA 1982, ss 2–5 (other supply contracts) and SGSA 1982, ss 7–10 (hire).
2   See 12.3.3.
3   Under SoGA ss 34–5: see 12.2.1.
4   UCTA 1977, s 6, 7; see 2.6.4.
5   See ch 14.

11.0.1   *Historical development of the implied terms*

Prior to the middle of the 19th century it seems that the attitude of the common law was epitomised by the maxim 'caveat emptor' – let the buyer beware. There was little legal protection for the buyer of goods unless he expressly contracted for it. Even in the late 17th century the principle of caveat emptor was recognised[1] and under the growing influence of the free market economic theories prevalent from the end of the 18th century the principle became enshrined in law so that in *Smith v Hughes*[2] Cockburn CJ could say:

'I take the rule to be, that where a specific article is offered for sale, without express warranty or without circumstances from which the law will imply a warranty – as where, for instance, an article is ordered for a specific purpose – and the buyer has full opportunity of inspecting and forming his own judgment, if he chooses to act on his own judgment, the rule caveat emptor applies.'

The approach is justified by McCulloch:

'The free ordinary competition of the producers is the only principle on which reliance can ordinarily be placed for securing superiority of fabric as well as cheapness. Wherever industry is emancipated from all sorts of restraints, those who carry it on endeavour, by lessening the cost, or improving the fabric of their goods, or both, to extend their business, and the intercourse that subsists among the different classes of society is so very intimate that an individual who should attempt to undersell his neighbours by substituting a showy and flimsy for a substantial article, would be very soon exposed[3].'

Such an approach might be justifiable in an age where goods were generally simple and were normally traded at markets, where buyers had the opportunity to examine goods before buying. However, the industrial revolution led to great changes in the number and complexity of goods sold, to the involvement of many more individuals in the purchase of complex items, and, with improvements in transport and communication, to different ways of doing business. Sellers and buyers were often some distance apart, rather than dealing face to face. At the same time, sellers came to recognise that it was in their commercial interests to support their products in the interests of goodwill[4].

The law came to recognise these changes in mercantile practice and expectations, and from the late 18th century caveat emptor was in decline. By the 1860s it had been significantly eroded[5], as indeed, can be seen even in the quote from *Smith v Hughes* cited above. The courts were prepared to imply terms into contracts for the sale of unascertained goods bought by description, where the buyer had not seen the goods, requiring the goods to correspond with description and to be of merchantable quality. Where the buyer bought specific goods, he was taken to rely on his own judgment and to that extent caveat emptor continued to apply subject to the qualification that if the buyer made known to the seller the purpose for which he required the goods, there would be an implied term that the goods would be fit for that purpose.

The basis for the implication of these terms was that they accorded with the legitimate expectations of the parties – a reasonable buyer would naturally expect an honest seller to sell goods of at least a minimum saleable quality, and a reasonable seller would know that, so that there was no need for the undertaking of quality to be expressed – and their development can be seen as, in effect, one aspect of the common law's protection of good faith values[6].

The Sale of Goods Act 1893 purported to codify the existing common law. However, either accidentally or deliberately, the Act made profound changes to the existing law in this area and further eroded the principle of caveat emptor, by extending the protection of implied terms relating to the goods to contracts for the sale of specific as well as unascertained goods. Moreover, until 1973, the Act only required goods to be merchantable where they were sold by description; in order to give buyers the protection of merchantability the courts were therefore forced to give 'sale by description' an extended meaning. Some cases decided prior to 1973 must therefore be treated with caution when considering the current provisions.

The Supply of Goods (Implied Terms) Act 1973 made further changes, introducing a definition of 'merchantable quality' and restricting the freedom of sellers to exclude the implied terms; similar restrictions applicable to all types of supply contract are now contained in the Unfair Contract Terms Act 1977. Similar terms had been implied into contracts of hire purchase since the Hire Purchase Act 1938, and in 1982 the Supply of Goods and Services Act extended similar implied terms to other types of supply contract[7].

The Sale of Goods Act 1979 made no further changes to the implied terms. However, by that time doubts were being expressed about their suitability for application to modern transactions and, in particular, their ability to meet the needs of consumers. In 1979 the Government therefore referred to the Law Commission the question whether any changes should be made to the implied terms and, in 1987, the Law Commission published a report recommending changes to both the content of the implied terms and the remedies for their breach[8]. The Commission's recommendations, with one significant amendment, were eventually implemented by the Sale and Supply of Goods Act 1994[9] which replaced the former requirement that goods be of merchantable quality with a requirement that they be of satisfactory quality[10]. However, even before the 1994 Act was passed the European Commission had initiated consideration of Europe wide reform of 'consumer guarantees' covering much the same area. That process led to the completion in 1999 of the EC Directive on Consumer Guarantees[11]. As a result, further reform to UK law is likely to be necessary in the near future to implement the Directive.

As a result of developments over the last century in business (as opposed to private) sales the principle of 'caveat emptor' is therefore now almost vestigial, at least in consumer contracts, and substantially eroded even in commercial contracts[12]. Nevertheless, the SoGA 1979 still states that it is the basic principle in sales law[13].

The discussion of the implied terms which follows concentrates on the terms in the context of sale contracts; however unless otherwise stated it applies equally to the equivalent terms in other supply contracts.

1 See Atiyah, *The Rise and Fall of Freedom of Contract*, p 178, although it seems that this was a principle of the common law rather than the law merchant: see Goode, *Commercial Law* (2nd edn, 1995), p 188 ff and the sources cited.
2 (1871) LR 6 QB 597; see 2.4.1.
3 McCulloch, *Principles of Political Economy* (1864) p 215.
4 See Llewellyn, *Cases and Materials on the Law of Sales* (1930) p 204.
5 See Atiyah, *The Rise and Fall of Freedom of Contract*, pp 474–79.
6 See Harrison, *Good Faith in Sales*, ch 3.
7 Although the Act did not apply to Scotland until extended by the Sale and Supply of Goods Act 1982.
8 Law Commission Report 160, 'Sale and Supply of Goods'.
9 A previous attempt had been made in the Consumer Guarantees Bill 1989 but some provisions of the Bill were opposed by the government. The 1994 Act was introduced as a private member's bill but had government support.
10 The Law Commission had proposed a requirement that goods be of 'acceptable quality': see 11.2.3.
11 Directive 1999/44/EC on certain aspects of the sale of consumer goods and associated guarantees (1999) OJ L 171/12, 7 July 1999.
12 See the comments of Lord Steyn in *Slater v Finning* [1997] AC 473 at 488 [1996] 3 All ER 398 at 410.
13 Section 14(1); see also SoG(IT)A, s 10 (1); SGSA, ss 4(1) and 9(1).

11.0.2 *Overview of implied terms*

Sections 13 and 14 of the SoGA set out three implied terms which apply to most sales; s 15 contains additional terms which apply when the sale is by sample, although in some respects the terms in s 15 overlap those in the other sections. Effectively the terms in ss 13 and 14 lay down a graduated series of duties, offering the buyer increasing levels of protection according to the amount of information given to the seller. First there is an implied condition under s 13 that the goods should correspond with their description; the more detailed the description, the greater the protection this will give the buyer. However, goods may correspond with their description and still be defective; s 14(2) therefore implies a term that the goods should be of satisfactory quality. The assessment of whether goods are of satisfactory quality take account of a number of factors, including whether they are fit for their normal purpose. However, that does not guarantee that the goods will be fit for the buyer's particular purpose. Section 14(3) therefore implies a third term, that where the buyer's purpose is made known to the seller, the goods should be reasonably fit for that purpose.

The distinction between the three terms is not always clear cut. As Lord Wilberforce explained in *Ashington Piggeries Ltd v Christopher Hill* 'It is well known that there is a good deal of overlapping between them, so that this subdivision is artificial and gives rise to difficulty[1].' In essence the implied terms together require the goods supplied to conform to the buyer's legitimate expectations. Thus the same set of facts may allow the buyer to complain of a breach of two, or even all three implied terms. In addition, the buyer may be able to add a claim for breach of an express term and/or a misrepresentation.

1   [1972] AC 441 at 489, [1971] 1 All ER 847 at 871, HL. See also the comments of Diplock LJ in *Teheran-Europe Co Ltd v ST Belton (Tractors) Ltd* [1968] 2 QB 545, [1968] 2 All ER 886 at 893.

11.0.2.1   *When is conformity to be judged?*

There is authority that the conformity of the goods with the implied terms should be judged at the time of delivery[1]. The better view[2], however, seems to be that the time at which the conformity should be assessed is when risk passes from seller to buyer[3]. So long as the goods are at the seller's risk he must bear the risk of any damage to them or deterioration in their quality. Once risk has passed such risk falls on the buyer. If the concept of 'risk' is to be meaningful it must be the case that the goods' conformity with the contract is judged when risk passes. In many cases risk will pass at the time of delivery, so that the goods' conformity will be judged at delivery, but risk may pass before delivery and when it does conformity should be judged at the earlier time.

It is in any case clear that the conformity of the goods is judged once and for all at the appropriate time. Similarly, in contracts of hire and hire purchase the goods are required to be of satisfactory quality and fit for the buyer's purpose at the commencement of the hire; they are not guaranteed free from defects for the whole of the contract period.

1   *Viskase Ltd v Paul Kiefel GmbH* [1999] 1 All ER (Comm) 641, holding that the place of delivery is where the seller's fitness undertaking is performed for the purposes of determining jurisdiction under the Civil Jurisdiction and Judgments Act 1982 and the Brussels Convention on Jurisdiction and the Enforcement of Judgments in Civil and Commercial matters, 1968.
2   See *Benjamin's Sale of Goods* (5th edn, 1997) para 11-062.
3   See ch 16.

11.1   Goods must correspond with the description

Section 13 of the Act implies a condition that where goods are sold by description they will correspond with the description. Furthermore, if the sale is by sample as well as by description, it is not sufficient for the bulk to correspond with the sample if the goods do not also correspond with the description[1]. The implied condition in s 13 applies to all sales, regardless of the status of either buyer or seller; however, where the buyer does not deal as a consumer within the meaning of the Unfair Contract Terms Act 1977[2], the seller may be able to exclude the condition, or liability for its breach.

Section 13 is deceptively simple. In many ways it is the most difficult of the implied terms, largely as a result of the way the Sale of Goods Act 1893, and subsequent decisions interpreting it, altered the common law. As a result, it is sometimes difficult to reconcile s 13 with developments in the common law.

Where a buyer wishes to bring a claim for breach of the implied terms in s 13 two questions must be answered: (a) was the sale a sale by description and, if so, (b) what was the description by which the goods were sold?

1   See 11.4.
2   See 2.6.4.

11.1.1 *Sale by description*

Clearly where S sells unascertained generic or future goods, the sale must be by description: the terms of the description will define the goods which are to be sold, and it seems that at common law the requirement that goods should correspond with their description was limited to sales of unascertained goods. However, the 1893 Act made no distinction between unascertained and specific goods in this context and, moreover, as originally enacted it applied the condition in s 14, that goods should be merchantable, only where the goods were sold by description. As a result, the courts tended to extend the category of 'sale by description' in order to protect buyers. In *Varley v Whipp*[1] it was held that, where S sold specific goods which B had not seen, the sale was a sale by description, and in *Grant v Australian Knitting Mills Ltd*[2] it was held that a sale could be by description even though the buyer had seen the goods:

> 'There is a sale by description even though the buyer is buying something displayed before him on the counter; a thing is sold by description, though it is specific, so long as it is sold not merely as the specific thing, but as a thing corresponding to a description, eg: woollen undergarments, a hot water bottle, a second hand reaping machine[3].'

The position is now put beyond doubt by s 13(3) of the 1979 Act which provides that 'a sale is not prevented from being a sale by description by reason only that, being exposed for sale or hire, they are selected by the buyer'. Moreover, the goods may describe themselves: for instance, in *Beale v Taylor*[4] a '1200' badge on a secondhand car was held to be part of the description of the car. Similarly, the use of descriptive words on the packaging of goods may be sufficient to make the sale a sale by description. This approach seems to be entirely justified in an age when mass produced goods are sold pre-packaged so that the buyer has no alternative but to rely on the specification claimed for the goods. As a result, most types of sale are capable of being sales by description if a description is applied to the goods.

1   [1900] 1 QB 513.
2   [1936] AC 85, PC.
3   Ibid per Lord Wright at 108.
4   [1967] 3 All ER 253, [1967] 1 WLR 1193, CA.

11.1.2   *Were the goods sold by reference to the description?*

Although the category of sales which may be sales by description has been extended by a combination of the Sale of Goods Acts and the decisions on them, a sale is not necessarily a sale by description, so as to bring the implied term in s 13 into play, merely because descriptive words are used in negotiations or in the contract; and even if the sale is by description, not all the descriptive words used will be part of the description for the purposes of s 13. The implied condition only applies where the goods are sold by description, and if the buyer complains that a statement made about the goods was false he will only succeed in a claim under s 13 if he can show that that statement formed part of the description by reference to which the goods were sold. Recent decisions show a tendency to adopt a restrictive approach to s 13; in older cases, however, the courts adopted a broader approach, and the cases are not easy to reconcile.

We have already seen that, in general, not all the statements made about goods during pre-contract negotiations will be terms of the contract: some may be mere puffs, or sales talk, of no legal significance, and others may be mere representations. Those distinctions are preserved by s 13, so that statements not intended to form part of the contract will not be part of the description by which the goods are sold[1]. Effectively, therefore, s 13 requires goods to correspond with the terms of the contract. Its significance lies in the fact that the term implied by s 13 is a condition, so that if the goods do not correspond to the description, the buyer is entitled to reject them.

In fact, it seems that descriptive words may become terms of the contract and yet not form part of the description by reference to which the goods are sold for the purposes of s 13. In that case, the express term may be classified as innominate, allowing the court to prevent the buyer rejecting the goods if the breach is only slight.

The crucial question is therefore whether the goods were sold by reference to the description in question, and that will depend on the intentions of the parties. Similar factors to those considered in relation to the question whether statements form terms of the contract will be relevant[2]. In particular, it will be relevant to consider whether the buyer could reasonably be expected to rely on the statement in question. In *Harlingdon & Leinster Ltd v Christopher Hull Fine Art Ltd*[3] S sold a painting, described as being by the German expressionist painter Gabriele Munter. The painting had been so described in a 1980 auction catalogue and S, who specialised in other areas of the fine art market, relied on the catalogue. He made clear to B, who did specialise in German expressionist painting, that he had no relevant expertise, and B bought the painting for £6,000. It later transpired that the painting was a fake, worth about £50–£100, and B tried to reject on the grounds that the painting did not comply with its description. The Court of Appeal held that there could not be a sale by description unless the description was influential in the sale, so as to become an essential term of the contract, and so there could not be a sale by description where the parties could not reasonably expect the buyer to rely on the description. The court was clearly influenced by the fact that the attribution of artistic works is not an exact science, and that anyone dealing in fine art is taking a calculated risk. On that basis, and on the facts of the case, the decision is perfectly justifiable. However, it does appear to open up the possibility that sellers might seek to contract out of the implied term under s 13 by disclaiming expertise, possibly evading the restrictions of the Unfair Contract Terms Act.

It seems that goods are only 'sold by description' where the description in question identifies the commercial characteristics of the goods to be sold. In *Ashington Piggeries Ltd v Christopher Hill Ltd*[4] Lord Diplock said that:

'The description by which unascertained goods are sold is, in my view, confined to those words in the contract which were intended by the parties to identify the kind of goods to be supplied. It is open to the parties to use a description as broad or narrow as they choose. But ultimately the test is whether the buyer could fairly and reasonably refuse to accept the physical goods proffered to him on the ground that their failure to correspond with that part of what was said about them in the contract makes them goods of a different kind from those he had agreed to buy. The key to s 13 is identification[5].'

Although these words relate specifically to unascertained goods, they seem to be of general application; indeed, it could be argued that 'description' should be construed more narrowly in the case of specific goods. The words must identify the kind of goods to be supplied, rather than simply identify the particular item. In *Reardon Smith Line Ltd v Yngvar Hansen-Tangen*[6] the Privy Council held that a statement in a contract to build a ship that the ship would be No 354 built at a particular shipyard was not part of the contractual description of the ship, so that the buyer was not entitled to reject a ship which conformed to all the specifications of the contract but had been built under a different number at a different yard. Lord Wilberforce explained that s 13 is concerned with words which identify 'an essential part of the description of the goods'[7].

However, although this test may be simple to state, since it depends on the intentions of the parties, it is difficult to apply. As Lord Diplock indicated in *Ashington Piggeries*, the parties may intend to describe the goods in broad terms, or in minute detail. Thus in *Re Moore & Co and Landauer & Co*[8] it was held that goods did not comply with their description when the contract called for 3,000 tins of fruit to be packed 30 tins to a case, and the seller delivered the correct number of tins, but some packed 24 tins to a case; and in *Bowes v Shand*[9] it was held that a statement about the date of shipment of goods was part of the description. These and similar decisions have often been criticised but requiring exact correspondence with all aspects of the contractual description can be justified in the context of large scale commercial transactions in unascertained, bulk commodities[10]. Such an approach may be less appropriate in other contexts[11]. In *Reardon Smith*, Lord Wilberforce described some of the older cases as 'excessively technical and due for fresh examination'[12]. However, he recognised that in contracts for the sale of unascertained future goods every element of the description might be vital as defining the contract goods, and the need for certainty in large scale transactions might outweigh the need for flexibility. The real problem is the classification of the implied term in s 13 as a condition, which in the past meant that once a statement was found to be part of the contractual description, even a small deviation would allow the buyer to reject the goods and escape the contract. As a result of the changes made by the Sale and Supply of Goods Act 1994 a non-consumer buyer may no longer reject goods on the grounds of a breach of the implied condition in s 13 where the breach is so slight that rejection would be unreasonable[13]. The result in *Re Moore and Landauer* would therefore probably now be different: the seller would still be in breach but the buyer would not be entitled to reject. However, it probably would still be reasonable for the buyer to reject in a case like *Bowes v Shand* in view of the special commercial context of that case.

1   See eg *Oscar Chess Ltd v Williams* [1957] 1 All ER 325, [1957] 1 WLR 370, CA.
2   See 2.5.1.
3   [1991] 1 QB 564, [1990] 1 All ER 737, CA.
4   [1972] AC 441, [1971] 1 All ER 847, HL.

5   At 503–504, 883–884.
6   [1976] 3 All ER 570, [1976] 1 WLR 989.
7   At 577, 999.
8   [1921] 2 KB 519, CA.
9   (1877) 2 App Cas 455; see 30.1.3. It seems that the decision is still good law: see *Bunge Corpn v Tradax SA* [1981] 2 All ER 513, [1981] 1 WLR 711, HL.
10   See Bridge [1991] LMCLQ 52 at 59; Sealy and Hooley, *Text and Materials in Commercial Law* (2nd edn, 1999) at 356.
11   The issue here is effectively the same as that considered in ch 10 of whether time stipulations should be regarded as essential in commercial contracts: see 10.2.1.
12   At 576, 998.
13   See 12.1.

11.1.3   *Breach of the implied term*

If the seller delivers goods of a totally different kind from those contracted for, the goods clearly do not correspond to their description. Thus in *Wallis Son and Wells v Pratt and Haynes*[1] there was a breach where under a contract for the sale of English sanfoin seed the seller delivered giant sanfoin. Such cases might be regarded as cases of fundamental breach, and a court will be reluctant to construe an exclusion clause as covering such a case unless clear words are used[2].

Where the goods are described in detail, the goods must correspond to every element of the description by reference to which they are sold. Any discrepancy between the goods and the description, other than a de minimis one, will be a breach of contract. In *Arcos v Ronaasen*[3] the buyer ordered half-inch thick timber staves for making barrels; most of the staves delivered varied in thickness from half to nine sixteenths of an inch, but were perfectly fit for the buyer's purpose. Nevertheless, the buyer was held entitled to reject. As Lord Atkin said:

> 'A ton does not mean about a ton, or a yard about a yard. Still less when you descend to minute measurements does half an inch mean about half an inch. If a seller wants a margin he must, and in my experience does, contract for it . . . No doubt there may be microscopic variations which businessmen, and therefore lawyers, will ignore . . . But apart from this consideration the right view is that the condition of the contract must be strictly performed[4].'

Although, as a result of the restrictions on the right to reject introduced by the Sale and Supply of Goods Act 1994 the outcome in this case would probably now be different, it would still be open to the court to find a breach of the implied condition on these facts.

This approach can be criticised as over-strict and uncommercial. Business people do not normally reject in such circumstances. In fact it is clear that the buyers in *Arcos* rejected in order to avoid the effects of a fall in the market for timber and, moreover, that the court was aware of this. The decision is therefore criticised for encouraging bad faith behaviour and *Arcos* was no doubt one of the cases Lord Wilberforce had in mind in *Reardon Smith* as 'due for fresh examination'. The case is perhaps best seen as an example of the traditional non-interventionist approach to commercial contracts, favouring commercial certainty. If the parties have included a term in their contract it must be there for a reason. On this approach, therefore, the more precise the description of the goods, the more precisely they must correspond.

In addition, liability for breach of the implied condition is strict: the seller is liable regardless of his responsibility for the breach.

1   [1911] AC 394, HL; see also *Nichol v Godts* (1854) 10 Exch 191; mixture of hemp and rape oil
    supplied under a contract for foreign refined rape oil.
2   It may also be that in such a case a buyer would not be held to have accepted the goods before he
    was aware of the breach: see Treitel, *Law of Contract* (10th edn, 1999) p 758; Atiyah, *Sale of
    Goods* (10th edn, 2000) pp 77–78.
3   [1933] AC 470, HL.
4   At 479.

11.1.4 *Description and quality*

The cases discussed above clearly indicate that goods may be free from defects
and fit for the buyer's purpose and still fail to correspond with the contract
description. Equally, goods may comply with the description and yet be defective
or unfit for the buyer's purpose. In such cases there will often be a breach of the
conditions implied under ss 14(2) (satisfactory quality) and 14(3) (fitness for
purpose), but in some respects the scope of those sections may be narrower than
that of s 13. The implied terms in s 14 only apply where the seller sells in the
course of a business; in addition, there may be exclusions of liability covering the
s 14 conditions but not the condition in s 13. It is therefore necessary to consider
the relationship between the condition in s 13 and those in s 14.

The important question is to decide whether goods which are defective in some
way comply with the contract description. The modern tendency is to construe s 13
narrowly, leaving questions of quality to be dealt with under s 14. Thus in *Ashington
Piggeries*[1] a contract for the supply of herring meal called for meal of 'fair average
quality'. The House of Lords held that that statement was not part of the description
for the purposes of s 13. However, the line between description and quality may be
difficult to draw, depending on commercial practice in particular trades, and in
appropriate cases a statement may be relevant to both description and quality[2].

The problem is particularly difficult where goods are contaminated. In *Ashington
Piggeries* the contract was for the supply of herring meal to be used for making
mink food. S supplied herring meal which had been treated with a preservative
which reacted with the meal to produce a toxin fatal to mink. B argued that
contaminated meal did not correspond with the description 'herring meal' but four
members of the House of Lords held that the meal was still properly described as
'herring meal': the contamination did not change its nature. Again, however, the
line may be difficult to draw. In previous cases[3] it had been held that contamination
could mean that goods failed to match their description. Lord Wilberforce observed
that questions of contamination and correspondence with description could, 'if
pressed to analysis, be a question of an Aristotelian character'[4]. Such 'metaphysical
discussions' were inappropriate to a commercial dispute: 'the test of description,
at least where commodities are concerned, is intended to be a broader, more
commonsense, test of a mercantile character'[5].

In *Ashington Piggeries* the House of Lords therefore rejected a contention that
'herring meal' implicitly meant 'non-toxic herring meal'. However, on occasion
words of description may carry an implication: for instance, in a case where a bull
was sold as a 'pure bred polled Angus bull', it was held that the descriptive words
were 'meaningless unless intended to convey the impression that the animal might
be used to get this class of stock'. The description thus implied that the bull could
be used for breeding, and a bull which was incapable of breeding failed to
correspond with the description[6]. In contrast, words of description which have a
technical or special trade meaning will be interpreted in accordance with that

meaning. This may effectively narrow the description: for instance, a contract to supply safety goggles was not broken when the seller supplied goggles made of 'safety glass' which splintered in use: safety glass had a technical meaning and did not guarantee that the goggles would be safe[7].

1 [1972] AC 441, [1971] 1 All ER 847.
2 See *Toepfer v Continental Grain Co* [1974] 1 Lloyd's Rep 11 ('Hard Durum Wheat'); *Toepfer v Warinco AG* [1978] 2 Lloyd's Rep 569 'fine ground' soya meal.
3 See *Robert A Munro & Co Ltd v Meyer* [1930] 2 KB 312 (bone meal containing high proportion of cocoa husks); *Pinnock Bros v Lewis and Peat Ltd* [1923] 1 KB 690 (copra cake containing castor oil).
4 At 487.
5 Ibid.
6 *Cotter v Luckie* [1918] NZLR 811.
7 *Grenfell v Meyrowitz Ltd* [1936] 2 All ER 1313, CA.

11.1.5 *Exclusion of liability*

The seller may seek to exclude or limit liability for breach of the s 13 term, perhaps in order to avoid the effects of decisions such as *Arcos v Ronaasen* and *Re Moore and Landauer*. It may be possible to qualify the description by appropriate wording, as suggested by Lord Atkin in *Arcos* in the passage quoted above[1]. A clause excluding liability for breach of the implied term is likely to be construed *contra proferentem* at common law[2]. It is unlikely that a court would accept an interpretation of an exclusion which would enable the seller to deliver goods of a wholly different type to that contracted for[3]. Moreover any term in the contract which seeks to exclude or restrict the implied condition in s 13, or liability or the remedies for its breach, will be subject to s 6 of the Unfair Contract Terms Act 1977. Such terms will be wholly ineffective as against a buyer who deals as a consumer, and in other cases will be subject to a test of reasonableness. The seller may seek to exclude liability by preventing the sale being a sale by description; for instance, by applying no description to the goods, or perhaps by preventing the buyer relying on any description, for instance by making clear that he has no expertise, as in the *Harlingdon and Leinster* case. It is not clear if such statements would be subject to s 6. In *Harlingdon and Leinster*, Slade LJ thought that there had been no exclusion of s 13; the sale simply was not one by description[4]; but in *Hughes v Hall*[5] it was held that a term in a contract 'sold as seen' prevented the sale being one by description[6] and was subject to s 6.

1 Above, 11.1.3.
2 See 2.6.2.
3 See *Vigers Bros v Sanderson Bros* [1901] 1 KB 608.
4 [1990] 1 All ER 737 at 753, CA; above 11.1.2. See Snaith, (1990) NLJ 1672.
5 [1981] RTR 430.
6 This was doubted by the Divisional Court in *Cavendish-Woodhouse Ltd v Manley* (1984) 82 LGR 376.

11.2 The goods must be of the correct quality

Section 14(1) of the 1979 Act provides that:

> 'Except as provided by this section and section 15 and subject to any other enactment, there is no implied condition or warranty about the quality or fitness for any particular purpose of goods supplied under a contract of sale.'

The Act thus restates the common law principle of caveat emptor. However, s 14 goes on to provide that where goods are sold in the course of a business there are two implied conditions, that goods should be of satisfactory quality (s 14(2)) and reasonably fit for the buyer's purpose (s 14(3)). The effect, as noted above, is substantially to erode the concept of caveat emptor, especially in consumer sales where the conditions cannot be excluded. Prior to 1893 terms about quality were only implied where goods were sold unseen by the buyer; the 1893 Act apparently attempted to reflect that by limiting the implied condition that goods should be merchantable to cases where the goods were sold 'by description'. However, with the expansion of the category of 'sale by description' the implied condition was extended. It now applies to all sales where the seller sells in the course of a business.

11.2.1 Sale in the course of a business

Unlike the implied condition that goods should correspond with their description, the implied conditions in s 14 only apply where the seller sells in the course of a business, which includes 'a profession and the activities of any government department or local or public authority'[1]. Prior to 1973 the merchantable quality term applied only where the seller dealt in goods of the same description as the contract goods and the fitness term where the goods were 'of a description which it is in the course of the seller's business to supply', so that the implied terms only applied where the goods sold were of a type which the seller regularly supplied. The wording was changed by the Supply of Goods (Implied Terms) Act 1973 following a report of the Law Commission[2]. The intention was to extend the application of the implied terms to all business sales so as to increase consumer protection[3]. However, the same phrase, 'in the course of a business', appears in a number of other statutes in which it has repeatedly been given a narrower interpretation so that a sale will only be regarded as being in the course of a business where either (a) the transaction is an integral part of the business or (b) there is sufficient regularity of similar transactions. Thus it has been held that for the purposes of the Trade Descriptions Act 1968 a courier who sold the car he used in his business was not selling in the course of a business[4].

This restrictive approach may be justified under the Trade Descriptions Act since the Act imposes criminal liability. However, in *R&B Customs Brokers v UDT Finance Ltd*[5] the Court of Appeal held that the same test should be used to determine whether a buyer acted in the course of a business, and therefore whether the buyer dealt as a consumer, for the purposes of the Unfair Contract Terms Act 1977, with the result that a freight forwarding company which bought three cars over a period of five years was not acting in the course of a business when buying a car.

The decision in *R&B Customs Brokers* widened the definition of 'consumer' in the 1977 Act and thus the scope of consumer protection. If the same approach were to be applied under s 14 of the 1979 Act, however, it would restrict the scope of the implied terms and therefore of consumer protection. In appropriate circumstances the first transaction by a business could be 'integral' to and therefore in the course of a business. Equally, a one-off transaction with a view to profit could be in the course of a business, because the transaction would *be* the business. It is also clear that the last sale by a business being wound up can be in the course of a business[6]. Nevertheless the *R&B* approach would mean that occasional sales by a business of equipment the business does not normally deal in would not be 'in the course of a business'.

In *Stevenson v Rogers*[7] the Court of Appeal had to consider the meaning of 'in the course of a business' in s 14 of the 1979 Act, in just this type of case. R, a fisherman, sold his trawler. He had previously sold just one other vessel. The buyer brought a claim that the vessel was unmerchantable and R argued that there was no implied term of merchantability because the sale was not in the course of a business. The Court of Appeal adopted a purposive approach to the interpretation of the provision and, after a careful review of the legislative history[8], held that the expression 'in the course of a business' in s 14 should be given a wide interpretation so that any sale by a business is a sale 'in the course of a business' for the purposes of s 14. The narrow interpretation adopted in *R&B* would effectively re-introduce the requirement of regularity of transactions which the 1973 amendment had been intended to remove. The sale of the trawler was therefore a sale in the course of a business for the purposes of s 14, to which the implied terms applied.

The decision in *Stevenson* is to be welcomed. Its effect is that the implied quality and fitness terms now apply to all sales other than purely private sales. However, it does leave a number of questions unanswered. The Court of Appeal was bound by, but distinguished the decision in *R&B* on the basis that it was concerned with the interpretation of a different statute and with the status of the buyer. This is hardly convincing. Consumer status under the 1977 Act requires both that the buyer does not act in the course of a business and also that the seller does so[9]. It would be surprising if the expression 'in the course of a business' were to be given a different meaning when it appears twice in the same section of the same Act. Logically, therefore, the question whether the seller acts in the course of a business under the 1977 Act should be determined by the *R&B Customs Brokers* test. But the controls on exclusion clauses in sale contracts now contained in the 1977 Act had their origins in the Supply of Goods (Implied Terms) Act 1973, just as did the expression 'in the course of a business' in SoGA, s 14. It is submitted, therefore, that the same approach should be used to determine whether a sale is 'in the course of a business' under both Acts. Moreover the Unfair Contract Terms Act definition of consumer dealing, and presumably therefore the *R&B* definition of 'in the course of a business', is imported into the Sale of Goods Act for certain purposes, raising the possibility that the phrase will effectively have a different meaning for the purposes of different sections of the same Act. The law is therefore in need of clarification and it is submitted that *Stevenson* is to be preferred to *R&B Customs Brokers*.

---

1   Section 61. It is an offence for a business seller to pose as a private seller in any advertisement: Business Advertisements (Disclosure) Order 1977, SI 1977/1918.
2   Law Commission No 24, Exemption Clauses in Contracts. The Commission's report drew heavily on the earlier report of the Moloney Committee on Consumer Protection (1962, Cmnd 1781).
3   Ibid para 31, note 29; para 46.
4   *Davies v Sumner* [1984] 3 All ER 831, [1984] 1 WLR 1301, HL. Contrast *Havering London Borough Council v Stevenson* [1970] 3 All ER 609 where a car hire firm which regularly sold off cars in its fleet after one or two years was selling in the course of a business for the purposes of the Trade Descriptions Act. The Act applies to any person who 'in the course of a trade or business' applies a false trade description to goods. It was recognised that a one off venture in the nature of a trade with a view to profit could also be a sale in the course of a trade because the transaction itself constituted a trade.
5   [1988] 1 All ER 847, [1988] 1 WLR 321, CA discussed fully at 2.6.4.2; see also *Peter Symmons & Co v Cook* (1981) 131 NLJ 758.
6   *Buchanan-Jardine v Hamilink* 1983 SLT 149.
7   [1999] QB 1028, [1999] 1 All ER 613; see Sealy [1999] CLJ 276; Brown (1999) 115 LQR 384; de Lacey (1999) 62 MLR 776.
8   Following *Pepper v Hart* [1993] AC 593.
9   UCTA, s 12(1): see 2.6.4.2.

11.2.1.1 *Sales through an agent*

Where a private seller uses a business as his agent to sell goods, the buyer may rely on the agent's reputation and expect a higher standard from the goods than he would on a private sale. Section 14(5) therefore provides that in such a case the implied terms in s 14 apply in the same way as if the principal were selling in the course of a business, unless the buyer knows that the agent is acting for a private seller, or reasonable steps are taken to inform him of that fact. Where the agency is disclosed the principal is therefore liable as if he were a business seller. In the case of an undisclosed agency both principal and agent are liable on the implied terms, in accordance with ordinary agency rules[1].

1   *Boyter v Thompson* [1995] 2 AC 628, [1995] 2 All ER 135, HL. See 5.3

11.2.2 *'Goods supplied under the contract'*

Section 14 applies to the 'goods supplied under the contract'. This widens the scope of liability beyond merely the goods which are sold under the contract. Thus there was a breach when soft drinks were supplied in a defective bottle which exploded, even though the bottle itself was returnable and was not 'sold'[1]. The section applies to all goods supplied in purported performance of the contract. In *Wilson v Rickett, Cockerill & Co*[2] S contracted to supply Coalite; an explosive detonator was included with the Coalite supplied. It was held that the goods were unmerchantable: the consignment as a whole was unmerchantable, even though there was nothing wrong with the Coalite itself and the detonator was a perfectly good detonator.

1   *Geddling v Marsh* [1920] 1 KB 668, a case under what is now s 14(3).
2   [1954] 1 QB 598, [1954] 1 All ER 168.

11.2.3 *Goods must be of satisfactory quality*

Section 14(2) of SoGA 1979, now states that:

> 'Where the seller sells goods in the course of a business, there is an implied term that the goods supplied under the contract are of satisfactory quality'.

This implied term is classified as a condition in England and Wales[1].

This section, which applies to all contracts made after 3 January 1995, was introduced by the Sale and Supply of Goods Act 1994. It replaces the former s 14(2) which provided that where the seller sold goods in the course of a business there was an implied condition that the goods supplied under the contract should be of 'merchantable quality'. That provision, in turn, had its roots in the recognition by the common law during the 19th century that a buyer of goods expected them to meet at least a minimum standard of quality and the seller knew that. As Lord Ellenborough observed in a case concerning a contract for sale of 12 bags of 'waste silk', 'The purchaser cannot be supposed to buy goods to lay them on a dunghill'[2]. The buyer's expectations were given effect by recognising that even in the absence of any express undertaking as to the quality of the goods, the contract contained an implied term that they should be of merchantable quality. The Sale of Goods Act 1893 followed the common law and s 14(2) implied into the contract of sale a condition that the goods supplied under the contract should be of merchantable quality[3].

The 1893 Act offered no guidance as to the meaning of 'merchantable quality' beyond stating[4] that 'quality' includes 'state or condition'. It seems that 'merchantable' meant no more or less than 'saleable'; however, as early as 1910 it was recognised that the requirement was difficult to apply to contracts for machinery and that the expression 'merchantable quality' was 'more appropriate . . . to natural products such as grain, wool or flour than to a complicated machine'[5].

The case law under the 1893 Act developed two tests of 'merchantability'. The first, the 'acceptability' test, regarded goods as merchantable if their actual state was such that a reasonable buyer, fully aware of all the facts, including any hidden defects, would buy them without a reduction of the price or special terms[6]. The second emphasised the 'usability' of the goods: goods would be merchantable provided they would be used by a reasonable buyer for any purpose for which goods of the contract description would ordinarily be used[7]. In *Brown v Craiks*[8] B ordered fabric, intending to use it to manufacture dresses. The description used in the contract was a wide one, capable of applying to both dressmaking and industrial fabric; the price was high for industrial fabric, but not so high as to be unrealistic. S delivered fabric which matched the contract description but which, although suitable for industrial uses, was not suitable for dressmaking. The House of Lords held, applying the 'usability test' that the fabric was merchantable.

It is not clear how far, if at all, the 'usability' and 'acceptability' tests differed; in many cases they would produce the same result[9]. The 'acceptability' test was perhaps more favourable to the buyer, and there was a tendency to adopt that test in consumer, and the 'usability' test in commercial cases. The concept of 'merchantability' thus remained both flexible and difficult to apply, and in 1976 Ormrod LJ observed that since 1893:

'the word [merchantable] has fallen out of general use and largely lost its meaning, except to merchants and traders in some branches of commerce. Hence the difficulty today of finding a satisfactory formulation for a test of merchantability. No doubt people who are experienced in a particular trade can still look at a parcel of goods and say "those goods are merchantable" or "those goods are merchantable but at a lower price" distinguishing them from "job lots" or "seconds". But in the absence of expert evidence of this kind it will often be very difficult for a judge or jury to make the decision except in obvious cases'[10].

In 1973, therefore, a statutory definition of 'merchantable quality' was introduced[11]. It was carried through into s 14(6) of the 1979 Act, which provided that:

'Goods of any kind are of merchantable quality . . . if they are as fit for the purpose or purposes for which goods of that kind are commonly bought as it is reasonable to expect having regard to any description applied to them, the price (if relevant) and all the other relevant circumstances.'

This definition was widely regarded as an amalgam of the 'usability' and 'acceptability' tests. Nevertheless, the requirement of merchantability, and the 1973 definition, were criticised[12]. In particular it was felt, partly as a result of some decisions apparently hostile to consumer interests in the 1970s, that the test was inappropriate for consumer purchases. It was argued that 'merchantable' meant 'fit for sale' and it was pointed out that consumers do not buy goods to sell them. Moreover, it was felt that the definition of 'merchantable' placed too much emphasis on the goods being usable and failed to take adequate account of the fact that consumers, quite legitimately, expect more; for instance, that goods should be free of so-called 'minor' or 'cosmetic' defects. Finally, it was feared that the reference to 'reasonable expectations' might effectively allow a seller to lower the standard of merchantability, by showing that, for instance, new cars generally suffer from teething troubles and that therefore such problems must reasonably be expected, or even that, because a particular make had a particularly bad reputation, the standard expected of it was lower than for other makes[13].

These objections are not entirely convincing: the requirement that goods be 'merchantable' in the sense of 'saleable' could be interpreted as meaning that they are fit to be sold to, not by, the buyer, and in several cases during the 1980s the courts showed that they were capable of applying the test of merchantability in such a way as to take account of consumer expectations. However, in 1987 the Law Commission accepted these criticisms and therefore recommended that the test of 'merchantable quality' be replaced by a new formulation. The Commission proposed that the new requirement should consist of a generally applicable statement of the required quality standard, supplemented by a list of factors which might be taken into account when assessing whether goods meet that standard. They considered three options for the general standard: a qualitative standard based on a single adjective such as 'good' or 'sound' quality; a 'neutral' standard based on a single adjective such as 'proper' or 'appropriate' quality; or a standard of acceptability, and ultimately favoured this last option. Thus they recommended that the goods supplied should be required to be of 'acceptable quality'.

The Commission's recommendations were broadly accepted. However, in the Consumer Guarantees Bill introduced in 1989 to implement the proposals the general test was replaced by a requirement that goods should be of satisfactory quality, and this formulation was preferred in a DTI consultation paper, 'Consumer Guarantees', published in 1992. Apparently it was felt by consumer groups that 'satisfactory' quality imposes a higher standard than would 'acceptable' quality: consumers might accept goods which were not satisfactory and the 1994 Act therefore adopted the test of 'satisfactory quality'.

The requirement that the goods should be of 'satisfactory quality' in s 14(2) is amplified by new ss 14(2A) and 14(2B) which contain a definition of 'satisfactory quality', similar to that of merchantable quality previously contained in s 14(6), and, in accordance with the Law Commission's recommendations, a list of factors to be considered when deciding whether goods are of satisfactory quality. Section 14(2A) provides that:

> 'goods are of satisfactory quality if they meet the standard that a reasonable person would regard as satisfactory, taking account of the description of the goods, the price (if relevant) and all the other relevant circumstances.'

Section 14(2B) states that:

> 'The quality of goods includes their state and condition and the following (among others) are in appropriate cases aspects of the quality of goods—

(a) fitness for all the purposes for which goods of that kind are commonly supplied;
(b) appearance and finish;
(c) freedom from minor defects;
(d) safety; and
(e) durability.'

It is worth noting that the matters included in the list in s 14(2B) are not absolute requirements, but merely factors to be considered '*in appropriate cases*'. Thus, for example, goods are not required to be durable, but goods which are not sufficiently durable may be regarded as unsatisfactory. In making an assessment of quality the court must consider all the circumstances of the case, including the factors in the list. Thus, for instance, goods with minor or cosmetic defects might be considered 'satisfactory' if sold at a lower than normal price. The test would seem to be whether a reasonable person would regard the goods as unsatisfactory in light of the defects and of all the other circumstances.

The changes made by the 1994 Act have been welcomed, especially by consumer representatives. However, some commentators have questioned whether the changes will bring any significant improvement to the law[14]. First, it should be noted that much of the uncertainty surrounding the test of 'merchantable quality' stemmed from the fact that it was a broad, flexible test whose application could vary according to the facts of individual cases. 'Satisfactory quality' is no more precise a formulation; indeed, any general test must be flexible[15]. Some commentators have even questioned the wisdom of attempting to set out any statutory definition of the required quality standard[16]. It has also been pointed out that the abandonment of 'merchantable quality' severs UK law from that of a number of Commonwealth jurisdictions which still have requirements of merchantable quality, and therefore from a potentially valuable source of explanatory case law[17]. Above all, there will necessarily be some uncertainty as to the meaning of 'satisfactory quality' until a sufficient body of case law applying the new provisions has grown up. There is as yet only one reported first instance decision in which the new provisions were considered in any detail, and, it is submitted, the result in that case would have been the same under the old law[18].

In fact, one may doubt whether the new formulation will make any significant difference to the outcome in many cases. In many cases the assessment of quality may be more or less instinctive and it is clear that the Law Commission saw its proposals as involving a change of emphasis rather than a complete abandonment of the old law. Moreover, there is a substantial body of case law on the meaning of 'merchantable quality' and many of the factors included in the list in s 14(2B) were taken into account by the courts in deciding cases on the meaning of 'merchantable quality'. The most likely effect of the inclusion of the list in s 14(2B) will be to focus attention on the factors listed, especially in consumer disputes which may be decided at the level of the county court or, often, settled by negotiation without recourse to litigation.

It seems quite likely, therefore, that the courts will continue to refer to some cases decided under the old law, at least for guidance, in applying the new test of 'satisfactory quality'. The experience of the courts applying the statutory definition of 'merchantable quality' introduced in 1973 may well be instructive. In *Rogers v Parish (Scarborough) Ltd*[19] the Court of Appeal described the statutory definition as 'clear and free from technicality'[20] and observed that reference to the pre-1973 case law would only be appropriate in 'exceptional cases'. However, in *Aswan*

287

Engineering Establishment Co v Lupdine Ltd[21] a differently constituted Court of Appeal relied heavily on the older case law and expressed the view that s 14(6) had not been intended to change the law laid down in those cases. Whilst the 1994 changes represent a more radical departure from the prior law than did the 1973 definition, it seems unlikely that the old case law will be jettisoned altogether. Significantly in the one reported case in which the new provisions have been considered the court was referred to a number of cases decided before 1994 but found them not to be 'of much assistance'[22].

1 SoGA, s 14(6).
2 *Gardiner v Gray* (1815) 4 Camp 144.
3 Although at that time the condition applied only where the goods were sold by description.
4 Section 62 of the 1893 Act; s 61 of the 1979 Act prior to the 1994 amendment.
5 Per Farwell LJ in *Bristol Tramways v Fiat Motors Ltd* [1910] 2 KB 831 at 840, CA.
6 See *Grant v Australian Knitting Mills Ltd* (1933) 50 CLR 387 per Dixon J; *Bristol Tramways v Fiat Motors Ltd* per Farwell LJ; *Henry Kendall & Sons v William Lillico & Sons Ltd* [1969] 2 AC 31, HL, per Lords Pearce (at 118), Guest (at 108) and Wilberforce (at 126).
7 *Cammell Laird & Co Ltd v Manganese Bronze and Brass Co Ltd* [1934] AC 402, HL; *Henry Kendall & Sons v William Lillico & Sons Ltd* [1969] 2 AC 31, per Lords Reid (at 77) and Morris (at 98).
8 [1970] 1 All ER 823, [1970] 1 WLR 752, HL.
9 See *Henry Kendall & Sons v William Lillico & Sons Ltd; Cehave NV v Bremer Handelsgesellschaft mbH.*
10 *Cehave NV v Bremer Handelsgesellschaft mbH* [1976] QB 44 at 80, CA.
11 By SoG(IT)A, 1973.
12 Professor Bridge described it as 'quite useless to any decision maker': [1991] LMCLQ 52 at 56.
13 See 'Merchantable Quality – What does it Mean?' Consumers' Association (1979) p 32.
14 See *Atiyah's Sale of Goods* (10th edn, 2000) p 181; Bridge, Sale of Goods (1997) p 304, *Benjamin's Sale of Goods* (5th edn, 1997) para 11-057.
15 See Atiyah, *Sale of Goods* (10th edn, 2000) p 181; Adams and Brownsword (1988) 51 MLR 481.
16 Bridge [1991] LMCLQ 52 at pp 56–57.
17 See *Atiyah's Sale of Goods* (10th edn, 2000) p 157.
18 *Thain v Anniesland Trade Centre* 1997 SLT 102, Sh Ct, discussed below 11.2.4.4. The requirement of satisfactory quality has been applied in other cases, but without any discussion or analysis. In *Danka Rentals Ltd v Xi Software* (1998) 17 Tr LR 74 the court found that a photocopier which went 'wrong in almost every conceivable respect' and was a 'complete disaster' was not of satisfactory quality without considering the meaning and effect of the new provisions. See also *Albright & Wilson UK Ltd v Biachem Ltd* [2000] All ER (D) 530.
19 [1987] QB 933, [1987] 2 All ER 232.
20 Per Mustill LJ at 942, 235.
21 [1987] 1 All ER 135; see 11.2.4. See also the view of Lord Denning in *Cehave NV v Bremer Handelsgesellschaft mbH* at 62.
22 In *Thain v Anniesland Trade Centre*, above, note 18. In *Albright & Wilson UK Ltd v Biachem Ltd* [2000] All ER (D) 530 Eady J held that goods were unsatisfactory without considering the wording of the new provisions but by following cases decided prior to 1973.

11.2.4 Applying the test of satisfactory quality

The core of the new test is that goods should meet the standard which a reasonable buyer would regard as satisfactory. The test is not whether a reasonable person would regard the goods as satisfactory but whether the goods supplied, with all faults and defects, comply with an objectively satisfactory standard for goods of the same description and price. As has been noted, application of this test in a particular case will depend on all the facts of the case. In many cases the test will be difficult to apply, especially in relation to complex machinery and consumer goods. However, as noted earlier, many of the factors referred to in the new s 14(2B) were considered by the courts in applying the test of merchantable quality and cases decided under the old law may therefore offer some guidance as to the way the new test will be applied.

11.2.4.1   *Fitness for all common purposes*

'Fitness for all purposes for which goods of the kind in question are commonly supplied' is now, 'in appropriate cases' an aspect of the quality of the goods. This marks a significant change from the pre-1995 law. Cases decided prior to 1973 established that where goods of a particular description were commonly bought for a range of purposes, they would be merchantable provided they were fit for a least one of those purposes. Thus in *Kendall v Lillico*[1] B bought groundnut extract and used it to make food which he sold to the owner of a game farm, who fed it to his stock. The groundnuts used in the extract had been affected by a mould which produced a toxin poisonous to the birds, which died. However, groundnut extract was often used to make cattle food and the extract supplied to B could safely have been used for cattle food. The House of Lords therefore held that the extract was merchantable. Similarly, in *Sumner Permain v Webb*[2] B bought tonic water, intending to sell it in Argentina. S supplied tonic water which contained a higher concentration of salicylic acid than was permitted in Argentina, and B argued that the tonic was therefore unmerchantable. However, the tonic could be sold in most other countries, and the Court of Appeal therefore held that it was merchantable.

The statutory definition of merchantable quality introduced in 1973 provided that goods would be of merchantable quality if they were 'as fit for the purpose or purposes for which goods of that kind' were commonly bought as it was reasonable to expect. However, in *Aswan Engineering Establishment Co v Lupdine Ltd*[3] the Court of Appeal held that the statutory definition had not been intended to change the law laid down prior to 1973, so that goods with more than one common purpose were merchantable provided they were fit for at least one of those purposes. The case concerned a contract to supply plastic pails which were used to contain damp-proofing compound which was exported to Kuwait. On arrival in Kuwait the pails were stored, stacked five or six high, in a container on the quayside for several days. During this time the temperature inside the container reached as high as 70 degrees celsius. In those conditions the pails collapsed under their own weight and the buyers claimed that they were unmerchantable on the grounds that they were unfit for export to Kuwait, which was one of the normal purposes for which such goods were supplied. The effect of the Court of Appeal's interpretation was to prevent the buyers' claim succeeding. Although the interpretation was difficult to reconcile with the language of the statute the result on the facts of the case therefore seems fair. Beyond the facts of the particular case, however, the effect of this interpretation was that where goods had more than one common purpose a buyer buying them for one particular purpose was required to make his particular purpose known to the seller in order to rely on the implied condition in s 14(3) that the goods should be reasonably fit for his particular purpose.

The new provision therefore marks a significant change. It seems that the Law Commission intended to reverse the effect of the decision in *Aswan v Lupdine*[4]. It should no longer be possible for a seller to claim that goods are of satisfactory quality where they are fit for only one of the common purposes for which such goods are supplied. Indeed, it would now seem to be possible for the buyer to claim that the goods are unsatisfactory on the grounds that they are not fit for all their common purposes even if they are fit for the purpose for which he requires them. However, the new Act does not impose an absolute requirement that goods must be fit for all their common purposes and a court faced with similar facts to those in *Aswan* could still reach the same result by a number of routes. There seems no reason why goods which are fit for most of their common purposes but not for one particular purpose should not be considered 'satisfactory' in a particular case in light of the description applied to them or the contract price. Alternatively, on the facts of *Aswan* the court might find that storage of the pails in the extreme circumstances of that case was not a common purpose.

1   [1969] 2 AC 31, [1968] 2 All ER 444; see also *B S Brown & Son Ltd v Craiks Ltd* [1970] 1 All ER 823, HL, above 11.2.3.
2   [1922] 1 KB 55.
3   [1987] 1 All ER 135, [1987] 1 WLR 1, CA.
4   Law Commission Report 160, 'Sale and Supply of Goods' (1987) paras 3.31–3.36.

11.2.4.2   *Appearance and finish and freedom from minor defects*

One of the main reasons for the introduction of the new statutory formulation was that the statutory definition of merchantable quality, with its emphasis on 'usability', did not correspond with the expectations of consumers who want goods not only to be usable but also to be free of 'minor' or 'cosmetic' defects. Appearance and finish are therefore both included in s 14(2B) as 'aspects of quality'. However, it is clear that even under the old law, minor defects which did not prevent the goods being used for their common purpose could still render them unmerchantable, especially where the buyer was a consumer. This is clearly demonstrated in a line of cases from the 1980s concerned with consumer purchases of motor cars. In *Rogers v Parish (Scarborough) Ltd*[1] B bought a new Range Rover for £16,000. It suffered from a number of 'minor' defects, including misfiring, engine noise, leaking oil seals and scratches to the paintwork. The Court of Appeal held that the car was unmerchantable. Mustill LJ said that the purpose for which cars are bought would include 'not merely the driver's purpose of driving the car from one place to another but of doing so with the appropriate degree of comfort, ease of handling and reliability and, one may add, pride in the vehicle's outward and interior appearance[2]'. Similarly, in *Shine v General Guarantee Corpn*[3], the court emphasised that goods could be unmerchantable despite being 'usable'. In that case the buyer had bought a second-hand Fiat X-19. It had at some time been totally immersed in water so that the manufacturer's anti-corrosion warranty was avoided. The Court of Appeal held that the car was unmerchantable; as Bush J observed 'a car is not just a means of transport: it is a form also of investment (albeit a deteriorating one) and every purchaser of a car must have in mind the eventual saleability of the car as well as, in this particular case, his pride in it as a specialist car for the enthusiast'[4]. Similarly again, in *Bernstein v Pamson Motors (Golders Green) Ltd*[5] Rougier J rejected the argument that a new car was merchantable despite a defect which was easily repairable. In that case the engine of a new Nissan Laurel seized after only 140 miles or so due to the presence in an oilway of a blob of sealant which blocked the supply of oil to the camshaft.

In these cases, and especially in *Rogers* and *Shine*, the courts seem to have been willing to take account of the expectations of consumers and the outcome of these cases would almost certainly be the same under the new law. Even in a commercial case 'minor' or 'cosmetic' defects could make goods unmerchantable, especially if they were manufactured goods bought for resale[6]. However, there were cases the other way. For instance, in *Millars of Falkirk Ltd v Turpie*[7] a new car was delivered with a leak in the power steering system; it would cost £25 to fix and the seller offered to repair the leak. The buyer (a solicitor) declined that offer and immediately sought to reject. The court held the car was merchantable despite the leak. In a commercial case the court would be even more unwilling to hold that minor defects made goods unmerchantable, especially in a sale of commodities or raw materials which, even if defective, often have a commercial resale value. The buyer in such a case may seek to reject for economic motives – to escape a bad bargain. Thus in *Cehave v Bremer*[8] the Court of Appeal held that citrus pulp pellets which had been damaged by overheating and were 'far from perfect', but which could still be used for the buyer's intended purpose, were merchantable.

The motive for decisions such as these seems to have been to prevent the buyer rejecting where, in the court's opinion, to do so would be unreasonable. The difficulty was that prior to the 1994 reforms the implied term that goods should be merchantable was classified as a condition so that if the buyer sought to reject a finding of unmerchantability would automatically permit rejection. In *Cehave v Bremer* the court found that an express term requiring the goods to be loaded in 'good condition' had been broken, but that term was 'innominate' and its breach only entitled the buyer to claim damages.

Section 15A of the Act now restricts the right of a non-consumer buyer to reject for breach of implied condition where the breach is so slight that rejection would be unreasonable[9]. In a case such as *Cehave v Bremer* the court could therefore now find the goods unsatisfactory but still refuse to allow rejection, restricting the buyer to a claim for damages. This option would not be available, however, in a consumer case such as *Millars*. It seems likely that the Law Commission had such cases in mind when it recommended the inclusion of express reference to appearance and finish and freedom from minor defects. However, there is no guarantee that were similar facts to those in *Millars* to arise the outcome would be any different under the new law. Section 14 does not impose an absolute requirement that goods should be free from such defects[10], but only makes finish and freedom from minor defects aspects of quality to be taken into account 'in an appropriate case'. It would still be possible for a court which considered that the buyer was behaving unreasonably in trying to reject to find that the goods were in satisfactory condition notwithstanding the presence of 'minor' defects[11].

1 [1987] QB 933, [1987] 2 All ER 232, CA.
2 [1987] 2 All ER 232 at 237.
3 [1988] 1 All ER 911; see Brown (1988) 104 LQR 520.
4 At 915.
5 [1987] 2 All ER 220.
6 See eg *Jackson v Rotax Motor and Cycle Co* [1910] 2 KB 937, CA.
7 1976 SLT 66.
8 [1976] QB 44.
9 SoGA, s 15A; see 12.2.
10 See Law Commission Report 160, para 3.42.
11 See Adams and Brownsword (1988) 51 MLR 481.

11.2.4.3 *Safety*

Again inclusion of specific reference to 'safety' as an aspect of quality seems to do little other than to confirm the approach taken by the courts prior to 1995, when it is clear that defects which made goods unsafe would generally have made them unmerchantable. For instance, in *Bernstein v Pamson Motors*[1] Rougier J, holding that the car was unmerchantable despite the seller's argument that the defect was easily repairable and therefore 'minor', emphasised the potentially disastrous effects of a car seizing whilst being drive at speed.

1 [1987] 2 All ER 220 at 229.

11.2.4.4 *Durability*

As explained earlier, the better view[1] seems to be that the time at which the quality of the goods must be assessed is when risk passes from seller to buyer[2]. Although there were dicta in some pre-1995 cases to the effect that merchantability was a 'continuing term'[3], this was the position prior to 1995 and it remains the position now. It is recognised, however, that defects present in goods at the time of supply might not manifest themselves until some time later. Moreover, buyers, and especially consumers, reasonably expect that goods will not only be usable at the moment of supply but, in the absence of accidental damage or other special circumstances, will continue in that state for a reasonable period thereafter.

This expectation was reflected in pre-1995 case law which established that goods would be unmerchantable if, at the time of transfer of risk, they were in such a condition that they would wear out or break down earlier than would reasonably be expected[4]. In the commercial context it was established that where goods were to be transported, especially in international sales where long transport might be involved, the goods must be shipped in such a condition that they would be able to survive the transport, so that there would be a breach if say, tomatoes were shipped so ripe that they would be expected to go off before reaching their destination[5].

The position is now confirmed by s 14(2B). The Law Commission considered making it a separate statutory requirement that goods should be reasonably durable but ultimately rejected this option. Instead s 14(2B) states that in 'an appropriate case' durability is an aspect of quality to be considered when deciding if goods meet the standard that a reasonable person would consider satisfactory.

It must be emphasised that, just as under the old law, quality and durability are assessed at the time when risk passes from seller to buyer. The requirement is not that goods should remain of satisfactory quality for a reasonable time but that at the time of transfer of risk they should be in such a condition that they will deteriorate no more rapidly than might reasonably be expected[6]. The new law does not specify a 'life expectancy' for goods. As the Law Commission observed, the proper life expectancy will vary from case to case. Account must be taken of natural deterioration due to wear and tear, and therefore of the way in which the goods are treated. In addition, 'different types of goods have different life expectancies; and different grades of the same type of goods also (and quite properly) have different life expectancies[7]'. Although 'durable' may not seem a wholly appropriate word it is clear that the requirement applies both to manufactured, 'durable' goods and to perishables such as foodstuffs.

It will often be difficult to assess whether goods are sufficiently durable to be regarded as 'satisfactory'. For the buyer the problem is often one of proof. First, he must establish that the goods broke down earlier than might reasonably be expected. A court might take into account such factors as statements of expected durability in trade association codes of practice[8], 'use by' and 'best before' dates and advertising claims in deciding what would be a reasonable life expectancy for goods. Second, the buyer must prove that the goods broke down or wore out as a result of a defect present at the time of transfer of risk. The fact that they wore out or broke down earlier than might reasonably be expected may be prima facie evidence that they were not in satisfactory condition at that time, but may be countered by evidence of misuse etc.

The problems of applying the requirement of durability and the test of satisfactory quality in general are illustrated by the decision in *Thain v Anniesland Trade Centre*[9], the first reported case on the new provisions. The buyer purchased a second-hand Renault which was some five years old and had done some 80,000 miles. She paid £2,995 which was found to be a reasonable price for a car of that age and mileage. After about two weeks she noticed a noise from the gear box which proved to be caused by wear in the differential bearing. She claimed that the car was unsatisfactory on the grounds that it was not reasonably fit for its purpose and was not sufficiently durable. Her claim failed. There was no evidence that the gear box had begun to fail at the time of supply. At that time the car was perfectly usable. The court accepted that the gear box was already worn as a result of the car's age and mileage and that as a result it could fail at any time. However, that lack of durability did not make the car unsatisfactory because, on the facts, durability was not a quality which a reasonable person would expect. To put it another way, the buyer of a second-hand car knows, and accepts the risk that the car may have some hidden defects appropriate to its age which may require repair sooner or later. The court emphasised that the buyer here had declined the option to purchase an extended warranty on the vehicle.

Thain lays down no general rule. Indeed, as the court recognised 'cases relating to quality tend . . . to turn on their own facts'. The court recognised that the result would have been different had the car been new, and suggested that a new car could reasonably be expected to last for at least the duration of the guarantee period without a major component failure. What the decision illustrates is that the factors listed in s 14(2B) are not absolute requirements, and that the outcome of a particular case will depend on the interplay of different factors. No doubt one might say that at the time it was sold the car in *Thain* was not 'durable', as evidenced by its breakdown. However, that lack of durability did not make the car unsatisfactory in light of the other circumstances of the case including the price, the description of the car as second-hand and its age and mileage. It is interesting, too, to compare *Thain* with cases decided under the 'old law'. The case bears a striking similarity to *Bartlett v Sidney Marcus Ltd*[10], discussed below, in which it was held that a secondhand car was merchantable provided that at the time of sale it was driveable[11].

There is one further consequence of durability being an aspect of quality at the time of transfer of risk. Where goods are insufficiently durable the breach of contract occurs at the time risk passes to the buyer, not later when the defect appears. Thus in many cases a buyer who succeeds in a claim that goods were unsatisfactory because they were insufficiently durable may be unable to reject them due to the passage of time[12]. Moreover, the limitation period for any claim in respect of the breach will run from the time of sale so that in an extreme case the buyer may find his claims barred altogether[13].

1   See *Benjamin's Sale of Goods* (5th edn, 1997) para 11-062.
2   See ch 16.
3   See *Lexmead (Basingstoke) Ltd v Lewis* [1982] AC 225 per Lord Diplock at 276.
4   *Lexmead (Basingstoke) Ltd v Lewis* [1982] AC 225.
5   *Mash and Murrell v Joseph I Emanuel Ltd* [1961] 1 All ER 485, [1961] 1 WLR 862; see 33.1.3.

6 Law Commission 160, 'Sale and Supply of Goods' (1987) para 3.52.
7 Ibid, para 3.49.
8 The Law Commission rejected the option of making express statutory reference to codes of practice but recognised that they could be relevant in an appropriate case: para 3.50.
9 1997 SLT 102, Sh Ct.
10 [1965] 2 All ER 753, [1965] 1 WLR 1013; see below 11.2.4.5.
11 Contrast the decision in *Crowther v Shannon Motor Co* [1975] 1 WLR 30.
12 See 12.2.1.3.
13 See eg *Parasram v Witter Towbars Ltd* (1993) unreported, Lexis transcript.

11.2.4.5 *Price and description*

'Price and description' were expressly referred to in the statutory definition of 'merchantable quality' and it seems almost certain that they will be taken into account in assessing whether goods are of satisfactory quality in the same way as they were under the old law. In general terms they may raise or lower the quality standard to be expected of the goods. They may also qualify the relevance of the factors listed in the new s 14(2B).

In general, a higher standard will be expected from higher priced goods. Similarly descriptions such as 'luxury' or 'deluxe' may raise expectations, whilst goods described as 'seconds', 'shop-soiled', 'ex-display' or 'second-hand' may be expected to be of a lower standard. This approach was clearly demonstrated in a number of cases concerned with 'merchantable quality'. Thus in *Rogers v Parish (Scarborough) Ltd*[1] the Court of Appeal held that a new Range Rover which suffered from a series of 'minor' defects was unmerchantable, and Mustill LJ emphasised the importance of both price and description.

> 'In the present case the car was sold as new. Deficiencies which might be acceptable in a second-hand vehicle were not to be expected in one purchased as new. Next, the description "Range Rover" would conjure up a particular set of expectations, not the same as those relating to an ordinary saloon car, as to the balance between performance, handling, comfort and resilience. The factor of price was also significant. At more than £14,000 this vehicle was, if not at the top end of the scale, well above the level of an ordinary family saloon. The buyer was entitled to value for his money[2].'

Similarly, in *Shine v General Guarantee Corpn*[3] the Court of Appeal emphasised the importance of description: the buyer 'thought he was buying an enthusiast's car, a car of the mileage shown and at the sort of price cars of that age and condition could be expected to fetch, a car described as "a nice car, good runner, no problems" . . . What he in fact was buying for the same price was . . . potentially a "rogue car" and irrespective of its condition it was one which no member of the public, knowing the facts, would touch with a barge pole unless they could get it at a substantially reduced price[4]'.

Description and price may also be relevant to the purposes for which the goods are commonly bought. In general, the wider the description applied to goods, the wider the range of purposes for which the goods would commonly be bought; but the price may indirectly indicate the intended purpose or determine the quality to be expected. The result in *Brown v Craiks*[5] might have been different if the price of the fabric had been unreasonably high for industrial fabric: the price would then have indicated that the fabric contracted for was not industrial fabric[6]. A lower price, or a description such as 'second-hand', 'shop-soiled' or 'seconds' may all lower the standard to be expected of goods and qualify the extent to which they can be expected to be durable or free from minor or cosmetic defects. In *Bartlett v Sidney Marcus Ltd*[7] the Court of Appeal held that a second-hand car 'was merchantable provided that it was in usable condition, even though it was not perfect[8]' so that where B bought a car for a slightly reduced price, knowing that the clutch was defective, the car was merchantable even though the defect was more serious than had been thought. Even now that the law places less emphasis on 'usability' the buyer of second-hand goods must expect a certain amount of wear and tear, varying according to the age of the goods, the price and so on[9], as the decision in *Thain*, above, illustrates.

Often the same facts will give rise to a claim under s 13 and s 14(2). Section 14(2A) refers to 'the description of' the goods, not the description by which they are sold. This may therefore allow the court to take into account under s 14(2) descriptions which do not form part of the contractual description for the purpose of s 13. However, a court may be reluctant to allow a claim which fails under s 13 to succeed under s 14(2). In *Harlingdon & Leinster Ltd v Christopher Hull Fine Art Ltd*[10] the court rejected a claim that the painting was unmerchantable by virtue of the wrong attribution. The court held that paintings are normally bought for their aesthetic value and as an investment, with a view to resale. The aesthetic value of the painting in the case was not affected by the attribution; and the painting was still saleable, albeit for very much less than the plaintiffs had expected (and less than they had paid). Cases such as *Shine* and *Rogers* which are really 'consumer' cases raise very different considerations from a case such as this one. Clearly the court felt that the plaintiffs should be taken to have assumed the risk of the attribution being false, and were not prepared to allow them to succeed in a claim under s 14 where the s 13 claim had failed.

1 [1987] QB 933, [1987] 2 All ER 232, CA.
2 [1987] QB 933 at 944, [1987] 2 All ER 232 at 237.
3 *Shine v General Guarantee Corpn* [1988] 1 All ER 911; see Brown (1988) 104 LQR 520.
4 At 915.
5 [1970] 1 All ER 823, HL above 11.2.3.
6 See *H Beecham & Co Pty Ltd v Francis Howard & Co Pty Ltd* [1921] VLR 428.
7 [1965] 2 All ER 753, [1965] 1 WLR 1013.
8 Per Lord Denning at 755.
9 See *Business Application Specialists Ltd v Nationwide Credit Corpn Ltd* [1988] RTR 332, CA.
10 [1990] 1 All ER 737, above 11.1.2.

11.2.4.6 *Other factors*

The list of factors in s 14(2B) is not intended to be exclusive and in appropriate cases other factors may be relevant. For instance, cases under the old law had established that packaging and instructions could be relevant when assessing merchantability. In *Niblett v Confectioners' Materials Ltd*[1] B bought a quantity of tins of condensed milk. The tins were labelled 'Nissly Brand'. Nestle obtained an injunction to prevent the resale of the tins under that label on the grounds that the labels infringed their copyright. The Court of Appeal held that as the tins could not be resold under their original labels, they were unmerchantable. In *Wormell v RHM Agriculture (East) Ltd*[2] the Court of Appeal recognised that inaccurate or misleading instructions might make goods unmerchantable, although they found that the instructions in question in that case were not misleading.

It would be surprising if similar cases were decided differently under the new law and in *Albright & Wilson UK Ltd v Biachem Ltd*[3] it was held at first instance, following *Niblett* (and without any reference to the wording of s 14(2)), that inaccurate documentation was capable of making goods unsatisfactory. The result is plainly correct but the basis of the decision is not clear. Of course, instructions may be relevant to safety: potentially hazardous goods may be of satisfactory quality if supplied with full accurate instructions and warnings, but unsatisfactory otherwise[4] and the lack of documentation in *Albright* made the goods unsafe. However, lack of proper instructions or warnings may make goods unsatisfactory even though they are not unsafe and it is perhaps unfortunate that the Law Commission did not include such matters in the list of factors to be considered by the court.

In some cases fitness for immediate use may also be a relevant factor. However, the Law Commission expressly declined to make this an absolute requirement. In some cases goods may be satisfactory even though they are not immediately usable, if they can be made usable by doing something that the parties would expect to be done to the goods; for instance, assembling self-assembly furniture. Under the old law it was held that pork chops infected with trichinae, which made them dangerous to eat, were merchantable because they would be safe if cooked properly before eating[5]. This is an extreme case. In contrast, in *Grant v Australian Knitting Mills Ltd*[6] B bought a pair of woollen underpants which contained traces of sulphites which caused him dermatitis. The sulphites could have been removed by washing but the underpants were held unmerchantable: a buyer would not normally be expected to wash new underpants before wearing them. Ultimately, as the Commission recognised, suitability for immediate use, taking account of what a buyer may reasonably be expected to do with the goods, is an aspect of fitness for purpose[7].

New goods are often supplied with a manufacturer's warranty. In *Rogers v Parish* the Court of Appeal held that the manufacturer's warranty given with a new Range Rover should not be taken into account when deciding whether the vehicle was merchantable. 'Can it really be right to say that a reasonable buyer would expect less of his new Range Rover with a warranty than without one? Surely the warranty is an addition to the buyer's rights, not a subtraction from them, and, it may be noted, only a circumscribed addition. . . [8]' However, in other cases the availability of an express warranty given by the supplier has been held relevant when assessing merchantability[9].

1   [1921] 3 KB 387.
2   [1987] 3 All ER 75, [1987] 1 WLR 1091. See generally McLeod (1981) LQR 550.
3   [2000] All ER (D) 530.
4   Law Commission 160, 'Sale and Supply of Goods' (1987) para 3.45.
5   *Heil v Hedges* [1951] 1 TLR 512. The case is criticised by Atiyah, *Sale of Goods* (10th edn, 2000) p 172.
6   [1936] AC 85, PC.
7   Para 3.64.
8   [1987] 2 All ER 232 Per Mustill LJ at 237.
9   See *Eurodynamics Ltd v General Automation Ltd* (6 September 1988, unreported), QBD: computer software.

11.2.5 *When is quality to be assessed?*

As already noted[1], the question whether goods are of satisfactory quality is assessed by reference to their condition at the time risk passes from seller to buyer. However, in making that assessment, account must be taken of the defect, even though it is not known to the parties at that time. In *Kendall v Lillico*[2], a merchantable quality case, a majority of the House of Lords thought that it was also necessary to take into account knowledge acquired between the sale and the trial which might show that the defect could easily be remedied and which might therefore make the goods merchantable. In that case the knowledge in question was knowledge that the poisoned groundnut extract could safely be used for some animal food in small quantities: a reasonable buyer with full knowledge of the facts would have known that fact and therefore still have purchased the goods. However, this aspect of the case has been much criticised: as Atiyah observes, even a very slight defect, if hidden, can make goods dangerous and 'in circumstances like these it is precisely the fact that the condition is hidden which constitutes the danger, and therefore the defect in the goods[3]'. Essentially this is a question of fitness for purpose: on the facts of *Kendall* the goods were not fit at the time of supply and therefore should not be regarded as merchantable or, under the new law, satisfactory. There is nothing in the new law to change the reasoning of the majority in *Kendall* but it is to be hoped that it would not be followed.

1   Above 11.0.2.1.
2   [1969] 2 AC 31, [1968] 2 All ER 444.
3   Atiyah, *Sale of Goods* (10th edn, 2000) p 174.

11.2.6   *Exceptions*

Liability for breach of the implied condition that goods should be of satisfactory quality is strict: it is no defence for the seller to show that he was not responsible for the defect, or even that he was unaware of it[1]. Moreover, the seller's right to exclude the implied term, or remedies for its breach, is severely restricted by s 6 of the Unfair Contract Terms Act 1977[2].

However, in two situations the implied condition is excluded by the SoGA itself. Section 14(2C) provides that the implied term:

'does not extend to any matter making the quality of goods unsatisfactory—
(a) which is specifically drawn to the buyer's attention before the contract is made,
(b) where the buyer examines the goods before the contract is made, which that examination ought to reveal.'

This largely reproduces two exceptions contained in the old law; however, the wording has been slightly changed and the new exclusions may therefore be slightly wider than the old which referred only to 'defects' drawn to the buyer's attention or which he ought to have discovered.

The first exception comes close to creating a duty of disclosure: the seller cannot be liable in respect of any matter disclosed to the buyer. Note that for the seller to avoid liability on this basis the matter in question must be specifically drawn to the buyer's attention. The Act does not, however, require it to be the seller who makes the disclosure, provided that the seller can show that the matter was drawn to the buyer's attention.

The second exception only applies where the buyer examines the goods. It must be stressed that there is no obligation on the buyer to examine at all; and if the buyer makes only a cursory examination, his right to complain about matters which that examination could not be expected to reveal is unaffected[3]. However, if the buyer is given the opportunity to examine the goods and leads the seller to believe he has done so, he may be estopped from denying that he has made a full examination, and so will be bound by defects which a full examination would have revealed[4].

Where goods are acquired on hire purchase or credit sale the contract will not be made until the application for credit is approved, and the contract signed, by the finance company. If the buyer is allowed to take possession of the goods and becomes aware of defects before the contract is signed, it may be argued that the exception applies, so that the buyer cannot complain that the goods are unmerchantable[5].

1   *Frost v Aylesbury Dairy Co* [1905] 1 KB 608, CA.
2   See 2.6.4.
3   *Godley v Perry* [1960] 1 All ER 36, [1960] 1 WLR 9 (the case actually concerned a similar provision under s 15).
4   This would explain the difficult case of *Thornett and Fehr v Beers & Son* [1919] 1 KB 486. The case was decided under a slightly differently worded provision which referred to 'defects which *such* examination ought to have revealed'.
5   See *R & B Customs Brokers Ltd v United Dominions Trust Co* [1988] 1 All ER 847, [1988] 1 WLR 321; the Court of Appeal did not decide whether this argument was correct.

11.3   The goods must be fit for the buyer's purpose

Section 14(3) implies a further condition, that where the buyer, expressly or by implication, makes known to the seller 'any particular purpose for which the goods are being bought' the goods supplied under the contract will be reasonably fit for the buyer's purpose 'except where the circumstances show that the buyer does not rely, or that it is unreasonable for him to rely, on the skill or judgment of the seller'.

Like the implied condition that goods be of satisfactory quality, the condition of fitness for purpose only applies where the seller sells the goods in the course of a business, but where that requirement is fulfilled it applies to all goods supplied under the contract. The considerations discussed above in relation to s 14(2) therefore apply here[1].

1   See 11.2.1; 11.2.2.

11.3.1   *Particular purpose*

Section 14(3) only applies where the buyer makes known to the seller the 'particular purpose' for which the goods are bought. However, the purpose may be made known expressly or impliedly, for instance as a result of previous transactions[1]. Often the contract may be negotiated through agents; in that case it is sufficient for the buyer to indicate his purpose to the seller's agent authorised to receive notification of the purpose. Where goods are bought on hire purchase or conditional sale from a finance company, the buyer's contract is with the finance company; however, the buyer will negotiate the transaction through a dealer who will sell the goods to the finance company. In such a case it is sufficient if the buyer indicates his purpose to the dealer[2].

Often the buyer will not indicate his purpose, or will do so only in general terms. However, he may still be able to rely on s 14(3). 'Particular purpose' refers to the purpose indicated by the buyer, rather than any special purpose[3], so that if the buyer indicates a range of purposes the goods must be reasonably fit for any reasonably foreseeable purpose within that broad range. Reasonable fitness is clearly a flexible standard, like satisfactory quality, and many of the factors relevant to quality, such as durability, minor defects and warnings, will be relevant to a claim under s 14(3). Since the standard is flexible, the more precisely the buyer specifies his purpose, the more closely the goods must fit that purpose. Thus where goods are bought for their normal purpose, the buyer will be held to have impliedly made his purpose known to the seller and will be able to rely on s 14(3)[4].

'The fact that, by the very terms of the sale itself, the article sold purports to be for use for a particular purpose cannot possibly exclude the case from the rule that, where goods are sold for a particular purpose, there is an implied warranty that they are reasonably fit for that purpose[5].'

In such a case the condition of fitness for purpose adds nothing to the condition of merchantability, and the buyer will be unlikely to succeed in a claim under s 14(3) if he could not establish a claim under s 14(2)[6].

If the buyer does want the goods to be fit for a special purpose, however, he must indicate it. In *Griffiths v Peter Conway Ltd*[7] B bought a Harris tweed coat. She had hyper sensitive skin and suffered an allergic reaction which an ordinarily sensitive person would not have suffered, but as she had not made her special condition known to S, it was held that the coat was reasonably fit for the purpose indicated.

Griffiths was distinguished in *Ashington Piggeries*[8] where the food manufacturer (M) made a claim under s 14(3) against his supplier (S) who had supplied contaminated herring meal. S knew that the meal was to be used for making animal feed rather than fertiliser, but not that the feed was for mink; however, although the contaminated meal was poisonous to all animals, it was only fatal to mink. Nevertheless, it was held that M had sufficiently indicated his purpose as being for use in the manufacture of animal feed. M's actual purpose – making food for mink – fell within that broad range of purposes, and was not an unforeseeable use. The House of Lords described *Griffiths v Conway* as a 'highly special case' and distinguished it on the basis that Mrs Griffiths' condition was virtually unique to her, whereas the food in this case was poisonous to all animals. The meal was therefore not reasonably fit for the purpose indicated by M. The approach is similar to the approach to remoteness of damage in contract: the meal was generally unsuitable for the purpose indicated – making animal food – and that unsuitability caused the death of the mink. However, this approach seems to place a heavy burden on the seller, and Lord Diplock dissented on this point, arguing that the seller should not be held liable where the information supplied was insufficient to allow him to exercise his skill and judgment.

Griffiths was however followed in *Slater v Finning*[9]. S supplied a camshaft for installation in the engine of B's fishing vessel, *Aquarius II*. The camshaft failed in use, as did two further, identical replacements, causing considerable losses to B's business. B claimed damages to compensate for those losses on the grounds that the camshaft supplied was not reasonably fit for the purpose indicated. Expert evidence however established that the fault was caused by an idiosyncrasy in the *Aquarius II* which resulted in excessive wear to the camshaft when in use. The *Aquarius'* engine, fitted with an identical camshaft, worked satisfactorily in another vessel. B argued that the camshaft was nevertheless unfit for the purpose indicated, ie: for installation in the *Aquarius II*. The House of Lords rejected that claim. Where a person buys goods without indicating that he requires them for any special purpose the seller is entitled to assume that they are required for their normal purpose. Here B had not indicated any special features of the *Aquarius II* and S was therefore entitled to assume that it was a normal vessel, for which, as the evidence showed, the camshaft would have been suitable.

Essentially cases such as *Slater* and *Griffiths* raise the question who should bear the risk of the goods proving unsuitable for the buyer's purpose because of unknown idiosyncrasies. The point is illustrated by an example given by Lord Griffiths in argument in *Slater*. If a person buys a new tyre for his car, specifying the make and model and the seller supplies a tyre suitable for that make and model of car but, because of an unknown defect in the steering of the buyer's particular car, the tyre wears out prematurely, who should bear the risk? The answer is that that risk falls on the buyer. The alternative, as Lord Steyn explained, would require the seller in such a case to carry out expensive and time consuming checks in every case. 'Considerations of everyday commerce militate against the adoption of the argument. It also seems to lead to an unjust result[10].' The seller may be required to make enquiries if he is aware that goods may be unsuitable for some buyers[11] but he cannot be expected to do so where the risk is wholly unforeseeable. As Lord Steyn concluded:

> 'Outside the field of private sales the shift from caveat emptor to caveat venditor in relation to the implied condition of fitness for purpose has been a notable feature of the development of our commercial law. But to uphold the present claim would be to allow caveat venditor to run riot[12].'

1 *Manchester Liners Ltd v Rea* [1922] 2 AC 74, HL.
2 SoGA, s 14(3)(b); the supplier will be a credit broker for the purposes of the Consumer Credit Act 1974: see 24.3.1; 26.4.
3 *Kendall & Sons v Lillico & Sons Ltd* [1969] 2 AC 31, [1968] 2 All ER 444, HL.
4 *Priest v Last* [1903] 2 KB 148; *Grant v Australian Knitting Mills Ltd* [1936] AC 85, PC.
5 Per Collins MR in *Priest v Last* at 153.
6 See per Nicholls LJ in *Aswan*.
7 [1939] 1 All ER 685, CA; and see *Ingham v Emes* [1955] 2 QB 366, [1955] 2 All ER 740, CA.
8 *Ashington Piggeries Ltd v Christopher Hill Ltd* [1972] AC 441, [1971] 1 All ER 847.
9 [1997] AC 473, [1996] 3 All ER 398.
10 [1997] AC 473 at 485, [1996] 3 All ER 398 at 407.
11 See *Manchester Liners Ltd v Rea* [1922] 2 AC 74, HL.
12 [1997] AC 473 at 488; [1996] 3 All ER 398 at 410.

11.3.2 *The buyer must rely on the seller*

Section 14(3) is subject to two provisos: the buyer must in fact rely on the seller's skill or judgment and it must be reasonable for him to do so.

Reliance is a question of fact. Prior to 1973 the buyer had to prove that he did rely on the seller, but reliance will now be presumed unless the seller raises the issue and proves that the buyer did not rely on him. As Lord Wright explained:

> 'The reliance will seldom be express: it will usually arise by implication from the circumstances; thus to take a case like that in question, of a purchase from a retailer the reliance will in general be inferred from the fact that a buyer

goes to the shop in the confidence that the tradesman has selected his stock with skill and judgment'[1].

In general if the buyer has indicated his purpose it will be difficult for a retail seller to disprove reliance by a consumer buyer, or for a manufacturer to disprove reliance by a customer. On the other hand, there may be no reliance if the buyer selects goods himself, or orders by a trade name, or knows that the seller can only supply goods of one particular type or from one particular source. For instance, in *Wren v Holt*[2] B bought Holden's beer from a tied public house. The beer was contaminated by arsenic. B gave evidence that he knew that the public house sold only Holden's beer, and that he drank there because he liked Holden's beer. A claim that the beer was unfit under s 14(3) failed on the basis that B had not relied on S.

Where S manufactures goods for B, B may provide a specification, or details of how the goods are to be made up. However, he may still be held to rely on S to actually manufacture the finished item or select appropriate components. He may therefore make a claim under s 14(3) if the finished product proves defective due to any matter within the area of reliance. In *Ashington Piggeries* the mink breeder supplied the recipe for the mink food, but relied on the food manufacturer to make up the formula. The breeder was entitled to complain that the food was not reasonably fit for his purpose because it was poisonous as a result of a contaminated ingredient, rather than because of an error in the breeder's formula[3].

Clearly reliance depends on the relative expertise of the parties; thus where the seller neither has nor claims any relevant expertise, the court may find that the buyer did not rely on him, or that it was unreasonable to do so. For instance 'Where a foreign merchant . . . buys by description goods . . . for resale in his own country, of which he has no reason to suppose the English seller has any special knowledge, it flies in the face of common sense to suppose that he relies on anything but his own knowledge of the market in his own country and his own commercial judgment as to what is saleable there[4]'. Similarly, where buyer and seller are both dealers in the type of goods sold it may be that the buyer relies on his own judgment rather than on the seller. However, there is no absolute rule to that effect; in *Kendall v Lillico*[5] both B and S were animal food dealers and members of the same trade association. S argued that that indicated that B did not rely on him; B argued that it indicated reliance because he would rely on the good reputation of a member of the association. The majority of the House of Lords held that reliance was a question of fact in each case; on the facts here B had relied on S, because the goods in question were new to the market and B relied on S 'not to sell anything he knew was rubbish'.

In *R and B Customs Brokers Ltd v United Dominions Trust Ltd*[6], B agreed to take a car on conditional sale, and was allowed to take possession of it before the sale contract was signed. As a result B became aware that the roof of the car leaked before the contract was made. The Court of Appeal held, nevertheless, that B was still relying on the skill or judgment of the garage which had supplied the car to repair the leak.

1 Per Lord Wright in *Grant v Australian Knitting Mills Ltd* [1936] AC 85 at 99.
2 [1903] 1 KB 610, CA. Contrast *Manchester Liners Ltd v Rea* [1922] 2 AC 74 where the buyers might have suspected, but did not know, that the sellers had only one source.
3 See also *Cammell Laird & Co Ltd v Manganese Bronze and Brass Co Ltd* [1934] AC 402, HL.
4 *Teheran-Europe Co Ltd v S T Belton (Tractors) Ltd* [1968] 2 QB 545 per Diplock LJ at 560–61.
5 [1969] 2 AC 31, [1968] 2 All ER 444.
6 [1988] 1 All ER 847, [1988] 1 WLR 321.

11.3.3 *Reliance must be reasonable*

The second proviso to s 14(3) is that there is no condition that the goods will be fit for the buyer's purpose even if the buyer does rely on the seller if it was unreasonable to do so. The requirements that the buyer indicate his purpose and that his reliance on the seller be reasonable are linked. If the buyer does not sufficiently indicate his purpose he cannot reasonably rely on the seller to supply goods suitable for it[1].The reasonableness of reliance is also likely to be closely linked to the fact of reliance; where reliance would be unreasonable, the court may often find that the buyer did not, in fact, rely on the seller. The reasonableness of reliance therefore probably depends on the relative expertise of the parties. It will generally be unreasonable for the buyer to rely on the seller if the latter makes clear that he has no expertise in relation to the goods in question. Thus a disclaimer, similar to the one used by the seller in *Harlingdon & Leinster Ltd v Christopher Hull Fine Art Ltd*[2] may allow the seller to avoid liability under s 14(3) as well as under s 13.

1   *Slater v Finning* [1997] AC 473; [1996] 3 All ER 398 at 408, per Lord Steyn.
2   [1991] 1 QB 564, [1990] 1 All ER 737, CA.

11.3.4 *The relationship between satisfactory quality and fitness for purpose*

Where goods are bought for their normal purpose, the implied conditions of satisfactory quality and fitness for purpose will overlap: if the goods are unfit for their normal purpose, both conditions will be broken, and in practice in such a case buyers plead breach of both conditions. Where goods with more than one common purpose were bought for one of those common purposes the buyer was formerly able to rely on s 14(2) only if the goods were not fit for any of their common purposes. If they were only unfit for his particular purpose he could not rely on s 14(2) and could only invoke s 14(3) if he had made his particular purpose known to the seller[1]. However, as a result of the changes made by the Sale and Supply of Goods Act 1994 the buyer in such a case may now be able to claim that the goods are not of satisfactory quality on the grounds that they are not fit for all their common purposes, and hence succeed under s 14(2) even though he has not made known to the seller his particular purpose. As suggested above, if a claim under s 14(2) fails in such circumstances, a claim under s 14(3) is unlikely to succeed.

Unlike s 14(2), s 14(3) is not expressly excluded where defects are pointed out to the buyer or the buyer examines the goods[2]. In many cases the fact that the buyer is aware of a defect or has examined the goods may indicate that he does not rely on the seller, and so prevent him relying on s 14(3). However, in some cases the buyer may still rely on the seller: for instance, the seller might point out a defect but assure the buyer that the goods will be fit for his purpose despite it.

1   *Aswan Engineering Establishment Co v Lupdine Ltd* [1987] 1 All ER 135, [1987] 1 WLR 1; above
     11.2.4.1.
2   See 11.2.6.

11.4   Sales by sample

Where goods are sold by sample SoGA s 15 implies two conditions into the contract. They are:

(a) that the bulk will correspond with the sample; and
(b) that the bulk will be free from any defect making their quality unsatisfactory which would not be apparent on a reasonable examination of the sample.

The terms implied by s 15 apply to all sales by sample, whether or not in the course of a business. However, it will be unlikely that goods will be sold by sample other than in the course of a business.

11.4.1 When is a sale 'by sample'?

Section 15(1) provides that a sale is a sale by sample 'where there is an express or implied term in the contract to that effect in the contract'. Often the contract will expressly provide that goods are sold by sample; if there is no such provision, it will be necessary to construe the contract to discover the intentions of the parties. A sample may be shown to the buyer and yet the contract not be a sale by sample. The sale will be by sample where the sample 'is to present to the eye the real meaning and intention of the parties with regard to the subject matter of the contract which, owing to the imperfections of language, it may be difficult or impossible to express in words. The sample speaks for itself'[1]. Thus goods are sold by sample where the sample is used to define what is being sold, in the same way that a description defines essential qualities of the goods. A sale may be by sample and description: for instance a contract for '500 pure wool suits, in accordance with sample supplied' would be a sale by both sample and description.

1 Per Lord MacNaghten in *Drummond v Van Ingen* (1887) 12 App Cas 284 at 297, HL.

11.4.2 The bulk must correspond with the sample

It is an implied condition that the bulk actually delivered will correspond with the sample[1]. This is effectively the equivalent of the implied condition in s 13 that goods will correspond with their description. Correspondence must be exact, subject to de minimis variations. If the goods do not correspond, it is no defence for the seller to point out that they could easily be made to correspond[2].

In addition, on delivery of the goods the seller is bound on request to give the buyer a reasonable opportunity of examining the goods and comparing the bulk with the sample[3].

1 Section 15(2)(a).
2 *E and S Ruben Ltd v Faire Bros & Co Ltd* [1949] 1 KB 254.
3 SoGA, s 34(2); see 12.2.1. Prior to the passing of the Sale and Supply of Goods Act 1994 it was an implied term, under s 15, that the seller should afford the buyer a reasonable opportunity of comparing bulk with sample.

11.4.3 The bulk must be free from hidden defects

The second implied condition where goods are sold by sample is that the bulk should be free from any defect making the quality of the goods unsatisfactory which would not be apparent on a reasonable examination of the sample[1]. This is essentially the equivalent of s 14(2) but unlike the implied term that the goods must be of satisfactory quality, the term is excluded even where the buyer does not examine the goods, if an examination would have revealed the defect[2]. However, the term is only excluded as regards defects which would have been revealed by a reasonable examination. In *Godley v Perry*[3], B bought a consignment of plastic toy catapults after a sales visit during which he was shown a sample. He tested it by pulling back the elastic. In fact the catapults were made of a brittle plastic and could break in use leaving a hard jagged edge. It was held that the defect was not discoverable on a reasonable examination: it could have been discovered by breaking the sample, but in the circumstances it was not reasonable for the buyer to test the sample to destruction.

1   Section 15(2)(b).
2   Section 14(2C)(c).
3   [1960] 1 All ER 36, [1960] 1 WLR 9.

11.5   Excluding the implied terms

As we have seen, the seller's power to exclude the implied terms, or liability for their breach, is severely restricted by the Unfair Contract Terms Act 1977 and the Unfair Terms in Consumer Contracts Regulations 1999[1]. In particular, where the buyer is a consumer, any term in a contract which seeks to exclude the terms is ineffective[2]. Where the buyer does not 'deal as a consumer' such a term will be effective provided it satisfies the test of reasonableness.

An assessment of reasonableness for this purpose will take account, in particular, the factors listed in Sch 2 to the 1977 Act[3]. A total exclusion of the implied terms or liability for their breach is unlikely to be considered reasonable, and such blanket exclusions are rare. More commonly the contract will seek to limit or exclude some of the remedies for breach of the terms, or offer a limited warranty – perhaps limiting the seller's liability to repair of the goods – in substitution for the implied terms. The reasonableness of such terms will depend in part on the adequacy of the rights given to the buyer in substitution for the implied terms. In *AEG (UK) Ltd v Logic Resource Ltd*[4] a contract term which warranted goods 'free of defects caused by faulty materials and bad workmanship' but provided that the buyer's only remedy for breach of that warranty was to have the goods repaired by the seller and excluded the statutory implied terms was held unreasonable. Important factors included that under the 'warranty' the goods had to be returned to the seller for repair, at the buyer's expense, and that the buyer had been given inadequate notice of what was considered to be a serious restriction on his rights.

As explained earlier, under many arrangements commonly used to finance the supply of goods such as hire purchase and finance leasing, the goods are supplied to the customer by a finance company which acquires them from a manufacturer or supplier[5]. It is common for such financing suppliers to seek to exclude the implied terms by a blanket exclusion of the implied terms. In *R&B Customs Brokers Ltd v UDT*, for instance, where goods were supplied under a hire purchase contract the contract provided that the supplier 'does not let the goods subject to any warranty or condition whether express or implied as to condition description quality or fitness for any particular purpose at all'. Dillon LJ, obiter, indicated that he was inclined to hold the exclusion reasonable partly because the supplier as a finance company had never had possession of or inspected the goods. This may seem to reflect the commercial reality of the situation but it leaves the purchaser of the goods without protection unless he can obtain an express warranty from the manufacturer or (actual) supplier of the goods. In subsequent cases the courts have tended to reject Dillon LJ's approach. There is no absolute rule that it is reasonable for a financing supplier to exclude the implied terms, and in several cases such exclusions have been held unreasonable[6]. The finance company is then left to pursue a claim for an indemnity against its supplier.

There are however other ways in which a seller may effectively exclude the implied terms and, possibly, escape the controls in the Unfair Contract Terms Act. For instance, a disclaimer of expertise may prevent the sale being one by description and prevent the buyer relying on the seller; by pointing out defects, the seller may prevent the buyer arguing that they make the goods unsatisfactory.

1   See 2.6.3.
2   UCTA, ss 6 and 7; see 2.6.4.
3   See 2.6.4.4.
4   [1996] CLC 265; see Bradgate (1996) 60 MLR 582. See also *Stag Line Ltd v Tyne Ship Repair Group Ltd, The Zinnia* [1984] 2 Lloyd's Rep 211.
5   See 8.2.4.3.
6   See *Lease Management Services Ltd v Purnell Secretarial Services Ltd* [1994] CCLR 127, *Sovereign Finance v Silver Crest Furniture Ltd* [1997] CCLR 76, *Danka Rentals Ltd v Xi Software* (1998) 17 Tr LR 74.

11.6   Implied terms are absolute

As we have seen, liability for breach of the statutory implied terms is strict in that the seller is liable even though he was unaware of the defect and took all reasonable care. Thus where goods reach the ultimate consumer via a distribution chain from manufacturer to wholesaler to retailer, the retailer will be primarily liable to the consumer for any defects in the goods, even though they may ultimately be due to the default of the manufacturer. This may involve a retailer in extensive liability if, for instance, the goods injure the consumer. The problem is caused by the fact that there is no privity of contract between consumer and manufacturer.

In theory the retailer can seek redress from the wholesaler for breach of the contact between them, leaving the wholesaler, in turn, to sue the manufacturer, so that liability is passed back up the distribution chain. However, whereas the retailer cannot exclude his liability to the consumer, the wholesaler and manufacturer deal with business customers and can exclude or limit their liability for breach of the implied terms provided their exclusions are considered reasonable[1]. In addition, the chain of contractual liabilities may break down if one of the parties becomes insolvent or cannot be traced. As a result, other routes have been provided to enable injured consumers to seek redress direct from manufacturers[2].

1   See 2.6.4.1.
2   See ch 13.

11.7   Other implied terms

In accordance with the general principles of contract law, a court may imply further terms into a contract of sale where such terms are necessary to give effect to the intentions of the parties. In addition, further terms about quality or fitness for purpose may be annexed to a contract by custom or trade usage[1]: for instance it may be an implied term where goods are ordered from a manufacturer of goods of that description, that the goods will be of the manufacturer's own make[2] and will be supplied under his normal brand label[3].

1 SoGA, s 14(4); the alleged custom must satisfy the common law requirements for incorporation of customary terms: see 2.5.4.
2 *Johnson v Raylton* (1881) 7 QBD 438, CA.
3 *Scaliaris v E Ofverberg & Co* (1921) 37 TLR 307, CA.

11.8 The EC Consumer Guarantees Directive[1]

A long-standing policy objective of the European Community is the 'protection and information of consumers' and to this end the European Commission has for some time held the view that there is a need for action to strengthen and harmonise the rights of consumers who purchase defective products in order to protect their economic interests. This need became stronger with the completion of the Single Market, when it was felt that there was a need to strengthen consumers' confidence in, and thus encourage their participation in, the Single Market. In 1993 the Commission published a 'Green Paper on Guarantees for Consumer Goods and After Sales Service[2]' in which it canvassed opinions on the desirability and most appropriate form of harmonisation of the law relating to consumer guarantees. Following extensive consultation a Directive on this subject was finalised in 1999[3]. The final text of the Directive differs significantly from the proposals in the original Green Paper. The Directive must be implemented no later than 1 January 2002.

The core of the Directive is in art 2 which requires that where consumer goods are sold to a consumer they should be 'in conformity with the contract'. The conformity requirement is broadly analogous to the requirements in ss 13–15 of the Sale of Goods Act but there are significant, although subtle differences between the two requirements and, more importantly, the Directive is more limited in its application than are the implied terms. Consumer goods are defined as 'any moveable item[4]'. A consumer is defined, as under the Unfair Terms Directive[5], as 'any natural person who, in the contracts covered by [the] Directive is acting for purposes which are not related to his trade, business or profession[6]'. A 'seller' is 'any natural or legal person who, under a contract, sells consumer goods in the course of his trade, business or profession[7]'. The Directive is stated to apply to certain types of contracts – contracts for the sale of goods to be manufactured[8] and contracts for goods to be installed by the seller[9] – which might in English law be categorised as contracts for work and materials, but it is not clear whether it applies to other forms of supply contract, such as hire purchase.

The definition of consumer creates few problems but the definition of 'seller' may generate difficulties similar to those addressed in cases such as *Stevenson v Rogers*[10]. It is quite clear that private sales fall wholly outside the scope of the Directive, whereas, as we have seen, goods sold privately are required in English law to comply with the description by which they are sold[11]. Moreover, since the Directive only applies where the seller sells the goods in the course of 'his' business, it may be that its application is limited to cases where the goods are of a type the seller regularly sells as was the position in English law prior to 1973.

The Directive requires the goods delivered to be in conformity with the contract at the time they are delivered[12]. Goods are presumed to be in conformity with the contract if they:

'(a) comply with the description given by the seller and possess the qualities of the goods which the seller has held out . . . as a sample or a model;

(b) are fit for any particular purpose for which the consumer requires them and which he has made known to the seller at the time of conclusion of the contract and which the seller has accepted;

(c) are fit for the purposes for which goods of the same type are normally used; and

(d) show the quality and performance which are normal in goods of the same type and which the consumer can reasonably expect given the nature of the goods and taking into account any public statements on the specific characteristics of the goods made about them by the seller, the producer or his representative . . . [13]'.

The conformity requirement is subject to certain restrictions. There is deemed to be no lack of conformity if at the time the contract was concluded the consumer was aware or could not reasonably be unaware of the lack of conformity, or, if goods are made from the consumer's own materials, if the lack of conformity originates in the materials[14]. It is also possible for the seller in certain circumstances to escape liability for advertising and other statements of the manufacturer[15]. Subject however to these limitations, exclusion or restriction of the conformity requirement is ineffective[16].

It seems clear that the presumption of conformity raised by the goods' correspondence with these requirements is rebuttable. For instance, although the Directive does not say so the goods would presumably not conform to the contract if not in accordance with its express terms. Broadly speaking, however, the aspects of conformity in the Directive seem to correspond to the cumulative requirements of the implied terms in SoGA, ss 13–15. Earlier drafts required that the goods satisfy the consumer's 'legitimate expectations', and it has been suggested above that the implied terms create, in effect, a requirement that goods correspond to the buyer's legitimate expectations. There are however a number of differences between the language of the Directive and that of the implied terms. In particular, notwithstanding the provisions of paragraph (d) above, the Directive seems to place greater emphasis on fitness for purpose as an aspect of conformity, to the exclusion of other factors, than English law has done since the reforms of 1994. Those reforms were intended to enhance consumer protection. The language of the Directive appears, however, to have been based on that of the Vienna Convention on Contracts for the International Sale of Goods, which is intended for application to commercial contracts. It is perhaps unfortunate that more consideration was not given to the special needs and expectations of consumers. The terms of the Directive are sufficiently broad and flexible that in most cases they will produce results similar to those produced by application of the SoGA implied terms. Adoption of the conformity test in substitution for the existing implied terms in consumer cases would however seem to be a potentially retrograde step for the UK in light of the concerns which motivated the 1994 reforms.

1   See Twigg Flesner and Bradgate (2000) Web JCLI; Shears Zollers and Hurd [2000] JBL262.
2   See generally Bradgate (1995) Consumer LJ 94.
3   Directive 1999/44/EC of the European Parliament and of the Council of 25 May 1999 on certain aspects of the sale of consumer goods and associated guarantees (1999) OJ L 171/12, 7 July 1999.
4   Art 1(2)(b). There are exclusions for goods sold by execution or authority of law and water and gas, unless put up for sale in limited quantities.
5   Directive 93/13/EEC; OJ L 95 21/4/93. See 2.6.5.1.

6 Art 1(2)(a).
7 Art 1(2)(c).
8 Art 1(4).
9 Art 2(5).
10 [1999] QB 1028, [1999] 1 All ER 613. See 11.2.1.
11 SoGA, s 13.
12 Art 2(2).
13 Art 2(2).
14 Art 2(3).
15 Art 2(4).
16 Art 7.

Chapter 12

The Buyer's Remedies

12.0 Introduction

If the seller commits a breach of any of his obligations under the contract, the buyer is entitled to damages for any losses that breach causes him. In addition, some breaches allow the buyer to reject the goods and terminate the contract. Other remedies may also be available: the rules of the common law apply to contracts for the sale of goods[1] and the rights to claim specific performance[2] and to claim interest, or to recover money paid in the event of a total failure of consideration[3], are specifically preserved by the Sale of Goods Act 1979; and where the buyer has paid the price in advance, rejection of the goods will give rise to a restitutionary claim on the grounds that there is a total failure of consideration. However, the buyer's basic remedies under the Act are the right to reject the goods, to terminate the contract and to claim damages.

As explained in the preceding chapter, the EC Consumer Guarantees Directive[4] must be implemented by January 2002. The directive provides for four remedies to be available to the consumer where goods are not in conformity with the contract: repair or replacement of the goods, rescission of the contract and reduction of the price payable. The remedies available under the directive therefore differ in a number of respects from those available in existing domestic law and implementation of the directive will therefore raise a number of difficult questions. Detailed discussion of the directive will be postponed until the end of this chapter.

1   SoGA, s 62(2).
2   SoGA, s 52.
3   SoGA, s 54.
4   Directive 1999/44/EC of the European Parliament and of the Council of 25 May 1999 on certain aspects of the sale of consumer goods and associated guarantees (1999) (OJ L 171/12, 7 July 1999).

12.1 The right to reject

The buyer's duties under the contract of sale are to accept and pay for the goods. By rejecting the goods the buyer refuses to perform his duty to accept them. Where the buyer rejects before paying for the goods he will normally also refuse to pay. Such a refusal to perform would normally be a breach of contract but rejection may be justified in three situations. First, the contract may give the buyer an express right to reject: for instance, some stores allow consumers to return goods if they are dissatisfied with them, even where there is no breach of contract. Second, the Act expressly gives the buyer a right to reject in certain circumstances: for instance, if the seller delivers the wrong quantity of goods[1]. Third, the Act provides that the buyer is entitled to reject where the seller is in breach of a condition. Although the Act does not define 'condition', it distinguishes between 'conditions' and 'warranties' and s 11(3) of the Act provides that:

> 'whether a stipulation in a contract of sale is a condition, breach of which may give rise to a right to treat the contract is repudiated, or a warranty, breach of which may give rise to a claim for damages but not to a right to reject the goods and treat the contract as repudiated depends in each case on the construction of the contract'.

It seems clear from this that breach of a condition gives the buyer the right to reject the goods whilst breach of a warranty does not[2]. As previously noted, express terms of the contract may be classified as innominate terms[3]; the buyer's right to reject the goods for breach of such a term will depend on the seriousness of the breach and its consequences[4]. Where any express or implied term properly classified as a condition is broken, however, the buyer is entitled under the Act to reject the goods. Significantly, the implied terms in ss 13–15 of the Act are classified by the Act as 'conditions', so that the buyer is entitled to reject the goods if the seller is in breach of any of those terms, or of any express term properly classified as a 'condition'.

Rejection is not necessarily the same as refusal of delivery: the buyer may reject either on or after delivery. However, the right to reject for breach of condition is subject to several restrictions. First, the right is lost if the buyer has, or is deemed to have, accepted the goods. Some cases[5] suggest that the buyer may be deemed to have accepted the goods and thus lose the right to reject very soon after the goods are delivered, although some of the relevant cases might now be decided differently as a result of changes made by the Sale and Supply of Goods Act 1994. Second, the right of a non-consumer buyer to reject for breach of the statutory implied conditions is now excluded where the breach is so slight that rejection would be unreasonable[6]. Third, commercial contracts may include terms which restrict or exclude the buyer's right to reject[7]. However, even if the right to reject is excluded, unavailable or lost on one of these grounds, the buyer will still be entitled to claim damages for any losses caused by the seller's breach.

Rejection is a potent remedy, especially if the buyer rejects before paying for the goods, when it is essentially a self-help remedy; however, if the buyer rejects after paying the price, or if he wishes to claim damages for any additional losses caused by the breach, he may need the assistance of the court. The court may also be involved if the seller challenges the buyer's rejection.

Since rejection involves a refusal by the buyer to perform his obligations under the contract, a rejection which is not justified, either by the terms of the contract or because of a breach by the seller, amounts to a breach by the buyer, entitling the seller to claim damages. Disputes about quality and rejection thus often involve mutual allegations of breach: the buyer rejects, and the seller claims damages for non-acceptance; the buyer defends alleging that his rejection was justified because the seller was in breach, often on the grounds that the goods were defective. The seller may reply either that he was not in breach, or that, if he was, the buyer is not entitled to reject, for instance because the goods have already been accepted. In all but the clearest cases such a situation is fraught with uncertainty, and the parties to commercial contracts therefore tend to prefer to deal with such disputes by negotiation.

1   SoGA, s 30: see 10.3.
2   See also s 61, which defines 'warranty'.
3   Above 2.5.5.
4   *Cehave NV v Bremer Handelsgesellschaft mbH* [1976] QB 44, [1975] 3 All ER 739, CA; see 9.2.3.
5   See *Bernstein v Pamson Motors (Golders Green) Ltd* [1987] 2 All ER 220; cf *Truk (UK) Ltd v Tokmakidis GmbH* [2000] 1 Lloyd's Rep 543, below 12.2.1.3.
6   SoGA, s 15A.
7   Such a provision would be ineffective in a contract with a person who deals as a consumer by virtue of s 6 of the Unfair Contract Terms Act 1977: see 2.6.4.1.

12.1.1   *Rejection and termination*

The right to reject is often treated as if it were merely a form of the general right to terminate a contract for breach. Thus in *Kwei Tek Chao v British Traders and Shippers Ltd*[1] Devlin J said that '[a] right to reject is merely a particular form of the right to rescind . . . ; and a rightful rejection . . . is a rescission which brings the contract to an end'[2]. This treatment is no doubt influenced by the fact that rejection involves the buyer returning the seller's performance and, where he has already paid for the goods, may result in him recovering his own. However, the better view is that rejection involves the buyer refusing to perform his obligation to accept the goods and is therefore properly regarded as a specific example of the right to withhold performance. Thus s 11(3)[3] seems to recognise that breach of condition gives the buyer two rights: (a) to reject the goods, and (b) to treat the contract as repudiated, in which case he will be entitled to terminate the contract. The relationship between these two rights is examined further below[4]. However, it seems that although once the goods have been delivered the buyer cannot terminate the contract without first rejecting the goods, the two rights can be exercised separately, so that the buyer can reject without terminating. Moreover, in certain situations the Act clearly gives the buyer the right to reject but not to terminate: for instance, when the seller delivers the wrong quantity of goods[5].

1   [1954] 2 QB 459.
2   [1954] 2 QB 459 at 480. It seems that Devlin J was using the term 'rescission' here to refer to the process of termination for breach of contract. The use of 'rescission' in this sense was disapproved by the House of Lords in *Johnson v Agnew* [1980] AC 367 at 393. Note, however, that one of the remedies available under the EC Consumer Guarantees Directive is 'rescission' of the contract.
3   Above 12.1.
4   Below 12.1.3.1.
5   Above 10.3.

12.1.2   *Effecting a rejection*

If the buyer wishes to reject, he is not necessarily obliged physically to return the goods to the seller's premises, but must make them available for collection at the delivery point. However, the buyer must be able to return the goods to the seller: the right to reject may be lost if, as a result of the buyer's conduct, restitution is impossible. Moreover, the buyer must clearly indicate his intention to reject:

if not, his conduct may be interpreted as acceptance of the goods. For instance, in *Lee v York Coach and Marine*[1] the buyer's solicitors sent letters indicating that the buyer had the right to reject and asking the seller to repair the goods: the letters were held to be insufficient to amount to a rejection.

1   [1977] RTR 35, CA.

12.1.3 *The effects of rejection*

The effect of a lawful rejection is to put the parties in the same position as if the seller had not delivered. The buyer is therefore entitled to withhold payment, and, if he has already paid, may be able to recover the payment by means of a restitutionary claim. Unless the seller is entitled to and does make a replacement delivery, the buyer is entitled to damages for non-delivery[1] and in any case may claim damages for any losses caused by the defective delivery, or by the rejected goods, including damage to property, personal injury, and, in a consumer case, possibly inconvenience and vexation.

On rejection, property in the goods revests in the seller; the buyer has no lien over the goods or right to retain them to secure payment of any sums due from the seller. The risk of loss of, or damage to, the goods must also revest in the seller, and the buyer will be liable only as an involuntary bailee. However, between delivery and rejection the risk of loss will generally be on the buyer, raising the question whether the buyer can reject if the goods have been damaged between delivery and rejection. It seems clear that if the damage is due to the very defect for which the buyer rejects – for instance, if a new car delivered with defective brakes is damaged when, as a result, it runs into a wall – the buyer's right to reject is unaffected. Equally, if the goods are damaged due to the buyer's negligence, he should be liable for that damage and, indeed, may be held to have accepted the goods. However, the effect of accidental damage is unclear. In *Head v Tattersall*[2], decided prior to the 1893 Act, it was held that B could reject a horse, under an express right to reject in the contract, even though it had been accidentally injured prior to rejection, but it is not clear if the case has survived the Act or if it applies to rejection for breach of condition[3].

1   See 12.3.1.
2   (1871) LR 7 Exch 7.
3   See *Benjamin's Sale of Goods* (5th edn, 1997) para 6.010, where it is argued that the risk should fall on the buyer; contrast Sealy (1972) 31 CLJ 225; and see Hudson in Feldman and Meisel (eds) *Corporate and Commercial Law: Modern Developments* (1996).

12.1.3.1 *A right to cure?*

The right to reject is probably more important to consumers than to commercial buyers. Commercial buyers, especially in large-scale commodity dealings, rarely reject for defects of quality, but instead accept the goods subject to an allowance against the price, and quality disputes decided by arbitration are often decided on that basis. Even defective goods normally have a resale value and it will generally be easier for the buyer, with access to a local market, than for the seller to arrange for their resale. In other cases, including consumer transactions, the buyer may be happy to allow the seller to 'cure' his breach by replacing or repairing the goods after rejection, either for the sake of a good trading relationship, or because the terms available from the seller are better than those available elsewhere. Similarly, sellers in practice will often not stand on their strict rights, and will not take the point that the buyer has 'accepted'. Thus, where goods prove defective, the seller may often attempt to repair the goods and, if that attempt proves ineffective, ultimately replace them, or refund the price even though, according to the terms of the Sale of Goods Act, the buyer may be taken to have accepted them. The contract may expressly give the seller the right to repair or replace defective goods. Subject to what is said below, such a provision may be subject to the Unfair Contract Terms Act, and therefore ineffective against a buyer who deals as a consumer and subject to a test of reasonableness in other cases[1]. In the absence of such a provision, however, although 'cure' may be common practice, it is not clear whether there is a legal right for either party to a domestic sale to insist on cure. In contrast, some other jurisdictions do give the seller a right to cure[2] and there is a right to cure in certain international supply contracts[3].

Some commentators argue that English law recognises a similar right for the seller to 'cure' based on the distinction, mentioned above, between withholding performance and terminating the contract[4]. It is argued that since the effect of rejection is to put the parties in the same position as if the seller had not delivered, the seller is entitled to make a replacement delivery provided that the time for performance has not expired and that the seller has not otherwise repudiated the contract. The form which 'cure' would take would vary according to whether the contract was for unascertained or specific goods. Under a contract for unascertained goods the seller could 'cure' by delivering replacement goods matching the contract description; under a contract for specific goods the seller could only 'cure' by repairing the goods. However, despite occasional dicta[5], there is only limited support for this view in the case law. The leading case, *Borrowman, Phillips & Co v Free and Hollis*[6], concerned a contract to sell a cargo of maize. The seller tendered a cargo without the shipping documents required by the contract, which the buyer rejected; the seller then tendered a second cargo with shipping documents, and it was held that the buyer was bound to accept. Most of the other cases cited in support of a right of 'cure' are, like *Borrowman*, concerned with documentary sales[7] and there is no reported case in which a seller who has actually delivered goods under a simple domestic sale contract has been held to be entitled to make a second delivery after the buyer has legitimately rejected them as not conforming to the contract. The nearest example is *Longbottom v Bass Walker*[8], which concerned a domestic contract for the sale of 147 pieces of cloth. The buyers purported to terminate the contract for delay and Atkin LJ observed that, if a delivery had included defective pieces, the buyers' 'only remedy would have been to return the defective pieces as the sellers could claim the right to deliver the full quantity of contract goods during the contract period'[9]. However, this comment was clearly obiter; moreover, the contract in question expressly permitted the seller to deliver the goods in instalments: different considerations may apply where instalment deliveries are not sanctioned by the contract, since a right to 'cure' in such a case would be tantamount to requiring the buyer to accept instalment delivery, contrary to SoGA s 31(1).

One difficulty with the view that there is a general right of cure is that SoGA s 11(3) expressly recognises that breach of a condition may entitle the buyer to treat the contract as repudiated. Of course, the buyer is not obliged to treat the contract as repudiated; he may reject the goods without terminating the contract, in which case there would be nothing to prevent the seller tendering a replacement delivery. However, if the buyer is entitled to treat the contract as repudiated, and does so, the contract is at an end and there is no room for a right of cure. The proponents of a right of cure point out that s 11(3) does not say that a breach of condition will always give rise to a right to treat the contract as repudiated, but only that it 'may' do so, but it is not clear how much significance should be read into this[10]; the use of 'may' could be explained on other grounds – for instance, because where the contract is severable a breach of condition by the seller does not necessarily entitle the buyer to treat the contract as repudiated[11] – and the section also says that breach of warranty 'may', rather than 'does', give rise to a claim for damages.

One must conclude, therefore, that the extent to which the existing law recognises a general right for the seller to cure a breach of condition by replacing a rejected delivery is unclear; this was the view of the Law Commission in 1983[12]. In any case, it seems that even if such a right does exist, its scope would be limited in many cases. First, any re-tender must be made before the time for delivery has expired; second, the buyer clearly does have a right to terminate the contract where the seller's conduct is repudiatory including, perhaps, where the seller's initial breach destroys the buyer's confidence in his ability or willingness to perform[13]. In many consumer contracts and contracts for sale of specific goods, the time for delivery is likely to have expired by the time the buyer rejects, so that it will be too late to re-tender; and a breach of implied condition may be taken to have destroyed the buyer's confidence, at least in a consumer contract.

There are arguments in favour of recognising a general right of cure. First, it would accord with existing commercial (and consumer) practice. Second, it would prevent the buyer using a breach as an excuse to escape a contract which has become economically unattractive. It is difficult to see how a consumer who rejects defective goods and is offered an exact replacement is prejudiced. Against this, it is argued that recognition of a general right to cure would seriously weaken the bargaining power of buyers, especially consumers, faced with defective goods, for whom an absolute right to demand a refund is a powerful bargaining counter, while the right of a commercial buyer to escape a contract for breach of condition is now restricted by the limitations imposed by the Sale and Supply of Goods Act 1994 on the right to reject where the breach is slight[14].

In 1983 the Law Commission favoured introduction of a statutory right to cure in consumer contracts, to allow the seller to cure where refusal of cure would be unreasonable[15], but in its final report on the subject in 1987 the Commission decided against introducing such a right which might weaken the rights of consumers[16] and would be inappropriate in many commercial transactions and would raise a number of consequential problems. It is likely, however, that the issue will have to be reconsidered in the near future, for under the EC Consumer Guarantees Directive the seller is effectively given a right to cure by repair or replacement. Moreover, the seller has extensive rights to cure under the Vienna Convention on Contracts for the International Sale of Goods, which it is expected the UK will ratify at some date in the not too distant future.

The discussion thus far has been about the existence and extent of a right for the seller to cure a defective tender after rejection by the buyer, and thus prevent the buyer terminating the contract. 'Cure' may also describe two other situations. First, a buyer faced with defective goods may elect not to reject them but to allow the seller to repair them; the effects of an attempt to repair on the buyer's right to reject are discussed below[17]. Second, where the buyer lawfully terminates the contract and then seeks damages, the seller may effectively have a right to cure by virtue of the rules on mitigation of damages. If, after rejection, the seller offers to deliver replacement goods and the buyer refuses that offer, he may be held to have unreasonably failed to mitigate[18], unless the initial breach was sufficient to destroy his confidence.

1   See *AEG (UK) Ltd v Logic Resource Ltd* [1996] CLC 265; 11.5.
2   See eg United States Uniform Commercial Code 2-508.
3   There is a right to cure in international contracts governed by the Uniform Law on International Sales (art 44) or the Vienna Convention on Contracts for the International Sale of Goods (arts 34, 37, 46 and 48): see 33.2.11. It may also be that a limited right to cure in international sales exists in English law: see below.
4   See Goode, *Commercial Law* (2nd edn, 1995) p 363; Beale, *Remedies for Breach of Contract* (1980) p 91; Carter, *Breach of Contract* (2nd edn, 1991) para 102; Apps [1994] LMCLQ 525; Atiyah, *Sale of Goods* (10th edn, 2000) p 501, 508. Contra, see *Benjamin's Sale of Goods* (5th edn, 1997) para 12-031; Ahdar [1990] LMCLQ 364; Bradgate and White, 'Rejection and termination in contracts for the sale of goods' in Birds, Bradgate and Villiers (edn) *Termination of Contracts* (1995); Bridge, *The Sale of Goods* (1997) p 199.
5   See eg Lord Devlin [1966] CLJ 192; Lord Goff in *Motor Oil Hellas (Corinth) Refineries SA v Shipping Corpn of India, The Kanchenjunga* [1990] 1 Lloyd's Rep 391 at 399.
6   (1878) 4 QBD 500, CA.
7   See eg *Ashmore & Son v CS Cox & Co* [1899] 1 QB 436; *EE & Brian Smith (1928) Ltd v Wheatsheaf Mills Ltd* [1939] 2 KB 302; *Agriculotres Federados Argentinos Sociedad Co-operativa Ltda v Ampro SA Commerciale Industrielle et Financière* [1965] 2 Lloyd's Rep 157; *SIAT di dal Ferro v Tradax Overseas SA* [1980] 1 Lloyd's Rep 53, CA.
8   [1922] WN 245.
9   [1922] WN 245 at 246.
10 See *Benjamin's Sale of Goods* (5th edn, 1997) para 10-028.
11 See 12.2.3.
12 Law Commission WP No 85, 'Sale and Supply of Goods' (1983) para 2.38.
13 Goode, *Commercial Law* (2nd edn, 1995) p 366.
14 SoGA 1979, s 15A; see 12.2.
15 Law Commission WP No 85 *Sale and Supply of Goods* (1983).
16 Law Commission Rep 160, *Sale and Supply of Goods*, para 4.13; contrast the view of Ahdar [1990] LMCLQ 364.
17 See 12.2.1.2.
18 See *Payzu Ltd v Saunders* [1919] 2 KB 581, CA.

12.2   Loss of the right to reject

The right to cure, if it exists, arises after the buyer has rejected the goods and prevents the buyer immediately terminating the contract for breach of condition. However, the buyer is not obliged to reject the goods: he may keep them and simply claim damages for the breach, treating the breach of condition as if it were a breach of warranty, and in practice the buyer will often do so.

The contract may include terms restricting the right to reject. Such terms are ineffective against a person who buys the goods 'as a consumer'[1], but may be valid against a non-consumer. In the absence of such a term, any breach of condition gives the buyer a right to reject the goods; however, there is a danger that that right may be exercised in bad faith, for instance by using a minor defect in the goods to justify rejecting the goods and terminating the contract. In such situations in the past, the courts, failing to draw any distinction between rejection of the goods and termination of the contract, may often have been forced to hold that there was no breach of condition, in order to prevent the buyer rejecting. However, SoGA, s 15A, introduced by the Sale and Supply of Goods Act 1994, now provides that where a breach of condition is so slight that rejection would be unreasonable, a buyer who does not deal as a consumer may not reject but must treat the breach as a breach of warranty[2]. 'Deals as consumer' is defined in the same way as under the Unfair Contract Terms Act[3]. Significantly, this restriction only restricts the right to reject for breach of the implied conditions in SoGA, ss 13–15 and therefore does not apply to breaches of express conditions. However, the court can effectively control the right to reject for breach of express term by classifying the term as an innominate term rather than a condition. The right to reject for breach of such a term would depend on the application of the *Hong Kong Fir* test[4]. It should be noted that the emphasis of s 15A is different from that of the *Hong Kong Fir* test: under s 15A the right to reject is excluded where the breach is slight, whereas under the *Hong Kong Fir* test the right would only be available if the breach were serious.

In addition, the right to reject may be lost by operation of law if the buyer has 'accepted the goods or part of them'[5]; in that case the buyer is entitled only to damages for breach of warranty. This restriction applies to both consumer and non-consumer buyers. It is therefore vital to know when the buyer has 'accepted' the goods.

1   Unfair Contract Terms Act 1977, s 6; above 2.6.4.1.
2   In *Truk (UK) Ltd v Tokmakidis GmbH* [2000] 1 Lloyd's Rep 543 it was held that paintwork defects which would cost 4153 DM to rectify, on a vehicle costing some 550,000 DM were so slight that it would be unreasonable to reject on account of them.
3   SoGA, s 61(5A). See 2.6.4.2.
4   [1962] 2 QB 26, [1962] 1 All ER 474, CA; see 2.5.5; 2.9.3.
5   Section 11(4).

12.2.1 *Acceptance*

Section 35 of the Sale of Goods Act 1979 provides that the buyer may be deemed to have accepted the goods, and thus lost the right to reject, in three situations:

(a) where he expressly intimates his acceptance;
(b) where he does some act 'inconsistent with the seller's ownership'; and
(c) where after a reasonable period he retains the goods without indicating that he rejects them.

However, the Act provides that where the seller tenders delivery he is bound on request to afford the buyer a reasonable opportunity of examining the goods for the purpose of ascertaining whether they are in conformity with the contract and, in the case of a sale by sample, of comparing the bulk with the sample[1] and, where the buyer has not examined the goods before delivery, he will not be deemed to have accepted them by express intimation or inconsistent act until he has had a reasonable opportunity of examining them for those purposes[2]. A buyer who deals as a consumer cannot be deprived of this right to examine by any contract term, waiver or otherwise[3]. This restriction does not apply to the third type of acceptance, by lapse of time, but the Act provides that, in deciding whether a reasonable time has elapsed, account must be taken of whether the buyer has had a reasonable opportunity of examining the goods[4].

1   SoGA, s 34.
2   SoGA, s 35(2).
3   SoGA, s 35(3).
4   SoGA, s 35(3).

12.2.1.1 *Express intimation*

Generally, the buyer will only be taken to have expressly accepted goods if clear words of acceptance are used[1]. The signing of a delivery note should generally be treated merely as an acknowledgment of delivery, but a signature on an appropriately worded delivery note could amount to acceptance, provided the person signing the note had authority to accept the goods. It will therefore be necessary to construe the facts, and the words of any 'acknowledgment', in order to decide their effect.

Prior to the passing of the Sale and Supply of Goods Act 1994, the right to examine the goods did not apply to acceptance by express intimation; where goods arrived prepackaged or in sealed containers, a buyer who signed a suitably worded delivery note could therefore lose the right to reject even though any defects were undiscoverable. A buyer dealing as a consumer will now not lose the right to reject in such a case unless he is first offered a reasonable opportunity to examine the goods[2]. However, the right to examine may be excluded as against a non-consumer buyer so that a non-consumer buyer might still lose the right to reject in such circumstances if he were to sign a delivery note which contained a waiver or exclusion of the right to examine the goods. The Law Commission recommended that exclusion of the right of a non-consumer buyer to examine the goods should be valid subject to a test of reasonableness under the Unfair Contract Terms Act 1977[3]. However, there is no provision to that effect in the 1994 Act and although a restriction in the contract on the right to examine would be subject to the 1977 Act, a waiver of the right in the delivery note itself would appear to fall outside that Act's control.

1 See *Varley v Whipp* [1900] 1 QB 513, where the buyer's 'grumbling' letter arranging a meeting with the seller to discuss a solution was held not to be an acceptance.
2 'Dealing as a consumer' is defined for this purpose as under the Unfair Contract Terms Act 1977: SoGA, s 61(5A). See 2.6.4.2.
3 Law Commission 160 *Sale and Supply of Goods* (1987) para 5.24.

12.2.1.2 *Inconsistent act*

In many cases the goods will have become the buyer's property on, or soon after, delivery. It is therefore difficult to understand how the buyer's acts can be 'inconsistent with the seller's ownership'. However, in *Kwei Tek Chao v British Traders and Shippers Ltd*[1] Devlin J explained that property in the goods initially passes conditionally, subject to the buyer's right to reject, so that in the meantime the seller retains a 'reversionary interest': the buyer is therefore deemed to accept the goods if he does any act inconsistent with that interest. Probably, this means no more than 'inconsistent with rejection'[2].

The cases suggest that the buyer may lose the right to reject on this basis in two classes of case: (a) where he has 'affirmed' the contract by dealing with the goods, and (b) where the physical return of the goods is impossible as a result of the buyer's conduct. Thus, acts such as selling or any other dealing with the goods, consuming them so that they cannot be returned, using them more than necessary to check their conformity with the contract and even, perhaps, repairing or attempting to repair or asking the seller to repair them, could all be regarded as acts inconsistent with the seller's ownership.

However, none of these acts can amount to acceptance unless the buyer has first had a reasonable opportunity of examining the goods[3].

Thus the buyer will not lose the right to reject on this basis until:

(a) the goods have been delivered to him; and

(b) he has had an opportunity after delivery to inspect them; and

(c) after that opportunity to examine he does an act inconsistent with rejection.

It seems that the place for examination of the goods is the place of delivery[4], so that if goods for resale are delivered by the seller direct to the buyer's customer, with no chance for the buyer to inspect[5], the resale will not bar rejection on this basis[6].

It has been clear since 1967[7] that the buyer is entitled to an opportunity to examine the goods before he can be taken to have accepted them by inconsistent act. Nevertheless, prior to the passing of the Sale and Supply of Goods Act 1994 the buyer could lose the right to reject on this basis even though he was physically able to return the goods to the seller. For instance, if goods were delivered to the buyer and he then resold them without inspecting them, he might be taken to have accepted them so that if his customer then rejected them, he would be left with a consignment of defective goods on his hands. Similarly, a buyer who agreed to the seller attempting to repair the goods might be taken to have accepted them and be unable to reject even if the repair proved unsuccessful. The position is now modified by SoGA, s 35(6), which provides that the buyer is not to be taken to have accepted the goods '*merely* because (a) he asks for, or agrees to, their repair by or under an arrangement with the seller, or (b) the goods are delivered to another under a sub-sale or other disposition'. It should be noted, however, that this limitation does not apply where the buyer attempts to repair the goods himself or to have them repaired independently of the seller. Moreover, a buyer who resells or deals with the goods or seeks their repair could still be deemed to have accepted them by virtue of the delay in rejection caused as a result.

In international sale contracts the seller often performs by delivering documents representing the goods[8]. In that case the buyer will not lose his right to reject the goods if they prove defective on arrival merely because he deals with the documents, for instance by pledging them, unless the defect or other breach of contract was apparent on the face of the documents. Effectively, therefore, in such a case the buyer has a right to reject the documents and a second right to reject the goods themselves for breaches not apparent on the documents[9].

1   [1954] 2 QB 459; approved by the Court of Appeal in *Gill & Duffus SA v Berger & Co Inc* [1983] 1 Lloyd's Rep 622, CA.

2   See Goode, *Commercial Law* (2nd edn, 1995) p 371.

3   SoGA, s 35(2).

4   *Perkins v Bell* [1893] 1 QB 193, CA.

5   As in *Mollings & Co v Dean & Son Ltd* (1901) 18 TLR 217.

6   The buyer could lose the right to reject by lapse of time: see 12.2.1.3.

7   Cases decided before 1967 must be treated with some caution because prior to then it had been held that an inconsistent act could amount to acceptance even if done before the buyer had an opportunity to inspect: *Hardy & Co Ltd v Hillerns and Fowler* [1923] 2 KB 490. The law was clarified by the Misrepresentation Act 1967.

8   See 33.2.2.

9   *Kwei Tek Chao v British Traders and Shippers Ltd* [1954] 2 QB 459.

12.2.1.3 *Lapse of time*

The buyer will be deemed to have accepted the goods if, after the lapse of a reasonable time, he retains the goods without intimating that he rejects them. Since the law allows the buyer a reasonable time before being deemed to accept the goods, a contract term which fixes a time limit for rejection or notification of claims will be subject to the Unfair Contract Terms Act, if the time allowed is less than would be a reasonable time for rejection, taking account especially of the nature of the goods[1]. Such a term will be ineffective against a consumer, but may be valid against a non-consumer if it is judged reasonable. In making an assessment of reasonableness the court must therefore consider whether the time allowed for rejection is reasonable and, if not, if the restriction is nevertheless reasonable in all the circumstances – for instance, because the contract provides for other remedies, or because of the price paid.

Where no time limit is fixed, the buyer loses the right to reject after the lapse of a reasonable time. There must come a time when the seller is entitled to regard the transaction as closed and assume that he is safe from a claim for a refund. However, what is reasonable will be a question of fact depending on the circumstances of the individual case[2] and an appeal court will therefore generally be slow to interfere with a finding of a trial judge on the issue. The Law Commission considered but decided against introducing a fixed time limit for rejection: different types of goods would need different time limits:

> 'What is "reasonable" in one case may not be reasonable in another; and in determining what is reasonable it appears that the interests of both the buyer and the seller may be taken into account. The existing provision is therefore not directed to what is reasonable for either the buyer or the seller to the exclusion of the other, and permits (although of course it does not guarantee) a result which is fair to both parties. A more rigid provision, if intended to apply to all types of goods, would almost inevitably create certainty at the expense of justice'[3].

In deciding what is reasonable the following may all be relevant.

1. The nature of the goods: are they complex, necessitating a longer period for adequate testing, or perishable, in which case the buyer must decide quickly whether to reject?
2. The conduct of the parties: for instance, if the seller attempts repair, or assures the buyer that the goods will be alright, or if the parties attempt to negotiate a settlement[4], the time may be extended. As noted above, the Act now provides that the buyer is not deemed to have accepted defective goods 'merely' because he agrees to an attempt by the seller to repair them[5], but the Act does not prevent the buyer being deemed to have accepted by virtue of the time taken to repair. On the other hand, as the Law Commission observed, 'it would clearly be wrong if the clock remained running while (for example) the goods were with the seller being repaired. By the time the repair was finished the reasonable time might have run out, and the buyer would then be unable to reject the goods even if they had not been properly repaired'[6].
3. The custom of the particular trade.
4. Market conditions: the right to reject will be lost more quickly if the market price is subject to rapid fluctuation.

In essence, it seems that the assessment of what is a reasonable time depends on the reasonable (or legitimate) expectations of the parties, which will take account not only of the circumstances known to them at the time of sale but also of their subsequent dealings.

The lapse of time rule may prejudice consumers, particularly where defects are not immediately apparent. Time begins to run from the date of delivery and in

Bernstein v Pamson Motors (Golders Green) Ltd [7] it was held that 'reasonable time' means an objectively reasonable period to try out the goods, not necessarily a reasonable time to discover the defect. In that case the buyer bought a new car which seized up within three weeks of purchase due to a blob of sealant in the lubrication system. The buyer had driven only 142 miles, having been ill for part of the period. Rougier J held that the car was unmerchantable, but that the buyer was too late to reject, although he was entitled to damages. Emphasising 'from the point of view of the seller . . . the commercial desirability of being able to close his ledger reasonably soon after the transaction is completed', Rougier J observed that 'What is a reasonable time in relation to a bicycle will hardly suffice for a nuclear submarine'[8].

On the facts the decision seems harsh. The general approach may, however, be defended. Rougier J considered that in making the assessment of what is reasonable the court must consider both the seller's interest in 'closing his ledger' and the buyer's interest in having time to examine the goods to check their conformity with the contract. This is consistent with treating the rule as a 'legitimate expectations' rule: the reasonable buyer knows that the seller wants to be able to close the transaction and therefore, acting reasonably, does not expect to have an open-ended period to evaluate the goods; the reasonable seller knows that the buyer needs time to examine the goods and therefore cannot legitimately expect that the deal is closed until that time has elapsed.

In fact the decision in *Bernstein* may be criticised for not applying the objective test strictly enough by taking account of subjective factors unknown to the seller, because in making his assessment of what was reasonable, Rougier J discounted the period of Mr Bernstein's illness[9]. The main criticism of the decision, however, is in its application of the law to the facts. Was it really reasonable for the seller to consider the deal closed after three weeks in the case of a sale of a new car?

One clear implication of the decision in *Bernstein* is that where goods are affected by a latent defect, the buyer may lose the right to reject before he is aware of either the defect or the right and the decision has therefore been criticised as being inconsistent with the requirement that goods had to be reasonably durable at the time of sale to be considered merchantable. The Law Commission, however, firmly rejected the idea of introducing a long-term right of rejection in sale contracts on the grounds that such a right could only be justified if the buyer were required to give the seller credit for his use of the goods[10]. The buyer's position is nevertheless somewhat ameliorated by SoGA, s 35(5), inserted by the Sale and Supply of Goods Act 1994, which provides that the factors which are material in assessing whether a reasonable time has elapsed so as to bar rejection include whether the buyer has had a reasonable opportunity of examining the goods for the purpose of 'ascertaining if they are in conformity with the contract'. This seems to shift the perspective from which reasonableness is to be assessed to that of the buyer. It would not, however, guarantee that a case on the same facts as *Bernstein* would now be decided differently. First, time still begins to run from the date of delivery. Second, it is not clear whether the test is a wholly objective or a partly subjective one: in other words, does it require an assessment whether *this particular buyer* has had a reasonable opportunity to examine the goods – so that, for instance, a court could take into account the fact that, as in *Bernstein*, the buyer had been ill and unable to use the goods – or whether the time elapsed is sufficient for a hypothetical reasonable buyer to check the goods? It is submitted that there are sound reasons for leaving out of account factors personal to the particular buyer unless they are know to the seller. Third, the section gives the buyer a reasonable time to evaluate the goods generally, not to discover the particular defect. In fact, the language used is very close to that of the submission made on behalf of the successful defendants in *Bernstein*.

What is clear is that *Bernstein* lays down no absolute rule. It merely involves a finding of fact that in a particular case three weeks was a reasonable time to test a car. Even before the 1994 reforms there were cases which adopted an approach more favourable to the buyer. In a Canadian case[11] a local authority purchased a computer system to be used to store its housing records. During the first eight months of use it proved inadequate and various attempts were made to repair it, before the buyer rejected it. However, even after rejection, the buyer continued to use the system for a further seven months while attempting to negotiate a settlement. It was held that the buyer could still reject. The system was complex, and a longer time was therefore required to determine if it was fit, or could be made fit, for the purpose for which it was ordered. The behaviour of the parties was also relevant. Continuing to use the system, thereby minimising the buyer's losses, was commercially reasonable behaviour in the circumstances; the buyer's housing records had all been transferred to the system and it could not afford to purchase another. Two English cases decided since the 1994 reforms may also be instructive. In *Peakman v Express Circuits Ltd*[12] a machine was delivered on 20 November and rejected on 18 December 1995. Defects in the machine were apparent immediately on delivery, and the supplier attempted to fix them. The Court of Appeal refused to interfere with a finding that the buyer had not accepted the goods after attempting to use them for four weeks. The court emphasised that there must be a reasonable time for the buyer to try out the goods and decide whether to keep them, and also emphasised, as in *Bernstein*, that the complexity of the goods is relevant. It is submitted that the approach is entirely consistent with the suggestion, above, that acceptance is concerned with the seller's legitimate (reasonable) expectations. Where, as here, the seller knows that the goods are initially defective and attempts to repair them, he cannot reasonably believe that the buyer has had a reasonable opportunity to evaluate them.

A similar line can be discerned in *Truk (UK) Ltd v Tokmakidis GmbH*[13], in which the lapse of six months between delivery of a vehicle and rejection was held not to be too long. As the seller knew, the buyer bought the vehicle for resale. The defect was only discovered when it was identified by a potential buyer. Whilst recognising that *Bernstein* was a somewhat harsh decision on its facts, the judge[14] took a generally similar line on several points. He emphasised that (as was held in *Peakman*) what is in issue is whether the buyer has had a reasonable time to examine the goods generally, not a reasonable time to discover the particular defect, and that therefore, when latent defects appear some time after sale, it may be too late to reject. This may, however, cut either way: the fact that a particular defect was patent and could have been discovered in a short time will not reduce the time allowed for examination if a reasonable time to examine the goods generally would be longer. The judge held that, had the buyer purchased the goods for its own use, a reasonable time for examination might have been one to two months. He recognised, however, that where goods are bought for resale, defects are often not discovered until the goods are resold and that a longer period ought therefore to be allowed for examination in such a case so that a reasonable time would be the time taken to resell the goods plus a further reasonable period for the buyer to decide whether or not to reject them. The language used in the judgment is of the actual time taken to resell the goods. However, it seems that what the judge had in mind was the time the parties anticipated it would take to sell the goods. On the facts of the particular case, it was clear that the parties had anticipated that resale might take six months. The approach is therefore consistent with the suggestion made earlier, that the law is effectively concerned with the legitimate expectations of the parties. Even after expiry of a reasonable time to examine the goods, the buyer may be entitled to a further reasonable period to determine what action to take – ie whether to accept or reject them – before he is deemed to have accepted them. The length of that period will depend, amongst other things, on the dealings between the parties. Here there were negotiations between the parties for a further seven months before the buyer finally rejected the goods. It was held that he had not accepted.

1 See *R W Green v Cade Bros Farms Ltd* [1978] 1 Lloyd's Rep 602 (seven-day limit for notifying defects in seed potatoes unreasonable); *Knight Machinery (Holdings) Ltd v Rennie* 1995 SLT 166 (requirement in contract for sale of printing machinery for notice of rejection to be given within seven days held unreasonable).
2 Section 59.
3 Paragraph 5.19.
4 See *Hammer and Barrow v Coca Cola* [1962] NZLR 723 (retention for 25 days whilst parties attempted to negotiate).
5 SoGA, s 35(6).
6 Law Commission 160 *Sale and Supply of Goods* (1987) para 5.30.
7 [1987] 2 All ER 220.
8 [1987] 2 All ER 220 at 230.
9 See Hwang [1992] LMCLQ 334.
10 Paragraph 5.6.
11 *Public Utilities Commission of City of Waterloo v Burroughs Business Machines Ltd* (1974) 52 DLR (3d) 481, Ont CA.
12 (1998) unreported, CA.
13 [2000] 1 Lloyd's Rep 543.
14 His Honour Raymond Jack QC.

12.2.2 *Rejection of part*

Prior to the passing of the Sale and Supply of Goods Act 1994, unless the contract was severable, the buyer lost the right to reject under s 11(4) when he 'accepted the goods or part of them'. This rule applied even where only some of the goods were defective. The only exception was that where the seller delivered goods of the contract description mixed with goods of a different description, s 30(4) gave the buyer the option of rejecting only the non-conforming goods, creating a curious distinction between breaches relating to description and those relating to other matters such as quality. Outside this anomalous case, rejection was therefore an 'all or nothing' remedy: the buyer who, deliberately or by virtue of the Act, accepted any of the goods, was deemed to accept them all, unless a term of the contract allowed partial rejection. Commercial contracts often do permit partial rejection; in fact, they often prevent the buyer rejecting all the goods where only some are defective. Moreover, even in the absence of a contractual right of partial rejection, the seller would often allow the buyer to reject only part of the goods as part of a negotiated settlement.

The law therefore encouraged the buyer to reject and was both out of step with commercial practice and inefficient. The position is now modified by SoGA, s 35A, which provides that where the buyer has the right to reject the goods by reason of a breach which affects some or all of them, but accepts some of them, he does not thereby lose the right to reject the rest, provided that where some of the goods are unaffected by the breach he accepts all of them. The special rule in s 30(4) has been repealed. Thus where all of the goods are affected by the breach the buyer may choose to reject some or all of them; where only some of the goods are affected by the breach he may: (a) reject all of the goods; (b) reject all of the goods affected by the breach and keep the remainder; or (c) reject some of the defective goods and keep the remainder, including all those unaffected by the breach.

The right of partial rejection is subject to two limitations. First, it is subject to the overriding rule that a non-consumer buyer should not reject at all where the breach is so slight that rejection would be unreasonable[1]. Second, where the buyer accepts some of the goods forming part of a commercial unit, he is deemed to accept all of the goods comprised in that unit[2]. He may therefore not reject goods forming part of a 'commercial unit', defined as 'a unit division of which would materially impair the value of the goods or the character of the unit'[3]. As illustrations of this restriction, the Law Commission suggested that the buyer would not be allowed to reject one shoe from a pair, one encyclopaedia from a set, or a defective component from a motor car[4].

1   SoGA, s 15A.
2   SoGA, s 35(7).
3   SoGA, s 35(7).
4   Law Commission 160 *Sale and Supply of Goods* (1987) para 6.12.

12.2.3   *Instalment contracts*

The buyer's rights to reject and terminate the contract are modified where the contract is severable. Section 11(4) of SoGA, which excludes the buyer's right to reject where he accepts the goods or part of them, only applies where the contract is 'not severable'. On general principles, if the contract is, or the obligations of the parties under the contract are, severable, a breach by either party in relation to one severable part of their obligations will not necessarily affect other severable obligations under the contract, or the contract as a whole. In particular, a breach by one party of a severable obligation will not entitle the other wholly to refuse to perform his obligations.

In deciding whether the contract is severable, the first question will be to decide if there is one contract or several. This will depend on the documents and the language used. If there are several contracts, a breach in relation to one contract will have no legal effect on any of the other contracts. However, the situation may be difficult to analyse: the seller may send a customer a set of terms of trading and indicate that all orders are to be placed on those terms; similarly, parties who trade together regularly may agree 'streamlined' procedures allowing the buyer to place orders on terms fixed in advance, possibly under a 'master' agreement. This is likely to be the case where parties use electronic media such as fax, or computer communication such as e-mail or electronic data interchange (EDI) to place orders. Alternatively, there may be a 'requirements' contract under which the buyer agrees that he will order all his requirements for goods of a particular type from the seller, and the seller agrees to meet those orders at a stated price[1]. Under such arrangements, each individual order is likely to be regarded as creating a new, separate contract of supply. In contrast, if the parties contract for the supply of a fixed quantity of goods to be delivered over a period as required by the buyer, there is likely to be one single contract. Similarly, if a number of items are ordered in one document, there is likely to be one contract, even if the items are of several different descriptions. If on the proper construction of the arrangement there is one contract, a statement that each delivery should be treated as a separate contract is likely to be treated only as making it a severable contract[2].

If there is one contract, it is necessary to decide whether or not it is severable. The Act suggests that a contract will be severable if it provides for 'the sale of goods to be delivered by stated instalments, which are to be separately paid for'[3]. However, it is clear that this is not an exhaustive definition of a 'severable' contract, and where the contract allows for delivery by instalments, a court is likely to favour treating the contract as severable, in order to apply the more flexible rules which apply to severable contracts. Thus it has been held that contracts which provided for delivery of the contract goods as required by the buyer[4], in instalments to be determined by the seller[5], or for delivery in instalments to be paid for by monthly account[6], were severable.

The rights of the buyer under a severable contract are not entirely clear: there is some ambiguity in the language of the Act. It is clear that the buyer is not prevented from rejecting goods delivered in one instalment simply because he has accepted a previous instalment and this was the position even before the 1994 reforms. Clearly, therefore, the buyer can reject an individual defective instalment, either on general principles or by virtue of the right of partial rejection in s 35A. It may then be possible for the seller to tender a replacement delivery, but if not there will be an overall short delivery under the contract as a whole, for which the buyer can claim damages[7]. In addition, the right of partial rejection under s 35A applies to each instalment of a severable contract, so that where only some of the goods in an individual instalment are defective, the buyer may reject some or all of the defective goods and keep the rest.

The second, more difficult, question is whether the buyer can terminate the whole contract on the grounds of a breach in relation to one or more individual instalments. Section 31(2) provides that where a contract is severable:

'and the seller makes defective deliveries in respect of one or more instalments . . . it is a question in each case depending on the terms of the contract and the circumstances of the case whether the breach is a repudiation of the whole contract or whether it is a severable breach giving rise to a claim for compensation but not to a right to treat the whole contract as repudiated'.

It is therefore clear that a breach in relation to one or more instalments can amount to a repudiation of the whole contract, allowing the buyer to terminate it. It will do so if it is 'so serious as to go to the root of the contract'[8]. In *Maple Flock Co Ltd v Universal Furniture Products (Wembley) Ltd* [9] the Court of Appeal suggested that the seriousness of a breach should be assessed by reference to (a) the ratio of the breach to the contract as a whole, and (b) the likelihood of its being repeated. In that case S contracted to sell 100 tons of rag flock by instalments of one and a half tons each. Fifteen acceptable deliveries were made; the sixteenth was contaminated, but the next two were acceptable. B then repudiated the contract for the breach in relation to the sixteenth delivery. A further four deliveries, all acceptable, were made and rejected, and S then sued. It was held that B was in breach of contract. Only one instalment out of 22 had been defective and there was very little likelihood of repetition. In contrast, in *Robert A Munro & Co Ltd v Meyer*[10] the contract was for sale of 1,500 tons of bonemeal to be delivered by weekly deliveries of 125 tons. After half the goods had been delivered it was discovered that each consignment was contaminated with cocoa husks. It was held that this breach amounted to a repudiation of the whole contract, allowing the buyer to terminate. Thus, 'if the breach is of such a kind or in such circumstances as reasonably to lead to the inference that similar breaches will be committed in relation to subsequent deliveries, the whole contract may then and there be regarded as rescinded'[11].

Section 31(2) refers to 'defective deliveries'. In *Regent OHG v Francesco of Jermyn Street* it was held that the section also applies to short deliveries so that a short delivery of one suit in one instalment under a severable contract for the supply of 62 suits by instalments was insufficient to amount to a repudiation of the whole contract. The buyer was not entitled to treat the short delivery under the contract as a whole as a ground for rejecting the whole contract quantity[12].

Although the test in *Maple Flock* is easy to state, it is (like the *Hong Kong Fir*[13] test) uncertain and difficult to apply. Except in the clearest cases, such as *Munro v Meyer*, where one party commits a breach in relation to one instalment, the other terminates the contract at his peril: if the court holds that the breach was not a repudiation of the whole contract, the party who terminated the contract will be liable for having wrongfully repudiated[14].

Even if the *Maple Flock* test is satisfied, it is not clear whether s 31(2) allows the buyer to reject goods delivered in previous instalments and already accepted. The language of the section, referring to 'repudiation' of the contract suggests that the buyer may terminate the contract from the time of breach, and this would be consistent with the normal analysis of termination of contracts for breach. However, the position is not entirely clear[15]. The buyer may be able to reject instalments already accepted if he can show that his acceptance of them was conditional on the remaining deliveries being acceptable.

1 See eg *Percival v LCC Asylum Committee* (1918) 87 LJKB 677; *Great Northern Rly Co v Witham* (1873) LR 9 CP 16.
2 See *Robert A Munro & Co Ltd v Meyer* [1930] 2 KB 312.
3 Section 31(2).
4 *Jackson v Rotax* [1910] 2 KB 937, CA.
5 *Regent OHG v Francesco of Jermyn Street* [1981] 3 All ER 327.
6 *H Longbottom & Co Ltd v Bass Walker & Co Ltd* [1922] WN 245.
7 The buyer cannot treat such short delivery as a ground for repudiating the whole contract: *Regent OHG v Francesco of Jermyn Street* [1981] 3 All ER 327, below.
8 Per Donaldson J in *Warinco AG v Samor SPA* [1977] 2 Lloyd's Rep 582 at 588.
9 [1934] 1 KB 148, CA.
10 [1930] 2 KB 312.
11 *Millar's Karri and Jarrah Co (1902) v Weddel, Turner & Co* (1908) 14 Com Cas 25 at 28, per Bigham J.
12 The shortfall would now be regarded as so slight that rejection would be unreasonable under SoGA, s 30(2A)(a), above 10.3.
13 *Hong Kong Fir Shipping Co Ltd v Kawasaki Kisen Kaisha* [1962] 2 QB 26, [1962] 1 All ER 474, CA: see 2.5.6.
14 The difficulties are well illustrated by the facts of *Warinco AG v Samor SPA* [1977] 2 Lloyd's Rep 582; on appeal [1979] 1 Lloyd's Rep 450, CA.
15 See Atiyah, *Sale of Goods* (8th edn, 1990) pp 493–494; contrast the view in the 10th edn (2000) p 507.

12.2.4 *Other supply contracts*

The concept of 'acceptance' is unique to contracts of sale. There is no equivalent to s 11(4) in the legislation governing other contracts for supply, where the buyer's rights to terminate the contract depend on general contractual principles. Thus a person who acquires goods under contracts such as hire purchase, hire or barter is entitled to reject the goods and terminate the contract if there is a breach of condition, including any of the statutory implied conditions, but loses the right to terminate if he affirms the contract. Crucially, a person will not be taken to have affirmed a contract until he is aware of the breach and the right to terminate. As a result, when goods affected by latent defects are supplied under contracts other than sale, the person acquiring the goods cannot be deemed to have affirmed the contract until the defect becomes apparent. Moreover, 'affirmation is a matter of election. A man only affirms a contract when he knows of the defects and by his conduct elects to go on with the contract despite them'[1]. Thus a person who acquires goods under a contract other than sale has a more extensive right to reject goods than does the buyer under a sale. In *Farnworth Finance Facilities Ltd v Attryde*[2] A entered into a hire purchase agreement to acquire a motor cycle, which proved defective. After using it for four months and driving 4,000 miles, during which time attempts were made to repair it, he terminated the contract. It was held that he had not affirmed the contract. The decision is in sharp contrast to that in *Bernstein*, above.

It seems unfair that the buyer's rights should depend on the fine and often technical distinctions between sales and other supply arrangements. This is recognised to some extent by s 14(1) of the Supply of Goods (Implied Terms) Act 1973, which provides that s 11(4) of the 1979 Act does not apply to a conditional sale agreement where the buyer 'deals as a consumer' within the definition of that expression in the Unfair Contract Terms Act 1977[3]. However, having considered the difference between acceptance and affirmation, the Law Commission, in its 1987 report, recommended that there should be no change in the present position and, notwithstanding the amendments made to the law on acceptance in sale, there are still significant differences between the two regimes.

There is a second difference between rejection under a sale contract and termination of other supply contracts. If a buyer who has already paid the price rejects goods under a sale contract, he is entitled to recover the price as money paid for a consideration which has wholly failed. However, where the hirer under a hire or hire purchase agreement terminates the contract, he will only be able to recover payments made if there is a total failure of the consideration for which they were paid. Where the hirer has had the use of the goods for a period, he will normally be unable to establish that there is a total failure, and he will thus be limited to a claim for damages in which he will have to prove his loss. Damages will be based on the cost of hiring equivalent goods, which will often be the same as the payments made under the contract, with a deduction for the value of the use the hirer has had from the goods: where the defect is serious, that may result in the hirer recovering very nearly the whole of his payments[4].

1 Per Lord Denning in *Farnworth Finance Facilities Ltd v Attryde* [1970] 1 WLR 1053 at 1059, CA.
2 [1970] 2 All ER 774, [1970] 1 WLR 1053, CA.
3 See 2.6.4.2.
4 See *Charterhouse Credit Co Ltd v Tolly* [1963] 2 QB 683, [1963] 2 All ER 432, CA; *UCB Leasing Ltd v Holtom* [1987] RTR 362, CA.

12.3 Damages for breach

If the seller commits any breach of contract the buyer may claim damages for any losses the breach causes him. Where the breach is of a condition, the buyer has the additional option to reject the goods and terminate the contract, but he is entitled to damages whether he rejects or accepts.

In any case, the buyer's claim is for damages for breach of contract and the rules generally applicable to such claims apply[1]. In particular, the buyer must prove that his loss was caused by the breach and was not too remote, and he must take reasonable steps to mitigate his loss. Any term in the contract limiting the amount of damages payable will be subject to the legal controls on exclusion and limitation clauses. A term providing for payment of liquidated damages on breach will be subject to the rule against penalties, and will be enforceable only if it is a genuine attempt to pre-estimate the loss[2]. However, the general contract rules are somewhat modified by the Sale of Goods Act, which lays down special rules for cases of non-delivery, late delivery and breach of warranty of quality.

1 See generally 2.10.
2 See 2.10.2.

12.3.1 *Damages for non-delivery*

If the seller fails to deliver, he totally fails to perform his obligations under the contract. The buyer is therefore released from his obligations to accept and pay for the goods. If the price has been pre-paid, the buyer may recover it by way of a claim for money had and received in which there will be no need to prove loss or mitigation. However, if the buyer has suffered additional losses, for instance because he has had to buy replacement goods at a higher price, he must bring a claim for damages for non-delivery. The amount of any prepayment can be included as part of the buyer's damages, but the losses claimed must be proved and the buyer must take reasonable steps in mitigation.

The measure of damages for non-delivery is 'the estimated loss directly and naturally resulting, in the ordinary course of events, from the seller's breach of contract'[1], which is effectively the same measure as that provided for by the first limb of the rule in *Hadley v Baxendale*[2]. However, the rule is modified by SoGA, s 51(3), which provides that:

> 'Where there is an available market for the goods in question the measure of damages is prima facie to be ascertained by the difference between the contract price and the market or current price of the goods at the time or times when they ought to have been delivered or (if no time was fixed) at the time of the refusal to deliver'.

This 'market price rule' is effectively an aspect of the rule that the plaintiff must mitigate his loss. Where goods of the contract description are available in the market, the buyer can mitigate his loss by buying replacement goods in the market, and he is expected to do so. If he fails to do so, he must take the risk of any increase in the market price. Conversely, if he manages to reduce his loss, either by making a particularly favourable deal or by postponing his purchase and taking advantage of any fall in the market, he is entitled to keep the benefit of the bargain. The buyer may speculate on the market, but entirely at his own risk[3].

1 SoGA, s 51(2).
2 (1854) 9 Exch 341.
3 See *Kaines (UK) Ltd v Osterriechische Warrenhandelsgesellschaft* [1993] 2 Lloyd's Rep 1.

12.3.1.1 *Date of assessment*

The date of assessment of damages under s 51(3) is the date of the breach: the buyer is expected to go into the market immediately and make a replacement purchase. However, a court is likely to apply this requirement flexibly: the buyer must be allowed a reasonable time to assess the situation, and if he acts reasonably and delays entering the market, for instance in order to attempt to negotiate with the seller, he is unlikely to be penalised if the market price increases.

Where the seller commits an anticipatory breach by indicating, before the time for delivery, that he does not intend to perform, the buyer has a choice whether to accept the breach and terminate the contract at once, or to keep the contract alive and wait for performance. In the latter case, damages remain to be assessed by reference to the market price at the date for actual delivery. If the buyer accepts the anticipatory breach and terminates, damages are still assessed by reference to the date fixed for actual delivery; however, the buyer is under a duty to mitigate his loss and if the market price rises between the date of termination and the contractual delivery date, the buyer's damages may be assessed at the earlier date if the seller proves that by delaying the buyer unreasonably failed to mitigate his loss[1].

The application of these rules in a market context is well illustrated by the decision in *Kaines (UK) Ltd v Osterreichische Warrenhandelsgesellschaft*[2]. On 3 June the plaintiffs contracted to buy from the defendants 600,000 barrels of Brent crude oil for September delivery. The defendants repudiated the contract and the plaintiffs accepted that (anticipatory) repudiation on 18 June. The market price at that date was 24 cents per barrel higher than the contract price; on the following day it was 26 cents per barrel higher. The price rose and fell throughout June, reaching a low point on 25 June, when it was 10 cents per barrel lower than the contract price. However, the plaintiffs did not buy a replacement cargo until 29 June, by which time the market had risen again and the market price was 75 cents per barrel higher than the contract price. The plaintiffs initially claimed damages assessed by reference to the 29 June price. The defendants argued that the damages should be fixed by reference to the date for delivery in September (which would be purely nominal, as the plaintiffs had produced no evidence of the price at that date); alternatively, they argued that damages should be calculated by reference to the lowest market price between the date of breach and the date of the plaintiffs' replacement purchase, on the basis that, having failed to make an immediate purchase, the plaintiffs were under a continuing duty to mitigate their loss and should have bought when the market reached its lowest point on 25 June, in which case damages would be nominal. The Court of Appeal, applying the rules summarised above, held that the correct date for assessment of damages was 19 June. Damages for anticipatory breach are normally assessed by reference to the market price at the date for delivery but the plaintiff is under an immediate duty to mitigate. On the facts, because of the volatility of oil prices, the plaintiffs should not have delayed making a replacement purchase but should have taken immediate steps to mitigate their loss by entering the market. If the plaintiffs chose to delay making a replacement purchase after that date they were speculating for their own benefit and at their own risk:

> 'if a buyer fails to take advantage of an available market to buy in a substitute cargo at an appropriate time, whether the seller's breach is anticipatory or not, the buyer's decision is (in the vernacular) down to him: it is not a decision from which the seller can either suffer or profit'[3].

1　*Melachrino v Nickoll and Knight* [1920] 1 KB 693.
2　[1993] 2 Lloyd's Rep 1; see Bridge [1994] JBL 152.
3　[1993] 2 Lloyd's Rep 1 at 11, per Bingham LJ.

12.3.1.2　*'Available market'*

Section 51(3) only applies where there is an 'available market'. Most of the cases on the meaning of this phrase have been concerned with sellers' claims for damages for non-acceptance but the principles seem equally applicable in this context. Early cases regarded a market as a geographical place in which goods were traded[1]. However, modern cases place emphasis on the availability of a source of supply of goods of the contract description and the balance of supply and demand between buyers and sellers. If the goods are unique, there cannot be said to be an 'available market' and it has been held that there is therefore no 'available market' for secondhand cars, because each car is unique[2]. Even if there is a market for goods of the contract description, it must be available to the buyer: it must be geographically accessible, and be such that a person in the buyer's position could buy in it[3].

The existence of an available market will often be a question of fact, dependent on the evidence available to the court. The meaning of 'available market' was considered in the context of a seller's claim for non-acceptance under a large-scale commodity contract in *Shearson Lehman Hutton Inc v Maclaine Watson & Co Ltd (No 2)*[4]. The existence of an available market is likely to be in issue where the buyer has not made a replacement purchase, or is alleged to have bought at a price higher than that in the market. Where there is no actual attempt to purchase, there will only be an available market on the date in question if there were then 'sufficient traders potentially in touch with each other to evidence a market'[5] in which a purchase could be made. However, there may be an available market if goods of the contract description were available, even if it would not be possible to replace the whole contract quantity in one purchase[6]. It has been held that there is no available market unless the price of goods is fixed by supply and demand[7], and, in the context of a buyer's claim, demand must not exceed supply[8].

1　See eg *Dunkirk Colliery Co Ltd v Lever* (1878) 9 Ch D 20 at 25, per James LJ.
2　*Lazenby Garages Ltd v Wright* [1976] 2 All ER 770, [1976] 1 WLR 459, CA. This seems to ignore the fact that there are fairly standard values for particular common models, depending on age, condition etc.
3　See *The Texaco Melbourne* [1994] 1 Lloyd's Rep 473.
4　[1990] 1 Lloyd's Rep 441.
5　[1990] 1 Lloyd's Rep 441 at 447, per Webster J.
6　*Garnac Grain Co Inc v H M F Faure & Fairclough Ltd* [1968] AC 1130n, [1967] 2 All ER 353, HL.
7　*Charter v Sullivan* [1957] 2 QB 117, [1957] 1 All ER 809, CA.
8　*W L Thompson Ltd v Robinson (Gunmakers) Ltd* [1955] Ch 177, [1955] 1 All ER 154.

12.3.1.3　*The measure of damages*

If there is an available market, the buyer's damages are assessed objectively, by reference to the price at which a person in the buyer's position could have bought in the market at that date. No account is taken of subjective factors special to the buyer, such as lack of expertise, which might result in him paying a higher price[1]. Assessment of the 'market price' on a given date will depend on evidence: it will often be the case that a range of prices was available. In large-scale commodity dealings, it may be necessary to take into account the price at which goods could be obtained within a few days of the breach, in order to take account of the price available from sellers who were in the market on the date in question but could not be contacted then because of communication difficulties.

The market price rule is a prima facie rule; it may be displaced where it would be inappropriate[2], and it has been suggested that it will not apply in any case where the parties must have contemplated that it would not provide adequate compensation for a breach of contract[3]. However, it is well established that the rule is not displaced merely because the buyer has contracted to resell the goods at more, or less, than the market price at the date of delivery. In *Williams v Agius*[4] B contracted to buy a cargo of coal for 16s 3d per ton and contracted to resell it at 19s per ton. By the time of the date for delivery the market price had risen to 23s 6d and S failed to deliver. When B sued for damages for non-delivery, S argued that the damages should be assessed by reference to B's resale price, rather than the higher market price, but the House of Lords held that the resale should be disregarded: B was entitled to be put in the same position as if the contract had been performed, and in order to fulfil his contract B would have to buy at the market price. Equally, if B failed to fulfil the resale contract, the sub-buyer would have been entitled to damages fixed by reference to the market price. It is clear that the same rule would apply if B had contracted to resell at a price higher than the current market price. Generally, therefore, the buyer will not be entitled to recover the profits he would have made on a lost resale where there is an available market for the goods: the buyer could have avoided those losses by buying replacement goods in the market[5].

1   *Shearson Lehman Hutton Inc v Maclaine Watson and Co Ltd (No 2)* [1990] 1 Lloyd's Rep 441.
2   See eg *The Texaco Melbourne* [1994] 1 Lloyd's Rep 473, HL.
3   *W L Thompson Ltd v Robinson (Gunmakers) Ltd* [1955] Ch 177.
4   [1914] AC 510, HL.
5   The rule ignoring actual resale transactions may be justified in a market context where it promotes certainty and speedy resolution of disputes, avoiding the need for lengthy investigation of facts. Under the Vienna Convention on Contracts for the International Sale of Goods, however, damages are assessed by reference to the actual price paid by the buyer under any substitute transaction: CISG, art 75.

12.3.1.4   *Special damages*

However, the buyer is entitled to claim 'special damages' where they would be available under the general law, and profits on a lost resale may be recoverable in exceptional circumstances where they are not too remote. In *R & H Hall Ltd v W H Pim Jr & Co's Arbitration*[1] B contracted to buy a cargo of wheat for 51s 9d per quarter, and resold the same cargo whilst it was at sea for 56s 9d per quarter. S failed to deliver and at the date for delivery the market price for similar wheat was 53s 9d per quarter. The House of Lords held that B was entitled to recover the lost profit on his resale. *Williams v Agius* was not cited, but the two cases can be reconciled. A crucial factor in *Hall v Pim* was that B had contracted to resell the specific cargo he bought from S; he therefore could not buy replacement goods in the market place to fulfil his resale contract. Moreover, the contract between S and B made express provision for such a resale: it was found that there was at least a 50/50 chance of resale whilst the cargo was afloat, so that B's resale, and inability to perform his contract if the goods were not delivered, was foreseeable and not too remote. It may also be significant that in *Wiliams v Agius* the seller sought to evade the market price rule in order to reduce the damages payable for his own (deliberate) breach.

It seems that in order to rely on *Hall v Pim* the buyer must show:

(i) that he contracted to resell the same goods he bought from the seller as specific goods;

(ii) that he entered into the resale contract before the date for delivery; and

(iii) that his loss from inability to perform that contract was not too remote: it must have been foreseeable by the seller as a reasonable probability that the buyer would resell the goods as specific goods; the loss will also be too remote if the resale price is 'extravagant'.

Other losses may be recoverable as special damages, provided they are not too remote. Thus, if goods are bought for resale, the buyer may be able to claim compensation for damage to goodwill and loss of future business from his customer[2]. Where goods are bought for use, the buyer may be able to claim damages in respect of profits he would have made from use of the goods had they been delivered, but such a claim will rarely succeed where there is an available market, since they could be avoided by making an alternative purchase in the market.

1   (1927) 30 Ll L Rep 159.
2   *GKN Centrax Gears Ltd v Matbro Ltd* [1976] 2 Lloyd's Rep 555, CA.

12.3.1.5   *No available market*

Where there is no available market, for instance where goods are specially manufactured for the buyer, the buyer's damages are prima facie the difference between the contract price of the goods and their value at the date for delivery. In the absence of a market for the goods the buyer must supply other evidence of their value at the date when they should have been delivered. Where he has contracted to resell the goods, the resale price may be evidence of their value, provided the price is not unusually high. The buyer must mitigate his loss and, although it may not be possible to buy identical goods in the market, he should buy the nearest equivalent; if the alternative is more expensive, he will be entitled to recover the extra costs incurred provided he acted reasonably[1]. If the goods were bought for use, the buyer may be able to recover damages in respect of profits lost as a result of the non-availability of the goods; the damages must not be too remote[2] and the buyer must take reasonable steps to mitigate his loss: for instance by hiring a temporary replacement until he can purchase an alternative.

1   *Blackburn Bobbin Co v Allen* [1918] 1 KB 540.
2   *Victoria Laundry (Windsor) Ltd v Newman Industries Ltd* [1949] 2 KB 528, [1949] 1 All ER 997, CA.

12.3.2   *Damages for late delivery*

If the goods are not delivered on time in accordance with the contract, it must first be decided whether the time for delivery was of the essence[1]. If it was, the buyer may treat the contract as repudiated and, if he does so, the position is as if the seller had not delivered at all and the buyer may claim damages for non-delivery. However, even if the buyer does not terminate the contract, late delivery is a breach of contract for which he is entitled to damages.

There is no indication in the Sale of Goods Act of how damages for late delivery should be assessed, and so general contractual principles must be applied. If the goods were intended for use in the buyer's business, he may recover damages in respect of the loss of profit caused by their non-availability, provided the loss is not too remote. If the goods were to be used for some specially lucrative purpose, the buyer will only be able to claim a sum equal to the profit he would have made using them for their normal purpose, unless his special purpose was reasonably foreseeable by the seller at the time of the contract[2].

If the goods were intended for resale, the basic measure is the difference between the value of the goods at the contract delivery date and their value at the date of actual delivery[3]: ie the amount (if any) by which the value has fallen and which the buyer has lost by the delay in reselling. If there is an available market for goods of the contract description, the value will be assessed by reference to the market price at the relevant date. It is not clear whether in this context account can be taken of any actual resale by the buyer in fixing the damages. In *Wertheim v Chicoutimi Pulp Co*[4] the Privy Council held that account should be taken of the fact that the buyer had managed to resell the goods at more than the market price current at the date of delivery. B contracted to buy a cargo of wood pulp at 25s per ton. By the contract delivery date the price had risen to 70s per ton, but delivery was delayed and by the time the goods were delivered the price had fallen back to 42s 6d per ton. However, the buyer had managed to resell the pulp at 65s per ton, and the Privy Council held that he was entitled to the difference between the market price at the contract delivery date (70s) and the actual price at which he had resold the goods (65s) by way of damages. The decision was explained on the basis that, when dealing with a case of late delivery, as opposed to non-delivery, the court can examine the facts and see what did happen rather than hypothesise about what might have happened, and that to disregard the buyer's resale would overcompensate him. However, in the later case of *Slater v Hoyle & Smith Ltd*[5], a case concerned with delivery of defective goods, the Court of Appeal refused to follow *Wertheim* and applied the straightforward 'difference in value' rule. The argument that the court can, and should, consider the buyer's actual actions applies equally to a case of defective delivery as it does to one of late delivery, and the two cases are therefore difficult to reconcile. Most commentators prefer the approach in *Slater* to that in *Wertheim*, arguing that the court should either disregard the resale altogether and apply the difference in value rule, as in *Slater*[6], or take the resale fully into account, in which case the buyer has suffered no loss at all: he has sold the goods at the same price as if they had been delivered on time[7]. However, *Slater* was not followed, and, indeed, was questioned in a recent Court of Appeal decision on defective delivery[8], so that the questions whether and to what extent the court can take account of the buyer's actual dealings with the goods when assessing damages remain unclear.

In practice, it seems that buyers rarely seek to claim from their sellers consequential losses caused by delay in delivery[9]. Often the contract will exclude the seller's liability for such losses; alternatively, there may be force majeure or similar clauses which extend the time for delivery where delays are caused by circumstances outside the seller's control. Where the contract is for a particular item to be manufactured and supplied by the seller, delay in delivery may be covered by a liquidated damages clause.

1   See 10.2.1.
2   *Victoria Laundry (Windsor) Ltd v Newman Industries Ltd* [1949] 2 KB 528, [1949] 1 All ER 997, CA; *Cory v Thames Ironworks Co Ltd* (1868) LR 3 QB 181.
3   *Elbinger Actiengesellschaft v Armstrong* (1874) LR 9 QB 473.
4   [1911] AC 301.
5   [1920] 2 KB 11, CA.
6   See *MacGregor on Damages* (16th edn, 1997) para 857; *Benjamin's Sale of Goods* (5th edn, 1997) para 17-038.
7   Burrows, *Remedies for Torts and Breach of Contract* (2nd edn, 1994) p 146.
8   *Bence Graphics International Ltd v Fasson (UK) Ltd* [1997] 1 All ER 979, below 12.3.3.
9   See Beale and Dugdale, 'Contracts between businessmen' (1975) 2 BJLS 45.

12.3.3   *Damages for delivering defective goods*

If the seller delivers defective or substandard goods, the buyer may reject them if the defect amounts to a breach of a condition. If he does so, subject to the possibility discussed earlier that the seller may have a limited right to make a replacement tender[1], the position is as if the seller had not delivered and the buyer is entitled to damages for non-delivery. In addition, he may be entitled to damages for any loss or damage caused by the defective goods prior to rejection, provided they are not too remote and subject to the duty to mitigate.

However, even where the buyer does not, or is not entitled to, reject the goods, for instance because he has accepted them, because the breach is so slight that rejection would be unreasonable or because the defect amounts to a breach of warranty but not a breach of condition, he is still entitled to damages for breach of warranty. Such damages are assessed in accordance with SoGA, s 53, which allows the buyer either to sue for damages or to set up his claim in diminution or extinction of the price[2]. Thus the buyer may exercise a measure of self-help, by simply withholding part or all of the price, and if the seller sues for the price, the buyer may set up the defects as a defence reducing his liability, and any clause in the contract which seeks to restrict or exclude this right will be subject to the Unfair Contract Terms Act 1977[3]. His claim for damages may completely extinguish his liability to pay, even if it is too late to reject. If the buyer's damages exceed the price, he may claim the excess in separate proceedings or by means of a counterclaim in the seller's action for the price[4].

According to s 53(2), 'the measure of damages for breach of warranty is the estimated loss directly and naturally resulting, in the ordinary course of events, from the breach of warranty'. This is simply the ordinary contract measure under the first limb of the rule in *Hadley v Baxendale*[5]. However, according to s 53(3):

> 'In the case of breach of warranty of quality such loss is prima facie the difference between the value of the goods at the time of delivery to the buyer and the value they would have had if they had fulfilled the warranty'.

Although the section refers to 'breach of warranty of quality', it is assumed that the measure applies to any claim for damages where the goods are defective or for breach of any of the statutory implied terms in ss 13–15 of the Act. The rationale is that where the seller delivers goods which are defective or below the contract standard, the goods will still have a value; the buyer can sell the goods delivered and damages under s 53(3) will allow the buyer to buy replacement goods of the required standard. However, the measure will be easier to apply where there is an available market for the goods, and especially to commodities, where the market may be able to price goods of different qualities or standards. In other cases the damages will have to be assessed by reference to other factors: for instance, the contract price, or the price at which the buyer had contracted to resell the goods, may be evidence of the value of the goods as warranted; alternatively, the cost of repair may be taken as the measure of the buyer's loss provided that it is not unreasonable to have the goods repaired[6]. Damages are generally to be assessed as at the date of delivery. However, a later date may be appropriate in the case of latent defects which the buyer could not discover immediately on delivery.

Where the 'difference in value' rule in s 53(3) applies, the price the buyer obtains on a resale is generally ignored[7]. The rule is, however, only a prima facie rule. It therefore does not apply in all cases and will be displaced when inappropriate. The difficulty is to know when it will be displaced and, in particular, how the special rule in s 53(3) relates to the more general principle in s 53(2).

Where the buyer's losses exceed the difference in value, he may be able to recover them as 'special damages'. Section 54 expressly provides that 'special damages' may be recovered for breach of a sale contract where such damages would be recoverable at common law. 'Special damages' are generally assumed to be damages which would be recoverable under the second limb of the rule in *Hadley v Baxendale*[8]. The buyer may therefore recover 'special damages' to compensate for any additional losses, provided that they can be shown to have been caused by the goods[9] and not too remote, and subject to the duty to mitigate[10]. Thus special damages may be awarded for the profits which would have been made on a resale, provided that it was foreseeable that the goods would be resold, and either that the defect could not be discovered prior to resale or that the buyer could not buy replacement goods to fulfil his resale contract[11]. Damages may also be awarded for loss of further orders[12], and to indemnify the buyer against damages payable to his customer[13].

Where goods are bought for use, damages may cover loss of profits which would have been earned by their use[14]; in *George Mitchell (Chesterhall) Ltd v Finney Lock Seeds Ltd*[15] S delivered to B, a farmer, seed which did not comply with the contract description. The breach was not discoverable until the crop came up and the plaintiff's damages included lost profits and the wasted expenditure involved in clearing the valueless crop. Damages may also be awarded for damage to the buyer's other property[16], for personal injuries to the buyer[17] and, in consumer cases at least, may be awarded for inconvenience and, possibly, disappointment. In *Bernstein v Pamson Motors (Golders Green) Ltd*[18] it was held that B had accepted an unmerchantable car and therefore could not reject it; however, he was entitled to damages which included the costs of returning home after his car broke down and £150 as compensation for a 'totally spoilt day, comprising nothing but vexation'[19]. This is not an exhaustive list: damages may be recoverable for any special losses suffered, subject to the general rules applicable to such claims in contract.

It is more difficult to know when the difference in value rule will be displaced because the buyer's losses are less than are recoverable on the difference in value basis. In *Slater v Hoyle & Smith Ltd*[20] there was a contract for sale of 3,000 pieces of unbleached cotton of a specified quality. The buyers had already contracted to sell 2,000 pieces of bleached cotton of the same quality to a customer to use to manufacture shirts. The cotton delivered was found to be not of the contract quality and the buyers claimed damages for breach of warranty of quality. They had, however, managed to use some of the cotton delivered by the seller in partial fulfilment of their contract with their customer, under which the price was higher than the current market value of the substandard cotton. The Court of Appeal held that the buyers were nevertheless entitled to damages based on the difference between the value of the cotton as warranted and the actual market value of the cotton delivered and that no account was to be taken of the sums received on the resale contract. According to Scrutton LJ:

> 'If the buyer is lucky enough, for reasons with which the seller has nothing to do, to get his goods through on the sub-contract without a claim against him, this in principle cannot affect his claim against the seller any more than the fact that he had to pay very large damages on his sub-contract would affect his original seller'[21].

In *Bence Graphics International Ltd v Fasson (UK) Ltd*[22], however, the majority of the Court of Appeal refused to follow *Slater*. S supplied B with vinyl film for use in the manufacture of marking decals for containers. As S knew, B's customer required the decals to last for at least five years and it was an express term of the contract that the vinyl film supplied would last for at least five years. S in fact supplied a substantial quantity of film which, due to a defect in manufacture, was defective and degraded in use so that decals made from it lasted for considerably less than five years. The defect was not discovered until B had used much of the defective film to manufacture decals which it had supplied to its customer. B claimed damages for breach of warranty. At the time of the action it had received only one claim for compensation from its customer, which it had settled. The trial judge found that the difference in value between film of the contract quality and the film actually delivered was £564,328.54 and awarded damages in that sum. The majority of the Court of Appeal, however, held that the rule in s 53(3) was only a prima facie rule and was subject to the more general rule in s 53(2) that the buyer's damages should be the loss directly and naturally arising. Since the parties had contemplated that the film would be used to manufacture decals which would be sold, the loss they would have anticipated arising from a breach would be the amount of B's liability to its customer. Otton LJ attempted to distinguish *Slater* on the grounds that *Slater* involved a resale of the very goods supplied by the seller, whereas here B had used the goods supplied by S to manufacture a new product, and that the seller in *Slater* did not know that the goods were to be resold. Auld LJ, however, was prepared to go further and questioned whether *Slater* was rightly decided.

The decision in *Bence* has been criticised[23]. It is submitted, however, that, although the reasoning of the majority is not entirely convincing, the outcome on the facts was correct. To have awarded B damages assessed by reference to the identified difference in value would have given it a windfall by compensating it for a loss it had not suffered. The goods were not bought for resale as a commodity but as raw materials for use in a manufacturing process. It is no doubt true that, had the defect been known at the time of delivery, the goods would have been worth little or nothing. Had B been claiming damages in respect of unused stock, the full difference in value measure might have been appropriate. Once, however, B had used the goods for their intended purpose and sold the products for full value, to award the difference in value would effectively give it the use of those raw materials for free. It may be argued that the result gave S a windfall by allowing it to claim full payment having rendered a contract performance of lower quality than contracted for. This problem stems from the fact that contract damages are compensatory and assessed by reference to the buyer's loss. It might be resolved if the court were to develop power to award restitutionary damages allowing the seller to profit from rendering a substandard performance[24], or if English law were to recognise a separate right of price reduction. It should be borne in mind, however, that S would anyway be liable to indemnify B against claims received from its customer.

The real difficulty created by *Bence* is to know when the difference in value rule in s 53(3) will be displaced. The great advantage of the rule is its certainty, which is especially important in relations to market transactions such as those in the commodity trades[25]. The transaction in *Bence* was not such a contract. It is submitted that where goods are purchased as commodities for trade the court should be slow to accept that the difference in value rule is displaced.

1 See 12.1.3.1 above.
2 SoGA, s 53(1).
3 See *Stewart Gill v Horatio Myer* [1992] QB 600, [1992] 2 All ER 257; see 2.6.4.1.
4 SoGA, s 53(4).
5 (1854) 9 Exch 341.
6 See the discussion of *Ruxley Electronics and Construction Ltd v Forsyth* [1996] AC 344, [1995] 3 All ER 268 at 2.10.3.4.
7 *Slater v Hoyle & Smith Ltd* [1920] 2 KB 11, CA.
8 (1854) 23 LJ Ex 179; see 2.10.3.
9 See eg *Beoco Ltd v Alfa Laval Co Ltd* [1994] 4 All ER 464; see 2.10.3.1.
10 SoGA, s 54.
11 *Molling & Co v Dean & Son Ltd* (1901) 18 TLR 217.
12 *GKN Centrax Gears Ltd v Matbro Ltd* [1976] 2 Lloyd's Rep 555, CA.
13 See eg *Godley v Perry* [1960] 1 All ER 36, [1960] 1 WLR 9. The buyer need not have satisfied his customer's claim before seeking an indemnity against his liability: *Total Liban SA v Vitol Energy SA* [1999] 2 All ER (Comm) 65.
14 *Cullinane v British Rema Manufacturing Ltd* [1954] 1 QB 292, [1953] 2 All ER 1257, CA.
15 [1983] 2 AC 803, [1983] 2 All ER 737, HL.
16 *Bostock & Co Ltd v Nicholson & Sons Ltd* [1904] 1 KB 725.
17 *Godley v Perry* [1960] 1 All ER 36, [1960] 1 WLR 9.
18 [1987] 2 All ER 220.
19 See *Ruxley Electronics and Construction Ltd v Forsyth* [1996] AC 344, [1995] 3 All ER 268: see 2.10.3.4.
20 [1920] 2 KB 11, CA.
21 [1920] 2 KB 11 at 23.
22 [1998] QB 87, [1997] 1 All ER 979, CA.
23 See Treitel (1997) 113 LQR 188.
24 This possibility seems to have been rejected by the House of Lords in *Attorney General v Blake* [2000] 4 All ER 385; see 2.10.3.
25 See Bridge [1998] JBL 259.

12.4 Other remedies

Although the buyer's principle remedies for breach of contract by the seller are rejection and damages, other remedies generally available in contract may also be available. We have already seen that, where the price is prepaid, the buyer may recover it by means of a restitutionary claim for money had and received if the seller's breach gives rise to a total failure of the consideration for which the price was paid. The restitutionary claim is particularly important in the event of a breach of the implied term, in s 12 of the Act, that the seller has a right to sell the goods[1].

SoGA, s 52 gives the court a discretion to order specific performance in any action for breach of contract to deliver specific or ascertained goods. Specific performance can never be awarded in respect of goods which are unascertained[2]. However, even if the jurisdiction to award specific performance is available, the court will generally be reluctant to exercise it in relation to a commercial contract. Specific performance is generally only ordered where damages would not provide the plaintiff with an adequate remedy, so that specific performance of a contract for the sale of goods will rarely be ordered unless the goods are unique[3].

Where the seller is guilty of misrepresentation, the buyer may claim damages or rescind the contract on the basis of the misrepresentation[4]. The remedies for misrepresentation may sometimes be more favourable to the buyer than those for breach of contract; in particular, it seems that delay alone will not bar the right to rescind for misrepresentation, whereas it may amount to acceptance, barring the right to reject for breach of condition. However, a court would probably be unwilling to allow rescission where the right to reject had been lost[5], and unless the misrepresentation can be shown to have been fraudulent, the court is likely to exercise its discretion under the Misrepresentation Act 1967 to refuse rescission and award damages in lieu[6].

Where the property in the goods has passed to the buyer and he is entitled to immediate possession of the goods, he may also be entitled to sue in tort for wrongful interference with the goods, and he may therefore sue in tort on this basis if the seller wrongfully fails to deliver. In such an action the court has an option to order specific delivery of the goods, or to award damages based on the value of the goods. Although damages are not restricted by the market price rule, a court is unlikely to award more in an action for wrongful interference than it would award in an action for non-delivery and so a court would probably take the market value of the goods as evidence of their value. However, a claim for wrongful interference can be brought when a claim for non-delivery would not be available, for example against a third party who interferes with the goods, such as a carrier who refuses to deliver them, or against the seller if the seller remains in possession after the sale to the buyer and resells the goods to a second purchaser so as to give the second purchaser a good title[7].

1   See 14.1.1.
2   *Re Wait* [1927] 1 Ch 606. Cf *Sky Petroleum Ltd v VIP Petroleum Ltd* [1974] 1 All ER 954, where the court granted an injuction to restrain breach of a requirements contract for the supply of petrol, but in special circumstances.
3   The reluctance of the courts to order specific performance is illustrated by *Cohen v Roche* [1927] 1 KB 169 (no specific performance of contract for antiques); *Société des Industries Métallurgiques SA v Bronx Engineering Co Ltd* [1975] 1 Lloyd's Rep 465 (machinery); and *CN Marine Inc v Stena Inc, The Stena Nautica* [1982] 2 Lloyd's Rep 323 (ship).
4   See 2.4.2.1.
5   See *Leaf v International Galleries Ltd* [1950] 2 KB 86.
6   Misrepresentation Act 1967, s 2(2).
7   See ch 17.

12.5   The EC Directive on Consumer Guarantees[1]

The remedial scheme provided for by the Consumer Guarantees Directive where goods supplied are not in conformity with the contract differs in a number of significant ways from that under the existing Sale of Goods Act. Article 3 provides for four remedies to be available to the consumer: (i) repair of the goods; (ii) replacement of the goods; (iii) rescission of the contract; and (iv) price reduction. Earlier drafts of the directive provided for the consumer to choose between these remedies but the final version arranges them in a hierarchy. Article 3(3) provides that:

'In the first place the consumer may require the seller to repair the goods or he may require the seller to replace them, in either case free of charge, unless this is impossible or disproportionate.

A remedy shall be deemed disproportionate if it imposes costs on the seller which, in comparison with the alternative remedy, are unreasonable taking into account:

- the value the goods would have if there were no lack of conformity;
- the significance of the lack of conformity; and
- whether the alternative remedy could be completed without significant inconvenience to the consumer.

Any repair or replacement shall be completed within a reasonable time and without any significant inconvenience to the consumer taking account of the nature of the goods and the purpose for which the consumer required the goods'.

The consumer may demand rescission or price reduction only if: (a) he is entitled to neither repair nor replacement; or (b) the seller has not completed repair or replacement within a reasonable time; or (c) the seller has not completed repair or replacement without significant inconvenience to the consumer[2]. The consumer is not entitled to rescission at all if the lack of conformity is 'minor'[3]. Further remedies – most notably, from an English perspective, damages – may be provided for in domestic law.

Overall, this scheme seems to be much less favourable to the consumer than the existing Sale of Goods Act scheme. Most notably, whereas under domestic law (subject to the comments earlier in this chapter about a right for the seller to cure[4]) a consumer buyer who receives goods not in conformity with the contract has an absolute right to reject them and demand a refund, under the directive rejection (rescission) becomes, in effect, the remedy of last resort, available only where repair or replacement is unavailable or unsuccessful and never in the case of minor defects. It will be recalled that, under existing English law, the consumer buyer's right to reject is not restricted in cases where the seller's breach is slight[5].

The primary remedies under the directive are repair and replacement. The buyer has no legally enforceable right to repair or replacement under existing domestic law, and it may therefore be argued that the directive thus increases consumer rights in this respect. However, the consumer's rights to repair and replacement under the directive are not absolute: they are subject to the test of 'disproportionality'. In effect, therefore, they are available at the seller's option and it might be better to regard them as giving the seller, rather than the buyer, a right to insist on cure. As noted earlier, the existence of a right of seller cure in English law is open to doubt[6]. The better view is that no such right exists.

Were the UK to adopt the remedial scheme of the directive in substitution for the existing scheme under the SoGA, it would significantly reduce consumer rights. In particular, by removing the consumer's existing right to demand a refund, it would remove the consumer's most potent weapon in any dispute with the supplier[7]. Perhaps the major criticism of the remedial scheme is its complexity. Consumers need clear and certain rights which can be asserted effectively without legal advice. Much of the language of the directive – 'disproportionate', 'unreasonable', 'significant inconvenience', 'appropriate' – is open-textured, so that it will be difficult to predict its application in any particular case. This in itself will hinder a consumer in negotiations with a recalcitrant supplier.

The reason for this preference of the supplier's interests seems to have been concern that consumers might exercise their rights unreasonably. Suppliers expressed concern that rescission of the contract would leave them with defective goods on their hands and that consumers might seize on minor defects and use them as pretexts for rescinding contracts for reasons unconnected with the defects.

Whilst there is some merit in the argument that rescission is economically inefficient, especially where repair is possible, it is submitted that this is a price worth paying for ensuring that consumers, who are generally at a disadvantage when dealing with suppliers, have simple and effective rights.

There are other significant differences between the directive and English law. Most importantly the remedies under the directive are available for up to two years from the date of delivery of the goods[8]. At first, this seems to be very much to the consumer's advantage. The point has been made earlier that the right to reject in English law may be lost in a relatively short time as a result of deemed acceptance and that this runs counter to the recognition that durability is an aspect of quality[9]. However, the long-term rights available under the directive are qualified in several ways. First, it should be borne in mind that rescission will often not be available at all. Second, repair and, especially, replacement are likely to be regarded as 'disproportionate' if sought a long time after delivery. Third, the directive permits member states to require the consumer to notify the supplier of any lack of conformity within two months of discovering it[10] and to provide for any refund payable to the consumer in the event of rescission to be reduced to take account of his use of the goods[11].

We should also note that the remedy of price reduction provided for in the directive is currently not available in English law, although it is a feature of many civil law systems. English law does permit the buyer to claim damages and to set up the claim for damages in diminution or extinction of the price, but the remedy of price reduction is conceptually different from that of damages. It must be noted, however, that the differences may be of little practical importance in consumer cases.

It is suggested, therefore, that the remedial scheme of the directive is, overall, less favourable to the consumer than the existing SoGA regime. It remains to be seen how the UK will implement the directive. As explained previously, the directive is a 'minimum harmonisation' measure, so that it would be open to the UK to retain existing rules which provide for a higher level of consumer protection. The difficulty is that although the directive's regime is less favourable to the consumer overall, in some respects it is more favourable – for instance by giving the consumer at least a limited legal right to demand repair, and by providing for a long-term right of rejection in some cases. It therefore would not be possible for the UK simply to retain its present regime and ignore the directive. On the other hand, a synthesis of the two regimes would be very difficult to achieve. The best method of implementation may therefore be to introduce the directive as a free-standing scheme alongside the existing Sale of Goods Act. The alternative would seem to be wholesale revision of the Act and its replacement – perhaps by a new Consumer Sales Act – based, at least in part, on the directive.

1 See Twigg Flesner and Bradgate (2000) 2 Web JCLI.
2 Article 3(5).
3 Article 3(6).
4 See 12.1.3.1.
5 See 12.2.
6 See 12.1.3.1.
7 Compare the New Zealand Consumer Guarantees Act under which, as under the directive, the consumer's primary remedies are repair or replacement but the consumer is always entitled to demand a refund if the goods are affected by a serious fault, including where the fault is such that no reasonable consumer would have bought the goods had they known of the fault.
8 Article 5(1).
9 See 12.2.1.3.
10 Article 5(2).
11 Recital 15.

Chapter 13

Manufacturers and Product Liability

13.0 Introduction

The statutory implied terms in contracts for the supply of goods offer extensive protection to a person who purchases goods which prove to be defective. As we have seen, breach of the implied terms may entitle the buyer to reject the goods and claim damages for any losses caused by the breach, including for personal injuries and damage to other property, as well as for the reduced value of the defective goods themselves. A defect in a complex, modern product may cause widespread damage resulting in extensive consequential losses. Subject to proving that the losses were caused by a breach of contract, the immediate purchaser of the goods can recover damages in respect of all such losses. However, being based on the statutory implied terms, the claim lies in contract and, as a result, is a claim against the immediate supplier of the goods. The protection of implied terms is limited by the doctrine of privity of contract, and the terms therefore give the buyer no rights against the manufacturer of the goods, or anyone else involved in the distribution of the goods.

The principle of the supplier's contractual liability for defective goods developed during the nineteenth century, at a time when products were less complex and suppliers might reasonably be expected to be aware of the quality and capabilities of the goods they supplied. In an era of highly technical products and mass marketing techniques, it may be less reasonable to expect the supplier to be fully aware of the capabilities and qualities of the products he sells, and it might seem more rational and equitable that liability for losses caused by defective products should fall on the manufacturer, who is responsible for their production and, perhaps more significantly, through advertising and promotion, for creating customer demand and expectations. This has been recognised in the United States:

'The world of merchandising is no longer a world of direct contract; it is rather a world of advertising, and when representations expressed and disseminated in the mass communications media and on labels (attached to the goods themselves) prove false and the user or consumer is damaged by reason of his reliance on the representations, it is difficult to justify the manufacturer's denial of liability on the ground of the absence of technical privity. Manufacturers make extensive use of newspapers, periodicals and other media to call attention, in glowing terms, to the qualities and virtues of their products, and this advertising is directed at the ultimate consumer, or at some manufacturer or supplier who is not in privity with them'[1].

Indeed, although, as a result of the efforts of consumer organisations and advisers, consumers are now generally aware of their contractual rights against suppliers, the natural expectation of a purchaser of a defective product would probably be that the manufacturer should be responsible for repairing or replacing it and providing compensation for any losses. Often manufacturers do undertake to support their products, for instance by means of guarantees, in order to enhance their commercial reputation; but in the absence of such voluntary support, the purchaser's primary legal rights at present lie against the supplier.

In some jurisdictions the position has been modified by statute[2]. In England, however, the position remains that the manufacturer is not normally liable to the ultimate consumer for the quality of the goods he produces. The Law Commission was urged when it undertook its review of the doctrine of privity to create a special regime to give consumers direct rights of action against manufacturers of defective goods, but declined to do so. The Commission was concerned that the issue needed special consideration and that any proposals it might make might conflict with initiatives from other organisations[3]. However, although the subject has been considered at both the domestic and European levels, to date the law remains unchanged. In 1992 a consultation document issued by the Department of Trade and Industry[4] proposed that manufacturers should be jointly and severally liable with retailers for the quality of goods, but the proposals have been taken no further. Similar proposals were contained in the European Commission's 1993 Green Paper on Consumer Guarantees[5], which led to the Consumer Guarantees Directive[6], but the final text of the directive imposes liability solely on the retailer[7].

1 *Randy Knitwear Inc v American Cyanamid Co* 181 NE 2d 399 (1962), per Fuld J in the Court of Appeals of New York.
2 See eg the New Zealand Consumer Guarantees Act under which a manufacturer of household goods is held to guarantee that: (a) the goods are of acceptable quality; (b) repairs and spares will be available for a reasonable time; and (c) the goods correspond with their description.
3 See Law Commission 242 *Privity of Contract: Contracts for the Benefit of Third Parties* (1996) para 7.55. It may be possible for a consumer in certain circumstances to acquire direct rights against a manufacturer by virtue of the general privity reform in the Contracts (Rights of Third Parties) Act 1999: see para 7.54 of the Law Commission report.
4 DTI, *Consumer Guarantees: A Consultation Document* (1992).
5 Green Paper on Guarantees for Consumer Goods and After Sales Services, European Commission (1993) Com(93)509.
6 Directive 1999/44/EC of the European Parliament and of the Council of 25 May 1999 on certain aspects of the sale of consumer goods and associated guarantees (1999) (OJ L 171/12, 7 July 1999).
7 The Directive does, however, require the Commission to review the operation of the directive not later than 7 July 2006 and requires such review to consider the case for introducing direct producer liability: art 12.

13.0.1 *The limitations of contract claims*

The main restriction on the effectiveness of contractual liability under the implied terms is the doctrine of privity: a claim can only be brought by one contracting party against the other party to the contract. A simplified distribution chain might involve the following parties:

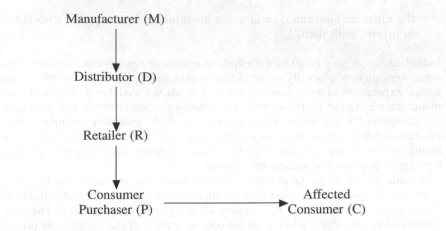

The absence of privity between P and M does not mean that M can avoid all liability for losses caused by the goods. Each person in the distribution chain incurs contractual liabilities to his immediate customer. Thus liability for any losses caused by a defective product can be passed back up the distribution chain by a series of claims for contractual indemnity. However, the chain of indemnities suffers from several weaknesses. Where P buys goods 'as a consumer', R cannot exclude or limit his contractual liability by reference to any contract term or notice[1]. However, R does not buy the goods as a consumer, and so D can exclude, or limit, his liability to R for breach of the statutory implied terms, provided the exclusion satisfies the test of reasonableness[2]. R may thus find that he is unable to claim an indemnity against his liability to P. Similarly, M may exclude or limit his liability to D by an appropriate term in the contract between them. The position is similar under the Consumer Guarantees Directive. It provides that where the final seller is liable to a consumer because of a lack of conformity resulting from an act or omission of another party in the distribution chain, he shall 'be entitled to pursue remedies' against that party. However, the nature of the remedies and the manner in which they may be exercised is a matter for national law[3] so (unless the UK introduces a special scheme) the retailer's right of redress will be subject to the same limitations as at present.

In addition, the indemnity chain is only as strong as its weakest link. If one of the parties in the chain cannot be traced, or becomes insolvent, the chain will break; if the retailer is insolvent, the consumer's contractual rights will be worthless.

The position of the second affected consumer, C, may be even weaker. If C buys the goods second hand from P, C may have some protection under the contract of sale, although if P does not sell in the course of a business, that protection will be extremely limited[4]. If C receives the goods as a gift from P, C has no contractual rights against anyone. The weakness of P's position is illustrated by *Daniels and Daniels v R White & Sons Ltd and Tabard*[5]. Mr Daniels purchased a bottle of lemonade from Tabard, a retailer. The lemonade was contaminated with carbolic acid and, as a result, both Mr White and his wife became ill after drinking it. Mr Daniels was able to recover damages in respect of his injuries from Mrs Tabard, on the basis that the lemonade was not merchantable. However, since Mrs Daniels was not party to the contract of sale, she could not claim compensation on that basis, and was forced to pursue a claim against the manufacturer in negligence, in which she failed.

The position is the same under the Consumer Guarantees Directive. Although earlier proposals would have enabled the 'consumer guarantee' of the quality of goods sold to be enforced not only by the initial purchaser but also by subsequent owners of the goods[6], the final text of the directive gives rights only to the initial purchaser.

There are ways in which C might be given a direct right of action on the contract of purchase. For instance, if P buys goods as a gift for C, C may be able to enforce the contract of sale under the Contracts (Rights of Third Parties) Act 1999 if either the contract expressly provides for him to do so or if, on its proper construction, it is intended that C should be able to enforce. Thus the Law Commission suggested that if P informs R that goods are being bought as a gift for C and the contract requires R to deliver them to C, a court might conclude that C is intended to be able to enforce the contract including by demanding goods of satisfactory quality and so on[7]. Alternatively, it may be possible for C to establish that P bought the goods as his agent, or, if P purported to act as agent, to ratify P's contract[8]. It may be possible for P to assign to C the benefit of his rights against R under the contract of sale[9]. It may also sometimes be possible for P to recover compensation for losses suffered by C, particularly in light of the House of Lords' decision in the *Linden Gardens* case[10]. The strength of these various arguments is however uncertain. In many cases none of them will apply. As the law stands, therefore, a consumer in C's position will often have no contractual rights of his own.

1 Unfair Contract Terms Act 1977, ss 6, 7; see 2.6.4.1.
2 Unfair Contract Terms Act 1977, ss 6, 7; see 2.6.4.1.
3 Article 4.
4 See 11.2.1.
5 [1938] 4 All ER 258.
6 See Green Paper on Guarantees for Consumer Goods and After Sales Services, European Commission (1993) Com(93)509.
7 Law Commission 242 *Privity of Contract: Contracts for the benefit of Third Parties* (1996) para 7.41, 7.42.
8 See 4.7.
9 See 2.7.
10 *Linden Gardens Trust Ltd v Lenesta Sludge Disposals Ltd* [1994] 1 AC 85, [1993] 3 All ER 417; see 2.7.

13.0.2 *Alternatives to contract claims*

Because of the limitations imposed on the effectiveness of contractual product liability by the doctrine of privity, the law has developed other methods to allow persons to recover damages for losses caused by defective products. In certain situations it may be possible to establish privity via an implied contract; alternatively, damages may be recoverable in tort, where the absence of privity will be irrelevant.

However, a contractual claim, and particularly one for breach of the statutory implied terms in the contract supply, offers the claimant a number of advantages. First, as noted earlier, a claim for breach of implied term will often be relatively easy to establish: in particular, a claim for breach of the implied term that goods should be of satisfactory quality only requires the claimant to prove the facts that the goods were sold in the course of a business, were defective, and that the defect caused his loss. Second, liability for breach of the implied terms is strict, and cannot be excluded as against a consumer. Third, the damages awarded in a claim for breach of contract may include damages for economic losses, including the reduced value of the defective goods themselves. Therefore, where the claimant can rely on a contractual claim, and especially on the implied terms, he will do so.

13.1 Tortious product liability

It was established in *Donoghue v Stevenson*[1] that, in certain circumstances, a manufacturer owes a duty of care to the ultimate user of his products, and may therefore be held liable in negligence if, as a result of negligence in manufacture, the product is defective and causes loss or injury to the consumer. In addition, a manufacturer may now incur strict liability in tort under the Consumer Protection Act 1987, implementing the 1985 European Product Liability Directive[2]. The liabilities are not co-extensive, and it is therefore necessary to consider both.

1   [1932] AC 562.
2   85/374/EEC.

13.1.1 *Liability in negligence*

Early attempts to hold manufacturers liable in tort for injuries caused by their products[1] were largely unsuccessful. Unless the product was inherently, or by its nature, dangerous, or the manufacturer was guilty of fraud, the manufacturer's only liability was in contract, and it was feared that wider liability would open the 'floodgates of litigation'.

The 'contract fallacy' was exploded in *Donoghue v Stevenson*[2], where Lord Atkin said:

> 'a manufacturer of products, which he sells in such a form as to show that he intends them to reach the ultimate consumer in the form in which they left him with no reasonable possibility of intermediate examination, and with the knowledge that the absence of reasonable care in the preparation or putting up of the products will result in an injury to the consumer's life or property, owes a duty to that consumer to take reasonable care'[3].

The decision in *Donoghue v Stevenson* was of profound importance in product liability law. '[T]he case was a recognition on the part of the judiciary of the age of mass manufacture and standardised products, an age in which the economic position of the retailer was vitally changed'[4]. Since many modern products are supplied pre-packaged, there is often little or no chance for them to be examined between leaving the manufacturer and reaching the consumer. The manufacturer will only escape liability if an intermediate examination was probable, rather than possible[5], so that he can rely on the probability of that examination to reveal the defect. 'The essential point [is] that the article should reach the consumer or user subject to the same defect as it had when it left the manufacturer'[6].

A claim in negligence is not limited by privity. A claim may be brought by a consumer-purchaser of the product, a remote purchaser, such as a second-hand buyer, a person who receives the product as a gift, a person who uses the product or even by a third party bystander injured by the product. The manufacturer's negligence may be a failure to take care in manufacture, resulting in a particular product being defective, as in *Donoghue v Stevenson* itself; alternatively, the manufacturer may be held liable for a failure to take care in design of the product, including a failure to carry out adequately careful research[7]; for a failure to carry out effective tests; for a failure to provide an effective warning of dangers[8]; or a failure to recall a product, or issue appropriate warnings if a danger becomes apparent after the product has been put into circulation[9].

Liability is not limited to the manufacturer: other parties in the distribution chain may be held liable if they can be shown to have been negligent. In *Fisher v Harrods Ltd*[10] the defendants were held liable as retail distributors for marketing a jewellery polish without first taking care to test it and establish that it, and its packaging, were safe; in *Goodchild v Vaclight*[11] importers responsible for putting goods into circulation without first testing them adequately were held negligent.

1   See eg *George v Skivington* (1869) LR 5 Exch 1; *Heaven v Pender* (1883) 11 QBD 503, CA.
2   [1932] AC 562.
3   [1932] AC 562 at 599.
4   Borrie and Diamond, *The Consumer, Society and the Law* (4th edn, 1981) p 35.
5   *Haseldine v C A Daw & Son Ltd* [1941] 2 KB 343, [1941] 3 All ER 156, CA.
6   Per Lord Wright in *Grant v Australian Knitting Mills Ltd* [1936] AC 85 at 106–107, PC.
7   *Vacwell Engineering Ltd v BDH Chemicals Ltd* [1971] 1 QB 88, [1969] 3 All ER 1681.
8   *Vacwell Engineering Ltd v BDH Chemicals Ltd* [1971] 1 QB 88, [1969] 3 All ER 1681; *Fisher v Harrods Ltd* [1966] 1 Lloyd's Rep 500.
9   *Walton and Walton v British Leyland (UK) Ltd, Dutton Forshaw (North East) Ltd and Blue House Lane Garage Ltd* (12 July 1978, unreported): see Miller and Harvey, *Consumer and Trading Law, Cases and Materials* (1985) p 159.
10   [1966] 1 Lloyd's Rep 500.
11   [1965] CLY 2669.

13.1.2   *Limitations on negligence liability*

However, despite the significance of negligence liability, and its extension since *Donoghue v Stevenson*, it is subject to a number of limitations which may restrict its effectiveness in the context of product liability. The manufacturer, or other defendant, can only be held liable where he has failed to take reasonable care, and the claimant must prove that failure to take care. The burden of proving negligence may be difficult, and expensive, to discharge. In some cases, particularly of manufacturing defects, the claimant may be able to rely on the principle res ipsa loquitur to transfer the burden of proof onto the defendant. In such cases it may be difficult for the manufacturer to avoid liability, unless he can show how the defect occurred. The manufacturer will have to show not only that he took reasonable care to establish a safe system of production and quality control to avoid defects, but also that the employees responsible for implementing that system, for whom the employer is vicariously liable, took reasonable care in implementing that system.

Where the complaint is that the product was negligently designed, the claimant's position will be considerably weaker. Expert evidence will be necessary to establish negligence, and the courts may be reluctant to impose liability for negligent design which would involve 'second guessing' executive decisions on the cost-benefit balance of different design options.

A second difficulty facing the claimant is the need to establish a causal link between the defendant's negligence and his own loss or injury. However, in this respect the claimant is in no worse position than if his claim was in contract. In practice, the difficulty of establishing causation often defeats product liability claims relating to products such as medicines and drugs.

Since the action is one for common law negligence, the manufacturer can rely on any of the defences normally available in tort: for instance, the manufacturer may be able to rely on the partial defence of contributory negligence if the claimant disregards warnings, misuses the goods, or continues to use them after a danger becomes apparent. Such facts may also be held to break the chain of causation or, in extreme cases, even allow the manufacturer to rely on the defence of volenti non fit injuria.

A further restriction on the efficacy of an action in negligence is that, although damages may be awarded for personal injuries or damage to property, damages will generally not be awarded for purely economic losses. In *Muirhead v Industrial Tank Specialities Ltd*[1] electric pumps manufactured by the defendants were fitted at the plaintiff's lobster farm. Due to failure of the pumps, the plaintiff lost his stock of lobsters and his business was out of operation for several weeks. The plaintiff succeeded in a claim for damages for the loss of the lobsters; however, a claim for lost profits on expected sales was unsuccessful.

It now seems clear that damages will rarely be awarded in negligence in respect of the reduced value of the defective product itself, or for the cost of repairs, even where they are necessary to make the product safe. In *Murphy v Brentwood District Council*[2] (a buildings liability case) Lord Keith observed that to impose liability on the manufacturer for such costs would 'open an exceedingly wide field of claims, involving the introduction of something in the nature of a transmissible warranty of quality'[3]. The restriction on claims for economic loss may lead to difficult questions as to the categorisation of the claimant's claim, particularly where a defect in one part of a product damages another part: for instance, the bursting of a defective tyre may cause a car to crash. In *Aswan Engineering Establishment Co v Lupdine Ltd*[4] Lloyd LJ tentatively suggested that in such a case the car would be regarded as a separate item of property, and thus the plaintiff's claim would be not be for economic loss, even though the tyre was part of the original equipment supplied with the car[5]. However, in *Murphy v Brentwood District Council* the House of Lords regarded it as unrealistic to regard a single item, manufactured and supplied by one person, as a 'complex structure' in which different parts are regarded as individual pieces of property.

1 [1986] QB 507, [1985] 3 All ER 705, CA; see also *Simaan General Contracting Co v Pilkington Glass Ltd (No 2)* [1988] QB 758, [1988] 1 All ER 791.
2 [1990] 2 All ER 908, HL.
3 [1990] 2 All ER 908 at 921.
4 [1987] 1 All ER 135, [1987] 1 WLR 1, CA.
5 [1987] 1 All ER 135 at 152–153.

13.1.3 Strict product liability

The need to prove negligence in order to recover damages from the manufacturer of a defective product can pose difficulties for the injured claimant. In the US the problem was overcome by the courts recognising that the manufacturer of a defective product which causes personal injury or damage to property is strictly liable for that damage. Although now set out in s 402A of the Second Restatement of Torts, which has been adopted by 45 of the 50 states, this principle of strict product liability was developed by the courts, and was justified on the policy basis that the manufacturer is the more appropriate party to bear the loss caused by defective products and, by insuring and passing on to their customers the costs of insurance, to spread that loss. Initially, the manufacturer's liability was based on a continuing contractual warranty, running with the goods[1] but it is now generally regarded as an absolute duty imposed in tort[2].

Strict tortious liability for defective products was introduced in the UK by Pt I of the Consumer Protection Act 1987. It should be noted, however, that liability under the Act exists alongside liability in negligence; in some cases a common law claim may succeed where a claim would not be available under the Act. In many cases it is to be expected that claimants will pursue statutory and common law claims in the alternative. What follows is an outline of the legislation; for detailed coverage the reader should refer to one of the specialist texts on the subject[3].

1   *Escola v Coca Cola Bottling Co of Fresno* 24 Cal App 2d 453, 150 P 2d 436 (1944); *Henningsen v Bloomfield Motors* 32 NJ 358, 161 A 2d 69 (1960).
2   *Seely v White Motor Co* 45 Cal Rptr 17 (1965); *Greenwood v Yuba Power Products* 59 Cal 2d 57, 27 Cal Rptr 697 (1963).
3   See Stapleton, *Product Liability* (1994); Howells, *Comparative Product Liability* (1993); Clark, *Product Liability* (1988); Fairest, *The Consumer Protection Act* (1987); and see Bradgate and Savage (1987) NLJ 929, 953, 1025, 1049.

13.1.4   *The Consumer Protection Act 1987 (CPA)*

Part I of the 1987 Act was passed to implement the European Community's 1985 Directive on product liability[1]. A declared objective of the directive was to harmonise the laws of member states in order to promote the free movement of goods within the Community and remove a potential obstacle to free competition. However, in order to obtain members' agreement to the provisions of the directive, it was necessary to include in it optional provisions. Different states have adopted different approaches to the optional elements, substantially undermining the objective of achieving harmonisation[2]. The optional derogations were, however, reviewed in 1995 by the European Commission, and with one exception have been retained[3]. In 1999 the Commission initiated a further review of the directive's operation by publishing a Green Paper[4] inviting comments on a number of issues, including some of the optional derogations.

Although Pt I of the Consumer Protection Act (CPA) is intended to implement the EC directive, the wording of some of its provisions differs significantly from that of the directive, and it has been suggested that it does not fully implement it. However, s 1 of the Act provides that:

> 'This part shall have effect for the purpose of making such provision as is necessary to comply with the ... Directive and shall be construed accordingly'.

The courts may therefore be able to interpret the Act so as to comply with the directive even where it does not appear to do so on its face.

A claim may be brought under the Consumer Protection Act by any person who is injured by a 'defective' product. 'Product' includes goods and electricity[5]. Where a component or raw material incorporated in a finished product is defective, both the component and the finished product are potentially defective. The definition of 'product' raises the difficult question, discussed earlier, whether computer software is a product for the purposes of the Act[6].

A product is defective for the purposes of the Act if its safety, including not only the risk of personal injury but also the risk of damage to other property, is 'not such as persons generally are entitled to expect'[7]. In assessing the safety of the product, the court is to take into account all the circumstances, but the Act refers specifically to a number of factors, including all aspects of the marketing of the product, the use of any mark in relation to the product, instructions and warnings, and what might reasonably be expected to be done with the product and the time when the product was supplied by its producer[8]. This last factor allows the court to take account of the 'state of the art' at the time of supply: the Act provides that 'nothing in this section shall require a defect to be inferred from the fact alone that the safety of a product which is supplied after that time is greater than the safety of the product in question'. It is clear that a product may be defective for the purposes of the Act as a result of a manufacturing defect, defects in design, or as a result of a failure to provide adequate instructions or warnings.

The Act imposes primary liability for defects on the 'producer' of the product, which includes[9]:

(a) the manufacturer of a finished product or of a component;

(b) a person who won or abstracted the product; and

(c) in relation to goods which were neither manufactured nor abstracted, any person responsible for an industrial or other process to which any essential characteristic of the product is attributable.

In addition, liability is imposed on:

(d) 'any person who, by putting his name on the product or using a trade mark or other distinguishing mark in relation to the product, has held himself out to be the producer' of it; this could include, for instance, a supermarket selling 'own brand' goods;

(e) any person who imported the product into the European Community; and

(f) in certain circumstances, any person who supplied the product unless he is able to identify one of the persons liable under (a)–(d) above, or his own supplier, in response to a request from a person who suffers damage caused by the product[10].

In many cases there may be more than one potential defendant liable under the Act in respect of the same damage. In that case, liability is joint and several.

The original text of the directive excluded from its scope primary agricultural produce[11]. The Act therefore imposed no liability on any person in respect of 'defects' in agricultural produce or game which had not undergone any 'industrial process' at the time that person supplied it to another[12]. However, partly as a result of concerns over food safety raised by a number of recent food scares, the directive was amended in 1999 to remove this exemption so that it does now cover agricultural produce even if at the time of supply it has undergone no processing[13]. Thus, for instance, a farmer who supplies meat infected with BSE would now potentially be liable as a producer of a defective product[14]. The amendment must be implemented by member states by 4 December 2000.

The Act sidesteps the problems of privity and foreseeability which may restrict the right to sue in contract and tort respectively. Any person injured by a defect in a product may sue. A claim may be brought in respect of death or personal injuries or damage to private property[15]; however, no claim may be brought in respect of damage to business property, or for 'pure' economic losses. In particular, the Act provides that no claim may be made for the loss of or damage to the defective product itself, 'or for the loss of or damage to the whole or any part of any product which has been supplied with the product in question comprised in it'[16]. Questions of the classification of damage, similar to those which arise in negligence, are therefore likely to arise under the Act.

Although liability under the Act is strict, a number of defences are available to a defendant. It is a defence to show:

(a) that the defect is attributable to compliance with domestic or EC legislative requirements; or

(b) that the defendant did not supply the product; or

(c) that the product was not manufactured or supplied in the course of a business; or

(d) that the defect did not exist at the time the product was put into circulation; or

(e) in the case of components, that the defect constitutes a defect in the finished product and was attributable to the design of the finished product or to compliance with instructions given by the manufacturer of the finished product[17].

In addition, defences available in a tort action, including contributory negligence and volenti non fit injuria, are available in a claim under the Act. However, liability cannot be excluded or limited by reference to any notice or contract term[18].

The most controversial aspect of the Act is the inclusion of a 'development risks' defence. This was one of the optional elements in the directive. The British government appears to have chosen to include the defence in order to avoid damaging the competitiveness of British industry and discouraging the development of new products. The Act provides that it is a defence to show:

'that the state of scientific and technical knowledge at the relevant time was not such that a producer of products of the same description as the product in question might be expected to have discovered it if it had existed in his products while they were under his control'[19].

This defence could be particularly important in relation to innovative, high-technology products and new drugs. However, it is not restricted to such areas[20].

The inclusion of the development risks defence is controversial for two reasons. First, as a matter of general policy, it undermines the principle of strict liability and lowers the level of consumer protection provided. The Pearson Committee, which recommended the introduction of a system of strict product liability in the UK in 1977, opposed the inclusion of such a defence, on the grounds that:

'to exclude development risks from a regime of strict liability would be to leave a gap through which, for example, the victims of another Thalidomide disaster might easily slip'[21].

Second, it has been argued that the wording of the UK legislation is more favourable to the producer than that of the directive. The directive permits the producer to be exempted if 'the state of scientific and technical knowledge at the time he put the product into circulation was not such as to enable the existence of the defect to be discovered'[22]. The directive therefore seems to be concerned with the state of scientific and technical knowledge generally, whereas the CPA refers to what a producer of similar products might be expected to discover. The European Commission therefore brought proceedings against the UK government for failing properly to implement the directive. The ECJ, however, held that the Commission had not established that the UK legislation would not achieve the same effect as the directive[23]. The provision in s 1(1) of the Act requiring the court to construe the Act so as to implement the directive was particularly important in this regard.

The ECJ took the opportunity to offer some guidance on the operation of the development risks defence. It confirmed that the defence is not concerned with the state of knowledge in the particular industry but with the state of scientific and technical knowledge generally, 'including the most advanced level of such knowledge'[24]. However, the court agreed with the Advocate General that knowledge is only relevant for the purposes of the defence if it is 'accessible' to European product manufacturers. This somewhat undermines the strict approach taken to the relevant standard of knowledge, although with the development of the Internet relevant knowledge will become increasingly accessible, regardless of the place where it is published. There are other difficulties. For instance, it is not clear what standard of knowledge a producer is required to act on. Scientific knowledge develops and changes over time. New ideas are introduced to challenge established knowledge; some are rejected, others become generally accepted. The court's decision therefore leaves the application of the defence little clearer than it was previously. The Commission has expressly sought feedback on the operation of the development risks defence in its 1999 Green Paper on the directive.

The basic limitation period for claims under the Act is three years from the date of damage or injury; however, since damage may not be immediately apparent, for instance in the case of injuries caused by products such as drugs, an alternative period of, effectively, three years from the date when the defendant knew, or could reasonably have known of the claim[25], is provided. Since a product may remain in circulation for many years, in order to protect manufacturers from 'open-ended' liability, there is a long-stop provision which effectively prevents any claim being brought more than ten years after the product was put into circulation[26].

---

1 85/374/EEC.
2 For a discussion of the differences in implementation see Howells, 'Product Liability: A Global Problem' (1987) 29 Managerial Law 1; 'Implication of the Implementation and Non-Implementation of the EC Products Liability Directive' (1990) 41 NILQ 22.
3 See the Commission report COM (95) 617.
4 COM (99) 36 Final.
5 CPA, s 1(2).
6 See 8.1.4; see Whittaker (1989) 105 LQR 125.
7 CPA, s 3.
8 CPA, s 3(2).
9 CPA, s 1(2)(a).
10 CPA, s 2(2).
11 Article 1. Member states were given the option to impose liability for such produce.
12 CPA, s 2(4).
13 Directive 99/34/EC.
14 Other defences might be available in appropriate cases.
15 CPA, s 5(3); no claim may be brought for property damage of £275 or less.
16 CPA, s 5(2).
17 CPA, s 4.
18 CPA, s 7.
19 CPA, s 4(1)(e).
20 See Newdick, 'The Development Risk Defence of the Consumer Protection Act 1987' (1988) 47 CLJ 455.

21 Cmnd 7054 (1977).
22 Article 7(e).
23 *EC Commission v United Kingdom* (C 300/95) [1997] All ER (EC) 481; see Hodges (1998) 61 MLR 560; Mildred and Howells (1998) 61 MLR 570.
24 [1997] All ER (EC) 481 at 495.
25 Limitation Act 1980, s 11A(4), s 14(1A).
26 Limitation Act 1980, s 11A(3).

13.1.5 *Evaluation of strict liability*

At the time of writing, over twelve years after it came into force, there are still no reported cases on the 1987 Act. It is not clear if this merely reflects the normal delays of civil litigation or indicates an unwillingness on the part of claimants or defendants to litigate the Act. Whatever the reason for it, the lack of case law makes it difficult to evaluate the impact of the Act. The initial introduction of strict product liability caused some disquiet amongst British manufacturers, who pointed to the experience of the US, where product liability awards have been so high that some manufacturers have been unable to obtain adequate insurance cover. For instance, in *Grimshaw v Ford Motor Co*[1], a case concerned with a Ford Pinto motor car found to be defective in design due to the location of the petrol tank, the plaintiff was awarded $2,842,000 compensatory damages plus $3,500,000 punitive damages; and in 1986, Ford apparently faced product liability claims for total sums in excess of $4bn[2]. Some manufacturers have responded by withdrawing products from the market altogether, and there have been some moves to return to a fault-based system.

It has been argued that the American experience does not necessarily provide an accurate indication of what may happen in the UK. In the US, unlike in England, personal injury actions are heard by juries, who are responsible for assessing damages; they naturally tend to sympathise with claimants. In addition, American courts may award punitive damages, which go beyond what is required to compensate the claimant. Moreover, the American contingency fee system, which allows a lawyer to take a case for an agreed proportion of the damages if the claim succeeds is thought to encourage litigation and lawyers to seek higher awards. In the past these have been significant differences between the American and English systems. However, the litigation culture in the UK is changing. Contingency fees where the lawyer receives a percentage of the damages are still prohibited in England, but English lawyers are now permitted to take cases on a conditional, 'no win, no fee' basis[3]. Punitive damages are not normally awarded at present, but in 1997 the Law Commission recommended that the courts should be given power to award punitive damages where the defendant's actions 'deliberately and outrageously' disregard the claimant's rights[4]. Such damages would perhaps be available where a defendant deliberately marketed a product known to be unsafe.

Nevertheless, the impact of the 1987 Act so far seems to have been less drastic than manufacturers initially feared. It is still necessary for the claimant to prove a causal link between the defect in the product and his loss or injury, and in many cases that may be difficult and expensive to establish. Further, it has been argued that the combination of the definition of 'defective', with its reference to the 'expectations' of 'persons generally', and the availability of the development risks defence may

351

mean that the standard imposed by the Act is little stricter than that imposed in negligence. If that view is correct, the Act has done little more than reverse the burden of proof.

1   119 Cal App 3d 757 (1981); the punitive damages were reduced from $125m on appeal.
2   See (1986) NLJ 645.
3   Courts and Legal Services Act 1990, s 58, as amended by the Access to Justice Act 1999, s 27.
4   Law Commission 247 *Aggravated, Exemplary and Restitutionary Damages* (1997). The Commission specifically drew on the relevant US legislation: see para 5.46, note 32.

13.1.6   *Legislative control and breach of statutory duty*

English law has for some time imposed a degree of legislative control on product safety standards. Part II of the Consumer Protection Act 1987, replacing earlier legislation[1], gives the Secretary of State extensive powers to make regulations to ensure that goods are safe by controlling the content, design, composition, packaging and so on of goods, including orders restricting their availability for sale or requiring prescribed information to be supplied with them[2]. The Act contains wide enforcement powers, allowing the Secretary of State to prohibit altogether the supply of types of goods, or to require warnings to be supplied with them[3]. Other powers are delegated to local authorities acting through their authorised officers, who may (inter alia) issue notices suspending the supply of goods for up to six months, and apply for orders for the forfeiture of goods which breach regulations[4]. It is a criminal offence to contravene regulations made under the Act[5]. Any person injured as a result of a breach of regulations made under the Act may bring a civil claim for damages on the basis of breach of statutory duty[6].

   The 1987 Act also introduced a 'general safety requirement', making it a criminal offence to supply goods which are not 'reasonably safe' having regard to all the circumstances[7]. This provision was intended to catch unsafe goods not covered by specific regulations. It has now largely been replaced by the General Product Safety Regulations 1994[8]. The regulations implement an EC directive[9] which complements the directive on product liability; where they apply s 10 of the 1987 Act is disapplied. The regulations apply to new and second-hand products, but only to products intended for or likely to be used by consumers. They impose an absolute duty on producers not to place a product on the market unless 'it is a safe product'[10]. A product is safe if 'under normal or reasonably foreseeable conditions of use' it presents no risk, or only 'the minimum risks compatible with the product's use, considered as acceptable and consistent with a high level of protection for the safety or health of persons'[11], and in assessing whether a product is thus 'safe', account is to be taken of a range of factors, including the characteristics of the product, its packaging, presentation and labelling, instructions for assembly, maintenance, use and disposal, its effect on other products with which it will foreseeably be used and 'the categories of consumers at serious risk when using the product, in particular children'. Producers are also required to provide consumers with the relevant information to enable them to assess and guard against risks inherent in the product which are not immediately obvious and to adopt measures to keep themselves informed of risks which the product might present and take appropriate steps to avoid them[12]. As under Pt I of the 1987 Act, 'producer' is given an extended definition, to include manufacturers, own branders, those who recondition products, importers responsible for bringing into the Community products manufactured outside it, and others in the distribution chain 'insofar as their activities may affect the safety properties of the product'[13]. Other distributors are subject to different duties under the Regulations, including a duty to act with due care and not to supply products which they know, or should presume, to be dangerous[14]. The regulations are enforceable by means of the mechanisms for enforcement of the 1987 Act, including prohibition notices and notices to warn[15].

1 Consumer Protection Acts 1961, 1971; Consumer Safety Act 1978.
2 CPA, s 11.
3 CPA, s 13.
4 CPA, ss 14–16.
5 CPA, s 12.
6 CPA, s 10.
7 CPA, s 41(1).
8 SI 1994/2328. See Howells [1994] LMCLQ 479; Cartwright (1995) 58 MLR 222.
9 Council Directive 92/59.
10 Regulation 7.
11 Regulation 2.
12 Regulation 8(1).
13 Regulation 2(1).
14 Regulation 9.
15 Regulation 11.

13.2 Contract-based liability

The law of negligence and the system of strict liability under the 1987 Act provide extensive protection for a person who suffers injury or damage to property caused by a defective product. However, neither system allows recovery in respect of purely economic losses; in particular, the cost of repairing a defective product is likely to be categorised as 'economic' and be irrecoverable in tort. Similarly, the claimant will be unable to recover in tort where his complaint is that the product simply fails to perform as expected. Such claims are regarded as being essentially the province of contract law. However, in some circumstances it may be possible for a consumer or user of a product to establish a direct contractual link with the manufacturer even though he did not buy direct from him.

13.2.1 *Guarantees*

Many products are supplied with a guarantee or warranty from the manufacturer. Typically, the guarantee provides that if the goods prove defective within a certain period, the manufacturer will repair or even replace them. The provision of such a guarantee may often be an important selling point in favour of the goods. Where there is such a guarantee, it may be that its provisions are contractually enforceable by the buyer. However, the status of guarantees at common law has always been unclear[1]. Where the buyer knows of the guarantee at the time of purchase, the guarantee may be a collateral contract, the consideration for which is provided by entering into the principle contract to purchase the goods. This analysis cannot apply where the consumer is unaware of the guarantee at the time of purchase although where, as often happens, the consumer returns a guarantee registration card, that may be interpreted as providing consideration for the manufacturer's promises in the guarantee.

Even where the guarantee is contractually enforceable, it will not provide the same protection as is available under the contract of sale. The contract created by the guarantee is not one of sale and the statutory implied terms are not part of it. Often the consumer will only have the rights expressly provided by the guarantee so that, for instance, he may have to bear the costs of returning the goods to the manufacturer for repair.

Although many manufacturers do offer guarantees with their products, there is no legal requirement to do so, and there is little control over the terms included in the guarantee. In the past, guarantees often contained exclusions which sought to protect the manufacturer against liability in negligence. Such guarantees often took away more than they gave. Section 5 of the Unfair Contract Terms Act 1977 now prevents a term in a guarantee excluding liability for any losses caused by a product which proves defective whilst in consumer use as a result of negligence in manufacture[2], and a guarantee is required to contain a clear indication that the buyer's statutory rights are unaffected by it[3]. However, there is no requirement that the guarantee must give any particular rights to the consumer[4]. In its 1992 consultation document, Consumer Guarantees, the DTI proposed that manufacturers' guarantees should be legally enforceable, and that manufacturers and retailers should be jointly and severally liable to honour them, but opposed requiring a guarantee to be given or prescribing the content of guarantees:

> 'Such an approach would, in the Government's view, be unnecessarily bureaucratic and run the risk of creating loopholes that could be exploited by manufacturers seeking to avoid taking responsibility for the quality of their products. . . . Such matters are best left to market forces operating in a free competitive environment'[5].

The same approach is taken by the EC Consumer Guarantees Directive[6]. It provides that a guarantee shall be binding on the person providing it in accordance with its terms and any advertising[7]. When the directive is implemented the question of the legal enforceability of guarantees will therefore be settled[8]. 'Guarantee' is defined as:

> 'any undertaking by a seller or producer to the consumer, given without extra charge, to reimburse the price paid or to replace, repair or handle consumer goods in any way if they do not meet the specifications set out in the guarantee statement or in the relevant advertising'.

The directive therefore has no application to the insurance type extended warranty which the consumer is required to pay for[9]. The giving of a guarantee remains optional, but if one is given it must: (i) state that the consumer has rights under national sales law as appropriate and that those rights are unaffected by the guarantee; and (ii) set out in 'plain intelligible language' the scope and main terms of the guarantee[10]. The content of the guarantee is otherwise a matter for the guarantor. The objective, as in existing domestic law, is to impose the minimum level of regulation to ensure the consumer is not misled whilst avoiding any unnecessary restriction on competition.

1   'Guarantees' are distinguished from the extended warranties often sold with motor cars and electrical goods. In those cases the consumer pays for the warranty. There is therefore no doubt that the warranty is contractual. Such warranties are generally a form of insurance, and the consumer's contract is with the insurer or a financial institution rather than with the retailer who sells the warranty.
2   See 2.6.4.1.
3   Consumer Transactions (Restrictions on Statements) Order 1976, SI 1976/1813.
4   The Consumer Guarantees Bill 1990, promoted by the National Consumer Council, would have made it a legal requirement that certain classes of consumer product should contain a clear statement of whether they had the benefit of a 'Consumer Guarantee', and would have prescribed the terms required to be included in a 'Consumer Guarantee'. However, the Bill would not have

made it a requirement that all goods should have a guarantee, nor that such guarantee should include statements about quality or performance of the goods. The Bill was opposed by the government and did not become law.

5 DTI 'Consumer Guarantees A Consultation Document' (1992) p 5.
6 Directive 1999/44/EC on certain aspects of the sale of consumer goods and associated guarantees.
7 Article 6.
8 Although the Directive does not say so it is assumed that the intention is that guarantees should be contractually binding. The Directive says nothing about the mechanics of enforcing rights under the guarantee.
9 See Twigg-Flesner [1999] Consum LJ 177.
10 Article 6(2). The consumer is entitled on demand to have the guarantee made available in writing or 'another durable medium': art 6(3).

13.2.2 *Collateral contracts and manufacturer's claims*

The customer's expectations of a product are often profoundly influenced by the claims made for the product by the manufacturer in promotional and advertising material. If the product fails to perform in accordance with those claims, the customer may make a claim against the supplier, relying on the contract of supply, and the manufacturer's claims may be relevant as part of the contractual description, or to the standard required in order for the goods to be of satisfactory quality. As noted earlier, the same is true under the EC Directive on Consumer Guarantees[1].

The manufacturer's statements may also be regarded as giving rise to a collateral contract between manufacturer and ultimate consumer: in that case, the consumer can enforce that contract and obtain damages direct from the manufacturer if the product fails to perform as promised. In *Shanklin Pier Ltd v Detel Products Ltd*[2] the plaintiffs were visited by a sales representative from the defendants, who extolled the virtues of the defendants' paint and claimed that, if used to paint the plaintiffs' pier, it would last at least three years. On the strength of that claim, the plaintiffs instructed their contractors to purchase and use the defendants' paint. Within three months it was necessary to repaint the pier. Although the contract for supply of the paint was not between the plaintiffs and defendants, it was held that the defendants' representations gave rise to a collateral contract, entitling the plaintiffs to claim damages.

However, although the device of the collateral contract is well established, the courts have generally been reluctant to invoke it in this context. The claimant must establish that all the requirements for the creation of a valid contract are satisfied: in particular, he must prove that the defendant's claim was intended to be contractually binding, and that he has provided consideration for that promise. Consideration will generally be provided by entering into the contract to purchase the defendant's product. However, where the manufacturer's claim is made in general advertising material, rather than directly to the claimant as in *Shanklin*, it will be difficult to establish that it was intended to be contractually binding. Of course, a manufacturer's advertising claim was held to be a contractual promise in *Carlill v Carbolic Smoke Ball Co*[3], but modern advertising claims are rarely couched in such precise terms, and are more likely to be construed as 'mere puffs'. In *Lexmead (Basingstoke) Ltd v Lewis*[4] the defendants' advertising literature claimed that a towing hitch manufactured by the defendants 'requires absolutely no maintenance, it is foolproof'. The Court of Appeal held that the language was not intended to be contractual: it was a mere puff, and so gave rise to no contractual liability.

Nor are the manufacturer's statements likely to give rise to liability in tort. If the claimant can establish that the manufacturer's claim was fraudulent, he may recover damages in deceit[5]; but where fraud cannot be proved, the relationship between manufacturer and consumer is unlikely to be close enough to give rise to a duty of care in negligence. In *Lexmead v Lewis* the Court of Appeal rejected the plaintiff's claim that the defendant manufacturers owed a duty of care in relation to their advertising claims:

> 'We cannot regard the manufacturer and supplier of an article as putting himself into a special relationship with every distributor who obtains his product and reads what he says or prints about it and so owing him a duty to take reasonable care to give him true information or good advice . . . To make such statements with the serious intention that others will or may rely on them . . . is not, in our opinion, enough to establish a special relationship with those others or a duty to them'[6].

The House of Lords in *Lexmead* left open the question whether a duty of care would exist in such a situation, but in view of recent developments in the tort of negligence generally[7], it is unlikely that a duty of care could be established[8].

The position therefore remains that, in general, it is the seller, not the manufacturer, who is primarily liable for product quality. It has been suggested here that in modern commercial conditions this is inappropriate. The significance of brands in modern commercial activity means that in many cases consumers look to manufacturers rather than retailers as guarantors of quality. Moreover, as consumers are encouraged to make use of the European Single Market and the opportunities offered by e-commerce, it may often be easier for a consumer to pursue a claim against a multinational manufacturer than against a supplier in another country[9]. It seems, however, that the question of manufacturer liability is not closed. Under the Directive on Consumer Guarantees the European Commission is required to review and report on the Directive's operation no later than July 2006, and is expressly required to report on the case for introducing direct producer liability[10].

1 Article 2(2)(d). The seller can in certain circumstances avoid liability for such statements: art 2(4). See 11.8.
2 [1951] 2 KB 854, [1951] 2 All ER 471; see also *Wells (Merstham) Ltd v Buckland Sand and Silica Ltd* [1965] 2 QB 170, [1964] 1 All ER 41.
3 [1893] 1 QB 256. See also *Bowerman v ABTA Ltd* [1996] CLC 451.
4 [1982] AC 225, CA; the point was not pursued in the House of Lords.
5 *Langridge v Levy* (1837) 2 M & W 519.
6 [1982] AC 225 at 264, CA, per Stephenson LJ.
7 See *Caparo Industries plc v Dickman* [1990] 2 AC 605, [1990] 1 All ER 568; *Murphy v Brentwood District Council* [1991] 1 AC 398, [1990] 2 All ER 908, HL.
8 For more detailed discussion of manufacturer's liability for misrepresentations in advertising, see Bradgate (1991) Anglo-Am LR 155.
9 It may be arguable that in some cases the consumer will be able to enforce guarantee rights arising under the contract of sale against all retailers forming part of a particular distribution network: see Twigg-Flesner [1999] JBL 568.
10 Article 12. See also the comments of the Law Commission, Report 242 *Privity of Contract: Contracts for the Benefit of Third Parties* at para 7.55.

Chapter 14

The Duty to Pass a Good Title

14.0 Introduction

Section 12 of the Sale of Goods Act 1979 implies three terms into the contract of sale: first, a condition that the seller has a right to sell the goods; second, a warranty that the goods are free from undisclosed encumbrances; and, third, a warranty that the buyer should enjoy quiet possession of the goods[1]. These implied terms can never be excluded or limited by any contract term[2] and the first of them is so absolutely fundamental that a breach may involve a total failure by the seller to perform the contract. The approach of the courts to this condition has been so different from that adopted in relation to the other statutory implied conditions in ss 13–15 that it deserves to be considered separately.

1 Similar terms are implied into hire purchase contracts by s 8 of SoG(IT)A 1973 and into other contracts for the supply of goods by s 2 of SGSA 1982. There are more limited terms in contracts such as hire and rental involving the transfer of possession, but not ownership, of the goods, implied by virtue of s 7 of SGSA 1982.
2 Unfair Contract Terms Act 1977, s 6, which applies to the terms in sale and hire purchase contracts; the exclusion of the terms in other supply contracts is restricted by UCTA, s 7.

14.0.1 'Property', 'title' and 'the right to sell'

We have seen that the transfer of property from seller to buyer is the essence of a contract of sale. Legally, it is the transfer of property which distinguishes sale from other transactions[1], and it has been said that 'the whole object of a sale is to transfer property from one person to another'[2]. Practically, many important consequences follow from the transfer of property[3].

Despite the legal and practical importance of the transfer of property, the language used by the Act in this connection is far from clear. The Sale of Goods Act uses the terms 'property', 'title' and 'owner', but only defines the first, and that only incompletely[4]. Section 12 is headed 'implied terms about title etc' but actually uses the word 'title' only in connection with the situation where the seller contracts to sell a limited title to the goods. In other situations, the primary requirement of s 12 is that the seller should have 'the right to sell the goods'.

It has been suggested[5] that 'ownership' refers to the 'absolute legal interest' in goods, and that when the Act refers to 'property' it refers to a title to the absolute legal interest. A contract for the sale of goods is therefore a contract by which the seller agrees to transfer to the buyer such title as he has to the absolute legal interest in the goods. However, 'title' is a relative concept. Two titles to the legal interest in any particular goods can exist at any one time, one based on ownership and another based on possession. So long as the owner of goods is in possession of them, the two titles are merged. But if A's goods are in the possession of B, both A and B have titles to the goods – A's based on ownership, B's on possession. As between them A's title is superior, but if the goods are stolen from B by C, B's possessory title is sufficient to enable B to recover the goods[6]. A person in possession of goods therefore always has a title to them, which he can sell, and a sale will transfer his title to the buyer. However, as a general rule a seller can transfer to his buyer no better title than he himself has[7]. The main effect of s 12 is to require the seller to transfer the best title to the absolute interest, and if the seller transfers less than the best title to the absolute legal interest in the goods, so that someone has a title superior to that received by the buyer, the seller is in breach of contract. However, even with this clarification, a number of questions relating to the application and effect of s 12 remain unanswered.

1   See 8.1.2.
2   Atkin LJ in *Rowland v Divall* [1923] 2 KB 500 at 505, CA.
3   See 15.0.1.
4   SoGA, s 61(1): see 8.1.2.
5   See Battersby and Preston (1972) 35 MLR 268; Ho [1997] CLJ 571. See 8.12; 9.0.
6   At common law C could not resist B's claim by asserting that A had a superior title – sometimes explained in Latin by saying C could not set up the *jus tertii* (third party right) – but this rule was abolished by the Torts (Interference with Goods) Act 1977, s 8, which does permit C to set up A's title in certain circumstances.
7   Expressed in Latin as *nemo dat quod non habet*. See ch 17.

14.1   The seller's right to sell the goods

SoGA, s 12 implies into a contract of sale a condition that 'in the case of a sale [the seller] has a right to sell the goods and in the case of an agreement to sell he will have such a right at the time when the property is to pass'. The term requires that the seller should have a right to sell, rather than that the seller should be the owner of the goods. Thus there is no breach if goods are sold by an agent with authority to sell the goods. Conversely, there is a breach even though the seller is the owner of the goods, if for any reason he has no right to sell them. In *Niblett v Confectioners' Materials Co Ltd*[1] S contracted to supply B with cans of condensed milk. The cans supplied bore labels with the brand name 'Nissly'. The Nestlé company successfully sought an injunction to prevent B selling the cans under that label, on the grounds that the label infringed their trademark. B had to remove the labels and sell the cans without labels, at a considerable discount. It was held that there was a breach of s 12(1): at the time of the passing of property, S had no right to sell the goods. 'If a vendor can be stopped by process of law from selling he has not the right to sell'[2].

The implied condition requires the seller to have a right to sell the goods at the time property is to pass. There is not necessarily a breach where the seller contracts to sell goods he does not own at the time of the contract, provided he does have a right to sell at the time property is to pass. Thus, for instance, S could contract to buy a cargo of goods at sea and then, before property passes to him, contract to resell that cargo to B. Similarly, under a conditional sale the requirement is that the seller should have a right to sell at the time when the condition is fulfilled and property is to pass to the buyer[3]. There is no breach, provided that S does have a right to sell at the time property is to pass to B[4]. Moreover, it seems that even if there is a breach because the seller has no right to sell at the time property is to pass, if the seller later acquires title to the goods, that title is fed through to the buyer, curing the breach of contract[5]. In *Microbeads AC v Vinhurst Road Markings Ltd*[6] B bought goods and was then sued for infringement of patent by X. The patent had been granted to X after the property in the goods passed to B; in contrast to *Niblett*, there was therefore no breach of the implied condition in s 12(1): S had a right to sell at the time of the contract and at the time property passed.

1   [1921] 3 KB 387, CA.
2   *J Barry Winsor & Associates Ltd v Belgo Canadian Manufacturing Co Ltd* (1976) 76 DLR (3d) 685.
3   See Bridge, 'The Title Obligations of the Seller of Goods' in Palmer and McKendrick (eds), *Interests in Goods* (2nd edn, 1998). Similarly, under a contract of hire purchase there is a statutory implied term that the supplier should have the right to sell at the time when property is to pass.
4   The seller may however be in breach of a separate express or implied term that he is owner of, or has property in, the goods at the time of the contract: see *Barber v NWS Bank Ltd* [1996] 1 All ER 906.
5   *Butterworth v Kingsway Motors Ltd* [1954] 2 All ER 694, [1954] 1 WLR 1288.
6   [1975] 1 All ER 529, [1975] 1 WLR 218, CA.

14.1.1   *The effect of breach*

The implied term in s 12(1) is a condition, so that breach allows the buyer to reject the goods and terminate the contract. However, it has been held that, in contrast with breaches of the other implied conditions, where the seller commits a breach of s 12 by selling goods to which he has no title, s 11(4) of the Act has no application, so that the buyer will not lose the right to reject on the grounds that he has accepted the goods.

The leading authority for this proposition is *Rowland v Divall*[1]. In that case B bought a car for £334 in May. In June B resold the car to X for £400. In September it transpired that the car had been stolen from O, who reclaimed it from X. B refunded the £400 paid by X and then claimed from S a refund of the £334 on the basis that there had been a total failure of consideration as a result of the breach of condition. S admitted liability for breach, but argued that there was no total failure as B and X had, between them, had some four months' use of the car and that as B could not return the car, he could not reject it. The Court of Appeal upheld B's claim and allowed a him total refund, on the ground that there was a total failure of consideration. The exact basis of the decision is, however, not clear. We have seen that rejection of goods for breach of condition allows the buyer to recover payments made on the basis of total failure of consideration. However, that claim is dependent on the buyer's rejection of the goods, and the right to reject is lost where the buyer has accepted the goods. In *Rowland v Divall* it might seem that B had accepted the car, either by lapse of time or by inconsistent act as a result of reselling to X. However, the Court of Appeal held that there could be no acceptance in the circumstances.

The three members of the Court of Appeal offered different explanations for this result. Bankes LJ held that the breach was so fundamental that there could be no acceptance: B had got nothing of what he had paid for, 'namely a car to which he would have title'. Scrutton LJ pointed out that B's inability to return the car was the result of it having been repossessed by its true owner, and was therefore the direct consequence of S's breach: 'it does not lie in the defendant's mouth to set up as a defence to the action his own breach of condition' Atkin LJ, having observed that 'the whole object of a sale is to transfer property from one person to another' said 'the buyer paid the money in order that he might get the property, and he has not got it'. He argued that s 11(1)(c) of the 1893 Act, the equivalent of s 11(4) of the 1979 Act which prevents rejection where the buyer has accepted the goods, could not apply because, since the 'whole object of a sale' is to pass title, where no title passed, the transaction was not a sale, and s 11(1)(c) only applied to sales. The court thus held that the breach of s 12 automatically resulted in a total failure of consideration, not dependent on rejection.

Both the reasoning and the result are open to criticism[2]. It is not clear why the right to reject for breach of s 12 should not be subject to the rules on acceptance just as any other breach of condition. How, for instance, is the breach more serious than if the car had suffered a serious mechanical defect resulting in its total destruction after four months? The reasoning of Atkin LJ will not stand up to scrutiny. A contract of sale is defined in SoGA, s 2(1) as one where the seller agrees to transfer the property in goods to the buyer. The fact that he fails to do so does not alter the classification of the contract as a sale. Moreover, according to the analysis suggested earlier, the seller's basic undertaking under s 2(1) is to transfer such title as he has to the general property interest in the goods. The seller in *Rowland* had done that. He was in breach of the implied condition in s 12. Finally, if we accept the reasoning that the contract was not a sale, and therefore not subject to s 11(1)(c), it was for the same reason not subject to s 12.

The result also seems unjust: B appears to have got something (four months' use of the car) for nothing[3]. By finding that there was a failure of consideration, the court ignored that benefit as not the one contracted for. However, the principle of *Rowland v Divall* has been extended and applied to allow the hirer under a hire purchase contract to recover payments made under the contract without any allowance for use or depreciation, even though, in principle at least, a hire purchase contract is initially a hire, under which the hirer pays for the use of the goods[4]. The principle was recently applied and, arguably, extended further in *Barber v NWS Bank Ltd*[5]. B agreed to acquire a car from a finance company under a conditional sale agreement which provided that property would pass when he had paid the price in full but that 'until such time the property in the goods shall remain vested in the [seller]'. After 18 months B discovered that the car was subject to a prior hire purchase agreement and that the finance company had therefore not owned it at the time the contract was made. Since this was a conditional sale agreement, the statutory implied term required that the company should have the right to sell at the time when property was to pass: there was therefore no breach of the implied term. The Court of Appeal held, however, that the assertion in the contract that 'property . . . shall remain vested in the [seller]' amounted to an express term that the seller had property at the time of the contract. That term was classified as a condition and, on breach of it, 'on established authorities[6]' B was entitled to recover all sums paid under the agreement.

The buyer's claim for breach of the s 12 condition is not limited to recovery of the price paid: where he has incurred additional expenses, they can be recovered. Thus in *Warman v Southern Counties Car Finance Corpn Ltd*[7] B took a car on hire purchase. After seven months it was discovered that the supplier did not have title to it, and it was repossessed by its true owner. B recovered not only the instalments he had paid under the agreement, but also the costs of insuring the car, minor repairs to it and the costs of defending the claim bought by the true owner.

Where goods are stolen, they may often be resold several times before the true owner discovers them and seeks to repossess them. The dispossessed owner (O) is entitled to sue in conversion any person who has dealt with the goods, but he will normally seek to recover them from the person in possession, the most recent purchaser (P). If O succeeds, P will then sue his vendor (V1), relying on s 12; V1 will, in turn, sue his own vendor (V2), and so on back up the chain of contracts until the chain breaks. Where goods are stolen, the chain will normally break with the thief, so that the loss will ultimately rest with the person who acquired the goods from the thief[8].

1   [1923] 2 KB 500.
2   Professor Bridge is particularly critical: see *The Sale of Goods* (1997) pp 391–398.
3   Contrast *Hunt v Silk* (1804) 5 East 449, where a tenant who took a lease of land from a landlord with no title to the property and no right to grant a lease, was unable to recover his rental payments because he had had the use of the property. Professor Treitel argues that the decision in *Rowland v Divall* is justified because the plaintiff was a dealer, buying for resale, and it was therefore essential for him to acquire a marketable title: Treitel, *The Law of Contract* (10th edn, 1999) p 981. See also Bridge, 'The Title Obligations of the Seller of Goods' in Palmer and Mckendrick (eds), *Interests in Goods* (2nd edn,1998) p 318.
4   *Karflex v Poole* [1933] 2 KB 251; *Butterworth v Kingsway Motors Ltd* [1954] 2 All ER 694, [1954] 1 WLR 1286.
5   [1996] 1 All ER 906.
6   [1996] 1 All ER 906 at 912, per Sir Roger Parker. *Rowland v Divall* was cited in argument but not in the judgment.
7   [1949] 2 KB 576, [1949] 1 All ER 711.
8   See *Butterworth v Kingsway Motors Ltd* [1954] 2 All ER 694, [1954] 1 WLR 1286,where P obtained an indemnity from V1 against the costs of fighting O's claim; V1 in turn obtained an indemnity from V2 against all his liabilities to P and his own costs of fighting P's claim; but note *Bankamerica Finance Ltd v Nock* [1988] AC 1002, [1988] 1 All ER 81, HL where V1 joined in V2 as second defendant to the action and the court made a Sanderson order for costs, requiring V2 to pay P's costs directly. Since V2 was insolvent, P had to bear his own costs.

14.1.2   *Proposals for reform*

The rule in *Rowland v Divall* has been criticised by many commentators. Since the buyer is allowed to recover the full price paid under the contract without account being taken of his use of the goods and any benefit he has received from them, he appears to be unjustly enriched. On the other hand, the buyer is exposed to claims by the true owner and, if the defect is discovered, his title may be unmarketable, for fear of liability under s 12 to his buyer. In 1966 the Law Reform Committee considered the problem and proposed reform, recommending that in a claim under s 12(1) the buyer should be required to give credit to his seller for his use and enjoyment of the goods[1]. The Law Commission tentatively supported such a proposal in its 1983 working paper[2]. However, in 1987 the Commission produced its final report on *Sale and Supply of Goods* and recommended, contrary to its previous views, that there should be no such reform[3]. Two factors were particularly influential. First, it was felt that valuation of the buyer's use and enjoyment of the goods would be difficult; secondly:

'although it may at first sight seem odd that a buyer should have prolonged use of an article and yet still be entitled on termination of the contract to recover its full purchase price, we have now concluded that it is no answer to this to make the buyer pay the seller for the use of someone else's goods. By definition a breach of the implied term as to title means that the goods were not the seller's to sell. What rightful claim does the seller have, therefore, to payment for the buyer's use and possession of the goods?'[4].

1   Law Reform Committee 12th Report *Transfer of Title to Chattels* (Cmnd 2958) (1966).
2   Law Commission WP 85 *Sale and Supply of Goods* (1983); see also Law Commission Report 121 *Pecuniary Restitution on Breach of Contract* (1983).
3   Law Commission 160 *Sale and Supply of Goods* (1987).
4   Law Com 160, para 6.4.; see also Birks, *An Introduction to the Law of Restitution* (1989) p 248; Goff and Jones, *The Law of Restitution* (4th edn, 1993) p 464. Despite the Law Commission's rejection of reform, the question of reversing *Rowland v Divall* was raised again by the Department of Trade and Industry in 1994: DTI *Transfer of Title: sections 21 to 26 of the Sale of Goods Act 1979* (1994).

14.1.3   Scope of the Rowland v Divall rule

Given that *Rowland v Divall* remains good law, what is its scope? The s 12 term requires the seller to have a right to sell the goods. The failure of consideration identified in *Rowland* seems to arise from the fact that the buyer does not acquire ownership of the goods. In certain circumstances, however, a buyer may acquire a good title to goods, and thus become owner, even though the seller had no right to sell them. For instance, in *Butterworth v Kingsway Motors Ltd*[1] H took goods on hire purchase terms from O. In breach of the terms of the hire purchase agreement, H sold the goods to S before completing the payments under the agreement. S resold the car to B, who used it for 11 months. During that time H continued to make payments under the hire purchase agreement. However, 11 months after B bought the car, O discovered the truth and repossessed the car; B successfully sued to recover the price he had paid to S; eight days later H made the final payment under the hire purchase agreement. Pearson J held that when H made the final payment, she acquired title and her title 'fed' that of S. He left open the question whether B would have succeeded had he made his claim after title was 'fed through' in this way. Similarly, there are situations in which, as an exception to the general rule, statutory rules may result in a buyer acquiring a better title than his seller had[2].

It is artificial to regard such cases as involving a total failure of consideration in the absence of rejection. In *Niblett v Confectioners' Materials Co Ltd*[3] Atkin LJ thought there would be no breach of s 12(1) in such a situation, but more recently, in *R v Wheeler*[4], the Court of Appeal, although not deciding the point, seems to have assumed that a buyer who innocently bought stolen goods in market overt[5], and thus acquired a good title to them, could nevertheless have rejected them for breach of s 12(1). It is submitted that this is the correct approach: there is still a breach of s 12(1) in such cases because the seller has no right to sell the goods[6]. However, *Rowland v Divall* could be distinguished as regards the available remedies on the basis that since, despite the seller's breach, the buyer acquires a good title in such a case, albeit that he does not acquire that title from the seller, there is no failure of consideration unless the buyer can and does reject the goods. The result would be that where the seller has no right to sell but the buyer nevertheless acquires a good title to the goods the buyer would be entitled to damages and to reject the goods, but that the right to reject would be lost if the buyer has accepted the goods. Similar reasoning could apply to a situation such as that in *Niblett v Confectioners' Materials*, where the seller has no right to sell but the buyer does acquire title. More difficult problems arise if the goods are consumable and are consumed by the buyer. He then acquires a title to them, not from the seller but by virtue of his consumption; and it is his consumption, rather than repossession by the original owner, which prevents restitution. However, he may still be liable to the original, dispossessed owner in conversion, so that to deny him a remedy against a seller might be unjust. Even if he is deemed to have accepted the goods, he should still be entitled to recover damages which could include the conversion damages paid to the dispossessed owner[7].

1   [1954] 2 All ER 694.
2   See ch 17.
3   [1921] 3 KB 387 at 401.
4   (1990) 92 Cr App Rep 279; see Brown (1992) 108 LQR 221. See also *Barber v NWS Bank Ltd* [1996] 1 All ER 906, above, 14.1.1, although the decision there depended on the court's interpretation of s 27(6) of the Hire Purchase Act 1964.
5   Under SoGA, s 22. The market overt rule has now been abolished by the Sale of Goods (Amendment) Act 1994: see 17.5.
6   See Atiyah, *Sale of Goods* (10th edn, 2000) pp 104–105; Goode, *Commercial Law* (2nd edn, 1995), p 298. There is a breach of the warranty in s 12(2) in such a case.
7   See Atiyah, *Sale of Goods* (10th edn, 2000) p 108, who suggests that the solution would be to allow the buyer to seek a contribution from the seller as joint tortfeasor.

14.2   Implied warranties

In addition to the implied condition in s 12(1) there are two implied warranties under s 12(2) of the Act. Since they are only warranties, breach gives rise only to a claim for damages.

14.2.1   *Freedom from encumbrances*

SoGA, s 12(2)(a) implies into a contract of sale a warranty that 'the goods are free and will remain free until the time when the property is to pass from any charge or encumbrance not disclosed or known to the buyer before the contract is made'. In practice this provision is generally of little importance. Encumbrances on goods generally are either possessory (liens and pledges) or must be registered[1]. The warranty seems to create a duty to disclose registered encumbrances of which the buyer does not have actual notice.

Such an encumbrance would impair the marketability of the buyer's title. The warranty is therefore broken by the mere existence of an undisclosed encumbrance; even if the buyer's enjoyment of the goods is not disturbed by the encumbrance holder.

1   Under the Companies Act 1985 or Bills of Sale Acts 1878–1882: see 22.0.3.1, 22.0.3.2.

14.2.2   *Quiet possession*

Section 12(2) implies a second warranty, that 'the buyer will enjoy quiet possession of the goods except so far as it may be disturbed by the owner or other person entitled to the benefit of any charge or encumbrance' disclosed or known to the buyer before the contract is made. It seems that there will be a breach if the buyer is disturbed in possession by a wrongful act of the seller or any person claiming through him, or by a lawful act of any other person, including a true, dispossessed owner of the goods[1]. There is nothing in the wording of the section to prevent the seller being held liable where the buyer's possession is disturbed by a wrongful act of a third party, but it has been accepted that the seller would not be liable in such a case[2].

Often, breach of this warranty will also involve a breach of the implied condition under s 12(1). However, unlike the implied condition, the warranty of quiet possession is a continuing warranty. Thus in *Microbeads AG v Vinhurst Road Markings Ltd*[3] the buyer of a machine was 'disturbed' by a person who had acquired a patent in respect of the goods after they had been sold to the buyer[4]. There was no breach of the condition in s 12(1) because the seller had a right to sell at the time property passed, but there was a breach of the warranty for quiet possession. Moreover, the buyer's right of action in respect of breach of warranty does not arise until he is disturbed, so that the limitation period does not begin to run against him until that time.

1 *Mason v Burningham* [1949] 2 KB 545, [1949] 2 All ER 134, CA.
2 *The Playa Larga* [1983] 2 Lloyd's Rep 171.
3 [1975] 1 All ER 529, [1975] 1 WLR 218, CA.
4 The patent had been applied for but not granted at the time of the sale.

14.3 Exclusion of liability

The implied terms in s 12 can never be excluded or limited by any contract term, regardless of whether the buyer deals as a consumer or in the course of a business. However, the seller may effectively avoid liability for breach of the implied warranties if he discloses any relevant encumbrance or charge before the contract is made. Moreover, s 12(3) provides that where 'there appears from the contract or is to be inferred from its circumstances an inference that the seller should transfer only such title as he or a third party may have' the implied terms in s 12(1) and s 12(2) are excluded and replaced by two restricted warranties that the seller has disclosed all encumbrances known to him but not to the buyer and that the buyer's possession will not be disturbed by the seller or by anyone claiming through him. This provision will apply, for example, where goods are sold by sheriff's officers or bailiffs who cannot be sure that goods they have seized from a debtor are the debtor's unencumbered property; however, it is not restricted to such situations and it seems that it is perfectly possible for a seller expressly to contract to sell only such title as he has. It is difficult to see how this can be reconciled with the absolute prohibition on the exclusion of the implied terms.

Chapter 15

The Passing of Property

15.0   Introduction

The Sale of Goods Act 1979 contains a detailed code, set out in ss 16–19, concerned with the transfer of property from seller to buyer. There are no provisions equivalent to these in the legislation applying to other contracts of supply, and it seems that under such contracts property will pass at common law when the parties intend it to pass. Some contracts, including hire purchase and work and materials, may include express terms dealing with the passing of property, but, in the absence of such terms, the intention of the parties must be inferred from the circumstances. In most cases this is likely to lead to results similar to those which would be reached under the statutory rules in the Sale of Goods Act.

One of the most striking features of the rules of English law concerned with the passing of property is that, contrary to the natural expectation, property is not necessarily linked either to delivery or possession. Thus the buyer can become owner of the goods before they are delivered to him and, conversely, the seller can retain property after delivery to the buyer. It can be argued that the provisions of the Act, based on rules developed by the common law prior to 1893, are unsuited to modern business conditions. Cranston has described them as 'highly technical, prejudicial to consumers and out of touch with what happens in practice'[1], whilst they appear to have been outpaced by modern developments in commercial practice so that their application can cause great practical difficulties.

1   Cranston, *Consumers and the Law* (2nd edn, 1984) p 166.

15.0.1   *The significance of property*

We already noted the conceptual importance attached by the law to the passing of property. The transfer of property from seller to buyer also has a number of important practical consequences in English law, as the following illustrations show:

(a) S delivers goods to B but before B pays for the goods he becomes insolvent. If property has passed, S is an unsecured creditor in B's insolvency, but if property has not passed, S is entitled to assert his property rights and repossess the goods.

(b) B pays for goods before they are delivered but, before delivery, S becomes insolvent. B can only claim the goods if property has passed to him; if not, he is an unsecured creditor.

(c) S agrees to sell goods to B but, before delivery, they are accidentally damaged. The passing of property will generally determine the passing of risk of loss or damage to the goods, so that if property has passed, B will have to pay for the goods.

(d) S agrees to sell goods to B, but B refuses to accept delivery. If property has passed, B may be able to sue for the price; if not, S may only be entitled to sue for damages for non-acceptance, in which case he must seek to mitigate his loss[1].

(e) S agrees to sell goods to B, and delivers them but, before paying for them, B sells them to X. If property had passed to B, S will be unable to recover the goods from X; but if property was still in S at the time of the sale to X, S may be able to recover them – the general rule is that only the owner of goods can dispose of them to another so as to pass a good title. However, there are exceptions to this general rule which may protect X even if B was not the owner of the goods at the time of the sale to X[2].

In English law the answers to the questions raised by all the above illustrations depend primarily on the location of property. English law therefore adopts a conceptual approach: the answers to the various questions flow from the essential concept of 'property'. In contrast, the US Uniform Commercial Code adopts a functionalist approach, offering a specific solution to each question. Such an approach allows the solution to each question to be based on considerations of policy and may avoid some of the difficulties of the English approach. However, the great merit of a conceptual approach is that it provides a basis for the resolution of new problems as and when they arise; moreover, as we shall see, in many situations English law adopts a pragmatic approach and modifies the conceptual approach by taking account of such factors as delivery and possession.

1 See 18.2.1; 18.2.2.
2 See 17.4.

15.0.2 *The classification of goods*

The distinctions drawn by the Sale of Goods Act between 'existing' and 'future' goods and between 'specific' and 'unascertained' goods have already been noted[1]. Those distinctions are crucial in the context of passing of property.

The Act does not define 'existing' goods but, by default, they must be goods which are not 'future goods'. It will be recalled that 'future' goods may be goods which are not yet in existence at the time of the contract, such as a crop to be grown, or a machine to be constructed by the seller, or goods which are in existence but not owned or possessed by the seller at the time of the contract. A contract for the sale of future goods cannot be intended to pass property to the buyer at the time of the contract, and must initially therefore be an agreement to sell[2].

'Specific goods' are goods 'identified and agreed upon at the time the contract of sale is made'[3], and 'unascertained goods' are therefore any goods which are not specifically identified and agreed upon at the time the contract is made. As we have seen, a contract may be for wholly unascertained goods, where the contract simply describes the goods in generic terms – for example '100 tons of potatoes' – or for sale of 'quasi-specific goods', that is unascertained goods from a specified source – for instance, 100 tons of potatoes to be grown on a particular field or 1,000 tons of grain from the cargo of a named ship. Many commercial contracts are for sale of unascertained goods and, particularly in international commodity trading, for sale of unascertained goods from a named source, such as a particular ship. In 1995 the Sale of Goods Act was amended by the addition of two new sections, 20A and 20B, dealing with contracts for sale of unascertained goods from an identified bulk source. Such contracts must therefore now be considered separately from those for wholly unascertained goods.

Even where the contract is for the sale of unascertained goods, the goods to be used in performance of the contract must be identified at some stage before property can pass: the goods then become 'ascertained'. However, although some rules may apply to both specific and ascertained goods, it must be stressed that goods are categorised as 'specific' or 'unascertained' at the time of the contract. If the contract is for unascertained goods, the rules applicable to specific goods have no application, even though the goods become ascertained at some later stage.

It has been suggested earlier[4] that both existing and future goods may be specific or unascertained. However, it is clear that the rules on passing of property applicable to contracts for specific goods cannot apply to specific future goods.

1   See 8.1.4.1.
2   SoGA, s 5(3).
3   SoGA, s 61(1).
4   See 8.1.4.1.

15.1   The statutory scheme

The rules about the passing of property are set out in ss 16–19 and 20A–B of the Sale of Goods Act, under the heading 'Transfer of property as between seller and buyer'. We have already seen that a contract for the sale of goods is a contract for the transfer of the general property in the goods. It seems that the effect of the provisions in ss 16–19 is to effect a transfer from the seller to the buyer of such title as the seller has to the absolute legal interest in the goods.

The basic rule is contained in s 17, which provides that property is to pass when the parties intend it to pass, and s 19 reinforces this provision by providing a specific example of party intention, where the seller reserves a right of disposal until a condition is fulfilled. However, because the parties often do not express their intention, s 18 sets out five rules of presumed intention, which may be used to ascertain the intention of the parties about the passing of property 'unless a different intention appears'. The rules in s 18 can therefore be excluded, expressly or impliedly, by the contrary intention of the parties.

Both ss 17 and 18 are subject to s 16, which provides that 'Subject to section 20A . . . where there is a contract for sale of unascertained goods no property in the goods is transferred to the buyer unless and until the goods are ascertained'. Section 20A was introduced by the Sale of Goods (Amendment) Act 1995. It deals with contracts to sell unascertained goods from a designated bulk source, and provides that, in certain circumstances, a buyer who contracts to buy unascertained goods from a designated bulk may acquire an undivided share in the bulk. Such a buyer thus acquires a property interest in the whole bulk by becoming a tenant in

367

common of the bulk. However, he acquires no property in any particular goods until the goods for his contract are ascertained.

Subject to the qualification in s 20A, the rule in s 16 is absolute and cannot be excluded, even by agreement of the parties. 'A contract to sell unascertained goods is not a contract of sale but a promise to sell'[1].

The overall effect of ss 16–20A is thus that, except in the case of a contract to sell goods from bulk, no property can pass until the goods to be used in performance of the contract are ascertained. If the contract goods are specific or ascertained, property will pass when the parties intend it to pass. If they do not expressly or impliedly indicate their intention, it will pass in accordance with the rules of presumed intention in s 18.

1 Per Lord Loreburn in *Badische Anilin Fabrik v Hickson* [1906] AC 419, HL.

15.1.1 *Equitable property interests*

As a general rule a contract to create or transfer an interest in property will, if specifically enforceable, immediately give rise to an equitable interest in the property[1]. It is generally assumed, however, that this principle has no application to contracts for the sale of goods. In *Re Wait*[2], Atkin LJ observed that ss 16–19 of the Sale of Goods Act 1893 contained a set of rules concerned with the transfer of property from seller to buyer which 'appear to be complete and exhaustive statements of the legal relations both in law and equity'[3]. He therefore concluded that the buyer under a contract for the sale of goods acquires no equitable interest in the goods prior to the transfer of property in accordance with the Act. He recognised that the parties may, expressly or impliedly, agree to create equitable rights, but no equitable rights are created by the mere fact of the agreement to sell.

These comments are generally read as indicating that a contract for the sale of goods creates no equitable property rights. However, *Re Wait* was concerned with a contract for sale of unascertained goods and it may be that Atkin LJ's comments should be restricted to that particular situation. Lord Hanworth MR, who agreed with Atkin LJ in the result in *Re Wait*, seems to have concerned himself only with contracts for sale of unascertained goods. In *The Aliakmon*[4] Lord Brandon commented that 'there is much force in the observations of Atkin LJ in *Re Wait*'[5] and quoted from them with approval. However, he also recognised that those views were, strictly, obiter and, since it was unnecessary for him to express a concluded view on the point, indicated that he was giving only his provisional view. More recently, in *Re Goldcorp Exchange Ltd (in receivership)*[6], the Privy Council held that the buyers in that case, who had contracted to buy bullion, acquired no equitable interest in any goods by virtue of their contracts. However, the contracts in that case were for wholly unascertained goods and Lord Mustill, giving the opinion of the Privy Council, said only that no equitable interest could arise in such a case[7].

It is therefore not conclusively settled that a contract for the sale of goods can never give rise to an equitable interest prior to the passing of property. However, the creation of an equitable property interest out of a contract to transfer a legal interest normally depends on the contract being specifically enforceable. The court has only a limited discretion to award specific performance of a contract for the sale of goods, and that discretion is rarely exercised. As a result, it may be that even if a contract for the sale of goods can give rise to an equitable property interest, it will do so only in exceptional cases where the contract would be specifically enforceable.

1   See *Holroyd v Marshall* (1862) 10 HL Cas 191.
2   [1927] 1 Ch 606, CA.
3   [1927] 1 Ch 606 at 636.
4   *Leigh and Sillivan Ltd v Aliakmon Shipping Co Ltd* [1986] AC 785, [1986] 2 All ER 145.
5   [1986] AC 785 at 812, [1986] 2 All ER 145 at 151.
6   [1995] 1 AC 74, [1994] 2 All ER 806.
7   [1995] 1 AC 74 at 96, [1994] 2 All ER 806 at 819.

15.2   Establishing the intention of the parties

Section 17(1) of the Act provides that 'Where there is a contract for the sale of specific or ascertained goods the property in them is transferred to the buyer at such time as the parties to the contract intend it to be transferred' and s 17(2) provides that 'For the purpose of ascertaining the intention of the parties regard shall be had to the terms of the contract, the conduct of the parties and the circumstances of the case'. In 1940 it was said that 'as the parties seldom express any such intention, or perhaps even think of it, the intention will generally be a matter of inference from the terms of the contract'[1]. In many cases this is still probably true: in particular, in many consumer sales the parties, and especially the buyer, probably give little or no thought to the passing of property, even though it may have significant legal consequences. A consumer contract will normally make express provision for the passing of property only where payment is postponed: in that case the contract will normally defer the passing of property until the price is paid, making the contract a conditional sale.

Even in non-consumer transactions the parties may give little thought to the passing of property. However, since the late 1970s there has been increased awareness of the advantages offered by a conditional sale arrangement, particularly in protecting the seller against the consequences of the buyer becoming insolvent. In *Aluminium Industrie Vaassen BV v Romalpa Aluminium Ltd*[2] the Court of Appeal recognised that a term expressly reserving ownership of goods supplied under a sale contract could give the seller effective property rights which could be exercised in the event of the buyer becoming insolvent, even where the parties expected the buyer to consume the goods in his business, or resell them, before paying for them. As a result, the insertion of such 'retention of title clauses' in contracts of sale has become commonplace, and such a clause is included in most sets of standard terms of trading.

In theory, the parties can agree to make the passing of property dependent on any condition. However, the most common condition imposed is that property will not pass until the buyer has paid for the goods and, possibly, paid other sums due to the seller. The right of the seller to impose such a condition is emphasised by s 19 of the Act, which provides that:

> 'Where there is a contract for the sale of specific goods, or where goods are subsequently appropriated to the contract, the seller may, by the terms of the contract or appropriation, reserve the right of disposal of the goods until certain conditions are fulfilled.'

Where such a condition is imposed, no property passes to the buyer, notwithstanding delivery of the goods to the buyer, until the condition is fulfilled. However, such a condition will only be effective if imposed before the property has passed to the buyer: any attempt to impose a condition after property has passed will be ineffective. In *Dennant v Skinner and Collom*[3] B bought several vehicles at auction. After they had been knocked down to him, B offered to pay by cheque, and the auctioneer insisted that, before taking the vehicles, B should sign a certificate that no property in them would pass to him until the cheque was cleared. However, property passes in an auction sale when the goods are knocked down to the buyer; the vehicles were thus already B's property and it was therefore held that the certificate was ineffective to prevent property passing.

Where the contract is for specific goods, property will pass, in the absence of a contrary intention, at the time of the contract. However, where the contract is for unascertained goods, no property can pass until the goods for the contract are ascertained, and property will not normally pass until goods are 'unconditionally appropriated to the contract'[4]. It seems that in such a case the seller can therefore reserve a right of disposal at any time up until the goods are appropriated to the contract, and this is consistent with the wording of s 19, which makes clear that the seller can reserve a right of disposal 'by the terms of the appropriation'. An appropriation subject to a reservation of title will not be 'unconditional'. Such a reservation will therefore be effective to prevent property passing, even if it is not contained in the contract and, indeed, even if the imposition of the condition is a breach of contract[5].

Even where there is no express reservation of a right of disposal, the circumstances may impliedly indicate the intention of the parties as to the passing of property. Section 19(2) provides an example of a situation where the reservation of a right of disposal is implied in the context of an international sale: 'Where goods are shipped and by the bill of lading the goods are deliverable to the order of the seller or his agent, the seller is prima facie to be taken to reserve the right of disposal'. However, other circumstances may lead to the inference that a right of disposal has been reserved. Thus an express provision about the passing of risk may be taken to indicate that property is not intended to pass until the goods are paid for, because property and risk normally pass together; and, similarly, a provision requiring the buyer to insure the goods after delivery may indicate that risk has passed and therefore suggest that property has been retained by the seller. Alternatively, although the fact that goods are sold on credit may not be enough alone to indicate that property is reserved, it may lead to that inference if the other circumstances indicate that that was the intention of the parties. In *Dobson v General Accident Fire and Life Assurance Corpn Ltd*[6] S sold jewellery and allowed B to pay by means of a building society cheque. The cheque had been stolen and was dishonoured on presentation. The Court of Appeal held that it was implicit in the circumstances that the property in the jewellery was only intended to pass in return for a valid cheque.

The question of implied reservation of ownership is particularly important in international sales, and we examine the question further below in that context[7].

1 Per Lord Wright in *Ross T Smyth & Co Ltd v Bailey Son & Co* [1940] 3 All ER 60 at 66, HL.
2 [1976] 2 All ER 552.
3 [1948] 2 KB 164, [1948] 2 All ER 29.
4 SoGA, s 18, r 5; see 15.2.3.2.
5 *Gabarron v Kreeft* (1875) LR 10 Exch 274; see Bradgate [1988] JBL 477; *Benjamin's Sale of Goods* (5th edn, 1997) para 5-104.
6 [1990] 1 QB 274, [1989] 3 All ER 927.
7 See 33.1.4; 33.2.9.

15.2.1   *Rules of presumed intention*

Where there is no express or implied indication of the parties' intention as to the passing of property, property will pass in accordance with the five rules of presumed intention laid down by s 18. The first three rules apply to contracts for the sale of specific goods. The fourth applies where goods are supplied on approval or sale or return, or similar terms. The fifth rule applies to contracts for the sale of unascertained goods or future goods by description. However, it must be stressed that these 'rules' only apply in the absence of an express or implied indication of the intention of the parties. In many cases the same result could be reached either by inferring the intention of the parties, or by applying the 'rules' in s 18.

15.3   Contracts for the sale of specific goods

Section 18 contains three rules dealing with the passing of property in specific goods.

15.3.1   *Rule 1: specific goods in a deliverable state*

Rule 1 provides that:

> 'Where there is an unconditional contract for the sale of specific goods in a deliverable state the property in the goods passes to the buyer when the contract is made, and it is immaterial whether the time of payment, or the time of delivery, or both be postponed'.

Although the rule is subject to contrary intention, it expressly indicates that such intention is not to be inferred merely from the fact that the time of delivery, or of payment, is deferred[1]. However, it has been said that 'In modern times very little is needed to give rise to the intention that the property in specific goods is to pass only on delivery or payment'[2] and the rule will be relatively easy to displace in such cases.

Rule 1 only applies where the contract is 'unconditional'. The case of *Varley v Whipp*[3] seems to suggest that a contract which contains 'conditions', ie important terms, is not 'unconditional'[4], but this cannot be correct: if it were, s 18, rule 1 would hardly ever apply, since the term implied by s 12(1) of the Act is a condition and now cannot be excluded in a domestic sale, unless the seller contracts to sell only a limited title[5] and the other statutory implied conditions cannot be excluded from consumer contracts[6]. The better view, therefore, is that 'unconditional contract' simply means that the passing of property is not subject to a condition, such as a retention of title pending payment.

Rule 1 only applies to specific goods. It was suggested earlier that future goods may be regarded as specific for certain purposes, but it is clear that future goods cannot be governed by rule 1. If they were, the seller would be in breach of the implied condition in s 12 of the Act. The parties therefore cannot intend property in future goods to pass when the contract is made and there must, implicitly, be a contrary intention that property should not pass at least until the goods are acquired by the seller, so that rule 1 is excluded. Contracts to sell future goods by description are governed by rule 5; contracts to sell specific items to be

371

acquired by the seller are not governed by any of the rules of implied intention. Subject to the comments made earlier[7], where there is a contract for the sale of specific future goods to be acquired by the seller, it may be possible to argue that the buyer acquires an equitable interest in the goods as soon as they are acquired by the seller, at least if the goods are unique so that the contract would be specifically enforceable. Alternatively, it may be that in an appropriate case the proper inference is that the parties intend property to pass to the buyer as soon as the goods are acquired by the seller.

The most important limitation on the application of rule 1 is that it only applies where the contract is for sale of specific goods in a deliverable state. Goods are in a deliverable state when they are in 'such a state that the buyer would under the contract be bound to take delivery of them'[8]. This expression has been given a restricted meaning: goods may be in a deliverable state even though they are defective, so that the buyer would be entitled to reject them. The goods are not in a deliverable state where the seller has agreed to do something to them before the seller is to take delivery under the contract: for instance, if B agrees to buy a second-hand car provided it is resprayed, the car is not in a deliverable state until it has been resprayed. The point is illustrated by the decision of the Court of Appeal in *Underwood Ltd v Burgh Castle Brick and Cement Syndicate*[9], where S contracted to sell a condensing engine weighing 30 tons. The machine was bolted to a concrete bed, and the contract required S to deliver it 'free on rail'. It was therefore necessary for S to detach the machine from its bed and dismantle it for loading. During this process the machine was damaged. It was held that property had not passed: the machine was not in a deliverable state at the time of the contract. 'A deliverable state does not depend upon the mere completeness of the subject matter in all its parts. It depends on the actual state of the goods and the state in which they are to be delivered by the terms of the contract'[10]. However, the same result could have been reached on the basis that the terms of the contract indicated the intention of the parties, that property was not to pass until the goods were loaded 'free on rail'.

The facts of *Underwood* illustrate one important consequence of rule 1. Risk of loss of, or damage to, the goods normally passes at the same time as property[11]. Thus, where rule 1 applies, risk of loss will normally pass to the buyer at the time the contract is made, even though delivery is postponed. Therefore, if the goods are accidentally damaged before delivery, the buyer will bear the risk[12]. The seller in possession will be a bailee and will therefore be liable for any loss caused by his negligence; but unless he is responsible for delaying delivery[13], he will bear no liability for purely accidental damage. Rule 1 may therefore have a particularly adverse impact on consumers: property purchased but not yet delivered is unlikely to be covered by the buyer's household insurance; it may well be covered by the seller's insurance, and certainly could be covered at little extra cost to the seller.

1 Reflecting *Tarling v Baxter* (1827) 6 B & C 360, where both delivery and payment were deferred but property, and risk, passed when the contract was made.
2 Per Diplock LJ in *R V Ward Ltd v Bignall* [1967] 1 QB 534 at 545, CA.
3 [1900] 1 QB 513.
4 It was necessary to find that property had not passed under s 18, r 1: if property had passed, as the law stood in 1900, the buyer would have lost the right to reject the goods.
5 See 14.3.
6 See ch 11 and 2.6.4.1.
7 See 15.1.1.
8 Section 61(5).

9   [1922] 1 KB 343, CA; see also *Philip Head v Showfronts Ltd* [1970] 1 Lloyd's Rep 140.
10   [1922] 1 KB 343 at 345, per Bankes LJ at 345.
11   SoGA, s 20.
12   As in *Tarling v Baxter* (1827) 6 B & C 360.
13   SoGA, s 20(2); see 16.1.2.

15.3.2   *Rule 2: specific goods not in a deliverable state*

Rule 2 is the converse of rule 1: it applies where the goods are not in a deliverable state at the time the contract is made:

> 'Where there is a contract for the sale of specific goods and the seller is bound to do something to the goods for the purpose of putting them into a deliverable state, the property does not pass until the thing is done and the buyer has notice that it has been done'.

Thus, in the example given in 15.3.1, property in the car would not pass until it had been resprayed *and* the buyer had notice of that fact. The requirement that the buyer have notice provides some measure of protection, since it allows the buyer to arrange insurance on the goods, if he so wishes. It should be noted, however, that the Act does not require the seller to give notice, it is enough that the buyer has notice.

Where a buyer does agree to buy specific goods, but asks the seller to do something to them, such as respray a car, prior to collection, the circumstances must be examined closely to decide if the agreement is that the seller must do something to the goods prior to the buyer taking delivery, or that the seller will sell the goods as they are and then do something to them.

15.3.3   *Rule 3: specific goods to be weighed (etc) to fix price*

Rule 3 applies where the contract is 'for the sale of specific goods in a deliverable state but the seller is bound to weigh, measure, test or do some other act or thing with reference to the goods for the purpose of ascertaining the price'. In that case, property does not pass until the required act has been done and the buyer has notice that it has been done. The rule only applies where the weighing (etc) is to be done by the seller, rather than by the buyer or a sub-buyer[1] and only where the weighing etc is for the purpose of fixing the price, rather than (say) testing for quality. However, where goods have to be tested for quality it may be possible to infer an intention that property is not to pass until after testing.

1   *Nanka-Bruce v Commonwealth Trust* [1926] AC 77, PC.

15.3.4   *Rule 4: goods supplied on approval or sale or return*

Rule 4 applies where goods are delivered to the buyer 'on approval or on sale or return or other similar terms'. In those cases property passes to the buyer:

> '(a) when he signifies his approval or acceptance to the seller or does any other act adopting the transaction; or

(b) if he does not signify his approval or acceptance to the seller but retains the goods without giving notice of rejection then, if a time has been fixed for the return of the goods, on the expiration of that time, and if no time has been fixed, on the expiration of a reasonable time'.

Rule 4 applies to three different types of transaction. Goods are delivered on approval when the buyer wants to check them for quality, or assess their suitability for his purpose, before buying. Goods are delivered on 'sale or return' terms where the buyer is unsure about his ability to resell them and wants freedom to return some or all of the goods. Strictly, neither arrangement is a sale, or agreement to sell, at the time of delivery. The initial contract between the parties involves a bailment of the goods coupled with the grant by the prospective seller to the prospective buyer of an option to buy the goods on the terms specified in the contract. The seller is therefore committed to sell if the buyer wants the goods, but the buyer is not committed to buy unless and until he indicates his acceptance of the goods, either expressly or by implication. If the buyer adopts the transaction by doing one of the acts stipulated by rule 4, he accepts the seller's offer, so that a contract of sale comes into existence and, at the same time, property in the goods passes to him. The arrangements offer security for both parties: the buyer is protected against the commercial risk of buying goods which are not fit for his purpose, or which he cannot sell; the seller is protected against the buyer's insolvency because, until the transaction is adopted by the buyer, the goods are the seller's property. Generally, the agreement will fix a time limit for the return of the goods: if they are retained beyond that time, property will pass to the buyer, subject to any agreement to the contrary, and the buyer will be bound to pay for the goods[1].

It may be important to distinguish sale or return/approval arrangements from other types of commercial transaction which may be outwardly similar but have different legal consequences. First, it should be emphasised that where goods are delivered on approval/sale or return, they are delivered in response to a request from the 'buyer'. If goods are delivered without such prior request, they are unsolicited and the recipient may, in some circumstances, be entitled to treat them as a gift[2]. As a result the practice of delivering unsolicited goods, which was once a popular form of 'inertia selling', is no longer common.

An approval/sale or return arrangement may be superficially similar to a conditional sale agreement. However, under a conditional sale the buyer is committed to buy the goods: the seller may repossess them in the event of non-payment but the buyer has no right to return them[3]. Property will not pass until the condition, normally payment of the price, is fulfilled. If the transaction is really a sale on approval/sale or return[4] then, in the absence of an express reservation of ownership, property will pass to the buyer automatically under rule 4, regardless of payment.

A person who receives goods on approval/sale or return terms may appear to be in a similar position to an agent. The classification of the arrangement may affect the rights of third parties who deal with the 'buyer'. All the terms of the arrangement must be examined to decide into which category it falls. The fact that the parties describe it as 'sale or return' will not be conclusive[5], but if the 'buyer' is allowed to deal freely with the goods and their proceeds and retain any profit he makes, the transaction is likely to be regarded as a true sale or return arrangement[6]; if the 'buyer' must account to the 'seller' for proceeds of resales, and is remunerated by receiving a percentage of the profits, the arrangement is more likely to be regarded as agency[7].

Many retail stores offer to exchange goods if the customer is dissatisfied or if, for example, articles of clothing do not fit. Such arrangements are not 'sale or return' transactions caught by rule 4: they are sales from the outset, so that property normally passes to the buyer at the time the contract is made, but subject to the buyer's express right to return the goods.

Where rule 4 applies, property may pass to the 'buyer' in any of the following four ways.

(a) The buyer indicates his approval or acceptance of the goods.
(b) The buyer does any act adopting the transaction. The buyer may adopt the transaction by dealing with the goods, for instance by reselling or pledging them[8], or by using them for longer than necessary to assess their suitability. However, the buyer will not be deemed to have adopted the transaction if he is prevented from returning the goods by circumstances outside his control[9].
(c) The buyer retains the goods, without rejecting them, beyond any time limit fixed for their return.
(d) Where no time limit is fixed, the buyer retains the goods beyond a reasonable time without rejecting them. What is reasonable will obviously depend on the circumstances of the case: for instance, a shorter time will be reasonable where the goods are perishable or the market for the goods is subject to fluctuation.

Even if the buyer does not expressly adopt the transaction he will, in effect, impliedly do so if he retains the goods beyond the time for their rejection without giving notice of rejection. The requirements for a valid notice of rejection were considered by the Court of Appeal in *Atari Corpn (UK) Ltd v Electronics Boutique Stores (UK) Ltd*[10]. S supplied goods to B, a retailer, under a sale or return arrangement which required B to pay in full for the goods by 30 November 1995 but gave B full rights of sale or return until 31 January 1996. Sales were poor and on 19 January 1996 B gave notice to S that it no longer intended to stock the goods, that it was recovering unsold items from its retail outlets and that, once they were recovered, it would compile a list of the items to be returned. S argued that this was ineffective as a notice of rejection because it did not specify which goods were being returned. The Court of Appeal rejected this argument. The requirements for a valid notice of rejection and the consequences of service of such a notice will depend on the terms of the agreement between the parties. Adopting a commercially realistic interpretation of the arrangement here, the court concluded that the contract between them did not require a detailed inventory for a valid notice of rejection, which would be difficult for the buyer to prepare in a case such as this, where goods had been distributed to and sold at a number of retail outlets. The terms of an effective rejection notice may be prescribed by the sale or return agreement, which may provide for the goods to be returned, to be made available for return, or simply for notice of rejection to be given by a prescribed date, but in the absence of any such requirement all that is required is a clear indication that the buyer rejects the seller's offer. The notice must specify the goods to which it relates, but unless otherwise agreed, it is sufficient if it refers to them by generic description. Service of such a notice brings to an end the buyer's right to possess and deal with the goods. The buyer does not have to physically return the goods to the seller unless the agreement so prescribes, but on rejection he must make the goods available for collection by the seller in accordance with the express or implied terms of the original supply agreement. The fact that the buyer in *Atari* did not have the goods immediately available for collection by the seller did not invalidate the notice of rejection, although if the buyer does not make the goods available for collection after serving notice of rejection he may be liable to the seller for wrongful interference with goods.

The buyer will not be deemed to have adopted the transaction by retaining the goods if he is prevented from returning them by forces outside his control. In *Re Ferrier*[11] B was prevented from returning the goods at the time fixed in the contract because they were seized, along with B's property, by a sheriff's officer who retained them for four weeks. Subsequently, B became bankrupt and his trustee in bankruptcy claimed that property had passed as a result of the retention of the goods, but it was held that B's failure to return the goods in the circumstances did not amount to retention of the goods so as to adopt the transaction.

Like all the rules in s 18, rule 4 can be excluded by contrary intention. Thus, for instance, the seller can supply goods on sale or return terms but add a reservation of ownership, so that property will not pass to the buyer until the price is paid[12].

1 The contract may require earlier payment for the goods: see *Atari Corpn (UK) Ltd v Electronics Boutique Stores (UK) Ltd* [1998] 1 All ER 1010.
2 Consumer Protection (Distance Selling) Regulations 2000, SI 2000/2334, regs 24–25.
3 Atiyah, *Sale of Goods* (8th edn, 1990) p 298 suggested that a sale subject to retention of title may be regarded as a sale on 'similar terms' to a sale on approval/sale or return. However, whilst similar principles may apply in some situations, sales subject to retention of title are not governed by s 18, r 4. See the comments in the 10th edn (2000) p 325.
4 But see *Weiner v Gill* [1906] 2 KB 574, CA, below.
5 *Weiner v Harris* [1910] 1 KB 285, CA.
6 *Re Nevill* (1871) 6 Ch App 397.
7 *Weiner v Harris* [1910] 1 KB 285.
8 *Genn v Winkel* (1912) 107 LT 434, CA. If the buyer delivers the goods to his customer on sale or return terms, he does not adopt the transaction until his customer adopts it.
9 *Elphick v Barnes* (1880) 5 CPD 321.
10 [1998] 1 All ER 1010; see Adams (1998) 61 MLR 432.
11 [1944] Ch 295.
12 *Weiner v Gill* [1906] 2 KB 574, CA.

15.4 Contracts for unascertained goods

The rules governing the passing of property under contracts for the sale of unascertained goods are probably the most important for practical purposes. The overriding rule in relation to such contracts is that in s 16, that under a contract for sale of unascertained goods, 'no property in the goods is transferred to the buyer unless and until the goods are ascertained'. Subject to this, the passing of property under contracts for sale of unascertained goods is governed by the fifth rule in s 18, which provides that:

> 'where there is a contract for the sale of unascertained or future goods by description, and goods of that description in a deliverable state are unconditionally appropriated to the contract, either by the seller with the assent of the buyer, or by the buyer with the assent of the seller, the property in the goods then passes to the buyer'.

Like the other rules in s 18, rule 5 is a rule of presumed intention and can therefore be excluded or varied by the parties. However, they cannot contract out of the fundamental rule in s 16 that no property can pass until the goods are ascertained. Since the same act will often both ascertain the goods and appropriate them to the buyer's contract, the parties can in effect postpone the passing of property but cannot advance it.

The rules in s 16 and s 18, rule 5 apply both to sales of wholly unascertained generic goods and to contracts to sell 'quasi-specific' goods – ie unascertained goods from a designated bulk source. However, their application to contracts for unascertained goods from a designated bulk source is now modified by ss 20A and 20B of the Act, and it will therefore be convenient to consider such contracts separately from contracts for wholly unascertained goods.

15.4.1 *No property can pass in unascertained goods*

Subject to the qualification in s 20A, where goods are sold from a designated bulk, the rule in s 16 that under a contract for the sale of unascertained goods no property in any particular goods can pass to the buyer until the goods are ascertained is absolute, 'for how can we speak of someone having bought goods if we cannot tell what it is that he has bought'[1]. 'Common sense dictates that the buyer cannot acquire title until it is known to what goods the title relates'[2]. The rule, which is long established, cannot be varied by agreement for '[i]t makes no difference what the parties intended if what they intend is impossible': as is the case with an immediate transfer of title to goods whose identity is not yet known[3]. There is no definition of 'ascertained' in the Sale of Goods Act, but it has been said that it means 'identified in accordance with the agreement after the time a contract of sale is made'[4].

The importance of the principle in s 16 is illustrated by the decision of the Privy Council in *Re Goldcorp Exchange Ltd*[5]. A company invited members of the public to buy gold and other bullion as an investment. Customers paid for bullion and received a certificate of ownership, which indicated the amount of bullion purchased and gave them the right to call for delivery of that quantity on seven days' notice. In the meantime, the company would store the bullion for them. Customers were told that bullion would not be set aside for individual customers but would be kept as part of the company's general trading stock; however, they were also promised that the company would at all times maintain a sufficient stock to satisfy its obligations to customers. The company broke this last promise; it went into insolvent liquidation and it was found that there was insufficient bullion to meet the claims of customers. Moreover, the bullion in stock was claimed by a bank which had taken a floating charge over the assets of the company. The customers claimed to be entitled to a share in the bullion, but their claim failed. They had acquired no property in any bullion because their contracts were for the sale of unascertained goods and the contract left the company free to supply them from any source. The same facts prevented the customers claiming an equitable interest in the bullion, by way of trust or otherwise. There can be no effective declaration of trust unless the property subject to the trust can be identified[6]. The Privy Council refused to infer a declaration of trust over the company's existing stock, as that would have inhibited the company's freedom to deal with its stock and been inconsistent with the terms of the contract. Nor could the claimants succeed in a claim for specific performance, for the same reason that their contracts were for unascertained goods[7]. They were simply unsecured creditors in the company's insolvency.

Where a buyer of unascertained goods pays for them prior to delivery he is therefore in a precarious position. He can acquire no property in any goods until the goods are ascertained. In some cases it may be possible to claim that the purchase money is held on trust for the purchaser, but only if it can be shown that the money was paid to be applied only for a specific purpose. Such a claim succeeded in *Re Kayford Ltd*[8], where a mail order supplier (unilaterally) established a trust account into which it paid moneys received from customers who ordered goods. However, in the absence of clear evidence of an intention to create a such trust, the courts are likely to be slow to infer such an intention in a normal commercial situation. An attempt by the buyers in *Re Goldcorp* to assert an equitable interest in the purchase money failed. A finding that the seller held customers' payments on trust would inhibit its ability to use the funds in its business. Moreover, the courts are generally reluctant to recognise such equitable interests in commercial transactions for they may bind third parties who may be unaware of them and subvert the prescribed order for distribution of assets on insolvency.

1   Goode, *Proprietary Rights and Insolvency in Sale Transactions* (2nd edn, 1989) p 17.
2   Per Lord Mustill in *Re Goldcorp Exchange Ltd* [1995] 1 AC 74 at 90, [1994] 2 All ER 806 at 814.
3   Per Lord Mustill in *Re Goldcorp Exchange Ltd* [1995] 1 AC 74 at 90, [1994] 2 All ER 806 at 814.
4   Per Atkin LJ in *Re Wait* [1927] 1 Ch 606 at 630.
5   [1995] 1 AC 74, [1994] 2 All ER 806; see Sealy [1994] CLJ 443; McKendrick (1994) 110 LQR 509.
6   See per Oliver J in *Re London Wine Shippers Ltd* [1986] BCC 121 at 137. There may therefore be a declaration of trust where goods are sold from a designated bulk, but not in the case of a sale of wholly unascertained goods.
7   SoGA, s 52: see 12.4.
8   [1975] 1 All ER 604, [1975] 1 WLR 279.

15.4.2   *Appropriation*

Section 16 is restrictive: under a contract for the sale of unascertained goods no property can pass until the goods to be used in performance of the contract are ascertained. However, s 16 does not say when property will pass: subject to the requirement that the goods must have been ascertained, property will pass when the parties intend it to, and in the absence of an express or implied indication of their intention, when goods of the contract description in a deliverable state are unconditionally appropriated to the contract by one party with the assent of the other, under s 18, rule 5. The same rule applies to contracts for the sale of future goods by description, including goods to be manufactured or grown by the seller.

It seems that 'description' here has the same meaning as has been given to it in recent cases under s 13, where 'description' relates to words which define essential characteristics of the goods. Thus, in order to pass property, the goods appropriated to the contract must be of the type to be sold under the contract. As under s 18, rule 1, goods are in a deliverable state when there is nothing to be done to the goods by the seller before the buyer can be required to take delivery.

The most important, and difficult, aspect of rule 5 is the requirement that the goods must be 'unconditionally appropriated' to the contract. Goods are appropriated to the contract when one party irrevocably indicates his intention to use those goods in performance of the contract, so that those particular goods are 'irrevocably earmarked' for the contract. Normally, the seller is responsible for appropriating goods to the contract; once he has done so, he is committed and cannot tender other goods in performance of the contract without the buyer's consent. In international contracts for sale of goods on CIF terms the seller is normally required to send the buyer notice of appropriation. Such a notice identifies the goods to be used in performance of the contract, and enables the buyer to deal with them, for instance by reselling them. However, appropriation does not necessarily pass property in the goods: it will only do so if it is unconditional and the other requirements of rule 5 are satisfied.

It has been said that the law on appropriation is 'not straightforward'[1]. The meaning of 'appropriation' was considered by Pearson J in *Carlos Federspiel & Co SA v Charles Twigg & Co Ltd*[2]. S contracted to manufacture and supply a consignment of bicycles to B, an importer in Costa Rica. The contract required S to ship the goods 'free on board'[3]. B paid for the goods in advance, but before they were completed, S went into receivership. The bicycles were completed and packed in crates bearing the buyer's name, but were then unpacked and the receiver refused to deliver them. B argued that property had passed: the goods had been appropriated to the contract when they were packed in the crates. Pearson J rejected that contention:

> 'To constitute an appropriation of the goods to the contract the parties must have had, or be reasonably supposed to have had, an intention to attach the contract irrevocably to those goods so that those goods and no others are the subject of the sale and become the property of the buyer'[4].

Generally, 'appropriation' will be the last act the seller has to do to perform the contract; here the last act would be the shipment of the goods. Until that time the seller might reasonably expect to be entitled to change his mind and allocate the bicycles in the crates to another contract. The acts of crating and labelling the bicycles could be regarded merely as aspects of the internal administration of the seller's business. The same rule would apply to a sale of specific future goods. 'A tradesman often finishes goods, which he is making in pursuance of an order given by one person, and sells them to another'[5].

In reaching his decision, Pearson J was forced to distinguish *Aldridge v Johnson*[6]. In that case B agreed to purchase a quantity of barley and sent 200 sacks to S for S to fill. S filled 155 sacks with barley, but then emptied them again before becoming insolvent. It was held that property had passed to B when the grain was placed in the sacks. Pearson J explained this as a case where S had made constructive delivery of the goods to B by putting the grain in the sacks. It should be remembered that appropriation will only pass property if it is assented to by the other party; where, as is often the case, the buyer assents in advance to the seller selecting the goods for the contract, the decisive question is: 'To what act of appropriation has the buyer assented?' In *Aldridge v Johnson* B had assented to S delivering by filling the sacks; in *Federspiel v Twigg* B assented to S shipping the goods.

In *Hendy Lennox (Industrial Engines) Ltd v Grahame Puttick Ltd*[7] generator sets were set aside on the seller's premises and marked with the names of the customers for whom they were intended. Staughton J held that that was insufficient to appropriate them to contracts with the named customers. However, he held that the generators were appropriated to the contracts when the sellers sent the customers invoices and delivery notes including the serial numbers of the generators to be delivered to them[8]. Thereafter, the sellers could not substitute other generators for those identified in the invoices and delivery notes; all that remained was for the buyers to take delivery.

Rule 5 provides one example of appropriation. Where the seller delivers goods to the buyer, or to a carrier or bailee for transmission to the buyer, without reserving a right of disposal, he is taken to have unconditionally appropriated the goods to the contract[9]. However, like all the rules in s 18, this is only a prima facie rule; it is displaced by contrary intention and, in particular, it does not apply if the seller reserves a right of disposal. Moreover, it is subject to the overriding rule that the goods for the buyer must be ascertained. In *Healy v Howlett & Sons*[10] S, a fish merchant based in Dublin, contracted to sell 20 cases of mackerel to B, a fishmonger in Billingsgate. S had two other customers for mackerel and loaded 190 cases of mackerel on a train for Holyhead to satisfy all three contracts; he gave instructions to the rail company at Holyhead to divide up the consignment into three separate parcels for the three customers; however, the train was delayed and by the time it reached Holyhead, the mackerel had deteriorated. B refused to pay and it was held that no property passed to B until 20 cases were appropriated to B's particular contract at Holyhead; indeed, prior to that time the 20 cases delivered to B formed an unascertained part of the whole consignment. Moreover, it would seem that even if S had loaded only 20 cases for B, the result would have been the same: the goods were consigned to S's own order at Holyhead, so that loading could not be regarded as an unconditional appropriation.

In contrast, in *Wardar's (Import and Export) Co Ltd v W Norwood & Sons Ltd*[11], S contracted to sell 600 cartons of frozen kidneys out of 1,500 cartons held in a cold store, and gave B a delivery note to obtain the kidneys. B's representative arrived at the cold store to find 600 cartons stacked on the pavement awaiting collection. It was held that the 600 cartons were appropriated to B's contract when the representative presented the delivery note and was told that the cartons on the pavement were for his contract.

In both these cases the same act makes the goods for the buyer's contract 'ascertained' and appropriates those goods to the contract. This will often be the case where the contract is to sell an unascertained part of an identified bulk. In such a case the goods for the buyer's contract can become ascertained by exhaustion, if the remainder of the bulk is discharged or delivered so that only the quantity required for the buyer's contract is left[12]. In *The Elafi*[13], Mustill J held that as soon as the buyer's goods were ascertained by exhaustion, property passed to the buyer because that was what the parties intended: there was no need for a separate appropriation.

Even where the contract is for the sale of wholly unascertained goods, the same act may both ascertain the goods and appropriate them to the contract. The act of appropriation identifies the goods to be used in satisfaction of the contract, and commits the seller to use those goods; once the goods are thus identified they will, by definition, be ascertained. However, 'appropriation' does not always pass property. In international sales on CIF terms the seller is often required to send the buyer notice of appropriation, indicating the goods to be delivered under the contract. Such a notice may refer to goods forming part of a larger bulk: for instance, S might contract to sell 500 tons of wheat and 'appropriate' to the contract 500 tons forming part of a larger bulk on board a named ship. In that case the notice commits S to deliver 500 tons of wheat from that ship; however, the wheat for the particular contract is still unascertained, and, indeed, no particular 500 tons have yet been appropriated to the contract.

Furthermore, even if the appropriation ascertains the goods for the contract, it will only pass property if it is 'unconditional', ie if the seller does not reserve a right of disposal until some condition is fulfilled[14]. Thus, for instance, even though the seller delivers the goods to a carrier for transmission to the buyer, no property will pass if the seller reserves ownership[15]; and if goods are shipped, the seller is prima facie presumed to reserve the right of disposal if he takes the bill of lading to his own order[16]. This is not a conclusive presumption: it may be rebutted if the circumstances of the case indicate that no right of disposal was reserved[17]; conversely, the fact that the bill of lading is in the seller's name may indicate that the goods are not yet appropriated to the contract at all.

The final requirement in rule 5 is that if the seller makes the appropriation, it must be assented to by the buyer; if the buyer makes the appropriation, as, for instance, where S agrees to sell ten cases of wine from his cellar and allows B to select the cases, the seller must assent. However, the Act makes clear that assent may be given expressly or impliedly, and may be given before the appropriation. In most cases the seller will make the appropriation; where the buyer orders goods to be dispatched to him, he will normally be taken to have impliedly assented in advance. The important question in such a case is to decide what act of appropriation has been assented to: only that act will be effective to pass property. For instance, in an international contract on fob terms, as in *Carlos Federspiel v Twigg*[18], the buyer assents to the goods being appropriated on shipment; if B orders goods by mail order, he impliedly assents to S appropriating goods to the contract by posting them[19].

Where the contract is for wholly unascertained goods, and is silent as to the mode or place of delivery, it may not be possible to infer advance assent. In that case an appropriation by either party will only be effective if the other subsequently assents. However, if one party has notice of the other's appropriation he may be held to have assented if he fails to object[20].

1 Per Lord Mustill in *re Goldcorp Exchange Ltd* [1995] AC 74 at 90, [1994] 2 All ER 806 at 814.
2 [1957] 1 Lloyd's Rep 240.
3 See 33.1.
4 [1957] 1 Lloyd's Rep 240 at 255.
5 Per Heath J in *Mucklow v Mangles* (1808) 1 Taunt 318.
6 (1857) 7 E & B 885; see also *Langton v Higgins* (1859) 4 H & N 402.
7 [1984] 2 All ER 152, [1984] 1 WLR 485.
8 [1984] 1 WLR 485 at 489, 495.
9 SoGA, s 18, r 5(2).
10 [1917] 1 KB 337.
11 [1968] 2 QB 663, [1968] 2 All ER 602, CA.
12 See 15.2.3.1.
13 *Karlshamns Oljefabriker v Eastport Navigation Corpn, The Elafi* [1982] 1 All ER 208.
14 By SoGA, s 19; see 15.1.1.
15 SoGA, s 18, r 5.
16 SoGA s 19(2), see 15.1.1.
17 As in *The Parchim* [1918] AC 157, PC; see 33.1.4 where this question is considered further.
18 [1957] 1 Lloyd's Rep 240, above.
19 See *Badische Anilin und Soda Fabrik v Basle Chemical Works, Bindschedler* [1898] AC 200, HL.
20 *Pignataro v Gilroy* [1919] 1 KB 459.

15.5   Sale of unascertained goods from a designated bulk

The rules just described also apply where the contract is for the sale of unascertained goods from a designated bulk source, as for instance to sell a quantity forming part of the cargo of a named ship. However, their application is now modified by ss 20A and 20B of the Sale of Goods Act, introduced by the Sale of Goods (Amendment) Act 1995.

15.5.1   *The position prior to 1995*

Prior to 1995, the rule in SoGA, s 16 meant that where a buyer contracted to buy a quantity of goods forming part of a larger bulk, he could acquire no property in any goods until the goods to be used in performance of his contract were separated out and thus ascertained. In *Re Wait*[1] W bought 1,000 tons of wheat about to be loaded on the MV 'Challenger' and, before loading, resold 500 tons of the wheat from Challenger to P. P paid for the wheat before the ship arrived, but, before it arrived and discharged its cargo, W became bankrupt. P claimed to be entitled to 500 tons of wheat, but his claim failed. The goods were still unascertained because the wheat for P's contract still formed part of the bulk cargo aboard the Challenger. The fact that the goods were unascertained prevented property passing; it also prevented P obtaining a decree of specific performance[2] or any equitable interest in the wheat. He was left to claim as an unsecured creditor in W's bankruptcy.

The court rejected the argument that an agreement to sell part of a specified bulk gave the buyer an equitable interest in the goods. Although it is possible to create an equitable interest expressly, by declaration of trust, clear words are needed to indicate an intention to declare a trust and, where the goods form an unascertained part of a larger bulk, any declaration of trust is likely to fail for lack of certainty of subject matter[3]. A declaration that a specified quantity of goods forming part of a larger, identified, bulk is held on trust will only create an equitable proprietary interest in the bulk if it can be found that the parties intended to create a tenancy in common of the whole bulk[4].

The position was similar if two or more buyers entered into separate contracts with the same seller. For instance, in *Re Wait* even if P and another buyer, say Q, had each agreed to buy 500 tons from the Challenger, so that between them they had agreed to buy the whole of the cargo, the goods for neither of their contracts would have been ascertained, and no property would have passed[5], unless it could be found on the facts that the buyers had agreed to become tenants in common of the whole bulk. Normally, such an inference would be impossible since it would mean that each purchaser acquired not a specified quantity of goods but a share in the bulk which might be greater or less than the actual amount purchased if the bulk contains more or less than it is thought to contain.

The position of a buyer of unascertained goods from bulk was in some ways better than that of a buyer of wholly unascertained goods. A buyer could acquire a share in a bulk if he contracted to buy a specified share or proportion, of the goods held in bulk, say 'half of the cargo of the MV Challenger', rather than a particular quantity. Such an agreement would give rise to a tenancy in common, the buyer (in this example) owning an undivided half share in the whole bulk, but such arrangements, involving a risk that the actual size of the bulk may be greater or less than expected, are commercially unattractive. A tenancy in common might also arise if the goods of two owners were mixed[6] so as to create a bulk, so that if, say, S agreed to sell part of a particular bulk to B and separated out the goods for B's contract but then returned them to the bulk, S and B would own the bulk as tenants in common. A tenancy in common was therefore found in *Re Stapylton Fletcher Ltd*[7]. Wine merchants sold wine to customers but retained it in store for the customers. Detailed records were kept of the wine bought by each customer and customers' wine was kept totally separate from the company's own stock. However, customers' wine was stored in stacks by type and vintage and individual cases were not marked with the names of individual customers. It was nevertheless held that the wine was sufficiently ascertained to enable property to pass when it was separated from the company's trading stock for storage. Property then passed in accordance with the intention of the parties, inferred from the terms of the arrangement, that the customers should own it as tenants in common with other buyers of the same type and vintage.

A buyer of goods from bulk might also acquire a title by estoppel. Where a person who has contracted to sell goods from bulk represents that the buyer's goods have been set aside and the buyer relies on that representation, the seller may be estopped from denying the truth of his representation[8]. However, the effect of the estoppel will only be to prevent the seller defending a claim for damages for wrongful interference with the buyer's goods; it will not actually give the buyer any proprietary interest in goods and therefore will not bind any third party[9]. Estoppel will therefore give the buyer no protection if the seller becomes insolvent.

Finally, where the contract was for the sale of goods from a designated bulk, it was possible for the buyer's goods to be ascertained by exhaustion. In *The Elafi*[10] S agreed to sell to B 6,000 tons of copra from a cargo of 22,500 tons aboard a named ship. The remainder of the cargo was sold to other buyers. B then agreed to buy a further 500 tons from one of those buyers, so that he had agreed to buy 6,500 tons of the cargo in all. The ship discharged 16,000 tons of copra in Hamburg, leaving just 6,500 tons, the quantity due to B. Part of that remaining cargo was then damaged by sea water. Mustill J held[11] that B's goods were ascertained by exhaustion when the 16,000 tons was discharged. All of the remaining cargo was then due to B, so that property could then pass to B, allowing him to claim in tort against the carrier. Goods are sufficiently ascertained for the purposes of s 16 if one buyer agrees to buy the whole of a particular bulk, even though he acquires it under separate contracts or from different sellers: 'What is needed for ascertainment is that the buyer should be able to say "Those are my goods"; this requirement is satisfied if he can say "All those are my goods" '[12].

1 [1927] 1 Ch 606 at 630, CA; see Davies [1991] JBL 105.
2 SoGA, s 52; see 12.3.
3 But see *Hunter v Moss* [1994] 3 All ER 215, [1994] 1 WLR 452. It may be that *Hunter* depends on a special rule applicable only to shares, not goods: see *Re Harvard Securities Ltd* [1997] 2 BCLC 369 at 383.
4 See per Lord Mustill in *Re Goldcorp Exchange Ltd* [1995] 1 AC 74 at 91, [1994] 2 All ER 806 at 815.
5 See *Re London Wine Shippers Ltd* [1986] PCC 121.
6 *Indian Oil Corpn Ltd v Greenstone Shipping* [1988] QB 345, [1987] 3 All ER 893; *Aldridge v Johnson* (1857) 7 E & B 885.
7 [1995] 1 All ER 192, [1994] 1 WLR 1181.
8 *Knights v Wiffen* (1870) LR 5 QB 660.
9 *Re Goldcorp Exchange Ltd* [1995] 1 AC 74, [1994] 2 All ER 806.
10 *Karlshamns Oljefabriker v Eastport Navigation Corpn, The Elafi* [1982] 1 All ER 208.
11 Following *Wait and James v Midland Bank* (1926) 31 Com Cas 172.
12 Per Mustill J in *Karlshamns Oljefabriker v Eastport Navigation Corpn, The Elafi* [1982] 1 All ER 208 at 215. The case involved a claim against a carrier. The position might have been different if the buyer had been claiming against the seller: it would then have been necessary to decide which seller supplied which goods. Commercial practice in futures dealing in commodities is to allocate sellers to buyers leaving them to arbitrate disputes.

15.5.2 *The Sale of Goods (Amendment) Act 1995*

With the modern trend to bulk storage and carriage of goods, contracts for the sale of goods from bulk became more common, especially, but not solely, in the commodity trades. The rule in SoGA, s 16, as applied in *Re Wait*, meant that the law in such situations was out of step with commercial expectations. Traders would buy and sell goods from bulk, and purport to pledge them to banks under financing arrangements, in the expectation that they were acquiring property in them. Indeed, in some other legal systems a buyer from bulk did acquire a property interest.

Thus, for instance, under the US Uniform Commercial Code[1] a person who contracts to buy goods from bulk becomes a tenant in common of the bulk. Under English law a buyer who contracted to buy goods from bulk and paid for them before delivery would normally acquire no property in any goods and would therefore be left as an unsecured creditor with little chance of recovery if, as happened in *Re Wait*, the seller became insolvent before separation of the buyer's goods from the bulk. He might also find himself bearing the risk of loss of or damage to the goods but, having no property interest in them, be unable to sue any person who negligently damaged them.

Although *Re Wait* was decided in 1927, and was frequently criticised[2], its implications did not cause great concern until the 1980s. Indeed, according to one leading oil company at the time, 'many buyers and sellers are either ignorant of these legal problems, or ignore them, so that much commerce is proceeded as if the transfer of title to part of a bulk were possible'[3]. In 1985, however, a case decided in Rotterdam by a Dutch court applying English law[4] brought the problem to the attention of the commodity trades, and one of the trade associations asked the Law Commissions to review the law. Following extensive consultation and a review of the law in England and in other jurisdictions, the Commissions concluded that English law was out of step with commercial expectations and, in this regard, inferior to the law of other jurisdictions. Prompted partly by concern that traders might choose other, more favourable, legal systems to govern their contracts, the Commissions therefore proposed reform[5]. Their objectives were to protect the pre-paying buyer of unascertained goods from a designated bulk source whilst, at the same time, not restricting trade in bulk goods. Moreover, they were concerned not to impose administrative burdens on insolvency practitioners responsible for administering property in the event of insolvency. In order to achieve these objectives, they recommended the insertion of two new sections, 20A and 20B, into the Sale of Goods Act. The essence of the Commissions' proposals was that a person who contracts to buy a specified quantity of goods from a designated bulk source and who pays some or all of the price should become a tenant in common of the bulk. The Commissions' recommendations were accepted and were implemented by the Sale of Goods (Amendment) Act 1995[6].

1   Section s 2–105(4).
2   See eg Goode, 'Ownership and Obligation in Commercial Transactions' (1987) 103 LQR 433.
3   Quoted in Law Commission Report 215 *Sale of Goods Forming Part of Bulk* (1993) para 3.3.
4   *The Gosforth* (20 February 1985, unreported): see Davenport [1986] LMCLQ 4.
5   Law Commission 215, Scot LC 145 *Sale of Goods Forming Part of Bulk* (1993); see Bradgate and White [1994] LMCLQ 315.
6   See Burns (1996) 56 MLR 260; Ulph [1996] LMCLQ 93.

15.5.2.1   *The buyer's undivided share*

Section 20A of the Sale of Goods Act now applies where there is a contract for the sale of a specified quantity of unascertained goods and:

'(a) the goods or some of them form part of a bulk which is identified either in the contract or by subsequent agreement between the parties; and
(b) the buyer has paid the price for some or all of the goods which are the subject of the contract and which form part of the bulk.'

Where the section applies, then (unless the parties agree otherwise): (a) property in an undivided share in the bulk is transferred to the buyer; and (b) the buyer becomes an owner in common of the bulk as soon as the conditions in paras (a) and (b), above, are satisfied, or at such later time as the parties may agree.

The buyer does not at this stage own any particular goods. He will acquire property in a quantity of goods in accordance with the normal rules in ss 16 and 18, rule 5 when the goods to be supplied to him are ascertained by separation from the bulk and appropriated to his contract. However, the property interest created by s 20A is sufficient to protect him against the seller's becoming insolvent before ascertainment of his goods.

Three requirements must be satisfied before s 20A can apply: (a) the contract must be for the sale of goods from an identified bulk source; (b) the contract must be for sale of a specified quantity of goods; and (c) the buyer must pay some or all of the price.

(a)   The contract must be for the sale of goods from an identified bulk source
The bulk from which the goods are to be supplied may be identified in the contract, or by later agreement between the parties[1]. Section 20A can therefore apply to a contract to supply goods from a designated bulk, and to a contract which is initially for wholly unascertained goods, provided that a bulk from which the goods are to come is subsequently identified. It will therefore cover the type of situation, common in international commodity trading, where a seller agrees to sell wholly unascertained goods and subsequently gives the buyer a 'notice of appropriation' identifying a particular vessel from which the goods are to be supplied.

'Bulk' is defined in the Act as:

'a mass or collection of goods of the same kind which —
(a) is contained in a defined space or area; and
(b) is such that any goods in the bulk are interchangeable with any other goods therein of the same number or quantity'[2].

The Law Commission suggested as examples of a 'bulk' within this definition:

(a) a cargo of wheat in a named ship;
(b) a mass of barley in an identified silo;
(c) the oil in an identified storage tank;
(d) cases of wine (all of the same kind) in an identified cellar;
(e) ingots of gold in an identified vault;
(f) bags of fertiliser in an identified storehouse;
(g) a heap of coal in the open at a specified location; and
(h) a roll of carpet from which a specified length is to be supplied[3].

The Commission expressly stated that the definition was intended to exclude a seller's general stock, in order not to inhibit a trader's right to deal with his stock in order to supply customers as he sees fit. By its nature, a trader's stock fluctuates from time to time as goods are manufactured, bought and sold. A trader who contracts to supply goods from his general stock is not normally committing himself to use his existing stock to fulfil the contract. It is submitted, however, that it cannot be an absolute rule that a sale from stock is never covered by s 20A. Where the seller has indicated that the goods to be supplied are to come from his existing stock *and nowhere else* (for instance, where the seller's stock is limited and irreplaceable), the stock could be regarded as a 'bulk' for the purposes of the Act.

(b)   The contract must be for sale of a specified quantity
The new rules only apply where the buyer contracts to buy a specified quantity of goods such as '1,000 tonnes of grain' or '100 gallons of oil'. They do not apply to contracts for the sale of a share of a bulk, expressed as a proportion, percentage or fraction. It is now expressly provided that a contract to sell an undivided share in goods *is* a contract for the sale of goods, to which the SoGA applies[4], but a person who agrees to buy 'half' of the cargo of a named ship acquires an undivided share in accordance with the general law, not under s 20A. The difference between this type of arrangement and contracts to purchase specified quantities is especially important where the bulk is found to contain a greater or smaller quantity than was originally thought. The buyer of an undivided share will share, pro rata, in any gain or shortfall, whereas s 20A contains provisions which seek to ensure that the risk of any gain or shortfall is borne first by the seller.

(c)   The buyer must pay some or all of the price
In order to take the benefit of s 20A, the buyer must have paid some or all of the price. Where he has paid only part of the price, the size of the share to which he becomes entitled is determined by the quantity of goods paid for, rather than the quantity contracted for[5]. Payment of part of the price is to be treated as payment for a corresponding part of the goods[6].

Once all three requirements are satisfied, the buyer acquires property in an undivided share in the bulk and therefore becomes an owner in common of the bulk with the seller and/or other buyers, unless the parties agree otherwise. In accordance with the general principle that property passes when the parties intend it to pass, s 20A permits the parties to agree to defer the vesting of the buyer's interest. Thus, for instance, if B contracts to buy 1,000 tonnes of grain from a particular silo and pays half of the price, but S reserves property until payment in full, B will acquire no property, the parties' express agreement ousting the rule in s 20A.

A tenancy in common of goods may take effect either in law or equity. The Law Commission described the tenancy in common created by s 20A as 'a special type of co-ownership, in relation to which the normal rules of co-ownership would be too restrictive'[7]. Although the position is not entirely clear, the better view is that it is a legal tenancy in common, albeit in many respects one sui generis[8].

1   SoGA, s 20A(1)(a).
2   SoGA, s 61(1) inserted by SoG(A)A 1995, s 2.
3   Law Commission 215, para 4.3.
4   Sale of Goods Act 1979, s 61(2).
5   Section 20A(3).
6   Section 20A(6).
7   At para 4.15.
8   Law Commission 215, para 4.15; see Ulph [1996] LMCLQ 93.

15.5.2.2   *The size of the buyer's share*

The effect of s 20A is to make the buyer owner of an undivided share of the bulk, which must be expressed as a fraction, or proportion, of the whole. However, it is assumed that by contracting for sale of a specified quantity the parties intend the seller to take the risk of any variation in the bulk quantity. The Act therefore contains a complicated scheme of rules to quantify the size of the buyer's share. According to s 20A(3):

'. . . the undivided share of a buyer in a bulk at any time shall be such share as the quantity of goods paid for and due to the buyer out of the bulk bears to the quantity of goods in the bulk at that time'.

Thus if S agrees to sell to B 500 gallons of oil from a tank containing 1,000 gallons, B becomes tenant in common with S, and they own the oil in the ratio 1:1. B is therefore entitled to an undivided half share of the whole bulk.

The size of any buyer's share depends on the ratio of the amount due to the buyer to the actual amount in the bulk at any time. The *proportion* of the bulk owned by any particular buyer may therefore fluctuate if goods are removed from the bulk, but the effect of s 20A(3) is that the quantity represented by the buyer's share will remain constant. Thus, in the above example, if S removes 250 gallons (as he is entitled to do), leaving 750 gallons in the tank, the bulk is owned jointly by S and B in the ratio 1:2. B's share of the bulk is now two thirds, but that still represents 500 gallons, the quantity due to him under his contract.

Section 20A(3) is particularly important where the bulk initially contains less, or more, than the parties thought, or where goods are lost or stolen from the bulk. So long as B removes none of the goods due to him and there remains at least sufficient oil in the tank to satisfy his contract, the fractional size of his share fluctuates, but the quantity of oil due to him remains constant. The effect is therefore that the risk of any deficiency in, or loss from, the bulk is borne first by S. In contrast, if B had originally contracted to buy a half share of the oil in the tank then so long as neither party removed any goods, B would always own a half share of the oil in the tank but the quantity represented by that share might fluctuate as a result of loss etc of oil. B would then share the risk of any loss of goods from the bulk.

The position is the same if there are several buyers, so long as the quantity in the bulk is at least sufficient to satisfy all of their contracts. Section 20A(4) governs the situation where there is more than one buyer and there are insufficient goods to satisfy all the buyers' claims[1]. It provides that where the aggregate of the shares of all the *buyers* calculated in accordance with s 20A(3) would exceed the quantity of goods actually in the bulk, each buyer's share is reduced proportionately so that the aggregate of the undivided shares is equal to the whole bulk. Suppose, therefore, that S sells 500 gallons to B and 250 gallons each to C and D from a bulk thought to contain 1,000 gallons but which is subsequently discovered in fact to contain only 800 gallons. Their shares calculated in accordance with s 20A(3) would be 10/16, 5/16 and 5/16. Since it is mathematically impossible for them collectively to own more than 16/16, the presumptive shares of B, C and D are reduced proportionately, by s 20A(4), so that they still own the 800 gallons in the ratio 2(B): 1(C): 1(D). As against each other they therefore own shares representing 400, 200 and 200 gallons respectively. The proportionate shares of the buyers inter se thus remain constant. It is clear, however, that s 20A(4) is no more than a device to prevent the new rules creating a mathematical impossibility. The new provisions draw a sharp distinction between property and contract rights and s 20B(3)(c) states that nothing in ss 20A or 20B affects 'the rights of any buyer under his contract'. B, C and D therefore remain contractually entitled to demand delivery from S of the full amount due to each of them, and each may sue for short delivery if he receives less than the quantity contractually due. So long, therefore, as S remains solvent the contractual rights remain paramount. Moreover, as against each other, B, C and D are entitled to take delivery of the quantity due to them under their respective contracts.

1 If there is only one buyer but insufficient in the bulk to satisfy his contract, he will own the whole bulk, subject to any agreement to the contrary. If there was insufficient to satisfy his contract when it was made, the contract will actually be for specific goods unless it can be argued that the contract is void for mistake, either at common law or under SOGA s 6: see 16.2. If the shortfall arises after the contract is made his goods will be appropriated to his contract by exhaustion: see 15.5.2.3. below.

15.5.2.3 *Delivery of goods from bulk*

So long as the goods remain in bulk, the buyer remains a tenant in common of the whole bulk but does not own any particular goods. Once the particular goods to be delivered to him are ascertained by separation from the bulk property in them will pass to the buyer in accordance with the normal rules applicable to contracts for unascertained goods, either by their being unconditionally appropriated to his contract, or otherwise in accordance with the intention of the parties. However, as noted earlier[1], since under a contract for sale of goods from bulk the seller can only supply in performance of his contract goods from the designated bulk, the rule at common law was that the buyer's goods could be ascertained by exhaustion where the quantity in the bulk was reduced to, or to less than, the quantity due to the buyer under his contract[2]. This rule is now confirmed by s 18, rule 5(3), which provides that where there is a contract for the sale of goods from a bulk identified either in the contract or by later agreement and the bulk is reduced to, or to less than, the quantity due to the buyer under his contract then, provided that the buyer is the only buyer to whom goods are then due out of the bulk, the remaining goods are to be taken as being appropriated to the buyer's contract and property in them passes to the buyer. The same rule applies even if the buyer's entitlement arises under two or more separate contracts so long as he is entitled to the whole of the goods remaining in the bulk[3].

As noted earlier, where the buyer pays for only part of the goods due to him under his contract, the size of his share is determined by the quantity paid for. Any delivery to him of goods from the bulk is then treated first as being in respect of the goods represented by his undivided share[4].

1 See 15.5.1.
2 *Karlshamns Oljefabriker v Eastport Navigation Corpn, The Elafi* [1982] 1 All ER 208.
3 As in *The Elafi*: see s 18, r 5(4).
4 Section 20A(5).

15.5.2.4 *Dealings with goods in bulk*

At common law, where a tenancy in common arises each co-owner is entitled to a share in the whole of the co-owned property, and requires the consent of the other co-owners to deal with all or any part of it. The Law Commissions recognised that this rule would be inappropriate in a commercial context where it is vital that each co-owner should be able to deal freely with his share of the goods. SoGA, s 20B therefore contains provisions to facilitate dealings in goods in bulk. It provides that each person who becomes a co-owner by virtue of s 20A is deemed to consent to:

'(a) any delivery of goods out of the bulk to any other owner in common of the bulk, being goods which are due to him under his contract; and

(b) any removal, dealing with, delivery or disposal of goods in the bulk by any other person who is an owner in common of the bulk *in so far as the goods fall within that co-owner's undivided share in the bulk at the time of the removal, dealing, delivery or disposal*' (emphasis added).

For the purposes of this section, 'delivery' is given an extended meaning and includes 'such appropriation of goods to the contract as results in property in the goods being transferred to the buyer'[1]. Thus when goods are separated out from the bulk and appropriated to the buyer's contract, they are deemed to be delivered for this purpose.

Section 20B(2) further provides that no cause of action accrues against any person who acts in accordance with the deemed consents and s 20B(3) provides that (in the absence of a contract provision to the contrary) nothing in the Act is to require any buyer from bulk to compensate any other buyer from the same bulk for any shortfall in the quantity he receives.

The effect of s 20B(1)(a) is that any buyer is entitled to remove the quantity due to him under his contract, even if he in fact takes more than the amount represented by his share calculated in accordance with the rules in s 20A, for instance because the bulk contains less than it was thought to contain. For instance, suppose that S sells 500 gallons of oil each to B and C from a bulk thought to contain 1,000 gallons but which in fact contains only 800 gallons. B and C own the bulk in the ratio 1:1. The quantity represented by each of their shares is 400 gallons. However, each is deemed by s 20B(1)(a) to consent to the other taking delivery of the quantity due to him under his contract. C remains contractually entitled to demand delivery of 500 gallons from S. The position appears to be the same if B has only paid for part of the quantity contracted for, in which case his share in the bulk under s 20A would be less than 50%, for under s 20B(1)(a) C is deemed to consent to B taking delivery of the quantity due to him *under his contract*.

The effect of s 20B(1)(a) as between the co-owning buyers can be summarised as 'first come, first served'. A co-owning buyer who takes delivery of goods from the bulk is entitled to retain them, even if it later proves that the bulk is inadequate to supply the shares of all the co-owners. The Law Commissions considered, and deliberately rejected, the options of requiring a buyer who took delivery in such a situation to return some of the goods, or to compensate any other buyer. Such a scheme would be unnecessarily complex, would burden insolvency practitioners and would be commercially unattractive[2].

Section 20B(1)(a) does not apply to a seller who remains a co-owner, since it only applies where a co-owner removes goods 'due to him *under his contract*'. Delivery of goods to the original seller is covered by s 20B(1)(b), under which each person who has become a co-owner by virtue of s 20A is deemed to consent to any 'removal, dealing with, delivery or disposal of goods in the bulk' by any other co-owner 'so far as the goods fall within that co-owner's undivided share' at the time of the transaction. So if S contracts to sell to B 500 gallons from a bulk thought to contain 1,000 gallons but which in fact contains only 800 gallons, the bulk is owned by B and S in the ratio 5:3. B consents to S withdrawing the quantity which falls within his undivided share – in this case, 300 gallons, so that S will be liable to B if he withdraws more than that amount.

Section 20B(1)(b) also covers the situation where any tenant in common – seller or buyer – sells or otherwise deals with his share of the bulk. Each co-owner is deemed to consent to every other dealing with the goods so far as they fall within that co-owner's undivided share. This provision may prove problematic where, for any reason, the seller has sold more shares than the bulk can support. Suppose, for instance, that, as above, S sells 500 gallons of oil each to B and C from a bulk thought to contain 1,000 gallons but which, in fact, contains only 800 gallons. If B contracts to resell to D 'my share' in the bulk, D will acquire B's interest in the goods in accordance with the common law. Suppose, however, that B contracts to resell to D the 500 gallons thought to be due to him under his contract. The quantity represented by B's share is only 400 gallons. C is deemed to consent to B dealing with the goods only insofar as the goods fall within B's undivided share. However, so long as the goods remain in bulk D will only acquire a property interest if the requirements of s 20A are satisfied. If so, he will become a co-owner in accordance with the rules in s 20A and the size of his share will be determined in accordance with s 20A(3) and (4) and applying the formula in s 20A(4) D will be entitled to an equal share in the bulk with C. As a result D's interest after the sale will be the same as B's before it. A resale by B of the quantity presumed to be due to him under his contract will therefore be covered by the deemed consent in s 20B(1)(b), even if that quantity exceeds the quantity actually represented by B's undivided share. Moreover, since D here becomes a co-owner by virtue of s 20A, he will be covered by s 20B(1)(a) so that, as between C and D, each is deemed to consent to the other taking delivery of the quantity due to him under his contract.

The objective of s 20B is to facilitate dealings in goods in bulk and, in the event of the seller's insolvency, to enable an insolvency practitioner to distribute the goods to the buyers interested in the bulk in accordance with their contractual entitlements, without the need for complicated adjustments. However, difficult problems may arise where a seller has, whether fraudulently or inadvertently, sold more shares than the bulk can support. For instance, suppose that S sells to B and C 500 gallons each from a bulk believing it to contain 2,000 gallons but which in fact contains only 1,000 gallons. The sales therefore exhaust S's property interest in the goods. If S now contracts to sell a further 500 gallons to D, can D take a share in the bulk? The answer will depend on the application of SoGA, s 24, which contains an exception to the general rule *nemo dat quod non habet* and which is considered in Chapter 17. Suffice it to say here that D's entitlement will depend, inter alia, on whether he acted in good faith and without notice of S's lack of property. In order to determine whether D is entitled to a share in the bulk it may therefore be necessary to investigate the circumstances surrounding the sale to him, something which the Law Commissions were keen to avoid.

1   Section 61(2).
2   Law Commission Report 215, paras 4.22–4.32. It remains possible for the parties to vary this rule by mutual agreement and provide contractually for adjustment of shares inter se in the event of shortfall.

15.5.2.5   *Evaluation*

Sections 20A and 20B offer some protection to a buyer who contracts to buy goods from bulk and to that extent have improved the law, especially in relation to commercial dealings from bulk in the commodity and similar trades. However, the scope of the sections is limited. They have no application where the contract is for wholly unascertained goods and no agreement is made to satisfy the contract from any particular bulk source. The buyers in *Re Goldcorp* would therefore not be protected by the new provisions. Indeed, since a sale from stock is generally not a sale from bulk, the provisions will rarely protect consumers, something which the

Law Commissions expressly recognised[1]. Given the growth in mail order and distance selling of all kinds, especially boosted by the development of e-commerce, there is an urgent need to devise some method to protect consumers and others who contract for wholly unascertained goods and pay for them prior to delivery in order to boost and maintain commercial confidence[2]. However, any such protection must be considered in the context of the general law of insolvency and not merely as part of the law of sale.

More generally, the provisions in ss 20A and 20B leave a number of questions still to be worked out. There is, for instance, no express provision for the situation where some of the goods in the bulk are damaged or deteriorate. Section 20B(3)(c) does say that nothing in ss 20A or 20B is to affect the rights of any buyer under his contract, so that as against the seller each remains entitled to receive goods which conform to his contract. The sections, however, make no provision for the rights of the buyers against each other in such a case. Presumably, the 'first come, first served' principle applies and any buyer who receives defective goods will be left to his contractual rights against the seller. In particular, oversales, where a seller for any reason sells more shares than a bulk can support, will give rise to difficult problems which remain to be worked out. It may be that in such situations the provisions do not achieve the Law Commission's objective of practical simplicity.

1   Law Commission Report 215, para 4.3
2   A consumer who pays for goods by credit card may in some circumstances be protected by s 75 of the Consumer Credit Act 1974: see 26.5.1.

Chapter 16

Risk, Frustration and Mistake

16.0   Introduction: the meaning of 'risk'

Where ownership or possession of property is transferred, the question arises who should bear the risk of any loss of or damage to the property? There are important rules in the Sale of Goods Act designed to answer that question.

'Risk' in this context has a very limited meaning. Any commercial operation involves risks. Some of those risks may be allocated between the parties by the terms of the contract. For instance, in a sale, the seller bears the risk that the goods are of satisfactory quality, but, where the buyer does not deal as consumer, he may exclude his liability under the implied quality term and throw this risk onto the buyer[1]. In general the buyer bears the risk of defects in the goods: caveat emptor, except in so far as he is protected by the terms of the contract. Thus the buyer bears the risk that the goods might not be suitable for his purpose, unless he has made his purpose known to the seller and reasonably relied on the seller's skill or judgment[2]. The seller bears the risk that the buyer may not pay; each party takes the risk that changes in market conditions may make the contract less profitable than anticipated.

The 'risk' we are concerned with here is the risk of deterioration of or damage to the goods; it includes accidental damage and damage caused by third parties[3]. If such risk falls on the seller, he cannot deliver the goods if they are destroyed, or deteriorate or are so damaged that they become of unsatisfactory quality . He must find replacement goods in order to perform his contract; if the contract is for specific goods, he will be unable to use other goods, and, unless the goods can be repaired and delivered in time to perform the contract, he will be unable to deliver. If the risk falls on the buyer, he must take delivery and accept and pay for the goods even though they have deteriorated, been damaged or even destroyed.

Essentially, therefore, the allocation of risk of loss or damage to one party means, commercially, that that party should insure the goods against such loss. It also means that that party must perform his obligations under the contract, despite the deterioration, etc, in the goods. If he fails to do so, he will be liable for breach of contract, unless his performance is excused. Whether or not performance is excused depends on the rules relating to frustration of the contract, which are closely connected to the rules concerned with the passage of risk, and deal with deterioration etc of the goods between the making of the contract and the passing of risk which makes performance of the contract impossible. Where the deterioration occurs before the contract is made, there is no question

392

of 'risk'; however, the relevant rules, the equivalent of those applying to cases of mistake, are closely linked to those concerned with frustration, and are therefore examined below.

1   Unfair Contract Terms Act 1977, s 6; see 2.6.4.1.
2   SoGA, s 14(3); see 11.3.
3   See generally Sealy, '"Risk" in the Law of Sale' [1972] 31 CLJ 255.

16.1   The transfer of risk

The general rule in English law is that the risk of loss of or damage to property falls on its owner. The rule is often expressed in Latin as *res perit domino*. The Sale of Goods Act adopts this principle and applies it to sale transactions so that risk of loss, damage or deterioration passes from seller to buyer together with property:

> 'Unless otherwise agreed, the goods remain at the seller's risk until the property in them is transferred to the buyer, but when the property in them is transferred to the buyer the goods are at the buyer's risk whether delivery has been made or not'[1].

Risk is therefore linked to ownership, regardless of possession, and it is important to remember that the rules on passing of property mean that ownership and possession can be, and often are, separated.

In order to decide who bears the risk of loss in any particular case, it is therefore essential first to decide if property has passed; the location of risk was at issue in many of the cases concerned with the passing of property examined in Chapter 15[2]. If S sells specific goods to B to be collected later, property will pass to B when the contract is made; the goods will therefore be at his risk from that time and if S's premises are destroyed in a fire, B must still pay for the goods. Conversely, if S delivers goods subject to a retention of title, prima facie he also retains the risk of loss or damage. If S sells unascertained goods, no property can pass to B until the goods are ascertained and therefore S bears the risk of loss up to that time. Where goods are delivered on approval or on sale or return terms, they remain at the seller's risk until the buyer adopts the contract; if the goods are accidentally damaged before then, the buyer is entitled to return them[3].

In many cases the natural expectation might be that the risk of loss or damage would fall on the person in possession of the goods. The linking of risk and ownership, coupled with the complex and sometimes artificial nature of the rules concerned with the passing of property, means that the risk of loss is often thrown onto a person who is not insured against it. However, the rule in s 20, res perit domino, is only a prima facie rule: it is modified in a number of situations with the result that the law does, to some degree, take account of fault and possession in allocating risk.

1   SoGA 1979, s 20.
2   Eg *Healy v Howlett* [1917] 1 KB 337; *Underwood Ltd v Burgh Castle Brick and Cement Syndicate* [1922] 1 KB 343, CA; *Wardar's (Import and Export) Co Ltd v Norwood & Sons Ltd* [1968] 2 QB 663, [1968] 2 All ER 602, CA; *Philip Head v Showfronts Ltd* [1970] 1 Lloyd's Rep 140.
3   *Elphick v Barnes* (1880) 5 CPD 321.

16.1.1   *Contrary intention*

The rule in s 20 is expressed to apply 'unless otherwise agreed'. It is therefore always possible to make provision in the contract for the allocation of risk. Where goods are supplied on conditional sale terms, including where goods are supplied subject to a retention of title clause, it is common for the contract to provide, expressly, that, although property does not pass to the buyer until payment, the goods are to be at the buyer's risk from delivery. Often the contract will expressly require the buyer to insure the goods: provided that he bears the risk of loss he has sufficient insurable interest to claim under a policy of insurance[1]. Similarly, hire purchase contracts will normally provide that the goods supplied are at the buyer's risk from the time of delivery.

Even if the basic rule is not expressly excluded, the court may be able to find that the circumstances impliedly indicate a contrary agreement to exclude it. In the common forms of international sale contracts there are established commercial customs as to the time when risk passes. Thus in a sale on fob terms it is presumed that the parties intend the risk to pass on loading[2], and in cif contracts risk passes to the buyer as from the time the goods are shipped, even though property may not pass, and even though the contract is not made, until later[3]. An implied intention as to the passing of risk may also be found in a particular contract. Thus in a sale of specific goods where delivery is postponed it may be possible to infer that the passing of risk is also postponed. In *Sterns Ltd v Vickers Ltd*[4] S owned 200,000 gallons of spirit, which was stored in a storage tank by T, a bailee. S agreed to sell 120,000 gallons of the spirit to B and gave him a delivery order for that quantity, and T accepted that delivery order. However, B did not arrange to collect the spirit immediately but postponed delivery for several months; when he did draw off the spirit it was found that it had deteriorated, and B claimed that it was unmerchantable. Until the contract quantity was drawn off, no property could pass to B because the contract goods were unascertained. However, the Court of Appeal held that risk passed to B when T accepted the delivery order: S had then done everything he had to do to fulfil his obligations under the contract and thereafter T held the spirit on behalf of S and B in the proportion 8:12.

Sterns Ltd v Vickers Ltd shows that risk can pass, on the basis of implied agreement, even where the goods form an unascertained part of an identified bulk[5]. The principle of that case has been approved by the House of Lords[6]; however, it was stressed that *Sterns* was exceptional:

> 'It is difficult to see how a parcel is at the buyer's risk when he has neither property nor possession except in such cases as *Inglis v Stock* and *Sterns v Vickers* where the buyer had an interest in an undivided part of a bulk parcel on board a ship or elsewhere, obtained by attornment of the bailee to him'[7].

The principle could not apply where the goods remain wholly unascertained. Thus in *Healy v Howlett*[8] S loaded 190 boxes of fish on a train and consigned them to his own order; the fish deteriorated before the seller instructed the railway company to allocate 20 boxes to the buyer's contract. The fish was still at the seller's risk at the time of deterioration: at that time the seller had not yet appropriated any of the fish to any particular contract. In *Sterns*, S had appropriated the contents of the storage tank to his contract with B and given B the means to obtain delivery.

Provided that he had paid at least part of the price, the buyer in *Sterns v Vickers* would now own an undivided share in the spirit in the tank by virtue of SoGA, s 20A. Where s 20A applies it is not clear whether risk passes to the buyer when he acquires his undivided share, or only later when he acquires property in particular goods by ascertainment and appropriation. There is nothing in the new provisions, or in the Law Commissions' proposals on which they are based, to deal specifically with the point. Applying the principle of *res perit domino,* and on the authority of *Sterns,* it could be argued that risk of loss should pass to the buyer from the time when he acquires his undivided share. However, SoGA, s 20B(3) states that 'Nothing in this section or section 20A . . . shall . . . (c) affect the rights of any buyer under his contract'. In their report the Commissions explained that:

> 'The interim co-ownership of the bulk is intended to be without prejudice to the buyers' contractual rights. They would still be entitled to delivery of goods which conformed to the contract in quantity and quality.'

The better view therefore seems to be that the seller alone bears the risk of any loss of or damage to the goods in bulk, notwithstanding the buyer's acquisition of an undivided share, until particular goods are delivered to the buyer by being appropriated to his contract, at which time their conformity with the contract is assessed[9]. Risk might pass to the buyer before separation of his goods from the bulk, in accordance with *Sterns v Vickers,* if the buyer is responsible for delivery being delayed and that delay causes the loss of or damage to the goods. If the whole bulk is destroyed or is so damaged or deteriorated that the goods cease to conform to the contract the contract may be frustrated, as discussed below[10].

1 *Inglis v Stock* (1885) 10 App Cas 263, HL; see 35.1.3.
2 See 33.1.5.
3 See 33.2.10.
4 [1923] 1 KB 78.
5 See also *Inglis v Stock* (1885) 10 App Cas 263.
6 In *The Julia* [1949] AC 293, [1949] 1 All ER 269.
7 Per Lord Porter at [1949] AC 293, 312, [1949] 1 All ER 269, 276. It might be better to explain *Sterns* as a case where the arrangement indicated an implied intention that risk was to pass to the buyer.
8 [1917] 1 KB 337, see 15.5.2.
9 Cf *Benjamin's Sale of Goods* (5th edn, 1997) para 6-045.
10 See 16.2.1.

16.1.2 *Risk where delivery is delayed*

Section 20 recognises two other situations where the normal rule on risk is modified. Where delivery is delayed through the fault of either party, 'the goods are at the risk of the party at fault as regards any loss which might not have occurred but for such fault'[1]. Thus if on Monday S sells specific goods to B and agrees to deliver them to B's home on Wednesday, property prima facie passes to B at the time of sale. However, if S fails to deliver as agreed, he bears the risk of any loss 'which might not have occurred but for' the delay.

The application of s 20(2) is illustrated by *Demby Hamilton & Co Ltd v Barden*[2]. S agreed to sell to B 30 tons of apple juice, to correspond with an agreed sample. S crushed the apples and put the juice in casks to await collection. It was not yet appropriated to the contract because the contract required B to give directions as to delivery to B's customers. B delayed in giving instructions for delivery, and when the juice was collected it was discovered that the juice had 'gone off'. It was held that property had not passed to B, but, applying s 20(2), that B should bear the risk of the deterioration which had resulted from his delay.

It seems clear that s 20(2) applies to impose on the party in default the risk of deterioration and accidental damage to the goods. It is not clear who bears the burden of proof that the loss in question was caused by the delay. The section refers to 'loss which might[3] not have occurred but for the delay'. It is not clear if this throws the burden on the party on default to prove that the delay did not cause the loss, or if it merely reduces the burden on the innocent party. In *Demby*, Sellers J did not decide the point but said that 'I think that all the facts and circumstances have to be looked at in very much the same way as a jury would look at them in order to see whether the loss can properly be attributed to the failure of the buyer to take delivery'[4]. However, he did add that even though s 20(2) throws the risk of such losses on the party in default, the innocent party must act reasonably and avoid loss if possible. Presumably, a failure to act reasonably to avoid the loss will break the causal link between the default and the loss[5]. In *Demby,* S could not sell the juice to another customer: in order to correspond with the agreed sample, all of the juice for B had to be made from the same batch of apples.

1   SoGA, s 20(2).
2   [1949] 1 All ER 435.
3   The first draft of the 1893 Act had 'would' rather than 'might'.
4   [1949] 1 All ER 435 at 438.
5   Where the seller is left in possession of the goods, as in *Demby,* he is entitled to charge the buyer a reasonable amount for his care and custody of the goods, and the buyer must compensate him for any losses caused by the failure to take delivery: SoGA, s 37.

16.1.3   *Duties as bailee*

Section 20(3) provides that 'Nothing in this section affects the duties or liabilities of either seller or buyer as bailee or custodier of the goods of the other party'. Thus if S sells specific goods for later delivery, even if property and risk pass at the time of the contract, the seller is a bailee of the goods until delivery, and owes the duties of a bailee. Similarly, if goods are delivered subject to a retention of title, even if risk is retained by the seller, the buyer is in the position of a bailee[1].

A bailee is normally only liable for loss caused by his negligence[2]. A bailee is thus not liable for wholly accidental damage to the goods or for deterioration which could not be avoided by taking reasonable care. However, the burden is on the bailee to prove that he did take reasonable care, and a bailee may be vicariously liable for the acts of his employees or agents to whom the goods are entrusted. Moreover, the bailee must abide by the terms of the bailment: if he deviates from the agreed terms, he is strictly liable for loss. Thus if S agrees to store goods for B pending delivery and agrees to keep them in his shop, he is strictly liable for any loss if he stores the goods, instead, in his warehouse.

If the buyer fails to take delivery at the date fixed by the contract, the seller's position is not clear. He may be regarded as an involuntary or gratuitous bailee, and therefore owe a lower duty of care than a voluntary bailee. However, the Act allows the seller in such a case to charge a reasonable sum for his care of the goods[3], and the better view seems to be that he should be regarded as a voluntary bailee[4]. The seller must therefore take reasonable care of the goods; but the buyer must bear the risk of loss or damage caused by the delay but not caused by the seller's negligence.

Although the position is not clear, it is submitted that a failure by one party, acting as bailee, to take care of the goods only entitles the other to claim damages in respect of the damage to the goods. Thus if the seller remains in possession of the goods after risk has passed to the buyer, and the goods are damaged due to the seller's negligence, the buyer cannot reject the goods or refuse to pay. In such a situation, risk will already have passed to the buyer, and the seller may be regarded as having made constructive delivery of the goods. Section 20(3) merely preserves the liability which would arise in bailment at common law.

1   A person who receives goods on sale or return, or on approval, is also a bailee. However, a careless act which damages the goods may operate to adopt the transaction and pass property and risk.
2   See generally 8.2.4.
3   SoGA, s 37.
4   See *Benjamin's Sale of Goods* (5th edn, 1997) para 6-019; *Chalmers' Sale of Goods* (18th edn, 1981) p 158.

16.1.4   *Goods in transit*

Transport exposes the goods to special risks: for instance, they may be damaged in an accident, or deteriorate due to delay. It is therefore important to decide who bears the risk of such losses. The position is covered by ss 32–33, which further modify the rules relating to the passing of risk where the goods are damaged whilst being carried to the buyer.

Section 32(1) provides that where the seller is 'authorised or required', in pursuance of the contract of sale to send the goods to the buyer, 'delivery of the goods to a carrier . . . for the purpose of transmission to the buyer is prima facie deemed to be a delivery of the goods to the buyer', so that the seller will then have fulfilled his basic duty to deliver under s 27 and the buyer will be deemed to be in possession. In addition, delivery to the carrier may appropriate the goods to the contract and pass property, and therefore risk, unless the seller reserves a right of disposal[1].

Thus where s 32 applies, the carrier is deemed to be the buyer's agent, and the goods are at the buyer's risk while in transit. However, this is a prima facie rule: where the contract provides for delivery at some specified place, the seller does not deliver until the goods are handed over at that place; if he employs a carrier to get the goods to the delivery point, the carrier is the seller's, not the buyer's, agent, s 32 does not apply[2] and the goods are at the seller's risk until they reach the delivery point. It is therefore crucial, when considering who bears the risk of damage or deterioration in transit, to decide what is the delivery point under the contract. For instance, where goods are sold 'free on board' (FOB) the seller delivers the goods by loading them onto a ship for transmission to the buyer[3]; the buyer bears the risks of sea transport. However, until the goods cross the ship's rail, the goods are at the seller's risk, so that if the goods are damaged while being transported by road to the port, the risk falls on the seller: s 32(1) has no application.

Where the seller does deliver, in accordance with s 32(1), by delivering the goods to a carrier for transmission to the buyer, and the seller arranges the contract of carriage, s 32(2) requires him to make such contract as is 'reasonable having regard to the nature of the goods and the circumstances of the case'. If the seller fails to make a reasonable contract and the goods are lost or damaged in transit, the buyer may decline to treat delivery to the carrier as delivery to himself[4]: in that case, the seller has not delivered until the goods reach the buyer, so that they can be rejected if the effect of the damage is to make them not of satisfactory quality; alternatively, the buyer may claim damages for the seller's breach.

Failure to make a reasonable contract therefore puts the risk of loss in transit on the seller. The contract may be unreasonable because, for instance, the seller selects an unreasonably slow method or route, the carrier's facilities are unsuitable for the goods, or the terms of the contract are unreasonable or unusual. In *Thomas Young & Sons v Hobson*[5] S contracted to sell goods 'free on rail'. S contracted with the railway company for the goods to be carried at owner's risk; they could have been carried at carrier's risk for the same price, subject to examination by the railway company. It was held that the contract was unreasonable.

In addition, where goods are carried by sea, the seller must provide the buyer with sufficient information to enable the buyer to insure the goods in transit; if not, the goods are at the seller's risk during transit[6].

Where the seller agrees to deliver the goods, at his own risk, at some place other than where they are at the time of the sale – for instance, because he agrees to deliver them at the buyer's premises – s 32(1) cannot apply: the carrier is the seller's agent to make delivery. However, s 33 provides that 'the buyer must nevertheless (unless otherwise agreed) take any risk of deterioration in the goods necessarily incident to the course of transit'. This provision is probably only of limited application in modern conditions. As Professor Goode observes:

> 'at the time of the case law from which s 33 was derived, travel and transportation were much more hazardous affairs. Everyone knew that the roads were badly built, that a coach was liable to be held up by highwaymen, that sailing ships might be diverted and sunk in a storm'[7].

Modern transport is generally faster and safer; refrigeration and sophisticated packaging may protect the goods in transit. Moreover, it should be noted that the section only protects the seller against deterioration caused by the ordinary risks of transit: it will not protect him in respect of loss caused by his own carelessness.

Even where goods are at the buyer's risk in transit, whether under s 32 or s 33, it should be remembered that if goods are despatched in such a condition that they cannot survive the ordinary rigours of transport, they are not of satisfactory quality[8].

1   SoGA, s 18, r 5(2).
2   See *Dunlop v Lambert* (1839) 6 Cl & Fin 600, HL.
3   See 33.1.2.
4   It seems that this applies even if the loss is not caused by the seller's breach.
5   (1949) 65 TLR 365, CA.
6   See s 32(3); 33.1.5.
7   Goode, *Commercial Law* (2nd edn, 1995) p 265.
8   *Mash and Murrell Ltd v Joseph I Emanuel Ltd* [1961] 1 All ER 485, [1961] 1 WLR 862. It is assumed that this principle applies to the situation covered by s 33: see *Benjamin's Sale of Goods* (5th edn, 1997) para 6-015.

16.1.5 *Risk and rejection*

The provisions concerned with the passing of risk are primarily concerned with its passage from seller to buyer. However, where the buyer lawfully rejects the goods, for instance, for breach of condition, the effect may be to pass the risk of loss back to the seller. Although the position is not clear, it seems that the fact that the goods have deteriorated or been accidentally damaged after delivery will not prevent the buyer rejecting them, either in accordance with an express term of the contract or for breach of condition[1]. Thus it seems that where risk passes to the buyer, it does so conditionally, subject to his right to reject the goods.

The Law Commission considered whether this rule should be changed so as to prevent rejection unless the goods were in substantially the same state as when delivered. However, it was pointed out that the condition of the goods might change before rejection even though the buyer acted reasonably: for instance, perishable goods deteriorate constantly; and some goods, such as carpets or furniture kits, must be fitted or assembled to be used. A limitation on rejection would adversely affect the interests of consumers in such cases, and it was therefore recommended that there should be no change in the existing law[2].

If the buyer does reject, risk reverts to the seller. However, the buyer will be a bailee of the goods until they are collected and must take reasonable care of them.

The EC Directive on Consumer Guarantees is similarly silent on questions of risk[3]. It is possible for member states implementing the directive to provide for any refund due to the buyer in the event of rescission of the contract to be reduced to take account of any use the consumer has had of the goods[4]. It is not clear if such reduction could extend to accidental damage to the goods whilst in the buyer's possession. The directive also fails to deal with the important question who bears the risk of loss of or damage to the goods where they are returned to the seller for repair in accordance with its provisions. The logic of the principle *res perit domino* might suggest that, as between the seller and the consumer buyer, the buyer should bear the risk of loss whilst the goods are in transit *to* the seller, unless they are collected by the seller's agent. Whilst they are in the seller's possession for repair the seller will be liable as a bailee for negligent loss of or damage to the goods. The seller should also owe the buyer a duty of care in returning the goods after repair, although the buyer would remain at risk of purely accidental loss.

1   *Head v Tattersall* (1871) LR 7 Exch 7; above 12.1.3. Similarly, accidental damage will not prevent the buyer returning goods delivered on approval or sale or return terms: *Elphick v Barnes* (1880) 5 CPD 321.
2   Law Commission Report 160 *Sale and Supply of Goods* (1987), para 5-40.
3   Directive 1999/44/EC of the European Parliament and of the Council of 25 May 1999 on certain aspects of the sale of consumer goods and associated guarantees (1999) (OJ L171/12, 7 July 1999). See 12.5.
4   Recital 15.

16.1.6   *Property, risk and insurance*

The general rule in English law is that risk of loss is linked to property rather than to possession. However, it is possible for risk to be separated from both. In commercial contracts the possibility that risk may fall on a person who has neither property nor possession can cause difficulties, as is illustrated by the decision in *The Aliakmon*[1]. B agreed to buy a cargo of steel coils carried by sea, on terms which effectively meant that risk passed to B as from shipment but that S retained property and the right to possession until payment. It was discovered that the coils had been damaged in transit due to negligent stowage. The risk of that loss fell on B under the contract of sale; however, the House of Lords held that in order to sue in negligence for damage to goods, a plaintiff must have either property in the goods or the immediate right to possession. B was therefore not entitled to sue the carrier in negligence.

The actual result in *The Aliakmon* would now be different as a result of the Carriage of Goods by Sea Act 1992[2]; however, outside the particular context of carriage by sea the decision remains good law and therefore if, for instance, goods are damaged during land transport, the buyer who bears risk but has no property in the goods is still unable to sue. There are ways in which the difficulties can be evaded: for instance, the contract of sale could require the seller to sue for the buyer's benefit or assign his right of action to the buyer. However, such arrangements will be impracticable in many commercial situations. More importantly, the buyer could protect himself by insurance: a person to whom risk of loss has passed has sufficient interest in the goods to insure them[3], and commercial buyers often will have insurance in such situations. Even so, it might be said that the rule throws the cost of insurance onto the wrong party and effectively allows the carrier, or other person responsible for damaging the goods, to make a windfall by reason of the arrangement between buyer and seller.

In consumer transactions, on the other hand, the buyer to whom risk has passed will probably not be insured against loss or damage to goods not in his possession. The problem for consumers is not the separation of property and risk, but the rule which links them. Atiyah has described the 'technical legal position' as 'grotesque'[4] and Cranston describes the rules as to risk as 'highly artificial . . . and at the same time . . . highly unjust to consumers in some aspects of their application'[5].

The problem may be illustrated by two examples. Suppose first that B visits a furniture store, chooses an 'ex-display' dining suite, and agrees that the store should deliver it the next day. The suite being specific goods, property and risk pass to B immediately. Without any negligence on the part of the store[6], it is destroyed by fire during the night: B bears the risk of loss of the suite and therefore must pay for it.

Now suppose that B agrees to buy a new refrigerator, to be delivered by S the next day. S sells similar refrigerators to two other customers and uses an independent contractor to deliver the goods. Three identical refrigerators are loaded. B's goods are initially unascertained; normally delivery of the goods to the carrier would be delivery to B, and would appropriate goods to the contract[7] but no property can pass until the goods for B's contract are ascertained[8]. If the delivery van crashes while there are at least two refrigerators on board, S bears the risk of loss; however, if the van crashes after two refrigerators have been delivered, B's refrigerator may be ascertained by 'exhaustion'[9], and property and risk will pass to B.

The results produced by application of the rules are so arbitrary and so contrary to the expectations of most buyers that a court would probably strive to reach some other result, for instance, by finding an implied intention that either property, or risk, should not pass until delivery. However, if the normal 'rules' are strictly applied, consumer buyers could be severely prejudiced. Most household insurance policies would probably not cover goods lost in the circumstances described above, whereas the supplier's insurance probably would cover the goods even after property has passed to the buyer.

The problem should not be overstated. Situations such as those described are rare. Moreover, either through ignorance of the strict legal position, or in order to retain customer goodwill, most suppliers would probably not require the buyer to pay for goods lost in such circumstances[10], but would claim on their own insurance. In theory the insurance company could then claim to be subrogated to the retailer's right to claim the price from the buyer[11]; in practice the insurer might not seek to exercise that right. Moreover, the retailer's insurance might be construed as extending to cover the buyer's interest in the goods[12]; in that case the insurer would not be entitled to exercise subrogation rights against the buyer[13].

The law on the passing of risk is artificial; it is out of step with commercial and consumer expectations. There is no conceptual reason for linking risk to ownership and a rule linking risk, instead, to possession, in accordance with the expectations of commerce, has much to commend it.

1 [1986] AC 785, [1986] 2 All ER 145; see further 32.4.3.
2 See 32.5.5.
3 *Inglis v Stock* (1885) 10 App Cas 263, HL; see 35.1.3.
4 Atiyah, *Sale of Goods* (10th edn, 2000) p 354.
5 Cranston, *Consumers and the Law* (2nd edn, 1984) p 169.
6 The store is a bailee; it is therefore liable for negligent damage.
7 SoGA, s 18, r 5.
8 *Healy v Howlett* [1917] 1 KB 337.
9 *Karlshamns Oljiefabriker v Eastport Navigation Corpn* [1982] 1 All ER 208.
10 See the survey cited by Cranston in *Consumers and the Law* (2nd edn, 1984) at p 170.
11 See 35.7.2.
12 This will be possible if the policy covers property 'in trust or on commission': see *Waters and Steel v Monarch Fire and Life Assurance Co* (1856) 5 E & B 870: see 35.1.5.
13 *Petrofina (UK) Ltd v Magnaload Ltd* [1984] QB 127, [1983] 3 All ER 35; see 35.7.2.

16.2 Mistake and frustration

The rules allocating risk between buyer and seller deal with the question whether the seller can deliver goods after loss or damage and require the buyer to accept and pay for them. If the goods are damaged whilst at the seller's risk, he cannot deliver them in performance of the contract. He may be able to repair the goods and deliver them, or deliver a replacement. However, if neither of those alternatives is possible, the seller will be unable to deliver and will therefore be in breach of contract, unless his performance is excused; whether or not it is depends not on the rules relating to risk but on the connected rules dealing with mistake and frustration.

A contract of sale can be affected by mistake or frustration in the same way as any other contract. However, the Sale of Goods Act contains special provisions, in ss 6 and 7, which deal with mistake and frustration in one particular, limited, class of circumstances, where specific goods have 'perished'. Section 6 applies where there is a contract for the sale of specific goods and, without the knowledge of the seller, the goods have perished before the contract is made. It is therefore concerned with a particular case of mistake[1] and where it applies it makes the contract void. Section 7 applies where there is a contract for the sale of specific goods and, between the making of the contract and the passing of risk from seller to buyer, the goods perish without the fault of either party. It therefore deals with circumstances which would normally be regarded as frustrating the contract and where it applies the contract is avoided.

Where ss 6 and 7 apply, the normal common law rules concerned with mistake and frustration are excluded; the effect on the contract of circumstances which fall outside the scope of ss 6 and 7 depends on the general common law and statutory rules concerned with mistake and frustration[2] which may be more flexible than those concerned with perishing.

1 The section is thought to be based on the famous case of *Couturier v Hastie* (1856) 5 HL Cas 673; it is argued that it is based on a misunderstanding of the basis of the decision in that case: see Atiyah (1957) 73 LQR 349; Atiyah, *The Sale of Goods* (10th edn, 2000) p 93 ff.
2 See 2.4.1, 2.9.4.

16.2.1 *Specific goods*

Both ss 6 and 7 apply only to contracts to sell specific goods. In *Howell v Coupland*[1], decided before the 1893 Act, the court gave an extended meaning to 'specific'. S contracted to sell 200 tons of potatoes to be grown on specified fields but, due to disease, only 80 tons were produced on those fields and B sued for non-delivery in respect of the shortfall. The Court of Appeal treated the contract as one for sale of specific goods; the crop failure made performance impossible, because the contract allowed S to deliver potatoes from the specified fields, and no others. Performance was therefore excused.

However, the contract in *Howell v Coupland* would not be for specific goods within the statutory meaning of that expression: the contract goods were not identified and agreed upon at the time the contract was made[2]. A similar contract had to be considered in *Sainsbury Ltd v Street*[3], where S agreed to sell B the crop of barley, estimated at 275 tons, to be grown on a particular field. McKenna J held that the contract was not for the sale of specific goods and so ss 6 and 7 were inapplicable, but that the decision in *Howell v Coupland* depended on the presumed intention of the parties and survived the Act either as an example of a sale of goods subject to a contingency to be fulfilled[4] or as a rule of the common law, preserved by s 62(2) of the Act[5].

It is not clear whether future goods can ever be specific for the purposes of ss 6 and 7; a contract to sell a specified item, such as a second-hand car or a piece of antique furniture, to be acquired by the seller from someone else for the purposes of resale to the buyer, would appear to be a contract to sell specific goods to which ss 6 and 7 can apply. If not, the court could apply the common law rules on mistake and frustration, or decide the case according to the presumed intention of the parties, as in *Howell v Coupland* and *Sainsbury v Street*.

Deciding the case according to the presumed intention of the parties offers greater flexibility than is possible on a strict reading of the statutory provisions. In *Sainsbury v Street* there was a bad harvest and the field only produced 140 tons; however, the price of barley rose substantially, and S therefore sold the 140 tons to another buyer at a higher price than that agreed with B. When B sued for non-delivery, S argued that the contract was avoided by virtue of s 7 and *Howell v Coupland*. McKenna J held that the parties must have intended that, in such circumstances, S should offer B the option of buying the goods actually produced on the terms originally agreed. S would not be liable in respect of the shortage.

These decisions depend on the construction of the contract. Alternative interpretations may be possible in particular cases: if on the proper construction of the contract the seller warrants that the contract quantity will be produced, he will be liable if there is a shortfall. Alternatively, the contract may be construed as allocating the risk of partial, or total, failure to the buyer, if on its proper construction he has contracted to pay the contract price no matter what quantity of goods are produced: the contract is then effectively a sale of a 'chance', and if less than the anticipated quantity is produced, the buyer must still pay the agreed price.

What is clear is that ss 6 and 7 cannot apply to contracts to sell unascertained goods. The rationale behind the sections is that the seller is excused liability for non-performance where performance is made impossible because of circumstances outside his control. Where the contract is for wholly unascertained goods the seller can offer alternative goods even if the goods he intended to use for the contract are destroyed[6]. Where the contract is to sell unascertained goods from an identified source, such as part of the cargo of a named ship, performance may become impossible if the source is wholly destroyed: for instance, if the named ship is sunk. In that case the seller may be excused performance but the case will depend on the general rules relating to mistake and frustration, not on ss 6 and 7. If the seller has contracted to sell all of the goods from a named bulk source to several buyers, and only part of the bulk is destroyed, it seems that the seller cannot argue that any of the contracts are frustrated[7]. Thus if the seller delivers to any particular buyer less than the quantity due under that buyer's contract, the seller will be in breach of contract, unless the contract contains express – or, possibly, implied – terms permitting the seller to allocate the available goods between buyers.

As already noted, the allocation of risk where a buyer acquires an undivided share in goods forming part of a bulk under SoGA, s 20A is not clear. If risk passes to the buyer when he acquires his undivided share, any subsequent damage to or loss of the goods will have no effect on the rights of the parties. If, however, as suggested earlier, risk of loss remains with the seller until goods are ascertained and appropriated to the particular buyer's contract, difficult questions may arise if the goods in the bulk deteriorate or are lost or damaged before delivery. If the whole of the bulk is destroyed or lost, any contracts to supply goods from it will be frustrated in accordance with normal contract principles. If, however, only part of the bulk is damaged or destroyed the position is unclear. Section 20B(3)(c) states that nothing in ss 20A or 20B shall 'affect the rights of any buyer under his contract'. This could be read as indicating that the seller remains absolutely liable in such a case to supply goods of the right quality in the right quantity. Such a reading would be harsh. It might also give rise to difficult questions of fact. Suppose, for instance, that S contracts to sell 500 tonnes of grain to each of B and C from a bulk thought to contain 1,000 tonnes. B takes delivery of 500 tonnes and then, some time later, when C calls for delivery of his goods, it is found that only 300 tonnes remain. S's liability may depend on whether the deficiency arose before or after the delivery to B. If before, S will bear the risk and be liable to C for short delivery; if after the delivery to B, the goods will have become C's property as a result of ascertainment by exhaustion and the risk of loss will fall on C. It is submitted that the solution to such problems should depend on the intention of the parties. It may therefore be possible in an appropriate case to find an implied term, similar to that in *Sainsbury v Street*, which would release the seller from his delivery obligation as regards that part of the goods lost or damaged but allow the buyer to demand delivery of the remainder. Such a term would not contradict s 20B(3)(c): the buyer's contractual rights would not be affected by anything in s 20A or s 20B, but by the implied term which would define and be part of those rights.

1   (1876) 1 QBD 258.
2   See *Re Wait* [1927] 1 Ch 606 at 631, per Atkin LJ.
3   [1972] 3 All ER 1127, [1972] 1 WLR 834.
4   SoGA, s 5(2).
5   SoGA, s 62(2).
6   A contract to sell wholly unascertained goods might be frustrated if, for example, the only source of the particular goods was wholly destroyed or became unavailable.
7   See *J Lauritzen AS v Wijsmuller BV, The Super Servant Two* [1990] 1 Lloyd's Rep 1, CA; above 2.9.4.

16.2.2   *The goods must have perished*

Sections 6 and 7 only apply where performance is made impossible because the goods have 'perished'. There are very few decisions on the meaning of 'perish' in this context. Clearly, goods which are totally and irretrievably destroyed have 'perished'. In *Horn v Minister of Food*[1] S contracted to sell a quantity of potatoes; however, before delivery the potatoes were affected by rot and became unfit for consumption. Morris J held that they had not perished: they could still be described as 'potatoes'[2].

However, cases from other areas, including insurance law, suggest a wider meaning and indicate that deterioration less than total destruction may amount to 'perishing'. The leading case is *Asfar v Blundell*[3], where a ship carrying a cargo of dates sank in the Thames. The owner claimed on a policy of insurance which allowed recovery if the dates had perished. The dates were recovered from the river, a 'pulpy mass' soaked in water and impregnated with sewage. The insurers argued that they were still dates and had not perished: they could be used to distil alcohol. The court rejected that argument which 'might commend itself to a body of chemists, but not to businessmen. We are dealing with dates as a subject matter of commerce . . . [The] test is whether, as a matter of business, the nature of the thing has been altered'[4]. On this basis an item has perished if it is 'so changed in its nature as to become an unmerchantable thing which no buyer would buy and no honest seller would sell'[5].

It is generally accepted that this approach is correct[6]. However, it does give rise to a potential difficulty. 'Merchantable' effectively means 'saleable', and defining 'perishing' in terms of loss of saleability or non-compliance with description causes ss 6 and 7 to overlap the implied terms in ss 13–14 of the Act. Although they now require the goods delivered to be of 'satisfactory' rather than 'merchantable' quality[7], it seems clear that the quality standard has not been lowered, and that goods which would be 'unmerchantable', and therefore be held to have perished, would not be of satisfactory quality if the seller actually delivered them. Normally, if S delivers goods which are not of satisfactory quality, B can reject and, in addition to recovering the price (if prepaid), claim damages for non-delivery, if the market price has moved, and for consequential losses, all on the basis of the breach of the implied terms. However, if the goods are held to have perished, S can argue that the contract is void (s 6) or avoided (s 7) so that, in either case, his liability is limited to refunding the price[8]. Suppose, for instance, that a retailer sells a pack of chilled food which, without fault on the retailer's part, has deteriorated so as to be unfit to eat. The customer eats it and becomes ill. If s 6 applies, the contract is void and the retailer is not liable for the customer's illness.

A court would presumably strive to avoid such a result. One way to do so would be to adopt a more restricted interpretation of 'perished', as in *Horn v Minister of Food*. An alternative would be to treat ss 6 and 7 as rules of presumed intention which can be excluded by contrary intention[9]; it might then be argued that the seller cannot rely on either section where he actually delivers the goods, on the grounds that he then impliedly warrants that they are of satisfactory quality under s 14(2)[10]. This approach is supported by the decision of the Australian High Court in *McRae v Commonwealth Disposals Commission*[11], where it was held that a provision equivalent to s 6 was inapplicable because the seller had warranted the existence of the goods. However, the wording of ss 6 and 7 appears to be absolute, leaving no scope for contrary intention[12]. Moreover, in a New Zealand case[13] the court held, without considering the relationship between s 6 and s 14, that s 6 could apply, to make the contract void, where the seller had delivered the goods.

It is clear that goods may be held to have perished in other circumstances. In *Barrow, Lane and Ballard Ltd v Phillip Phillips & Co Ltd*[14] S contracted to sell 700 bags of nuts. It was held that the contract was void under s 6 when it was discovered that 109 bags had been stolen before the contract was made. However, this approach also causes potential problems. Stolen property may be recovered and in some cases there may be a good chance of it being recovered relatively quickly: have the goods perished in such a case? If the goods are unavailable for performance of the contract at the time fixed for delivery, making performance impossible, the seller should be excused, either by virtue of ss 6 and 7, or by virtue of common law mistake or frustration; however, since the consequences of applying the statutory rules differ from those which apply to other cases of mistake and frustration, it may be necessary to decide which rules are applicable.

1 [1948] 2 All ER 1036.
2 The decision is widely criticised: see eg Atiyah, *The Sale of Goods* (10th edn, 2000) p 101; strictly, the comments on s 7 were obiter as on the facts risk was held to have passed to B.
3 [1896] 1 QB 123, CA.
4 [1896] 1 QB 123 at 127, per Lord Esher.
5 [1896] 1 QB 123 at 128; see also the views of Lopes LJ (at 130) and Kay LJ (at 132).
6 See eg *Benjamin's Sale of Goods* (5th edn, 1997) para 1-127; Goode, *Commercial Law* (2nd edn, 1995), pp 271–272.
7 See 11.2.3,
8 'Perish' clearly assumes that the goods have deteriorated, so that ss 6 and 7 cannot apply where the goods never were of the right quality: for instance, where manufactured goods are unsatisfactory due to manufacturing or design defects. See Atiyah *The Sale of Goods* (10th edn, 2000) p 96.
9 See Atiyah, *The Sale of Goods* (10th edn, 2000) pp 96–97; *Benjamin's Sale of Goods* (5th edn, 1997) para 1-130.
10 See *Chalmers' Sale of Goods Act* (18th edn, 1979) p 99.
11 (1950) 84 CLR 377.
12 See Treitel, *The Law of Contract* (10th edn, 1999) p 260.
13 *Rendell v Turnbull & Co* (1908) 27 NZLR 1067. The case involved a seller's claim for damages for non-acceptance and the buyer's counterclaim for damages. However, the buyer's only loss was economic, based on the increased market price of similar goods.
14 [1929] 1 KB 574.

16.2.3 *Perishing of part*

As *Barrow, Lane and Ballard Ltd v Phillips*[1] illustrates, where part of the contract goods are lost, the whole contract may be void under s 6 or avoided under s 7. However, in cases falling outside the statutory rules, the courts have been able to reach more flexible, and equitable, results. Thus, in *Sainsbury v Street*[2], where only part of the expected crop was produced, there was an implied term in the contract that S should offer B the crop which was produced, but that S would not be liable for non-delivery of the goods which were unavailable. A court might strive to reach the same result in cases covered by the statutory provisions, and again this would be possible if the rules in ss 6 and 7 were treated as rules of presumed intention, which could therefore be excluded by a contrary intention[3].

If the rules are treated as subject to contrary intention, it appears that if part of the goods perish, the position is as follows:

(a) S is not liable for non-delivery of the full contract quantity[4]; but
(b) S is required to offer B those goods which are available[5]; but
(c) B cannot be required to take the reduced quantity which is available and is not in breach if he rejects them[6].

1 [1929] 1 KB 574.
2 [1973] 3 All ER 1127.
3 See Atiyah, *The Sale of Goods* (10th edn, 2000) pp 99–100.
4 *Howell v Coupland* (1876) 1 QBD 258, CA.

5   *Sainsbury Ltd v Street* [1973] 3 All ER 1127.
6   *Barrow, Lane and Ballard Ltd v Phillip Phillips & Co Ltd* [1929] 1 KB 574.

16.2.4   *Goods perish before the contract is made*

Section 6 applies where the goods have perished before the contract 'without the knowledge of the seller'. A seller who knows that the goods have perished but nevertheless contracts to sell them should not be able to escape liability for non-delivery, and if the seller purports to sell goods which he knows to have perished, he will be liable for damages for non-delivery[1].

Where s 6 does apply, and the goods have perished without the seller's knowledge, the contract is void. However, as we have noted, it seems that, despite its wording, the section only establishes a prima facie rule, which can be excluded by contrary intention. Thus it may be excluded if the seller expressly or impliedly warrants that the goods exist, as was held to happen in *McRae v Commonwealth Disposals Commission*[2]. As we have noted, there are difficulties in reconciling this approach with the wording of s 6, and it has been suggested that *McRae* could be explained on the basis that the goods in that case (a shipwreck) had not perished, but had never existed[3]. However, the court reached its decision on the basis that the equivalent of s 6 could be excluded by contrary intention. In any case, it will be rare that the seller will be held to warrant that the goods exist[4].

Where the parties enter into a contract whose performance is impossible but the case falls outside the scope of s 6, the rights of the parties will depend on the application of the common law rules relating to mistake.

1   *Bell v Lever Bros Ltd* [1932] AC 161 at 217, HL, per Lord Atkin.
2   (1950) 84 CLR 377.
3   An alternative, where the seller is held to warrant that the goods exist, would be to treat that warranty as creating a collateral contract, but there are also difficulties with that approach. Further alternatives would be to hold the seller liable for damages for negligent or fraudulent misstatement.
4   See Wright J in *Barrow, Lane and Ballard Ltd v Phillip Phillips & Co Ltd* [1929] 1 KB 574 at 582.

16.2.5   *Goods perish after the contract is made*

Section 7 applies where there is a contract for the sale of specific goods and, between the making of the contract and the passing of risk to the buyer, the goods perish. Its application is therefore restricted: it will only apply where the parties expressly or impliedly exclude the operation of the normal rule, in s 18, rule 1, that in a contract for specific goods property and risk pass when the contract is made, or where the contract is covered by s 18, r 2 or r 3.

Section 7 has no application if the perishing is due to the fault of either party. It is the equivalent of frustration, and generally a party cannot rely on self-induced frustration. Thus if the goods are destroyed because S is negligent in his storage of them, S will be liable for non-delivery.

Where s 7 does apply, the contract is avoided. Thus the seller is not required to deliver the goods and the buyer need not pay. If the price has been pre-paid, the seller must refund it. Other losses lay where they fall. In other cases of frustration not covered by s 7, the common law and statutory rules concerned with frustration will apply. In particular, the court may have power, under the Law Reform (Frustrated Contracts) Act 1943 to apportion between the parties the losses caused by frustration[1]. Thus, for instance, if the seller incurs expenses putting goods into a deliverable state and the contract is then frustrated, for example by an export embargo, the court may allow the seller to retain all or part of any pre-payment to offset his costs[2].

In practice, the consequences of events which might frustrate the contract are often covered by express provisions in the contract. For instance, force majeure clauses may apply where performance is impeded or made impossible by events outside the parties' control, such as weather, strikes, embargoes, war and so on. Indeed, even where there are no such provisions, the parties are unlikely to invoke either the general rules of frustration or mistake, or those contained in ss 6 and 7 of the Sale of Goods Act. Where the goods are destroyed, the parties will normally seek to negotiate a settlement: for example, the seller may offer alternative goods and the buyer accept them, enabling the parties to preserve their trading relationship without resort to technical and somewhat arbitrary legal rules.

1 See 2.9.4.
2 Law Reform (Frustrated Contracts) Act 1943, s 1(2).

Chapter 17

Title Conflicts in Sale Transactions

17.0   Introduction

It is of the essence of a capitalist economy that property should be freely alienable and circulate within the economy. An inevitable consequence in a society which allows private ownership of property and encourages trade, is that disputes will arise involving competing claims to items of property. Such disputes are more likely to arise in relation to goods than land. Land is static and title to land is recorded in documentary form. Dealings in land are normally preceded by thorough investigation of the documentary title. The volume of dealings in goods and the need for free alienability of property means that the documentary recording of title to goods is generally impracticable. With the increase in commercial activity and the increased mobility of modern society, the scope for title conflicts has increased.

There is therefore a tension between the desires to protect private ownership of property and to promote the alienability of property. That tension is reflected in the law. As Denning LJ (as he then was) put it:

'In the development of our law, two principles have striven for mastery. The first is for protection of property: no one can give a better title than he himself possesses. The second is for the protection of commercial transactions; the person who takes in good faith and for value without notice should get a good title. The first principle has held sway for a long time, but it has been modified by common law itself and by statute so as to meet the needs of our own times'[1].

Disputes may arise in a number of ways. A seller may sell goods but retain title to secure payment of the price. If the buyer resells the goods before paying for them, the seller may seek to recover them from the sub-buyer. Alternatively, the owner of goods may entrust them to a bailee to store, or to an agent to deal with on his behalf. If the bailee or agent sells the goods, the owner may wish to recover them from the person in possession. Or, in the simplest case, goods may be stolen from their owner who, upon discovering them, will seek to recover them from the person in possession; however, the person in possession may have bought them in good faith, either direct from the thief or, more likely, after several intermediate transactions. In these cases the conflict involves competing claims to the absolute ownership in the goods – ownership. Conflicts can equally arise where the person in possession claims only a limited interest: for instance, the goods may have been pledged to him as security for a loan.

In each of these cases the competing claimants are both innocent victims of the dishonesty, or commercial incompetence, of another – the thief, dishonest agent or insolvent buyer. In theory, each of the claimants has an alternative personal claim against someone: the dispossessed owner will generally have a claim for conversion against anyone who deals with his property so as to deny his title, and, in the case of a resale by a buyer who has not paid for the goods, or by a bailee or agent, there may be a claim for breach of contract. Equally, the person in possession will generally have a contractual claim against his immediate supplier for the refund of the price paid, and damages[2]. In practice those claims may be worthless. The dispossessed owner's claim lies against a thief or other rogue, or against a buyer who, having failed to pay for the goods, will almost certainly be insolvent. Even if the true 'rogue' can be traced, he is unlikely to be worth suing. The person in possession may be in a better position: if he did not buy direct from the 'rogue', his claim for breach of contract may lie against an identifiable and solvent defendant. However, if he succeeds in that claim, the loss is merely transferred to another innocent party; if each innocent purchaser sues his vendor for breach of contract, the loss will be passed back up the chain of transactions until it falls on the first innocent purchaser, who bought the goods from the rogue.

Ultimately, therefore, the law must decide which of two innocent parties should bear the loss. 'Whatever the solution, an innocent party suffers: the original owner of the property; the innocent purchaser; or a merchant who has bona fide dealt with it'[3]. The solution offered by the law is 'all or nothing'. As indicated by Denning LJ in the quotation above, the allocation of loss has shifted over time. The original principle was *nemo dat quod non habet* – no one can give a better title than he himself has – so the original dispossessed owner could always recover his property, throwing the loss on the bona fide purchaser. The growth of commercial activity and the need to protect bona fide purchasers in order to encourage confidence in transactions, and therefore trade, led to that principle being modified, and a number of exceptions were developed, first by the common law and then by statute. Where one of those exceptions applies the bona fide purchaser takes precedence over the original owner, so that the loss is effectively thrown onto the latter.

From time to time it has been suggested that a preferable solution would be to apportion the loss between the two victims:

> 'The relevant question in this sort of case . . . is . . . which of two innocent parties shall suffer for the fraud of a third. The plain answer is that the loss should be divided between them in such proportion as is just in all the circumstances. If it be pure misfortune, the loss should be borne equally; if the fault or imprudence of either party has caused or contributed to the loss, it should be borne by that party in the whole or in the greater part'[4].

However, such suggestions have gone unheeded. A dispossessed owner may bring a claim in tort for wrongful interference with goods against any person who deals with the goods so as to deny his title to them. In practice, having traced the goods, the dispossessed owner will normally seek to recover them from the person in possession. Liability for wrongful interference is strict, so that if the person in possession refuses to deliver them up in response to a claim from the dispossessed owner, he is liable, unless he can establish that he has acquired title to the goods by means of one of the exceptions to the *nemo dat* rule.

Other claims may be possible. For instance, the owner may bring a claim for damages against anyone who handled the goods, including the person who dispossessed him. Alternatively, he may be able to make a restitutionary claim against the person who dispossessed him and, by tracing, claim any asset bought with the proceeds of the goods. The claim for wrongful interference against the person in possession tends, however, to be the most attractive option. It is simple to establish and lies against a solvent and easily identifiable defendant. Above all, liability is strict: the defendant is liable if he has dealt with the goods or refuses to deliver them up, even though he honestly and reasonably believes that he owns them. Recovery of the goods is not guaranteed. If the claim succeeds, the court has a discretion as to the form of judgment: it may order the defendant to deliver up the goods to the claimant; alternatively, it may make an order giving the defendant the option of delivering up the goods or paying their value in damages; or it may order the defendant to pay damages[5]. The only mitigation, from the point of view of the defendant, is that the court can order the claimant to pay an allowance in respect of any improvement to the goods[6]. Conversely, the original dispossessor will often be difficult to trace and, probably, worthless.

A person in possession of goods, faced with a demand for their return by a person claiming to be their true owner, is therefore faced by a dilemma. If he refuses to comply with the demand, he may incur liability in conversion; if he wishes to contest the claim, he must trace the series of transactions by which the goods came into his possession in order to see if any of them fall within any of the exceptions to the 'nemo dat' rule.

1   *Bishopsgate Motor Finance Corpn Ltd v Transport Brakes Ltd* [1949] 1 KB 322, [1949] 1 All ER 37, CA.
2   Under s 12 of the Sale of Goods Act or the equivalent provisions in other legislation; see 14.1.
3   Hahlo, 'Sale of Another Person's Property' (Quebec Civil Code Revision Commission).
4   Devlin LJ in *Ingram v Little* [1961] 1 QB 31 at 38, CA.
5   Torts (Interference with Goods) Act 1977, s 3(2).
6   Torts (Interference with Goods) Act 1977, s 3(7).

17.0.1   *The basic principle: nemo dat quod non habet*

The basic common law principle, nemo dat quod non habet, is preserved by s 21(1) of the Sale of Goods Act 1979, which provides that:

> 'subject to this Act, where goods are sold by a person who is not their owner, and who does not sell them under the authority or with the consent of the owner, the buyer acquires no better title to the goods than the seller had, unless the owner of the goods is by his conduct precluded from denying the seller's authority to sell'.

Section 21 therefore makes clear that the basic rule is subject to exceptions. Indeed, two exceptions are recognisable in s 21(1): agency ('under the authority or with the consent of the owner[1]') and estoppel ('the owner of the goods is by his conduct precluded from denying the seller's authority to sell'). Two further exceptions are contained in s 21(2), which provides that nothing in the Act affects the provisions of the Factors Act allowing a person to dispose of goods as if he were their owner, or the validity of certain common law and statutory powers of sale, or sales under a court order. Finally, a further three exceptions are set out in ss 22–25 of the Act: sales by sellers with voidable title (s 23), by sellers in possession (s 24) and by buyers in possession (s 25). A fourth exception, which applied where goods were sold in market overt and was contained in s 22 of the Act, was abolished by the Sale of Goods (Amendment) Act 1994.

There is little or no discernible policy linking the different exceptions. In several situations it seems that the title of the original dispossessed owner is defeated where he has voluntarily parted with possession of the goods. However, it is clear that that is not a general principle: in some situations the original owner will be defeated even though he did not voluntarily part with possession; conversely, even if he did voluntarily relinquish possession, he is entitled to recover the goods even from a bona fide purchaser unless the purchaser can bring himself within the wording of one of the particular exceptions. Some of the exceptions overlap and the person in possession will often seek to rely on several of the exceptions as alternatives. Additional difficulty is caused by the fact that further exceptions are contained in other legislation and, especially, in the Factors Act 1889, the provisions of which overlap to some extent with those of the Sale of Goods Act. It has therefore been said that the relevant provisions of the Sale of Goods Act and the Factors Act should be read together as a single code[2].

In recent years a number of proposals for reform of this area have been made. Most recently, a discussion document published by the Department of Trade and Industry in 1994 suggested, as one option for simplification of the law, the abolition of the separate exceptions to the nemo dat rule and their replacement by a general rule that where the owner of goods voluntarily entrusts them to, or acquiesces in their possession by, a third party, an innocent purchaser of the goods should acquire a good title to them[3].

1   It may be that 'consent' refers also to the situation where a buyer who has not yet obtained possession resells the goods with the seller's assent so as to defeat the seller's lien: see SoGA, s 47; below 18.3.3.
2   Per Megaw LJ in *Worcester Works Finance Ltd v Cooden Engineering Co Ltd* [1971] 3 All ER 708 at 713.
3   *Transfer of Title: sections 21 to 26 of the Sale of Goods Act 1979: A Consultation Document* (1994).

17.0.2   *Good faith and notice*[1]

The various exceptions to the nemo dat rule apply only in favour of a person who acquires the goods in good faith without notice of the rights of the original owner. It is clear that the test of 'good faith' is subjective. Section 61(3) of the Act provides that 'A thing is deemed to be done in good faith within the meaning of this Act when it is in fact done honestly, whether it is done negligently or not'[2]. All that is required under this head, therefore, is that the buyer acts honestly.

The Sale of Goods Act contains no definition of 'notice'. However, it is generally said that the concept of constructive notice has no place in commercial transactions[3] and that 'notice' in this context therefore means 'actual notice'. Thus s 29(3) of the Hire Purchase Act 1964, for the purposes of a group of sections which create an exception to the nemo dat rule, defines 'notice' as 'actual notice'. However, it seems that the position is not so simple as this would suggest. It is established that there is no general duty on a buyer of goods in a commercial context to investigate his vendor's title or 'to scrutinise commercial documents such as delivery notes with great care'[4], but it is also said that actual notice is assessed objectively, not subjectively: 'if by an objective test clear notice was given, liability cannot be avoided by proof merely of the absence of actual knowledge'[5]. Obviously, in deciding what facts were known to a buyer of goods, the court must draw inferences from the facts. A buyer will be treated as having notice of any facts to which it can be shown he deliberately turned a blind eye. A person will also be treated as having notice of a fact if he knows of circumstances which 'must lead a reasonable man applying his mind to them, and judging from them, to the conclusion that the fact is so'[6], but a buyer will not be treated as having notice merely because the circumstances of his purchase were suspicious. It is not clear, however, whether in cases where the buyer knows facts which would provide notice to a reasonable person he can nevertheless establish that he did not have actual notice by proving that he, subjectively, honestly did not draw the reasonable inference from them. It seems that the statement that there is no place for 'constructive notice' in commercial law may mean no more than that there is no duty on a buyer, in the ordinary course of things, to investigate his seller's title[7].

There is in fact a considerable degree of overlap between the concepts of 'good faith' and 'notice' as interpreted by the courts. Thus evidence of facts which would make a reasonable person suspicious may be taken as evidence of dishonesty and therefore of lack of good faith, or as indicating that the buyer must have had notice of the seller's lack of title, or both. Moreover, under two of the exceptions to the nemo dat rule there is a further requirement that the disposition to the buyer seeking to rely on the exception must have been 'in the ordinary course of business'. This requirement too has been interpreted so that, in effect, circumstances which would make a reasonable buyer suspicious will mean that the disposition is not in the ordinary course of business.

Under all but one of the exceptions to the nemo dat rule[8] the burden of proving good faith and lack of notice lies on the person seeking to rely on the exception. It can at least safely be said that where the circumstances of the case are suspicious the court will look critically at a claim of good faith and lack of notice and that the evidential burden will consequently be harder to discharge.

1   See generally Ulph, 'Good Faith and Due Diligence' in Palmer and McKendrick (eds), *Interests in Goods* (2nd edn, 1998); Harrison, *Good Faith in Sales* (1997) ch 8.
2   See also *Dodds v Yorkshire Bank* [1992] CCLR 92 (a case under Hire Purchase Act 1964, Pt III, below 17.4.3). 'Good faith' is not defined in the Factors Act 1889.
3   See, in a different context, the statement by Lindley LJ in *Manchester Trust v Furness, Withy & Co* [1895] 2 QB 539 at 545.
4   *Feuer Leather v Frank Johnston & Sons* [1981] Com LR 251.
5   Per Neill J in *Feuer Leather v Frank Johnstone & Sons* [1981] Com LR 251 at 257.
6   Per Lord Tenterden in *Evans v Truman* (1830) 1 Mood & R 10 at 12.
7   See Harrison, *Good Faith in Sales* (1997) p 237.
8   The exceptional case is the exception under s 23 where the buyer acquires goods from a seller with a voidable title: below 17.4.1.

17.1   Agency

We have already considered the importance of the role of agents in commercial activity, and it is clearly important that a person buying goods dealing with an agent should get good title to the goods. Section 21 merely makes clear that the common law rules are preserved, and a person who buys goods from an agent acting for the owner of the goods will get a good title to them provided the transaction was within the agent's actual or apparent authority[1].

Conversely, if the agent deals with the principal's property outside the scope of his actual and apparent authority, the principal will be able to recover the goods from the purchaser. If the agent is given possession of goods and authorised to sell on stipulated terms – for instance, at not less than a stated price – he may be held to have apparent authority to sell on other terms merely by virtue of being in possession of the goods[2]; but if there is no apparent authority, the principal can recover the goods. However, in most cases the agent will be a mercantile agent who has wide powers under the Factors Act 1889, to bind his principal by dispositions of the principal's property. The powers of mercantile agents under the Factors Act are expressly preserved by s 21(2) of the Sale of Goods Act.

1   See generally ch 4.
2   *Fry and Mason v Smellie* [1912] 3 KB 282, CA.

17.1.1   *Mercantile agents*

During the eighteenth and nineteenth centuries a great deal of trade was carried on through factors, agents who sold goods for their principals. Factors generally contracted in their own names without disclosing the principal's identity and often also traded on their own behalf. Effectively, therefore, a factor was a professional agent who traded in goods.

A person dealing with a factor would often be unaware of whether the factor was acting on his own behalf or for a principal. The certainty of commercial transactions required that persons dealing with a factor should be able to rely on the factor's authority. It was established at common law that a person who bought goods from a factor would take a good title regardless of unknown limitations on the factor's authority, but factors might dispose of goods other than by means of sale, in which case the common law protection was unavailable.

In 1823 the first of a series of Factors Acts was therefore passed to extend the protection of persons dealing with factors, by treating a factor who dealt with the goods in his own name as the owner of the goods for certain purposes, because 'the law is highly injurious to the interests of commerce in general'[1]. A series of Factors Acts followed during the nineteenth century, culminating in the Factors Act 1889, which remains in force[2]. Essentially, the effect of the legislation was both to confirm and extend the common law protection of persons dealing with factors. Section 2(1) of the 1889 Act provides that:

> 'When a mercantile agent is, with the consent of the owner, in possession of goods or of the documents of title to goods, any sale, pledge or other disposition of the goods made by him when acting in the ordinary course of business as a mercantile agent, shall, subject to the provisions of this Act, be as valid as if he were expressly authorised by the owner of the goods to make the same; provided that the person taking under the disposition acts in good faith, and has not, at the time of the disposition, notice that the person making the disposition has not authority to make the same.'

Changes in commercial practice mean that the nineteenth-century type of factor is rarely found today; however, businesses and professional agents still sell goods on behalf of other people, and such agents are likely to be regarded as 'mercantile agents'. The Sale of Goods Act is expressed to be without prejudice to the provisions of the Factors Act 1889[3]. However, in order for a person dealing with a mercantile agent to claim the protection of the Factors Act, a number of requirements must be fulfilled.

1   Preamble to the Factors Act 1823.
2   The history of the legislation is described by Lord Goff in *National Employers' General Mutual Insurance Association Ltd v Jones* [1990] 1 AC 24, [1988] 2 All ER 425, HL.
3   SoGA, s 21(2)(a).

17.1.1.1 *The agent must be a mercantile agent*

Section 2 of the Factors Act applies to dispositions of goods by mercantile agents. 'Mercantile agent' is defined in s 1 of the 1889 Act as:

> 'a mercantile agent having in the customary course of his business as such agent authority either to sell goods or to consign goods for the purpose of sale, or to buy goods, or to raise money on the security of goods'.

Where a person in possession of goods belonging to another disposes of them, it may be necessary to examine the arrangement between the owner and the possessor closely in order to decide if the possessor is an agent or is in possession on his own behalf. If the possessor is held to be in possession under a sale or return agreement, rather than as an agent, a person dealing with him will not be protected by the Factors Act; normally, he will take a good title because any disposition of the goods by the person in possession will adopt the sale or return transaction, passing property from the original owner to the possessor and through him to the disponee. However, if the sale or return arrangement contains a retention of title in favour of the original supplier until the goods are paid for, a person who deals with the possessor will be at risk: the possessor's disposition will not pass title from the original owner and, if the possessor does not pay the owner, the owner will be entitled to repossess the goods from the disponee, even though he acted in good faith[1].

A mercantile agent must be in business to sell, or otherwise deal with goods on behalf of other people. Thus a car hire company which acquired cars on hire purchase terms was not a mercantile agent when, from time to time, it sold off cars from its fleet and used the proceeds of sale to pay off the hire purchase debts[2]. Although the cars were not its property, the hire company sold on its own behalf; its business did not include the sale of goods on behalf of other people. However, a person may be a mercantile agent even though he acts for only one principal[3], and though the transaction in question is his first as a mercantile agent, provided that he is in business as a mercantile agent at the time he receives the goods in question[4].

1   *Weiner v Gill* [1905] 2 KB 172; contrast *Weiner v Harris* [1910] 1 KB 285, CA, where the arrangement was held to be an agency so that the third party disponee was protected.
2   *Belvoir Finance Ltd v Harold G Cole Ltd* [1969] 2 All ER 904, [1969] 1 WLR 1877.
3   *Lowther v Harris* [1927] 1 KB 393.
4   *Heap v Motorists' Advisory Agency Ltd* [1923] 1 KB 577.

17.1.1.2 *The agent must be in possession of the goods or of documents of title to them*

The rationale for the protection of persons dealing with mercantile agents is the appearance created by the agent's possession of the goods. The disponee is therefore only protected by the Factors Act where the agent is in possession of the goods at the time of the sale or other disposition; it is insufficient that the agent was in possession at some earlier time, for instance when he showed the goods to the disponee[1]. The Act provides that the agent is in possession where the goods, or documents of title, are in his actual possession or are held 'by any other person subject to his control or for him or on his behalf'[2].

It is sufficient for the purposes of the Act that the agent has possession of documents of title relating to the goods. A wider category of documents is recognised as 'documents of title' for this purpose than for the purposes of the common law. For the purposes of the Act, 'documents of title' includes bills of lading, warehouse certificates, delivery warrants and orders and 'any other document used in the ordinary course of business as proof of the possession or control of goods' or 'authorising or purporting to authorise' the possessor of the documents to receive or transfer the goods they represent[3]. However, it has been held that a car log book was not a document of title[4] and presumably the same would apply to the modern car registration document which does not purport to identify the owner of the vehicle but merely its registered keeper.

1 *Beverly Acceptances Ltd v Oakley* [1982] RTR 417, CA.
2 Factors Act 1889, s 1(2).
3 Factors Act 1889, s 1(4).
4 *Folkes v King* [1923] 1 KB 282, CA; but the log book was, and thus, presumably, the registration document is, required if the sale of a car is to be in the ordinary course of business: *Pearson v Rose and Young Ltd* [1951] 1 KB 275, CA.

17.1.1.3 *The agent must have obtained possession with the consent of the owner*

Since the rationale underlying the protection of persons dealing with mercantile agents is that the true owner of the goods has consented to the creation of a situation where the agent appears to be their owner, the owner is only bound where he has consented to the agent's possession. However, consent is rebuttably presumed so that the onus is on the owner to prove that he did not consent to possession[1]. Moreover, provided that the owner consented to possession, it is irrelevant that the agent obtained that consent by deception[2].

If the owner consents to the agent's initial possession, the withdrawal of consent has no effect on any subsequent disposition by the agent unless the disponee knows that consent has been withdrawn[3].

1 Factors Act 1889, s 2(4).
2 *Folkes v King* [1923] 1 KB 282, CA, confirmed in *Pearson v Rose and Young Ltd* [1951] 1 KB 275, CA.
3 Factors Act 1889, s 2(2).

17.1.1.4 *Possession must have been given for some purpose connected with sale*

It has been held that the owner is only bound by the agent's dispositions if he has consented to the agent having possession of the goods in his capacity as a mercantile agent, for one of the purposes mentioned in s 1 of the Act[1]. It is sufficient that the goods are deposited with the agent for some purpose preparatory to sale, such as to receive offers; but if the goods are given to the agent for some other, unconnected purpose, such as repair, the owner will not be bound by any disposition unless one of the other exceptions to the nemo dat rule applies.

From the point of view of the third party who deals with the agent, this distinction may appear unrealistic. If the agent does in fact deal in goods of the kind in question, the third party is equally deceived by the agent's possession, whether the owner left the goods for sale or for (say) repair. However, the distinction is well established; it can perhaps be understood in the historical context of the legislation when factors would be unlikely to combine that business with other activities such as repair or storage. The rule underlines the tendency of the law to protect the dispossessed owner.

1   *Pearson v Rose and Young Ltd* [1951] 1 KB 275, CA; *Astley Industrial Trust Ltd v Miller* [1968] 2 All ER 36.

17.1.1.5   *The sale or other disposition must be in the ordinary course of business of a mercantile agent*

This requirement has been interpreted as meaning that the agent must act in the way a mercantile agent would act if he was dealing in an authorised transaction[1]. Thus it is irrelevant that the agent is acting without the owner's authority, or that he acts dishonestly, purporting to act as principal, or that the particular transaction is one which would not be normal for an agent in the particular trade. In *Oppenheimer v Attenborough* A, a diamond merchant, pledged to P diamonds belonging to O. Evidence was produced that, by custom, diamond merchants did not pledge gems. Nevertheless, it was held that the transaction was in the ordinary course of business because it was effected in the way in which a mercantile agent would do business.

It seems, therefore, that what is required is that the agent should act –

'in such a way as a mercantile agent in the ordinary course of business as a mercantile agent would act, that is to say, within ordinary business hours, at a proper place of business and in other respects in the ordinary way in which a mercantile agent would act, so that there is nothing to lead the [disponee] to suppose that anything is done wrong'[2].

On this basis the requirement that the sale be in the ordinary course of business overlaps to some extent with the requirement that the disponee must act in good faith.

What is in the ordinary course of business will be a question of evidence in each case. It has been held that a sale of a car without its logbook[3] (or, presumably, registration document), or ignition key[4], would not be in the ordinary course of business. However, these clearly cannot be regarded as absolute rules: it has been held that the absence of a car log book did not take the sale of a new car outside the ordinary course of business[5] and even in sales of second-hand vehicles circumstances might arise where the seller could explain the absence of the registration document: for instance, by explaining that the vehicle had only recently been acquired by the previous owner and that a new registration document had not yet been received.

416

1   *Oppenheimer v Attenborough* [1908] 1 KB 221, CA.
2   *Oppenheimer v Attenborough* [1908] 1 KB 221 at 230, per Buckley LJ.
3   *Pearson v Rose and Young Ltd* [1951] 1 KB 275, CA.
4   *Stadium Finance Ltd v Robbins* [1962] 2 QB 664, [1962] 2 All ER 633, CA.
5   *Astley Industrial Trust Ltd v Miller* [1968] 2 All ER 36, CA.

17.1.1.6   *The disponee must act in good faith and take the goods without notice of the agent's lack of authority*

The law is generally reluctant to divest an owner of his property, and generally does so only in favour of persons who acquire property in good faith. Thus a person dealing with a mercantile agent is only protected where he acts in good faith and without notice of the agent's lack of authority.

The Factors Act places the burden of proof on the disponee to prove that he did act in good faith[1]; however, the test is subjective, so that provided he did act in good faith it is irrelevant that a reasonable person would have thought the circumstances suspicious.

1   *Heap v Motorists' Advisory Agency Ltd* [1923] 1 KB 577.

17.1.1.7   *Effect of agent's disposition*

Where a mercantile agent deals with goods in a transaction protected by the Factors Act, the owner of the goods is bound by the transaction whether he authorised it or not. If the agent sells the goods, the buyer gets a good title, extinguishing that of the original owner, so that any person who subsequently acquires an interest in the goods is protected against any claim by the original owner. Where the agent deals with the goods other than by way of sale, for instance by pledging them, the owner is bound by the disposition. Thus, for instance, in the case of a pledge, the owner can only repossess his property by redeeming the pledge.

Although commercial conditions have changed, so that the historical justification for the mercantile agency rule no longer exists, the justice of the rule seems clear. The owner who entrusts his property to an agent is better placed than the person who buys from the agent to assess the agent's honesty, and the owner should therefore bear the risk of the agent's dishonesty. However, in modern conditions, and hedged about as it is with restrictions, it may be doubted if the rule now provides adequate protection for third parties who deal with agents.

17.2   Estoppel

Section 21 provides that the nemo dat rule applies 'unless the owner of the goods is by his conduct precluded from denying the seller's authority to sell'. This preserves the common law principle of estoppel: if goods are sold by someone who is not their owner, the buyer nevertheless gets good title if the owner of the goods is estopped from denying the seller's right to sell. It seems that where the facts give rise to an estoppel, the buyer gets a good title to the goods, extinguishing the title of the estopped owner[1].

In *Lickbarrow v Mason*[2] Ashurst J said that:

'whenever one of two innocent parties must suffer for the fraud of a third, he who has enabled such person to occasion loss must sustain it'.

This dictum might suggest a broad role for estoppel, and the other exceptions to the nemo dat rule listed in ss 21–25 of the Sale of Goods Act might be regarded as particular instances of situations where the dispossessed owner loses his title to goods because his conduct allows another to appear to be the owner. However, the courts have given a very restricted interpretation to the 'estoppel' exception in s 21. As a result, estoppel, and in particular the dictum of Ashurst J, tend to be invoked as arguments of last resort, where other exceptions are not available.

Estoppel arises where the owner (O) is precluded by his conduct from denying the seller's (S) authority to sell. It is therefore clear that O will be estopped where his conduct makes it appear that S is an agent with authority to sell: in other words, a sale by an agent with the apparent authority[3] of the owner will pass a good title. However, the language of s 21 is wider than 'apparent authority': it also includes cases where O's conduct makes it appear that S is the true owner of the goods, which may be described as cases of 'apparent ownership'. There is an important difference between the two classes of case. In cases of apparent agency, or apparent authority, the buyer (B) will only get good title if he deals with S in a manner consistent with S's apparent authority. An agent's authority to deal with his principal's property is often limited. However, the owner of property normally has an unfettered power to deal with it, and in cases of apparent ownership B will get good title to the goods provided S acts in a way consistent with him being the owner.

An estoppel is generally created by a representation by the person estopped, which is relied on by the person to whom it is made. The same is true under s 21. Although the section refers to the owner being precluded 'by his conduct' from denying the seller's right to sell, it is clear that O's representation may be made by words or by conduct. It is sometimes said that there is a further class of 'estoppel by negligence'. It is not clear that this is a separate category[4]; however, cases where the estoppel arises from negligence give rise to special problems, and they therefore deserve separate consideration.

1   *Eastern Distributors Ltd v Goldring* [1957] 2 QB 600, [1957] 2 All ER 525, CA. The buyer acquires the title of the party estopped: if he was not the owner of the goods, the buyer cannot become owner by estoppel. See *Battersby and Preston* (1972) 35 MLR 268 .
2   (1793) 6 East 22n.
3   See 4.2.
4   See Atiyah, *Sale of Goods* (10th edn, 2000) p 372, where it is argued that cases of 'estoppel by negligence' really involve a negligent failure to report facts or to correct a previous representation by a third party, such as S himself. Either case may be regarded as involving an implied representation by O. See 17.2.2.

17.2.1   *Estoppel by representation*

The basis of estoppel is a representation by O that S has the right to sell the goods. The representation may be made by words or by conduct, provided it is clear and unequivocal. In *Eastern Distributors Ltd v Goldring*[1] O was the owner of a van. As part of a hire purchase fraud he signed hire purchase forms in blank, for completion by S, allowing S to appear to be owner of the van. The purpose of the arrangement was to enable S to sell the van to a finance company so that, in effect, O could raise money on the security of the van. S used the signed form to sell the van to the finance company (B), even though the jointly planned fraud fell through. It was held that by signing the forms in blank, O was estopped from denying S's right to sell the van; he was therefore estopped from recovering it from B2, who had bought it from B. Similarly, in *Shaw v Metropolitan Police Comr*[2] O gave his car to S, together with a signed letter saying that he had sold it to S and the vehicle transfer notification form signed in blank. It was held that O had made a clear representation that S had the right to sell the car, which would have raised an estoppel. However, the contract between S and B provided for title to pass to B on payment; B had not paid, and so S had not 'sold' the car but had only agreed to sell. The Court of Appeal held that estoppel in s 21 only operated where the goods were sold, so that on the facts O was entitled to recover the car.

A representation will only give rise to an estoppel if it is voluntary. Thus in *Debs v Sibec Developments Ltd*[3] O was not estopped when he signed a document acknowledging that he had sold his car (a Mercedes worth over £57,000) at gunpoint, and following threats against himself and his family. This decision is probably correct in principle; however, O's state of mind when parting with his property is irrelevant to the effect his representation has on the third party, B who relies on it.

As noted above, a representation may be made by conduct. For instance, if O stands by and watches as S contracts to sell his (O's) property, O will be estopped[4]. However, it is well established that O will not be estopped merely because he voluntarily parts with possession of his property[5]; generally something further by way of a positive representation is needed to create an estoppel.

1   [1957] 2 QB 600, [1957] 2 All ER 525, CA.
2   [1987] 3 All ER 405, [1987] 1 WLR 1332, CA.
3   [1990] RTR 91.
4   See the similar decision in *Spiro v Lintern* [1973] 3 All ER 319, [1973] 1 WLR 1002, CA; see 4.3.
5   *Farquharson Bros & Co v C King & Co* [1902] AC 325, HL.; *Central Newbury Car Auctions Ltd v Unity Finance Ltd* [1957] 1 QB 371, [1956] 3 All ER 905, CA; *Mercantile Bank of India Ltd v Central Bank of India Ltd* [1938] AC 287.

17.2.2   *Estoppel by negligence*

It is often said that an estoppel may be raised by negligence. However, it is clear that a claim of estoppel by negligence will only rarely succeed. It seems that negligence will create an estoppel where it amounts to a representation, as where O negligently fails to disclose information to B, thus impliedly representing that S has the right to deal with the goods[1], and such negligence will only create an estoppel where O owes B a duty of care. Thus it is well established that a person who is careless with his property and leaves it unattended can recover it even from a bona fide purchaser.

'If I lose a valuable dog and find it afterwards in the possession of a gentleman who bought it from somebody whom he believed to be the owner, it is no answer to me to say that he would never have been cheated into buying the dog if I had chained it up, or put a collar on it, or kept it under proper control. If a person leaves a watch or a ring on a seat in the park or on a table at a cafe and it ultimately gets into the hands of a bona fide purchaser it is no answer to the true owner to say that it was his carelessness and nothing else that enabled the finder to pass it off as his own'[2].

There was therefore no estoppel in *Central Newbury Car Auctions Ltd v Unity Finance Ltd*[3], where S offered to take a car on hire purchase and, contrary to normal hire purchase practice, O allowed him to take away the car together with its log book before the hire purchase proposal was accepted; the log book contained a clear warning that the person named in it was not necessarily the legal owner of the car. Denning LJ gave a strong dissenting judgment, arguing that O had been negligent to the point of recklessness. He accepted that neither carelessness nor parting with possession of goods would alone be enough to raise estoppel; however, here O had voluntarily parted with both the goods and the recognised means of transferring them.

The modern tendency is to approach cases of estoppel by negligence in accordance with the general principles of negligence, so that O will only be estopped if he owes a duty of care to B and is in breach of that duty. In view of the general trend in the modern law of negligence, this approach is likely to restrict the scope of estoppel by negligence. In *Mercantile Credit Co Ltd v Hamblin*[4] O asked S to help her get a loan on the security of her Jaguar car. O signed in blank the forms presented to her by S, believing them to relate to a loan application; in fact they were hire purchase forms which made it appear that S owned the car and that it had been let to O on hire purchase. S used the forms to sell the car to B, a finance company, which believed it was entering into a hire purchase contract with O. The Court of Appeal held that O owed B a duty of care but that, on the facts, she was not in breach of that duty: she knew the dealer socially and it was reasonable for her to rely on him[4]. Moreover, even if O had been negligent, it was S's fraud, not her negligence, which caused B's loss.

In *Moorgate Mercantile Co Ltd v Twitchings*[5] the House of Lords went further. Both O and B were finance companies. Both were members of Hire Purchase Information (HPI), a trade association set up by finance companies to keep a register of hire purchase agreements relating to motor vehicles, and to give information to the police, finance companies and motoring organisations in order to try and minimise hire purchase frauds. B received a hire purchase proposal in respect of a car, and, in accordance with usual practice, made a search of the HPI register in order to make sure that the vehicle was not subject to a subsisting hire purchase agreement. There was no agreement registered, and B therefore accepted the proposal, buying the car. In fact it transpired that the car was owned by O, which had let it on hire purchase but, contrary to normal trade practice[6], had not registered the agreement. By a bare majority the House of Lords held that, even though O and B were both members of HPI, O owed B no duty of care, so that O was not estopped.

This approach was reaffirmed in *Debs v Sibec*[7]. Because of the threats made by the robbers, O did not report the loss of his car for over a month after it was taken away. During that time it was sold several times before coming into the hands of B, a dealer, who had searched the HPI register before buying the car. It was held that even if O was negligent in failing to report the robbery, that did not estop him from recovering the car: he owed no duty of care. There was evidence that even if O had reported the robbery immediately, the fact would not have appeared on the HPI register at the time of the first resale; a duty of care to register would therefore extend to each purchaser in the chain of resales. Moreover, Simon Brown J emphasised that the real cause of B's loss was not any negligence by O, but B's reliance on his vendor's trustworthiness.

A duty of care to avoid causing economic loss by negligence will only be imposed where there has been an assumption of responsibility by the defendant such as to create a special relationship between himself and the claimant[8]. The courts may be willing to recognise such an assumption of responsibility towards one individual or a defined and limited class of persons, but are unlikely to do so where the duty would be owed to an indeterminate class of potential claimants. In *Moorgate v Twitchings* there was a relatively close relationship between the parties, as members of HPI, but a duty of care would have been owed to all members of HPI. Since *Moorgate* was decided, a second asset reference agency, Experian, has been established and the registers operated by both HPI and Experian may be searched, on payment of a fee, by members of the public. It is therefore unlikely that, should similar facts arise in the future, a duty of care would be recognised.

In a 1994 consultation document[9] the Department of Trade and Industry recommended that the specific decision in *Moorgate* should be reversed by legislation. However, these proposals have not been implemented. Even if they were, the decision in *Moorgate* and the general trend of the law of negligence suggest that, in the absence of very special facts, such as those in *Mercantile Credit v Hamblin*, it will be very difficult to establish estoppel by negligence in the future.

This approach seems to go too far in protecting the original owner. As Lord Denning has said:

> 'the courts, in favouring the original owner at the expense of the innocent purchaser, have run counter to the needs of a commercial country'[10].

By allowing the owner of goods to be recklessly careless with them and yet recover them from a bona fide purchaser, the law allows the owner to act with flagrant disregard for the effect of his conduct on others. The reasonable man locks his door when he goes out; he foresees that if he leaves the door open, he may be burgled, and that if the video is stolen someone is likely to be persuaded to buy it. The policy of the law may be to encourage care in buyers, but in many cases the owner will be better placed than the buyer to prevent the loss. Moreover, even where the buyer has exercised care, as in *Moorgate*, he is still unprotected.

Where the owner voluntarily parts with possession, the case for protecting the bona fide purchaser is even stronger.

> 'Theft, and to some extent loss, have the unpredictability of lightning, and there is relatively little the owner can do to protect himself against them. It is of his own free will, on the other hand, that the owner parts with possession of goods of his own to another by way of loan, lease, deposit, pledge etc and he has every opportunity of investigating the integrity of that person before doing so. It is only fair and equitable, therefore, that the risk should fall on him rather than on the innocent purchaser. The fact that he has, in the first instance, voluntarily parted with possession swings the delicate balance of equity in [the purchaser's] favour'[11].

1　See Atiyah, *Sale of Goods* (10th edn, 2000) p 372.
2　*Farquharson Bros & Co v C King & Co* [1902] AC 325 at 335, HL, per Lord MacNaghten.
3　[1957] 1 QB 371, [1956] 3 All ER 905, CA.
4　The court distinguished *Eastern Distributors Ltd v Goldring* [1957] 2 QB 600, (above, 17.2.1) on the basis that O here was not party to the fraud; this was therefore not a simple case of estoppel by representation.
5　[1977] AC 890, [1976] 2 All ER 641, HL.
6　98% of hire purchase agreements relating to vehicles were registered.
7　[1990] RTR 91.

8   See generally *Henderson v Merrett Syndicates Ltd* [1995] 2 AC 145, [1994] 3 All ER 506; *White v Jones* [1995] 2 AC 207, [1995] 1 All ER 691; *Williams v Natural Life Health Foods Ltd* [1998] 2 All ER 577.

9   *Transfer of Title: sections 21 to 26 of the Sale of Goods Act 1979: A Consultation Document* (1994).

10   *Central Newbury Car Auctions Ltd v Unity Finance Ltd* [1957] 1 QB 371 at 381.

11   Hahlo, *Sale of another person's property.*

17.3   Sellers in possession

Possession often gives the appearance of ownership, and a person who buys goods will normally rely on the appearance created by possession. However, we have seen[1] that possession and property are separate and that, in the context of a sale transaction, property may pass before or after physical possession of the goods. The Sale of Goods Act therefore contains several provisions designed to protect persons who buy goods from persons who no longer, or do not yet, own them. Some of those provisions mirror similar provisions contained in the Factors Act 1889. For most purposes the two sets of provisions are identical; however, the provisions of the Factors Act are wider than those of the Sale of Goods Act in some respects.

A person who has sold goods to a customer may remain in possession of them after the sale; if the seller sells the goods a second time, to a second buyer, a title conflict arises between the two buyers. The following diagram represents the situation:

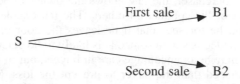

Either buyer may have a personal claim against S for breach of contract or, in some circumstances, for conversion. However, where S is insolvent that claim will be worthless. It is then vital to know which buyer has stronger title to the goods.

The Sale of Goods Act gives S a lien over the goods in his possession to secure payment of the price[2]; so long as the price is unpaid and S retains possession, he is entitled to exercise his lien by withholding delivery. If S is entitled to a lien over the goods and resells them, B2 takes good title to the goods in preference to B1, even if title has already passed to B1, for instance under s 18, rule 1[3]. Such a resale may be a breach of S's contract with B1, entitling B1 to sue S for breach of contract; however, in certain circumstances the Act allows S to terminate the contract with B1, and in those circumstances S may resell without incurring liability for breach of contract[4].

If S remains in possession after he has been paid, he has no statutory right of resale under the Act. However, if he resells the goods he may nevertheless pass a good title to B2. His power to do so will depend primarily on the question whether title has already passed to B1 under the first contract. If title remains in S, for instance, under an express or implied term in the contract with B1, or because that contract is covered by s 18, rule 2 or 3, S can continue to deal with the goods as owner and if he resells so as to pass title to B2, B2 becomes owner of the goods. However, where the goods were specific, or where S is unable to find replacement goods for his contract with B1, B1 will have a claim against S for damages for non-delivery.

The position is more difficult if title has passed to B1 under the first sale. In that case the nemo dat rule prima facie means that B1 has a stronger title than B2 to the goods, leaving B2 with a mere claim for breach of contract against S. However, a statutory exception to the nemo dat rule protects B2, and where its requirements are fulfilled, the positions are reversed: B2 then takes a good title to the goods; B1's title is extinguished and B1 is left with a personal claim against S for breach of contract or conversion.

The position is governed by s 24 of the Sale of Goods Act 1979, which provides:

> 'Where a person having sold goods continues or is in possession of the goods, or of documents of title to the goods, the delivery or transfer by that person, or by a mercantile agent[5] acting for him, of the goods or of the documents of title under any sale, pledge or other disposition thereof, to any person receiving the same in good faith and without notice of the previous sale, has the same effect as if the person making the sale or transfer were expressly authorised by the owner of the goods to make the same'.

A similar provision is contained in s 8 of the Factors Act 1889; however, the Factors Act provision is slightly wider, in that it also protects a person who receives the goods under any 'agreement for sale, pledge or other disposition'. Both sections have several features in common with s 25 of the Sale of Goods Act and s 9 of the Factors Act, which apply to dispositions by a person who, having agreed to buy goods, acquires possession of them[6] before property passes. Decisions under those provisions may therefore be relevant to the construction of s 24 of the Sale of Goods Act and s 8 of the Factors Act and vice versa.

Section 24 only applies where S 'continues or is in possession' of the goods at the time of the sale to B2. Section 1(2) of the Factors Act provides that a person shall be deemed to be in possession of goods or documents of title to goods where they are 'in his actual custody or are held by any other person subject to his control or for him or on his behalf'. S may therefore be in possession for the purposes of s 24 where he has constructive possession of goods which are in the physical control of a third party, such as a bailee, on his behalf[7]. Conversely, it seems that, provided S remains continuously in physical possession of the goods, it is not necessary for him to be in possession as seller. In *Pacific Motor Auctions Pty Ltd v Motor Credits Ltd*[8] S, a dealer, transferred cars to B1, a finance company, under a financing arrangement, but retained possession to sell the goods as B1's agent. The Privy Council held that s 24 nevertheless applied, even though S was in possession not as seller, but as B1's agent and bailee. This decision was followed by the Court of Appeal in *Worcester Works Finance Ltd v Cooden Engineering Ltd*[9], where S transferred ownership of a car to B1, a finance company, representing that it was to be let on hire purchase to a customer who did not in fact exist. S therefore remained in possession of the car, and it was held that the continuity of physical possession was sufficient to allow B2, who subsequently took the car from S, to get a good title under s 24.

These cases were concerned with the situation where S 'continues in possession'. Section 24 also applies where S 'is in possession'. A literal reading of this expression, in line with that in *Pacific Motor Auctions* and *Cooden*, would suggest that S would have a power to pass a good title whenever goods he had sold came back into his possession, and would expose a buyer to extensive risk if, for instance, he returned

423

goods to the original seller for repair; this might be particularly serious in a case such as the sale of new cars, where the buyer may be required to return the car to the original seller for servicing. However, it has been held that if S once loses possession, B2 is not protected if S later recovers possession of the goods in some other capacity[10]. The Court of Appeal in *Cooden* suggested that 'is in possession' refers to the situation where S sells future goods, so that he is not in possession of the goods at the time of the contract, but they come into his possession at a later date.

The Court of Appeal in *Cooden* also rejected a contention that S's possession of the goods must be lawful. The section focuses on physical possession and the continuity of possession; it is not necessary that S be in possession with B1's consent.

In order for B2 to take priority over B1 under s 24, B2 must take delivery of the goods or transfer of documents of title to the goods under a sale, pledge or other disposition, and he must act in good faith. 'Disposition' has been given a wide interpretation, so that it applied where B2, who had initially supplied the goods to S but had not been paid, repossessed them with S's consent[11]. However, there must be some transfer of a proprietary interest in the goods, rather than merely of possession, and it has been held that, in accordance with the definition of 'delivery' in s 61 of the Act, 'delivery' must involve a voluntary act. Thus it was held in a case decided under s 25 of the Act that there was no delivery by B1 to B2 where B2 seized goods without the consent of B1[12].

In *Nicholson v Harper*[13] it was held that B2 would only be protected if he took actual, rather than merely constructive, delivery of the goods. However, in *Gamer's Motor Centre (Newcastle) Pty Ltd v Natwest Wholesale Australia Pty Ltd*[14] the High Court of Australia, considering the New South Wales equivalent of s 25, held that constructive delivery would suffice, and in *The Saetta*[15] Clarke J preferred that reasoning to that in *Nicholson v Harper*. There could thus be delivery to B2 where the goods remained continuously in the possession of the same person but the capacity in which he held them changed so that after the disposition he held them as bailee for B2. *Nicholson v Harper* was explained in *Gamers* as a case where there was neither constructive nor actual delivery. It may perhaps be regarded as a special case because the goods were throughout in the possession of B2, warehouse proprietors, initially as bailee for S and then for an interest of their own, and there was nothing beyond the disposition itself to indicate any change in the nature of their possession. A better explanation for the decision may therefore be that, although constructive or symbolic delivery may be sufficient for the purposes of ss 24 and 25, there must be some (voluntary) act of delivery over and above the disposition itself[16]. However, the position in English law remains unclear.

Provided B2 acts honestly, he will be in good faith even though he acts negligently[17]. However, where he does not immediately take delivery of the goods, he must act in good faith both when he makes the contract and when he takes delivery of the goods.

Where B2 buys the goods and the requirements of s 24 are fulfilled, B2 takes title to the goods, extinguishing B1's title. Where B2 takes the goods under 'any other disposition' the nature of B2's interest will depend on the nature and effect of the disposition. For instance, where B2 takes the goods under a pledge, B1 owns the goods subject to the pledge. However, if B2 takes the goods under a conditional sale agreement he will acquire no title until the condition is fulfilled[18].

1 Chapter 15.
2 SoGA, ss 41–43; see 18.3.1.
3 SoGA, s 48(2).
4 SoGA, s 48(3), (4); see 18.3.4.
5 'Mercantile agent' in this context effectively has the same definition as it has under the Factors Act: SoGA, s 26.
6 Discussed below 17.4.2.
7 *City Fur Manufacturing Company Ltd v Fureenbond (Brokers) London Ltd* [1937] 1 All ER 799; *Forsythe International (UK) Ltd v Silver Shipping Co Ltd, The Saetta* [1994] 1 All ER 851 (a case decided under s 25).
8 [1965] AC 867, [1965] 2 All ER 105, PC.
9 [1972] 1 QB 210, [1971] 3 All ER 708, CA. The court preferred *Pacific Motor Auctions* to the earlier Court of Appeal decision in *Eastern Distributors Ltd v Goldring* [1957] 2 QB 600, [1957] 2 All ER 525.
10 *Mitchell v Jones* (1905) 24 NZLR 932.
11 *Worcester Works Finance Ltd v Cooden Engineering Ltd* [1972] 1 QB 210.
12 *Forsythe International (UK) Ltd v Silver Shipping Co Ltd, The Saetta* [1994] 1 All ER 851.
13 [1895] 2 Ch 415; see also *Ladbroke Leasing (South West) Ltd v Reekie Plant Ltd* 1983 SLT 155.
14 (1987) 163 CLR 236
15 [1994] 1 All ER 851. See also *Michael Gerson (Leasing) Ltd v Wilkinson* [2000] 35 LS Gaz R 37, in which the Court of Appeal has accepted that constructive delivery will suffice for the purposes of s 24.
16 See Skelton [1994] LMCLQ 19. It is possible to identify such an act in *Gamers* where B1 delivered to B2 a document acknowledging that it held the goods as bailee for B2.
17 SoGA, s 61(3).
18 *Re Highway Foods International Ltd* [1995] BCC 271, [1995] BCLC 209.

17.3.1 Oversales from bulk

Section 24 may be important where goods are sold from bulk and the seller, deliberately or otherwise, contracts to supply two or more buyers from the bulk and sells a greater quantity of goods than the bulk can supply.

If at the time when a contract is made with any particular buyer there are sufficient goods in the bulk to supply that buyer and all previous buyers with their contract quantities in full, there is no problem. All the buyers will become tenants in common of the bulk by virtue of s 20A and their shares, and rights against each other, will be determined by the provisions of ss 20A and 20B[1].

Difficulties may, however, arise if at the time of the sale to a particular buyer the quantity in the bulk is insufficient to supply that buyer and all previous buyers in full. In effect, the seller is then contracting to sell the same goods twice. In that case the last buyer can only become a tenant in common if he can rely on s 24. In order to do so he must establish that (a) at the time of the contract the seller was in possession of the goods or a documents of title thereto, and (b) he took delivery of the goods or documents of title.

The first of these requirements will normally cause no difficulty. It will clearly be satisfied if the goods are in the actual possession of the seller, as where they are held in the seller's warehouse. It will also be satisfied if the goods are in the physical possession of a third party provided either that the seller holds a document of title, as where the goods are in the possession of a carrier but the seller holds a bill of lading, or the third party holds the goods as bailee for the seller so that the seller is in constructive possession of the goods, as where the goods are held in the warehouse of a third party.

The second requirement may be more difficult. Clearly, there is no problem if the seller is in actual possession of the goods and the buyer takes actual delivery of the goods by their being separated from the bulk and appropriated to his contract.

Similarly, the section is satisfied if the seller is in possession of a document of title and delivers that document to the buyer, as where the seller in possession of a bill of lading in respect of part of a bulk cargo delivers the bill to the buyer. It seems that the section will also be satisfied if the seller in possession of a document of title delivers a different document of title[2]. The position is a little more difficult if the seller at the time of the contract is in actual possession of the goods – eg because they are in his warehouse – and delivers to the buyer a document of title, such as a delivery order. On its face, it seems that the section requires that where the seller is in possession of goods he must deliver the goods to the buyer if the latter is to be protected by s 24. However, if, as has been held[3], a buyer who takes constructive delivery of goods is protected by s 24, this difficulty is overcome. By giving the buyer a delivery order, the seller can be said to make constructive delivery of the goods, which will enable the buyer to rely on s 24[4].

Suppose, therefore, that S contracts to sell 500 gallons of oil to each of B1 and B2 from a bulk containing 1,000 gallons, and then contracts to sell a further 500 gallons to B3. B3 will be entitled to rely on s 24, and will therefore become owner of an undivided share in the bulk provided that he can satisfy the requirements of that section, and this was the intention of the Law Commissions when they proposed the 1995 reforms to the SoGA[5]. It must be borne in mind, however, that in order to rely on s 24, B3 must establish that he acted in good faith and without notice of the previous sales. In cases of oversales it will therefore be necessary to investigate the circumstances surrounding the sale in order to determine whether any particular buyer is entitled to a share in the bulk. It seems that this was not what the Commissions intended and may give rise to very difficult factual questions when the issue arises.

1   See 15.6.2.
2   *D F Mount Ltd v Jay and Jay (Provisions) Ltd* [1960] 1 QB 159, [1959] 3 All ER 307.
3   *Forsythe International (UK) Ltd v Silver Shipping Co Ltd, The Saetta* [1994] 1 All ER 851; see 17.3.1.
4   See Gullifer [1999] LMCLQ 93.
5   Law Commission 215, Scot LC 145 *Sale of Goods Forming Part of Bulk* (1993) para 4.18.

17.4 Buyers in possession

A person who has bought goods may resell them; indeed, a commercial buyer will often buy goods expressly for the purpose of resale; alternatively, the buyer may resell them in order to raise funds. This may be particularly likely if the buyer is in financial difficulties, when goods may be resold in order to try to stave off insolvency. Thus S, the seller, sells goods to B1, who in turn resells to a sub-buyer, B2, as follows:

$$S \xrightarrow{\text{First Sale}} B_1 \xrightarrow{\text{Second Sale}} B_2$$

If B1 fails to pay, S may, of course, sue B1 for the price. However, if B1 cannot be traced, or is insolvent and not worth suing, S may seek to recover the goods from B2. He can do so if he can establish that B1 had no title to the goods at the time of the resale to B2, unless B2 can take advantage of an exception to the nemo dat principle. There are two exceptions which are specifically intended to protect a person, such as B2, who buys goods from a person who has bought, or agreed to buy them.

17.4.1   *Sale under a voidable title*

Section 23 of the Sale of Goods Act provides that:

> 'When the seller of goods has a voidable title to them, but his title has not been avoided at the time of the sale, the buyer acquires a good title to the goods, provided he buys them in good faith and without notice of the seller's defect of title'[1].

The section therefore applies where B1 acquires goods from S in circumstances which entitle S to avoid the transfer to B1 and recover the goods. B2 is nevertheless protected, provided that the goods are sold to him before S avoids the transfer.

Typically, this exception is invoked where S transfers goods to B1 under a contract which is voidable for misrepresentation or duress. The most common case is where B1 agrees to buy goods and pays with a cheque which is subsequently dishonoured: he is then guilty of misrepresentation because when he pays by cheque he impliedly represents that it will be honoured on presentation. In such cases B1 is often a confidence trickster who cannot be traced or is not worth suing. Provided he resells the goods to B2 before S rescinds the contract, B2 gets a good title if the requirements of s 23 are fulfilled.

However, if the transaction between S and B1 was wholly void, B2 is not protected by s 23, and will generally be wholly unprotected. The distinction between void and voidable contracts is therefore crucial, and S may well try to establish that his contract with B1 was wholly void on the grounds of mistake. The issue arises, typically, where B1 fraudulently obtains goods from S by masquerading as some other person, X, and pays with a worthless or stolen cheque. In such cases the contract between S and B1 will be void for mistake if S can establish that he intended to contract with X, rather than with B1. However, although it may be possible to establish such a mistake where the parties do not make the contract inter praesentes[2], where they deal face to face, it will generally be presumed that S intends to contract with the person physically in his presence, so that there will be no mistake[3].

In *Ingram v Little*[4] B1 agreed to buy a car from S and offered to pay by cheque, falsely giving his name as 'P G M Hutchinson' and giving an address. S was initially reluctant to take a cheque, and insisted on checking the address given for 'P G M Hutchinson' in the telephone directory before releasing the car. The address in the directory matched that given by B1; however, it turned out that B1 was not Hutchinson, and the cheque was stolen. The car was discovered in the possession of B2, to whom B1 had sold it. A majority of the Court of Appeal held that the contract was void for mistake, so that S could recover it. However, *Ingram* must be regarded as an exceptional case. In *Lewis v Averay*[5] S sold his car to B1, who falsely claimed to be Richard Greene, a well-known actor of the time, and paid with a cheque signed 'R A Green'. It was held that the contract was voidable for misrepresentation, but not void for mistake; S had intended to contract with B1, the person in his presence, not with Greene the actor. B2, who had bought the car from B1, had therefore acquired a good title.

It is not easy to reconcile *Ingram* with *Lewis*[6], and Lord Denning in *Lewis* went so far as to say that *Ingram* was wrongly decided. It is submitted that *Lewis*, which protects the bona fide purchaser, is to be preferred, and that it represents the general rule in such cases. Mistake of identity will rarely be established where the parties deal face to face.

The distinction between 'void' and 'voidable' transactions is always difficult to draw[7], and it seems harsh that B2's rights should depend on it. Concentration on the technical question 'void or voidable?' disguises what is essentially a policy question, as Devlin LJ, who dissented in *Ingram v Little*, recognised:

'the dividing line between voidness and voidability is a very fine one . . . Need the rights of the parties in a case like this depend on such a distinction? The great virtue of the common law is that it sets out to solve legal problems by the application to them of principles which the ordinary man is expected to see as sensible and just. Here the common law, instead of looking for a principle that is simple and just depends on theoretical distinctions. The relevant question in this sort of case is not whether the contract was void or voidable, but which of two innocent parties shall suffer for the fraud of a third'[8].

In 1966 the Law Reform Committee proposed that the distinction between void and voidable contracts should be abolished in this context[9]. B2 would then be equally protected in either case.

Even where the contract is only voidable, not void, B2 is only protected if the requirements of s 23 are satisfied. In particular, he must acquire the goods in good faith before S rescinds the contract with B1. Curiously, under s 23, unlike the other nemo dat exceptions, the burden of proof is on the dispossessed owner to establish that the buyer did not act in good faith[10]. Rescission is normally effected by notifying the other contracting party, or by obtaining a court order. In the typical case, where B1 is fraudulent, it will normally be impossible for S to contact B1. However, in *Car and Universal Finance Co Ltd v Caldwell*[11], where S was defrauded into selling a car in return for a worthless cheque, it was held that S had effectively rescinded the contract by notifying the police and the AA of the loss of the car and asking them to look out for it; he was therefore able to recover the car from B2, who bought the car after the police had been notified. This decision severely prejudices the position of B2 and it has been suggested that it should be reversed[12]. However, its effect is limited because in such a case B will often be protected under the separate exception in SoGA, s 25[13].

Section 23 can protect remote purchasers, who acquire the goods from B2. B2 is not protected if he does not acquire the goods in good faith. However, if B2 resells the goods to B3, B3 may take advantage of the section if he acquires the goods in good faith before S avoids the original transaction.

1 The section only protects a buyer; however, a similar rule applies at common law and will protect a person who takes under another disposition.
2 See *Cundy v Lindsay* (1878) 3 App Cas 459, HL; contrast *King's Norton Metal Co Ltd v Edridge, Merrett & Co Ltd* (1897) 14 TLR 98, CA.
3 See 2.4.1; see also *Citibank NA v Brown Shipley & Co Ltd* [1991] 2 All ER 690.
4 [1961] 1 QB 31, [1960] 3 All ER 332.
5 [1972] 1 QB 198, [1971] 3 All ER 907; see also *Phillips v Brooks* [1919] 2 KB 243.
6 It is sometimes suggested that the crucial factor in *Ingram* was that S checked the telephone directory, proving that S intended to deal with Hutchinson: see Treitel, The Law of Contract (10th edn, 1999) p 276.

7   See 4.7.1 and 28.4.3.
8   [1961] 1 QB 31 at 42, [1960] 3 All ER 332 at 351.
9   12th Report, Cmnd 2958 (1966) para 15 in Diamond *A Review of Security Interests in Property*
     (1989, DTI), see 17.7. In *Lewis v Averay* Lord Denning expressed the view that a mistake of
     identity never makes the contract void, but only voidable.
10 In its 1994 Consultation Document, *'Transfer of Title: sections 21 to 26 of the Sale of Goods
     Act 1979'*, the DTI recommended that the burden of proof be reversed.
11 [1965] 1 QB 525.
12 Law Reform Committee, 12th Report, Cmnd 2958 (1966) para 15 in Diamond *A Review of Security
     Interests in Property* (1989, DTI), see 17.7.
13 *Newtons of Wembley Ltd v Williams* [1965] 1 QB 560, [1964] 3 All ER 532, CA.

17.4.2   Sale by a buyer in possession

Section 25 of the Sale of Goods Act provides that:

> 'Where a person having bought or agreed to buy goods obtains, with the
> consent of the seller, possession of the goods or the documents of title to the
> goods, the delivery or transfer by that person, or by a mercantile agent acting
> for him, of the goods or documents of title, under any sale, pledge or other
> disposition thereof, to any person receiving the same in good faith and without
> notice of any lien or other right of the original seller in respect of the goods,
> has the same effect as if the person making the delivery or transfer were a
> mercantile agent in possession of the goods or documents of title with the
> consent of the owner'.

This is broadly equivalent to the exception in s 24. However, there are several
significant differences in wording. Like s 24, it repeats an exception contained in
the Factors Act 1889[1]; once again, the Factors Act exception is slightly wider,
extending protection to a person who receives the goods under any 'agreement for
sale, pledge or other disposition'.

The significance of s 25 is that it applies where B1, who has agreed to buy goods
but to whom property has not yet passed, resells them to B2. It is therefore of the
utmost importance where goods are supplied under conditional sale agreements
under which S retains title until he is paid for the goods. Since the decision in the
Romalpa[2] case in 1976, it has become common practice for sellers who extend
credit to their customers to reserve title until payment, even where it is anticipated
that the goods will be resold before payment in order to raise funds to pay the
price. In practice, S will not seek to enforce his retention of title unless B1 is
insolvent. If B1 has resold the goods to B2, then, provided the requirements of
s 25 are satisfied, B2 gets good title, and S will be unable to recover them, leaving
S with a (practically worthless) personal action for the price against B1, unless he
can claim rights to other property under his retention of title clause[3].

However, s 25 only applies where B1 is a person who has 'bought or agreed to
buy' goods from S. It is therefore essential to classify the supply arrangement
between S and B1. Section 25 does not apply if the contract between S and B1 is
one for work and materials[4], agency[5] or sale or return[6]: in each of those cases, B1
is not a person who has 'bought or agreed to buy'. These distinctions may be
difficult to draw. The most difficult distinction, however, will generally be that
between conditional sale and hire purchase. It is well established that the hirer
under a hire purchase agreement is not a person who has 'agreed to buy'[7], so that
B2 is not protected by s 25 if B1 held the goods on hire purchase. Indeed, hire

429

purchase was conceived as a way of enabling a supplier to avoid his customer reselling the goods and transferring a title under s 25. In *Forthright Finance Ltd v Carlyle Finance Ltd*[8] the Court of Appeal held that the essential distinction between sale and hire purchase is that the buyer under a sale contract is contractually obliged to pay the price in full. Thus a contract which required the buyer to pay the full price for goods by instalments, and provided that, on payment in full, title to the goods would pass – subject to the buyer's option *not* to take title – was a contract of sale, not hire purchase. The reality of the transaction was that the buyer was committed to pay for the goods and the option not to take title was unlikely to be exercised. The court recognised that the form of the contract had been devised to evade the operation of s 25. Nevertheless, where under a conditional sale agreement the price is payable by instalments, the agreement closely resembles hire purchase; s 25(2) therefore provides that s 25 does not apply to a sale by a person who has agreed to buy goods under a conditional sale agreement which is a consumer credit agreement as defined by the Consumer Credit Act 1974 and under which the price is payable by instalments[9]. Section 25 therefore does *not* apply to sales where the seller is in possession of the goods under a contract of hire purchase or under certain types of conditional sale agreement. However, where a person to whom a motor vehicle is let on hire purchase or supplied under a conditional sale agreement resells the vehicle, a further, special exception to the nemo dat rule, created by Pt III of the Hire Purchase Act 1964, may apply[10].

In order for s 25 to apply, B1 must be in possession of the goods, or the documents of title to them, at the time of the sale to B2; however, constructive possession will suffice, so that B2 was protected by s 25 in a case where S delivered goods direct to B2 at B1's request: B1 was in constructive possession through S[11]. Furthermore, in contrast to the position under s 24, B1 must be in possession of the goods or documents of title with the consent of S. A thief therefore cannot pass a good title under s 25. However, a confidence trickster can: it is irrelevant that B1 obtains S's consent by deception and, moreover, once B1 has possession with S's consent, withdrawal of that consent has no effect unless B2 knows of it[12]. Thus a person who has bought goods under a voidable contract has 'agreed to buy', and can pass a good title, even if S has rescinded the contract prior to the resale[13].

B2 is protected by s 25 where he takes delivery of the goods in good faith under any sale, pledge or other disposition. In these respects s 25 is identical to s 24, and the discussion of these matters in relation to s 24 is equally applicable here[14]. Where goods are sold by S to B1 on conditional sale terms subject to a reservation of title until payment, B2 will be able to rely on s 25 unless he has notice both of the reservation of title and the fact that the price remains unpaid. In *The Saetta*[15] S supplied fuel bunkers to B1 for use aboard a ship chartered by B1 from B2. When B1 defaulted in payment of hire under the charter B2, the owner of the ship, took possession of it and the bunkers. B2 was aware that B1 had not paid for the bunkers and evidence showed that while some bunker suppliers included reservation of title clauses in their contracts, others claimed a maritime lien over the bunkered vessel and only 'a few suppliers' had neither a reservation of title nor a lien. It was argued that in those circumstances B2 must have known that S would be likely to have a reservation of title or some similar right, but it was held that, in the absence of actual knowledge of the reservation of title, that was insufficient notice to deny B2 the protection of s 25[16].

There is one significant difference between ss 24 and 25. Whereas a sale by a seller in possession under s 24 has the same effect as if 'the delivery or transfer were expressly authorised by the owner' of the goods, a sale by a buyer in possession under s 25 has the same effect as if the buyer 'were a mercantile agent in possession of the goods or documents of title with the consent of the owner'. The courts have given these words a potentially restrictive interpretation. In *Newtons of Wembley Ltd v Williams* the Court of Appeal held that, as a mercantile agent can only pass good title if he acts in the ordinary course of business as a mercantile agent, s 25 requires the buyer in possession to act as a mercantile agent acting in the ordinary course of business would act. On the facts of the case, this caused no problem: B1 had sold a car in an established street market in Warren Street, and the requirement was fulfilled. However, it is difficult to see how a person who is not a mercantile agent can act as if he were one. A mercantile agent must sell from business premises, during business hours and so on; but if B1 is a private individual he will not have business premises. It might have been better had s 25 been interpreted as meaning that a sale by B1 has the same effect as a sale by a mercantile agent who is acting in the course of business[17].

There is a further difficulty in the wording of s 25. It provides that a sale by a buyer who obtains possession of the goods with the consent of 'the seller' has the same effect as if he were 'a mercantile agent in possession of the goods or documents of title with the consent of the owner'. On its face this would suggest that if S is not the owner of the goods, a sale by B1 under the terms of s 25 will still pass a good title to B2, extinguishing the title of the true owner[18]. However, in *National Employers Mutual General Insurance Association Ltd v Jones*[19] the House of Lords rejected that reading of the Act. In that case S was a thief who stole a car from O, the true owner, and sold it to B1[20]. B1 could not acquire title under the Act, but B1 then resold to B2, and it was argued that B2 acquired good title by virtue of s 25: B1 had agreed to buy, and had acquired possession with the consent of S; his resale therefore had the same effect as if he were a mercantile agent authorised by O. The Court of Appeal[21] rejected that argument by reading s 25 and s 9 of the Factors Act as applying only where the initial seller had property in the goods. The House of Lords reached the same result, but by different reasoning, relying primarily on the history and general policy of the Factors Acts, and on the fact that the sale by a buyer in possession has the same effect as if the buyer were a mercantile agent. A sale by a mercantile agent only deprives the owner of property, under the Factors Act, s 2, if the owner entrusts the agent with possession of the goods. Therefore, B1 could only pass title to B2 under s 25 of the Sale of Goods Act (or Factors Act, s 9) if he was entrusted with the goods by their owner.

The reasoning in *Jones* is not entirely convincing. It appears to involve a departure from the clear, literal wording of the section and it is difficult to see why two different words in the same section of a statute should be given the same meaning. Sir Denys Buckley, dissenting in the Court of Appeal, observed that there might be sound policy reasons why the first buyer from the thief should not be protected, but subsequent buyers, who do not deal with the thief, should be. However, similar wording appears in s 24 of the Act, where there would be no good reason to prefer the second over the first buyer, since both buy from the thief. Moreover, the language of s 25 does suggest that it is only the title of the original seller which is overridden[22]. Whatever the merits of the reasoning, the effect of the *Jones* decision is clear: a person who buys stolen goods can now never acquire a good title to them and is always at risk of their being repossessed by the original owner.

1   Factors Act 1889, s 9.
2   *Aluminium Industrie Vaasen BV v Romalpa Aluminium Ltd* [1976] 2 All ER 552, [1976] 1 WLR 676; see 18.4.1.
3   See 18.4.3; 18.4.5.

4   *Dawber Williamson Roofing Ltd v Humberside CC* (1979) 14 BLR 70.
5   *Shaw v Metropolitan Police Comr* [1987] 3 All ER 405, [1987] 1 WLR 1332, CA.
6   Normally B2 will be protected because the sale by B1 will adopt the transaction, passing title to B1 and thus to B2. However, if S retains title under a sale or return transaction, it has been held that B2 will not get title on B1's resale: *Weiner v Harris* [1910] 1 KB 285, CA. See generally Taylor [1985] JBL 390.
7   *Helby v Matthews* [1895] AC 471, HL.
8   [1997] 4 All ER 90.
9   This provision did not apply in *Carlyle,* where the price of the goods meant that the agreement was not a consumer credit agreement as defined by the Consumer Credit Act: see ch 25.
10   See 17.4.3.
11   *Four Point Garage Ltd v Carter* [1985] 3 All ER 12.
12   Factors Act 1889, s 2(2).
13   *Newtons of Wembley Ltd v Williams* [1965] 1 QB 560, [1964] 3 All ER 532, CA.
14   Above 17.3.
15   *Forsythe International (UK) Ltd v Silver Shipping Co Ltd, The Saetta* [1994] 1 All ER 851.
16   Strictly, the finding was obiter, since Clarke J had already found that the transaction fell outside s 25 on other grounds.
17   See *Benjamin's Sale of Goods* (5th edn, 1997) para 7-078 and Atiyah, *Sale of Goods* (10th edn, 2000) p 407.
18   Various alternative interpretations of the provision had been proposed: see Cornish (1964) 27 MLR 472; Battersby and Preston (1975) 38 MLR 77; Atiyah, *Sale of Goods* (7th edn) pp 302–303; *Benjamin's Sale of Goods* (3rd edn, 1987) para 533.
19   [1990] 1 AC 24, [1988] 2 All ER 425.
20   This is a simplified version of the facts; in reality there were several resales.
21   [1987] 3 All ER 385, CA.
22   See the arguments of Battersby (1991) 54 MLR 752, which have persuaded me to alter the views expressed in the first edition of this book.

17.4.3   *Sales of vehicles let on hire purchase*

As noted above, s 25 has no application where goods are sold by a person to whom they are bailed under a hire purchase agreement, because such a person is not a person who has 'agreed to buy'[1], and for this purpose, 'consumer' conditional sale agreements where the price is payable by instalments are equated with hire purchase[2]. However, it was recognised that this might work injustice on a person who might acquire such goods in ignorance of the hire purchase agreement and later find them repossessed by the finance company which had supplied them. A special statutory exception to the nemo dat rule was therefore introduced by the Hire Purchase Act 1964[3]. It applies where motor vehicles held under hire purchase agreements are sold by the hirer before property has passed to him. The provisions are complex, but their effect is to protect the first private purchaser of the vehicle, provided he acts in good faith.

The provisions are very restricted in scope. First, they apply only to motor vehicles, even though many other categories of goods may be supplied on hire purchase. Secondly, they apply only where a vehicle has been bailed under a hire purchase agreement, or supplied under a conditional sale agreement. Thus, for instance, if a car is let under a leasing arrangement, the provisions do not apply (and the buyer has no protection if the goods are sold). Thirdly, they only apply in favour of a person who buys, agrees to buy or takes the vehicle on hire purchase: other dispositions are not protected. Fourthly, they do not protect a 'trade or finance purchaser', which means a purchaser who carries on business wholly or partly of purchasing vehicles for resale or providing finance by purchasing cars to let them on hire purchase or to agree to sell them under conditional sale agreements[4]. It has been held that a person who dealt in cars in his spare time was not a private purchaser for this purpose, even when he bought a car for his own use[5]. Although a dealer cannot be protected by the provisions, the first private purchaser is protected even though the vehicle has passed through the hands of one or more dealers.

In order to be protected by the provisions, the private purchaser must acquire the vehicle in good faith. As under the other nemo dat exceptions, the test of good faith is subjective, so that provided the purchaser is honest he is protected[6]. If the first private purchaser is not in good faith, neither he nor any subsequent purchaser is protected. This may cause problems for a purchaser who did not himself buy directly from the defaulting hire-purchaser: his protection depends on the bona fides of the first private purchaser. However, in such a case he may rely on a series of presumptions[7], the effect of which is that provided that he can show that he or one of his predecessors in title acquired the vehicle in good faith, he gets good title unless the bailor can establish either (i) that the first private purchaser did not act in good faith, or (ii) that there was no disposition of the vehicle by the original bailee – for instance, because the vehicle was stolen from him – or (iii) that there is a break in the chain of title between the first private purchaser and the claimant.

The provisions of the Hire Purchase Act offer a measure of protection to private purchasers of vehicles supplied under hire purchase or conditional sale agreements. However, their scope is limited. Trade dealers, who cannot rely on the provisions, must protect themselves. In 1938 the finance companies responsible for supplying vehicles on hire purchase and similar terms established an organisation, the Hire Purchase Bureau, to receive and hold details of hire purchase and similar agreements affecting vehicles. Initially, the register of agreements kept by the Bureau could be searched by the finance houses who were its members. Gradually, however, the range of the Bureau's activities was expanded[8]. It is now a commercial organisation, Hire Purchase Information plc, and a second organisation, Experian, operates a similar register. The two organisations share information and their registers, which contain much information other than that relating to finance agreements, can be inspected by members of the public. Since hire purchase and conditional sale are, effectively, methods of providing secured finance for the supply of goods, these registers can be seen as a form of private sector register of security interests. However, it has been held that a company which fails to register an agreement owes no duty of care to another which searches and relies on the register[9]. A memorandum of agreement between the finance houses and motor dealers requires finance houses to register their agreements promptly, but a non-party, including a private purchaser, will not be protected by that agreement. The result is that a company which fails to register an agreement will incur no liability to a purchaser who checks the register before buying a vehicle. Conversely, given that there is no duty to investigate title in transactions relating to goods, and the definition of 'notice' in the Hire Purchase Act as 'actual notice'[10], a private buyer who can rely on the Hire Purchase Act provisions suffers no penalty if he purchases a vehicle without searching the register and thus fails to discover details of a registered agreement.

1 *Helby v Matthews* [1895] AC 471, HL.
2 SoGA, s 25(2).
3 Hire Purchase Act 1964, Pt III, ss 27–29. For a general discussion of this and related areas see Davies (1995) 15 LS 14.
4 Hire Purchase Act 1964, s 29(2).
5 *Stevenson v Beverley Bentinck Ltd* [1976] 2 All ER 606, [1976] 1 WLR 483, CA.
6 *Dodds v Yorkshire Bank Finance* [1992] CCLR 30 CA.
7 Hire Purchase Act 1964, s 28.
8 See generally Davies [1995] JBL 36.

9 *Moorgate Mercantile Ltd v Twitchings* [1977] AC 890, [1976] 2 All ER 641, HL; see 17.2.2.
10 Hire Purchase Act 1964, s 29(3).

17.5 Sales in market overt

Until 1994 the Sale of Goods Act contained a further exception, in s 22, which provided that where goods were sold in market overt, a buyer who bought them in good faith would get a good title to them. The exception was subject to a number of limitations. It only applied to sales in open, publicly constituted markets, established by Royal Charter, statute[1], or long-established custom and to sales from the ground floor of shops in the City of London[2]. A sale in a market had to be in accordance with the customs or usages of the market and in any case the sale had to take place between sunrise and sunset[3].

The market overt rule had little in common with the other exceptions to the nemo dat rule but had a long history[4]. Historically, it encouraged trade and vigilance: most sales took place in open, public markets and fairs. A dispossessed owner could be expected to visit his local market and look out for his goods. However, by the 1990s it was widely seen as anachronistic and it was finally abolished[5] in relation to contracts made on or after 3 January 1995 by the Sale of Goods (Amendment) Act 1994. The reason for its abolition seems to have been concern that it could facilitate the disposal of stolen goods: as a result of the decision in *National Employers' General Mutual Insurance Association Ltd v Jones*[6] it was the only nemo dat exception which could protect a bona fide purchaser of stolen goods. In particular, the rule facilitated the sale of stolen works of art and antiques which are often sold in long-established markets[7].

It cannot be denied that the market overt rule was anachronistic. It is no longer true that most trade takes place in markets and the speed and ease of modern transport undermines the justification for the rule that the dispossessed owner can protect himself by looking out for his goods at the local market: the goods may be at the opposite end of the country, and sold, before he knows they are gone. Similarly, the special status of the City of London was hard to justify in modern conditions. However, abolition of the rule leaves even innocent purchasers of stolen goods wholly unprotected. Since the owner of stolen property will often be insured against theft, the ability to recover stolen property will often benefit the insurer rather than the dispossessed owner and it might therefore have been better to extend the protection of the bona fide purchaser[8]. However, such extension might have had the effect of further raising premiums for theft insurance[9].

1 *Bishopsgate Motor Finance Corpn Ltd v Transport Brakes Ltd* [1949] 1 KB 322, [1949] 1 All ER 37, CA. For a general discussion of the market overt rule see Davenport and Ross, 'Market Overt' in Palmer and McKendrick (eds), *Interests in Goods* (2nd edn, 1998).
2 *The Case of Market Overt* (1596) 5 Co Rep 836. See Pease (1915) 31 LQR 270.
3 *Reid v Metropolitan Police Comr* [1973] QB 551, [1973] 2 All ER 97, CA.
4 The earliest known case is from 1291.
5 Reform had previously been recommended by the Law Reform Committee in 1966: 12th Report, Cmnd 2958 (1966).
6 [1990] 1 AC 24, [1988] 2 All ER 425.
7 In some quarters it has been suggested that it might have facilitated the sale of stolen goods at events such as car boot sales, but it is unlikely that such sales would have been regarded as sales in market overt.
8 The Law Reform Committee recommended in 1966 that a similar rule be extended to all retail sales.
9 See Battersby (1991) 54 MLR 752.

17.6   Special powers of sale

There is a final group of exceptions, preserved by s 21(2)(b) of the Sale of Goods Act 1979, which provides that nothing is to affect 'the validity of any contract of sale under any special common law or statutory power of sale or under the order of a court of competent jurisdiction'. This takes in a wide range of transactions and allows a buyer to take good title under such transactions, notwithstanding the nemo dat rule. Common law powers include the power of a pledgee to sell goods pledged with him[1]. Statutory powers include those of sheriffs and bailiffs to sell goods of debtors seized under writs or warrants of execution, and of bailees to sell goods bailed with them[2]. A sale may also be made by an officer of the court acting under a court order. Such an order might be made where, for instance, the parties are in dispute over ownership of perishable goods, to prevent the goods deteriorating, leaving the parties to fight over the proceeds of sale.

1   See 22.1.1.5.
2   The bailee is required to give notice to the owner, requiring him to collect the goods, before selling: Torts (Interference With Goods) Act 1977, s 12.

17.7   Limitation

The dispossessed owner may also be effectively deprived of his property by the rules on limitation of actions. The right to bring an action in respect of any act of conversion is barred after six years from the first act of conversion[1] and the owner's title is extinguished[2]. The only exception is that there is no limitation period where the owner is deprived of goods by theft or other offences of dishonesty[3], unless the goods come into the hands of a bona fide purchaser. In that case, the owner's title is extinguished six years after the bona fide purchase.

1   Limitation Act 1980, s 3(1).
2   Limitation Act 1980, s 3(2).
3   Limitation Act 1980, s 4.

17.8   Conclusion

The nemo dat principle itself is simple but some of the law surrounding it and its exceptions is outdated and much is highly technical and illogical.

> 'Statutory protection for the bona fide purchaser has developed in a piecemeal and haphazard fashion; and some of the relevant provisions have been so drafted and interpreted as to make their application depend not on principles of equity or justice but on fine technicalities which have little rhyme and less reason[1].'

The present law requires the courts to draw fine distinctions between transactions which may have similar practical effects. Moreover, concentration on the detailed and technical rules obscures the policy issues which are raised by title conflicts, which require the court to choose not just between two innocent parties, but between two competing principles – protection of property and security of transactions. A more subtle solution to such problems would be to apportion the loss between the two parties, according to the extent of their respective responsibility for it, as suggested by Lord Devlin.

Another factor which might be considered relevant is the availability to the parties of insurance cover. Most owners insure their cars, and other valuable property, against theft and possibly against other loss occasioned by dishonesty. An innocent purchaser who buys a stolen car or other property in good faith and in ignorance of it being stolen is unlikely to be insured against the loss he suffers by having to return the property. As a result, the dispossessed owner will often claim for his loss on his insurance policy, leaving his insurer, who is subrogated to his rights, to sue the bona fide purchaser[2]. Insurance against bad debts is also available to sellers of goods. At present the law seems to throw the risk of loss caused by fraud on the party least likely to be insured against it.

Reform of this area of law has been mooted on four occasions in the last 30 years. In 1966 the Law Reform Committee considered and rejected Lord Devlin's proposal to apportion losses, pointing out that where there had been a chain of transactions the apportionment of loss between all the parties in the chain would be a particularly difficult task[3]. The Committee made its own proposals for reform, but they were rejected, for fear of encouraging dishonesty by facilitating the disposal of stolen goods. In 1971 the Crowther Committee on Consumer Credit[4] recommended abolition of some of the technical distinctions which the present law draws between similar supply arrangements, such as conditional sale and hire purchase, allowing the innocent purchaser the same protection in each case.

The matter was considered again in 1989 by Professor Diamond in his Review of Security Interests in Property[5], carried out for the Department of Trade and Industry. The review was primarily concerned with reform of the law relating to security over personal property. The report recommended that all security devices, including conditional sale, hire purchase, finance lease, should be treated alike and that non-possessory securities should require protection by registration. Such reform would necessitate –

> 'a clear statement of the rights of innocent purchasers of the goods subject to the security interest . . . It would be an unacceptable hindrance to trade if buyers from dealers in such goods, whether at the manufacturing, wholesale or retail level, were expected to search in the register of security interests'[6].

The report therefore made two sets of proposals. The first, regarded as the minimum required by the proposed security reforms, recommended that an innocent purchaser should always take free of any security interest, regardless of its nature, except that in the case of motor vehicles the present position should be maintained and trade purchasers should be required to search the register of security interests, and would only take free of unregistered interests.

However, Professor Diamond recommended an alternative set of 'better reforms', which would go considerably further. 'There should be a general principle in the law that applies wherever the owner of goods has entrusted goods to, or acquiesced in their possession by another person', so that any disposition of the goods by the possessor in favour of an innocent purchaser would confer a good title on the purchaser, to the extent that the owner could have conferred title[7]. This would only apply where it would appear to a reasonable purchaser that the possessor's disposition was in the ordinary course of business, but this requirement would not apply to a sale by the possessor of consumer goods[8], removing some of the difficulties created by the decision in *Newtons of Wembley Ltd v Williams*[9]. Such a broad principle would cover the cases currently covered by ss 23–25 of the Sale of Goods Act and also many cases of agency and of apparent ownership. It would remove the artificial distinctions currently drawn between void and voidable contracts, and between similar transactions such as hire purchase, conditional sale and finance leasing. Professor Diamond also proposed that ss 8–9 of the Factors Act 1889, duplicating the exceptions in ss 24–25[10], and the decision in *Car and Universal Finance Ltd v Caldwell*[11] should be repealed: rescission of a voidable contract would have no effect on the innocent purchaser, who would be protected unless the dispossessed owner had repossessed the goods[12].

Professor Diamond's proposals go considerably further in the protection of the bona fide purchaser than the courts have so far been prepared to go. They would simplify and rationalise the law and were generally well received[13]. However, neither they nor the remainder of his recommendations have so far been implemented and in January 1994 a further, brief, consultation document was issued by the Consumer Affairs division of the Department of Trade and Industry, inviting views on the desirability of reform. Its core proposal was for replacement of the detailed exceptions in ss 21–25 of the Sale of Goods Act with a broad principle, along the lines recommended by Professor Diamond, that where the owner of goods has entrusted them to or acquiesced in their possession by another person, an innocent purchaser of the goods should acquire a good title to them, which might apply only to dispositions appearing to be in the ordinary course of business or extend to all sales of consumer goods. An alternative, more limited, option considered in the discussion document was the extension of the principle in Pt III of the Hire Purchase Act[14] to all goods held on hire purchase, conditional sale or lease, or covered by a bill of sale. However, the document allowed only a very short time for responses and to date the only modern reform to the nemo dat rule has been the abolition of the market overt rule.

1　Report of the Crowther Committee on Consumer Credit, Cmnd 4596 (1971) para 4.2.8.
2　As in *National Employers Mutual General Insurance Association Ltd v Jones* [1990] 1 AC 24, [1988] 2 All ER 425, HL.
3　Law Reform Committee, 12th Report, Cmnd 2958 (1966).
4　Above, note 1.
5　DTI, *A Review of Security Interests in Property* (1989).
6　Paragraphs 13.5.1, 13.5.2.
7　Paragraph 13.6.3.
8　Paragraph 13.6.4.
9　[1965] 1 QB 560, [1964] 3 All ER 532, CA.
10　Paragraph 13.6.10.
11　[1965] 1 QB 525.
12　Paragraph 13.6.6.
13　They were welcomed by a Memorandum approved by both the Law Society and the Law Reform Committee of the General Council of the Bar ('Comments on "A Review of Security Interests in Property"', The Law Society, 1989), save that the Memorandum disagreed with the proposal to abolish the distinction between voidable contracts and those void for mistake, on the grounds that the distinction encourages sellers to take reasonable care to confirm the identity of their buyers. However, it is not clear that the present law encourages effective precautions.
14　Above 17.4.3.

Chapter 18

Buyer's Duties and Seller's Remedies

18.0   The buyer's duties under a contract of sale

Section 27 of the Sale of Goods Act provides that 'It is . . . the duty of the buyer to accept and pay for [the goods] in accordance with the terms of the contract'. However, it is clear that this does not give a complete picture: the buyer is also under a duty to take delivery of the goods[1] and further duties may be imposed by the terms of the contract. In particular, in large or international transactions, the buyer may often have to perform extra duties, such as giving notices of readiness, or nominating ships to carry the goods, which are necessary to enable the seller to fulfil his duties[2].

1   SoGA, s 37.
2   See ch 33.

18.0.1   *The duty to pay the price*

The buyer's duty to pay the price is clearly fundamental, since the essence of the contract of sale is the exchange of property in the goods for the price. Normally, the buyer's payment obligation will be defined by the terms of the contract. If the contract does not fix a price, the buyer must pay a reasonable price[1]; however, the fact that no price has been agreed may often indicate that the parties have not entered into a binding contract. Normally, the contract will fix the price and contain additional provisions, for instance, allowing the buyer a discount for early payment, or requiring interest to be paid if payment is made late. It is now a statutory implied term in certain sale contracts that interest is payable on the price in the event of late payment[2].

Similarly, the contract will normally fix the time for payment. If the contract is silent, the general rule is 'cash on delivery': the buyer must be ready and willing to pay when the seller is ready and willing to deliver[3]. In practice this rule is almost always varied in commercial contracts, where it is normal for the buyer to be allowed credit. Even where the contract does fix the time for payment, the prima facie rule is that 'stipulations as to time of payment are not of the essence'[4] so that late payment is a breach of contract but not normally a repudiatory breach. Therefore, if the buyer does not pay on time, the seller may be entitled to claim interest if the contract provides for it, or damages for any losses caused by the late payment[5], but normally may not terminate the contract. However, s 48(3) of the Act allows the seller to terminate the contract and resell the goods if either (a) the goods are perishable, or (b) the buyer fails to pay within a reasonable time of the seller serving notice of his intention to resell the goods; effectively, therefore, time is of the essence where the goods are perishable, or where the seller serves notice to complete. Of course, the contract may expressly make the time for payment 'of the essence', or give the seller an express right to resell[6]. In addition, the seller is entitled to withhold delivery of the goods until the buyer is ready to pay[7], and may exercise his lien over the goods, provided they are still in his possession[8].

The contract may also define how payment is to be made. If the contract does not fix the place for payment the general rule is that a debtor must seek out his creditor to make payment[9], and payment will normally be due at the seller's place of business. Payment is normally required to be made in cash; however, the contract may provide for payment to be made in some particular way, for instance by means of bill of exchange or letter of credit, and international sale contracts normally do define the method of payment to be used. The contract may impliedly allow payment to be made other than in cash, and it will normally be implied that the buyer can pay by cheque. Payment by cheque or other bill of exchange normally operates only as a conditional discharge of the buyer's obligation to pay the price, so that if the bill is dishonoured, the seller's right to claim payment from the buyer revives. Alternatively, the seller may sue on the bill[10]. However, it has been held that payment by credit card will normally operate as an absolute discharge of the buyer's liability; the seller's only right then is to claim payment from the credit card company and, if for any reason the credit card company fails to pay, the seller has no right to claim payment from the buyer[11].

The contract may allow the buyer to pay the price by instalments. In that case instalments are payable in accordance with the terms of the contract and the contract may be subject to the Consumer Credit Act 1974[12].

1   SoGA, s 8(2); see 8.1.3.1.
2   Late Payment of Commercial Debts (Interest) Act 1998, below 18.0.1.1.
3   SoGA, s 28.
4   SoGA, s 10(1).
5   *President of India v La Pintada Compania Navigacion SA* [1985] AC 104, [1984] 2 All ER 773, HL.
6   SoGA, s 48(4); see 18.3.4.
7   SoGA, s 28.
8   SoGA, s 41; see 18.3.1.
9   *The Eider* [1893] P 119, CA.
10 See 28.1.2.
11 *Re Charge Card Services Ltd* [1989] Ch 497, [1988] 3 All ER 702, CA.
12 See 26.6.4.

18.0.1.1 *Interest*

Where goods are supplied on credit terms, the seller is in a relatively weak bargaining position if the buyer fails to pay at the due date. He may refuse to enter into further contracts or withhold credit from the buyer until the outstanding debt is settled, but that will only be possible if a continuing relationship is contemplated, and even then it may be commercially impractical if the buyer is a major customer.

The rationale for not treating the time for payment as of the essence is that late payment can generally be adequately compensated by a payment of interest.

However, prior to 1998, interest on late payments was only available in limited circumstances. It was established in 1893 that the court had no power at common law to award damages to compensate for late payment of a debt[1]. The courts were given statutory power in 1934 to award interest on debts for which judgment was given[2] and in 1982 on sums paid after the commencement of proceedings but before judgment[3]. Once a creditor commenced proceedings for a debt, therefore, he was entitled to interest on the debt whether the debtor paid before or after judgment. But where the debtor paid late but before commencement of proceedings the creditor had no right to interest or compensation. In 1978 the Law Commission recommended creation of a general statutory right to interest[4], but their recommendation was not implemented.

In 1984 the House of Lords recognised a limited exception to the general common law rule, permitting the court to award damages under the second limb of the rule in *Hadley v Baxendale*[5] if the creditor can prove that late payment has caused him special damage, provided that such damage was in the reasonable contemplation of the debtor at the time the contract was made[6]. Whilst recognising the harshness of the general rule, and calling for its reform, however, their Lordships felt it was too well established to be changed. The result was that, in most cases, a debtor could withhold payment due under a contract with impunity and so, in effect, obtain an extended period of interest-free credit, provided that he paid before the commencement of proceedings.

By the 1990s there was widespread concern that there was a culture of late payment under which debtors deliberately withheld payment of their debts to their own financial advantage, and that this had a particularly adverse effect on small businesses, who lacked the bargaining power, when dealing with larger trading partners, to insist on a contractual right to interest. The problem was recognised both in the UK and in Europe, where late payment was seen as an obstacle to the Single Market. In 1998, therefore, the Late Payment of Commercial Debts (Interest) Act 1998 was passed, making interest payable on debts arising under contracts for the supply of goods or services which are paid late, regardless of the issue of proceedings. The rationale of the legislation was explained by the Minister for Small Firms when introducing the legislation, as follows:

> 'Paying late is wrong and unfair. Any business that pays late as a matter of course is effectively saying that it is acceptable to abuse the provision of trade credit and the good faith of its suppliers'[7].

The Act's immediate objective is to provide an incentive for the debtor to make prompt payment, whilst also compensating the creditor for being deprived of use of the money during the period of default. More generally, however, it is hoped that, by encouraging prompt payment, the Act will lead to a change in business culture so that late payment becomes less common. An EC directive on the same subject was published in June 2000[8]. The provisions of the two instruments are broadly similar.

The effect of the 1998 Act is that it is an implied term of a contract for the sale or supply of goods or supply of services where both parties act in the course of business that debts created by the contract carry simple interest[9]. So where the buyer under a sale contract fails to pay at the due time, the seller is entitled to interest under the Act. The Act only applies where both parties act 'in the course of a business'. That phrase will no doubt give rise to the same difficulties in this context as it has in others[10]. It is submitted that, given the objectives of the Act, the wider interpretation favoured in *Stevenson v Rogers*[11] will maximise the Act's application and should be preferred. Interest under the Act runs from the date specified in the contract for payment, or, if none is specified, from the day after the last day of the period of 30 days commencing with either the date of the supplier's performance or the date on which the debtor has notice of the amount due or claimed to be due[12].

The statutory right to interest would be worthless if it could simply be excluded. The courts are therefore given power to strike down contract terms which seek to exclude or evade the Act. First, any contract term which purports to exclude or vary the right to statutory interest is void unless the contract provides a 'substantial remedy' for late payment[13] in the light of circumstances when the relevant terms were agreed. A contractual remedy is regarded as 'substantial' for this purpose unless (a) it is insufficient either for compensating the supplier for late payment or for deterring late payment and (b) 'it would not be fair or reasonable to allow the remedy be relied on to oust or . . . vary' the statutory right[14]. In assessing whether it would be fair or reasonable to allow a contract provision to oust or vary the statutory right, the court is directed to consider, in particular:

'(a) the benefits of commercial certainty;
 (b) the strength of the bargaining positions of the parties relative to each other;
 (c) whether the term was imposed by one party to the detriment of the other (whether by the use of standard terms or otherwise); and
 (d) whether the supplier received an inducement to agree to the term'[15].

These are broadly similar to the factors the court is required to consider when making the assessment reasonableness under Sch 2 to the Unfair Contract Terms Act 1977, but the requirement to consider 'the benefits of commercial certainty' may mean that a provision which might otherwise be judged unfair will be upheld.

Second, any term (whether in the buyer's standard terms or otherwise) which purports to postpone 'the time at which a qualifying debt would otherwise be created' by the Act, shall be valid only if it satisfies the test of reasonableness in the Unfair Contract Terms Act[16]. The intention appears to be to prevent the parties simply agreeing to postpone the date for payment so as to defer the date when the right to interest starts to run under the Act, but the section is not clearly drafted. If this is its effect, the result is that a contract term providing for payment more than 30 days after delivery will be subject to a test of reasonableness[17].

The parties are thus free to agree to the payment of interest on terms more generous than the statutory right, but any provision less favourable to the supplier is subject to the court's discretionary control. Withholding payment may, however, be legitimate in some circumstances. For instance, the buyer may claim to be entitled to exercise a right of set-off, or may withhold payment because of defects in the goods, or to put pressure on the supplier to settle a dispute. Partly in order to provide for this type of situation, the Act gives the court a wide discretion to remit the right to statutory interest, in whole or in part, 'where by reason of the conduct of the supplier' (before or after creation of the debt) the 'interests of justice' so require.

The rate of interest payable under the Act is to be fixed by order by the Secretary of State from time to time[18]. The Act is to be brought into force in stages. At present, it applies only to contracts made between small business suppliers, defined as businesses with 50 or fewer employees, and (a) large businesses, (b) UK public authorities, or (c) other small businesses[19].

The 1998 Act addresses a longstanding defect in English commercial law. Whether it will be effective either to deter late payment or to help change the culture of late payment remains to be seen. The rate of interest prescribed by the Act is generous. However, the language of the Act is complex and many of its provisions are open-textured, giving considerable discretion to the courts. The application of the Act in any situation is therefore uncertain. One may question whether a business which lacks the bargaining power to insist on a contractual provision for interest will have the power to take enforcement proceedings against a debtor who ignores the new Act, especially given the potential for costly litigation created by the Act's various discretionary provisions[20].

1   *London Chatham and Dover Rly Co v South Eastern Rly Co* [1893] AC 429.
2   Law Reform (Miscellaneous Provisions) Act 1934, s 3 (1).
3   Supreme Court Act 1981, s 35A or County Courts Act 1984, s 69, inserted by Administration of Justice Act 1982.
4   Law Commission's Report on Interest 1978 (Law Com no 88).
5   (1854) 9 Exch 341.
6   *President of India v La Pintada Compania Navigacion SA* [1985] AC 104, [1984] 2 All ER 773.
7   Hansard HC Debs 5 May 1998, col 591.
8   Directive 2000/35 of June 29, 2000, on combating late payment in commercial transactions.
9   Sections 1–2. Consumer credit agreements and contracts intended to operate by way of mortgage, pledge, charge or other security are excluded from the Act and there is power for the Secretary of State by order to exclude other classes of contract: s 2(5).
10 See 2.6.4.2 and 11.2.1.
11 [1999] 1 All ER 613; see 11.2.1.
12 Section 4. Special provision is made for advance payments, when the period runs from the day after the date on which the obligation to which the advance payment relates is performed: s 11.
13 Section 8.
14 Section 9(1).
15 Section 9(3).
16 Section 14.
17 This seems to be the effect of the corresponding provision of the EC directive, art 3.3. Under the directive a term varying the statutory right is not to be enforceable if, considering all the circumstances 'including good commercial practice', the term is 'grossly unfair to the creditor'.
18 Section 6. The initial rate has been fixed at 8% per annum over Bank of England base rate prevailing from time to time: Late Payment of Commercial Debts (Rate of Interest) Orders 1998, SI Nos 2480 and 2765. The EC directive requires the rate to be set at least six percentage points over the main refinancing rate of the European Central Bank, or, for states nor participating in economic and monetary union, above the rate set by its national central bank.
19 Late Payment of Commercial Debts (Interest) Act 1998 (Commencement No 1) Order 1998, SI 1998/2479; Late Payment of Commercial Debts (Interest) Act 1998 (Commencement No 2) Order 1999, SI 1999/1816; Late Payment of Commercial Debts (Interest) Act 1998 (Commencement No 4) Order 2000, SI 2000/2740. It is expected that the Act will be extended to all business suppliers by 2002.
20 See Hann (1998) 148 NLJ 1676.

18.0.2   *The duty to take delivery*

Section 37 of the Act gives the seller certain remedies if the buyer fails to take delivery of the goods within a reasonable time. It is therefore clear that the buyer is under an obligation to take delivery of the goods, at the place and time fixed for delivery by the contract. Often the contract may require the buyer to take delivery when required to do so by notice served by the seller. However, the time for the buyer to take delivery is not normally of the essence, so that the buyer's failure to take delivery on time will allow the seller to claim damages but not to terminate the contract, unless by failing to take delivery the buyer indicates that he intends to repudiate the contract. There is an exception, however, in the case of perishable goods[1], when the time for taking delivery is normally of the essence. In addition, if delivery is delayed due to the buyer's default, he will bear the risk of any loss of or damage to the goods 'which might not have occurred' but for his fault[2].

1   *Sharp v Christmas* (1892) 8 TLR 687, CA.
2   SoGA, s 20(2).

18.0.3   *The duty to accept the goods*

Although the Act states that it is the buyer's duty to accept the goods, it does not define 'acceptance' in this context. It seems that the buyer commits a breach of his duty to accept if he wrongfully rejects the goods, so that a buyer who rejects is in breach unless the rejection is justified by a prior breach of contract by the seller[1]. 'Acceptance' is therefore not necessarily the same thing as 'taking delivery': the buyer may accept the goods but then fail to take delivery, or take delivery but then wrongfully reject the goods. However, in many cases a failure to take delivery will also constitute a wrongful rejection, for instance, if the buyer fails to take delivery at the prescribed time and makes clear that he will not take delivery at all. Wrongful rejection by the buyer amounts to a repudiatory breach, entitling the seller to terminate the contract.

1   See 12.1.

18.1   The seller's remedies

If the buyer fails to perform his obligations under the contract, the seller has a range of remedies to choose from. If the buyer indicates an intention to repudiate the contract, the seller may accept that repudiation and terminate the contract. He is then released from his obligations under the contract. In addition, if the buyer is in breach of contract, for instance, by failing to take delivery, or failing to accept the goods, the seller is entitled to claim damages for any loss he suffers as a result of the breach. As an alternative, in certain circumstances he may bring a liquidated claim against the buyer for the price, if the buyer fails to pay.

Both the claim for damages and the claim for the price are personal claims; they may be appropriate where the buyer will not perform his obligations. However, in many cases the buyer fails to perform because he cannot do so, for instance because he is insolvent. In that case a personal claim is of little or no value. The Act gives the seller a number of real remedies, which will often be more advantageous because they can be exercised as a means of self-help and can be exercised against the goods themselves. These remedies are therefore particularly important where the buyer is insolvent. Furthermore, the terms of the contract will often supplement the statutory real remedies by including a retention of title clause, giving the seller extended protection against the buyer's insolvency.

18.2   Personal remedies

Two personal monetary claims are available to the seller: a claim for the price and a claim for damages.

18.2.1   *The claim for the price*

Where available, the action for the price offers the seller a number of advantages. Since it is a liquidated claim, there is no need for the seller to prove loss, or to mitigate his loss. Moreover, as a liquidated claim it offers procedural advantages[1]. However, s 49 of the Sale of Goods Act allows the seller to bring a claim for the price only where either (a) the property in the goods has passed to the buyer or (b) 'the price is payable on a day certain irrespective of delivery'. It seems that in order for payment to be due 'on a day certain' the contract must fix the date for payment, or provide a formula which allows it to be defined without reference to the actions of the parties[2], so that the common formulae which make payment due 'x days after delivery' or 'x days after invoice date' do not require payment on 'a day certain'.

If the requirements of s 49 are not satisfied, the seller cannot claim the price even if it is the buyer's wrongful refusal to take delivery which prevents property passing[3]. In that case he is restricted to a claim for damages for non-acceptance. However, if the requirements of s 49 are satisfied, the seller can claim the price, together with interest if that is payable under the contract, and claim additional damages for any loss he suffers as a result of the failure to pay[4] or the buyer's failure to take delivery at the proper time[5].

The restrictions imposed on the claim for the price by s 49 create a dilemma for the seller. In a claim for damages for non-acceptance, he must mitigate his loss, normally by seeking to resell the goods. However, if he resells the goods, he puts it out of his power to perform the contract with the original buyer, and therefore loses the right to claim the price[6]. Moreover, even an attempt to resell may be treated as terminating the contract, causing property to revest in the seller: in that case the claim for the price may be extinguished. On policy grounds, it might be preferable to allow the seller to claim the price wherever the buyer is better placed to resell the goods, and restrict him to a claim for damages where he can more easily resell.

1   See 2.10.2.
2   *Henderson and Keay Ltd v A M Carmichael Ltd* 1956 SLT (Notes) 58, OH ('prompt payment cash against invoice' not 'a day certain').
3   *Colley v Overseas Exporters* [1921] 3 KB 302.
4   SoGA, s 54.
5   SoGA, s 37(1).
6   *R V Ward v Bignall* [1967] 1 QB 534, [1967] 2 All ER 449, CA.

18.2.2   *Damages for non-acceptance*

Where the buyer wrongfully refuses to accept and pay for the goods, the seller may bring an action against him for damages for non-acceptance[1]. Where he cannot claim the price under s 49, this is the only claim available to the seller; however, even where a claim for the price is available, he may choose to claim damages instead.

The claim for damages for non-acceptance mirrors the buyer's claim for damages for non-delivery, and is governed by similar principles[2]. Since it is a claim for damages, the normal rules relating to damages claims apply: the seller must prove his loss, take reasonable steps to mitigate his loss, and cannot recover in respect of losses which are too remote. Prima facie the measure of damages is 'the estimated loss, directly and naturally resulting, in the ordinary course of events, from the buyer's breach'[3]. However, where there is an available market for goods of the contract description, the seller's damages are prima facie assessed, in the same way as damages for non-delivery, by reference to the market price, and the seller is entitled to the difference between the contract price and the market price at the date of the buyer's breach[4]. The seller is expected to mitigate his loss by seeking an alternative buyer for the goods in the market. Thus if the market price at the date of breach is higher than the contract price, the seller is prima facie entitled to no damages. The market price rule is, however, only a prima facie rule. It will be displaced wherever its application would be inappropriate. The governing principle is that the damages for non-acceptance are 'the estimated loss, directly and naturally resulting, in the ordinary course of events, from the buyer's breach'[5].

The existence of an available market is assessed in the same way as on a claim for non-delivery[6]. However, on a seller's claim, there will be no available market if supply exceeds demand: in that case, the seller may argue that the buyer's breach has deprived him of a sale, and claim as damages the profit he would have made on a sale to the buyer[7]. Even if the seller manages to sell the goods to another customer, there is no reason to suppose that 'the second customer was a substituted customer, that, had all gone well, the [seller] would not have had both customers, both orders, and both profits'[8]. On the other hand, if demand exceeds supply, the replacement contract is an alternative: the seller could not have satisfied both.

In principle, if there is an available market, the actual price at which the seller resells is irrelevant, so that if he manages to sell at more than the market price, he is still entitled to damages assessed by reference to the market price[9]. However, in practice the resale price may provide strong evidence of the market price and in *Shearson Lehman Hutton Inc v Maclaine Watson & Co Ltd (No 2)*[10] Webster J held that if the seller offers the goods for resale on the day of breach, there is an available market if there is one actual buyer at a fair price, implying that the price at which the goods are resold will normally be taken as the market price.

Where there is no available market, the seller's damages must be assessed differently. Prima facie he is entitled to damages to compensate for the lost profits he would have made had the buyer accepted and paid for the goods. However, he must take reasonable steps to mitigate, for instance by trying to find an alternative customer. Where the goods are unique, it may be necessary to modify them in order to try to sell them: the costs of modification will be recoverable provided the seller acts reasonably.

In either case, the seller may be able to claim special damages in respect of any other losses suffered as a result of the buyer's breach[11]. Thus damages may be recovered for such items as wasted expenditure, storage costs, advertising costs incurred in trying to resell the goods and reasonable expenses incurred in modifying the goods for resale.

1 SoGA, s 50(1).
2 See 12.3.1.
3 SoGA, s 50(2).
4 SoGA, s 50(3).
5 *Bem Dis A Turk Ticaret S/A TR v International Agri Trade Co Ltd* [1999] 1 All ER (Comm) 619.
6 See the discussion at 12.3.1, above.
7 *W L Thompson v Robinson (Gunmakers) Ltd* [1955] Ch 177, [1955] 1 All ER 154; contrast *Charter v Sullivan* [1957] 2 QB 117, [1957] 1 All ER 809, CA.
8 Hamilton LJ in *Re Vic Mill* [1913] 1 Ch 465 at 473.
9 *Campbell Mostyn (Provisions Ltd) v Barnett Trading Co* [1954] 1 Lloyd's Rep 65.
10 [1990] 1 Lloyd's Rep 441.
11 SoGA, s 54.

18.2.3   *Damages for wrongful failure to take delivery*

If the buyer delays in taking delivery but ultimately accepts the goods, the seller cannot claim for non-acceptance. However, he may incur losses as a result of the failure to take delivery at the proper time. He may recover damages in respect of such losses under s 37 of the Sale of Goods Act, which also allows him to make a reasonable charge for care and custody of the goods. In effect, damages are awarded under s 50 where the buyer's breach is repudiatory; damages are awarded under s 37 in cases of non-repudiatory late delivery.

18.3   Real remedies

Section 39 of the Sale of Goods Act gives an unpaid seller the following three rights:

'(a) a lien on the goods, or right to retain them for the price while he is in possession of them;
(b) in case of the insolvency of the buyer, a right of stopping the goods in transit after he has parted with the possession of them; and
(c) a right of resale.'

These rights arise automatically, by implication of law, and may be exercised against the goods themselves and even though property has passed to the buyer. Where property has not passed to the buyer, the seller can withhold delivery, stop the goods in transit and resell them by virtue of being owner; however, such acts may be a breach of contract vis-à-vis the buyer. It is therefore expressly provided that the seller has a right to withhold delivery, co-extensive with the rights of lien and stoppage, even where property has not passed[1]. Curiously, the Act does not give the seller a right, vis-à-vis the buyer, to resell where property has not passed, so that although he can pass a good title to the second buyer, he may commit a breach of contract vis-à-vis the original buyer. However, it seems that the statutory right of resale will be interpreted as applying both where property has passed to the buyer before the resale, and where it has not[2].

The statutory rights are given to an 'unpaid seller'. The seller is 'unpaid' until the whole of the price has been paid or tendered and, where payment is made by a bill of exchange or negotiable instrument as a conditional payment, he is unpaid if the condition is not fulfilled[3]. Thus if B buys goods and pays by cheque, S is an unpaid seller if the cheque is dishonoured.

In practice the seller's statutory rights against the goods are often of little value in modern transactions. The seller will therefore often seek to provide himself with extra protection by including a retention of title clause in the contract of sale.

1   SoGA, s 39(2).
2   See Atiyah, *The Sale of Goods* (10th edn, 2000) p 448; *Benjamin's Sale of Goods* (5th edn, 1997) para 15-011; *R V Ward Ltd v Bignall* [1967] 1 QB 534, [1967] 2 All ER 449, CA. The contract may give the seller an express right of resale.
3   SoGA, s 38.

18.3.1   *The unpaid seller's lien*

The right of lien allows the seller to withhold delivery, even if property has passed to the buyer, until he is paid. However, it is very restricted. It is only available where either (a) the goods are not supplied on credit, or (b) if the goods were supplied on credit, the credit period has expired, or (c) the buyer is insolvent[1]. Moreover, since a lien is a possessory remedy, it is lost if the buyer or his agent gets possession of the goods with the seller's consent[2], if the goods are delivered to a carrier or bailee for transmission to the buyer without reserving a right of disposal[3] or if the seller waives his right[4], for instance by assenting to a resale[5]. However, provided the seller retains physical possession of the goods, he is entitled to exert his lien even if he is in possession (as will normally be the case) as bailee for the buyer.

The right of lien will generally be of very limited value in modern, domestic commercial transactions. Goods are often supplied on credit, so that they come into the buyer's possession before expiry of the credit period. The lien may be of value where goods are delivered in instalments, allowing the seller to withhold a delivery until earlier ones are paid for[6], since the lien continues until the whole of the contract price is paid. However, even this will not be possible if the contract is severable: in that case, the lien is applied severably to each severable instalment[7].

1   Section 41(1); 'insolvent' is defined for these purposes in SoGA, s 61(4).
2   SoGA, s 43(1)(b).
3   SoGA, s 43(1)(a).
4   SoGA, s 43(1)(c).
5   Under SoGA, s 47; see 18.3.3.
6   *Re Edwards, ex p Chalmers* (1873) 8 Ch App 289.
7   *Longbottom & Co Ltd v Bass Walker & Co* [1922] WN 245, CA.

18.3.2   Stoppage in transit

The seller loses his lien if he delivers the goods to the buyer or to a carrier who is not his own agent for transmission to the buyer. However, if the buyer becomes insolvent while the goods are in transit, the unpaid seller has the right to stop the goods in transit and, by so doing, recover possession and his lien until payment[1]. The right is exercised by the seller taking possession of the goods or giving notice to the carrier[2]; it is lost when the transit ends and the goods are delivered to the buyer or his agent[3]. The right of stoppage in transit will rarely be of much practical value in a modern, domestic transaction when goods are unlikely to be in transit for any length of time.

1   SoGA, s 44.
2   SoGA, s 45.
3   SoGA, s 46; for this purpose it seems that the carrier is not to be regarded as the buyer's agent.

18.3.3   Effect of resale by the buyer

The buyer may resell the goods before they come into his actual possession. However, the seller's rights of lien and stoppage are unaffected by such a resale, and can therefore be asserted even against the sub-buyer, unless the seller assents to the resale[1]. There is no need for the seller to notify the sub-buyer of his assent to the resale, but he will not be taken to have assented merely because he knows of the resale and does not object to it. The seller's conduct will only be interpreted as assenting to a resale if it indicates an intention to renounce his rights against the goods, and this will be a question of fact[2].

The seller's rights are also defeated if he delivers a document of title to goods, such as a bill of lading, to the buyer and the buyer transfers it to another person who takes it in good faith and without notice of the seller's rights[3].

1   SoGA, s 47(1); the seller may also lose his rights if one of the nemo dat exceptions applies in favour of the buyer.
2   Contrast *Mordaunt Bros v British Oil and Cake Mills Ltd* [1910] 2 KB 502 (no assent) with *D F Mount Ltd v Jay and Jay (Provisions) Ltd* [1960] 1 QB 159, [1959] 3 All ER 307 (assent). An important factor in the latter case was that the seller knew that the buyer needed to resell the goods in order to pay for them.
3   SoGA, s 47(2).

18.3.4   *The right to resell the goods*

Where the seller exercises his lien or stops the goods in transit, the contract of sale remains in force for performance. If the buyer still fails to pay, the seller may seek to recoup his losses by reselling the goods and, if he does so, the new buyer gets a good title to the goods, even if title had passed to the original buyer[1]. Such a resale will be a breach of the seller's contract with the first buyer unless he has a right to resell. The seller has such a right if the buyer repudiates the contract: the seller may then accept the breach and terminate the contract by reselling. In addition, the Act gives the unpaid seller a right of resale where the goods are perishable, or where the seller gives notice of his intention to resell the goods and the buyer does not tender the price within a reasonable time[2]. Effectively, the Act makes the time of payment of the essence in such cases.

In addition, the seller may include in the contract an express right to resell the goods if the buyer defaults in payment. Where the seller exercises such a right, the contract with the original buyer is terminated[3]. In all these cases, if the seller resells, he does so for his own benefit: he is therefore entitled to any profit made on the resale[4]. However, he may claim damages for any losses he suffers as a result of the buyer's failure to pay.

1   SoGA, s 48(2). This may offer the second buyer wider protection than s 24.
2   SoGA, s 48(3).
3   SoGA, s 48(4); the Act uses the word 'rescinded'.
4   *R V Ward Ltd v Bignall* [1967] 1 QB 534, [1967] 2 All ER 449, CA.

18.4   Retention of title clauses

It has become commonplace for sellers to supply goods to their customers on credit terms. However, credit involves the risk that the debtor will default in payment. The buyer will rarely simply refuse to pay; he may withhold payment where he alleges that the goods are defective, or that the seller has been guilty of some other breach of contract, but in that case the seller can sue for the price, or for damages for non-acceptance, and the buyer will raise the alleged breach as a defence in that action. More commonly, the buyer fails to pay because he is unable to do so, normally because of financial difficulties. If the buyer is insolvent the seller's personal claims will often be worthless.

Where a debtor becomes insolvent, some other person takes over the management of his property and distributes it in order to discharge the debtor's liabilities. Individuals may be declared bankrupt, and their estates collected and distributed by a trustee in bankruptcy. Companies may be wound up by a liquidator. Alternatively, a secured creditor will often have the right to appoint an administrative receiver to take over management of the company and realise assets to pay the appointing creditor[1]. Although a receiver does not wind up the company, and, indeed, his actions may result in the disposal of sufficient assets to pay off the creditor and 'turn the company around', in many cases the appointment of a receiver is merely a prelude to the appointment of a liquidator. A further alternative, introduced by the Insolvency Act 1985, is the appointment of an administrator, although an administrator is not concerned to pay off creditors, and the aim of appointing an administrator is to avoid insolvency[2].

The order for distribution of assets in insolvency, which is prescribed by statute, is broadly the same in each kind of proceeding and requires the assets to be used to meet the costs of the insolvency procedure itself and the claims of preferential creditors, including the Revenue's claim for unpaid taxes, social security contributions and certain debts due to employees, and of secured creditors before those of unsecured creditors[3].

No creditor can be paid unless the claims of all the creditors in prior classes have been met in full. If there are insufficient assets to meet the claims of all the creditors in a particular class, each receives a rateable proportion of the sum due to him.

Companies can create floating charges which cover all their property, including property acquired after creation of the charge[4]. Banks lending to companies will often take a floating charge over the whole of a company's assets and undertaking as security and in practice lenders secured by floating charges will lend up to the full value of the borrower's assets so that, if the borrower makes default on his debt to the secured lender, most or all of his assets will go to meet the claims of the preferential and secured creditors, leaving little or nothing for unsecured creditors. Thus 'unsecured creditors rank after preferential creditors, mortgagees and the holders of floating charges and they receive a raw deal'[5]. The unpaid supplier of goods will normally be an unsecured creditor; often he will see the goods he supplied sold off to meet the claims of other creditors.

A personal claim is therefore of little value to a creditor if the debtor is insolvent. However, a real claim to a specific item of property will allow the creditor to claim that piece of property in priority to other creditors. Subject to certain statutory exceptions, only property belonging to the insolvent can be applied in payment of the insolvent's debts. The statutory real rights of the unpaid seller may therefore give some protection against the buyer's insolvency, but where the goods are supplied on credit, those rights will be of very limited value and so suppliers of goods have sought to extend their protection by appropriate contract terms.

The simplest form of protection for the supplier is to retain property in the goods until he is paid: in that case, in the event of default he may be able to recover the goods themselves as his property. There are many well established means of reserving property: for instance, the goods may be supplied on hire, or hire purchase terms. However, such arrangements contemplate that the goods themselves may be returned to the supplier; they are therefore inappropriate for many commercial supply contracts where the intention is that the buyer should resell the goods supplied, or use them in his business, in order to earn his profits.

A conditional sale also involves a reservation of property, and under a typical consumer conditional sale it will be assumed, as in the case of hire purchase, that the debtor will retain the goods, unaltered. The decision of the Court of Appeal in the *Romalpa* case[6] of 1976, however, demonstrated that a conditional sale agreement could be effective even where the goods were supplied on the understanding that they would be consumed or resold. By supplying goods on conditional sale terms, subject to a reservation of property, suppliers could therefore protect themselves against their customers becoming insolvent.

1   For a general description of company insolvency procedures see Boyle and Birds', *Company Law* (3rd edn, 1995) ch 17.
2   See 22.0.1.1.
3   A receiver discharges his functions by paying off his appointing creditor; he is therefore not concerned with the claims of unsecured creditors. However, in practice there will often be little or nothing left after payment of the secured creditors, and liquidation will follow the receivership.
4   See 22.2.2.3.
5   Per Templeman LJ in *Borden (UK) Ltd v Scottish Timber Products Ltd* [1981] Ch 25, [1979] 3 All ER 961.
6   *Aluminium Industrie Vaasen BV v Romalpa Aluminium Ltd* [1976] 2 All ER 552, [1976] 1 WLR 676, CA.

18.4.1   *The Romalpa case*

In the *Romalpa* case a Dutch company (S) supplied aluminium foil to an English company (B) on terms which provided that the foil remained S's property until B had paid all debts due to S. Until then, B was required to store the foil separately from its own property and, although B was allowed to manufacture new products using the foil, it was required to transfer such manufactured products to S 'as surety' and, if it resold any new products manufactured with the foil, it was to assign to S the right to receive payment.

B became insolvent and a receiver was appointed. However, prior to insolvency B had sold a quantity of foil and the price of that foil, £35,152, was paid by the buyer to the receiver. B owed S over £122,000 and S now claimed to be entitled to the proceeds of sale of the foil it had supplied. It should be noted that the parties had not contemplated the possibility of B reselling the foil itself, and so no provision was made for this eventuality in the contract of sale. S therefore argued that a right for B to resell foil should be implied into the contract, and that a necessary corollary of that was that B was under an implied duty to account for the proceeds of any sales of foil. The Court of Appeal held that the parties must have intended B to have a right to resell the foil, and so such a right must be implied. B conceded that, until resale, B held the foil as bailee for S, and the Court of Appeal held that the contract therefore created a fiduciary relationship between S and B. As a result, B was accountable to S as a fiduciary for the proceeds of sale of the foil which therefore belonged to S.

The Court of Appeal did not regard its decision as significant but as confined to its own particular facts, and leave to appeal to the House of Lords was refused. However, the commercial world reacted differently. Professor Goode wrote: 'It is doubtful whether any case decided this century has created a greater impact on the commercial law'[1], and it rapidly became commonplace for sellers to include similar clauses, which have become known as retention of title, or '*Romalpa*', clauses in their contracts of supply. There is now a wide variety of such clauses in common use[2]. Sellers may simply retain title to the goods they supplied until payment, either for the goods themselves, or of other sums. However, they may seek to go further and claim the proceeds of any resale of the goods, as in *Romalpa* or, where the goods are used in a manufacturing process, claim rights over new products manufactured from the goods.

The widespread use of retention of title clauses has potentially serious consequences for secured creditors: a successful claim under a retention of title clause allows the supplier to reclaim the goods, their proceeds or product, and the pool of assets available to meet the claims of other creditors is therefore diminished. Receivers and liquidators therefore responded by developing a series of arguments to challenge the effectiveness of retention of title claims.

One argument commonly put forward is that the clause has not been effectively incorporated into the contract of supply and is therefore ineffective. This may not always be necessary. Where the contract is for unascertained goods, it may be possible for the seller to impose a simple retention of title after the contract is made, since s 19 of the Sale of Goods Act permits him to reserve a right of disposal by the terms of the contract or the appropriation of goods to the contract[3]. However, the more extensive rights claimed by some retention of title clauses will only be effective if incorporated in the contract in accordance with ordinary principles of contract law[4].

A retention of title claim will only succeed if the assets claimed by the seller are his property under the terms of the clause. Thus the receiver may argue that the goods claimed by the seller are not the seller's property; if the seller claims proceeds of a resale, the receiver may argue that the clause gives him no rights in respect of proceeds. Essentially, this argument depends on the proper construction of the contract and the ability to identify goods as the seller's property.

Even if the seller can establish that the clause does give him rights to the property in question, the receiver may argue that those rights are less than full ownership, and that, instead, they create a security interest. In the case of a corporate buyer, it will be argued that the clause gives rise to a charge, which, if created by the company, will be void against a liquidator or creditor of the company unless it is registered[5]. In the case of an unincorporated buyer, it will be argued that the contract requires registration under the Bills of Sale Acts 1878–1882[6]; effectively, any clause which would be regarded as creating a company charge will be registrable as a bill of sale if created by an individual. However, retention of title claims are less important in individual bankruptcies than in corporate insolvency because, since individuals cannot create floating charges, the position of trade creditors in bankruptcy is less precarious than in corporate insolvency[7].

The charge argument is the most contentious of those put forward. Where it is argued that a clause creates a charge over assets claimed by the seller, the argument is that, notwithstanding the language of the clause, the effect of the clause is to allow the asset in question to become the buyer's property, subject to the grant of a charge back to the seller[8]. In many ways the argument is artificial: the intention of the seller, at least, is almost certainly to avoid creating a charge, in order to avoid the registration requirement. It will generally be wholly impractical for the seller to register a charge every time he supplies goods to a customer subject to a retention of title, and clauses are almost never registered. Moreover, even if the seller registers a charge, it will generally rank in priority behind any floating charge granted to the buyer's bank, and will therefore fail to achieve the seller's objective. However, the effect of a contract in law depends on the construction of the contract, which is a matter for the court.

There is now an extensive body of case law concerned with the effect of retention of title clauses, but the law has developed in piecemeal fashion and it remains difficult to predict whether any particular clause will be effective. Many of the cases are difficult to reconcile, and it seems that to a large degree each case will turn on its own facts and on the terms of the particular contract: 'the decision in any particular case may have depended on how the matter was presented to the court, and, in particular, may have depended on material concessions by counsel'[9]. As a result, this area has been described as 'a maze if not a minefield'[10].

451

1 *The Times*, 11 May 1977.
2 For discussion of the various types of clause and of commercial practice, see Spencer [1989] JBL 220 and Wheeler, *Reservation of Title Clauses: Impact and Implications* (Oxford, 1991). Wheeler found that 92% of companies in her survey used a retention of title clause. In the receivership of Leyland Daf in the early 1990s there were over 400 retention of title claims: see *Lipe Ltd v Leyland Daf Ltd* [1993] BCC 385.
3 See 15.1.1; see Bradgate [1988] JBL 477. Insolvency practitioners nevertheless tend to challenge retention of title claims on the basis of failure to incorporate the clause in the contract.
4 See 2.5.2.
5 Companies Act 1985, s 395; since the clause is void against a creditor, it is also void against a receiver. Provisions making significant changes to the companies charges system are contained in Pt IV of the Companies Act 1989, but it seems unlikely that those provisions will ever be brought into force. See 22.0.3.2.
6 See 22.0.3.1.
7 Prior to 1985, a retention of title clause would almost certainly have been ineffective against an individual because of the rule of reputed ownership which applied in bankruptcy; see the Report of the Review Committee on Insolvency and Practice (1982) Cmnd 8558, ch 23.
8 Gregory (1990) 196 LQR 550 argues that it may be possible for the seller to 'reserve' a charge: such a charge is not created by the company and is therefore not registrable, but see *Stroud Architectural Systems Ltd v John Laing Construction Ltd* [1994] BCC 18, below 18.4.2.
9 Per Robert Goff LJ in *Clough Mill Ltd v Martin* [1984] 3 All ER 982, [1985] 1 WLR 111, CA.
10 Per Staughton J in *Hendy Lennox Ltd v Grahame Puttick Engines Ltd* [1984] 2 All ER 152, [1984] 1 WLR 485.

18.4.2   *The seller claims the original goods*

By s 17 of the Sale of Goods Act, the passing of property from seller to buyer depends on the intention of the parties, and s 19 allows the seller to impose a condition on the passing of property. By imposing a retention of title clause, the seller imposes such a condition, and it was therefore assumed until 1984 that a simple retention of title clause which retained title to the goods supplied by the seller until payment would be effective, and the point was conceded in *Romalpa*.

In *Clough Mill Ltd v Geoffrey Martin* this assumption was challenged. S supplied yarn to B, a company which made fabric. The contract of sale provided that S retained title to all the goods supplied under that particular contract until the whole of the contract price was paid. B was required to store S's yarn separately from its own until it was paid for. The parties anticipated that B would use the yarn in its business before paying for it, and the clause therefore provided that S was to be the owner of new products made from its yarn, and have rights over the products similar to those over the yarn.

B went into receivership and when S claimed to be entitled to recover yarn it had supplied and not been paid for, the receiver argued that the clause did not retain property, but allowed property to pass to B subject to a charge back to S. The essence of the argument was that the purpose of the clause was to provide S with security against non-payment. In the earlier case of *Re Bond Worth Ltd*[1] Slade J had said that 'any contract which, by way of security for payment of a debt, creates an interest in property defeasible on payment of such debt, must necessarily be regarded as creating a charge'[2]. The receiver argued that the contract of sale gave B extensive rights which were inconsistent with S still owning the yarn.

These arguments succeeded at first instance[3] but were rejected by the Court of Appeal, which emphasised that the purpose of the contract is not conclusive of its effect. The seller could secure himself in many ways which would not create a charge, including by supplying on hire purchase or by means of lease. The court distinguished *Re Bond Worth* on the basis that the clause in that case reserved 'equitable and beneficial ownership'. It therefore allowed property to pass to the buyer. Here, however, the contract simply prevented any property from passing to B, so that B never had anything to charge.

The reasoning in *Clough Mill*[4] is rather unsatisfactory. In particular, the bare assertion that property never passed seems to beg the question, which was 'Did the clause effectively reserve property?', and the court failed to address the difference between a retention of title clause which allows the buyer to consume and resell the goods supplied, and the traditional conditional sale agreement. However, the decision clearly establishes that a simple retention of title clause, reserving title to the goods in their original form until they are paid for, will be effective. Equally, it seems that a clause which reserves 'equitable and beneficial ownership' will be ineffective: it allows legal title to pass to the buyer, subject to the immediate grant back by the buyer of equitable rights, defeasible on payment of the price, and so gives rise to a charge[5].

1   [1980] Ch 228, [1979] 3 All ER 919.
2   [1980] Ch 228 at 248.
3   [1984] 1 All ER 721, [1984] 1 WLR 1067.
4   [1984] 3 All ER 982, [1985] 1 WLR 111, CA.
5   *Re Bond Worth Ltd* [1980] Ch 228. Gregory (1990) 106 LQR 550 argues that the reasoning in the case is inconsistent with the decision of the House of Lords in *Abbey National Building Society v Cann* [1990] 1 All ER 1085, but *Re Bond Worth Ltd* was followed in *Stroud Architectural Systems Ltd v John Laing Construction Ltd* [1994] BCC 18. In *Westdeutsche Landesbank Girozentrale v Islington London Borough Council* [1996] AC 669 at 706, [1996] 2 All ER 961 at 989 Lord Browne-Wilkinson observed that: 'A person solely entitled to the full beneficial ownership of money or property, both at law and in equity, does not enjoy an equitable interest in that property. The legal title carries with it all rights. Unless and until there is a separation of the legal and equitable estates, there is no separate equitable title. Therefore to talk about [the owner] "retaining" its equitable interest is meaningless', tending to support the *Re Bond Worth* analysis.

18.4.2.1   *Indentification*

A simple clause, such as that in *Clough Mill*, only protects the seller so long as he can identify the goods as his property under the retention of title clause. If the goods are so altered as to become a different item, they will be irrecoverable. The difficult question is to know when goods will have been so altered. In *Re Peachdart Ltd*[1] S supplied leather used to make handbags. Although there was evidence that the leather remained identifiable throughout the manufacturing process, so that S could prove that a particular bag was made with leather from a particular contract, Vinelott J held that the parties must have intended that the leather would cease to be S's property as soon as it entered the manufacturing process. Similarly, in *Model Board Ltd v Outerbox Ltd*[2], where cardboard was printed and made up into cardboard boxes, it was held that the seller's title to the board had been extinguished. In both cases the goods no longer had any significant value as raw material after entering the manufacturing process.

The seller's ownership will also be terminated if his goods are used in a manufacturing process and become irreversibly mixed with other goods. Thus in *Borden (UK) Ltd v Scottish Timber Products Ltd*[3] S lost title to resin when it was mixed with wood chips to make chipboard. However, if the seller's goods are affixed to other property but can be detached without damaging either item, they will not lose their identity, and the seller can recover them[4].

A receiver may also seek to resist the seller's claim for recovery where the seller cannot identify goods as his property because they have been mixed or confused with other similar goods belonging to the buyer in the buyer's warehouse: for instance, where S supplies bottles of wine and B stores them together with other, similar bottles which are already his property. The law relating to ownership of such mixtures is not clear[5]. In general it seems that where the mixing is innocent, the contributing owners own the mixed fund as tenants in common. Where the goods are wrongfully mixed by one party, older cases suggest that the innocent owner is entitled to the whole mixture[6] but it seems that the modern rule is that the parties own the mixture as tenants in common, and the innocent party is generally entitled to recover from it a quantity equivalent to his input[7]. However, it seems that the innocent party can only claim a share in the mixture if he can prove that his goods are still in it[8]; this might be difficult where, for instance, goods have been mixed in a warehouse and deliveries have been made from the warehouse from time to time. Such a rule would allow the wrongdoer to profit from his wrong, and it would seem fairer to place the burden of proof on the wrongdoer to prove that the innocent party's goods are no longer in the mixture[9]. A retention of title clause will often require the buyer to store the seller's goods separately from his own; if the buyer fails to comply and mixes or confuses the goods with others so as to prevent their identification as the seller's property, his act will be wrongful and the seller should be able to recover his share from the mixture without proving that he owns any particular item.

1   [1984] Ch 131, [1983] 3 All ER 204.
2   [1993] BCLC 623; see Hicks [1993] JBL 485. See also *Chaigley Farms Ltd v Crawford, Kaye & Grayshire Ltd* [1996] BCC 957 (livestock supplied to abattoir ceased to be supplier's property on slaughter). Contrast the similar New Zealand case *Re Weddell New New Zealand Ltd* [1996] 5 NZBLC 104,055 (livestock supplied to abattoir); *New Zealand Forest Products v Pongakawa Sawmill Ltd* [1991] 3 NZLR 112, [1992] 3 NZLR 304 (CA) (logs sawn into timber), in which the seller's interest survived processing. See Sealy [1997] CLJ 28.
3   [1981] Ch 25, [1979] 3 All ER 961, CA. See also *Ian Chisolm Textiles Ltd v Griffith* [1994] BCC 96.
4   *Hendy Lennox (Industrial Engines) Ltd v Grahame Puttick Ltd* [1984] 2 All ER 152, [1984] 1 WLR 485.
5   See McCormack (1990) 10 LS 293; Birks, 'Mixtures' in Palmer and McKendrick (eds) *Interests in Goods* (2nd edn, 1998).
6   See *Sandeman & Sons v Tyzack and Branfoot Steamship Co Ltd* [1913] AC 680, HL.
7   *Indian Oil Corpn v Greenstone Shipping SA* [1988] QB 345, [1987] 3 All ER 893.
8   *Ian Chisolm Textiles Ltd v Griffith* [1994] BCC 96; see Goode, *Proprietary Rights and Insolvency in Sale Transactions* (2nd edn, 1989) p 91.
9   This could be done by applying a rule similar to that in *Re Hallett's Estate* (1879) 13 Ch D 696, presuming the buyer to use his own property before the seller's. See Birks, above, n 5.

18.4.3   *Retention of title to secure all sums due*

In order to avoid problems of identification, a seller may include a term in the contract that the goods supplied remain his property until all goods supplied by him have been paid for. The clause in *Clough Mill* retained title to all the goods supplied under the particular contract until the whole contract price was paid. If the buyer pays part of the price under such a contract but the seller exercises his right of repossession, he may repossess goods the buyer has paid for. The Court of Appeal considered this problem and, obiter, suggested possible solutions. According to Lord Donaldson MR, the seller's right to repossess and resell continues 'until' he has been paid, so that he can only recover and resell sufficient to discharge the outstanding price, any excess realised on a resale would belong to the buyer. Robert

Goff LJ suggested a more complex analysis. If the buyer repossesses while the contract remains in force, an implied term prevents him reselling more than necessary to discharge the outstanding price; he therefore cannot retain any profit made by reselling. However, if the contract is terminated, for instance because the buyer repudiates it and the seller accepts the repudiation, the seller may repossess and resell free of any such implied term[1]. If he repossesses goods for which the buyer has paid, he must refund the price on the grounds of a total failure of consideration; however, he will be entitled to claim damages from the buyer for any loss caused by the buyer's failure to pay, and can set off that claim against his liability to make a refund. In most cases the approach of Lord Donaldson and of Robert Goff LJ will produce the same result[2].

The seller's clause may go further than that in *Clough Mill* and retain title to goods supplied until the buyer has paid for them and for goods supplied, or other debts incurred, under other contracts[3]. The effect of such a clause is that, so long as any debt is outstanding from the buyer to the seller, property in the goods covered by the clause remains in the seller even if the buyer has paid for those goods. Property in the goods is thus used to secure payment of other debts and the effect closely resembles that of a charge. It has been argued that such clauses should therefore be construed as creating charges[4]. If the buyer and seller regularly do business on such terms, the buyer could pay for goods and yet never own any of them, so long as he owes the seller anything[5].

The House of Lords considered such a clause in *Armour v Thyssen Edelstahlwerke AG*[6]. Goods had been supplied to a Scottish company under an all moneys clause and, relying on a series of Scottish decisions[7], the company's receiver argued that the effect of the clause was to allow property to pass to the buyer subject to the grant back of a security interest to the seller. However, the House of Lords rejected this argument, adopting a similar line to that taken in *Clough Mill*: the clause prevented property passing until its conditions were fulfilled[8]; the buyer therefore never owned the goods and could not grant any security over them.

The decision leaves a number of questions unanswered. In particular, the problem mentioned above, that the seller may repossess goods already paid for, arises here. In principle it would seem that if the seller does repossess goods which have been paid for, because of non-payment of a debt arising under a separate contract, he must refund the price paid for the goods on the basis of total failure of consideration[9]. However, this would seem to undermine the purpose of the clause. It is unfortunate that, unlike the Court of Appeal in *Clough Mill*, the House of Lords decided not to offer guidance on this difficult point.

1 It is difficult to see how the seller can repossess and resell without terminating the contract: see *R V Ward Ltd v Bignall* [1967] 1 QB 534, CA, above 18.3.4, and see Atiyah, *The Sale of Goods* (10th edn, 2000) p 479.
2 See Bradgate (1991) 54 MLR 726.
3 Including possibly debts due to other businesses: see *Armour v Thyssen Edelstahlwerke AG* [1991] 2 AC 339, [1990] 3 All ER 481, HL.
4 See Goodhart and Jones (1980) 43 MLR 489; Goodhart (1986) 49 MLR 96; Davies [1985] LMCLQ 49. See also the view of Professor Diamond in his 'Review of Security Interests in Property' (1989) DTI para 17.12.
5 Note that property in goods supplied under such a clause only remains in the seller so long as debts are outstanding. If the account between the parties is clear, property in all goods supplied prior thereto will pass to the buyer.
6 [1991] 2 AC 339, [1990] 3 All ER 481, HL; Bradgate (1991) 54 MLR 726, cf Mance [1992] LMCLQ 35.
7 *Emerald Stainless Steel Ltd v South Side Distribution Ltd* 1982 SC 61; *Deutz Engines Ltd v Terex Ltd* [1984] SLT 273.

8   See Goode, *Proprietary Rights and Insolvency in Sale Transactions* (2nd edn, 1989) p 101.
9   Goodhart and Jones (1980) 43 MLR 489; Bradgate (1991) 54 MLR 726; contrast McCormack [1989] Conv 92.

18.4.4   *Claims to manufactured products*

In many cases the buyer will use the goods in a manufacturing process before paying for them; often that will be anticipated by both parties. Where the goods have been used in that way and the buyer becomes insolvent, the seller may attempt to lay claim to the manufactured product, and a retention of title clause often includes an express claim to such products.

The first question in such a case is whether the manufacturing process has resulted in the loss of S's goods. If they can be recovered in their original form, S can recover them on the strength of a simple retention of title to the original goods. Thus where diesel engines were supplied and fitted into generator sets, S could recover them even though they had been connected by bolts, pipes and wires and disconnection would take several hours: the engines were still identifiable as separate items of property, had not been irreversibly incorporated into the generators and could be detached from them without damage[1].

However, if the manufacturing process results in the original goods being consumed, or losing their identity, the seller's title will be extinguished. In *Borden (UK) Ltd v Scottish Timber Products Ltd*[2] S supplied resin which was used in the manufacture of chipboard. S claimed that its retention of title to the resin allowed it to trace the resin into the finished product and claim a share of the chipboard. The Court of Appeal rejected that claim, emphasising the difficulties which it would create in quantifying the size of the parties' shares in the chipboard[3]. The intention of the parties in such a case will normally be presumed to be that the buyer manufactures new products for his own benefit.

In *Re Peachdart Ltd*[4] Vinelott J went further. S supplied leather to be used by B to make handbags. It was held that when pieces of leather entered the manufacturing process, it was intended that they should cease to be S's property, even though the leather remained identifiable.

In order to avoid such problems, the seller may include an express claim to products manufactured using his goods. However, such a claim is likely to be regarded as creating a charge. The clause in *Clough Mill*[5] contained such a provision, and the Court of Appeal, obiter, considered its effect. Since the seller expressly or impliedly authorises the use of his goods in the manufacture of the new product, ownership of the new product depends on the intention of the parties. Whilst in theory it is open to the parties to make any agreement they please about the ownership of new products, so that they could agree that such products belong to the seller as soon as they come into existence, in practice it will be presumed that the intention is that new products should initially belong to the buyer. The court emphasised that the new product will normally be worth more than the value of the seller's materials included in it: the buyer, or other suppliers of raw materials, may have contributed components and the buyer will have contributed labour. To recognise the seller as owner of the whole new product would therefore be to give him a windfall profit. The expectation of the parties would normally be that the seller's interest in the product should be limited to payment of the sum due to him for his goods and defeasible on such payment, and so a clause which provides that new products are to belong to the seller will normally be construed as creating a charge to secure that payment[6].

If the seller seeks to avoid this conclusion by expressly claiming only a proportionate share in the new product, he expressly recognises that he has only a limited interest in the product to secure payment of the outstanding debt, and so is likely to be regarded as having only a charge over the product[7].

Where goods are incorporated into real property so as to become fixtures, the seller's rights will clearly be terminated: the goods then cease to exist as such and become part of the realty.

1   *Hendy Lennox (Industrial Engines) Ltd v Grahame Puttick Ltd* [1984] 2 All ER 152, [1984] 1 WLR 485.
2   [1981] Ch 25, [1979] 3 All ER 961, CA.
3   See Bridge LJ at 970–971.
4   [1984] Ch 131, [1983] 3 All ER 204.
5   [1984] 3 All ER 982, [1985] 1 WLR 111, CA.
6   This view is supported by *Borden (UK) Ltd v Scottish Timber Products Ltd* [1981] Ch 25, [1979] 3 All ER 961: see per Templeman LJ ([1979] 3 All ER 961 at 973). See also *Specialist Plant Services Ltd v Braithwaite* [1987] BCLC 1, CA.
7   *Kruppstahl v Quittman* [1982] ILRM 551.

18.4.5   Resale of the goods and claims to proceeds

The buyer of goods subject to retention of title may resell them before paying the seller. If so the buyer's customer will normally be able to rely on s 25 of the Sale of Goods Act[1], and will thus acquire a good title to the goods, provided that he takes the goods in good faith without notice of the rights of the original seller. It seems that he will only be denied the protection of s 25 if he knows of the seller's retention of title and that the seller is still unpaid[2]. The seller will therefore be unable to recover the goods from the sub-buyer. In fact the buyer's customer will often not have to rely on s 25. The possibility that the buyer will resell the goods before paying for them will often be anticipated by the parties to the original contract, and the buyer will have an implied, if not an express, right to do so, so that he will sell as the seller's agent[3]. In such a case, unable to recover the goods from the sub-buyer, the seller may try to claim instead the proceeds of the sub-sale as representing his goods. Such a claim succeeded in *Romalpa* itself, where the Court of Appeal held that the buyer had an implied right to resell the foil, subject to an implied duty to account for the proceeds in equity. However, although several attempts have been made in subsequent cases to establish a similar claim to proceeds, none has succeeded.

In order to succeed against a receiver or liquidator, the seller must establish a proprietary claim to the proceeds of sale. He must therefore establish that the goods were sold by the buyer on his behalf and the proceeds of sale received by the buyer in a fiduciary capacity. If so, he may be able to trace his property in the goods into the proceeds of sale. In practice, a claim will only succeed where goods have been sold prior to insolvency and the proceeds received afterwards. Where the proceeds are received prior to insolvency, they will normally have been paid into the buyer's general bank account, which will almost certainly be overdrawn.

The first obstacle for the seller to overcome will be to establish that the buyer effected the sale and received the proceeds in a fiduciary capacity. In *Romalpa* the contract provided that goods manufactured from the seller's foil should be held by the buyer for the seller as 'fiduciary owner'. Moreover, the receiver conceded that the buyer held the foil as bailee for the seller pending payment. The Court of Appeal therefore concluded that, when re-selling the foil, the buyer acted as the seller's agent, and that as a result of the bailment and agency relationships between them there was a fiduciary relationship between the parties. That relationship entitled the seller to trace its property into the proceeds of sale in accordance with the principle of *Re Hallett's Estate*[4], that where property is disposed of by a fiduciary the proceeds of sale are received in a fiduciary capacity and are, in equity, the property of the beneficiary. Subsequent decisions have refused to follow this line, and it has proved impossible to establish a fiduciary relationship. It was assumed in *Romalpa* that the relationships between principal and agent and bailor and bailee are fiduciary. However, agents[5] and bailees[6] are not necessarily fiduciaries, and the classification of the relationship in a particular case depends on the intention of the parties, to be derived from the terms of their contract and the surrounding circumstances, so that references in the contract to the buyer selling as 'agent' or holding the goods as 'bailee' are not conclusive[7].

Generally, it seems that a fiduciary relationship will be held to be inconsistent with the express terms of the contract and the essential nature of the transaction as a sale of goods on credit terms. In particular, if the buyer holds proceeds of sale as a fiduciary he will be required to keep them separate from his own funds and will be unable to use them for his own benefit in his business. The fact that the buyer is allowed credit, implying that he is to be free to use the proceeds of sale in his own business, will therefore tend to indicate that the relationship is not a fiduciary one[8]. Moreover, a fiduciary would normally be required to keep his principal's property separate from his own. Thus the fact that the buyer is not required to keep the seller's goods separate from his own before resale[9] or to keep proceeds of sale separate from his own money[10] will similarly tend to indicate that a fiduciary relationship is not intended. Even if the contract does impose such a requirement, the court may regard it as a sham if it appears that the parties did not intend it to be complied with.

Above all, if the buyer is a fiduciary, he is liable to account to the seller for the whole of the proceeds of any resale, including any profit he makes. However, the expectation of the parties will normally be that the seller should receive only such amount as is owed to him under the original contract of sale, and that the buyer will keep the profit.

It thus seems that, notwithstanding the *Romalpa* decision, the courts will be reluctant to recognise that a retention of title clause gives rise to a fiduciary relationship so as to give the seller a proprietary claim to proceeds of sale. The normal expectation will be that, where the buyer is allowed to resell before payment, he does so for his own benefit[11]. This approach is entirely consistent with developments in the general law of agency[12].

If there is no fiduciary relationship, any rights the seller has to proceeds, including rights under an express requirement in the contract for the buyer to account, or a purported assignment of claims to proceeds[13], will be construed as being in the nature of a charge since the normal assumption will be that the parties only intend the seller to receive an amount equal to the unpaid debt, rather than the whole of the proceeds, and that his interest in the proceeds should cease on payment of the price of the goods. In *Tatung (UK) Ltd v Galex Telesure Ltd*[14] Phillips J went further and suggested that even if a fiduciary relationship is established, it may be construed as entitling the seller to a charge over the proceeds, which will be void if unregistered. This possibility was not considered by the Court of Appeal in *Romalpa*.

Even if not construed as a charge, such an assignment will be defeated if, as is often the case, the buyer has entered into a factoring arrangement in respect of its book debts. That was the case in *Compaq Computers Ltd v Abercorn Group Ltd*[15], where it was held that if there are multiple equitable assignments of the same chose in action, such as the buyer's book debts, priority of the assignments is determined in accordance with the rule in *Dearle v Hall*[16]. This gives priority to the first assignee to give notice of his assignment to the debtor. The seller will rarely have given such notice nor, in practice, be able to do so, whereas, since it is a factor's business to take assignments of debts, it will have established procedures to give such notice to debtors.

Strictly speaking, *Romalpa* remains good law and authority for the proposition that an unpaid seller may be able to trace into the proceeds of any resale of his goods. However, subsequent decisions have distinguished *Romalpa* all but out of existence[17]. The grounds on which they have done so are often unconvincing. For instance, the argument, accepted in several cases, that a requirement for the buyer to hold proceeds of sale in a fiduciary capacity, would be inconsistent with the grant of credit to the buyer was considered and rejected in *Romalpa*. In the absence of some authoritative clarification of the law, therefore, all that can be said with certainty is that at present the courts seem reluctant to give effect to a claim to proceeds of sale. In *Compaq Computers Ltd v Abercorn Group Ltd*[18] a comprehensively drafted clause required the buyer to store the goods as bailee and agent for the seller, to account in full for the proceeds of any resale and to keep such proceeds in a separate bank account. It was nevertheless held that the clause created no more than a charge over the proceeds of any resale: the seller's interest in the proceeds was limited to the amount of the outstanding debt due from the buyer and was defeasible on payment of that debt. 'It is hard to conceive of a seller's claim to proceeds having a better chance of success than this one; unless of course the transaction ceases to be a sale'[19].

1 See 17.4.2. The sale to the sub-buyer must purport to transfer property: if it too is subject to a retention of title, the original seller will be able to recover the goods unless the sub-buyer has paid for them: *Re Highway Foods International Ltd* [1995] BCC 271, [1995] BCLC 209.
2 See *Forsythe v Silver Shipping Co Ltd, The Saetta* [1994] 1 All ER 851, where it was held that knowledge that retention of title clauses and similar securities were almost universal in the particular trade was insufficient to constitute notice of the seller's rights: see 17.4.2.
3 This is a limited agency: the buyer has no authority to create privity of contract between the seller and sub-buyers.
4 *Knatchbull v Hallett* (1879) 13 Ch D 696.
5 *Boardman v Phipps* [1967] 2 AC 46 at 127; see *Triffit Nurseries v Salads Etc Ltd* [1999] 1 All ER (Comm) 110; affd [2000] 1 All ER (Comm) 737.
6 *Henry v Hammond* [1913] 2 KB 515.
7 *Hendy Lennox (Industrial Engines) Ltd v Grahame Puttick Ltd* [1984] 2 All ER 152, [1984] 1 WLR 485; *Re Andrabell Ltd* [1984] 3 All ER 407.
8 *Hendy Lennox* [1984] 2 All ER 152; *Re Andrabell Ltd* [1984] 3 All ER 407.
9 *Hendy Lennox* [1984] 2 All ER 152, [1984] 1 WLR 485; *Re Andrabell Ltd* [1984] 3 All ER 407.
10 *Re Andrabell Ltd*; *Re Peachdart Ltd* [1984] Ch 131, [1983] 3 All ER 204.
11 *E Pfeiffer Weinkellerei-Weineinkauf GmbH & Co v Arbuthnot Factors Ltd* [1988] 1 WLR 150.
12 See 6.2.1.8.
13 *E Pfeiffer Weinkellerei-Weineinkauf GmbH & Co v Arbuthnot Factors Ltd* [1988] 1 WLR 150; *Re Weldtech Equipment Ltd* [1991] BCC 16.
14 (1988) 5 BCC 325. See also Farrar and Chai [1985] JBL 160.
15 [1991] BCC 484.
16 (1823) 3 Russ 1; see 27.3.1.
17 See de Lacy (1991) 54 MLR 736.
18 [1991] BCC 484; see Sealy [1992] CLJ 19.
19 Hicks [1992] JBL 398 at 411.

18.4.6 Administration orders

Even if the seller has a valid retention of title clause, his right to rely on it may be restricted where an administration order is made. Administration is a procedure introduced by the Insolvency Act 1985, whereby an insolvency practitioner is appointed as administrator to take over the running of a company in order to try to save it from insolvency[1]. The Insolvency Act 1986 now provides that where an application for an administration order is made, no steps may be taken to repossess goods supplied under a retention of title agreement until the hearing of the application or, if an order is made, while the order remains in force[2]. The repossession of goods supplied under hire purchase, conditional sale and chattel leasing contracts is also frozen. There is power for the administrator to apply to the court for an order allowing him to sell goods covered by such an agreement, but if such an order is made, the court must order that the proceeds of sale be used to discharge sums due to the supplier under the supply contract[3].

1   See 22.0.1.1.
2   Insolvency Act 1986, s 10(1), s 11(3).
3   Insolvency Act 1986, s 15.

18.4.7   *Conclusion*

In view of the case-by-case development of the law on retention of title clauses, and the wide variety of different clauses in common use, it is unlikely that it will ever be possible to predict with complete certainty that a particular clause is or is not effective. Some broad, impressionistic conclusions can, however, be drawn from the cases. A retention of title to goods supplied, either under a simple or an 'all moneys' clause is likely to be upheld; any attempt by the seller to claim rights over the proceeds of sale of the goods or products made from them is likely to be construed as a charge and therefore fail unless registered.

The cases on the subject are difficult to reconcile, and there are clear differences of approach to different types of claim. Thus, whereas the Court of Appeal in *Clough Mill* and the House of Lords in *Armour v Thyssen* were prepared to take a claim to the goods in their original form at face value, when considering claims to proceeds of sale and manufactured products, the courts have tended to disregard the words of the particular clause as not reflecting the presumed intentions of the parties.

In many respects retention of title clauses are artificial. The use made in these cases of concepts such as agency, bailment and fiduciary relationship, is sometimes inconsistent with established law on those subjects. However, the willingness of the courts to make use of established concepts in order to achieve a particular aim has been one of the hallmarks of the common law in general and of commercial law in particular. As Robert Goff LJ remarked in *Clough Mill*, 'concepts such as bailment and fiduciary duty must not be allowed to be our masters but must rather be engaged as the tools of our trade'[1]. The recognition of the validity of retention of title clauses may therefore be regarded as a leading modern example of the willingness of commercial law to adapt to and accommodate new commercial practices, and it is probably no more artificial than hire purchase. It does, however, raise a number of policy issues[2]. Some commentators have argued that 'freedom of contract' should allow the parties to reach any agreement they like about the passing of property, but this disregards the fact that retention of title clauses affect third parties. By inserting a retention of title clause, a supplier of goods can improve his position in the event of his buyer becoming insolvent and effectively 'jump the queue' prescribed by statute, depleting the pot of assets available for distribution to other creditors. This form of protection is not available to all creditors: in particular, suppliers of services cannot use retention of title clauses, so that a successful retention of title clause reduces even further the chance of those creditors recovering anything in the debtor's insolvency. In *Borden (UK) Ltd v Scottish Timber Products Ltd* Templeman LJ was 'unwilling to imply a term or invoke the aid of equity to produce a result which other creditors of the buyers might justifiably regard as a fraudulent preference'[3]. Above all, a retention of title clause gives security without publicity. The bank's floating charge must be registered and its existence can be discovered by other potential creditors by searching in the appropriate register. The 'absence of any provisions requiring disclosure of reservation of title clauses is unsatisfactory and should be remedied as soon as possible'[4].

However, exactly the same objections can be directed at hire purchase, finance leasing and other arrangements. This is the heart of the problem. Conditional sale, hire purchase, equipment leases and similar arrangements are all intended to provide a person supplying goods on credit with security against non-payment but the law adopts a formalistic approach and treats different security arrangements in different ways. In 1971 the Crowther Committee recommended that a more substantive approach should be adopted and that all security arrangements should be subject to a registration requirement[5] and a similar line was taken by Professor Diamond in his 1989 report[6]. He recommended the establishment of a new 'notice filing' registration system, applicable to all security devices, including retention of title, hire purchase, conditional sale and chattel leases for a period of three years or more, and the drawing of a distinction between purchase money security interests, 'taken by a supplier of goods to secure payment of their price, or by a lender of the money used to pay for them'[7] and other securities. All security interests would be subject to the 'notice filing' requirement, but instead of having to register each individual transaction, the creditor would merely have to register in advance a general notice 'to put on record that a named debtor may have created a security interest in favour of a named creditor' and indicating the nature of the property covered by the interest[8]. This would have clear advantages in the case of retention of title, where there will often be a series of contracts between the same parties and registration of each individual transaction is quite impracticable.

Purchase money security interests would benefit from special priority rules and would take priority even over prior registered security interests affecting the same property. Simple retention of title clauses, retaining title to the goods supplied until their price is paid, or transferring the seller's claim to be paid to the proceeds of sale of the goods themselves, would be regarded as purchase money securities[9] and would therefore take priority over (say) a bank's floating charge. Clauses retaining property in goods until sums other than their price are paid, such as was approved by the House of Lords in *Armour v Thyssen*[10] or transferring the seller's claim to new products made with the goods, would be subject to the normal priority rules and would thus normally be deferred to a prior floating charge[11]. Interestingly, therefore, the distinction proposed by Professor Diamond between purchase money and more extensive securities differs from that drawn by the courts in the decided cases where 'all moneys' clauses are, but proceeds clauses generally are not, effective.

Recognising that his proposals would involve far reaching reform, Professor Diamond made a second set of proposals for reform to the existing company charges system, which he recommended should be implemented immediately, pending implementation of his main proposals. Under those proposals, the status of retention of title clauses would have been clarified by expressly requiring products and 'all monies' clauses to be registered as charges.

Professor Diamond's main proposals would rationalise and greatly improve the existing law; they would meet many of the objections to the recognition of retention of title clauses, overcoming the objection that they create security without publicity. The proposed distinction between 'simple' and more 'complex' retention of title clauses has much to recommend it. Even his more limited proposals would clarify the law. However, neither set of reforms seems likely to be implemented in the foreseeable future. In 1994 the DTI issued a consultation document seeking views on possible reforms to the Companies Charges legislation[12]. One option canvassed was the establishment of a notice filing system, which could extend to retention of title clauses, replacing the current legislation. Another was less radical reform to the present system, and in this context the document considered whether the status of retention of title clauses should be clarified. The only options identified, however, were requiring clauses which extend to new products and/or proceeds of sale to be registered, effectively codifying the present law, and exempting all retention of title clauses from registration. Curiously, the distinction proposed by Professor Diamond was not mentioned.

International reform seems no more likely. Although retention of title is common throughout Europe and beyond, there are significant differences between the treatment of retention clauses in different jurisdictions[13]. In the 1970s both the European Community and the Council of Europe commenced work on attempts to harmonise laws on retention of title. Neither attempt came to anything[14]. In 1995 the European Union opened for signature a Convention on Insolvency Procedures, and in 1999 published a draft Regulation based on the Convention. However, neither the Convention nor the draft Regulation deals with retention of title. They provide for mutual recognition of insolvency proceedings but on the whole do not deal with substantive aspects of insolvency law, and expressly provide that proceedings in one state will not affect rights based on a retention of title clause in relation to goods in another jurisdiction[15]. It has been suggested that the fundamental differences between legal and business cultures make harmonisation difficult, if not impossible[16]. Within the European Union efforts at harmonisation have been hampered by a reluctance to interfere with national property and insolvency laws. Perhaps significantly, although the European Commission's first draft of the Directive on late payment of commercial debts recognised the need for common treatment of retention of title clauses and would have required member states to recognise a simple retention of title clause[17], even this limited provision was removed from the final text[18].

1   [1984] 3 All ER 982 at 987.
2   See Ahdar [1993] LMCLQ 382.
3   [1979] 3 All ER 961 at 973, CA. A transaction effected out of a desire to improve the position of a particular creditor in the event of insolvency is a preference and may, in certain circumstances, be set aside: see now s 239 of the Insolvency Act 1986.
4   Report of the Cork Committee on Insolvency Law and Practice (1982) Cmnd 8558, para 1639.
5   Report of the Committee on Consumer Credit (1970) Cmnd 4596, para 1640. The proposal was supported by the Report of the Cork Committee on Insolvency Law and Practice (1982) Cmnd 8558.
6   Prof A L Diamond 'A Review of Security Interests in Moveables' (1989) DTI.
7   Paragraph 11.5.9.
8   Paragraph 11.2.3.
9   Paragraphs 17.8, 17.9.
10 [1991] 2 AC 339, [1990] 3 All ER 481, HL.
11 Paragraphs 17.10, 17.11, 17.14.

12 Company Law Review: Proposals for Reform of Part XII of the Companies Act 1985.
13 See Monti, Nejman and Reuter [1997] ICLQ 866.
14 See Goode (1980) 1 Co Lawyer 185; Latham [1982] JBL 81; Monti, Nejman and Reuter [1997] ICLQ 866. The Council of Europe completed a draft convention on retention of title in 1983 but work went no further.
15 Article 7(1).
16 Monti, Nejman and Reuter [1997] ICLQ 866.
17 The provision excluded instalment payment conditional sales.
18 See Directive 2000/35 of June 29, 2000, on combating late payment in commercial transactions.

Chapter 19

Contracts for the Supply of Services

19.0 Introduction

We have already noted the increasing economic importance of the provision of services, both within the domestic economy and as a valuable export. The provision of services is itself an important commercial activity but many services are provided in the course of other commercial transactions. A wide range of very different transactions involve a supply of services, including contracts for the installation, servicing and repair of industrial and domestic plant and equipment; the servicing and repair of vehicles; contracts for professional services, including legal, accountancy and financial advice and services; domestic and leisure services, such as the provision of holidays, hotel accommodation and entertainments; and even contracts for private medical care. Contracts of agency, for the provision of banking facilities, and for the carriage and warehousing of goods, which may all form vital ancillary parts of commercial sale contracts, are all contracts for the supply of services; some of them are examined in more detail elsewhere in this book[1].

Whereas the Sale of Goods Acts have provided a detailed code to regulate contracts for the sale of goods since 1893, contracts for the supply of services have until comparatively recently received little parliamentary attention. Until 1982 they were left to be regulated by the common law, and a detailed body of case law has grown up to define the obligations of the parties to some of the more common contracts for the supply of services. However, the Supply of Goods and Services Act 1982 (SGSA) now applies to all contracts involving the supply of services. If a contract involves the supply of goods as well as services it must first be construed in order to decide if it is really a contract for the sale of goods[2]. Where a contract involves the supply of goods and services but is not a sale, the Act implies terms requiring the goods to correspond with their description, be of satisfactory quality, fit for the buyer's purpose and correspond with any sample, in the same way as in any other contract for the supply of goods[3]. In addition, Pt II of the 1982 Act applies equally to contracts for the supply of services alone, such as professional advice, and to the service element of contracts of work and materials. It implies into such contracts three terms:

(a) that the service will be performed with reasonable skill and care[4];
(b) that, where no time for performance is fixed, the work will be carried out within a reasonable time[5]; and
(c) that where no consideration is fixed by the contract, a reasonable charge will be paid[6].

464

The Act was intended merely to codify the existing common law, and it is clear that, in view of the standard of reasonableness adopted by all three implied terms, the Act is flexible: what is reasonable in any particular case will be a question of fact. However, defining contractual obligations in statutory form offers one advantage, in that it focuses attention on the supplier's obligations to customers and clients, offering a clear and easily accessible statement of the essential duties. This may be particularly advantageous to consumers, in that it may make it easier for them to assert their rights, and reduces the scope for them to be 'fobbed off' by unscrupulous suppliers.

Plainly, the 1982 Act does not provide a complete statement of the rights and obligations of parties to contracts for the supply of services, and the statutory implied terms will normally be supplemented by express terms and by terms implied at common law. In the case of the more common types of contract there are extensive bodies of case law defining the obligations of the parties.

Some business activities have been subjected to additional control, where that has been deemed necessary in the public interest. Thus the activities of solicitors, estate agents and the providers of financial services are regulated by statute[7]. In other cases, the activities of service providers are subject to self-regulatory control by trade associations or professional organisations; in some cases self-regulation has been encouraged by the government, as an alternative to legislative control[8].

1   See Pt II (Agency) and Pt IV (Banking).
2   See 8.2.2.
3   See ch 11.
4   SGSA 1982, s 13.
5   SGSA 1982, s 14.
6   SGSA 1982, s 15.
7   The Solicitors Act 1974, Estate Agents Act 1979 and Financial Services and Markets Act 2000 respectively.
8   See eg the regulation of banking services by the Banking Code of Practice, below ch 29.

19.0.1   *The scope of the 1982 Act*

As noted above, Pt II of the SGSA 1982 applies to all contracts involving the supply of services, including those for professional services and those which involve the supply or bailment of goods[1]. However, a contract of apprenticeship or employment is not a contract for the supply of services for the purposes of the Act[2].

There is power for the Secretary of State to make orders exempting particular classes of service from the application of one or more of the implied terms[3]. This power has been exercised to exclude the application of s 13, which implies a term requiring services to be performed with reasonable skill and care, in relation to advocates, arbitrators, company directors[4], directors of building societies and members of the committees of management of societies registered under the Industrial and Provident Societies Act 1975[5].

1   SGSA, s 12(3).
2   SGSA, s 12(2).
3   SGSA, s 12(4).
4   The Supply of Services (Exclusion of Implied Terms) Orders 1982, SI 1982/1771; SI 1985/1.
5   The Supply of Services (Exclusion of Implied Terms) Order 1983, SI 1983/902.

19.1   The service must be performed with reasonable care and skill

Section 13 of the SGSA provides that:

> 'In a contract for the supply of a service where the supplier is acting in the course of a business, there is an implied term that the supplier will carry out the service with reasonable skill and care'.

Like the implied terms requiring goods to be of satisfactory quality and fit for the buyer's purpose, the term is only implied where the supplier is acting in the course of a business. However, a similar term will probably be implied into non-business contracts at common law, and the fact that the supplier does not act in the course of a business will simply be a factor which affects the standard of care reasonably to be expected of the supplier. It is clear that, even if no term is implied, even a gratuitous supplier of services is subject to a duty of care in negligence requiring him to exercise reasonable care[1].

The standard adopted is the common law negligence standard. It is flexible, allowing the court to take account of all the circumstances of the case in deciding what is reasonable. There are countless authorities illustrating what may be reasonable for a particular trade or profession in particular circumstances. In general the supplier is expected to 'exercise the ordinary skill of an ordinary competent man exercising that particular art'[2]. However, if the supplier of the service claims any special skill, expertise or specialism, that claim may raise the standard of what is reasonable.

Thus, for instance, a solicitor may be in breach if he fails to register a land charge[3]. Carpet layers were in breach when they left the carpet in such a condition that it presented an obvious danger to persons using the premises[4]; but in another case, carpet layers were not in breach when they failed to lay the carpet so that the pattern was centralised[5].

However, where the service involves the provision of advice, it may be difficult to establish liability, especially if the advice is of a somewhat speculative nature. For instance, 'the valuation of land by trained, competent and careful professional men is a task which rarely, if ever, admits of a precise conclusion. Often beyond certain well-founded facts so many imponderables confront the valuer that he is obliged to proceed on the basis of assumptions. Therefore he cannot be faulted for achieving a result which does not admit of some degree of error'[6]. In *Luxmoore-May v Messenger May Baverstock*[7] a provincial firm of auctioneers undertook to research a painting for a client who intended to put it up for auction. The auctioneers consulted Christies, but failed to attribute the paintings to the artist Stubbs. As a result, the paintings were sold for less than one hundredth of the price they fetched five months later when attributed to Stubbs. The auctioneers were not liable. The valuation of paintings by unknown artists 'pre-eminently involves an exercise of opinion and judgment . . . it is not an exact science'[8].

As these cases illustrate, the supplier of services does not normally undertake that the services will be fit for any particular purpose or achieve a particular result.

> 'The law does not usually imply a warranty that he will achieve the desired result, but only a term that he will use reasonable care and skill. The surgeon does not warrant that he will cure the patient. Nor does the solicitor warrant that he will win the case'[9].

Thus where the supplier of services contracts to make a finished product, it may be vital to decide if the contract is one for the sale of the finished item, in which case there will be an implied term that the finished product should be of satisfactory quality and fit for the buyer's purpose, or a contract for services involving the supply of work and materials. In the latter case, whilst the materials used must be of satisfactory quality and fit for purpose, the supplier's undertaking is that he will exercise reasonable skill and care in carrying out the work. He will therefore not be liable for any defect in the finished product unless it is caused by his negligence or by the use of defective materials.

However, there is no reason why the supplier should not expressly undertake that he will achieve a particular result, and it may be possible to imply such a term in a particular case. In *Greaves & Co Contractors Ltd v Baynham, Meikle & Partners*[10] contractors were engaged by an oil company to build a warehouse for the storage of barrels of oil and sub-contracted the design of the building, including the floors, to a firm of structural engineers. The engineers were informed that stacker trucks carrying barrels of oil would be running over the floors. After the warehouse opened, cracks began to appear in the floor, caused by vibrations produced by the stacker trucks. On the facts of the case it was held that there was an implied term that, if the work was completed in accordance with the design, the floor would be reasonably fit for use by loaded stacker trucks. Indeed, in a construction or similar contract it may be that a term that the finished product will achieve its purpose will generally be implied at common law. Similarly, in *IBA v BICC Construction Ltd*[11] a majority of the House of Lords held that the defendant structural engineers, who had designed a television mast, would have been liable for its collapse even if they had not been negligent. Lord Scarman said:

> 'The extent of the obligation is, of course, to be determined as a matter of construction of the contract. But in the absence of a clear, contractual indication to the contrary, I see no reason why one who in the course of his business contracts to design, supply and erect a television aerial mast is not under an obligation to ensure that it is to be reasonably fit for the purpose for which he knows it is intended to be used. . . . I do not accept that the obligation of the supplier of an article is to be equated with the obligation of a professional man in the practice of his profession'[12].

This approach may indicate an unwillingness on the part of the courts to allow the often fine distinction between contracts of sale and contracts for work and materials to prejudice the position of a customer where a finished product is supplied. However, since the implied term in these cases arises at common law, it will be excluded if it is contrary to the express terms of the contract, and such exclusion would seem to be outside the scope of the Unfair Contract Terms Act 1977; even if covered by the Act, the exclusion will be effective, even against a consumer, provided it is reasonable[13].

It is clear that such a term will rarely be implied in a contract for professional services of a speculative nature: for instance, it has been held that a surgeon will not be taken to have warranted the success of an operation unless he does so expressly and clearly[14].

A person who has contracted to supply services to another may use third party sub-contractors to fulfil his obligations under the contract. Often it will be anticipated when the principle contract is made that sub-contractors will be used. Examples include building contracts, where it may be anticipated that specialist sub-contractors may be used, contracts for the carriage of goods and package holiday contracts. If the service is not performed with the required standard of care it may be necessary to consider the liability of both the contractual supplier (the main contractor) and the actual supplier (the sub-contractor). Clearly, if the sub-contractor is negligent he may be liable in the tort of negligence. If the main contractor acts as agent for the customer when arranging the sub-contract there may be a direct contract between customer and sub-contractor, under which the contractor will also owe a contractual duty of care. Alternatively, it may be possible for the customer to enforce the contract between the main and sub contractor as one made for his benefit[15] if on its proper construction it was intended that he should have a right to enforce it.

The customer, may however, wish to pursue a claim against the main contractor. It will then be necessary to determine whether the main contractor's undertaking is one to perform the service, or merely one to act as the customer's agent and arrange for others to perform the service. Which it is will depend on the proper construction of the main contract. If it is properly construed as merely an undertaking to arrange for others to provide services, the contractor's only obligation will be to exercise reasonable care in the selection of sub-contractors[16]. Where, however, the contractor's obligation is to supply the services in question, the contractor undertakes that the services will be performed with reasonable skill and care, so that if the sub-contractor performs negligently, the main contractor may be held personally liable for any loss the customer suffers. The main contractor will be held to have undertaken a personal liability where sub-contracting is not reasonably contemplated by the customer[17]. Personal liability may, however, also be undertaken even where it was anticipated that the service would be performed by a third party[18].

It has been suggested that the negligence standard of care imposed on suppliers of services is not high enough and that they should be subject to strict liability. However, such a change would present difficulties in defining the range of services to be subject to strict liability: it was thought that some professionals such as architects and designers might be deterred from supplying advice if they were to be strictly liable for its accuracy, whilst many businesses supplying services may be small, with few fixed assets, and therefore less able than manufacturers of goods to insure against liability[19]. These arguments are not entirely convincing. As we have seen, the courts have effectively distinguished between two different categories of service supplies already, and the possibility of imposition of strict liability on designers and architects at common law does not seem greatly to have affected their willingness to supply their services. The third argument, relating to the size of the supplier's business, has some force, but it disregards the fact that primary liability for supplying defective goods falls not on the manufacturer, but on the supplier, who may have resources little greater than the supplier of services.

1   See eg *Chaudhry v Prabhakar* [1988] 3 All ER 718, CA, above, 6.2.1.2.
2   *Bolam v Friern Hospital Management Committee* [1957] 2 All ER 118 per McNair J.
3   *Midland Bank Trust Co Ltd v Hett Stubbs and Kemp* [1979] Ch 384, [1978] 3 All ER 571; *Bell v Peter Browne & Co* [1990] 3 All ER 124.
4   *Kimler v William Willett Ltd* [1947] KB 570, [1947] 1 All ER 361, CA.
5   *CRC Flooring v Heaton* (8 October 1980, unreported); see Lawson, 'The Quality of Services Supplied: Guidance from the Court of Appeal' (1984) NLJ 39.
6   Per Watkins J in *Singer and Friedlander Ltd v John D Wood & Co* (1977) 243 Estates Gazette 212 at 213.
7   [1990] 1 All ER 1067, [1990] 1 WLR 1009, CA.
8   Per Slade LJ at 1076; see also *Stafford v Conti Commodity Services Ltd* [1981] 1 All ER 691 (broker's advice on commodity futures market).
9   Per Lord Denning MR in *Greaves & Co Contractors Ltd v Baynham, Meikle & Partners* [1975] 3 All ER 99 at 103, CA.
10 Above, note 9.

11 (1980) 14 BLR 9.
12 (1980) 14 BLR 9 at 47.
13 Unfair Contract Terms Act 1977, s 3. A court might be inclined to regard such a clause as unreasonable in a consumer contract.
14 *Thake v Maurice* [1986] QB 644, [1986] 1 All ER 497, CA.
15 Under the Contracts (Rights of Third Parties) Act 1999: see 2.7.2.
16 *Wilson v Best Travel Ltd* [1993] 1 All ER 353.
17 *Rogers v Night Riders* (a firm) [1983] RTR 324, CA (minicab services); *Stewart v Reavell's Garage* [1952] 2 QB 545, [1952] 1 All ER 1191 (garage services).
18 See *Wong Mee Wan v Kwan Kin Travel Services Ltd* [1995] 4 All ER 745, PC (package holiday); *Jarvis v Swans Tours Ltd* [1973] QB 233, [1973] 1 All ER 71, CA. Package holidays are now covered by the Package Travel, Package Holidays and Package Tours Regulations 1992, SI 1992/3288, implementing an EC Directive (EC) 90/314, under which 'the tour organiser is liable to the consumer for the proper performance of the obligations under the contract, irrespective of whether such obligations are to be performed by that other party or by other suppliers of services' without prejudice to any liability of the actual provider of the services.
19 Royal Committee on Civil Liability and Compensation for Personal Injury (Cmnd 7054) (1978).

19.1.1 *Contract and tort*

The standard of liability imposed in contract on suppliers of services by the 1982 Act is the same as that imposed in the tort of negligence. Thus the same act may give rise to liability in both contract and tort, and that may sometimes offer advantages to the customer: in particular, the limitation period in contract begins to run from the date of breach, whereas that in tort runs from the date of damage. In *Midland Bank Trust Co v Hett Stubbs and Kemp*[1] solicitors failed to register a land charge to protect an option granted to their client, the plaintiff. The owner of the property sold the property and the plaintiff's option was overridden. It was held that the client's tortious action in negligence was not barred until six years after the property was sold.

In recent years the courts have preferred to leave the rights and duties of parties who are in a contractual relationship to be governed by the terms of their contract[2]. In *Tai Hing Cotton Mill Ltd v Liu Chong Hing Bank Ltd*[3] Lord Scarman, giving the opinion of the Privy Council, said:

> 'Their Lordships do not believe that there is anything to the advantage of the law's development in searching for a liability in tort where the parties are in a contractual relationship. This is particularly so in a commercial relationship'[4].

More recent cases have tended to explain and distinguish the *Midland Bank* case as one where there was a continuing breach of duty, and where the solicitors' initial breach could have been remedied at any time prior to the eventual sale of the property[5]. Thus where solicitors were negligent in drafting a restrictive covenant in a contract of employment, the plaintiff client suffered loss when the contract was executed, not when the covenant proved ineffective; the initial contract was 'defective' and the client therefore suffered loss at that time when he received a less valuable service than he bargained for[6]. Similarly, when insurance brokers negotiated contracts of insurance for clients and, due to non-disclosure by the brokers, the contracts were voidable, the plaintiffs suffered loss when the voidable contracts of insurance were concluded, not at the later date when they were avoided by the insurers[7]. However, where a lender advances money on the basis of a negligent valuation of property offered as security he does not suffer loss so that his cause of action against the value accrues until the amount outstanding on the loan exceeds the value of the security[8].

In all these cases the plaintiff's claim was for purely economic loss. Where the breach of contract causes physical damage to property or personal injury, a cause of action in tort will not accrue until the damage or injury occurs[9], so that it will offer advantages to the claimant.

However, the House of Lords considered the question of the concurrent liability in contract and tort of suppliers of services in *Henderson v Merrett Syndicates Ltd*[10]. Following an extensive review of the law, Lord Goff, with whom the rest of the House agreed, held that where the requirements for imposition of a tortious duty of care are satisfied, such a duty may be imposed even where the parties are in a contractual relationship. He expressly approved the decision in *Midland Bank v Hett Stubbs and Kemp* and explained that in *Tai Hing* the Privy Council was concerned with the question whether a more extensive duty could be imposed in tort than was imposed by the contract between the parties. Managing agents acting for 'names' in the Lloyd's insurance market therefore owed both a tortious and a contractual duty of care to the 'names' for whom they acted, and the names were free to pursue their claims either in contract or in tort, taking the benefit of any procedural advantage of either cause of action.

1 [1979] Ch 384, [1978] 3 All ER 571.
2 *Tai Hing Cotton Mill Ltd v Liu Chong Hing Bank Ltd* [1986] AC 80, [1985] 2 All ER 947, PC.
3 [1986] AC 80.
4 [1986] AC 80 at 107.
5 *Bell v Peter Browne & Co* [1990] 2 QB 495, [1990] 3 All ER 124.
6 *D W Moore & Co Ltd v Ferrier* [1988] 1 All ER 400, [1988] 1 WLR 267, CA.
7 *Iron Trades Mutual Insurance Co Ltd v J K Buckenham Ltd* [1990] 1 All ER 808; *Islander Trucking v Hogg Robinson & Gardner Mountain* [1990] 1 All ER 826.
8 *First National Commercial Bank plc v Humberts* [1995] 2 All ER 673, CA; *Nykredit plc v Edward Erdman Group (No 2)* [1998] 1 All ER 305.
9 *Pirelli General Cable Works Ltd v Oscar Faber & Partners* [1983] 2 AC 1, [1983] 1 All ER 65, HL; *London Congregational Union Inc v Harriss & Harriss* [1988] 1 All ER 15, CA.
10 [1995] 2 AC 145, [1994] 3 All ER 506; see 6.2.1.2.

19.1.2 *Exclusion of liability*

Liability for breach of the statutory implied term requiring the service to be performed with reasonable care and skill may be excluded or limited by an appropriate term in the contract, subject to the restrictions imposed by s 2 of the Unfair Contract Terms Act 1977. Any attempt to exclude liability for death or personal injury caused by a breach of the implied term in SGSA s 13 will be wholly ineffective; liability for other types of damage may, however, be excluded or limited provided that the exclusion satisfies the test of reasonableness. In contrast, the implied terms relating to the quality etc of goods supplied under contracts of supply can never be excluded where the buyer deals as consumer[1].

1 Unfair Contract Terms Act 1977, ss 6, 7; see 2.6.4.1.

19.1.3 *Remedies*

Whereas the implied terms relating to the quality etc of the goods supplied under a contract of supply are classified as conditions, the implied term that services be performed with reasonable care and skill is simply classified as a 'term'. It is therefore an 'innominate' term and the claimant's remedy in the case of a breach depends on the seriousness of the breach and of its consequences. He will only be entitled to terminate the contract if the breach deprives him of substantially the whole of the benefit it was intended that the contract should provide[1]. In other cases the claimant is limited to a claim for damages. Even where the contract is terminated, sums paid under the contract can only be recovered where there is a total failure of the consideration for which they were paid.

1   See 2.9.3.

19.2   Time for performance

Section 14 of the Supply of Goods and Services Act 1982 provides that where the parties have not agreed a particular time for performance of the service, and the time for performance cannot be ascertained by reference to previous dealings, or calculated by reference to the terms of the contract, there is an implied term that the service will be performed within a reasonable time. This simply restates a common law rule. It probably embodies two requirements: that the work should be started within a reasonable time, and that it should then be completed within a reasonable time from commencement.

What is 'reasonable' is a question of fact, depending on all the circumstances of the case. Expert evidence of the time a reasonably competent supplier would require to complete the work may be required. The test is objective. In *Charnock v Liverpool Corpn*[1] a garage took eight weeks to complete a vehicle repair which should have been completed in five weeks at most. The garage was short-staffed and was giving priority to manufacturers' warranty work. The Court of Appeal held that the garage was in breach of contract.

1   [1968] 3 All ER 473, [1968] 1 WLR 1498.

19.3   A reasonable price

If the contract does not fix the consideration for the service, or provide an agreed means for determining it, and the consideration cannot be determined by reference to a course of dealing between the parties, there is an implied term that a reasonable charge will be paid. Under a contract for services there is no requirement that the consideration be money.

Although it may seem unwise to enter into a contract without knowing the likely charge, a great many contracts are made on that basis. For instance, solicitors and other professionals often do not agree a fee before commencing work, although an hourly rate may be agreed. Similarly, if a car is sent for repair, the cost of the work may not be known in advance, because it will depend on the time taken. In order to avoid disputes, the customer can set an upper limit on the charge, so that the supplier must contact the customer and obtain approval before exceeding the limit. Alternatively, the customer may seek an estimate or a quotation for the work. An estimate is normally regarded as an approximation of the likely cost: the actual cost may be higher or lower, but the estimate will provide a yardstick by which to assess the reasonableness of the actual charge and if the actual charge is much higher than the estimate, the supplier will have to justify it. In contrast, a quotation is likely to be regarded as a binding statement of the price to be charged[1]: in that case the supplier takes the risk of increases in raw material or labour costs. However, if the customer requests extra work, there will be a variation of the contract, and the quotation may be exceeded.

What is a reasonable charge is a question of fact. If the customer feels that the charge is excessive, he should dispute it at once. If he pays and then disputes the charge later, his consent to the charge will be evidence that it was reasonable, unless he can establish that he did not consent: for instance, because he paid under duress.

1   *Croshaw v Pritchard and Renwick* (1899) 16 TLR 45.

19.3.1   *Interest*

The customer must pay for the services supplied in accordance with the terms of the contract. Contracts for the supply of services, either alone or together with goods, are covered by the Late Payment of Commercial Debts (Interest) Act 1998. Thus where supplier and customer act in the course of a business it will be an implied term of the contract that interest is payable on the price if not paid at the proper time[1].

1   See 18.0.1.1.

Part IV

Financing the Transaction

Chapter 20

Financing the Transaction

20.0 Payment methods

A person who acquires goods or services under a contract must pay for them. Assuming that the contract is not one of exchange or barter, the buyer's obligation will be to make a money payment. As explained elsewhere, an obligation to make a money payment can be satisfied by other means: for instance, if the buyer is owed money by the supplier, it may be possible to set off one debt in partial or total satisfaction of the other, or the contract may be varied to permit the buyer's obligation to be satisfied in other ways. These possibilities aside, however, there are broadly speaking four ways in which the buyer's obligation can be satisfied. The first and most obvious is by cash payment. Cash payment will, however, often be inconvenient or impracticable. The commercial world has therefore developed a range of alternative means by which payment obligations can be satisfied. Broadly speaking, these fall into three categories. First, the buyer may satisfy his obligation by giving a promise, separate from the contract of supply, to pay at a later date, as where he gives a promissory note. Second, the buyer may give an order to a third party to make payment, as where he gives a bill of exchange for the price. Third, the buyer may get a third party either to make payment, or to give an undertaking to pay at a future date, as where goods are 'paid for' by credit card, or, in international transactions, by letter of credit.

20.1 Financing, credit and security

There is naturally a tension between the interests of buyers and sellers, whether of goods or services. The buyer will normally want credit; he may be unable to pay on delivery, and need to use or resell the goods or services provided by the seller in order to earn the money to pay for them. Even where the buyer can pay on delivery, credit will improve the buyer's cash flow, allowing funds to be retained within his business for the duration of the credit period. On the other hand, where the seller does not know the buyer, or has doubts about the buyer's willingness or ability to pay, the granting of credit may be an unacceptable option. Even where the seller knows and trusts the buyer, the seller will wish to allow the shortest possible credit period for, just as extended credit benefits the buyer's cash flow, early payment benefits the seller's. The ingenuity of commerce is nowhere better illustrated than in the wide range of mechanisms it has devised to reconcile these competing interests of buyers and sellers.

Whether or not the seller provides the buyer with credit ultimately depends on the relative bargaining power of the parties. If the buyer has sufficient bargaining power, or if other suppliers are willing to offer credit, the seller may have no choice but to allow credit or lose a sale. Conversely, the buyer may be prepared to borrow from some other source in order to finance the transaction: if he can pay cash on delivery, he may be able to negotiate favourable terms with the seller, such as a reduction in the price for cash.

The seller or anyone else who grants the buyer credit will probably want some security as protection against the buyer's failure to pay; he may insist on a third party guarantee, or require the buyer to grant security over existing property. Where the contract is for the supply of goods, the goods themselves may be used as security with the seller retaining some proprietary interest in them by supplying on hire purchase or conditional sale terms, or subject to a retention of title[1]. However, although security may protect the seller against the buyer's failure to pay, none of those arrangements meets the seller's desire for early payment. If the buyer is unable or unwilling to pay cash on delivery, either from his own resources or by obtaining credit elsewhere, the conflicting desires of seller for early payment and buyer for extended credit can only be reconciled by some mechanism which allows the seller to seek immediate payment from some third party. One possibility is for the seller to sell the goods to a third party such as a finance house, and leave the third party to supply the goods on credit terms to the buyer. This arrangement is common in hire-purchase, conditional sale and equipment leasing[2]. The alternative is for the seller to supply the goods or services direct to the buyer and then sell the right to receive payment to a third party for immediate cash payment.

In the following chapters we will consider these various alternatives. In Chapters 21 to 26 we will examine the nature, development and regulation of the various transactions involving the supply of credit and granting of security. In Chapters 27 and 28 we will examine some aspects of the second alternative, before moving on to consider, in Chapters 29 and 30, the commercial activities of the most important suppliers of credit and other financial accommodation, the banks.

1   Strictly speaking, a sale subject to a retention of title is a conditional sale, but in practice the term 'conditional sale' tends to be used to describe a transaction similar to hire purchase where the price is paid in instalments and where the goods in question are not expected to be consumed or resold. See 8.1.2.
2   See ch 8; 21.1.2.

Chapter 21

Credit and Security

21.0 Introduction

The word 'credit' is used in a variety of senses. Many are concerned with the notion of 'trust' or reputation. In a commercial context, 'credit' may be used to refer to a person's financial status or reputation for solvency, as when a person is described as a 'good credit risk', indicating an evaluation of their ability to pay their debts. Alternatively, we may speak of a person's account being 'in credit' at the bank, by which we mean simply that a balance in their favour, representing a sum of money owing to them, is shown in the bank's records. In its legal sense, however, 'credit' is used to describe a variety of arrangements by which one person provides financial accommodation to another. Credit, in this sense, is vital to modern commercial activity and in both consumer and commercial transactions, credit facilities play a key role in financing the acquisition of goods and services or supporting general business activity. According to the Cork Report on Insolvency Law and Practice[1], 'credit is the lifeblood of the modern industrialised economy'. Many businesses rely on credit facilities to operate. A business will often first have to spend money in order to make a profit, and a business which does not have sufficient capital to finance its spending must seek credit facilities, usually from banks, finance houses or fellow traders. Furthermore, as a business expands, so too does its need for credit facilities.

An adequate supply of credit is vital to a healthy economy. 'The provision of credit for trade and industry stimulates production and encourages enterprise. Credit also tides individuals and companies over difficult times'[2]. In recent times, UK financial institutions have often been criticised for failing to make adequate supplies of credit available to business, or for doing so only on unsuitable terms[3]. However, over-supply of credit can be as dangerous as under-supply. First, excessive availability of credit can fuel demand in the economy and thus generate inflation. From time to time, therefore, governments have taken steps to control the availability of credit, for instance by imposing regulatory controls such as requirements for the payment of minimum deposits, or, as the more recent tendency has been, by altering interest rates. Secondly, the availability of credit may encourage individuals, especially consumers, to take on financial commitments beyond their means. As Galbraith points out:

> 'The process of persuading people to incur debt and the arrangements for them to do so, are as much a part of modern production as the making of the goods and the nurturing of wants[4].'

It has therefore been found necessary to impose controls on the way in which credit is sold and marketed.

1   (1982) Cmnd 8558, para 10.
2   Oditah, *Legal Aspects of Receivables Financing* (1991) p 1.
3   The Review of Banking Services in its report on Competition in UK Banking (2000) concluded that there was no shortfall in the provision of debt finance to small businesses (para 5.7) but that there was shortage of small scale risk capital for such businesses (ch 6) which could stifle growth.
4   J K Galbraith, *The Affluent Society* (1970) p 167.

21.1   Types of credit

Credit can be supplied in a number of ways. Professor Goode has defined it in broad terms as 'the provision of a benefit (cash, land, goods, services and facilities) for which payment is to be made by the recipient in money at a later date'[1]. Similarly, the Consumer Credit Act 1974 states that 'credit includes a cash loan, and any other form of financial accommodation'[2]. Broadly speaking, therefore, 'credit' is supplied whenever payment of a debt is contractually deferred. Within this broad definition, however, credit arrangements can be classified according to two different classifications which, respectively, contrast lender, or loan, credit with vendor, or sales credit, and fixed sum with 'revolving' credit.

Loan credit involves a creditor advancing money to a borrower, on terms which require the borrower to repay the money, together, normally, with interest and charges, at a later date. The debtor therefore benefits by having the use of the sum advanced, the creditor from the payment of interest. Common examples include bank loans and overdrafts. Sale credit involves the supplier of goods or services agreeing to defer payment of the price. Again the debtor benefits from the deferment by having the use of the money which would otherwise be paid to the creditor. Many common commercial supply arrangements, including conditional sale and hire purchase, involve sale credit. Both loan credit and sale credit may be, and are, used to finance the purchase of goods and services. The crucial difference between them is that, in the case of loan credit, the goods or services are supplied separately from the credit, normally by a different supplier, whereas in the case of sale credit, both goods or services and credit are supplied by the same person. Although a loan creditor may want to know what the credit will be used for, and indeed may impose contractual restrictions on the debtor's use of the money advanced, the debtor is practically (if not legally) free to use the credit as he wishes. Loan credit is therefore more flexible than sale credit.

Loan credit may appear to be more expensive, because the debtor will be required to pay interest on the loan. However, both forms of credit involve the creditor in risk and expense and he will therefore make a charge to compensate him for (a) the loss of the use of the amount of the credit for the credit period, (b) the possible effects of inflation, and (c) the risk that the debtor may default in repayment. In the case of sale credit, these charges may be disguised, for instance by the simple expedient of charging more to credit than to cash customers.

The second classification, distinguishing fixed sum from revolving credit, cuts across the first. Under a *fixed* sum credit arrangement, a fixed amount is drawn by the debtor and is repaid over a stated period. The credit arrangement comes to an end on completion of the repayments. An example is a personal loan. Where credit is provided through a *revolving* facility, the creditor is not given a fixed amount but is provided with a line of credit upon which he can draw. An upper limit is fixed and the debtor can make one or more drawings of any amount provided that at any time the total amount outstanding does not exceed the limit. He is not obliged to use the full facility. Each drawing reduces the amount of the credit facility and, as the debtor repays amounts to the creditor, the facility is replenished. Thus bank loans and hire purchase arrangements involve fixed sum credit, whilst overdrafts and credit card arrangements provide revolving facilities.

The commercial world has been astute to develop new means of supplying credit, often in response to, and as a way of avoiding, restrictions on the use of existing types of credit imposed from time to time either to protect debtors or to further government economic policy. The point remains that all of these arrangements, whether for loan or sale, fixed sum or revolving credit, serve the same commercial purpose and involve the supply of credit, but until 1974 different forms of arrangement were treated differently. In particular, the law distinguished between loan and sale credit and, as a result, credit law became confused and irrational. The Crowther Committee recognised this in 1971:

> 'it is to us of the highest importance to recognise that they are, in fact, two aspects of the same thing – the transfer of purchasing power from one set of persons to another set of persons, against a promise to repay the principal with interest'[3].

The Consumer Credit Act 1974 was passed to implement recommendations of the Crowther Committee and to provide protection for consumer debtors. As a result the law does now treat both types of arrangement alike for certain purposes. The Act defines 'credit' in broad terms and applies equally to loan and sale, fixed sum and revolving credit[4].

The following paragraphs describe the principal forms of credit transaction in more detail; the 1974 Act is considered in Chapters 24 to 26.

1   *Commercial Law* (2nd edn, 1995) p 637. In *Dimond v Lovell* [2000] 2 All ER 897 the House of Lords (subject to some reservations on the part of Lord Hobhouse) approved another, similar definition by Professor Goode that, for the purposes of the Consumer Credit Act 'credit is extended whenever the contract provides for the debtor to pay, or gives him the option to pay, later than the time at which payment would otherwise have been earned under the express or implied terms of the contract' (see Goode, *Consumer Credit Legislation* (1999) vol I, para 443). See also *Grant v Watton (Inspector of Taxes)* [1999] STC 330 at 345, per Pumfrey J.
2   Section 9(1).
3   Report of the Committee on Consumer Credit (Cmnd 4596) (1971), para 1.1.2.
4   See below, ch 24.

21.1.1 *Loans*

As we have already seen, a loan is simply an arrangement whereby a debtor is advanced a sum of money which is repaid over a period of time. The debtor agrees to repay the loan, together with interest and any charges, either at the end of the loan period or by instalments of fixed amounts over the period of the loan. The rate of interest will be fixed according to the prevailing market rate at which lending institutions are advancing funds and such factors as the degree of risk for the creditor. Normally, the creditor will ask why the loan is required but, in practice, where funds are transferred directly to the debtor, little control can be exercised over how the loan is used.

The banks are one of the main sources for loans both to individuals and commercial organisations. In the case of individual personal advances, funds may be transferred by way of personal loan or overdraft. A personal loan merely involves the transfer of a fixed sum loan to the account of the debtor and the opening of a loan account which is debited initially with the amount advanced plus interest charges. The loan account operates until the debt has been extinguished over the fixed period.

Banks may also provide overdrafts as a means of allowing customers to overdraw on their current accounts up to a maximum debit balance. As noted above, overdrafts therefore provide a revolving credit facility under which the amount of the credit fluctuates according to how much is paid into and withdrawn from the account at any one time. Overdrafts are intended as a facility for customers whose cash flow varies from time to time; they are not normally used to finance specific transactions.

In recent years there has been a shift from overdraft to fixed-term lending for small businesses[1]. For individuals, too, personal loans have become increasingly popular because, unlike hire purchase and credit sale, they can be used to finance the purchase of services, such as holidays or home improvements, as well as goods.

The banks have tended to be the main source of loan finance for both individual and corporate borrowers[2]. Building societies, too, provide loan finance facilities. Their core business remains the provision of secured loans to finance house purchases, but since the Building Societies Act 1986 they are permitted to provide a wider range of credit facilities. Nevertheless, their lending tends to be to private individual debtors rather than to businesses[3].

Other institutions involved in lending are finance houses and moneylending firms. Finance houses expanded considerably with the growth of hire purchase and a great part of their business is still the provision of instalment credit finance. They tend to be subsidiaries of banks, large retailers and manufacturers, and other financial institutions. Such institutions have, however, diversified considerably into such activities as credit card operation, personal loans, and leasing.

Moneylending firms specialise in making cash loans to individuals, often at rates of interest in excess of the current market rate. The activities of moneylenders caused considerable concern in the late nineteenth century. A House of Commons Select Committee on Moneylending in 1898 considered that:

> 'the system of moneylending by professional moneylenders at high rates of interest is productive of crime, bankruptcy, unfair advantages over other creditors of the borrower, extortion from the borrower's family and friends, and other serious injuries to the community'.

Moneylenders were subjected to increasing regulation by a series of Moneylenders Acts. Under this legislation they had to have an annual licence, moneylending contracts were required to be evidenced in writing, the true rate of interest had to be stated, restrictions were placed on advertising and canvassing for business, and the courts were given the power to reopen unconscionable bargains[4]. Many of the provisions in the Moneylenders Acts formed the model for the Consumer Credit Act which now regulates moneylending along with other credit transactions.

1   *Competition in UK Banking* (2000) para 5.26.
2   The Review of Banking Services in the UK found that the traditional banks had 46% of the market for personal loans for consumer customers; other 'established' banks had a further 13% and converted building societies 16%: see *Competition in UK Banking* (2000) para 4.31. The high street banks had some 90% of the market for lending to small- to medium-sized businesses: para 5.18.

3   In recent years several former building societies have converted into banks for commercial reasons:
    see 29.0.3. The Review of Banking Services in the UK found that traditional building societies
    accounted for only 1% of consumer personal loans: *Competition in UK Banking* (2000) para 4.31.
4   See Moneylenders Act 1927.

21.1.2   Sale credit

As we have seen, one factor which distinguishes loans or lender credit from sale or
vendor credit is that although a loan may be advanced for the purchase of identifiable
goods, the loan and the goods are supplied separately by two different people.
In the case of sale credit, the person who supplies the goods also supplies the
credit. However, the legal reality of the situation may not be immediately
apparent. For example, in a typical hire purchase transaction a customer identifies
the goods he requires and negotiates with the dealer. The dealer sells the goods to
a finance company with which the dealer may be associated or have arrangements,
and the finance company enters into a hire purchase contract with the customer:
thus both the goods and the credit are supplied by the finance company under a
single contract, although the customer negotiates with, and the goods originate
from and are despatched by, the retailer. The principal forms of vendor/sale credit
agreement have already been described in order to contrast their legal incidents
with those of a simple sale of goods[1]. The following sections concentrate on the
credit aspects of these transactions.

1   Above 8.2.1; 8.2.4.

21.1.2.1   *Hire purchase*

As we have seen, the hire purchase transaction became popular in the late nineteenth
century. By 1891 there were probably one million agreements in existence and in
that year the Hire Trades Protection Association was formed[1]. Once the House of
Lords[2] accepted the theoretical basis of the hire purchase contract as a bailment, or
hire, with an option to purchase, it flourished as a means of instalment credit which
provided the creditor with effective security against the debtor's default or wrongful
disposal of the goods. With the mass production of cars, radios, radiograms, vacuum
cleaners and other household appliances, the hire purchase contract provided the
means by which consumers could enjoy the use of such goods immediately, paying
for them over two or three years.

   The hire purchase contract assumed its present three-cornered shape in the
1920s. Retailers could not provide the extensive credit facilities necessary to
satisfy demand for the more expensive consumer goods, and finance houses
were established to finance the supply of such goods. They developed from
three sources: companies formed in the 1860s, originally to finance the purchase
of specialised coal wagons for the railway and colliery companies; American
companies which, having financed a consumer credit boom in the US expanded
their activities to the UK; and finance houses established by UK manufacturing
companies to support the market in their own goods. They began to play an
increasingly important role in the supply of goods on instalment payment terms.
Apart from cash transactions, a seller did not sell directly to customers, but to
the finance company which then hired to the customer with an option to
purchase.

Since such transactions were not regarded as loans on security of the goods, the restrictive provisions of the Moneylenders Acts and Bills of Sale Act were not permitted to inhibit the growth in hire purchase. Thus, the hire purchase transaction was free from control other than that under the general law of contract, which undoubtedly contributed to its popularity amongst the finance houses. Consumers also derived benefit, as the Crowther Committee observed:

'There can be little doubt that this by-passing of the Moneylenders Acts has been in the interests of consumers as a class, since otherwise the great extension of credit to ordinary households, and the higher material standards of living based upon it, would not have been possible'[3].

However, the Committee proceeded to identify the inevitable corollary of that proposition, that consumers were subjected to abuses and deprived of the comprehensive protections which such Acts were intended to afford. A particular abuse was the 'snatch back' of goods by a company for a trivial default by the customer when nearly all the instalments had been paid. The goods would then be disposed of by the hiring company without any compensation to the hirer for the amount paid, making a considerable profit for the hiring company.

Public opinion and pressure from social reformers resulted in the passing of the Hire Purchase Act 1938, intended to attack some of the worst abuses in the hire purchase business. Basic formalities were introduced for hire purchase contracts within a financial limit and restrictions were placed on the remedies for default by a customer. There followed a series of statutes gradually extending protection, culminating in the Hire Purchase Act 1965, many of the provisions of which are now contained in Consumer Credit Act.

1   See The Report of the Committee on Consumer Credit (the Crowther Committee) (Cmnd 4596) (1971) p 43.
2   *Helby v Matthews* [1895] AC 471, HL.
3   (Cmnd 4596) (1971) p 44.

21.1.2.2   *Conditional sale agreements*

As we have seen, a conditional sale agreement is a contract for the sale of goods under which the seller retains the property in the goods until payment of the price or performance of other specified conditions, normally as security for payment of the price. A sale of goods subject to a retention of title is a conditional sale[1] but where the price is payable by instalments, the practical effect of a conditional sale may be very similar to that of hire purchase. At common law there were significant legal differences between the two transactions; in particular, the fact that the buyer under a conditional sale agreement could dispose of them and pass a good title to a good faith purchaser[2] encouraged the development of the hire purchase contract. However, the tendency of modern legislation is largely to ignore the conceptual distinction between the two transactions and treat them alike[3].

1   See 18.4.
2   *Lee v Butler* [1893] 2 QB 318.
3   Supply of Goods (Implied Terms) Act 1973, s 14(1): see 12.2.4; Sale of Goods Act 1979, s 25(2): see 17.4.2.

21.1.2.3   *Credit sale*

What distinguishes credit sale from conditional sale and hire purchase is that the seller does not reserve the property in the goods. Such agreements have become increasingly popular with large department stores and mail order firms supplying goods which either do not have a high value or depreciate rapidly. There is no point in reserving the property in goods if such goods have a limited resale value.

21.1.2.4   *Rental agreements*[1]

Although not strictly a form of instalment credit, the Crowther Committee considered that where goods are supplied under long-term hiring contracts, hire may effectively be an alternative to purchasing the goods on credit, and therefore recommended that rental agreements should be treated as a form of vendor credit. In much the same way that hire purchase benefited from being relatively free of statutory control until 1938, rental agreements emerged as an alternative to hire purchase when the latter became subject to greater control. Indeed, such agreements remained relatively free from legislative control until the passing of the Consumer Credit Act 1974.

1   See 8.2.4.

21.1.3   **Hybrid transactions**

By the 1960s a third type of credit transaction was developing, which did not fit easily into the category of lender or vendor credit. The Crowther Committee termed these 'hybrid transactions', since they were closely tied to the supply of goods or services but retained some of the flexibility of pure loans. One reason for the development of such transactions was the growth of a market for the provision of finance tied to the supply of services, for which hire purchase and conditional sale were clearly inappropriate; however, they were also used to finance the supply of goods. Typically, finance houses would provide personal loans to customers of retailers with whom they had pre-existing arrangements. Thus the customer entered into two separate contracts, one with the retailer for the sale of goods or supply of services and the second with the finance house for a loan. This contrasts with hire purchase, where the finance house supplies both goods and credit and one attraction of such loan arrangements for finance houses was that, at common law, they could not be held responsible for the quality of goods and services supplied[1]. Other 'hybrid' credit arrangements include budget accounts and check trading. Budget accounts are operated by individual retailers, or by finance houses (sometimes subsidiaries of the retailer) on their behalf. A customer with a budget account pays an agreed fixed monthly (or other periodic) amount to the credit of the account; he is then allowed to buy goods or services from the retailer, on credit, up to a specified multiple of the monthly payment. Credit is therefore provided to the customer by the retailer or finance house. Under check trading arrangements credit is extended in the form of vouchers or trading checks, each carrying a specific value, which can be used at retail outlets which have arrangements with the check trading company. The retailer is paid by the check company, less a commission, and the customer pays the check company by instalments.

1   The finance house would now be liable for the quality of goods or services by virtue of Consumer
    Credit Act 1974, s 75: see 26.4.

21.1.3.1   *Credit cards*

One increasingly popular way for consumers to obtain credit is by using a credit
card. Credit cards were first introduced in the US in the 1930s by organisations
such as oil companies and hotels, for use by their customers, who could use them
to pay for goods or services provided by the issuing organisation. In-house cards
issued by individual retailers for use at their own establishments are still common;
however, the most common form of card today is issued by a financial institution
such as a bank and is not restricted to any particular supplier but can be used to pay
for goods and services in a wide range of retail outlets. The first such credit card in
the UK was the Barclaycard, launched by Barclays Bank in the 1960s; since then
the use of credit cards has grown considerably to the point where, today, most
financial institutions issue at least one such card, they are used worldwide, and
account for approximately 10% of consumer spending in the UK[1].

A credit card facility is a form of revolving or 'running account' credit whereby
the card issuer, normally a financial institution, allows the cardholder to use the
card during a monthly accounting period to pay for goods and services and/or to
draw cash, up to a prescribed credit limit, interest being payable on the amount
outstanding at the end of the monthly accounting period.

Card issuers generally belong to one of two card payment organisations, Visa or
Mastercard. Retailers are recruited to accept cards by 'merchant acquirers', who act
on behalf of card issuers. The terms of membership of the payment organisations
require all members to accept credit card transactions from retailers recruited by or
on behalf of other members of the payment organisation, whilst retailers must accept
all cards issued by any member of the payment organisation to which the issuer by
whom the retailer was recruited belongs. Thus, for example, a retailer recruited on
behalf of a card issuing member of the Visa organisation must accept all Visa cards.
When a card is used to pay for goods or services in a face-to-face transaction, the
cardholder signs a voucher for the amount of the price, authorising the retailer to
claim payment from the card issuer or merchant acquirer. The retailer presents the
voucher to the merchant acquirer who recruited him and obtains payment for the
goods or services, less a charge payable to the merchant acquirer. The merchant
acquirer then presents the voucher to the issuer and in turn obtains payment, less a
handling fee payable to the issuer. The retailer thus obtains less than the full amount
of the voucher when goods are paid for by credit card, and retailers are now permitted
to charge higher prices to customers paying by credit card. The card issuer collects
all the vouchers and, at the end of the monthly accounting period, sends the cardholder
an account for payment. Under the terms of most common cards the cardholder is
required to pay a minimum amount of the outstanding balance on his account each
month; interest is charged only on any outstanding balance. However, since the
cardholder is not required to pay off the whole balance, the credit period is not fixed.
Many cardholders now choose to pay off their accounts in full each month in order
to avoid paying interest; the cardholder thus obtains a short period of interest-free
credit. To compensate for the loss of interest caused by this tendency, most card
issuers now charge an annual fee for use of their card. The cardholder may thus pay
an annual fee for use of the card, an excess to the retailer who accepts the card and
interest on the balance on his account if he fails to discharge it in full.

The contract between credit card issuer and cardholder is regulated by the Consumer Credit Act 1974. Under the Act the cardholder's liability for unauthorised use of the card if it is lost or stolen is limited to a maximum liability of £50[2]. Where the card remains in the cardholder's possession he is not liable for unauthorised use at all[3]. The risk of fraudulent or unauthorised use of a card is thus passed to the card issuer. That risk is particularly significant in 'card not present' transactions, as when the card is used to pay for goods or services in a mail order, telephone or Internet transaction. A person using the card for such a transaction will be required to supply details of the card to confirm its validity but, since the card is not produced, the retailer does not obtain the cardholder's signature. A consumer now has an automatic right to have his account re-credited and any payment cancelled where his card is used fraudulently in connection with a distance contract, even if the card is lost or stolen[4]. The standard terms of contract used by the card issuer and merchant acquirers normally contain a 'charge back' clause, under which sums paid to the retailer in respect of a transaction must be reimbursed (by deduction from sums payable to the retailer) if the cardholder successfully challenges liability for a transaction on the grounds that he did not authorise it[5]. The risk of unauthorised use in these cases thus falls on the retailer.

The use of credit cards was subjected to judicial analysis for the first time in the case of *Re Charge Card Services Ltd*[6]. In this case the Court of Appeal considered a simplified transaction in which retailers, in this case garages, were recruited direct by the card issuer without the intervention of a merchant acquirer. However, the basis of the court's analysis is probably applicable to the more common scheme described above. The court considered that the underlying scheme is established by two separate contracts. The first is made between the credit company and the seller: the seller undertakes to accept payment by use of the card from anyone holding the card and the credit card company agrees to pay to the supplier the price of goods or services supplied less a discount. The second contract is between the credit card company and the cardholder: the cardholder is provided with a card which enables him to pay the price by its use and in return agrees to pay the credit company the full amount of the price charged by the supplier[7]. A third bilateral contract is created when the cardholder/buyer purchases goods or services from the seller. In the words of Sir Nicolas Browne-Wilkinson V-C:

> 'Tendering and acceptance of the credit card in payment is made on the tacit assumption that the legal consequences will be regulated by the separate underlying contractual obligations between the seller and the credit company and the buyer and the credit company . . . In the circumstances, credit cards have come to be regarded as substitutes for cash: they are frequently referred to as "plastic money". The credit card scheme provides advantages to both seller and purchaser. The seller is able to attract custom by agreeing to accept credit card payment. The purchaser, by using the card, minimises the need to carry cash and obtains at least a period of free credit during the period until payment to the card company is due'[8].

The Court of Appeal went on to hold that a supplier accepts payment by card in substitution for payment in cash, so that the cardholder's liability for the price is unconditionally discharged.

> 'One way of looking at the matter is to say that there was a quasi-novation of the purchaser's liability. By the underlying scheme, the company had bound

the garage to accept the card and authorised the cardholder to pledge the company's credit. By the signature of the voucher all parties became bound: the garage was bound to accept the card in payment; the company was bound to pay the garage; and the cardholder was bound to pay the company. The garage, knowing that the cardholder was bound to pay the company and knowing that it was entitled to payment from the company which the garage itself had elected to do business with, must in my judgment be taken to have accepted the company's obligation to pay in place of liability on the customer to pay the garage direct"[9].

Credit cards must be distinguished from other plastic cards and similar arrangements in common use. Purchases on budget accounts are now often made using a plastic account card. They involve a supply of credit, and may have many features in common with credit cards. However, the terms on which the card is held, requiring the cardholder to make a fixed monthly payment, are different from those which apply to a credit card and where the account is operated by the retailer there are only two parties to the transaction. Charge cards, such as Diners Card and American Express, also involve the grant of credit. However, in contrast to the position with a standard credit card, the cardholder is required to repay the whole outstanding balance on his account at the end of each accounting period.

Cheque guarantee and debit cards, on the other hand, do not necessarily involve the grant of credit. A cheque guarantee card is issued by a bank and involves the bank giving an undertaking that any cheque in respect of which the card is used will be paid by the bank provided certain conditions set out on the card are complied with[10]. A debit card allows the cardholder to pay for goods or services, or to withdraw cash, directly from his bank account, either by signature of a voucher or directly, by means of an electronic funds transfer authorised by signature or by use of a personal identification number (PIN)[11]. Debit cards are therefore issued for use with current accounts and are used largely as an alternative to cheques. As with credit cards, the individual banks and other financial institutions who issue cards are members of larger networks, the main ones being Switch, Visa and Mastercard. They are structured similarly to credit card networks, with retailers being recruited by merchant acquirers. The procedures for use of and contractual analysis of debit card arrangements are broadly similar to those for credit cards, described above. The main difference is that there is no monthly statement or request for payment. The cardholder's signature acts as his mandate to the bank to debit his account with the amount of the transaction as well as his authority to pay the retailer, and on receipt of his mandate his account is debited directly. Use of a cheque guarantee or debit card does not necessarily involve a right on the part of the cardholder to overdraw his account and therefore does not necessarily involve any grant of credit[12].

There have recently been trials of so-called 'digital cash' cards, such as Mondex, designed especially for small scale transactions, such as paying car parking charges. Usage of such cards is so far at a very low level. It is anticipated, however, that with the development of e-commerce, they may become more common. The various systems differ in their detail. The essential point for present purposes is that the cards are pre-paid: that is to say, the card holder 'charges' the card with 'cash' in return for a payment. The amount of cash so loaded is recorded on a chip on the card. When the card is used for payment, the amount of the transaction is deducted from the card and credited to the retailer. Payment is thus direct by an electronic transfer of value and, since the card is pre-paid, there is no element of credit from the customer's point of view.

1 See Office of Fair Trading *Connected Lender Liability: A Review by the Director General of Fair Trading of section 75 of the Consumer Credit Act* (March 1994) p 13. In 1997 UK-issued credit cards were used for 1,252 million transactions, worth £67,623m (source: Association for Payment Clearing Services, *Yearbook of Payment Statistics* (1998)).

2 Consumer Credit Act 1974, s 84. See 26.5.2.

3 Consumer Credit Act 1974, s 83.

4 Consumer Protection (Distance Selling) Regulations 2000, SI 2000/2334, reg 21, implementing Directive 97/7/EC on the Protection of Consumers in respect of Distance Contracts. In August 2000 credit card issuers announced new security measures to be used where cards are used for card not present transactions, designed to reduce the risk of fraud by requesting additional information from the person authorising the transaction in order to ensure that that person is the legitimate cardholder.

5 Such clauses may be open to challenge as unreasonable under the Unfair Contract Terms Act 1977, or possibly on other grounds: see Brownsword and MacGowan (1997) 147 NLJ 1806 and Brownsword and Howells (1999) 19 LS 287.

6 [1989] Ch 497, [1988] 3 All ER 702.

7 The contract normally provides that the card remains the property of the card issuer. The issuer may therefore recover and retain the card if it suspects that is being used by an unauthorised person: *Tony Mekwin MTV & Co v National Westminster Bank plc* [1998] CCLR 22.

8 [1988] 3 All ER 702 at 768.

9 [1988] 3 All ER 702 at 772. See also [1989] JBL 339.

10 *First Sport Ltd v Barclays Bank plc* [1993] 3 All ER 789. See 30.1.

11 See 30.3.3.

12 See 26.5.

21.2   Security

Anyone providing credit to a debtor must face the prospect that the debtor may fail to pay his debt. The debtor may simply refuse to pay, but, in the absence of dishonesty, payment will normally only be refused where the debtor disputes liability, perhaps on the basis of an alleged breach of contract by the creditor or of a dispute as to the interpretation of the contract. The contract itself may contain provisions, such as those allowing discounts or requiring payment of interest, or restricting rights of set-off, designed to encourage the debtor to perform promptly and minimise the debtor's ability to refuse performance on the grounds of any alleged breach by the creditor. Ultimately, however, if the debtor refuses to perform his obligations the creditor may have to resort to legal action to enforce payment. More serious, from the creditor's point of view, is the risk that the debtor is unable to pay. A debtor who is unable to pay his debts is insolvent. Several procedures are prescribed by law to deal with the estates of insolvent individuals and companies, but the different procedures share several important characteristics. Normally, the property of the insolvent debtor vests in a third party such as a trustee in bankruptcy, receiver or liquidator, whose job it is to collect the insolvent debtor's property and realise it in order to pay the debtor's creditors. In each case the order in which debts must be paid is prescribed by law. Generally, the costs of the insolvency procedure and the claims of preferential and secured creditors rank before the claims of unsecured creditors and the basic principle is that the insolvent's assets should be distributed on a *pari passu* basis, so that creditors with equal ranking claims share equally in the assets, each receiving the same proportion of their claim. Litigation against an insolvent debtor is pointless; in any case, court proceedings against the debtor are normally stayed in insolvency proceedings. The result is that an ordinary creditor is most unlikely to receive payment in full if his debtor becomes insolvent; at best he will normally receive a 'dividend' representing a proportion of the debt due to him and, in many cases, will receive nothing or very little.

A potential creditor can guard against the risk of a debtor's insolvency by making appropriate checks on the debtor's creditworthiness before granting credit; he may, for instance, take up bank references or use a credit reference agency to check for outstanding debts and court judgments against the debtor, and such checks may be sufficient for a creditor lending only a small amount. However, although such checks are valuable, their effectiveness is limited. Creditworthiness may be difficult to assess, especially in times of recession when unforeseen financial catastrophes may strike individuals and companies. In order to guard against the risk of the debtor's inability to pay, a creditor lending a substantial amount will therefore want to take security for payment of the debt. There are many different security arrangements but essentially they all serve the same purpose: 'to improve the creditor's chance of getting paid or of receiving whatever else the debtor is required to do by way of performance'[1]. The taking of security may also improve the chances of the debtor performing his obligations even where he is not insolvent:

'In most situations the last thing the creditor wants is to have to enforce his security. His prime objective is that the contract he has entered into with the debtor should be performed. The debtor's fear that the security may be enforced, or a threat by the creditor to enforce the security, will often be enough to ensure that a debtor who is having difficulty in fulfilling all his contract will give priority in performance in favour of a secured creditor'[2].

However, the main purpose and advantage of security is to guard against, and improve the creditor's position in the event of, the debtor's insolvency.

1   Diamond, *A Review of Security Interests in Property* (1989) para 3.2.
2   Diamond, *A Review of Security Interests in Property* (1989) para 3.3(a).

21.2.1   *Types of security*

The ingenuity of the commercial community is well illustrated by the variety of arrangements it has developed to fulfil the creditor's desire for security. Broadly speaking, however, a creditor wishing to take security has a choice between taking real or personal security.

Real security involves the creditor taking, or being given, some proprietary right over property of the debtor. There are a number of real security arrangements: in some cases the debtor voluntarily grants rights to the creditor, in others the creditor's rights arise as a matter of law; in some cases the creditor must take or have possession of the property over which the security exists, in others the creditor may have security over property without taking possession of it. The creditor's rights vary according to the nature of his security, but generally real security gives him a right either to retain or take possession of the debtor's property or, ultimately, to have it sold and the proceeds of sale applied to satisfy his debt.

Personal security involves some third party surety entering into a separate contract with the creditor to assure the creditor of the debtor's performance and answer for the debtor's failure to perform, for instance by guaranteeing payment of a debt or indemnifying the creditor against losses caused by the debtor's failure to perform.

Clearly, a creditor will only accept personal security provided by a creditworthy and financially sound person or institution. Personal security is only as good as the creditworthiness of the third party surety. In contrast, the value of real security depends primarily on the value of the property over which the creditor has security. In practice the two forms of security are often combined: a debtor may be required to provide real security over property and one or more third party sureties for his performance, whilst personal security may be reinforced by requiring the surety to provide real security for performance of his obligations. Thus, for instance, a small company seeking bank finance may be required to give the bank a charge over its assets (real security) and arrange for its borrowing to be guaranteed by its directors (personal security) who in turn may be required to secure their guarantees by granting the bank mortgages over their homes (real security).

21.2.2 *Quasi-security*

In addition to formal security arrangements there are a number of other devices which provide a creditor with some measure of protection against his debtor's non-payment. Some, such as contractual rights of set-off, give merely personal rights against the debtor[1]. Others give the creditor proprietary rights. In particular, many of the common forms of vendor credit agreement, such as hire purchase and conditional sale, involve the creditor/supplier retaining property in the goods supplied until payment. The purpose of such a property retention is to provide the creditor/seller with security against the debtor's failure to pay. The terms of the supply contract may give the creditor the right to re-take possession of the goods in the event of any default by the buyer, and since the goods remain the property of the creditor/supplier, they will not fall into the debtor's estate if he becomes insolvent; instead, they will belong to the creditor/supplier, who may therefore recover them free of the claims of other creditors by reason of his ownership. Title retention arrangements are therefore intended to, and do, serve much the same purpose as genuine security arrangements. However, the tendency of English law is to distinguish between such arrangements and formal proprietary securities; they therefore avoid many of the controls which are imposed on formal proprietary securities[2], and they may be termed 'quasi security' arrangements.

1   See Goode, *Legal Problems of Credit and Security* (2nd edn, 1988) p 4.
2   See 22.0.3.

21.3 Policy considerations

The legal treatment of credit and security involves the balancing of a number of interests. First, and most obviously, the interests of the creditor must be balanced against those of the debtor. This is particularly important where, as is often the case, there is an imbalance of bargaining power between creditor and debtor. Debtors may need protection against one-sided or unfair contract terms, excessive interest rates and other charges or unjust exercise by secured creditors of their security rights; they may also need to be provided with information about the contract, its terms and their rights.

Second, where a debt is secured by personal security the interests of the third party surety must also be considered and balanced against those of both debtor and creditor. In some cases the surety may need protection from both of them.

Third, wherever real security is given the interests of the secured creditor must be balanced against those of the debtor's other, unsecured creditors. Enforcement of his security by the holder of real security gives the secured creditor priority over the debtor's other creditors and, by removing the asset used as security from the pool of assets available to satisfy the claims of other creditors, depletes that pool. The recognition of real security rights thus undermines the principle of *pari passu* distribution of assets in insolvency and it has therefore been found necessary to impose restrictions on the creation and enforcement of real security rights in order to achieve an appropriate balance between the interests of all creditors.

The preferential treatment of secured creditors in insolvency has most often been justified on the basis that it improves the flow of credit and thus assists commerce. Security reduces a creditor's exposure to the risk of the debtor's insolvency and may thus incline a lender to make finance available to borrowers to whom it would otherwise not lend, or to make credit available at a lower rate of interest than it otherwise would, reflecting the reduced risk involved. By reducing the risk of insolvency, security also reduces the need for credit monitoring, and thus reduces the transaction costs of supplying credit. In recent years, however, the justifications for the favoured treatment of secured creditors have begun to be questioned. Real security effectively depletes the pot of assets available for distribution to general creditors in the event of the debtor's insolvency, many of whom will be unable, for various reasons, to obtain similar protection for themselves. Moreover, in so far as the alternative to taking security is more careful credit monitoring, it may be argued that creditors should be encouraged to adopt more responsible lending policies and undertake some supervision of their debtors. A secured creditor has less incentive to undertake credit monitoring and, safe in the knowledge that he is protected by his security, may be willing to allow a debtor to over-extend himself financially. The favoured treatment of secured creditors has thus been criticised as unfair and economically inefficient[1].

Such criticisms, concerned with the effect of security on third parties, raise difficult issues of the order of priority of claims in insolvency. If they are to be addressed at all it can only be in the context of a thorough review of insolvency law. Security is too well established to be abolished. The law has, however, sought to protect the interests of debtors, sureties and third parties. The common law itself developed rules for the protection of certain categories of debtor and surety, but its effectiveness was limited by its adherence to the principle of freedom of contract. The main controls are now statutory. In particular, the Consumer Credit Act 1974 regulates the rights and liabilities of creditors against certain categories of debtors and sureties while the Bills of Sale Acts 1878–1890, Companies Act 1985 and Insolvency Act 1986 contain important restrictions on the effectiveness of certain types of real security. We will consider the different types of security arrangement and their effectiveness in Chapters 22 to 23 before examining the protection afforded to consumers by the 1974 Act in Chapters 24 to 26.

---

1   See Ziegel (1990) 28 Alberta L Rev 739; Finch (1999) 62 MLR 633 and the sources there cited.

Chapter 22

Real Security

22.0 Introduction

As noted in the previous chapter[1], there are a number of ways in which a debtor can use property to provide security to a creditor, including by transactions such as conditional sale, hire purchase and lease. The law, however, recognises only four true real security devices: lien, pledge, charge and mortgage[2]. Other arrangements which perform a security function are generally not regarded as creating true security interests. According to Professor Goode, 'A security interest is a right given to one party in the asset of another party to secure payment or performance by that other party or a third party'[3]. This definition reflects the present law. It has two aspects. First, a right or interest not given to secure payment of a debt or performance of an obligation cannot be a security interest in law[4]. Second, a true security interest is granted by a debtor over his own property, whereas hire purchase and similar arrangements involve the reservation of ownership, by a supplier of goods, albeit that the purpose of the reservation is to provide the supplier with security[5]. Professor Goode therefore refers to such arrangements, and other arrangements which perform a security function, as 'quasi-securities'.

In contrast, in his 1989 report, Professor Diamond defined real security as:

> 'A right relating to property, the purpose of which is to improve the creditor's chance of getting paid or of receiving whatever else the debtor is required to do by way of performance of the contract'[6].

Professor Diamond's definition (made in the context of a report recommending reform of the existing law) thus emphasises function over form and recognises that although title reservation arrangements are not currently regarded as security interests in the strict legal sense, their commercial function is to provide security by reserving to the supplier real rights in property.

The commercial effects of both 'true' security interests and title reservation securities are the same: first, the protection of the creditor against the insolvency of his debtor, the property rights created by the security allowing him to claim the property covered by the security in priority to other creditors of the debtor; and, second, 'coercion' of the debtor, the threat of enforcement of the security acting as an 'encouragement' to the debtor to perform his obligations to his creditor[7]. There have therefore been frequent calls for reform and rationalisation of the law of real security, some of which are considered below[8]. To date such calls have gone unheeded.

1   Above 21.2.1.
2   See *Re Cosslett (Contractors) Ltd* [1998] Ch 495 at 508, [1997] 4 All ER 115 at 126, per Millett LJ.
3   Goode, *Legal Problems of Credit and Security* (2nd edn, 1988).
4   *Re Cosslett (Contractors) Ltd* [1998] Ch 495 at 508, [1997] 4 All ER 115 at 125, per Millett LJ.
5   Goode, *Legal Problems of Credit and Security* (2nd edn, 1988) p 1.
6   Diamond, *A Review of Security Interests in Property* (1989) para 3.2.
7   At para 3.3.
8   See 22.3.

22.0.1   *The categorisation of security interests*

Although there are only four main types of real security interest, there are a number of variants of each type, and real securities can therefore be categorised in several ways, as legal or equitable, consensual or non-consensual, registrable or unregistrable and possessory or non-possessory. These various categorisations overlap. Thus, for instance, the lien of an unpaid seller of goods or of a person who does work on a chattel is a non-consensual, legal, possessory security: it arises automatically without the consent of the debtor, exists at common law, and depends on the creditor having possession of the goods to which it relates. In contrast, a floating charge is an equitable, consensual, non-possessory, registrable security.

The most important distinction is that between possessory and non-possessory securities which corresponds to a large degree with that between non-registrable and registrable securities. Pledges and (most) liens are possessory securities; mortgages and charges are non-possessory. Possessory securities were developed first but suffer from a number of disadvantages. In particular, a possessory security depends on the creditor's possession of the asset to which the security relates and it is therefore inflexible and unsuitable for use in relation to assets which the debtor needs to use in his business. As Professor Bridge observes, 'The only effective security over productive assets is non-possessory in nature: the debtor must be free to use those assets in the ordinary course of trade'[1]. There are other disadvantages, too, to possessory security.

> 'Possession by the creditor is inconvenient and expensive; the debtor is likely to need the asset either to sell or run its business; the turnover of assets may be too large or rapid to allow of constant physical movement. In addition, of course, intangible assets do not lend themselves to the delivery of possession'[2].

Despite these differences, all real securities share some characteristics which derive from the fact that the creditor has real rights in the secured asset. In particular, although the rights of a creditor vary according to the nature of his security interest and the terms of any contract between him and the debtor, all security interests give the creditor the same basic rights. First, they give the creditor the right, already noted, to claim that asset, or, more correctly, its proceeds, and have them applied to discharge his debt in priority to the debtor's other creditors. Second, since the creditor has property rights in the secured asset, he can assert his security rights not only against the debtor but also against any person who subsequently acquires the asset or an interest in it, unless that person can rely on an exception to the rule nemo dat quod non habet. Professor Goode refers to these rights, which are characteristic of real security, as the rights of preference and pursuit[3]. However, it should be emphasised that they derive from the proprietary nature of the creditor's interest, rather than from its nature as a security interest. Significantly, a creditor secured by a title reservation arrangement has the same rights.

1   Bridge [1992] JBL 1.
2   Goode (1984) 100 LQR 234 at 235.
3   *Commercial Law* (2nd edn, 1995) p 673.

22.0.1.1 *Restrictions on the creditor's rights*

As noted in the previous chapter[1], the recognition of security interests requires the interests of the creditor to be balanced with those of the debtor and of other creditors of the debtor. It has been found necessary to impose restrictions on the enforcement by secured creditors of their rights in order to protect the interests of both debtors and other creditors, and in some cases these restrictions apply not only to 'true' security interests but also to some types of 'quasi securities', such as title reservation arrangements. Thus the Consumer Credit Act 1974 imposes restrictions on the rights of the creditor to take steps to enforce the agreement and to enforce any security provided by the debtor[2]. The same restrictions apply to the right of creditors who supply goods on hire purchase or conditional sale terms to recover the goods[3] and where the debtor has paid at least one third of the total sum due under a hire purchase or conditional sale agreement, the creditor cannot recover possession of the goods without a court order[4].

The Consumer Credit Act is intended to protect individual debtors. Important restrictions on the enforcement of security by creditors of companies are imposed by the Insolvency Act 1986 in the interests not only of the debtor company but also of its other creditors. Section 8 of the Act allows the court to make an administration order, placing the management of the company in the hands of an insolvency practitioner called an administrator. Such an order may be made where the court is satisfied that the company is, or is likely to be, unable to pay its debts as they fall due and the making of an order is likely to achieve certain objectives, including the survival of the company and all or part of its undertaking as a going concern or a more advantageous realisation of the company's assets than might be achieved in a liquidation. For present purposes, the importance of the administration procedure is that once an application for an order has been made, no steps can be taken without the consent of the court, or of the administrator after his appointment, to enforce any security over any property of the company or to repossess goods supplied on hire purchase or conditional sale terms, subject to any reservation of title or under a lease capable of lasting for more than three months[5].

1   Above, 21.3.
2   Consumer Credit Act, s 87; see 26.6.
3   Consumer Credit Act, s 87(1)(c).
4   Consumer Credit Act, s 99.
5   Insolvency Act 1986, s 10.

22.0.2 *Creation of security interests*

With the exception of certain liens and statutory charges, 'true' security interests are consensual so that no security interest can be created without the consent of creditor and debtor[1]. However, agreement alone is not necessarily sufficient to create a valid security interest. Where formalities are prescribed by law, the agreement must be in the prescribed form. Thus, for instance, a legal mortgage, which consists of a transfer of ownership to the creditor subject to the debtor's equity of redemption, must be in the form prescribed by law for the transfer of the type of property mortgaged: a mortgage of land must be made by deed[2] and mortgages of goods must be in the form prescribed by the Bills of Sale Acts[3].

An agreement or transfer will be of no effect unless it relates to identifiable property over which the debtor has the right to create security. At common law, therefore, an agreement to mortgage future property was ineffective 'merely because there is nothing to transfer'[4]. It was settled in *Holroyd v Marshall*[5], however, that, provided that it is specifically enforceable, an agreement to transfer property to be acquired by the debtor at a future date is effective in equity, for:

> 'if a vendor or mortgagor agrees to sell or mortgage property, real or personal, of which he is not possessed at the time, and he receives the consideration for the contract, and afterwards becomes possessed of property answering the description in the contract, there is no doubt that a Court of Equity would compel him to perform the contract, and that the contract would, in equity, transfer the beneficial interest to the mortgagee or purchaser immediately on the property being acquired[6].'

Moreover, the effect of a such a transaction is that the creditor's interest in the property vests retrospectively, as from the date of the creation of the security.

The extent of a creditor's interest in the security property depends on the amount of the secured debt. Thus where security is given for payment of a debt, the creditor has no interest in the security property until he has advanced the credit.

1   Some quasi securities can be created by unilateral action: for instance, a seller of goods may unilaterally impose a condition on the passing of property: see 18.4.1.
2   Law of Property Act 1925, s 85; see 22.2.1.1.
3   See 22.0.3.1.
4   Lord Westbury LC in *Holroyd v Marshall* (1862) 10 HL Cas 191 at 210.
5   Ibid.
6   Per Lord Westbury LC (1862) 10 HL Cas 191 at 211.

22.0.2.1   *Perfection of security interests*

Once the conditions set out above for creation of a valid security are fulfilled the security property may be bound in the hands of the debtor[1]. However, this is not enough to make the creditor's interest binding on third parties so as to allow the creditor to claim the asset in priority to other creditors. That requires that the creditor's interest be perfected.

There are three ways in which a security interest may be perfected. Possessory security interests – pledges and liens – are perfected by the taking of possession. No more is needed because the fact of the creditor's possession makes clear that the debtor does not enjoy unfettered rights of disposition over the security property. However, the development of non-possessory securities in the form of mortgages and charges required the development of some means of giving notice of the security to third parties who might otherwise be misled by the debtor's continued possession into believing him to be the unencumbered owner of the security property. The solution was to require non-possessory securities to be registered, and, thus, as a general rule, non-possessory securities must be perfected by registration.

The main systems of registration of non-possessory securities are examined below, but there is one class of non-possessory security which may be perfected without registration. A debtor may give security over a debt owed to him by a third party by assigning it to his own creditor by way of mortgage or charge. It is settled that where there are successive assignments of the same debt, priority goes to the first assignee to give notice to the debtor according to the 'rule in *Dearle v Hall*[2]'. To take a simple illustration, suppose that A is owed money by B, and first grants a mortgage of that debt to C and then assigns the same debt to D. Priority as between C and D goes to the first to notify B of his assignment. Thus if D is the first to give notice he takes priority, even though his assignment was the second in time, provided only that he took his assignment without notice of the prior assignment in favour of C. The rule is particularly important where there are competing claims to the same debt by a mortgagee or charge holder and a factor. Thus in *Compaq Computers Ltd v Abercorn Group Ltd*[3] a retention of title clause in a contract for the sale of goods permitted the buyer to resell the goods supplied but purported to give the original seller rights to the proceeds of the buyer's resale. The buyer had also entered into a factoring agreement by which it assigned its future book debts to a factoring company. The seller and factor both claimed rights to the proceeds of resales and it was held that the retention of title clause constituted a charge on the proceeds of the resales, but that in any case priority between the seller and factor's assignments should be determined according to the rule in *Dearle v Hall*. The result was that the factor, which had given notice of its assignment to the buyer's customers, took priority over the unpaid seller[4]. The rationale for the rule is that if an assignment is notified to the debtor, a potential later assignee of the same debt can discover the prior assignment by enquiring of the debtor; however, the rule is often criticised as archaic and impractical[5]; it 'was developed in order to govern priorities between successive assignees of a trust fund [and] has been pressed into service in different and inappropriate context with predictably unhappy results'[6]. The rule is therefore effectively excluded where the first assignment is registered, since registration acts as notice of the assignment. Most assignments of debts by way of security are registrable, either under the Bills of Sale Acts or the Companies Act 1985. However, as the *Compaq Computers* case illustrates, registrable assignments are not necessarily always registered.

1 Goode, following the Uniform Commercial Code, speaks of the creditor's interest 'attaching' to the security property: see Goode, *Legal Problems of Credit and Security* (2nd edn, 1988) p 27.
2 (1823) 3 Russ 1.
3 [1991] BCC 484; see [1992] CLJ 19; above 18.4.5.
4 The retention of title seller had not registered its charge: if it had done so, the act of registration would have acted as notice to the factor, excluding the rule.
5 See eg Goode (1984) 100 LQR 234 at 241–244.
6 Millett J (1991) 107 LQR 679.

22.0.3 *Registration of security interests*

Possession of property creates the appearance of ownership. Where a person is allowed to possess the property of another, his possession may create a misleading impression of wealth and lead creditors to advance credit to him in the mistaken belief that the property in question and its proceeds will be available to satisfy any claim they may have against him. The rule of reputed ownership was formerly applied in bankruptcy proceedings to protect creditors thus misled. According to this rule, goods in the possession of a bankrupt in the course of his trade or business with the consent of their owner fell into the bankrupt's estate and were therefore available to meet the claims of the bankrupt's creditors. However, the rule was never applied to company insolvencies and was abolished in 1985.

As already noted, the creation by a debtor of non-possessory security interests creates a similar risk that third parties may be misled. Security assets in the possession of the debtor may be owned by him but be subject to a security interest in favour of a particular creditor. In order to guard against potential future creditors being misled by the appearance of unencumbered ownership created by the debtor's continued possession of assets over which he has granted security, non-possessory security interests are required to be registered. Later creditors can be expected to search the appropriate register and those who do will discover the existence of the security. Registration provides notice of the security interest to the whole world and therefore perfects the creditor's security: a registered security will therefore be binding on later creditors, whereas failure to register a registrable security may render it ineffective against them.

The main registration systems are those created by the Bills of Sale Acts 1878–1891 for securities created by individuals and the Companies Act 1985, for securities created by companies. However, there are also a number of special registers for security interests in certain types of property, including ships[1], aircraft[2], farming stock and machinery[3] and intellectual property rights[4].

1 Merchant Shipping Act 1894, s 31; Merchant Shipping Act 1988, Sch 3.
2 Civil Aviation Act 1982, s 86; Mortgaging of Aircraft Order 1972, SI 1972/1268.
3 Agricultural Credits Act 1928, ss 8 and 14.
4 Trade Marks Act 1994, s 25; Patents Act 1977, s 33; Registered Designs Act 1948, s 19.

22.0.3.1 *Bills of Sale Acts*

There are currently two main Bills of Sale Acts in force: the Bills of Sale Act 1878 (BoSA 1878) and the Bills of Sale (Amendment) Act 1882 (BoS(A)A 1882), as amended by the Bills of Sale Acts 1890 and 1891. Those Acts replaced earlier legislation[1] whose purpose was, like the reputed ownership rule, to protect other potential creditors against secret dispositions of property. They therefore applied not only to security transactions but to all transactions under which a person disposed of goods but remained in possession of them. However, the Acts applied not to transactions as such but to the documents in which they were recorded. Partly as a result of these origins, the current legislation is therefore complex and, to modern eyes, archaic and anomalous.

The definition of a bill of sale is contained in s 4 of the 1878 Act, which provides that it includes:

> 'bills of sale, assignments, transfers, declarations of trust without transfer, inventories of goods with receipt attached thereto, or receipts for purchase moneys of goods, and other assurances of personal chattels as security for any debt, and also powers of attorney, authorities or licences to take possession of personal chattels as security for any debt, and also any agreement, whether intended or not to be followed by the execution of any other instrument, by which a right in equity to any personal chattels or to any charge or security thereon, shall be conferred . . .'

The legislation distinguishes between absolute and conditional, or security, bills. A 'security bill' is one given to secure the payment of money. Absolute bills of sale are governed solely by the 1878 Act. The 1882 Act only applies to security bills, but applies to them the provisions of the 1878 Act, except in so far as they are inconsistent with its own provisions. The two Acts therefore have to be read together in relation to security bills. However, they have very different objectives. The 1878 Act, like its predecessors, was:

> 'designed for the protection of creditors, and to prevent their rights being affected by secret assurances of chattels which were permitted to remain in the ostensible possession of a person who had parted with the property in them . . . The purpose of the 1882 Act was essentially distinct. It was to prevent needy persons being entrapped into signing complicated documents which they might often be unable to comprehend, and so being subjected by their creditors to the enforcement of harsh and unreasonable provisions'[2].

This difference in function is apparent in the requirements imposed by the Acts and by the sanctions for non-compliance with those requirements. All bills of sale must be registered at the Filing and Record Department of the Central Office of the Royal Courts of Justice within seven days of their creation[3]. Failure to register makes an absolute bill void against other creditors[4] and a security bill void for all purposes[5]. The 1882 Act also requires security bills to be in a form prescribed by the Act and contained in a deed[6] attested by one or more credible witnesses[7], and provides that a bill not in the prescribed form is void[8]. The Act recognises that compliance with these requirements might be especially cumbersome for securities of low value, but, rather than exempting them from its requirements, simply provides that security bills of sale given in consideration of any sum under thirty pounds are void[9]. The 1882 Act also imposes restrictions on the right of a creditor to seize, take possession of or sell goods covered by a security bill[10].

A number of arrangements are exempted from the Bills of Sale Acts, including 'transfers of goods in the ordinary course of business of any trade or calling' (which must be the trade of the transferor), 'bills of sale of goods in foreign parts or at sea' and documents such as bills of lading and delivery orders 'used in the ordinary course of business as proof of the possession or control of goods, or authorising or purporting to authorise, either by indorsement or delivery, the possessor of such document to transfer or receive goods thereby represented'[11]. The most important exceptions, however, are created by the definition of 'bills of sale'. To modern eyes an almost perverse feature of the legislation is that it applies not to transactions but to documents: wholly oral agreements are therefore unregulated[12]. Possessory securities clearly fall outside the mischief of the Act, and a document recording a possessory security is not a bill of sale. The definition of 'personal chattels' in the Act[13] excludes intangible property, including choses in action. The Acts therefore do not apply to documents giving security over debts, although s 344 of the Insolvency Act provides that a general assignment of book debts by way of security is registrable as if it were an absolute bill of sale. Finally, the Acts do not apply to securities created by companies, but the Companies Act effectively imports the definition bills of sale, providing that certain securities created by companies which, if created by individuals would be registrable as bills of sale, are registrable as company charges.

The Bills of Sale Acts are widely regarded as anachronistic. Their language is archaic and they are surrounded by a mass of technical case law. Bridge, commenting on the definition of 'bill of sale' in the 1878 Act, observes that 'there is no principle here or anything that conceptually links together the various instances of a bill of sale; it is a mere catalogue'[14]. Moreover, compliance with the formal and procedural requirements of the Acts is cumbersome. As a result, lenders rarely take mortgages of or charges over personal chattels from individuals. One effect of the legislation is thus to restrict the availability of credit to individuals and unincorporated businesses. In particular, the requirement of the 1882 Act that a security bill contain a schedule specifically describing the property covered by the bill[15], effectively prevents unincorporated debtors giving non-possessory security over property to be acquired in the future; even if it were possible to describe such property the Act provides that a bill which relates to property not owned by the grantor at the time of its execution is void against creditors other than the grantor[16]. These restrictions do not apply to corporate debtors, which therefore have greater and more flexible powers to create security, and the difference between the borrowing powers of individuals and companies thus created has probably contributed significantly to the popularity of the corporate form as a business medium.

The Bills of Sale Acts have had one further, significant effect. Businesses have gone to great lengths to seek security arrangements which fall outside the scope of the Acts, and the desire to avoid the Bills of Sale Acts thus contributed to the development of common transactions such as hire purchase, conditional sale and sale and lease back.

1   Bills of Sale Acts 1854 and 1866.
2   Per Lord Herschell LC in *Manchester, Sheffield and Lincolnshire Rly Co v North Central Wagon Co* (1888) 13 App Cas 554 at 560; see also Lord Halsbury LC in *Charlesworth v Mills* [1892] AC 231 at 235.
3   BoSA 1878, s 10; BoS(A)A 1882, s 8.
4   BoSA 1878, s 8.
5   BoS(A)A 1882, s 8.
6   BoS(A)A 1882, s 4; Schedule.
7   BoS(A)A 1882, s 10.
8   BoS(A)A 1882, s 9.
9   BoS(A)A 1882, s 12.
10 BoS(A)A 1882, s 7.
11 BoSA 1878, s 4.
12 *Newlove v Shrewsbury* (1888) 21 QBD 41.
13 BoSA 1878, s 4.
14 [1992] JBL 1 at 4.
15 BoS(A)A 1882, s 4.
16 BoS(A)A 1882, s 5.

22.0.3.2   *Companies Acts*

The Bills of Sale Acts do not apply to dispositions by companies, but Pt XII of the Companies Act 1985 contains provisions which require most, but not all, mortgages and charges created by companies to be registered. The provisions, which reproduce provisions contained in the Companies Act 1948, are widely perceived as having a number of defects, and in recent years there have been several calls for reform. Part IV of the Companies Act 1989 contains provisions, based in part on recommendations made by Professor Diamond in his 1989 Review of Security Interests in Property, intended to replace those in Pt XII of the 1985 Act. However, they in turn have met with some opposition from practitioners and it is now clear that the provisions of Pt IV of the 1989 Act will not be brought into force as a whole. In 1994 the DTI issued a consultative document[1] which sought views on several options for reform; in 1995 it announced that, in light of response to the consultation, it would retain the main provisions of the 1985 Act, albeit possibly with some modifications based on the 1989 provisions

Section 395 of the Companies Act requires particulars of certain classes of charge created by companies to be delivered to the Registrar of Companies within 21 days of their creation. There is no definition of 'charge' for these purposes, save that 'the expression "charge" includes mortgage'[2]. At present, therefore, determination whether any particular security requires registration depends on the application of the common law definition of 'charge'[3] and there is a considerable body of case law considering the effect of various types of transaction. The 1989 Act would introduce a statutory definition by providing that '"charge" means any form of security interest (fixed or floating) over property, other than an interest arising by operation of law'[4], but this provision would merely replace disputes about whether a particular transaction creates a 'charge' with similar disputes about whether they constitute a 'security interest'. It seems that the expression 'security interest' could include interests which are not charges at common law and in its 1994 consultation the DTI questioned not only whether this definition is appropriate but also whether any definition is required.

The Act only requires a charge created by a company to be registered if it falls within one of the following categories:

'(a) a charge for the purpose of securing any issue of debentures;
(b) a charge on uncalled share capital of the company;
(c) a charge created or evidenced by an instrument which, if executed by an individual, would require registration as a bill of sale;
(d) a charge on any land, wherever situate, or any interest therein, but not including a charge for any rent or other periodical sum issuing out of land;
(e) a charge on book debts of the company;
(f) a floating charge on the undertaking or property of the company;
(g) a charge on calls made but not paid;
(h) a charge on a ship or aircraft or any share in a ship; or
(i) a charge on goodwill or on any intellectual property'[5].

Thus when considering whether any particular transaction requires registration a court must first consider whether it creates a charge at common law and then whether the charge so created falls into any of the listed categories. There are several significant omissions from the list of registrable charges, including charges on shares and insurance policies[6].

The Act requires that particulars of a registrable charge must be delivered to the Registrar of Companies within 21 days of its creation[7]. The Registry staff then check the particulars and issue a certificate of registration which is conclusive evidence of registration and compliance with the statutory formalities[8].

The Register of Company Charges is a public document, open for inspection on payment of a small fee. The purpose of registration is therefore to give notice of the existence of charges over company property to other potential creditors; registration gives constructive notice of the charge and the registered particulars and therefore perfects it. However, registration does not determine priority as between successive chargees of the same asset, although because registration constitutes constructive notice of the charge, it may be relevant to the question of priorities[9]. Moreover, as a result of the 21-day period allowed between creation of a charge and its registration, the Register does not even fulfil its primary function: the picture of the financial status of a company it gives at any time to a potential creditor searching the register may be up to three weeks out of date. Potential creditors may therefore delay advancing funds until at least 21 days after registration of their own securities in order to ensure that no other, prior charge over the same assets is registered.

Unlike the Bills of Sale Acts, Pt XII of the Companies Act is concerned solely with the protection of third party potential creditors of the company, not of the company itself. Failure to register a registrable charge therefore means that it is void against a liquidator or any creditor[10] of the company 'so far as any security on the company's property or undertaking is conferred' by it[11] but the security remains fully effective against the company itself and against any purchaser of the affected property. The statutory obligation to register is imposed on the company which creates the charge and if the charge is not registered within the 21-day period the company and every officer of it in default is liable to a fine. Particulars of a charge may, however, be delivered to the registry by any person interested in it and the drastic consequences of non-registration – denying the charge effect in the very situation in which the creditor is likely to want to rely on it – means that in practice chargee creditors undertake the registration of securities granted to them[12].

1 *Company Law Review: Proposals for Reform of Part XII of the Companies Act 1985*; see 22.3.
2 Section 396(4).
3 See 22.2.2.
4 Section 395(2).
5 CA 1985, s 396.
6 The DTI's 1995 announcement contemplated some modification to the list in s 396. The 1989 Act would have replaced the list with the following:
   (a) a charge on land or any interest in land . . . ;
   (b) a charge on goods or any interest in goods, other than a charge under which the chargee is entitled to possession either of the goods or of a document of title to them;
   (c) a charge on intangible moveable property of any of the following descriptions:
       (i) goodwill,
       (ii) intellectual property,
       (iii)book debts (whether book debts of the company or assigned to the company),
       (iv)uncalled share capital of the company or calls made but not paid;
   (d) a charge for securing an issue of debentures; or
   (e) a floating charge on the whole or part of he company's property.
   (CA 1989, s 93). This list largely reproduces the categories of charge in the existing s 395 but there are some, potentially significant, changes in wording. Nevertheless, it would still not cover all types of company charge or financing arrangement.
7 Full details of the registration procedure are beyond the scope of this book; see Boyle and Birds, *Company Law* (2nd edn, 1995) ch 7.
8 Under the 1989 Act reforms the Registrar's certificate would no longer be conclusive. This particular aspect of the 1989 provisions was opposed by practitioners and it is clear that in any future reform of the law the Registrar's certificate will remain conclusive.
9 See 22.2.2.5.
10 It has been held that for this purpose a receiver represents the creditor who appoints him and an unregistered charge is therefore void as against a receiver: *Clough Mill Ltd v Geoffrey Martin* [1984] 1 WLR 1067 at 1081, reversed on other grounds [1984] 3 All ER 982, [1985] 1 WLR 111.
11 CA 1985, s 395(1).
12 Under the relevant provisions of the 1989 Act, a failure to register a registrable charge would make it void against an administrator or liquidator of the company and against 'any person who for value acquires an interest in or right over the property subject to the charge' so that unregistered charges will not be binding on purchasers of the charged property.

22.0.4 *Classifying security interests*

As already noted, there are many ways of achieving security, but not all constitute 'security interests' in the strict sense. Where parties enter into an arrangement whose purpose and effect is to provide one of them with security, the agreement may therefore have to be construed and classified in order to decide if it is registrable under the Bills of Sale Acts or Companies Act. Even if an agreement does constitute a 'security interest' in this sense, it will be necessary to go further and decide what type of security interest it creates – mortgage, charge, pledge or lien? To take a simple example, as will appear below, the deposit of an asset with a creditor in return for an advance could be consistent with the creation of a pledge or of an equitable charge or mortgage. Finally, if the agreement constitutes a charge, it will often be necessary to go further still and decide exactly what type of charge it creates, in order to decide if it is registrable under the Companies Act.

Classification of an interest is relevant to other questions besides registrability. Certain securities must be created or evidenced in a prescribed form, while the rights of the creditor on the debtor's default, the rights of the debtor against the creditor, priority as between creditors and the tax and accounting treatment of the parties may all depend on the classification of the security. These are all essentially questions of policy. What publicity should be required for the creation of a valid security? As between debtor and creditor, who should be entitled to any surplus from the proceeds of the security asset after repayment of the secured debt? As between competing creditors, who should gain priority, especially in the event of the debtor's insolvency? However, these issues are rarely, if ever, addressed overtly by the courts when classifying security arrangements.

22.0.4.1 *Security or quasi security?*

The ingenuity of the commercial world in developing new security devices seems almost limitless. Much of this creativity has been directed to using new and wider classes of assets as security, so that it is now possible to use real and personal, tangible and intangible property, including book debts, or receivables, intellectual property, insurance policies and their proceeds, present and future property, fixed plant and machinery, stock in trade. However, an even greater amount of creativity has been directed to creating security arrangements which avoid the various, often cumbersome, legal restrictions imposed on security interests for the protection of debtors and third parties. In particular, creditors have gone to great lengths to devise arrangements which provide the flexibility of non-possessory security without the need to register.

It is well established that an arrangement does not constitute a security interest merely because it is intended to, and does, provide the creditor with some measure of 'security' against the debtor's default. It has been suggested[1] that 'true' security interests share certain features; in particular, they must give 'real', as opposed to purely personal, rights, and must be granted by the debtor rather than being reserved by the creditor, for the purpose of securing payment of a debt or some other contractual obligation. Some security arrangements, such as contractual rights of set-off, can therefore be excluded from the category of 'security interests' on the grounds that they give only personal rights against the debtor, even though their effect may be to restrict the debtor's ability to use a particular asset, or reduce its value in the debtor's hands and thus adversely affect the debtor's liquidity and, ultimately, even solvency. For instance, in *Re Cosslett (Contractors) Ltd*[2] a contract for the performance of land reclamation works provided that plant and machinery brought onto site by the contractor could not be removed without the consent of the employer, and that if the contractor became insolvent the employer could retain the plant and use it to complete the works. It was held that the employer's right to retain possession was not a security at all, since it did not secure performance of the contractor's obligations but merely allowed the employer to complete the works in the contractor's place.

There are many common arrangements, however, which provide the creditor with real rights in an asset, similar to and sometimes even more potent than those enjoyed by a creditor with a true 'security interest'. The classification of such arrangements may often be the subject of dispute and a matter of considerable legal complexity, requiring careful consideration of the details of the arrangement. For instance, as already noted, title reservation devices such as hire purchase and conditional sale are commonly used by supplier-creditors. Such arrangements may be excluded from the category of 'security interests' on the grounds that they are reserved by the creditor, not granted by the debtor: the debtor does not own the asset until the price is paid, and therefore has nothing over which to grant security[3]. Yet this approach can be criticised as over-simplistic. It ignores the difficult policy question whether such arrangements should be permitted to provide the benefits of non-possessory real security without publicity. Moreover, under some arrangements the assertion that the creditor's rights are reserved can be challenged. A contract of hire purchase imposes strict limitations on the rights of the hirer in relation to the goods; in particular he may neither dispose of them nor consume or destroy them. In contrast, where a retention of title clause is included in a commercial contract for the supply of goods for resale or consumption which gives the buyer extensive rights to deal with the goods before paying for them, it may seem artificial, in view of the extensive rights granted to the buyer, to regard the seller as reserving ownership. The transaction could equally be analysed as allowing property in the goods to pass to the buyer, subject to a grant back of a security interest to the seller, and, indeed, such an analysis has been applied to some forms of retention of title[4]. In most cases, however, the courts are happy to treat such transactions as involving a reservation by the supplier.

Title reservation arrangements can also be used, in effect, as a means of securing loan credit. A prospective debtor who owns goods may sell them, either direct or through an intermediary, to a lender who then re-supplies them to the debtor under a conditional sale, hire purchase or similar transaction. In some cases the goods may never leave the possession of the debtor. The analysis and classification of such transactions is rather more difficult, requiring the court to consider the overall effect of the whole arrangement between the parties.

Similar, but more acute, problems of classification may arise in relation to dealings in receivables. A simple assignment of a debt clearly does not constitute a security, and it is established that a contract for the block-discounting of book debts or other receivables[5] does not create a security interest, but such arrangements may not only serve the same function as a charge on receivables but even be drafted in such a way as to give the discounter the advantages of a charge. For instance in *Lloyds and Scottish Finance Ltd v Cyril Lord Carpets*[6] a company sold its book debts to a discounter under a series of contracts. The terms of the contracts provided for: the company to receive 80% of the face value of the debts immediately; the company to collect the debts as agent for the discounter and to provide the discounter with post-dated cheques representing the instalments due in respect of debts it would collect, thus (effectively) guaranteeing payment by its debtors; and the discounter to pay the company the balance of the face value of the debts, less a charge, on their collection. The effect of the contract was therefore very much as if the company had charged its book debts in favour of the discounter, but it was held to be a genuine block discounting arrangement.

1   Goode, *Legal Problems of Credit and Security* (2nd edn, 1988); above 22.0.
2   [1998] Ch 495, [1997] 4 All ER 115.
3   See *Clough Mill Ltd v Martin* [1984] 3 All ER 982, [1985] 1 WLR 111, CA, see 18.4.2; *Armour v Thyssen* [1990] 3 All ER 481, HL, see 18.4.3.
4   Eg *Re Bond Worth Ltd* [1980] Ch 228; *Stroud Architectural Systems Ltd v John Laing Construction Ltd* [1994] BCC 18; see 18.4.2.
5   See 27.3.2.
6   (1979) [1992] BCLC 609.

22.0.4.2   *The method of classification*

Classification of an agreement requires the court to look at the substance of the agreement and not merely its form, and 'the substance must, of course, be ascertained by a consideration of the rights and obligations of the parties, to be derived from a consideration of the whole of the agreement'[1]. The task of the court, then, is to identify the true legal effect of the agreement in question by considering its terms and the rights and obligations of the parties. The 'label' attached to an agreement by the parties is not conclusive of its effect: the court 'looks at the written agreement, in order to ascertain from its terms whether it amounts to a transaction of the legal nature which the parties ascribe to it'[2]. On the other hand, the court can only ignore the terms of the agreement if it is a 'sham'[3]. Application of this test is often difficult. It requires detailed consideration of the terms of the agreement and there is an extensive body of case law concerned with the classification of security agreements. Moreover, the problem is not made any easier by the variety of language that has been used: substance, truth, reality, genuine are 'good words'; disguise, cloak, mask, colourable device, label, form, artificial, sham, stratagem and pretence are 'bad names'[4].

The proper approach to problems of classification was considered by the Court of Appeal in *Welsh Development Agency Ltd v Export Finance Co Ltd*[5]. A company, Parrot Corpn Ltd, exported computer disks and entered into an agreement with Export Finance Co (Exfinco) to finance its operations. Under a master agreement Exfinco made a standing offer to purchase disks from Parrot for sale to Parrot's customers; that offer could be accepted from time to time by Parrot invoicing a customer. The terms of the agreement then provided for Parrot to sell the disks to customers as undisclosed agent for Exfinco. Sales to customers were subject to a retention of title in favour of Exfinco and customers made payments into a bank account in Parrot's name but controlled by Exfinco. One of the questions for the court was whether, notwithstanding its form, the agreement in fact created a charge on the disks in favour of Exfinco.

The court reviewed the principles applicable to such questions. It is settled that an agreement does not constitute a security interest in law merely because its purpose is to provide a creditor with security: the law is concerned with the legal nature of transactions, not with their economic effect:

'Just as it is possible to increase the amount of cash available to a business by borrowing, buying on hire-purchase or credit sale terms, factoring book debts or raising additional share capital, all with different legal incidents, so it is possible to achieve security for an unpaid purchase price in different ways with different legal consequences'[6].

The task of the court is to ascertain the intention of the parties as indicated by the terms of their agreement. The court may, however, disregard the terms of the agreement if it is a 'sham':

'The court must consider whether or not the documents really mask the true transaction. If they do . . . the court must have regard to the true position, in substance and in fact, and for this purpose tear away the mask or cloak that has been put upon the real transaction'[7].

However, it is rarely argued, and less often established, that an agreement is a sham:

'For acts or documents to be a "sham", with whatever legal consequences follow from this, all the parties thereto must have a common intention that the acts or documents are not to create the legal rights and obligations which they give the appearance of creating'[8].

Such an intention may be found if, for example, it is established that, in fact, the parties did not abide by the agreement in practice, so that their conduct, in effect, amounts to a variation of the agreement. However, the court must not approach documents recording the transaction 'in a sinister desire to impute to them something which they do not contain'[9]. An agreement is not a sham merely because its purpose is to avoid statutory requirements for the registration of bills of sale or company charges – 'malice is not to be attributed to a person who so carries out a transaction that it remains outside the law'[10] – or to achieve priority over a prior security interest or to evade restrictions in a prior security agreement on transactions such as factoring or block discounting[11].

Where an agreement is not a 'sham', the task of the court is to construe the agreement in order to determine its legal effect and therefore its substance. The intention of the parties must be ascertained from the terms of the agreement, but the language of the agreement as a whole must be construed against its commercial background, including the commercial objectives of the parties in order to determine its meaning.

'The substance of the parties' agreement must be found in the language they have used; but the categorisation of a document is determined by the legal effect which it is intended to have, and if when properly construed the effect of the document as a whole is inconsistent with the terminology which the parties have used, then their ill-chosen language must yield to the substance'[12].

Thus the fact that an agreement states that it is by way of security does not mean that it creates a security interest in law; nor does the use in an agreement of language appropriate to a secured loan, such as 'advance', 'repayment' and 'credit line'[13], mean that an agreement is for a secured loan. Individual terms are not conclusive. Thus if a transaction purports to be a sale it will not be construed as a charge merely because some of its terms would be consistent with a charge, provided that they are not inconsistent with its being a sale[14].

Applying these principles to the facts of the case, the Court of Appeal in the *Exfinco* case concluded that the agreement before them did not create a charge. There was no suggestion that the agreement was a sham, and although some of the terms of the agreement would more commonly be found in an agreement for a secured loan than in a contract of sale, none of them was inconsistent with the transaction being a sale, whereas the agreement did, expressly, provide for a sale of the goods by Parrot to Exfinco and provide for Exfinco to have the rights of a seller against overseas customers.

1 Per Lord Herschell in *Helby v Matthews* [1895] AC 471 at 475.
2 Staughton LJ in *Welsh Development Agency Ltd v Export Finance Co Ltd* [1992] BCLC 148 at 186.
3 See *Re Japan Leasing (Europe) plc* [1999] BPIR 911.
4 Per Staughton LJ in *Welsh Development Agency v Export Finance Co Ltd* [1992] BCLC 148 at 185.
5 [1992] BCLC 148.
6 Per Lord Donaldson MR in *Clough Mill Ltd v Geoffrey Martin* [1984] 3 All ER 982 at 994, [1985] 1 WLR 111 at 125, CA.
7 Per Lord Hanworth MR in *Re Geo Inglefield Ltd* [1933] Ch 1 at 17.
8 Diplock LJ in *Snook v London and West Riding Investments Ltd* [1967] 2 QB 786 at 802.
9 Per Lord Hanworth in *Re Geo Inglefield* [1933] Ch 1 at 22.
10 *Re Geo Ingelfield* [1933] 1 Ch 1 at 23, per Hanworth MR. Eve J also recognised that there could be legitimate reasons for seeking to avoid registration (at 6). See also *Welsh Development Agency v Export Finance Co Ltd* [1992] BCLC 148 at 188, per Staughton LJ.
11 As in *Welsh Development Agency Ltd v Export Finance Co Ltd* [1992] BCLC 148.
12 Per Millett LJ in *Orion Finance Ltd v Crown Financial Management Ltd* [1996] 2 BCLC 78 at 84.
13 *Lloyds & Scottish Finance v Cyril Lord Carpets* [1992] BCLC 609. Contrast *Orion Finance Ltd v Crown Financial Management Ltd* [1996] 2 BCLC 78, where the use of words connoting security, such as 'security', 'charge' and 'encumber' seems to have been influential in the decision that a financing arrangement was a charge.
14 *Lloyds and Scottish Finance Ltd v Cyril Lord Carpets Sales* [1992] BCLC 609; *Welsh Development Agency Ltd v Export Finance Co Ltd* [1992] BCLC 148.

22.1 Possessory security

The common law recognises two forms of possessory security, the pledge and the lien. Strictly, it should be noted that not all liens depend on possession, and that some are equitable or statutory in origin; moreover, it may be argued that a true common law lien is not a security in the true sense, since at common law it gives the lienee no real rights but merely a personal right against the lienor to retain possession of property. However, a lien is generally regarded as a form of possessory security and the exercise of a lien can give the lienee many of the practical advantages of a security interest and so it is considered here.

Both pledge and lien are of ancient origin but although more modern, non-possessory security arrangements are generally more flexible and may be more advantageous for the parties, possessory securities remain important, especially because they avoid the registration requirements to which most non-possessory securities are subject.

Both pledge and lien depend on the secured creditor having possession of the property held as security; both may be lost if the creditor loses possession. Much of the law on pledges and liens is concerned with the degree of control required to amount to 'possession' in law and the effects of the creditor's loss of possession. It is important to note that *actual* possession is not necessary for the creation or continuance of either a pledge or a lien; constructive possession will suffice. A person has *actual* possession of goods if he has actual physical control of them and the intention to control them. A person has *constructive* possession of goods if, although they are in the physical possession of a third party, that person holds them on his behalf and he has the right to take immediate possession of them. Thus, if goods are held by a bailee, the bailor has constructive possession provided that he has the right to call for the immediate delivery of the goods. Constructive possession can be transferred: if goods owned by A are stored in B's warehouse, B holds them as bailee for A and they are in A's constructive possession. A can transfer constructive possession of the goods to C by arranging for B to attorn to C, acknowledging that he now holds the goods on C's behalf. Similarly, A could transfer possession of goods in his own possession to C by attorning and acknowledging that he holds the goods as bailee for C.

It is sometimes said that possession may also be 'symbolic' where a person holds, not the goods themselves, but some symbol which represents them[1]. However, although the concept appears to be recognised in some cases, it is not used consistently. Thus, for instance, delivery of a key to premises in which goods are stored is sometimes said to give symbolic possession of the goods; but it seems better to treat this as giving actual possession if possession of the key gives unrestricted access to the premises and thus to the goods themselves[2]. Possession of a document of title to goods is also sometimes said to give 'symbolic possession' of the goods[3], but the only document of title to goods recognised by the common law is the bill of lading and it has been suggested that a bill of lading should be treated as containing an attornment by the carrier who issues it in favour of any person to whom it is transferred[4], so that a person in possession of a bill of lading should be regarded as in constructive possession of the goods to which it relates. The better view, therefore, seems to be that there is no separate category of 'symbolic *possession*' but that *constructive* possession may be symbolically transferred by delivery of some symbol, such as a small sample of a bulk[5], intended to represent the goods and indicating that the transferor makes himself a bailor for the transferee.

1   See Bell, *Modern Law of Personal Property in England and Ireland* (1989) p 57.
2   See *Ward v Turner* (1752) 2 Ves Sen 431, per Lord Hardwicke. In *Hilton v Tucker* (1888) 39 Ch D 669 delivery of a key to a room was said to give 'constructive possession' of the room's contents.
3   See Bell, *Modern Law of Personal Property in England and Ireland* (1989) p 59.
4   See Goode, *Commercial Law* (2nd edn, 1995) p 49.This does not mean that the carrier is a bailee for a consignee named in or transferee of the bill of lading: see *The Future Express* [1993] 2 Lloyd's Rep 542.
5   See *Re Cole* [1964] Ch 175.

22.1.1   *Pledge*

The pledge is the oldest form of real security; indeed, the pledge, or 'vadium', was known to the Romans[1]. It is a form of consensual security, created by delivery of goods by one person, the pledgor, to another, the pledgee, by way of security. The pledgee thus has possession of the goods; in addition, he has a right to sell the goods in the event of the pledgor's default. Professor Goode has therefore described the pledge as 'the most powerful form of security interest known to English law'[2].

Since it involves a deposit of goods, a pledge is a type of bailment[3] and it is generally said that the pledgee thus acquires a 'special property' in the goods, although this was doubted by Lord Mersey in *The Odessa*[4], who observed that the pledgee has only limited rights to use and no right to consume the goods[5], and that his power of sale is circumscribed by law[6] and, in effect, exercised on behalf of and by virtue of the authority of the pledgor. Nevertheless, the pledgee does have real rights in the pledged goods, enforceable against third parties.

A pawnbroker provides cash advances to individuals secured by the deposit of goods by way of pledge. Such pledges are often referred to as 'pawns', the words 'pledge' and 'pawn' being used almost interchangeably. Pawns have been subject to statutory control since 1604[7]. Pledges given to secure consumer credit agreements are now regulated by the Consumer Credit Act 1974[8], which uses the word 'pawn' to refer to the article deposited and 'pledge' to refer to the pawnee's rights over that article[9].

1   See Palmer and Hudson in Palmer and McKendrick (eds) *Interests in Goods* (2nd edn, 1998).
2   Goode, *Commercial Law* (2nd edn, 1995) p 644.
3   See per Holt CJ in *Coggs v Barnard* (1703) 2 Ld Raym 909 at 913, Court of Kings Bench; see also per Bowen LJ in *Re Hardwick, ex p Hubbard* (1886) 17 QBD 690 at 698.
4   [1916] 1 AC 145.
5   See below 22.1.1.2.
6   See below 22.1.1.5.
7   (1604) 1 Jac I, c 21.
8   See ch 24.
9   Consumer Credit Act, s 189. See McLeod [1995] JBL 155.

22.1.1.1 *Creation*

A pledge is created by the pledgor delivering property to the pledgee with the intention of creating a pledge. It is said that the pledgee's possession must be lawful, but that means only that the pledgor must consent to his possession, and the owner of goods may be bound by a pledge created by a third party without his consent if any of the exceptions to the nemo dat rule apply.

(a) The transfer of possession
Much of the case law on pledges is concerned with the transfer of possession required to create a pledge. Physical delivery of the actual goods to the pledgee, so that the pledgee takes actual possession of them, will clearly suffice, but a pledge can also be created by 'constructive delivery'. Thus a pledge may be created by the pledgor depositing with the pledgee a document of title to the goods. The only document of title recognised for this purpose at common law is a bill of lading[1], although other classes of documents may be recognised as documents of title by local custom or under particular legislation[2], and a wider class of documents of title is recognised for the purposes of the Factors Act 1889, so that a mercantile agent may have greater power to create a binding pledge by depositing documents than would his principal[3]. The creation of a pledge by deposit of a document of title is common in the financing of international sales where a buyer of goods may pledge them to a bank as security for an advance of funds by depositing the bill of lading with the bank[4]. Deposit of a document other than a document of title will create no more than a pledge of the document. So deposit of a delivery order relating to goods will not create a pledge of the goods. Where goods are held by a third party bailee for the pledgor, a pledge can also be created by the pledgor ordering the bailee to hold the goods to the order of the pledgee and the bailee then attorning to the pledgee[5]. Thus, for instance, if goods are held in a warehouse, their owner can make a valid pledge of them by giving the pledgee a delivery order, provided that the order is acknowledged by the bailee attorning to the pledgee.

Possession of goods sufficient to create a pledge of them may also be created by the pledgor giving to the pledgee a key giving access to and control of them, provided that the key gives the pledgee exclusive control over the goods. Thus, for instance, a pledge of goods in a warehouse can be created by giving the pledgee a key giving direct access to the warehouse. However, all that is required is that the pledgee should have the exclusive *legal* right to control the goods; it is irrelevant that the pledgor may wrongfully interfere with the pledgee's access to and control of the goods, so that a valid pledge can be created of goods held in premises of a third party, or even of the pledgor himself. In *Hilton v Tucker*[6] C agreed to lend D £2,500 on the security of certain prints and engravings, to be stored in a particular room in a building owned by T. The goods were deposited and D then informed C that the key to the room was held by T 'at your disposal'. It was held that a valid pledge of the prints and engravings had been created by the delivery of the key to T, to hold on C's behalf, even though under the terms of the agreement, D also had access to the prints and engravings for limited purposes such as cleaning them. In *Wrightson v McArthur*[7] a valid pledge was created when goods were set aside in a locked room in the pledgor's premises and the key was given to the pledgee. The pledgor gave the pledgee a licence, which the court held to be irrevocable, to have access to the premises in which the room was.

A valid pledge can also be created over goods which remain in the physical possession of the pledgor, if he attorns to the pledgee so as to make himself a bailee of the goods for the pledgee. However, a court is likely to require clear evidence of such a change in status; for instance, evidence that the pledgee pays the pledgor a rental for storing the goods may indicate the change in status[8]. Where the pledgor's attornment is contained in a written document, the document will be a bill of sale and thus be registrable as such. In *Dublin City Distillery v Doherty*[9] whiskey was kept in a bonded warehouse to which there were two keys, one held by the distillery and the other by Customs and Excise officials. Both keys were needed to obtain access to the whiskey. The distillery purported to pledge the whiskey to C by entering details of the pledge in its stock books and giving C invoices and delivery warrants. The House of Lords held that no valid pledge had been created. Since one of the keys to the warehouse was held by the Customs and Excise, control of the whiskey was shared by the distillery and the Customs and a delivery warrant would therefore only be effective if signed by both of them. In any case, however, any pledge created here would have been registrable as a bill of sale, since it depended for its creation on the delivery warrants which purported to transfer possession to the whiskey.

Lord Waddington explained in the *Dublin Distillery* case that where the pledgor attorns to the pledgee the attornment operates as a constructive delivery of the goods to the pledgee followed by a re-delivery by the pledgee to the pledgor, to hold as bailee. However, at common law where goods pledged form part of a larger bulk, they must be physically separated in order to confer a pledge on the pledgee. An attornment in respect of part of bulk, without separation, may estop the pledgor from denying that the goods have been delivered to the pledgee, but the rights thus created will be purely personal rights binding only the pledgor[10]. It is not clear how this rule is affected by the Sale of Goods (Amendment) Act 1995. Under that Act a person who contracts to buy a quantity of goods forming part of a designated bulk and pays for some or all of the goods acquires an undivided share in the bulk[11]. It is not clear whether this undivided share could be pledged by attornment or by deposit of a document of title. For instance, a person who contracts to buy part of a bulk consignment of goods being carried by sea may receive a bill of lading covering the goods purchased. If he has paid the price of his goods he will acquire an undivided share in the cargo as a whole. The position is not clear but it is arguable that the deposit of the bill of lading with a bank as security for an advance may create a valid pledge of that undivided share[12], especially since the 1995 Act was partly motivated by a concern to protect the position of banks which took bills of lading relating to goods in bulk as security.

(b)   Pledges and the Bills of Sale Acts

A mere agreement to deliver goods by way of pledge is ineffective to create a pledge[13]. If the agreement gives the 'pledgee' the right to take possession of the goods, it will be registrable as a bill of sale. However, an executory contract to pledge goods as security for an advance to be made in the future is not registrable because it gives the 'pledgee' no right to take possession but requires the pledgor to deliver the goods[14] and such an agreement will give rise to a valid pledge provided that the goods are deposited within a reasonable time of the agreement and the advance. Thus in *Hilton v Tucker*[15] the sequence of events was that C agreed to provide the loan on the security of the prints and then advanced half of the loan. Two days later D wrote to C confirming that he had placed the pictures in the locked room and deposited the key to be held to C's order. It was held that delivery of the key to the third party completed a valid pledge of the pictures. Where a valid pledge is created by deposit of goods, a document setting out the rights of pledgor and pledgee is not registrable as a bill of sale.

(c)   What can be pledged?

Only those things capable of being reduced to possession and transferred by delivery can be pledged. The use of pledges is thus, effectively, limited to goods and negotiable instruments[16]. A chose in action cannot be pledged. Security over intangible property must therefore be created by charge or mortgage. The deposit of a share certificate may be a pledge of the certificate but not of shares it represents; however, it may create an equitable mortgage of the shares[17].

(d)   Form of a pledge

No particular form is prescribed for the creation of a valid pledge at common law: all that is required is the deposit of the security asset. However, where the pledge is regulated by the Consumer Credit Act 1974, the pledgee must give a pawn receipt in the form prescribed by the Act[18] and must hold a consumer credit licence. Failure to provide a pawn receipt is an offence[19]. An unlicensed pledgee commits an offence[20] and cannot enforce the pledge without an order of the Director General of Fair Trading[21].

1   See *Meyerstein v Barber* (1866) LR 2CP 38.
2   See *Official Assignee of Madras v Merchant Bank of India* [1935] AC 53 where it was found that receipts given by a railway company were documents of title under relevant Indian legislation.
3   See 22.1.1.3.
4   See 34.2.6.
5   *Dublin Distillery v Doherty* [1914] AC 823.
6   (1888) 39 Ch D 669.
7   [1921] 2 KB 807.
8   See *Official Assignee of Madras v Merchant Bank of India* [1935] AC 53.
9   [1914] AC 823.
10   *Maynegrain Pty Ltd v Compafina Bank* [1982] 2 NSWLR 141.
11   Sale of Goods Act 1979, s 20A: see 15.5.2.
12   See Gullifer [1999] LMCLQ 93 at 103.

13 *Meyerstein v Barber* (1866) LR 2 CP 38 at 51 per Willes J. But see Palmer and Hudson in Palmer and McKendrick (eds), *Interests in Goods* (2nd edn, 1998) p 645.
14 *Ex p Hubbard* (1886) 17 QBD 690.
15 (1888) 39 Ch D 669.
16 See chs 27–28. Thus a bill of exchange marked 'not negotiable' or a cheque crossed 'A/c payee' cannot be pledged: Bills of Exchange Act 1882, ss 81, 81A.
17 *Harrold v Plenty* [1901] 2 Ch 314; see 22.2.1.2. Contrast the position of a share warrant to bearer, which is negotiable: *Carter v Wake* (1877) 4 Ch D 605.
18 Consumer Credit Act 1974, s 114.
19 Consumer Credit Act 1974, s 115.
20 Consumer Credit Act 1974, s 39.
21 Consumer Credit Act 1974, s 40.

22.1.1.2 *Effect of a pledge*

The effect of a pledge is to make the pledgee a bailee of the pledged asset. The pledgee therefore owes the pledgor a duty of care in respect of the pledged asset, but that duty can be modified by contract, and commercial pledges will normally be governed by express agreements which limit the pledgee's duty of care and may also require the pledgor to insure the pledged asset and to pay any costs of storing it.

A pledge also gives the pledgee a 'special property' in the pledged asset – a proprietary interest but less than full ownership, limited to the value of the secured debt. It seems that the pledgee may deal with his interest – for instance, by assigning or sub-pledging it – without destroying the pledge[1]. He is entitled to use goods pledged with him, but does so at his own risk:

'If the pawn be such as it will be the worse for using, the pawnee cannot use it, as cloaths, etc but if it be such as will be never the worse, as if jewels for the purpose were pawn'd to a lady, she might use them. But then she must do it at her peril, for whereas, if she keeps them lock'd up in her cabinet, if her cabinet should be broke open, and the jewels taken from thence, she would be excused; but if she wears them abroad, and is there robb'd of them, she will be answerable'[2].

The pledgee has sufficient interest to insure the pledged property and to sue a third party who damages it.

The pledgor retains the general property in the pledged asset and can therefore deal with it, subject to the pledge.

1 This point was left open in *Donald v Suckling* (1866) LR 1 QB 585: below 22.1.1.4.
2 Per Holt CJ in *Coggs v Barnard* (1703) 2 Ld Raym 909; cf *The Odessa* [1916] AC 145 at 159, per Lord Mersey.

22.1.1.3 *Pledges and the nemo dat rule*

If a person purports to pledge goods which he does not own, the pledge will be binding on the owner of the goods if the pledgee can rely any of the exceptions to the nemo dat quod non habet rule[1]. Thus, for instance, a valid pledge of goods, binding on the owner of the goods, may be made by a mercantile agent or a seller or buyer in possession of the goods[2], and a pledge of documents of title relating to goods has the same effect as a pledge of the goods[3]. The category of documents recognised as documents of title for this purpose is wider than that recognised at common law so that, for instance, a pledge by a mercantile agent of a delivery order relating to goods may create a valid pledge of the goods, even though a pledge of the same document by the owner of the goods would not do so.

1   See ch 17. The pledgor would be in breach of an implied term in the pledge that he had a right to create a pledge.
2   Factors Act 1889, ss 2(1), 8, 9.
3   Factors Act 1889, s 3.

22.1.1.4 *Loss of possession*

The pledgee's security is destroyed if he surrenders possession of the pledged goods to the pledgor[1] but not if he merely delivers them to the pledgor for a limited purpose, in which case the pledgor holds the goods as a bailee for the pledgee who therefore remains in possession[2]. This is commonly done in the context of international sales, where the buyer of goods may deposit documents of title to the goods, such as bills of lading, with a bank as security for an advance of the price. The bank will release the documents to the buyer to enable him to sell the goods and redeem the pledge, but will do so on the terms of an arrangement known as a 'trust receipt', the effect of which is to allow the buyer to take possession of and sell the goods as agent, and receive the proceeds of sale as trustee, for the bank, so that the bank remains in (constructive) possession of the goods until they are sold and its security is therefore preserved[3].

The pledgee's security is only destroyed if he consents to the pledgor recovering possession. The security remains intact if the pledgor recovers possession without the pledgee's consent, or by fraud[4]. Difficulties arise if the pledgor recovers possession by fraud and then purports to deal with the goods, for instance by reselling or repledging them. The original pledgee may be bound by such disposition if any of the exceptions to the nemo dat rule applies, so that, for instance, he may be bound if the pledgor is a mercantile agent to whom the goods are entrusted for sale[5].

The pledge is not necessarily destroyed by the transfer of possession to a third party. In *Donald v Suckling*[6] D pledged debentures with C as security for payment of a bill of exchange. Before maturity of the bill C deposited the debentures with X as security for a loan of more than the value of the bill. D argued that the effect of this was to destroy the pledge, but this argument was rejected by the Court of Queen's Bench. Blackburn J and Cockburn CJ seem to have thought that C's conduct may have been a breach of contract, but agreed that it was not sufficiently inconsistent with the pledge to destroy it. The position might be different if there was an express or implied term that the pledgee should remain in possession of the pledged property, or if the pledgee purported to deal with more than his own interest in the goods, for instance by purporting to sell them as owner. The effect of C's pledge here was to pledge his own interest in the debentures, so that X acquired no better right to them than C had. D would therefore be entitled to recover them by tendering the amount of the bill of exchange to C, since that tender would destroy C's interest and with it both his and X's right to retain the debentures.

1   *Ryall v Rolle* (1750) 1 Atk 165.
2   *Reeves v Capper* (1838) 5 Bing NC 136.
3   See *Re David Allester* [1922] 2 Ch 211.
4   *Mocatta v Bell* (1857) 24 Beav 585.
5   *Lloyds Bank Ltd v Bank of America* [1938] 2 KB 147.
6   (1866) LR 1 QB 585.

22.1.1.5 *Enforcement*

The pledgor can redeem the pledge by repaying the secured debt at any time. However, at common law the pledgee is entitled to sell the pledge in order to realise his security if the debtor fails to pay the secured debt either at the due date or, if no date was fixed, on reasonable notice[1]. If the sale realises more than the outstanding debt the excess is held on trust for the pledgor[2]; however, if the sale realises less than the debt, the balance remains due from the pledgor as a personal debt.

The pledgee's right to enforce the pledge is restricted where the Consumer Credit Act applies. A pawn regulated by the Act is redeemable at any time within six months of its being taken[3] so that the pledgee cannot realise his security within that period, and the pledgee must in any case give notice to the pledgor of his intention to sell before doing so cannot be realised[4].

1   *Re Hardwick* (1886) 17 QBD 690.
2   See *Mathew v TM Sutton Ltd* [1994] 4 All ER 793. The court therefore has an equitable jurisdiction to order the pledgee to pay interest on any surplus if the pledgee delays in accounting to the pledgor.
3   Section 116 (1).
4   Consumer Credit Act 1974, s 121(1).

22.1.1.6 *Termination of the pledge*

The interest created by a pledge is terminated if the pledgor pays, or tenders payment of, the secured debt, if the pledgee waives his rights, for instance by releasing the pledge to the pledgor, or if the pledgee commits a breach of the pledge inconsistent with its continuation. For instance, in *Cooke v Hadden*[1] a pledge of champagne was destroyed by the pledgee's drinking it.

1   (1862) 3 F & F 229.

22.1.2 *Lien*

A lien is simply a right to retain property belonging to another until some obligation is performed[1]. In *Tappenden v Artus*[2] Diplock LJ described it as 'primitive' and explained that:

> 'The common law lien of an artificier is of very ancient origin, dating from a time when remedies by action upon contracts not under seal were still at an imperfect stage of development . . . Like a right of action for damages, it is a remedy for breach of contract which the common law confers upon an artificier to whom the possession of goods is lawfully given for the purpose of his doing work upon them in consideration of a money payment'[3].

These comments were concerned with the nature of the common law lien. Other types of lien exist. An equitable lien is a form of non-possessory security, similar to a charge. A lien may be given expressly, by contract. Statute may confer a right of lien on a creditor: for instance, an unpaid seller of goods has a lien over the goods while they are in his possession until the price is paid[4]. A maritime lien is a right to detain a ship and its cargo for payment of charges relating to the ship, such as salvage or seaman's wages; like an equitable lien it is a form of non-possessory security.

Notwithstanding its primitive nature, the common lien remains an important and potent security for certain classes of creditor and the following paragraphs are mainly concerned with common law liens.

1   See per Grose J in *Hammonds v Barclay* (1802) 2 East 227.
2   [1964] 2 QB 185.
3   [1964] 2 QB 185 at 194.
4   SoGA, ss 41–43: see 18.3.1.

22.1.2.1   *The common law lien*

Like a pledge, a lien is a possessory security. However, it differs from a pledge in a number of respects.

(a) A pledge is created by the delivery of goods or other property for the purpose of creating a security. In contrast, a lien is simply a right to retain property previously delivered to the person asserting the lien (the lienee) for some other purpose[1]. The existence of a lien therefore does not depend on delivery.
(b) A lienee has no proprietary interest in the property to which the lien relates but only a right to detain the property. It provides a defence to a claim for wrongful interference with the property by a person who would otherwise be entitled to possession[2]. A lienee therefore has no right at common law to sell the property covered by the lien (although such a right is now given by statute[3]) and has no right in the property which can be transferred to any third party.

Partly as a result of these limitations, it may be doubted whether a lien is a true security interest at all but there is no doubt that a lien can and does serve a security function.

A lien may be general or particular. A particular lien allows the debtor to retain possession of goods or documents as security for payment of debts which relate to the property retained; a general lien allows the creditor to retain possession of any property of the debtor until any debt due from the debtor is paid. Common law liens are normally particular, but a common law lien may be extended to a general lien by the express or implied terms of any contract between lienor and lienee, or by established custom, and solicitors, bankers, factors, insurance brokers and stockbrokers have all been recognised as having general liens as a matter of custom. A general lien is obviously advantageous to the lienee, providing greater and more flexible security than a particular lien. It may, however, also offer advantages to the lienor. A lienee who has only a particular lien may be reluctant to release the property to which it relates until debts relating to that property are paid; but if he has a general lien, he will be more willing to release goods to the lienor without immediate payment, as long as he has possession of other goods of the lienor, or will do so at some future date. However, although the courts recognise these advantages, they are generally reluctant to recognise general liens which may prejudice the interests of other creditors of the lienor[4] and clear evidence will be required to establish such a lien on the basis of custom.

1   *Re Cosslett (Contractors) Ltd* [1998] Ch 495 at 508, [1997] 4 All ER 115 at 126, per Millett LJ.
2   See *Tappenden v Artus* [1964] 2 QB 185 at 195.
3   Torts (Interference with Goods) Act 1977, s 12.
4   See *Rushforth v Hadfield* (1805) 6 East 519, especially per Le Blanc J (at 528); contrast the attitude in *Kirkman v Shawcross* (1794) 6 Term Rep 17.

22.1.2.2   *Creation of liens*

Common law liens are granted to practitioners of a relatively limited number of trades or callings who do work on, or perform services in relation to, the property of others. An innkeeper has a lien for the cost of the guest's food and board over the guest's belongings brought to the inn; a common carrier has a lien for carriage charges over the goods carried; an artificier who does work on the goods of others has a lien on the goods, but only for repairs or improvements to the goods, not for maintenance[1]; a professional who produces or works on documents for a client is entitled to a lien on the documents; and a ship's master has a lien on cargo for the payment of freight[2]. Such liens therefore arise as a result of contracts for the performance of work or services. However, as Diplock LJ explained in *Tappenden v Artus*[3], their existence does not depend on any contract term but the terms of the contract between the parties may prevent a lien arising[4].

As Bell observes, the list of common law liens now has 'an archaic flavour' and 'seems somewhat arbitrary'[5], and it is difficult to discern any linking thread in the list. At common law, practitioners of common callings were obliged to provide their services to anyone who requested them; the grant of liens to innkeepers and common carriers, therefore, compensated to some extent for that obligation. In other cases the lien seems to have been recognised to encourage the performance of services, especially where the service provider would normally only be paid on completion of the work.

A lien arises where the lienee (a) has property of the lienor in his possession and (b) does work or performs services which give rise to a lien. The lienee's possession of the lienor's property must be lawful both when he receives the property and when he does the work which gives rise to the lien. A particularly difficult question which has troubled the courts on many occasions is whether the owner of goods is bound by a lien created by a third party without his consent: for instance, where goods are let on hire purchase, is the owner bound by a repairer's lien if the hirer has the goods repaired? The cases on this point were reviewed in *Tappenden v Artus*, where Diplock LJ sought to explain the relevant principles in terms of agency. The position seems to be as follows:

(a) The owner of goods is bound by any lien created with his authority, and if the owner expressly or impliedly authorises a person to do an act which gives rise to a lien, he will be bound by that lien. Thus if the owner expressly or impliedly authorises another to have goods repaired, he is bound by any lien which arises as a result of the repair. Diplock LJ rejected as erroneous the statement in *Pennington v Reliance Motor Works Ltd*[6] that the owner would only be bound where he had expressly authorised the repair.

(b) The hirer under a hire purchase contract has implied authority to use the goods and do other acts reasonably incidental to their use, including to have them repaired[7], and the same must be true of contracts of conditional sale.

(c) If the person in possession of the goods has actual or apparent authority to do the act which gives rise to the lien, a contractual restriction on his power to create a lien will only be effective to prevent a lien arising if the lienee has notice of the restriction. In *Ablemarle Supply Co v Hind*[8] a contract for the hire purchase of a taxi purported to exclude the authority of the hirer to create any lien over the vehicle, but it was held that that exclusion was ineffective against a garage which acquired a lien over the taxi for repairs to it. The repairer was aware of the hire purchase agreement but not of its terms and, as Diplock LJ explained in *Tappenden v Artus*, the hirer therefore had apparent authority to have the taxi repaired and the owner could not rely on a secret limitation on the terms on which he could do so.

(d) The position is different if the lienor has no authority from the owner of the goods to do the act which gives rise to the lien. Thus in *Bowmaker Ltd v Wycombe Motors Ltd*[9] the owner of a car was not bound by a lien where the hirer took the car for repair after the hire purchase agreement had been terminated, and the position would presumably be the same if (say) a contract of hire or hire purchase excluded the right of the hirer to have the goods repaired. However, such exclusion would almost certainly have to be express[10] and even an express limitation may be ineffective against a repairer who knows of the hire contract but not of its terms, who might be able to argue that the hirer had 'usual authority', in the *Watteau v Fenwick*[11] sense, to have the goods repaired.

The analysis of the cases in *Tappenden v Artus* does much to clarify the law but it leaves some questions unanswered. Since the owner was bound in *Ablemarle v Hind* on the basis of apparent authority, the result would presumably have been different had the repairer not known of the hire purchase contract[12]. Moreover, the rationale for holding the owner of goods bound by a repairer's lien created without his authority is that he benefits from the repair work; however, the same is true even if the repairs are wholly unauthorised, as where the owner has prohibited the work or the repairs are authorised by a thief, yet in such cases it seems clear that the owner is not bound by any lien.

1 *Hatton v Car Maintenance Co Ltd* [1915] 1 Ch 621; *Re Southern Livestock Products Ltd* [1964] 1 WLR 24.
2 A person who salvages goods or vessels at sea also has a lien, but this derives from maritime law.
3 [1964] 2 QB 185.
4 See eg *Wilson v Lombank Ltd* [1963] 1 WLR 1294: provision for credit; *Forth v Simpson* (1849) 13 QB 680: contract permitted 'lienor' to remove the goods from the 'lienee's' possession.
5 *Modern Law of Personal Property in England and Ireland* (1989) p 139.
6 [1923] 1 KB 127.
7 See *Singer Manufacturing Ltd v London and South West Rly Co* [1894] 1 QB 833 where it was held that the hirer of a sewing machine had implied authority to take the machine with him when he travelled and therefore to create a lien in favour of a railway company with whom it was deposited.
8 [1928] 1 KB 307.
9 [1946] KB 505.
10 The court rejected an argument that the right to have the goods repaired was impliedly excluded in *Tappenden v Artus*.
11 See 4.4.
12 On the facts of the case, the owner was aware of the hirer's arrangements for repair and storage of the vehicle and assented to them. It might therefore have been possible to find an estoppel on this basis.

22.1.2.3 *Effects of a lien*

The lienee holds the property of the lienor in his possession as bailee, and therefore owes the lienor a duty of care, subject to any contract term restricting or modifying that duty.

The lien depends on the lienee continuing in possession. It is therefore lost if the lienee loses possession, either to the lienor or to a third party. In *Hatton v Car Maintenance Ltd*[1] the plaintiff entered into a contract with the defendants by which they agreed to store her car, maintain and repair it, and provide her with a driver, who was deemed to be the agent of the defendants. The car was kept at the defendants' premises but the plaintiff was allowed to take it whenever she wished. It was held that her freedom to take possession of the car at will meant that any lien which would otherwise have arisen was lost. Although the driver was the agent of the defendants for some purposes, he was not in possession of the car when he drove it, since he did so under the plaintiff's instructions. However, the lienee may be able to release goods into the physical possession of the lienor without losing his security. In *Albemarle v Hind*[2] the defendants garaged, serviced and repaired taxis. They allowed the driver to take the taxis to ply for hire on condition that they remained 'in pawn' and were returned each night. It was held that the defendants' lien was preserved: the effect of the agreement was that when the taxis were taken out by the owner he held them as bailee for the defendants.

1   [1915] 1 Ch 621.
2   [1928] 1 KB 307; see also *Allen v Smith* (1862) 12 CBNS 638.

22.1.2.4   *Lienee's rights*

At common law the lienee's only right is to retain possession of the goods until the debt for which they are held is settled, and a sale of the goods is a conversion. However, several classes of lienee have statutory powers of sale. An unpaid seller of goods has the right in certain circumstances to terminate the contract and resell the goods[1] and a more general power of sale is given to bailees by the Torts (Interference with Goods) Act 1977. Under s 12 of the 1977 Act, a bailee in possession of uncollected goods has a right to sell them where the bailor is in breach of an obligation to take delivery or give directions as to delivery of the goods, or cannot be traced. The bailee must first give the bailor notice, in the prescribed form, of his intention to sell goods or obtain the authority of the court to sell[2], and where there is any dispute between bailee and bailor over any payment claimed by the bailee – for instance, where the owner of goods disputes liability for repair charges – the bailee can only sell with the authority of the court.

A power of sale may also be reserved by the lienee's contract. The inclusion of such a power in the contract is not inconsistent with the classification of the security as a lien and so does not change the nature of the lienee's interest into a charge, provided that the original interest was in the nature of a lien[3].

Where the lienee sells by virtue of a statutory power of sale, the sale must be effected in accordance with any procedure prescribed. Subject to that, the effect of a sale by a lienee is broadly equivalent to one by a pledgee. The sale must be reasonable and may be held unreasonable if at an undervalue. If the proceeds of the sale exceed the debt the lienee must account to the lienor for the surplus, but if the proceeds are insufficient to satisfy the debt, the lienor remains liable for the outstanding balance.

A lien is included within the definition of 'security' for the purposes of the Insolvency Act 1986, s 248(b), so that the lienee's right to enforce the lien is restricted if an administration order is made. The effect is that if the administrator seeks the return of property held by a lienee, the latter can only retain it with the approval of the court[4].

1   See 18.3.4; see also Innkeepers Act 1878, s 1, authorising an innkeeper to sell at public auction after advertising the sale.
2   Section 13.

3 *Great Eastern Railway Co v Lord's Trustee* [1909] AC 109; *Re Hamlet International plc* [1999]
2 BCLC 506 (freightforwarders' contractual lien included power of sale); cf *Re Cosslett*
(Contractors) Ltd [1998] Ch 495, [1997] 4 All ER 115, where the creditor was held *not* to have a
lien over property in its possession and a contractual right of sale was construed as creating a
floating charge: see 22.0.4.1.
4 See *Bristol Airport v Powdrill* [1990] Ch 744, [1990] 2 All ER 493. The case actually concerned the
statutory power of an airport authority to detain aircraft under the Civil Aviation Act 1982, s 88.

22.1.2.5 *Termination of lien*

The lienor can normally only terminate the lien and recover the goods by tendering
the amount of the debt which it secures. However, in certain circumstances the
lienor is excused from having to make a tender. First, as we have seen, the lienee's
interest is lost if he loses possession of the goods, and once lost, the lien is not
revived even if the lienee later recovers possession[1]. This may be seen as an instance
of the lienee waiving his lien; it will also be waived if the lienee agrees to accept
alternative security. The lien may also be lost if the lienee commits a serious breach
of the terms on which he holds the goods, for instance, by delivering them to a
third party. The lienor may be excused from making a tender if the lienee fails to
provide him with details of the amount due, or insists on asserting a lien for an
amount greater than that which is due. However, the court will probably be reluctant
to find that the lien is lost in this last way in the absence of clear evidence. In
Albemarle Supply Co Ltd v Hind[2] taxis were garaged with the defendants, who
cleaned, fuelled and repaired them and charged these costs to an account. When
the owner of the taxis sought to recover them, the defendants demanded payment
of the whole balance on the account, but also supplied full details of the individual
charges. The costs of fuel and cleaning could not be the subject of a lien but Scrutton J
held that the owners were not excused from tendering the amount due in respect of
repairs; the defendants had not refused to release the taxis and had supplied the
owners with information from which they could calculate the amount to be tendered
to release the lien.

1 *Pennington v Reliance Motor Works Ltd* [1923] 1 KB 127; cf *Euro-Commercial Leasing Ltd*
   v Cartwright and Lewis [1995] 2 BCLC 618 (solicitors' lien), where a distinction seems to
   have been drawn between liens over chattels and liens over chose in action (see at 620).
2 [1928] 1 KB 307.

22.2 Non-possessory security

We have already noted the advantages offered to both creditor and debtor by non-
possessory securities. In particular, since they do not depend on the creditor taking
possession, they allow a debtor to use intangible and even future property as security.
Historically, the common law was not prepared to recognise non-possessory
security; however, the courts of equity did so and non-possessory securities are
now more important than possessory.

There are two main non-possessory securities, the mortgage and the charge.
A mortgage involves the outright transfer of ownership of property by the debtor
to the creditor, subject to a right for the debtor to 'redeem' the mortgaged property,
by repaying the secured debt with interest as appropriate, and having the property
re-transferred to him. In contrast, a charge involves no transfer of ownership but is
a mere incumbrance on the debtor's property which gives the creditor the right to

have the mortgaged property appropriated for payment of the secured debt. Although the theoretical difference between the two transactions is clear, however, the distinction may often be difficult to draw in practice. The terms 'mortgage' and 'charge' are often used almost interchangeably[1] and the expression 'charge' may be used to refer to an equitable mortgage[2].

For many important purposes the two transactions are assimilated; for instance, 'charge' includes 'mortgage' for the purposes of the Companies Act 1985. However, the distinction may still be important for the purposes of specific legislation[3]; moreover, the remedies available to a mortgagee (which include the right of foreclosure) are more extensive than those available to a chargee, although the latter are often extended by express terms in the charge, and it may therefore be necessary to decide whether a security is a mortgage or charge in order to identify the remedies available to the creditor.

1   See the comments of Slade J in *Re Bond Worth Ltd* [1980] Ch 228 at 250.
2   See per Buckley LJ in *Swiss Bank Corpn v Lloyds Bank Ltd* [1982] AC 584 at 594–595; Goode, *Legal Problems of Credit and Security* (2nd edn, 1988) p 15.
3   See eg *London County and Westminster Bank Ltd v Tompkins* [1918] 1 KB 515.

22.2.1   *Mortgages*

A mortgage is both a flexible and, because of the remedies available to the mortgagee to enforce his security, highly potent security.

At common law a mortgage of property involves a transfer of ownership to the mortgagee subject to an agreement for the property to be re-transferred to the mortgagor on discharge of the debt secured by the mortgage. Equity, however, regarded the mortgagee's obligation to re-transfer the mortgaged property as specifically enforceable and therefore, recognising the reality of the transaction, regarded the mortgagor as continuing to own a proprietary interest in the property, an equity of redemption, by virtue of which he was entitled to redeem the mortgage and obtain a re-transfer of the mortgaged property at any time, even after his contractual right to redeem had terminated. The equity of redemption was a proprietary interest which the mortgagor could deal with, so that in effect equity came to regard the mortgagor as owner of the mortgaged property, subject to the mortgage.

22.2.1.1   *Creation of mortgages*

Since a mortgage involves a transfer of ownership, there is no generally prescribed form for its creation; in principle, a valid mortgage can be created by any transaction appropriate to transfer ownership of the mortgaged property. However, this principle is modified in a number of cases.

The Law of Property Act 1925 requires a legal mortgage of land to take the form either of a demise for a term of years absolute, subject to a proviso for cesser on redemption, or a charge by deed expressed to be by way of legal mortgage[1].

In contrast, no formality is generally[2] required for the creation of a mortgage of personalty. The Sale of Goods Act rules on the transfer of property do not apply to a mortgage of goods[3] and the transfer of ownership of goods by way of mortgage therefore depends on the intention of the parties[4]. In practice, however, an agreement for mortgage of chattels would probably be recorded in writing for evidential purposes, in which case the document would constitute a security bill of sale and have to be in the prescribed form and be registered.

A mortgage of an equitable interest in any property must be in writing[5] and where a mortgage of any type of property is granted to secure the debt of someone other than the mortgagor, under an agreement regulated by the Consumer Credit Act 1974, the Act requires the mortgage to be in writing[6]. Finally, a legal mortgage of a chose in action must be by written assignment of the chose, and notice of the assignment must be given to the debtor[7]. A general assignment of book debts, or of a class of debts, is also required to be registered under the Bills of Sale Act 1878[8].

1 LPA 1925, ss 85–87.
2 Mortgages of intellectual property rights must be in writing: Patents Act 1977, s 30(5); Copyright Designs and Patents Act 1988, s 90(3); Trade Marks Act 1994, s 24(4). Mortgages of ships and aircraft must be in the form prescribed by statute and be registered in accordance with the appropriate statutory scheme: Merchant Shipping Act 1894, s 31; Merchant Shipping Act 1988, Sch 3; Civil Aviation Act 1982, s 86; Mortgaging of Aircraft Order 1972, SI 1972/1268.
3 SoGA, s 61(4).
4 It is not clear if delivery is needed, but delivery could in any case be constructive: see Bell, *Modern Law of Personal Property in England and Ireland* (1989) p 323.
5 LPA, s 53(1)(c).
6 Consumer Credit Act 1974, s 105(1), (6).
7 LPA 1925, s 136; see 27.3.1.
8 Insolvency Act 1986, s 344; see 22.0.3.1.

22.2.1.2 *Legal and equitable mortgages*

A mortgage may be legal or equitable. A mortgage of an equitable interest in property must be equitable but a dealing with a legal interest which is ineffective to create a legal mortgage may nevertheless create an equitable mortgage.

An equitable mortgage is created where the parties enter into a binding contract to create a legal mortgage. The contract must be one which would be specifically enforceable, but all that this requires in this context is that damages would be an insufficient remedy for the creditor if the debtor failed to perform his contract. A contract to create a mortgage of land must be in writing signed by both parties[1]. For other types of property no formality is required for the creation of a binding contract. In effect, therefore, all that is necessary is that the creditor should have advanced the credit which is to be secured by the mortgage[2] because 'a mere claim to damages or repayment is obviously less valuable than a security in the event of a debtor's insolvency[3]'. A deposit of documents of title by the debtor with the creditor may be evidence of a contract to create a mortgage and therefore be sufficient to constitute an equitable mortgage of property other than land[4] if that is the intention of the parties. Where the documents relate to goods, the deposit will probably be construed as intended to create a pledge of the goods, but a deposit of documents of title to intangible property, such as share certificates, is more likely to be construed as intended to create a mortgage[5].

A present assignment by way of mortgage of property to be acquired by the mortgagor in the future has no effect at law; however, it operates as a contract to assign the property when acquired and therefore, provided that the mortgagee has advanced the credit secured by the mortgage so that the agreement is specifically enforceable[6], creates an equitable mortgage of the property as soon as it is acquired in accordance with the principle of *Holroyd v Marshall*[7].

1   Law of Property (Miscellaneous Provisions) Act 1989, s 2(1).
2   *Rogers v Challis* (1859) 27 Beav 175.
3   Per Buckley LJ in *Swiss Bank Corpn v Lloyds Bank Ltd* [1982] AC 584 at 595.
4   A deposit of title deeds is ineffective to create an equitable mortgage of land by virtue of the Law
     of Property (Miscellaneous Provisions) Act 1989, s 2(1): *United Bank of Kuwait Ltd v Sahib*
     [1997] Ch 107, [1996] 3 All ER 213.
5   *Harrold v Plenty* [1901] 2 Ch 314.
6   *Tailby v Official Receiver* (1888) 13 App Cas 523.
7   (1862) 10 HL Cas 191; see 22.0.2.

22.2.1.3   *Rights of the mortgagee*

A mortgage of personalty vests the mortgaged property in the mortgagee but the
mortgagor's equity of redemption compels him to permit the mortgagor to redeem
the mortgage at any time, even after the contractual redemption date. However, if
the mortgagor fails to redeem the mortgage at the due date the mortgagee may
seek to enforce the mortgage. Four methods of enforcement are generally available:
foreclosure, possession, sale and the appointment of a receiver. All derive from the
fact that the mortgagee is strictly, in law, owner of the mortgaged property. They
may be supplemented by express powers in the contract creating the mortgage.
However, the Consumer Credit Act 1974 restricts the mortgagee's power to enforce
his security for breach of an agreement regulated by the Act[1]. Where the 1974 Act
does not apply, the mortgagee's power to take possession of goods assigned under
a bill of sale is regulated by the Bills of Sale (Amendment) Act 1882, which specifies
the circumstances in which the mortgagee may take possession and allows the
mortgagor to apply to the court for an order restraining seizure[2].

Foreclosure is an especially potent remedy, not available to any other security
holder. Its effect is to terminate the mortgagor's equity of redemption and vest the
mortgaged property in the mortgagee. The secured debt is extinguished. Where
the value of the mortgaged property exceeds the secured debt foreclosure will give
the mortgagee a windfall, and its availability is therefore restricted. It is only
available by order of the court and the mortgagee cannot apply for an order unless
the mortgagor has failed to redeem the mortgage within a reasonable time after the
mortgage has become due. The court will normally first make an order nisi,
providing for foreclosure unless the debtor redeems the mortgage within a stated
time. If the debtor fails to do so, the mortgagor must then return to court to obtain
an order absolute. In practice, therefore, mortgagees may prefer to rely on their
other remedies.

Any mortgagee may apply to the court for an order for sale[3]. A mortgage will
normally, however, give the mortgagee an express power of sale but even in the
absence of an express power, a right of sale may be implied either at common law
or under statute. A power of sale on giving reasonable notice is implied at common
law in a mortgage of intangible property[4] and s 101 of the Law of Property Act
1925 gives the mortgagee a power of sale where the mortgage is created by deed.
However, the exercise of the statutory power of sale is restricted by the Act.
Moreover, it is not clear whether a mortgagee of goods has any implied power of
sale at common law or under statute. It was held in *Re Morritt*[5] that the statutory
power of sale in the Conveyancing Act 1881, equivalent to that in s 101 of the
1925 Act, was inconsistent with the Bills of Sale (Amendment) Act 1882 and
therefore inapplicable to mortgages of goods, and it seems that the position is the
same under the 1925 Act. Three members of the Court of Appeal in that case[6]

thought that a mortgagee of goods in possession of them would have an implied power of sale at common law, but this has since been doubted[7], while two other members of the court (Lopes LJ and Lord Esher MR) held that a power of sale was implied in a mortgage of goods effected by a security bill of sale by virtue of the language of s 7 of the 1882 Act[8].

The proceeds of sale are applied to extinguish the secured debt; any surplus is held for the debtor, who remains liable for any shortfall. The debtor therefore has an interest in the outcome of the sale as, indirectly, do other creditors of the debtor. It is established, however, that in exercising his powers under the mortgage the mortgagee is entitled to act in his own best interests. He owes a duty, which arises in equity, to the mortgagor and to any other person interested in the equity of redemption, such as a subsequent incumbrancer or a surety[9], to use his powers 'for the sole purpose of securing repayment of the moneys owing under his mortgage and a duty to act in good faith'[10]. He will therefore be in breach of duty if he exercises his powers for some purpose other than securing repayment of moneys due under the mortgage[11]. In addition, if he exercises his power of sale, he must exercise reasonable care to obtain a proper price[12]. This duty arises in equity, although the standard of care required is the same as would be required in common law negligence[13]. However, he may choose if and when to sell according to his own interests[14]. He therefore incurs no liability if he could have obtained a higher price by deferring a sale, and has no liability for any decline in the value of the property prior to taking possession[15].

In practice, a mortgagee will often prefer to appoint a receiver, or receiver and manager, especially where the mortgaged property is a business. The receiver's primary function is to manage the mortgaged property, receive income from it and apply it in payment of interest and repayment of capital due under the mortgage. To this end, a receiver appointed under a mortgage has limited statutory powers to manage the property and receive its income[16]. In practice, the terms of the mortgage will give the receiver more extensive powers to manage and receive income from the mortgage property, carry on any business and realise any or all of the mortgaged property, and will normally make the receiver agent of the mortgagor in exercising these functions. In exercising his powers, the receiver's primary duty is 'to try and bring about a situation in which interest on the secured debt can be paid and the debt itself repaid'[17]. However, like the mortgagee exercising a power of sale, he also owes equitable duties of good faith and due diligence to the mortgagor and others interested in the equity of redemption. Thus if he sells the property he owes the same duty as a mortgagor to obtain a proper price. Similarly, although he is not obliged to carry on any business previously carried on by the mortgagor, if he chooses to do so he owes an equitable duty of due diligence to take reasonable care in its management. So where a receiver appointed under a mortgage of a pig farm chose to carry on the business, it was held that he could be liable to the mortgagee for breach of this duty where he failed to obtain discounts on pig food which were readily available in the market[18].

1   Consumer Credit Act 1974, s 87.
2   BS(A)A 1882, ss 7, 7A; the Act therefore gives the mortgagee an implied right of seizure even where none is expressly given by the mortgage: *Watkins v Evans* (1887) 18 QBD 386.
3   Law of Property Act 1925, s 91.
4   *Deverges v Sandeman Clark & Co* [1902] 1 Ch 579; *Stubbs v Slater* [1910] 1 Ch 632.
5   (1886) 18 QBD 222.
6   Lindley, Bowen and Cotton LJJ.
7   In *Deverges v Sandeman Clark & Co* [1902] 1 Ch 579.

8 See 22.0.3.1.
9 *China and South Sea Bank Ltd v Tan* [1990] 1 AC 536, [1989] 3 All ER 839.
10 *Downsview Nominees Ltd v City Corpn Ltd* [1993] AC 295 at 317, [1993] 3 All ER 623 at 639 per Lord Templeman. See Berg [1993] JBL 213.
11 *Downsview Nominees Ltd v City Corpn Ltd* [1993] AC 295, [1993] 3 All ER 623.
12 *Cuckmere Brick Co Ltd v Mutual Finance Ltd* [1971] Ch 949; cf *Kennedy v de Trafford* [1897] AC 180.
13 *Medforth v Blake* [1999] 3 All ER 97.
14 *China and South Sea Bank Ltd v Tan* [1990] 1 AC 536, [1989] 3 All ER 839. The court has a discretion, however, on the application of the mortgagor or any other person interested in the mortgaged property, to order a sale, under the Law of Property Act 1925, s 91(2): see *Palk v Mortgage Services Funding plc* [1993] 2 All ER 481.
15 *AIB Finance Ltd v Debtors* [1998] 2 All ER 929.
16 Law of Property Act 1925, s 109.
17 *Medforth v Blake* [1999] 3 All ER 97 at 111, per Sir Richard Scott V-C.
18 *Medforth v Blake* [1993] 3 All ER 97.

22.2.2 *Charges*

According to Atkin LJ:

'where in a transaction for value both parties evince an intention that property, existing or future, shall be made available as security for the payment of a debt, and that the creditor shall have a present right to have it made available, there is a charge, even though the present legal right which is contemplated can only be enforced at some future date, and though the creditor gets no legal right of property, either absolute or special, or any legal right to possession but only gets a right to have the security made available by an order of the court'[1].

Unlike a mortgage or pledge, therefore, a charge involves the transfer neither of property nor possession; instead, it creates a mere incumbrance on property of the debtor, which gives the creditor the right to have that property realised and its proceeds applied to discharge the debt it secures. The interest created by the charge is, however, a property interest which the chargee can deal with, outright or by way of security.

A charge can be created over any class of property, real or personal, tangible or intangible, present or future[2]. Moreover, a charge can be created over a particular designated asset or over a whole class of assets of a particular kind, and may be either fixed or floating. A fixed charge attaches to the charged asset(s) immediately on its creation and therefore prevents the chargor dealing with the charged asset free of the charge without the consent of the chargee. A floating charge, however, is normally created over a class of assets specified by description, and 'hovers' or 'floats' over all assets of that description acquired by the debtor from time to time, but does not attach to any of them until it 'crystallises'. The effect is that the chargor remains free to deal with assets subject to the charge, so long as the charge has not crystallised. Floating charges are examined in more detail below[3].

The effect of a charge is merely to encumber the charged asset to the extent of the secured debt; a charge therefore could not exist at common law. A legal charge of real property can now be created by statute[4]. A charge of personal property must be equitable.

1 *National Provincial and Union Bank of England v Charnley* [1924] 1 KB 431 at 449. Similarly, Buckley LJ, in *Swiss Bank Corpn v Lloyds Bank Ltd* [1982] AC 584 at 595, observed that there is a charge whenever 'property is expressly or constructively made liable, or specially appropriated,

to the discharge of a debt or some other obligation, and confers on the chargee a right of realisation by judicial process, that is to say, by the appointment of a receiver or an order for sale'. See also Millett LJ in *Re Cosslett (Contractors) Ltd* [1998] Ch 495 at 508, [1997] 4 All ER 115 at 125.
2   *Holroyd v Marshall* (1862) 10 HL Cas 191.
3   22.2.2.3.
4   Law of Property Act 1925, ss 85–87.

22.2.2.1   *Creation of charges*

As indicated by Atkin LJ in the passage quoted above, the creation of a charge depends on the intention of the parties. A charge is therefore normally created by contract. The contract need be in no particular form and may even be wholly oral[1]. A charge of future property will be ineffective unless given for consideration, but a valid charge on existing assets may be created gratuitously provided it is created by deed. Moreover, 'no particular form of words is necessary for the purpose of creating a charge'[2]. The decision whether an agreement creates a charge therefore depends on the words used and their proper construction, and since the law is not concerned with subjective intentions, the parties may be found to have intended to create, and to have created, a charge, even though they did not realise it, if that is the effect of their acts or agreement.

> 'If upon the true construction of the relevant documents in the light of any admissible evidence as to surrounding circumstances the parties have entered into a transaction the legal effect of which is to give rise to an equitable charge in favour of one of them over the property of the other, the fact that they may have not realised this consequence will not mean that there is no charge. They must be presumed to intend the consequence of their acts'[3].

Thus 'a person may create an effective equitable charge over chattels by declaring that he holds them in trust for a creditor by way of security for the payment of a specified debt'[4]. An agreement to pay a debt out of a specified fund, or to hold a fund on trust to discharge a debt, may amount to a charge. In *Swiss Bank Corpn v Lloyds Bank Ltd* [5] the plaintiffs lent a sum in Swiss francs to enable the defendant to buy shares in an Israeli bank. The loan required Bank of England consent under the Exchange Control Act 1947, which was given subject to conditions. It was a condition of the plaintiffs' loan that the borrower should observe the Bank of England's conditions, which included that the shares should be held in a separate account and the plaintiffs' loan should be repaid from the proceeds of resale of the shares. The plaintiffs claimed that, as a result, they had an equitable charge over the shares to secure repayment of their loan, but the Court of Appeal and House of Lords held that no charge was created. An agreement between creditor and debtor to pay a debt out of a specific fund would create an equitable assignment of the fund and create a charge over it if it created a specifically enforceable contract to repay from that particular fund. Here, however, as Lord Wilberforce emphasised, the requirement to pay the debt out of the proceeds of the shares was imposed by the Bank of England for exchange control purposes, not to protect the creditor; it was not, as such, a requirement to repay the loan out of that fund but a requirement not to repay it out of any other funds.

Because a charge can be created without any special formality, difficult questions of construction can arise where it is alleged that the effect of a transaction is to create a charge. Sometimes, as in the *Swiss Bank* case, the creditor may argue that a charge is created in order to establish a prior claim to a particular asset; more often, however, it is a liquidator or receiver who argues that a transaction which creates a functional security gives rise to a charge and that the charge is void on the grounds of its non-registration under the Companies Act 1985. It is therefore necessary to examine the arrangement in order to ascertain whether it possesses the characteristics of a charge. In *Re Bond Worth Ltd*[6] Slade J said:

> 'any contract which, by way of security for payment of a debt, creates an interest in property defeasible on payment of such debt, must necessarily be regarded as creating a charge'[7].

This dictum has often been invoked in cases concerned with the effect of retention of title clauses. It cannot apply where the clause is effective to prevent property passing to the buyer, but in *Re Bond Worth* the clause, which reserved 'equitable and beneficial ownership', permitted property in the goods to pass to the buyer and sought to give the seller an equitable interest in them[8]. Similar reasoning applies where a seller seeks to establish a claim under a retention of title clause to the proceeds of goods sold by the buyer if, as is normally the case, the buyer sells on his own account and thus owns the proceeds of sale[9].

The problem of distinguishing a charge from other arrangements arises in a number of contexts. For instance, in *Re Cosslett (Contractors) Ltd,* discussed earlier[10], it was held that although the employer's right to retain possession of plant and equipment was not a security, its right to seize and sell plant and unused materials and apply the proceeds of sale towards satisfaction of sums due from the contractor was a charge, since it was a right given by contract to take possession of property and apply it towards satisfaction of a debt or other liability[11].

Particularly difficult classification questions arise where parties enter into secured financing arrangements such as sale and lease back, when the court must decide if the transaction involves a genuine sale or creates a charge over the property concerned. As we have seen[12] the court seeks to identify the legal nature of the arrangement by ascertaining whether its terms are consistent with the normal incidents of a sale or of a charge.

Romer LJ highlighted three essential differences between a charge and a sale in *Re Geo Inglefield Ltd*[13].

(1) Under a charge (or mortgage) the chargor is entitled to recover the property by returning any money received from the creditor. Under a genuine sale the buyer normally has no right to buy back the goods.
(2) If a mortgagee or chargee sells the charged asset, he is entitled to retain only so much of the proceeds as is required to discharge his debt and is accountable to the chargor for any surplus, whereas if a buyer resells at a profit, he is entitled to retain the profit.
(3) Conversely, if a sale by a mortgagee or chargee realises insufficient to discharge the debt, he can pursue the debtor for the shortfall, whereas if a buyer resells for less than he paid for the goods, he must bear the loss.

Despite this guidance, the line between sale and charge may be difficult to draw. The difficulty is that no one of the factors listed by Romer LJ is conclusive[14]. Everything therefore depends on the proper construction of the parties' agreement. In *Re Curtain Dream plc*[15] a company entered into a financing arrangement under which X Ltd agreed to provide it with a line of credit of £500,000. It was a term of the agreement that the company would invoice X Ltd for specified goods and would enter into a separate 'trading agreement' by which X Ltd purported to resell the same goods to the company, subject to a reservation of title in favour of X Ltd. It was held that the two contracts should be read together in order to determine the effect of the whole transaction, and that, properly construed, they created a charge over the goods. A crucial factor was that the company was contractually bound to re-purchase the goods 'sold' to X Ltd. In contrast, in *Welsh Development Corpn v Export Finance Co Ltd*[16], as we have seen, an arrangement by which a company sold goods to a financing company and then sold those goods to customers as the financing company's undisclosed agent was held not to create a charge, even though the overall effect of the arrangement was that the financing company was not entitled to retain the profit made on the sales to customers and could effectively recover any losses from the company. Similarly, in *Re Geo Inglefield Ltd*[17] itself, an agreement by which a company, which supplied goods to customers on hire purchase terms, sold the goods and the benefit of its hire purchase contracts to a discounter, on terms by which it guaranteed payment by customers of the outstanding hire purchase instalments was held not to create a charge.

A different classification question was raised in *Re Bank of Credit and Commerce International (No 8)*[18]. A bank which advanced money to a customer took security for the advance in the form of a document by which a director of the company purported to 'charge' the balance on his account with the bank for the liabilities of the company. It was argued that, notwithstanding its wording, the document could not operate as a charge. In *Re Charge Card Services Ltd*[19] Millett J indicated that such a charge could not be created because 'a charge in favour of a debtor of his own indebtedness to the chargor is conceptually impossible'[20]. The Court of Appeal in *Re BCCI (No 8)*[21] accepted this reasoning. In the House of Lords, however, Lord Hoffmann, with whom the rest of the House agreed, rejected the argument of conceptual impossibility. There is no doubt, of course, that a debt is a species of property which can be charged. The argument was that it would be impossible for the bank to realise its security in the normal way because it could not claim payment of the debt from itself. The House of Lords accepted this proposition but denied that it was fatal to classification of the interest as a charge. The bank could enforce its security in a different way, by an appropriate entry in its books reducing or cancelling the customer's credit balance.

Their Lordships' reasoning (which, strictly speaking, was obiter) appears to have been rooted in commercial pragmatism. Such 'charges' are common. The fact that equivalent security could be created in other ways was 'no reason for preventing banks and their customers from creating charges over deposits if, for reasons of their own, they want to do so[22]'. As Lord Hoffmann observed:

> 'In a case where there is no threat to the consistency of the law or objection of public policy, I think that the courts should be very slow to declare a practice of the commercial community to be conceptually impossible . . . [T]he law is fashioned to suit the practicalities of life and legal concepts like 'proprietary interest' and 'charge' are no more than labels given to clusters of related and self-consistent rules of law. Such concepts do not have a life of their own from which the rules are inexorably derived'[23].

1   A charge creates, rather than transfers, an equitable interest and therefore is not required to be in writing.
2   Per Bankes LJ in *National Provincial and Union Bank of England v Charnley* [1924] 1 KB 431 at 440.
3   Per Buckley LJ in *Swiss Bank Corpn v Lloyds Bank Ltd* [1982] AC 584 at 595–596.

4 Per Slade J in *Re Bond Worth Ltd* [1979] 3 All ER 919 at 940.
5 [1982] AC 584.
6 [1980] Ch 228.
7 [1980] Ch 228 at 248.
8 See also *Stroud Architectural Systems Ltd v John Laing Construction Ltd* [1994] BCC 18.
9 See 18.4.5.
10 [1998] Ch 495, [1997] 4 All ER 115.
11 Contrast *Re Hamlet International plc* [1999] 2 BCLC 506, above 22.1.2.4.
12 See 22.0.4.2.
13 [1933] Ch 1 at 27.
14 See per Millett LJ in *Orion Finance Ltd v Crown Financial Management Ltd* [1996] 2 BCLC 78 at 84.
15 [1990] BCLC 925.
16 Above 22.0.4.2.
17 [1933] Ch 1.
18 [1998] AC 214, [1997] 4 All ER 568.
19 [1987] Ch 150, [1986] 3 All ER 289; affd [1989] Ch 497, [1988] 3 All ER 702.
20 [1987] Ch 150 at 175, [1986] 3 All ER 289 at 308.
21 [1996] Ch 245, [1996] 2 All ER 121.
22 [1998] AC 214 at 227, [1997] 4 All ER 568 at 577.
23 [1998] AC 214 at 228, [1997] 4 All ER 568 at 578. Professor Goode has criticised the decision in strong terms: see (1998) 114 LQR 178; cf Calnan (1998) 114 LQR 174.

22.2.2.2 *Remedies*

A chargee is entitled to have the charged property applied to pay the debt secured by the charge, and may therefore apply to the court for an order for sale of the charged property or for the appointment of a receiver. In practice, however, where a charge is created deliberately by a formal agreement, the agreement will give the chargee powers of sale and to appoint a receiver without application to the court, and will spell out the powers of any receiver so appointed[1]. Where the charged property is sold, the chargee is entitled to have its proceeds applied towards or in satisfaction of the secured debt. The debtor remains liable for any shortfall but is entitled to any surplus. Unlike a mortgagee, a chargee has no right of foreclosure or to take possession of the charged property.

1 In the absence of such provision, the powers of the receiver will be as set out in Sch 1 of the Insolvency Act 1986. Where the charge is created by deed, powers of sale and appointment of a receiver are given by statute: Law of Property Act 1925, s 101.

22.2.2.3 *Fixed and floating charges*

As already noted, although a fixed charge allows the chargor to retain possession of and use the charged assets, it necessarily inhibits his freedom to dispose of those assets. While, therefore, a fixed charge could be given over assets such as plant and machinery which the chargor needed to retain and use, it could not be given over circulating assets, such as stock in trade and work in progress, in which a trading or manufacturing company might have much of its capital tied up. The floating charge was devised in the mid-nineteenth century to overcome the limitations of the fixed charge and allow such circulating assets to be used as security[1]. Professor Goode describes the floating charge as 'one of the most subtle creations of equity'[2] and a 'manifestation of the English genius for harnessing the most abstract concepts to the service of commerce'[3]. However, despite more than 100 years of history during which it has generated a substantial body of case law, many questions remain about the effects and even the nature of the floating charge.

The recognition of the floating charge followed from the decision in *Holroyd v Marshall*[4] that an effective mortgage could be created in equity over property to be bought in the future to replace existing mortgaged plant and machinery. However, the security recognised in *Holroyd v Marshall* was fixed. The floating charge was recognised in *Re Panama New Zealand and Australia Royal Mail Co*[5], in which a company created a charge on its 'undertaking and all sums of money arising therefrom and all the estate, right, title, and interest of the company therein' to secure an issue of debentures. It was held that the proper construction of the instrument was that it created a charge on all present and future property of the company but that the word 'undertaking' implied that the company could carry on its business and deal freely with its property in the ordinary course of business so long as instalments of interest on the debentures, and capital when repayable, were paid as due:

> 'But the moment the company comes to be wound up, and the property has to be realised, that moment the rights of [the chargee], beyond all question, attach'[6].

The effect, therefore, is that so long as the charge remains floating, it constitutes a security over a constantly changing fund: the chargor is free to deal with the charged assets in the ordinary course of business, including by disposing of them, without obtaining the express consent of the chargee, and any assets so disposed of are removed from the security; but as new assets are bought, they become subject to it. As Lord MacNaghten explained[7]:

> 'a floating charge . . . is ambulatory or shifting in its nature, hovering over[8] and so to speak floating with the property which it is intended to affect until some event occurs or some act is done which causes it to settle and fasten on the subject of the charge within its reach and grasp'.

The floating charge provides an effective way for trading and manufacturing companies to provide security and thus obtain finance. Its benefits are, however, largely unavailable to individuals. A document executed by an individual creating a charge would be a security bill of sale, and a security bill of sale must include a schedule describing the property included in it[9] and is generally void except as against the grantor insofar as it relates to property to be acquired by the grantor[10].

1 The history of the development of the floating charge is described by Pennington (1960) 23 MLR 630.
2 *Legal Problems of Credit and Security* (1988) p 46.
3 *Commercial Law* (2nd edn, 1995) p 731.
4 (1862) 10 HL Cas 191.
5 (1870) 5 Ch App 318.
6 Giffard LJ.
7 *Illingworth v Houldsworth* [1904] AC 355 at 358.
8 A floating charge is generally said to 'hover'. As Nourse J observed in *Re Woodroffe's Musical Instruments Ltd* [1986] Ch 366 at 378, '"hovering" carries an undertone of menace'.
9 Bills of Sale (Amendment) Act 1882, s 4; above 22.0.3.1.
10 Bills of Sale (Amendment) Act 1882, s 5. Section 6 creates some limited exceptions for growing crops and fixtures, plant and machinery brought to replace similar items included, in the original bill, as in *Holroyd v Marshall*, but these are of limited relevance to a typical floating charge.

22.2.2.4   *What interest is created by a floating charge?*

Over the years there has been extensive academic debate over the question whether the holder of a floating charge has an interest in the charged property prior to crystallisation of the charge. The earliest cases suggested that the effect of a floating charge was to create a fixed charge with licence for the chargee to deal with the charged property. Conversely, it is sometimes suggested that a floating charge holder has no interest in the charged property until the charge crystallises[1]. It is now generally accepted that the effect of a floating charge was accurately described by Buckley LJ in *Evans v Rival Granite Quarries*[2]:

> 'A floating security is not a future security; it is a present security, which presently affects all the assets of the company expressed to be included in it. On the other hand, it is not a specific security; the holder cannot affirm that the assets are specifically mortgaged to him. The assets are mortgaged in such a way that the mortgagor can deal with them without the concurrence of the mortgagee. A floating security is not a specific mortgage of the assets, plus a licence to the mortgagor to dispose of them in the course of his business, but is a floating mortgage applying to every item comprised in the security, but not specifically affecting any item until some event occurs or some act on the part of the mortgagee is done which causes it to crystallise into a fixed security'.

Nevertheless, the point is not absolutely settled. The question is not entirely academic. The fact that a floating charge holder acquires an interest in the charged property before crystallisation may explain why a person who takes a floating charge may gain priority over the holder of a prior, unregistered, floating charge of which he has no notice[3].

1   See eg Gough, *Company Charges* (2nd edn, 1995) p 332.
2   [1910] 2 KB 979 at 999.
3   For a list of the practical implications of treating the chargee's interest as proprietary, see Goode, *Legal Problems of Credit and* Security (2nd edn, 1988) p 50; contrast Bell, *Personal Property in England and Ireland* (1989) p 176 who argues that the issue is largely irrelevant.

22.2.2.5   *Priority of charges*

Where two or more charges affect the same property, it is necessary to decide which of them has priority. Most charges created by a company are registrable under the Companies Act 1985[1] and are void against a liquidator or creditor if not registered. A registered charge thus takes priority over an unregistered, registrable charge. However, provided a registrable charge is registered within 21 days of its creation, registration is irrelevant to the question of priorities.

A floating charge gives the chargor authority to deal with property covered by the charge in the ordinary course of business, which impliedly includes authority to create other, fixed, charges over the same property. A fixed charge therefore generally has priority over an earlier floating charge. However, the chargor generally has no implied authority to create prior ranking floating charges over the same property, so that where two floating charges affect the same property, provided both, if registrable, are registered, priority is given to the first to have been created[2].

Floating charges often include a provision known as a negative pledge, forbidding the chargor from creating any other prior ranking fixed or floating charge over the charged property. Such a provision deprives the chargor of authority to create any such charge, but it will only be effective against a creditor who has notice of it[3]. Registration of a charge does not give constructive notice of the negative pledge but, if details of it are included in the particulars of the charge registered at the Companies Registry, any other chargee who searches the register will have notice of the pledge. However, although the position is not clear, it seems that a later chargee who does not search the register will not be taken to have constructive notice of it[4].

1   Section 395. See 22.0.3.2.
2   This rule is varied where creation of prior ranking charges is expressly or impliedly permitted. Eg where a floating charge is taken over the whole of a company's assets it may be taken as impliedly permitting the creation of prior ranking floating charges over specific assets or classes of assets: *Re Automatic Bottle Makers* [1926] Ch 412.
3   *Wilson v Kellard* [1910] 2 Ch 306.
4   The Companies Act 1989 would introduce a new s 416(1) into the 1985 Act, under which registration would constitute constructive notice of those matters which are required to be registered under the Act. Details of a negative pledge are not required to be registered, but there is power for the Secretary of State to make regulations requiring other particulars to be registered, which could be exercised so as to require registration of negative pledges. If this were done, registration of a charge including details of any negative pledge would constitute constructive notice of the pledge.

22.2.2.6 *Fixed or floating charge?*

As we have seen, a floating charge offers a number of significant commercial advantages, allowing security to be given over assets such as stock in trade and work in progress. As *Re Panama* illustrates, a floating charge may even cover the whole business of the chargor. However, a fixed charge has a number of advantages over a floating charge.

First, all floating charges must be registered under the Companies Act[1], whereas some fixed charges are not registrable.

Second, a floating, but not a fixed, charge is void if created within 12 months before the commencement of winding up unless either the company was solvent when it was given or 'new value' was provided in exchange for the charge; and a charge given to a 'connected person' within two years before the commencement of winding up is void unless given for new value[2].

Third, as already outlined, a fixed charge may take priority even over an earlier floating charge.

Fourth, even if there is no prior ranking fixed charge, if the chargor becomes insolvent the claims of a floating charge holder are not met until the costs of the insolvency and the claims of any preferential creditors have been satisfied. A fixed charge holder is entitled to have the charged property appropriated to his claim in priority to all other claims.

On the other hand, a floating charge offers one significant legal advantage over a fixed charge. The holder of a floating charge may appoint an administrative receiver over the charged property[3], and as a result is entitled to receive notice of any petition for an administration order and, moreover, may effectively block an administration order by appointing an administrative receiver. It has therefore become common for the holders of fixed charges to take floating charges over the same property in order to gain the power to appoint an administrative receiver[4].

In view of these differences between fixed and floating charges, it may be important to decide whether a charge is fixed or floating. This involves application of the test outlined earlier[5] in order to ascertain the true effect of the transaction, by determining whether it has the characteristics of a fixed or floating charge. The characteristics of a floating charge were described by Romer LJ in *Re Yorkshire Woolcombers Ltd*[6], who said a charge is a floating charge:

'(1) If it is a charge on a class of assets of a company present and future;
 (2) if that class is one which, in the ordinary course of business, would be changing from time to time; and
 (3) if you find that by the charge it is contemplated that, until some future step is taken by or on behalf of those interested in the charge, the company may carry on its business in the ordinary way so far as concerns the particular class of assets.'

Later cases have emphasised, however, that these are only guidelines, not absolute rules. It is clear that a charge may be a floating charge even though it does not possess all of these characteristics. Thus, for instance, a charge over a class of assets which can decrease but not increase may be a floating charge[7] and a floating charge may be created over land[8]. The third aspect of the test, the chargee's freedom to carry on business with the charged assets, tends to be regarded as the most important indicator of the nature of the charge[9]. Even this, however, is only a guide. If the chargor enjoys complete freedom to use the assets as he pleases, the charge is almost certainly a floating charge. It is clear, however, that even if the charge imposes some restriction on the chargor's freedom to deal with the assets, it may still be a floating charge[10]. As Hoffmann J observed in *Re Brightlife Ltd*, most well drafted floating charges contain a negative pledge clause which imposes a restriction on the chargor's freedom to deal with the charged assets[11]. Conversely, it is not fatal to the classification of the charge as fixed that the chargee has some freedom to use the assets[12].

Since fixed charges generally give greater protection than floating charges, creditors will seek to take a fixed charge wherever possible. As noted earlier, it was assumed that, given the need for restrictions on the chargee's power to deal with the charged assets, there was an inherent difficulty in creating a fixed charge over assets of a type which in the ordinary way circulate in the course of business, such as stock in trade and book debts. In recent years this view has been challenged. In *Siebe Gorman & Co Ltd v Barclays Bank Ltd*[13] a company granted to the defendant bank a 'first fixed charge' over 'all book debts now and from time to time owing' to the company. The terms of the charge prohibited certain dealings by the company with its book debts and required them to be paid into the company's bank account with the defendants, over which the defendants had a lien. Slade J held that in view of the restrictions placed on the company's freedom to deal with its debts, the charge so created was a fixed charge. It is therefore possible to create a fixed charge over future book debts. However, despite a number of subsequent cases on the same point, it is still not clear when such a charge will be construed as fixed.

It is clear that description of a charge as 'fixed' is not conclusive[14]. Unless the agreement is a 'sham'[15], or was not followed in practice, the court will examine its terms in order to ascertain whether they are consistent with the characteristics of a fixed or floating charge. Later cases have shown that the crucial factor is the debtor's freedom to deal with the debts and their proceeds, but it is not clear what degree of freedom will be held inconsistent with the creation of a fixed charge. It is not necessarily inconsistent with a floating charge that there are some restrictions on the chargor's freedom; thus in *Re Brightlife Ltd*[16], where a charge on debts and their proceeds prohibited the chargor selling, factoring or discounting the debts but allowed it to pay debts it collected into its own bank account and then use the proceeds in its business, it was held that the freedom to deal with the proceeds of debts in this way was inconsistent with there being a fixed charge.

However, in *Re Atlantic Computer Systems plc*[17] a company granted a charge over future instalment payments due to it from customers under computer rental agreements. The charge contained no controls on dealings with the proceeds of the debts but was held to be a fixed charge. The case could perhaps be explained on the basis that the charge related to debts under existing leasing agreements, and therefore to existing, rather than future, debts, but that explanation was rejected in *Re Atlantic Medical Ltd*[18], where a similar charge which covered debts due under both existing rental agreements and any future agreements entered into to replace them was held to be a fixed charge.

If the creation of a fixed charge over book debts requires some restriction on dealings with their proceeds, it will generally be difficult for a chargee other than a clearing bank to take a fixed charge. The chargor will need to collect the debts and pay them into a current account in order to utilise their proceeds in its business. A bank can exercise control over proceeds by requiring them to be paid to an account held with itself, and it is significant that the chargee in *Siebe Gorman* was the chargor's bank[19]. A solution to this problem was found, however, by the chargee in *Re New Bullas Ltd*[20], where a charge over debts provided that (1) the chargor should pay debts into a specified bank account and (2) deal with the proceeds as directed by the chargee but (3) that if no such directions were given, the proceeds should be released from the fixed charge and be subject to a floating charge. It was held that the effect was to create a fixed charge over the debts until they were collected, but a floating charge over their proceeds.

Re New Bullas thus suggests that failure to restrict the chargor's freedom to deal with the proceeds of debts will not be fatal to the construction of a charge over book debts as fixed if the charge treats debts and their proceeds separately. This in turn suggests that it may even be possible to create a fixed charge over raw materials and work in progress if finished stock is treated separately[21]. R*e New Bullas* has, however, been strongly criticised, on grounds both of principle and policy[22]. In particular, it may distort the order of priorities on insolvency: since the charge over book debts is created as a fixed charge[23], it will rank higher in priority than if it were created as a floating charge over book debts, giving the chargee's claims priority over those of the preferential creditors. This will be important where, as is often the case, unrealised book debts are a significant asset in the insolvency. In *Royal Trust Bank Ltd v National Westminster Bank plc* Millett LJ observed: 'I do not see how it can be possible to separate a debt or other receivable from the proceeds of its realisation'[24].

However, this comment was obiter, and *Re New Bullas* has been followed in New Zealand[25].

The law is therefore unclear. There is clear authority that a fixed charge may validly be created over future book debts; however, it is still not clear when such a charge will be held to be created. This question has generated a considerable amount of case law in recent years, but so far without clarifying the issue. Indeed, it is difficult to see how the law could be clarified without an authoritative ruling from the House of Lords, which seems unlikely to happen in the context of insolvency litigation.

1 Companies Act, ss 95 and 395; see 22.0.3.2. It is generally assumed that a floating charge over part only of a class of assets is registrable.
2 Insolvency Act 1986, s 245.
3 Insolvency Act 1986, s 29(1).
4 Such charges have become known as 'lightweight floating charges'. Their effectiveness was upheld in *Re Croftbell* [1990] BCC 781. See generally Oditah [1991] JBL 49.
5 See 22.0.4.2.
6 [1903] 2 Ch 284 at 295.
7 *Re Bond Worth* [1980] Ch D 228 at 248, [1979] 3 All ER [1979] 919 at 954.
8 *Welch v Bowmaker (Ireland) Ltd* [1980] IR 251.
9 See per Millett LJ in *Royal Trust Bank Ltd v National Westminster Bank plc* [1996] BCC 613 at 619.
10 See *Re Brightlife Ltd* [1987] Ch 200; *Re G E Tunbridge Ltd* [1995] 1 BCLC 34; *Royal Trust Bank Ltd v National Westminster Bank plc* [1996] BCC 613; *Re Cosslett (Contractors) Ltd* [1998] Ch 495, [1997] 4 All ER 115; *Re Westmaze Ltd* [1999] BCC 441.
11 [1986] 3 All ER 673 at 677; see also per Millett LJ in *Re Cosslett (Contractors) Ltd* [1998] Ch 495 at 510, [1997] 4 All ER 115 at 127.
12 *Siebe Gorman & Co Ltd v Barclays Bank Ltd* [1979] 2 Lloyd's Rep 142; *Re Cimex Tissues Ltd* [1994] BCC 626.
13 [1979] 2 Lloyd's Rep 142; see also *Re A Company (No 005009 of 1987), ex p Copp* [1989] BCLC 13.
14 *Re Armagh Shoes Ltd* [1984] BCLC 405; *Re New Bullas* [1993] BCLC 1389.
15 See 22.0.4.2.
16 [1987] Ch 200.
17 [1992] 1 All ER 476.
18 [1992] BCLC 386; Bridge (1991) 107 LQR 394.
19 In *Oakdale (Richmond) Ltd v National Westminster Bank plc* [1997] 1 BCLC 63 it was held that restrictions in a fixed charge on book debts, including a requirement that they be paid into an account with the bank, were not anti-competitive contrary to art 85 (now art 80) of the Treaty of Rome.
20 [1992] BCC 251, [1992] BCLC 1389; see Bridge (1994) 110 LQR 340.
21 See Bridge (1994) 110 LQR 340.
22 See Goode (1994) 110 LQR 592; Worthington (1997) 113 LQR 562; cf Berg [1995] JBL 433.
23 A floating charge is defined by the Insolvency Act 1986 as 'a charge which *as created* is a floating charge': s 251.
24 [1996] BCC 613 at 618.
25 *Re Brumark Investments Ltd* [2000] 1 BCLC 353; see McLauchlan (1999) 115 LQR 365.

22.2.2.7 *Crystallisation of a floating charge*

A floating charge continues to 'float' unless and until some event occurs which causes it to 'crystallise'. It then 'descends' to catch the property then in the debtor's hands subject to it. The debtor's authority to deal with assets covered by the charge is then withdrawn and the charge becomes fixed, with the result that the chargee can only deal with the property subject to the charge. 'That which kept the charge hovering has now been released and the force of gravity causes it to settle and fasten upon the subject of the charge within its reach and grasp'[1].

Just as a charge is classified as floating because of the chargor's authority to deal with the charged property, it ceases to float when that authority is withdrawn. The authority is granted to enable it to carry on business, and its authority to deal with its property is therefore impliedly withdrawn, and the charge crystallises, if it goes into liquidation[2], even if it is solvent and is liquidated merely for reconstruction[3] or otherwise ceases trading[4]. The chargor's authority to deal with the property is also withdrawn if the chargee appoints a receiver[5] or takes possession of the charged property.

In *Re Brightlife Ltd*[6] Hoffmann J held that it is for the parties to agree what events will crystallise the charge. Crystallisation occurs because the parties have agreed it. Automatic crystallisation in the situations described above comes about by virtue of an implied term to that effect in the floating charge. The significance of this is that the terms of the charge can therefore exclude crystallisation where it would otherwise occur, However, crystallisation on cessation of business is 'of the essence of a floating charge'[7] and clear words will therefore be needed to exclude the normal rule[8]. The charge may also by its terms provide for crystallisation to occur in other situations. Typically, it may provide for the chargee to serve notice withdrawing the chargor's authority and crystallising the charge on the happening of any prescribed event. This is uncontroversial. However, a charge may also provide for automatic crystallisation on the happening of certain events, such as a creditor of the chargor levying execution or distress on its property, or purporting to create another, prior charge over the same property. Automatic crystallisation is attractive for the chargee, since it occurs without action on his behalf and therefore avoids any delay, but may prejudice third parties who acquire interests in the charged property and who will be bound by the interest of the chargee[9], since it may occur without their knowing, or even being able to know, of the fact of crystallisation. Automatic crystallisation clauses were therefore criticised by the Cork Committee[10] and by a number of commentators, but their validity has been upheld at first instance[11]. In *Re Brightlife Ltd* Hoffmann J was invited to hold automatic crystallisation clauses ineffective on grounds of public policy. However, having observed that public interest requires a balancing of the commercial benefits of the floating charge against the prejudice they cause to unsecured creditors, he concluded that 'arguments for and against the floating charge are matters for Parliament rather than the courts and have been the subject of public debate in and out of Parliament for more than a century' and that, in view of the 'limited and pragmatic interventions by the legislature', it was 'wholly inappropriate for the courts to impose additional restrictive rules on grounds of public policy. It is certainly not for a judge of first instance to proclaim a new head of public policy which no appellate court has even hinted at before'.

1 Hoffmann J in *Re Woodroffes' Musical Instruments Ltd* [1986] Ch 366 at 378.
2 *Re Panama New Zealand and Australia Royal Mail Co* (1870) 5 Ch App 318.
3 *Re Crompton & Co Ltd* [1914] 1 Ch 954.
4 *Re Woodroffes' Musical Instruments Ltd* [1986] Ch 366. In *Re Real Meat Co Ltd* [1996] BCC 254 at 260-261 Chadwick J considered that 'it is now beyond argument, at least in a court of first instance, that under the general law, the cessation of the chargor company's business causes an automatic crystallisation of a floating charge'.
5 *Evans v Rival Granite Quarries* [1910] 2 KB 979 at 999.
6 [1987] Ch 200.
7 Per Nourse J in *Re Woodroffes' Musical Instruments Ltd* [1986] Ch 366 at 377.
8 *Re The Real Meat Company Ltd* [1996] BCC 254.
9 But see Goode, *Legal Problems of Credit and Security* (2nd edn, 1988) p 90, *Commercial Law* (2nd edn, 1995), who argues that a third party without notice of crystallisation who acquires an interest in property subject to the charge takes free of it because the chargor has apparent authority to deal with the property.
10 Report of the Review Committee on Insolvency Law and Practice (1982) (Cmnd 8558), paras 1577–1579.
11 *Re Permanent Houses (Holdings) Ltd* [1988] BCLC 563; they were also approved, obiter, by Hoffmann J in *Re Brightlife Ltd*. They have been upheld in New Zealand (*Re Manurewa Transport Ltd* [1971] NZLR 909) and in Australia (*Stein v Saywell* (1969) 121 CLR 529) but rejected in Canada (*R v Consolidated Churchill Copper Corpn* [1978] 5 WWR 652). Section 100 of the Companies Act 1989 would allow the Secretary of State to make regulations providing for crystallisation to be ineffective until notice of it is filed at the Companies Registry.

22.2.3 Equitable liens[1]

Unlike a common law lien, an equitable lien is a non-possessory security. It is a right over the property of another person to have that property applied towards the satisfaction of a debt. It is therefore very similar to a charge; the main difference is that most equitable liens arise by operation of law and, as a result, are not required to be registered under the Bills of Sale or Companies Acts. Thus the unpaid vendor of land has a lien over the property to secure payment of the price, and a purchaser who pays before conveyance of the property has a similar lien over the property to secure repayment of the price if the transaction is not completed. Similar rights are given to the unpaid vendor and pre-paying purchaser of intangible personal property, but not to sellers and buyers of goods[2]. The unpaid seller does, of course, have a statutory lien over the goods, but that is a legal lien and subsists only so long as the goods remain in the seller's possession.

A non-possessory equitable lien created by agreement is likely to be treated as creating a charge[3] and therefore have to be registered if created by a company. If it relates to goods or book debts it will be registrable as a security bill of sale.

1   See Phillips, 'Equitable Liens: A Search for a Unifying Principle' in Palmer and McKendrick (eds) *Interests in Goods* (2nd edn, 1998).
2   *Re Wait* [1927] 1 Ch 606; above 15.2.3.1.
3   See *Re Welsh Irish Ferries Ltd* [1986] Ch 471.

22.3 Conclusion

The English law of real security can be, and has been, criticised, by commentators and judges alike. As Dillon LJ observed in *Welsh Development Association v Export Finance Corpn*[1], much of the law in this area is out of date; Professor Bridge has described it as 'antiquated'[2]. Its terminology is often outmoded, and it has failed to keep pace with developments in commercial financing, lending and security.

At the heart of the system, and of the problem, is the company charges system. Here, as we have seen, there are a number of unanswered questions and unsatisfactory answers. Issues such as the distinction between fixed and floating charges, whether it is possible to create a fixed charge over book debts, and the effectiveness of automatic crystallisation clauses, have all generated a considerable amount of litigation in recent years, generally without clarifying the law.

The objectives of the law in this area should be to facilitate borrowing, be clear and comprehensible and balance the interests of borrower, lender and the borrower's other actual and potential creditors. The present company charge system falls well short of these objectives. In 1989 Professor Diamond recommended a radical and general reform of security law, but also proposed that some reforms to the company charge system should be made regardless of the reception of his main proposals, and as a matter of urgency. Some of them formed the basis for provisions in Pt IV of the Companies Act 1989. As we have seen, those proposals have been shelved.

However, these proposals would not address the main criticisms of the system. Some would see the floating charge itself as pernicious, favouring the interests of large creditors. The recognition of fixed charges over circulating assets such as book debts only exacerbates the problem. However:

'the floating charge has become so fundamental a part of the financial structure on which the commercial and industrial system of the United Kingdom depends that its abolition can no longer be contemplated'[3].

In any case, it is recognised that abolition of the floating charge would only drive lenders to make greater use of quasi-security devices such as sale and leaseback, achieving much the same effect without the publicity created by registration.

The floating charge is only part of the larger problem, which is the proliferation of arrangements which perform a security function and the need to distinguish between them. As the Crowther Committee observed in 1971[4], by concentrating on the legal form rather than the commercial substance of agreements the law 'lacks any functional basis: distinctions between one type of transaction and another are drawn on the basis of legal abstractions rather than on the basis of commercial reality'. Those distinctions are often difficult to draw, the case law is complex and many of the cases are difficult to reconcile, yet the distinctions have important legal and practical consequences for the parties, their rights against each other and even for third parties. On them may turn the question whether a security is registrable, and therefore invalid if unregistered, or the nature of the creditor's rights in the event of the debtor's default, including the question of entitlement to any surplus received by a creditor who realises his security[5]. The sheer complexity of the law creates uncertainty and causes difficulties for businesses and their legal and financial advisers. For these reasons the Crowther Committee proposed that the law of secured lending should be reformed and rationalised, and that all functional security arrangements should be treated alike, as is done, for instance, in the United States[6].

The Crowther proposals for the functional treatment of consumer credit agreements produced the Consumer Credit Act 1974, but those for a Security and Lending Act were ignored and in 1989 Professor Diamond made almost the same criticisms of the existing law as were made by Crowther almost 20 years earlier[7].

'The English law of security is divided into rigid compartments, making the law fragmented and incoherent. Transactions essentially similar in nature are treated in very different ways . . . This can cause problems when an attempt is made to create a security interest, for a method must be chosen appropriate to the property concerned and the effect that is desired . . . It can also cause problems at the stage of enforcement, for different forms of security interest may have very different consequences . . . The compartmentalisation [of the law] inevitably gives rise to a law that is complex and uncertain . . . [P]erfectly legitimate business activities are in consequence attended with unnecessary expense and delay. Because issues are decided by reference to rules that evolved for different purposes the law is capable of acting unfairly and may fail to hold a just balance as between the parties'[8].

He, too, therefore proposed radical reform to the law. Its aim would not be to make it more difficult to take security, but, if anything, to make it easier to do so effectively. Like Crowther, he proposed a functional system, based on the model of the US Uniform Commercial Code, art 9. It would apply to all consensual securities[9], including hire purchase, conditional sale and retention of title agreements. Leases for three years or more would be included. Pledges, too, would be covered by the proposed scheme, although they would be exempt from some of its requirements. All securities would be treated broadly alike for most purposes.

The company charges system would be abolished. All non-possessory securities would be perfected by a 'notice filing' system: the creditor would not have to register individual transactions but simply a financing statement putting on record that a named debtor may have created a security interest in his favour and indicating the type of property affected. Such a system would not provide full details of security created, but would provide a warning to later creditors. Registration would not be compulsory, but priority between competing securities would be determined by priority of filing. However, purchase money security interests (PMSIs), including hire purchase conditional sale and some retention of title agreements[10], would be given special treatment, and would automatically have priority over all conflicting securities affecting the same property provided they had been perfected by filing. To avoid imposing unmanageable burdens, it would not be applicable to most security interests created by consumers, although interests over high value items such as cars would be covered. The register would be computerised to facilitate searching by creditors. Creditors secured by any form of security interest covered by the new law would have the same powers of enforcement, similar to those currently available to a mortgagee.

These are far-reaching proposals. In 1991 the Secretary of State for Trade and Industry announced that, in view of the complexity and cost of reform, they would not be implemented[11]. The DTI's 1994 consultation on the company charges system proposed, as one option, replacement of the existing system by a notice filing system, but the system envisaged was far more limited than that proposed by Professor Diamond. It would apply only to companies and would replace the existing system of registration of charges. It was aimed at facilitating the registration of securities rather than rationalising the law on a functional basis.

Of course, no system is a panacea. The quest for new security devices, extended rights and so on is likely to continue and will ever pose problems of classification for the law. The American system favoured by Crowther and Diamond has been criticised. Professor Gilmore, one of the main authors of the American system, said in 1981 that 'the sad truth is that personal property security law is well on its way to becoming as fragmented and quite as complex as ever it was in the bad old days before the Code'[12]. Nevertheless, Professor Diamond's proposals would greatly have improved the law. It is unfortunate that they have been shelved. Most common law jurisdictions have now, or are planning to, adopt legislation on the model of the American system. The failure to address the shortcomings of English security law is an indictment of our commercial law. As Professor Goode has written, 'the world moves on and we must move with it. As we enter the next millennium it is time for the unified personal property security interest to take hold in these islands'[13].

1 [1992] BCLC 148.
2 [1992] JBL 1 at 2.
3 Report of the Review Committee on Insolvency Law and Practice (1982) (Cmnd 8558), para 110.
4 Report on Consumer Credit (1971) (Cmnd 4596), para 1.3.6.
5 See eg the difficult questions this raises in relation to retention of title clauses: see 18.4.3.
6 By art 9 of the Uniform Commercial Code.
7 DTI, *A Review of Security Interests in Property* (1989).
8 At paras 8.24–8.29.
9 At para 9.32.
10 A simple retention of title clause retaining title to the goods supplied and any proceeds of their resale as security for the price of those goods would be treated as a PMSI for this purpose. More extensive clauses claiming rights in manufactured products or retaining title as security for other sums would be subject to the normal priority rules.
11 24 April 1991, *Hansard* HC Vol 189 col 482.

12 Gilmore, 'The Good Faith Purchase Idea and the Uniform Commercial Code: Confessions of a Repentant Draftsman' (1981) 15 Georgia LR 605. See also Ziegel (1990) 28 Alberta LR commenting on the Canadian system.

13 Goode, 'The Exodus of the Floating Charge' in Feldman and Meisel (eds),*Corporate and Commercial Law: Recent Developments*, p 203.

Chapter 23

Personal Security

23.0 Introduction

Personal security is provided by means of contracts of suretyship, by which one person, the surety, undertakes to be answerable for the contractual performance of another. Contracts of suretyship may be used to secure performance of any kind of contractual undertaking, but they are most commonly used to secure payment of debts. The surety arrangement may be constituted by one, two or three separate contracts. In a simple case there will be a contract between the creditor and debtor and a separate contract between creditor and surety, creating a tripartite relationship as shown in Fig 1.

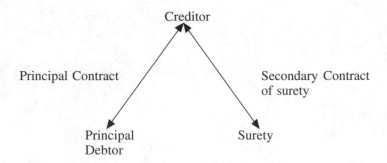

A number of variations on this model are possible. The relationship between debtor and surety may or may not be contractual. In that case the arrangement may be constituted by one contract to which creditor, debtor and surety are all parties, or there may be three separate contracts. The surety may contract with the creditor as if he were a principal debtor, but stand as a surety vis-à-vis the principal debtor[1]. The security may be provided at the request of creditor or debtor. Even in the absence of a contract between principal debtor and surety, however, the surety will have certain rights against the principal debtor. We must therefore consider separately the relationships between creditor and surety and between surety and principal debtor.

---

1   *Duncan Fox & Co v North and South Wales Bank* (1880) 6 App Cas 1 at 11, per Lord Selborne.

23.0.1 *Uses of suretyship*

Contracts of suretyship are commonly used to secure the payment of debts. Typical examples of their use are a parent guaranteeing a debt of a minor child, a company guaranteeing the debts of its subsidiary or of another company in its group, or directors of a company guaranteeing the company's debts. Guarantees are especially important in the context of international trade, where traders may have particularly strong concerns about the ability or willingness of their contractual partners to perform their obligations, or their own ability to enforce performance by litigation against an overseas defendant, and therefore seek a guarantee of performance from someone within the jurisdiction of their own national courts. Thus, to support exports, banks provide a variety of facilities which may be used to guarantee performance of contracts or payment[1], del credere agents guarantee that any third parties they introduce to their principals will perform their contractual obligations[2], and the UK government provides institutional support for exports by offering guarantees of payment to exporters through the Export Credits Guarantee Department.

A contract of suretyship may stand alone, in which case the creditor merely has the security of a personal, contractual, undertaking from the surety. Often, however, a contract of suretyship is reinforced by the surety providing real security to secure his undertaking. Security may also be provided by the surety simply providing security over his or her property to secure another's debt, but without entering into any personal undertaking to pay the debt[3]. For instance, directors of a company might charge their homes to secure a loan made to the company. In that case, if the company defaults the creditor has the rights of a chargee over the directors' homes, which may be appropriated to the payment of the company's debt, but has no right to pursue the directors personally for the amount of the debt or any shortfall after sale of the charged property. Nevertheless, the directors in such a case would be sureties of the company's debt and have the rights of sureties vis-à-vis both the creditor and the company.

1   See ch 34.
2   See 3.2.3.
3   *Smith v Wood* [1929] 1 Ch 14; *Re Conley* [1938] 2 All ER 127; *Re Bank of Credit and Commerce International (No 8)* [1998] AC 214, [1997] 4 All ER 568; see 22.2.2.1.

23.0.2 *Guarantees and indemnities*

A contract of suretyship may be either a guarantee or an indemnity. Unfortunately, neither word is used consistently. Both are used to describe arrangements other than suretyship. 'Guarantee' may mean a manufacturer's or supplier's undertaking about the quality of goods or services, which may or may not be contractual[1]; sometimes it may mean no more than 'term of a contract' or 'warranty'[2]. 'Indemnity' may mean 'recompense for any loss or liability which one person has incurred, whether the duty to indemnify comes from an agreement or not'[3]. The expression 'contract of indemnity' is often used to describe a particular type of insurance contract[4]. Within the context of suretyship the two words are often used almost interchangeably; strictly speaking, however, there is a fundamental difference between contracts of guarantee and contracts of indemnity. The surety's liability under a guarantee is secondary to and dependent on that of the principal debtor, whereas under an indemnity the surety undertakes a separate liability to the creditor, as principal. As Holroyd Pearce LJ explained in *Yeoman Credit Ltd v Latter*[5]:

> 'An indemnity is a contract by one party to keep the other harmless against loss, but a contract of guarantee is a contract to answer for the debt, default or miscarriage of another who is to be primarily liable to the promisee'.

Thus, to take a much cited illustration, if A agrees to supply goods to B on the strength of C's promise that 'if he does not pay you, I will', C undertakes a secondary liability for the price, dependent on B's, and therefore provides a guarantee; but if C's promise is 'I will see you paid', C is providing a separate undertaking as principal and therefore an indemnity[6].

Important legal consequences follow from the difference between the two types of transaction. Thus contracts of guarantee, but not indemnity, must comply with the formal requirements of the Statute of Frauds[7] and the distinction between the two was largely worked out in cases decided under that Act. Moreover, since a guarantor's liability is dependent on and defined by that of the principal debtor, a guarantor is not liable if the principal contract is invalid for any reason[8] but the liability of an indemnitor[9] is independent of that of the principal debtor and he therefore remains liable even if the contract between creditor and debtor is invalid[10]. For the same reason, release by the creditor of the principal debtor will also release a guarantor, but not an indemnitor[11].

Unfortunately, despite the legal consequences which follow from it, the distinction between a guarantee and an indemnity is often fine and difficult to draw. As Harman LJ observed in *Yeoman Credit Ltd v Latter*[12] it has 'raised many hair-splitting distinctions of exactly the kind which brings the law into hatred, ridicule and contempt by the public'. In drawing the distinction the court must examine the contract and 'have regard to its essential nature'[13]. The fact that a contract is described by the parties as a 'guarantee' or 'indemnity' is therefore not conclusive of its legal effect. In *Yeoman Credit Ltd v Latter* a finance company let a car to an infant. The defendant, an adult, entered into a separate contract described as a 'hire purchase indemnity and undertaking', by which he undertook to indemnify the finance company against 'any loss resulting from or arising out of' the hire purchase agreement and which defined the company's loss as the full amount which the hirer would have had to pay under the hire purchase contract to acquire the car, plus any expenses incurred by the company in exercising its rights under the contract, less any amount actually paid by the hirer. When the hirer defaulted, the finance company, which could not sue him under the hire purchase contract because of his infancy, claimed against the defendant under the 'indemnity'. The defendant argued that it was really a guarantee, that his liability therefore depended on that of the hirer, and that since the principal contract was void under the Infants Relief Act 1874, there was nothing for him to guarantee. The Court of Appeal concluded, however, that the contract was, as it purported to be, an indemnity under which the defendant undertook liability separate from that of the hirer. In effect, the contract required the defendant to ensure that the finance company received the full amount it expected to receive under the hire purchase contract and the defendant's rights and obligations under it were different in a number of respects from those of the hirer under the hire purchase contract. Moreover, all the parties knew that the hirer was an infant. The reason for requiring the defendant's indemnity was to ensure that the finance company would receive full payment if the hirer defaulted. A guarantee would not have provided that protection and the majority of the court[14] therefore concluded that the parties must be taken to have intended to create an indemnity, not a guarantee[15].

Essentially, the classification of the contract as a guarantee or indemnity therefore requires the court to ascertain the intention of the parties. The task of classification is made more difficult by the fact that the parties may, in effect, create a hybrid of the two types. Even where a contract is classified as one of guarantee, 'it is open to the parties expressly to exclude or vary any of their mutual rights or obligations which would otherwise result from its being classifiable as a guarantee'[16]. In other words, questions other than the application of the Statute of Frauds may be answered by reference to the express and implied terms of the contract rather than by classifying the contract as a guarantee or indemnity. As Lord Reid said, 'Parties are free to make any agreement they like and we must, I think, determine just what this agreement means'[17].

The problem of 'hybrid' surety contracts is illustrated by the case of *Heald v O'Connor*[18], in which the defendant 'guaranteed' the obligations of a company under a debenture. The debenture was void[19] and the defendant argued that his undertaking was also, therefore, void. The surety agreement was described as a 'guarantee' and provided that the guarantor would pay 'if and whenever the company makes default' but it also included what is sometimes referred to as a 'principal debtor clause', which provided that his liability should be 'as a primary obligor and not merely as a surety and shall not be impaired or discharged by reason of any time or other indulgence' granted by the creditor to the debtor company. Fisher J approached the question as one of construction of the contract. The assumption by the surety of primary liability is a hallmark of an indemnity but he held that the reference to the primary liability here was intended only to exclude the rule which would otherwise apply, that where the creditor agrees to extend the time for payment or otherwise varies the terms of his contract with the debtor, the surety under a guarantee is discharged from liability[20]. The remainder of the contract was consistent with its being properly construed as a guarantee. The defendant had agreed to pay those sums which the principal debtor could lawfully be called upon to pay but did not pay and as the principal contract was void, and no moneys were payable.

In the following paragraphs the word 'guarantee' will be used to refer to both guarantees and indemnities except where there are differences between them.

1 See 13.2.
2 See per Lord Diplock in *Moschi v Lep Air Services* [1973] AC 331 at 349.
3 *Chitty on Contracts* (28th edn, 1999) para 44-011.
4 See ch 35.
5 [1961] 1 WLR 828 at 831.
6 See *Birkmyr v Darnell* (1704) 1 Salk 27 at 28.
7 Section 4; see 23.1.1.3.
8 See *Coutts & Co v Browne-Lecky* [1947] KB 104; *Heald v O'Connor* [1971] 1 WLR 497.
9 Other writers use the word 'indemnifier' to refer to the person who gives an indemnity, but that seems more appropriate to describe a person who pays an indemnity than one who undertakes to do so. 'Indemnitor' has been used in the United States to describe a person who gives an indemnity and seems a more appropriate word. It is therefore used here.
10 *Yeoman Credit Ltd v Latter* [1961] 1 WLR 828.
11 See 23.1.4.1.
12 [1961] 1 WLR 828 at 835.
13 Per Holroyd Pearce LJ in *Yeoman Credit Ltd v Latter* [1961] 1 WLR 828 at 831.
14 Davies LJ dissented on this point.
15 See also *Wauthier v Wilson* (1912) 28 TLR 239.
16 Per Lord Diplock in *Moschi v Lep Air Services* [1973] AC 331 at 349.
17 *Moschi v Lep Air Services* [1973] AC 331 at 344.
18 [1971] 1 WLR 497.

19 By reason of s 54 of the Companies Act 1948.
20 See 23.1.4. Another effect of such a clause is to make the surety's obligation immediately enforceable without prior demand by the creditor: see *MS Fashions Ltd v Bank of Credit and Commerce International (No 2)* [1993] Ch 425, [1993] 2 All ER 769, CA; cf *Re Bank of Credit and Commerce International Ltd (No 8)* [1994] 3 All ER 565.

23.0.3   *Types of guarantee*

There are a number of different types of guarantee, classification depending on the nature of the obligation undertaken by the surety and therefore on the construction of the agreement in any particular case. The following distinctions are particularly important.

(a)   Discrete and continuing guarantees
A guarantee may be used to secure both fixed sum and running account credit. In the former case the guarantee is described as 'discrete': the guarantor guarantees the debtor's liability under one particular obligation and, once the contract of guarantee is concluded, he is only released from his obligation on payment of the whole of the guaranteed debt. Running account credit, such as an overdraft, is normally secured by a continuing guarantee. Such a guarantee normally takes effect as a standing offer which is accepted by the creditor each time an advance is made. The guarantor is liable for the sum outstanding from the debtor from time to time and is not released merely because the guaranteed account is in credit at any time. On the other hand, since the guarantee is a standing offer, the guarantor can normally bring his liability to an end at any time by revoking his offer, subject to any restrictions imposed by terms of the guarantee itself[1].

(b)   Demand and conditional guarantees
The terms of the guarantee may impose conditions which must be fulfilled before the guarantor can be required to make any payment under it: for instance, the creditor may be required to produce evidence of the principal debtor's default. More commonly, however, the guarantee will be payable on demand by the creditor.

1 Normally, the guarantee will require the guarantor to give notice, enabling the creditor to claim on the guarantee during the notice period. The effect of notice depends on the proper construction of the agreement: see *Bank of Credit and Commerce International Ltd v Simjee* [1997] CLC 135, below 23.1.3.

23.0.4   *Guarantees and bonds*

The distinction between demand and conditional undertakings is especially important in relation to certain types of instrument commonly used in international trading and in the construction industry to secure performance of contractual obligations, often other than the payment of money. Such instruments take a number of forms and are referred to by several names, including 'performance guarantees', 'performance bonds' and 'standby credits'. In each case a bank or other financial institution provides an undertaking – a 'bond' – normally in the form of a deed, to pay a sum of money on a specified event. Normally, the bond consists of a promise to pay a sum of money, but states that the party providing the bond shall be discharged if either the bond is satisfied or the party whose performance is secured performs its contract. In some cases the bank's undertaking is conditional, for instance on the production of a court judgment or a certificate that the contractor whose performance is secured is in breach of contract. However, in many cases the bank's undertaking is simply to pay on demand.

Under the type of bond used in international trade, the bank's undertaking is normally as a principal, rather than as a guarantor. Such arrangements perform the same function as guarantees but the bank's undertaking to pay is generally construed as independent of the underlying contract whose performance it secures; they have largely been equated with bankers' commercial credits and they are therefore considered further below[1]. The nature of the undertaking will, however, depend on the proper construction of the bond. The importance of the distinction is illustrated by *Trafalgar House Construction (Regions) Ltd v General Surety and Guarantee Ltd*[2], in which the House of Lords had to construe a typical form of bond used in the construction industry. The bond had been issued to secure performance by a sub-contractor employed on a construction contract, and consisted of an undertaking to pay a sum of money but provided that 'this obligation shall be null and void' if either (a) the sub-contractor performed its contract or (b) 'on default by the sub-contractor the Surety shall satisfy and discharge the damages sustained by the Main contractor thereby'. The Court of Appeal considered that the commercial purpose of the bond was to provide the main contractor with an immediate source of finance if the sub-contractor were in default, and therefore construed the 'surety's' undertaking as one of principal to pay the sum of the bond in the event of a breach of contract by the sub-contractor, without the main contractor having to prove it had suffered any loss or damage caused by the breach. The House of Lords unanimously rejected this interpretation and held that the undertaking was a genuine guarantee. The main contractor was therefore only entitled to demand payment if and to the extent that it had suffered damage as a result of the sub-contractor's breach. Although a guarantee will often be in the form of an undertaking by the guarantor to 'see to it' that the guaranteed obligation is performed[3], that is not always the case and the present undertaking was not in that form. Their Lordships were influenced by the fact that the bond was in a form which had been in use for over 150 years[4] but the key factor was that the language of the bond – for instance, referring to the provider of the bond as 'surety' – was consistent with its being a true guarantee[5].

1 See 34.3.
2 [1995] 3 All ER 737.
3 See *Moschi v Lep Air Services Ltd* [1973] AC 331, below 23.1.3.
4 Lord Jauncey was particularly critical of the archaic language used 'which is quite unnecessarily lengthy, which obfuscates its true purpose and which is likely to give rise to unnecessary arguments and litigation as to its meaning': [1995] 3 All ER 737 at 745.
5 Their Lordships were possibly concerned that interpreting the bond as an independent undertaking would provide the main contractor with an apparent windfall, unconnected to any loss they might suffer. A solution to this problem has now been found in relation to performance bonds: see *Cargill International v Bangladesh Sugar and Food Industries* [1998] 2 All ER 406, [1998] 1 WLR 461, below 34.3.

23.1 Relations between creditor and surety

'The law of guarantee is part of the law of contract'[1]. The general rules of contract law concerned with the creation and validity of contracts apply to suretyship contracts and the rights and obligations of creditor and surety are defined, primarily, by the terms of the contract between them. However, the general rules are modified in some respects in their application and are supplemented by some special rules applicable only to suretyship contracts.

1   Lord Diplock in *Moschi v Lep Air Services* [1973] AC 331 at 346.

23.1.1   *Formation of guarantees*

An effective and binding guarantee or indemnity must comply with the requirements for the creation of a valid contract; in addition, it may have to comply with special statutory formalities under the Statute of Frauds 1677 or the Consumer Credit Act 1974.

23.1.1.1   *Consideration*

If the surety's undertaking is to be binding it must either be supported by consideration moving from the creditor, or be contained in a deed.

Where the surety is provided before credit is advanced, consideration may be provided by the creditor promising to make the advance, in which case there is a bilateral contract between surety and creditor which binds the creditor to make the advance. It is more normal, however, for the surety's undertaking to be a unilateral one, where the surety's offer is accepted, and consideration for it is provided, by the creditor actually making the advance. In that case the creditor is not bound to make the advance, but if it does so, the surety is bound. The surety's promise can be revoked at any time before the credit is advanced. In either case it is irrelevant that the credit is provided to the debtor, not to the guarantor, and that the guarantor receives no benefit: the detriment to the creditor is sufficient consideration.

A guarantee given to secure an existing debt after the credit is advanced is prima facie ineffective because the advance itself is past consideration[1]. However, such a guarantee will be binding if contained in a deed or if the creditor provides fresh consideration. Consideration may be provided by the creditor either promising to forbear from suing the debtor or actually so forbearing at the request of the surety. A guarantee may be provided to an existing creditor to persuade it to make further advances and secure both the new advances and the existing debt. Thus, for instance, if a company has an overdraft of £50,000, the bank may agree to allow it to make further drawings in return for a guarantee of the whole overdraft by its directors. The bank's agreement to allow further drawings provides consideration for the guarantee both of those further drawings and of the existing debt[2].

1   *Astley Industrial Trust Ltd v Grimston Electric Tools* (1965) Sol Jo 149.
2   *Johnston v Nicholls* (1845) 1 CB 251.

23.1.1.2   *Offer and acceptance*

Where, as is normal, the surety's undertaking is a unilateral one, given in consideration of the creditor actually advancing credit, it is accepted by the advance and can be revoked at any time before credit is advanced. Where the guarantee is a continuing one of a revolving credit facility, it is necessary to decide whether the credit facility is entire or divisible. If it is entire, the surety is bound as soon as credit is first advanced. If, however, the credit facility is divisible, the surety's promise is treated as a standing offer, which is accepted each time a fresh advance is made, and which therefore can be revoked, as to the future, at any time. Thus, for instance, a guarantee of a bank overdraft is normally treated as a continuing guarantee of a divisible facility. As each drawing is made, the guarantor's liability is increased, but the guarantor can at any time put an end to his liability by revoking his guarantee, and he will have no liability in respect of borrowings after such revocation. Bank guarantees normally require the guarantor to give notice of revocation, and the balance of opinion favours the view that such a provision is binding on the guarantor[1], but there is no decided case on the point. Once credit has actually been granted to the debtor, the first advance may be regarded as providing consideration for the guarantor's promise to give notice. Where no credit has actually been advanced, the position is less clear. It may be that the mere making available of the overdraft facility could be regarded as sufficient consideration for the guarantor's promise to give notice, since that promise is clearly intended to protect the creditor by allowing it either to terminate the facility or to take alternative security.

1 Pagets' *Law of Banking* (11th edn, 1996) p 636; Chorley, *Law of Banking* (6th edn, 1974) p 341.

23.1.1.3 *Statute of Frauds 1677*

The Statute of Frauds was passed to prevent the making of fraudulent contractual claims by requiring certain classes of contract to be made, or evidenced, in writing. Many of its provisions have been repealed or replaced, but s 4, which applies to contracts of guarantee, remains in force. It provides that:

> 'no action shall be brought whereby to charge the defendant upon any speciall promise to answere for the debt, default or miscarriages of another person unlesse the agreement upon which such action shall be brought, or some memorandum or note thereof, shall be in writing, and signed by the party to be charged therewith or some other person thereunto by him lawfully authorised'.

The language (and spelling) of the section is archaic but its effect, as explained in case law, is that contracts of guarantee are not enforceable unless either made in writing or evidenced in writing and, in either case, signed by the guarantor or his agent. The expression 'to answer for' means 'to accept liability for[1]' or 'to be responsible for[2]'. Since the section only applies to contracts whereby one person agrees to 'answer for' the debt of another, it does not apply to contracts of indemnity by which the surety undertakes a personal, primary liability[3] and the distinction between contracts of guarantee and of indemnity was largely worked out in this context.

A guarantee which does not comply with the section is unenforceable, although it remains a valid contract and therefore can be made enforceable if a written memorandum of it is executed before proceedings are commenced. The impact of the section on modern commercial transactions is limited, since guarantees given to financial institutions are normally in writing and, indeed, on the institution's standard form. However, transactions do occasionally fall foul of the section; thus, for instance, where a debtor secured a loan to him by depositing with a bank the title deeds to property, title to which was registered in the names of his daughters, it was held that the deposit was by way of the daughters' guaranteeing the loan to their father and therefore unenforceable in the absence of a written memorandum[4].

The House of Lords explained in *Elpis Maritime Co Ltd v Marti Chartering Co Inc*[5] that the section can be satisfied either by a written agreement, signed by or on behalf of the guarantor, or by a written memorandum, signed by or on behalf of the guarantor, recording a prior agreement. The owners of a ship entered into a charterparty and during negotiations the charterers' agents orally agreed to guarantee certain payments under the charter. A written charterparty was then concluded, with a number of additional pages which included a written statement that the agents guaranteed payment of demurrage and freight. The agents signed the front sheet of the contract 'for and on behalf of charterers as brokers only' but signed the additional pages simply with their name. It was held that since there was a valid, pre-existing contract, there was sufficient memorandum to satisfy the section and it was irrelevant whether the brokers had signed the additional page as agents or on their own behalf. The section merely requires a written memorandum, signed by the person to be bound; it is not necessary that he should have signed on his own behalf. The result would have been different if there had been no pre-existing contract, since in that case it would have been necessary that the agents signed for themselves in order to make them party to the contract.

Where there is a written contract which complies with the requirements of the section, extrinsic, parol evidence may be adduced to explain its terms[6].

1   Per Lord Diplock in *Moschi v Lep Air Services Ltd* [1973] AC 331 at 347.
2   Per Lord Simon of Glaisdale [1973] AC 331 at 357.
3   *Birkmyr v Darnell* (1704) 1 Salk 27.
4   *Deutsche Bank Ltd v Ibrahim* [1992] 1 Bank LR 267.
5   [1992] 1 AC 21, [1991] 3 All ER 758.
6   *Perrylease Ltd v Imecar AG* [1988] 1 WLR 463.

23.1.1.4 *Consumer Credit Act 1974*

Section 105 of the Consumer Credit Act requires any security provided in relation to a regulated agreement[1] to be in writing, in the form prescribed by the section and regulations made under it[2] and signed by or on behalf of the surety. The section applies to guarantees and indemnities. A security which does not comply with the section is 'improperly executed' and cannot be enforced against the surety without an order of the court[3].

1   See ch 25.
2   Consumer Credit Agreements Regulations 1983, SI 1983/1553, as amended; Consumer Credit (Guarantees and Indemnities) Regulations 1983, SI 1983/1556.
3   See 26.1.

23.1.2 *Validity of the surety contract*

A contract of suretyship, like another contract, may be invalidated as a result of factors affecting its formation such as misrepresentation[1], duress or undue influence[2] or mistake[3]. However, in this context it is necessary to consider the effects not only of the conduct of the creditor, but also of the debtor.

1   See 2.4.2.
2   See 2.4.3.
3   See 2.4.1.

23.1.2.1   *Invalidity due to the conduct of the creditor*

A contract of suretyship may be avoided if it was obtained as a result of any duress, undue influence or misrepresentation by the creditor.

The contract may be set aside on the grounds of undue influence if it is shown that the creditor has actually exerted a dominating influence over the surety[1], but the relationship between creditor and surety will not normally give rise to a presumption of undue influence. Problems often arise where one customer of a bank is required to guarantee a loan to another customer. It is clear that the relationship between banker and customer does not normally give rise to a presumption of undue influence[2] but it may be possible to establish that a bank or other creditor exercised undue influence over a particular surety, for instance, if it is shown that the surety relied on the creditor for advice[3]. A surety owes no general duty to explain the terms of the guarantee[4] but if a bank which takes a guarantee from a customer offers an explanation of its terms it owes a duty of care to the customer not to misstate the effect of the guarantee and may be liable in damages if it is negligent in its explanation[5]. In 1992, following recommendations of the Review Committee on Banking Services Law and Practice[6], the banks introduced a voluntary code of practice to govern their dealings with private customers. Under the current version banks undertake to explain to sureties the nature of the liability they incur[7].

Similarly, a guarantee will be voidable if it is entered into as a result of misrepresentation by the creditor. Despite some early nineteenth century cases[8] to the contrary, it is now settled that a contract of suretyship, unlike a contract of insurance, is not a contract uberrimae fidei so as to impose a duty on the creditor to disclose to the surety material facts in his knowledge.

> 'There is not to be a duty on a bank to disclose too much to a guarantor or commercial life becomes impossible. In particular it is clear that a bank is under no obligation to disclose to a guarantor facts relating to the impecuniosity or past track record of a debtor, for it would be understood by a surety that the existence of financial problems on the part of the debtor was just the reason why a guarantee was being required'[9].

A limited duty of disclosure is recognised, however. Cases concerned with fidelity guarantees, where the surety guarantees the fidelity of an employee of the creditor, have established that the employer/creditor is under a duty to disclose any previous dishonesty of the employee; failure to do so is treated as an implied misrepresentation because the employer is taken to know that the surety contracts on the basis of an assumption that the employer believes the employee to be honest. This approach has been extended to other cases, so that the creditor is required to disclose to the surety any unusual features of the principal contract which make it different from that which the surety would naturally expect. Thus where a surety granted a power of attorney to a debtor to allow him to use the surety's Treasury stock as security for a loan, it was held that the bank providing the loan was under a duty to disclose to the surety that the terms of the loan agreement provided for the treasury stock to be sold and its proceeds used to repay the loan, since as a result there was not merely a risk, but a certainty, that the stock would be realised to repay the loan, and there was no incentive for the principal debtor to repay it[10]. In *Geest plc v Fyffes plc*[11] Colman J concluded, following a review of the case law and authority from Australia[12], New Zealand[13] and Canada[14], that the basis of the disclosure rule is that the contract is voidable for an implied misrepresentation by the creditor where in view of the nature of the contract and the conduct of the creditor 'a reasonable potential surety would naturally assume that the true state of affairs did not exist and that, had it existed, he would in all the circumstances necessarily have been informed of it'[15].

1　See 2.4.3.
2　*National Westminster Bank plc v Morgan* [1985] AC 686.
3　*Lloyds Bank Ltd v Bundy* [1975] QB 326.
4　*Barclays Bank plc v Khaira* [1992] 1 WLR 623.
5　*Cornish v Midland Bank plc* [1985] 3 All ER 513.
6　(1989) (Cmnd 622).
7　*The Banking Code*, para 3.14.
8　Eg *Railton v Matthews* (1844) 10 Cl & Fin 934.
9　Michael Burton QC in *Levett v Barclays Bank plc* [1995] 2 All ER 615 at 627. The surety may request such information. Under the Banking Code the banks warn customers that they may be asked to consent to the disclosure to the surety or their legal adviser of confidential financial information: para 3.14.
10　*Levett v Barclays Bank plc* [1995] 2 All ER 615; see Berg [1995] LMCLQ 331; see also *Hamilton v Watson* (1845) 12 CL & Fin 109 at 119.
11　[1999] 1 All ER (Comm) 672.
12　*Commercial Bank of Australia Ltd v Amadio* (1983) 151 CLR 447.
13　*Westpac Securities Ltd v Dickie* [1991] 1 NZLR 657.
14　*Toronto Dominion Bank v Rooke* (1983) 49 BCLR 168.
15　[1999] 1 All ER (Comm) 672 at 683.

23.1.2.2　*Invalidity due to the conduct of the debtor*

A guarantee transaction involves three parties. Of the three, the guarantor generally has least to gain from the transaction. The law has therefore been concerned to protect guarantors. Indeed, awareness of the inherent risk of fraud was the reason for the application of the Statute of Frauds to contracts of guarantee[1]. For much the same reason it is recognised that a guarantee may be invalidated by duress, undue influence or misrepresentation by the debtor. The problem typically arises where A, needing finance, exerts improper pressure or influence on B to persuade B to guarantee a loan or other financial accommodation provided to A by a creditor, C. Often, B will be required to provide further security over his/her property to secure the guarantee. The most common example of this situation in recent years has involved a wife providing a guarantee of a loan to her husband, often for the purposes of his business, by joining in a mortgage over the matrimonial home in which she has an interest. As Lord Browne-Wilkinson explained in the leading case of *Barclays Bank plc v O'Brien*[2], social changes have made this type of situation more common. Wealth is now more widely distributed through society. For many people, a large proportion is often tied up in the family home, which is often jointly owned. If the proprietor of a small business approaches a financial institution for a loan, it will generally want security. In many cases the main, or even only, significant capital asset over which security can be offered will be the family home, jointly owned by the applicant for finance and his/her spouse.

If A exerts improper pressure over B in order to procure his/her agreement to provide a guarantee, should the guarantee itself, a transaction between B and C, be affected? If so, on what basis? In a series of cases decided between 1979 and 1992 it was held that C was affected by A's misconduct where C appointed A his agent to obtain B's execution of the guarantee. However, the law was reviewed and clarified by the House of Lords in *Barclays Bank plc v O'Brien*[3], where it was held that A's undue influence, misrepresentation or duress gives B an equity, as against A, to have the guarantee set aside[4]. That equity binds the creditor, C, if either (i) A is the agent of C or (ii) C has actual or constructive notice of the facts giving rise to the equity. Agency will be rare. C will be taken to have constructive notice of B's equity where the facts are such as to put C on inquiry as to the circumstances in which B agreed to provide the security. This will be the case where C is aware that there is a close emotional relationship between A and B and the transaction is solely for the financial benefit of A. Thus where a wife guarantees her husband's debt, the bank is put on inquiry, and thus has constructive notice of any improper conduct by the husband, because:

'(a) the transaction is on its face not to the financial advantage of the wife; and (b) there is a substantial risk in transactions of that kind that, in procuring the wife to act as surety, the husband has committed a legal or equitable wrong that entitles the wife to set aside the transaction'[5].

As the House of Lords emphasised, the *O'Brien* principle is not restricted to wives standing surety for their husbands but applies to all cases 'where there is an emotional relationship between cohabitees' if the creditor is aware of their cohabitation[6] and in other cases where the creditor is 'aware that the surety reposes trust and confidence in the principal debtor in relation to his financial affairs'. It can therefore apply as between a non-cohabiting couple[7], and where parents stand surety for a loan to their child[8]; and in *Crédit Lyonnais Bank Nederland NV v Burch*[9] the Court of Appeal held that the principle applied where a junior employee gave an unlimited guarantee of her employer's liabilities, secured by a charge on her flat[10].

It must be emphasised that the bank's security is only invalidated if the principal debtor's conduct does give rise to some invalidating factor, such as misrepresentation or undue influence, and the creditor has notice (actual or constructive) of that fact. The creditor will only be held to have notice if both the requirements above are satisfied – ie the creditor is aware of the relationship between the parties *and* that the transaction is not to the financial advantage of the guarantor. However, it is clear that the more disadvantageous the transaction the more likely will be the inference that it must be the result of some improper pressure[11]. Conversely, if the transaction secured is for the benefit of the guarantor as well as the debtor, the creditor is not fixed with constructive notice of the debtor's misconduct even if the transaction was obtained by misrepresentation or undue influence. Thus it did not apply where undue influence was used by a husband to persuade his wife to execute a mortgage on their matrimonial home to secure a loan which, the creditor believed, was to be used to pay off the existing mortgage on the property and buy a holiday home[12].

The *O'Brien* principle thus protects the guarantor by attributing constructive notice of the principal debtor's wrongdoing to the creditor. However, the courts have been alert to the need to avoid imposing excessive burdens on creditors. The import of the doctrine of constructive notice into commercial transactions has always been resisted because of the uncertainty it would bring.

'In the law of commercial transactions certainty is important. It is particularly important in relation to security documents. It is in the interests both of lenders and borrowers that there should be this certainty. This certainty should not be undermined by deciding individual cases in a way that is believed not to cause injustice as between the parties to that transaction but which departs from the clear structure of the law as laid down in authority'[13].

Moreover, it has been recognised that the law must not make it impossible for family homes to be used as security. Creditors need to know what they should do in order to avoid being fixed with constructive notice of any wrongdoing: the structure of this type of transaction is:

'so commonplace, and the efficient funding of small businesses so dependent on its validity, that the parties, and in particular the lending institutions, must be entitled to proceed in accordance with a settled practice which is effective to secure the validity of the transaction while at the same time affording the wife the protection of proper legal advice'[14].

It is important that lending institutions should not be subject to excessive burdens which would be time consuming and expensive and thus increase the cost of borrowing.

In *O'Brien* Lord Browne-Wilkinson suggested that the creditor should require the guarantor to attend a private meeting with a representative of the creditor where he should be advised: (a) of the extent of his/her liability under the guarantee; (b) of the risk he runs; and (c) to take independent advice. He felt that these requirements would not be too onerous. The Code of Banking Practice already required banks taking guarantees to take similar steps[15]. A series of cases subsequent to *O'Brien,* however, seem to have set a lower standard for creditors. In *Royal Bank of Scotland v Etridge (No 2)*[16] the Court of Appeal reviewed the cases and summarised their effect in a series of propositions. Broadly speaking, it seems that the creditor will have done sufficient to avoid being fixed with constructive notice if it advises the guarantor to obtain independent legal advice. A private meeting with the bank is unnecessary. If the guarantor does obtain independent legal advice and a solicitor confirms that he has explained the nature of the guarantee and that the guarantor understands it, the creditor is entitled to rely on the solicitor's certificate to that effect[17]. It makes no difference for this purpose that the same solicitor is also acting for the creditor[18], or for the principal debtor[19], in the transaction. The creditor is entitled to rely on solicitors to be aware of and perform their professional duties. If a conflict of interest arises, the solicitor can be expected to recognise it and decline to act for the guarantor.

In general, therefore, the creditor is protected against being affected by notice of the debtor's improper conduct if it advises the guarantor to seek independent advice. The burden on the creditor is not particularly onerous and is in accordance with good banking practice[20]. If a solicitor certifies that he has advised the debtor the bank's protection is generally absolute. The only situation in which the bank will be held to have notice of improper conduct in the face of such a certificate is where it has evidence that the solicitor's certificate is false, or where the terms of the transaction are so disadvantageous to the guarantor that no competent independent solicitor could advise them to proceed with it[21]. The net result is that the burden of responsibility is effectively transferred from the creditor to the solicitor.

The *O'Brien* decision was generally welcomed as affording some protection to guarantors, whilst avoiding the need to strain law or facts in order to find an agency.

The decision in *Etridge* has done much to clarify the law and eases the position of creditors. However, the application of the concept of notice in this area has been criticised by some commentators. It has been suggested that the proper basis of the court's intervention in these cases is the unconscionability of the bargain[22], and the decision in *Burch*, lends some support to this view. It has also been suggested that the trend of the cases since *O'Brien* has made it to easy for creditors to avoid being affected by notice simply by advising the guarantor to seek independent advice. In 1998 Sir Peter Millett, now Lord Millett, expressing concern about the 'ritual reliance on the provision of legal advice', wrote that he had 'serious misgivings about the position we have reached in this country following . . . *O'Brien* . . . We have substituted an inappropriate bright line rule for proper investigation of the facts, and have failed the vulnerable in the process' and, noting that Australian courts have used the jurisdiction to grant relief from harsh and unconscionable bargains to deal with this type of situation[23], he commented that there was 'much merit in this approach'[24]. The English courts have not yet been prepared to go this far.

1   See above 23.1.1.3.
2   [1994] 1 AC 180 at 188, [1993] 4 All ER 417 at 422.
3   [1994] 1 AC 180, [1993] 4 All ER 417; see Berg [1994] LMCLQ 34.
4   See *TSB Ltd v Camfield* [1995] 1 All ER 951.
5   Per Lord Browne-Wilkinson [1994] 1 AC 180 at 196, [1993] 4 All ER 417 at 429.
6   [1993] 4 AU ER 417 at 431.
7   *Massey v Midland Bank plc* [1995] 1 All ER 929, CA.
8   *Avon Finance Ltd v Bridger* [1985] 2 All ER 281.
9   [1997] 1 All ER 144, CA.
10 Under the Banking Code banks now undertake not to take unlimited guarantees: para 3.14.
11 See *Crédit Lyonnais Bank Nederland NV v Burch* [1997] 1 All ER 144, CA.
12 *CIBC Mortgages plc v Pitt* [1994] 1 AC 200, [1993] 4 All ER 433.
13 Per Hobhouse LJ in *Banco Exterior Internacional v Mann* [1995] 1 All ER 936 at 945.
14 Per Stuart-Smith LJ in *Royal Bank of Scotland v Etridge (No 2)* [1998] 4 All ER 705 at 720.
15 See now the Banking Code, para 3.14.
16 [1998] 4 All ER 705; see Price (1999) 115 LQR 8; Giliker (1999) 62 MLR 609.
17 *Massey v Midland Bank plc* [1995] 1 All ER 929.
18 *Halifax Mortgage Services Ltd v Stepsky* [1996] Ch 207, [1996] 2 All ER 277.
19 *Massey v Midland Bank plc* [1995] 1 All ER 929; *Banco Exterior Internacional v Mann* [1995] 1 All ER 936; *Bank of Baroda v Rayerel* [1995] 2 FLR 376; *Barclays Bank plc v Thomson* [1997] 4 All ER 816.
20 See the Banking Code, para 3.14, in which the banks undertake to explain to potential guarantors the nature of the obligation they undertake and to encourage them to take independent legal advice. But see *Bank of Cyprus (London) Ltd v Markou* [1999] 2 All ER 707, where the bank failed to recommend independent advice.
21 *Crédit Lyonnais Bank Nederland NV v Burch* [1997] 1 All ER 144.
22 See Chen-Wishart [1997] CLJ 60; Tjio (1997) 113 LQR 10.
23 *Commercial Bank of Australia v Amadio* [1983] 151 CLR 447; Rickett (1998) 114 LQR 17; but see Gardner (1999) 115 LQR 1.
24 (1998) 114 LQR 214 at 220.

23.1.2.3   *Mistake*

A contract of guarantee will be held void if it is made on the basis of a fundamental mistake[1], including where the mistake is induced by the conduct of the debtor or another third party. In *Associated Japanese Bank (International) Ltd v Crédit du Nord* [2] A (the plaintiffs) and B entered into a sale and lease-back transaction in respect of four specified machines, and C (the defendants) guaranteed the rental payments due from B under the lease as 'sole or principal debtor'. In fact, the machines supposedly the subject of the sale and lease-back did not exist, and both A and C had been defrauded by B. Steyn J held that the guarantee contract was subject to an express or implied condition precedent that there was a valid lease of the machines, or, alternatively, that both A and C had contracted on the basis of a shared mistake that the lease related to existing machinery. The non-existence of the machinery made the guarantee essentially different from what it was reasonably believed to be, and, since it was induced by the fraud of B, C had reasonable grounds for their mistaken belief. The guarantee was therefore void.

1   See 2.4.1.
2   [1988] 3 All ER 902.

23.1.3   *The surety's obligation*

As we have seen[1], the nature and extent of the surety's obligation depends on the construction of the surety contract. In practice, its terms will generally be dictated by the creditor, normally a bank or other financial institution, and the contract will often be on the creditor's standard terms. As a result, contracts of surety will generally be construed strictly, contra proferentem, against the creditor, for the courts recognise that not only does the creditor control the terms of the contract, but the transaction is one from which the surety normally derives no benefit[2].

As the House of Lords recognised in *Moschi v Lep Air Services Ltd*[3], the parties are free to make any agreement they like. However, normally the obligation assumed by a guarantor is to 'see to it' that the principal debtor performs his contract. In *Moschi* the plaintiffs were freight forwarding agents who held a lien over goods owned by a company as security for moneys due to them from the company. In return for the plaintiffs' releasing the goods, the company agreed to pay the outstanding sum by weekly instalments and the defendant, a director of the company, guaranteed the performance by the company of its obligation to pay the instalments. The company made several defaults in payment which the plaintiffs accepted as a repudiation of the contract with the company. They terminated that contract, and then sued the defendant on his guarantee, claiming the full amount of the weekly instalments, less the amount already paid by the company. The defendant argued that he had merely guaranteed that each instalment would be paid when due, and that, since termination of the contract put an end to the company's obligation to pay future instalments, he could not be liable for instalments which would have fallen due after termination. The House of Lords unanimously rejected that interpretation of the guarantee. Although it would be possible for a guarantor merely to guarantee payment of each instalment, the normal interpretation of a guarantee would be that the guarantor promises to see that the principal debtor performs his contract. A default by the principal debtor therefore puts the guarantor in breach of his undertaking and makes him liable for damages[4].

As we have seen, the nature of the surety's obligation depends in part on the classification of the surety contract as a guarantee or indemnity, for whereas the liability of a surety under a guarantee is secondary to and dependent on that of the principal debtor, under an indemnity the surety undertakes a primary liability to compensate the creditor against any loss he suffers by entering the contract with the debtor. This distinction is crucial where the principal contract is invalid, for the surety under a guarantee can then incur no liability. The distinction, and the tendency of the court to construe contracts of suretyship strictly in favour of the surety, is illustrated by the case of *Coutts & Co v Browne-Lecky*[5], in which the defendants guaranteed repayment of the overdraft of an infant. The loan to the infant was void[6], and it was held that the guarantors therefore could not be held liable:

'There can be no suretyship unless there be a principal debtor . . . Nor can a man guarantee anybody else's debt unless there is a debt of some other person to be guaranteed'[7].

The decision in *Coutts* is open to criticism. All parties knew that the principal debtor was an infant, and that that was the reason for taking the guarantee. In line with the reasoning of the majority in *Yeoman Credit Ltd v Latter*[8], it would seem sensible for the surety's undertaking to have been construed as one to be liable for the debt even if the principal was not, ie as an indemnity, and therefore binding notwithstanding the infancy of the principal debtor. However, as we have seen, the contract in *Yeoman* was expressly described as an indemnity and contained terms consistent with that interpretation.

We have seen that a continuing guarantee of a revolving credit facility may be revoked at any time so as to put an end to the guarantor's liability. The effect of the guarantor's notice depends on the construction of the guarantee. It may operate to terminate the guarantor's liability altogether, so that unless a demand for payment is made during the notice period the guarantor ceases to be liable[9]. Alternatively, it may operate simply to terminate the continuing nature of the guarantee, freezing the guarantor's liability. In *Bank of Credit and Commerce International SA v Simjee*[10] a guarantee provided that it was to be a 'continuing security' but that it could be 'determined and the liability of the guarantor crystallised at the expiration of three months' notice'. The guarantor gave notice to terminate his liability and, when the creditor made no demand within three months, claimed that he was thereby discharged from all liability. The Court of Appeal rejected that interpretation. As the guarantee made clear, the guarantor's liability was 'crystallised' at the end of the notice period. Service of notice in such a case therefore limits the guarantor's liability to the amount outstanding on the debtor's account at the date the revocation becomes effective. Further advances to the debtor cannot thereafter increase the guarantor's liability, but any payments made by the debtor and credited to the account after that date will reduce the guarantor's liability, since such credits will be applied, in accordance with the rule of 'first out, first in' in *Clayton's Case*, to discharge the debtor's earlier borrowings first. In practice, the creditor will avoid this result by closing the guaranteed account when the guarantee is revoked and opening a new account for future dealings with the debtor.

Where the surety imposes a financial limit on his liability, and the amount of the principal debt is greater than the limit, it is important to decide whether he has guaranteed a fixed part of the debt, or the whole of the debt, subject to a financial limit. In the former case the part covered by the guarantee is treated as a separate debt; in the latter, the surety is taken as having guaranteed the whole debt subject to a financial limit. This has important consequences for the surety's right to be subrogated to any rights of the creditor against the debtor[11], or where the principal debtor is insolvent.

1 Above 23.0.2.
2 *Blest v Brown* (1862) 4 De GF & J 367.

3   [1973] AC 331.
4   This interpretation is criticised by Goode, *Commercial Law* (2nd edn, 1995) p 833.
5   [1947] KB 104.
6   By virtue of the Infants Relief Act 1874. The age of majority is now 18 and persons under that age are known as 'minors'.
7   Lord Selborne in *Lakeman v Mountstephen* (1874) LR 7 HL 17 at 24.
8   [1961] 2 All ER 294, above 23.0.2.
9   See *National Westminster Bank Ltd v Hardman* [1988] FLR 302, where the guarantee provided that it was to 'remain in force until determined by three months' notice'.
10 [1997] CLC 135.
11 See 23.2.1.2.

23.1.4 *Discharge of the surety*

A surety's obligations may be discharged in the same way as other contractual obligations, by performance (ie the surety paying to the creditor the sum due under their contract) or by frustration (although an obligation to pay money will rarely be frustrated) or as a result of the surety's acceptance of a repudiatory breach of contract by the creditor. A guarantor will also be discharged by any event which discharges the principal debtor, including performance of the principal contract. The effect of such discharge on a surety under a contract of indemnity will depend on the nature of the surety's undertaking. For instance, if the hirer under a hire purchase contract is given a right to terminate the early agreement by paying it off before the hire has run its full term, a surety who gave an indemnity in the form of that in *Yeoman Credit Ltd v Latter*[1] would not be discharged because his undertaking would be to see that the creditor received the full sum expected under the hire purchase contract[2].

Where a guarantee is in a deed, the guarantor may be protected by the old rule that any material alteration of a deed or other instrument made without the approval of all the parties makes it void[3]. However, an alteration will only have this effect if it is material and prejudices the guarantor. Thus where a standard form guarantee was altered by the insertion of an address for service of papers on the guarantor, its validity was unaffected. It was established that the alteration could not prejudice the guarantor[4].

In addition to the above, however, sureties are protected by a number of equitable rules under which a surety is automatically discharged from liability in a number of situations where the creditor does some act which adversely affects his rights.

1   Above 23.0.2.
2   If the surety relates to an agreement regulated by the Consumer Credit Act, the creditor cannot recover more from the surety than he could recover from the principal debtor: s 113.
3   *Pigot's Case* (1614) 11 Co Rep 26b.
4   *Raiffeisen Zentralbank Osterriech AG v Crossseas Shipping Ltd* [2000] 1 All ER (Comm) 76; see also *Co-operative Bank plc v Tipper* [1996] 4 All ER 366 – pencil amendment to standard form was not a final amendment.

23.1.4.1 *Prejudice of the surety's rights*

A surety enjoys certain rights against the debtor for whom he assumes liability[1] and any act by the creditor which could prejudice those rights will generally discharge the surety from liability. It is not necessary to prove that the surety's rights have actually been prejudiced: the possibility of prejudice is sufficient.

Some cases suggest that the basis of the rule is that it is an implied condition precedent to the surety's liability that his rights against the debtor will not be prejudiced; however, in *Crédit Suisse v Borough Council of Allerdale Borough Council*[2] Colman J explained it as a rule of equity that the creditor is precluded from relying on the guarantee. Whichever interpretation is correct, by allowing automatic discharge without proof of prejudice the rule conveniently avoids the difficult problem of proving actual prejudice[3].

> 'It is the clearest and most evident equity not to carry on any transaction without the knowledge of him [the surety] who must, necessarily, have a concern in every transaction with the principal debtor. You cannot keep him bound and transact his affairs (for they are as much his as your own) without consulting him'[4].

Thus an agreement by the creditor to release the debtor from liability also releases the surety, unless the creditor expressly reserves his rights against the surety. The explanation for this rule is that a surety who discharges the debtor's liability is entitled to claim an indemnity from the debtor. If the release were to deprive the surety of this right, his position, and the basis on which he assumed liability, would be adversely altered without his consent; but if he were entitled to the indemnity, the release of the debtor by the creditor would be of no practical benefit to the debtor. In the same way, any variation of the contract between the creditor and the debtor will release the surety unless the creditor consents to the variation[5]. The only exception is where the variation is either self-evidently insubstantial or to the benefit of the surety[6]. Thus an agreement by the creditor to give the debtor time to pay will discharge the surety[7], apparently because the surety could at any time pay off the debt and then claim an indemnity from the debtor or compel the debtor to perform his original obligation, raising similar problems to those raised where the debtor is discharged[8].

In *Moschi v Lep Air Services Ltd* [9] the guarantor argued that he was discharged where the creditor accepted a repudiatory breach by the debtor and terminated the contract. The House of Lords unanimously rejected that argument: 'It is only in the jurisprudence of Humpty Dumpty that the rescission of a contract can be equated with its variation'[10]. However, if the debtor accepts a repudiatory breach by the creditor and terminates the principal contract, the surety will also be discharged.

The surety will also be discharged by other acts of the creditor which would prejudice his rights, such as the release by the creditor of any security provided by the debtor or any co-surety, for those acts would prejudice the surety's rights of subrogation and contribution respectively. The creditor also owes the surety an equitable duty to respect his interests, and any breach of this duty may discharge the surety. There would be a breach, for instance, where the creditor fails to take the necessary steps to perfect any security given by the debtor, for instance by registering a bill of sale[11] or by negligently selling property held as security at an undervalue[12]. However, the creditor does not commit a breach merely by postponing the realisation of any security, even if as a result the security declines in value[13], and any breach will only discharge the surety to the extent that he is actually prejudiced by the creditor's breach, so that the effect of a breach will often be to reduce, rather than to extinguish, the surety's liability.

A contract of suretyship will often contain terms which modify the general rules on the discharge of the surety. A clause which provides that the surety is not to be discharged by any variation of the principal contract or indulgence granted by the creditor to the debtor would appear to be valid: effectively, it would convert the contract into an indemnity. The effect of a clause which excludes or restricts the creditor's equitable duty to the surety, or the surety's 'right' to be discharged for its breach, is less clear. It could be argued that such a clause is subject to a test of reasonableness under the Unfair Contract Terms Act. However, it is settled that the creditor's duties to respect the surety's interests arise in equity[14] rather than in contract or tort. Section 3 of the 1977 Act would therefore not apply unless the equitable duties were supplemented by express or implied contractual duties. It might be argued that s 2 of the Act, which applies to exclusions of liability for negligence, could apply. Negligence is defined to include breach of 'any *common law* duty to take reasonable care'[15], but it might be argued that in this context 'common law' means any duty which arises under the general law, in contrast with duties arising under contract or statute. However, the Act would still not apply unless it were also found that the clause in question restricted the creditor's liability, or any right or remedy of the surety in respect of such liability. Since it seems that the creditor's equitable duty does not sound in damages, it seems that the creditor has no 'liability' for breach and it is therefore likely that an exclusion or restriction of the equitable duty falls outside the 1977 Act[16]. However, such provisions may be caught by the Unfair Terms in Consumer Contracts Regulations 1999. The regulations apply to any contract between a natural person acting for purposes outside his trade, business or profession, and any person who is acting for purposes relating to his trade, business or profession. A guarantee given by one individual to secure a loan by a business creditor to another individual, as where a parent guarantees a loan to his or her child, would therefore seem to be covered by the regulations. It has been held by the European Court of Justice[17] that a contract whereby a son guaranteed a bank loan to his father's business was not protected by the door step selling directive[18]. However, that directive only applies where there is a contract for the supply of goods or services by a trader to a consumer. The only supply in the particular case was by the bank to the guarantor's father and was made for the purposes of his business. There is no such requirement in the unfair terms directive or the 1999 regulations, and it is submitted that they would therefore apply to a guarantee of a loan by a business creditor for the purposes of the principal debtor's business.

1 See 23.2.
2 [1995] 1 Lloyd's Rep 315; affd [1996] 2 Lloyd's Rep 241.
3 *Rees v Berrington* (1795) 2 Ves 540.
4 Per Lord Loughborough in *Rees v Berrington* at 543.
5 *Holme v Brunskill* (1877) 3 QBD 495.
6 Ibid.
7 *Samuell v Howarth* (1817) 3 Mer 272.
8 The surety is not discharged by the creditor's mere failure to enforce the debt promptly.
9 [1973] AC 331.
10 Per Lord Simon of Glaisdale at 355. 'Rescission' is used here to mean 'repudiation' or 'termination'.
11 *Wulff v Jay* (1872) LR 7 QB 756.
12 *Mutual Loan Fund Association v Sudlow* (1858) 5 CBNS 449.
13 *China and South Sea Bank Ltd v Tan Soon Gin* [1990] 1 AC 536.
14 *Watts v Shuttleworth* (1860) 5 H & N 235; *China and South Sea Bank Ltd v Tan Soon Gin* [1990] 1 AC 536.
15 Section 1(1)(b).
16 See generally *Chitty on Contracts* (28th edn, 1999) paras 42-075–76; Goode, *Legal Problems of Credit and Security* (2nd edn, 1988) pp 193–196.
17 *Bayerische Hypotheken-und Wechselbank AG v Dietzinger* (C-45/96) [1998] ECR I-1199.
18 Directive 85/577/EEC to protect consumers in respect of contracts negotiated away from business premises.

23.2 Surety's rights against the debtor and fellow sureties

Since a surety incurs liability on behalf of another person, the law gives the surety certain rights against the debtor whose liability he discharges. In addition, a surety has a right to receive a contribution from any other surety liable for the same debt.

23.2.1 *Surety's rights against the debtor*

A surety who has discharged the secured debt may have a right to be indemnified by the principal debtor. In addition, he is entitled to be subrogated to the rights of the creditor against the debtor.

23.2.1.1 *Indemnity*

A guarantor is entitled to be indemnified by the principal debtor where the guarantee is given at the debtor's request[1]. It is not clear whether the right to indemnity derives from an implied term in any contract between creditor and guarantor (or an implied contract between them) or is a restitutionary right given to avoid the unjust enrichment of the debtor. However, it seems that the guarantor has no right to indemnity where the guarantee is provided without any request from the debtor[2], as, for instance, where the guarantee is supplied at the request of the creditor. This occurs, for instance, where a dealer introduces a hire purchaser to a finance company and is required by the company to guarantee the hirer's obligations.

Although the position is not clear, it seems that an indemnitor has similar rights to be indemnified by the principal debtor where the surety is provided at the debtor's request, even though strictly an indemnitor's liability is as principal.

A surety has no right to be indemnified by the debtor until he has paid the creditor. However, once the secured debt has become due he is entitled to seek a declaration on a quia timet basis of his right to be indemnified and an order requiring the debtor to pay the debt[3], and if he is sued by the creditor he can claim an indemnity by bringing in the principal debtor as a third party in the proceedings.

1   *Re a Debtor* [1937] Ch 156.
2   *Owen v Tate* [1976] QB 402.
3   *Wolmershausen v Gullick* [1893] 2 Ch 514.

23.2.1.2 *Subrogation*

A surety who has paid the secured debt is entitled to be subrogated to the rights of the creditor against the debtor. This entitles him to take over and enforce against the debtor any securities held by the creditor, or to prove in the debtor's insolvency in place of the creditor. The right to subrogation is available even where the surety was provided without any request from the debtor.

The surety's right to subrogation does not arise until the secured debt has been paid in full. Difficult questions arise where the surety has guaranteed only part of the debt. It is necessary then to decide whether the surety has guaranteed the whole debt, subject to a limit on his liability, or has guaranteed a specified part of the debt. In the former case the surety is not entitled to any rights by way of subrogation until the whole debt is paid; however, if the proper construction of the surety is that the surety has guaranteed payment of a limited, fixed part of the debt, the surety is entitled to rights of subrogation as soon as his guaranteed part of the debt is paid[1].

The surety's right to subrogation arises in equity but it is bolstered by s 5 of the Mercantile Law Amendment Act 1856, under which he is entitled to have assigned to him 'every judgment, specialty or other security which shall be held by the creditor'.

Since the surety's right of subrogation allows him to take over any claims the creditor may have against any security provided by the principal debtor, the creditor owes the surety a duty of good faith in enforcing any security[2], which includes a duty if he exercises a power of sale over any security to take reasonable care to obtain a proper price[3]. Breach of the duty will reduce the amount of the guarantor's liability by the amount of his loss but will not automatically discharge the surety[4].

1   *Thornton v M'Kewan* (1862) 11 WR 140; *Goodwin v Gray* (1874) 22 WR 312; *Re Sass* [1896] 2 QB 12; *Re Butler's Wharf Ltd* [1995] 2 BCLC 43.
2   *China and South Sea Bank Ltd v Tan* [1990] 1 AC 536, [1989] 3 All ER 839.
3   *Cuckmere Brick Co Ltd v Mutual Finance Ltd* [1971] Ch 949; see 22.2.1.3.
4   *Skipton Building Society v Stott* [2000] 1 All ER (Comm) 257.

23.2.2   *Surety's rights against co-sureties*

Where there is more than one surety of the same debt, the creditor is free to obtain payment from any of them. Equity requires, however, that no one surety should be required to pay more than his fair share of the debt, and any surety who pays more than his fair share can therefore seek a contribution from the other(s)[1].

Where all the sureties are liable in the same amount, they should all contribute equally. The cases establish that where they are liable for different amounts the ratio of their contributions should be the same as that of the maximum liabilities they assumed[2]. However, it is not clear what this means. There are two bases of contribution recognised in the law of insurance where two or more insurers are liable for the same loss. The maximum liability basis apportions loss in the same ratio as the maximum amounts covered by the insurers' policies; the independent liability basis apportions it in the same ratio in which the insurers would have been liable for the actual loss suffered. It is not clear which basis should be adopted in cases of contribution between sureties. The difference between the two can be illustrated by example. Suppose that A and B both guarantee D's overdraft, A with a maximum liability of £10,000 and B with a maximum of £20,000. Under the maximum liability basis they would contribute to D's debt in the ratio 1:2, regardless of the amount of the debt. Under the independent liability basis the ratio of their contributions will depend on the amount of the debt. If D's debt is £10,000 or less, each would be liable for the whole debt and they would therefore contribute equally. If D's debt is any amount greater than £10,000 but less than £20,000, A's maximum liability would be £10,000 but B would be liable for the whole debt, so that if D's debt is £15,000 they should contribute in the ratio 2:3, A paying £6,000 and B £9,000. If D's debt is £20,000 or more, A will be liable for £10,000 and B for £20,000 and they will therefore contribute in the ratio 1:2. Some cases suggest that the maximum liability basis is used to determine contributions between sureties[3] but others seem to favour the independent liability basis[4]. The Court of Appeal has expressly stated that it is not bound by authority on the point[5]. Insurance law favours the independent liability basis for cases of indemnity insurance[6] and that basis would seem more appropriate in the present context.

The Civil Liability (Contribution) Act 1978 creates a statutory right to contribution where two or more parties are liable in respect of the same 'damage'. The Act does not apply to cases where more than one person is liable for the same debt. The Act clearly therefore applies where sureties guarantee a liability other than a debt and, in view of the analysis of a guarantor's liability in *Moschi v Lep Air Services* as a liability for damages[7], it seems that the Act would also govern rights of contribution between co-guarantors, even when the obligation guaranteed is a debt. Where the Act applies, the amount of contribution recoverable from a person is 'such as may be found by the court to be just and equitable having regard to the extent of that person's responsibility for the damage'[8].

1 *Dering v Earl of Winchelsea* (1787) 2 Bos & P 270. Where the guarantee is payable on demand the surety is entitled to contribution even if he pays without a demand, provided that there is an ascertained liability and payment is not 'officious': *Stimpson v Smith* [1999] 2 All ER 833.
2 *Ellesmere Brewery Co v Cooper* [1896] 1 QB 75.
3 *Ellesmere Brewery Co v Cooper* [1896] 1 QB 75; see the example given at 81.
4 See *American Surety of New York v Wrightson* (1910) TLR 603 at 613.
5 *Commercial Union v Hayden* [1977] QB 804 at 815, per Cairns LJ.
6 See 35.7.4.
7 This point was left open by the Court of Appeal in *Barclays Bank plc v Miller* [1990] 1 All ER 1040.
8 Section 2(1).

23.3 Letters of comfort

A letter of comfort is a means of reassuring a potential creditor that a debt will be repaid. It is often given by a company where credit is to be advanced to its subsidiary company, in lieu of a guarantee, or where a guarantee would be inappropriate, and contains statements that the giver is aware of the advance of credit and does not intend to relinquish control of the subsidiary. The use of letters of comfort has become increasingly common in recent years. Their effect depends on the exact wording used and the circumstances in which the letter is given. In *Kleinwort Benson Ltd v Malaysian Mining Corpn Bhd*[1] a creditor made a loan to a company on the strength of a letter of comfort from its parent which stated that:

> 'It is our policy to ensure that the business of [the subsidiary] is at all times in a position to meet its liabilities to you under the [loan agreement]'.

When the subsidiary went into liquidation the creditor sought payment of the debt from the parent company on the basis of the letter of comfort. After detailed analysis of the wording of the letter and the circumstances in which it was given the Court of Appeal, reversing the decision of Hirst J, held that the letter did not contain a contractual promise, but merely a statement of present intent. The parent had assumed at most a moral, not a legal, responsibility to the plaintiffs.

The *Kleinwort Benson* decision suggests that a letter of comfort may offer a creditor little real legal security and has been criticised. The letter of comfort was given in a commercial context and was relied on by the plaintiffs. However, the case does not lay down an absolute rule that a letter of comfort can never be binding. Everything will turn on the wording used and the factual context in which the letter is given. In *Kleinwort Benson* it was significant that during negotiations the parent company had been asked, and had refused, to provide a guarantee of the subsidiary's borrowing and that the creditor had charged a higher rate of interest than it would have charged if a formal guarantee had been given, to reflect the increased risk. In contrast, in *Re Atlantic Computers plc*[2] a letter of comfort which contained 'an expression of present intention by way of comfort only' was held to be a contractual warranty of the maker's present intention. In an Australian case in which a letter of comfort given in circumstances similar to those in *Kleinwort Benson* stated that 'it would not be our intention to reduce our shareholding in [the subsidiary] from the current level . . . during the currency of this facility. We would, however, provide your bank with ninety days notice of any decisions taken by us to dispose of this shareholding' it was held that there was a binding contractual undertaking to give notice of any disposal of the shares[3]. The wording in question was clearly stronger than that in issue in *Kleinwort Benson*, but the judge criticised the approach of the Court of Appeal as excessively technical: 'Courts will become irrelevant in the resolution of commercial disputes if they allow this approach to dominate their consideration of commercial documents'.

1   [1989] 1 WLR 379.
2   [1995] BCC 696. See also *Chemco Leasing SpA v Rediffusion plc* [1987] 1 FTLR 201.
3   *Banque Brussels Lambert SA v Australia National Industries* (12 October 1991, unreported): see (1991) JBL 282.

Chapter 24

The Regulation of Credit

24.0 Introduction

It has long been recognised that credit transactions have to be subjected to some control in order to protect consumers. There is a need for 'a strong level of protection in a market which for many centuries – perhaps even since ancient times – has been regarded by law makers as particularly sensitive. Buyer-seller interactions in credit markets are characterised by imbalances of information and bargaining strength between lenders and borrowers'[1]. For these reasons, the supply of credit to consumers is now subject to extensive statutory control under the Consumer Credit Act and regulations made under it.

1 OFT, *Consumer Credit Deregulation, A review by the Director General of Fair Trading* (1994) para 1.8.

24.1 The Crowther Committee Report

The 1974 Act was the product of the Crowther Committee Report of 1971. There was in fact already legislation in place governing aspects of the supply of credit to consumers, and there had been such legislation for some time. However, the pattern of control was incomplete, with different types of credit arrangement subject to different rules. The Crowther Committee considered that the existing law was deficient in the following respects[1].

(a) It lacked any functional basis, distinctions between different types of transaction being drawn on the basis of legal abstractions rather than on the basis of commercial reality.
(b) The law did not distinguish consumer from commercial transactions.
(c) There was an artificial separation between the law relating to lending and the law relating to security for loans.
(d) There was no rational policy relating to the rights of third parties.
(e) Many statutes were excessively technical.
(f) There was no consistent policy in relation to sanctions for infringement.
(g) 'The fact is that the present law relating to credit, based largely on legislation enacted in the last century, is unsuited to modern commercial requirements and fails to tackle everyday problems in a realistic manner'[2].

The Committee's suggested solution was a massive rationalisation of the law regulating all credit transactions. The Committee proposed two statutes: a Lending and Security Act to rationalise the regulation of security interests and conflicts between secured parties and a Consumer Sale and Loan Act which would regulate consumer credit transactions, including a requirement for those involved in the credit industry to be licensed. As we have seen[3], the first proposal was rejected by the government. The second produced the Consumer Credit Act 1974 (CCA 1974).

1 Report of the Committee on Consumer Credit (1971) Cmnd 4596, ch 4.
2 At 181.
3 See ch 22.

24.2 The Consumer Credit Act 1974[1]

The Consumer Credit Act received the Royal Assent on 31 July 1974, but because of its complexity and comprehensive scope it was not fully implemented until 1985, some 14 years after the Crowther Report on which it is based. It repealed much of the existing legislation regulating credit and replaced it with a framework of law based upon common rules and principles applicable to most credit and hire transactions. Many of the detailed provisions of the Act are technical and complex, but its underlying principles are clear. In essence, the Act seeks to control trading malpractices, redress bargaining inequality between consumers and traders and regulate the remedies for default[2]. To this end the Act imposes two levels of controls:

(a) over the credit industry generally, by the issue of licences, restrictions on advertising and canvassing and wide supervisory powers of the Director General of Fair Trading; and
(b) over individual agreements in relation to such matters as formalities, termination, cancellation and default.

It has been said that one of the strengths of the Act–

'is that it does not seek to meet its objectives through interventionist action such as interest rate capping or direct control of the substance of contracts. Rather, it explicitly endorses freedom of contract within a framework of rules designed to ensure openness: consumer protection is attained in large part through measures to ensure that full and truthful information about credit contracts is available to consumers'[3].

Nevertheless, the legal structure created by the Act is complex. Moreover, it is overlaid with a detailed superstructure of regulations dealing with such matters as the form of agreements and advertisements, calculation of interest rates and so on. Nor is this the whole story. Consumer credit agreements are subject to the general law of contract as well as rules applicable to specific types of agreement under the general law or under other legislation. So, for instance, a consumer conditional sale agreement will be regulated by CCA 1974 but will also be subject to the Sale of Goods Act 1979, as well as to the general law of contract. In particular, the terms of a consumer credit agreement may be subject to control under the Unfair Contract Terms Act 1977 and/or the Unfair Terms in Consumer Contracts Regulations 1999. Thus the terms of an agreement which complies with CCA 1974 may nevertheless be held to be unfair under the 1999 regulations[4].

There is also now an EU dimension to consumer credit law. An EC Directive on Consumer Credit was introduced in 1987[5] but since the 1974 Act already covered much the same ground, it required no significant amendment to UK law. Two further amending directives[6] have required minor amendments.

1   What follows is a broad examination of key issues. Inevitably, the Act contains a great deal of detail and readers are referred to Goode, *Consumer Credit Law* (2nd edn, 1989) and Guest and Lloyd, *Encyclopaedia of Consumer Credit Law* (looseleaf) for more detail. The Act is referred to hereafter as 'CCA 1974'.
2   See Crowther, ch 6.
3   OFT, *Consumer Credit Deregulation, A review by the Director General of Fair Trading* (1994) para 1.8.
4   See *Director of Fair Trading v First National Bank plc* [2000] 2 All ER 759.
5   Directive 87/102/EEC (OJ L 42/48).
6   90/88EEC (OJ L 2/6114); 98/7/EEC (OJ L 101/17).

24.3   The Director General

The Crowther Committee favoured the creation of a Consumer Credit Commissioner to oversee the legislation and act as an ombudsman in the field of consumer credit. It was decided, however, to extend the scope of the activities of the Director General of Fair Trading (DGFT) to cover credit and thus avoid unnecessary duplication of resources.

The principal role of the DGFT under the Act is in granting, renewing, varying, suspending and revoking licences. In addition, he is required to supervise the legislation, disseminate information and advice, and periodically review the operation of the Act. Thus he may advise industry groups of his views on the correct interpretation of particular disputed provisions in the legislation. He has, for example, engaged in an extensive dialogue with credit card companies over the application of some of the Act's provisions to their activities[1], and in 1997 issued guidelines to creditors offering credit to 'non-status borrowers' (ie borrowers with poor credit ratings who find it difficult to obtain credit), following discovery of evidence of the use of oppressive terms and irresponsible lending practices[2].

The proper approach to the exercise of these functions has been described as follows:

> 'In exercising its powers in relation to consumer credit, the Office of Fair Trading must keep in mind the balance between the legitimate interests of commercial organisations, the importance of credit in this modern economy, and its benefit to most consumers, and the difficulties experienced by some vulnerable consumers and the effect that these have on those individuals and on society in general'[3].

In 1994 the DGFT conducted an extensive review of the legislation as a whole, including consultation with industry and consumer groups, which resulted in the publication of a report containing a number of reform proposals[4], many of them intended to reduce the regulatory burden of the Act. However, in 1997 the government announced that it planned to make no changes to the law.

1   See 26.4.2.
2   See (1997) 17 Fair Trading 1.
3   Geoffrey Horton, Director of Consumer Affairs; see (1997) 17 Fair Trading 1.
4   OFT, 'Consumer Credit Deregulation, A review by the Director General of Fair Trading' (1994).

24.3.1 *Licensing*

In justifying the need for a system of licensing under the auspices of a regulatory body the Crowther Committee observed that the efficacy of the protective measures concerned with individual transactions is in practice limited–

> 'by the fact that a single individual may be unaware of his legal rights or unable or unwilling to exercise them; and the more unscrupulous type of credit grantor may well take the view that the occasional check on his malpractices by a determined consumer in an isolated transaction is not a serious deterrent, and is outweighed by the financial advantages he may derive from evading the law. There is thus a need for an agency to investigate trading practices, require production of accounts and records and, in the case of serious malpractice, suspend or revoke the offender's licence'[1].

As noted earlier[2], a licensing system operated under the Moneylenders Act 1927 but the system was decentralised, with no duty of enforcement placed on any particular agency. Thus, in practice, enforcement was practically non-existent.

Consistent with the comprehensive nature of CCA 1974, a licence is now required not only by those who provide credit or hire (rental) facilities, but also by those involved in ancillary credit businesses. Thus a licence is required to carry on a consumer credit business and a consumer hire business[3]. Local authorities and bodies empowered by a public general Act to carry on such a business are exempt, but in effect all businesses, in so far as their activities comprise or relate to the provision of credit or hire agreements caught by the Act (termed 'regulated agreements' under the Act) are required to be licensed. It is important to realise that the provision of credit or hire agreements need not be the principal business; if credit or hire agreements are made in the course of any business a licence will be required[4].

The Act identifies five categories of activity as ancillary credit businesses. Thus any business requires a licence in so far as it comprises or relates to one or more of the following activities:

(i)   credit brokerage;
(ii) debt-adjusting;
(iii) debt-counselling;
(iv) debt-collecting; or
(v)   the operation of a credit reference agency.

Credit brokerage relates to the business of introducing individuals to persons who provide either consumer credit or goods under consumer hire agreements. The definition under the Act is wide enough to include the activities of insurance agencies and mortgage brokers, solicitors and accountants arranging loans for clients, estate agents introducing prospective buyers to building societies as well as retail outlets which introduce their own customers to a finance house in order to finance the supply of goods or services[5].

Debt-adjusting relates to renegotiating, on behalf of a debtor/hirer, a debt incurred under a consumer credit or hire agreement. It also covers the situation where a debt is taken over, or otherwise liquidated, in return for payments by the consumer[6].

Debt-counselling is simply giving advice to debtors/hirers in respect of the liquidation of debts due under a consumer credit or hire agreement[7].

Debt-collecting is the taking of steps to procure payment of debts due under consumer credit or hire agreements[8].

A credit reference agency is a person carrying on a business comprising the furnishing of persons with information relevant to the financial standing of individuals, being information collected by the agency for that purpose[9].

1   At p 255.
2   See 21.1.1.
3   Section 21(1).
4   However, a person may not be treated as carrying on a credit or hire business simply because he occasionally enters into such a transaction, s 189(2): see *R v Roy Marshall* (1989) 90 Cr App Rep 73.
5   There is an exemption in s 146(5) for individuals acting as freelance collectors for check traders or agents for mail order.
6   Section 145.
7   Section 145.
8   Section 146.
9   Section 145.

24.3.2   *Licence applications*

There are two types of licence: standard licences and group licences. A standard licence is issued to a single person (including a company), or to a partnership or unincorporated body in the name of the partnership or body. It lasts for five years[1] and authorises the licensee to carry on the activities described by the licence[2]. The applicant for a licence must therefore specify in his application the types of consumer credit business for which he wishes to be licensed[3].

Group licences are of indefinite duration and are issued by the DGFT to cover persons operating in a particular business, if the public interest is better served by doing so, rather than by obliging the persons concerned to apply separately for standard licences. Group licences have, for example, been issued to the Law Society in respect of solicitors holding practising certificates, to the Institute of Chartered Accountants in respect of their practising members and to the National Association of Citizens Advice Bureaux covering bureaux registered with them. A person covered by a group licence may also apply for a standard licence; indeed, they must do so if their precise credit business activities are not covered by the group licence.

A person must be granted a licence if he satisfies the DGFT that he is a fit person to engage in activities covered by the licence, and the name or names under which he applies is or are not misleading or otherwise undesirable. Factors taken into account are whether the applicant, or persons associated with the applicant, have committed any offence involving fraud, dishonesty or violence or a breach of consumer law; practised discrimination on sex, colour, racial, ethnic or national grounds; or engaged in deceitful, oppressive, unfair or improper business practices (whether lawful or not)[4]. Specific factors in the former category include breaches of the CCA 1974 provisions, convictions under the Trade Descriptions Act 1968, or supplying goods not of satisfactory quality. Unfair or improper business practices include variation of the interest rate stated in an agreement, pressuring consumers into purchases by causing anxiety about their state of health, and failure to settle outstanding debts on cars taken in part-exchange[5]. The DGFT is not required to investigate the solvency or business competence of the applicant, although evidence of either may be taken into account in deciding whether to grant a licence.

The decision of the DGFT whether to grant a licence is based on information provided by the applicant on the application form and information supplied from such sources as local authority trading standards departments. If the DGFT decides not to issue a licence he must inform the applicant that he is 'minded to refuse'[6], giving his reasons and inviting representations. Where the only evidence against granting a licence consists of complaints, a former DGFT has outlined the problems involved in issuing a 'minded to refuse' notice:

> 'Counter statements designed to show that the complaint is misconceived may raise sufficient questions about the validity of the complaint that we are unable to make a finding of fact on the issues raised. In short, it is very difficult for me to arrive at a decision which is not favourable to the applicant in those cases which are comprised solely of complaints. Such cases are, however, very rare indeed, for we would try to obtain other supportive evidence to lend weight to the proposed case'[7].

If the DGFT remains unconvinced after considering representations from the applicant, an appeal may be made to the Secretary of State or the High Court on a point of law[8]. Alternatively, the DGFT can seek undertakings from the applicant in respect of future conduct and proceed to issue the licence.

Once the licence has been granted, the DGFT has the right to suspend or revoke it should he consider that, if it had expired, he would be 'minded to refuse' it[9]. The same procedure would then be followed as in an original application.

1   Consumer Credit (Period of Standard Licence) (Amendment) Regulations 1991, SI 1991/1817. Licences were originally granted for a period of 15 years.
2   Fees are payable for a licence, currently £175 for a company or partnership and £80 for a sole trader.
3   It was proposed in the 1994 review that this requirement should be removed and that all licences should cover all types of consumer credit business: OFT, *Consumer Credit Deregulation, A review by the Director General of Fair Trading* (1994).
4   Section 25(2).
5   See eg Annual Report of the Director General of Fair Trading 1981, p 21.
6   Section 27(1)(a).
7   Borrie, 'Licensing Practice Under the Consumer Credit Act' [1982] JBL 91, 95–96.
8   Section 34.
9   Section 32.

24.3.3   *Enforcement of licensing*

A person who engages in any activity for which a licence is required without holding a licence in respect of those activities commits an offence[1]. A more potent sanction, however, is that any agreement regulated by the Act which is made by an unlicensed business cannot be enforced without an order from the DGFT[2] unless it is a 'non-commercial agreement', not made in the course of a consumer credit business carried on by the creditor[3]. Where a customer introduced to a creditor by an unlicensed credit broker enters into a regulated agreement[4], the agreement will also be unenforceable even where the actual creditor is licensed[5]. This latter provision, in effect, introduced an element of self-policing into the licensing system. As Sir Gordon Borrie, a former Director General of Fair Trading, observed:

> 'Creditors who at one time may have used credit brokers with little thought as to whether they had sufficient integrity or knowledge or were sufficiently reputable intermediaries will now in their own interests ensure that their brokers do not engage in conduct that may make them likely candidates for revocation action'[6].

In deciding whether to make an order to allow enforcement of an unlicensed agreement, the DGFT may consider how far customers were prejudiced by the trader's conduct; whether he would have been likely to grant a licence if an application had been made; and the degree of culpability for the failure to obtain a licence.

1   Section 39(1). The offence is punishable by a fine of up to £5,000 or two years' imprisonment.
2   Section 40(1).
3   See s 189; *Hare v Schurek* [1993] CCLR 47.
4   Where a debtor introduced by a non-licensed broker enters into an agreement which is not regulated, the credit agreement is unaffected although any contract between the debtor and the broker is unenforceable: *Citibank Trust Ltd v Gregory* (20 January 1992, unreported).
5   Section 149.
6   Borrie *The Development of Consumer Law and Policy – Bold Spirits and Timorous Souls* (Hamlyn Lectures, 1984) p 87.

Chapter 25

Regulated Agreements

25.0 Introduction

As we have seen, the Consumer Credit Act (CCA) was intended to apply to all forms of credit agreement, and in principal it does so, although as will become apparent, its application to certain types of credit arrangement, and especially to credit and other cards, is problematic. Despite its wide scope however, the Act does not apply to all credit agreements. As its title suggests, its main purpose is the protection of consumers, but some consumer contracts fall outside its scope, whilst some business credit transactions are regulated by it[1].

The Act applies only to 'regulated agreements' which are defined as 'consumer credit agreements or consumer hire agreements, other than exempt agreement(s)'[2].

1 See below.
2 Section 189.

25.1 Consumer credit agreements

Unlike other consumer protection statutes, the 1974 Act makes no clear-cut distinction between consumer and business transactions. A consumer credit agreement is 'a personal credit agreement by which the creditor provides the debtor with credit not exceeding £25,000'[1]. A 'personal credit agreement' consists of 'an agreement between an individual (the debtor) and any other person (the creditor) by which the creditor provides the debtor with credit of any amount'[2]. 'Individual' is defined as including a partnership or other unincorporated body of persons not consisting entirely of bodies corporate[3]. The Act therefore regulates certain business credit transactions provided that the debtor is not a corporate body. In 1994 it was proposed that business borrowing and hiring should cease to be regulated by the Act[4], but those proposals were not accepted. Conversely, an agreement with an individual consumer is not regulated if the amount of credit exceeds £25,000.

Credit is defined in very broad terms as including 'a cash loan and any other form of financial accommodation'[5]. The Act therefore applies to the many different categories of credit transaction identified earlier. The three common forms of instalment credit – hire purchase, conditional sale and credit sale – are specifically defined in terms which, in principle, accord with the observations made in Chapter 21. A hire purchase agreement is one where goods are bailed in return for periodical payments and the property in the goods will not pass until one or more of the following occurs: (a) the exercise of an option to purchase; (b) the doing of any other specified act by any party to the agreement; or (c) the happening of any other specified event[6]. A conditional sale agreement is an agreement for the sale of goods or land under which the price is payable by instalments and the property is to remain in the seller until the required conditions are fulfilled[7]. A credit sale is defined on the same terms as a conditional sale except that property passes to the buyer immediately[8].

In order to decide if an agreement is regulated, the amount of credit supplied must be calculated. It is important to distinguish between the credit provided and the total charge for credit[9] which includes interest and other charges. The latter is not treated as credit and must therefore be excluded when calculating the amount of credit supplied under the agreement. Suppose, for example, that goods are supplied under a conditional sale agreement under which the buyer will make total payments of £32,000, including a deposit of £4,000 and interest of £3,000. The deposit is not advanced and the interest is part of the total charge for credit. Both must therefore be subtracted from the total sum payable, revealing that the amount of credit is £25,000 and that the agreement is within the CCA 1974[10].

1 Section 8. The limit was raised from £15,000 in 1998: Consumer Credit (Increase of Monetary Limits) Order 1998, SI 1998/996.
2 Section 8(1).
3 Section 189(1).
4 OFT, *Consumer Credit Deregulation: A Review by the Director General of Fair Trading* (1994).
5 Section 9(1). See *Dimond v Lovell* [2000] 2 All ER 897.
6 Section 189.
7 Section 189. An agreement for payment by instalments under which property will pass on completion of the payments unless the debtor elects *not* to acquire the goods is a conditional sale: *Forthright Finance Ltd v Carlyle Finance Ltd* [1997] 4 All ER 90: see 17.4.2.
8 Section 189.
9 Section 20.
10 The calculation of the amount of credit and the total charge can give rise to difficult questions: see eg *Apollo Leasing v Scott* [1986] CCLR 1 (inclusion of VAT); *Huntpast v Leadbeater* [1993] CCLR 15; *Humberclyde Finance Ltd v Thompson* [1997] CCLR 23 (insurance waiver premium part of the charge for credit).

25.1.1 *Classification of credit agreements under the Consumer Credit Act 1974*

For the purposes of its regulatory provisions, Pt II of the Act draws a series of distinctions between different types of agreement. In particular, it distinguishes between fixed-sum and running-account credit, restricted-use and unrestricted-use credit and debtor-creditor and debtor-creditor-supplier agreements. These categorisations cut across each other. They are fundamental to an understanding of the Act.

25.1.1.1 *Fixed-sum and running-account credit*

The Act distinguishes between fixed-sum and running-account credit[1]. Under a fixed-sum credit agreement, such as a loan or hire purchase agreement, a fixed amount of credit is advanced, and it is relatively easy to calculate the amount of credit[2].

Running-account credit is supplied under a facility such as an overdraft or credit card which allows the debtor to obtain cash, goods or services from the creditor or a third party (as in the case of a bank credit card) on credit, usually up to an agreed credit limit[3]. The credit limit is the maximum debit balance which is allowed to stand on the account during any agreed period, disregarding permissible temporary advances under the agreement which may exceed the maximum[4]. Under running-account credit agreements it may not be so easy to calculate the amount of credit since the amount may vary from day to day. Where the credit limit is fixed at £25,000 or less, the agreement will be regulated. Most personal credit cards set a monthly credit limit well below that figure, depending upon the credit rating of the individual debtor, and are therefore regulated.

An astute credit company might consider that one way of avoiding their agreements being classified as regulated would be either to set no credit limit or a credit limit in excess of £25,000. The Act, however, precludes such methods of avoidance by providing[5] that a running-account credit agreement will qualify as a regulated agreement if:

(a) the debtor cannot draw more than £25,000 at any one time;
(b) the agreement provides that if the debit balance rises above a given amount (currently £25,000 or less), the total charge for credit increases or some other condition favouring the creditor comes into operation; or
(c) at the time that the agreement is made it is probable, having regard to the terms of the agreement and any other relevant circumstances, that the debit balance will not at any time rise above £25,000.

Thus, if the accounting period for the credit agreement is set over a year with a credit limit of £30,000, it will still be a regulated agreement under (a) above if the debtor can only draw at any one time an amount up to £25,000. Alternatively, if the credit limit is set at £30,000 but there is a provision whereby interest will be charged at 3% above the usual rate should the debit balance exceed £25,000, the agreement will be regulated.

1 Section 10(1)(b).
2 In order to avoid doubt, the Act provides that 'the credit provided under a hire purchase agreement is fixed-sum credit . . . of an amount equal to the total price of the goods less the aggregate of the deposit and the total charge for credit' (s 9(3)).
3 Section 10(1)(a).
4 Section 10(3)(a).
5 Section 10(3)(b).

25.1.1.2 *Restricted- and unrestricted-use credit*

A restricted-use credit agreement is a regulated consumer credit agreement whereby credit is supplied to finance a specific transaction with the creditor or some third party, or to refinance an existing indebtedness of the debtor (whether to the creditor or to anyone else) and the debtor can use the credit only for that transaction[1]. Typical examples are hire purchase transactions and credit card purchases where credit funds are transferred directly to the supplier. Unrestricted-use credit is credit supplied under any other regulated agreement, its main feature being that the debtor can use the credit for any purpose. Under a restricted-use credit agreement, therefore, not only must it be expressly or impliedly agreed that the funds are to be used for one of the specified purposes, but the credit must be supplied in such a way that the debtor is not free to use them as he chooses. There must therefore be some practical restriction on the debtor's use of the funds, as when a loan to purchase a car is paid direct to the car dealer, or some supervision by the creditor of the use of the funds[2].

The distinction between restricted- and unrestricted-use credit is particularly important in relation to linked transactions, the canvassing of loan applications, and in distinguishing between debtor-creditor-supplier and debtor-creditor agreements.

1   Section 11(1).
2   Section 11(3). See *National Westminster Bank plc v Story* [1999] Lloyd's Rep Bank 261: the requirement is that the debtor is not free to use the credit as he chooses, not that he can only use the it for the stipulated purpose.

25.1.1.3   *Debtor-creditor supplier agreements/debtor-creditor agreements*

By distinguishing between these two types of agreement, CCA 1974 is effectively distinguishing between those agreements where the creditor also supplies the goods, or has a business arrangement with someone to supply the goods (debtor-creditor-supplier (d-c-s) agreements) and agreements where there is no connection between the creditor and the supplier of any goods or services purchased[1] (debtor-creditor (d-c) agreements).

A d-c-s agreement can involve two parties – the debtor/consumer and the creditor/ supplier – or three parties – the debtor/consumer, the creditor and the supplier of the goods and services. An example of the former would be the typical hire purchase or conditional sale agreement where the retailer sells goods to a finance company which enters into a credit transaction with the debtor under which it supplies the goods as well as the credit. The following would be examples of three party agreement d-c-s agreements.

(i)   A restricted-use credit agreement financing a transaction between a debtor/ consumer and a third party supplier, made by the creditor under pre-existing arrangements, or in contemplation of future arrangements between himself and the supplier[2]. This covers the situation where a finance house provides loans for the customers of a retailer to purchase goods or services, the customer being introduced to the finance house by the retailer under a formal arrangement. It also covers typical credit card transactions using cards such as Access or Barclaycard, where the credit company enters into a formal contract or has arrangements with the supplier whereby goods or services can be supplied to credit cardholders[3].

(ii) An unrestricted-use credit agreement which is made by the creditor under pre-existing arrangements between himself and a person (the supplier) other than the debtor, in the knowledge that the credit is to be used to finance a transaction between the debtor and the supplier. Thus if debtor A is buying a car from supplier B and requires finance, B might advise A to approach moneylender C, a credit company with whom B has an arrangement. C knows that the loan is for a particular transaction and advances the funds directly to A (thus rendering it unrestricted-use credit) who then pays for the car.

A d-c agreement is any credit agreement, such as a loan, which is not a d-c-s agreement. Such agreements are not tied to any specific supply transaction, the creditor having no business arrangement with a supplier of goods or services[4]. Thus if a bank advances funds to a customer for the purchase of a vehicle, it may be aware of who is supplying the vehicle but provided there is no business arrangement between bank and supplier, the loan will be a d-c agreement.

The Crowther Committee explained the rationale behind the distinction between d-c and d-c-s agreements in the following terms:

'Where goods are bought for cash provided by an independent lender there is no reason to regard the sale as any different from a normal cash sale, or to treat the loan as other than a normal loan. Where, however, the price is advanced by the seller or a connected lender the sale and loan aspects of the transactions are closely entwined. The connected lender and the seller, where not the same person, are in effect engaged in a joint venture to their mutual advantage and their respective roles cannot be treated in isolation'[5].

1   Sections 12 and 13.
2   Section 12(b).
3   The Act requires that there be arrangements, not an agreement, between creditor and supplier. A transaction financed by a credit card is therefore a three party d-c-s agreement even where the supplier was recruited by a merchant acquirer so that there is no contract between creditor and supplier: see 21.1.3.1.
4   Section 13.
5   Paragraph 6.2.24.

25.1.2   *Exempt agreements*

Certain types of credit agreement are removed from the scope of the legislation. These include mortgages given on land by certain specified bodies[1]. Also exempt are fixed sum debtor-creditor-supplier agreements (other than hire purchase or conditional sale agreements) where the number of payments to be made by the debtor does not exceed four and the payments are to be made within a period not exceeding twelve months beginning with the date of the agreement[2]. The objective of this provision is to exempt trade and domestic credit agreements where the supplier and the creditor may be the same person and the debt is extinguished quickly. As the Crowther Committee observed:

'We have not been aware of any special problems that arise in this area . . . Moreover we have been keenly conscious of the undesirability of trying to impose any form of regulation upon such an enormous number of largely informal transactions, unless it is strictly necessary to do so'[3].

Debtor-creditor-supplier agreements for running-account credit where all indebtedness is extinguished at the end of a specific accounting period are also exempt[4]. This exempts from the Act credit card agreements such as American Express or Diners' Club, where the debtor is required to clear the account at the end of each period, in contrast with those agreements where the debtor is merely required to pay a minimum amount at the end of a period, thus extending the credit period.

There is also an exemption, relating to 'low cost' debtor-creditor agreements, where the rate of interest does not exceed 1% above the highest base lending rate of any of the London Clearing Banks in operation on a date 28 days before the date on which the agreement was made. Certain non-commercial and small agreements are also given partial exemption from the Act[5].

1   Subject to the conditions laid down in Exempt Agreement Orders, these include local authorities, building societies, insurance companies, friendly societies, employers' and workers' organisations, charities, credit unions, land improvement companies or a bodies corporate specifically referred to in any public general Act. See s 16(1), Consumer Credit (Exempt Agreements) Order 1989, SI 1989/869 and Consumer Credit (Exempt Agreements) (Amendment) Order 1999, SI 1999/1956.
2   See note 1.
3   Paragraph 1.1.8.
4   Consumer Credit (Exempt Agreements) Order 1989, SI 1989/869, as amended.
5   See 25.2.

25.2   Consumer hire agreements

The Act also applies to consumer hire agreements, in order to prevent creditors circumventing its provisions by supplying goods under 'simple' hire rather than hire purchase or conditional sale agreements. A consumer hire agreement is an agreement made by a person with an individual (the hirer) for the bailment of goods where the agreement:

(a) is not a hire purchase agreement;
(b) is capable of lasting for more than three months; and
(c) does not require the hirer to make payments exceeding £25,000[1].

All consumer hire agreements are regulated agreements unless within the category of exempt agreements.

Where an agreement is of indefinite duration, terminable on notice by either party, it will be within the Act because it clearly is capable of lasting for more than three months.

Calculating the amount the hirer is required to pay is simply a matter of assessing the minimum contractual liability. For example, if an individual hires equipment under an agreement which sets a minimum rental period of two years and a monthly rental of £50, the total he is required to pay under the contract is £1,200 thus bringing the agreement within the Act.

The categories of consumer credit and consumer hire are not mutually exclusive. Where a hire agreement provides for payment of the hire charges to be deferred to a date later than when they would otherwise have been payable, the agreement will also be a credit agreement and, if regulated, subject to the provisions applicable to credit agreements as well as those applicable to hire[2].

1   Section 15.
2   *Dimond v Lovell* [2000] 2 All ER 897, HL.

25.2.1   *Exempt hire agreements*

The Secretary of State has the power to provide by order that CCA 1974 should not regulate consumer hire agreements where the owner is a body corporate authorised by or under any enactment to supply gas, electricity or water, or a public telecommunications operator, and the subject of the agreement is a meter or metering equipment[1].

1   See Consumer (Exempt Agreements) Order 1989, SI 1989/869, as amended.

25.3 Non-commercial and small agreements

The basic distinction in CCA 1974 is between regulated and exempt agreements. Non-commercial and small agreements fall between those categories in that they are partly regulated by the Act.

A non-commercial agreement is a consumer credit agreement or a consumer hire agreement not made in the course of a consumer credit or hire business carried on by the creditor or owner[1]. For example, a purely private transaction whereby an individual advances funds to another as a gesture of goodwill or friendship and not in the course of a business, would be classed as a non-commercial agreement. A person who occasionally enters into credit or hire transactions which would be regulated may be treated as not carrying on a consumer credit business; those agreements would therefore not be made in the course of a consumer credit business and would be non-commercial[2]. Such agreements are exempt from some of the formalities and cancellation provisions of the Act[3].

A small agreement is a regulated consumer credit or consumer hire agreement for credit or hire payments not exceeding £50[4]. Hire purchase and conditional sale agreements can never be small agreements but a credit-sale agreement where the credit does not exceed £50 would be. Small agreements are exempt from most of the provisions of the Act regulating formalities and cancellation rights.

1   Section 189(1).
2   See *Hare v Schurek* [1993] CCLR 47.
3   A non-commercial agreement is valid without an order of the DGFT, even though made by an unlicensed trader: CCA 1974, s 40(1).
4   It has been proposed that this figure should be increased to £150: OFT, *Consumer Credit Deregulation: A Review by the Director General of Fair Trading* (1994).

25.4 Multiple agreements

Although the Act draws distinctions between different categories of agreement, it recognises the possibility that a single agreement may be a hybrid containing features of two or more of the statutory types. To take a simple example, if a bank enters into a single agreement with a customer to provide him with an overdraft facility on his current account and at the same time to provide him with a personal loan, the overdraft facility is running account credit, the personal loan is fixed sum credit. Section 18 of the Act deals with these and similar arrangements, which it refers to as 'multiple agreements'. Although its provisions are far from clear, its broad effect is that where different 'parts' of a single agreement fall into different 'categories' of agreement, each 'part' is to be treated as separate agreement for the purposes of the Act. Where the agreement as a whole, or a single indivisible part of it, falls into more than one category it is to be treated as being an agreement in each of the categories.

Neither 'part' nor 'category' are defined by the Act, but it seems that 'part' refers to a section of the agreement which is capable of standing alone as a separate contract[1]. 'Category' seems to refer to the categories of agreement mentioned in the Act, such as consumer credit and consumer hire, restricted-use and unrestricted-use credit, and so on. So, in the example given, the agreement would be a multiple agreement. If the overdraft and loan facilities are in different 'parts' of the agreement, they will be regarded as separate agreements. If not, the agreement will have to comply with the requirements applicable to both restricted-use and unrestricted-use credit agreements. One consequence of this approach is to prevent creditors evading the Act's controls by tacking together separate facilities in a single contract to take the overall agreement outside the £25,000 credit limit. If the separate facilities are in different parts of the agreement and fall into different statutory categories, they will be treated as separate agreements for the purposes of the Act.

1 It may have a wider meaning: see *National Westminster Bank plc v Story* [1999] Lloyd's Rep Bank 261.

25.5 Linked transactions

Where goods are obtained on credit it is common for ancillary contracts, such as guarantees, insurance, or maintenance contracts, to be entered into at the same time. Any protection afforded in respect of the main transaction may be substantially undermined if the same protection is not extended to such ancillary or linked agreements, especially since such transactions are invariably used as a vehicle for imposing additional, and sometimes excessive, charges on a customer. CCA 1974 therefore introduced the concept of the 'linked transaction', which is entered into by a debtor, hirer or a relative of the debtor or hirer, and any other party who will often be, but need not be, the creditor[1]. Thus a transaction may be linked despite the fact that the parties to it are not the same as the parties to the main agreement.

A transaction is linked to a regulated agreement (the principal agreement), actual or prospective, if any of the following conditions are satisfied.

(a) It is entered into in compliance with a term of the principal agreement[2]. For example, if a finance house insists that the debtor under a hire purchase contract for electrical equipment enters into a maintenance agreement or an insurance contract with a specified firm, the maintenance or insurance contract would be a linked transaction. The linked transaction may be entered into with the creditor or with a third party and there need be no prior business relationship between the creditor and third party. The linked transaction may have been entered into by an 'associate' of the debtor, including a relative, spouse or business partner of, or company controlled by the debtor[3]. A transaction is only 'linked' on this basis if made after or at the same time as the principal agreement, since it must be entered into under a contractual requirement in the main contract. A transaction entered into before the principal agreement may be 'linked' but only in so far as it falls in one of the two categories below.

(b) It is a transaction financed, or to be financed, by a separate three party debtor-creditor-supplier agreement[4]. For example, where the holder of a credit card uses it to pay for a holiday, the contract between the cardholder and the holiday company is a linked transaction. Similarly, if a finance company with an arrangement with a furniture supplier grants a loan to the supplier's customer to enable them to buy furniture from the dealer, the contract for supply of the furniture would be 'linked'. Two-party d-c-s agreements do not involve linked agreements, since there is then only one contract for the supply of credit and goods or services[5].

(c) It is a transaction initiated by:
   (i) the creditor or owner, or his associate;
   (ii) a person who, in the negotiation of the transaction, is represented by a credit broker who is also a negotiator in antecedent negotiations for the principal agreement[6];

(iii) a person who, at the time the transaction is initiated, knows that the principal agreement has been made or contemplates that it might be made who initiated it by suggesting it to the debtor or hirer or his relative, who enters into it

    (i) to induce the creditor or owner to enter into the principal agreement, or

    (ii) for another purpose related to the principal agreement, or

    (iii) where the principal agreement is a restricted use credit agreement, for a purpose related to a transaction financed, or to be financed, by the principal agreement[7].

This provision is focused on transactions 'providing or facilitating a use of the goods or services acquired with the finance provided under the principal agreement' rather than those entered into 'as a condition of entry to the regulated agreement or as a term of it or for the purposes of it'. The following would be examples of linked transactions in this category.

(i)   An insurance contract which the creditor requires the debtor to enter into as a prerequisite of entry into the regulated agreement but which is not contractually required by a term of the regulated agreement would be linked to the regulated agreement.

(ii) A contract of insurance to cover health or the risk of cancellation taken out, at a holiday company's suggestion, by a holiday maker, would be a transaction linked to a regulated credit agreement for a holiday.

(iii) A contract for the supply of frozen food initiated by a food supplier who becomes aware that a consumer is buying a deep freeze on hire purchase from a dealer and sends a salesman to the consumer or his relative would be linked to the hire purchase contract since the supplier of the food knew of the credit agreement and suggested the transaction to the debtor for a purpose related to the supply of the freezer.

An agreement for the provision of security cannot be a linked transaction[8].

In general, a linked transaction entered into before the making of the principal agreement has no effect until that agreement is made[9]. However, in the case of an insurance contract, any contracts 'in so far as they contain a guarantee of goods' and any agreement for the opening of a deposit or current account, the linked transaction will have effect before the principal agreement is made[10].

As indicated above, the significance of a transaction being linked is that any withdrawal, cancellation or early settlement rights attached to the principal agreement extend to the linked transaction.

1 CCA 1974, s 19.
2 CCA 1974, s 19(1)(a).
3 See the definitions of 'relative' in s 189 and 'associate' in s 184.
4 CCA 1974, s 19(1)(b).
5 Eg hire purchase.
6 See 26.1.
7 CCA 1974, s 19(1)(c).
8 CCA 1974, s 19(1).
9 Section 19(3).
10 Consumer Credit (Linked Transactions) (Exemptions) Regulations 1983, SI 1983/1560.

Chapter 26

Control of Credit Agreements

26.0 Truth in lending

Disclosure is a favoured device for regulating business activity in the UK. The Consumer Credit Act 1974 embraces the disclosure philosophy by adopting the concept of 'truth in lending' and requiring businesses to comply with regulations on advertising, canvassing, quotations and the form and content of agreements. The objective of such regulations is to reduce the inequality of bargaining power between consumers and those offering credit or hire facilities by allowing the consumer to obtain an accurate picture of the nature and scope of facilities on offer.

26.0.1 *Advertising*

The advertising provisions of CCA 1974 apply to any advertisement published for the purposes of a business carried on by the advertiser indicating that he is willing to provide credit or to enter into an agreement for the bailment of goods by him[1]. The provisions extend to every form of advertising, in any medium[2]. They apply to advertisements for some forms of transaction not regulated by the Act: for instance, they apply to all advertisements for agreements secured on land, regardless of the amount of credit involved. There are, however, certain exemptions. The provisions only apply where the advertiser carries on a consumer credit or consumer hire business, or a business involving the provision to individuals of credit secured on land[3] and an advertisement will be exempt if it indicates either that the amount of credit advanced must exceed £25,000 and will not be secured on land, or that credit is only available to bodies corporate[4]. There is further power for the Secretary of State to make regulations exempting certain advertisements from the general requirements[5] and regulations have been made exempting advertisements by certain classes of business and for certain exempt agreements[6].

CCA 1974, s 44(1) enables the Secretary of State to make regulations covering the form and content of advertisements. The overriding requirement is that such advertisements convey a fair and reasonably comprehensive indication of the nature of the credit or hire facilities offered and their true cost. The regulations made under this provision[7] are detailed and complex, laying down what may be included in an advertisement, and how it should be presented and set out. The main rule is that information should be shown in a clear and legible manner and be presented 'together as a whole'. The charge for credit must be expressed as an annual percentage rate (APR), intended to provide a guide to the cost of credit and enable consumers to compare different facilities available. The APR must be prominently shown. The regulations divide controlled advertisements into three categories – simple, intermediate and full – and stipulate information which is required, prohibited or permitted to be included in advertisements in each category. For instance, a simple advertisement may include no more than the advertiser's name and occupation or its general nature. If more information, such as the price, is included, the advertisement will be an intermediate or full advertisement and must comply with the regulations applicable to those categories of advertisement. The inclusion of certain expressions is completely prohibited, whilst certain types of transaction must contain prescribed warning statements. Contravention of the regulations is an offence[8].

In his 1994 Review the Director General of Fair Trading concluded that regulatory control of advertisements is still required but that the current advertising regulations are excessively detailed and complex, creating difficulties and unnecessary expense for businesses seeking to comply with, and authorities which have to enforce, the regulations, whilst providing no significant benefits to consumers. He therefore recommended that the regulations should be much simplified[9].

CCA 1974 creates a number of further offences concerned with advertising. An advertiser commits an offence if an advertisement contains information which is false or misleading in a material respect[10], even if the misleading aspect does not relate to the credit element of the contract[11]. In one case a car dealer advertised '0% finance' on a car, but when a prospective purchaser enquired about the part exchange allowance available on it, he was told that a higher allowance would be given if he paid cash for the car rather than taking it on credit terms. It was held that the advertisement therefore contained a false or misleading statement, since it implied that a cash buyer would pay no more than a credit customer[12].

An advertiser also commits an offence if an advertisement indicates a willingness to provide restricted-use credit for the supply of goods or services, when the supplier is not selling or providing the goods or services for cash[13]. Thus, for example, a business engaged in mail order trading cannot disguise the financial disadvantage of credit by omitting the cash price of goods.

If an advertiser commits an offence, the publisher, deviser and any person who procured publication of the advertisement, may also commit an offence[14].

A person charged with contravention of the Act's advertising provisions may be able to rely on the due diligence defence in s 168 of the Act. In addition, a special defence is available to a person who published an offending advertisement in the course of his business provided that he received it in the course of business and had no reason to suspect that its publication would be an offence[15].

1   Section 43(1). See *Jenkins v Lombard North Central plc* [1984] 1 All ER 828.
2   Section 189(1).
3   Section 43(2), (4).
4   Section 43(3).
5   Section 43(5).
6   Consumer Credit (Advertisement) Regulations 1989, SI 1989/1125; Consumer (Exempt Agreements) Order 1989, SI 1989/869.
7   Consumer Credit (Advertisement) Regulations 1989, SI 1989/1125.
8   Section 167(2).
9   OFT, *Consumer Credit Deregulation: A review by the Director General of Fair Trading* (1994). Some regulatory control would, in any case, be required in order to comply with the EC Consumer Credit Directive (87/102/EEC).
10 Section 46.

11 *Rover Group Ltd v Sumner* [1995] CCLR 1.
12 *Metsoja v Pitt* [1990] CCLR 12. Compare *Ford Credit v Normand* 1994 SLT 318. The use of expressions such as '0% finance' is now restricted by the Consumer Credit (Advertisement) Regulations 1989, SI 1989/1125.
13 Section 45.
14 Section 47.
15 Section 47(2).

26.0.2 *Quotations*

Similar regulations to those covering advertisements have been made in respect of the form and content of quotations[1]. The regulations apply to both consumer credit and hire agreements and also to all agreements for the provision to individuals of credit secured on land. The regulations make no distinction between business and private customers. They deal with the situation where a trader receives a request from an individual asking for written information about the terms on which the trader will do business in respect of a particular transaction.

The information provided must include specific information including the APR, the amount of credit and credit limit, details of the payments which may be payable and the difference in treatment of cash and credit transactions.

In his 1994 Review the DGFT concluded that consumers rarely request quotations and that the detailed quotations regulations should therefore be repealed and replaced by extending the general offence of supplying false or misleading information to the situation where information is supplied in response to a request from a prospective customer.

1 Section 52(1) and Consumer Credit (Quotation) Regulations 1989, SI 1989/1126.

26.0.3 *Canvassing*

The CCA 1974 prohibits the canvassing of debtor-creditor agreements off trade premises. Canvassing means soliciting the entry of a consumer into a regulated agreement by making oral representations during a visit not previously arranged. Even where a visit is made in response to a previous request, an offence is still committed if the request was not in writing and signed by, or on behalf, of the person making it[1]. In essence, canvassing is off trade premises if the place the canvasser visits is not the place of business of the creditor/owner, a supplier, the canvasser or the consumer.

It is also an offence to send circulars to minors inviting them to borrow money, obtain goods on credit or hire, obtain services on credit or apply for information or advice on borrowing money or otherwise obtaining credit or hiring goods[2].

1 Section 49.
2 Section 50. See *Alliance and Leicester Building Society v Babbs* [1993] CCLR 77.

26.1 Formalities

There are few formal requirements for the creation of credit and hire agreements under the general law, other than those relating to contracts for the sale or other disposition of land or interests in land[1] and contracts of guarantee[2]. However, CCA 1974, Pts V–IX lay down detailed requirements relating to the form and content of regulated agreements. In general, the principles underlying these provisions are that[3]:

(a) agreements should be simple to understand and comply with;
(b) there should be sufficient flexibility to allow for those cases where information cannot be provided immediately;
(c) the required information should be kept within reasonable limits and made prominent by, for example, inclusion in an outlined area;
(d) the courts should have a general power to dispense with any requirements the breach of which was inadvertent and did not mislead; and
(e) sanctions for breach are tailored to the gravity of the offence.

The provisions do not apply to:

(a) non-commercial agreements[4];
(b) debtor-creditor agreements enabling the debtor to overdraw on a current account;
(c) debtor-creditor agreements to finance the making of payments arising on, or connected with, the death of a person[5]; and
(d) small debtor-creditor-supplier agreements for restricted use credit[6].

The sanctions for non-compliance with the statutory formal requirements are potentially severe. An agreement which does not comply with the formalities is 'not properly executed' and cannot be enforced against the debtor[7] or hirer unless either the court makes an enforcement order[8], or the debtor or hirer consents to enforcement[9]. This may have consequences beyond the relationship of debtor and creditor. In *Dimond v Lovell*[10] D's car was damaged in an accident caused by the negligence of L. While her car was undergoing repair, she hired a replacement from a car hire company specialising in 'accident hire'. The hire agreement provided for payment of the hire charges to be deferred until her claim for damages was resolved. It was held that the agreement was therefore a consumer credit agreement and, not being exempt, was regulated. It did not comply with the formalities applicable to regulated credit agreements and it was therefore unenforceable against D. D was therefore unable to recover damages from L to cover the costs of hire, for which D was not legally liable[11]. On the other hand, an improperly executed agreement is not void. Thus if the debtor takes delivery of goods under an improperly executed conditional sale agreement he is in possession as a person who has agreed to buy goods. Therefore if he resells the goods, even if he does so before the agreement is properly executed, his buyer may acquire a good title to the goods pursuant to s 25 of the Sale of Goods Act 1979[12].

Improper execution of an agreement means that the agreement is unenforceable against the debtor without a court order. The debtor may therefore obtain a benefit under the contract without having to pay for it. In *Dimond* the House of Lords rejected an argument that the hire company could claim payment from D on a restitutionary basis to prevent her being unjustly enriched at their expense. Acceptance of that argument would have undermined the policy of CCA 1974 that where the relevant formal requirements are not complied with the debtor should not have to pay. Theoretically, therefore, where an agreement is improperly executed the customer may be able to retain the credit or goods without payment. The court does, however, have power to permit enforcement. In deciding whether or not to make an enforcement order the court must consider the prejudice caused to the debtor by the improper execution and the degree of the creditor's culpability. A court would, therefore, probably be sympathetic to a creditor or owner seeking enforcement of an improperly executed agreement where the customer had not been prejudiced[13], especially where the breach was inadvertent or had been remedied[14]. If the court does make an enforcement order, it has extensive powers to impose conditions, including to reduce any amount payable by the debtor to compensate him for prejudice caused by the default[15] or to amend any agreement or security[16].

1   Law of Property (Miscellaneous Provisions) Act 1989, s 2.
2   Statute of Frauds 1677, s 4; see 23.1.1.3.
3   See Report of the Committee on Consumer Credit (1971) Cmnd 4596, pp 265–266.
4   See 25.2.
5   Eg payments of capital transfer tax or court fees relating to a grant of representation.
6   See 25.2.
7   This does not mean that there is no legal liability for other purposes: *R v Modupe* [1991] Crim LR 530.
8   Section 127(1). See 26.7.
9   Section 173 (3).
10 [2000] 2 All ER 897, HL.
11 It may be possible for the accident hire company to avoid this outcome by drafting the agreement so as to bring it within one of the categories of exempt agreements, but see *Zoan v Rouamba* [2000] 2 All ER 620, where such an attempt was unsuccessful.
12 *Carlyle Finance Ltd v Pallas Finance Ltd* [1999] 1 All ER (Comm) 659.
13 Section 127; see *Nissan Finance UK Ltd v Lockhart* [1993] CCLR 39.
14 Certain types of breach are irremediable: see 26.2.3.
15 Section 127(2); see *National Guardian Mortgage Corpn Ltd v Wilkes* [1993] CCLR 1; *Rank Xerox v Hepple* [1994] CCLR 1.
16 Section 136.

26.1.1   *Pre-contract information*

CCA 1974, s 55 enables regulations to be made requiring specified information to be disclosed to a prospective debtor or hirer before a regulated agreement is made. No regulations have been made under this section; however, most debtors and hirers will receive some information under the advertising and quotation regulations.

26.1.2   *Form and content*

Regulations[1] also require that a debtor or hirer is made aware in the agreement of his obligations and rights under CCA 1974, the amount and rate of the charge for credit and any remedies available. In particular, the debtor under a hire purchase agreement must be informed of his right of termination, and the limitation on the creditor's right of repossession where the goods are protected[2]. Such information as is required must, where appropriate, be given prominence and be easily legible and distinguishable. Any financial information must be presented as a whole in the agreement.

The agreement, in a form complying with the regulations, must be signed personally by the debtor or hirer and by or on behalf of the creditor or owner. Signature on a blank form with details provided at a later date is not sufficient.

It seems that, on the whole, compliance with the formal requirements of the regulations causes few difficulties for most businesses[3]. Most consumer credit and hire agreements are made on printed standard forms, drafted to comply with the regulations. Traders may apply to the Director General of Fair Trading for the formal requirements to be waived where it would be impracticable to comply, but it seems that such waivers are rarely sought[4].

One may question whether the formal requirements fulfil their objective of providing consumers with information. Credit contracts often contain many detailed provisions, often couched in complicated language and in small print. Such agreements are, of course, subject to the 1999 Unfair Terms in Consumer Contracts Regulations[5] and must therefore be expressed in plain, intelligible language.

1   Consumer Credit (Agreements) Regulations 1983, as amended, made pursuant to ss 60–61.
2   See 26.6.5.
3   But see *Dimond v Lovell* [2000] 2 All ER 897, above. Accident hire agreements have generated an enormous volume of litigation in recent years, much of it turning on compliance with the CCA formality requirements.
4   In *Dimond v Lovell* Sir Richard Scott V-C, in the Court of Appeal, took the view that any such waiver would operate prospectively only, and could not retrospectively validate an improperly executed agreement: [1999] 3 All ER 1 at 15.
5   See *Director of Fair Trading v First National Bank plc* [2000] 2 All ER 759; see 2.6.5.

26.1.3   *Copies of the agreement*

A person entering into a regulated agreement is entitled to receive one, and in some cases, two copies of the agreement. The most common situation is for a customer to sign an agreement at business premises and then, after checks on creditworthiness, for the creditor to sign at a later date. In that case, the customer must be given a copy of the unexecuted agreement[1] when first he signs it and also be supplied with a copy of the agreement once it has been signed by the creditor and thereby become executed. The second copy must be given to the customer within seven days of the agreement being made. The reason for requiring the consumer to be given two copies of the agreement is to allow him to compare the agreement he signed with the final, fully executed agreement to ensure that no changes are made to it after he signs.

Where the creditor or hirer has already signed, the customer's signature will convert the agreement into an executed agreement, of which the customer is entitled to one copy. No further copy would then be required.

Special rules apply where the agreement is secured on land. In that case the debtor is entitled to receive three copies of the agreement[2].

The debtor or hirer is also entitled to request a copy of the agreement or particulars of the sums paid or payable, during the currency of the agreement[3].

1   Section 62(1).
2   Section 58.
3   Sections 77–79.

26.2   Withdrawal and cancellation

A consumer credit agreement will normally be made by the consumer making an offer which is accepted by the creditor[1]. At common law the consumer is, of course, entitled to revoke his offer at any time before it is accepted[2]. CCA 1974 bolsters that common law right by giving the consumer an absolute right to withdraw from a prospective agreement at any time before the agreement is made, and supplements it by giving the consumer an additional right to cancel any agreement within a limited time after it is made.

1   Normally, the consumer makes an offer by completing and signing the creditor's standard form credit agreement and submitting it to the creditor, and the creditor accepts by signing the agreement in its turn, but an agreement may come into being at an earlier stage, as where the consumer's offer is accepted by conduct: see *Carlyle Finance Ltd v Pallas Industrial Finance Ltd* [1999] 1 All ER (Comm) 659.
2   See 2.3.1.

26.2.1   *Antecedent negotiations*

Entry into a formal regulated agreement will normally be preceded by some communication between the prospective debtor/hirer and the creditor or someone acting on the creditor's behalf. CCA 1974 refers to such pre-contract communications as 'antecedent negotiations' which are defined in s 56 as any negotiations with the debtor or hirer conducted:

(a)   by the creditor or owner;
(b)   by a credit broker in relation to goods which the broker supplies to the creditor to be supplied to the debtor under a two party d-c-s agreement; or
(c)   the supplier in a three party d-c-s agreement[1].

Negotiations begin when the negotiator and debtor or hirer first enter into communication, including by advertisements, and include all representations made by the negotiator to the debtor and any other dealings between them[2].

Thus if a consumer visits a car dealer and agrees to take a car on hire purchase under a hire purchase agreement with a finance house, the transaction is a two party d-c-s agreement under which the car dealer supplies the car to the finance house and arranges the credit agreement. Any advertisement by the car dealer and the consumer's negotiations with the dealer are therefore 'antecedent negotiations' under head (b). If the consumer agreed instead to buy the car from the dealer with the aid of a loan supplied by the finance house, the agreement would be a three party d-c-s agreement and the consumer's negotiations with the car dealer would be 'antecedent negotiations' under head (c).

In cases (b) and (c) the negotiator is treated as acting both on his own behalf and as agent for the creditor[3]. Effectively, therefore, in such cases a dealer who initiates a credit agreement is treated as the agent of the creditor so that the creditor is liable for the dealer's statements. Moreover, this statutory agency cannot be excluded: any agreement is void to the extent that it purports to make the negotiator agent for the debtor or to relieve the creditor from liability for the acts or omissions of the negotiator[4].

This statutory agency has its origins in narrower provisions in the Hire Purchase Act 1965[5]. It is particularly important because at common law the dealer is not normally regarded as the agent of the creditor in such a case[6], although he may have actual or apparent authority in a particular case[7]. Significantly, however, the statutory agency does not apply in cases where a dealer initiates a hire or leasing contract through a finance company. In such cases the finance company will only be bound by statements made by the dealer if the dealer has actual or apparent authority to act as the agent of the finance company.

1   Section 56(1).
2   Section 56(4).

3   Section 56(2).
4   Section 56(3).
5   HPA 1965, s 16.
6   *Branwhite v Worcester Works Finance Ltd* [1969] 1 AC 552; see below 26.4.
7   See eg *Lease Management Services Ltd v Purnell Secretarial Services Ltd* [1994] CCLR 127.

26.2.2   *Withdrawal*

Either party may withdraw from a prospective regulated agreement by giving to the other oral or written notice of his intention to withdraw[1]. However, the consumer debtor or hirer may also give notice to any credit-broker or supplier who acted as negotiator for the creditor in antecedent negotiations[2], or to any person who, in the course of a business carried on by him, acted on behalf of the consumer in any negotiations for the agreement[3]. The statute thus allows the consumer to give effective notice of withdrawal not only to the creditor or his agent, but also to his own agent, such as the solicitor who negotiated a loan on his behalf.

The Act further strengthens the consumer's right to withdraw by providing that any agreement is void if and to the extent that it purports to bind the consumer to enter into a regulated agreement[4].

The effect of withdrawal is the same as that of cancellation, considered below.

1   Section 57(1).
2   Section 57(3). 'Antecedent negotiations' are defined in s 56: see below.
3   Section 57(3)(b).
4   Section 59.

26.2.3   *Cancellation*

At common law both parties are bound once an agreement is concluded. However, in order to protect consumers against high pressure sales tactics of doorstep salesmen, the Hire-Purchase Act 1965 conferred on a hirer or buyer a right to cancel an agreement within a limited period after its conclusion where it was signed other than at appropriate trade premises, thus giving the consumer a 'cooling-off' period to reflect on the agreement and decide whether to proceed with it. CCA 1974 extends that right of cancellation to all regulated agreements where the antecedent negotiations include oral representations made in the presence of the customer by an individual acting as, or on behalf of, the negotiator, and the unexecuted agreement is signed by the debtor or hirer elsewhere than the business premises of the creditor or owner, any party to a linked transaction or the negotiator[1]. The provisions do not therefore apply to the situation where high pressure canvassing takes place at the customer's home but the agreement is then signed at business premises some time later; conversely, they do apply where negotiations take place at the creditor's premises but the debtor is allowed to take the agreement away to sign it. It is arguable that in such a case there is no danger of the debtor being pressurised into the agreement since he first seeks the creditor by visiting his premises, and has time for reflection before signing, and it has therefore been suggested that the law should be amended to provide that the agreement would not be cancellable where the antecedent negotiations take place on trade premises[2].

An agreement is only cancellable under these provisions where oral representations are made in the debtor's presence during 'antecedent negotiations'. 'Representation' is given a wider meaning under the Act than it has at common law, and is defined to include 'any condition or warranty, and any other statement or undertaking'[3]. Thus promissory statements as to the future, which could not be representations at common law, can be representations for the purposes of the Act. The intention is to protect the consumer who is subjected to sales talk[4]. The meaning of 'representation' was considered by the Court of Appeal in *Moorgate Services Ltd v Kabir*. The court held that a representation could be a statement of fact or opinion or a promise as to the future. It need not relate either to the credit agreement, or where the agreement involves the supply of goods, directly to the goods to be supplied, but may relate to ancillary matters. The only restriction is that a representation must be 'a statement which is capable of inducing the proposed debtor to enter into the contract'[5] or 'which is material to any of the matters being negotiated with the debtor or hirer and which is capable of influencing his judgment whether or not to enter into the agreement'[6].

The cancellation provisions do not apply to non-commercial agreements and small debtor-creditor-supplier agreements for restricted-use credit, nor to agreements secured on land[7], restricted-use agreements to finance the purchase of land, or bridging loans in connection with the purchase of land, when cancellation of agreements would cause practical difficulties, requiring, for instance, conveyancing transactions to be undone and registrations of charges on land to be cancelled.

If an agreement is cancellable, each copy of it must contain a notice in the prescribed form indicating the right of cancellation, how and when it may be exercised and the name and address of a person to whom notice of cancellation may be given. Where the circumstances require that a second copy of the agreement be given to the customer, the second copy must be sent by post. Where a second copy is not required, a separate notice containing the cancellation information must be posted to the customer within seven days of the agreement being made[8]. Failure to comply with these requirements means that the agreement is improperly executed and cannot be enforced[9].

The consumer can cancel at any time within the period beginning when he signs the unexecuted agreement and ending at the end of the fifth day following the day on which the consumer receives the second copy of the executed agreement, or the cancellation notice if no second copy is required[10]. Cancellation can be effected by giving notice, in any form, to the creditor or owner, their agent, any person specified in the agreement, a credit broker or supplier who was a negotiator in antecedent negotiations, or to any person who, in the course of business, acted on behalf of the consumer in any negotiations for the agreement[11]. If the notice is sent by post it is effective at the time of posting, even if it is never received[12].

On cancellation, the agreement and any linked transaction are treated as if they had never been made[13]. Any payments made are recoverable[14] and the customer must return any goods supplied[15]. Where, however, such goods have become incorporated into land or other goods, or supplied to meet an emergency, the cash price must be paid[16]. If, however, the goods are perishable, or have been consumed by use before cancellation, the customer is under no obligation to return them or pay the cash price[17]. The rationale of this provision is that the customer should not be deterred from exercising cancellation rights whilst in possession of perishable goods such as might be the case where a freezer is supplied together with frozen food. It is, however, unlikely that such goods would be delivered to the customer before the cancellation period expires.

The creditor must within ten days return to the consumer any goods given by the consumer in part-exchange, or pay the consumer a sum equivalent to the part-exchange allowance[18].

These provisions apply only to regulated consumer credit and hire agreements but consumers now have similar cancellation rights in a number of other situations[19].

1   Section 67.
2   OFT *Consumer Credit Deregulation: A review by the Director General of Fair Trading* (1994) OFT.
3   Section 189.
4   See Goode, *Consumer Credit Law* para 15-40.
5   *Moorgate Services Ltd v Kabir* [1999] CCLR 74, per Staughton LJ.
6   Per Beldam LJ.
7   Section 67(a).
8   Section 64.
9   Section 127.
10 Section 68.
11 Section 169.
12 Section 69(7).
13 Section 69(4).
14 Section 70 (sums paid by the debtor); s 71 (sums paid by the creditor; there are complicated provisions dealing with the recalculation of repayments where the debtor does not immediately repay in full any credit advanced).
15 Section 72.
16 Section 69(2), s 72(9).
17 Section 72(9).
18 Section 73. This requirement could create difficulties where the creditor has given a generous part exchange allowance in excess of the value of the part exchange goods but cannot return them.
19 Consumer Protection (Cancellation of Contracts Conducted away from Business Premises) Regulations 1987, SI 1987/2117, implementing Council Directive 85/577/EEC; Financial Services (Cancellation) Rules 1989; Consumer Protection (Distance Selling) Regulations 2000, SI 2000/2334 implementing Council Directive 97/7/EC. There are a number if significant differences between the various cancellation regimes.

26.3   Duty to provide information during the agreement

The debtor or hirer under a regulated agreement has a statutory right to require the creditor or owner to provide information as to the amounts paid under the agreement and amounts outstanding[1].

1   Sections 77–79; s 97.

26.4   Dealer/creditor liability

We have seen that where the supply of goods or services is financed by credit there are often three parties involved. The consumer may negotiate with a dealer who supplies goods or services to the consumer, but also arranges a contract between the consumer and a finance company to supply the consumer with credit to finance the transaction. Alternatively, the dealer may supply goods to the finance company for it to supply them to the consumer on hire purchase or similar terms. In both cases the consumer has a contract with the finance company, and in the second case may have no direct contractual relationship with the dealer. In both cases, however, the consumer often has direct contact only with the dealer who is responsible for negotiating the whole transaction.

The dealer could, of course, be liable to the consumer for any false statements he makes on the basis of fraud or negligent misstatement[1], or his statements might be interpreted as giving rise to a collateral contract[2]. At common law, however, the dealer's statements could only affect the contract between consumer and creditor so as to become terms of it or give rise to liability for misrepresentation if the dealer was acting as agent for the creditor when negotiating with the consumer. Generally there would be no such agency at common law.

The classic exposition of the situation was provided by Pearson LJ in *Mercantile Credit Co Ltd v Hamblin*[3] and approved by a majority of the House of Lords in *Branwhite v Worcester Works Finance Ltd*[4]:

> 'There is no rule of law that in a hire purchase transaction the dealer never is, or always is, acting as agent for the finance company. In a typical hire purchase transaction the dealer is a party in his own right, selling his car to the finance company, and he is acting primarily on his own behalf and not as a general agent for either of the two parties. There is no need to attribute to him an agency in order to account for his participation in the transaction. Nevertheless the dealer is to some extent an intermediary between the customer and the finance company and he may well have in a particular case some ad hoc agency to do particular things on behalf of one party or the other or it may be both of these two parties. For instance, if the car is delivered by the dealer to the customer after the hire purchase agreement has been conducted, the dealer must be making delivery as agent of the finance company'.

An actual or apparent agency may be found on the facts of a particular case. For instance, in *Lease Management Services Ltd v Purnell Secretarial Services Ltd*[5] the plaintiff negotiated a contract for the lease of a photocopier with a representative of Canon (South West) Ltd. The copier was actually supplied to the defendant company which let it to the plaintiff, but the defendant traded as 'Canon (South West) Finance' and the lease contract made it appear that the defendant company was part of the same group as Canon (South West) Ltd. The defendant was held to be estopped from denying that it was part of the same group as Canon (South West) Ltd or that that company was its agent when negotiating the lease. However, the general rule is that, unless the facts are exceptional, no agency will arise at common law[6], even where the dealer has a master contract with the finance house, and is allowed to use the finance house's pre-printed forms and take a commission from the finance house[7]. The finance company is therefore not liable for any statements or promises by the dealer to the consumer, the dealer has no authority to vary or terminate the contract on behalf of the finance house or to receive notice of termination, and the dealer would not necessarily be the agent of the finance company to receive payment of any pre-contract deposit.

Lord Wilberforce, dissenting in *Branwhite*, argued that the majority decision ignored mercantile reality. The Hire Purchase Act 1965 recognised that reality and laid down that in a hire purchase transaction the dealer should be treated as agent of the finance house[8]. As we have seen[9] the CCA follows that line and s 56 treats the dealer as the creditor's agent in negotiations antecedent to both two and three party d-c-s transactions[10].

In relation to two party d-c-s agreements the dealer/credit broker is said to be the creditor's agent when conducting negotiations 'in relation to goods sold or proposed to be sold by the credit broker to the dealer' to be supplied to the consumer under a two party d-c-s agreement[11]. It has been held, however, that the agency is not limited to the dealer's representations about the goods or the credit. If there are negotiations relating to the goods, all representations made during those negotiations are covered by the statutory agency. In *Forthright Finance Ltd v Ingate*[12] a consumer wanted to buy a new car and dispose of her old one, which was subject to an existing conditional sale agreement. During negotiations relating to the supply of the new car, the dealer/credit-broker agreed to buy the consumer's old car and use the proceeds to discharge the outstanding liability under the existing conditional sale agreement. The transaction was completed but the dealer failed to discharge the existing liability. The Court of Appeal held that a wide meaning should be given to the words 'in relation to the goods' to cover all negotiations forming part of the overall transaction. Even though there was a separate contract for the sale of the old car to the dealer, the dealer's undertaking was part of the transaction for the new car – without it the consumer would not have bought the new car – and was therefore made in the course of the statutory agency. The creditor was therefore liable for it. Thus, it seems, even undertakings or representations about matters collateral to the main contract will fall within the statutory agency provided that they can be said to form part of the overall 'transaction'.

Where the statutory agency applies there is therefore no need to consider whether the dealer had actual or apparent authority to act for the creditor at common law[13]. The creditor is bound by the statements and undertakings made by the dealer during negotiations and any attempt to exclude its liability for them is void[14]. However, in situations not covered by s 56, such as negotiations leading to an unregulated agreement or to the making of a hire or leasing contract it will still be necessary to decide if an agency can be found at common law.

1 Under the principle in *Hedley Byrne & Co Ltd v Heller & Partners* [1964] AC 465.
2 *Andrews v Hopkinson* [1957] 1 QB 229, [1956] 3 All ER 422.
3 [1965] 2 QB 242 at 269, CA.
4 [1969] 1 AC 552, [1968] 3 All ER 104. Lord Wilberforce delivered a powerful dissent: see 3.2.1.
5 [1994] CCLR 127; see also *Woodchester Leasing Equipment Ltd v Clayton and Clayton* [1994] CCLR 87, where an agency was found on the facts.
6 *Woodchester Leasing Equipment Ltd v British Association of Canned and Preserved Foods Importers and Distributors Ltd* [1995] CCLR 51.
7 *Mercantile Credit Co Ltd v Hamblin* [1965] 2 QB 242 at 269; and see *JD Williams & Co v McCauley, Parsons and Jones* [1994] CCLR 78.
8 HPA 1965, s 16.
9 See 26.2.1.
10 Section 56(2).
11 Section 56(1)(b).
12 [1997] 4 All ER 99.
13 See Goode, *Consumer Credit Law* (2nd edn, 1989) p 496; see ch 4 above.
14 Section 56(3).

26.4.1 *Joint and several liability*

We have seen that at common law in a typical three party transaction where the customer purchased goods from a seller with funds supplied by a connected creditor, the creditor incurred no liability for any defects in the goods or any other breach of contract by the seller. The Crowther Committee were concerned to expose the reality of the three way relationship. They considered that:

> 'To a considerable extent the finance house and the dealer are engaged in a joint venture. The finance house controls the contract documents used by the dealer in his instalment credit business. It competes keenly with other finance houses for the privilege of obtaining the dealer's credit business. On motor vehicle business it pays the dealer a substantial commission for

introducing a hire purchase contract, thus giving the dealer a positive incentive to procure the customer's signature to a hire purchase agreement instead of settling for cash. It provides general financial support for the dealer, the cost of which may be materially influenced by the volume of retail instalment credit business introduced to it by the dealer. When business is slack, the finance house will continually press the dealer to increase the volume of transactions put through . . .

If, with all the pressure for business exerted by the lender and the financial inducements the lender offers, the seller seeks to boost sales by making false representations, or supplies goods which are defective, is it right that the lender should be able to disclaim all responsibility and insist on repayments of the loan being punctually maintained? We do not think so . . .'[1].

The Committee went on to justify why the buyer's rights against a seller may be insufficient protection.

'The majority of the cases in which the buyer is likely to suffer are those where a seller is of doubtful repute and is able to continue in business only because of the financial support he receives from the lender. The buyer supplied with defective goods may find that to secure redress from such a seller he has to incur the worry and expense of litigation in which the burden of taking the initiative lies with him; and that in some cases the seller's financial position is so poor that it is doubtful whether he will be able to meet the judgment even if the buyer is successful. The buyer's difficulties of pursuing a claim against the seller are enhanced if, whilst wrestling with the financial problems of litigation, he has to go on paying the lender under the loan agreement. Problems of this kind are particularly prevalent in relation to agreements for the installation of central heating. There have been many cases where the supplier has either not delivered at all or has provided an ineffective heating system, and has then gone into liquidation before the consumer has been able to obtain redress, so that the consumer is left to meet a liability on a loan contract entered into with a third party'[2].

The Report therefore concluded:

'we therefore recommend that where the price payable under a consumer sale agreement is advanced wholly or in part by a connected lender the lender should be liable for misrepresentation relating to the goods made by the seller in the course of antecedent negotiations and for defects in title, fitness and quality of goods. Further, we consider that where the sale and the loan are made by separate contracts, the borrower should nevertheless have the right to set off against any sum payable by him under the loan contract any damages he is entitled to recover from the lender for breaches of the sale agreement by the seller.

In reaching this conclusion we have been influenced by the additional fact that if the delinquent seller is worth powder and shot it ought to be easier for the lender to put pressure on him to deal with the complaint than it is for the borrower. The lender is not likely to be so inhibited by expense of suing the seller; and in most cases proceedings by the lender would be unnecessary because the lender is in a position to say to the seller that future financing facilities will be withdrawn unless the seller attends to the complaint and takes greater care in the conduct of his business'[3].

The Committee's recommendations were implemented by CCA 1974, s 75, which provides that if the debtor under a three party d-c-s agreement made under or in contemplation of arrangements between the supplier and creditor has, in relation to a transaction financed by the agreement, any claim against the supplier in respect of a misrepresentation or breach of contract, he shall have a like claim against the creditor. The effect of s 75 is therefore to make the creditor under a three party d-c-s transaction jointly and severally liable with the supplier for any breach of contract or misrepresentation by the supplier.

The existence of this potential liability is a considerable protection for consumers against the unwillingness or inability of a supplier to meet a claim. It is particularly useful where the supplier has become insolvent. The extent of the creditor's liability may, of course, far exceed the amount of credit advanced. For example, if customer A buys furniture from supplier B to the value of £3,000 and pays a deposit of £150 on a credit card and the rest in cash, and B becomes insolvent before the furniture becomes A's property, the credit card company is liable to refund the full amount of £3,000. Similarly, if A buys a car for £5,000 from dealer B with the aid of a loan of £3,000 from creditor C and defects in the car cause an accident in which A is injured, C is jointly and severally liable to A for damages for breach of contract, which will include damages for A's injuries.

The effect of s 75 is that if the debtor has a claim against the supplier he has a 'like claim' against the creditor. In a Scots case[4] it was held that this meant that where a breach of contract by the supplier gave the debtor the right to terminate the supply contract, the debtor was also entitled to terminate the credit contract. The decision has however been criticised, and in *Jarrett v Barclays Bank plc*[5] the Court of Appeal held that 'like claim' must mean 'like cause of action' so that the supplier's breach of contract or misrepresentation will give the debtor a cause of action not only against the supplier but also against the creditor, albeit that the remedies available against them will differ; so, for instance, the fact that the consumer has a right to specific performance as against the supplier will not give him a right to specific performance against the creditor. The better view is therefore that where the consumer has a right to terminate or rescind his contract with the supplier, he is not entitled to terminate the credit agreement, but, having terminated the supply contract, he has a monetary claim against the supplier either for a refund of the price, or for damages, and can make a 'like claim' against the creditor for the same amount, which can be enforced by withholding payments due under the credit agreement. Where the debtor's claim is for breach of contract, however, it would seem that damages would not include compensation for sums, such as interest, payable under the credit agreement. Such sums would be recoverable where the debtor's claim is for misrepresentation[6].

Where a debtor does proceed against a creditor, the creditor is entitled to join the supplier as a party to the action and claim an indemnity from him[7].

Section 75 does not apply to non-commercial agreements[8] or to disputes where the claim relates to any single item to which the supplier has attached a cash price not exceeding £100 or more than £30,000[9]. By using the term 'any single item', the section imposes a somewhat arbitrary restriction on claims. For example, if a consumer buys a number of different items in one purchase but the items are separately priced, there would be no claim under s 75 in respect of any particular item with a price of £100 or less[10].

In 1993 the Deregulation Task Force established by the President of the Board of Trade recommended that s 75 should be amended so as to impose on the creditor 'second in line liability' under which the creditor would only be liable where the consumer had first unsuccessfully pursued the supplier. It was argued that this approach would be closer to that adopted in the EC Consumer Credit Directive[11]. However, this suggestion was rejected by the Director General of Fair Trading[12]. The directive permits member states to have stronger consumer protection measures. Moreover, in practice, consumers do normally pursue the supplier before the creditor but to require them to pursue hopeless claims would considerably weaken their protection.

1 Report of the Committee on Consumer Credit (1971) Cmnd 4596, para 6.6.22.
2 Paragraph 6.6.25.
3 Paragraphs 6.6.26–6.6.29.
4 *United Dominions Trust v Taylor* 1980 SLT 28.
5 [1997] 2 All ER 484.
6 See 2.4.2.1.
7 Section 75(2), (5).
8 See 25.2.
9 Section 75(3)(b); it was suggested in 1994 that the lower limit should be increased to £150 but in 1995 the DGFT favoured retention of the present limit: OFT, *Connected Lender Liability: A Second Review by the Director General of Fair Trading of s 75 of the Consumer Credit Act 1974* (1995).
10 See Goode, *Consumer Credit Law* (2nd edn, 1989) p 493.
11 Directive 87/102/EEC.
12 OFT, *Connected Lender Liability: A Review by the Director General of Fair Trading of s 75 of the Consumer Credit Act 1974* (1994).

26.5 The regulation of credit and other cards

The credit card is perhaps the most common form of financial accommodation used today. CCA 1974 contains some provisions specifically applicable to credit cards and credit card transactions. However, their scope is uncertain and some of the Act's general provisions can be applied to credit card transactions only with difficulty. This is perhaps unsurprising. When the Crowther Committee reported in 1971, credit cards were already in use, but their use has increased dramatically since then. Credit card turnover as a percentage of consumer spending increased eightfold between 1976 and 1991[1]. By 1998 there were 22.7 million cardholders in the UK, representing some 49% of the adult population[2]. Moreover, as explained in an earlier chapter[3], the structure of credit card transactions has changed considerably in that time, with the development of international credit card networks in which banks act as 'merchant acquirers', recruiting traders to accept credit cards on behalf of all banks that are members of the network. These developments have, in particular, created difficulties in applying CCA 1974, s 75 to credit card transactions. In addition, a number of different types of card have come into common use since the Act was passed, and the Act's application to them is uncertain.

1 See OFT, *Connected Lender Liability: A Review by the Director General of Fair Trading of s 75 of the Consumer Credit Act 1974* (1994).
2 Association of Payment Clearing Services, *Payments Market Briefing* (July 1999).
3 See 21.1.3.1.

26.5.1 *Credit tokens and credit token agreements*

CCA 1974 does not refer to credit cards as such, but to 'credit tokens' and 'credit token agreements'. A credit token is defined as a:

'card, cheque, voucher, coupon, stamp, form, booklet or other document or thing given to an individual by a person carrying on a consumer credit business who undertakes (a) that on production of it to the creditor he will supply cash, goods or services to the debtor on credit, or (b) that if it is produced to a third party who supplies cash, goods or services, he will pay the third party for them in return for payment to him by the individual'[1].

A 'credit token agreement', is a 'regulated agreement for the provision of credit in connection with the use of a credit token[2]'.

There is no doubt that credit cards issued by retailing organisations, banks, building societies and other similar organisations are credit tokens, issued under credit token agreements, as, too, are cheques and vouchers issued by institutions and used by the consumer to acquire goods up to the face value of the voucher. Since the card agreement is a regulated agreement, it must comply with the general requirements applicable to regulated agreements. Most credit cards can be used both to pay for goods or services and to draw cash, and can therefore be used to obtain restricted and unrestricted use credit, and the Act therefore assumes that credit card agreements are multiple agreements[3]. Charge cards are credit tokens but since the agreements under which they are issued are exempt agreements[4], they are not regulated and therefore not 'credit token agreements'. Cheque guarantee cards are not credit tokens because although they are issued under a consumer credit agreement, the issuer (the bank) does not undertake to pay for goods or services but to honour cheques drawn supported by the card[5].

The position of debit, EFTPOS and ATM cards is not clear[6]. A debit or EFTPOS card appears to fall within the definition of a 'credit token': the issuer undertakes to the holder that where goods are supplied to the holder on presentation of the card, the issuer will pay the supplier[7]. It may be noted that where a third party supplies goods or cash on presentation of a card, there is no need for there to be any credit element to the transaction for the card to qualify as a credit token (see (b) above)[8]. On the other hand, it may be argued that debit and EFTPOS cards are merely a means of payment, effectively a substitute for a cheque; the issuer undertakes not to pay for goods or services bought using the card, but to honour the cardholder's order to pay[9]. It might also be argued that, so long as the cardholder's account is in credit, the card issuer does not pay third parties who supply goods or services 'in return for payment to him by the [cardholder]' unless the bank is treated as paying in return for a payment to itself made by debiting the cardholder's account. It is therefore not clear whether a debit or EFTPOS card is a 'credit token'. Whatever the status of the card itself, a 'credit token agreement' must be an agreement for the provision of credit. However, the effect of s 14(3) is that where the issuer of a credit token undertakes to pay third parties who supply goods, services or cash on production of the token, there is a deemed provision of credit. The result is that if a debit or EFTPOS card is a credit token, it is issued under a 'credit token agreement'.

An ATM card can only be used to withdraw cash from an ATM, but the machine may be operated by the card issuer or by another bank. Where the card can be used to withdraw cash from third party ATMs, the analysis seems to be the same as for debit and EFTPOS cards, above – the third party pays cash on production of the card, the card issuer then pays the third party – so that the card is a credit token issued under a credit token agreement. Where, however, the card can only be used to withdraw cash from the issuer's machine, the issuer is undertaking that he will supply cash on presentation of the card. In that case the card is only a credit token if cash is supplied *on credit*[10] (see (a) above), so the card is not a credit token unless the holder can use it to overdraw his account. The card will only be issued under a credit token agreement if the agreement provides for it to be used to overdraw on the account.

The position is thus most unsatisfactory. EFTPOS, debit and ATM cards are now regular features of everyday life, and yet there is no settled understanding of their legal status. The use of such cards, unless in conjunction with an overdraft facility, involves little or no grant of credit – no more than when payment is made by cheque. In general, the credit period is a matter of days, at most. If they are credit tokens, subject to the Act, their treatment as such is in most cases anomalous. Charge cards, use of which allows the user to enjoy a longer, but limited, period of credit, are exempted from most of the Act's provisions. The position is further complicated by the fact that any cards today are 'multi-function' cards, capable of being used as debit, EFTPOS and ATM cards. For many purposes, however, the question whether a debit, EFTPOS or ATM card is a credit token issued under a credit token agreement will be irrelevant, because several key provisions of the CCA will not apply to them in any case.

1   Section 14(1).
2   Section 14(2).
3   See Example 16 in CCA 1974, Sch 2, Pt II.
4   Consumer Credit (Exempt Agreements) Order 1989, SI 1989/869; see 25.1.2.
5   See 36.1.
6   See generally the discussion in Sealy and Hooley, *Commercial Law, Text, Cases and Materials* (2nd edn, 1999) pp 742–747.
7   See *Paget's Law of Banking* (11th edn, 1996) ch 19; Sealy and Hooley, *Commercial Law, Text, Cases and Materials* (2nd edn, 1999) p 745.
8   See s 14(1)(b). In practice, purchases made with a debit card are not charged to the cardholder's bank account until after a few days so that there is generally an element of credit.
9   See Goode, *Consumer Credit Legislation* (looseleaf) para I 549.3.
10 Section 14(1)(a).

26.5.2 *Joint liability and credit cards*

It is generally accepted that where a credit card is used to acquire goods or services at an approved outlet, a three party d-c-s agreement is created and that, as a result, the card issuer is potentially jointly and severally liable with the supplier under s 75 of the Act. The credit card issuers, however, have been very reluctant to accept such liability and, over the years, have advanced a number of arguments to justify their refusal to accept liability. Many of these seem questionable or even spurious, but to date – no doubt to avoid setting an adverse precedent – none of these arguments has been tested in a reported case in the higher courts.

First, it has been argued that a card issuer is only liable for consumers' claims against businesses it actually recruited to accept its card. As explained elsewhere, many businesses are now recruited by merchant acquirers to accept cards issued by all members of a particular card network, so that there is normally a fourth party, the merchant acquirer, interposed between the card issuer and the business supplier and there is therefore no agreement between the bank and the supplier. However, this argument ignores the wording of s 12 of the Act, under which there is a three party d-c-s agreement where there are 'arrangements' between creditor and supplier and it is clear that there can be 'arrangements' even though there is no direct agreement. Moreover, it seems that merchant acquirers could be regarded as acting as agents for all card issuers in their network, in which case there would be a direct agreement between the card issuer and supplier.

A second argument arises from the fact that the transitional provisions applicable to s 75 make clear that the section applies only to agreements made after 1 July 1977. Card issuers have therefore argued that they have no liability on agreements funded by use of cards issued before that date[1]. The view of many commentators is that where a card is renewed a new agreement is created, so that the section would apply to cards renewed after 1977. A further interpretation is possible. Section 75 only applies to a d-c-s agreement as defined by s 12(1)(b) or 12(1)(c). The relevant provision appears to be s 12(1)(b), under which a d-c-s agreement is a restricted use credit agreement falling within s 11(1)(b), which refers to 'an agreement to finance a transaction between the debtor and a . . . supplier'. Such an agreement would seem to be created only when the card is used to buy goods or services. On this interpretation, therefore, s 75 would apply to all transactions financed by credit cards and made after 1977, regardless of the date of issue of the card. It must be conceded, however, that this interpretation would create difficulties in applying other provisions of the Act, and it is generally assumed that a single, regulated, credit token agreement is created when a card is issued, rather than new agreements being created each time the card is used[2].

A further argument was that s 75 did not apply where the credit card financed only part of a transaction, so that, for instance, where a consumer bought a holiday and paid the deposit by cheque and the balance by card, the section would not apply. However, s 75 does not seem to require that the transaction under which liability arises be financed in full by the debtor-creditor-supplier agreement.

It has also been argued that s 75 does not apply where credit cards are used to purchase goods or services outside the UK. If the interpretation of the Act suggested above were accepted, this argument might have some substance: in that case the d-c-s agreement in question would be made outside the UK and would not be subject to the Act. However, it seems unlikely that a court would accept such a denial of liability, especially since banks encourage consumers to use cards to make purchases abroad[3].

Finally, it has been argued that the card issuer is not liable where a card is used not by the principal debtor but by some second, authorised user, such as the cardholder's spouse, who is not a 'debtor' in the terms of the Act. However, it seems clear that in such a case the authorised user could be regarded as the agent of the cardholder so that the section would apply.

The legal arguments against liability therefore seem to lack substance, but the real question is whether card issuers should be liable for the defaults of retailers and other suppliers who accept their cards. The rationale for imposing liability on the creditor under s 75 was that creditors could be expected to exercise some control over the activities and solvency of suppliers with whom they had arrangements. In view of the growth of credit card networks, however, it is unrealistic to expect banks issuing credit cards to exercise such control, especially in an international market. The card issuers have therefore argued that, regardless of the arguments outlined above, they should not be liable under s 75 and that the imposition of liability is unreasonable and burdensome.

It is clear that the real fear of the card issuers is that they may be exposed to very extensive liability in some cases, either due to the insolvency of a supplier or where there are extensive damages claims for consequential losses, as, for instance, where a card is used to pay for private medical treatment which gives rise to a claim against the doctor. It must be noted, however, that if a card issuer does meet a claim it is entitled to claim an indemnity from the supplier[4], and the right to indemnity is normally reinforced by express contractual rights to claim a 'charge-back' from the supplier or merchant acquirer who recruited the supplier to recover sums paid to the cardholder. The only real problem for card issuers, therefore, is where either the supplier is overseas, in which case there may be practical difficulties enforcing any right to indemnity, or where the supplier is insolvent.

In light of these problems, in 1994 and 1995 the Director General of Fair Trading conducted an extensive review of the application of s 75 to credit cards[5]. He concluded that the present law is neither unclear nor ambiguous. He also rejected the argument of the card issuers that they should only be liable where the consumer has first brought an unsuccessful claim against the supplier. However, he concluded that the law should be amended to limit the amount of card issuer's liability to the amount debited to the card holder's account in respect of the transaction and that s 75 should only apply where the amount paid by credit card is between the financial limits for the application of s 75[6]. In return the card issuers agreed to accept liability on a voluntary basis for overseas transactions.

Whatever the merits of these various arguments, it is clear that s 75 does not apply to debit or EFTPOS cards. Because of the doubt over their status as 'credit tokens', in order to protect the banks from joint liability for goods and services paid for by debit card, CCA, s 187(3A) specifically provides that arrangements between a creditor and a supplier are to be disregarded if they are arrangements for the electronic transfer of funds from a bank current account.

1   In 1978 card issuers voluntarily agreed with the OFT to accept liability on cards issued before 1977, but only up to the amount of credit charged to the cardholder's account in respect of the transaction.
2   The credit token agreement is for both restricted- and unrestricted-use credit and is therefore a multiple agreement within s 18. The Act assumes that a restricted-use credit agreement is made when the card is issued: see example 16 in Sch 2, Pt II.
3   In *Jarrett v Barclays Bank plc* [1997] 2 All ER 484 the Court of Appeal held that a consumer bringing a claim against a credit card issuer under s 75 could bring proceedings in England notwithstanding that a foreign court had sole jurisdiction in relation to the consumer's claim against the supplier. The consumer's claim against the card issuer was based on the credit agreement and the 1974 Act. The case did not, however, address the question whether the card issuer has any liability in this situation. If the Act does not apply to overseas purchases the UK would need to amend it in order to implement the EC Consumer Credit Directive.
4   Section 75(2); above 26.4.1.
5   OFT, *Connected Lender Liability: A review by the Director General of Fair Trading of s 75 of the Consumer Credit Act 1974* (1994); OFT, *Connected Lender Liability: A Second Review by the Director General of Fair Trading of s 75 of the Consumer Credit Act 1974* (1995).
6   See 26.4.1

26.5.3   *Credit cards and their misuse*

CCA 1974 establishes a general rule that a debtor under a regulated agreement is not liable to the creditor for any loss arising from the use of the credit facility by another person not acting, or to be treated as acting, as the debtor's agent[1].

However, the misuse of credit tokens poses special problems. In the words of the Crowther Committee:

'If a card is lost or stolen through what may be a purely momentary carelessness on the part of the cardholder, some time may elapse before he discovers the loss. During that time, a fraudulent third party could easily run up accounts to the full amount of credit provided by the card; and if the card is valid for services such as air travel, entertainment and so on the unfortunate cardholder might well be presented with a crippling bill'[2].

The Act therefore contains special provisions specifically to deal with the problem of misuse of credit tokens.

A debtor cannot be liable for an unauthorised use of a credit token unless he has first accepted the token either by signing it or a receipt for it, or by using it[3]. It is an offence to supply an unsolicited credit token[4].

Once the debtor has accepted a credit token, his liability for its misuse depends, first, on whether the person who misused it acquired possession of the token with the debtor's consent, and, secondly, whether the debtor has notified the creditor of the lose of the token.

The general rule is that a debtor under a regulated agreement is not liable for losses caused by a third party other than one acting as his agent[5]. This does not, however, prevent the debtor under a credit token agreement being held liable 'to any extent' for losses caused by a person who obtained possession of the credit token with his consent[6]. If, however, the card is accidentally lost or is stolen, the debtor's liability is limited to £50 during the period the token is not in the possession of an authorised person[7] and the debtor is not liable for any loss arising after the creditor has been given oral or written notice that the token has been lost, stolen or 'is otherwise liable to misuse'[8].

These provisions only protect a person who is a debtor under a credit token agreement for losses arising as a result of misuse of a credit facility[9]. It was suggested above that debit, EFTPOS and ATM cards may be credit tokens. It is at least arguable, however, that such cards are not credit tokens at all, or are only so classified when used in conjunction with a credit facility. On the basis of the earlier analysis it seems that some ATM cards, at least, and possibly all ATM, debit and EFTPOS cards, fall outside the scope of these provisions; certainly that was the assumption of the Banking Review Committee in 1989[10]. As a result of the Committee's recommendations, however, the Banking Code[11] imposes a similar limit on the cardholder's liability in the event of loss or unauthorised use of such cards, subject to the qualification that the cardholder is not entitled to protection if he is shown to have been guilty of fraud or 'gross negligence'.

Recent years have seen an alarming increase in the volume of fraud involving credit and other plastic cards. In 1999 the total value of losses by fraud on all types of card was £189.4m. Over half of this involved credit cards[12]. Fraud may take several forms. The most common is misuse of a lost or stolen card, including where the card has been intercepted in the post. The fastest growing area of card fraud, however, is in relation to 'card not present' transactions, where card details are used without presentation of the card, to order goods or services by mail order, telephone, over the Internet and so on. A fraudster may obtain card details in various ways, including by intercepting legitimate transactions and recording the relevant details, or by copying them from copies of customers' credit card slips. Perhaps the most sophisticated form of fraud involves the manufacture of counterfeit cards, using details copied from genuine cards.

In order to protect consumers against these types of fraud the Consumer Protection (Distance Selling) Regulations 2000[13] contain special provisions which govern the fraudulent use of cards in connection with 'distance transactions' and modify the rules described above. A consumer is entitled to cancel any payment made, and have his account re-credited, where fraudulent use has been made of his payment card in connection with a 'distance contract' by another person who was 'not acting, or to be treated as acting, as his agent'[14]. Where the consumer alleges that unauthorised use has been made of his card the card issuer bears the burden of proving that use was authorised[15]. These provisions do not apply to cases of unauthorised use of a credit facility under a regulated consumer credit agreement covered by CCA 1974. However, 'payment card' is defined as including credit cards, charge cards, debit cards and store cards[16], so that the Regulations apply to types of card not covered by the 1974 Act. In addition, the rules of CCA 1974 are modified in relation to distance contracts, so that a consumer card holder cannot be held liable under that Act for any unauthorised use of his card in connection with a distance contract, even where the card has been lost or stolen and the loss not reported[17].

The overall effect of the provisions described above is that a cardholder will not be liable for unauthorised transactions using his card or its details, except where the card is lost or stolen, when his liability is limited to £50 in respect of face to face transactions. The consumer cannot be held liable for any unauthorised use of any type of card in connection with a distance contract.

The losses arising from credit card fraud therefore fall on the card issuers. In fact, however, they will generally have the right to recover some of their losses from the retailer who accepted the card. Most card issuers' standard terms include a 'charge-back' provision under which the card issuer is entitled to withhold payment, or recover it if payment has already been made, if the cardholder denies having authorised the use of his card in relation to a card not present transaction[18]. Loss is therefore shifted onto the retailer in such cases.

Credit and other payment cards have an important role to play in the development of electronic commerce. One of the factors inhibiting that development is thought to be consumer concern about security of payment details and the risk of fraud. In fact, as demonstrated above, in many cases any loss arising from such risks will fall not on the individual cardholder but on the card issuer or retailer[19]. Nevertheless, the need to challenge unauthorised payments and enter into a dispute with a card issuer may be a serious inconvenience to a cardholder. In an effort to allay cardholders' fears, the banks and card issuers are therefore developing new, more secure, 'smart' cards. No technology is likely, however, wholly to prevent fraud. The provisions of the CCA protecting cardholders from liability for card misuse are therefore especially important in the e-commerce environment.

1 Section 83(1). The rule does not apply to non-commercial agreements and in respect of loss arising from misuse of an instrument regulated by s 4 of the Cheques Act 1957.
2 Paragraph 6.12.5.
3 Section 66.
4 Section 51 and see *Elliott v Director General of Fair Trading* [1980] 1 WLR 977, [1980] ICR 629.
5 Section 83.
6 Section 84(2).
7 Section 84(1).
8 Section 84(3).
9 Section 83(1).
10 *Banking Services Law and Practice: Report of the Review Committee* (1989).
11 Paragraph 4.14–4.16; see 30.3.3.2.
12 *Association of Payment Clearing Services Yearbook 1999*.
13 SI 2000/2334.
14 Regulation 21.
15 Regulation 21(3).
16 Regulation 21(6).
17 Regulation 21(5).
18 For discussion of the effectiveness of such provisions see Brownsword and Macgowan (1997) 147 NLJ 1806.
19 Losses may then be passed back to cardholders generally through increased charges.

26.6   Termination and remedies

Credit and hire agreements, generally made on the creditor's or owner's standard terms, predictably contain a variety of clauses granting the creditor or owner specific rights and remedies in the event of default by the customer. Provided that such clauses comply with the general principles of contract, they are entirely legitimate at common law. Common clauses include:

(a)   acceleration clauses which require immediate payment of all of the outstanding balance in the event of breach;
(b)   clauses permitting termination by the creditor on the occurrence of specified events;
(c)   clauses seeking to fix the amount of any damages payable in the event of a breach; and
(d)   clauses giving the creditor the power to repossess the subject matter of the contract.

The Crowther Committee considered that one of the three primary tasks of consumer protection legislation should be to regulate the exercise of rights available to a creditor under the general law, either by imposing restrictions on the exercise of certain rights, such as the right to repossess goods, or by giving greater discretion to the courts to intervene and relieve debtors from liability in cases of default.

In general, CCA 1974 builds on reforms made by the Hire Purchase Act 1965, and places substantive and procedural restrictions on the use and abuse of certain common contract rights available to creditors while giving extra rights to debtors. The statutory provisions seek to strike a balance between consumers and creditors/owners. On the one hand, it is relatively easy for the business creditor to bear most of the risk in default cases by a combination of prudent insurance and pricing policy, thus spreading the burden over all his customers. On the other hand:

'the concept of risk spreading must not be taken too far. Every restriction on a creditor's remedy has to be paid for to the extent to which the creditor is not himself willing or able to absorb the loss or expense in which he is involved by the restrictions on him, this must be passed on to his customers. Hence the good customer is made to subsidise the bad. Moreover, the burden of bad debts bears particularly harshly on the small trader . . .'[1]

1   See Report of the Committee on Consumer Credit (1971) Cmnd 4596, para 6.1.16.

26.6.1   *Termination of consumer credit agreement – early discharge by debtor*

CCA 1974 allows a debtor to discharge his liability under a regulated agreement in advance of the date fixed for termination by making full payment of the amount due under the agreement[1]. Thus, for instance, a debtor who acquires funds elsewhere may use them to discharge his liability under a regulated agreement. This right cannot be excluded by any term in the contract[2]. It is exercised by serving a notice on the creditor and paying any sums due under the agreement. If a debtor takes advantage of this provision, he may claim a rebate in respect of charges for credit[3] and the statutory right to make early payment is supplemented by a right to require a creditor to provide a statement of the precise amount required to discharge the debt[4], taking account of any rebate due. A failure to comply with a request for such a statement means that the agreement cannot be enforced while the default continues, and the creditor commits an offence if the default continues for one month[5]. Any statement supplied must be accurate: a creditor who supplies an inaccurate statement commits a criminal offence[6] but the statement is binding on the creditor[7] so that if the figure quoted is too low the creditor is estopped from demanding the correct balance[8].

Early settlement of a debt also terminates any future liability of the debtor or his relative, under a linked transaction other than a contract of insurance or guarantee[9].

1   Section 94.
2   Section 173(1).
3   Section 95: Consumer Credit (Rebate on Early Settlement) Regulations 1983, SI 1983/1562.
4   Section 97.
5   Section 97(3). A statement referring to the right to discharge a debt early must be included in the agreement: Consumer Credit (Agreements) Regulations, SI 1983/1553.
6   Section 97(3); see *Home Insulations Ltd v Wadsley* [1989] BTLR 13.
7   Section 172.
8   A statement may give rise to an estoppel at common law even if not given in response to a statutory request: *Lombard North Central Ltd v Stobart* [1990] BTLR 105.
9   Section 96.

26.6.2   *Termination of consumer hire agreement by hirer*

A fixed term hiring agreement may commit the hirer to make rental payments amounting in total to as much as the hire purchase price of the goods, without any of the eventual advantages of ownership that hire purchase gives a debtor. In 1964 Sachs J observed:

> 'It is becoming increasingly apparent from cases which come before the courts, that there is a tendency on the part of some finance companies, at any rate, to try to use contracts of what I have referred to as simple hire in order to ensure that the hirer does not have the protection of the Hire Purchase Act. These contracts of hire to which finance companies are inclined, are simple only in the sense that technically they are not contracts of hire purchase. One has but to look at the contract in this particular case to see in its small print how far from simple it is, either from the layman's or indeed the lawyer's point of view. The sooner the legislature is apprised of this tendency and the sooner it takes in hand the problem, the fewer will be the occasions when finance companies are able to inflict on any unwary hirer hardships of the type that have become manifest in the present case'[1].

CCA 1974 attacks these problems. Section 101 gives the hirer, under a regulated consumer hire agreement, the right to terminate the agreement after at least 18 months have expired. This right exists even where the agreement may provide for a fixed term longer than 18 months. The hirer is required to give to the owner notice equivalent to the shortest period between two payments, or of three months, whichever is less.

In general, the statutory right to terminate is intended for consumer, as opposed to commercial, hirers. Thus the right does not apply to agreements: (a) which require the hirer to make payments which in total exceed £1,500 in any year; (b) where the hirer is hiring the goods for business purposes and he selects goods which are then acquired by the owner from another person at the hirer's request; or (c) where the hirer requires the goods to hire them out to other persons in the course of business[2]. It is worth pointing out that, in the case of the second and third categories, the hirer will generally be a corporate body, in which case the agreements would not in any event be regulated hire agreements.

1   *Galbraith v Mitchenall Estates Ltd* [1965] 2 QB 473 at 485, [1964] 2 All ER 653 at 659.
2   Section 101(7).

26.6.3   *Termination of hire purchase and conditional sale agreements by returning goods*

CCA 1974, s 99, continues a provision originally contained in the Hire Purchase Act allowing the debtor under a regulated hire purchase or conditional sale agreement to terminate it and return the goods. The debtor can exercise the right at any time before his final payment is due, by giving notice to the person entitled or authorised to receive the sums payable under the agreement.

The debtor must, of course, discharge any liability that accrued before the date of termination. In addition, the debtor must normally bring his total payments up to one half of the total price before he may terminate. The agreement may, however, provide for a smaller sum, or no sum at all, to be paid.

The court has a general discretion to order payment of a lesser part of the total price if it considers that such a sum would be sufficient to compensate the creditor[1]. The courts do not, however, have any discretion to extinguish obligations to pay arrears which are already due. The debtor must, of course, return the goods and, if he has failed to take reasonable care of them, the amount payable to discharge the agreement may be increased, in order to recompense the creditor.

As a general rule, the longer the agreement has been operational and thus the more payments that have fallen due, the more inappropriate termination under this provision becomes. In such circumstances debtors may consider refinancing by borrowing an amount sufficient to make early repayment under s 94 and thus assuming ownership of the goods. In some circumstances it may even be preferable for a debtor to wait for the creditor to initiate default procedures rather than terminate under s 99.

A decision to terminate may have to be made fairly swiftly if the agreement contains an acceleration clause. Such a clause is a contractual provision requiring immediate payment of all or part of the unpaid balance of the debt on the occurrence of a specific event. Thus, if the debtor is in default, all payments fall due under the acceleration clause and the debtor loses the right to terminate since s 99(1) specifically states that the debtor is entitled to terminate the agreement 'at any time before the final payment by the debtor . . . falls due'.

The use of acceleration clauses is justified on the basis that in their absence creditors would be required to bring a series of actions as each instalment falls due, or allow the agreement to expire by which time the possibility of recovery would be remote[2]. It could be argued that such clauses are in the nature of penalties and could therefore be struck down by the courts. However, the general view is that such clauses merely advance the time when the instalments fall due and on that basis cannot be attacked as penalties[3].

1   Section 100(3).
2   See R M Goode and J S Ziegel, *Hire Purchase and Conditional Sale* (1965) p 110.
3   See *Wadham Stringer Finance Ltd v Meaney* [1980] 3 All ER 789, [1981] 1 WLR 39; Goode, *Consumer Credit Law* (2nd edn, 1989) para 20.87.

26.6.4 *Termination by the creditor on the debtor's default*

Whilst the vast majority of consumer credit agreements are discharged by the debtor making full payment, some consumers do experience difficulties in meeting payments. A debtor who fails to make payments as due is in default.

In general, lower-income consumers are more likely to default than those from other income groups[1], simply because they have fewer resources with which to meet unforeseen changes in their financial position. In earlier times, it used to be considered that debtors in default had only themselves to blame and must take the consequences of their own recklessness or improvidence. Indeed, the Crowther Committee observed that:

> 'There are many, particularly in the low income group, who are not reckless so much as improvident. They lack the ability to budget or to manage their income. They have little or no sense of values and are not motivated by rational considerations in selecting their purchases. Such people will, for example, spend a slice of their income not on articles they really need but on other less important items, and they will spend regardless of whether they are getting value for money. Here again, legal protection tends to be largely ineffective'[2].

Modern techniques of persuasion in marketing and advertising goods, services and credit facilities only serve to make matters worse for such 'improvident' consumers. Indeed, it has been suggested that some consumers are seduced into a cycle of poverty by the attractions that credit offers, which only serves to exacerbate their financial plight[3].

The most frequently identified causes of default are illness and unemployment[4]. With increasing levels of unemployment, across all income groups, it may be expected that the level of default will increase. Ultimately, the most that the law can do in respect of such default cases is to mitigate the hardship by compassionate judicial control over the enforcement of debt and the repossession of goods held by the debtor. As the Crowther Committee observed:

> 'Given the characteristics of the typical honest defaulter, it is extremely difficult to devise administrative and legal measures for protecting him without depriving the much larger number of consumers, who use credit wisely, of its considerable benefits. The best policy beyond much question, is not to restrict or control the granting of credit, but to be more careful in assessing the ability of borrowers to carry the burden of repayment, and to be ready with policies of rescue and remedy for the minority for whom it brings difficulties'[5].

To that extent the business of credit reference agencies which give information on creditworthiness provides a useful means of preventing reckless or dishonest persons from gaining access to credit facilities.

Default by the debtor may take a variety of forms but, as indicated above, the commonest form is non-payment. The standard remedy for such default at common law would be for the owner to seek to recover the debt, with the agreed interest. For other breaches the creditor may claim damages for any losses the breach causes. If the debtor's breach is repudiatory, the creditor may terminate the contract and recover (i) any arrears outstanding at the date of breach and (ii) damages, which will include compensation for losses caused by the early termination equal to the amount of future instalments, less any resale value of the repossessed goods[6]. If, however, the breach is non-repudiatory, the creditor will only be entitled to recover those instalments in arrears at the date of the breach[7]. The failure to pay instalments on time or at all may not amount to a repudiatory breach; however, the agreement may contain a provision making prompt payment of each instalment 'of the essence'. The effect of such a clause is to make any late payment repudiatory, allowing the creditor to terminate the contract and claim repudiatory damages, however trivial the breach may appear to be[8].

Another common practice is to provide in the agreement that, in the event of the creditor terminating the agreement for default, the debtor will be required to make an additional payment. In effect, such clauses are used to compensate the creditor for the diminished value of goods he might repossess and are often described as compensation for depreciation, loss of profit or liquidated damages. We have seen that where the debtor exercises the statutory right to terminate, the Act stipulates a minimum payment of 50% of the total purchase price[9]. There is, however, no statutory control of minimum payment clauses in respect of termination otherwise than by the debtor. The primary weapon used by the courts to strike down such clauses is the rule against penalties[10]. In the leading case of *Bridge v Campbell Discount Co*[11] a clause which required the debtor in the event of termination following a repudiatory breach to pay all arrears of rental and 'by way of agreed compensation for depreciation of the vehicle such further sum as may be necessary to make the rentals paid and payable hereunder equal to two thirds of the hire purchase price' was held to be a penalty. The House of Lords considered that it was not a genuine pre-estimate of the loss.

An important consideration in such cases is often whether the hirer actually indicates that he is in breach of contract or whether he is exercising a contractual right to voluntarily terminate the agreement. In *Bridge* the hirer wrote: 'Owing to unforeseen personal circumstances I am sorry but I will not be able to pay any more payments . . . Will you please let me know when and where I have to return the car. I am very sorry regarding this but I have no alternative'. The Court of Appeal treated the letter as a notice of termination, whereas their Lordships considered it to be a notification of breach. This is significant because where an agreement is terminated without a breach the rule against penalties is not applicable at common law. In *Associated Distributors Ltd v Hall*[12] the Court of Appeal held that a clause requiring a minimum payment on a voluntary termination was not a penalty, since the creditor had no right to sue for damages where the hiring is terminated under a contractual right to return the goods. The payment was therefore in the nature of an amount payable simply in order to exercise the contractual option to return the goods. This caused Lord Denning in the *Bridge* case to observe:

> 'Let no one mistake the injustice of this. It means that equity commits itself to this absurd paradox: it will grant relief to a man who breaks his contract but will penalise the man who keeps it'[13].

Their Lordships in *Bridge* were evenly divided on whether, had they held that the letter from the debtor was a voluntary termination, they would have followed *Associated Distributors*[14]. The situation as it stands explains the court's relative unwillingness to hold that a debtor has exercised his voluntary right to terminate[15]. It should be stressed that where the debtor does terminate voluntarily and the agreement is caught by CCA 1974 only the statutory minimum payment will be payable. The above analysis will only therefore be relevant in respect of agreements not caught by the Act.

1 See Crowther Report, p 143.

2   Paragraph 6.1.7.
3   See Caplovitz, *Consumer in Trouble* (1974).
4   See Crowther Report, chs 3, 9 and National Consumer Council, *Consumer Credit* (1980).
5   Paragraph 3.7.17.
6   See *Yeoman Credit Ltd v Waragourski* [1961] 3 All ER 145, [1961] 1 WLR 1124, CA.
7   *Financings Ltd v Baldock* [1963] 2 QB 104, [1963] 1 All ER 433, CA.
8   See eg *Lombard North Central plc v Butterworth* [1987] QB 527, [1987] 1 All ER 267, CA.
9   See 26.6.3.
10 See 2.10.2.
11 [1962] AC 600, [1962] 1 All ER 385, HL.
12 [1938] 2 KB 83, [1938] 1 All ER 511.
13 [1962] AC 600 at 629, [1962] 1 All ER 385 at 399.
14 Viscount Simonds and Lord Morton of Henryton would have followed *Associated Distributors*;
     Lords Denning and Devlin would not. Lord Radcliffe expressed no opinion on the point.
     The same rule as in *Associated Distributors* has been applied in Scotland: *EFT Commercial
     Ltd v Security Change Ltd* 1993 SLT 128.
15 *United Dominions Trust v Ennis* [1968] 1 QB 54, [1967] 2 All ER 345, CA.

26.6.5   Repossession of goods under hire purchase or conditional sale agreements

The Crowther Committee considered that 'the importance of security in a transaction tends to be exaggerated, and repossession, whilst causing hardship to the debtor, is often of little value to the secured party'[1]. The Finance Houses Association pointed out in evidence to the Committee that only one car in 40 taken on hire purchase was repossessed, and that repossession was sought only where the owner found he had no other remedy[2]. In the case of some goods, such as household appliances, repossession may be uneconomic in view of the low resale value of the goods. However, repossession is considered valuable not so much because of the actual ability to repossess, as the psychological inducement it gives the consumer to maintain regular payment of the instalments. Furthermore, it may be argued that giving the creditor security in the goods effectively enables credit to be extended to those who, because of their income, would be unable to obtain it on their credit rating alone.

In order to protect debtors against the risk of repossession of goods by the creditor for breach of the agreement where the debtor has paid a considerable part of the total price, hire purchase legislation introduced the notion of 'protected goods'. Similar provisions are now contained in CCA 1974, s 90, which provides that under a regulated hire purchase or conditional sale agreement where the property in the goods remains in the seller, a creditor must obtain a court order to repossess goods from the debtor when the debtor is in breach of contract and has paid one third or more of the total purchase price[3]. Any installation charge included in the total purchase price is excluded for the purpose of calculating the one third payment[4].

Failure to comply with these provisions means that the regulated agreement, if not already terminated, terminates, and the debtor is released from all further liability and is entitled to recover from the creditor all sums paid by him under the agreement[5]. However, anecdotal evidence suggests that, despite the strong penalties for non-compliance, some creditors may be prepared to repossess protected goods where their resale value is sufficiently high.

Even where goods are not protected, the creditor under a regulated hire purchase or conditional sale agreement is not entitled to enter any premises to take possession of goods unless a court order[6] is obtained.

These provisions do not apply where the debtor voluntarily gives his consent at the time of repossession[7]. Similarly, s 90 only refers to recovery of possession from the debtor; thus, there may be no infringement where the creditor repossesses goods which the debtor has abandoned[8].

Section 90 also makes it clear that its provisions do not apply where the debtor has terminated, or terminates, the agreement. It must be apparent, however, that the decision to terminate was taken consciously knowing of the consequences[9], and that the debtor's notice amounts to an unequivocal notice of termination rather than, say, a request for help[10].

1 See 6.6.45.
2 See 6.6.47.
3 Section 90(1). The debtor need not be in actual possession. The section applies if the creditor repossesses goods which are in the actual possession of a third party who holds them as bailee for the debtor: *Kassam v Chartered Trust plc* [1998] RTR 220.
4 Section 90(2). Default charges are not part of the total price so where a debtor who has paid more than one third of the price the charging of default charges to the account cannot change the status of the goods as 'protected': *Julian Hodge Bank Ltd v Hall* [1998] CCLR 14.
5 Section 91.
6 Section 92.
7 Section 173(3).
8 See *Bentinck Ltd v Cromwell Engineering Co* [1971] 1 QB 324, [1971] 1 All ER 33, CA.
9 See *United Dominions Trusts (Commercial) Ltd v Ennis* [1968] 1 QB 54, [1967] 2 All ER 345, CA.
10 See *Chartered Trust plc v Pitcher* [1989] TLR 97.

26.6.6 *Creditor's notice before taking action*

Under CCA 1974 a creditor must give notice to a debtor before taking certain types of action to enforce their common law rights.

Where the creditor proposes to take action under the agreement as a result of the debtor's breach of a regulated agreement, a default notice must be served under s 87 before the creditor may:

* terminate the agreement;
* demand early payment of any sum;
* recover possession of any goods or land;
* treat any of the debtor's or hirer's rights as terminated, restricted or deferred; or
* enforce any security.

No notice is required before taking action to recover sums accrued due or damages, unless the creditor or owner is proceeding against a surety. Likewise, no notice is required if the creditor or owner wishes to rescind the agreement.

The purpose of this requirement is to give the debtor an opportunity to correct his breach. The debtor or hirer is allowed at least seven days from the date the notice is served to correct the breach. The notice must therefore specify the nature of the debtor's breach, any action to be taken by the debtor to remedy it and the consequences of failure to comply with it.

In *Woodchester Lease Management Ltd v Swain*[1] the debtor under a regulated hire agreement defaulted on one payment and the creditor served a default notice which overstated the amount the debtor needed to pay to remedy his default. The creditor argued that the inaccuracy did not prejudice the debtor, since if he paid in accordance with it he would be at no risk of further enforcement action. The Court of Appeal, emphasising that the purpose of the Act is to protect consumer debtors and that the creditor has access to information to ensure that the notice is accurate, rejected that argument. If accepted it would expose debtors to the risk of inaccurate default notices for sums far in excess of the amount actually owing. Subject to the possibility that the court may disregard *de minimis* errors, the creditor's default notice must be accurate.

A similar notice must be served where the creditor intends to take action when the debtor is not in breach to enforce a term of agreement[2] or to terminate the agreement[3].

1   [1999] 1 WLR 263.
2   Section 76.
3   Section 98.

26.6.7   *Repossession of goods on hire*

The provisions of s 92 prohibiting entry of premises to recover possession of goods also apply to regulated hire agreements. A further protection for hirers is that where the owner of goods does recover possession of the goods, the courts have a discretion to grant the consumer financial relief by ordering that the whole or part of any sum paid by the hirer to the owner shall be repaid and the obligation to pay the whole or part of any sum owed to the owner in respect of the goods shall cease[1].

1   Section 132.

26.7   Judicial control

CCA 1974 gives the courts extensive discretionary powers for the control and enforcement of regulated agreements. There is now a growing body of case law illustrating the exercise of these powers. However, most of the cases are decided at the level of the county court and it is difficult to identify clear principles.

When making any order the court has a wide discretion to impose conditions on or suspend any term of the order[1], or to include 'such provision as it considers just for amending any agreement or security in consequence of a term of the order'[2]. These provisions give the courts considerable flexibility in their handling of disputes and claims. The powers cannot, however, be used to suspend an order requiring a person to deliver up goods unless the court is satisfied that they are in that person's possession or control[3], nor, in the case of a consumer hire agreement, to extend the period for which the hirer is entitled to possession of the goods[4].

The following orders may be made.

(a)   Enforcement and time orders

Where an agreement is not properly executed[5] the creditor must obtain an enforcement order before taking any steps to enforce it. The court has a wide discretion on an application for an enforcement order to reduce or discharge sums payable by the debtor, hirer or any surety, to compensate for any prejudice caused to him by the creditor's default[6], or to dismiss the application if it considers it just to do so having regard to any such prejudice and its powers to impose conditions on the order or to vary the agreement[7].

A time order allows the court to require a debtor or hirer to pay 'any sum owed' by such instalments and at such times as the court considers reasonable having regard to the means of the debtor or hirer. In *Southern & District Finance Ltd v Barnes*[8] the Court of Appeal held that this only gives the court power to reschedule sums actually due and payable at the date of the order[9]. Where, however, the creditor has invoked an acceleration clause, the whole sum payable under the agreement will become due immediately, and the position is the same where a mortgagee claims possession of the mortgaged property. Although the section only expressly requires the court to consider the means of the debtor, an order can only be made where it is just to do so, and the court must therefore consider the creditor's interests in deciding whether to make an order. Thus it was not just to make an order where there was a long history of default and substantial arrears and the instalments the debtor could afford would not meet accruing interest[10]. Similarly, the court should not make a time order, at least in relation to a mortgage, where there is no prospect of the debtor ever resuming payments at the contract rate[11].

The court may also use a time order to require a debtor or hirer to remedy any breach (other than non-payment) within such period as it specifies. A time order may be made on the debtor's application following service by the creditor of an enforcement notice, but the court may also make an order, if it appears just to do so, on the creditor's application for an enforcement order or in an action to enforce the agreement[12].

(b)   Protection orders

The court may make orders protecting any property of the creditor or owner, or property subject to any security, from damage or depreciation pending the outcome of proceedings under the Act[13]. This includes orders restricting or prohibiting the use of the property or giving directions in respect of its custody.

(c)   Special powers in the case of hire purchase and conditional sale

On an application in respect of a regulated hire purchase or conditional sale agreement for an enforcement order, time order or in an action by the creditor for recovery of possession of the goods, the court may, if it appears just, make a return order or a transfer order[14].

A return order is an order for the return of the goods to the creditor; and a transfer order is an order requiring the debtor to return some of the goods to the creditor and vesting the remaining goods in the debtor[15]. A transfer order may only be made where the amount already paid to the creditor by the debtor exceeds the part of the total price referable to the transferred goods by at least one third of the unpaid balance of the total price. The reason for this restriction is to compensate the creditor for the return of used goods.

The debtor may, at any time before the goods enter the possession of the creditor, pay the balance of the total price and, subject to fulfilling any other necessary conditions, claim the goods notwithstanding any return or transfer order[16].

In the event of a debtor's failure to comply with either a return or transfer order, the creditor may invite the court to cancel the order and substitute an order for so much of the total price as is referable to the goods.

---

1   Section 135.
2   Section 136.
3   Section 135(2).
4   Section 135(3).
5   See 26.1.
6   Section 127(2).
7   Section 127(1).
8   (1995) 27 HLR 691.
9   See also *Ashbroom Facilities v Bodley* [1992] CCLR 31 and *J & J Securities v Lee* [1994] CCLR 44; cf *Cedar Holdings v Jenkins* [1988] CCLR 34 and *Cedar Holdings v Thompson* [1993] CCLR 7.

10 *First National Bank plc v Syed* [1991] 2 All ER 250.
11 *Southern & District Finance Ltd v Barnes* (1995) 27 HLR 691.
12 Section 129.
13 Section 131.
14 Section 133.
15 Section 133.
16 Section 133(4).

26.7.1 *Extortionate credit bargains*

We have seen that under the general law of contract the courts are reluctant to interfere in contractual relations on the grounds that the bargain struck between the parties was extortionate[1]. However, the Moneylenders Act 1900 gave the courts wide powers to reopen any transaction within the Act that was harsh and unconscionable and to: reopen accounts; relieve the debtor from payment of any sum in excess of what was judged to be fairly due for principal, interest and charges; order repayment of any excess; and set aside any security given. The Moneylenders Act 1927 laid down that there was a rebuttable presumption that an interest rate in excess of 48% per annum was excessive and the transaction was harsh and unconscionable.

CCA 1974[2] develops the principles originally laid down in those Acts, allowing the court to reopen a credit agreement where it finds the bargain extortionate. These powers may be exercised even in respect of an unregulated agreement, since a 'credit bargain' is defined as an agreement where credit of any amount is provided to an individual, together with any other transaction which must be taken into account in computing the total charge for credit[3].

The Act does not provide that any particular rate of interest is presumed extortionate but provides that a bargain is extortionate if it requires the debtor or a relative of his to make payments which are grossly exorbitant or otherwise grossly contravenes ordinary principles of fair dealing[4]. In deciding whether a bargain is extortionate, the court must have regard to any evidence relating to the following matters:

(a) interest rates prevailing at the time the agreement was made;
(b) the debtor's age, experience, business capacity and state of health;
(c) the degree to which the debtor was under financial pressure at the time he made the bargain, and the nature of such pressure;
(d) the degree of risk accepted by the creditor, having regard to the value of any security provided;
(e) the creditor's relationship with the debtor;
(f) whether or not a colourable cash price was quoted for any goods or services included in the credit bargain;
(g) in relation to a linked transaction, the extent to which the transaction was reasonably required for the protection of the debtor or creditor or was in the interest of the creditor; and
(h) any other relevant consideration.

If a bargain is extortionate the court can effectively rewrite it. It may extinguish liabilities, order repayment of sums paid and order accounts to be taken[5]. An order can be made which adversely affects the creditor even though it was not the creditor but a party to a linked transaction who received an unfair advantage under the original credit bargain.

The debtor or any surety may take proceedings to have the bargain reopened under these provisions or may raise the matter in any proceedings to which they are parties to enforce the agreement or any security or any linked transaction, or in any other proceedings where the amount paid or payable under the credit agreement is relevant[6].

These provisions were intended to give the courts wide power to relieve consumer debtors. Decided cases are of little precedent value, since each case will depend on its own special facts. It seems, however, that in general the courts have been reluctant to exercise the powers available to them. In *Ketley Ltd v Scott*[7] a lender advanced £20,500 to a prospective house purchaser at only a few hours' notice at a nominal annual rate of interest of 48%. The court rejected the borrower's argument that the bargain was extortionate, largely on the grounds of the borrower's conduct. Similarly, in *Wills v Woods*[8] Sir John Donaldson emphasised that the Act uses the word 'extortionate', not 'unwise', and that the jurisdiction seemed to contemplate at least a substantial imbalance in bargaining power, of which one party had taken advantage[9].

This approach is consistent with observations made by the draftsman of CCA 1974 that: 'it is likely that the courts will be sparing with relief. The bargain must after all be grossly exorbitant or unfair'[10]. A different approach has occasionally been adopted. In *Falco Finance Ltd v Gough*[11] a mortgage agreement permitted the debtor to pay a discounted rate of interest, but provided that, in the event of any default in payment, the right to the discount would be permanently forfeit. The full contractual rate would then be payable, increasing the monthly repayments from £324.75 to £449.75. The court held that this was an extortionate credit bargain, emphasising that the disproportionate increase in the interest rate was not connected to any loss suffered by the creditor. This, however, is a relatively isolated example. In 1991 the Office of Fair Trading published a report[12] reviewing the operation of these provisions and concluded that they had failed to perform their intended function. As the report noted, this is hardly surprising: 'exorbitant' is defined as 'grossly excessive' and the Act requires that the bargain be 'grossly exorbitant'. Moreover, in most cases the court was prepared to uphold bargains provided that the interest rate was not in excess of 48%, effectively importing the test from the old Moneylenders Acts. The report therefore recommended that the concept of the 'extortionate credit bargain' be replaced by that of the 'unjust credit transaction' and that in deciding whether a transaction is unjust the court should consider the following factors.

(a) Does the transaction involve excessive payments?
(b) Was any conduct of the creditor, whether lawful or not, deceitful, oppressive or otherwise unfair?
(c) Did the creditor act responsibly in checking the debtor's creditworthiness and ability to repay before entering the transaction?

It is clear that a transaction which might not be an extortionate credit bargain could be an unjust credit transaction; it would clearly be easier to show that a transaction requires 'excessive payments' than that it requires grossly exorbitant payments. The report further recommended that in order to relieve the debtor of the onus of applying for a transaction to be reopened, the OFT should have power to apply for a transaction to be reopened and the court should be given power to reopen a transaction of its own motion. However, although the recommendations were favourably received by the government, they have not been implemented and were not mentioned in the most recent review of the 1974 Act.

1   See ch 2.
2   Sections 137–140.
3   Section 137(2).

4   Section 138(1).
5   Section 139(2).
6   The decision of the Court of Appeal in *First National Bank plc v Syed* [1991] 2 All ER 250 suggests that the court may have power to reopen a bargain of its own motion: see per Dillon LJ at 252.
7   [1981] ICR 241.
8   (1984) 128 Sol Jo 222, CA. See generally Bentley and Howells (1989) Conv 164, 175.
9   Contrast *Castle Phillips & Co v Wilkinson* [1992] CCLR 83, where a secured loan to an inexperienced debtor at over three times the prevailing building society rate of interest was considered extortionate.
10 Bennion (1977) 121 Sol Jo 485.
11 [1999] CCLR 16.
12 OFT, *Unjust Credit Transactions* (1991).

26.7.2   Unfair terms

It must be borne in mind that the 1974 Act is not the only statutory control over consumer credit agreements. In particular, the Unfair Terms in Consumer Contracts Regulations 1999 may now apply to some of the terms. Indeed, in *Falco Finance Ltd v Gough*[1] the agreement was held to be unfair contrary to the 1994 Regulations then in force. The discounted interest rate was offered as an inducement to the debtor to enter into the contract, the benefit of which could be lost as a result of terms concealed in the small print, contrary to the requirement of good faith. This approach was confirmed in *Director General of Fair Trading v First National Bank plc*[2], where the Court of Appeal held that the regulations could apply to a consumer mortgage agreement and that a term which provided that, in the event of default, any outstanding instalments plus the unpaid capital balance would become immediately payable and be subject to interest at the contract rate until payment was imposed contrary to the requirement of good faith and was therefore unfair. The contract provided for interest to continue on any outstanding balance after judgment, whereas the court would have no power to award interest after judgment under the general law[3].

It must be recalled that the regulations do not permit the court to assess the fairness of any term which defines the main subject matter of the contract or of the adequacy of the price and remuneration as against the goods or services supplied. It would therefore not be possible for the court to use the regulations to invalidate an agreement simply because it provides for an excessively high rate of interest. However, the Court of Appeal in *First National Bank* held that the term there in question fell outside this exclusion. 'Peripheral' terms, including those concerned with the creditor's rights on default, therefore, will be subject to challenge under the regulations. It may be that the judges will feel more comfortable challenging such terms than in questioning the fairness of the core bargain, but it may be, perhaps, that as courts become more familiar with the exercise of discretionary powers to intervene in contracts that they will become more willing to exercise their powers under other legislation, including the 1974 Act.

1   [1999] CCLR 16, above.
2   [2000] 2 All ER 759.
3   County Courts (Interest on Judgment Debts) Order 1991, SI 1991/1184.

Chapter 27

Money and the Transfer of Obligations

27.0 Introduction

We saw earlier[1] that if the supplier is unwilling to give his customer credit, but the customer is unwilling to borrow to make immediate payment, the conflicting needs of the parties can only be accommodated by the supplier transferring to a third party the right to receive payment from the customer, in return for an immediate cash payment.

Broadly speaking, there are two mechanisms by which such a transfer can be effected – assignment and negotiation – but before examining them it is necessary to say something about the nature of money and property.

1 See ch 20.

27.1 The idea of money

Money is central to a developed capitalist economy, since it provides a universal means of exchange. Any token having an agreed exchange value might be regarded as money. However, for the lawyer, 'money' is some token issued by the state, denominated by reference to a unit of account and used as a universal means of exchange[1]. The pound sterling is therefore 'money', as indeed is the dollar, the franc or the mark. It is submitted that the Euro is 'money' although the ECU was not[2]. So-called 'digital cash' is not money. There have recently been experiments with several forms of digital cash, intended to be used for low value transactions, especially on-line transactions. All share certain characteristics. Most importantly, they are simply digital representations of value, which are paid for. Digital units are issued by a private individual, who undertakes to redeem them for money. They are therefore not issued by or with the authority of the state and are not 'money' in a legal sense.

Individual notes and coins have a dual status in law. They exist as objects, and may have a value as objects beyond their face value: for instance, as collectable items to a numismatist[3]. Additionally, notes and coins represent legal rights to claim their nominal value; indeed, sterling bank notes bear the words 'I promise to pay the bearer on demand the sum of . . . pounds'. Historically, one pound sterling represented the value of one pound in weight of gold. A pound is, of course, now worth considerably less, but in any case, by virtue of the Currency and Bank Notes Act 1954, a person presenting a bank note to the Bank of England for encashment

610

may no longer demand gold but is only entitled to demand its replacement by other notes and coins of equivalent value.

Individual notes and coins, when used as currency rather than as curios or collectable objects, are fungible: that is to say that one note is as good as another of the same denomination. When a person deposits money with a bank, he ceases to own the individual notes and coins deposited, which become the property of the bank. In return, he obtains a contractual right to repayment from the bank of the sum deposited, together with interest in accordance with the terms of the contract between himself and the bank. The depositor's right to repayment from the bank, like the rights represented by bank notes, is recognised in law as a type of property.

1 Mann, *The Legal Aspect of Money* (5th edn, 1992) p 8.
2 Ibid p 23.
3 See 8.1.3.

27.2 The classification of property

English law divides property into realty and personalty. Personalty is subdivided into chattels real – leaseholds – and pure personalty. Pure personalty can be further sub-divided into choses in possession and choses in action. Choses (things) in possession are those items of property which can be physically possessed – a television set, a refrigerator or a motor car would therefore be a chose in possession. Choses in action are 'personal rights of property which can only be claimed or enforced by action and not by taking physical possession'[1]. A debt is a legal right to demand a sum of money. The law recognises it as a type of property. However, the debt cannot be physically possessed but must be enforced, if necessary, by legal action. This is true even if the debt is evidenced in tangible form, for instance by a written contract. The physical document which evidences the legal right is separate from the legal right to payment, although the fact that the right is evidenced by a document may be important in some cases. Similarly, rights under a contract are property: a chose in action.

1 *Torkington v Magee* [1902] 2 KB 427 at 430.

27.3 The transfer of choses in action

Tangible property may be transferred physically. Choses in action are intangible and cannot be transferred by physical delivery. However, intangible rights are too valuable to be frozen, and the law has therefore developed two methods of transferring intangible property, by assignment and negotiation. Both methods play an important part in commercial activity.

27.3.1 *Assignment*

At common law, rights under a contract were regarded as purely personal and could not be transferred. Thus suppose that B buys goods from C and resells them to A. A now owes money to B, who owes money to C. B might wish to satisfy his debt to C by transferring the right to demand payment from A. At common law that was not possible, unless all three parties agreed to a novation of the contract between A and B to substitute C as a party in B's place.

Equity recognised that choses in action could be transferred by assignment. However, the assignee could be in no better position than the assignor and was therefore said to take 'subject to equities'. In the above example, equity therefore allowed B to transfer to C the right to payment; but if A had a claim against B, he would be able to assert that claim against C: for instance, B might have made a misrepresentation inducing A to buy the goods, giving A a right to rescind the contract or claim damages. In addition, an equitable assignee could only sue by joining in the assignor as a plaintiff in the action; however, the courts of equity were prepared to order the assignor to lend his name to such an action.

Since 1873 it has been possible to assign contract rights at law. The position is now covered by s 136 of the Law of Property Act 1925[1], which allows legal assignment provided that the assignment is made in writing and written notice is given to the debtor. The assignment must be absolute, not by way of charge, and must be of the whole debt, not of part. A legal assignment is still subject to equities. An equitable assignment is still possible, and an incomplete legal assignment will normally take effect as an agreement to assign and be enforceable as an equitable assignment. The main advantage of a legal over an equitable assignment is that a legal assignee may sue to enforce the obligation in his own name. Although an equitable assignee is not required to give notice of the assignment to the debtor, such notice will generally be desirable for a number of reasons. First, until such notice is given, the debtor is entitled to pay the assignor, and such payment will give him a good discharge for the debt. Second, the assignee takes the debt subject to equities arising before notice of assignment is given to the debtor; this may include a right to set off sums due under other contracts, provided the right to the sum set off arises before the notice of assignment is given. Third, notice will give the assignee priority over subsequent assignees of the same debt. It was held in *Dearle v Hall*[2] that where two assignees lay claim to the same debt, the first to give notice to the debtor gains priority, and the same rule applies even if one of the assignments is legal under the Law of Property Act[3]. Thus an equitable assignee who gives notice of his assignment to the debtor will take priority even over a later legal assignee.

Personal rights under a contract, such as the right to performance of a contract for personal services, are not assignable, and a contract may include terms prohibiting, or restricting, assignment. An assignment in breach of such prohibition or restriction is ineffective. Subject, however, to these limitations, contractual rights are generally transferable at law and in equity by assignment. The requirements for an effective assignment, whether at law or equity, limit its value in commercial operations. However, assignment forms the basis of a number of arrangements such as factoring by which businesses sell the rights to receive money which is or will in future be due to them and thus obtain finance against book debts or other 'receivables'.

1   Replacing s 25(6) of the Judicature Act 1873.
2   (1823) 3 Russ 1.
3   *E Pfeiffer Weinkellerei-Weineinkauf GmbH & Co v Arbuthnot Factors Ltd* [1988] 1 WLR 150; *Compaq Computers Ltd v Abercorn Group Ltd* [1991] BCC 484; see Sealy [1992] CLJ 19.

27.3.2   *Factoring*

Under a factoring arrangement, a business which has supplied goods or services to customers on credit will transfer to the factor the right to receive payment from those customers, in return for an immediate cash payment. The factor will pay a discounted price in return for undertaking the collection, and may make a retention until payment is received. The factor is effectively a professional debt collecting agency, often a subsidiary of a bank or other large commercial organisation. The name 'factor' derives from the activities of the eighteenth- and nineteenth-century agents, known as factors, who sold goods on behalf of their principals and occasionally lent them money on the security of the goods to be sold[1]. However, the activities of the modern factor are very different from those of the factor-agent, and they should not be confused.

Since the debt is transferred to the factor by assignment, the customer may set up against the factor any defences it would have to a claim by the supplier. The factoring agreement may be with or without recourse. Where the agreement is with recourse, the factor may require the supplier to compensate it in the event of non-payment by the customer. Where the factor agrees to bear the risk of non-payment, the agreement will be for 'non-recourse factoring'. Under such an arrangement the factor will clearly charge a higher price for its services to reflect the increased risk of non-payment.

The main terms of the factoring arrangement will normally be contained in a master agreement; that will operate as an equitable assignment of future debts and will only become a legal assignment if a written assignment is made after each debt arises. Often the factor will only require the assignor to notify it of sums due, and will rely on the equitable assignment. In order to overcome the difficulty that an equitable assignee cannot sue in his own name, the factoring agreement will normally contain a term appointing the factor the assignee's agent for the purpose of bringing proceedings against debtors. The suppliers' invoices will normally include a notice advising customers to make payment to the factor.

Factoring offers a number of advantages to the assignor business. It receives immediate payment of sums due to it, even though it may have granted credit to its customers. The sum received from the factor may be less than the face value of the debts, but that is likely to be reflected in an increase of the nominal price to the customer, as part of the cost of credit. In addition, the business avoids the expense of collecting debts itself; the factor undertakes the collection and, if necessary, the enforcement of payment and is able to take advantage of economies of scale, both in its internal organisation and in any court proceedings[2]. However, because factoring depends on assignment, it carries the weaknesses inherent in that mode of transfer. In particular, the need for notice to the debtor in order to constitute a legal assignment may leave the factor in an exposed position. It is rare for the parties to give the debtor express notice of the assignment; indeed, the assignor may well wish to keep its financial arrangements secret from customers. Until notice is given, the debtor may pay the supplier direct and equities, such as rights to set off sums due under other contracts with the supplier, may continue to arise which weaken the factor's title. If notice is not given, the factor may find that it loses priority to a subsequent assignee who does give notice.

1   See 3.2.3.
2   See Galanter, 'Why the Haves Come Out Ahead' (1974) 9 Law and Society Rev 95 and Zander, *Cases and Materials on the English Legal System* (8th edn, 1999) p 10 for a description of the advantages enjoyed by 'repeat players' in litigation.

27.3.2.1   *International factoring*

The importance of factoring as a means of financing international trade is reflected by the fact that in 1988 UNIDROIT adopted a draft convention on international factoring. The draft convention is intended to form part of the general move to harmonisation of international commercial law and supplements the Vienna Convention on International Sale of Goods[1]. It has not yet been ratified by the UK and can only be briefly outlined here.

The draft convention only applies to factoring of debts arising from international transactions, that is to say:

(a) where seller and buyer have their places of business in different states; and
(b) where either:
    (i) both states are parties to the convention; or
    (ii) both the contract of sale and the factoring contract are governed by the law of a state party to the convention.

The draft convention does not apply where the underlying contract of sale was a consumer contract and in any case it may be excluded by agreement of the parties to the factoring contract or the sale contract. The draft convention concentrates on the relationship between factor and customer, leaving the relationship between factor and supplier to be governed by domestic law. It largely mirrors the existing rules of English law. The debtor may raise against the factor any defence arising from the contract of sale, and any right of set-off arising before notice of assignment is given. However, where the customer discovers a breach of the contract of sale after paying the factor, the draft convention would not allow the customer to recover payment from the factor unless the factor had not yet paid the supplier, or the factor paid the supplier after becoming aware of the customer's claim[2].

1 See Goode [1988] JBL 347, 510.
2 Article 10.

27.3.2.2 *Discounting*

As an alternative to full factoring of its debts, a business may enter into an invoice discounting arrangement. Such an arrangement is commonly used to finance hire purchase and conditional sale transactions; the supplier transfers the right to receive payment from its customers to an organisation such as a finance house in return for an immediate cash payment, thus obtaining the cashflow benefits provided by factoring. As with factoring, there is generally a master 'block discounting' agreement under which the supplier agrees to offer future debts in a designated category. In contrast with a factoring arrangement, the debtor is not notified of the arrangement, so that there is neither a legal nor an equitable assignment of the debt. The supplier remains responsible for collecting the debts due from its customers, acting as agent for the finance house, so that it must bear the administrative costs associated with debt collection. The agreement will normally be 'with recourse', so that the supplier is required to guarantee payment by its customers or to indemnify the finance house against losses suffered as a result of purchasing the debts[1]. However, a discounting contract may be attractive because it will allow the supplier to retain control over debt collection and therefore maintain its relationship with customers. Since the finance house has no right to collect payment direct from the customer, it may be in a precarious position if the seller fails to remit payments, or becomes insolvent. In order to secure its position it may therefore take security from the seller, often in the form of bills of exchange or promissory notes for the amount of future instalment payments due from it[2].

1   It may be particularly difficult to distinguish a with recourse agreement from a charge: see eg *Lloyds and Scottish Finance Ltd v Cyril Lord Carpet Sales Ltd* [1992] BCLC 609; *Orion Finance Ltd v Crown Financial Management Ltd* [1996] 2 BCLC 78. See 22.0.4.1, 22.0.4.2.
2   See ch 28.

27.3.3   Negotiability

Although assignment provides the legal basis for factoring and other similar arrangements, its limitations would severely restrict its utility as a means of transferring intangible property in a commercial context and would have obstructed the development of modern commerce. Fortunately, mercantile practice recognised a second means of transferring certain types of intangible property, superior to assignment in most respects, which forms the basis of many modern commercial transactions and, in particular, much of the modern banking system.

Certain instruments were recognised by mercantile practice as being negotiable. An instrument is a document, such as a share certificate or cheque, which evidences the holder's entitlement to enforce a legal right. A negotiable instrument can be freely transferred by delivery or by delivery and any necessary indorsement, so that the legal obligation it evidences can be enforced by the lawful holder of the instrument. Such negotiation operates to transfer title to the obligation in both law and equity and, moreover, the transferee of a negotiable instrument may take free of equities and defects in the title of the transferor[1]. A negotiable instrument thus operates as a striking exception to the doctrines both of privity of contract and nemo dat quod non habet.

The law merchant recognised commercial practice and therefore admitted the concept of negotiability into law. At the present time two main classes of negotiable instrument are recognised by law: promises to pay, such as bank notes and promissory notes, and orders to pay, such as cheques and bills of exchange. The recognition of an instrument as negotiable in law depends on proof that it is negotiable, in the sense described above, by mercantile custom. There is therefore no objection, in theory, to new classes of instrument being accepted as negotiable provided a mercantile custom to that effect can be proved. In *Goodwin v Robarts*[2] the Court of Exchequer Chamber held that certain instruments issued by the Russian and Austro-Hungarian governments were negotiable, and Cockburn CJ said:

'The law merchant with respect to bills of exchange and other negotiable securities is . . . neither more nor less than the usages of merchants and traders in the different departments of trade, ratified by the decision of the courts of law, which, upon such usages being proved before them, have adopted them as settled law with a view to the interests of trade and the public convenience'[3].

Reliance on custom has been one of the strengths of English commercial law, lending the law the flexibility to adapt to changing business practices. However, the reported cases give no guidance as to the criteria which will be used to decide if a new instrument is 'negotiable'. In recent years a wide range of new commercial instruments has been introduced. The legal status of many of them is unclear. The Review Committee on Banking Services Law and Practice therefore recommended that a new statute governing negotiable instruments should lay down a list of guidelines to be taken into account in deciding the negotiable status of new instruments. However, that recommendation was not accepted by the government.

Amongst the other commercial documents recognised as negotiable are bearer bonds, share warrants payable to bearer and dividend warrants. Postal orders are instruments, but are not negotiable. Bills of lading are sometimes described as negotiable, but the description is inaccurate. A bill of lading may be transferred, but although the transferee may sometimes take advantage of estoppels not available to the transferor, the transfer is not free from equities[4]. Share certificates are instruments but are not negotiable because transfer can only be effected by completion of a stock transfer form and entry in the register of shareholders of the company concerned. It is possible to destroy an instrument's negotiability: for instance, if a cheque is crossed 'not negotiable' it may still be transferred but it ceases to be negotiable: a transferee will take subject to any defects in the title of the transferor[5].

Commercial custom determines whether a class of documents is negotiable. The question whether a particular document falls into that class is quite separate, and depends on the intention of the parties, objectively determined. A document acknowledging a debt and undertaking to repay it – an 'IOU' – is not a promissory note. In *Claydon v Bradley*[6] B signed a document acknowledging receipt of £10,000 'to be paid back in full by July 1'. It was held that the document was merely a receipt for the money lent. The parties could not have intended it to be negotiable, with the consequences that that would entail (including that it might be transferred to a third party who would take free of equities) and therefore could not be a promissory note.

1   See *Crouch v Credit Foncier of England* (1873) LR 8 QB 374; *Simmons v London Joint Stock Bank* [1891] 1 Ch 270 at 294 per Bowen LJ.
2   (1875) LR 10 Exch 337.
3   (1875) LR 10 Exch 337 at 346.
4   See 32.1.
5   It is also possible to destroy an instrument's transferability. For instance, a cheque drawn 'a/c payee only' is now neither negotiable nor transferable as a result of the Cheques Act 1992. Most standard cheques are printed with the words 'a/c payee only' and are therefore not negotiable. See 30.1.4.
6   [1987] 1 All ER 522.

Chapter 28

Bills of Exchange

28.0   Introduction

The law relating to bills of exchange is now contained in the Bills of Exchange
Act 1882 (BoEA 1882), which has been described as 'the best drafted Act of
Parliament ever passed'[1]. The Act, part of the great codification of commercial
law of the late nineteenth century, is very detailed and much of the law is highly
technical; what follows is only an overview of the law. However, bills of exchange
deserve some study not only for the important role they play in commerce, but
also as an important illustration of the concept of negotiability. Moreover, the
unconditional nature of the payment obligation created by a bill of exchange,
coupled with its negotiability, means that it can easily be manipulated for
fraudulent purposes. Many of the cases in this area raise the problem frequently
encountered by commercial law, which of two innocent parties should suffer
where a third has behaved fraudulently.

1   MacKinnon LJ in *Bank Polski v K J Mulder & Co* [1942] 1 KB 497 at 500. The Review Committee
    on Banking Services Law and Practice recommended a general review of the law relating to
    negotiable instruments to update the 1882 Act, but that recommendation was rejected in the
    Government's 1990 White Paper on Banking Services (1990) (Cmnd 1026).

28.1   The use of bills of exchange

A bill of exchange is an order by one person, the drawer of the bill, to another, the
drawee, to pay money to some person. The order may be to pay to a named person
or to the bearer of the bill, and the form used will affect the way in which the bill
can be transferred[1]. If the bill names a payee, the payee may be a named third party
or the drawer of the bill. Thus if S sells goods to B, payment to be by bill of
exchange, S will draw a bill on B for the price, naming S as the payee of the bill.
   The drawer of a bill is liable on it as soon as it is put into circulation[2]; however,
a drawee only becomes liable to honour the bill if it is presented to him for
acceptance and he accepts it[3]. If the bill is payable at some date in the future, it will
normally be presented for acceptance at a date prior to maturity, and in some cases
that may be necessary in order to fix the date when the bill is payable[4]. If the
drawee accepts the bill, he becomes liable to pay it at maturity[5]; if not, he is not
liable on the bill, although he may be liable to the drawer for breach of some
underlying contract requiring him to accept, and the bill is dishonoured.

Some bills are never presented for acceptance. If a bill is payable 'at sight' or 'on demand' it will be payable immediately when it is presented to the drawee, without the need for prior acceptance. On presentation it is either paid or dishonoured. A cheque is a bill of exchange payable on demand, drawn on a bank[6]; it is not presented to the bank for acceptance but merely for payment. A bill payable at a future date will normally be presented for acceptance because acceptance by the drawee will provide a second obligation to pay, and thus increase its security and marketability.

The essential characteristic of the bill of exchange is its negotiability. Thus the payee of the bill need not present it for payment, but can transfer it to a third party, perhaps for cash, or in satisfaction of some prior debt. The payee can therefore use a bill of exchange payable at a future date to raise cash immediately. The person in lawful possession of a bill is its holder; if certain conditions are fulfilled, the holder may qualify as a holder for value[7] or a holder in due course[8] and be in a particularly favoured position to enforce the bill.

Some examples of the use of bills of exchange may help illustrate their working.

If S sells goods to B, the price to be paid by bill of exchange, S will draw a bill on B for the price; by accepting the bill, B will become liable to pay it. If S has in turn bought goods from X and owes X their price, he can discharge the obligation to X by transferring to him the bill of exchange accepted by B.

A bill of exchange may be used where B buys goods and wants credit. If B wants 90 days' credit, S can draw on B a bill payable in 90 days. If B accepts the bill, S can then immediately sell, or discount, the bill, often with a bank or discount house[9] for an immediate cash payment, thus satisfying both B's wish for credit, and S's for immediate payment. Of course, S may not receive the full face value of the bill when he discounts it: a discount will be made to reflect the fact that it is not payable at once and also the possible risk of non-payment; S will take that into account when fixing the price for the goods.

Bills of exchange are extensively used in international trade where the buyer's desire for credit, coupled with the long transit times involved in sea transport, cause particular problems[10]. Where the price is payable by bill of exchange, S will draw a bill on B and send it to B together with the bill of lading and other documents covering the goods; the bill is then known as a 'documentary bill'. If B does not accept the bill of exchange, he is required to return the other documents to S, and if he retains them he acquires no title to the goods covered by the bill of lading[11].

Bills of exchange are often used in international trade in documentary credit transactions. We have seen that a bill payable at a future date may be discounted, and that its value will depend on the acceptor's credit standing. Its value can therefore be increased by having the bill accepted by someone with a good credit standing, such as a bank. S may therefore require B to open with a bank a documentary credit under which the bank will undertake to accept bills of exchange drawn on it by S[12]; the bank's acceptance will increase the discount value of the bills.

The use of bills in international transactions can give rise to particularly difficult conflicts of laws problems[13]. In 1988, in an effort to mitigate those problems, UNCITRAL adopted a Convention on International Bills of Exchange and International Promissory Notes. The convention is not yet in force.

Bills may also be used by persons wishing to raise loans, as a means of providing security. If D borrows from C, he may agree to accept bills of exchange drawn on him by C for the amount of the loan, or the instalments. C can then obtain repayment by presenting the bills for payment as they mature; alternatively, C can discount the bills for immediate cash payment. Again, the value of the bills may be increased by the acceptance of a bank or some similar organisation. D may therefore ask his bank to accept bills drawn by C; alternatively, he may arrange an acceptance credit with the bank, under which the bank agrees to accept bills drawn by D up to a maximum amount specified in the credit. D can then raise cash by discounting the bills with C. The terms of the agreement between D and the bank will require D to reimburse the bank when the bills are presented for payment, although they may allow D to draw further bills under the credit to raise cash to pay the bank, thus 'rolling over' the obligation to repay the bank and, effectively, extending the loan. Effectively, an acceptance credit allows a bank customer to borrow on the strength of the bank's commercial reputation. Of course, the bank will charge its customer a fee for providing the service.

1   See 28.3.
2   BoEA 1882, s 21(1), s 55; see 28.4.5.
3   BoEA 1882, s 17; see 28.5.1.
4   BoEA 1882, s 39; see 28.2.
5   BoEA 1882, s 54; see 28.4.5.
6   BoEA 1882, s 73.
7   BoEA 1882, s 27; see 28.3.2.2.
8   BoEA 1882, s 29; see 28.3.2.3.
9   See 29.1.2.
10 See 31.3.
11 Sale of Goods Act 1979, s 19(3), see 33.2.9.
12 See ch 34.
13 See eg *Montage GmbH v Irvani* [1990] 2 All ER 225.

28.1.1   *Unconditional nature of the payment obligation*

The payment obligation created by a bill of exchange is unconditional. This gives the bill a second characteristic, in addition to its negotiability, which makes it especially attractive as a means of payment in commercial transactions. The obligation to pay created by the bill of exchange is largely independent of any underlying transaction in connection with which it is drawn, so that the bill can be enforced, even by the original drawer, regardless of any alleged breach of the underlying contract. For most purposes, the bill is as good as cash. Thus if S delivers goods to B in return for a bill of exchange accepted by B, B cannot refuse to honour the bill on the grounds that the goods are defective:

> 'a bill of exchange or promissory note is to be treated as cash. It is to be honoured unless there is some good reason to the contrary: eg there is an arguable case based on total failure of consideration'[1].

This principle has repeatedly been asserted by the courts. The reason for it was explained by Lord Wilberforce:

> 'When one person buys goods from another it is often, one would think generally, important for the seller to be sure of his price: he may (as here) have bought the goods from someone else whom he has to pay. Bills of exchange are to be taken as deferred instalments of cash'[2].

Payment by bill of exchange thus gives the seller the desired assurance of payment: the buyer may not withhold payment of the bill on the grounds of alleged breaches of contract such as late delivery or defects in the goods. In the event that a dispute does arise, the use of a bill of exchange effectively adjusts bargaining power in favour of the seller: if he simply allowed the buyer credit, the buyer could withhold payment and negotiate a reduction in the price and, if sued, raise the alleged breach by the seller as a counterclaim in the proceedings. Where a bill of exchange is used, the buyer must satisfy the bill and then, if necessary, institute proceedings for damages. If the buyer fails to honour the bill, the court will normally refuse to allow him to raise the alleged breach as a counterclaim in an action on the bill, and the seller will be able to obtain summary judgment[3].

Clearly, defences based on the underlying contract should not be allowed to be raised in an action by a transferee of the bill: if they were, the marketability of bills and their commercial value would be greatly reduced. However, that does not appear to justify the attitude taken by the courts in cases where the claim on the bill is brought by the original payee responsible for the alleged breach. One justification appears to be that, if the buyer were allowed to raise alleged breaches of the underlying contract as defences to an action on the bill, there would be no benefit to the seller in taking a bill rather than allowing credit; in effect, the intentions of the parties would be defeated. However, this disregards the fact that a bill can be immediately discounted for cash. The real reason for the 'deep rooted concept of English law' that 'the bill is itself a contract separate from the contract of sale'[4] appears to be the fear that anything which undermines the separate status of the obligation created by the bill of exchange would create uncertainty and undermine the marketability of bills generally, and thus be damaging to commerce.

The only exceptions to the general rule recognised by the courts are where the breach gives rise to a total failure of consideration for which the bill was given, or a partial failure in a quantified amount[5]. Thus if S delivers defective goods and B lawfully rejects them, there is a total failure of consideration which will justify non-payment of a bill; similarly, if S delivers less than the contract quantity, but B keeps the goods delivered, there is a partial failure quantified by the proportional value of the shortfall, and non-payment may be justified. On the other hand, if S delivers goods which B accepts but alleges to be defective, B's claim is for unliquidated damages: he must honour the bill and claim damages by separate proceedings if necessary.

It should be noted that although a bill of exchange gives rise to an unconditional obligation to pay, where a bill is given in satisfaction of an existing obligation, it operates only as a conditional discharge of that obligation. Thus if S sells goods to B and B pays by bill of exchange (including a cheque) and the bill is dishonoured, S has the option of suing on the original contract of sale, since the giving of the bill does not satisfy B's obligation to pay unless and until it is honoured.

1   Per Lord Denning MR in *Fielding and Platt Ltd v Najjar* [1969] 1 WLR 357 at 361, CA.
2   *Nova (Jersey) Knit Ltd v Kammgarn Spinnerei GmbH* [1977] 2 All ER 463 at 470, HL.
3   Under CPR Pt 24; see *Fielding & Platt Ltd v Najjar* [1969] 2 All ER 150, [1969] 1 WLR 357, CA; *Montebianco Ind Tessili SpA v Carlyle Mills (London) Ltd* [1981] 1 Lloyd's Rep 509, CA. See 36.1.2.
4   Lord Russell of Killowen in *Nova (Jersey) Knit Ltd v Kammgarn Spinnerei GmbH* [1977] 2 All ER 463 at 480, HL.
5   Ibid.

28.1.2   Impact of the Consumer Credit Act 1974

The separate nature of the payment obligation created by a bill of exchange creates the possibility of abuse by an unscrupulous creditor. We have already noted that a postdated bill or promissory note may be given by the debtor under a credit agreement as a form of security. If the debtor (D) defaults on the loan, the creditor (C) can obtain payment by enforcing the bill of exchange, relying on the separate nature of the contract on the bill. Alternatively, C can obtain early repayment by discounting the bill with a third party, who can enforce the bill if necessary, and who will be able to ignore any defences D may have arising out of the contract with C, if he qualifies as a holder in due course. In either case it will be irrelevant to his liability on the bill that D is unable to pay, or, if the credit relates to the supply of goods or services, as for instance where goods are supplied on hire purchase, that he may have a complaint about the goods.

The Consumer Credit Act 1974[1] prohibits the taking of a negotiable instrument other than a cheque in payment of any sum due under a regulated credit agreement[2], or the taking of any negotiable instrument, including a cheque, as security for any sum due under a regulated credit agreement in order to prevent bills of exchange or promissory notes being used in the way just described to evade the controls the Act imposes on creditors' rights and remedies in the event of default. If a negotiable instrument is taken in breach of these provisions, it is unenforceable[3] and the fact that it was taken in breach of the Act constitutes a defect in title. However, a transferee of the instrument may take free of that defect and enforce the instrument as a holder in due course, unless it can be shown that he took the instrument with knowledge of the defect in the transferor's title[4].

CCA 1974 has no effect on the use of bills in contracts other than regulated credit agreements. It is extremely rare for consumers to use promissory notes or bills of exchange, other than cheques, in ordinary daily transactions. Suppose, however, that a consumer contracts for a builder to do work at his home and, on completion of the work, pays by cheque. Subsequently, he discovers that the work is unsatisfactory and stops the cheque. He does so at his peril. The payment obligation arising from the cheque is autonomous of the underlying contract, so that the builder can enforce that obligation free of the consumer's claim for breach of contract, and this rule has recently been confirmed and applied to payments by direct debit[5].

It is submitted that this is unfortunate. The treatment of the payment undertaking in a bill of exchange as autonomous of the underlying contract is justified on two bases: first, that a bill may be negotiated and come into the hands of a third party who will be unaware of any claims arising under the contract; and, second, because, as stated by Lord Wilberforce in *Nova v Kammgarn*[6], the bill is treated as equivalent to cash, and the payee should therefore be in no worse position than if he had been paid in cash. The first justification no longer applies to cheques, which are rarely negotiated; indeed, the standard cheque forms issued by banks to individuals nowadays are not negotiable[7]. It was suggested above that the reason underlying the second justification is to protect the negotiability of instruments. It is true that it has been recognised in a different context[8] that cheques are now generally used by individuals not for their negotiable character but as an alternative to cash, but consumers – and others – use cheques primarily for convenience, not to give an autonomous undertaking. In so far as the alternative for the consumer is to pay cash immediately, it can be argued that the autonomy rule leaves the drawer of the cheque in no worse position than if he had paid cash, and that the payee who agrees to accept a cheque should be no worse off than if he had insisted on cash payment. However, cheques are often used to provide immediate payment where cash is not available so that the alternative would actually be a supply on credit. Moreover, the autonomy rule is probably contrary to the natural expectations of most private cheque users who, if they gave the matter any thought at all, would probably expect that payment by cheque gives them a measure of protection against unsatisfactory performance, by allowing them to countermand the cheque if dissatisfied. In the absence of any likelihood of the cheque being negotiated, there would seem to be sound reasons for refusing to apply the rule developed for bills issued in a commercial context, and allowing the buyer to raise the seller's breach, and the resulting counterclaim for damages, as a defence to a claim on the cheque[9].

1   See ch 26.
2   For the meaning of 'regulated credit agreement' see 25.0.1.
3   Section 123.
4   Section 125.
5   *Esso Petroleum Co Ltd v Milton* [1997] 2 All ER 593. See 30.3.2.
6   [1977] 2 All ER 463, above 28.1.1.
7   See 30.1.3.
8   *D & C Builders Ltd v Rees* [1966] 2 QB 617, [1965] 3 All ER 837, CA.
9   The consumer's position is therefore stronger if he pays by credit card. In that case if the goods prove defective he may withhold payment to the card issuer relying on the issuer's concurrent liability for the breach of contract under s 75 of the Consumer Credit Act 1974: see 26.5.2.

28.1.3   *Historical development of bills of exchange*

Before turning to the substantive law relating to bills of exchange, it is worth making a brief examination of their history. Since the Bills of Exchange Act 1882 is a codifying statute, decisions in cases prior to the Act should only be referred to for guidance where the Act itself is ambiguous or unclear[1]. However, the history of the bill of exchange provides a classic illustration of the way English commercial law developed: mercantile custom became part of the lex mercatoria, which in turn was absorbed into the common law which, in its turn, was ultimately codified by statute:

> '[N]o more instructive chapter in legal history could be written than that which would tell in an adequate way the story of the development of mercantile law of which the law of bills is 'the most important branch'[2].

It seems that bills of exchange were originally developed in the thirteenth century for use in international trade[3] by the bankers of Lombardy, who carried on business all over Europe. Medieval merchants from different countries engaged in international trade would attend the great merchant fairs to do business. A merchant selling goods at such a fair would normally prefer to be paid in his own currency and, to satisfy that desire, the fairs were serviced by money exchangers who would carry out the business of currency exchange. Suppose that A sold goods to B. B could approach a money exchanger, X, and buy currency to pay A. However, carrying large amounts of cash was both cumbersome and dangerous. Instead, the money exchangers developed a practice of paying by giving the merchant a document addressed to a money exchanger in his own country (call him Y), instructing Y to pay the merchant the required sum. This was the original form of the bill of exchange; it was acceptable to merchants because of its convenience and because of the commercial reputation of the money exchangers.

A could take the document and present it to Y on his return to obtain payment; alternatively, if A needed funds for further business before his return home, he could sell the bill for cash, again relying on the commercial reputation of the money exchangers. From its inception, the bill of exchange therefore facilitated international trade. On payment, X would become indebted to Y. However, as the use of bills of exchange grew there would be a great volume of mutual business between X and Y and, rather than making payment in settlement of each individual transaction, they would merely strike an account between them at regular intervals, paying only the outstanding balance. The bill of exchange therefore laid one of the foundations of modern banking practice[4].

Since the lex mercatoria was a common system used all over Europe, the recognition of the mercantile custom that bills created legally enforceable obligations became a part of the law of England. It seems that, initially, bills were only enforced in transactions involving foreign merchants, but gradually their utility led to extended use and they were enforced in purely domestic transactions, first between traders, and finally between all parties regardless of status. With the absorption of the lex mercatoria into the common law, the law of bills of exchange became part of the common law, despite the fact that bills seem to contradict many basic common law principles. By 1602 bills were enforceable at common law[5] and although initially they were not transferred, transfer by indorsement was allowed by the mid-seventeenth century and by the end of the century their negotiability was recognised at common law.

Promissory notes developed alongside bills of exchange and became enforceable at common law in much the same way. Whereas a bill of exchange is an order by one person to another to pay money, a promissory note is simply a promise by one person to pay money to another. A bank note is a promissory note payable to bearer on demand. In 1702 it was held that a promissory note was not negotiable[6] but its negotiable status was restored by the Bills of Exchange Act 1704.

In the seventeenth century a third type of instrument came into use, modelled on the bill of exchange. Prior to the seventeenth century, merchants kept their gold and silver in the Royal Mint in the Tower of London. However, in 1645 Charles I forcibly 'borrowed' some £200,000 from the money deposited there and merchants began to look for a safer place to deposit their money. The London goldsmiths took gold on deposit for safekeeping, and paid depositers interest for the use of it; they were thus the forerunners of the modern banks. They would issue depositers with receipts for the sum deposited, which, it was eventually recognised, could be transferred, and over time adopted a practice of accepting instructions from depositers to repay all or part of the sum deposited to a third party, if so desired. The deposit receipt seems to be the ancestor of the modern bank note and the letter of transfer, modelled on the bill of exchange, developed into the modern cheque.

The concept of negotiability, developed through the bill of exchange and cheque, played a crucial part in the development of the modern banking system. A person who deposits money with a bank ceases to own the money and becomes owner of a debt, a right to demand payment from the bank. It is generally taken for granted that the customer can give orders to the bank, by cheque or other mandate, to pay to third parties sums from the debt owed to him and that the benefit of that order can be transferred. However, if not for the development of negotiability, such transfers could only be effected by assignment, subject to its limitations.

1   *Bank of England v Vagliano Bros* [1891] AC 107, HL.
2   Street, *Foundations of Legal Liability* p 323.

3   The history is traced in detail in Street, Foundations of Legal Liability, and Holden, *History of Negotiable Instruments in English Law* (1955).
4   See the description of the clearing system, below 30.1.5.
5   *Martin v Boure* (1603) Cro Jac 6.
6   *Clerke v Martin* (1702) 2 Ld Raym 757.

28.2   The requirements for a valid bill of exchange

Section 3 of the Bill of Exchange Act 1882 defines a bill of exchange as:

> 'an unconditional order in writing addressed by one person to another, signed by the person giving it, requiring the person to whom it is addressed to pay on demand or at a fixed or determinable future time a sum certain in money to or to the order of a specified person or to bearer'.

A cheque is defined as 'a bill of exchange drawn on a banker payable on demand'[1]. A document which does not satisfy the requirements of s 3 therefore cannot be a bill of exchange or a cheque.

Every element of the definition in s 3 is significant, and must be briefly examined.

(a)   Unconditional order
A bill must order payment; a document which merely requests the drawee to make a payment cannot be a bill of exchange. More significantly, the order to pay must be unconditional. Thus, for instance, an order to pay 'provided funds are available' or out of a specified fund is conditional[2], and does not qualify as a bill. However, where a bill is drawn with an indication of the fund to be debited, the order is unconditional; thus a cheque can be drawn on a particular account; the cheque gives the bank an order to pay together with an authority to reimburse itself by debiting the account on which the cheque is drawn.

(b)   In writing
A cheque or bill may be printed[3] and cheques and bills are normally drawn on printed forms, minimising the difficulties caused by the formal requirements of the Act. However, difficulties can still arise, especially where the printed form is altered. There is no requirement that the bill be drawn on any particular material and from time to time cases are reported in the news of cheques (particularly in favour of the Inland Revenue) being drawn on unusual materials, such as a cow or an item of underwear. More seriously, the requirement of writing could pose an obstacle to the development of electronic commerce. As the law stands, parties may make a contract instantaneously by sending electronic messages between their computers, but must use a written instrument if they want the advantages of paying by bill of exchange. However, this obstacle could be removed by the Secretary of State exercising the power under the Electronic Communications Act 2000 to modify the requirement that a bill of exchange be in writing[4].

(c)   Addressed by one person to another
As we noted above, there is no reason why the drawer cannot draw a bill in favour of himself as payee. However, the drawer and drawee may not be the same person: if A draws a 'bill' on himself, any holder may treat the document either as a bill or as a promissory note.

(d) Signed by the person giving it

A bill must be signed by the drawer. Until the bill is signed, the drawer cannot be liable on a document as a bill. However, there is no requirement that a person sign personally. The drawer may sign through an agent, as where a director of a company signs a cheque on behalf of the company. Generally, a person signing a bill assumes liability for its payment, but if a person signs adding words indicating that he does so on behalf of a principal, or in a representative character, the principal and not the agent is liable on the bill. This is only the case, however, if the signature makes clear that the signatory acts as agent; descriptive words are insufficient, so that a person who signs a company cheque as 'AB, director' would be personally liable on it[5]. In deciding whether a signature on a bill is that of the principal or agent, a court must adopt the interpretation 'most favourable to the validity' of the bill[6]. In *Elliott v Bax-Ironside*[7] directors had accepted a bill on behalf of a company. The drawer required the directors to indorse the bill personally, and they did so, signing the name of the company as well as their own names. They were held personally liable on the indorsement, on the basis that the company was already liable on the bill by virtue of the acceptance.

The justification for this rule seems to be that bills are negotiated and discounted on the basis of their appearance, the marketability of a bill depending on the creditworthiness of the persons against whom it may be enforced. A holder should therefore be able to enforce the bill against an apparent signatory, unless the bill makes clear that that person signed only as an agent. However, this does not extend to a forged signature. If the drawer's signature is forged, the drawer is not liable on the bill: no liabilities are incurred through a forged signature[8], although a bill upon which the drawer's signature is forged may still have some effect, since the acceptor and later indorsers of the bill may be liable on it.

'Signature' is not defined in the Act. In a different context it has been held that a facsimile signature applied with a rubber stamp is capable of being a 'signature'[9] and facsimile signatures are widely used on cheques. It is not clear whether a bill of exchange can be signed 'digitally'. It would be possible, however, for the Secretary of State to modify the signature requirement so as to permit the use of digital signatures, for use in connection with an 'electronic bill of exchange', by using his powers under the Electronic Commerce Act 2000[10].

(e) Payable on demand or at a fixed or determinable future time

A bill may be expressed to be payable on demand, 'at sight' or 'on presentation'; in each case it is payable on demand[11], so that the drawee is required to pay as soon as the bill is presented. A cheque is payable on demand. In addition, if a bill is accepted or indorsed after the time for payment, it is treated as payable on demand as regards the indorser or acceptor.

Commercial bills are commonly payable at some future date. The bill may expressly indicate the date for payment; alternatively, it may fix payment by reference to some event, provided that it is an event which must happen, rather than a contingent event[12]. Thus a bill payable '90 days after date' is valid and is payable 90 days after the date of the bill. A bill payable '90 days after sight' is payable 90 days after presentation for acceptance, and is valid; such a bill must be presented for acceptance to fix the date when it is payable. On the other hand, a bill expressed to be payable on, or a fixed period after, acceptance, would not be valid: acceptance is a contingent event since the drawee might dishonour the bill on presentation[13].

A more flexible approach was taken in two recent cases. In *Hong Kong & Shanghai Banking Corpn Ltd v GD Trade Co Ltd*[14] bills had been drawn using a printed form which provided that they were payable 'at .... sight'. The drawer had inserted the words '90 days after acceptance' between the words 'at' and 'sight' but using a type face too large for the space, with the result that the word 'sight' was partially overtyped. It was argued that the documents were not bills within the statutory definition because they were payable '90 days after acceptance' and therefore payment depended on a contingent event. The Court of Appeal explained that the rule requiring payment to be due on a determinable date is required because it is necessary for a number of purposes to determine the maturity date of the bill. A strict approach to the interpretation of bills is justified because they may be negotiated and thus come into the hands of third parties. For the same reason, their interpretation must depend on the words used on their face, not on surrounding circumstances (of which a third party would be ignorant). On the other hand, the court was entitled to adopt a commercially sensible approach to the interpretation of a bill which –

> 'is a document in daily use in hundreds of commercial transactions and, in the case of an instrument which has been drawn as a bill with the plain intention that it should take effect as such, the court should lean in favour of a construction which upholds its validity as a bill where that is reasonably possible'[15].

Applying this principle, it was apparent here that the drawer had not intended to delete the word 'sight', so the bills were payable 90 days after acceptance or sight. The court further suggested (without actually deciding) that if the bills were defective as drawn, the defect would have been cured by the terms of the drawee's acceptances, which in each case indicated the date at which payment would be due.

A similar approach was taken in *Novaknit Hellas SA v Kumar Bros International Ltd*[16]. A series of bills drawn under a sale contract were stated to be payable either '60 days from shipment' or '60 days from presentation of documents'. Under the sale contract the bills were to be presented for acceptance with shipping documents relating to the goods. On this basis the Court of Appeal held that bills payable '60 days from presentation of documents' had the same effect as if they had been made payable '60 days from sight', since the bills would be presented for acceptance at the same time as the shipping documents. The court further concluded that since shipment in each case was bound to occur before presentation of the documents and bill, those bills were not uncertain and were valid. With respect, the test ought to be whether the bill is valid as drawn and at that time shipment was necessarily a contingent event. However, the court's approach was pragmatic and perhaps indicates a desire not to permit technical points to be taken to avoid liability: the bills in question had all been accepted. The court went on to offer two further bases for holding the acceptors liable on the bills. First, as the court had suggested in the *Hong Kong and Shanghai* case, if the bills were initially uncertain, the uncertainty could perhaps have been cured when the drawee accepted indicating the date for payment. It was, however, not necessary to decide this point because the court concluded that if the acceptance did not cure any defect in the bills, the bills having been accepted payable on a determinable date took effect as promissory notes.

It has been held that a promissory note payable 'on or before[17]' or 'by[18]' a specified date is not valid, and the same would seem to apply to a bill.

(f)   The bill must order payment to, or to the order of, a specified person or to bearer

The bill may be payable to a named payee. If the bill is payable 'to X or order' the bill may be paid to X or a person nominated by X, so that the bill can be transferred. Even if the words 'or order' are omitted, the bill may still be transferred. However, if the bill is marked 'pay X only' it is not transferable, and only X can enforce payment. Where a cheque is crossed 'Account payee' it is not transferable[19].

Alternatively, the bill may be payable 'to bearer'. In that case the bill may be transferred by delivery, and any person to whom it is transferred may enforce it. However, an instrument payable, for instance, 'to cash' or 'to wages' is not a bill and so falls outside the Act[20].

(g)   The order must be to pay 'a sum certain in money'

The amount to be paid must be certain, although the bill may provide for payment by instalments, with interest at a stated rate, or in a foreign currency. An order to pay money and do some other act is not a valid bill.

In addition to the above, bills are normally dated. However, dating is not a statutory requirement, unless the bill is payable 'n days after date', in which case a date is required to fix the date for payment. Even in that case the absence of a date may not be fatal, since any holder may complete the date and, if the bill comes into the hands of a holder in due course the date so inserted is deemed to be the correct date[21]. The bill may also include a statement of the place where it is drawn: this may be important to categorise the bill as 'inland' or 'foreign', which is relevant in the event that the bill is dishonoured[22], and/or a statement of the place where it is payable, such as at a particular bank.

1   BoEA 1882, s 73.
2   BoEA 1882, s 3(3).
3   BoEA 1882, s 2.
4   Electronic Communications Act 2000, s 8; see 1.5.1.1. Other obstacles must be overcome in order to create an electronic bill of exchange: see 28.7.
5   BoEA 1882, s 26(1).
6   BoEA 1882, s 26(2).
7   [1925] 2 KB 301.
8   BoEA 1882, s 24.
9   *Goodman v J Eban Ltd* [1954] 1 QB 550, [1954] 1 All ER 763, CA.
10   See 28.7.
11   BoEA 1882, s 10.
12   BoEA 1882, s 11.
13   *Korea Exchange Bank v Debenhams (Central Buying) Ltd* [1979] 1 Lloyd's Rep 548.
14   [1998] CLC 238.
15   [1998] CLC 238 at 242.
16   [1998] CLC 971.
17   *Williamson v Rider* [1963] 1 QB 89, [1962] 2 All ER 268, CA.
18   *Claydon v Bradley* [1987] 1 All ER 522, [1987] 1 WLR 521, CA.
19   BoEA 1882, s 81A, inserted by the Cheques Act 1992; see 30.1.3.
20   *Orbit Mining and Trading Co Ltd v Westminster Bank Ltd* [1963] 1 QB 794.
21   BoEA 1882, s 12(1).
22   See 28.5.3.

28.2.1   *Incomplete bills*

A bill may still be effective even though, as drawn, it omits one or more of the statutory requirements. By virtue of s 20(1) of the Act, any person in possession of a bill has prima facie authority to complete the missing item; and if a person signs a piece of paper and 'delivers' it for conversion into a negotiable instrument, the act of delivery constitutes prima facie authority to complete the paper as a bill for any amount, using the signature as that of drawer, acceptor or indorser. This is a striking provision, clearly intended to protect third parties. However, the original signor is only liable on the bill as completed if it is completed within a reasonable time and in accordance with the authority actually given[1]; this might seem to undermine the protection given to third parties, who may take the bill with no idea that it has been completed in breach of authority. However, persons who become parties to the bill after its completion are fully liable on it and, moreover, if the bill comes into the hands of a holder in due course, it is conclusively presumed that the bill was completed within a reasonable time and in accordance with the signor's instructions[2]; the holder in due course can therefore enforce the bill according to its apparent tenor, regardless of the authority actually given by the original signor.

The liability of a person who signs a blank paper, including a blank cheque, under s 20 depends on the paper being 'delivered' for completion as a bill. Thus if a signed paper is stolen, the thief cannot convert it into a bill or cheque, and enforce it, because of his lack of authority. Moreover, since the paper is never delivered to the thief, even a holder in due course cannot rely on s 20 to enforce the bill against the signor. Similarly, if the signor delivers the paper to the agent for some purpose other than completion as a bill, s 20 has no application[3]. There is a clear parallel here with the exceptions to the nemo dat principle in the law of sale: a person is not liable on a bill or cheque merely because he is careless with his signature. However, as in sale, the principle of estoppel may make the signor liable even where s 20 is not applicable. In *Lloyds Bank Ltd v Cooke*[4] D signed a cheque and delivered it to A with instructions to complete it as a cheque for £250 in favour of P. A actually completed it in the sum of £1,000 to obtain a loan from P. As the original payee, P could not qualify as a holder in due course, and so could not rely on s 20 but as it had changed its position in reliance on the cheque, it was held that D was estopped from denying the validity of the cheque. However, in the later case of *Wilson and Meeson v Pickering*[5], the court refused to extend *Cooke* and held that such an estoppel would only arise where the signor intended to create a negotiable instrument. In this case, D had signed a cheque and crossed it 'not negotiable'; the court therefore held that no estoppel could arise.

1   BoEA 1882, s 20(2).
2   BoEA 1882, s 20(2).
3   *Smith v Prosser* [1907] 2 KB 735, CA.
4   [1907] 1 KB 794, CA.
5   [1946] KB 422, [1946] 1 All ER 394, CA.

28.3   Transfer of a bill of exchange

The essential characteristic of a bill is that it is negotiable. In other words, (a) it can be transferred without notice to the person(s) liable on it and (b) if certain conditions are fulfilled, the transferee may take the bill free of any defects in title of, or defences available against, the transferor. Not every transfer has this second effect, and the word 'negotiate' ought to be reserved for transfers which do. However, the 1882 Act uses the words 'negotiate' and 'negotiation' to refer simply to transfers. It has been suggested that the language of the statute should be amended, to draw a distinction between transfer and negotiation[1].

Some bills may not be transferred: a bill drawn 'pay X only' can only be enforced by X, and therefore cannot be transferred, and the position is the same if the bill is marked 'not transferable' or 'not negotiable'[2]. A cheque marked 'not negotiable' may be transferred, but not fully negotiated, so that the transferee can never acquire a better title than the transferor, but a cheque crossed with the words 'account (or a/c) payee', with or without the addition of the word 'only', is not transferable[3]. Most cheque forms are now printed with a crossing in this form and marked 'pay ..... only' and therefore are not transferable[4].

The method of transferring a bill depends on whether it is a bearer or order bill. A bearer bill may be transferred simply by delivery[5]. However, a bill drawn payable to a named payee must be indorsed in favour of the transferee and delivered to him in order to effect a full transfer[6]. An indorsement is normally written on the back of the bill itself, although it may also be written on a slip of paper attached to the bill, known as an 'allonge', and this may be done where the bill is transferred several times and the back of the bill becomes full. An indorsement may be 'special' or 'general'. In order to specially indorse a bill, the payee writes on it the name of the transferee and signs his own name; thus if a bill is drawn to 'T Smith', Smith can transfer the bill to D Jones by writing 'Pay D Jones, signed T Smith'. Jones can transfer the bill in the same way.

A general indorsement consists of the signature of the payee or holder: the bill is then converted into a bearer bill and can be transferred by delivery[7]. Thus Smith could also transfer the bill to Jones by simply signing it and delivering it to Jones; Jones could then transfer the bill by delivery. However, the Act allows any holder to convert a generally indorsed bill back into an order bill, simply by writing the name of a particular person above the last signature[8]. Thus Jones could take the bill from Smith, generally indorsed, and reconvert it to an order bill by adding 'Pay D Jones' over Smith's signature. This is important to guard against the theft of a bearer bill. It is not clear if a bill originally drawn to bearer can be 'closed' in the same way, by being specially indorsed, and academic views differ. The better view seems to be that a bill originally drawn payable to bearer always remains a bearer bill; if the drawer wishes to expose himself to the risks involved in drawing a bearer bill he should be able to do so[9].

An order bill may be transferred several times by a string of indorsements, unless it is restrictively indorsed. A restrictive indorsement is one such as 'Pay D Jones only', which prohibits further negotiation, or which indicates that it is transferred with limited authority to deal with it in a specified way, such as 'Pay Jones for the account of Smith'[10].

If an order bill is transferred without indorsement, the transfer operates only as an equitable assignment: the transferee therefore takes the bill subject to equities, and gains none of the benefits of a bill of exchange, except that the transferee has the right to have the bill indorsed in his favour to correct the defect[11].

A person who indorses a bill becomes liable on it and may have to pay the holder if it is dishonoured by the acceptor[12]. However, an indorser can exclude his own liability by indorsing the bill 'without recourse'.

1 Report of the Review Committee on Banking Law and Services (1989) (Cm 622) pp 224, 397. This recommendation is not to be implemented at the present time.
2 BoEA 1882, s 8.
3 BoEA 1882, s 81A inserted by the Cheques Act 1992: see 30.1.3.
4 It has been suggested that as a result they are not bills of exchange: see McLeod (1997) 113 LQR 133.
5 BoEA 1882, s 31(2).
6 BoEA 1882, s 31(3).

7   BoEA 1882, s 34.
8   BoEA 1882, s 34(4).
9   In *Miller Associates (Australia) Pty Ltd v Bennington Pty Ltd* [1975] 2 NSWLR 506 it was held that a bearer bill cannot be converted to an order bill by special indorsement; see Goode, *Commercial Law* (2nd edn, 1995) p 535; contrast Ellinger and Lomincka, *Modern Banking Law* (2nd edn, 1994) p 311. The Report of the Review Committee on Banking Law and Services recommended that the law be clarified by confirming that the view taken in *Miller* reflects English law.
10   BoEA 1882, s 35.
11   BoEA 1882, s 31(4).
12   BoEA 1882, s 55(2).

28.3.1   *Forged indorsements*

The requirement of indorsement for the transfer of an order bill makes it more secure against theft than a bearer bill. The Act provides that a forged or unauthorised signature, including an indorsement, is of no effect[1]. A distinction must be drawn between an unauthorised and a forged signature, since an unauthorised signature can be ratified. Unfortunately, the distinction may not always be easy to draw[2]. Thus if Jones steals a bill payable to Smith, and forges Smith's signature in order to transfer the bill to Hayes, Hayes gains no title: the forgery has no legal effect. Hayes therefore cannot retain the bill against Smith, or enforce it against any prior party, other than Jones, unless that party is estopped from setting up the forgery. Estoppel requires a representation by the person to be estopped. Clearly, if A, whose signature on a bill is forged, positively represents to B that the signature is genuine and B acts in reliance on that representation, A will be estopped from denying its truth. In *Greenwood v Martins Bank Ltd*[3] it was held that a customer of a bank who, having discovered that his signature had been forged on a number of cheques by his wife, failed to notify the bank on which they were drawn, was estopped from denying that the signatures were genuine. The customer's silence here was deliberate. In the circumstances, and in view of the relationship between customer and bank, that silence was held to amount to a representation that the signature was genuine. It is not clear, however, that silence will give rise to an estoppel in other circumstances. In order for it to do so, it must be deliberate and in circumstances such that there is a duty to speak. Silence is more likely to be negligent and, as seen in other contexts[4], negligence will only give rise to an estoppel where there is a duty of care owed by the party to be estopped to the party alleging estoppel. It has been held that a customer owes a bank a duty of care in the operation of a bank account[5], but the payee of a cheque owes no duty either to the drawer or drawee to take care of the cheque[6]. Imposition of a duty of care in relation to statements depends on there being an assumption of responsibility for the statement[7]. It may be arguable that once the holder of a bill is aware of its loss he is under a duty to notify the drawer, drawee/acceptor and any other prior parties of its loss, but it is difficult to see how a duty of care could be owed to subsequent parties: before they take the bill they will generally be unknown members of an indeterminate class; a statement or negligent omission made after they become parties will only give rise to an estoppel if they then act in reliance on it. So, if a bill is stolen from X and transferred to Y by means of a forged indorsement, and X becomes aware of the forgery, he may be estopped from denying the forgery if he fails to notify Y and Y acts to his detriment in reliance on the bill.

The forgery rule causes particular problems for banks which collect or pay bills on behalf of their customers: if the bank pays a person not entitled to enforce the bill, for instance because that bill has been transferred by a forged indorsement, it may be liable to the true owner of the bill and unable to debit its customer for the money paid out. Whilst a bank can be expected to know and check its customer's signature, it can hardly be expected to know the signatures of other parties who indorse a cheque. There is some statutory protection for banks which collect or pay cheques[8]; it has been suggested that there should be a similar protection in relation to persons paying or collecting other bills in cases of forged signatures[9].

A third party who takes a bill after a forged indorsement may be protected by s 7(3) of the Act, which provides that if a bill is payable to a fictitious or non-existent payee, it may be treated as payable to bearer[10]; it can therefore be transferred by delivery. This provision becomes important in cases where a bill is drawn for the purposes of fraud. If X draws a bill naming Y as payee, and then forges Y's signature to indorse the bill to Z, Z can acquire no title through the forged signature; but if the bill is treated as a bearer bill, Z may ignore the forgery and acquire title by delivery. Clearly, if there is no person with the name given in the bill – for instance, the bill is made payable to 'Batman' or 'Mickey Mouse' – the payee is fictitious. However, if a realistic name is used, it will generally be possible to find someone with that name. Suppose, for instance, that the payee is named as 'Bruce Wayne', is the payee fictitious if there is a real person named Bruce Wayne? The answer depends on the intention of the person drawing the bill. If the drawer of the bill intends the person named in the bill to receive payment, the payee is not fictitious; but if the drawer never intended the named payee to receive payment, the payee is fictitious even though there may be a real person of that name. Thus in *Bank of England v Vagliano Bros*[11] an employee drew bills on his employer, pretending that they had been drawn by real customers and made payable to those customers. The employer accepted the bills, and the clerk then sold them for cash by forging the signatures of the payees. The holders sought to enforce the bills against the employer as acceptor, and succeeded: the clerk had actually drawn the bills and he never intended the named payees to receive payment. The bills were therefore payable to fictitious payees, and could be treated as bearer bills. Similarly, in *Clutton v Attenborough*[12] an employee defrauded his employer by preparing a bill for his employer in favour of 'J Brett', on the basis that Brett had done work for the employer. The employer signed the bill as drawer and the clerk then sold the bill, forging the signature of J Brett. Again, it was held that the bill was a bearer bill: the employer intended 'J Brett' to receive payment, but the J Brett in question was someone who had done work for the employer. Although there may have been many people named 'J Brett', there was none who possessed the attributes of the Brett envisaged by the drawer of the bill. In contrast, in *Vinden v Hughes*[13] an employee got his employer to draw bills in favour of named customers; the employee then forged the customers' signatures to sell the bills for cash. It was held in this case that as the employer, the drawer of the bills, did intend the customers to receive payment, they were not bearer bills[14].

The decisions extending the meaning of 'fictitious' and 'non-existent' are clearly beneficial to innocent third parties who may take the bills in such cases. However, the test based on the drawer's intention, and involving the attributes of the payee to be considered, may require some difficult distinctions to be drawn. Moreover, in *Vagliano* it is difficult to see why the drawer's intention should be relevant at all: the employer was liable as acceptor, not drawer.

1 BoEA 1882, s 24.
2 See 4.7.1; 28.4.4.
3 [1933] AC 51, HL.

4 See *Moorgate Mercantile Co Ltd v Twitchings* [1977] AC 890, [1976] 2 All ER 641, HL; see 17.2.2.
5 *London Joint Stock Bank v Macmillan and Arthur* [1918] AC 777, HL; see 29.3.3.
6 *Yorkshire Bank plc v Lloyds Bank plc* [1999] 2 All ER (Comm) 153.
7 *Williams v Natural Life Health Foods Ltd* [1998] 2 All ER 577.
8 See 30.2.
9 *Report of the Review Committee on Banking Law and Services* (1989) (Cm 622), p 71.
10 BoEA 1882, s 7(3).
11 [1891] AC 107, HL.
12 [1897] AC 90, HL.
13 [1905] 1 KB 795.
14 In the Canadian case of *Boma Manufacturing Ltd v Canadian Imperial Bank of Commerce* (1996) 140 DLR (4th) 463 it was held that the drawer of a cheque is the person on whose account it is drawn, so that where an employee with authority to sign cheques signed cheques drawn on her employer's account payable in favour of real people whom she did not intend to receive payment, the payees were not fictitious, since the drawer, the employer, did intend the named payees to receive payment.

28.3.2 *Holders*

The holder of a bill is the person entitled to enforce it by presenting it for payment, and, in the event of dishonour, by taking enforcement proceedings. Payment to a holder operates to discharge the payer from liability on the bill; payment to anyone other than the holder cannot operate as a discharge. The Act defines the holder as the bearer of a bearer bill, or the payee or indorsee in possession of an order bill[1]. One effect of this definition is that a thief can be a holder of a bearer bill. The thief has no title to the bill, so that payment to him can be refused if the theft is known; but as holder the thief can transfer the bill to a third party who may qualify as a holder in due course and take a perfect title.

The Act recognises three different classes of holder, each with different rights. One essential characteristic distinguishing between the three classes is the giving of consideration for the bill. The Review Committee on Banking Law and Practice felt that the law in this area is unnecessarily complex, and recommended the abolition of the requirement of consideration for bills of exchange[2]. As the committee pointed out, the formal nature of the bill means that consideration is not necessary to prove the seriousness of the intention of the drawer and acceptor, who are primarily liable on the bill, to accept legal liability to pay. One effect of the Committee's recommendations would be to reduce the classes of holder to two. Recent decisions suggest that there may be a need for clarification of this area, but the government did not take up this recommendation in its 1990 White Paper.

1 Section 2.
2 At p 68.

28.3.2.1 *The holder*

The mere holder of a bill has very limited rights. He may:

(a) transfer it, by indorsement and/or delivery as necessary;
(b) insert the date of the bill if it is omitted[1]; and
(c) present it for payment.

In addition, every holder is rebuttably presumed to be a holder in due course. However, if it is proved that the bill was issued, accepted or negotiated due to 'fraud or duress or force and fear or illegality', the holder must prove that he is a holder in due course, by showing that the bill has subsequently been transferred for value in good faith[2].

1 BoEA 1882, s 12; see 28.2.
2 BoEA 1882, s 30.

28.3.2.2 *Holder for value*

When the holder presents the bill for payment, payment may be refused on the grounds of any defences available arising from any defects in his title or out of the original contract. In particular, since the rights and obligations created by a bill are contractual, the acceptor or other payer can refuse payment on the grounds that he received no consideration for it. The holder can then only enforce payment by showing that he provided consideration, and so qualifies as a holder for value. However, the meaning of 'consideration' in this context is wider than in the general law. The Act provides[1] that consideration may be provided in any of three ways. Any consideration sufficient to support a simple contract will suffice to support a bill: thus if a transferee of a bill pays cash for it, he is a holder for value. In addition, an antecedent debt or liability may provide consideration for a bill, although it would not normally provide consideration for a simple contract: thus if S sells goods to B for £100 and, one month later, B gives A a cheque for £100, the existing debt is good consideration for the bill and S is a holder for value. This appears to be an exception to the rule that past consideration is no consideration. The past debt in question must be owed by the person liable on the bill. In *Oliver v Davis*[2] P lent D £350; in return D gave P a postdated cheque for £400 and then persuaded D2 to give P a further cheque for £400. D2's cheque was stopped, and P sought to enforce it. D2 claimed that she had received no consideration, and P sought to rely on the loan previously given to D. It was held that that was insufficient: there was no connection between that and D2's cheque. If P had agreed with D2 that he would not enforce the debt against D1, he would have provided consideration. However, he had not done so: he did not know why D2 had given her cheque until it was stopped and in evidence he conceded that he had never agreed to release D1. In contrast, in *Diamond v Graham*[3], D lent money to H, but placed a stop on the cheque for the loan; H gave a postdated cheque for the amount of the loan to a friend, G, and arranged for G to give a cheque for the same amount to D. D then released the stop on his cheque to H. It was held that D could enforce G's cheque. D provided consideration by releasing the stop on his cheque in favour of H.

In addition, the Act provides that a holder may be taken to have given consideration for a bill if consideration has at any time been given for it[4]: in that case, the holder is a holder for value as against all persons who became parties to the bill before consideration was last given for it. A holder may therefore rely on consideration provided by a previous party to the bill to qualify as a holder for value. Suppose that A buys goods from B and accepts a bill of exchange drawn on him for the price. B then transfers the bill to C in settlement of an existing debt, and C gives the bill to her son, D, as a gift. D has given no value to C, but as against A and B can rely on the value given by C and so qualify as a holder for value. In *Diamond*, D could also rely on the fact that H had provided consideration for G's cheque by giving his own cheque in return. It has been held, however, that this section only applies after the bill has been negotiated, so that the original payee can only qualify as a holder for value if he himself provides value for this bill, and that the consideration must have been supplied by a person entitled to enforce the promise in the bill. Thus where an account holder instructed his bank to draw its own cheque in favour of a named payee, the payee could not qualify as a holder for value on this basis because, although the account holder gave value, the cheque had not been negotiated and, although the account holder had provided consideration, no consideration had been provided by a promisee of the bill[5].

The Act further provides that where a person has a lien on a bill, he is taken to be a holder for value to the extent of the lien[6]. Thus if X borrows £100 from Y and deposits with Y a bill for £1,000 as security for the loan, Y has a lien on the bill for £100 and is a holder for value to that extent.

Holder for value status enables a holder to enforce a bill even though the person against whom it is enforced received no consideration for it[7]. However, if there is any other defect in his title to the bill, the holder for value may fail: to enforce the bill free of all defects and equities, the holder must be a holder in due course[8].

1   BoEA 1882, s 27(1).
2   [1949] 2 KB 727, [1949] 2 All ER 353, CA; see also *Hasan v Willson* [1977] 1 Lloyd's Rep 431; *MK International Developments Ltd v Housing Bank Ltd* [1991] 1 Bank LR 74.
3   [1968] 2 All ER 909, [1968] 1 WLR 1061, CA.
4   BoEA 1882, s 27(2).
5   *MK International Developments Ltd v Housing Bank Ltd* [1991] 1 Bank LR 74.
6   BoEA 1882, s 27(3); see 22.1.2.
7   The Act does not define the rights of a holder for value.
8   If the recommendation of the Review Committee that the requirement that consideration be given for a bill be abolished, holder for value status would be abolished.

28.3.2.3   *Holder in due course*

A holder in due course is in a specially favoured position: he can enforce the bill regardless of defects in title of any previous party, and free of personal defences which would have been available between previous parties, such as partial or total failure of consideration[1]. Effectively, the holder in due course is the equivalent of the bona fide purchaser for value in the general law, and the status of holder in due course is recognised in law in order to promote the transferability of bills of exchange. The Act sets out the requirements which must be established in order for a holder to qualify as a holder in due course. As we have seen, every holder is prima facie presumed to be a holder in due course, so that it will normally be for the person resisting payment to show that the plaintiff is not a holder in due course; but if it is shown that the bill was drawn, accepted or negotiated as a result of fraud etc, the holder must establish his status by showing that the bill has since been transferred for value in good faith[2].

In order to qualify as a holder in due course, a person must be 'a holder who has taken a bill, complete and regular on the face of it, under the following conditions':

(a) that he became the holder of it before it was overdue, and without notice that it had previously been dishonoured, if such was the fact; and

(b) that he took the bill in good faith and for value, and that at the time the bill was negotiated to him he had no notice of any defect in title of the person who negotiated it[3].

A person seeking to enforce a bill must therefore satisfy each of the following requirements in order to qualify as a holder in due course.

(1) He must be a holder. Since no one can become a holder of a bearer bill through a forged indorsement, if an indorsement on a bearer bill is forged, no one who subsequently comes into possession of the bill can be a holder in due course; however, the transferee of a stolen bearer bill may do so.

Although the definition of 'holder' in s 1 of the Act includes the original payee of an order bill, it has been held that a holder in due course must be someone to whom the bill has been negotiated. Thus the original payee cannot qualify as a holder in due course[4]; however, in a later case it was held that the original payee who negotiated the bill to an indorsee and, after several further transfers, received it back by indorsement, could enforce the bill against the acceptor and drawer in the capacity of indorsee, and so qualify as a holder in due course[5].

(2) The bill must be complete and regular on its face at the time of its transfer. It has been held that 'face' includes the rear of the bill[6], so that a missing indorsement, or a discrepancy between the name of the payee and the name in which he indorses the bill, make it irregular. Further, although a person who receives an incomplete bill may have authority to complete it[7], he can never qualify as a holder in due course; however, if he completes the bill and transfers it to a third party, the third party can be a holder in due course, if the other requirements of s 29 are satisfied.

(3) The bill must not have been overdue at the time of its transfer. A bill is overdue when the time for payment has passed; if payable on demand, the bill is overdue when it has been in circulation 'for an unreasonable length of time'[8], which is a question of fact in each case. Banks will generally not pay cheques presented more than six months from the date of their issue, regarding them as 'stale' and requiring confirmation from the drawer before paying. However, a bill or cheque may be overdue even though it has been in circulation for less than six months; and equally a period of more than six months may not be unreasonable, so that the bill will not be overdue, according to the particular facts.

(4) The person seeking to enforce the bill must have taken it without notice that it has previously been dishonoured by non-acceptance or non-payment.

(5) The person seeking to enforce the bill must have taken it in good faith and without notice of any defect in the transferor's title. These two requirements are closely bound together. The doctrine of constructive notice is not applied to bills of exchange, and the Act provides that, provided a person acts honestly, negligence does not amount to bad faith[9]. In order to prove that a person did not take a bill in good faith, 'it is necessary to show that the person . . . was affected with notice that there was something wrong about it when he took it'[10]. However, there is no need to show that the person was aware of the exact nature of the particular wrong; and a person who suspects that something is wrong and deliberately ignores the fact, may be regarded as acting in bad faith or as having notice[11]. Furthermore, the mere fact that the circumstances would have made a reasonable person suspicious will tend to raise an evidential burden requiring the person asserting good faith to prove that he was not suspicious. Similarly, the fact that a bill was acquired at a gross undervalue may also be evidence of bad faith[12].

The transferor's title may be defective as a result of either the circumstances in which he acquired the bill, or those in which he transferred it. Section 29(2) provides that:

'the title of a person who negotiates a bill is defective within the meaning of this Act when he obtained the bill, or the acceptance thereof, by fraud, duress, or force and fear, or other unlawful means, or an illegal consideration, or when he negotiates it in breach of faith, or under such circumstances as amount to a fraud'.

(6) The person seeking to enforce the bill must have taken it 'for value'. It has generally been assumed that, although a person may rely on value given by a previous holder in order to qualify as a holder for value, in order to be a holder in due course the holder must himself have provided consideration. However, in *Clifford Chance v Silver*[13] the Court of Appeal held that it was enough that sufficient 'value' had been given to qualify as a holder for value, so that a holder could rely on value given by a previous party to the bill. The court relied on cases decided prior to the 1882 Act which used the expression 'bona fide holder for value without notice' rather than 'holder in due course'. The decision, made in the context of an appeal from an application for summary judgment and without detailed consideration of the point, is surprising. The holder in due course is generally thought to be, effectively, a bona fide purchaser, but the reasoning of the Court of Appeal would allow a donee of a bill to qualify as a holder in due course. Moreover, the language of s 29(1)(b) of the Act, providing that a holder is a holder in due course if 'he took the bill in good faith and for value', seems to imply that the good faith, and provision of value, must coincide with the holder's taking of the bill. However, a person who takes a bill in payment of a pre-existing debt or liability may qualify as a holder in due course, and it has been held that a holder who has a lien over a bill, sufficient to make him a holder for value[14] gives sufficient consideration to qualify as a holder in due course[15]. In addition, when a holder cannot rely on the presumption that he is a holder in due course he can establish his status by proving that value has at any time been given for the bill[16]. The decision in *Silver* therefore brings some consistency to this area[17].

Once a bill has passed into the hands of a holder in due course, defects in title are cured and any person deriving title through a holder in due course has the same rights as a holder in due course as regards previous persons who became parties to the bill before the holder in due course[18], even though he may know of a prior defect in title, such as fraud or duress[19]. Of course, the position is different if the transferee was party to the fraud.

1   BoEA 1882, s 38(2).
2   BoEA 1882, s 30(2).
3   BoEA 1882, s 29.
4   *R E Jones Ltd v Waring and Gillow Ltd* [1926] AC 670, HL.
5   *Jade International Steel und Eisen Stahl GmbH & Co KG v Robert Nicholas Steels Ltd* [1978] QB 917, [1978] 3 All ER 104, CA.
6   *Arab Bank v Ross* [1952] 2 QB 216, [1952] 1 All ER 709, CA.
7   BoEA 1882, s 20; see 28.2.1.
8   BoEA 1882, s 36(3).
9   BoEA 1882, s 90.
10 *Jones v Gordon* (1877) 2 App Cas 616 at 628, per Lord Blackburn.
11 *Raphael v Bank of England* (1855) 17 CB 161.
12 *Jones v Gordon* (1877) 2 App Cas 616.
13 [1992] 2 Bank LR 11; see Hitchens [1993] JBL 511.
14 Section 27(3), above 28.3.2.2.
15 *Barclays Bank Ltd v Astley Trust Ltd* [1970] 2 QB 527.
16 BoEA 1882, s 30(2), above.

17 If the recommendations of the Review Committee on Banking Law and Practice were implemented,
      the requirement that a holder in due course had taken the bill for value would be abolished.
18 BoEA 1882, s 29(3).
19 *May v Chapman* (1847) 16 M & W 355.

28.4 Liability on the bill

The liability created by a bill of exchange is essentially contractual: the bill gives
rise to a series of promises which can be enforced as contracts. As noted above, the
contracts thus created are largely independent of the underlying transaction in
connection with which the bill is given. Liability falls, primarily, on the acceptor
of the bill or, where the bill is dishonoured by the drawee, on the drawer. Thus the
person primarily liable on a cheque is the drawer, since a cheque is not accepted by
the bank on which it is drawn. However, any other party to the bill may incur
liability on it and have to pay compensation if the bill is not honoured. The basis of
liability on a bill is signature: as a general rule, any person who signs a bill, in any
capacity, becomes potentially liable on it.

28.4.1 *Capacity*

Since liability on a bill is contractual, no person can be made liable on a bill unless
he has capacity to incur contractual liability[1]. Thus a minor cannot be made liable
on a bill, and this applies even if the minor could be held liable on the underlying
contract. A company's capacity to become liable on a bill of exchange depends on
the power contained in its memorandum. Generally, however, a trading company
will have implied power to draw, accept and indorse bills of exchange.

A party to a bill who lacks capacity may not be held liable on it. However, the
bill remains fully valid and enforceable against other parties.

1   BoEA 1882, s 22.

28.4.2 *Liability depends on delivery*

Although the essential basis of liability is signature of the bill, the Act provides
that every contract on a bill is incomplete and revocable until delivery of the bill[1].
The only exception is that if a drawee of a bill accepts, and notifies the person
entitled to payment of that acceptance, the acceptance is then complete. 'Delivery'
involves the transfer of possession of the bill[2]; it can be actual or constructive, and
a bill can be delivered by an agent on behalf of his principal. In addition, delivery
may be absolute or conditional: for instance, if S sells goods to B for delivery at
some future date, B may give S a bill for the price, but deliver the bill conditionally
upon delivery of the goods.

The need for delivery would mean that a person who signs a bill or cheque
would be protected if the cheque or bill were stolen. However, the transferability
of bills would be severely undermined if a person seeking to enforce a bill was
required to prove delivery by prior parties. It is therefore rebuttably presumed that
the bill has been delivered by every person who has signed it[3], placing the burden
of proof on the person denying delivery. Even so, the position of anyone taking a
bill would be precarious: it would be impossible to rely on the appearance of the

bill if a signatory could escape liability by disproving delivery. The general policy of promoting the transferability of bills by protecting the bona fide transferee is therefore continued by a further conclusive presumption that, where the bill is in the hands of a holder in due course, it has been validly and unconditionally delivered by all prior parties to it[4]. The result is that if X signs a bill payable to bearer and loses it, if the bill comes into the hands of a holder in due course, X is liable and cannot escape liability by claiming that he did not deliver it.

1   BoEA 1882, s 21.
2   BoEA 1882, s 2.
3   BoEA 1882, s 21(3).
4   BoEA 1882, s 21(2).

28.4.3   *Liability depends on signature*

The overriding rule is that signature is the basis of liability on a bill[1]. Thus a person who signs a bill is prima facie liable on it; and a person who has not signed a bill, such as a transferor of a bearer bill by delivery, cannot be liable on it, although such a person may incur other liabilities[2].

A person may sign a bill, so as to incur liability on it, through an agent. However, as we have noted[3], a forged or unauthorised signature is wholly ineffective. It gives no right to retain the bill or enforce payment, and a person incurs no liability through a forged or unauthorised signature unless he is estopped from setting up the forgery or lack of authority. However, in line with the general law of agency, an unauthorised signature can be ratified and, if ratified, is wholly effective. It is therefore necessary to distinguish forgeries from unauthorised signatures.

(a)   Forgeries

If the drawer's signature is forged, the bill is wholly ineffective[4]; in contrast, if the drawee's signature is forged, the drawee is not liable but the bill is valid and the drawer is liable on it. Where an indorsement is forged, the bill is perfectly valid. However, the person whose signature is forged is not liable on it, and the effect of the forgery is to break the chain of title so that no one who takes the bill after the forgery can enforce it against any person who became party to it before the forgery. Suppose that B draws a bill on A, payable to himself, and A accepts. B then indorses to C; the bill is stolen by D, who forges C's signature to indorse it to E. The position is shown by the following diagram:

$$A \longrightarrow B \longrightarrow C \qquad (D) \longrightarrow E$$

$$\text{(Acceptor)} \quad \text{(Payee)} \quad \text{(Indorsee)}$$

E has no title to the bill and cannot enforce it against A, B or C. C is the true owner of the bill, and if he recovers it he is entitled to enforce it against A or B. However, an indorser is estopped from denying the validity of prior signatures[5]. Thus E can enforce the bill against D, if he can be found, and if E indorses the bill to F, F can enforce against E and D; but he cannot enforce against A, B or C. Since C's signature is forged, he can never be liable on the bill. The only exception is where C is estopped from setting up the forgery: such an estoppel may arise if C makes a positive representation that his signature is genuine[6] or where he is under a duty to disclose the forgery and, knowing of it, fails to do so. It has been held that a bank customer who discovers that forged cheques have been drawn on his account, owes a duty to the bank to disclose the forgery[7].

(b) Unauthorised signatures

Where a bill is signed by an agent it may be necessary to consider the liability of both the principal and the agent. The agent may either sign his own name, or sign the principal's name on his behalf[8], and these two situations must be distinguished.

The principal will be liable in either case, provided that the agent acts within the scope of his authority in signing the bill. Even if the agent acts outside his actual authority, the principal will be liable if the agent has apparent authority: the principal is then estopped from setting up the lack of authority. However, the Act provides that a 'procuration signature' operates as notice that the agent's authority is limited: where a bill is signed by procuration, the principal will therefore only be liable on a signature within the scope of the agent's actual authority[9]. The statement on the bill that it is signed 'by procuration' operates as a 'red flag' to warn anyone taking the bill that it has been signed by an agent who may have only limited authority. A bill is signed by procuration where it is signed 'P per pro A', or some similar formula is used. Unfortunately, it is not clear if this rule applies to every case where the fact that the bill has been signed by an agent is apparent on the bill, or only to cases where the formula 'per procurationem' (or its equivalents 'per pro' or 'p p') is used, or the bill is signed pursuant to a power of attorney[10].

A principal will also become liable on an unauthorised signature if he ratifies it.

(c) Agent's liability

If the agent signs the bill in his own name he may also be held liable on it unless the bill makes clear that he signs only in a representative capacity. Again, the intention is to protect third parties, who must rely on the appearance of the bill. If the agent is to avoid personal liability, it is not enough for him merely to add descriptive words: the bill must make clear that the agent is not undertaking personal liability[11]. Thus if a company director signs a bill drawn on the company, and adds the word 'director' after his signature, his signature could still be interpreted as making him personally liable on the bill. However, each case will depend on its circumstances. In *Bondina Ltd v Rolling Shower Blinds Ltd*[12] company directors signed company cheques in their own names without any qualifying words. The company became insolvent and the payee of a dishonoured cheque sued the directors as personally liable. The Court of Appeal held that in signing the cheque, which included printed details of the company's name and bank account number, the directors adopted all the printing on the cheque, and therefore made clear that the cheque was drawn by the company and that it was intended that only the company should incur liability on it. However, it should be borne in mind that the case concerned a cheque, and the party seeking to enforce it was the original payee. In modern practice, cheques are rarely negotiated and are used largely as an alternative to cash. Other bills are more likely to be negotiated, and less likely to include the sort of printed details normally found on a cheque.

In deciding if the agent who signs a bill has undertaken personal liability, the court seeks to determine, objectively, the intention of the agent. Section 26(2) of the Act provides that in deciding whether a signature is that of the agent or the principal, the court should adopt the interpretation most favourable to the validity of the bill. In *Rolfe Lubell & Co v Keith*[13] S supplied goods to B, a company, payment to be by a bill of exchange drawn on B for the price. In addition, S required the directors of the company to indorse the bills in their personal capacity. The defendant director indorsed the bill, but added the words 'for and on behalf of [the company]; director' after his signature with a rubber stamp. It was held, applying s 26(2), that the director was personally liable and the words added by the stamp should be ignored: the company was already liable on the bill, and therefore to treat the director's signature merely as that of his principal, the company, would add nothing to the validity of the bill.

The problem of agents' signatures is most acute where a company is a party to a bill, since it must sign by a human agent, normally a director. It is a statutory requirement that every company bill or cheque must include the name of the company in legible print or writing: if not, a person who signs the bill for the company is personally liable[14]. The company's name must be complete, so that where the director of a company accepted a bill of exchange on behalf of the company, but the bill omitted the word 'Limited' from the company name, the director was liable on the bill[15].

An agent who signs his principal's name, or who signs his own name but makes clear that he accepts no personal liability, will not be held personally liable on the bill. However, if the agent wrongly claims to be authorised to sign, or claims to be the principal, he may be liable for the tort of deceit or for breach of warranty of authority on ordinary agency principles.

1   BoEA 1882, s 23.
2   See below.
3   Above 28.3.1.
4   BoEA 1882, s 3, above 28.2.
5   BoEA 1882, s 55.
6   *Leach v Buchanan* (1802) 4 Esp 226.
7   *Greenwood v Martins Bank* [1933] AC 51.
8   BoEA 1882, s 91.
9   BoEA 1882, s 25.
10 See Goode, *Commercial Law* (2nd edn, 1995) p 567; *Byles on Bills of Exchange* (26th edn, 1988) p 68; contrast *Chitty on Contracts* (28th edn, 1999) para 33-041.
11 BoEA 1882, s 26(2).
12 [1986] 1 All ER 564, [1986] 1 WLR 517.
13 [1979] 1 All ER 860.
14 Companies Act 1985, s 349.
15 *Novaknit Hellas SA v Kumar Bros International Ltd* [1998] CLC 971.

28.4.4   *The meaning of 'forgery'*

In most respects an unauthorised signature and a forged signature have exactly the same effect. An important distinction between the two, however, is that an unauthorised signature can be ratified, so that it may be necessary to distinguish the two. The BoEA does not define either 'forgery' or 'unauthorised', but forgery is a criminal offence and 'forgery' is defined in the criminal law. At the time the BoEA was passed, the Forgery Act 1861 drew a distinction between a forgery and an unauthorised act, and an unauthorised signature did not amount to the criminal offence of forgery. However, under the Forgery and Counterfeiting Act 1981, 'forgery' is 'the making of a false instrument with the intent that [the maker] or someone else shall use it to induce somebody to accept it as genuine and . . . act to his own or any other person's prejudice'[1], and an instrument is false both if it purports to be made by a person who did not make it and if it purports to be made on the authority of a person who did not authorise it[2].

Court of Appeal authority suggests that 'forgery' in the BoEA should be interpreted in accordance with the definition current in the criminal law from time to time[3]. The result would appear to be that every unauthorised signature on a bill is now a forgery. However, that interpretation leaves no scope for the separate category of 'unauthorised' signatures which can be ratified. The following three situations are possible:

(a) A signs his own name, claiming to have P's authority to do so, but actually without authority;

(b) A signs P's name, claiming to have P's authority to do so, but actually without authority; or

(c) A signs P's name, and represents the signature to be P's own.

All three appear to constitute forgery under the Forgery and Counterfeiting Act. However, it is suggested that for the purposes of deciding whether A's signature can be ratified, cases (a) and (b) should be regarded as involving unauthorised but ratifiable signatures and only case (c) should be regarded as a forgery, on the grounds that in (c) A does not claim to have P's authority (the prime requirement for ratification in agency), but claims that he is P[4].

1   Forgery and Counterfeiting Act 1981, s 1.
2   Forgery and Counterfeiting Act 1981, s 9.
3   See *Kreditbank Cassel GmbH v Schenkers Ltd* [1927] 1 KB 826, CA, applying the Forgery Act 1913.
4   See *Brook v Hook* (1871) LR 6 Exch 89; see 4.7.1.

28.4.5   *Liabilities of parties to the bill*

As we have noted, the liabilities created by a bill are contractual. The undertakings of each party to a bill are defined by the Bills of Exchange Act. In addition, signature of a bill gives rise to certain estoppels, particularly against a holder in due course, relating to existing facts and events prior to the signature in question.

(a)   *Acceptor's liability*
In most cases the acceptor is the person primarily liable on a bill; the only exception is where the bill is an accommodation bill[1], in which case primary liability falls on the drawer. By accepting, the acceptor undertakes that he will pay the bill at maturity in accordance with the terms of the acceptance[2]. In addition, the acceptor is estopped as against a holder in due course from denying the drawer's existence, capacity and authority to draw the bill, the genuineness of the drawer's signature and the existence and capacity to indorse of the payee. However, there is nothing to prevent the acceptor denying that the payee's indorsement is genuine: estoppels relate to existing facts or prior events, not to the future.

(b)   *Drawer's liability*
The drawer's liability on a bill is normally secondary: the drawer does not undertake to pay the bill, but instead undertakes that the bill will be honoured by being accepted and paid in due course and, if not, that he will compensate the holder, or an indorser who pays the bill[3], provided that the necessary dishonour proceedings are taken[4].

The drawer's liability is not to pay the bill, but to pay compensation for its dishonour: this will normally include the value of the bill plus interest and the costs of enforcement[5]. In addition, the drawer is estopped from denying to a holder in due course the existence of the payee and his capacity to indorse the bill. The drawer can exclude his liability on the bill by drawing it 'without recourse'.

(c) Indorser's liability
By signing the bill, each indorser becomes a party to it and gives the same undertaking as the drawer[6]. Like the drawer, his liability depends on appropriate dishonour proceedings being taken, and like the drawer he can exclude personal liability by indorsing 'without recourse'. An indorser is estopped, as against a holder in due course, from denying the genuineness and regularity of the drawer's signature and of prior indorsements. In addition, the indorser is estopped from denying to all subsequent indorsees that the bill was valid at the time of his indorsement and that he had a good title to it at that time. One effect of this provision is to make the thief of a bill liable on it to subsequent indorsees. Take the following example:

$$A \longrightarrow B \longrightarrow C \qquad (D) \longrightarrow E$$

(Acceptor)   (Payee)   (Indorsee)

D steals the bill from C and indorses it to E by forging C's signature. We have already seen that neither D nor E has a valid title to the bill. E cannot enforce the bill against A, B or C. However, D is estopped from denying to E the validity of the bill and his title to it at the time of his indorsement, and so must compensate E.

(d) Other signatories
Any person who signs a bill other than as a drawer or acceptor is liable as if he were an indorser[7]. Suppose that S sells goods to B, a company, and B accepts a bill drawn on it for the price. S may require the directors of B to sign the bill in order to improve its marketability. If the directors do sign, they become liable as if they were indorsers. The same result can be achieved by making the directors into indorsers, either by actually indorsing the bill to them and having it indorsed back, or by simply converting their signatures into indorsements by filling in an indorsement to them above their signatures[8].

In addition, a person may sign a bill as a drawer, acceptor, or indorser for the purpose of increasing its marketability. For instance, if A wishes to borrow money, he can do so by drawing a bill on B, a person of good financial standing, and obtaining B's acceptance and then discounting the bill for cash. A person in B's position is an 'accommodation party', a person who becomes a party without receiving value and for the purposes of lending his name to the bill. Such a person would normally be able to avoid liability on the grounds that he received no consideration for his signature. However, as against a holder for value, an accommodation party cannot avoid liability on this basis, for the purpose of obtaining the signature of an accommodation party is to improve the marketability of the bill. An accommodation party can raise any other defences, such as fraud or duress, unless the bill is held by a holder in due course. The position of an accommodation party is rather like that of a guarantor of the bill to subsequent parties. However, the contract created by an accommodation signature is not formally one of guarantee. In most other legal systems, including under the American Uniform Commercial Code and the Uniform Law on Bills of Exchange and Promissory Notes, a similar result is produced by a person signing an 'aval'; however, an aval acts as a guarantee of the drawee's liability to all parties to the bill, including those prior to the signor of the aval[9].

Where a person accepts a bill as an accommodation party, as does B in the example above, the bill is an 'accommodation bill'. In that case, although the acceptor is liable on the bill to a holder for value, primary liability for payment falls on the drawer so that if the acceptor pays the bill, he is entitled to obtain an indemnity from the drawer[10].

(e) The transferor of a bearer bill
Since a bearer bill can be transferred without indorsement, the transferor does not need to sign the bill. If he does sign, he becomes a party to the bill and incurs the same liability as if he were an indorser. If he simply transfers by delivery, he does not become party to it. However, the act of transfer gives rise to certain warranties in favour of the immediate transferee. Provided the transferee is a holder for value, the transferor warrants that:

(i) the bill is what it purports to be: ie that it is a genuine bill or cheque; there is thus a breach if (say) the drawer's signature is forged;
(ii) that he has a right to transfer the bill: there is thus a breach if the transferor is a thief, or if the bill has previously been stolen and the transferor is not a holder in due course; and
(iii) that he does not know of any facts which make the bill worthless: for instance, that it has been stopped[11].

Since the transferor's liabilities are based on warranties, in the event of breach he is liable for damages. Normally, damages will be based on the value of the bill. However, since the transferor is not liable on the bill itself, his position may be better than that of an indorser: for instance, if the bill has been transferred as payment under a contract for the sale of goods, and the transferee sues for breach of warranty, the transferor may counterclaim damages for defects in the goods.

1 See *(d)* below.
2 BoEA 1882, s 54.
3 BoEA 1882, s 55(1).
4 See 28.5.
5 BoEA 1882, s 57.
6 BoEA 1882, s 55(2).
7 BoEA 1882, s 56.
8 BoEA 1882, s 20; see 28.2.1.
9 See *G&H Montage GmbH v Irvani* [1990] 2 All ER 225. In a 1990 White Paper following the recommendations of the Review Committee on Banking Law and Practice the government recommended that the 1882 Act be amended to recognise avals in English law: (1990) (Cmnd 1026).
10 BoEA 1882, s 59(3).
11 BoEA 1882, s 58.

28.5 Enforcement of the bill

The holder of a bill is entitled to enforce the undertakings given by the parties to it, as outlined above, if necessary by taking legal proceedings in his own name.

However, in order to enforce those obligations, the holder must comply with a number of requirements and his failure to do so may release some or all of the parties who would otherwise be liable on the bill. The rules governing the holder's duties in relation to enforcement are extremely detailed and technical; what follows is an outline. Broadly speaking, the holder must (a) present the bill (i) for acceptance and (ii) for payment; (b) in the event of dishonour, give notice of dishonour to prior parties; and (c) in the case of a foreign bill, have the dishonoured bill noted and protested by a notary public.

28.5.1   *Presentation*

It is only strictly necessary to present a bill for acceptance if it is payable 'n days after sight', in which case presentation is needed to fix the date for payment, or if it is expressly made subject to acceptance. There is no need to present for acceptance a bill payable on demand, such as a cheque[1]. However, in practice most bills other than cheques will be presented for acceptance, since acceptance increases the marketability and value of the bill.

A bill payable 'n days after sight' must be presented for acceptance or negotiated within a reasonable time[2]: the holder may not simply retain the bill. If the bill is not presented or negotiated within a reasonable time, the drawer and prior indorsers are released from liability: if the bill is dishonoured they are entitled to notice of that fact, and if they receive no such notice, they will, justifiably, assume that they are not to be held liable. Presentation is excused in certain circumstances, including where presentation is impossible, despite the exercise of reasonable diligence[3]. However, presentation is not excused merely because the holder believes the bill will not be accepted if presented.

Where presentation for acceptance is required, the bill must be presented to the drawee or his authorised representative (often a bank)[4]. If the drawee gives only a partial or qualified acceptance, the holder may treat the bill as dishonoured. However, he may elect to accept a partial acceptance without prejudicing his position: if the bill is drawn for £1,000 and the drawee accepts for £800, the holder may simply accept the partial acceptance and treat the bill as dishonoured as regards the balance; the drawer and prior indorsers are not prejudiced, since their liability is reduced by the amount paid. However, if the drawee gives a qualified acceptance, for instance by imposing a condition on payment, the holder must treat the bill as dishonoured unless the drawer and previous indorsers agree to the qualification. If the holder agrees to a qualified acceptance without the consent of prior parties, they are released from liability for the qualification might prejudice their position[5].

If the drawee does not accept the bill when it is presented for acceptance, it is dishonoured and the holder can immediately enforce payment against prior parties. The holder must immediately treat the bill as dishonoured, and give notice of dishonour: if not, he loses the right to enforce against prior parties[6].

Most bills must be presented for payment at the correct time and place. Failure to present for payment is excused in certain cases, including where presentation is impossible after the exercise of reasonable diligence[7] but subject to those exceptions, failure to present for payment at the proper time and place will release prior parties. Thus in *Yeoman Credit Ltd v Gregory*[8] a bill was accepted payable at the National Provincial Bank on a stated day; however, the drawee indicated to the indorsee that there were no funds available to pay it at the National Provincial Bank, and that it should be presented instead at the Midland Bank where he had funds. The holder therefore presented the bill on the due date at the Midland, but it was dishonoured.

On the next day it was presented at the National Provincial Bank, where payment was again refused. It was held that the indorser was released from liability: the bill had not been presented at the proper place at the proper time. Some cases decided before 1882 suggest that failure to present the bill for payment releases prior parties not only from liability on the bill but also from liability for the debt in respect of which they transferred the bill, but they are of doubtful authority[9].

Generally, the proper place for presentation will be the place for payment indicated in the bill, or the drawee's address as stated in the bill[10]. In fact, if a bill is accepted generally, there is no need to present the bill for payment in order to make the acceptor liable to pay it: he is obliged to seek out the holder and pay[11]. In practice, acceptance is often qualified so that payment is due at a particular place stated in the bill; generally the drawee's bank. In that case, the bill must be presented there in order to hold the drawee liable.

The bill must be promptly presented on the date for payment specified in the bill; if it is payable on demand, it must be presented for payment within a reasonable time[12]. The holder may present the bill in person, but it may be presented by an agent on his behalf; often the holder will authorise his bank to collect the bill on his behalf, as is done with cheques.

1 BoEA 1882, s 39.
2 BoEA 1882, s 40.
3 BoEA 1882, s 41(2).
4 BoEA 1882, s 41(1).
5 BoEA 1882, s 44.
6 BoEA 1882, s 42.
7 BoEA 1882, s 46(2).
8 [1963] 1 All ER 245, [1963] 1 WLR 343.
9 See *Soward v Palmer* (1818) 8 Taunt 277; *Peacock v Pursell* (1863) 32 LJCP 266. The cases can be explained on other grounds: see Goode, *Commercial Law* (2nd edn, 1995) p 558.
10 BoEA 1882, s 45(4).
11 BoEA 1882, s 52. Goode, *Commercial Law* (2nd edn, 1995) p 557 criticises this rule as 'arrant nonsense': the drawee may not know who is entitled to payment.
12 BoEA 1882, s 45(1)–(2).

28.5.2 *Notice of dishonour*

Where a bill is dishonoured by non-acceptance or non-payment, the holder may seek payment from any other party. However, in order to do so, the holder must within a reasonable time give notice of dishonour to every other party to be held liable[1]. The Act contains detailed rules specifying the timing and content of a notice of dishonour. Any person not notified of dishonour in accordance with the rules in the Act is released from liability, unless the bill is subsequently negotiated to a holder in due course, or unless notice is excused[2]: no notice is required to the drawer, for instance, where the drawee is under no obligation to the drawer to pay the bill: thus no notice of dishonour is needed where a bank fails to pay a cheque due to lack of funds. If a holder gives notice to a particular party, the notice protects intermediate parties in the liability chain. Suppose that A draws a bill, payable to himself on demand, on B and indorses it to C. C in turn indorses to D, and D presents the bill for payment but it is dishonoured. If D gives notice of dishonour to A and C, he can obtain compensation from either. If C pays the bill, he can in turn claim against A, relying on the notice of dishonour served by D.

1 BoEA 1882, s 49.
2 BoEA 1882, s 50.

28.5.3   *Noting and protesting*

The Act distinguishes 'inland' and 'foreign' bills and where the bill is a 'foreign bill' an additional step is required in order to provide adequate evidence of dishonour. A bill is an inland bill if:

(a) it is, or purports to be, drawn and payable in the British Isles; or
(b) it is, or purports to be, drawn in the British Isles on a person resident in the British Isles[1].

If the bill is a foreign bill, the holder must have it re-presented by a public notary; if the bill is then again dishonoured, the notary must note that fact on the bill and draw up a formal protest, which he signs in the presence of witnesses[2]. This procedure provides evidence of dishonour which is acceptable throughout the world but is cumbersome and in its 1990 White Paper the government recommended that it should be abolished[3].

1   BoEA 1882, s 4.
2   BoEA 1882, s 51.
3   (1990) (Cmnd 1026).

28.5.4   *Defences to a claim on a bill*

A bill of exchange creates contractual liability, but that liability is not absolute. A party to a bill may raise several defences against a person seeking to enforce the contract created by the bill. The effectiveness of those defences may depend on the relationship between the holder seeking to enforce the bill and the party trying to establish the defence. A distinction may be drawn here between immediate and remote parties. Suppose that A draws a bill on B, payable to C; B accepts, and C indorses to D. A and B are immediate parties in relation to each other, as are A (drawer) and C (payee) and C (indorser) and D (indorsee); the other relationships are remote.

The defendant to a claim on a bill may try to defend the claim and escape liability on the basis of the circumstances in which he became party to the bill: for instance because he accepted or indorsed the bill due to misrepresentation or duress, so that his contract is voidable; or, where the bill was given under another contract, for example as payment for goods or services, on the basis of a breach of that contract. Such defences are purely personal and cannot be raised against a remote party who is a holder in due course; moreover, as we have seen, the separation of the contract created by the bill from any underlying contract means that breach of the underlying contract only offers a defence to a claim by an immediate party if the breach gives rise to a total or partial failure of consideration[1].

Secondly, the defendant may admit his liability on the bill but argue that the plaintiff has no title to it: for instance on the grounds that the bill has been stolen or an indorsement forged.

Thirdly, the defendant may argue that he is not liable on the bill at all, for instance because his signature on the bill was unauthorised or forged, or because he had no capacity to incur liability on the bill. If the defendant can establish such a claim, he is not liable to anyone, unless he is estopped from asserting the forgery or lack of authority. Similarly, the defendant may escape liability if the bill has been altered in some way after he signed it.

Fourthly, the defendant may simply assert that there is no bill at all because one or more of the requirements in s 1 of the Act is unfulfilled. If such a claim is made out, there is no bill and no one can be liable on it.

Most of these defences have already been examined. However, in certain circumstances alteration of a bill may give rise to a defence, and we must briefly examine that now.

1   See 28.1.2.

28.5.5   *Alteration of a bill of exchange*

If a bill is materially altered, it is avoided as regards all persons who became party to it prior to the alteration[1] unless they consent to the alteration. The bill is not wholly nullified: it can be enforced, as altered, against the person responsible for the alteration and all subsequent parties: they are not prejudiced since they take the bill as altered and to hold them liable on the bill as altered accords with their expectations. However, to enforce the altered bill against prior parties would unfairly prejudice them: effectively they would be held liable on a contract they never made.

On the other hand, avoidance of the bill may prejudice a holder who takes the bill in good faith after the alteration. In order to protect such a bona fide purchaser, the consequences of alteration differ according to whether the alteration is apparent or not. If the alteration is apparent, the bill is avoided as regards prior parties. If it is not apparent, a holder in due course may enforce the bill against persons who became party to it before the alteration in accordance with its original terms. Suppose that A draws a bill for £9,000 in favour of B; B alters the words and numbers on the bill, so that it appears to be for £90,000 and indorses to C. If the alteration is apparent, C can enforce the bill for £90,000 against B, but cannot enforce against A at all; if the alteration is not apparent, C can enforce the bill for £90,000 against B or for £9,000 against A. If the alteration is apparent, the holder cannot complain that prior parties are released: he should have been aware of the alteration; if the alteration is not apparent, allowing the bill to be enforced according to its original tenor causes no prejudice to prior parties, and strikes a balance between their interests and those of the bona fide purchaser.

These rules only apply where the bill is materially altered. Any alteration to the date of the bill, the sum payable or the time or place of payment is material[2], as is alteration of the name of the payee[3]. Other alterations may be material if they affect the rights of the parties[4]. However, in order to be material, an alteration must be made after the bill is issued[5]. Moreover, an alteration only affects the validity of the bill if it is deliberately made. In *Hong Kong and Shanghai Banking Corpn v Lo Lee Shi*[6] a bank note was damaged when it was accidentally washed, dried, starched and ironed; part of the note's number was lost. It was held that the note had been materially altered, but the alteration was accidental and did not affect its validity.

Alteration poses a danger for an innocent third party who may purchase the bill in good faith, ignorant of a clever alteration, and then be unable to enforce it for its face value. A right of enforcement against the party responsible for the alteration is unlikely to be worth pursuing in most cases. In particular, the rule causes difficulties for banks in the payment of cheques: if the bank pays out on an altered cheque, it may have no right to debit the drawer's account with the sum paid, or, if the alteration was not apparent, it may only be entitled to debit the drawer with the amount of the cheque as drawn. The bank may be able to recover the sum paid out from the payee in an action for money paid under a mistake, but to do so it must act speedily;

the right of recovery will be lost if the payee has changed his position in reliance on the payment[7]. The position of the bank is mitigated to some extent by the fact that the drawer of a cheque owes the bank a duty of care to draw cheques so as not to facilitate alteration or forgery: if the customer draws the cheque negligently in breach of this duty, the bank may claim damages to cover the amount it pays out on the altered cheque[8]. However, this duty depends on the close (contractual) relationship between bank and customer: the drawer or acceptor of a bill does not generally owe a duty of care to subsequent holders when drawing or accepting[9].

1   BoEA 1882, s 64.
2   BoEA 1882, s 64(2).
3   *Slingsby v District Bank* [1932] 1 KB 544, CA; *Lumsden v London Trustee Savings Bank* [1971] 1 Lloyd's Rep 114.
4   *Koch v Dicks* [1933] 1 KB 307, CA.
5   *Foster v Driscoll* [1929] 1 KB 470, CA.
6   [1928] AC 181, PC.
7   See 30.2.2.
8   *London Joint Stock Bank v Macmillan and Arthur* [1918] AC 777.
9   *Schofield v Earl of Londesborough* [1896] AC 514, HL.

28.6   Discharge of a bill

As we have seen, a bill may be transferred several times so that there may be a number of parties potentially liable on it. The liability of all parties is brought to an end when the bill is discharged. Discharge of the bill should be distinguished from discharge of an individual party which may come about separately: for instance, a drawer or indorser may be discharged if the holder fails to give appropriate notice of dishonour, but the acceptor remains liable and the bill can be enforced against him by legal proceedings if necessary.

28.6.1   *Discharge by payment*

A bill may be discharged in a number of ways, but the primary method is by payment in due course by, or on behalf of, the acceptor or drawee[1]. A bill is paid in due course when it is paid:

(a) on or after maturity;
(b) to the holder;
(c) in good faith and without notice of any defect in the holder's title.

It is therefore clear that payment after maturity to a holder with a perfect title to the bill will discharge it. Equally, it is clear that if an order bill is lost or stolen and transferred by a forged indorsement, no one who becomes party to the bill after the forged indorsement can be a holder, and therefore payment to such a person, even in good faith, will not discharge the bill; the person entitled to the bill can still enforce payment. However, if a bearer bill is lost or stolen, payment to the finder or thief, or to a subsequent transferee, can be payment in due course, even though that person may have no title to the bill, provided that the payer acts in good faith and without notice of the lack of title; the person in possession of a bearer bill is the holder. Similarly, payment in good faith and without notice to a holder with defective title, for instance because he obtained the bill by fraud or duress, is payment in due course.

If the payer pays someone other than the holder, the bill is not discharged and the payer remains liable to pay the person genuinely entitled to payment. A bank paying a cheque in such a case may be protected by statute[2], but there is no similar protection for drawees of other bills. In such a case, the payer may be entitled to recover the money from the payee, as money paid under a mistake of fact, but the right to recover may be lost unless the payer acts swiftly. There is a general rule that if money is paid to an agent for his principal, including where money is paid to a bank for its customer[3], the right to recover it from the agent is lost if the agent has already paid it to the principal. There is, moreover, a special rule applicable to bills of exchange which may preclude recovery even where the recipient of the payment has not parted with it. The basis and precise ambit of the rule are unclear, but it seems that where the payer seeks to recover a payment on the grounds of a mistake in circumstances in which the payee is required by the Act to give notice of dishonour, the payer's claim for repayment will fail unless it is made immediately, on the same day payment is made. Thus in the leading case of *Cocks v Masterman*[4], where a bank mistakenly paid on behalf of its customer a bill on which the customer's acceptance had been forged, and discovered the mistake the next day, it was held that it was too late to recover payment. Dicta in the case suggest that the rule applied where the payer was negligent and thus prejudiced the payee by preventing him giving notice of dishonour, but in a later case it was said that the rule applies regardless of any negligence on the part of the payer[5] and it was even suggested that recovery might be barred even if sought on the same day as the payment was made although the Privy Council subsequently doubted that the rule was so strict[6].

The rule in *Cocks v Masterman*, precluding recovery unless it is claimed on the same day as payment, has been described as 'stringent'[7] and 'technical'[8]. It is clear that the strict rule only applies where the payee is required to give notice of dishonour, so that it does not apply where the bill itself is forged, and therefore a nullity[9], or where recovery of a payment under a cheque is sought because the cheque has been countermanded[10] where it seems that a mistaken payment may be recovered provided that notice of the mistake was given in reasonable time and the delay caused the payee no loss.

In *Barclays Bank v W J Simms, Son & Cooke (Southern) Ltd*[11] Robert Goff J suggested that the proper basis for the rule might be that recovery is precluded where the payee has changed his position after receipt of the payment, it being assumed that where the payee is required to give notice of dishonour, any delay in recovery, which delays his giving such notice, prejudices his position. The difficulty with this view is that the Act merely requires the holder of a bill to give notice of dishonour within a reasonable time after dishonour[12]. However, in *Lipkin Gorman v Karpnale Ltd*[13] the House of Lords recognised that there is a general defence of change of position in English law which will prevent a claim for recovery of money succeeding where it would be inequitable to allow recovery. This is more flexible than estoppel, since it may operate to prevent recovery only to the extent to which the payee has changed his position, whereas estoppel would prevent recovery altogether. Their Lordships did not seek to define the scope of the defence in *Lipkin Gorman* but it seems likely that it may now be possible to explain *Cocks v Masterman* and the rule which prevents recovery from an agent who has paid his principal as specific examples of the change of position defence[14].

The person primarily liable for payment of a bill is the drawee or acceptor. However, as we have seen, if the drawee or acceptor fails to honour the bill, the drawer or indorsers may be liable if the necessary proceedings on dishonour are taken. If the bill is paid by an indorser or by the drawer, the party making payment and all subsequent parties are discharged from liability, but the bill is not discharged and may still be enforced against prior parties. The only exception is that if an accommodation bill is paid by the drawer, it is discharged[15]. If the bill is paid by an indorser, he may either enforce the bill against prior parties, or cancel all later indorsements, reissue it and thus negotiate for value[16]; where the drawer pays, he may not reissue, but may enforce against the acceptor[17], unless it is an accommodation bill.

1 BoEA 1882, s 59.
2 Cheques Act 1957, s 60; see 30.2.3.
3 Eg *Gowers v Lloyds and National Provincial Foreign Bank Ltd* [1938] 1 All ER 766.
4 (1829) 9 B & C 902.
5 *London & River Plate Bank v Bank of Liverpool* [1896] 1 QB 7.
6 *Imperial Bank of Canada v Bank of Hamilton* [1903] AC 49, PC.
7 Per Lord Lindley in *Imperial Bank of Canada v Bank of Hamilton* [1903] AC 49 at 58.
8 Per Robert Goff J in *Barclays Bank v W J Simms, Son & Cooke (Southern) Ltd* [1980] QB 677 at 703.
9 *Imperial Bank of Canada v Bank of Hamilton* [1903] AC 49; *National Westminster Bank Ltd v Barclays Bank Ltd* [1975] QB 654.
10 *Barclays Bank v W J Simms, Son & Cooke (Southern) Ltd* [1980] QB 677. See Goode (1981) 97 LQR 254.
11 [1980] QB 677.
12 BoEA 1882, s 49(12); delay is in any case excused where the delay is caused by circumstances beyond the control of the party giving the notice: s 50.
13 [1991] 2 AC 548, [1992] 4 All ER 512.
14 As recognised by Lord Goff in *Lipkin Gorman* [1991] 2 AC 548 at 578-579; [1992] 4 All ER 512 at 533.
15 BoEA 1882, s 59(3).
16 BoEA 1882, s 59(2)(b).
17 BoEA 1882, s 59(2)(a).

28.6.2 *Discharge by other means*

Although payment is the primary method by which a bill is discharged, the bill, or an individual party, may also be discharged by cancellation, either of the bill or of the liability of a party[1], or by the holder renouncing his rights on the bill or against a party[2]. In addition, the bill is discharged if the acceptor is or becomes the holder of it at or after maturity[3] and, as we have seen, an apparent material alteration to a bill operates to discharge prior parties[4].

1 BoEA 1882, s 63.
2 BoEA 1882, s 62.
3 BoEA 1882, s 6.
4 BoEA 1882, s 64; above 28.5.5.

28.7 An electronic bill of exchange?

Banks have been at the forefront of the use of new technology in commercial operations. In recent years, as the commercial use of new technology has grown and businesses have placed an ever greater premium on speed, the possibility of creating an electronic bill of exchange, capable of instantaneous transmission between computer terminals, and thus removing the need to transfer possession of a piece of paper, with delays that entails, has been considered. As we have seen, in order to be recognised as a bill of exchange, a document must satisfy the formal criteria set out in the definition of a bill of exchange in s 1 of the 1882 Act[1]. Subject to the problems created by the requirements that a bill be in writing signed by the drawer being overcome by exercise of the powers in the Electronic Commerce Act 2000, there seems to be no reason why an effective bill of exchange could not be created using a computer and transmitted electronically from that computer to another, to be printed out and accepted[2]. However, whilst it seems perfectly possible in theory to produce an electronically generated bill of exchange, the simulation of all the aspects of a bill by electronic means, including its transfer, is more difficult. The bill of exchange gives rise to a string of contracts: each transferor incurs some legal liability and, where the bill is payable to order, each indorser incurs a contractual liability enforceable by all subsequent parties. Thus an electronic bill of exchange must be capable not only of being transferred, but also of being transferred so as to create similar contractual liabilities on the transferors. 'The creation of a multi-party contract, which can be readily transferred, which confers property rights on its "owner", and which is recorded by electronic means, remains a revolutionary concept'[3].

As with bills of lading[4], it has been suggested that this difficulty could be overcome by using a registry system. A central body or organisation would act as a depositary or registry, and dealings with the bill would be dealt with by sending messages to the registry, for it to record. Such a system could either be based on the deposit of an actual, paper-based bill, or be wholly electronic, with the initial bill being created electronically and recorded in the registry's computer system. Both systems were considered by the Review Committee on Banking Law and Practice, which recommended legislation to allow such systems to be set up[5]. The aim would be to replicate, so far as possible, the legal effect of a traditional bill of exchange. The depositary would create a record of ownership which would operate as proof of ownership of the obligation created by the 'bill'; if the depositary recorded a transfer, the transferee would have the same rights as an indorsee of a traditional bill, whilst the transferor would incur liabilities like those of an indorser. Such a deposit scheme would be based on a contract between members of the scheme; however, the legislation would provide for the bill to be transferred to non-members by simply producing a print-out of the dealings with the 'electronic bill' which could then be transferred in the traditional way. Obviously, the depositary would occupy a highly responsible position; the Committee therefore recommended that depositaries should be approved by the Bank of England or by the Treasury.

1 Above 28.2.
2 In America it has been held that a telex message in the correct form was a bill of exchange: *Chase Manhattan Bank v Equibank* 394 F Supp 352 (1975).
3 Ellinger, 'Electronic Funds Transfer as a Deferred Settlement System' in Goode (ed), *Electronic Banking, the Legal Implications* (1985) p 42.
4 See 32.4.4.
5 *Banking Services: Law and Practice*, Report by the Review Committee (1989) (Cmnd 622), paras 8.33–8.38. This recommendation was accepted by the government in its 1990 White Paper (1990) (Cmnd 1026).

Chapter 29

Banks and their Customers

29.0 The banks

The banking system plays an essential part in commercial activity in a developed economy. The modern bank provides a wide range of services to both business and private customers. The provision of such services is itself an aspect of commerce, and the activities of banks are an important contributor to the UK's invisible exports. In addition, banks provide essential services which underpin all other commercial activity, by facilitating payment for the goods and services traded, and by promoting the circulation of capital within the economy.

29.0.1 *The business of banking*

Banking is essentially concerned with the borrowing and lending of money. A depositor lends money to the bank, which in turn lends it to borrowers in search of loan capital. The bank charges its borrowers interest, which may be used to pay interest to the bank's depositors and produce a profit for the bank's owners. The bank thus effectively puts those in search of capital for investment or spending in touch with those with spare capital to invest, theoretically to the benefit of all three parties. It also creates spending power within the economy. A prudent bank will not lend out all of the money deposited with it, but will retain a proportion in order to meet depositors' calls for repayment, or unforeseen eventualities. However, if A deposits £100 with bank B, B may lend £90 to C. C may use that money to purchase goods or services from D, who will in turn deposit the money with bank E. E can then lend a proportion, say £81, to F, and the cycle can continue. C will hope to use the goods or services purchased from D to generate a profit with which to repay the money borrowed from B, together with interest. The banks therefore play a crucial role in commercial activity; moreover, because of their importance, any doubts about the stability of the banking system have a profoundly damaging effect on the economy and trade as a whole. The business of banking is therefore subject to regulatory control and supervision. Its economic importance is also reflected in the fact that it has been subject to two reviews in little over a decade. The first, the Review Committee on Banking Services Law and Practice, reported in 1989[1] and made a number of recommendations for reform of the law, including that relating to payment mechanisms, some of which were accepted by the government in a White Paper published in 1990[2]. In 1998 the government appointed

652

a second committee to undertake a further review of banking services, other than investment banking, concentrating on competition in UK banking, especially in relation to the supply of banking services to individuals and to small businesses. The review, published in 2000, concluded that there was a lack of effective competition in relation to the supply of banking services in certain key markets as a result of which 'neither personal nor small business customers are getting a fair deal from banks'[3], and recommended government action to enhance competition[4].

Banking today is, however, concerned with much more than the borrowing and lending of money. The pace of change in banking in recent years, driven by developments in technology and commercial practice, has been considerable. The range of services offered by the established banks has widened to include secured and unsecured lending to business and individuals, savings and investment advice, insurance, credit cards and a range of investment products. Many of these services are provided by other financial service providers – building societies, finance and discount houses, credit card companies and cheque cashers, to name but a few. Not all of them are 'banks' as a matter of law; some may be banks for some purposes and not for others.

1   *Banking Services: Law and Practice*, Report by the Review Committee (1989) (Cmnd 622).
2   White Paper on Banking Services (1990) (Cmnd 1026).
3   Treasury Press Release, 20 March 2000.
4   See *Competition in UK Banking* (2000).

29.0.2   The legal definition of 'banking'

There are several reasons why it may be necessary to decide whether a particular business is, as a matter of law, a 'bank' or carrying on the business of 'banking'. First, banking activities in the UK are currently regulated under the Banking Act 1987, which also restricts the use of the descriptions 'bank', 'banker' and 'banking business'. Second, a number of incidents attach to the relationship of 'banker' and 'customer' at common law. Third, several statutes refer to 'banks', 'banking' and 'bankers' without giving any comprehensive definition of these terms. The most important are the Bills of Exchange Act 1882 and Cheques Act 1957. Both contain provisions granting protection to 'banks' in certain prescribed circumstances, but the 1882 Act defines a bank as 'any body of persons, whether incorporated or not, who carry on the business of banking'[1], leaving open the question of what is 'the business of banking', and the 1957 Act is to be 'construed as one with' the 1882 Act[2].

1   Section 2.
2   Cheques Act 1957, s 6(1).

29.0.2.1   The definition under the Banking Act

The Act does not define the terms 'bank', 'banker' or 'banking business', nor does it regulate 'banking' as such. The Act regulates the activities of 'deposit taking' businesses. A business cannot accept deposits from the public unless it is authorised under the Act. An institution cannot describe or hold itself out as a 'bank' or 'banker', or as carrying on a 'banking business' unless it is authorised under the Act and satisfies certain criteria[1]. Those criteria are, however, concerned with factors such as management and capitalisation, not the function of the institution. The key function of a bank under the Act is therefore the taking of deposits, defined as

'. . . money paid on terms

   (a) under which it will be repaid, with or without interest or a premium, and either on demand or at a time or in circumstances agreed by or on behalf of the person making the payment and the person receiving it; and

   (b) which are not referable to the provision of property or services or the giving of security'[2].

Under the First EC Banking Directive[3], upon which the 1987 Act is partly based, a second factor is relevant, and banking is defined in terms of deposit taking and lending[4].

Several modern statutes define 'bank' by reference to authorisation under the 1987 Act. It is clear, however, that neither the definition in the 1987 Act nor that in the directive is determinative of a business's status as a bank at common law or for other purposes. Indeed, that is expressly recognised by s 69(4) of the 1987 Act, which provides that an institution not authorised under the Act may nevertheless establish that it is a bank or banker in order to take the benefit of any rule of law applicable to banks or bankers. In other words, an institution which is not a bank for the purposes of the 1987 Act may be a bank for other legal purposes.

1   See below 29.0.4.
2   Banking Act 1987, s 5(1).
3   Directive 77/780/EEC.
4   This definition is preferred by Professor Cranston, who observes that it 'accords with what banks have traditionally done': *Principles of Banking Law* (1997) p 9.

29.0.2.2   *The common law definition of banking*

The leading authority on the definition of 'bank' at common law is the Court of Appeal decision in *United Dominions Trust Ltd v Kirkwood*[1]. Lord Denning MR and Harman LJ differed in the result but, relying heavily on expert evidence given by senior members of the banking community, agreed that an essential aspect of banking was the collection and payment of cheques. Diplock LJ thought that the essential characteristic of banking was the receipt of deposits, 'that is to say, loans for an indefinite period upon running account, repayable as to the whole or any part thereof upon demand by the customer either without notice or upon an agreed period of notice[2]', but was also 'inclined to agree' that 'to constitute the business of a banker today' the banker must also undertake to pay cheques drawn on him by and collect cheques on behalf of his customer. Lord Denning and Diplock LJ agreed that there was sufficient evidence that UDT did collect and pay cheques on behalf of its customers as well as receiving deposits and making loans for it to be considered a bank. Lord Denning also felt that the commercial reputation of a business was a relevant factor, and would thus have recognised the plaintiffs as a bank on the grounds that they were regarded as such in the commercial sector. 'In any case of doubt it is permissible to look at the reputation of the firm amongst ordinary intelligent commercial men.' As one of the witnesses, representing one of the High Street banks, had said, 'It is so very difficult to describe what is a bank . . . I think the matter of reputation has to come into it'[3]. Diplock LJ was only prepared to take account of evidence of commercial reputation in so far as it provided indirect evidence of the activities carried on by the 'bank'.

The question came before the Court of Appeal again in *Re Roes' Legal Charge*[4]. There was no great evidence of the plaintiff lender's reputation, but evidence showed that it took current accounts, paid cheques drawn on it by customers, and collected cheques for customers. However, these activities were carried on on a very small scale when compared with the activities of institutions such as the clearing banks. The defendant argued that the plaintiff's banking business was negligible and that it was not a true bank. The Court of Appeal disagreed and held that the plaintiff was a bank. It carried on the activities of a bank, and it was irrelevant that it did so on a much smaller scale than other institutions. Provided the banking business carried on by an organisation is genuine, and is not negligible in comparison with the other activities of the organisation in question, the organisation may be regarded as a bank. Lawton LJ, giving the judgment of the court, declined, however, to define 'bank' in precise terms, saying, 'I have no intention whatsoever of attempting to define that which Parliament for so many years has decided not to define'[5].

These cases therefore establish that, at common law, the essence of banking is the receipt of deposits and the collection and payment of cheques on behalf of customers. The 1987 Act recognises that an institution which does not meet the statutory criteria to call itself a 'bank' may nevertheless be a 'bank' for certain other legal purposes. These cases indicate that an institution which takes deposits and *does* qualify as bank under the 1987 Act may nevertheless not be a bank at common law. The 1987 Act says that an institution may not describe itself as a bank unless it is authorised to take deposits. It does not follow that all authorised deposit takers are 'banks'.

It is submitted, however, that we should be wary of placing too much emphasis on *Kirkwood*. Indeed, it is probably wrong to attempt to find a single, all-purpose definition of 'bank' or 'banking'. The definition is likely to differ according to the context and the purpose for which a definition is necessary. Both *Kirkwood* and *Re Roes' Legal Charge* were concerned with the application of the Moneylenders Act 1900. Under that Act, now repealed by the Consumer Credit Act 1974, a loan was unenforceable if it was made by an unlicensed moneylender, unless the lender was a bank. Moreover an unlicensed lender committed a criminal offence. In both cases a loan had been made by an unlicensed lender and the borrower sought to resist repayment on that basis. The lender therefore sought to establish that it was a bank to recover its loan. In *Kirkwood* the lender was an established and respected institution which had made a large number of loans. A finding that it was not a 'bank' would have made those loans irrecoverable and exposed it to criminal liability. Conversely, the emphasis on deposit taking for the purposes of the 1987 Act is understandable, since the Act is concerned with the maintenance of public confidence and the protection of depositors.

What is it, though, which marks out a 'bank' from other financial institutions? The *Review of Banking Services in the UK,* published in March 2000, observed that 'banking products supply three main economic services: money transmission, debt and savings'[6]. Money transmission is vital to commercial activity: it provides the means of paying for goods and services and 'underpins economic life in the UK'[7]. It is submitted that this is correct: one distinguishing feature of banks is that banks take deposits from customers and undertake money transmission on their behalf – they make and collect payments. However, as the court in *Kirkwood* recognised, the business of banking changes over time. The emphasis placed by the court in *Kirkwood* on the collection and payment of cheques is no longer appropriate. The use of cheques as a means of making payments is declining and is expected to continue so to do. In 1998 they constituted less than one third of the volume of non-cash payments. New styles of banking, making use of telecommunications and the Internet, have developed. A business which operates over the Internet, receives deposits on behalf of customers by direct credit transfer, issues them with ATM and EFTPOS cards with which to withdraw cash and pay for goods and services and pays direct debits on their behalf is still a bank, even if it never issues nor collects a cheque.

1   [1966] 2 QB 431, [1966] 1 All ER 968, CA.
2   [1966] 2 QB 431 at 465, [1966] 1 All ER 968 at 986.
3   [1966] 2 QB 431 at 454, [1966] 1 All ER 968 at 979.
4   [1982] 2 Lloyd's Rep 370.
5   [1982] 2 Lloyd's Rep 370 at 382.
6   *Competition in UK Banking* (2000) para 1-14.
7   Ibid.

29.0.3   *The different types of bank*

The High Street banks are familiar to everyone. However, whilst they are particularly important, both in terms of size and the value of their activities[1], they represent only one of several types of banking business.

The clearing banks are all members of the Association for Payment Clearing Services (APACS), an unincorporated umbrella organisation which oversees the operation of the clearing systems which are central to the collection and payment of cheques and other bank payment orders[2]. They include the 'big four' High Street banks – Barclays, Lloyds TSB, HSBC[3] and NatWest – and other familiar names including Bank of Scotland, Royal Bank of Scotland, Standard Chartered Bank, Girobank, Co-operative Bank, Yorkshire Bank, Abbey National plc, Halifax plc and Northern Rock plc. They provide a wide range of banking services to private and business customers.

Many of the modern clearing banks developed from the joint stock banks of the eighteenth and nineteenth centuries. Until the 1960s they were many more in number, mergers between banks having been frowned upon, and, from 1918, subject to Bank of England and Treasury approval to avoid the concentration of banking business, and economic power. However, a report of the National Board for Prices and Incomes in 1967 cleared the way for further mergers. In recent years a number of factors have changed the face of mainstream banking. First, a number of other financial institutions, most notably building societies, have converted from mutual to public limited company status and thus become banks. Abbey National plc, Halifax plc and Northern Rock plc, all now members of APACS, are converted building societies. Second, an increasing number of non-UK banks have established a presence in the UK. Thus, for instance, Chase Manhattan Bank, Deutsche Bank and Bank of Tokyo Mitsubishi are all members of APACS. Third, a number of businesses established in other sectors, such as Sainsburys, Tesco and Virgin, for example, have established banking operations (often in partnership with established banks)[4]. Fourth, a number of banks have been established specialising in telephone and/or Internet banking. Often these are subsidiaries of established banking institutions.

As a result there are now a number of new providers of banking services in the UK. At the same time, there have been a number of mergers and take-overs in the sector. For example, the Trustee Savings Bank (originally established as a number of separate institutions under the Trustee Savings Banks Act 1817 to provide deposit account facilities for members of the working class who at the time were not welcomed by the commercial banks), having been floated on the stock exchange in 1985[5], merged with Lloyds Bank to form Lloyds TSB. The Midland, an established High Street bank, was taken over by Hong Kong and Shanghai Bank and, in 1999, changed its name to 'HSBC plc'.

The High Street banks are not the only providers of banking services. Building societies also borrow money from depositors and lend it to borrowers. Traditionally, their activities have been almost wholly concerned with lending money to private borrowers to finance house purchases by way of mortgage. Originally, they were friendly, or mutual, societies, founded by a group of individuals who pooled their resources to provide mutual financial assistance. They were regulated separately from banks and were unincorporated bodies, their assets being held on trust for their members. However, since 1980 the commercial banks have been free to compete on equal terms with building societies for mortgage business, and have increased their share of such business, whilst the Building Societies Act 1986 allowed building societies to provide a wide range of financial services to customers, including current accounts operated by cheque books. The Act also allowed building societies to transfer their assets to limited companies and thus assume corporate status[6]. A building society which does so effectively becomes a bank, since it ceases to be regulated as a building society and must obtain authorisation as a bank if it wishes to remain in business. As noted above, a number of former building societies have taken this option since it was made available. The functional distinctions between banks and building societies have thus become less clear and, although building societies' clients are still predominantly private individuals rather than businesses, they now compete directly for many types of business, and for some purposes their position is equated[7].

In contrast, the merchant banks mainly provide banking and financial services to business. Unlike the High Street banks, merchant banks do not have chains of provincial branches, but tend to trade from a small number of offices, predominantly in the City of London and overseas. Originally, they were particularly involved in the financing of international trade, and much of their business was concerned with the acceptance of bills of exchange, and with capital issues of shares and bonds. However, in recent years they have considerably expanded their range of services. They may offer current account facilities to customers, and a whole range of financial services and advice, particularly in relation to investment and in the context of take-overs and mergers.

Discount houses are highly specialist organisations, which offer a service to business by discounting, or buying at a discount, bills of exchange, financing that business by borrowing money in the short-term money markets. Money may be borrowed on the short-term market at low rates of interest, but is repayable on demand; this could place discount houses in difficulties if they had used the money borrowed to discount bills, but in that situation they have a unique right to resell bills of exchange to the Bank of England. In passing, it is worth noting that the Bank of England may use this system to influence such general economic factors as interest rates.

Other finance houses may offer facilities to businesses and individuals. Many provide credit facilities, by financing transactions such as hire purchase and equipment leasing and by factoring debts. They in turn raise the funds to finance such transactions by borrowing from the commercial banks and the public or by issuing bills of exchange. Many finance houses are wholly owned subsidiaries of the High Street banks.

1   In 1998 three UK High Street banks each made more profit than the UK's five major supermarket companies combined: see *Competition in UK Banking* (2000) p vii.
2   See ch 30.

3   Hong Kong and Shanghai Bank.
4   Sainsbury's bank is a joint venture with the Bank of Scotland; Tesco Personal Finance with the Royal Bank of Scotland.
5   The flotation was challenged by some investors with the banks but sanctioned by the House of Lords: see *Ross v Lord Advocate* [1986] 3 All ER 79, [1986] 1 WLR 1077, HL.
6   Sections 97–102.
7   Eg the statutory defences available to a banker under the Bills of Exchange Act 1882 and the Cheques Act 1957 are extended to building societies by Sch 8, Pt 4, para 3 of the Building Societies Act 1986. See 30.2.3; 30.2.5.

29.0.4 *The regulation and control of banking*

The banking system depends on confidence. Loss of that confidence may have a severely damaging effect on trade generally. Loss of confidence in an individual bank may lead to a 'run on the bank': depositors, worried about the safety of their investments, will seek to withdraw their money; if, as is almost certain, the bank has lent money, it may be unable to recover sufficient liquid funds to repay all investors at short notice. News of such difficulties is likely to lead more investors to seek to recover their money, creating a vicious circle which may lead to a failure of the bank. The failure of a bank may inflict great losses and financial hardship on business and individual investors. It may also shake public confidence in the banking system as a whole. Such a crisis occurred in the UK in the early 1970s, when a number of banking institutions found themselves in difficulties as a result of their lending policies. They had borrowed money on terms which allowed depositors to call for repayment at short notice; this allowed the banks to offer a lower rate of interest. However, they had lent on terms which did not allow the banks to recall the loans at short notice: they had 'borrowed short and lent long'. As a result, when a number of depositors sought repayment of their deposits in order to invest in more attractive schemes, the banks had insufficient liquid funds available to pay them. In order to avoid a banking collapse, the Bank of England, together with the major commercial banks, organised a financial 'lifeboat' or rescue package to save the threatened banks.

The crisis of the 1970s highlighted the need for some sort of oversight or regulation of banking businesses both to protect individual investors and to safeguard the general public interest. The Bank of England had historically exercised a measure of control, but the Banking Act 1979 created a formal and much stricter regime. The Act was passed in response partly to the earlier crisis, and partly to an EC directive[1] aimed at the harmonisation of laws of member states on the constitution and control of banks. Extensive supervisory powers were given to the Bank of England, and the only bodies allowed to take deposits from the public were the Bank of England itself, certain exempt institutions such as building societies and the Post Office Savings Bank, and those institutions either recognised as banks, or licensed to take deposits, by the Bank of England. The Act laid down criteria to be taken into account in deciding whether to recognise a bank or license a deposit taker, and allowed the Bank of England to demand information from, investigate and, if necessary, petition for the winding up of a deposit taker or bank. It also established a deposit protection scheme, into which all deposit taking institutions were required to pay, to provide a fund to compensate depositors in the event of a banking failure.

The 1979 Act was repealed and replaced by the Banking Act 1987 which established a new regulatory framework in response to the collapse of the Johnson Matthey Bank in 1984. The Act itself was amended in 1992 by regulations[2] introduced to implement the Second EC Banking Co-ordination Directive[3], whose objective is to enable banks established in one member state of the EC to open branches and trade in other member states. It requires that a credit institution which is duly authorised by appropriate regulatory authorities in the state where it is established to provide certain 'listed services' should be permitted to provide those services in other member states, and that primary responsibility for supervision of the activities of a credit institution should fall on the regulatory body in its home state. However, in order to prevent institutions evading regulation by establishing themselves in states with lighter or more lax regulatory regimes, the directive requires institutions to be established in the state where they carry on their principal business. An authorised institution which wishes to provide its services outside the state where it is established must give notice of the fact to its 'home' regulator. An institution which is not authorised in the state where it is established cannot provide listed services in another state.

The 1987 Act continued the supervisory role of the Bank of England. Following the collapse of Barings Bank in 1995, however, doubts were expressed about the bank's ability to carry out its supervisory role effectively and in 1998 the Bank of England Act transferred the bank's functions under the 1987 Act to a new regulatory body, the Financial Services Authority (FSA). The FSA was established in anticipation of the passing of the Financial Services and Markets Act 2000 (FSMA). When that Act is brought into force it will establish a single regulatory system for all financial services. The 1987 Act will be repealed. However, it is not expected that the FSMA will be brought fully into force before 2001 or 2002 and in the meantime the scheme under the 1987 Act will continue in force.

The Act does not seek to regulate the day-to-day activities of banks, but requires that all institutions taking deposits from the public must be authorised by the FSA unless they are exempt[4]. Amongst the exempt bodies are the National Savings Bank, friendly societies and Building societies, which are supervised separately under the Building Societies Act 1986, and credit institutions authorised in other member states of the EC. Institutions incorporated in the UK whose principal place of business is outside the UK may not apply for authorisation. In deciding whether or not to authorise an institution, the FSA must consider a number of factors, including whether the institution:

(a) is conducted in a prudent manner;
(b) has adequate capital and liquidity;
(c) makes adequate provision for doubtful debts and depreciation;
(d) maintains adequate accounting and other records; and
(e) has directors or controllers who are fit and proper people to be involved in the management of a deposit taking business[5].

The Act contains detailed definitions of 'deposit'[6] and 'deposit taking business'[7] in order to ensure that businesses taking deposits referable to the supply of goods or services are not caught by the Act[8].

An institution will not be considered to be conducted in a prudent manner unless it has an initial capital of at least 5m ECU and maintains own funds of at least that amount. The multi-tier system created by the 1979 Act has been abolished, but only institutions with assets of at least £5m can describe themselves as 'banks'.

Under s 1(1) of the Act, the FSA is charged with the general supervision of authorised institutions. In particular, the FSA has extensive powers to regulate the activities of authorised institutions, including to block changes in their ownership, require the submission of accountants' reports[9], appoint investigators[10], regulate advertisements for deposits[11] and, if necessary, petition for the winding up of an authorised institution[12]. The FSA has wide powers to gather evidence and require the production of documents[13]. A Board of Banking Supervision including the Chairman of the FSA, one other member of the FSA designated by the chairman, and six independent members has been established to assist the FSA in the exercise of its functions[14].

The regulatory system was unable to prevent the collapse of the Bank of Credit and Commerce International in 1991 or that of Barings Bank in 1995. Following the BCCI collapse the system was strongly criticised in a report by Bingham LJ (as he then was) in 1992[15], which made a number of recommendations to improve the system. Ultimately, however, as Bingham LJ recognised, 'supervisory arrangements can be no more effective than those who operate them: it is on the skill, alertness, experience and vigour of the supervisors, in the UK and abroad, that all ultimately depends'[16]. It is unlikely that any system of regulation can absolutely guarantee that a bank will never fail. The 1987 Act therefore establishes a depositors' protection fund to protect investors who may suffer loss in any collapse and which guarantees that in the event of a bank failure depositors will receive back 90% of any deposit, up to £20,000[17]. However, the Act gives the FSA and its officers and staff immunity from legal liability to any depositor for any acts or omissions done in the discharge of the FSA's supervisory functions under the Act, unless they can be shown to have acted in bad faith[18].

As we have already noted, the modern bank provides a range of services beyond merely taking deposits, making loans and operating current accounts. As the law stands, its other activities may be regulated under other legislation. For instance, consumer credit business will be subject to the Consumer Credit Act 1974[19] and investment advice and other financial services will be regulated under the Financial Services Act 1986. As explained above, the primary objective of the Financial Services and Markets Act 2000 is to replace the various different regulatory schemes applicable to financial services with a single regulatory scheme applicable to all financial services (with the important exception that the Consumer Credit Act will remain in force).

Under the 2000 Act anyone carrying on a regulated activity will require authorisation from the FSA[20], and it will be an offence to carry on such activities without authorisation[21]. 'Regulated activities' for the purposes of the Act include deposit taking and also dealing in investments, managing investments, providing financial advice and managing collective investment schemes[22]. Schedule 6 to the Act lays down certain 'threshold conditions' which must be satisfied by anyone seeking authorisation. They include that the person must have, in the opinion of the FSA, adequate resources in relation to the activity in question, taking into account, amongst other things, the provision made for liabilities and the manner in which risk is managed[23], and that the person satisfies the FSA that he is a 'fit and proper person[24]'. An authorised deposit taker must be a corporation or a partnership[25].

The Act provides no more than a framework. The details of the new scheme will be laid down in detailed regulations and guidance issued by the FSA indicating the manner in which it will exercise its new powers. It remains to be seen if the new scheme will provide more effective regulation of banking activity than the present one.

1   Directive 187/77/EEC.
2   Banking Co-ordination (Second Council Directive) Regulations 1992, SI 1992/3218.

3   89/646/EEC [1989] OJ L 386 1.
4   Section 3.
5   Schedule 3.
6   Section 5. See above 29.0.2.1.
7   Section 6.
8   See *SCF Finance Co Ltd v Masri (No 2)* [1987] QB 1002, [1987] 1 All ER 175 for an example of the interpretation of similar provisions in the 1979 Act.
9   Section 39.
10   Section 41.
11   Section 33(2).
12   Section 92.
13   Sections 39, 42. See *Bank of England v Riley* [1992] Ch 475, [1992] 1 All ER 769; *A v B Bank* [1993] QB 311, [1992] 1 All ER 778.
14   Section 2(1).
15   Inquiry into the Supervision of the Bank of Credit and Commerce International, 1992.
16   Ibid.
17   Section 50. 'Depositor' means the person who made the initial deposit so that an assignee of a depositor is not protected by the scheme: *Deposit Protection Board v Dalia* [1994] 2 AC 367, [1994] 2 All ER 577, HL.
18   Section 1(4). It is in any case unlikely that a duty of care in negligence would be owed to a depositor at common law: see *Yuen Kun Yeu v A-G of Hong Kong* [1988] AC 175; *Davis v Radcliffe* [1990] 1 WLR 821. It may, however, be possible to hold the bank liable in the tort of misfeasance in public office in relation to its exercise of its supervisory powers, although the requirements of the tort are difficult to satisfy: see *Three Rivers District Council v Bank of England (No 3)* [2000] 3 All ER 1, where the House of Lords left the point open for further argument.
19   See chs 25 and 26.
20   Section 19.
21   Section 23.
22   Schedule 2.
23   Schedule 6, para 4.
24   Schedule 6, para 5.
25   Schedule 6, para 1(2).

29.1   Banks and their customers

Our primary concern is with the role of banks in the financing of commercial operations, particularly in relation to making and collecting payments for goods and services. However, whilst the collection and payment of cheques and other payment orders is a central feature of the service provided by banks to their customers, it is only one part of the banker-customer relationship. The services provided by banks to their customers are themselves an aspect of commerce and, although detailed coverage of them is outside the scope of this book, we must briefly consider the nature of the relationship between banks and their customers.

29.1.1   *The changing nature of banking business*

'The banking system in this country evolved under the proud aegis of Victorian commercial prosperity'[1]; however, in recent years the nature of banking business, and the relationship between banks and their customers, has undergone radical change.

Until the twentieth century, only a privileged minority of the population, predominantly the landed gentry, professionals and businessmen, held bank accounts. By 1988, it was estimated that 89% of the adult population of the UK held a bank account[2] and that there were some 33 million private bank customers in the UK[3]. Many factors have contributed to this expansion in the use of banking services: the increased prosperity of society as a whole and the modern preference of employers to pay wages and salaries by cheque or direct credit transfer have probably been major factors. In addition, banks now offer a wide range of ancillary services to private customers; if the number of persons who make use of those services without holding a bank account is included, the number of bank 'customers' is probably even higher. The customer base of banks has therefore widened considerably in recent years.

Other developments have contributed to radical changes in the nature of banking services. The lifting of credit controls led to the expansion of credit, the provision of which to both business and consumers is now a major part of the banks' business. The development of new technology has introduced new methods of doing banking business, both within the banking system itself, where automated clearing systems such as BACS and CHAPS have been introduced, and externally, with the widespread use of automated teller machines (ATMs) for cash withdrawals and 'electronic funds transfer at point of sale' (EFTPOS) systems for paying for goods and services. These are now well established and familiar. More recently, developments in telecommunications and computer technologies have made possible the development of wholly new ways of delivering banking services. The High Street banks now offer customers the option of telephone and/or Internet banking services, whilst some specialist telebanking businesses have been established. Although customer take-up of these services is currently relatively low, they are expected to grow in significance in the coming years. One side-effect of these developments has been a reduction in the size of the traditional bank branch networks, as banks have closed smaller, less profitable, branches in order to maximise profits, leaving customers without easy access to a local branch to rely on electronic, telephone and Internet banking services.

A third factor affecting the role of banks and the services they provide has been the increase in competition in the provision of certain services. As was noted above[4], the Building Societies Act 1986 freed the building societies to compete with the banks for 'traditional' banking business, whilst the changes to financial services law enabled the banks to offer a wide range of financial services to customers. In the period from 1995 to 2000 there were 21 new entrants into the UK personal banking market[5]. Some of these were new businesses, including banking subsidiaries established by retailers such as Sainsburys and Marks & Spencer and insurance and other financial services companies, such as Scottish Widows and Prudential, and specialist Internet and telephone banking undertakings. Others were former building societies which converted from mutual to public limited company status. Yet others were subsidiaries or UK branches of established foreign banks. Nevertheless, in its report *Competition in UK Banking* in 2000 the Review Committee concluded that although there were signs of improvement in the personal banking services market, there was still a failure of competition, especially in relation to the provision of basic banking services. In so far as new banks are former building societies, they do not significantly increase the provision of banking services since they were free to provide such services prior to conversion. Many of the new entrants to the markets are actually joint ventures between established banks and other, non-banking businesses. Moreover, the Committee found that the new entrants had been selective about the services they provide[6]. Relatively few of them have, at least to date, chosen to provide basic current account services. Above all, the continuing trend of mergers and take-overs has tended to counteract the competition enhancing effects of these developments.

Despite these developments, there remains a significant minority of the population which does not have a bank account. Restrictions on the transferability of cheques, introduced in the Cheques Act 1992, have made it difficult for individuals without a bank account to cash cheques[7]. The tendency to increasing use of electronic payments exacerbates that difficulty. The government is therefore keen to encourage the development of appropriate banking services for low income consumers and in 2000 indicated its intention to develop a 'universal bank', possibly with the co-operation of the High Street banks, using the Post Office network to provide counter services.

1   *Banking Services: Law and Practice*, Report by the Review Committee (1989) (Cmnd 622) para 2.16.
2   Cmnd 622, para 2.20.
3   Cmnd 622, para 1.06; the figure excludes holders of building society accounts.
4   Above 29.1.2.
5   *Competition in UK Banking* (2000) para 4.89.
6   *Competition in UK Banking* (2000) para 4.91.
7   See McLeod (1997) 113 LQR 133.

29.1.2   *The range of banking services*

Although, as we have seen, the principal business of banking remains the taking of money on deposit from customers and the collection and payment of cheques and other payment orders on their behalf, banks now offer a wide range of ancillary services to domestic and business customers. They may provide loans, secured or unsecured, both for businesses and for domestic customers, including loans for specific purposes, such as home mortgages or for the purchase of particular items, or more general facilities such as overdrafts. They may offer the use of a variety of plastic cards, including credit cards and cash withdrawal or EFTPOS cards. They offer a wide range of financial and other advice: for instance, on investment, tax and wills, and a range of financial services, including stockbroking, unit trusts and insurance. They may act as trustees or executors of wills. They offer extensive services to business clients, including factoring of debts[1], discounting of bills[2], letter of credit facilities[3] and advice on export markets[4]. More traditionally, they may provide credit references for customers, or offer safe deposit facilities for the storage of documents and valuables.

The expansion in the range of services offered by banks, together with the increased competition for business and the expansion of the customer base has led to changes in the structure of banks and in the relationship between banker and customer. Many of the services provided by the bank will be provided through subsidiary companies; at the same time, the close relationship between banker and customer has been eroded; banks have begun to market themselves and their products aggressively and 'The bank manager has perforce moved away from his role as the trusted financial adviser, the man of business, to that of the salesman of a whole range of products and services'[5].

1   See 27.3.2.
2   See 28.1.
3   See ch 34.
4   See Pt V.
5   *Report of the Review Committee on Banking Services Law and Practice*, para 2.31.

29.1.3 *Who is a 'customer'?*

The word 'customer' is used in both the Bills of Exchange Act 1882 and the Cheques Act 1957, and it may be important to know who is a customer, in particular in order to decide if a bank can rely on the statutory defences available under the Acts to banks paying and collecting cheques[1]. However, neither statute defines 'customer', and in order to decide who is a customer for these purposes we must turn to the common law. Our main concern is with the bank's central functions of taking deposits and collecting and paying cheques, and in that context it has been held that a person becomes a customer as soon as he opens an account with the bank[2]. It is irrelevant that the amount of money deposited is small, or that few transactions are conducted on the account. Thus if a person takes a cheque to a bank, opens an account and pays in a cheque for collection, he becomes a 'customer', even if that is the only transaction conducted on the account: 'duration is not of the essence'[3]. This rule is particularly significant in the context of the statutory defences available to banks which collect and pay cheques[4]. However, a person for whom the bank carries out a casual service is not a 'customer': if a bank cashes a cheque for someone who does not have an account with the bank, the bank is treated as buying the cheque, so that when it collects payment, it does so for itself, and not for a customer.

The classification of a person as a bank 'customer' may also be important at common law where certain incidents attach to the banker-customer relationship, taking effect as implied terms of the contract. Many of the services offered by banks are, however, now available to persons who do not have deposit or current accounts with the bank: for instance, credit cards, loans, financial services are all offered generally, and a customer might therefore be defined as any person who has a contractual relationship with the bank under which the bank provides any service. Where a person who is not a 'customer' in the sense described earlier has a contract with a bank for the provision to him of some limited banking services, the contract may nevertheless attract some of the common law incidents of the banker-customer relationship. On the other hand, some of those incidents will not be appropriate to cases where the customer does not have a current or deposit account with the bank.

1 See 30.2.3; 30.2.5.
2 *Ladbroke & Co v Todd* (1914) 30 TLR 433; it may be that a person becomes a customer even earlier, as soon as the bank agrees to open the account: *Woods v Martins Bank* [1959] 1 QB 55, [1958] 3 All ER 166.
3 Lord Dunedin in *Taxation Comrs v English Scottish and Australian Bank Ltd* [1920] AC 683.
4 See 30.2.3; 30.2.5.

29.1.4 *The basis of the relationship*

The basis of the relationship between the bank and its customer is the contract between them which arises when the customer opens an account, and at common law its main incidents take effect as implied terms of that contract. It also draws, however, on a range of other legal concepts including agency, trusts, property and bailment. A bank may also incur legal responsibilities even to non-customers, for instance in the general law of negligence.

There is surprisingly little statutory regulation of the relationship; moreover, until recently, although the banks frequently used express contract terms to govern the supply of individual ancillary services, such as credit cards, cash cards, loans etc, the terms of the central contract created by opening an account were rarely set out expressly. Instead, 'the banker-customer relationship has been largely left to implied contract, whose terms have been elucidated by a patchwork of judicial decisions'[1]. Traditionally, the incidents of the banker-customer relationship have been derived from judicial recognition of mercantile expectations and banking practice: 'a man who employs a banker is bound by the usage of bankers'[2]; however, whilst this approach may have been appropriate at the time when banking services were largely used by businessmen, the increasingly widespread consumer use of banking services in modern times calls for a greater degree of regulation. In addition, the lack of either a statutory framework or even an express contract means that many bank customers – and some bankers – may be left ignorant of their rights and liabilities. In *Turner v Royal Bank of Scotland plc*[3] Sir Richard Scott V-C recognised this when he observed that 'Ordinary customers do not read *Paget* or any other banking textbooks' and continued:

> 'The law holds a person contractually bound by an established usage even if he does not know of it. But it cannot become an established usage unless it is notorious. How can a banking practice be notorious if the existence of the practice is kept from customers'[4].

In other words, a customer will be bound by the usage of banks if it is 'notorious' not only amongst bankers, but also 'among the customers, the ordinary members of the public who open accounts with banks'[5].

The Review Committee on Banking Services Law and Practice considered these problems. It rejected the idea of imposing a model contract on banks[6], since that would stultify competition. Instead it proposed a system of self-regulation, based on banks adopting and complying with a code of best practice, to be monitored by the banking ombudsman, with the option of legislative regulation if self-regulation proved ineffective. In its 1990 White Paper the government accepted the proposal for self-regulation but without the reserve option of legislation and a Code of Practice, entitled 'Good Banking', was eventually introduced on 16 March 1992[7]. An independent committee[8] was established to review the code and a second edition was published in March 1994. A third edition was published in 1998 and came into effect on 31 March 1999. Compliance with the code is voluntary, but it is widely adopted. Some 160 lenders subscribe to the code, which governs relations between subscribers and their personal (not business) banking customers and covers all aspects of the relationship other than the provision of mortgages (which are covered by a separate Code of Mortgage Lending Practice published by the Council of Mortgage Lenders) and certain investment services. The code establishes minimum standards for its subscribers: they remain free to adopt higher standards. Subscribers undertake to make copies of the code available to customers[9] and to comply with the law and with other relevant codes of practice affecting their business[10]. Compliance with the code is monitored. Subscribers have a 'Code Compliance Officer' and complete a 'Statement of Compliance' each year.

The heart of the code is contained in eleven 'key commitments' by which subscribers promise customers that they will:

- act fairly and reasonably in dealings with customers;
- ensure that all services and products comply with the code;
- provide customers with information and services and products in plain language and offer help if there is anything the customer does not understand;

- help customers choose products or services which fit their needs;
- help customers understand the financial implications of mortgages, other borrowing, savings and investment products and card products;
- help customers understand how their accounts work;
- have safe, secure and reliable banking and payment systems;
- ensure that procedures followed by their staff reflect the commitments of the code;
- correct errors and handle complaints speedily;
- consider cases of financial difficulty and mortgage arrears sympathetically and positively; and
- ensure that all services and products comply with relevant laws and regulations.

In accordance with these commitments the code provides that on becoming a customer, and at any time on request, the customer will be given 'clear, written information explaining the key features of the bank's main products and services', and details of tariffs, interest rates and charges[11]. All written terms and conditions will be fair in substance and will set out the customer's rights and responsibilities clearly and in plain language[12] and procedures for notifying the customer of changes to the terms of the contract are laid down[13].

The legal status of the code is unclear. It is generally assumed that it is not legally binding but the latest version is expressed in terms of promises, and it is at least arguable that as between a customer and a bank which subscribes to the code it could take effect as part of the bank-customer contract, at least if the bank publicises its adherence to the code, except in so far as it is excluded by express terms of that contract. Alternatively, it may be argued that the code is evidence of banking practice[14] so that its provisions may be reflected by implied terms in the contract. It is difficult, however, to see how that argument could succeed as against a bank which does not subscribe to the code, since it can be argued that by not subscribing it effectively indicates that it is not undertaking the obligations in the code. The code is considered by the Banking Ombudsman in deciding cases referred to him and will similarly be taken into account by the Financial Services Ombudsman under the new regime established by the Financial Services and Markets Act 2000. In addition, the Financial Services Authority has indicated that it will require observance of 'high ethical standards' when deciding whether to authorise, or continue the authorisation of, an institution under the Banking Act[15]. It is assumed that an institution which subscribes to the code but fails to observe it would not meet these standards and it may also be argued that a non-subscriber whose standards fall significantly below those of the code thereby fails to observe 'high ethical standards'.

Of course, certain terms in the banker-customer contract are subject to regulation under the general law, either under the Unfair Contract Terms Act or the Unfair Terms in Consumer Contracts Regulations[16].

1   Report of the Review Committee on Banking Services Law and Practice, para 2.07.
2   *Hare v Henty* (1861) 10 CBNS 65 at 77, per Willes J. This has not always been the case: see *Lloyds Bank Ltd v Savory & Co* [1933] AC 201, HL, where compliance with banking practice was held to be inadequate to constitute reasonable care: below 30.2.5.
3   [1999] 2 All ER (Comm) 664.
4   [1999] 2 All ER (Comm) 664 at 670.
5   [1999] 2 All ER (Comm) 664 at 670.
6   Such a model contract was produced by the Office of Fair Trading: see Appendix L to the Committee's report.
7   See Morris [1992] LMCLQ 474. An earlier draft code published in December 1990 had been strongly criticised by consumer groups.
8   The Code of Banking Practice Review Committee, now the Independent Review Body for the Banking and Mortgage Code.

9   The text of the code is available at the British Bankers' Association website at www.bba.org.uk.
    Copies can be obtained from banks which subscribe to it.
10 Banking Code, para 5.12.
11 Banking Code, para 2.1.
12 Paragraph 2.9.
13 Paragraphs 2.12–2.14.
14 In some cases the courts appear to have taken the code into account as evidence of good practice:
    see *Barclays Bank plc v O'Brien* [1994] 1 AC 180; *Royal Bank of Scotland plc v Turner* [1999]
    2 All ER (Comm) 664.
15 Bank of England Statement of Principles, 1993.
16 See 2.6.5.

29.2   Incidents of the banker-customer relationship

As we have seen, the opening of an account gives rise to the relationship of banker
and customer. The normal incidents of the relationship were described by Atkin LJ
in *Joachimson v Swiss Bank Corpn*[1]:

> 'The bank undertakes to receive money and to collect bills for its customers'
> account. The proceeds so received are not to be held in trust for the customer,
> but the bank borrows the proceeds and undertakes to repay them. The promise
> is to repay at the branch of the bank where the account is kept, and during
> banking hours. It includes a promise to repay any part of the amount due
> against the written order of the customer addressed to the bank at the branch
> ... The customer on his part undertakes to exercise reasonable care in executing
> his written orders so as not to mislead the bank or facilitate forgery'.

1   [1921] 3 KB 110 at 127, CA.

29.2.1   *The customer is a creditor of the bank*

Essentially, the relationship is one of debtor and creditor: the customer lends the
money deposited to the bank, and in return acquires the contractual right to
repayment, which may be due either at some specified future date, in the case of a
term deposit, or on demand in the more common case of a current or ordinary
deposit account[1]. In some cases, particularly for higher interest rate deposit accounts,
the terms of the agreement may call for a period of notice to be given before
withdrawing funds. However, generally in such a case the money is still repayable
on demand, subject to a loss of interest in the event of failure to give notice.
The relationship can be reversed: if the account is overdrawn the customer becomes
the debtor, the bank the creditor.

The fact that the relationship is one of debtor-creditor has certain implications.
Most notably, it means that, on depositing money with the bank, the customer ceases
to own the money. In the event that the bank becomes insolvent, the customer's only
right to repayment is as an ordinary unsecured creditor: the bank does not hold a
fund as property for him. When the bank makes payments in accordance with the
customer's instructions, for instance when it honours his cheques, it does so from its
own resources; it then reimburses itself the sum paid out by debiting the customer's
account and thus reducing the amount of its debt to the customer.

1   *Foley v Hill* (1848) 2 HL Cas 28.

29.2.1.1   *Repayment*

It is an implied term of the banker-customer contract that the bank will repay the money lent to it by the customer, and honour the customer's instructions to make payments to third parties. When such payments are made, the bank is entitled to reimburse itself by debiting the customer's account in accordance with the customer's mandate – the instruction to make payment. Such instruction can be given by cheque, by other written order, such as a standing order or direct debiting authority, or by the use of an ATM or EFTPOS card. If the bank makes a payment without the customer's mandate, it has no authority to debit his account, although this rule is modified by statutory provisions designed to protect banks paying cheques[1]. On the other hand, failure by the bank to honour the customer's mandate and make payment is a breach of contract for which the bank may be liable in damages[2]. Furthermore, where a cheque is returned unpaid, the wording on the cheque, such as 'refer to drawer', may be defamatory, allowing the customer to claim damages in defamation[3].

The customer may withdraw the mandate, for instance by 'stopping', or countermanding, a cheque[4]. Notice of countermand must be given to the branch on which the cheque is drawn[5] and is not effective until it reaches the teller or ledger clerk. In *Curtice v London City and Midland Bank*[6] the customer countermanded a cheque by letter to the bank which, due to the bank's error, was not removed from the bank's letter box until after the cheque had been paid. It was held that the cheque had not been effectively countermanded (although the bank might have been liable in negligence). The Banking Code requires banks to give customers information about how and when they may countermand cheques and other payment instructions[7].

The demand for payment must be made at the branch where the account is drawn, and if a bank pays a cheque elsewhere it is treated as buying the cheque, which it then presents on its own behalf. The demand must also be made during business hours, and the bank is entitled to refuse payment if there are insufficient funds to honour the order, or if the cheque is 'stale': it is normal practice to regard a cheque as stale if it is presented more than six months after the date when it was drawn.

A failure to honour a cheque is justified in certain circumstances. The bank may be compelled by law to dishonour the customer's cheque. A person who has obtained a court judgment against another may apply for a garnishee order to enforce the judgment debt. Such an order requires a person who owes money to the judgment debtor to pay it instead to the judgment creditor. A garnishee order may be made in favour of a judgment creditor in respect of the debt owed by a bank to its customer and if such an order is made it may prevent the bank honouring the customer's mandate. Similarly, a person with a claim against another may apply to the court, during or before commencement of proceedings, for a freezing injunction[8] to prevent the defendant moving or disposing of assets so as to frustrate any judgment which may be made against him. If such an order is made and served on the bank, it too may restrict or prevent the bank honouring its customer's mandate. Finally, restraint orders made in certain types of criminal proceedings may prevent the customer dealing with his bank account[9].

In other circumstances the bank's duty to obey the customer's mandate may be overridden by its other duties to the customer or to third parties. For instance, the bank owes a duty of care to its customer and may be in breach of that duty if it honours cheques drawn in circumstances where it has reasonable cause to suspect that the customer is being defrauded[10].

The bank's obligation to obey the customer's mandate may also be restricted if the bank exercises its right to combine accounts. Where a customer holds more than one account with the same bank, the bank has an implied right to combine those accounts. The right will normally be exercised where one account is overdrawn and the other in credit: by combining the two accounts, the bank may reduce or even cancel the customer's indebtedness on the overdraft. The bank may therefore be entitled to dishonour a cheque drawn on an account which is in credit, where the same customer holds a second, overdrawn account, and the combined sum in the two accounts is insufficient to meet the amount of the cheque. The exercise of the right may benefit the customer: for instance, if C holds two accounts, one overdrawn in the sum of £100, the other in credit in the sum of £500, and draws a cheque for £200 on the first account, the bank will honour it because there are sufficient funds in the two accounts taken together to meet the cheque. More often, the right is exercised for the bank's benefit, particularly where the customer is insolvent.

The right to combine accounts can be exercised in respect of different classes of account, and in respect of accounts held with different branches of the same bank. It has been explained on the basis that 'in truth, as between banker and customer, whatever number of accounts are kept in the books, the whole is really but one account[11]'. However, it is probably more accurate to say that although there may be a number of separate contracts between the bank and an individual customer, there is only one relationship of debtor and creditor between them. The right was examined by the House of Lords in *National Westminster Bank Ltd v Halesowen Pressworks and Assemblies Ltd*[12]. Earlier cases had explained the right on the basis of the bank having a lien over money deposited with it. However, as noted above, money deposited with the bank becomes the bank's property, and it cannot exercise a lien over its own property; their Lordships therefore explained that the proper basis of the right is that it is a form of set-off. Thus, as explained in a recent case, exercise of the right allows the bank to assess the overall indebtedness of itself and the customer[13]. The bank was therefore able to exercise its right of combination in respect of the customer's accounts, even after a seizure order had been made in respect of the customer's assets under the Drug Trafficking (Offences) Act 1986.

The right to combine accounts is limited in three situations[14]:

(a) where the bank and customer have agreed to keep accounts separate; such agreement may be explicit, but is often implied; thus where a customer has a loan account and a current account, it is normally implied that the two should be kept separate as long as the customer's business is trading normally;

(b) where a particular fund is deposited with the bank for a specified purpose of which the bank has notice[15]; and

(c) the bank cannot combine the customer's private account with an account held in his name as trustee; however, the bank may combine an account held by a nominee or trustee with one held by the beneficiary personally, but the status of the account as a nominee account must be clear and indisputable: the bank may not combine accounts merely on the basis of an arguable case that one is held as a nominee account for the benefit of the holder of the other[16].

1   See 30.2.3.
2   See 30.1.
3   See 30.1.
4   It is not clear whether the customer is entitled to countermand a cheque which has been supported by a cheque guarantee card: see 30.1.
5   *Burnett v Westminster Bank Ltd* [1966] 1 QB 742, [1965] 3 All ER 81.
6   [1908] 1 KB 293, CA.

7   Banking Code, para 2.1.
8   See 36.1.2.1.
9   Orders may be made under the Drug Trafficking Act 1994, s 26; the Criminal Justice Act 1988, s 77; and the Prevention of Terrorism (Temporary Provisions) Act 1989, s 13(8).
10 *Barclays Bank Ltd v Quincecare Ltd* [1992] 4 All ER 363; below 29.3.2.
11 Malins V-C in *Re European Bank, Agra Bank Claim* (1872) 8 Ch App 41 at 44.
12 [1972] AC 785, [1972] 1 All ER 641, HL.
13 *Re K* [1990] 2 QB 298, [1990] 2 All ER 562.
14 *Greenwood Teale v William, Williams, Brown & Co* (1894) 11 TLR 56.
15 *Barclays Bank Ltd v Quistclose Investments Ltd* [1970] AC 567, [1968] 3 All ER 651, HL.
16 *Uttamchandani v Central Bank of India* (1989) 133 Sol Jo 262, CA; *Bhogal v Punjab National Bank* [1988] 2 All ER 296, CA.

29.2.2   The bank's duty of care

As noted by Atkin LJ in *Joachimson*[1], the bank undertakes to collect bills and cheques, and other payments, for its customer. In making and collecting payments, the bank acts as its customer's agent and certain incidents of a principal-agent relationship are superimposed on the basic debtor-creditor relationship. Clearly, the bank is not normally in a fiduciary position, because the funds deposited with it are its own property, not the customer's. However, the bank does owe the customer a duty of care in the performance of its functions, including in collecting and paying cheques. Such a duty of care arises as an implied term of the contract, either at common law, or by virtue of s 13 of the Supply of Goods and Services Act 1982.

1   Above 29.3.

29.2.2.1   Duties in paying cheques

A number of cases have considered whether the banker's duty of care requires it to dishonour cheques drawn by agents in suspicious circumstances. The difficulty for the bank is that if it does dishonour a cheque in such a case, it is potentially exposed to liability for wrongful dishonour if the agent was in fact acting properly; on the other hand, if the agent abuses his authority to draw cheques by drawing on his principal's account for his own purposes, the principal may seek to hold the bank liable in negligence for honouring the cheques. In the past it has been suggested that the bank's duty in such cases extended to making 'such enquiries as may be appropriate and practical if the bank in question has, or if a reasonable banker would have, grounds for believing that authorised signatories are misusing their authority for the purpose of defrauding the principal'[1]. However, more recent cases seem to set the duty of care lower, recognising that banks deal with a very high volume of cheques and that the older cases may impose an unrealistically heavy burden on banks, and therefore subordinating the duty of care to the central duty to obey the customer's mandate. Thus in *Barclays Bank Ltd v Quincecare Ltd*[2] Steyn J suggested that a bank would be negligent if it obeyed the mandate where the circumstances were such as to put it on inquiry and provide reasonable grounds for suspecting that an attempt was being made to defraud the customer; the appropriate standard was that of the ordinary prudent banker, bearing in mind that the basis of the bank's dealings with its customer is trust rather than disbelief. The standard of care expected was further explained by the Court of Appeal in

Lipkin Gorman v Karpnale[3]. A solicitor had misappropriated the funds of his firm by drawing cheques on the partnership account to obtain cash which he used in gambling. The bank honoured the cheques, even though it knew of the solicitor's gambling and the way the cheques were drawn and paid was unusual. The Court of Appeal held that the bank was not liable in negligence: it would only be in breach of its duty of care if the circumstances were such that no reasonable cashier would pay without consulting a superior, and no superior would make payment without querying the cheque. It would not be reasonable to expect the bank to suspect a solicitor.

> 'The principle obligation is upon the bank to honour its customer's cheques in accordance with its mandate or instructions. There is nothing in the contract, express or implied, which would require a banker to consider the commercial wisdom or otherwise of the particular transaction . . . To a large extent the banker's obligation under such a contract is largely automatic or mechanical. Presented with a cheque drawn in accordance with the terms of that contract, the banker must honour it save in what I would expect to be exceptional circumstances'[4].

As Parker LJ observed in the same case, however, each case will depend on its own facts: the crucial question in each case is whether the bank has shown the required standard of care:

> 'Expressions . . . such as that a paying bank must pay under its mandate save in extreme cases, or that a bank is not obliged to act as an amateur detective, or that suspicion is not enough to justify failing to pay according to the mandate . . . are no more than comments on particular facts or situations and embody . . . no principles of law'[5].

He suggested, however, that it would be negligent for a bank to continue to pay out on cheques without inquiry in circumstances where a reasonable banker would have reasonable grounds for believing that a fraud was being committed[6]. If the banker is to be held liable, it must be established that a reasonable and honest banker, knowing of the facts, 'would have considered that there was a serious or real possibility albeit not amounting to a probability that its customer might be being defrauded' but 'the customer cannot, of course, rely on matters which a meticulous ex post facto examination would have brought to light'[7]. On the facts of the case the court concluded that the bank was not in breach of duty. Although it remains difficult to define precisely the standard of care required of a banker, it seems clear that the standard of care expected of the reasonable banker in these recent cases is lower than that required by the earlier cases, recognising the dilemma for bankers which an excessively high standard creates. Essentially, such cases raise the question of the extent to which the bank can be expected to police the customer's account and supervise the actions of the customer's agent. The answer suggested by recent cases seems to be that the principal having placed his trust in the agent, and placed him in a position to commit the fraud, must bear the loss unless the circumstances are exceptional.

1   Per Brightman J in *Karak Rubber Co Ltd v Burden (No 2)* [1972] 1 All ER 1210 at 231; and see *Selangor United Rubber Estates Ltd v Cradock (No 3)* [1968] 2 All ER 1073, [1968] 1 WLR 1555.
2   [1992] 4 All ER 363.
3   [1992] 4 All ER 409, [1989] 1 WLR 1340.

4   [1992] 4 All ER 409 at 421, per May LJ.
5   [1992] 4 All ER 409 at 440.
6   [1992] 4 All ER 409 at 439.
7   [1992] 4 All ER 409 at 441.

29.2.2.2   *Liability as a constructive trustee*

A bank which pays or receives payment of a cheque may also incur liability as a constructive trustee if it has either received trust funds or assisted in a breach of duty by a fiduciary, including an agent, a company director or even an employee. The liability is a personal one, to account to the victim of the breach of trust, although if the bank holds funds it may also be susceptible to a proprietary claim to those funds. Unfortunately, despite – or perhaps because of – a string of recent cases in which such liability has been considered, it remains difficult to state precisely when a bank will be held liable. In particular, it is not clear what degree of knowledge of the breach of trust is required before the bank can be held liable. In *Baden Delvaux*[1] Peter Gibson J suggested that there were five possible degrees of knowledge as follows: (a) actual knowledge; (b) wilfully shutting one's eyes to the obvious; (c) wilfully and recklessly failing to make such inquiries as a reasonable person would make; (d) knowledge of circumstances which would indicate the facts to an honest and reasonable person; and (e) knowledge of circumstances which would put an honest and reasonable person on inquiry. However, although this categorisation may be useful in some cases, later cases have emphasised that the categories are not watertight[2]. Broadly, the first three categories can be regarded as covering cases of 'actual notice', while the last two cover cases of 'constructive notice'. The crucial question, then, is whether constructive notice in either sense will suffice to give rise to liability as a constructive trustee.

   Such liability can be imposed in three different situations: first, where the bank receives trust funds and, knowing them to be trust funds, applies them for its own benefit (now termed liability for 'inconsistent dealing'); second, where the bank knowingly receives trust property for its own benefit in breach of trust ('knowing receipt'); and, third, where although it does not receive funds for its own benefit it knowingly assists in a breach of trust ('dishonest assistance')[3]. Although the distinction between 'knowing receipt' and 'dishonest assistance' has not always been observed in the cases, it seems that the degree of knowledge required to hold a bank liable may depend on the basis on which it is held liable.

(a) Knowing receipt
It is now generally accepted that a bank will only be held liable on this basis where it receives money for its own, and not merely for its customer's, benefit[4]. Liability may therefore be imposed where the bank uses money received to pay off or reduce the customer's overdraft. The bank's liability is a personal one, to account for the funds received, although a proprietary claim may also be available. It is, however, not clear what degree of knowledge is required to make it liable on this basis. Dicta in some cases suggest that it will be liable if it has constructive or actual notice of the breach of trust[5] (ie knowledge in any of the five categories above) but others suggest that liability will only be imposed in cases of dishonesty or where the bank has 'actual notice'[6] (ie knowledge in the first three categories above), at least in a commercial context where the courts have generally been reluctant to introduce concepts of constructive notice. In the most recent authority

on the point, Nourse LJ suggested, that rather than basing liability on different categories of knowledge or notice, the test should be whether the recipient's knowledge was such as to make it unconscionable for him to retain the benefit of the receipt[7], but this test would be no easier to apply to the facts of any particular case[8].

(b) Dishonest assistance

A bank may be held liable on this basis even where it has not received funds for its own benefit if, for instance, it has provided assistance to a fiduciary who commits a breach of his fiduciary obligations. A bank may therefore be held liable on this basis if it collects or pays cheques drawn by a fiduciary in breach of his obligations. A claim may thus be brought where, for instance, a company director or employee has embezzled funds from the company or employer, when the bank's 'deep pockets' may make it a particularly attractive target for the victim seeking redress. The bank's liability is a personal one, to account, so that it can be held liable even if it no longer holds the property in question (although it is said to be held liable as a 'constructive trustee').

The standard of knowledge required to give rise to liability on this basis was considered by the Privy Council in *Royal Brunei Airlines Sdn Bhd v Tan*[9], a case not concerned with a bank. Prior to this case the balance of opinion favoured the view that the defendant would only be held liable if he was dishonest or had actual notice of a breach of trust; indeed, in *Polly Peck International plc v Nadir (No 2)*[10] Scott LJ took the view that the question was already settled. As Millett J observed in *Agip v Jackson*, 'there is no sense in requiring dishonesty on the part of the principal while accepting negligence as sufficient for his assistant'[11]. The Court of Appeal in *Agip*[12] seems to have taken the view that constructive notice would suffice, but their Lordships in *Tan* favoured the view that a person who does not receive trust property will only be held liable as a constructive trustee for assisting in a breach of trust where he is dishonest. They preferred the test of 'dishonesty' to that of knowledge which gives rise to difficult questions as to the type of knowledge required to found liability, and therefore rejected the use of the *Baden Delvaux* scale in this context. However, the test of 'dishonesty' favoured by their Lordships is objective, not subjective, involving consideration of what an honest person would do in the circumstances.

> 'An honest person does not participate in a transaction if he knows that it involves a misapplication of trust assets to the detriment of the beneficiaries. Nor does an honest person in such a case deliberately close his eyes and ears or deliberately not ask questions, lest he learn something he would rather not know, and then proceed regardless'[13].

It is difficult to see how this test of dishonesty differs significantly from the test of 'notice' in the first three categories in the *Baden Delvaux* scale. Their Lordships also explained that a person who is dishonest in this sense may be held liable even though the person primarily responsible for the breach of trust is not 'dishonest'. Conversely, a person who is negligent but not dishonest may be held liable to the beneficiaries in negligence if the circumstances give rise to a duty of care, but will not be liable as a constructive trustee.

The decision in *Tan* has gone some way to clarifying the law. Although a decision of the Privy Council, it has been approved by the Court of Appeal[14]. Difficult questions may still arise in applying the test of 'dishonesty', but it seems right that a bank should not be held liable where it is neither dishonest nor in breach of a contractual or tortious duty[15].

1   *Baden Delvaux and Lecuit v Société Général pour Favoriser le Développement du Commerce et de l'Industrie en France SA* [1992] 4 All ER 161, [1993] 1 WLR 509.
2   See per Scott LJ in *Polly Peck International plc v Nadir (No 2)* [1992] 4 All ER 769.
3   *Barnes v Addy* (1874) 9 Ch App 244.
4   Per Millett J in *Agip (Africa) Ltd v Jackson* [1990] Ch 265, [1992] 4 All ER 385 (reversed on other grounds); Millett (1991) 107 LQR 71; *Polly Peck International plc v Nadir (No 2)* [1992] 4 All ER 769.
5   Per Millett J in *Agip (Africa) Ltd v Jackson* [1990] Ch 265 at 291; *El Ajou v Dollar Land Holdings plc* [1993] 3 All ER 717.
6   *Eagle Trust plc v SBC Securities* [1992] 4 All ER 488; *Cowan de Groot Properties Ltd v Eagle Trust plc* [1992] 4 All ER 700; see also per Scott LJ in *Polly Peck International plc v Nadir (No 2)* [1992] 4 All ER 769 at 777; *Eagle Trust plc v SBC Securities Ltd (No 2)* [1996] 1 BCLC 121; *Twinsectra Ltd v Yardley* [1999] Lloyd's Rep Bank 438, CA; *Bank of America v Arnell* [1999] Lloyd's Rep Bank 399.
7   *Bank of Credit and Commerce International (Overseas) Ltd v Akindele* [2000] 4 All ER 221.
8   It has been suggested that the recipient should be liable in all cases, regardless of knowledge, subject to the defence of change of position: see Lord Nicholls in Cornish, Nolan, O'Sullivan and Virgo (eds) *Restitution Past, Present and Future* (1998).
9   [1995] 2 AC 378, [1995] 3 All ER 97, PC.
10 [1992] 4 All ER 769; see also the views of Vinelott J in *Eagle Trust plc v SBC Securities* [1996] 1 BCLC 121.
11 [1990] Ch 265 at 293.
12 [1992] 4 All ER 451 at 467. See also *Selangor United Rubber Estates Ltd v Cradock (No 3)* [1968] 2 All ER 1073.
13 Per Lord Nicholls [1995] 2 AC 378 at 389, [1995] 3 All ER 97 at 106.
14 *Satnam Ltd v Dunlop Haywood Ltd* [1999] 3 All ER 652; see also *Brinks Ltd v Abu Saleh (No 3)* (1995) Times, 23 October.
15 See generally Birks [1992] LMCLQ 218; Fennell (1994) 57 MLR 38 and see *Lipkin Gorman v Karpnale Ltd* [1992] 4 All ER 409.

29.2.2.3   Duties in relation to other banking services

The duty of care discussed above arises as an implied term of the banker-customer relationship from the performance of the bank's basic functions in paying and collecting cheques. The fact that the parties are in a contractual relationship does not preclude the imposition of concurrent liability in tort[1], but it is clear that the court will not impose more onerous duties in tort than would be imposed by the contract[2]. The express and implied terms of the contract must therefore be the primary source of duties between bank and customer. As already noted, terms may be implied to reflect the usages of bankers. Otherwise, terms are implied in accordance with the general law. Thus a term will only be implied if it is necessary to give business efficacy to the contract.

Recently, it has become common practice for banks constantly to revise their range of 'products', including the launching of new accounts, and banks have come in for criticism for failing to notify customers of new accounts offering more favourable terms than their existing accounts. For instance, a customer may have money in an old account when the bank is offering a better rate of interest to new customers. Under the Banking Code, banks undertake to inform personal customers if a particular account is superseded, because such accounts are no longer opened or because the account in question is no longer actively promoted[3] and, at least once a year, to send the customer a summary of all its products with details of interest rates for comparison[4]. However, in the absence of an express undertaking, or special facts from which an implied undertaking can be inferred, there is no duty at common law to advise a customer of the opening of new accounts[5].

The bank may incur further duties of care, either in contract or in tort, if it performs other functions. Thus if it stores property for the customer, it incurs a duty of care as bailee; similarly, if it offers advice to a customer, it owes a duty to exercise reasonable care in giving that advice[6].

Such duties are not limited to customers: thus a bank owes a duty of care in accordance with basic tortious principles when it offers investment advice[7], or provides a credit reference on one of its customers[8]. However, provided that bank fulfils its duty of care at the time of giving its advice it has no continuing duty to keep its advice under review[9].

1   *Henderson v Merrett Syndicates Ltd* [1995] 2 AC 145, [1994] 3 All ER 506; see 6.2.1.2.
2   *Tai Hing Cotton Mill Ltd v Liu Chong Hing Bank Ltd* [1986] AC 80, [1985] 2 All ER 947, PC.
3   Banking Code, para 2.17.
4   Banking Code, para 2.16.
5   *Suriya & Douglas v Midland Bank plc* [1999] 1 All ER (Comm) 612.
6   *Cornish v Midland Bank plc* [1985] 3 All ER 513, CA. See also *Box v Midland Bank Ltd* [1979] 2 Lloyd's Rep 391, where a bank was held to owe duty of care when making representations to an applicant for a loan.
7   *Woods v Martins Bank Ltd* [1959] 1 QB 55, [1958] 3 All ER 166.
8   *Hedley Byrne v Heller & Partners* [1964] AC 465, [1963] 2 All ER 575, HL.
9   *Fennoscandia Ltd v Clarke* [1999] 1 All ER (Comm) 365.

29.2.2.4   Fiduciary duties

The bank may also incur extra duties: for instance, if it acts as a trustee, it owes fiduciary duties as any other trustee. However, in the absence of such additional duties, the bank is not a fiduciary. Thus the relationship between bank and customer does not give rise to a duty of disclosure[1] or to a presumption of undue influence[2]. However, a fiduciary relationship giving rise to a presumption of undue influence may arise in special circumstances, for instance if the bank offers advice on a transaction from which it derives a benefit, or if the customer relies on the bank so that it acquires a dominating influence over him[3].

1   *Suriya & Douglas v Midland Bank plc* [1999] 1 All ER (Comm) 612.
2   *National Westminster Bank Ltd v Morgan* [1985] AC 686, [1985] 1 All ER 821, HL.
3   *Lloyds Bank Ltd v Bundy* [1975] QB 326, [1974] 3 All ER 757, CA.

29.2.3   The customer's duty of care

The customer, too, owes a duty of care to the bank. However, the duty is severely limited. The customer owes a duty to inform the bank of forgeries, or fraud relating to his account, of which he becomes aware[1] and owes a duty to take reasonable care in drawing cheques so as not to facilitate alteration or fraud, and is liable for any loss caused to the bank as a result of a breach of that duty. Thus in *London Joint Stock Bank Ltd v Macmillan and Arthur*[2] the customer drew cheques by filling in the amount in figures and signing the cheque, leaving a clerk to fill in the amount of the cheque in words. A cheque payable to bearer was drawn for £2; the clerk fraudulently inserted the words 'one hundred and twenty pounds' and inserted the figures '1' before and '0' after the figure 2. The customer was held negligent and failed in an action to recover the extra £118 paid out by the bank on the altered cheque. However, this duty is limited: in another case, where the customer left a space between the name of the payee and the words 'or order', a rogue, a partner in the firm of Cumberbatch and Potts, was able to insert 'per Cumberbatch and Potts' in the space, so that the cheque was payable to the payee through Messrs Cumberbatch and Potts; the rogue then indorsed the cheque to a nominee. It was held that the bank had no authority to pay out on the altered cheque, and was unable to debit the customer's account: the customer had not been in breach of duty[3].

It seems clear that the customer's duty of care is unlikely to be extended. In *Tai Hing Cotton Mill Ltd v Liu Chong Hing Bank Ltd*[4] the plaintiff company employed a clerk who, over a period of six years, fraudulently drew cheques by forging the signature of the company's managing director and obtained a sum of $HK5.5m. In 1978 a new accountant began checking the company's bank statements against its accounts and discovered the fraud. The company brought a claim against three banks to recover the sums paid out on the forged signatures, and the banks argued that the customer had been negligent in failing to check bank statements and was therefore estopped from denying that the bank statements were accurate. The Privy Council held that the tortious duty of care on a customer is limited to those duties already identified in *Greenwood* and *MacMillan and Arthur*; moreover, the Privy Council emphasised that in view of the contractual relationship between a bank and its customers, a duty of care in tort could only be imposed where the court would imply a term requiring care to be taken. There was no need to imply a term requiring the customer to check bank statements in order to give business efficacy to the banker-customer contract which, the Privy Council stressed, was the business of the bank. The remedy was for banks to insert express terms requiring the checking of statements into their contracts with customers. Such terms would have to be clear and unambiguous if they were to make the bank statements conclusive evidence of the state of the customer's account[5]. The insertion of new terms would require clear notice to the customer, from which the court could infer the customer's consent to the new terms, and would have to be supported by consideration moving from the bank to the customer. New terms cannot be incorporated into the contract by merely printing them on the inside cover of a cheque book[6].

Tai Hing represents judicial recognition of the balance of bargaining power between banks and their customers. However, the effect of the decision is to leave the bank exposed to liability in the event of frauds on the customer's account, even though those frauds might be difficult or even impossible to detect without expensive security measures. It has therefore been suggested that the position should be modified by allowing a bank sued in debt or damages as a result of an unauthorised payment to raise contributory negligence by the customer as a partial defence where that negligence is so serious that it would be inequitable that the bank should be liable for the full amount[7]. Such an approach would introduce a measure of flexibility into this area and allow the court to apportion liability for loss caused by fraud in accordance with the relative responsibility of bank and customer; it would probably lead to a different result on the facts of *Tai Hing*, but of course it would still be for the courts to decide what conduct of the customer does amount to negligence. In 1993, however, the Law Commission recommended that contributory negligence should only be a defence in cases where the bank is liable for breach of a duty to take care[8]. Where the bank is sued for breach of its mandate by making an unauthorised payment its liability is strict so that the defence would be unavailable.

1   *Greenwood v Martin's Bank Ltd* [1933] AC 51, HL.
2   [1918] AC 777.

3   *Slingsby v District Bank Ltd* [1932] 1 KB 544, CA.
4   [1986] AC 80, [1985] 2 All ER 947, PC.
5   All three banks involved in the case had express terms relating to checking and/or approval of bank statements. However, those terms were held to be insufficiently clear and unambiguous to raise a duty of care or prevent a challenge to the statements.
6   *Burnett v Westminster Bank Ltd* [1966] 1 QB 742, [1965] 3 All ER 81.
7   Report of the Review Committee on Banking Services Law and Practice, para 6.14.
8   Law Com 219 *Contributory Negligence as a Defence in Contract* (1993) para 5.20.

29.2.4   *The bank's duty of confidentiality*

A bank necessarily acquires a great deal of information about its customers' business, financial and personal dealings. Much of that information may be sensitive, or of such a nature that the customer would prefer it not to be disclosed, to potential competitors, or to third parties generally. Furthermore, the commercial relationship between bank and customer, incorporating as it does certain elements of an agency relationship, requires there to be trust between customer and bank. The law recognises those requirements and therefore recognises that the bank owes a duty of confidentiality to its customer. The classic exposition of the duty was by the Court of Appeal in *Tournier v National Provincial and Union Bank of England*[1]. In that case the customer got into financial difficulties and, in the course of a conversation with the customer's employer, the bank manager disclosed to the employer that the customer's account was overdrawn, and that the customer had dealings with bookmakers. As a result, the customer lost his job. It was held that the bank was in breach of its duty of confidentiality in disclosing the information.
    The ambit of the duty was explained by Atkin LJ:

> 'It clearly goes beyond the state of the account, that is whether there is a debit or a credit balance, and the amount of the balance. It must at least extend to all transactions that go through the account, and to the securities, if any, given in respect of the account; and in respect of such matters it must, I think, extend beyond the period when the account is closed, or ceases to be an active account . . . [T]he obligation extends to information obtained from other sources than the customer's actual account if the occasion upon which the information was obtained arose out of the banking relations of the bank and its customers . . .'[2].

The duty therefore covers all information received by the bank as a result of the banker-customer relationship. It has recently been held, however, that the bank commits no breach if it discloses information to a person who might be expected already to be aware of it, even, apparently, if at the time of the disclosure that person has forgotten the information[3].
    Whether or not this restriction is correct, the duty is subject to a number of exceptions. In *Tournier* Bankes LJ recognised four categories of exception justifying disclosure of information which would otherwise be covered by the duty:

(a) where disclosure is compelled by law;
(b) where there is a public duty to disclose the information;
(c) where the bank's own interests require disclosure; and
(d) where the disclosure is expressly or impliedly authorised by the customer.

The decision in *Tournier* remains the definitive statement of the ambit of the banker's duty of confidentiality and its exceptions. However, there are doubts about the extent of the duty. In *Tournier* Scrutton LJ did not agree with all of the points made by Atkin LJ, and modern developments in banking practice and business have raised further doubts about the ambit of the duty, for instance whether it extends to information acquired by the bank's commercial subsidiaries carrying on non-banking business, such as estate agency, or to other financial institutions[4], and the exceptions to it. Because of those doubts, the Review Committee on Banking Law and Services suggested that the duty of confidentiality should be clarified by being placed on a statutory footing. However, in its 1990 White Paper the government stated that 'the present *Tournier* rules are very clear as they stand, they have worked well and they are well understood by bankers'[5] and proposed instead that the voluntary code of banking practice should explain the duty of confidentiality and its exceptions. This proposal was taken up and the Banking Code now restates the duty, and the circumstances in which the bank will disclose information, largely in terms of the *Tournier* formula[6].

1   [1924] 1 KB 461, CA.
2   [1924] 1 KB 461 at 485.
3   *Christofi v Barlcays Bank plc* [1999] 2 All ER (Comm) 417.
4   See Goode, 'The Banker's Duty of Confidentiality' [1989] JBL 269.
5   At p 16.
6   Banking Code, para 4.

29.2.4.1 *Compulsory disclosure and the public interest*

The first two of the *Tournier* exceptions are clearly connected. At the time of the *Tournier* decision, there were probably only two situations in which disclosure could be required by law; however, in recent years a number of statutes have created powers to order disclosure, generally in order to assist the detection of criminal activities and in 1989 the Review Committee on Banking Services Law and Practice identified 20 statutes under which disclosure could be compelled[1], including the Bankers' Books Evidence Act 1879 (s 7), the Income and Corporation Taxes Act 1970 (ss 481–513), the Companies Act 1985 (ss 434–435, for the purposes of investigations by the Department of Trade and Industry) and the Drug Trafficking Offences Act 1986. The Bank of England can also require disclosure of such information as it may reasonably require for the performance of its supervision of authorised deposit taking institutions[2].

The ambit of the second exception has always been unclear: for instance, it is not clear if it allows disclosure in any case where the bank knows, or suspects, that a crime has been committed. Obviously, as the number of cases where disclosure can be compelled under the first exception expands, the need for the second is somewhat eroded. The Review Committee therefore recommended that the second exception be abolished, but in its 1990 White Paper the government rejected this proposal, pointing out that the first exception covers cases where disclosure is compulsory whereas the second applies to permit disclosure at the bank's discretion, and emphasising the public interest in detecting crime:

'The increasing sophistication of financial crime means that there may well be cases in which a banker wishes to disclose information in the public interest, but he may be uncertain whether there is a specific statutory gateway for him to do so'[3].

It is clear that a duty of confidentiality is generally capable of being overridden by requirements of the public interest[4].

Should a bank disclose to its customer that it has been ordered to disclose information relating to the customer? It has been held that there is no contractual requirement for a bank to disclose to its customer an application to inspect the customer's account made under s 9 of the Police and Criminal Evidence Act 1984, nor, generally, to oppose the application[5]. However, in *Robertson v Canadian Imperial Bank of Commerce*[6] a bank was served with a court order requiring it to produce a customer's bank statements in civil proceedings. The Privy Council observed that 'In the ordinary way a customer in good standing could reasonably expect, if only as a matter of courtesy and good business practice, to be told that a subpoena had been received', but recognised that there might be circumstances in which the bank would be entitled for its own protection, or compelled by public duty, not to disclose the application. In so far as there was a duty on the bank to disclose the application, it was not an absolute duty but only one to use its best endeavours to contact its customer. The bank might be under a duty in an appropriate case to inform the court if documents were produced without the customer's knowledge, although on the facts of this case the customer was unable to show that the bank's failure to do so had caused him any loss.

1 Report of the Review Committee, Appendix Q.
2 Banking Act 1987, s 39; see *A v B Bank* [1992] 1 All ER 778, where it was held that the duty of disclosure imposed on the bank overrode an injunction prohibiting disclosure of documents.
3 At p 16.
4 *Parry-Jones v Law Society* [1969] 1 Ch 1, [1968] 1 All ER 177, CA.
5 *Barclays Bank plc v Taylor* [1989] 3 All ER 563, [1989] 1 WLR 1066, CA.
6 [1994] 1 WLR 1493.

29.2.4.2 *Commercial factors justifying disclosure*

The third exception is more controversial. It clearly will justify disclosure where, for instance, a bank sues its customer for repayment of sums advanced on overdraft, or where the customer sues the bank for dishonouring a cheque, and the bank needs to disclose the state of the account in its pleadings in order to support its case. It may also have a wider ambit: for instance, in *Sunderland v Barclays Bank*[1] it was held that the bank was entitled to disclose to the customer's husband that the customer's account was overdrawn in order to protect its commercial reputation when the customer unjustifiably complained that her cheques had been dishonoured. Certain dicta in the recent case of *Christofi v Barclays Bank plc* could be read as suggesting that it is for the bank to decide what is in its own interests. The customer's husband had been made bankrupt and the trustee in bankruptcy had registered a caution on property owned by the customer. The caution was warned off. In discussions with the trustee in bankruptcy the bank, which had a charge on its customer's property, disclosed that the caution had been warned off, as a result of which the trustee re-registered it. The Court of Appeal held that there was no breach on the facts because the trustee must be taken to have known that the caution had been warned off (he would have been notified by the Land Registry). However, Chadwick LJ indicated that disclosure might in any case have been justified as being in the bank's interest:

'... some banks might take the view that their commercial interests were best served by not telling a claimant that his claim is unprotected ... other banks

... might take a wider view of their commercial reputation ... Which view is to be taken in particular circumstances is of course a matter for the commercial judgment of the bank'[2].

This should not be taken as indicating that the bank has an unfettered discretion as to what its interests require. Indeed, it is questionable whether this falls within the scope of the exception recognised in *Tournier*, where Bankes LJ spoke of the bank's interests 'requiring' disclosure, suggesting that disclosure is only permitted where it is necessary in the bank's interests.

However, recent developments in the nature of banking business have created doubts about the extent of this exception: for instance, many banks now carry out a range of ancillary services, such as estate agency, insurance and financial services. Disclosure to a separate company, even though it may be a wholly owned subsidiary of the bank, clearly would involve a prima facie breach of the duty of confidentiality, because of the separate corporate identity of the subsidiary company[3]. A bank might wish to disclose information to subsidiaries, or to other divisions of the bank, for a wide range of purposes, including to assist in the marketing of the bank's services, and it is unclear if such disclosure would be covered by the rule permitting disclosure in the bank's interests, or on the basis that the customer gives implied consent to such disclosure, within the fourth exception. The Banking Code provides that banks will not use this exception to justify the disclosure of customers' accounts, names or addresses to any third party, including other companies within the same group, for marketing purposes.

Similar problems arise in relation to the practice of banks giving credit references on customers and the provision of information about customers to credit reference agencies. A business considering giving credit to a new customer may well wish to know if the customer is a safe credit risk, and it will generally be prudent to seek information about the potential customer's financial standing. The business may therefore ask its own bank to approach the new customer's bank and obtain a reference on the customer's financial viability. Banks normally comply with requests for such references on their customers provided the requests are made by another bank, and it has been assumed that the customer gives implied consent to the bank giving such references when he opens the account. However, this view seems to have been rejected by the Court of Appeal in *Turner v Royal Bank of Scotland plc*[4]. The bank there argued that the giving of credit references was justified by an implied term in the contract giving effect to the established usage of bankers. The Court of Appeal rejected that contention. There could not be an implied term based on a practice of which customers in general were ignorant. The giving of references in respect of personal customers is now covered by the Banking Code, under which banks undertake to tell the customer if they provide references and, where a reference is requested, only to give it if the customer gives written consent[5]. The bank giving such a reference owes a duty of care to the recipient of the reference[6] but may also owe a duty of care to its customer[7] and may be liable to its customer in defamation if it gives an unsatisfactory reference without justification. Such references are therefore normally couched in guarded language and are given subject to disclaimers of liability[8].

The expansion of credit in the economy has led to the growth in numbers of credit reference agencies whose function is to provide information about prospective borrowers to lenders. The activities of such agencies are subject to the supervision of the Data Protection Registrar and the Director General of Fair Trading under the Consumer Credit Act 1974[9]. Obviously, the banks are a major source of information about potential borrowers and their financial standing, and the question arises whether the disclosure of information about customers to credit reference agencies is justified within the *Tournier* exceptions. Many customers may feel some disquiet about such information being disclosed without their express consent; on the other hand, the government is anxious to encourage prudence in lending and borrowing, including proper use of credit reference agencies. Under the Banking Code the bank undertakes to its customer only to disclose information to credit reference agencies: (a) if it relates to an undisputed debt owed by the customer to the bank, no satisfactory proposals for payment have been made and 28 days' notice has been given to the customer; or (b) with the customer's consent[10].

1 [1938] 5 Legal Decisions Affecting Bankers 163.
2 [1999] 2 All ER (Comm) 417 at 425.
3 See *Bank of Tokyo v Karoon* [1987] AC 45n, [1986] 3 All ER 468, CA.
4 [1999] 2 All ER (Comm) 664.
5 Banking Code, para 4.5.
6 *Hedley Byrne & Co Ltd v Heller & Partners* [1964] AC 465, [1963] 2 All ER 575.
7 See *Spring v Guardian Royal Assurance plc* [1995] 2 AC 296, [1994] 3 All ER 129, where an employer was held to owe a duty of care to an employee when giving a reference.
8 Such disclaimers are only effective to the extent that they are reasonable under s 2 of the Unfair Contract Terms Act 1977: *Smith v Eric S Bush* [1990] 1 AC 831, [1989] 2 All ER 514, HL.
9 Section 25; see 24.3. The use of personal data held by the bank is also regulated by the Data Protection Act 1998. Under the Banking Code, banks undertake to explain to customers their right under Data Protection legislation to have access to their personal records held on computer files: para 4.4.
10 Banking Code, para 8.3.

29.3 Termination of the relationship

As we have seen, the bank has the authority of its customer to make payments in accordance with its mandate, and to collect payments for the customer's account, subject to the customer's right to withdraw the bank's mandate to make any individual payment by making an effective countermand of the relevant payment order[1]. In addition, the bank's mandate is, of course, terminated by the termination of the relationship of banker and customer, which may come about in a number of ways.

The relationship may be terminated automatically, in accordance with its terms. Thus, for instance, where the customer holds a fixed term deposit account, the relationship is terminated at maturity of the term. In other cases, the relationship may be determined by the parties. Where the terms of the contract place no restriction on repayment, as in the case of an ordinary current account, the sum deposited is repayable on demand, and the customer can terminate the relationship by demanding repayment and closing the account. However, the customer will not terminate the relationship by merely withdrawing the sum standing to the credit of the account without indicating an intention to close the account.

The bank can also terminate the relationship. However, as Atkin LJ explained in *Joachimson v Swiss Bank Corpn*[2], payments made by or to the customer may be in the process of collection for a period of several days, and closure of the account without notice might embarrass the customer, who might find his payment orders dishonoured as a result. The bank may therefore only terminate the relationship by giving notice to the customer. Where the Banking Code applies, the bank undertakes to give at least 30 days' notice before closing the customer's account, except in 'exceptional circumstances' such as fraud[3]. At common law, unless otherwise agreed, the bank must give reasonable notice. What is reasonable will be a question of fact in each case; the customer must be given sufficient notice to allow him to rearrange his affairs. In *Prosperity Ltd v Lloyds Bank Ltd*[4] one month's notice was held to be inadequate: the customer was an insurer who had instructed clients to make payments direct to his bank account. It has been held that, where an account is overdrawn, the bank does not terminate the relationship by demanding repayment, so that the bank may continue to charge compound interest on the sum outstanding on the account[5].

In addition, since the relationship is a personal one, it is terminated by the death or bankruptcy of the customer, or by the liquidation of a corporate customer or of the bank.

1   Above 2.5.2.
2   [1921] 3 KB 110 at 127, CA.
3   Banking Code, para 2.11.
4   (1923) 39 TLR 372.
5   *National Bank of Greece SA v Pinios Shipping Co* [1990] 1 AC 637, [1990] 1 All ER 78, HL.

29.4   Resolution of disputes

Obviously, disputes may arise in the course of the relationship between a bank and its customers. Such disputes will generally be dealt with in the first instance by a complaint to the local branch manager, and the vast majority of disputes will be settled by negotiation between bank and customer, either at branch or higher level. Under the Banking Code, banks undertake to inform customers of their procedures and how to use them[1].

If negotiation fails to achieve a satisfactory resolution of a dispute, either party may seek legal redress through the courts. However, the amount involved in the vast majority of banking transactions, particularly those involving individual, private customers, will be small, and will probably not justify incurring the legal costs of litigation. For such disputes there is now an alternative to litigation, via ombudsman schemes. Despite the similarity of the services provided by banks and building societies, particularly to private customers, there are currently two separate schemes for the different types of institution, but this will change in the near future when the Financial Services and Markets Act 2000 comes into force.

The Banking Ombudsman scheme was established in 1986[2]. Membership of the scheme is wholly voluntary[3] but banks which subscribe to the Banking Code are required to belong to the scheme or to the separate Building Society Ombudsman Scheme or to one of two approved arbitration schemes[4]. The ombudsman can hear claims brought by individuals, including traders, partnerships and even small companies (whose turnover does not exceed £1m per annum). The ombudsman has wide powers to investigate disputes and obtain information; he may seek to promote a settlement of the dispute, and, in the absence of agreement, may make recommendations for settlement on appropriate terms, including the payment of an award of up to £100,000, which may be binding on the bank concerned. The ombudsman is not bound to decide cases strictly according to law but will decide according to 'what is, in his opinion, fair in all the circumstances', taking into account, inter alia, 'general principles of good banking practice and any relevant code of practice'[5].

In contrast, the Building Society Ombudsman scheme was established under statute[6] and membership of the scheme is compulsory. However, the Building

Society Ombudsman has no power to make binding awards, and a building society may decline to comply with an award if it makes public its reasons for so doing.

Both ombudsmen have power to investigate and adjudicate in a wide range of disputes arising between customer and financial institution. To date, the biggest single class of complaint submitted to both ombudsmen has related to disputed automatic teller machine (ATM) transactions.

When the Financial Services and Markets Act 2000 comes into force, both the existing banking and building society ombudsmen schemes will be abolished. In their place the Act will establish a single Financial Services Ombudsman Scheme, covering all aspects of the financial services industry regulated by the Act. It is expected that the scheme will operate in much the same way as the existing schemes. It will be open both to private individuals and small businesses, which are expected to be defined as businesses with a turnover of less than £1m per annum *and* less than five employees. The ombudsman will have authority to decide cases in accordance with what he considers 'fair and reasonable', taking account not only of law but also of codes of practice and, it is proposed, 'good industry practice'. He will have power to award compensation up to a maximum of £100,000, and his decisions will be binding on the firm, but not on the customer who will retain the option of pursuing a claim before the court if dissatisfied with the ombudsman's decision.

1   Banking Code, paras 5.5, 5.6
2   See generally Seneviratne, James and Graham (1994) 13 CJQ 213.
3   The Review Committee on Banking Law and Services recommended that the Banking Ombudsman Scheme should be placed on a statutory footing: Report of the Review Committee, recommendation 15(1). However, this recommendation was rejected in the government's 1990 White Paper on Banking Law and Services.
4   Banking Code, para 5.9.
5   Terms of reference, para 14.
6   Pt IX of the Building Societies Act 1986.

Chapter 30

Bank Payment Orders

30.0 Payment orders

We have seen that a bank is its customer's debtor, and is obliged to obey the customer's orders to repay money or to make payments to third parties[1]. The customer may give such orders in a number of ways: by cheque, by orders to make payments through the bank giro credit transfer system, such as standing orders, direct debits and credit transfers, or by using electronic systems such as automated teller machines (ATMs) or electronic funds transfer (EFT).

The number of payments made through the banking system increased considerably during the twentieth century. Between 1988 and 1998 the number of payments through all systems, excluding credit and charge cards, increased from 5,234 million to 7,955 million[2], an increase of over 50%. Until recently, the most important bank payment method was the cheque. The Review Committee on Banking Law and Services reported that the number of cheques used increased approximately twelvefold between 1915 and 1987. The use of cheques is now in decline. In 1998, for the first time, the volume of cheque payments was exceeded by 'automated payments', including direct debits, direct credits and standing orders. Much of the decline in cheque usage can be attributed to the increased consumer use of plastic ATM and debit cards to obtain cash and to pay for purchases. The volume of debit card transactions, in particular, is growing significantly, with an increase from 10 million to 1,736 million transactions between 1988 and 1998[3]. On the other hand, cheques remain, for the present, the single most frequently used payment method and they continue to be widely used for business-to-business payments. These trends are expected to continue. In particular, it is anticipated that the use of direct payment methods, especially direct debits, and debit cards, especially for e-commerce, will grow. Nevertheless, cheques remain a vitally important part of commerce, and are likely to continue to play an important role, especially for higher value and business settlements, into the twenty-first century.

Most orders to make payments to third parties are processed through the clearing system. Orders are paid and collected by the banks of the payer and payee, the banks acting as agents for their respective customers. The clearing system facilitates the presentation and payment of individual payment orders: instead of paying each one individually, a daily account is drawn up showing all the mutual credits and debits between the participants; by setting off the debits against the credits, a balance of the net sum due from each participant to each of the others is produced, and only that balance is actually transferred between the banks, by a transfer between their accounts at the Bank of England. At present there are three different clearing systems in operation in Great Britain. Each system is operated by a separate company. In order to make use of the services of a clearing system, a financial institution must be a member of the system, membership being dependent on the institution satisfying certain criteria concerned, inter alia, with supervision and the volume of clearing business handled by the institution. Institutions which are not members of a particular system, including non-member UK-based institutions and overseas institutions, may make use of its facilities by employing member institutions as their agents. The three systems operate under the overall control of the Association for Payment Clearing Services (APACS), an unincorporated body set up in 1985 whose membership consists of all the members of the individual clearing systems.

The four systems currently in operation are:

(a) the Cheque and Credit Clearing Company Ltd, which handles bulk paper-based payment orders, including cheque clearances;
(b) the Clearing House Automated Payment System (CHAPS)[4]; CHAPS is an electronic system allowing same-day settlement of individual orders; originally it was only available for orders to pay sums in excess of £10,000 but it is now available for all payments without a lower financial limit;
(c) Bankers Automated Clearing Services Ltd (BACS), which operates a computerised settlement system for high volume[5], low value payments such as direct debits, standing orders, credit transfers for salary and wages payments etc.

Each of the different payment systems has its own legal rules and poses particular legal problems. We will examine the giro system and electronic funds transfer briefly below[6]. First, however, we must examine the law relating to cheques, not only because of the continuing importance of cheques in commercial activity, but also because the law relating to cheques is more developed than that relating to other instruments or payment systems.

1   See above 29.3.1.1.
2   Association for Payment Clearing Services, *Key Facts and Figures* (1999).
3   Ibid.
4   A separate system for individual high value payments within the City of London was abolished in 1995.
5   On a 'peak day' BACS handles up to 41 million transactions: Review Committee on Banking in the UK, *Competition in UK Banking* (2000) para 3.10.
6   At 30.3.2; 30.3.3.

30.0.1   *Regulation of payment networks*

The systems described above play a vital role in commercial and economic activity. 'Money transmission is a vital part of everyday life. Money flows continually between individuals, businesses and government; paying for goods and services for example, or in the form of taxes and wages[1].' In its report, *Competition in UK Banking*, the Review Committee on Banking in the UK subjected the operation of these systems to close scrutiny. It concluded that they tend to operate in an anti-competitive way. Non-members are at a significant disadvantage compared to members, and the rules on membership tend to inhibit new entrants to the market.

It also criticised the cost to customers of using some of the systems and some aspects of their operation, which it described as 'slow and inflexible'[2]. The committee concluded that reform of the systems was needed in the interests of competition and customers, and recommended the establishment of a payment systems commission (Paycom) to licence participants and oversee the operation of the payment systems, including ATM and credit card networks. The government indicated that it intends to accept and act on these proposals.

1   *Competition in UK Banking* (2000) para 3.1.
2   Paragraph 3.130.

30.1   Cheques

As we saw earlier, cheques were developed from the model of the bill of exchange and a cheque is defined as 'a bill of exchange drawn on a banker, payable on demand'[1]. Although there are certain special rules applicable to cheques but not to other types of bill of exchange, in general the law relating to bills applies to cheques. However, in many ways cheques are used very differently from other types of bills of exchange, and for this reason the Review Committee on Banking Law and Services recommended that the law relating to cheques should be separated from the general law relating to bills by passing a new 'Cheques and Bank Payment Orders Act'. This recommendation was not accepted by the government.

A cheque represents an order from the customer to the bank to pay money in accordance with the terms of the cheque. The customer may use the cheque either to withdraw cash or to make payment to a third party. The bank makes the payment out of its own funds and recoups the sum paid out by debiting the customer's account and so reducing the amount of its debt to the customer. Unlike other bills of exchange, a cheque is not presented to the drawee, the bank, for acceptance. The bank is therefore not legally obliged to the payee to honour the cheque. However, as we have noted earlier[2], provided there are sufficient funds credited to the account to meet them, the bank has a legal duty to its customer to honour cheques drawn on the account, unless the order to pay is countermanded before payment is complete[3] or the bank is prevented from making payment by some legal compulsion such as a garnishee order or freezing injunction[4].

The position of the bank is modified where the cheque is backed by a cheque guarantee card. Under a scheme drawn up by members of APACS, the banks undertake that they will honour any cheque, up to a stated maximum value, backed by such a card provided certain conditions are met. It is clear that, despite the name 'guarantee card', the bank's liability where a card is used is not as a guarantor or surety. The card constitutes an offer, by the bank, of a unilateral contract by which it undertakes to pay the cheque if the conditions are satisfied. That offer is conveyed to the payee by the drawer of the cheque acting as the bank's agent. It is clear that provided that the conditions on the card are met, the bank must honour the cheque even though there are insufficient funds in the customer's account. In *First Sport Ltd v Barclays Bank plc*[5] the Court of Appeal had to consider the bank's liability where the card was presented by someone other than the authorised signatory. Although the facts of the case were unclear, it seems that the card and a cheque book had been stolen and the card was used to guarantee a cheque taken from the stolen cheque book. The signature on the card had been altered but the alteration was not apparent, so that the signature on the card matched that on the cheque. The card set out five conditions to be satisfied on its presentation (see below), but also contained a statement that it could only be used by the authorised signatory. The bank argued that it had no liability to honour a cheque drawn by anyone other than the authorised signatory, but the Court of Appeal, despite a strong dissent by Kennedy LJ, held that it was bound. The majority held that, on the proper construction of the card, it was not a condition of the bank's offer that the card be used only by the authorised signatory: if it was, there would be no need to require the retailer to compare the signature on the card with that on the cheque. The tenor of the card was therefore that the retailer had to concern himself with appearances. Moreover, although only the authorised signatory had the bank's actual authority to convey the offer contained in the card, the effect of the wording on the card was to give apparent authority to any person in possession of the card to make that offer on behalf of the bank. The bank also argued that its offer only related to 'cheques' but that since a forged signature is a nullity[6] the 'cheque' in this case was not a bill of exchange and therefore not a cheque covered by the card. The majority also rejected that argument, refusing to give the word 'cheque' on the card its technical legal meaning. 'I would understand a cheque within the meaning of the bank's terms to be that which a reasonable seller would regard as such'[7].

From the perspective of commercial convenience there is much to be said for the decision of the majority in *First Sport*, which upholds the effectiveness of cheque guarantee cards. The conditions on the card in that case do suggest that the retailer was required to guard only against apparent forgeries, whereas the fraud in the particular case was undetectable. However, the reasoning used by the court is questionable. Apparent authority must be based on a representation by the 'principal' rather than the agent[8]. The bank here was held to have given apparent authority to the person presenting the card by virtue of the wording of the card; but that representation was only passed on to the retailer by the act of the person in possession presenting the card. The decision therefore comes close to permitting an apparent authority to be based on the false, and fraudulently self-serving, statement of the apparent agent. However, it is clear that the nature and extent of the bank's liability will depend on construction of the actual words used. The conditions now commonly include: (a) that the details on the cheque match those on the card – this normally means that the cheque must be on a printed form issued by the card issuing bank; (b) that the cheque is signed *by the person whose signature appears on the card* in the presence of the payee; (c) that the signature on the cheque matches that on the card; (d) that the card number is written on the back of the cheque by the payee; and (e) that only one cheque guaranteed by the card is used in respect of any particular transaction. The first three requirements are clearly intended to guard against fraud or use of the card by a thief; the fourth is intended to ensure that the payee does examine the cheque and card; and the fifth ensures that the financial limit on the bank's liability is not evaded by the customer drawing more than one cheque for one transaction. The card contains an expiry date which imposes a time limit on the bank's liability. The italicised words have been added since the decision in *First Sport* in an attempt to avoid the results of that decision. If a card is stolen from the cardholder and the cardholder's signature forged on a cheque, the conditions are not satisfied and the bank is not liable to honour the cheque. If, however, the card is stolen before it is signed by the cardholder and the thief signs the card, the position is not clear. It can be argued that if the thief signs a cheque, the cheque is signed by the person whose signature appears on the card; alternatively, it might be argued that since the signature on the card is not the thief's genuine signature, a cheque signed by the thief is not signed by the person whose 'signature' appears on the card.

The contract between the bank and customer under which the card is issued requires the customer not to issue cheques backed by the card unless there are adequate funds to meet them, and prevents the customer countermanding cheques supported by the card. It is generally assumed that this latter obligation is binding on the customer who, having authorised the bank to give its undertaking to pay the cheque on his behalf, is bound to indemnify the bank if it makes payment, so that any attempt by the customer to countermand a cheque supported by the card would be ineffective[9]. The bank can therefore ignore any purported countermand and, if it pays the cheque, debit the customer's account.

The bank has a legal obligation to its customer to honour cheques drawn on the account provided there are funds available to meet the cheque. Difficulties may arise where the customer draws a cheque against sums paid into the account before they are credited to the account. A bank is entitled to dishonour a cheque unless sufficient funds are credited to the customer's account to meet it when presented; there will generally be a lapse of time between a sum being paid in and it being credited to the customer's account, but a bank is entitled to a reasonable period in which to credit the account with sums paid in[10]. In fact, sums paid in are generally credited to the customer's account before they are actually cleared; if effects paid in, such as cheques, are subsequently dishonoured, the account will be debited with the appropriate amount. Whether or not a customer is entitled to draw cheques against uncleared effects is a question of fact, dependent on the intentions of the parties[11]; normally, deposit slips include a notice indicating that the bank reserves the right to refuse to pay cheques drawn against uncleared effects, but the bank may allow individual customers to draw against uncleared effects according to the branch manager's knowledge of the individual customer's credit record and reliability. The Banking Code requires banks to provide customers with information about when funds can be withdrawn against cheques paid into the customer's account[12]. If a customer is normally allowed to draw against uncleared effects, such practice may indicate the intention of the parties and override the notice on deposit slips.

If a bank wrongfully dishonours a cheque when there are funds available to meet it, the bank is liable to the customer for breach of contract. Until 1996 the rule was that the wrongful dishonour of a business customer's cheque would be presumed to cause the customer financial loss by implying that he is not creditworthy and thus damaging his reputation[13], but that no such presumption applied in the case of a private customer who could therefore recover only nominal damages unless he could prove that the wrongful dishonour caused him loss[14]. However, in *Kpohraror v Woolwich Building Society*[15] the Court of Appeal reconsidered the rule and concluded that the distinction between business and personal customers was no longer justified. As Evans LJ observed[16], an individual's credit rating is now as important for personal transactions such as mortgages, hire purchase and general banking, as it is for business purposes. It is now well known that records are kept of individuals' credit ratings and it is to be expected that if a person's cheque is dishonoured his ability to obtain credit will be damaged. If a cheque is wrongfully dishonoured, the customer is therefore entitled to damages for breach of contract without proof of loss, and regardless of his status as a business or personal customer. A customer who suffers actual quantifiable loss as a result of dishonour may recover additional damages to compensate for that loss, provided that it is not too remote in accordance with the general principles governing damages for breach of contract.

A bank which dishonours a cheque may also incur liability to its customer in defamation. Dishonoured cheques are normally returned to the payee with an indication of the reason for dishonour written or stamped on the face of the cheque. Words which incorrectly indicate that the drawer has insufficient funds credited to his account to meet the cheque will be defamatory, and it has been held that the words 'Refer to drawer' are therefore defamatory[17]. Banks therefore tend to give vague or ambiguous reasons for non-payment in an effort to avoid liability for defamation[18].

1 Bills of Exchange Act 1882, s 73.
2 See 29.3.1.1.
3 See 29.3.1.1; 30.1.5.
4 Formerly known as 'Mareva' injunctions: see 36.1.2.1.
5 [1993] 3 All ER 789.
6 Bills of Exchange Act 1882, s 24; see 28.4.3.
7 Per Bingham MR [1993] 3 All ER 789 at 800.
8 See 4.2.3.
9 See Ellinger and Lomnicka, *Modern Banking Law* (2nd edn, 1994) p 483.
10 *Marzetti v Williams* (1830) 1 B & Ad 415, where it was found as a fact that a delay of four hours was unreasonable.
11 *Rolin v Steward* (1854) 14 CB 595; *A L Underwood Ltd v Bank of Liverpool* [1924] 1 KB 775, CA.
12 Paragraph 1.1.
13 *Rolin v Steward* (1854) 14 CB 595.
14 *Gibbons v Westminster Bank Ltd* [1939] 2 KB 882.
15 [1996] 4 All ER 119.
16 [1996] 4 All ER 119 at 124.
17 *Jayson v Midland Bank Ltd* [1968] 1 Lloyd's Rep 409, CA.
18 In an Irish case, *T E Potterton Ltd v Northern Bank Ltd* [1993] 1 IR 413, it was held that a bank which dishonours a cheque owes a duty of care to the payee when notifying the reason for dishonour, so that the bank could be liable where the stated reason misled the payee in relation to the prospects of the cheque being paid and the drawer's solvency. It is not clear, however, that an English court would recognise a duty of care in this situation: see Ellinger [1995] JBL 583.

30.1.1   *The use of cheques*

As we have noted, cheques may be used by the customer both to withdraw cash from the account, and to make payments to third parties. In either role, the cheque is a bill of exchange and as such is governed by the law applicable to bills, as modified by special provisions applicable to cheques. However, as we noted above, cheques tend to be used differently from other bills. In particular, although a cheque is a negotiable instrument, cheques are rarely negotiated in modern practice (except where a cheque is drawn in favour of a person who has no bank account, in which case the payee may negotiate the cheque in order to obtain cash). In general, cheques are used merely as a convenient alternative to cash[1]. The negotiability of a cheque can be restricted by crossings, but crossings are not fully understood by most cheque users. It has therefore been argued that the negotiability of cheques in modern practice serves little purpose and generally only facilitates fraud. This has led some commentators to argue that the law of cheques should be separated from that governing bills[2]. The Review Committee on Banking Law and Services recommended that a new form of payment instrument, a bank payment order, should be created and given statutory status[3]. Such a payment order would be non-transferable, and therefore give protection against some forms of fraud. However, this recommendation was not accepted by the government[4] on the grounds that it might cause greater confusion about the use of cheques. The government expressed a preference for clarifying the law relating to cheques in general, and in particular to the problems of crossings on cheques, and some of the proposed changes were made by the Cheques Act 1992.

1   As recognised, for other purposes, by the Court of Appeal in *D & C Builders Ltd v Rees* [1966] 2 QB 617, [1965] 3 All ER 837.
2   See Cranston, *Principles of Banking Law* (1997) p 279.
3   Report of the Review Committee, Recommendation 7(7).
4   White Paper on Banking Law and Services, para 5.3.

30.1.2   *Payment of cheques*

The payee of a cheque may obtain payment of the sum ordered by the cheque in any one of three ways. As a bill of exchange, the cheque can be presented to the drawee for payment in cash. Thus the payee can take the cheque and present it in person to the bank upon which it is drawn. Presentation must be at the branch where the drawer's account is held[1]. In most cases this will be impractical and instead the payee will use his own bank as agent to present the cheque on his behalf. In this case the cheque is presented to the drawee bank through the clearing system, and the amount of the cheque is credited to the payee's account by his bank. As a further alternative, the payee may transfer the cheque to a third party in return for an immediate cash payment, in the same way that other bills are discounted. A cheque may be discounted in this way to a bank, which therefore buys the cheque and presents it for payment on its own behalf as holder. Since it is now possible for a person to pay effects to the credit of his account at another branch, or even at a different bank from the one where his account is held, this method of obtaining payment, by discounting, is generally used by payees who do not have bank accounts. It is much less common now than formerly since most standard cheque forms are now printed in such a way that they are not transferable[2].

Although the payee may have a choice as to which method to use to obtain payment of a cheque drawn in his favour, that choice may be restricted by a crossing or other marking on the cheque.

1   Bills of Exchange Act 1882, s 45(4).
2   As a result of the Cheques Act 1992: see 30.1.3. This causes problems for payees who do not have bank accounts: see McLeod (1997) 113 LQR 133.

30.1.3   *Crossings on cheques*

As noted above, as a bill of exchange, a cheque is normally negotiable; but negotiability exposes the holder or payee to the risk of theft or fraud. Crossings or other writing on a cheque may be used to restrict the transfer, or method of presentation, of a cheque, and thus as a protection against fraud or theft. The effect of a crossing will depend on the form of the crossing.

The simplest form of crossing is a general crossing. A cheque may be crossed generally by drawing two parallel lines across its face; the words 'and company' (or any abbreviation such as '& Co') may be added between the lines[1]. Many cheques are printed with such crossings on them. If a cheque is generally crossed it must be presented for payment through a bank account: the holder cannot present it in person for cash. Alternatively, a cheque may be specially crossed, in which case the name of a particular bank is added between the crossing lines. The effect of a special crossing is that the cheque may only be presented for payment through the bank named in the crossing.

A cheque crossed generally or specially may be additionally crossed with the words 'not negotiable'. The effect of such a crossing is to prevent the negotiation of the cheque. It does not, contrary to the expectation of some cheque users, prevent the transfer of the cheque, but means that, if the cheque is transferred, the transferee can acquire no better title than the transferor had[2]. 'Everyone who takes a cheque marked "not negotiable" takes it at his own risk, and his title to the money got by its means is as defective as his title to the cheque itself'[3].

Cheques are often crossed with the words 'Account payee only'. Prior to 1992, the effect of such a crossing was not entirely clear, but the better view was that (contrary to the belief of many cheque users) it did not prevent the transfer of the cheque[4], although it might act as a warning to the collecting bank that the cheque should only be collected for the account of the named payee and as a 'red flag' to anyone to whom the cheque was transferred. The effects would be (a) that a transferee of the cheque would not be able to qualify as holder in due course[5] and (b) that a bank which collected the cheque for anyone other than the named payee would not be protected by the statutory provisions which protect collecting bankers and would be liable in conversion if it collected it for anyone other than the true owner. A cheque could be made non-transferable if it were expressly marked 'not transferable' or made payable to a named payee 'only' rather than to the named payee 'or order'[6].

The position has now been changed by the Cheques Act 1992, which inserted a new s 81A into the Bills of Exchange Act 1882 to bring the law into line with common expectations by providing that a cheque crossed 'account payee' or 'a/c payee', with or without the addition of the word 'only', is not transferable. Many banks now issue private customers with books of cheques printed with the crossing 'account payee only'. As a result, most standard printed cheques are now, in effect, non-transferable. A customer who wants a transferable cheque can, of course, ask the bank for a book of uncrossed cheque forms. Alternatively, it is possible for the customer to restore the transferability of an 'a/c payee only' cheque by cancelling the printed crossing. It remains possible to make cheques non-transferable by drawing them marked 'not transferable' or payable to a named payee 'only'.

A bank which pays a crossed cheque other than in accordance with the crossing may be liable to the true owner of the cheque for any loss caused by its payment[7]. The only exception is that where a cheque is presented for payment and does not appear to be crossed or to have a crossing which has been obliterated or altered in a way not authorised by the Act, the bank incurs no liability if it pays the cheque in good faith and without negligence. In addition, if the bank pays other than in accordance with a crossing, it may not debit its customer's account, since it has no authority to pay other than in accordance with the crossing[8]. A cheque may be crossed by the drawer; in addition, the holder of a cheque may cross it, or alter the crossing so as to make it more restrictive[9]. Thus a holder may cross an uncrossed cheque, or convert a general crossing to a special one; and the banker to whom a cheque is specially crossed may add the name of another bank to act as its agent in presenting the cheque. Such an alteration, which further restricts the payment of the cheque, cannot prejudice the position of the drawer or of any prior party. However, subject to this exception, a crossing is a material part of the cheque[10], so that if the crossing is altered, the cheque may be avoided by an apparent alteration to the crossing[11]; if the alteration is not apparent, the bank may pay in accordance with the apparent tenor of the cheque.

The 1992 Act was intended to help protect against fraud. It was generally welcomed by consumer groups: it is obviously unsatisfactory that the law should fail to accord with the expectations and understanding of cheque users. However, it has been pointed out that it will impose a burden on the banking system without giving significant benefits to the drawers of cheques[12]. A paying bank cannot be sure at the time of payment that the cheque is being collected for the named payee, while a collecting bank will no longer be able to collect a cheque drawn 'a/c payee only' for itself as holder in due course[13]. Moreover, now that 'a/c payee only' cheques are the norm, most cheques are effectively non-transferable. This creates problems for the small but significant minority of the population who do not have a bank account[14]. The reform will prevent some forms of cheque fraud: a person who steals a cheque will not be able to indorse it, either to himself for collection or to an innocent third party (provided the third party is aware of the law). The Act will not, however, prevent a thief cashing a stolen cheque by opening an account in the name of the payee, or by altering the name of the payee.

It will be recalled that the Review Committee on Banking Law and Services recommended the introduction of a wholly new non-transferable payment order to deal with some of the problems of cheque fraud. The government rejected that proposal, preferring to reform the law of cheques. Ironically the effect of the 1992 Act and the commercial response to it is that for all practical purposes standard cheques have become non-transferable payment orders[15].

1   Bills of Exchange Act 1882, s 76.
2   Bills of Exchange Act 1882, s 81.
3   Per Lord Lindley in *Great Western Rly Co v London and County Banking Corpn* [1901] AC 414 at 424.
4   *National Bank v Silke* [1891] 1 QB 435; cf *Dungravin Trust (Pty) Ltd v Imperial Refrigeration Co (Pty) Ltd* [1971] 45 ALR 300.
5   See 28.3.2.3.
6   See 28.3. Marking an uncrossed cheque 'not negotiable' may also make it non-transferable; see *Hibernian Bank v Gysin and Hanson* [1939] 1 KB 483.
7   Bills of Exchange Act 1882, s 79.
8   *Bobbett v Pinkett* (1876) 1 Ex D 368.
9   Bills of Exchange Act 1882, s 77.
10 Bills of Exchange Act 1882, s 78.
11 Bills of Exchange Act 1882, s 64; see 28.5.5.
12 Ellinger (1992) 108 LQR 15.
13 Hooley [1992] CLJ 432; see 30.2.5.
14 See McLeod (1997) 113 LQR 133. Partly to meet the needs of such payees a new form of 'cheque cashing' business has developed. A cheque casher will buy a crossed cheque for cash. The cheque casher will normally take additional steps to ensure that the cheque will not be dishonoured: see McLeod (1997) 113 LQR 133.
15 It may be argued that, as a result, they are no longer bills of exchange in any real sense: see McLeod (1997) 113 LQR 133.

30.1.4   *The clearing system*

As noted above[1], there are actually three different clearing systems, set up to deal with different types of payment order. We are here concerned with the cheque clearing system.

A cheque must be presented for payment to the bank on which it is drawn at the branch where the drawer's account is held[2]. When a customer pays in a cheque drawn in his favour at his bank, the bank acts as his agent to present the cheque for payment. Presentation is effected through the clearing system[3]. The system was developed in the eighteenth century. Banks collecting cheques drawn on other banks for their customers would send messengers to other banks with a bundle of cheques for payment. The messengers adopted a practice of meeting together and exchanging cheques for payment. The meeting place became the clearing house. For over 150 years this was at 10 Lombard Street, but in the late 1980s it was moved to premises in Goodman's Fields. Cheques are taken to the central clearing house and there exchanged to be presented for payment.

Most cheques and other paper-based payment orders are presented through the general clearing system[4]. The payee of a cheque pays it in at his bank for collection; as an alternative, the payee may pay it in at any other bank, since, under a series of agreements, the banks have agreed to act as each other's agents in collecting cheques for customers, using the bank giro system. The branch where the cheque is paid in will credit the customer's account and then send the cheque to its clearing department in London for collection. The clearing department will then pass it, in the clearing house, to the clearing department of the drawee bank. The cheque is there processed by computer – details of the drawee's bank and account number are encoded on the cheque in magnetic ink, and the amount of the cheque is normally copied onto it in magnetic ink to allow computerised processing – in order to pass a message to the drawer's bank to debit his account, and to calculate the amount due to the payee's bank. Settlement between the drawer's and payee's bank takes place at this stage: the two banks will produce a list of mutual credits and debits representing effects processed that day; the debits and credits are set off against each other to produce a settlement figure and settlement is effected by a transfer between the accounts of the two banks at the Bank of England.

In *Barclays Bank Ltd v Bank of England*[5] it was held that, for the purposes of s 45 of the Bills of Exchange Act 1882, a cheque had to be physically presented at the branch of the drawer's bank where his account is held, where the decision whether or not to honour the cheque would be taken by checking the details on the cheque, including the signature, and that there are funds available to meet it[6]. Physical transmission of the cheque to the drawer's branch was therefore required to complete the process. This requirement prevented the use of electronic methods of cheque presentation, or 'truncation', of cheques. There was concern that this caused unnecessary delays in the process of cheque clearance and placed British banks at a disadvantage vis-à-vis their continental counterparts, who were already making use of cheque truncation and electronic presentation. The Review Committee on Banking Services Law and Practice recommended that the law be changed to permit cheque truncation[7] and in 1996 regulations[8] were introduced to make the necessary amendments to the Bills of Exchange Act. A bank may now publish details of an address at which all cheques drawn on it may be presented for payment and a cheque presented at that address is deemed to have been presented at the proper address for the purposes of the Act[9]. The need for physical presentation at the branch where the drawer's account is held is therefore removed. Moreover, the Act now provides that a cheque may be presented electronically by a message containing details of the 'essential features' of the cheque (the sort code of the bank on which it is drawn, account number, cheque number and amount for which it is drawn)[10]. The paying bank is entitled to request physical presentation of the cheque – for instance, if it suspects that the cheque is forged or has been altered[11].

The objective of the 1996 regulations was to permit electronic presentation of cheques and to speed up the process of cheque clearing. The banks have developed a computerised data exchange system to allow for the exchange of digitised cheque information[12]. In fact, however, full truncation has not been introduced and most cheques are still physically presented, albeit at the paying bank's clearing centre rather than at the branch where the drawer's account is held. As a result, the clearing cycle still normally takes three days. If the cheque is not honoured for any reason, the drawer's bank must return it to the payee's bank at the branch where his account is held before the end of the third day of the cycle. Since the cheque will already have been credited to the payee's account and included in the settlement between the banks, adjustments will have to be made to both accounts to take account of the dishonour[13].

Where the payee banks with the bank on which a cheque is drawn there will be no need for the cheque to pass through the whole clearing process. If the cheque is drawn on a different branch from that where it is paid in, it will have to be sent through the system to the bank's clearing centre. Where payee and drawer have their accounts at the same branch and the cheque is paid in there, the whole process will be dealt with within the branch.

1   See 30.0.
2   Bills of Exchange Act 1882, s 45.
3   The system and its development are described by Bingham J in *Barclays Bank Ltd v Bank of England* [1985] 1 All ER 385 at 387.
4   The procedure is different where drawer and payee both use the same bank.
5   [1985] 1 All ER 385.
6   In practice this may be a formality. The computerised processing of the cheque will check the availability of funds and the cheque will only be considered by the branch manager if the computer shows there are insufficient funds. Only cheques over a certain value will be checked for regularity.
7   Report of the Review Committee on Banking Law and Services, p 56. The recommendation was accepted by the government: White Paper on Banking Law and Services, para 5.13.
8   Deregulation (Bills of Exchange) Order 1996, SI 1996/2993.
9   BoEA 1882, s 74A.
10 BoEA 1882, s 74B.
11 BoEA 1882, s 74B(3). Such a request does not amount to a dishonour of the cheque: s 74B(4).
12 Known as 'Inter Bank Data Exchange' (IBDE), set up in 1996.
13 The Review of Banking Services in the UK was particularly critical in its report of the length of time taken to clear payments in the UK system, arguing that it compares unfavourably with the systems in other countries and causes unnecessary costs to bank customers: see *Competition in UK Banking*, paras 3.131–3.135.

30.2   The legal position of banks involved in clearing

As we have noted, although cheques are rarely negotiated in modern practice, their negotiable status creates great potential for fraud. Where cheques are presented for payment through the clearing system, both paying and collecting banks may be exposed to legal liabilities. A bank which pays a cheque without its customer's mandate generally has no right to debit the customer's account, but it may incur liability for wrongful dishonour if it dishonours a cheque drawn on it. Moreover, a bank which pays or collects a cheque for someone other than the true owner may incur liability to the true owner. The enormous increase in the use of banking facilities and cheque use, coupled with the change in the relationship between banks and their customers, in recent years, has greatly increased the risk of liability. However, a number of defences may be available to paying and collecting banks in order to protect them against liability.

30.2.1   *The paying bank*

A bank on which a cheque is drawn must not pay other than in accordance with the customer's mandate and must only pay exactly in accordance with the mandate.

Prima facie, therefore, it has no right to debit its customer's account if it pays a cheque in any of the following situations:

(a) if the drawer's signature is forged, or unauthorised;
(b) if the cheque has been materially altered without the drawer's authority[1];
(c) if it pays an order cheque to a person whose title depends on a forged indorsement;
(d) if it pays after an effective countermand by the customer; or
(e) if it pays to anyone other than the true owner, for instance if the cheque is stolen from the true owner.

In addition, if it makes payment other than to the true owner of the cheque, the bank may be held liable in conversion to the true owner. It is sometimes said that a bank may incur double liability in such cases, by being liable to the true owner in conversion and unable to debit the customer's account. However, it seems that the bank will only be liable in conversion where it makes, or is deemed to have made, payment in due course and so discharges the cheque and destroys its value[2]. This will be the case when the cheque is drawn, or indorsed, to bearer: any bearer of such a cheque is the holder of it, and only payment to the holder is payment in due course[3]. In this case, since the cheque is paid to the holder, the bank's payment is a payment in due course and discharges the drawer from liability to the holder; the bank should therefore be entitled to debit the drawer's account, since otherwise he would be unjustly enriched. This could be achieved, notwithstanding the lack of mandate for the payment, by allowing the bank to be subrogated to the rights of the holder of the cheque, whose claim its payment extinguishes[4].

Where the cheque is payable to order, neither a thief nor any person claiming through him can be a holder and therefore payment to such a person, whose title must rest on a forged indorsement, will not be payment in due course; the cheque will therefore remain enforceable by the true owner. However, if the bank in good faith and in the ordinary course of business makes such a payment to a person whose title depends on a forged or unauthorised indorsement, it is deemed to have paid in due course, and thus discharges the cheque[5].

If this analysis is correct, the bank should never incur double liability. Where it pays someone other than the true owner, its liability will depend on whether the cheque was payable to bearer or to order. Where the cheque was payable to bearer, the bank will be liable to the true owner, but entitled to debit the customer's account. Where the cheque was payable to order, the bank may only debit the customer's account if it is deemed to have paid in due course, but where the payment is not deemed to be in due course, will incur no liability to the true owner.

In most cases, therefore, the greatest risk to a paying bank is of liability to its customer for payment contrary to the mandate. Liability both for breach of mandate and for the tort of conversion is strict; however, a number of limited defences are available to a paying bank at common law, and these are supplemented by three statutory provisions designed to protect paying banks. As a result, the bank may avoid liability to both the true owner and the customer.

---

1   See 28.5.5.
2   See Ellinger, *Modern Banking Law*, pp 287–289.
3   See 28.6.1; if the holder satisfies the other requirements and qualifies as a holder in due course he will be the true owner of the cheque: see 28.3.3.2.
4   See Goode, *Commercial Law* (2nd edn, 1995) p 619.
5   Bills of Exchange Act 1882, s 60: see 30.2.3.

30.2.2   *Common law restrictions on the bank's liability*

The bank's position vis-à-vis its customer may be modified by many of the rules we have already examined. Thus although it has no mandate to debit the customer's account on the strength of a forged or unauthorised signature, it may be able to do so if the customer is estopped from setting up the forgery for lack of authority, either as a result of an express or implied representation[1] or as a result of a breach of the customer's duty of care[2]. As we have seen, the customer's duty of care is extremely limited[3]: it has been said that it does not extend to care of the cheque book[4]. A notice is normally included on the inside cover of a cheque book, warning the customer to take care of the cheque book and not to keep any cheque card with the book, but that is probably insufficient to make it a term of the contract that the customer should take care in safeguarding the cheque book. The Banking Code[5] emphasises that 'the care of your cheque book . . . is essential . . . Please ensure that you do not keep your cheque book and cards together'. However, even if it can be argued that the Code is contractually binding on the bank, it would be difficult to argue that it is so binding on the customer. Moreover, the relevant passage uses the language of a request ('please ensure that . . .') and would seem to be inappropriate to impose a contractual obligation. Cheque cards are normally issued subject to express conditions of use which include an express requirement that the customer take care of the card and cheques. Where the customer negligently fails to take care of either in breach of such a contract, his negligence may give rise to an estoppel, but since the bank's liability for breach of mandate is strict, it cannot provide a partial defence of contributory negligence[6].

Where the bank makes a payment which discharges a liability of the customer, the bank may be entitled to recover the amount paid from the customer even if the payment was outside its mandate: the bank is entitled to be subrogated to the rights of the recipient of the payment, otherwise the customer would be unjustly enriched[7].

Where a cheque is altered it is void, except that a holder in due course may enforce it in accordance with its original tenor where the alteration is not apparent[8]. If the bank honours a cheque which has been materially altered it therefore, prima facie, has no right to debit its customer's account[9]. The customer may be estopped from relying on the alteration if it was facilitated by the way he drew the cheque[10]. Alternatively, it may be that if the bank makes payment to a holder in due course it is entitled to debit the customer in accordance with the original mandate. On this basis, if a cheque is altered so as to increase the amount, the bank would have no mandate to debit the customer the altered amount but, if it could establish that it made payment to a holder in due course it might be possible to argue that it had thereby discharged a liability of its customer and should be entitled to debit the customer the amount for which the cheque was originally drawn, on the basis that the holder could have enforced the cheque against the customer for that amount. The bank is therefore entitled to be subrogated to the claim against it on the basis described above. However, this may be doubted. Even if correct, it will be of very limited application. Since most cheques are now drawn so as to be non-transferable, they cannot be negotiated and as a result no one can qualify as a holder in due course.

Where the bank makes an unauthorised payment, it may be able to recover the sum paid from the payee or from his bank, as money paid under a mistake[11]. Where the money is paid to the recipient's bank, it can be recovered from the collecting bank at any time before it releases the funds to its customer; where the money is in the hands of the recipient customer, it is recoverable unless the recipient received the payment in good faith and even then provided he has not changed his position following receipt so that repayment would be inequitable[12]. The most obvious type of mistake will be where the bank pays on a cheque bearing a forged signature, wrongly believing that it has its client's mandate to pay.

The basis of recovery is restitutionary. The bank cannot recover on this basis if its payment was authorised, as, for instance, where it has its customer's mandate but does not intend to pay because there are insufficient funds standing to the credit of the customer's account[13], and discharges a debt owed by the customer. The payee will then be taken to have provided consideration for the payment and/or to have changed position by discharging the debt.

1   *Brown v Westminster Bank Ltd* [1964] 2 Lloyd's Rep 187.
2   *Greenwood v Martins Bank Ltd* [1933] AC 51, HL; above 29.3.3.
3   *Tai Hing Cotton Mill Ltd v Liu Chong Hing Bank Ltd* [1986] AC 80, [1985] 2 All ER 947, PC.
4   See *Bank of Ireland v Evans Trustees* (1855) 5 HL Cas 389; *Lewes Sanitary Steam Co Ltd v Barclay & Co Ltd* (1906) 95 LT 444. Similarly, it has been held that there is no implied contractual or tortious duty of care which requires a customer who buys travellers' cheques to take care of them: *El Awadi v Bank of Credit and Commerce International SA* [1990] 1 QB 606, [1989] 1 All ER 242.
5   Paragraph 4.8.
6   See 2.10.3.1 and 29.3.3; Law Com 219, Contributory Negligence as a Defence in Contract Law (1993).
7   *B Liggett (Liverpool) Ltd v Barclays Bank Ltd* [1928] 1 KB 48; but see Goff and Jones, *The Law of Restitution* (5th edn, 1998) p 156.
8   See 28.5.5.
9   *Yorkshire Bank plc v Lloyds Bank plc* [1999] 2 All ER (Comm) 153.
10 *London Joint Stock Bank v Macmillan and Arthur* [1918] AC 777, HL; see 29.3.3.
11 The money may now be recovered whether the mistake was one of fact or law: *Kleinwort Benson Ltd v Lincoln City Council* [1998] 4 All ER 513.
12 See *Barclays Bank Ltd v W J Simms Ltd* [1980] QB 677, [1979] 3 All ER 522; *Lipkin Gorman v Karpnale Ltd* [1991] 2 AC 548, above 28.6.1.
13 *Lloyds TSB plc v Independent Insurance Co Ltd* [1999] 1 All ER (Comm) 8.

30.2.3   *Statutory defences for the paying banker*

The common law thus gives the paying bank a limited degree of protection against liability in respect of payments made without its customer's mandate. However, as we have seen, where the bank pays someone other than the true owner, it will normally either be liable to the true owner or be unable to debit its customer's account; yet this is the very situation where the bank is least likely to be at fault. After all, if a cheque is stolen and presented for payment by the thief, or by someone claiming title through him, the bank is unlikely to have any means of checking the identity of the person on whose behalf the cheque is presented for payment if it is presented through the clearing system. For this reason, there are a series of statutory defences which provide the paying bank with a considerable measure of protection against liability in this situation. Unfortunately, the law is unnecessarily complicated by the fact that the protection has developed in a piecemeal fashion: protection is provided by three different provisions which overlap to some degree and yet which provide protection subject to different criteria. For this reason it has been recommended that the three defences be consolidated and be based on similar criteria[1].

The first of the existing provisions is contained in s 60 of the Bills of Exchange Act 1882. This provision, which derives from one originally in s 19 of the Stamp Act 1853, protects the paying banker where it makes payment to a person who has no title to the cheque because his title depends on a forged or unauthorised indorsement; a bank paying such a cheque, either through the clearing system or over the counter, has no way of checking the validity of prior indorsements made by persons other than its own customer. The section does not apply if, for instance, a person steals a cheque payable to order and obtains payment by pretending to be the payee. In order to obtain the protection of the section, the bank must pay the cheque in good faith and in the ordinary course of business. If the section applies, the bank is deemed to have paid the cheque in due course and is thus entitled to debit its customer's account. The importance of s 60 is now reduced, since most cheques are now drawn 'a/c payee only' and are therefore non-transferable, rather than payable 'to order' as required by s 60.

As an alternative, the bank may be able to rely on the defence provided by s 80 of the Bills of Exchange Act 1882, which derives from s 9 of the Crossed Cheques Act 1876. This provision recognises that where a cheque is presented for payment through the clearing system, the paying bank has no way of verifying the identity of the person on whose behalf it is collected. The section therefore provides that where a bank pays a generally or specially crossed cheque in accordance with the crossing and acts in good faith and without negligence, it is placed in the same position as if it had paid the true owner. It will be recalled that a generally crossed cheque requires payment to be made through a bank, a specially crossed cheque requires payment to be made through a named bank. The effect of s 80 is that the paying bank is only concerned to see that payment is made to a bank in accordance with the crossing. It therefore protects the bank in cases where it pays a stolen cheque in ignorance of the theft. Section 80 offers wider protection than s 60, since it entitles the bank to debit its customer's account and protects it against liability to the true owner. Moreover, if the cheque has come into the hands of the true payee prior to payment, s 80 also protects the drawer in the same way, so that he is discharged from liability. The true owner is therefore left to pursue the recipient of payment in an action for money had and received. Section 80 only applies where the bank pays a crossed cheque, but by an amendment introduced by the Cheques Act 1992 a crossed cheque includes 'a cheque which under s 81A or otherwise is not transferable'. The effect of this amendment is unclear. On one reading it extends the effect of s 80 to uncrossed but non-transferable cheques; however, an alternative and perhaps more likely reading of the section would be that it simply makes clear that s 80 applies to crossed but non-transferable cheques[2].

There is clearly a large measure of overlap between the protection offered by s 60 and s 80. It is therefore surprising that they depend on different criteria. In particular, it is unclear whether there is any difference between the requirement in s 60 that the paying bank should act in the ordinary course of business and that in s 80 that it should act without negligence. There are dicta that the two requirements are not the same[3] but, in view of the interpretation given to negligence in this and similar contexts, it is likely that a banker will often be negligent if he fails to act in accordance with ordinary banking practice[4]. However, a bank may be outside the ordinary course of business even if it is not negligent: many of the cases on 'ordinary course of business' are concerned with such matters as payment of cheques outside normal banking hours. The Review Committee on Banking Law and Services therefore recommended that the requirement that the bank act in the ordinary course of business be removed and that all the statutory defences be available where the bank acts in good faith without negligence, and this recommendation was accepted by the government[5].

There may be a further difference between ss 60 and 80. Both sections allow the bank to debit its customer's account, but it is not clear that both protect the bank against liability to the true owner in conversion. Section 80 provides that, where its requirements are fulfilled, the bank 'shall be entitled to the same rights and be placed in the same position as if payment . . . had been made to the true owner'. This seems sufficient to protect the bank against liability to the true owner. In contrast, where the requirements of s 60 are fulfilled, the bank is deemed to have paid in due course, thus discharging the cheque. It is therefore entitled to debit its customer's account but it is not clear if it is protected against liability to the true owner. One might expect that if s 60 were intended to provide such protection it would use the same language as s 80. The difference in wording may be explained by the fact that the two sections are derived from provisions in two separate earlier pieces of legislation[6], but it may nevertheless be that s 60 does not protect the bank against the true owner. Where s 60 applies, it is the fact that the bank is deemed to have paid in due course which discharges the cheque and thus gives rise to a potential conversion claim: where s 60 does not apply, the true owner will be entitled to recover the cheque and enforce it. On this interpretation the effect of s 60 would therefore be to put a bank which pays an order cheque payable on demand into the same position as a bank which pays a bearer cheque: it is entitled to debit its customer's account but remains liable to the true owner of the cheque[7]. Section 60, unlike s 80, applies to cases where the cheque is paid over the counter as well as where it is paid through clearing, and where an order cheque is paid over the counter the bank is exposed to the same risk as where it pays a bearer cheque.

Further protection is offered by s 1 of the Cheques Act 1957. The Act was passed on the recommendation of the Committee on Cheque Indorsements[8] to remove the need for cheques to be indorsed at the counter when presented for payment or paid in for collection. It provides that if a bank pays a cheque in good faith and in the ordinary course of business, it incurs no liability by reason only of the absence of, or irregularity of, an indorsement, and is deemed to have paid in due course. The protection of the section is extended, by s 1(2), to certain other instruments, including 'cheques' made payable to cash[9]. Section 1 alone offers no protection in the case of a forged indorsement: the bank must then rely on s 60 of the 1882 Act. Moreover, it seems that the Act only applies to remove the need for an indorsement by the person presenting the cheque for payment; it will not protect the bank if one indorsement in a chain is missing: payment of a cheque in such circumstances would almost certainly be negligent and not in the ordinary course of business. Although the 1957 Act was intended to remove the need for indorsements, a circular issued in 1957 by the Committee to Clearing Bank Managers requires indorsements in certain circumstances, including where the cheque is presented for cash payment at the counter or where the cheque has a receipt for payment attached. A bank which paid in contravention of the circular would not be acting within the ordinary course of business and so would be unprotected by s 1.

1 Report of the Review Committee on Banking Law and Services, para 7.26; the recommendation has been accepted by the government.
2 Contrast Hooley [1992] CLJ 432 at 434.
3 *Carpenters' Co v British Mutual Banking Co* [1938] 1 KB 511, CA (Mackinnon LJ dissenting); *Baines v National Provincial Bank Ltd* (1927) 32 Com Cas 216.
4 See Ellinger, *Modern Banking Law* (2nd edn, 1994) p 379.
5 White Paper, Annex 5, para 5.9.
6 Section 60 from s 19 of the Stamp Act 1853; s 80 from the Crossed Cheques Act 1876.
7 Contrast Goode, *Commercial Law* (2nd edn, 1995) pp 611–612.
8 Cmnd 3 (1956).
9 Such instruments are not bills, since no payee is named, and are therefore not cheques.

30.2.4   *The collecting bank*

A bank which collects a cheque through clearing may also be exposed to liability. If it collects the cheque for anyone other than its true owner, it may be liable in conversion to the true owner; damages for conversion will normally be the face value of the cheque[1]. Alternatively, where the bank has received payment, the true owner may waive the tort of conversion and sue the bank instead for the amount of the cheque in an action for money had and received. However, where the bank collects the cheque for its customer, it will not be liable for money had and received if it pays the funds out to the customer, or otherwise changes its position, before the true owner's claim is brought. Liability in both actions is strict. Since the measure of recovery is the same in both actions, in most cases the true owner will prefer the action in conversion.

The bank's liability is to the true owner of the cheque. Where a cheque is stolen from the payee, the true owner will be the payee. However, where a signed cheque is stolen from the drawer, or where the drawer's signature is forged, or placed on the cheque without authority, the drawer will be the true owner.

The basis of the bank's liability is collection of the cheque on behalf of a person who has no title to it. The perilousness of the bank's position can be appreciated by considering that the bank will be liable to the drawer if it collects a cheque for the named payee where the cheque was obtained by duress or misrepresentation and the drawer has rescinded the contract prior to collection.

1   This is criticised by Ellinger and Lomnicka, *Modern Banking Law* (2nd edn, 1994) p 505, who point out that the cheque might not be honoured on presentation, so that the true owner may obtain a windfall. Where the cheque has been altered before being presented for collection the bank is liable but only for nominal damages, on the grounds that the alteration renders the cheque void (BoEA 1882, s 64) and therefore worthless: *Smith v Lloyds TSB Group plc* [2000] 2 All ER (Comm) 693.

30.2.5   *Defences available to the collecting banker*

At common law a bank collecting cheques for its customers is therefore exposed to a considerable legal risk. It would clearly be impractical for a bank always to verify its customer's title to a cheque before collecting it. As in the case of the paying bank, the common law position is therefore modified by a statutory defence. Section 4 of the Cheques Act 1957, based on provisions in previous legislation[1], provides that:

> 'Where a banker in good faith and without negligence –
> (a) receives payment for a customer of an instrument to which this section applies; or
> (b) having credited the customer's account with the amount of such an instrument, receives payment thereof for himself;
> and the customer has no title, or a defective title, to the instrument, the banker does not incur any liability to the true owner of the instrument by reason only of having received payment thereof'.

The section applies to cheques (including cheques which are not transferable as a result of s 81A of the Bills of Exchange Act 1882 or otherwise) and a number of other instruments, including 'cheques' made payable to cash[2].

Section 4 clearly covers both the normal situation, where the bank collects a cheque for the customer[3], and the situation where the bank receives payment for itself. As we have seen[4], it is normal practice for a bank to credit a customer's account with the value of cheques paid in before collecting them through clearing. In *Capital and Counties Bank v Gordon*[5] it was held that wherever a bank credited a customer's account before collection, it collected the cheque for itself as a holder for value. However, more recent cases[6] show that there is no such general rule: the bank will only be taken to be collecting for itself where the customer is allowed, by express or implied agreement, to draw against the cheque before it is cleared. In addition, where the customer has an existing overdraft, the bank has a lien on uncleared cheques to secure the amount of the overdraft, and is therefore deemed to be a holder for value to the extent of its lien[7]. It is clear that the bank can collect a cheque for itself and its customer jointly[8], for instance where a customer with an existing overdraft pays in a cheque for more than the amount of the overdraft. On the other hand, if the bank pays cash for the cheque over the counter, whilst it clearly gives value for the cheque, it is not protected by s 4 since it gives value without crediting the customer's account. In that case, the bank collects the cheque for itself as a holder for value, even though the customer may not actually indorse the cheque to the bank[9], and will only be protected if it qualifies as a holder in due course (and thus becomes the true owner). It will never be able to do that if the customer's title depends on a forged signature or indorsement.

At first sight the section, referring to the bank 'having received payment', appears to protect the bank against claims for money had and received, but not for conversion; however, it has been held that the section applies to all necessary acts involved in the collection of the cheque's value, and therefore, if the requirements of the section are fulfilled, the bank is protected against all liability[10].

Where the bank does not collect the cheque for itself, it is only protected if it collects for a customer. The meaning of 'customer' has largely been developed in this context. As we have seen, a person becomes a customer as soon as an account is opened[11], including where a cheque is paid in by a new customer to a new account opened for that purpose. The bank is not protected if it collects a cheque on a casual basis for someone without an existing or new account; however, it is rare today for banks to collect cheques other than for customers. As we have noted, a bank may collect a cheque as agent for another. The collecting agent is entitled to the protection of the section, provided that it can fulfil its conditions[12].

In order to obtain the protection of s 4, the collecting bank must act in good faith and without negligence. A number of cases have considered the meaning of 'negligence' in this context. The statute does not give rise to a duty of care owed by the bank to the owner of the cheque. The bank must prove that it acted without negligence in order to obtain the protection of the Act. The reference to 'negligence' causes one difficulty. There are dicta, most notably of Diplock LJ in *Marfani & Co Ltd v Midland Bank Ltd*[13], to the effect that even where the bank fails to establish that it was not negligent it can nevertheless claim the protection of s 4 if it can establish that its negligence did not cause the true owner's loss, so that, for instance, if the bank is held to have been negligent in failing to make inquiries of the customer, the bank may avoid liability if it proves that even if such inquiries had been made, the customer would have given convincing answers, satisfactory to a reasonable banker. The better view, however, is that causation is irrelevant and that if the bank cannot establish that it acted without negligence, it is denied the protection of s 4, even though the negligence did not cause the loss[14]. This must be correct. The s 4 defence is likely to be invoked where, for instance, a cheque is stolen. The purpose of the 'no negligence' requirement is to ensure that bankers collecting cheques do take reasonable precautions to guard against assisting fraud. If the bank which fails to take reasonable precautions can always escape liability by showing that reasonable precautions would make no difference the objective would be frustrated. Almost by definition it may be assumed that the clever fraudster will have a clever answer for the bank's inquiry. The difference between the two positions may, however, not be that great in practice. If the bank cannot discharge the burden of proving that it was not negligent it may have difficulty in establishing that taking the proper level of care would have made no difference. To put it another way, to fail to take precautions which it can be proved would have been ineffective is probably not negligent.

In general, negligence will be judged by the standards of ordinary reasonable banking practice, which, obviously, may change from time to time, but the court is not bound to accept current practice. In *Lloyds Bank Ltd v E B Savory & Co* Lord Warrington said that:

> 'the standard by which the absence, or otherwise, of negligence is to be judged must in my opinion be ascertained by reference to the practice of reasonable men carrying on the business of bankers, and endeavouring to do so in such a manner as may be calculated to protect themselves and others against fraud'[15].

However, it will rarely be the case that the court will hold established banking practice to be negligent, and more recently the test has been described as follows:

> 'Where the customer is in possession of the cheque at the time of delivery for collection, and appears on the face of it to be the "holder", ie: the payee or indorsee or the bearer, the banker is in my view entitled to assume that the customer is the owner of the cheque unless there are facts which are known, or ought to be known, to the banker which would cause a reasonable banker to suspect that the customer is not the true owner'[16].

Although it is sometimes suggested that these statements reveal two different approaches to the question of whether a bank has acted negligently, it is submitted that the test in both cases depends primarily on current banking practice, subject to the caveat that, in an extreme case, the court may find current practice to be unsatisfactory. More significantly:

> 'What facts ought to be known to the banker, and what facts are sufficient to cause him reasonably to suspect that the customer is not the true owner, must depend on current banking practice, and change as that practice changes. Cases decided thirty years ago, when the use by the general public of banking facilities was much less widespread, may not be a reliable guide to what the duty of a careful banker . . . is today'[17].

The cases suggest that a bank may be held negligent when the circumstances are such that a reasonable banker would be put on inquiry that the customer's title may be defective. The bank will therefore be negligent if it ignores facts which would make a reasonable banker suspicious, or if it fails to take reasonable care to obtain information which a reasonable banker would obtain, and which would reveal that the circumstances are suspicious. The negligence may therefore relate either to the manner in which the cheque is drawn or paid in, or the manner in which the customer's account is opened; the two classes of case are connected.

It has been held that a bank is negligent if it collects cheques without inquiry for the account of an agent payable to, or drawn by the agent on his principal[18]; for an employee payable to, or drawn by, the employee on his employer[19]; or, for the owner of a company, cheques payable to the company[20]. Of course, these are not absolutes: the circumstances of the case may show that the situation is perfectly innocent, as, for instance, where the bank collects a salary cheque drawn on an employer's account by the accounts clerk. In all these cases the bank's negligence lay in collecting cheques without inquiry where the circumstances should have put the bank on inquiry. It would probably also be negligent to collect a cheque for a customer without requiring an indorsement where an indorsement would be required in accordance with the 1957 circular.

For much the same reason, if a bank collects a cheque crossed 'a/c payee only' for the account of someone other than the named payee, it will be difficult for a bank to establish that it was not negligent. The Cheques Act 1992 does not, however, abolish s 4. The bank might avoid liability if it could establish that the two names were identical or nearly so, and that it had taken appropriate steps to confirm the identity of the account holder when opening the account[21]. In *Honourable Society of the Middle Temple v Lloyds Bank plc*[22] an English bank collected a cheque as agent for a Turkish bank. The cheque was crossed 'a/c payee only'. It had in fact been stolen and indorsed in favour of the Turkish bank's customer. Rix J held, first, that it would in principle be possible for the English (collecting agent) bank to rely on the s 4 defence. It would normally be reasonable for a bank collecting a cheque as agent for an overseas principal to assume that the principal had taken appropriate steps to confirm the identity of its customer and ensure that it collected the cheque for the true owner. On the facts, however, Lloyds were unable to do so. They had taken no steps to bring the effect of the Cheques Act 1992 to the attention of the Turkish bank and were not entitled to assume that they understood the (new) significance of the 'a/c payee only' crossing[23].

The bank may also be denied the protection of s 4 where its negligence prevents it having information which would enable it to appreciate that the circumstances surrounding the collection of the cheque are suspicious. In particular, a bank may be negligent if it fails to obtain references on a new customer when opening an account. In *Lloyds Bank Ltd v E B Savory & Co* a bank opened an account for a woman customer without first asking her the name of her husband's employer; the bank was held negligent, and therefore liable when it collected cheques drawn by the husband on his employer as part of a fraud[24]; had the bank known the identity of the husband's employer, it might have appreciated that the circumstances surrounding the payment in were suspicious. However, in recent years it has become common for people to change their jobs much more frequently than was the case when *Savory* was decided; it has been held that a bank is under no duty to keep up to date with changes in the customer's employment[25], so that the duty to obtain details of the customer's employment on opening the account may be of limited value.

In contrast to *Savory*, in *Marfani & Co Ltd v Midland Bank Ltd*[26], an employee of the plaintiffs defrauded them of money by opening an account in the name of one of their major clients; the bank required the employee to provide a reference before opening the account, and the employee, who had clearly prepared his position in advance, obtained a reference from an existing customer of the bank who knew him in his assumed name. The bank was held to be entitled to the protection of s 4:

it had acted without negligence and in accordance with current banking practice in obtaining a reference from an existing customer.

In recent years great concern has been expressed about the ease with which a bank or building society cheque account can be opened, and the possibilities for fraud this creates: a person may steal a cheque and open a bank account, into which the cheque is paid, and later withdraw the money, and, in some cases, produce no more identification than a letter bearing his name. In some cases reported in the press, the account has been opened on the strength of the name on the envelope in which the stolen cheque was delivered[27]. The value of references for new customers has been doubted[28] but the Review Committee on Banking Law and Practice recommended in its report[29] that a code of best banking practice should require banks to follow satisfactory procedures on opening accounts to enable them to ascertain the identity of new customers, including obtaining references. The original draft code recommended that where possible the bank should arrange a face-to-face meeting with new customers, and that solid evidence of identity, in the form of a document such as a passport or full driving licence, should be required. However, the current version of the Code merely states that:

'4.6 When you first apply to open an account we will tell you what identification we need to prove identity. This is important for your security and is required by law'[30].

A bank which is unable to rely on the statutory defence in s 4, for instance because it is unable to show that it acted without negligence, may nevertheless raise the contributory negligence of the true owner of the cheque as a partial defence to a claim[31].

1 Crossed Cheques Act 1876, s 12; Bills of Exchange Act 1882, s 82.
2 Section 4(2).
3 Including where it collects as agent for another bank: *Honourable Society of the Middle Temple v Lloyds Bank plc* [1999] 1 All ER (Comm) 193; see Hooley [1999] CLJ 128.
4 Above 30.1.
5 [1903] AC 240, HL.
6 See eg *A L Underwood Ltd v Bank of Liverpool* [1924] 1 KB 775, CA; *Westminster Bank Ltd v Zang* [1966] AC 182.
7 Bills of Exchange Act 1882, s 27(3); above 28.3.2.2.
8 *Barclays Bank Ltd v Astley Industrial Trust Ltd* [1970] 2 QB 527, [1970] 1 All ER 719.
9 Cheques Act 1957, s 2.
10 *Capital and Counties Bank v Gordon* [1903] AC 240, HL.
11 Above 29.2.3.
12 *Honourable Society of the Middle Temple v Lloyds Bank plc* [1999] 1 All ER (Comm) 193; see Hooley [1999] CLJ 128.
13 *Marfani & Co Ltd v Midland Bank Ltd* [1968] 2 All ER 573 at 583, [1968] 1 WLR 956 at 976; see also per Cairns J at 980, 584; per Rix J in *Honourable Society of the Middle Temple v Lloyds Bank plc* [1999] 1 All ER (Comm) 193 at 226.
14 *Lloyds Bank Ltd v E B Savory & Co* [1932] 2 KB 122 at 148 per Greer LJ; affd [1933] AC 201 at 233 per Lord Wright; *Thackwell v Barclays Bank plc* [1986] 1 All ER 676.
15 *Lloyds Bank Ltd v E B Savory & Co* [1933] AC 201 at 221.
16 Per Diplock LJ in *Marfani & Co Ltd v Midland Bank Ltd* [1968] 1 WLR 956 at 972.
17 Per Diplock LJ [1968] 1 WLR 956 at 972.
18 *Marquess of Bute v Barclays Bank Ltd* [1954] 1 QB 202, [1954] 3 All ER 365; *Midland Bank Ltd v Reckitt* [1933] AC 1, HL.
19 *Lloyds Bank Ltd v E B Savory & Co* [1933] AC 201. *Morison v London County and Westminster Bank Ltd* [1914] 3 KB 356, CA.
20 *A L Underwood Ltd v Bank of Liverpool* [1924] 1 KB 775, CA.
21 See the government White Paper *Banking Services Law and Practice* (1990) (Cmnd 1026), para 5.6.
22 [1999] 1 All ER (Comm) 193; Hooley [1999] CLJ 128.
23 On the facts there were also circumstances which should have put Lloyds on inquiry.

24 It would now be unlawful discrimination to require only women to state their partner's employment; given the change in work patterns in recent years, it would probably be necessary for the bank to obtain such information from both male and female customers.
25 *Orbit Mining and Trading Co Ltd v Westminster Bank Ltd* [1963] 1 QB 794, [1962] 3 All ER 465, CA.
26 [1968] 1 WLR 956.
27 This, of course, is the type of fraud which the 1992 Act does not guard against.
28 See Ellinger and Lomnicka, *Modern Banking Law* (2nd edn, 1994) p 520.
29 Paragraph 6.26.
30 The bank is required to take certain steps to confirm the customer's identity in order to comply with the Money Laundering Regulations 1993, SI 1993/1933.
31 Banking Act 1987, s 47.

30.2.6   *Bank acting as paying and collecting banker*

As we have seen, various statutory defences may be available to a bank which pays or collects a cheque on behalf of a customer, but the availability of those defences depends on different conditions. It may happen that the same bank acts in both capacities, collecting a cheque on behalf of one customer and paying on behalf of another. The cheque may be drawn on the payee's own branch, or may be paid at one branch and collected by another. It seems that in such a case, a bank may only establish a defence by satisfying the conditions of the defence relevant to the capacity in which it is sued: thus if it is sued as collecting banker, it must satisfy the requirements of s 4 of the Cheques Act 1957; if sued as paying banker it must satisfy the requirements of s 60 or s 80 of the 1882 Act. In the more likely case where it is sued in both capacities, it must satisfy the requirements of both relevant sections[1].

1   *Carpenters' Co v British Mutual Banking Co Ltd* [1938] 1 KB 511; cf *Gordon v London City and Midland Bank Ltd* [1902] 1 KB 242.

30.3   Other payment orders

Although cheques remain the most commonly used method of giving orders to a bank to make payments to third payments, a number of other payment methods are available, and their use is increasing. They include travellers' cheques, payments made through the bank giro system and payments made through electronic funds transfer systems. The importance of these systems, especially electronic funds transfer, is likely to increase in coming years. However, at present the law relating to these systems is relatively undeveloped. What follows is therefore a brief outline of their use, and of some of the legal problems to which their use may give rise.

30.3.1   *Travellers' cheques*

Travellers' cheques are widely used by travellers, including holidaymakers and businessmen, as a means of paying for goods and services and obtaining cash. Travellers' cheques are issued by banks and, although several different forms are in use, in general they resemble either bills of exchange drawn on, or promissory notes issued by, the bank which issues them. In the former case the bank is ordered, and in the second promises, to pay a sum of money to the payee named in the cheque. Travellers' cheques normally have space for two signatures and, in order to guard against theft or fraud, the traveller is required to sign the cheques once when collecting them from the bank and then to countersign them when issuing them to the payee; the bank is ordered, or promises, to pay the amount of the cheque only if the two signatures match.

The legal status of travellers' cheques is unclear. Arguably the order, or promise, to pay is conditional on the two signatures corresponding so that travellers' cheques are not cheques, bills of exchange or promissory notes[1]. However, even if this view is correct, they are widely regarded and treated by the commercial world as negotiable, and it is therefore suggested that they are negotiable instruments by commercial usage[2]. Thus even if not technically bills of exchange, travellers' cheques can be transferred by indorsement and delivery, or by simple delivery, according to the manner in which they are drawn, and a transferee who qualifies as a holder in due course can take free of any defects in the title of his transferor, and enforce payment of the cheque.

The rights of the traveller against the bank which issues travellers' cheques normally depend on the terms of the contract under which the cheques are issued. Since the bank only undertakes to pay if the two signatures on the cheque match, if the cheques are lost or stolen before they have been countersigned the traveller is normally entitled to a refund of their face value; the bank will suffer no loss, since it is entitled to refuse payment; any loss will therefore have to be borne by the holder of the traveller's cheque who accepts it from the thief; he must safeguard his position by insuring that the signature and countersignature do correspond. The traveller who seeks repayment will generally be required to indemnify the bank against loss, which may arise if the traveller has in fact countersigned the cheques before loss; the contract signed by the traveller at the time of purchasing the cheques will normally contain such an indemnity. In *Braithwaite v Thomas Cook Travellers' Cheques Ltd*[3] the contract expressly made the traveller's right to a refund subject to the proviso that he should have 'properly safeguarded each cheque against loss or theft'. The traveller was allowed to take the cheques without signing them; after a long day, he went out drinking with friends, carrying the still unsigned cheques in a plastic bag. At the end of the evening he travelled home on the underground and fell asleep. The cheques were lost or stolen, and it was held that his conduct constituted a failure properly to safeguard the cheques; he was therefore precluded from recovering their value. However, in *El Awadi v Bank of Credit and Commerce International SA*[4] there was no such express provision in the contract, although the contract provided that 'any claim for a refund shall be subject to approval by the issuer'. It was held that the traveller was entitled to a refund even though the cheques, which had been signed but not countersigned, were stolen as a result of his negligence; the contract gave the bank a right to refuse a refund if the traveller was in breach of any of his contractual obligations, but in line with the general approach to customers' duties of care, the court refused to imply a term requiring the traveller to take care of the cheques, or limiting his right to a refund. In addition, Hutchison J took the view that it would normally be an implied term of a contract for the sale of travellers' cheques that the traveller should be entitled to a refund in the event of loss. In reaching this decision, Hutchison J took into account the defendants' advertising material which emphasised the security advantages of travellers' cheques over cash and the availability of refunds, and the fact that as the cheques had not been countersigned, the bank could protect itself against loss by checking that the signatures and countersignatures matched.

The facts of *Braithwaite* could give rise to a different problem. If the cheques were stolen and the thief both signed and countersigned them and then transferred them to a bona fide transferee, could the transferee enforce them against the bank? The position has been considered in America. In one case it was held that, as the two signatures were forgeries, the holder could not enforce[5]; however, in the second it was held that the cheques were complete at the time of the theft because they contained the amount to be paid and the bank's acceptance, and so could be enforced against the bank[6]. It has been suggested that the latter view is more likely to represent English law[7]. Such an approach seems commercially desirable: a person to whom a travellers' cheque is transferred can only safeguard against fraud by checking that the two signatures correspond; where the loss is caused by the negligence of the traveller in this way, the loss should fall either on the traveller or on the bank. The effect of *El Awadi* is that, in the absence of express contract terms, such a loss will fall on the bank which, after all, charges for the provision of travellers' cheques (and thus can pass the risk of such loss on to other customers).

1   Bills of Exchange Act 1882, s 3(1); above 28.2; but see Goode, *Commercial Law* (2nd edn, 1995) p 625 for the contrary view.
2   See *Chitty on Contracts* (28th edn, 1999) para 34-174.
3   [1989] QB 553, [1989] 1 All ER 235.
4   [1990] 1 QB 606, [1989] 1 All ER 242.
5   *City National Bank of Galveston v Amercian Express Co* 7 SW 2d 886 (1928).
6   *Amercian Express Co v Anadarko Bank and Trust Co* 67 P 2d 55 (1937).
7   *Chitty on Contracts* (28th edn, 1999) para 34-184.

30.3.2   *Automated payments*

As already noted, the use of cheques, although still significant, is in decline. Recent years have seen rapid growth in the use of alternative payment methods, notably automated payment systems, comprising standing orders, direct credits and direct debits. The volume of such payments more than doubled in the period 1988–98 and their use is expected to continue to increase for regular payments including salary and wages payments, savings, mortgage and council tax payments, utility bills, subscriptions and so on.

Payments may be initiated either by the payer or payee. Credit transfers are initiated by the payer. They include standing orders, used for regular, repeated payments such as savings, and direct credits which allow a business to use one form to order its bank to make payments to a number of different payees, such as a list of creditors or salary payments to employees. In contrast, direct debits are initiated by the payee, who obtains an authority from the payer to order the payer's bank to pay such sums as the payee may demand from time to time. Direct debits are used where regular payments will have to be made, but where the amount of the payment may vary from time to time.

Automated payments are promoted as convenient for all concerned. Payment is made directly from the payer's to the payee's bank account, via the clearing system, without the need to write, send or pay in a cheque. Where repeated payments have to be made, a standing order or direct debiting mandate allows regular payments to be made on the strength of one written authority. Automated payments may also offer the payer some protection against fraud. Except in the case of direct debits, the order to pay is given direct to the payer's bank. There is thus no risk of the payee altering the amount of the order and both parties are protected against the risk of loss or theft of the payment order. Direct debits do expose the payer to the risk that an unauthorised payment may be taken due to fraud or error, especially since in 2000 the banks introduced a new scheme, 'Auddis'[1], under which a direct debit can be set up without the customer's signature. The system is intended to be used for telephone and internet contracts. However, a business is only allowed to originate payments through the direct debit system if it is first approved by a major bank or building society and the payer is protected by the 'direct debit guarantee' by which the bank undertakes that on the customer's request it must immediately re-credit the customer's account with the amount of any direct debit challenged as unauthorised. Automated payments are also convenient for the banks involved; in particular, the payee's bank does not have to present any instrument for payment; the payee's account will not be credited until the payment is received, so that if the order is dishonoured, for instance due to lack of funds, there is no need to debit the payee's account.

Standing orders, direct credits and direct debits are all cleared through the computerised BACS[2] system. On a peak day (such as a wages day), the system may handle up to 45 million transactions. In the case of standing orders, payment is initiated by the payer's bank compiling a computerised list of payments to be made on a particular date and sending it to the BACS clearing centre, either electronically by telecommunications, or via a computer bureau. The paying bank's instructions are processed at the clearing centre by a computer which produces further lists to be sent to the banks of the intended payees, giving details of the accounts to be credited, the amounts to be paid and the identities of the payers. The procedure for direct credits is similar, except that the originator can prepare the list of payments and send it to the BACS clearing centre, either directly or via its own bank. In the case of direct debits, the payment is initiated by the payee, who compiles an initial list containing details of the customers to be debited, their bank accounts and the amounts to be debited. The list is then processed at the BACS centre which prepares further lists to be sent to the banks of the various payers and payees containing details of the payments to be made and credited. The accounts of payer and payee are debited and credited simultaneously. Settlement between the banks is effected by transfer of net balances between their accounts at the Bank of England.

Although the system is partly computerised, the clearance of payments through BACS takes three days before the payee's account is credited at his branch. The Review of Banking Services in the UK was particularly critical of this aspect of the system, observing that:

> 'The rhythm of the UK payment system often seems to reflect the nineteenth century more than the twenty first . . . [A]spects of the payments cycle still bear witness to the work habits of a nineteenth century bank clerk[3]'.

Delays create costs for businesses, especially small businesses, making it hard for them to manage their financial affairs effectively.

Because of the delay involved in the use of BACS, a second system, known as CHAPS[4], was introduced in 1984 to provide a fully computerised same-day clearing system. The system was originally used only for payments of at least £10,000 but since 1993 it has been possible to use it for payments of any amount and in 1999 payments of less than £10,000 made up 40% of CHAPS payments by volume. However, fees for using CHAPS are relatively high, so that it is not a substitute for BACS, where high volume frequent payments have to be used. Each participating bank has a computer terminal, or 'gateway', which can be used to gain access to the British Telecom communications network; terminals in individual branches are linked to the bank's gateway, and, in order to make a payment, the payer's bank merely sends a message from its gateway, which is directed to the payee's bank's computer gateway. The system has a high level of security, all messages being authenticated and encrypted. Banks which participate in CHAPS may allow other, non-participating banks, and even individual approved customers, to have access to their computer gateways and thus to use CHAPS.

There is as yet relatively little authority on the legal status and effect of the various automated payment systems. The better view is that the paying and recipient banks act as agents for their respective customers to make and receive payment[5], and the payer's bank is only entitled to debit his account if it acts in accordance with his mandate, as given in the relevant payment order. It seems that the mandate is revocable at any time until payment is complete. However, it is not clear when a payment made through the giro system is complete. The Review Committee on Banking Services Law and Practice recommended that new legislation should define the time of completion of payment[6], but at that time UNCITRAL was working on a Model Law on International Credit Transfers and, since the problem of the timing of completion of payment is particularly acute in the international context, the government therefore decided to wait for UNCITRAL to complete its work. The Model Law was finalised in 1992 and provides that a credit transfer is complete when the beneficiary's bank credits the beneficiary's account[7].

Where payment is made through one of the automated systems, no property passes from payer to payee, unlike in the case of cheque and bill payments. Instead, completion of the payment results in the reduction in value of a chose in action owned by the payer – the debt due from his bank – and a corresponding increase in value of a chose in action, or the creation of a new chose in action, owned by the payee. It has been held that a direct debit does not operate as an assignment of funds from the payer to the payee[8], so the payee acquires no interest in the funds transferred until the payment is complete. The effect of a direct debit as between payer and payee was considered further by the Court of Appeal in *Esso Petroleum Co Ltd v Milton*[9]. M was the licensee of a petrol station. He was required by his contract to pay for petrol supplies by direct debit. Finding himself in dispute with the owner of the station, Esso, he cancelled his direct debit mandate, leaving a sum of almost £170,000 for petrol supplied by Esso but not paid for. When Esso sued for that amount, M argued that he had claims for breach of contract which he was entitled to set off against Esso's claim. As we have seen, a bill of exchange gives rise to a payment undertaking which is independent of the underlying transaction in respect of which it is given[10]. The majority of the Court of Appeal held that the same rule applies to a direct debit, with the result that M was not entitled to set off his claims against Esso's claim for payment. In effect, a payer who has agreed to pay by direct debit for goods or services to be supplied is in the same position as if he had given postdated cheques. With respect, this is unconvincing and the reasoning of Simon Brown LJ, who dissented, is to be preferred. As he pointed out, direct debits are not necessarily used as a substitute for cheques, and therefore for cash, but as a substitute for credit. A bill of exchange and a cheque both give rise to an autonomous undertaking by the drawer to pay. There is no such undertaking in the case of a direct debit, which is simply an authority by the payer to the payee to demand payments from his bank, and an authority to the bank to accept those demands. Moreover, the autonomy of the bill of exchange is justified by its negotiability. Direct debits are not negotiable. However, Balcombe LJ expressly rejected the suggestion that negotiability is the reason for the autonomy principle and justified it instead on the basis of allocation of commercial risk, the intention being to put the supplier in the same position as if he had received cash.

It has been argued above that the autonomy rule should no longer be applied as a matter of course to cheques[11]. It is therefore regrettable that it has now been extended to direct debits. It would be especially unfortunate if the decision in *Esso* were to be extended to the consumer context[12]. Direct debits are 'marketed' aggressively as 'convenient'; it might come as a surprise to a consumer to discover that by giving a direct debit instruction he also gives up any right to withhold payment and thereby put pressure on the supplier in the event of any breach of contract.

 1 Automated direct debit information system.
 2 Bankers' Automated Clearing Services: see 30.0.
 3 *Competition in UK Banking* (2000) para 3.130.
 4 Clearing House Automated Payment System: see 30.0.
 5 Ellinger and Lomnicka, *Modern Banking Law* (2nd edn, 1994) p 441 ff.
 6 Report of the Review Committee, Recommendation 12(2).
 7 Article 19(1).
 8 *Mercedes Benz Finance Ltd v Clydesdale Bank plc* [1997] CLC 81.
 9 [1997] 2 All ER (Comm) 593. See Hooley [1997] CLJ 500; Tettenborn (1997) 113 LQR 374.
10 See 28.1.1.
11 See 28.1.2.
12 Both Balcombe and Thorpe LJJ in the majority seem to have recognised that the principle applied in *Esso* might not apply to all direct debit cases.

30.3.3   *Electronic funds transfer*

Banks have been at the forefront of the introduction of new technology into commercial activity, principally through the introduction of electronic funds transfer (EFT) systems. EFT is used to describe a number of different systems in which the instruction to a bank to make a payment to the credit of a particular payee or account, or to debit a specified account, is given by electronic means, normally through computer systems. The introduction, and increasing use, of electronic banking has been described as 'the new dynamic for change on today's banking scene'[1]. However, the rapid development of new technology for use in banking transactions poses a number of novel legal problems. Some of these are common to all EFT systems; in particular, difficult questions arise in deciding when an EFT payment is complete and thus incapable of countermand. As we have seen, it has been proposed that this particular problem should await an international solution.

The BACS and CHAPS systems described above are both EFT systems. However, in many cases where payments are made via those systems, the customer's instruction to the bank to make payment is given in writing. Special difficulties arise where the customer's mandate is given electronically. EFT systems involving an electronic instruction from the customer are already in widespread use in automated teller machines (ATMs) used for cash withdrawals and electronic funds transfer at point of sale (EFTPOS) systems used for payment for goods and services, and their use is expected to continue to grow during the coming years. The legal problems raised by these systems are increasingly being recognised and were extensively considered by the Review Committee on Banking Services Law and Practice, and must briefly be discussed.

1   Report of the Review Committee on Banking Law and Services, para 9.01.

30.3.3.1 *Customer initiated electronic transactions*

The first ATMs were introduced in the UK in 1967. The systems currently in use involve the customer using a plastic card, issued by the bank, in conjunction with a four-digit personal identification number (PIN) to withdraw cash from, order statements, request account information and make deposits at automated teller machines. The cards currently in use bear a strip of magnetic tape upon which certain information is encoded. When the customer uses the card to withdraw cash, he inserts the card into the ATM machine and keys in his PIN; the machine then uses the information on the magnetic tape to verify the PIN given by the customer, and, provided the correct PIN has been keyed in, allows the customer to withdraw cash or transact other business. A number of banks, building societies and other institutions have entered into reciprocal arrangements to allow their customers to use their ATM cards in each others' machines. In 1986 the Link Interchange Network Ltd (LINK) was established to manage the development of the ATM network. All of the major ATM operators are members.

EFTPOS systems have been introduced more recently. Such systems allow card holders to use plastic EFTPOS cards to pay for goods and services. At the point of sale, such as the supermarket check-out, the customer presents the card, which is used to authorise the transfer of funds direct from the customer's bank account to the supplier's account. The supplier passes the card through an electronic reader, connected via a computer system to the EFTPOS clearing system, and thus gives the instruction to make the payment. The customer authorises the transaction either by signing a slip similar to that used to authorise credit card transactions, or by keying in a PIN on a keypad at the point of sale.

Payments made via EFTPOS systems still have to be cleared through the banking system and, like cheques (surprisingly), take three days to clear. The contractual network which underpins the use of EFTPOS and debit cards has been explained elsewhere[1]. The retailer will be in a contractual relationship with the card issuer or a merchant acquirer and as a result will have the benefit of a direct undertaking from the issuing bank to make payment in accordance with the transaction slip, less any charge. The use of the card coupled with the customer's signature and/or any associated PIN provides the bank with the customer's mandate to make payment to the supplier and debit the customer's account. The terms of the card agreement will forbid the customer countermanding the payment instruction once given.

ATMs are already widely used, having overtaken cheques as the most common means of making cash withdrawals from bank accounts in 1987. In 1998 there were 1.9 billion ATM transactions worth a total of £98bn[2]. EFTPOS and debit cards are expected to overtake cheques as a means of paying for goods and services in the near future. The use of debit cards – including EFTPOS and other cards – increased over 25-fold between 1989 and 1998, when there were 1,736 million transactions[3]. In both systems, where the transaction is authorised by use of a PIN, the bank's mandate to make payment is provided by the customer keying in the correct PIN.

The possibility was discussed earlier that ATM and EFTPOS cards may in certain circumstances be regarded as credit tokens and therefore subject to some of the provisions of the Consumer Credit Act 1974[4]. Subject to that possibility, the use of ATM and EFTPOS systems is subject to almost no statutory regulation, and there has been little common law consideration of the legal problems they pose. In general the use of such cards has been governed almost entirely by express contract terms. These terms are drawn up by the banks and tend to be one sided, favouring the interests of the bank. Moreover, the terms upon which different banks and building societies issue such cards tend to be broadly similar, so that a customer has little choice but to accept the terms on offer. Although some terms of such contracts would, possibly, be subject to the test of reasonableness in s 3 of the Unfair Contract Terms Act 1977, the effectiveness of such terms has never been considered in court. Such terms would now be subject to the Unfair Terms in Consumer Contracts Regulations 1999[5]. Most disputes between customers and their banks or building societies are dealt with by the ombudsmen, who to date have been reluctant to declare such terms unreasonable and therefore unenforceable[6].

ATM and EFTPOS systems give rise to a number of special legal problems, concerning the effectiveness of the mandate given by the PIN, privacy and the security of the system, liability in the case of card loss and liability for losses caused by system failure, such as the failure to make a payment. However, it is argued that premature legal regulation of electronic banking services might restrict technological development. The Review Committee on Banking Services Law and Practice therefore recommended a two-tier approach to the regulation of such systems, with a minimum level of statutory regulation supplemented by a code of best practice[7]. The government accepted this proposal but legislation has not been introduced and the matter is dealt with in the Banking Code.

1   See 21.3.1.
2   APACS Payments Market Briefing, July 1999.
3   Ibid.
4   See 26.5.1.
5   See 2.6.5.
6   See eg the 1987–88 Report of the Building Society Ombudsman, p 14; see Morris [1992] LMCLQ 227.
7   Report of the Review Committee, para 9.30.

30.3.3.2   *Authentication, privacy and security*

The principal difficulty is that of providing satisfactory authentication of the customer's instructions to the bank. In most cases, this is provided by the customer inserting the correct PIN into the computer terminal, and the computer checking the PIN against the information contained in the magnetic strip on the card. However, many commentators have argued that PIN systems are less secure against fraud than handwritten signatures. A customer may, contrary to the bank's instructions, make a written record of the PIN, and even keep it with the card. A thief who obtains the card and the PIN may use it to obtain cash and goods or services; further, it seems that it is possible for the data encoded on magnetic strips to be altered, or for cards to be forged[1]. Information may be obtained from cards by various means, of varying degrees of sophistication, ranging from passing them through dummy card readers to simply collecting discarded copies of transaction slips. Two reports by the National Consumer Council[2] highlighted the particular problem of 'phantom withdrawals', where a customer finds that his account has been debited with sums drawn from an ATM, for which the customer denies liability. Between 1986 and 1989 the Banking Ombudsman received over 900 complaints about allegedly phantom withdrawals; significantly, none of them was decided in favour of the customer.

A customer wishing to challenge a debit made to his account on the strength of an alleged ATM or EFTPOS transaction faces a number of difficulties. In particular, the terms of use of the card may well purport to make the bank's computerised record of transactions conclusive; even if there is no such term, or it can be challenged by the customer, he may be faced with the further difficulty of persuading a court to accept his oral evidence over that of the bank's computer[3]. Some commentators have urged that the burden of proof in relation to disputed transactions should be placed on the bank. However, that would often be an impossible burden to discharge and might encourage fraud[4]. The Review Committee therefore rejected such a solution, instead recommending that a code of practice should provide for EFT systems to meet minimum standards with regard to authorisation procedures and security, that institutions should undertake a commitment to improve their systems to take advantage of more secure authentication procedures as they become technologically possible[5], and take steps to make the computer systems themselves secure against outside interference[6] and to improve privacy at computer terminals to prevent anyone reading the customer's PIN when it is keyed in to the terminal[7]. It proposed that legislation should be introduced to prohibit the unsolicited mailing of EFT cards to customers[8], and to limit the liability of customers for loss due to fraudulent misuse of ATM and EFT cards.

Many of these matters are dealt with by the Banking Code. It provides that cards, other than replacements for existing cards, will only be issued to customers who request them[9]. PINs will be issued separately from cards and cardholders will be given the option to choose their own PINs[10]. Customers are advised to take care of their cards PINs and passwords, advised of appropriate security steps[11] and informed of the procedures for notifying loss of a card or disclosure of a PIN[12]. The Code contains detailed provisions dealing with liability for loss. Card issuers undertake to refund the value of transactions charged to the customer's account, together with interest and any charges, as a result of misuse where a card has not been received by the customer[13]. In other cases, cardholders will only be liable (a) for misuse which takes place before the issuer is notified that the card has been lost or the PIN is known by someone else, and (b) in any case, for losses up to a maximum of £50. However, this limitation on cardholders' liability is subject to an important qualification: the Code provides that cardholders will be held liable for all losses if they have acted fraudulently and 'if you have acted with gross negligence which has caused losses you may be liable for them'[14]. Examples of 'gross negligence', according to the Code, include failing to observe the security measures for PIN and card suggested in the Code if that failure has caused the loss. This limitation could create a significant gap in the cardholder's protection; for instance, a customer might be said to have acted with gross negligence by writing down the PIN 'without making a reasonable attempt to disguise it'[15]. It seems extreme to categorise such conduct as 'gross negligence'.

These provisions must now be read subject to the provisions of the Consumer Protection (Distance Selling) Regulations 2000[16], which provide that a consumer has an automatic right to have any payment cancelled where his card is used fraudulently, without his authority, in connection with a distance contract[17]. Those provisions only apply, however, in favour of a consumer where the card is misused in connection with a distance contract. In other cases the customer's rights depend entirely on the provisions of his contract with the bank and of the banking code. It is clear, therefore, that cardholders may be held liable, under the provisions of the Code, for losses in circumstances in which they would not be held liable under the Consumer Credit Act for losses caused by misuse of a credit card where, for instance, cardholders are only liable for use of their cards by third parties who acquire possession of the card with the holder's consent and not where they are merely negligent[18].

Finally, the Code provides that the bank will refund the amount of any transaction together with any interest and charges where faults have occurred in ATM's or 'associated systems used', provided that they were not obvious or advised by a message or notice at the time of use[19]. The bank's liability is, however, limited to making the appropriate refund. Liability for any consequential losses caused by a fault, such as losses caused by a failure to remit funds to the payee in an EFTPOS transaction, is therefore not covered by the Code.

It remains to be seen whether these measures will provide sufficient protection for cardholders. Although modelled on the provisions of the Consumer Credit Act, they provide significantly less protection for cardholders in a number of areas and it may yet therefore prove necessary to consider legislative control.

1 See the Report of the Review Committee on Banking Services Law and Practice, para 10.05.
2 *Banking Services and the Consumer* (1983); *Winning and Losing at Cards* (1985).
3 Although in *Judd v Citibank* 435 NYS 2d 210 (1980) an American court did reject the computer's evidence in favour of that of the customer.
4 The practice of the ombudsman is to require the bank to show that the machine was operating correctly at the relevant time and that there was no human error, but then to transfer the burden of proof to the customer: see Morris [1992] LMCLQ 227 at 242.
5 Recommendation 10.1.
6 Recommendation 10.5, 10.6.
7 Recommendation 10.4.
8 Recommendation 10.2.
9 Banking Code, para 3.9.
10 Paragraph 3.10.
11 Paragraph 4.8.
12 Paragraph 4.10.
13 Paragraph 4.12.
14 Paragraph 4.16.
15 Paragraph 18.2.
16 SI 2000/2334; see 26.5.3.
17 Regulation 21.
18 Consumer Credit Act 1974, s 84(2); see 26.5.2.
19 Banking Code, para 4.12.

Part V

International Trade

Chapter 31

The Nature and Structure of International Trade

31.0   Introduction

It is not enough for a business to trade in its own domestic market; modern businesses strive to export into foreign markets. Such international trade has advantages both for the exporting business, which may increase its profits by exploiting a second market and protect itself against the collapse of its home market, and, moreover, for the national economy of the exporting business. By exporting its own goods and services, a country can earn income necessary to finance the acquisition of goods and services which it cannot produce at home and must import. Industrialised nations may be heavily dependent on imports of raw materials and foodstuffs; less developed countries depend on exports of raw materials and minerals to finance imports of finished products and services. If the value of exports exceeds that of imports, there will be a net inflow of wealth into the country, and vice versa. Governments therefore attach great significance to national balance of payment figures and are keen to encourage exports by providing various incentives including tax concessions, advice and even financial assistance to exporters[1].

Trade has been carried on across national boundaries since ancient times. However, in modern times the volume of international trade has increased dramatically and, in particular, since the Second World War, as communications and transport have improved, there has been a great expansion. The UK's share of world trade has declined in recent years, but it nevertheless remains significant. In 1998 the total value of exports from the UK was £351,163m[2]. The nature of international trade has also changed. Whereas in earlier times traders dealt in exotic items and then in rare raw materials, sales of manufactured goods are now an increasingly significant factor. In 1998 the total value of British exports of goods was £164,132m; of that sum, £141,961m represented sales of finished and semi-finished goods.

Consideration of the volume of sales gives only a partial picture, however. The export trade involves the provision of both goods and services, the latter ranging from large-scale construction work to services such as insurance. Even the law itself may become an export commodity: thus it is recognised that the high reputation of London's commercial arbitrators may bring in valuable arbitration business. There are signs that the UK economy is becoming a 'service economy', increasingly dependent on 'invisible' exports of services. In 1998 the total value of invisible exports (including investment earnings) was £187,031m, of which services accounted for £60,070m. Since 1993 the exports of goods have made up roughly half the value of exports from the UK.

The international sale of goods nevertheless remains a vitally important transaction. It raises special legal problems which have largely been solved by a combination of legal pragmatism and commercial ingenuity:

> 'it is here that the ingenuity of financier and businessperson in developing instruments that will answer emerging commercial needs reaches its highest point'[3].

In this area commercial law can be seen at its most flexible as it has had to respond to and accommodate within its structures the special devices created by the business community to facilitate their dealings. Moreover, many of the problems raised by an international sale are shared by, for instance, international construction contracts. We will therefore concentrate on the international sale transaction.

1   Such as the Export Credits Guarantee Scheme operated by the UK government.
2   See Central Statistical Office, *UK Balance of Payments* (The Pink Book) (1999).
3   Goode, *Commercial Law* (2nd edn, 1995) p 879.

31.1   Different trading structures

The business wishing to trade abroad may make use of a number of mechanisms. It may sell direct to its foreign customer, or it may establish a network of representatives on foreign soil and supply its goods through them; such representatives may be agents, distributors or franchisees[1]. Alternatively, and increasingly, the exporter may establish itself in the territory of the state to which it wishes to export. The corporation, possessing a legal personality separate from that of its shareholders, facilitates such action and the so-called multinational corporation has become an increasingly common and important phenomenon. Many such multinationals are household names, such as ICI, General Motors, Ford and BP. The multinational corporation has been defined as 'a combination of companies of different nationality connected by means of shareholdings, management control or contract and constituting an economic unit'[2]. Typically, a company based in (say) the UK will establish a subsidiary in (say) Spain; the subsidiary may purchase goods from its parent for sale in the host market; or it may even manufacture there itself. A detailed study of such multinationals is beyond the scope of this work, and the reader is referred to the standard works on company law. However, they play an important role in international trade. Their size and wealth gives them great economic power, which often exceeds that of many states[3]. A decision by a parent company to close a subsidiary in one country and transfer production to another elsewhere may have a catastrophic impact on employment and the economy of the subsidiary's host country; and there is always the likelihood that the subsidiary, controlled from above, will favour the interests of its parent state to those of its host when the two conflict. At the same time, their size and legal complexity makes it difficult for the law to deal with the special problems they create. It has been said that there is 'no simple solution for the problem of the relationship to states, the world of states or an organised world community'[4]. Obviously, if decisions are effectively taken by the parent company, it will be difficult for the legal system of the subsidiary's host state to exercise any real control; an international response is needed, but 'on the international level, no effective regulation of multinationals is established yet'[5].

However, even where the exporter does make use of representatives in the importing state, he will still be involved in a sale, either to his distributor, franchisee or subsidiary in order for them to effect a resale, or to his customer either direct or through an agent. The rules which we examine below will therefore continue to be relevant.

1 See ch 3 above.
2 Schmitthoff, *Nationalism and Multinational Enterprise* (Hahlo, South and Wright (eds)) (1973), p 24.
3 A fact tacitly recognised by Staughton LJ in *Cargill International SA v Bangladesh Sugar and Food Industries Corpn* [1998] 2 All ER 406, a case arising out of a dispute between a state trading corporation and a subsidiary of a major international commodity trader, where (at 416), he opened his judgment with the words: 'If my heart ruled my head I would award the $526,000 to the state corporation of Bangladesh and not to an arm of the Cargill empire'.
4 Friedman, *Transnational Law in a Changing Society* (1977) p 79.
5 *Schmitthoff's Export Trade* (9th edn, 1990) p 322. Note, however, that guidelines have been published by the OECD, and that EC proposals for the creation of a 'European Company' may solve some of the difficulties of multinationals within the EU.

31.2 The nature of international trade law

This book is essentially concerned with private law, and in this section we are therefore concerned with the private law of international trade which governs the relationships between the parties involved in transactions for the international sale and supply of goods and services. As already noted, our main focus will be on international sale transactions. The use of the word 'transactions' here is deliberate. As will be seen, a typical international sale transaction involves a network of interlocking contracts made between a number of different parties, including for the carriage of the goods to their destination, their insurance in transit and the financing of the transaction. We are therefore concerned with the legal relationships, primarily, but not solely, contractual, between these parties.

The term 'international trade law' is also used to describe a quite different body of rules, which governs the relationships between states and seeks to regulate the use by states of tariffs, quotas and other measures to restrict imports. That body of law, concerned with the workings of such international instruments and institutions as the General Agreement on Tariffs and Trade and, now, the World Trade Organisation, is really a feature of public international law and is therefore outside the scope of this book.

It should also be emphasised that the expression 'international trade law' refers to the law which applies to international trade transactions. It is the trade, not the law, which is international. As explained below, there has in recent years been a general trend to the harmonisation of the national laws applicable to international transactions but for the most part the law remains essentially national. We are here primarily concerned with the English law applicable to international transactions. This is not mere chauvinism. English law has long had a high reputation in the international trading community as being especially well suited to the needs of commerce, and a great many contracts are made subject to English law, even when neither of the parties to it is English. In particular, many of the standard term contracts used in international transactions include a choice of law clause under which the contract is subjected to English law and disputes are to be litigated in the Commercial Court in London.

The expression 'international trade' covers a wide range of transactions. On the whole we are not here concerned with consumer transactions (although it is, of course, becoming increasingly common for consumers to make cross-border purchases, something which the development of e-commerce will facilitate). Even so, not all international sale transactions are alike. There is a world of difference between the type of transaction which is common in the commodity trades, where bulk cargoes are bought and sold by traders and a single cargo may be resold several times in the course of the journey to its destination, and a contract between (say) a UK importer and a Turkish manufacturer for the sale of (say) a consignment of T-shirts, and yet, in theory, the same legal rules apply to both.

In practice the treatment of the two contracts just described would be very different. A striking feature of international trade is the extensive use of standard form contracts for the various contracts of sale, carriage, insurance and payment. In particular, the commodity trades have prepared standard forms for use by their members so that contracts for the sale of bulk cargoes of commodities such as grain and oil are normally made on standard terms. As discussed elsewhere, those standard terms have come to have a settled meaning as a result of judicial interpretation, and the courts will generally be reluctant to disturb a settled interpretation of such a contract. The terms of the contract will often cover all aspects of the transaction and modify or even exclude many of the standard default rules of general sales law. Since they are prepared by trade associations of which both buyer and seller are normally members, and since the parties to such contracts are generally of equal bargaining power, such terms are not open to the same objections as the standard terms used by individual businesses when dealing with other traders or consumers. In effect, they become a private law for parties trading on the terms. The result is that when considering the rights and obligations of the parties to a typical large-scale commodity contract the general rules of sales law are for many practical purposes irrelevant, the parties' rights and obligations being defined, instead, by the terms of the contract.

31.2.1 *Principles of international trade law*

International trade law, and particularly that governing the large-scale dealings which characterise the commodity and similar markets, is 'pure' commercial law. There is no direct consumer involvement and it is assumed that the parties engaged in international trade have sufficient commercial experience and bargaining power to look after their own interests. In this context, therefore, certain values are at a premium. Particular emphasis is placed on certainty and predictability. Transactions take place against the background of a market in which prices may fluctuate rapidly. The quantities traded are such that even a small movement in a market price can result in a huge profit or loss. Traders therefore need to be able to make speedy decisions about their rights. That in turn requires, it is assumed, that the law should be clear, consistent and predictable. Features of international trade law therefore include a preference for certainty over flexibility[1]; a reluctance to disturb settled rules[2], and a willingness to adapt legal doctrine, if necessary, to accommodate commercial practice[3].

1 See eg *Bunge Corpn v Tradax SA* [1981] 2 All ER 513, above 10.2.1.
2 See eg *Effort Shipping Co Ltd v Linden Management SA, The Giannis NK* [1998] AC 605, [1998] 1 All ER, HL, below 32.6.5; *Aries Tanker Corpn v Total Transport Ltd, The Aries* [1977] 1 All ER 398, below 32.2.1.2.
3 See eg *New Zealand Shipping Co Ltd v Satterthwaite Ltd* [1975] AC 154, [1974] 1 All ER 1015, below 32.7. The best example is perhaps the treatment of documentary credits: see ch 34.

31.3 When is a sale international?

It might seem obvious that a sale should be categorised as an international or export sale when the goods in question are delivered outside the home state of the seller. However, such a categorisation might be misleading. Suppose that A, based in London, sells goods to B, based in Southampton. B immediately resells to C in New York and requires A to deliver the goods direct to New York. Although the transaction between A and B involves delivery outside the UK, it does not involve many of the special problems of international sales; for instance, should A have to resort to legal proceedings to obtain payment, he can do so without the procedural difficulties involved in suing a foreign defendant. In deciding whether a sale is international, the law therefore generally focuses on the places of business of the parties to the contract. This is the approach taken both by harmonised international sale law[1], and by domestic law, which excludes 'international supply contracts' from the ambit of the Unfair Contract Terms Act[2]. Thus the contract described above would not be regarded as an export contract; by contrast, in the inverse situation where A sells to B in New York, who requires A to deliver direct to C in Manchester, there would be an export sale, even though the goods never leave the UK.

1   See eg the United Nations Convention on Contracts for the International Sale of Goods (1980) art 1.
2   Section 26. See below 33.0.

31.3.1 *The special problems of international sales*

The export sale raises a number of special problems – physical, commercial, political and legal – not normally encountered in the simple domestic transaction. In order to combat those problems, commercial people have developed, and the law has recognised, a number of special contracts and devices so that the international sale involves a number of legal considerations different from those posed by the domestic transaction. However, where the contract between the parties is governed by English law the obligations of the parties will still depend to a large degree on the rules contained in the Sale of Goods Act.

(a) Physical problems
The first difficulty is that the parties to the contract will be separated by distance and, quite possibly, by language. The latter may pose difficulties in the negotiation of the contract and translation may lead to less than perfect results[1]. The former may also hinder negotiation, although the continuous improvement of communications has largely removed that difficulty. However, the physical separation of the parties does mean that goods are likely to be in transit between buyer and seller for a long period of time. Long distance transport is expensive; moreover, although some freight is carried by air, most goods for export from the UK are carried by sea, and such transport is hazardous, exposing the goods to the perils of the sea and also the possibility of their deterioration in transit due to the time taken. Where goods are exported to a landlocked country, some part of the journey will necessarily be by road or rail. The logistical problems of organising transport may then be so much the greater, although the increasing use of containers makes multimodal transport easier and reduces the need to unload and reload goods.

The large scale of many export/import transactions can also pose special problems, particularly in the commodity trade where goods may be stored and transported in bulk, and where parties may wish to trade in cargoes whilst they are in transit in order to take advantage of market movements.

(b) Commercial problems

Any seller is concerned that his buyer should be creditworthy. Where the parties to the contract are based in different states, the seller may find it difficult to obtain a credit reference on his buyer, at least where he deals with a new customer. In the absence of assurances as to the creditworthiness of a trading partner, a business will seek some form of security. A seller will wish to retain control of the goods until he is paid; a buyer to avoid payment until he is assured of delivery. This conflict of interests, common to all sales, is particularly acute in the context of international trade, where long transit times may extend the period of risk for a party who advances credit. The seller will therefore seek some means of retaining control of the goods until he has some satisfactory assurance of payment; he is unlikely to be satisfied even with a guarantee from a financial institution in the buyer's country, because of the problems of transnational litigation. There is the additional question of how the seller is to be paid. The parties must take account of possible fluctuations in currency exchange rates which may render what was a perfectly good deal unprofitable.

(c) Political problems

Most governments are keen to encourage exports and discourage imports. An exporter must therefore take into account the possibility that there may be restrictions on the import of his goods: a quota for imports may be imposed, or there may be a tariff on imports. To a large degree those difficulties have been reduced by international agreements[2], but the exporter must take them into account, together with the possibility that a change in economic conditions or in government policy may lead to a change in tariffs or quotas. Furthermore, he is at the mercy of other changes in government policy; for instance, the government of his buyer's state may impose a ban on certain imports in order to protect their own industry or prohibit imports from a certain source in order to exert political pressure. There is a particular risk of such changes where the government of the importing state is known to be unstable. Changes of government and therefore of policy may result in the imposition of disguised controls, as where, for instance, a government imposes stringent health standards on imported goods. In certain situations controls may be imposed on exports: for instance, during the 1980s the US government imposed restrictions on the export of modern technology for fear that it might come into the hands of Eastern bloc states. Finally, the possibility of nationalisation by a foreign government, although less likely today than it was until relatively recently, remains a risk for businesses dealing with certain countries.

(d) Legal problems

If an international contract breaks down, litigation may be particularly hazardous. First, there may be problems deciding what law governs the contract; such questions are dealt with by the rules of private international law ('conflict of laws'). The parties to a commercial contract are generally free to stipulate which law should govern their contracts, and it is common for international contracts to include a choice of law clause. As we have noted, many international contracts currently adopt English law, reflecting the high standing of both English law and its practitioners, and the importance of London as a commercial centre.

Secondly, there may be procedural difficulties in suing a foreign defendant and enforcing a judgment against him. It must be decided which country's courts have jurisdiction over the dispute, and a well-drafted contract will contain an express provision dealing with this point. If a contract is governed by the law of a state other than that whose courts have jurisdiction, it may be necessary to call evidence to prove the relevant foreign law. Even if these problems are avoided, if a judgment is obtained against a defendant in a foreign jurisdiction there may be legal and practical difficulties in enforcing it.

These procedural and enforcement difficulties have to some extent been ameliorated by the Convention on Jurisdiction and the Enforcement of Civil and Commercial Judgments 1968, which facilitates the enforcement of judgments in the courts of different member states of the European Community and is implemented in the UK by the Civil Jurisdiction and Judgments Act. In other cases other legislation may assist, but transnational litigation is not lightly to be embarked upon.

Thirdly, the application to international transactions of the ordinary rules of English commercial law may pose difficulties. Thus, for instance, prior to 1995 the modern trend towards shipment of goods in bulk in the commodity trades caused difficulties when the rules of the Sale of Goods Act are applied[3]. A typical international transaction involves a complex network of contracts between a number of parties. Such arrangements are not easily reconciled with the English doctrines of privity and consideration.

Fourthly, the international sale will normally impose extra duties on the parties: who is to arrange carriage and insurance? Who is to be responsible for arranging export clearance, paying customs duties, obtaining licences and so on?

1   For an example see *Aluminium Industrie Vaassen BV v Romalpa Aluminium* [1976] 2 All ER 552, [1976] 1 WLR 676; and see *Harvey v Ventilatorenfabrik Oelde GmbH* (1988) 8 Tr L 138.
2   Eg the General Agreement on Tariffs and Trade (GATT). The imposition of tariffs and similar restrictions on trade between members of the EU is prohibited by arts 9–37 of the Treaty of Rome, which provide for the free movement of goods within the EU.
3   These problems are now largely resolved by ss 20A and 20B of the Sale of Goods Act 1979, inserted by the Sale of Goods (Amendment) Act 1995: see 15.5.2.

31.3.2   *Overcoming the problems of international trade*

Commercial ingenuity has devised mechanisms and processes to overcome many of these problems; some have required a flexible response from the law in order to accommodate them within the framework of existing legal rules and concepts.

Many of the physical and financial problems are overcome by entering into other contracts alongside the international sale contract. Thus there will be contracts dealing with the carriage and warehousing of the goods, and insurance against loss or damage in transit. Agents are extensively employed to overcome the difficulties of geographical and linguistic separation. The 'man on the spot', familiar with local customs and practices, can negotiate the contract, examine goods prior to shipment, arrange carriage, insurance and warehousing, and receive the goods on unloading. The international sale transaction is thus likely to involve a complex network of contracts all linked to the hub contract of sale.

The contract of sale itself is likely to include special terms to deal with some of the other potential problems. Thus there will be terms which:

(a) identify the payment mechanism to be used;
(b) specify the currency of payment;
(c) allocate responsibility for obtaining licences, customs clearances, the payment of duties etc;
(d) provide for the effect of occurrences outside the control of the parties: strikes, embargoes, refusal of licences and other government action, storms and other acts of God[1]; and
(e) specify the system of law to be applied to disputes arising from the contract and the forum to which such disputes shall be referred; often the parties will opt for commercial arbitration in preference to litigation in court.

Many international sale contracts will be made on standard terms, often prepared by trade associations on behalf of their members[2]. However, even where the parties do not use standard terms, they are likely to make use of certain standard types of contract arrangement which due to long commercial usage have attained a special status and legal recognition. Thus a sale on 'FOB' (free on board) or 'CIF' (cost, insurance, freight) terms defines the obligations of the parties and has recognised legal consequences[3].

Most striking of all, commerce has designed special devices to overcome the problems of credit and security in the international context, and allow dealings in goods even while they are in transit. The key to the solution of these problems is the use of documents to represent the goods and one document in particular, the bill of lading, has a special commercial significance and a unique legal status, which enables it to be used to sell and pledge goods in transit. Making use of the bill of lading, special payment mechanisms have been developed to meet the difficulties of giving credit to a trading partner in a different state; the most significant of these is the documentary credit, which seeks to overcome the problem of mutual distrust by giving the seller a right of recourse against an accessible and viable target, a bank in his own country.

Thus in the law of international sale we see a number of special features resulting from the special problems of international sales. The transaction itself is dynamic, involving a network of connected contracts and a number of parties; extensive use is made of documents; and in the law of international sale we see a clear example of the development of commercial law as a pragmatic response to commercial practice to facilitate and encourage trade. We will examine the first two of these features below before turning to an examination of the legal incidents of the standard sale contracts and payment mechanisms. The third is a thread running throughout this section. However, before turning to an examination of international transactions, we must say something about the sources and development of international trade law.

1   Such clauses are often known as force majeure clauses.
2   Eg the GAFTA terms prepared for the Grain and Feed Trade Association; for a list of standard commodity contracts see *Schmitthoff's Export Trade* (9th edn, 1990) p 73.
3   See below 33.1 (FOB contracts) and 33.2 (CIF).

31.4   The sources and development of international trade law

We are primarily concerned with English law relating to international sale contracts. When such a contract is governed by English law it is governed by the general law of sale as laid down in the English law of contract, the Sale of Goods Act 1979, and judicial decisions on that statute. It is true that some special rules have been developed which apply only to international sale contracts, and that in places the rules of the general law of contract are modified in order to accommodate commercial practices. Nevertheless, all of those rules are a part of the domestic law of England. Similarly, if a contract is governed by German law, Dutch law or US law, it will be the domestic law of those states which is applied. The legal consequences of a contract may thus depend on the national law applicable to it.

Obviously this is not entirely satisfactory. The position is not ameliorated by the fact that the rules of private international law, or conflicts of law, which are applied to decide which system of law should apply to a dispute, are also a part of domestic law and differ from state to state. The parties to an international transaction can provide some measure of certainty by including a choice of law clause in their contract, and they frequently do so[1], but agreement may not always be possible and insistence by one party on its own domestic law may be an obstacle to the negotiation of the contract. There are therefore obvious attractions in the idea of an international law governing international transactions. In fact, many of the rules of commercial law have a common root. In medieval times, when trade was developing in Europe, disputes between merchants were generally decided under the rules of the law merchant. These rules, being based on the customs and expectations of merchants, were common throughout Europe. However, in the early seventeenth century, during Sir Edward Coke's tenure of the office of Chief Justice of the Court of King's Bench, the work of the specialist commercial tribunals was taken over by the English common law courts. As a result, the rules of the old law merchant tended to become integrated with those of the common law, and English commercial law thus began to diverge from that of the civil law countries.

1   See above 31.3.0.

31.4.1   *Harmonisation of international trade law*

Ironically, in recent years there has been growing pressure for harmonisation of the legal rules applying to international trade. So far as trade within Europe is concerned, the EC obviously plays an important role. The central objectives of the EC as defined in the EC Treaty are concerned with the promotion of the free circulation of goods and services within the community, and include:

(a) the elimination of customs duties and restrictions;
(b) the establishment of a common customs tariff and common commercial policy;
(c) the abolition of obstacles to freedom of movement for persons, services and capital;
(d) the institution and implementation of a policy to ensure that competition is not distorted; and
(e) the approximation of the laws of the member states to the extent required for the functioning of the Community.

In recent years the EC has promulgated a number of directives having an impact on commercial transactions[1] as well as directives on company law and banking. However, whilst the impact of the EC on English commercial law will no doubt continue to grow, and EC competition law may be particularly important in relation to transactions within Europe, the EC has otherwise so far had little impact on the law relating to international trade transactions.

Other harmonisation initiatives have come from inter-governmental and other international agencies. In a report in 1993 the Secretary General of UNCITRAL identified 28 organisations, including agencies of the United Nations and inter-governmental and non-governmental bodies engaged on work harmonising aspects of international trade law[2]. Significantly, the list did not include the EC. The most important organisations involved in harmonisation are probably the following.

UNCITRAL: the United Nations Commission on International Trade Law
UNCITRAL was established in 1966 under the aegis of the United Nations, specifically to help remove obstacles to international trade. To this end its mandate is to prepare and promote conventions and model laws, to encourage wider acceptance of international trade terms and practices, to disseminate information and to collaborate with and promote the work of other international agencies working in the field. UNCITRAL has 36 members elected by the UN General Assembly. It is responsible for a number of important international legal instruments, including the 1980 Vienna Convention on Contracts for International Sale of Goods; the 1978 Hamburg Rules designed to regulate the carriage of goods by sea[3], a convention on international bills of exchange and promissory notes[4], and model laws on international credit transfers[5] international commercial arbitration[6], and e-commerce[7].

UNIDROIT: the International Institute for Unification of Private Law
The work of UNIDROIT is concerned with the whole of private law and not solely with commercial law. It has a dual function, drafting conventions and conducting research. It has nevertheless been responsible for a number of important international trade law texts. In 1967 it produced the Hague Convention, a Uniform Law on International Sales, which was incorporated into English law by the Uniform Laws on International Sales Act 1967. More recently, it has prepared conventions on agency in the international sale of goods[8], international factoring[9] and international finance leasing[10] and published the Principles of International Commercial Contracts[11].

ICC: The International Chamber of Commerce
The ICC was founded in 1919 to promote trade by opening markets and encouraging the free flow of capital. It represents the international commercial community and is involved in international trade law on a number of levels. It maintains links with national governments and international organisations and makes representations on behalf of its members to the international formulating agencies both to initiate work and respond to their proposals. It carries out comparative legal studies on topics of interest to its members and provides an arbitration service for the settlement of disputes. As a non-governmental organisation it cannot formulate laws or conventions as such, but it has produced numerous documents designed to promote uniformity of international commercial practice. Of particular importance are the Uniform Customs for Documentary Credits (UCP)[12] establishing a legal framework for documentary credits, and INCOTERMS (International Rules for the Interpretation of Trade Terms), which is effectively a directory of definitions of trade terms[13]. Both are widely used.

Several different harmonisation techniques are available to these and other agencies. A convention is an international legal instrument to which states subscribe.

By so doing they undertake a legal obligation to other states party to the Convention to introduce domestic laws to implement it. A model law is more flexible: as its name suggests, it is intended to provide a model which states may use for their domestic laws on the relevant topic, but imposes no obligation to do so. An alternative technique is the production of uniform rules or model contracts. These are aimed primarily at traders rather than at governments and only acquire legal force if incorporated into individual contracts.

1 Eg Directive 85/374/EEC concerning liability for defective products: see 13.1.4.
2 *Current activities of international organisations related to the harmonisation and unification of international trade law*, Report of the Secretary General to the United Nations Commission on International Trade Law, 1 July 1993.
3 See 32.2.1.
4 United Nations Convention on International Bills of Exchange and International Promissory Notes 1988; see 28.1.
5 UNCITRAL Model Law on International Credit transfers 1992; see 30.3.2.
6 UNCITRAL Model Law on International Commercial Arbitration 1985; see also the UNCITRAL Arbitration Rules. See 36.2.2.4.
7 UNCITRAL Model Law on Electronic Commerce 1996; see 1.5.1.
8 Geneva Convention on Agency in the International Sale of Goods: see 3.3.
9 See 27.3.2.
10 See 8.2.4.3.
11 See 1.4.4.
12 See 34.1.
13 See 33.0.

31.4.2 *The desirability of harmonisation*

Despite the benefits of harmonisation, described above, not everyone is convinced that it is either desirable or practicable. Harmonisation, especially by convention, can be a slow process. The drafting of the convention may take a considerable time, as attempts are made to accommodate the demands of individual states and produce a compromise between their various interests and legal systems. Work on the Vienna Convention on Contracts for the International Sale of Goods took 12 years; the UNIDROIT Convention on International Finance Leasing took 14. There will then be a further delay whilst states decide whether or not to ratify, largely on the basis of considerations of their own national interest. States often tend to wait for the reactions of others before committing themselves. Normally, a convention will provide that it is not to come into force until it has received a stated number of ratifications. Thus it was eight years before the Vienna Convention came into force[1]. The UNCITRAL Convention on International Bills of Exchange and Promissory Notes was completed in 1988 but has not yet attracted sufficient ratifications to come into force.

There are often criticisms, too, of the finished article. Writing in the *Law Quarterly Review* in 1990 Sir John (now Lord) Hobhouse, an experienced judge of the Commercial Court, questioned the value of harmonisation of central areas of international trade law. Modern conventions –

'are inevitably and confessedly drafted as multi-cultural compromises between different schemes of law. Consequently they will have less merit than most of the individual legal systems from which they have been derived. They lack coherence and consistency. They create problems about their scope. They introduce uncertainty where no uncertainty existed before. They probably deprive the law of those very features which enable it to be an effective tool for the use of international commerce'[2].

Nevertheless, there is no doubt that there is a growing trend towards harmonisation, although in many cases the promulgation of model codes for voluntary adoption by traders, along the lines of the UCP and INCOTERMS, is perhaps a more promising way to seek harmonisation than by use of conventions, and it is perhaps significant that for recent projects UNCITRAL has tended to use model laws rather than conventions. Thus in 1987 the Law Commission published its report on Sale and Supply of Goods and concluded that it might be desirable not to introduce legislative changes to the law of commercial sales because of the likelihood of increasing legislative input from international agencies[3]. Such input is likely to become more significant as new methods of doing business are introduced. Most of the international law-formulating organisations have recently turned their attention to the legal problems of e-commerce. Data in electronic form flow speedily across national boundaries, and the need for a standard legal response in this area is obvious. UNCITRAL, the ICC and the EC all have groups working on aspects of e-commerce and, as detailed elsewhere[4], UNCITRAL and the EC have produced important legal instruments dealing with aspects of the subject[5].

1   It has not yet been ratified by the UK: see 33.2.11.
2   Hobhouse 'International Conventions and Commercial Law: the Pursuit of Uniformity' (1990) 106 LQR 530. Contrast the views of Sir Johan (now Lord) Steyn in 'A Kind of Esperanto' in Birks (ed), *The Frontiers of Liability* (1994) vol 2.
3   Law Commission Report 160, *Sale and Supply of Goods* (1987) (Cmnd 137), para 1.15.
4   See 1.5.1.
5   Work on e-commerce has largely superseded the earlier work on electronic data interchange. That too led to the production of several harmonised legal instruments, including the International Organisation for Standardisation's Trade Data Elements Directory (UNTDED) and Trade Data Interchange Directory (UNTDID) and the ICC's Uniform Rules of Conduct for Interchange of Trade Data by Teletransmission (UNCID).

31.5   Outline of a typical transaction

It has already been suggested that the international sale transaction is actually a composite of several contracts, with the sale contract itself at its heart. It will be helpful at this point to outline the stages in a typical transaction.

1.   The parties enter into the sale contract. This will define the obligations of the parties, including the payment mechanism to be used and responsibility for transport, insurance and other arrangements, identify the system of law which will govern the contract and so on. Assuming that English law applies to the formation of the contract, the normal rules relating to formation of contracts will apply and a series of messages may be exchanged before a legally binding contract is concluded.

The parties may often deal through agents; in particular a confirming house may be used by the buyer to place his order with the seller. A confirming house is a reliable and creditworthy business in the seller's country which can place the purchase order on behalf of the buyer, giving the buyer the advantage of its local knowledge and expertise and, possibly, the seller the security of a reliable and creditworthy debtor. The exact relationship of seller (S), buyer (B) and confirming house (C) will depend on the instructions given to the confirming house by its overseas client[1].

(a) C may act simply as an agent of the B, placing an order on its behalf and creating privity of contract between S and B[2]: Fig. 1.

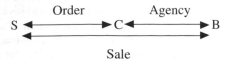

Fig 1

(b) C may buy from S in its own name and resell to B. In this case there are two contracts of sale and no privity between S and B: Fig 2.

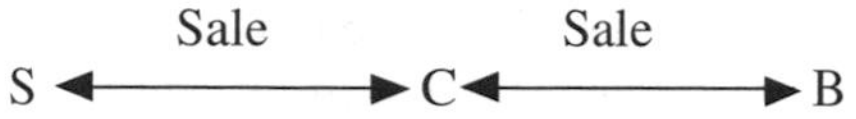

S ←————————→ C ←————————→ B

Sale   Sale

Fig 2

(c) C may be instructed to buy from S on B's behalf but not to create privity between S and B. This creates the relationship known in some countries as a commission agency. The effect in English law is that there is a contract of sale between S and C but no privity between S and B[3]: Fig. 3. Thus S can only look to C for payment and only C can enforce the contract against S. However, the relationship between B and C is that of principal and agent so that C is not strictly liable for the conformity of the goods with the contract but is only liable as an agent on his duty to exercise reasonable care[4]. C is remunerated by commission rather than by reselling to B at a profit.

S ←————————→ C ←————————→ B

Sale   Agency

Fig 3

(d) C may be instructed to order goods from S on B's behalf so as to create privity between S and B, but to add its confirmation to the order. The result is that there is a contract of sale between S and B and a collateral contract between S and C under which C effectively guarantees B's performance of the contract[5]: Fig 4.

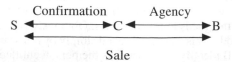

Fig 4

(e) In some cases C may take on additional duties on behalf of B and act as a freight forwarder: see below.

2. Depending on the terms of the contract B may have to make payment or set up the agreed payment mechanism. For instance, if payment is to be by documentary credit B will have to arrange to open the credit and notify S of its opening[6].

3. S or B must make shipping arrangements according to the terms of the contract. This may involve obtaining export licences, booking shipping space, getting the goods to port, obtaining customs clearances and getting the goods loaded onto

the nominated ship. Often a freight forwarder may be employed to make shipping arrangements. The freight forwarder will have specialist knowledge of shipping and carriage as well as customs requirements. It often may not be clear whether the freight forwarder acts as principal supplying services to his client (S or B) or merely makes carriage and other arrangements as agent on the client's behalf. The distinction may be important, for example, if the goods are damaged or lost: if the forwarder acted as agent he will only be liable if he failed to show the standard of care expected of an agent; whereas if he acted as principal he may be liable as carrier to his client and have a contract with the actual carrier in his own right[7].

The transport of goods will often involve several stages. Unless S and B have premises actually at ports, the goods will have to be transported, normally by land, to the port of loading, and then transported from the port of unloading to the buyer's premises. The goods may have to be warehoused along the way: for instance at the port of loading prior to actual loading. This may involve several contracts. Of course, the freight forwarder can be instructed to make all the necessary contracts on behalf of his principal, but it is easier if just one contract can be made to cover the whole of the transportation. In recent years there has been a growing trend towards such multi-modal transport, assisted by the increasing use of containers. Containerised cargoes can be handled much more quickly at ports, reducing delays and therefore allowing shipowners to increase the use and profitability of their vessels. They can also be transported from door to door direct: for instance, if S contracts to sell a load of machinery to B, an overseas customer, he can load the machinery into a container which can be taken direct to an export port by lorry or rail, loaded onto a ship, transported to the appropriate port of import and then carried by road or rail to B's premises, without any need to open the container. Thus instead of a series of contracts for carriage of goods by road, sea and rail, one contract for 'multi-modal carriage' can be made to cover all the stages of the journey. Freight forwarders may still be employed to make container transport arrangements, or to act as contracting carriers who employ sub-contractors to perform some or all of the contract, and where a shipper wishes to transport less than a full container load of goods the forwarder or container company, as appropriate, may load goods from several clients together in one container to make up a full container load. The shift to containerised and multi-modal transport throws up a number of special legal problems which are only now beginning to be answered[8].

4.   The goods will be carried to their destination. Where this is not B's place of business, as will often be the case, B will have to arrange to collect them from the ship or a warehouse at the port, pay all necessary import duties and arrange for the transport of the goods to his premises. Obviously B needs some means of collecting the goods. This can be achieved simply by S instructing the carrier to deliver to B and B identifying himself as the person entitled to delivery, for instance by producing a delivery order from S.

However, in many cases B will want more than simply to receive the goods. He will want to obtain control of them as soon as possible: in some cases he may want to resell them before they actually arrive at the port of destination; in others he may need to use the goods as security to finance their price. S will be unwilling to release the goods until he has received payment or some satisfactory assurance of payment, but B will be unwilling to pay without some assurance that the goods conform to the contract and are in satisfactory condition. B will also want details of the goods in advance of their arrival in order to prepare the necessary papers for customs clearance and so minimise the time the goods themselves are held at the port on arrival. Moreover, where the goods are at B's risk during transit, B will want some assurance that he is protected against their deterioration or loss during the transit.

These conflicting interests are accommodated by the extensive use of documents in international trade. Indeed, where goods are sold under a CIF contract the documents are so important that the contract has been described as 'a contract for the sale of goods to be performed by the delivery of documents'[9]. However, documents also perform a vital role in other types of international sale contract, especially where the seller makes transport arrangements. S will deliver documents which allow B to satisfy himself that the goods conform to the contract and to take control of them on arrival and B will pay the price, or release payment, in return for those documents. Thus, for instance, S may be required to deliver a policy of insurance covering the goods against loss during transit; an invoice giving details of the goods and their price for use in clearing the goods through customs; a certificate of quality or origin confirming the conformity of the goods with the contract of sale. However, the most important document in many cases, and certainly the most interesting, is the bill of lading which fulfils three functions:

(a) it provides evidence of the terms of a contract of carriage by sea between the shipper of goods and the carrier; in certain circumstances that contract can be transferred to a transferee of the goods[10];

(b) it operates as a receipt for the goods from the carrier and provides evidence of their condition at the time of loading; and

(c) it operates as a document of title to the goods so that transfer of the bill of lading may transfer ownership of the goods.

It is true that, for various reasons, the use of bills of lading has declined in recent times. Nevertheless, bills of lading are still commonly used in many situations and many of the problems of the most common international sale contracts cannot be understood without an understanding of the nature and role of the bill of lading. Moreover, 'The bill of lading is a creation of mercantile custom, a typical institution of international trade'[11] and 'The bill of lading has had a long and distinguished history. It has served the commercial community well. Indeed, it might be regarded as one of the most remarkable products of the mercantile genius'[12]. It therefore justifies study as an illustration of the way in which commercial law develops in response to mercantile practices.

1 See 3.2.3 above and *Schmitthoff's Export Trade* (9th edn, 1990) p 296 et seq; *Bowstead and Reynolds on Agency* (16th edn, 1996) para 9-019; *Benjamin's Sale of Goods* (5th edn, 1997) paras 23-274 et seq.
2 See above 3.2.3.
3 *Ireland v Livingstone* (1872) LR 5 HL 395.
4 Although the position is not entirely clear: see the dissenting judgment of Diplock LJ in *Anglo-African Shipping Co of New York v J Mortner Ltd* [1962] 1 Lloyd's Rep 610, CA.
5 C's liability is not necessarily restricted to payment of the price: see eg *Sobell Industries Ltd v Cory Bros & Co* [1955] 2 Lloyd's Rep 82, where C was held liable for damages for B's non-acceptance of the goods. Contrast the liability of the confirming bank under a confirmed documentary credit, below 34.1.4.
6 See ch 34.
7 See generally *Schmitthoff's Export Trade* (9th edn, 1990) p 302 et seq.
8 See *Schmitthoff's Export Trade* (9th edn, 1990) ch 28 and the UN (Geneva) Convention on International Multimodal Transport of Goods (1980).
9 Bankes LJ in *Arnold Karberg & Co v Blythe, Green, Jourdain & Co* [1916] 1 KB 495 at 610, CA; see below 33.2.2.
10 See below 32.5.5.
11 *Schmitthoff's Export Trade* (9th edn, 1990) p 561.
12 Sir Anthony Lloyd, 'The Bill of Lading: Do We Really Need It?' [1989] LMCLQ 47 at 48.

Chapter 32

Bills of Lading and Contracts of Carriage

32.0 Contracts of carriage

Where goods are sold pursuant to an international sale contract, it will generally be necessary for one of the parties to arrange for them to be transported to their destination. For many types of goods the appropriate mode of transport will be by sea.

Where that is the case, one option is for the party responsible for arranging carriage to charter a ship to carry the goods. A charterparty is essentially a contract for the hire of a ship and a charterparty will therefore normally only be appropriate where the volume of goods to be carried is sufficiently large to justify the hire of a whole vessel (unless the charterer intends to contract to carry goods for others and effectively re-sell part of the vessel's capacity). Where a vessel is chartered to carry cargo, the parties may enter into either a time or a voyage charterparty. Under a time charterparty the vessel is hired to the charterer for a fixed period of time, during which the charterer may use it for as many voyages as can be made during the charter period. A time charter might therefore be used where a series of shipments have to be made over a period of time as where, say, a buyer contracts to buy the whole production of a particular mine for a fixed period. Under a voyage charter the ship is hired for a specific voyage. In both cases the shipowner retains control of the vessel and responsibility for providing its crew and supplies. A further type of charter, the bareboat charter, involves the hire of a vessel without crew, so that the charterer is responsible for the provision of crew and management of the vessel. It is therefore not a contract of carriage as such, although the charterer might use the vessel to carry goods or to provide a carrying service for others.

Where the quantity of goods to be carried is insufficient to justify chartering a whole vessel the alternative is to arrange carriage for the goods as part of the cargo of a vessel travelling to the port of destination. The carriage contract may take one of several forms. Goods are often nowadays carried pursuant to a waybill contract under which the carrier undertakes to deliver the goods to a named consignee at the port of destination. Where, as is increasingly common, goods are carried in containers, the contract may provide for carriage not only by sea but possibly even 'door to door', utilising other methods such as road and/or rail, in which case the goods will be carried pursuant to a contract for 'multi-modal' transport. However, legally the most important, and interesting, arrangement is for carriage pursuant to a bill of lading.

'The bill of lading is a commercial document with a long history. Beginning as a bailment receipt for goods, it has developed into a receipt containing the contract of carriage and acquired, in time, a third characteristic, that of a negotiable document of title'[1].

The bill of lading was in use as early as the sixteenth century; indeed, it appears to have evolved from a practice originated in the Adriatic port of Trani in the eleventh century, where local law required ships' masters to keep a book of lading recording details of all cargoes loaded[2] and over time it has acquired special commercial significance and the unique legal status outlined in the previous chapter[3].

The modern practice on issue of a bill of lading was described by Devlin J in *Heskell v Continental Express Ltd*[4]. The shipper of goods for export, who might be either seller or buyer, normally acting through a freight forwarding agent, would find out when a ship was sailing to the intended port of destination, book space on the ship for his goods (if necessary) and deliver the goods to the ship. Normally, advance shipping arrangements would be made through a loading broker, an agent acting on behalf of the carrier. The shipper, or his agent, would receive a mate's receipt for the goods, and would then prepare a bill of lading giving details of the goods shipped. The draft bill of lading would be presented to the carrier, who would check the goods against it, and then sign it, making any appropriate amendments, and issue it to the shipper in exchange for the mate's receipt.

In more recent times the practice has changed. Mates' receipts are rarely used nowadays. Instead, the shipper sends the goods to port with a shipping note or dangerous goods note containing details of the goods, and a signed copy of that is issued to the shipper as a receipt. Often, information and bookings are sent to the shipping line by computer; generally, the bill of lading is prepared by the carrier by computer from the information supplied to him[5].

After receiving the bill of lading the shipper will forward it, normally by airmail, to the port of discharge to enable the goods to be collected from the ship on arrival. If he is the buyer of goods, he will ship them to his own order and will forward the bill to his own office or representative at the port of discharge; if he is the seller of goods, or resells them whilst they are in sea transit, he will forward them to his buyer, or, if payment is to be by documentary credit, to the buyer's bank[6].

It should be noted that even where goods are carried pursuant to a charterparty, bills of lading will normally be issued, although, as will be seen below, the status of the bill may differ where it is issued under a charterparty.

1 'Bills of Lading', Report by the UN Conference on Trade and Development (1971).
2 See Urbach, 'The Electronic Presentation and Transfer of Shipping Documents' in Goode (ed) *Electronic Banking – the Legal Implications* (1985).
3 See 31.5.
4 [1950] 1 All ER 1033, 83 Ll L Rep 438.
5 For a full description of shipping procedures, see Dockray, *Cases and Materials on the Carriage of Goods by Sea* (1987) pp 3–13.
6 See ch 34.

32.1 The bill of lading as a document of title[1]

The purpose of a document of title to goods is to enable an owner of goods to deal with them, for instance by selling or pledging them, even though they are in the physical possession of a bailee, by dealing with the document. In order to be a document of title to goods at common law a document must therefore be such that its transfer is effective to transfer constructive possession of the goods. Professor

Goode has described three requirements for a document to be recognised as a document of title at common law:

(a) it must be issued by a bailee of the goods, so that it operates as an advance attornment to any transferee;
(b) it must relate to identified goods; and
(c) there must be a custom recognising that transfer of the document transfers constructive possession of the goods[2].

At the end of the eighteenth century, in *Lickbarrow v Mason*[3], it was recognised that by mercantile custom the bill of lading is a document of title. The decision opened the way for goods to be sold and pledged whilst afloat and 'laid the foundation for the financing of overseas trade and the growth of commodity markets in the 19th century'[4] and thus for much of modern international trade.

> 'A cargo at sea in the hands of the carrier is necessarily incapable of physical delivery. During this period of transit and voyage, the bill of lading by the law merchant is universally recognised as its symbol, and the indorsement and delivery of the bill of lading operates as a symbolical delivery of the cargo . . . It is a key which in the hands of a rightful owner is intended to unlock the door of the warehouse, floating or fixed, in which the goods may chance to be'[5].

In theory, there is no reason why other documents could not be recognised as documents of title at common law, provided a sufficiently certain mercantile custom to that effect can be proved. However, over the years the courts have shown themselves remarkably reluctant to recognise any other class of documents as possessing the status of documents of title[6], although certain warehouse warrants and delivery orders have been given the status of documents of title by statute[7].

Confusingly, a wider class of documents is defined as 'documents of title' by the Factors Act 1889, s 1(4)[8]. However, where that section applies, the transfer of the 'document of title' only operates to allow a disposition to pass title under a statutory exception to the 'nemo dat' rule[9]. As between seller and buyer, only the transfer of a bill of lading is effective to transfer constructive possession, and therefore ownership, of goods in the possession of a bailee. Other documents, such as delivery orders or sea waybills, may be used in certain situations and may have certain advantages over the bill of lading in certain circumstances, but the unique status of the bill of lading as a document of title means that only a bill of lading will meet the needs of the parties where the consignor or consignee wishes to be able to deal with the goods whilst they are at sea, as is often the case for instance in the bulk oil and other commodity trades[10].

As noted above, transfer of a bill of lading may operate to transfer constructive possession of the goods to which it relates. Transfer of the bill is not, as such, necessary to transfer property in goods. Property in goods may be transferred pursuant to a contract of sale without the seller being in possession. Transfer of the bill of lading may, however, operate to transfer property in, as well as constructive possession of, the goods it covers.

Transfer of the bill will only transfer constructive possession if: (a) the goods to which it relates are identifiable; (b) the bill is transferable; and (c) it is transferred in the proper manner. Where the bill relates to goods which form part of a larger bulk, transfer of the bill cannot transfer constructive possession, and no property in any particular goods can pass, until the goods to which the bill relates are separated out so as to be identifiable, although where the bill is transferred pursuant to a contract of sale the buyer may acquire an undivided share in the bulk if the conditions of s 20A of the Sale of Goods Act 1979 are satisfied[11].

Transferability of the bill depends on its wording. A bill of lading may be transferable, like a bill of exchange, either by indorsement and delivery, or by delivery alone. If no consignee is named in the bill it may be transferred by simple delivery to the intended transferee; effectively, the carrier undertakes to deliver the goods to any person producing the bill. Alternatively, the bill may be made out to a named consignee (who may be the shipper or some other person, such as the person to whom the shipper has sold the goods). If the bill makes the goods deliverable 'to XYZ or order', it may still be transferred, but with the difference that the bill must now be transferred by indorsing the name of the transferee and delivering the bill to him. If, however, the bill simply names a consignee and does not contain the words 'or order', or includes words such as 'not transferable' or 'not negotiable', it is said to be a 'straight consigned bill' and the carrier can only deliver the goods to the named consignee. Thus where goods are shipped under a 'straight consigned bill' the consignee cannot deal with them during transit.

The simple transfer of the bill of lading only transfers constructive possession of the goods, giving the transferee the right to demand delivery of them from the carrier. The transfer will also transfer ownership of the goods to which the bill relates if the transferor so intends. Thus if he assigns the bill of lading to his bank by way of pledge to secure an advance of money to pay for the goods, the bank acquires constructive possession, sufficient to create a pledge, but does not acquire ownership. It may be necessary to examine all the circumstances surrounding the transfer of the bill in order to decide if the transferor intended to transfer ownership. In *The Kronprinsessan Margareta*[12] S shipped goods and took a bill of lading in B's name, but retained the bill. It was held that, on the facts of the case, S did not intend to transfer property in the goods[13].

The bill of lading retains its status as a document of title at common law so long as the goods to which it relates remain in the possession of the carrier. The goods may therefore be transferred by transfer of the bill of lading even after they have been landed if they remain in the carrier's possession, for instance because he has a lien over them for freight and they are held in a warehouse to the carrier's order[14]. The bill ceases to be a document of title at common law once the goods have been delivered by the carrier to the person presenting the bill: it is then said to be 'spent'.

The bill of lading is often described as 'negotiable': this description must be treated with care:

> 'it is well settled that "Negotiable" when used in relation to a bill of lading, means simply transferable. A negotiable bill of lading is not negotiable in the strict sense; it cannot, as can be done by the negotiation of a negotiable instrument, give to the transferee a better title than the transferor has got'[15].

1   See generally Dromgoole and Baatz in Palmer and McKendrick (eds) *Interests in Goods* (2nd edn, 1998).
2   *Proprietary Rights and Insolvency in Sales Transactions* (2nd edn, 1989) p 61.
3   (1794) 5 Term Rep 683. It is not clear if a bill which shows only that goods have been received for shipment is a document of title at common law: see *Diamond Alkali Export Corpn v Bourgeois* [1921] 3 KB 443; cf *The Marlborough Hill* [1921] 1 AC 444; *Ishag v Allied Bank International Fuhs and Kotalimbora* [1981] 1 Lloyd's Rep 92.
4   Per Diplock LJ in *Barclays Bank Ltd v Customs and Excise Comrs* [1963] 1 Lloyd's Rep 81 at 88.
5   Eg s 146(4) of the Port of London Act 1968.
6   Per Bowen LJ in *Sanders v Maclean* (1883) 11 QBD 327 at 341.
7   See eg *Farina v Home* (1846) 16 M & W 119. Limited customs were recognised in *Kum v Wah Tat Bank* [1971] 1 Lloyd's Rep 439, PC (mate's receipts in trade between Sarawak and Singapore)

and *Mercantile Banking Co of London v Phoenix Bessemer Steel Co* (1877) 5 Ch D 205 (certain delivery orders).
8   Sale of Goods Act 1979, s 61(1).
9   See above 17.1.1.2.
10 As to whether other documents could be regarded as documents of title, see Bridge [1993] JBL 379.
11 See 15.5.2.
12 [1921] 1 AC 486.
13 Contrast *The Parchim* [1918] AC 157, where S was held to have retained the bill of lading to protect his lien and property had passed to B.
14 *Barber v Meyerstein* (1870) LR 4 HL 317.
15 Per Lord Devlin in *Kum v Wah Tat Bank* [1971] 1 Lloyd's Rep 439 at 446, PC. Contrast Debattista, *Sale of Goods Carried by Sea* (2nd edn, 1998) ch 2; cf Tettenborn [1991] LMCLQ 538.

32.2   The bill of lading as evidence of the contract of carriage

The bill of lading normally contains the terms of the contract for the carriage of the goods loaded under it. The terms may be set out in full on the bill itself, or incorporated by reference[1]. They will generally be the standard terms of the individual carrier, except in so far as varied by special requirements or bargaining power of the shipper.

Strictly speaking, the bill of lading is not itself the contract of carriage. Normally, the contract will be concluded between the shipper and the carrier, either when space on the vessel is booked or when the goods are presented and accepted for loading, before the bill of lading is issued; and on ordinary contract principles, terms contained in the bill are incapable of affecting a contract already made[2]. The better view is that, as between shipper and carrier, the bill of lading is 'a receipt for goods, stating the terms on which they were delivered to and received by the ship, and therefore excellent evidence of those terms, but it is not a contract'[3]. In *The Ardennes*[4] mandarin oranges were shipped for carriage to London, and it was orally agreed that they should be carried direct in order to arrive before an expected rise in import tax on mandarins. In fact the carriers went via Antwerp so that the mandarins arrived late, after the tax increase. The shippers sued and the carriers attempted to rely on a clause in the bill of lading which allowed them to deviate from the agreed route. It was held that the clause in the bill was not part of the contract, which had already been concluded before the bill was issued.

However, a contract of carriage has a special legal status because, where the goods to which it relates are transferred, as where they are sold, the shipper's rights *and liabilities* arising under the contract of carriage may also be transferred to the transferee[5]. It is therefore settled that, as between the carrier and a third party, such as a consignee of the goods or indorsee of the bill of lading the bill provides conclusive evidence of the terms of the contract of carriage, for the third party has no way of knowing what the terms of the contract are, other than by reference to the bill of lading[6].

Special problems arise where a bill of lading is issued under a charterparty, and the terms of the bill conflict with those of the charterparty. The contract between the charterer and shipowner is contained in the charterparty, which is conclusive as between the two of them; but as between shipowner and a third party, the terms in the bill of lading are again conclusive, unless they expressly incorporate the terms of the charterparty[7].

The result is that whilst the contract of carriage may be transferred to a consignee or indorsee of a bill of lading, the transferee may actually take the benefit of rights which were not available to the transferor.

1　As where a so-called 'short form' bill of lading is used.
2　See eg *Olley v Marlborough Court Hotel Ltd* [1949] 1 KB 532; above 2.5.2.
3　Per Lord Bramwell in *Sewell v Burdick* (1884) 10 App Cas 74 at 105.
4　*The Ardennes (Cargo Owners) v SS Ardennes* [1951] 1 KB 55, [1950] 2 All ER 517.
5　Carriage of Goods by Sea Act 1992; see 32.6.5.
6　*The Emilien Marie* (1875) 44 LJ Adm 9; and see below 32.3.
7　For a full discussion see *Benjamin's Sale of Goods* (5th edn, 1997) para 18-016.

32.2.1　*The terms of the contract of carriage*

As has been noted, the contract of carriage, as evidenced by the bill of lading, will normally be on the standard terms of business of the carrier. It became apparent in the early part of the twentienth century that, in order to prevent abuse of the carrier's dominant bargaining position, the terms of the contract of carriage should be regulated by law; this was particularly important because, as has been noted, the contract of carriage could bind consignees and indorsees of bills of lading not party to the original negotiations. Moreover, because of the international nature of sea carriage there was seen to be a need for international uniformity in conditions of sea carriage. As a result of these pressures, a series of international conventions have been formulated to regulate the terms under which goods are carried by sea (and, indeed, similar conventions govern other modes of international freight transport).

In 1921 the International Law Association began work on a set of uniform rules and, at a convention in Brussels in 1924, the Hague Rules were adopted. Inter alia, the rules fixed the irreducible minimum obligations of the sea carrier, allowing him certain contractual protections and prohibiting further exclusions of liability. Those rules were given effect in English law by the Carriage of Goods by Sea Act 1924. In 1968 the Hague Rules were revised and the revised rules are now known as the Hague-Visby Rules; they are incorporated into English law by the Carriage of Goods by Sea Act 1971. Since then there has been a further, and more radical, revision of the law, resulting in the Hamburg Rules adopted by a UN conference in 1978. However, the UK has not ratified the Hamburg Convention so that the Hamburg Rules are not part of English law. Where a contract is governed by English law the Hague-Visby Rules will therefore normally apply. The rules are stated to apply to every bill of lading relating to the carriage of goods between ports in two different states if:

(a)　the bill of lading is issued in a contracting state;
(b)　the carriage is from a port in a contracting state; or
(c)　the contract of carriage expressly adopts the rules or any national legislation
　　giving effect to them[1].

Thus the parties may choose to subject their contract to the Hague-Visby Rules even where they would not automatically apply by virtue of their own terms. Moreover, the Carriage of Goods by Sea Act 1971 extends the application of the rules to all carriage from a port in the UK, whether or not the carriage is between two different states[2]. The Act also applies the rules to any contract evidenced in a bill of lading or a non-negotiable transport document (such as a sea waybill) which expressly adopts the rules[3]. The result is that the rules will apply to any contract for the carriage of goods from a UK port, whether for export or merely for coastal transport, and to any other contract governed by English law which expressly adopts them. Thus most contracts for sea carriage under a bill of lading will be governed by the Hague-Visby Rules and the 1971 Act; however, there may be some cases where goods are shipped from a foreign state not party to the Hague-Visby Rules and the parties choose English law to govern their contract where the contract will be governed solely by the common law.

Where the rules do apply, they apply 'in relation to and in connection with the carriage of goods by sea'[4], and not to (say) road transport prior to loading on ship. It has been held that this formula meant that the rules applied where goods were stored briefly at Le Havre during a broken voyage from Shoreham to Jeddah[5].

The Hague-Visby Rules stipulate the obligations of the parties to the contract of sea carriage and provide the carrier with certain limitations on liability. Detailed consideration of the rules is beyond the scope of this work[6]; however, some mention should be made of the basic obligations of the parties.

1   See article X.
2   Section 1(3).
3   Section 1(6). Note that a bill of lading will often expressly adopt the rules by reference. In many cases this is unnecessary because the rules apply automatically. The practice of incorporating the rules by a 'clause paramount' was essential under the Hague Rules.
4   Article III(8).
5   *Mayhew Foods Ltd v Overseas Containers Ltd* [1984] 1 Lloyd's Rep 317.
6   For detailed discussion see Wilson, *Carriage of Goods by Sea* (3rd edn, 1998); *Schmitthoff's Export Trade* (9th edn, 1990) p 595; Goode, *Commercial Law* (2nd edn, 1995) ch 36.

32.2.1.1   *Carrier's obligations*

At common law the sea carrier's basic obligations were: (1) to supply a seaworthy vessel; (2) to proceed without undue delay; (3) not to deviate unreasonably from the agreed route; and (4) to take care of the cargo. Those obligations are qualified in some respects by the Hague-Visby Rules as follows.

1.   The duty to provide a seaworthy vessel at common law required that the vessel be fit both to put to sea and to receive the goods; it had to remain fit up to the time of putting to sea. The meaning of 'seaworthiness' was the subject of much case law analysis, and the term was ultimately classified as an 'intermediate stipulation', so that the shipper's remedies in the event of breach would depend on the seriousness of the breach and its consequences[1]. Article III of the Hague-Visby Rules repeats the obligation and defines it more or less in line with the common law definition; however, the obligation is modified to one to exercise 'due diligence' to make the vessel seaworthy and to properly man, equip and supply it.
2.   The rules say nothing specifically about the duty to proceed without undue delay but the carrier's liability for breach is subject to the general limitations on carrier's liability in art IV.
3.   At common law it is breach of contract for the carrier to deviate from the agreed route, other than in certain limited circumstances for the purposes of saving life or communicating with a vessel in distress, averting danger to the ship or cargo, or where deviation is made necessary by the cargo owner's breach of contract. Unjustified deviation is regarded as a fundamental breach of contract which gives the cargo owner the option to treat the contract as repudiated, in which case the carrier is deprived of the protection of any exclusion or limitation clauses in the contract. The duty is effectively restated in the Hague-Visby Rules, which provide, in art IV(4) that a deviation to save or attempt to save life or property, or a reasonable deviation, shall not be treated as a breach of the rules or of the contract of carriage.

4. At common law the carrier is liable for the cargo as if he were a common carrier and is therefore liable for any loss unless caused by act of God, the Queen's enemies or inherent vice in the goods. In practice this obligation was always restricted by exclusions in the contract of carriage, and the Hague-Visby Rules now provide extensive protection against liability[2], including that the carrier is not to be liable for loss caused by the act or neglect of the ship's master or of the carrier's servants in the navigation or management of the ship[3], and place a financial limit on the carrier's liability, dependent on the weight of the cargo or the number of packages[4]. The contract may not provide the carrier with greater protection against liability than provided by the rules, although the contract may increase his liabilities[5]. The protections granted by the rules apply to any action against the carrier arising from the contract of carriage, whether framed in contract or tort[6], and extend to protect the carrier's servants or agents[7].

1   *Hong Kong Fir Shipping Co v Kawasaki Kisen Kaisha* [1962] 2 QB 26, [1962] 1 All ER 474, CA.
2   Article IV(1), (2), (3).
3   Article IV 2(a).
4   Article IV(5).
5   Article III(8); art V.
6   Article IV, Bis (1).
7   Article IV, Bis (4).

32.2.1.2 *Shipper's obligations*

At common law the shipper's basic obligations are: (1) to pay freight; (2) to pay general average contributions; (3) not to ship dangerous goods; and (4) to collect the goods on arrival. They are little modified by the Hague-Visby Rules.

1. 'Freight' is the agreed fee for the carriage of the goods. At common law the carrier is only entitled to receive freight on safe arrival of the goods. However, this obligation is normally modified by the contract so that freight is prepaid; the bill of lading will normally provide that freight is payable on shipment of the goods and the payment will then normally be 'advance freight' which (subject to exceptions) the carrier is entitled to retain even if the goods do not arrive at their destination[1].
    Where freight is not pre-paid it is payable on delivery of the goods by the consignee or indorsee of the bill of lading or any person who takes delivery[2]. Provided that the goods reach their destination, freight must be paid even though the goods arrive damaged or the handling of the goods otherwise gives rise to a claim against the carrier. The shipper, consignee or indorsee by whom freight is payable may not withhold payment or set off his claim against payment due[3]. The only exception is where the goods arrive so damaged that they are commercially no longer the same cargo.
    Other sums may be payable. For instance, if the goods are carried at the shipper's instructions, or in his interests, to some place other than the agreed destination, 'back freight' may be payable. The carrier has a lien over goods in his possession for sums due to him in respect of those goods, including freight.
2. Liability to pay General Average Contributions[4] arises where some part of the vessel or its cargo is sacrificed to preserve the remainder from some peril of the sea: for instance, part of the cargo or the ship's equipment may be jettisoned in a storm. Where this happens, all the cargo owners and the vessel owners are treated as being party to a common venture, and are required to contribute ratably

to the loss, so that a loss, incurred to protect the interests of all, is not borne by one alone. All cargo owners are required to pay general average contributions under the terms of their contracts of carriage; the liability is governed by the internationally agreed York Antwerp Rules, which, although not having force of law, are generally adopted by contract. The cargo owners will normally be covered against liability for general average by their policies of marine insurance.

The carrier is entitled to exercise a lien over the goods in his possession to secure payment of general average contributions.

3.   The shipper must not ship dangerous goods without informing the carrier of their nature. 'Dangerous goods' has been given a wide meaning. Goods are dangerous if they are liable to cause damage either to the vessel or to other cargo. Such damage need not be direct. The shipper's liability is strict. So there was a breach where the shipper unknowingly shipped a cargo of groundnut extract infested with khapra beetle, as a result of which the remainder of the ship's cargo had to be dumped at sea[5]. If such goods are shipped without the carrier's knowledge, the carrier may offload, destroy or render them harmless, without compensation to the cargo owner[6]. The shipper remains liable for any damage done by the goods.

4.   The shipper (if he ships goods to his own order) or consignee/indorsee must arrange to collect the goods on arrival. If he fails to do so, the carrier may warehouse the goods and charge him for the warehousing.

1   *Compania Naviera General SA v Kerametal Ltd, The Lorna I* [1983] 1 Lloyd's Rep 373. If the goods do not arrive, the carrier may be liable for their loss, but he is still entitled to retain advance freight.
2   See 32.5.2; 32.5.5.
3   *Dakin v Oxley* (1864) 15 CBNS 646; *Aries Tanker Corpn v Total Transport Ltd, The Aries* [1977] 1 All ER 398; *Bank of Boston Connecticut v European Grain and Shipping Ltd* [1989] 1 All ER 545.
4   See generally *Schmitthoff's Export Trade* (9th edn, 1990) p 607 ff.
5   *Effort Shipping Co Ltd v Linden Management SA, The Giannis NK* [1998] AC 605, [1998] 1 All ER, HL.
6   Hague-Visby Rules, art IV(6).

32.2.2   The Hamburg Rules

By the late 1960s there was some dissatisfaction with the Hague Rules which was only marginally eased by their amendment by the Visby Protocol. In particular, it was felt that the exemptions from liability granted to the carrier, and especially the exemption from liability for loss caused by the negligence of the carrier's servants and agents in navigation, were excessively generous and inappropriate in modern conditions, and the limitation of the rules to contracts of carriage under bills of lading was anachronistic in view of the increased use of other carriage documents. More generally, there was a feeling that the rules tended to favour the interests of the carrier over those of the cargo owner and therefore of developed over less developed countries. For these reasons, UNCITRAL established a group to draft a more modern and fairer set of rules. The result was the Hamburg Rules, adopted in 1978, which came into force in 1992[1].

In many ways, the Hamburg Rules are an improvement on the Hague-Visby Rules. They are wider in scope, applying to all contracts of carriage and not just those under a bill of lading. Time limits for claims and financial limits on carrier's liability are increased. Whereas under the Hague-Visby Rules the carrier is only liable for goods from the time loading commences to the time unloading is completed, leading to difficult problems of application, under the Hamburg Rules the carrier is liable for the goods throughout the period he is in charge of them. More importantly, the rules provide a conceptual basis for the carrier's liability. The Hague-Visby Rules prescribed no conceptual basis for the carrier's liability but provided a long list of situations in which the carrier would not be liable. Under the Hamburg Rules the carrier is liable for loss or damage unless he can show that 'he, his servants or agents took all measures that could reasonably be required to avoid the occurrence [which caused the loss] and its consequences'[2]. The carrier is therefore no longer exempt from liability for loss caused by negligence of the ship's master or crew. The basis of liability is 'presumed fault': the burden of proof is on the carrier to establish that any loss occurred without negligence on his part[3]. The only exception to this general rule is where loss is caused by fire, when the burden of proof is on the claimant to prove either that the fire was caused by the carrier's or crew's fault or neglect, or that the loss was caused by such fault or neglect in extinguishing the fire[4].

The other major improvement of the Hamburg Rules is that they expressly provide for the situation where the carrier arranges for a sub-contractor to perform part or all of the carriage contract. The rules distinguish between the 'contractual carrier' and the 'actual carrier'. The contractual carrier is fully liable, subject to the exemptions in the rules, for any loss of or damage to the goods during the period of the carriage, even if actually due to the default of the sub-contractor[5]. The only exception is where the contract of carriage expressly provides that part of it will be performed by a named sub-contractor and excludes the contractual carrier's liability for loss, damage or delay caused during that part of the carriage[6]. The provisions of the Convention about carrier's liability apply equally to the sub-contractor in relation to carriage performed by him so that if the cargo owner sues the sub-contractor, the latter is entitled to rely on the rules. The cargo owner thus always has an identifiable target against whom to bring a claim in the event of loss or damage.

Despite these and other improvements, the Hamburg Rules have been strongly criticised in some quarters. In particular, it is said that in places the drafting is unclear or confused and that their introduction would create uncertainty and 'cast aside the results of half a century of expensive litigation and pave the way for another half century of legal debate on a new and different regime'[7]. They have been strongly opposed by carriers and their representatives, who argue that the rules favour cargo owners and their interests[8]. Many of the criticisms of the rules are probably overstated[9]. However, since some states still retain the original, unamended Hague Rules, whilst others cling to the Hague-Visby Rules, the coming into force of the Hamburg Rules has further eroded the international uniformity which the original Hague Rules sought to create[10].

1 See generally Tetley [1979] LMCLQ 1.
2 Article 5.1.
3 See the Common Understanding appended to the Rules.
4 Article 4(a).
5 Article 10.
6 Article 11.
7 BIMCO Bulletin 1/88, p 9025.
8 No state with significant sea carrying interests has yet adopted the rules; 10 of the first 26 states to ratify are landlocked.
9 See generally Waldron [1991] JBL 305.
10 In 1998 a Bill for a new Carriage of Goods by Sea Act was introduced into the US Congress. It would create a new carriage regime in the US not based on any of the current international regimes. See Asiriotis and Tsimplis [1998] [LMCLQ] 126; Sturley [1999] LMCLQ 519; Asiriotis and Tsimplis [1999] LMCLQ 530.

32.3   The bill of lading as a receipt

On arrival at the port of destination, the carrier must deliver up the goods shipped to the holder of the bill of lading. 'A ship must deliver what she receives, as she received it'[1]. The carrier is liable for any loss of or damage to the goods whilst in transit, subject to the protection of any exclusion clauses in the bill of lading, and therefore in the event of any dispute between carrier and bill of lading holder relating to short delivery or delivery in damaged condition, it will be essential to establish the quantity and condition of the goods which were loaded. In addition, the shipper may wish to sell or otherwise deal with the goods whilst they are at sea; he will need to provide some evidence of their condition to any prospective buyer who cannot physically examine them whilst afloat. The bill of lading provides evidence of the quantity and condition of goods at the time of shipment[2] and therefore satisfies both these requirements. Since such evidence may be admissible against him in the event of a claim for loss of or damage to the cargo, the carrier will attempt to ensure that the statements as to the quantity and condition of the goods on loading say as little as possible.

Where the Hague-Visby Rules apply to a contract of carriage, the shipper is entitled to demand[3] that the carrier issue a bill of lading showing: (a) leading marks necessary to identify the goods; (b) the quantity of goods loaded; and (c) the apparent order and condition of the goods on loading.

The 'leading marks' should normally be stamped or otherwise marked on the goods themselves and must be such as to remain legible throughout the voyage. The quantity of goods loaded may be stated by reference to the number of packages/ pieces or to the weight or quantity of the goods. The carrier is only obliged to use one measure of quantity: thus, for example, he might record the number of packages and add words such as 'weight unknown'. Moreover, the carrier is only required to issue a bill containing the statements required by the rules if the shipper requests one[4]. Thus unless the shipper specifically requests otherwise, the carrier may issue a bill with a general reservation such as 'weight, quantity and contents unknown', in which case any statement of weight or quantity in the bill has no evidential effect.

The statement of apparent order and condition of the goods refers to the external appearance of the goods; the carrier is not expected to make statements as to the quality of the goods loaded. Where the bill states that the goods are in 'Apparent good order and condition', it is said to be 'clean'; if the statement of condition is qualified in any way (eg 'some loaded in damp condition' or 'some containers leaking'), the bill is said to be 'claused'. The shipper will normally require a clean bill, since a claused bill may not be acceptable to his buyer and will certainly not be acceptable to the buyer's bank where payment is by documentary credit[5]. However, it is enough that the bill records that the goods are loaded in apparent good condition; a bill which indicates that the goods were subsequently damaged will be regarded as 'clean'[6].

In addition, the bill will state the date when the goods were shipped or, if a received for shipment bill is issued, when they were received for shipment. The date of shipment is an important element in the description of the goods[7].

The bill of lading is issued by the carrier, but, as noted above[8], it is based on information supplied by the shipper, either directly by computer, or by the shipper drawing up a bill on a form supplied by the carrier and then presenting it to the carrier for signature. It is essential that the bill of lading is signed by or on behalf of the carrier, as the statements contained in the bill may be binding upon him.

In recent years there has been increasing interest in the use of computers and electronic trade data interchange (edi) for the preparation and issue of bills of lading, with a view to speeding up trade. The need for a signature is one obstacle to that development; 'electronic signatures' are technologically possible, but their legal status is unclear. The Secretary of State now has power to make regulations validating the use of electronic signatures under the Electronic Commerce Act 2000, but this only applies where the requirement for a signature is imposed by or under statutory or other legislative scheme[9]. Interestingly, the 1980 UN Convention on International Multimodal Transport of Goods allows a multimodal transport document to be signed 'by mechanical or electronic means', if not inconsistent with the law of the country where the document is issued[10].

If a claim is brought against the carrier for short delivery or for damage to the goods in transit, he will normally find it difficult to contradict the statements in the bill of lading. Different rules apply according to whether or not the Hague-Visby Rules apply to the contract of carriage, the identity of the claimant, and whether the claim relates to short delivery or damage/deterioration. In general, however, the carrier is bound by the statements in the bill of lading once it has come into the hands of a third party who takes it in good faith.

1 Per Lord Sumner in *Bradley v Federal Steam* (1927) 27 Ll L Rep 395 at 396.
2 A received for shipment bill provides evidence of the goods' condition when received for shipment. It may therefore not be acceptable to a buyer or bank since the carrier does not become liable for the goods until they are shipped.
3 Article III.
4 *The Mata K* [1998] 2 Lloyd's Rep 614.
5 See UCP 500 (1993) art 32; see below 33.0.1; 34.2.
6 *The Galatia* [1980] 1 All ER 501, [1980] 1 WLR 495, CA; see Schmitthoff [1979] JBL.
7 See 33.1.3.
8 See 32.0.
9 Parties may agree between themselves that a digital signature should be effective and binding, as is done under the BOLERO system: see 32.5.4.
10 Article 5.3. UCP 500 (1993) requires a transport document to be signed or 'authenticated' by the carrier or master or the agent of either. This would seem to be capable of including authentication by electronic signature.

32.3.1 *Bills governed by the Hague-Visby Rules*

Where the Hague-Visby Rules apply, the statements in the bill of lading are prima facie evidence of the quantity and condition of the goods at the time of loading; they may be contradicted if the carrier can produce rebutting evidence. However, once the bill has been transferred to a third party acting in good faith, the statements in the bill of lading provide irrebuttable evidence against the carrier[1]. The transferee's position is better than that of the original shipper since, unlike the shipper, he has no information as to the state of the goods at the time of loading other than that stated in the bill.

1 Article III, r 4.

32.3.2 *Bills governed by the common law*

In cases where the Hague-Visby Rules do not apply, the position in English law is now governed by the common law as modified by the Carriage of Goods by Sea Act 1992. In the hands of the original shipper, statements in the bill as to condition and quantity of goods loaded are prima facie evidence. However, once the bill comes into the hands of a third party, statements as to the condition of the goods are binding on the carrier. A statement that the goods were loaded in good order and condition raises an estoppel against the carrier preventing him from denying that the goods were in good order at the time of loading and therefore from denying that damage occurred during transit[1]. If the statement of receipt in good order is qualified in any way, the bill of lading is not clean, and the carrier may refer to the qualification to show the true condition at the time of loading. Thus where a received for shipment bill of lading referred to a ship's receipt, the bill was not clean and the carrier could refer to the receipt which indicated the true condition of the goods at the time of loading[2]. The qualification on the bill 'reasonably convey[ed] to any businessman that if the ship's receipt was not clean the statement in the bill of lading as to apparent order and condition could not be taken as unqualified'[3]. The common law estoppel operates only in favour of a transferee of the bill of lading for value who must act on the statement in the bill, without knowledge of its untruth; since the effect of the statement is to raise an estoppel, the transferee must show that he relied on it. However, in most cases 'the mercantile importance of clean bills is so important that the fact that he [ie the consignee] took the bill of lading which is in fact clean, without objection, is quite sufficient evidence that he relied on it'[4].

The position in relation to statements as to the quantity of goods loaded is different. In *Grant v Norway*[5] it was held that a ship's master has no authority at common law to sign a bill of lading for goods not actually loaded, so that if the bill overstates the quantity loaded, or if no goods are loaded at all, the carrier may dispute the statement in the bill. The decision is difficult to reconcile with the general rule on the liability of a principal for his agent's fraud[6], and its effect is to make the bill of lading 'least useful precisely where the representations on its face are most likely to produce the largest possible loss to endorsees who are in the worst possible position to monitor the shipment of the goods'[7]. Section 3 of the Bills of Lading Act 1855 attempted to resolve this difficulty by making the bill of lading in the hands of a consignee or indorsee conclusive evidence of shipment against the person signing the bill. However, where the bill was signed by the ship's master, the section only made the bill conclusive against the master, not the carrier. Section 3 has therefore been repealed and replaced by s 4 of the Carriage of Goods by Sea Act 1992, which provides that a bill of lading which represents goods to have been shipped or received for shipment and has been signed by the master or other person with the express, implied or apparent authority of the carrier to sign it, shall, in favour of a person who becomes holder of the bill in good faith, be conclusive evidence against the carrier of the shipment, or receipt for shipment, of the goods. The effect is that the carrier is bound by statements in the bill both as to the condition and quantity of the goods. However, s 4 applies only to bills of lading as defined in the Act. It therefore does not apply where a carriage document other than a bill of lading is issued. Furthermore, the definition of 'bill of lading' in the Act excludes 'straight consigned bills' under which a bill of lading is made out in favour of a named consignee, without the addition of the words 'or order' and is thus not transferable[8]. In that case the consignee's rights will depend on the common law, so that statements as to the condition but not as to the quantity of the goods will be binding on the carrier. Where the bill of lading contains an inaccurate statement of the quantity of goods loaded, the consignee's only remedy will be to sue the master or other signatory of the bill personally for breach of warranty of authority[9]. Alternatively, he will, in many cases, have an action against his seller for breach of the contract of sale. Even where s 4 of the 1992 Act does apply, it may be possible for the carrier to escape liability to a consignee where the bill is a received for shipment bill, since in that case the bill will only be evidence of receipt for shipment and not actual shipment.

In practice the evidential value of the bill of lading is often undermined by the practice of carriers entering reservations on the bill. The bill may contain a term such as 'weight, number and quantity unknown'. The effect of such a term is to cancel out the evidential effect of any statement in the bill of the weight, number or quantity of goods loaded so that such statements cannot be relied upon against the carrier[10]. Such statements are particularly important where goods are shipped in containers. The carrier will normally receive the container loaded and sealed and will thus have no way of checking its contents. Note that the inclusion of such a reservation does not necessarily mean that the carrier will escape liability for short delivery. The claimant will, however, be unable to rely on the statement in the bill and will therefore have to prove by other means the quantity loaded.

The carrier is generally not estopped by statements of leading marks. Their purpose is to identify the goods, and the carrier may contradict any part of the statement of leading marks which does not relate to the commercial identity of the goods. In *Parsons v New Zealand Shipping Co*[11] the bill of lading misstated the leading marks on a number of frozen lamb carcasses. Misdescription made no difference to the commercial identity or value of the carcasses, but the buyer of the cargo attempted to sue the carrier on the grounds of a failure to deliver the carcasses identified in the bill of lading. The claim was entirely without merit and was brought because the price of lamb had fallen; the court allowed the carrier to adduce extrinsic evidence to show that the carcasses delivered to the buyer were those identified in the bill of lading. In *Cox v Bruce*[12] the leading marks quoted in the bill of lading indicated goods of a higher quality than those actually loaded. The court held that the carrier was not estopped by the statement in the bill because the master of the ship signing the bill of lading had no (usual) authority to make statements as to the quality of goods loaded.

As noted above, the carrier prepares the bill of lading from information supplied by the shipper. If that information is inaccurate the carrier may be estopped from denying its accuracy and be held liable to the consignee for loss of or damage to the cargo. However, in such a case the carrier is entitled to an indemnity from the shipper.

1 *Compania Naviera Vasconzada v Churchill and Sim* [1906] 1 KB 237. The estoppel extends to prevent the carrier alleging that the packaging was defective or inadequate: *Silver v Ocean Steamship Co Ltd* [1930] 1 KB 416, CA, although Greer LJ doubted that the estoppel extended to the adequacy of the original packaging.
2 *Canadian and Dominion Sugar Co Ltd v Canadian National (West Indies) Steamships* [1947] AC 46, PC.
3 Per Lord Wright [1947] AC 46 at 54.
4 *Silver v Ocean Steamship Co Ltd* [1930] 1 KB 416 at 428, CA, per Scrutton LJ at 428.
5 (1851) 10 CB 665.
6 See above 4.2.3. In *The Nea Tyhi* [1982] 1 Lloyd's Rep 606 Sheen J found it impossible to reconcile *Grant* with *Lloyd v Grace, Smith & Co* [1912] AC 716, HL; see Reynolds (1967) 83 LQR 193.
7 Debattista [1986] LMCLQ 468 at 469.
8 Carriage of Goods by Sea Act 1992, s 1.
9 *Rasnoimport v Guthrie* [1966] 1 Lloyd's Rep 1; see 5.2. Contrast *Heskell v Continental Express Ltd* [1950] 1 All ER 1033, where no goods were loaded at all: as a result there never would have been a contract with the carrier even if the signature of the bill of lading had been authorised and so no damages were recoverable from the agent.
10 *New Chinese Antimony Co Ltd v Ocean Steamship Co Ltd* [1917] 2 KB 664; *The Mata K* [1998] 2 Lloyd's Rep 614; *River Guara (Cargo Owners) v Nigerian National Shipping Line Ltd* [1998]

QB 610; cf *A-G of Ceylon v Scindia Steam Navigation Co Ltd* [1962] AC 60, PC where the
statement 'weight, contents and value unknown' did not affect the evidential effect of a statement
as to the quantity of bags loaded. It is not clear whether the words 'said to contain', commonly
entered on bills of lading where sealed containers are loaded, has the same effect: see per
Phillips LJ in *The River Gurara* at 626.
11   [1901] 1 KB 548, CA.
12   (1886) 18 QBD 147, CA.

32.3.3   *Indemnities*

If the shipper intends to sell or otherwise deal with the goods whilst they are at sea,
he will be anxious that he does not receive a claused bill, which will not be acceptable
to a potential buyer or his bank. Equally, the carrier will be anxious not to issue a
clean bill for damaged goods, since he will be estopped by the statement of condition
in the bill. Where goods are loaded in obviously damaged condition, the shipper
may be tempted to ask for a clean bill of lading and to offer the carrier an indemnity
against liability to the consignee. However, it has been held that such an indemnity is
unenforceable by the carrier as it amounts to a contract to defraud the consignee[1].
The position is different where there is a genuine dispute between shipper and carrier
about the condition of the goods and whether or not the bill should be claused.

1   See *Brown Jenkinson v Percy Dalton (London) Ltd* [1957] 2 QB 621, [1957] 2 All ER 844, CA.

32.4   Delivery of the goods

Where goods are carried under a bill of lading the carrier is under a fundamental
obligation to deliver up the goods against presentation of a genuine bill of lading.
It is this obligation which underpins the status of the bill as a transferable document
of title. The carrier is entitled to a lien over the goods to secure payment of sums
due to him but, provided that all charges in respect of the goods have been paid,
the carrier must deliver up the goods to a person who presents the bill, and a
failure to do so will be a breach of contract.

Delivery of the goods without production of the bill of lading is a breach of
contract, and if the goods are delivered to a person who is not entitled to receive
them[1], the carrier also commits the tort of conversion. Liability in both cases is
strict, in the sense that it is no defence for the carrier to establish that he reasonably
believed the person to whom delivery was made to be entitled to it[2]. 'It is perfectly
clear law that a shipowner who delivers without production of the bill of lading
does so at his peril'[3].

The converse of this is that the carrier is entitled to refuse to deliver the goods
without production of the bill of lading, even if the person who requests delivery is
in fact entitled to receive them[4].

The unique commercial advantage of a bill of lading is that the consignee or
indorsee can use it to deal with the goods by reselling or pledging them before they
reach their destination. The seller under an international sale contract is obliged to
forward the bill of lading (and other documents) to his buyer with reasonable dispatch[5].
However, even where the seller fulfils that obligation, the increased speed of modern
sea transport means that often the bill of lading arrives after the goods reach the port
of destination. Without the bill, the buyer is not entitled to demand delivery and the
carrier is at risk if he releases the goods. In order to avoid goods thus being tied up at

the port because the bill of lading is not available on arrival, the practice has grown up of the carrier releasing the goods to the consignee without presentation of a bill of lading, in return for the consignee agreeing to indemnify the carrier against any liability he thereby incurs. Strictly speaking, the carrier who releases the goods against such an indemnity commits a breach of contract vis-à-vis the consignee or indorsee entitled to delivery under the bill of lading contract. The Privy Council has, however, held that such indemnity contracts are enforceable[6]. Thus where the person who takes delivery is the true indorsee or consignee, the carrier will be in breach of contract but the damages for breach will be nominal. Where delivery is made to a person other than the true consignee or indorsee, the carrier will be liable to the true owner but will be entitled to claim an indemnity.

Where the carrier delivers against an indemnity, he commits a deliberate breach of contract and knowingly takes a commercial risk[7]. It has recently been held that the carrier is also liable for breach of contract and conversion if the goods are released against a forged bill of lading, even if the forgery is not reasonably detectable[8], in the same way that a bank which pays a forged cheque is strictly liable to its customer. A forged bill is a nullity. This seems harsh. It exposes the carrier to a dilemma. If an apparently genuine bill is presented, the carrier will be entitled, and indeed obliged, to withhold delivery if the bill is in fact a forgery. On the other hand, if he refuses delivery and the bill later turns out to be genuine, the carrier will be liable to the presenter of the bill for breach of contract. It may be possible for the carrier to exclude liability for breach where delivery is effected as a result of fraud in such cases, but clear words will be needed because any such exclusion is contrary to the fundamental obligation to deliver up the goods to the holder of a genuine bill[9]. The argument for holding the carrier liable in such a case is that the carrier is best placed to guard against such fraud by devising forms which are proof against forgery and/ or checking the bill presented and the signature on it[10].

The carrier does not bear all risk of fraud, however. Traditionally, bills of lading have been issued in sets of three. It is well established that only one copy of the bill must be presented in order to obtain delivery of the goods and the carrier is entitled to deliver to the first person who presents a bill[11]. The practice of issuing multiple copies was originally adopted to facilitate resale of the goods afloat at a time when communications were slow. In modern conditions it facilitates fraud. The shipper may, for instance, sell or pledge the goods but deliver to the buyer or pledgee only one copy of the bill and then use one of the other copies to obtain delivery of the goods from the carrier. The carrier incurs no liability in such a situation and the buyer/pledgee is left to pursue the fraudulent shipper. It is for the buyer or pledgee of the goods in such a situation to guard against fraud by ensuring that he obtains all three copies of the bill. As long ago as 1882, Lord Blackburn observed:

> 'I have never been able to learn why merchants and shipowners continue the practice of making out bills of lading in parts . . . I suspect [that] merchants dislike to depart from an old custom for fear that the novelty may produce some unforeseen effect'[12].

He added that he expected that the practice would continue. It does to the present day.

1   *The Stettin* (1888) 14 PD 142; *Sze Hai Tong Bank v Rambler Cycle Co Ltd* [1959] AC 576, [1959] 3 All ER 182, PC.
2   *Motis Exports Ltd v Dampskibsselskabet AF 1912 A/S* [1999] 1 All ER (Comm) 571; affd [2000] 1 All ER (Comm) 91; see Todd [1999] LMCLQ 499.
3   Per Lord Denning in *Sze Hai Tong Bank v Rambler Cycle Co Ltd* [1959] AC 576 at 586, [1959] 3 All ER 182 at 184, PC.

4   *Trucks and Spares Ltd v Maritime Agencies (Southampton) Ltd* [1951] 2 All ER 982, WN 297;
    Kuwait Petroleum Corpn v I & D Oil Carriers Ltd, The Houda [1994] 2 Lloyd's Rep 541.
5   *Sanders Bros v Maclean & Co* (1883) 11 QBD 327, CA.
6   *Sze Hai Tong Bank v Rambler Cycle Co Ltd*, above note 3.
7   It is most unlikely that an exclusion clause would be construed so as to cover the deliberate
    breach involved in delivering the goods without production of the bill of lading.
8   *Motis Exports Ltd v Dampskibsselskabet AF 1912 A/S* [1999] 1 All ER (Comm) 571; affd [2000]
    1 All ER (Comm) 91.
9   Ibid; cf *Chartered Bank of India, Australia and China v British Steam Navigation Co Ltd* [1909]
    AC 369.
10 This reasoning is criticised by Todd [1999] LMCLQ 499.
11 *Glyn Mills Currie & Co v East and West India Dock Co* (1882) 7 App Cas 591.
12 *Glyn Mills Currie & Co v East and West India Dock Co* (1882) 7 App Cas 591 at 605.

32.5   Alternatives to bills of lading

Notwithstanding the reluctance to disturb settled practices, the use of bills of lading
in some modern situations creates a number of legal and practical problems, giving
rise to what has been described as a 'bill of lading crisis'[1].

The problem caused by the delayed arrival of the documents has already been
mentioned. The rule that goods can only be delivered against a genuine bill of lading
means that where goods are sold or pledged, modern communication methods such
as fax cannot be used to send the bill of lading to the buyer/pledgee: the fax copy will
not be an original. The practice of releasing goods against an indemnity (no doubt
often together with production of a faxed copy of the bill) provides a workable
solution to this problem but it is less than ideal, involving a degree of risk for the
carrier and undermining the commercial security of the bill of lading. Likewise, the
continued practice of issuing bills in sets of three facilitates fraud. Finally, where
goods are shipped in bulk under a single bill of lading, the shipper or consignee may
have difficulties dealing with the cargo. A bill of lading can only be used to transfer
the whole cargo to which it relates and therefore cannot be used if it is desired to sell
parts of the cargo to different buyers.

As a result of these and other problems there has in recent years been a considerable
decline in the use of bills of lading as buyers, sellers and carriers have sought
alternative carriage documents. However, none of the alternatives in use offers the
unique qualities of the bill of lading and, where it is intended to resell the cargo
afloat, a bill of lading will generally still be required. Moreover, a seller is only
entitled to tender a document other than a bill of lading where the contract of sale
permits him to do so

1   Ramberg, 'The Multimodal Transport Document' in Schmitthoff and Goode (eds) *International
    carriage of goods: some legal problems and possible solutions* (1988).

32.5.1   *Waybills*

Waybills have traditionally been used for air freight and in recent years it has
become increasingly common for bills of lading to be replaced for short voyages
by sea waybills. It is estimated that in the 1980s they were used for 70% of North
Atlantic sea freight traffic. The waybill may set out the terms of the contract of
carriage and operates as a receipt for the goods; however, the Hague-Visby Rules
do not apply to it unless expressly adopted by its terms[1]. Moreover, the waybill is
not a document of title to the goods; there is no need to present the waybill in order

to obtain the release of the goods, which instead are released only to the consignee named in the waybill. Goods carried under a waybill may therefore not be sold during transit and waybills are generally used for short voyages (for instance within Europe), for container transport and for export where the goods are not to be resold during transit. Their great advantage is that there is no need for the consignee to wait for the arrival of the waybill in order to collect the goods.

1   In contrast, the Hamburg Rules do apply to waybills: see 32.2.2.

32.5.2   Delivery orders

Ship's or merchant's delivery orders are frequently used where goods are carried in bulk in order to break up the bulk and allow it to be resold in smaller quantities than those covered by bills of lading. Delivery orders may be issued by carriers or by holders of bills of lading, who may be owners of the cargo, or freight forwarders who ship cargoes on behalf of several shippers under one bill of lading (to obtain preferential freight rates).

A ship's delivery order is issued either by the carrier, or by the holder of the bill of lading. When issued by the carrier, it amounts to an undertaking by the carrier to deliver the goods to the person named in the order, who therefore acquires the rights of a bailor of the goods vis-à-vis the carrier. When issued by the bill of lading holder it amounts to an order by that person (who is entitled to delivery of the goods) to the carrier to deliver the goods to the person named in the order. That person acquires no rights against the carrier unless the carrier assents to the order and thus attorns to the person named in the order. However, such a ship's delivery order may be acceptable to a buyer under a CIF contract[1]. A merchant's delivery order, on the other hand, is a personal undertaking by the bill holder, or an order to his agent, to deliver goods to the person named in the order. It gives the holder no property rights in respect of the goods in English law.

Prior to 1995, a buyer who received a delivery order in respect of goods forming part of a larger bulk consignment obtained no proprietary rights in respect of any part of the cargo, even if he had paid for it; indeed, the position was the same even if he received a bill of lading[2]. In *The Gosforth*[3] B agreed to buy a bulk cargo of citrus pellets from S and received a bill of lading in respect of the goods, but did not pay for them. B resold the pellets to 13 sub-buyers and arranged for an agent to divide the cargo between the sub-buyers on arrival in Rotterdam. The agent issued the sub-buyers with delivery orders in respect of their shares of the bulk cargo, but on arrival of the cargo S, who was still unpaid, exercised rights under Dutch law to arrest the cargo. The sub-buyers claimed to be entitled to the cargo in priority to S, but were held to have no property rights in it. They had received only merchants' delivery orders, which confer no property rights in either English law (which governed the contract of sale) or Dutch law; moreover, the goods remained in bulk, so that the sub-buyers would have acquired no property rights even had they received bills of lading. The situation would now be governed by s 20A of the Sale of Goods Act. Having paid for goods forming part of an identified bulk, each sub-buyer would be entitled to a property interest in the form of an undivided share in the bulk.

1   See below 33.2.3.
2   Sale of Goods Act 1979, s 16; *Re Wait* [1927] 1 Ch 606. See above 15.2.3.1.
3   (20 February 1985, unreported); see Davenport [1986] LMCLQ 4.

32.5.3   *Multimodal transport and containerisation*

One of the most significant developments in carriage in the second half of the twentieth century was containerisation. Goods can now be carried by road, rail, air, sea and inland waterway in metal containers of a standard size and specification[1]. Standardisation facilitates cargo handling: with the use of specialised (but standard) equipment, containers can be loaded and unloaded quickly and easily and transferred direct from ship to train or lorry and vice versa. As a result, cargo handling has become much faster and less labour intensive than in the past. Goods in containers can be carried on deck, increasing the cargo capacity of ships. Containers themselves can be sealed, offering protection against theft of or damage to the goods inside. Storage is facilitated, since the containers can be stored outdoors, and stacked several high, without the need for warehouse facilities, the containers themselves providing security and protection from the elements.

The container may be loaded by the exporter or by a container operator or freight forwarder. An exporter who has sufficient goods to fill a container (a 'full container load' (FCL)) may obtain a container – normally on hire from a container operator or freight forwarder – and fill ('stuff') it. For smaller quantities the exporter will deliver goods to the container operator as a 'less than container load' (LCL) and the operator will consolidate it with other smaller loads to make up a container load.

Containerisation has brought many benefits. It has also given rise to some awkward legal problems. Although the use of a sealed container may help protect the goods against petty theft, it by no means prevents theft. It is not unknown for whole containers to be stolen. Of more legal significance, where goods are delivered to a carrier in a sealed container the carrier has no way of checking the contents. If on arrival it is found that some of the contents are missing or are damaged, the carrier may have difficulty in establishing when the loss or damage occurred. Because of the evidential difficulties thus created, carriers taking custody of a sealed container will normally enter appropriate reservations such as 'weight, quantity and contents unknown' on any bill of lading or other document issued to the shipper. However, the legal effect of some reservations is uncertain[2].

Containerisation has also facilitated and prompted a growth in 'multimodal' or 'combined' transport operations. Traditional sea carriage contracts covered the goods from port to port, leaving the importer and exporter to make separate arrangements to move the goods from the exporter's premises to port of loading, and from the port of discharge to the importer's premises. It is obviously much simpler if the whole carriage from door to door can be arranged with one carrier.

Multimodal transport arrangements raise a number of legal questions[3]. Through carriage could be arranged in several different ways. The shipper could employ an agent such as a freight forwarder to enter on his behalf into a separate contract with the carrier responsible for each leg of the journey. Alternatively, the agent may itself carry out part of the carriage, and contract for the other legs of the journey as the shipper's agent. Or, alternatively again, the shipper may contract with one carrier who contracts as a principal to carry the goods for the whole journey but who then sub-contracts performance of one or more parts of the carriage to other specialist carriers. The nature of the arrangement will be crucial if any of the goods are lost or damaged in transit, because it will determine who is the party contractually liable for the loss or damage. Where there are several separate contracts arranged through an agent and goods are damaged in transit, it will be necessary to determine when damage occurred in order to determine who is liable for it.

It will therefore be preferable to arrange for through carriage by a single carrier who will undertake responsibility for the whole journey. It will, however, still be necessary to determine the extent of the carrier's liability and which, if any, legal regime governs it. Where goods are delivered into the hands of a sea carrier, a through bill of lading may be issued, pursuant to which the carrier undertakes to carry the goods to their destination. However, the more modern tendency is for the carrier to issue a 'multi-modal' or 'combined' transport document covering the whole journey. The legal status of both through bills and multi-modal transport documents is uncertain. First, it is not clear if they qualify as documents of title so that their transfer can also transfer ownership of the goods to which they relate. At common law the only document recognised as a document of title is a shipped bill of lading issued by a sea carrier[4]. Many through bills and multi-modal transport documents will, of necessity, be issued prior to shipment and will therefore be, at best, received for shipment documents. Thus even if issued by a sea carrier, they will not qualify as a document of title under the established custom. And yet such documents are now widely used. The importance of multi-modal transport was recognised by the 1990 edition of INCOTERMS, which for the first time included terms for use where multi-modal transport is contemplated. This has been continued in the latest revision, INCOTERMS 2000. Similarly, the 1993 revision of the Uniform Customs and Practice for Documentary Credits provides for multi-modal transport documents to be acceptable to banks under documentary credit arrangements[5]. Since the recognition of the bill of lading as a document of title depends on commercial practice, it would be possible for a court to hold that received for shipment bills and multimodal transport documents are now documents of title by commercial practice[6].

If an action is brought against the carrier, the next question will be to determine the extent of his liability, if any, for the goods. Whereas there are established international regimes governing the liability of land, air and sea carriers for the goods they carry, the details of the schemes differ. The first thing to note is that the Hague-Visby Rules only apply as a matter of law to 'contracts of carriage covered by a bill of lading or any similar document of title'[7]. Thus a multimodal transport document is only subject to the rules if it is a 'bill of lading' or 'other similar document of title'[8], or if it expressly incorporates the rules. Second, even if the rules apply, they only apply to the period of carriage by sea[9]. Any period before or after the sea carriage therefore falls outside the rules and the parties are free to make their own contractual arrangements as to liability in relation to such carriage. Where goods are lost or damaged in transit, it may therefore be necessary to determine when the loss or damage occurred in order to determine what terms should apply to the loss.

Various attempts have been made to overcome these problems by introducing some standardisation of multimodal transport contracts. In 1975 the ICC produced a set of Rules for Combined Transport Documents. These only have legal force if contractually adopted by the parties, but are in fact widely adopted. The rules apply to documents issued by combined transport operators and provide that the issuer undertakes legal responsibility for the whole of the carriage, including the acts of sub-contractors. Special rules govern the situation where the goods are lost or damaged but it is not known at what point in the journey loss or damage occurred. Where the timing of loss is known, the rules adopt a network solution to the problem of liability, whereby the carrier's liability is determined in accordance with the rules which would apply to the stage of the carriage during which the loss or damage occurred.

The ICC Rules are widely used but are voluntary. In 1980 the UN produced an International Convention on International Multimodal Transport of Goods but insufficient states ratified the Convention to bring it into force and it lapsed. In 1991 the United Nations Commission on Trade and Development (UNCTAD) and the ICC jointly published a set of rules to regulate multimodal carriage contracts. Like the ICC Rules, the rules have no independent legal force and only apply if expressly adopted in a contract. Also like the ICC Rules they adopt a 'network' system of liability, under which the operator's liability for loss or damage is determined in accordance with any statutory or conventional rules which would have applied to that stage of transit alone. Thus if loss occurs during sea carriage, the sea carrier is liable on the terms of the Hague-Visby Rules (regardless of the argument that the contract was for multimodal, not sea, transport). Even were these rules to be adopted, therefore, it would still be necessary in some cases to establish at what stage in the carriage loss or damage occurred.

1 Containers are normally manufactured to a standard size (normally 8 feet wide by 8 feet high by 20 or 40 feet long) and specification laid down by the International Standards Organisation.
2 See *The River Gurara, River Gurara (Cargo Owners) v Nigerian National Shipping Line Ltd* [1998] QB 610, above 32.3.2.
3 See Faber [1996] LMCLQ 503.
4 *Lickbarrow v Mason* (1794) 5 Term Rep 683.
5 See ch 34.
6 The Privy Council recognised in *The Marlborough Hill* [1921] 1 AC 444 that a received for shipment bill could be a document of title for certain purposes.
7 Article 1(1)(a).
8 Where the Hague-Visby Rules do not apply as a matter of law it would be possible for the parties expressly to subject the contract to the rules.
9 See *Mayhew Foods Ltd v Overseas Containers Ltd* [1984] 1 Lloyd's Rep 317.

32.5.4 *Electronic alternatives*

As noted above, it is vital that shipping documents are available at the port of destination when the cargo arrives, in order to obtain its release; however, 'with the increasing complexities of international trade, correct documents have even less chance today of being in the right place at the right time than ever before'[1]. Many factors contribute to delays: the greater speed of modern sea transport is one; another is the need for documents to be presented to, and inspected by, a number of intermediaries. Where goods are to be paid for by means of documentary credit, the documents must be presented to, and carefully checked by, the buyer's bank[2]; they may also have to be checked by customs authorities at the port as well as by the buyer.

An attempt to speed up the process has been made by substituting the waybill for the bill of lading where possible. However, the waybill is still a paper document and travels no faster than the mail. Modern electronic communications, via fax and computer, are virtually instantaneous. It would greatly facilitate international trade operations if such communications could be used for the transmission of cargo information and documentation and some progress has already been made in the computerisation of the waybill. Many traders still, however, prefer the security of a bill of lading, and where goods are to be resold at sea, or where the goods are to be used as security to obtain finance for their purchase, a bill of lading will normally be necessary. In particular, the bulk commodity trades are likely to continue to need a bill of lading or some equivalent possessing similar characteristics. There has therefore been a considerable amount of research into the possibility of producing an 'electronic bill of lading'. Various possibilities have been explored. One scheme contemplated the development of a central registry system for bulk cargoes. Shipping documents would be deposited with the registry (either in paper form or electronically) and changes in ownership would be notified to and recorded at the registry without the need for the documents themselves to be retransmitted to each new buyer of the cargo. However, a pilot registry scheme, SEADOCS, established during the 1980s, was abandoned. In 1990 the International Maritime Committee (CMI) adopted a set of rules for electronic bills of lading, but they were not taken up by the commercial community.

Several international legal instruments now make provision for electronic alternatives to paper documents. In particular, INCOTERMS 2000, like the 1990 revision before it, permits edi equivalents to be used in place of paper carriage documents. The Hamburg Rules recognise that a document can be signed electronically (although they seem to still require a paper document). The problems of equipment compatibility have largely been solved by the development of the Internet. If electronic alternatives to shipping documents are to be developed, however, a number of other legal and technical obstacles must still be overcome[3]. Electronic documents must be acceptable to customs and government authorities. Above all, traders and banks must be convinced that electronic documents offer as much security as their paper equivalents. The most promising scheme is BOLERO, a system developed by a consortium including the Society for Worldwide Interbank Telecommunications (SWIFT) and the Through Transport Club. It therefore has the support of business organisations, banks and carriers. The basis of the scheme is 'functional equivalence'. It does not create an electronic bill of lading as such, but creates a network of contracts which, so far as possible, replicate the legal and commercial functions of the traditional bill of lading. All members subscribe to a multi-party contract by which they agree that, as between them, electronic messages shall be legally valid, they will not deny having sent a message bearing their electronic signature and that they will be bound by an electronic document bearing their electronic signature[4]. Messages are authenticated and encrypted using a public key/private key system[5], with public keys being held in a central registry. Dealings with cargoes are handled by a second registry to which details of each transfer are sent. The system must be able not only to effect transfers of ownership of goods but also ensure that the transferee has the benefit of the contract of carriage. On each transfer of goods the registry therefore sends out messages to the new owner and to the carrier, effecting a novation of the carriage contract. The first 'live' transaction through BOLERO was effected in February 2000.

BOLERO currently offers the most promising prospect for the development of an electronic bill of lading. It is not a panacea. Above all, it is a closed system: since it is based on contract, it cannot bind or be used by outsiders who are not part of the BOLERO network. In addition, as things currently stand, it is not clear that electronic documents would satisfy the requirements of the Uniform Customs and Practice for documentary credits where a contract provides for payment by documentary credit[6]. However, BOLERO has the support of the international banking community. A number of leading banks are already members of the BOLERO network and it is anticipated that the next revision of the UCP will provide for the use of electronic shipping documents. It may be, therefore, that the days of the paper bill of lading are numbered.

---

1   Urbach, 'The Electronic Presentation and Transfer of Shipping Documents' in Goode (ed), *Electronic Banking – the Legal Implications* (1985).

2   See below ch 34.
3   See Faber [1996] LMCLQ 232.
4   Full details of the system are available at the BOLERO web site: www.bolero.net.
5   See 1.5.1.2.
6   See ch 34.

32.6   Claims against the carrier

We have seen that the carrier is responsible for the care of the goods during their transport, and that if they are lost or damaged the carrier will be liable, subject to the terms of the contract of carriage and any applicable scheme of liability. Under the most common forms of international sale contract, however, risk of loss of or damage to the goods passes to the buyer from the time the goods are shipped[1]. Thus, if the goods are damaged or lost during transit, it will be the buyer who bears the loss and who will therefore wish to claim against the carrier in respect of that loss; but where the contract of carriage has been made between the seller and the carrier[2], the doctrine of privity of contract would prevent the buyer, as a stranger to that contract, from bringing a contractual claim against the carrier at common law.

There is no such problem for many civil law systems, where a contract may confer benefits on third parties if made for their benefit[3]. The buyer's inability to claim against the carrier for damage to the goods would obviously be a serious inconvenience to commerce, and, moreover, would make English law unattractive to international traders. The doctrine of privity has now, of course, been relaxed by the Contracts (Rights of Third Parties) Act 1999, s 1 of which enables a person for whose benefit a contract is made to enforce the contract in certain circumstances[4]. However, s 6(5) of the Act expressly excludes contracts of carriage from the Act. It states that s 1 'confers no rights on a third party in the case of (a) a contract for the carriage of goods by sea . . . except that a third party may in reliance on that section avail himself of an exclusion or limitation of liability in such a contract'. 'Contract for the carriage of goods by sea' is defined broadly to include a contract contained in a bill of lading, waybill or 'corresponding electronic transaction' or under which an undertaking is given in a ship's delivery order. The situation presently under consideration is therefore outside the scope of the 1999 Act. The reason for this is that a special statutory modification of the privity doctrine for contracts of carriage was already effected by the Carriage of Goods by Sea Act 1992.

In fact, an attempt to evade the problem of privity had been made as long ago as 1855, in the form of the Bills of Lading Act 1855, which provided for the right to sue under the contract of carriage to be transferred to the consignee or indorsee of a bill of lading. In addition, the common law devised ways to evade the privity rule by enabling a consignee or indorsee in certain situations to rely on concepts of agency, assignment, tort or implied contract in order to make a direct claim against the carrier for damage to the goods during transit. However, the 1855 Act proved defective in a number of respects and recent case law revealed that, in a number of situations, a buyer of goods would be unable to claim against the carrier either at common law or under the 1855 Act. Following recommendations from the Law Commission, the 1855 Act was therefore repealed and replaced by the Carriage of Goods by Sea Act 1992. The common law exceptions to the privity rule remain available, and it will therefore be convenient briefly to consider them and the 1855 Act before examining the 1992 Act.

1   See below 33.1.5 and 33.2.10.
2   Note that in some cases it will be the buyer who makes the contract with the carrier: see below 33.1.
3   Although note that the status of the doctrine in Scots law is unclear.
4   See 2.7.2.

32.6.1   The Bills of Lading Act 1855

Section 1 of the Bills of Lading Act 1855 operated to transfer rights of suit and liabilities under a contract of carriage to:

> 'Every consignee of goods named in a bill of lading, and every endorsee of a bill of lading, to whom the property in the goods therein mentioned shall pass upon or by reason of such consignment or indorsement . . . as if the contract contained in the bill of lading had been made with himself'.

The section thus linked the transfer of contractual rights and liabilities to the passing of property in the goods. Leaving aside the fact that the bill of lading is only evidence of the contract of carriage, this wording meant that s 1 did not apply in a number of common situations. First, it could not apply where the property in the goods did not pass to the consignee or indorsee named in the bill, so that it did not apply where:

(a) the bill of lading was indorsed by way of security (for instance to a bank) rather than to transfer ownership[1];
(b) the bill of lading was transferred to an agent of the seller to collect the goods and issue delivery orders in favour of buyers[2];
(c) goods were exported under a leasing contract rather than a sale.

Moreover, the wording of the section required the property in the goods to pass 'upon or by reason of such consignment or indorsement'. Several different interpretations of these words were suggested. According to the narrow view, the Act only applied where the property in the goods passed at the same time as the consignment or indorsement[3]. This would mean that the section would not apply where the bill of lading was indorsed subject to a retention of title, so that property only passed on payment[4] or where s 19(3) of the Sale of Goods Act 1979 applied; when goods were shipped in bulk, in which case property would not pass until the buyer's goods were separated from the bulk[5]; or where title passed prior to shipment, as for instance where oil is shipped and title passes at the hose connection on shore.

   Alternatively it was suggested that the Act could apply wherever property passed under a contract pursuant to which the bill of lading was indorsed to the buyer[6], but in *The Delfini*[7] the Court of Appeal rejected that interpretation and favoured a middle view according to which the Act would apply where the consignment or indorsement was an essential link in the chain of events by which property passed to the buyer even though it was not the immediate cause of the passing of property. Although this avoided some of the difficulties of the narrow view, it still meant that the section would not apply where property passed before, or independently of, consignment or indorsement of the bill, as in *The Delfini*, where cargo was discharged from the ship against an indemnity from the shipper, so that property passed to the consignee before the bill of lading reached him and the court held that s 1 therefore did not apply.

Moreover, on any interpretation of the Act, it could not apply where the goods were shipped under a document other than a bill of lading, such as a waybill, or where the buyer received a delivery order rather than a bill, and probably not where the bill was made out to bearer or indorsed in blank[8].

1   *Sewell v Burdick* (1884) 10 App Cas 74, HL.
2   As in *The Julia* [1949] AC 293, [1949] 1 All ER 269, HL.
3   See Scrutton, *Charterparties and Bills of Lading* (19th edn, 1984) p 27.
4   As in *The Aliakmon* [1986] AC 785, [1986] 2 All ER 145, HL.
5   SoGA 1979, s 16: see 15.2.3.1.
6   Carver, *Carriage by Sea* (13th edn, 1982) p 98; *Sewell v Burdick* (1884) 10 App Cas 74; *The San Nicholas* [1976] 1 Lloyd's Rep 8; *The Sevonia Team* [1983] 2 Lloyd's Rep 640.
7   *Enichem Amic SpA v Ampelos Shipping Co Ltd* [1990] 1 Lloyd's Rep 252, CA; Reynolds (1990) 106 LQR 1.
8   See *The Elafi* [1982] 1 All ER 208, [1981] 2 Lloyd's Rep 679.

32.6.2   *Implied contract*

A long line of authority recognises that in certain situations a contract on the terms of the bill of lading may arise by implication between the carrier and the person who presents the bill of lading to collect the goods. Commonly known as 'Brandt contracts', after the leading case of *Brandt v Liverpool, Brazil and River Plate Steam Navigation Co Ltd*[1], such contracts had been recognised in a series of cases dating back at least as far as 1811[2]. In the earliest cases it was recognised that where a carrier delivered goods up to a person who presented the bill of lading, that person became liable to the carrier for any unpaid charges such as freight[3] or demurrage[4]. The rationale of the rule was that the carrier has a lien over goods in his possession to secure payment of any such charges; by releasing the goods he released that lien, and the court was prepared to imply a promise by the recipient to discharge the outstanding liability. Such a contract could be implied in circumstances where s 1 of the 1855 Act would not apply, as, for instance, where the recipient of the goods acquired only a security interest over them[5]. Later cases recognised that such an implied contract could also bind the carrier so that where, as in *Brandt* itself, the recipient presented the bill of lading and paid any outstanding charges in order to release the goods, an implied contract arose between carrier and recipient on the terms of the bill of lading, which allowed the recipient to claim against the carrier for any loss of or damage to the goods in transit, subject to the exceptions of liability and other terms of the bill of lading.

Brandt contracts have been implied in many situations where the recipient could not rely on s 1 of the Bills of Lading Act, including, for instance, where the goods had been carried in bulk and were released in exchange for a delivery order[6]. However, it was recognised that 'the boundaries of the doctrine are not clear'[7] and that 'the doctrine of *Brandt v Liverpool Steam Navigation Co Ltd* is far more often pleaded than established'[8] and a number of recent decisions have restricted its scope. In *The Aramis*[9] a bulk cargo of linseed expellers had been shipped under several bills of lading. When the ship arrived at Rotterdam, agents acting on behalf of the various buyers of parts of the bulk presented bills of lading to obtain the release of the goods but it was found that there was insufficient cargo to satisfy all the bills of lading, probably because of over-delivery at the previous port of discharge. No cargo at all was delivered under one bill, and very little under the other. The buyers who had paid for the goods sued the carriers.

They could not rely on s 1 of the Bills of Lading Act and instead based their claim on a *Brandt* contract. However, the evidence was that no sums were due to the carrier at the time the goods were discharged and the Court of Appeal therefore held that the facts did not support the implication of a contract; there must be something more than the mere delivery up of goods to a person presenting a bill of lading for the court to infer that the parties intended to create a new contract. Here the parties' actions could be explained by reference to their existing obligations, without the need to imply a fresh contract. The Court of Appeal recognised that the implication of a contract would be convenient and commercially sensible, but held that that was insufficient to justify implication.

The device of the implied contract has been extensively used in other commercial contexts[10]. The approach in *The Aramis* is difficult to reconcile with that taken in other cases, and it has been suggested that the Court of Appeal applied the wrong test for implying a contract by treating the question as one of implication in fact rather than in law[11]. Nevertheless, it seems likely that the decision will restrict the future use of *Brandt* contracts. It is common for freight to be pre-paid and it seems it will be difficult to imply such a contract where the carrier has no lien because no sums are due to him. It also seems that it will be impossible to claim on a *Brandt* contract where no goods are delivered at all.

The Aramis was distinguished and an implied contract was found to exist in *The Captain Gregos (No 2)*[12], even though the buyer obtained delivery of the cargo without presenting a bill of lading and without paying freight. However, the facts of the case were very special. The buyer had agreed to buy a cargo of oil and, in accordance with the contract of sale, obtained delivery of the cargo against a letter of indemnity. It was held that a contract on the terms of the bill of lading, including the Hague-Visby Rules, had to be implied between buyer and carrier in order to give business reality to the situation. The buyer had bought the whole cargo and, under the terms of the sale contract, property had passed to him before discharge and without delivery of the bill of lading. Moreover, the contract of sale expressly authorised the seller to arrange carriage of the goods on normal terms, so that the buyer had assented in advance to carriage subject to the Hague-Visby Rules. In *The Gudermes*[13], however, the Court of Appeal refused to find an implied contract despite considerable co-operation between the parties in arranging and effecting for the delivery of cargo by transhipment between two vessels at sea, and stated that a contract will only be implied if the parties' actions are 'consistent only with there being a new contract implied, and inconsistent with there being no such contract'[14].

---

1 [1924] 1 KB 575.
2 *Cock v Taylor* (1811) 13 East 399.
3 *Cock v Taylor* (1811) 13 East 399.
4 *Stindt v Roberts* (1848) 17 LJQB 166.
5 See *Allen v Coltart* (1883) 11 QBD 782.
6 *Cremer v General Carriers* [1974] 1 All ER 1, [1974] 1 WLR 341.
7 Per May LJ in *The Elli 2* [1985] 1 Lloyd's Rep 107 at 115, CA.
8 Per Staughton J in *The Aliakmon* [1983] 1 Lloyd's Rep 203 at 207.
9 [1989] 1 Lloyd's Rep 213.
10 See eg *New Zealand Shipping Co Ltd v Satterthwaite Ltd, The Eurymedon* [1975] AC 154, [1974] 1 All ER 1015, PC; *Pyrene & Co Ltd v Scindia Steam Navigation Co Ltd* [1954] 2 QB 402, [1954] 2 All ER 158.
11 Treitel, 'Bills of Lading and Implied Contracts' [1989] LMCLQ 162.
12 [1990] 2 Lloyd's Rep 395.
13 [1993] 1 Lloyd's Rep 311; see White and Bradgate [1993] LMCLQ 483.
14 Per Staughton LJ [1993] 1 Lloyd's Rep 311 at 320.

32.6.3   *Tort claims against the carrier*

We have noted earlier that the carrier is obliged to deliver the goods covered by a bill of lading to the first person to present the bill but that if he delivers the goods without presentation of the bill he does so at his own risk. The modern practice of delivering up goods without production of a bill of lading in return for an indemnity where the bill is not available on the goods' arrival leaves the carrier exposed to a claim in conversion if the person who receives the goods is not in fact entitled to them. A claim in conversion can be brought by any person with an immediate right to possession of goods; there is no need that he be their owner; however, a buyer of goods carried as part of a bulk cargo will be unable to make a claim in conversion until his goods are separated from the bulk, for until that time he has no immediate right to possession of any identifiable goods.

Where the goods are lost or damaged during transit due to the carrier's negligence, it may be possible for the consignee to bring a claim for damages in the tort of negligence. The traditional view was that the buyer of goods could only bring such a claim where he could show that property in the goods had passed to him at the time the damage occurred[1]. This view was challenged in *The Irene's Success*[2], where Lloyd J held that the relationship between the carrier and a buyer of goods on CIF terms to whom risk, but not property, had passed was sufficiently close to justify imposition on the carrier of a duty of care to the buyer. However, the House of Lords reasserted the traditional view in *The Aliakmon*[3] and held that in order to claim in negligence for damage to goods a plaintiff must show that, at the time of the damage, he had 'either the legal ownership of or a possessory title to the property concerned'. Thus the buyer under a CIF contract to whom risk, but not property, had passed, was unable to sue the carrier in negligence for damage caused to the goods during carriage. Although it is not entirely clear, it seems that the reference to 'possessory title' refers to an immediate right to actual possession. If this is correct, a buyer of goods carried as part of bulk will never be able to bring a claim in negligence, since he will have neither ownership of nor a 'possessory title' to any identified goods[4]. In *The Aliakmon* the carrier had actual possession and was entitled to a lien over the goods in respect of unpaid charges, so that the buyer had no right to demand them, and the seller had never released his right to possession: the buyer presented the bill of lading as agent for the seller.

The decision in *The Aliakmon* may be justified on policy grounds, on the basis that to allow an action in negligence in such cases would allow the buyer to evade the limitations on the carrier's liability in the bill of lading and Hague-Visby Rules[5]. In the Court of Appeal, Robert Goff LJ had suggested that this problem might be overcome by allowing a claim in tort subject to the terms of the bill of lading, but this view was rejected both by Lord Donaldson MR in the Court of Appeal and by Lord Brandon giving the judgment of the House of Lords, who felt that the Hague-Visby Rules were too complex to synthesise into a duty of care.

1   See *Margarine Union GmbH v Cambay Prince Steamship Co Ltd* [1969] 1 QB 219, [1967] 3 All ER 775.
2   *Schiffart und Kohlen GmbH v Chelsea Maritime Ltd* [1982] QB 481, [1982] 1 All ER 218.
3   *Leigh and Sillivan Ltd v Aliakmon Shipping Co Ltd* [1986] AC 785, [1986] 2 All ER 145; see Clark [1986] CLJ 386.
4   Where the requirements of s 20A of the Sale of Goods Act 1979 are satisfied the buyer's ownership of an undivided share in the bulk will now be sufficient to enable him to sue for damage to the goods, but only in respect of damage which is proved to have occurred *after* he acquired his share in the bulk.
5   See Adams and Brownsword, 'The Aliakmon and the Hague Rules' [1990] JBL 23.

32.6.4 *Claims by the shipper*

The shipper of the goods is, of course, normally[1] party to the contract of carriage and therefore entitled to enforce it, but where the goods are sold before damage occurs, the shipper has no interest in suing the carrier. Moreover, because damages for breach of contract are compensatory, the general rules of contract law would prevent the shipper claiming more than nominal damages. However, an exception to that general rule is generally thought to have been created in the nineteenth century in *Dunlop v Lambert*[2]. In that case it was held that where goods are shipped and sold so that risk of loss passes to the buyer whilst property remains with the seller, then in the event of damage the shipper may claim for the full extent of the damage. The seller is then accountable to the buyer for the money recovered.

At the time this rule was developed, the person to whom a bill of lading was transferred had no right of action. The bill of lading had only recently been recognised as a document of title. The rule was reconsidered by the House of Lords in *The Albazero*[3]. Lord Diplock explained the rule as an –

> 'application of the principle . . . that in a commercial contract concerning goods where it is in the contemplation of the parties that the proprietary interests in the goods may be transferred from one owner to another after the contract has been entered into and before the breach which causes loss or damage to the goods, an original party to the contract, if such be the intention of them both, is to be treated in law as having entered into the contract for the benefit of all persons who have or who may acquire an interest in the goods before they are lost or damaged, and is entitled to recover by way of damages for breach of contract the actual loss sustained by those for whose benefit the contract is entered into'[4].

Similar rules are recognised in other areas of commercial law: for instance in relation to insurance[5].

The House felt that, with the passing of the Bills of Lading Act 1855 and developments in the law of negligence giving the buyer in such a situation a personal right of action against the carrier, the need for the rule was reduced. In this case the plaintiffs had sold goods to a company in the same group; the bill of lading had been transferred and the buyer had acquired rights under s 1 of the Bills of Lading Act. The ship and its cargo were lost but the buyers failed to bring a claim within the time period allowed by the contract and the plaintiffs therefore sought to rely on *Dunlop v Lambert*. The House of Lords held that the rule in that case was inapplicable on the facts where the buyer had acquired a personal right to sue under s 1 of the Bills of Lading Act. However, the rule was not abolished, and it is clear that a similar rule allowing a contractor to claim damages for losses suffered by a third party survives in other contexts[6].

Where the Carriage of Goods by Sea Act 1992 applies to vest rights of suit in the buyer of goods, the seller's rights under the contract of carriage are now extinguished[7]. There is therefore no question of the seller suing on the strength of *Dunlop v Lambert* where the 1992 Act applies. It is not clear, however, if the seller is excluded by the reasoning in *The Albazero* where the buyer has a claim only on the basis of a *Brandt* contract or where the buyer may bring a claim in negligence. It would seem that the reasoning of the House of Lords would be equally applicable in both those cases[8].

1   A seller who ships goods may not always be party to the contract of carriage: see eg *Pyrene & Co Ltd v Scindia Steam Navigation Co Ltd* [1954] 2 QB 402, [1954] 2 All ER 158; below 33.1.
2   (1839) 6 Cl & Fin 600, HL: see the decision in *Panatown Ltd v Alfred McAlpine Ltd* [2000] 4 All ER 97.
3   [1977] AC 774, [1976] 3 All ER 129.
4   [1977] AC 774 at 847.
5   See ch 35.
6   *Linden Gardens Trust Ltd v Lenesta Sludge Disposals Ltd* [1994] 1 AC 85, [1993] 3 All ER 417; *Darlington Borough Council v Wiltshier Nothern Ltd* [1995] 3 All ER 895, CA. See 2.7.
7   Section 2(5): see 32.5.5.
8   In the light of the House of Lords' decision in *Panatown Ltd v Alfred McAlpine Ltd* [2000] 4 All ER 97 (see 2.7.1), it would seem that the availability of a negligence action would not exclude the seller's claim, but the position is not clear.

32.6.5 *The Carriage of Goods by Sea Act 1992*

Cases such as *The Aramis*[1], *The Aliakmon*[2], *The Delfini*[3] and *The Albazero*[4] highlighted significant gaps in the protection of buyers of goods carried by sea where the goods were lost or damaged in transit and, by the late 1980s, it was apparent that in a number of situations the buyer would have no right of redress against the carrier. In *The Aliakmon* Lord Brandon[5] suggested that a buyer might protect himself by requiring the seller to sue on the contract of carriage on his behalf, or by taking an assignment of the seller's rights. However, this would rarely be commercially practicable; the seller might be unwilling to sue for the buyer's account, and assignment would require notice to be given to the carrier. Moreover, in either case, the buyer would have only those rights available to the seller under the contract of carriage, and would not have the benefit of the estoppels which normally operate in his favour under the Hague-Visby Rules[6]. It is difficult to see how an assignment could be used where goods carried in bulk are sold to several buyers.

Although the buyer would often be protected by insurance covering loss or damage during transit, it was recognised that English law was out of step with commercial expectations and, in 1991, following extensive consultation with traders, the Law Commissions recommended reform[7]. The Law Commissions' proposals were implemented by the Carriage of Goods by Sea Act 1992[8].

One possible way to resolve the difficulties identified in the case law would be to link the right to sue on the contract of carriage with risk, so that the person who bore the risk of loss or damage would be entitled to sue in respect of it. However, the Commissions rejected that solution. Instead, s 2(1) of the Act provides that:

'. . . a person who becomes –
(a) the lawful holder of a bill of lading;
(b) the person who (without being an original party to the contract of carriage) is the person to whom delivery of the goods to which a sea waybill relates is to be made by the carrier in accordance with the contract; or
(c) the person to whom delivery of the goods to which a ship's delivery order relates is to be made in accordance with the undertaking contained in the order,
shall (by virtue of becoming a holder of the bill or, as the case may be, the person to whom delivery is to be made) have transferred to and vested in him all rights of suit under the contract as if he had been a party to that contract'.

The Act only protects the 'lawful holder' of a bill of lading. A holder must have possession of the bill, either as consignee or as a result of the completion, by delivery, of an indorsement, or the transfer of a bearer bill[9], but there is no need for the holder to be a purchaser or to have property in the goods. A person is to be regarded as a 'lawful holder' wherever he has taken the bill 'in good faith'. 'Good faith' is not defined, but in *The Aegean Sea*[10] Thomas J interpreted 'good faith' narrowly as requiring merely honesty:

> 'In the commercial context of bills of lading the meaning of the term good faith should be clear, capable of unambiguous application and be consistent with the usage in other contexts and countries'[11].

The Act thus breaks the link between contract rights and property which was the weakness of the 1855 Act and solves most of the problems highlighted by recent cases. A person who buys part of a bulk cargo acquires rights to sue in relation to that part of the cargo[12]. A person such as a bank to whom goods are consigned, or a bill of lading transferred only by way of security, also acquires rights of suit under the Act. The Act applies even where a bill is transferred after the goods to which it relates have been delivered by the carrier, provided that the transfer of the bill is made in pursuance of arrangements made before the bill became spent or as a result of rejection by the person to whom the goods were delivered[13]. The buyer in *The Delfini* would therefore be protected.

The Act applies to a wider range of documents than the 1855 Act, including waybills and ship's delivery orders, and gives power to the Secretary of State to make regulations applying the Act's provisions, modified as appropriate, to cases where 'a telecommunications system or other information technology' is used to effect transactions corresponding to those effected through the issue and transfer of paper documents[14], so that if an electronic alternative to a bill of lading is introduced, the Act can be applied to it. However, there are situations in which the Act will not apply. A straight consigned bill of lading, in which the goods are consigned to a named consignee and the bill is not transferable, is not a bill of lading for the purposes of the Act[15], but is treated as a waybill and is therefore covered. On the other hand, it is not clear if the Act applies to all or any multimodal transport documents, which may not be 'bills of lading' or to bills issued under a charterparty, since the rights transferred by the Act are those 'contained in or evidenced by the bill'[16], but where a bill is issued under a charterparty the contract of carriage is contained in the charter, not in the bill. The Act does not apply to merchant's delivery orders, and its definition of ship's delivery orders includes documents containing an undertaking by the carrier[17], so that it excludes ship's delivery orders issued by the bill of lading holder. Holders of such documents who wish to pursue the carrier will therefore still have to establish an implied contract or a tortious right of action.

The statutory transfer of rights effected by s 2(1) also operates to extinguish: (a) any rights to sue previously vested in any person by virtue of that section; and (b) where a bill of lading is transferred by the shipper of goods, any rights of the shipper to enforce the contract of carriage[18]. The first limb of this rule is unsurprising but the second means that although there may be situations where the original shipper may have a legitimate interest in suing the carrier after transfer of the bill – for instance in respect of losses caused by delay in loading – he will have no right of action. The Act provides that where rights of suit are vested in one person by virtue of the Act but another person with 'any interest or right in or relation to the goods' suffers loss, the person in whom rights of suit are vested may sue for the benefit of the person who suffered loss[19]. However, this section would not apply in the case where the shipper divested by the Act of a personal right to sue suffers loss as a result of the carrier's breach of contract, since the shipper will normally have no 'interest or right in or in relation to' the goods. In such a case the shipper may be forced to seek an assignment of rights from the person in whom they are vested.

Under the 1855 Act a person to whom rights of suit under the contract were transferred also became subject to the same liabilities in respect of the goods as if he had been an original party to the contract of carriage. The 1992 Act takes a similar line. Section 3 provides that where rights of suit are vested in a person by the operation of s 2, that person also becomes 'subject to the same liabilities . . . as if he had been a party to the contract of carriage'[20]. However, in order to avoid exposing banks, to whom goods might be consigned or bills transferred by way of security, to liability under the contract of carriage, the Act provides that a person to whom rights are transferred becomes liable on the contract only if he: (a) takes or demands delivery of the goods; (b) makes a claim under the contract; or (c) took or demanded delivery before the rights became vested in him[21]. Banks taking shipping documents as security will therefore not normally be exposed to liability on the contract of carriage unless they attempt to enforce that contract in one of the ways described.

In contrast to the position where rights are transferred, the original shipper of goods remains liable on the contract even where the Act operates to impose liabilities on another person[22]. The Act makes no specific provision, however, for the situation where an intermediate holder of a bill of lading becomes liable on the contract but then transfers the bill. The Act expressly provides that in such a case the intermediate holder's rights to enforce the contract are extinguished[23]. No provision is made for the effect on the holder's liabilities, no doubt because the Law Commission did not anticipate such a situation. No one can become liable on a bill of lading unless he attempts to enforce the carriage contract in one of the three ways described above. In *The Berge Sisar*[24], however, exactly such a situation arose. The case concerned the sale and carriage of a cargo of propane. Following arrival of the vessel, the buyer of the cargo took delivery of a small quantity from the carrier for the purposes of sampling and, on discovering that it was not of the contract quality, resold it. The carrier sought to claim for corrosion damage caused to the vessel by the cargo, and it was accepted that, by taking delivery of a quantity for sampling, the buyer had become liable on the contract. The Court of Appeal held by a majority[25], however, that by re-transferring the bill of lading the buyer had divested itself of liability under the contract. A factor which seems to have weighed heavily with the majority of the court was that that was the position under the 1855 Act[26], and in the absence of any clear indication to the contrary, it was assumed that it was not intended to change the law. The reasoning of the majority has been criticised[27] and there are obiter dicta in a first instance decision that once liabilities are vested in a transferee they are not divested by a subsequent transfer[28]. It may be argued that the policy of the Act is that it is the taking of steps to enforce the carriage contract which triggers liability under the Act. Against this it may be argued that the requirement of enforcement is intended to restrict the transfer of liabilities and that the intention is that, in general, liabilities should be linked to rights of suit. It should be borne in mind that, since the original shipper is never divested of liability under the contract, the carrier will normally have the choice of two potential defendants against whom the contract can be enforced. At any rate, it may be that the situation is not as unlikely as might be thought. For instance, if the buyer under a sale contract takes delivery of the goods but rejects them for breach of the sale contract and re-transfers the bill of lading to the seller, rights of suit are re-vested in the seller[29]. Is the buyer divested of liability under the contract by the transfer? In *The Berge Sisar* Millett LJ suggested that a holder of a bill of lading would only become irrevocably liable on the carriage contract if the nature of the steps he takes to enforce that contract 'preclude any further dealing with the goods'[30] but he does not seem to have had this situation in mind.

There is no doubt that, overall, the 1992 Act makes a significant improvement to the law. However, there are some curious gaps in its documentary coverage and some of its provisions, especially those affecting the original shipper, are surprising and potentially unfair. As *The Berge Sisar* illustrates, it leaves some questions unanswered. It remains to be seen whether it will prove a totally satisfactory response to the problems of modern carriage practices.

1 [1989] 1 Lloyd's Rep 213.
2 [1986] AC 785, [1986] 2 All ER 145.
3 [1990] 1 Lloyd's Rep 252.
4 [1977] AC 774, [1976] 3 All ER 129.
5 [1986] AC 785 at 819.
6 See above 32.3.1.
7 Law Com 196, 'Rights of Suit in Respect of Carriage of Goods by Sea' (1991).
8 See generally Bradgate and White (1993) 56 MLR 188.
9 Section 5(2).
10 *Aegean Sea Traders Corpn v Repsol Petroleo SA, The Aegean Sea* [1998] 2 Lloyd's Rep 39.
11 [1998] 2 Lloyd's Rep 39 at 60.
12 Section 2(3).
13 Section 2(2).
14 Section 1(5).
15 Section 1(2).
16 Section 5(1).
17 Section 1(4).
18 Section 1(5).
19 Section 2(4).
20 Compare the Contracts (Rights of Third Parties) Act 1999, which gives the third party a limited right to enforce the contract but does not expose him to liability.
21 Section 3(1).
22 Section 3(3). The position was the same under the 1855 Act: see *Effort Shipping Co Ltd v Linden Management SA, The Giannis NK* [1998] AC 605, [1998] 1 All ER, HL.
23 Section 1(5).
24 *Borealis AB v Stargas Ltd, The Berge Sisar* [1999] QB 863, [1998] 4 All ER 821.
25 Millett and Schiemann LJJ, Sir Brian Neill dissenting.
26 *Smurthwaite v Wilkins* (1862) 11 CBNS 842.
27 Reynolds [1999] LMCLQ 161.
28 *Aegean Sea Traders Corpn v Repsol Petroleo SA, The Aegean Sea* [1998] 2 Lloyd's Rep 39, per Thomas J.
29 Section 2(2)(b).
30 [1999] QB 863 at 885, [1998] 4 All ER 821 at 837.

32.7 Tort claims against third parties

The doctrine of privity also gives rise to problems where goods are damaged by someone other than the carrier as, for instance, where stevedores to whom the carrier has sub-contracted the loading or unloading of the goods damage them during the loading or unloading of the vessel, or the carrier sub-contracts performance of all or part of the carriage contract to a third party, as may happen

under contracts for multimodal carriage of goods. In that case the cargo owner –
whether buyer or seller – may wish to pursue a claim against the sub-contractor,
either because the carrier is not liable for the loss, or to evade restrictions on the
carrier's liability.

At common law the cargo owner has no contractual claim against the sub-contractors.
It might now be possible to argue that a contract between carrier and a stevedore is
a contract to confer a benefit on the cargo owner, and that the cargo owner is
entitled to enforce that contract under the Contracts (Rights of Third Parties) Act
1999. Since the carrier-stevedore contract is not a contract for the carriage of goods
by sea, it is not within the category of contracts excluded from the Act[1]. The question
whether the cargo owner is entitled to enforce the contract would therefore depend
on whether, on its proper construction, the parties to that contract intended it to
be enforceable by the cargo owner. The Law Commission did not expressly
consider this situation in its report, but it is worth noting that the Commission
took the view that the presumption of enforceability could be rebutted where the
parties have deliberately set up a chain of contracts, and that therefore, for
instance, the employer under a building contract would not have a direct right of
action against a sub-contractor employed by the main contractor[2]. The same
argument would appear to apply as between cargo owners and sub-contractors
such as stevedores.

This may in any case be of little significance because, as owner of the goods, the
cargo owner will be entitled to sue the stevedores, or other sub-contractors, in the
tort of negligence if the goods are damaged by their failure to take reasonable care.
The availability of the tort action raises similar policy issues to those which
influenced the House of Lords in *The Aliakmon*: by suing in tort the plaintiff may
evade any restrictions on liability in the carriage contract between itself and the
carrier – indeed, that may well be the very reason for suing the sub-contractor
rather than the carrier – and any similar restrictions on liability in the contract
between carrier and sub-contractor. In *Scruttons Ltd v Midland Silicones Ltd*[3],
where goods were damaged during unloading due to the negligence of stevedores,
the House of Lords held that the doctrine of privity prevented the stevedores relying
on the exceptions contained in a bill of lading. A solution to this problem was
found, however, in *The Eurymedon*[4], where the Privy Council managed to construe
the facts as giving rise to a contract between the goods' owners and the stevedores.
The exclusion clause in the carriage contract expressly purported to protect the
stevedores, and the contract was expressed to be made by the carrier as agent for
any employees or sub-contractors as well as on his own behalf. The Privy Council
held that the contract therefore amounted to an offer by the owners to the stevedores,
via the carriers as agents, to exempt them from liability if they unloaded the goods;
the stevedores accepted that offer by unloading the goods; performance of their
contract with the carriers was good consideration for the promise by the goods
owners.

The reasoning in *The Eurymedon* has been criticised. However, the result is
wholly justifiable in terms of commercial pragmatism and convenience, and the
decision has been approved and applied in a number of subsequent decisions[5] so
that it may be taken to be settled law. It has become common practice to include
clauses worded along the lines of that in *The Eurymedon* – termed '*Himalaya* clauses'
– in contracts of carriage. It may be, however, that it would no longer be necessary to
adopt the reasoning of the Privy Council in order to allow the stevedores to rely on
the exclusion clause. The wording of the *Himalaya* clause makes clear that it is
intended to protect the stevedores, and they would therefore now be able to take the

protection of the exclusion by virtue of the 1999 Act. It will be recalled that although contracts of carriage are generally excluded from the Act there is an exception which permits a third party to rely on 'an exclusion or limitation of liability in such a contract'[6]. Similar reasoning would protect other sub-contractors sued in tort for negligent damage to the goods.

The 1999 Act will not, however, resolve all the problems created by privity in this context. There may be other clauses in the carriage contract on which the sub-contractor may wish to rely, such as arbitration, jurisdiction and choice of law clauses. The 1999 Act only permits a third party to take the benefit of 'exclusion and limitation' clauses. Where the third party wishes to take the benefit of an exclusion or limitation clause in the carriage contract and the contract provides for reference of disputes to arbitration, the third party will be treated as a party to the arbitration agreement and will therefore be entitled to enforce, and be bound, by it[7]. This will not, however, permit the third party to enforce a free-standing arbitration clause, and jurisdiction and choice of law clauses fall wholly outside the Act. In order to rely on such clauses, the sub-contractor must therefore rely on the common law. It has been held that a *Himalaya* clause purporting to give third parties the benefit of 'all exceptions, limitations, provisions, conditions and liberties herein' did not entitle sub-contractors to take the benefit of an exclusive jurisdiction clause in the carriage contract[8]. On the other hand, a sub-contracting carrier may be able to enforce jurisdiction and other clauses in the sub-contract against the cargo owner by virtue of the doctrine of bailment on terms, according to which a bailor is bound by the terms of any sub-bailment if he has expressly or impliedly agreed to his bailee making a sub-bailment on those terms[9], but this reasoning would not protect a sub-contracting stevedore who does not become a bailee of the goods.

Notwithstanding two statutory reforms in the last decade, the doctrine of privity continues to create difficulties in relation to contracts for sea carriage, and the common law still has a role to play in countering them.

1   This reasoning would not apply where the claim arises from the carrier's decision to sub-contract the carriage of the goods.
2   Law Commission 242 (Cmnd 3329), 'Privity of Contract: Contracts for the Benefit of Third Parties' (1996) para 7.18.
3   [1962] AC 446, [1962] 1 All ER 1.
4   *New Zealand Shipping Co Ltd v Satterthwaite Ltd* [1975] AC 154, [1974] 1 All ER 1015.
5   *Port Jackson Stevedoring Pty Ltd v Salmond and Spraggon Pty Ltd* [1980] 3 All ER 257, [1981] 1 WLR 138, PC; *The Mahkutai* [1996] AC 650, [1996] 3 All ER 502, PC; see also *Glebe Island Terminals Pty Ltd v Continental Seagram Pty Ltd* [1994] 1 Lloyd's Rep 213, NSW CA. The approach of the courts in those cases makes an interesting contrast with that in *The Aramis* and *The Aliakmon.*
6   Contracts (Rights of Third Parties) Act 1999, s 6(5).
7   Contracts (Rights of Third Parties) Act 1999, s 8.
8   *The Mahkutai* [1996] AC 650, [1996] 3 All ER 502, PC.
9   See *The Pioneer Container* [1994] 2 AC 324, [1994] 2 All ER 250.

Chapter 33

International Sale Contracts

33.0 Introduction

A striking feature of English international trade law is that, on the whole, there is no special body of rules applicable to international, as opposed to domestic, sales. The UK is a party to the Hague Conventions on Contracts for the International Sale of Goods, which are given effect in English law by the Uniform Law on International Sales Act 1967. Under that Act contracts governed by English law are governed by the Uniform Laws if the contract so provides. Contracts never do. Thus where an international sale contract is governed by English law it is governed by the general law of contract and the Sale of Goods Act 1979. The parties are therefore free to agree the terms of their bargain, subject to the general law, and, indeed, are subject to less restriction than the parties to a domestic contract since the Unfair Contract Terms Act 1977 does not apply to international supply contracts where the contracting parties have their places of business in different states[1] and:

(a) the goods are to be carried from the territory of one state to another;
(b) the acts constituting offer and acceptance were done in different states; or
(c) the contract requires the goods to be delivered to a state other than that where offer and acceptance took place[2].

Thus the parties are free to allocate responsibility for arranging carriage or insurance or obtaining customs clearances etc to fix the method of payment, to stipulate for the buyer to accept a document other than a bill of lading or to agree any other terms. However, mercantile practice has developed a number of standard contract 'formulae' for international sales. The duties of the parties under these contracts are well known; they are set out in detail in INCOTERMS, a directory of trade terms, published by the International Chamber of Commerce[3]. In English law INCOTERMS have no legal force as such, but the parties may expressly incorporate them into their contract. The parties may therefore define their duties in 'short hand' form by contracting according to one of the common formulae as defined by INCOTERMS. If the parties fail to define their obligations expressly or by reference to INCOTERMS, their basic duties will be defined by the common law. The courts have recognised mercantile practice and the legal incidents of the most common standard contracts are now well established.

The result is that where the parties use one of the standard formulae, their respective obligations are both commercially and legally defined. Commercially, the formula used may define the obligations of the parties, eg to arrange carriage or insurance, and indicate what is included in the price. Legally, it may define the time and place of delivery and, most importantly, the passing of property and risk.

Amongst the most common formulae in use are the following.

(a) *'Ex works' (exw)*

An ex works contract imposes the least obligation on the seller. He must supply goods which conform to the contract and make them available for collection at his own premises. The buyer must arrange the collection and transport of the goods. The quoted price is thus the price at the seller's 'factory gate'.

(b) *'Free along side' (FAS)*

The seller must supply goods conforming to the contract and make them available to the buyer at a port nominated by the buyer for loading on board ship. The buyer must make the shipping arrangements; the seller must make arrangements and pay all costs necessary to place the goods alongside ship.

(c) *'Free on board' (FOB)*

In this case the seller must not only supply the goods, but also bears responsibility for seeing that they are shipped at the port named in the contract. The buyer normally arranges carriage[4] but the seller must see that the goods are loaded on the ship and pay the costs of loading.

An FOB or FAS contract may not be 'international': for instance, if Y contracts to sell goods to Z in New York, he may contract to purchase goods from X in England to fulfil his contract. It may be convenient for him to arrange for X to sell the goods 'FOB Southampton' to place them on board ship to fulfil his contract with Z.

(d) *'Cost-insurance-freight' (CIF)*

Under a CIF contract the seller must not only supply the goods, but must also arrange contracts for their carriage and insurance during transit to the port named in the contract, the cost of which is included in the contract price. The seller then sends the relevant contract, carriage and insurance documents to the buyer, who pays on receipt of the documents and uses them to collect the goods on arrival. As an alternative, the contract may be 'c & f' (cost and freight), in which case the seller arranges carriage but the buyer arranges his own insurance. This may be preferable where the buyer is a regular importer and has a block insurance policy available.

(e) *'Delivered ex ship' (DES)*

Under an ex ship, or 'arrival', contract the seller only fulfils his obligations when the goods have actually reached the named port of destination and been unloaded and released to the buyer. The seller must arrange and pay for carriage and insurance and pay all the costs of loading and unloading.

The formulae set out above are used where the contract contemplates carriage by sea. The parties may agree on other formulations; where goods are to be carried by road, rail or air, there are different, sometimes similar, formulae (such as 'free on rail') and the increasing use of containerised multimodal transport has led to the development of newer formulae such as 'free carrier' (FCA) and 'carriage and insurance paid to' (CIP), introduced for the first time in 1990[5]. Even where the parties do use sea transport and one of the standard contract formulae, they remain free to modify their obligations under the contract; the formula then simply defines what is included in the price. For instance, the seller under an FOB contract could agree to arrange insurance, or under an ex works contract, to arrange delivery to the buyer's premises. In those cases the buyer must pay extra above the contract price for the extra services provided by the seller.

1   Where the contract is made through an agent, it is the place of business of the principal, not the agent, which is relevant for this purpose: *Ocean Chemical Transport Inc v Exnor Craggs Ltd* [2000] 1 All ER (Comm) 519, CA.
2   Unfair Contract Terms Act 1977, s 26. The Unfair Terms in Consumer Contracts Regulations 1999 will apply if the buyer is a consumer, as defined.
3   The latest edition is INCOTERMS 2000.
4   See below 33.1.
5   See above 32.4.3.

33.0.1   *Seller's obligations in relation to bills of lading*

Under CIF and certain types of FOB contract the seller must arrange carriage of the goods and forward the shipping documents to the buyer to enable him to collect them. More commonly, where payment is by documentary credit, the documents are forwarded to the buyer's bank, which holds them as security for advancing the price to the buyer. Unless the contract of sale allows the seller to tender some other document, such as a delivery order or waybill, he must tender a bill of lading in respect of the goods. If the contract is silent, the law requires that a bill of lading tendered under the contract should have the following characteristics.

(a) It must be a shipped bill, ie showing that the goods have been loaded, rather than a 'received for shipment' bill: the buyer, or his bank, needs a guarantee that the goods have been loaded in accordance with the contract, and an indication of their condition at the time of loading (which may be crucial in the event of a claim against the carrier); a received for shipment bill gives neither.

(b) It must be 'clean' as opposed to 'claused': ie it must state, without qualification, that the goods have been loaded in apparent good condition. INCOTERMS explains that any notation on the bill which would indicate that the goods had not been, as far as the carrier could ascertain, received in good order and condition, would make the bill 'unclean' and thus unacceptable to a bank under a documentary credit[1]. The Uniform Customs and Practice for Documentary Credits defines a clean bill as one 'which bears no clause or notation which expressly declares a defective condition of the goods and/or the packaging'[2]. As will be seen, the condition of the goods at the time of loading is crucial: at that moment, risk of loss or damage will normally pass to the buyer, and the carrier will become liable for loss or damage during transit. A 'claused' bill may indicate that the goods were not in accordance with the contract of sale at the time of loading. Buyers, and their bankers, may have to make speedy decisions whether to accept a bill of lading. Any qualification as to the condition of the goods at the time of loading will therefore make the bill unacceptable[3]. The strict legal test of a clean bill is that it should contain no indication of damage to the goods at the time of loading. However, a broader test of 'commercial acceptability' is also recognised. In *The Galatia*[4] the seller tendered a bill of lading in respect of a cargo of sugar. The bill indicated that the cargo had been loaded in good condition but subsequently damaged by fire and the water used to extinguish it. It was accepted by the Court of Appeal that the test of a clean bill is that it should be 'a document that would ordinarily and properly have been accepted in the trade as being an appropriate document'. However, despite evidence that the notation on the bill in the present case made it commercially difficult to deal with, there was no evidence of a trade custom that notation of damage after loading made a bill 'unclean'. It was therefore held that the bill in question was 'clean' and had to be accepted.

(c) It must show that the goods were shipped in accordance with the contract: ie at the correct place and time.

(d) It must cover the goods for the whole period of transport. Since the bill of lading gives the buyer rights against the carrier in respect of loss, etc of the goods during transport, it is crucial that it governs the whole period: if not, the buyer would have no claim in respect of damage etc occurring during the period not covered by the bill.

(e) It must identify the goods to which it relates so that transfer of the bill can transfer the relevant goods.

(f) It must cover only the goods intended for the particular buyer. Suppose that S ships a bulk cargo of grain for three different buyers. He may take three (or more) bills of lading, so that each buyer can receive a bill relating to his own share of the cargo. (In practice, the seller might well take more than three bills, allowing each buyer to break up his share of the cargo and resell it in smaller parcels.) If he takes only a single bill of lading, he cannot tender it to any of the buyers. He must then issue each buyer with a delivery order, provided the relevant sale contracts allow that.

1   INCOTERMS 1990, para 19.
2   UCP 500 (1993) art 32. The same requirement that the document be 'clean' applies to other shipping documents presented under a contract governed by INCOTERMS or a credit governed by the UCP.
3   See *Hansson v Hamel and Horley Ltd* [1922] 2 AC 36, HL.
4   [1979] 2 All ER 726, [1980] 1 WLR 495; affd [1980] 1 All ER 501, CA; see Schmitthoff [1979] JBL 164.

33.1   FOB contracts

The FOB contract has a long history; examples can be found as early as the beginning of the nineteenth century[1]. The contract developed in an era when it was customary for a merchant to charter a ship and travel with it to trade at various ports; the merchant would require the persons from whom he bought goods to place them 'free on board' his vessel. Since then, the nature of international trade has changed drastically. The improvement in communications means that merchants no longer travel with their ships and contracts are negotiated and concluded at a distance. The growth of alternative carriage arrangements, notably the CIF contract, has meant a decline in the use of FOB arrangements. However, the form does remain widely used. Its popularity fluctuates from time to time, according to a number of economic and political factors. Under an FOB contract the buyer may exercise control over the choice of carrier, but must also bear the risk of changes in the cost of carriage and is responsible for making carriage arrangements. Thus sellers will prefer FOB contracts at times when carriage costs are high or likely to fluctuate, or when shipping space is scarce, as was the case during the First and

Second World Wars, when FOB contracts gained in popularity. Governments may also put pressure on buyers to choose the FOB form: a buyer under an FOB contract may nominate a carrier from his own country, thus favouring the domestic economy; if a foreign carrier is used, as is likely to be the case under a CIF contract, the cost of carriage will represent an outflow of funds from the domestic economy. Where governments act as buyers, they are therefore likely to favour the FOB form. Moreover, as noted above, an FOB contract may be made between a buyer and seller in the same state, where the buyer purchases goods for resale to a customer overseas (and where he may intend to resell on either FOB or CIF terms).

It is difficult to define an FOB contract because many different variants exist; as Devlin J put it, the FOB contract has become a 'flexible instrument[2]' and this flexibility probably explains the longevity of the FOB form. The essential obligations of the parties to an FOB contract were described in *Wimble, Sons & Co v Rosenberg*[3]. The seller must put on board ship goods which conform to the contract and must pay all charges in connection with loading. The seller is not obliged to book shipping space in advance; the buyer must nominate the ship to carry the goods and notify the seller of the nomination in time to allow the seller to deliver the goods on board. The costs of carriage are for the buyer's account[4].

However, the parties may, and frequently do, modify their obligations under an FOB contract. In particular, the relationship between seller, buyer and carrier may vary according to the nature of the arrangements made. In *Pyrene and Co Ltd v Scindia Steam Navigation Co Ltd*[5] Devlin J recognised three situations.

(a) B designates a ship on which S is required to load the goods. There is no prior contractual arrangement between B and the carrier. S delivers the goods to the ship and puts them on board in return for a bill of lading, either in his own name or showing B as consignor. In either case, S forwards the bill of lading to B and, according to Devlin J, S makes the contract of carriage and is a party to it. Devlin J described this as a 'classic' FOB contract.

(b) S may undertake additional duties. Under this type of FOB contract, S undertakes to arrange the carriage, and possibly insurance. S places the goods on board ship and receives a bill of lading in his own name, which he forwards to B in return for payment. S is clearly a party to the contract of carriage in this case, and the contract is very similar to a CIF contract[6]; however, the contract price excludes carriage costs so that if they increase, B must pay extra.

(c) Alternatively, B may make the contract of carriage in advance. In this case S puts the goods on board ship in exchange for a mate's receipt, which he forwards to S who uses it to obtain a bill of lading.

The *Pyrene* case concerned a contract of this third type. S had contracted to sell a fire tender to the Indian government 'FOB London'. B made the shipping arrangements in advance. During loading, the tender was dropped and damaged. Since risk had not yet passed to B, S sued the carrier for the damage and the carrier sought to rely on the limitations of liability in the Hague Rules (which governed contracts of carriage at that time). It was argued that S was not bound by that limitation because of lack of privity between S and the carrier. The case thus illustrates another aspect of the privity problem considered in the previous chapter. Devlin J held that the rules applied to the loading as well as the actual voyage. He then turned to the question whether S was bound by the contract of carriage. He held that, although B had made the contract, it must have been intended that it would bind and benefit S and had therefore been made on his behalf: it was necessary to load the goods in order to fulfil S's duty to deliver the goods on board, and he must therefore be in a contractual relationship with the carrier. Alternatively, it might have been possible to find an implied contract between S and the carrier based on the acts of delivering the tender to the rail and lifting it aboard.

The *Pyrene* decision is not without difficulties. However, the result seems desirable in line with the more recent judicial tendency to seek to prevent the evasion of contractual exclusions of liability by an action in tort. According to Devlin J, under a classic FOB contract S becomes party to the contract of carriage whether he takes the bill of lading in his own name or in that of B. The explanation appears to be that since S must arrange for the goods to be loaded in order to fulfil his delivery obligation, he must enter into some arrangement with the carrier to have the goods loaded. He is therefore party to the contract of carriage to that extent.

In *Ian Stach Ltd v Baker Bosley Ltd*[7] Diplock J said that under a 'classic' FOB contract the buyer 'has the right and responsibility of selecting the port [and] of making arrangements for shipping'. This appears to fit more easily into Devlin J's third category than his first and some writers use the term 'classic FOB' to describe that type of contract[8]. However, although the terminology is not always consistently used, Devlin J's classification has been widely adopted by courts and in textbooks and has been approved by the Court of Appeal[9]. It will therefore be followed here, but it is worth noting that modern changes in practice have led to a decline in the use of the 'classic' FOB form. The improvement in international communications probably means that it is now much easier than formerly for the buyer to book shipping space for goods in advance; equally, it is probably the case that unless advance arrangements are made it will often be difficult to obtain shipping space on board the vessel of choice. Thus it may be that the third type of contract recognised in *Pyrene* has replaced the 'classic' as the norm.

Under both the first two types of contract described in *Pyrene* the seller will be responsible for making the contract of carriage. Difficult questions may arise as to whether he does so on his own behalf, as principal, or as agent for the buyer; this in turn will depend on the contract between buyer and seller. The capacity in which the seller acts may have important consequences: for instance, if he acts as principal, a failure to obtain carriage space in accordance with the contract of sale will amount to a failure to deliver; if he acts as agent, he will only incur liability if he has failed to exercise reasonable care to arrange carriage. The question whether the seller acts as principal or agent may also be important in relation to the passing to the buyer of property and risk. However, the contract of sale will rarely make the seller's status explicit; instead, it will be necessary to draw inferences from all the circumstances of the case. Whether the goods are shipped to the order of the buyer or seller will be an important factor, but as will be seen below[10], not a conclusive one.

1 See generally Sassoon [1967] JBL 32.
2 In *Pyrene and Co Ltd v Scindia Navigation Co Ltd* [1954] 2 QB 402, [1954] 2 All ER 158.
3 [1913] 1 KB 279.
4 A requirement that the seller provide freight pre-paid bills of lading is therefore inconsistent with an FOB contract: *Glencore Grain Rotterdam BV v Lebanese Organisation for International Commerce* [1997] 4 All ER 514, CA.
5 [1954] 2 QB 402, [1954] 2 All ER 158.
6 See below 33.2.
7 [1958] 2 QB 130 at 139.
8 See for instance Atiyah, *The Sale of Goods* (10th edn, 2000); Day and Griffin, *The Law of International Trade* (2nd edn, 1993).
9 In *The El Amira and El Minia* [1982] 2 Lloyd's Rep 28, CA.
10 See 33.1.4.

33.1.1 *Duties of the parties under an FOB contract*

In view of what has been said, it is clear that the duties of buyer and seller under an FOB contract are largely defined by their contract. The contract must always be consulted to determine such matters as the place and time of loading, the price and the means of payment. In addition, the contract may define the basic duties of the parties. However, in the absence of express terms in the contract, the basic duties of the parties depend on commercial practice as recognised by the law.

Under a 'classic' FOB contract the buyer must[1]:

(a) nominate a ship to carry the goods;
(b) notify the seller of the nomination in time for him to fulfil his obligations; and
(c) pay the price in accordance with the contract.

If the contract is of the more modern type, as in *Pyrene v Scindia*, the buyer will first have to secure shipping space and make a contract of carriage with the carrier. Where payment is to be by documentary credit, it may be necessary for the buyer to notify the seller of the opening of the credit before the time for loading. Where the contract provides for payment by documentary credit, the seller is entitled to see the credit opened before shipping the goods[2].

The seller must:

(a) deliver to the port of loading goods which comply with the contract of sale and arrange for them to be loaded on the ship nominated by the buyer;
(b) pay all charges in connection with the loading up to the time the goods cross the ship's rail;
(c) provide the buyer with information necessary to enable him to insure the goods in transit[3]; and
(d) deliver the shipping documents to the buyer to enable him to collect the goods from the ship.

1 See *Schmitthoff's Export Trade* (9th edn, 1990) p 16 for a full list of the duties of the parties.
2 *Glencore Grain Rotterdam BV v Lebanese Organisation for International Commerce* [1997] 4 All ER 514, CA.
3 Sale of Goods Act 1979, s 32(3); 33.1.5 below.

33.1.2 *Nomination of an effective vessel*

Under a 'classic' FOB contract this will be the first duty to be performed; nomination will normally be for the buyer. The port of loading may be specified by the contract; if not, the buyer may nominate both port and vessel[1]. Alternatively, the contract may allow the seller to nominate the port; in that case he must notify the buyer of his nomination in time for the buyer to perform his obligation and nominate a ship[2].

The duty is to nominate an 'effective vessel': ie one ready and able to carry the goods in accordance with the contract of sale. Thus the vessel must be available to load the contract goods at the time and place fixed by the sale contract. Although there is no obligation on the buyer to book space in advance, the need to ensure that an effective vessel is available to carry the goods means that he will generally do so.

Where the contract allows a choice of ports or a period during which loading may take place, the buyer may nominate a ship at any of the specified ports loading at any time within the contract period. Thus a contract for sale 'FOB Dutch port, October shipment' would be satisfied by a nomination of a ship loading at Rotterdam on 28 October[3]. However, the buyer must give the seller sufficient notice of his nomination to allow the seller to perform his obligations. This may be particularly important where the contract allows the buyer a choice of port. Thus, for instance, in the above example the nomination might not be effective if given on 27 October. The contract will often stipulate the amount of notice of nomination to be given. Such provisions will generally be construed as conditions, so that a failure to give sufficient notice will allow the other party to terminate the contract[4].

A nomination is not irrevocable. If the buyer nominates a ship which proves unable to load the goods, the buyer may substitute a fresh nomination, provided there is time to do so in accordance with the contract. However, if the buyer fails to nominate an effective ship, the seller may terminate the contract[5]. He is then released from his obligations under the contract and may sue for damages for non-acceptance[6]. However, since failure to load will generally prevent property in the goods passing to the buyer[7], the seller will not be able to claim the price unless the contract makes the price payable on 'a day certain'.

1   *Boyd & Co Ltd v Louis* [1973] 1 Lloyd's Rep 209.
2   *Bunge Corpn v Tradax Export SA* [1981] 2 All ER 513, [1981] 1 WLR 711, HL.
3   *J & J Cunningham v R A Munro & Co Ltd* (1922) 28 Com Cas 42.
4   *Bunge Corpn v Tradax Export SA* [1981] 2 All ER 513, [1981] 1 WLR 711, HL.
5   *Bunge Corpn v Tradax Export SA* [1981] 2 All ER 513, [1981] 1 WLR 711, HL.
6   *Colley v Overseas Exporters* [1921] 3 KB 302.
7   Below 33.1.4.

33.1.3   *Delivery of the goods*

Once the buyer has nominated an effective vessel, the seller must arrange to load the goods on that vessel in accordance with the contract of sale. The goods themselves must comply with the express and implied terms of the contract, including the implied terms as to quality, fitness for purpose and compliance with description. The description of goods has been given a wide interpretation in international sale contracts, particularly those concerned with bulk commodities, where such things as date of shipment may be crucial in allowing the goods to be identified. The country of origin will probably be part of the description of the goods, as will the date of loading. In *Bowes v Shand*[1], for instance, the contract called for a cargo of '600 tons of Madras rice to be shipped at Madras during March and April'. The seller tendered a cargo most of which had been loaded during February. The buyer was held entitled to reject; Lord Cairns CJ observed that 'Merchants are not in the habit of placing upon their contracts stipulations to which they do not attach some value'[2]. Although the 'excessively technical' approach to what forms part of the contractual description has been criticised[3], it seems that that criticism is unlikely to apply in the context of international sale contacts for bulk commodities.

The goods must be of satisfactory quality and reasonably fit for the buyer's purpose, in accordance with s 14 of the Sale of Goods Act. In an FOB contract the point of delivery is when the goods cross the ship's rail, when risk of loss prima facie passes to the buyer; that is therefore the moment when the quality of the goods is to be assessed. However, the goods will not be of satisfactory quality if at the time of loading they are not in such a condition as to be able to survive carriage of the expected duration under normal conditions[4]. The packaging forms part of the goods, so that if the goods are damaged or deteriorate during transit due to defective or inadequate packaging, the seller will be liable. Where the seller makes the carriage arrangements, his liability may also be extended to cover loss or damage in transit if he does not make a reasonable contract with the carrier[5]. Generally, however, the risk of damage or deterioration in transit will be borne by the carrier or the buyer. Any apparent defect in the goods or their packaging will be noted on the bill of lading at the time of loading. If the bill is clean but the goods arrive damaged, the buyer will claim against the carrier.

The seller must see that the goods are loaded on the ship and pay all charges in connection with loading. Once the goods cross the ship's rail, the seller is deemed to have fulfilled the obligation to deliver the goods and, prima facie, property in and risk of loss to the goods pass to the buyer. If the goods are damaged during loading it may thus be crucial to decide whether or not they had crossed the rail at the time of damage. As we have seen, the result of *Pyrene v Scindia* is that loading is treated as part of the sea-carriage, so that the Hague-Visby Rules will apply to the loading operation and will bind the seller in respect of damage before the goods cross the rail[6]; nevertheless, the prospect of legal rights and liabilities shifting as the goods swing over the rail on a crane has rightly been described as 'absurd'[7].

The goods must be loaded during the contract period, and, in order to fulfil his obligation, the seller must ensure that the goods are delivered to the port in time for loading to take place. Where a contract called for goods to be shipped FOB during January and the seller delivered goods to the port 15 minutes before dockers stopped work on 31 January, it was held that he had not performed his obligation and the buyer was entitled to reject[8].

On completion of the loading, the seller must obtain the relevant shipping documents and forward them to the buyer. Under a 'classic' FOB contract, the seller will receive a bill of lading, which must be a clean, shipped bill. Under the more modern type of FOB, where the buyer books shipping space in advance, the seller will receive a mate's receipt.

1   (1877) 2 App Cas 455.
2   (1877) 2 App Cas 455 at 463.
3   By Lord Wilberforce in *Reardon Smith Line v Ynguar Hansen Tangen* [1976] 3 All ER 570 at 576, [1976] 1 WLR 989 at 998; above 11.1.2.
4   *Mash & Murrell Ltd v J Emmanuel* [1962] 1 All ER 77n, [1982] 1 WLR 16n.
5   Below 33.1.5
6   See also *Thermo Engineers v Ferrymasters* [1981] 1 All ER 1142, [1981] 1 WLR 1470.
7   By Devlin J in *Pyrene v Scindia* [1954] 2 QB 402 at 417.
8   *All Russian Co-Operative Society v Benjamin Smith* (1923) 14 Ll L Rep 351, CA.

33.1.4   *Passing of property in FOB sales*

The rules in ss 16–19 of the Sale of Goods Act on the passing of property apply to FOB contracts just as they do to any other sale contract. Thus no property can pass until the contract goods are ascertained (s 16). Subject to that restriction, the passing of property is dependent on the intention of the parties (s 17) and the seller may reserve a right of disposal (s 19). In the absence of any other indication of intention, the property will pass in accordance with the rules in s 18. The intention of the parties is to be determined from all the circumstances of the contract; the use of the FOB term may raise certain presumptions as to the intentions of the parties, based on commercial practice. However, it will be necessary to examine all the circumstances of the case, and the form of the bill of lading, and the parties' dealings with it, will be particularly important.

It is worth recalling the three types of FOB contract identified by Devlin J in the *Pyrene* case. Under the classic form, the seller places the goods on board the ship nominated by the buyer; there is no prior arrangement between buyer and carrier, so that the seller makes the contract of carriage. Under the extended form of contract, the seller undertakes additional duties, including the arrangement of the contract of carriage; thus in this case too the seller makes the contract of carriage. Under the third type, the buyer makes the contract of carriage in advance. In the first two cases the seller receives a bill of lading; it may be to his order or to that of the buyer. In the third case, the seller receives only a mate's receipt; however, the name on the receipt may well be an indicator of the parties' intentions as to the passing of property.

In general it is presumed that where the parties contract on FOB terms the intention is that property shall pass on shipment when the goods cross the ship's rail.

> '[T]he ship's rail is the dividing line to which lawyers and businessmen attach equal importance. The ship's rail determines not only the charges which have to be borne by the seller or buyer respectively, but it is also the legal test adopted for the performance of the contract, viz the passing of property, the delivery of the goods and the passing of risk, except where a different intention of the parties is evident. The ship's rail is thus the legal frontier between the seller's and buyer's lands . . .'[1].

The general rule can be displaced. Where the contract is for the sale of specific goods, it might be argued that property could pass at the time of the contract, in accordance with s 18, r 1 of the Sale of Goods Act. However, the use of the term 'FOB' will generally be sufficient to exclude that rule and it will take strong evidence to displace the presumption that property is not to pass until shipment. If property passed prior to shipment, the seller might be in some difficulty if the goods were to be damaged prior to shipment, for it is assumed that risk of loss normally passes to the buyer only when the goods cross the ship's rail: thus the seller would bear the risk of loss but not have the required property interest to found a claim for negligence in respect of damage to the goods, unless it were held that risk of loss had also passed to the buyer at the same time as property. Where the contract is for the sale of unascertained goods, the general rule has been explained on the basis that the loading of the goods is the last act to be done by the seller in performance of the contract, and therefore amounts to an appropriation for the purposes of s 18, r 5 of the Sale of Goods Act[2]. However, it is possible for the contract to provide for the passing of property at an earlier stage: for instance, it is common practice for property in liquid cargoes such as oil to pass when the cargo passes a hose connection at the port of loading.

It is rather easier to establish that the passing of property has been delayed until some later point in time than the loading of the goods. Where goods are loaded in bulk for several buyers, no property in any particular goods can pass until the goods for each buyer have been ascertained, in accordance with s 16 of the Sale of Goods Act, although individual buyers may become tenants in common of the bulk if the requirements of s 20A of the Sale of Goods Act are satisfied[3]. Alternatively, the passing of property may be deferred if that is the intention of the parties, particularly if the seller reserves property until he is paid for the goods. Section 19 of the Sale of Goods Act allows the seller to impose a reservation of title, and s 19(2) creates a presumption that if the seller takes a bill of lading in his own name, he intends to reserve property until the price is paid. Clearly, this can only apply to those FOB contracts where the seller does receive a bill of lading (ie the 'classic' form or where the seller undertakes extra duties), but it may be possible to raise a similar inference under a modern FOB contract if the seller takes a mate's receipt showing himself as the shipper; in any event, in such a case the buyer will be unable to obtain a bill of lading without the co-operation of the seller, so that the seller will have practical protection.

In the past some doubts have been expressed as to whether or not s 19(2) could apply to an FOB contract, it being argued that the seller having contracted to pass property at the time of shipment could not then break his contract by reserving ownership[4]. However, s 19(2) appears to have been based on a number of nineteenth-century cases, many of which concerned FOB contracts[5] and commercial practice has recognised that the seller may take the bill of lading in his own name as security for the price. The matter appears to have been settled by the decision of the Court of Appeal in *Mitsui & Co Ltd v Flota Mercante Grancolombiana SA*[6] confirming that a reservation of ownership until payment of the price in full is no breach by an FOB seller, unless there is some express provision to the contrary in the contract of sale.

However, even where the seller does take the bill of lading in his own name, s 19(2) only raises a presumption which may be displaced by the other facts of the case. Thus in *The Parchim*[7], where the seller took a bill of lading in his own name but risk impliedly passed under the contract on shipment, the Privy Council held that property passed on loading. Where the seller takes the bill of lading in his own name, three interpretations are possible.

1. The goods may not be appropriated to the contract. The seller may decide to use them for some other contract and substitute others for his contract with the particular buyer.
2. The goods are appropriated to the contract, but subject to a condition that property is not to pass until payment.
3. The goods are appropriated to the contract and become the buyer's property on loading, but the seller retains the bill of lading to retain constructive possession of the goods and therefore a lien to secure payment[8]. However, this interpretation is unlikely to be adopted where the seller needs to use the goods as security to raise finance himself, for instance to finance his own purchase. In such a case he will need the general property in goods to pledge with a bank, and a lien will be inadequate for his needs.

Equally, the court may find an intention that property shall be retained by the seller even where the bill of lading is in the buyer's name, especially if the price is not payable until after loading and the seller retains the bill of lading[9]. The cases in this area are difficult to reconcile and it is probably impossible to extract any universal principle. As a general rule, where the seller takes the bill of lading in his own name he is likely to be treated as reserving property.

Where there is a reservation of ownership under s 19, a further question arises as to whether the seller must release the bill of lading, and therefore the goods, to the buyer if the buyer tenders the price. In *Wait v Baker*[10] the seller who had reserved ownership refused the buyer's tender of the price and resold the goods to a third party. It was held that no property had passed to the first buyer and so he was unable to claim the goods. However, the decision appears to have been motivated by a desire to protect the third party; such a person would now gain a good title by virtue of s 24 of the Sale of Goods Act (or s 8 of the Factors Act)[11] and the better view appears to be that where the seller reserves property to secure the price, property passes when the buyer tenders the price, when the condition attached to the passing of property is satisfied[12].

The law in this area is far from clear. The difficulty stems, in part, from the failure to recognise that the question whether property has passed may be asked for a number of different reasons and, for reasons of commercial convenience, it may be desirable to give different answers to the question according to the context in which it is asked.

1　Schmitthoff, *Legal Aspects of Export Sales* (1953) p 43.
2　*Carlos Federspiel & Co SA v Charles Twigg & Co Ltd* [1957] 1 Lloyd's Rep 240.
3　See 15.5.2.
4　Carver, *Carriage by Sea* (13th edn, 1982); British Shipping Laws, para 1620.
5　Eg *Wait v Baker* (1848) 2 Exch 1.
6　[1989] 1 All ER 951, [1988] 1 WLR 1145.
7　[1918] AC 157.
8　See eg *Browne v Hare* (1859) 4 H & N 822; *The Sorfareren* (1915) 114 LT 46.
9　*The Kronprinsessan Margareta* [1921] 1 AC 486, PC.
10　(1848) 2 Exch 1.
11　See 17.3.
12　*Mirabita v Imperial Ottoman Bank* (1878) 3 Ex D 164, CA.

33.1.5　*Risk in FOB sales*

As in domestic sale contracts, the general rule in s 20 of the Sale of Goods Act 1979 applies to FOB contracts and risk prima facie passes with property so that risk normally passes to the buyer when the goods are put across the ship's rail. Thus in *Pyrene & Co Ltd v Scindia Steam Navigation Co Ltd*[1] the tender was at the seller's risk when it was dropped during loading prior to crossing the ship's rail. In *J & J Cunningham v R A Munro & Co Ltd*[2] the contract called for the sale of a cargo of bran FOB Rotterdam for October shipment. The seller delivered the bran to the port on 14 October but the buyer nominated a ship loading at Rotterdam on 28 October, by which time the bran had deteriorated due to overheating. The bran was still at the seller's risk and the buyer was therefore entitled to reject the goods.

However, even where property does not pass to the buyer on loading, risk normally will pass. This will apply even where goods shipped for the buyer form an unascertained part of a larger bulk; once the goods are shipped, the seller has fulfilled his obligation to deliver the goods and nothing remains to be done by him under the contract. The buyer has an insurable interest in the goods from the time of shipment[3]. If the contract varies the seller's duties, it may therefore vary the point at which risk passes: for instance, if the contract is for the goods to be delivered 'free on board stowed', the seller's duties are not complete until the goods are safely stowed, so that risk may not pass until that point[4].

Risk of loss may also remain with the seller by virtue of the provisions of s 32 of the Sale of Goods Act. Section 32(3) provides that:

> 'where goods are sent by the seller to the buyer by a route involving sea transit under circumstances in which it is usual to insure, the seller must give to the buyer such notice as will enable the buyer to insure them during their sea transit'.

If the seller fails to supply such information, the goods are at his risk during the sea transit. It has been argued that s 32(3) can have no application to FOB sales because the contract requires the seller to deliver the goods 'free on board' and delivery to a carrier is normally deemed to be delivery to the buyer[5]. However, in *Wimble, Sons & Co v Rosenberg*[6] the Court of Appeal held by a majority that s 32(3) did apply to a contract on FOB terms. The seller sold goods FOB Antwerp and had the right to nominate the vessel. Goods were shipped on 24 August, the ship sailed on 25 August and sank on 26 August; the buyer received the bill of lading three days later. He had not insured the goods and refused to pay, relying on s 32(3). Buckley and Vaughan Williams LJJ agreed that s 32(3) was applicable, but Buckley LJ agreed with Hamilton LJ that on the facts the buyer had sufficient information to insure and thus the seller was not in breach. All that is required is that the buyer should know the nature and value of the goods and the ports of loading and discharge. The FOB buyer will normally have that information so that, although s 32(3) does apply to FOB contracts, it will rarely impose any serious obligation on the seller.

Section 32(2), however, may be more important. That section applies where the seller makes a contract of carriage on behalf of the buyer – ie in cases of 'classic' FOB and where the seller takes on additional duties – and requires him to make 'such contract as is reasonable having regard to the nature of the goods and the other circumstances of the case'. If the seller fails to do so, and the goods are lost or damaged during transit, the buyer may either decline to treat delivery to the carrier as delivery to himself (so that the seller has failed to deliver) or claim damages from the seller. What is reasonable will depend on all the circumstances of the case, including what is usual in the trade. Thus, for example, if the seller sells frozen food on FOB terms, he must clearly arrange for carriage in a ship with refrigeration facilities; the seller may also be liable under this section if he makes a contract on unusual terms[7] or for carriage by an unusual route.

Conversely, risk may pass to the buyer prior to shipment. In *Cunningham v Munro* it was suggested that if the goods deteriorate because of the buyer's delay in giving the seller shipping instructions, or because the buyer induces the seller to deliver goods to the port before the goods can be loaded, for instance by nominating a ship which does not load at the time indicated, the buyer would be liable for such deterioration; he would be entitled to reject the goods for non-compliance with the implied conditions as to quality etc in the Sale of Goods Act, but would be liable to the seller in damages for the deterioration.

1   [1954] 2 QB 402, [1954] 2 All ER 158.
2   (1922) 28 Com Cas 42.
3   *Inglis v Stock* (1885) 10 App Cas 263.
4   For discussion of the effect of such provisions see Reynolds [1994] LMCLQ 119.
5   Sale of Goods Act, s 32(1).
6   [1913] 3 KB 743.
7   See *Thos Young & Sons v Hobson* (1949) 65 TLR 365, CA.

33.2   CIF contracts

The CIF (cost, insurance and freight) contract has been in use since at least the middle of the nineteenth century (although initially known as 'c f & i'). As Lord Wright observed in 1940: 'It is a type of contract which is more widely and more frequently in use than any other contract used for the purposes of sea-borne commerce'[1]. It overtook the FOB contract in popularity early the twentieth century (although, as noted above, the relative popularity of the two forms has fluctuated from time according to economic and other factors), and although the 'container revolution' has led to the development of other forms of arrangement, it remains of great importance, and its special features give it advantages which mean that new forms of contract for container traffic are likely to seek, so far as possible, to simulate it.

Under a CIF contract the seller is required to arrange the carriage of the goods and their insurance in transit, and the cost of those arrangements is included in the contract price (so that the buyer is not concerned with fluctuations in freight rates or insurance premiums). The seller obtains a bill of lading and a policy of insurance and forwards them to the buyer, together with an invoice for the price, and the buyer pays on receipt of the documents.

The popularity of the CIF form can be explained by the many advantages it offers to the parties. The buyer has the advantage of knowing from the date of the contract the exact price he must pay to obtain the goods: the contract price includes freight and insurance. More importantly, the use of documents to perform the contract and represent the goods allows the parties to deal with the goods afloat. Thus the buyer may resell the goods before they arrive, and it is common for some items, particularly bulk commodities, to be resold many times whilst afloat; alternatively, the documents may be pledged to a bank as security for an advance of the price. The use of documents facilitates the involvement of financial institutions; the documents can be transferred direct to the buyer's bank as security for the advance of the price: the bank will be willing to take up and hold documents where it would not be prepared to take possession of the goods themselves and normally, where payment is to be by bankers' documentary credit, this is what happens. This, in turn, allows the seller to be assured of payment and to receive the price as soon as the documents are received, without waiting for the arrival of the goods. Indeed, he is assured of payment even if the goods are damaged or never arrive at all for he is entitled to be paid on presentation of the documents[2]; the buyer is generally protected against such losses by the bill of lading, giving a contractual right against the carrier, and the policy of insurance, covering most accidental losses.

1   *Ross T Smyth & Co Ltd v T D Bailey, Son & Co* [1940] 3 All ER 60, HL.
2   See *Manbre Saccharine Co v Corn Products Co* [1919] 1 KB 198; below 33.2.10.

33.2.1   *CIF and FOB compared*

We have noted above that an FOB seller may sometimes arrange freight and insurance. However, even where that is the case, there are important differences between an FOB and a CIF contract.

1.   Under an FOB contract the buyer bears the risk of fluctuations in freight rates and insurance premiums.
2.   A CIF contract is always an export contract.
3.   The CIF seller can fulfil his contract by tendering to the buyer goods already afloat; indeed, he can buy goods afloat in order to fulfil his contract with the buyer. As a result, a CIF contract cannot be frustrated by an export ban. The FOB seller must ship goods in satisfaction of the contract.
4.   The named port in a FOB contract is the port of shipment; under a CIF contract the named port is the port of destination.
5.   Since the seller makes the arrangements for carriage and insurance, s 32(3) of the Sale of Goods Act cannot apply to a CIF contract.

33.2.2   *The importance of documents*

As we noted above, documents play a central role in the CIF contract and it is this that gives the contract its special characteristics. The seller performs the contract by tendering to the buyer the bill of lading, insurance policy and invoice (together with any other documents required by the contract, such as a certificate of quality or origin). These documents represent the goods, and protect the buyer against most risks of loss during transit. They enable him to deal with the goods before they arrive at the port of destination. Transfer of the bill of lading operates as constructive delivery of the goods and may pass to the buyer title to the goods, the right to obtain possession, and rights of action against the carrier in the event of loss, delay etc; the policy of insurance gives protection against the perils of the sea. The importance of the documents is illustrated by the rule that allows the seller to tender documents even after the goods they represent have been damaged or lost[1]. Similarly, if the documents conform to the contract, the buyer must accept them; if he rejects them he is in breach of contract even if the goods themselves do not comply with the contract when they arrive[2], although if the documents have been accepted, the buyer may reject the goods themselves if they prove defective[3].

> 'All that the buyer can call for is delivery of the customary documents. This represents the measure of the buyer's rights and the extent of the vendor's duty. The buyer cannot refuse the documents and ask for the actual goods, nor can the vendor withhold the documents and tender the goods they represent'[4].

This emphasis on documents led Scrutton J to describe the CIF contract as 'a sale of documents relating to goods'[5]. However, whilst this description offers a clear indication of the importance of the documents, it might be misleading; the contract is still one for the sale of goods, to which the Sale of Goods Act applies. The buyer does have rights in relation to the goods themselves, and this led Bankes and Warrington LJJ in the Court of Appeal in the same case to suggest that the contract might more properly be called 'a contract for the sale of goods to be performed by the delivery of documents'[6].

1   *Manbre Saccharine Co v Corn Products Co* [1919] 1 KB 198.
2   *Berger & Co Inc v Gill & Duffus SA* [1984] AC 382, HL.
3   *Kwei Tek Chao v British Traders and Shippers Ltd* [1954] 2 QB 459.
4   Per McCardie J in *Manbre Saccharine Co v Corn Products Co* [1919] 1 KB 198 at 202.
5   *Arnhold Karberg & Co v Blyth, Green Jourdain & Co* [1915] 2 KB 379 at 388.
6   [1916] 1 KB 495 at 510, 514, CA.

33.2.3   *Duties of the parties*

Not surprisingly, in view of the commercial significance of CIF contracts, there is a substantial body of case law concerned with the rights and duties of the parties and a number of judges have set out definitions of those duties under a typical contract[1]. In an often quoted judgment in *Biddel Bros v E Clement Horst Co*[2], Hamilton J set out the duties as follows:

> 'A seller under a [CIF] contract . . . has firstly to ship at the port of shipment goods of the description contained in the contract; secondly to procure a contract of affreightment, under which the goods will be delivered to the

destination contemplated in the contract; thirdly to arrange for an insurance upon the terms current in the trade which will be available for the benefit of the buyer; fourthly to make out an invoice . . . ; and finally to tender these documents to the buyer so that he may know what freight he has to pay and obtain delivery of the goods if they arrive, or recover for their loss if they are lost on the voyage. It follows that against tender of these documents , the bill of lading, invoice and policy of insurance . . . the buyer must be ready and willing to pay the price'.

We must examine these duties in more detail, but before doing so, a number of points must be noted. Although the list of duties offered by Hamilton J represent the basis of a typical CIF contract, and is reflected in INCOTERMS, the duties in any individual contract may vary from this model. The parties are always free to add to or vary the duties by express terms:

'It is a trite observation that what is sometimes called a true FOB or a true CIF contract is a comparative commercial rarity. Contracts vary infinitely according to the wishes of the parties to them'[3].

Thus the contract may impose additional duties on the seller: for instance to pay any commission due to a confirming house (when the contract may be designated 'CIF & c'), or to supply additional documents such as certificates of origin or quality; or the contract may reduce the seller's duties: a 'c & f' contract is much the same as a CIF contract except that the seller does not arrange insurance. Alternatively, the contract may provide for it to be performed by the seller tendering other documents than those mentioned by Hamilton J: for instance, where goods are shipped and carried in bulk it is common for the contract to provide for the seller to provide the buyer with a delivery order instead of a bill of lading, or, if the seller insures goods under a floating block policy, (where the policy covers any goods the seller owns afloat and notifies to the insurer from time to time), a certificate of insurance rather than a policy. However, certain characteristics are essential to a CIF contract, and if the contract purports to vary them, it may cease to be a CIF contract at all. In *The Parchim*, for example, a contract described as 'CIF' was said to have 'far more of the characteristics of a contract FOB than it has of a contract CIF'[4].

The court will endeavour to construe a contract which uses the 'CIF' designation as a CIF contract, and if it contains terms which contradict that designation, for instance, providing for the goods to be at the seller's risk until arrival, it may be possible to disregard them as repugnant and meaningless. However, where that is not possible, the contract will cease to be CIF A leading example is *The Julia*[5], where a cargo of rye was sold 'CIF Antwerp'. The contract made the sellers liable for the condition of the grain on arrival and for any deficiency in the quantity delivered, and provided for payment against delivery orders and certificates of insurance. The sellers sent to their agent in Antwerp a delivery order, which the agent undertook to honour, together with a notice that the buyers had a share in an insurance covering the bulk cargo. The buyers paid for those documents, but the goods were never delivered to them because the ship was diverted to Lisbon at the outbreak of the Second World War and the goods were sold there. The House of Lords held that the contract was not a CIF contract at all. Under a CIF contract the buyer gets documents representing the goods, allowing him to deal with them while afloat, but here the buyers never obtained such documents: the agent's delivery order, unlike a ship's delivery order, gave no property rights to the buyers so that the sellers retained property and possession until the goods were discharged from the ship. Moreover, the sellers undertook responsibility for the condition and quantity of the goods on arrival, indicating that the contract was really an arrival, or 'ex ship', contract. Consequently, since the goods never had arrived, the sellers had failed to perform and the buyers were entitled to a refund of the price.

Although the characteristics of a CIF contract have been set out in judicial decisions, those decisions are based on commercial custom and practice. It would therefore seem that the essentials of the contract could be varied by evidence of changes in commercial practice: in view of the changes being brought about by technological and other developments, that may be important in the future, but 'the evidence of a modifying custom must be clear indeed ere the well-known incidents of such a bargain as a CIF contract can be changed'[6].

Finally, it should be noted that the seller's duties may be performed in a different sequence from that identified by Hamilton J. Under modern conditions the seller may well arrange the contracts of carriage and insurance prior to shipping the goods.

1   See eg Lord Blackburn in *Ireland v Livingston* (1872) LR 5 HL 395 at 406; Lord Atkinson in *Johnson v Taylor Bros* [1920] AC 144 at 155; Lord Wright in *Ross T Smyth & Co Ltd v T D Bailey, Son & Co* [1940] 3 All ER 60 at 67, HL.
2   [1911] 1 KB 214 at 220.
3   Per Roskill LJ in *Concord Petroleum Corpn v Gosford Marine Panama SA, The Albazero* [1975] 2 Lloyd's Rep 295 at 302, CA.
4   [1918] AC 157 at 164, PC.
5   *Comptoir d'Achat et de Vente du Boerenbond Belge SA v Luis de Ridder Limitada* [1949] AC 293, [1949] 1 All ER 269, HL.
6   McCardie J in *Manbre Saccharine Co v Corn Products Co* [1919] 1 KB 198 at 206.

33.2.4   *Goods afloat*

Although Hamilton J speaks of the seller being under a duty to ship the goods, as indeed do other judges and INCOTERMS, this is not strictly accurate. It must be remembered that the seller can fulfil a CIF contract by tendering goods already afloat, which he has either shipped himself, or bought from some other person. All that is required therefore is that the seller should appropriate to the contract goods which:

(a) have been shipped;
(b) comply with the terms of the contract; and
(c) are covered by a contract of carriage to the port of destination and by a policy of insurance.

Some goods must have been shipped: the contract is not satisfied if the seller tenders documents relating to goods to be shipped, or which have never been shipped[1]; but there is no need for the shipper personally to have shipped the goods or to do so after making the contract. Equally, there is no need for the seller to make the contracts of carriage or insurance personally: where goods are carried under a bill of lading, the transfer of the bill operates to transfer the contract of carriage to the transferee[2] and a policy of marine insurance may be assigned[3].

1   *Hindley & Co v East India Produce* [1973] 2 Lloyd's Rep 515.
2   Carriage of Goods by Sea Act 1992, s 2; above 32.5.5.
3   Marine Insurance Act 1906, s 50(3).

33.2.5 *Appropriation of goods to the contract*

In the light of what we have said above, it will be apparent that there are at least four possible sequences in which the seller may fulfil the obligations imposed by the CIF contract.

(a) 1. Contract of sale between S and B.
   2. S ships goods in performance of that contract and makes insurance arrangements.
   3. S tenders to B documents relating to the goods shipped.
(b) 1. S ships goods and arranges insurance.
   2. S makes contract with B.
   3. S tenders to B documents relating to the goods already shipped.
(c) 1. Contract of sale between S and B.
   2. S purchases goods shipped by X to perform the contract with B.
   3. S tenders to B documents relating to the goods purchased from X.
(d) 1. S purchases goods afloat shipped by X.
   2. S makes contract with B.
   3. S tenders to B documents relating to the goods purchased from X.

Even in cases of type (a), unless the goods are specific, it will be necessary for S at some stage to appropriate goods to the contract with B. Specific goods are rarely sold under CIF terms, so that appropriation is generally necessary; indeed, it will often be an express requirement of the contract that the seller should send a notice of appropriation, in order to inform the buyer which goods are to be used for his contract, and thus enable him to make arrangements to resell them or otherwise deal with them. In the present context, 'appropriation' means that the goods are nominated or earmarked for use for the contract with B; appropriation only passes property to B if it is unconditional, and under CIF contracts the seller normally appropriates goods to the contract subject to the condition that property will only pass on payment of the price. Once goods are appropriated to the contract, S cannot use them for any other contract nor without B's consent use any other goods for the contract with B[1].

Where S ships the goods after making the contract of sale (case (a) above), the shipment may itself serve as appropriation, but this is unlikely unless there is some indication from the facts that it is intended by S, for instance because the bill of lading is taken to B's order. Generally, appropriation takes place by S sending to B a notice of appropriation; alternatively, the goods are appropriated to the contract when S tenders to B the documents relating to those goods.

Where S ships goods for the particular contract with B (case (a) above), the goods must comply at the time of shipment with all terms of the contract of sale. Thus they must be of satisfactory quality and fit for the buyer's purpose, including being in such condition that they can survive the voyage under ordinary conditions[2] and comply with the contract description, including any requirements in the contract as to the date or place of shipment[3]. In cases where S does not ship goods for the particular contract with B (types (b)–(d) above), but appropriates to the contract goods already afloat, the goods appropriated to the contract must have complied with the contract terms at the time they were loaded.

1   Where the contract is initially for unascertained goods a notice of appropriation relating to a bulk cargo will identify the source from which the buyer's goods are to come for the purposes of s 20A of the Sale of Goods Act.
2   *Mash & Murrell Ltd v J Emmanuel* [1962] 1 All ER 77n, [1962] 1 WLR 16n.
3   *Bowes v Shand* (1877) 2 App Cas 455, HL.

33.2.6 *Tender of documents*

In cases where S personally ships goods for the contract with B (types (a) and (b) above), S makes arrangements for the carriage and insurance of the goods; where S buys goods afloat, those arrangements are made by someone else and taken over by S. In either case, S must perform the contract with B by transferring to B documents representing the goods and the contracts of insurance and carriage. Unless the contract has varied the normal requirements, S must tender a bill of lading, policy of insurance and commercial invoice. Where there is no separate notice of appropriation, the tender of documents will appropriate the goods they represent to the contract.

The documents must exactly satisfy the contract. If not, the buyer may reject them. The following requirements must be satisfied.

(a) The bill of lading

(i) The bill of lading must be clean: it must show the goods were shipped in good order and condition. It will only indicate the apparent condition of the goods at the time of loading, not their quality. Where the buyer wants an assurance of quality, he will contract for the seller to provide a surveyor's report or certificate of quality.

(ii) It must show that the goods were loaded at the time and place required by the contract of sale.

(iii) It must be a shipped bill. The carrier is liable for loss during carriage and a shipped bill gives evidence of the condition of the goods at the date of shipment. A 'received for shipment bill' offers no evidence of the condition of the goods at the time shipment takes place and the carrier's liability commences.

(iv) It must be transferable: the buyer may want to resell or pledge the goods whilst they are afloat.

(v) It must cover only the goods intended for the buyer: if the bill covers a greater quantity, the buyer cannot deal with the goods he purchases.

(vi) It must be evidence of a valid contract of carriage from the port of loading to the port of destination, on terms usual at the time of shipment[1]. In *Arnhold Karberg & Co v Blyth, Green Jourdain & Co*[2] the seller tendered a bill of lading relating to carriage on a German ship; the outbreak of the First World War made that contract illegal and void, so that it was held the bill did not relate to a valid contract. The bill of lading must be such as to give the buyer an enforceable claim against the carrier in respect of damage to the goods. It must also cover the whole period of shipment. In *Hansson v Hamel & Horley*[3] the contract was for a sale CIF Yokohama. The goods were to be shipped from Norway. In fact the goods were shipped from Norway to Hamburg and then transshipped for carriage to Japan. The seller tendered a bill covering the carriage from Hamburg only. It was held that the buyer was entitled to reject the documents: the bill did not cover the whole voyage, and thus did not give the buyer full protection in respect of damage to the goods. It is irrelevant for this purpose that the goods arrive undamaged: the buyer might wish to sell the goods in transit, so the documents must comply with the contract when tendered.

(b) The policy of insurance

(i) The policy of insurance must relate to a contract of insurance which is valid and enforceable at the time the documents are tendered. Thus there will be a breach if the policy is voidable by the insurer on the grounds of misrepresentation or non-disclosure, or for breach of warranty[4].

(ii) The policy must cover all the usual risks. It is not clear if the risks covered must be those usual at the time of the contract of sale or at the time the policy is issued. In *Groom v Barber*[5] it was said that the policy must cover risks usually covered at the time of the contract of sale, but in that case the policy had been issued prior to the contract of sale. The better view would seem to be that the relevant time is normally the date of the policy.

(iii) The policy must be assignable, so that the buyer can take the benefit, and transfer the benefit if he deals with the goods. This means that the seller must tender a policy: a certificate of insurance is not assignable under the Marine Insurance Act[6], although the contract may expressly allow the seller to tender a certificate rather than a policy.

(iv) The policy must cover only the goods sold to the buyer. Thus where the seller is a merchant with a floating block policy, he will need to contract to tender a certificate.

(v) The policy must cover the goods for the entire voyage.

The purpose of tendering a policy of insurance is to protect the buyer against loss of or damage to the goods during the voyage. The seller must tender the policy even though the goods have already arrived undamaged: the buyer will normally have to pay on tender of the documents and may wish to resell the goods before examining them. The policy provides an assurance that he will be compensated if the goods have deteriorated in transit. Of course, if the goods are damaged due to a risk not covered by the policy and for which the carrier is not liable, the buyer must bear the loss (as happened in *Groom v Barber*); in contrast, if the policy does not meet the contract requirements, the buyer may reject it even though the goods arrive undamaged. The point is that the documents tendered to the buyer must be saleable. In general, since the seller makes insurance arrangements under a CIF contract, s 32(3) of the Sale of Goods Act can have no application to such contracts[7].

(c)   The invoice
S must tender to B an invoice for the inclusive CIF price. The invoice identifies the goods and will be used by B to clear the goods through customs. Where the freight is not pre-paid, it will be paid by B on arrival of the vessel. In that case, the invoice must discount the cost of freight, otherwise B would have to pay twice.

1   *Tsakiroglou v Noblee Thorl Gmbh* [1962] AC 93, [1961] 2 All ER 179, HL.
2   [1915] 2 KB 379 at 388.
3   [1922] 2 AC 36, HL.
4   See 35.3; 35.4.1.
5   [1915] 1 KB 316.
6   *Diamond Alkali Export Corpn v Bourgeois* [1921] 3 KB 443.
7   *Law and Bonar v British American Tobacco Co Ltd* [1916] 2 KB 605.

33.2.7   *The time of tender*

The seller must tender the documents in accordance with the terms of the contract. Since the tender of documents is the seller's principle duty under a CIF contract, where the contract stipulates a time for tender, that stipulation is a condition and the buyer is entitled to terminate for a late tender[1]. If the contract does not fix a time for tender, the seller is only obliged to tender the documents 'promptly', as soon as possible after shipment or appropriation. It is not clear if the buyer can terminate for the seller's failure to tender the documents 'promptly'. Generally, the documents will be forwarded by air, but, as noted elsewhere, it is becoming increasingly common for documents to arrive after the goods, creating problems of delay in unloading, and leading to a search for some acceptable method of electronically transmitting the relevant documents. The seller is not under an obligation to ensure that the documents reach the buyer before the vessel[2].

1   *Toepfer v Lenersan-Poortman NV* [1980] 1 Lloyd's Rep 143, CA, but contrast *Sanders v Maclean* (1883) 11 QBD 327, CA.
2   *Sanders v Maclean* (1883) 11 QBD 327, CA.

33.2.8   *The buyer's duties*

If the documents accord with the contract, the buyer must accept them and pay the price in accordance with the contract. Often the contract will require payment by documentary credit, in which case the documents will be presented to a bank, which will arrange payment[1]. If the documents are in order, the buyer must accept them, and cannot justify a rejection on the basis that the goods themselves do not conform with the contract[2]. The only exceptional case in which the buyer can reject documents which are good on their face and therefore apparently in accordance with the contract, is where the documents themselves are not genuine, as, for instance, where a bill of lading is falsely dated to show that goods were loaded during the period required by the contract when that was in fact not the case. The explanation for this exception is that the seller is under an implied obligation to tender documents which conform to the contract and which are themselves genuine. A wrongful rejection of the documents by the buyer is a repudiation of the contract which the seller can accept as releasing him from his remaining obligations under the contract. The buyer is then in breach of contract even though it may later be discovered that, had the seller not terminated, he would have been unable to perform the contract himself, or that the buyer would have been entitled to reject the goods. Such factors may, however, be taken into account on the assessment of damages for the buyer's breach[3]. The rule is intended to promote certainty. The shipping documents will often be presented to banks in connection with letters of credit for payment, and the bank cannot be expected to examine the goods: it must base its decision to accept the documents on the documents themselves.

This does not mean that the condition of the goods themselves is irrelevant. It was held in *Kwei Tek Chao v British Traders & Shippers Ltd*[4] that even if the buyer accepts the documents, he has a separate right of rejection in relation to the goods themselves. However, after accepting the documents the buyer may only reject the goods for defects not apparent on the face of the documents. Thus if the buyer accepts a bill of lading showing the goods were damaged at the time of loading, or were loaded late, he may not reject the goods themselves on that ground. But if the bill of lading is apparently in good order, the buyer may reject the goods on the grounds of defects which were not apparent, for instance, because the goods do not match the contract description, and it is irrelevant that he has accepted the documents, for instance by using them to resell the goods. In practice, the buyer will generally have paid for the goods on acceptance of the documents and will therefore not seek to reject the goods themselves, but will accept them and claim damages for breach of warranty. However, where the defective state of the goods is concealed by the fraud of the seller or his predecessor in title, the buyer may claim additional damages to cover any losses he would have avoided had he known of the breach and rejected the documents. Thus in *Kwei Tek* the goods were shipped outside the contract period but that fact was concealed on the bill of lading. The buyer was entitled to reject the goods when they arrived, despite having accepted the documents. Moreover, by that time the market price of the goods at their destination had fallen. The buyer was held entitled to the difference between the contract price and the market price at the date of arrival of the goods: if the bill of lading had been properly dated, he would have rejected the bill and avoided that loss.

In contrast, where the documents reveal some defect or breach of contract but the buyer purports to reject the goods for some other reason, he may not then justify the rejection by reference to the defect apparent on the documents[5]. It is not clear if this rule is based on a type of estoppel or waiver, or is an analogy with the rules on acceptance in the Sale of Goods Act[6]. It only applies where the breach is apparent on the face of the documents: it is not enough that they raise a doubt about the state of the goods[7].

In *Kwei Tek* the false dating of the bill of lading concealed the fact that the goods themselves did not conform to the contract, having been loaded outside the contract period. Had the bill been genuine, the buyer would have rejected it and avoided the fall in the market. The position is different if the seller tenders false documents but the goods themselves do conform to the contract – for instance, if the bill of lading is falsely dated but the goods were loaded during the contract period. The buyer is then entitled to reject the documents if the falsity is discovered, but if he accepts the documents he has no right to reject the goods and may recover only nominal damages for breach of contract as a result of the tender of false documents[8] for had there been no breach the seller would have presented a genuine bill of lading and the buyer would have accepted it. He would therefore not be able to recover damages in respect of any fall in the market price of the goods. However, if the buyer could show that the seller was aware that the documents were false, there seems no reason why he should not claim damages for fraud, which would seek to put him in the same position as if the documents had not been tendered; he would then be able to recover damages in respect of any fall in the market price.

If the buyer does reject the documents tendered by the seller, it is not clear if the seller can retender either the same documents or an alternative cargo. In *Kwei Tek* it seems that Devlin J was of the opinion that the buyer was entitled to reject documents not conforming to the contract, and terminate the contract. On the other hand, *Borrowman, Phillips & Co v Free & Hollis*[9] is generally cited as authority for the proposition that the seller can retender, provided that there is still time to do so within the contract period. However, in that case the sellers had served notice of intention to tender a particular cargo, but had not actually tendered the documents, and although there is support for the proposition that the seller may retender in other cases[10], the position remains unclear.

1 See ch 34.
2 *Berger v Gill & Duffus SA & Co Inc* [1984] AC 382, HL.
3 Ibid; for discussion of the problems caused by this case see Treitel [1984] LMCLQ 565.
4 [1954] 2 QB 459.
5 *Panchaud Frères v Etablissements General Grain Co* [1970] 1 Lloyd's Rep 53, CA.
6 See *Glencore Grain Rotterdam BV v Lebanese Organisation for International Commerce* [1997] 4 All ER 514, CA. See 12.2.1.
7 *Procter & Gamble Manufacturing Corpn v Peter Cremer GmbH & Co* [1988] 3 All ER 843.
8 *Procter & Gamble Philippine Manufacturing Corpn v Kurt A Becher* [1988] 2 Lloyd's Rep 21; see Treitel [1989] LMCLQ 457.
9 (1878) 4 QBD 500, CA.
10 See eg *Ashmore v Cox* [1899] 1 QB 436; *Smith v Wheatsheaf Mills* [1939] 2 KB 302; *SIAT v Tradax Overseas SA* [1980] 1 Lloyd's Rep 53, CA; see generally 12.1.3.1.

33.2.9 *The passing of property in CIF sales*

As with FOB contracts, the passing of property rules in the Sale of Goods Act apply to CIF contracts and govern the passing of property. Thus where the contract goods are part of a larger bulk, no property in any particular goods can pass until the buyer's goods have become ascertained, by virtue of s 16[1], but where the contract is for goods from a bulk source which is identified either in the contract or subsequently, including by the terms of a notice of appropriation, the buyer may acquire an undivided share in the bulk if the requirements of s 20A are satisfied[2]. Subject to that restriction, the general rule is that property passes according to s 17, when the parties intend it to pass. However, 'Since the parties seldom express any such intention or perhaps even think of it, the intention will generally be a matter of inference from the terms of the contract, the conduct of the parties and the circumstances of the case'[3].

It has been said that 'it seems to me impossible to lay down a general rule applicable to all CIF contracts'[4] so that in every case it will be necessary to examine all the circumstances, and decided cases offer no more than guidance. Property could pass at any one of several stages of the transaction. Where the contract is for specific goods, property could pass at the time the contract is made. In the more common case where the contract is for unascertained goods, property could pass on shipment if the goods are then ascertained. Alternatively, property could pass when the seller sends notice of appropriation of a particular cargo to the buyer. However, as noted above, notice of appropriation is generally presumed not to pass property, it being assumed that the appropriation is impliedly subject to the condition that property is not to pass until payment. Where the seller takes a bill of lading to his own order there is a statutory presumption that he intends to reserve a right of disposal[5]. However, as in the case of FOB contracts, the name on the bill of lading is not always decisive; dealings with the bill will be relevant, as will all the other circumstances.

In fact, where, as is normally the case, the buyer is to pay for the goods on receipt of the documents, the court will generally infer that the parties intend property to pass only on payment[6], provided the goods are then ascertained, and that presumption will be difficult to displace. In *Ginzberg v Barrow Haematite Steel Co Ltd*[7] the bill of lading was delayed and, to assist the buyers, who were anxious to obtain possession of the goods, the sellers let them have a delivery order. It was held that property had not passed to the buyers: it was well known that the sellers did not normally allow buyers credit, and that reinforced the general presumption. This is reflected in s 19(3) of the Sale of Goods Act, which provides that where the seller draws a bill of exchange on the buyer for the price, and forwards that to the buyer together with the bill of lading, the buyer may not retain the bill of lading if he does not honour the bill of exchange; and if he wrongfully retains the bill of lading, no property will pass to him.

However, whilst there is a general presumption that property is not intended to pass until payment, it may be displaced by appropriate facts. In *The Albazero*[8] the buyers and sellers were companies in the same group. The sellers took a bill of lading in their own name and indorsed it in favour of the buyers and despatched it to them before payment. The goods were damaged in transit and, since an action by the buyers was time barred under the contract of carriage, the sellers sought to argue that property had not passed, in order to claim themselves. The House of Lords held that, despite the general rule, the property had passed so that the sellers could not claim.

1 *Re Wait* [1927] 1 Ch 606, CA.
2 See 15.5.2. It is not clear whether the requirements are satisfied where the contract requires for payment by documentary credit and the seller has received notification of the opening of a conforming credit. It has been said that the opening of a credit operates as a conditional discharge of the buyer's payment obligation: see Lord Denning in *W J Alan & Co v EL Nasr Export and Import Co* [1972] 2 QB 189 at 212. It is submitted, however, that the opening of a credit does not amount to 'payment' for the purposes of s 20A, since the bank is not unconditionally obliged to pay. The policy of s 20A is to protect the buyer against loss caused by the seller becoming insolvent after the buyer has paid. Until documents are presented under the credit, the bank providing the credit is not obliged to pay.
3 Per Lord Wright in *Ross T Smyth & Co Ltd v T D Bailey, Son & Co* [1940] 3 All ER 60, HL.
4 Per Atkin J in *Stein Forbes & Co County Tailoring Co* (1916) 86 LJKB 448 at 449.
5 Sale of Goods Act, s 19(2).
6 *The Miramichi* [1915] P 71.
7 [1966] 1 Lloyd's Rep 343.
8 [1977] AC 774, [1976] All ER 129, HL.

33.2.10   The passing of risk in CIF sales

CIF contracts are an exception to the general rule in s 20 of the Sale of Goods Act which links the passing of risk to the passing of property. Whereas property passes under a CIF contract at the time the buyer pays and takes up the documents, the goods are deemed to be at the buyer's risk from the time of shipment. Where the seller ships goods for the buyer, risk passes at the time of shipment[1]; where the contract is made after shipment, risk passes at the time of the contract but retrospectively, so that the goods are deemed to have been at the buyer's risk since the time of shipment[2]. This might seem hard on the buyer, but in fact imposes little hardship. The buyer takes the benefit of the contract of carriage and policy of insurance and is therefore able to claim, either under the contract or the policy, in respect of most damage or loss from the time of shipment. Moreover, the rule 'is convenient in eliminating difficult questions of proof of the time goods were lost or damaged while at sea'[3]. However, the buyer is exposed to risks not covered by the contract of carriage or insurance: thus in *Manbre Saccharine v Corn Products Ltd*[4] the goods were lost when the ship was sunk during the First World War. The policy of insurance did not cover war risks, but because the terms of the policy were usual at the time the contract was made, the buyer would have had to pay for the goods whilst receiving nothing; in fact the buyer escaped liability because the seller failed to tender the correct documents.

As already noted, s 32(3) of the Sale of Goods Act does not apply to a CIF contract. Section 32(2) does apply, but adds nothing to the seller's essential obligation under a CIF contract. *Mash & Murrell v Joseph Emmanuel* applies to CIF contracts, so that the seller may be said to bear the risk of loss or deterioration caused by the state of the goods at the time of loading. However, the correct legal analysis of the position is that the seller bears such loss because the goods shipped are not of satisfactory quality at the time of shipment and the seller has therefore failed to fulfil one of his essential obligations.

In *Groom v Barber*[5] the court considered the logical implications of the rule that risk passes as from shipment. On 20 August 1914 the seller declared the cargo of a named ship to his buyer; in fact, unknown to the seller, the ship had been sunk by enemy action on 6 August. On 21 August the sinking became public knowledge and the buyer refused to pay. Atkin J held that, since risk passed from shipment, it was irrelevant that the goods were lost at the time the documents were tendered, and the seller had made a valid tender; the buyer was bound to pay. In *Manbre*

Saccharine Co v Corn Products Co McCardie J went further and held that the seller was entitled to tender documents relating to a cargo which he knew to be lost. These decisions may be a logical extension of the rules relating to the passing of risk in a CIF contract, but they raise difficult questions, in particular as to whether the seller can appropriate to a contract goods which are already lost.

Loss of or damage to the goods may occur at six different stages of the transaction.

1. Loss/deterioration after the buyer has paid the price is clearly for the buyer's account. The goods are the buyer's property and at his risk.
2. Loss/deterioration after tender of documents is also for the buyer's account, unless the buyer is entitled to reject the documents (eg as not conforming to the contract) and throw the loss back on the seller.
3. If the goods are lost or deteriorate after the goods have been appropriated to the contract, the seller may still tender the documents: once goods have been appropriated to the contract the seller is not entitled to tender any others.
4. If the goods are lost after shipment but before they have been appropriated to any particular contract, can the seller appropriate them to a contract and require the buyer to pay? In this situation the seller is not yet committed to using any particular goods for the buyer's contract. There are judicial dicta[6] which suggest that he can appropriate the lost cargo; the buyer is, after all, protected by the policy of insurance and contract of carriage against most losses. However, the balance of academic opinion suggests that the seller cannot appropriate a lost cargo[7] for, if he could, he would effectively be able to have the best of both worlds, by waiting to see how the market behaved: if the market rose, the seller would tender documents relating to the lost cargo; if it fell, the seller could buy an alternative cargo for his customer's contract and claim on the insurance in respect of the lost goods.
5. Goods are lost after the contract is made but before shipment. Here the position is clear: the seller cannot ship any goods and so cannot fulfil his contract using the 'lost' goods.
6. The goods are lost after shipment, but before the contract of sale: can the seller make a contract to sell lost goods? Logical extension of *Manbre Saccharine and Groom v Barber* would suggest that he can. Again, there is no decided authority and academic opinion differs. A contract to sell specific goods would be void in such a case, by virtue of s 6 of the Sale of Goods Act and a contract for unascertained goods from a designated source, as where the seller contracts to sell part of the cargo of a named vessel already lost, would be void for mistake at common law in such circumstances. Alternatively, the seller might be held impliedly to warrant the existence of the goods at the time of the contract; and if the seller knows of the loss he may be held to have fraudulently misrepresented his belief that the goods exist. If the goods exist at the time the contract is made but have already deteriorated, the position is equally unclear; in practice, there would be very great difficulty in proving that the goods had deteriorated after shipment but before the contract; but if the contract is for the sale of specific goods and the goods have deteriorated at the time of the contract, it would seem that the seller is in breach of the implied undertaking that they are of satisfactory quality at the time the contract is made.

1   *Johnson v Taylor Bros* [1920] AC 144.
2   *Comptoir D'Achat et de Vente du Boerenbond Belge SA v Luis de Ridder Limitada* [1949] AC 293, [1949] 1 All ER 269, HL.
3   Feltham, 'The Appropriation to a CIF contract of goods lost or damaged at sea' [1975] JBL 273.

4   [1919] 1 KB 198.
5   [1915] 1 KB 316.
6   In *Re Olympia Oil & Cake Co and Produce Brokers Ltd* [1915] 1 KB 233.
7   See *Benjamin's Sale of Goods* (5th edn, 1997) 19-074; Goode, *Commercial Law* (2nd edn, 1995) p 953; contrast Feltham [1975] JBL 273.

33.3   The Vienna Convention

UNIDROIT first started work on the harmonisation of the law of international sales in 1929. With the interruption caused by the Second World War its work did not bear fruit until 1964, when two conventions, the Uniform Laws on Formation of Contracts and on International Sale of Goods, were adopted at the Hague. The Hague Conventions proved unattractive both to states and to traders. They were ratified by only nine states, and were seen by developing and less developed nations as unfairly favouring the interests of Western developed nations. The UK ratified the Hague Convention subject to the permitted reservation that they should only apply to a contract if expressly adopted by the parties. The Conventions are given effect in English law by the Uniform Laws of International Sales Act 1967, which allows parties to contracts governed by English law to choose to apply the Uniform Law to their contract[1]. There is no reported English or Scots case in which the Uniform Law was adopted.

When UNCITRAL was established in 1966 it made harmonisation of sales law one if its initial projects. It was decided that the Hague Conventions were unlikely to win wide acceptance and work therefore started on a new harmonisation. In light of the experience of the Hague Conventions, an attempt was made to involve a wider and more representative Working Group in the drafting process in order to produce a text which would be 'capable of wider acceptance by countries of different legal, social and economic systems[2]'. The result was the Convention on Contracts for the International Sale of Goods, adopted in Vienna in 1980, and variously known as 'the Vienna Convention' or 'the CISG'. The Convention came into force on 1 January 1988 after receiving ten ratifications. By 1999 it had been ratified by 56 nations, including the US, 12 members of the EU and almost all of the UK's main trading partners. The UK has not, however, ratified the Convention[3].

There is not space here to offer more than a brief outline of the Convention's provisions[4]. It applies to contracts for the sale of goods where the parties have their places of business in different states, provided that either (a) both states are contracting parties to the Convention or (b) the rules of private international law lead to the contract being governed by the law of a state party to the Convention[5]. It is not applicable to consumer contracts nor to contracts for the sale of shares, negotiable instruments and other choses in action, ships, vessels, aircraft, hovercraft or electricity[6]. There is provision for the parties to a contract to exclude the application of the Convention, or any part of it, to their contract[7] but, unlike under the Hague Convention, the parties must contract out of, rather than contract into, its provisions.

The Convention deals with both the formation of the contract and with the obligations and remedies of the parties under the contract. However, although it does contain rules applying to the passing of risk under the contract, the Convention does not deal with the passing of property. Under most common international sale contracts the passing of property depends on well understood customary rules.

The obligations of the parties under the contract are not dissimilar to those under English law. The seller must deliver goods of the quantity, quality and description required by the contract[8] and the goods must be 'fit for the purposes for which goods of the same description would ordinarily be used'[9]. Other provisions reflect those of ss 14(3) and 15 of the Sale of Goods Act 1979. However, the remedies available in the event of breach of contract differ in some respects from those available in English law. The buyer has a right to avoid the contract in the event of a 'fundamental breach' of contract[10] but also has a right to demand repair or replacement of the goods delivered[11]. Moreover, in certain circumstances the seller has a right to 'cure' defective performance[12]. A breach of contract by either party is fundamental –

> 'if it results in such detriment to the other party as substantially to deprive him of what he is entitled to expect under the contract, unless the party in breach did not foresee and a reasonable person of the same kind in the same circumstances would not have foreseen such a result'[13].

The Convention provides for either party to recover damages in the event of breach by the other[14]. The assessment of damages is broadly similar to that under the Sale of Goods Act, although in the case of an actual resale by the seller, or replacement purchase by the purchaser, damages are assessed by reference to the actual price obtained or paid, as opposed to the hypothetical price used in applying the market price rule[15]. Moreover, where the seller delivers defective goods, the Convention entitles the buyer to claim a reduction of the price in the same proportion that the value of the goods actually delivered bears to the value of the goods as they should have been[16].

Since it has not been ratified by the UK, the Convention does not apply to contracts governed by English law (unless the parties adopt it by express reference in their contract). This does not mean that it is irrelevant to English lawyers or UK importers and exporters. It may apply to contracts involving UK traders where conflict of laws rules lead to the application of a contracting state rather than the law of England.

Views on whether the UK should ratify are divided. A consultation by the DTI in 1989 produced an equivocal response from the business and legal communities. Critics of the Convention claim that its introduction would introduce uncertainty into English law. Since the Convention does not deal with all aspects of international sale contracts, it would be necessary to resort to rules of domestic law, which might not fit easily with the rules of the Convention, to resolve questions relating to the validity of the contract and the passing of property. It is argued that many of the provisions of the Convention are less certain in their application than the corresponding provisions of English law. In particular, it is argued, the fundamental breach test which determines when a party is entitled to terminate the contract is less certain in its application than the bright line rule produced by the classification of terms into conditions and warranties. More importantly, the Convention does not deal expressly with the common forms of international sale contract such as those on CIF and FOB terms, to which some of its provisions are not easily applicable. Thus the editors of *Benjamin's Sale of Goods* observed that:

> 'its often vague or open textured terminology would, if it were to displace the present relatively settled English judge-made rules governing contracts on such terms, be a source of considerable (and regrettable) uncertainty'[17].

There is some force in these and similar criticisms, although in some cases they appear to have been overstated. Close examination of the provisions of the

Convention suggests that in many areas they are closer to the existing rules of English law than may at first appear. Whilst it is true that the Convention does not provide a complete code for international sales, the coherence of existing domestic law is probably overstated, especially in view of the various amendments which have been made to the Sale of Goods Act in recent years. The bright line distinction between conditions and warranties in English law has been significantly weakened by the recognition of the intermediate category of 'innominate' terms and the introduction of limitations on the right to reject goods for breach of condition in s 15A of the Sale of Goods Act[18]. The 'fundamental breach' test in the Convention in fact appears to be very similar to the test for determining when a contract may be terminated for breach of an innominate term. In so far as the Convention's provisions are not appropriate to CIF and FOB contracts it should be borne in mind that none of the Convention's provisions is mandatory. It is open to the parties to exclude or modify them by agreement and it is likely that the Convention would have little impact on the types of contract used for large-scale commodity trading where the use of detailed standard terms would exclude many of the Convention's provisions. Introduction of the Convention would create a measure of uncertainty, but introduction of any new legislation necessarily causes some uncertainty.

We noted at the start of this chapter that English law has no special body of rules applicable to international sales. It has a body of common law rules, based on mercantile practice, but most of its rules were not devised for international transactions and certainly not for modern trading conditions. The Vienna Convention is a modern law designed specifically for international contracts. Professor Goode has commented that the Convention 'is not a comprehensive convention . . . nor is it perfect. But it is for the most part better than our own Sale of Goods Act'[19]. There is now a significant and growing body of case law from courts around the world, interpreting and applying the Convention[20]. So long as the UK is not a party, its courts have no chance to influence the interpretation of the Convention. In 1998 the new Labour government undertook a new consultation on the desirability of ratifying the Convention and indicated that, in light of responses, it will in due course ratify, once Parliamentary time can be found for the legislation necessary to implement the Convention. It seems unlikely that the UK can forever remain aloof from the Convention as the number of states party to it grows[21].

---

1 Section 1(3).
2 See Nicholas (1989) 105 LQR 201 at 203.
3 The text of the Convention and other documentation is available at the UNCITRAL website at www.un.or.at.uncitral.
4 There is now an extensive literature on the Convention. See in particular Honnold, *Uniform Law for International Sales under the 1980 United Nations Convention* (2nd edn, 1990); Schlectreim, *Commentary on the UN Convention on the International Sale of Goods, 1980* (1998); Bridge, *The International Sale of Goods: Law and Practice* (1999) ch 2. Full details of material on the Convention can be found on the UNCITRAL website.
5 Article 1(1). States which ratify the Convention are permitted to exclude its operation in situation (b): art 95.
6 Article 2.
7 Article 6.
8 Article 35(1).
9 Article 35(2)(a).
10 Article 49.
11 Article 46.
12 Articles 37, 48.
13 Article 25.
14 Article 74.
15 See 12.3.1.3; 18.2.2.

16 Article 50; compare the rule in s 53 of the Sale of Goods Act 1979: see 12.3.3.
17 Preface to the 4th edn, 1992; see Feltham [1991] JBL 413.
18 See 12.2.
19 *Commercial Law in the Next Millennium* (1998) p 95.
20 The case law is published in summary form by UNCITRAL as 'Case Law on UNCITRAL Texts' or CLOUT.
21 See eg the views of Sir Johan Steyn in 'A Kind of Esperanto' in Birks (ed), *The Frontiers of Liability* (1994) vol 2.

Chapter 34

Financing International Trade

34.0 Introduction

As already noted, international sales where the parties are in different countries, separated by long distances and where the goods are in transit for long periods pose special problems. Sellers will be reluctant to part with the goods until they are assured of payment, whilst buyers will be reluctant to part with the price until they have control over the goods. The problem is further exacerbated if, as is often the case, the buyer wants credit. Where the parties have dealt together before, they may have developed trust in each other and the seller may be prepared to supply the goods 'on open account' – ie simply on credit for payment at a later date. In most cases, however, the seller will want some assurance of performance, if only to protect him against the risk of the buyer's insolvency. Several mechanisms have been developed to try to reconcile these conflicting interests. One option is for the seller to supply the goods on credit and retain title until the price is paid; but a retention of title is of limited effectiveness where the goods have been delivered and are located in some other country: if the seller repossesses them he may be forced to sell them in unfavourable conditions in foreign territory. The seller would much prefer payment of the price to a right to reclaim the goods. An alternative is to use the bill of lading in conjunction with a bill of exchange; indeed, bills of exchange are the most commonly used payment mechanism in international trade. Under a simple system, the seller draws a bill of exchange on the buyer for the price of the goods, and presents it to the buyer with the bill of lading and other contract documents; the bill of exchange is then known as a 'documentary bill'. The buyer accepts the bill, promising to pay it at some future date; if the buyer declines to accept the bill of exchange, he may not retain the bill of lading[1] and no property passes if he does. The buyer thus gains the benefit of a period of credit, since he is not required to pay the bill until it matures. The seller, on the other hand, may sell the bill, at a discount, to a bank and thus obtain immediate payment, albeit of less than the full face value of the bill. To guard against the risk of the buyer failing to accept the bill of exchange, the seller may employ a bank to act as his agent under a 'documentary collection' arrangement. In that case the bill of exchange and shipping documents are sent to a bank in the buyer's country, possibly acting as agent for the seller's own bank, with instructions only to release the shipping documents to the buyer on his acceptance of the bill of exchange.

However, this system still offers the seller only limited security. The buyer may fail to honour a bill, even after acceptance[2] and in that case the seller, having discounted the bill, will be liable on it and may be sued by the bank to which he discounted it, unless he did so 'without recourse'. The only advantage then is that the seller can bring an action against the buyer on the bill, rather than on the underlying contract, and the buyer will generally be unable to raise any breaches of the contract of sale as a defence to that action[3]. Further, on discounting the bill the seller will almost always receive less than its face value, the amount of the discount depending on the buyer's creditworthiness.

Far better for the seller is a system which gives some guarantee of payment by a person of recognised creditworthiness, such as a bank[4]. Such a guarantee gives the beneficiary the assurance of payment from an institution with an established credit reputation. A number of different guarantee arrangements have been developed; the most important in the context of international sales of goods is the documentary credit, also known as a 'letter of credit' or 'banker's commercial credit'.

So far we have been concerned with the seller's desire to be assured of the buyer's performance. The buyer may have similar concerns about the seller, and want some assurance of performance. In recent years a number of new instruments, such as performance bonds, have been developed to secure the performance of obligations other than the payment of money. They share many of the legal characteristics of the documentary credit. We will examine them briefly below, after considering the law relating to documentary credits.

1   Sale of Goods Act 1979, s 19(3), above 33.2.9.
2   See 28.5.
3   The seller may seek summary judgment under CPR Pt 24: *Nova (Jersey) Knit Ltd v Kammgain Spinnerei GmbH* [1977] 2 All ER 463, [1971] 1 WLR 713. See 28.1.2.
4   Banks offer a wide range of services to businesses engaged in international trade, including offering advice through a trade development service to put potential exporters in touch with potential markets, advising on currency rates and economic conditions, offering foreign currency accounts and providing direct financial assistance, by discounting bills of exchange or by acting as factors and purchasing debts due from customers.

34.1   The nature of documentary credits

Where the contract of sale calls for the buyer to pay by documentary credit, the buyer is required to enter into an arrangement with a bank whereby the bank gives the seller an undertaking to pay the price due under the contract provided that certain conditions are fulfilled. The bank's undertaking is legally enforceable, thus giving the seller the required assurance of payment. Where the bank with which the credit is opened does not have a branch in the seller's country, the credit may be confirmed by a bank there, giving the seller the added security of a target not only creditworthy but also within the jurisdiction. Once the credit is open, the seller can ship the goods and present the shipping documents required under the contract to the bank. Provided those documents comply with the instructions given to the bank by the buyer, the bank will pay the seller; according to the contract, payment may be due in cash, immediately or at some future date, or may be made by the bank accepting a bill of exchange drawn on the buyer, or by it agreeing to negotiate a bill drawn on the buyer without recourse to the seller[1]. The buyer may put the bank in funds to pay for the goods before the contract is made: in that case, the documents can be released to the buyer to obtain the goods; alternatively, the buyer may agree to repay the bank at some future date; until then the bank has the security given by possession of the bill of lading and has a pledge of the goods.

The documentary credit offers a number of advantages to all the parties involved in the transaction. The seller has the security offered by a promise of payment given by a bank: he is almost certain of payment, although in *Mitsui & Co Ltd v Flota Mercante Grancolombiana SA*[2] Staughton LJ observed that 'even the most copper-bottomed letter of credit sometimes fails to produce payment' and the Court of Appeal therefore held that a seller who had retained title on shipment still retained title even though it had received 80% of the contract price and the balance was secured by a documentary credit. Moreover, the bank's obligation under a documentary credit is as a principal, not simply as a guarantor. The buyer may use this assurance of payment to negotiate favourable purchase terms, such as an extended credit period or a discounted price. Both parties may obtain the benefit of improved cashflow. The bank will charge the buyer a fee for providing the credit, and is secured against the buyer's default by holding the bill of lading and by the security rights conferred by its contract with the buyer.

The buyer is exposed to some risk, because the documents will be presented to the bank rather than to him; if the documents are taken up, the seller will be paid and, whilst the buyer may reject the goods themselves when they arrive, he will be in a weak position having to claim back money already paid. It is thus essential for the buyer to give the bank precise instructions specifying exactly the documents which must be presented to obtain payment. If the bank pays without receiving the correct documents, it will be unable to claim reimbursement from the buyer.

Because of the advantages it offers, the documentary credit is in widespread commercial use. It was first used around 150 years ago, and although its popularity has fluctuated, influenced by the relative market strengths of buyers and sellers (since buyers must pay to open a documentary credit facility) and other economic factors, in general its use has increased, assisted by the increased uncertainty generated by international economic and political conditions since the Second World War. As a result, documentary credits are now so widely used that they have been described as 'the life-blood of international commerce'[3] and 'the classic FOB and CIF contracts of the textbooks providing for cash against documents without the intervention of the banker are now probably the exception rather than the rule'[4].

Documentary credits are significant for at least two other reasons. The customs relating to their use are set out in the Uniform Customs and Practice for Documentary Credits (UCP) published by the International Chamber of Commerce. The UCP are now widely used by banks throughout the world and may be said to represent the most successful attempt at harmonisation of international commercial law. Secondly, the documentary credit is the creation of the mercantile community. A documentary credit transaction gives rise to a number of contractual relationships which are difficult to fit into the traditional framework of contract law. However, the documentary credit and the obligations to which it gives rise have been recognised and enforced by the courts and it is now unthinkable that they should be declared unenforceable merely because they do not fit the conceptual legal framework.

1   So that the bank will not claim against the seller if the buyer fails to pay: see 28.4.5.
2   [1989] 1 All ER 951, [1988] 1 WLR 1145, CA.
3   By Kerr LJ in *Harbottle v National Westminster Bank Ltd* [1978] QB 146.
4   Per Diplock J in *Ian Stach Ltd v Baker Bosley Ltd* [1958] 2 QB 130 at 137.

34.1.1   *The Uniform Customs and Practice for Documentary Credits*

The first version of the UCP was published by the ICC in 1933. Since then it has been revised and updated on a regular basis by the ICC's Commission on Banking Techniques and Practice, in conjunction with various other international and commercial organisations, to take account of developments in banking practice (and the law). The current version, UCP 500, was published in 1993[1]. In 1984 UNCITRAL recommended its use for documentary credit transactions and its use is now almost universal. The ICC keeps the UCP under review and publishes answers to queries on their operation and issues guidance on problems which arise under them.

Despite their wide use, the better view is that in English law the UCP only apply to a credit if expressly incorporated into it by reference, and this is consistent with the language of the UCP[2]. In practice, credits are normally opened using standard bank documentation which will expressly subject the contract to the UCP. It must be emphasised that even if it could be argued that the UCP are so widely used as to have become customary, and capable of being implied into contracts without express reference, they have no independent legal force and take effect only as terms of the contracts into which they are incorporated. It is therefore possible for the express terms of a particular credit to modify or exclude the provisions of the UCP. A court will, however, strive to interpret the terms of the contracts arising under a credit in a manner which is consistent with the UCP[3]. It follows that the UCP should be interpreted in the same way as any other contract, albeit bearing in mind that they are a standard term document. In recent cases the courts have clearly adopted a purposive, commonsense approach to the interpretation of provisions of the UCP, taking account of background information as to the reasons why particular changes to the wording were adopted and so on[4]. In the event of a dispute, the court may receive evidence of banking practice, although it will not necessarily follow practice[5].

In recent years there has been a marked increase in the volume of litigation arising out of documentary credit operations[6] – hardly surprising given the financial amounts which are often in issue. It is reported that at least half of all documents presented under documentary credits are rejected on first presentation. Against this background, in 1997 the ICC launched a special dispute resolution system, 'DOCDEX', to provide a 'rapid, cost effective, expert-based dispute resolution mechanism for documentary credit practice'[7]. This is effectively a specialist arbitration system making use of the special expertise of members of the ICC's Commission on Banking Technique and Practice[8].

1   See Ellinger [1994] LMCLQ 377.
2   *Harlow and Jones Ltd v American Express Bank Ltd* [1990] 2 Lloyd's Rep 343, a case concerned with the ICC Uniform Rules for Collections, might suggest that the UCP would be implied into credits as customary terms, unless expressly excluded, but art 1 of the UCP seems to require express incorporation; see also *Royal Bank of Scotland v Cassa di Risparmio dell Province Lombard* [1992] 1 Bank LR 251.
3   See *Forestal Mimosa Ltd v Oriental Credit Ltd* [1986] 2 All ER 400; *Credit Agricole Indosuez v Generale Bank* [1999] 2 All ER (Comm) 1016 at 1024.
4   See eg *Seaconsar Far East Ltd v Bank Markazi Jomhouri Islami Iran* [1999] 1 Lloyd's Rep 36, below 34.2.2; *Kredietbank Antwerp v Midland Bank plc* [1999] 1 All ER (Comm) 801, below 34.2.3. See Bennett [1999] LMCLQ 507.
5   See *Banco Santander SA v Bayfern Ltd* [2000] 1 All ER (Comm) 776, where there was evidence of differences in banking practice.
6   See the Preface to UCP 500.
7   Foreword to the Rules for Documentary Credit Dispute Resolution.
8   It is understood that, to date, relatively few disputes have been referred to the system.

34.1.2   *Types of documentary credit*

The UCP define a documentary credit as follows:

'any arrangement, however named or described, whereby a bank (the "Issuing Bank") acting at the request and in accordance with the instructions of a customer ("the Applicant")

(i) is to make payment to or to the order of a third party ("the Beneficiary") or is to pay or is to accept and pay bills of exchange (Draft(s)) drawn by the Beneficiary or

(ii) authorises another bank to effect such payment, or to accept and pay such bills of exchange (Draft(s)), or

(iii) authorises another bank to negotiate,

against stipulated document(s), provided that the terms and conditions of the credit are complied with'.

A number of different arrangements fall within this definition. The credit itself may provide for any of four modes of payment:

1. 'payment at sight': the bank undertakes to pay the seller cash on presentation of the documents;
2. 'deferred payment': the bank undertakes to pay the seller cash at some future date, eg '90 days after shipment';
3. 'acceptance credit': the bank undertakes to accept bills of exchange drawn on it by the seller; those bills are likely to be term bills, payable at a future date, but the seller may discount them for cash;
4. 'negotiation credit': the bank undertakes to negotiate bills of exchange drawn by the seller; the issuing bank will have no recourse to the seller; the advising bank may have recourse to the seller unless it has confirmed the credit.

In addition, a wide range of different credits is in use.

A standby credit is not a true documentary credit but is governed by the UCP. Under a documentary credit the bank enters into a commitment as principal to pay the beneficiary; under a standby credit the bank typically enters into an obligation to pay if the bank's customer defaults; it therefore has more in common with a guarantee or performance bond and is examined briefly below[1].

A revolving credit is used where two parties trade together on a regular basis. The bank undertakes to pay sums due to the beneficiary from time to time, subject to a ceiling fixing the maximum amount which may be outstanding on the credit at any time. The bank's customer then repays sums paid by the bank from time to time, so reducing the customer's debt and therefore increasing the amount available for the beneficiary to draw on.

It will often be the case that S contracts to sell goods to B and enters into a separate contract to acquire those goods; S will then need to pay his supplier, X. If B is to pay by documentary credit, S could simply assign the benefit of the credit: rights under a documentary credit are assignable by complying with the requirements of s 136 of the Law of Property Act. However, this is not entirely satisfactory: X, as assignee, will take subject to any defects in S's title; more importantly for practical purposes, the sum due from S to X will generally be less than the price payable by B to S. If S assigns the benefit of the credit, he must assign it in its entirety. To avoid this problem, S may require B to open a transferable credit. This is:

'a Credit under which the Beneficiary (First Beneficiary) may request the bank authorised to pay, incur a deferred payment undertaking, accept or negotiate . . . to make the Credit available in whole or in part to one or more other Beneficiary(ies) (Second Beneficiary(ies))'[2].

Under the UCP, unless otherwise stated, each credit can be transferred only once[3]: ie if S transfers it to X, X cannot transfer it to Y. However, as the definition indicates, S can transfer less than the full value of the credit to X; and if S acquires goods from both X and Y, S can split the benefit of the credit and transfer part to each. The transferable credit is therefore a valuable instrument. However, it may only be transferred if the conditions set out in UCP, art 54 are satisfied, including that the bank requested to make the transfer must have agreed in advance to transfer to the particular second beneficiary[4].

As an alternative, S could arrange to enter into a back to back credit. Under this arrangement, S applies for a separate credit to finance the purchase from X, but uses the credit opened in his favour by B to finance that credit. The credit in favour of X is therefore dependent on the credit in favour of S.

Although these different arrangements all have different characteristics, no great legal significance attaches to them. However, two further distinctions are of great importance; these are the distinctions between revocable and irrevocable and between confirmed and unconfirmed credits.

Under a revocable credit, the bank is free to revoke its undertaking to pay the beneficiary at any time before payment is due. Moreover, it has been held that the bank is under no obligation to notify the beneficiary that the credit has been revoked[5], and, in light of developments in the general law of negligence, it seems unlikely that a tortious duty of care would be imposed on a bank to notify the revocation of a credit[6]. A seller of goods may therefore ship goods, only to find that the credit has been revoked and he has no assurance of payment. In such a case the seller would be left simply with a right of action against the buyer for the price, or for damages for breach of contract. In fact, it is the practice of banks to notify revocation of credits, but the revocable credit offers the beneficiary little security and has been described as 'practically worthless'[7]. The 1993 Revision of the UCP reverses the rule in previous revisions of the UCP and now provides that all credits are presumed irrevocable unless expressed to be revocable[8].

A seller who has sufficient bargaining power is likely to insist on the buyer opening an irrevocable credit. Once the bank has advised the beneficiary of the opening of an irrevocable credit, it comes under an irrevocable obligation to pay provided the correct shipping and other documents are presented. It may not revoke its undertaking to pay, even if its customer requests it to do so, unless there is clear evidence of fraud[9].

The issuing bank normally arranges for the beneficiary to be advised of the opening of the credit by an 'advising (or correspondent) bank' in his own country, and the issuing bank may also arrange for the advising bank to pay the beneficiary. Where the credit is unconfirmed the advising bank is under no obligation to the beneficiary; it acts solely as agent for the issuing bank both in advising the opening of the credit and in accepting drafts or otherwise paying the beneficiary. However, if the credit is confirmed by the advising bank, it enters into a separate obligation to pay the beneficiary and adds its undertaking to that of the issuing bank. If it pays the beneficiary it is entitled to be reimbursed by the issuing bank. The beneficiary thus gains a number of advantages: confirmation provides a second undertaking to pay; the confirming bank will be within the beneficiary's own country, and therefore be likely to have his confidence; and, in the event that payment is not made, it will be easier for the beneficiary to take proceedings against the confirming bank within the jurisdiction. It follows, of course, that a bank will only confirm a credit if the credit is irrevocable.

1   See 34.3.
2   UCP, art 48(a).
3   UCP, art 48(g).

4 *Bank Negara Indonesia 1946 v Lariza (Singapore) Pte Ltd* [1988] AC 583, [1988] 2 WLR 374; see Schmitthoff [1988] JBL 49; Godwin [1990] JBL 48.
5 *Cape Asbestos Co Ltd v Lloyds Bank Ltd* [1921] WN 274.
6 See *Bank of Nova Scotia v Hellenic Mutual War Risks Association (Bermuda) Ltd* [1990] 1 QB 818, [1989] 3 All ER 628, CA.
7 Per Bailhache J in *Cape Asbestos*.
8 Article 6(c).
9 *Discount Records Ltd v Barclays Bank Ltd* [1975] 1 All ER 1071, 1 WLR 315; see below 34.1.5.

34.1.3 *Outline of a documentary credit transaction*

In a typical documentary credit transaction the following stages will occur.

1. S and B enter into a contract of sale requiring payment by documentary credit; the contract will specify the type of credit required.
2. B instructs his bank ('the issuing bank') to issue the credit.
3. S is notified that the credit is opened. Notification may be given by the issuing bank; if that bank does not have a branch in the seller's country, it will instruct another bank with a branch there to give the notification ('the advising bank'). If the credit is to be confirmed, the advising bank will be required to add its confirmation.
4. Provided that the credit conforms to the contract of sale, S ships the goods.
5. S presents the shipping documents to the advising bank. Provided that they are in accordance with the instructions given to the bank, it will arrange for S to be paid according to the terms of the credit. Payment will generally be made locally, through the advising bank, either as agent for the issuing bank or, where it has confirmed the credit, in accordance with its own undertaking to S.
6. The bank may hold the documents pending payment by its customer, B, or may release the documents to allow B to deal with the goods, subject to the customer giving the bank security over the goods.

34.1.4 *The contracts created by a documentary credit transaction*

The undertakings of the issuing and confirming banks in a documentary credit transaction give rise to legal obligations which, despite the difficulties of accommodating them within the conceptual framework of the law of contract, are regarded as contractual in nature. A contract of sale financed by a confirmed credit thus gives rise to a network of contracts between the parties, represented by the diagram below. We must now examine the stages in the credit transaction, and those relationships, in more detail.

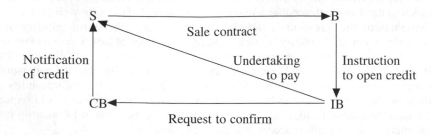

34.1.5   *The contractual nature of the banks' undertakings*

Since a revocable credit can be revoked without even notice to the seller, it is clear that the notification of a revocable credit amounts to less than an offer which can only be effectively revoked if revocation is notified to the offeree. However, if the credit is irrevocable, we have seen that the courts will not allow revocation at all: the bank is under a binding obligation to the seller. As the UCP provide: 'An irrevocable credit constitutes a definite undertaking of the issuing bank . . .'[1] and that undertaking is recognised and given legal force by the courts. Similarly, if the credit is confirmed, 'such confirmation constitutes a definite undertaking of . . . the confirming bank'[2], which again is legally enforceable. But what is the legal basis of these obligations? It has been held that the mere notification of the opening of a credit does not constitute the bank a trustee of any funds[3] and it is generally assumed that the banks' undertakings are contractual. However, this analysis gives rise to a number of problems and there have been numerous academic attempts to reconcile the bank's undertakings with traditional contract concepts. Two issues, in particular, cause difficulties.

(a)   When does an irrevocable credit become irrevocable? The point has never been authoritatively decided and there are conflicting dicta suggesting that the relevant time is when the beneficiary relies on the credit by shipping goods in accordance with the contract of sale[4] or earlier, as soon as the bank notifies the beneficiary that the credit is open[5]. This latter view accords more closely with commercial expectations, but it is difficult to see how the beneficiary accepts the bank's offer, or provides consideration, at this stage: there appears to be no more than an unaccepted offer of a unilateral contract.

(b)   More generally, what consideration does the beneficiary provide for the undertakings of the issuing and confirming banks? There clearly are contracts between the buyer and the issuing bank, and between the issuing and confirming banks, but the seller/beneficiary is a stranger to those contracts and cannot rely on consideration provided by the parties to them[6]. The making of the contract of sale cannot provide consideration for any contract with the banks, since it is already concluded and would therefore be past consideration. In the light of the decision in *The Eurymedon*[7], a possible explanation is that the beneficiary provides consideration by shipping goods in performance of the contract of sale. However, some commentators feel that the reasoning in *The Eurymedon* is not conceptually satisfactory, and in any case, that analysis would not explain how the banks' obligations become irrevocable prior to shipment, as they seem to do.

Several attempts have been made to explain documentary credits using existing legal concepts[8] such as assignment or novation[9], agency[10] or estoppel. It has also been suggested that the contracts created by documentary credits should be regarded as sui generis and enforceable without consideration[11]. This may well be the best explanation: the question is largely academic, since the enforceability of a documentary credit has never been challenged on the basis of lack of consideration[12]. As already noted, the system of documentary credits is so well established and so important for international commerce that it is unthinkable that a court would interfere in its workings. It seems likely that if a challenge to the enforceability of documentary credits were to be mounted, commercial pragmatism would require the court to uphold them, even 'at the cost of forcing the facts to fit uneasily into the marked slots of offer, acceptance and consideration'[13].

1 Article 9(a).
2 Article 9(b).
3 *Morgan v Larivière* (1875) LR 7 HL 423.
4 *Urqhart Lindsay & Co Ltd v Eastern Bank Ltd* [1922] 1 KB 318.
5 *Dexters Ltd v Schenker & Co* (1923) 14 Ll L Rep 586.
6 It might now be possible to argue that the contract between the applicant and the issuing bank for the opening of a credit in favour of the beneficiary is a contract for the benefit of the beneficiary which the beneficiary is entitled to enforce by virtue of the Contracts (Rights of Third Parties) Act 1999. However, this would seem to be excluded by art 3(b) of the UCP, which provides that: 'A beneficiary can in no case avail himself of the contractual relationships existing between the banks or between the Applicant and the Issuing Bank'.
7 *New Zealand Shipping Co Ltd v A M Satterthwaite & Co Ltd* [1975] AC 154, [1974] 1 All ER 1015, PC.
8 See Gutteridge and Megrah, *The Law of Bankers' Commercial Credits* (7th edn, 1984) ch 4; see Todd, *Documentary Credits and Bills of Lading* (3rd edn, 1998) pp 263–282.
9 McCurdy, (1922) 35 Harv LR 539, 583.
10 Gutteridge and Megrah, *The Law of Bankers' Commercial Credits* (7th edn, 1984) p 36.
11 *Benjamin's Sale of Goods* (5th edn, 1997) para 23-115; Ellinger, *Documentary Letters of Credit* p 122; Goode *Abstract Payment Undertakings* in Cane and Stapleton (eds) *Essays for Patrick Atiyah* (1991); Treitel, *The Law of Contract* (10th cdn, 1999) pp 139–140.
12 The point was taken in *Dexters Ltd v Schenker & Co* (1923) 14 Ll L Rep 586, but was abandoned at trial.
13 Per Lord Wilberforce in *The Eurymedon* [1975] AC 154 at 167, [1974] 1 All ER 1015 at 1020.

34.1.6 *The banks' obligations are autonomous*

It is a fundamental characteristic of the contractual obligations created by the documentary credit that, although they are created as a result of the contract of sale, they are autonomous of it. As the UCP put it[1]:

'Credits, by their nature, are separate transactions from the sales or other contract(s) on which they may be based and banks are in no way concerned with or bound by such contract(s) even if any reference whatsoever to such contract(s) is included in the credit'.

This independence is recognised by the courts. Provided that the beneficiary satisfies the requirements of the credit by presenting the required documents, he is entitled to payment even if it is alleged that he is in breach of the sale contract. In *British Imex Industries Ltd v Midland Bank Ltd*[2] the plaintiffs had entered into a contract to purchase goods and had opened a confirmed credit in favour of the sellers. A dispute then arose out of the sale contract and the plaintiffs sought an injunction to prevent the sellers drawing on the credit. The Court of Appeal refused such an injunction, Jenkins LJ observing that:

'the opening of a confirmed letter of credit constitutes a bargain between the banker and the vendor of goods, which imposes on the banker an absolute obligation to pay, irrespective of any dispute there may be between the parties as to whether the goods are up to the contract or not. An elaborate commercial system has been built up on the footing that banker's commercial credits are of that character and in my judgment it would be wrong for the court in this present case to interfere with that established practice'.

Nor, save in exceptional circumstances, can the buyer obtain an injunction against the bank to prevent it paying under the credit. In *Discount Records Ltd v Barclays Bank Ltd*[3] B contracted to buy a quantity of records from S. Boxes delivered under the contract were found to contain goods very different from those required by the contract: some were empty, others contained cassettes and eight track cartridges. B sought an injunction to prevent the bank paying under the credit. Megarry J refused the injunction, stressing the separation of the payment obligation from the underlying contract of sale, and observing that the commercial value of the documentary credit system lies in the certainty created by the credit: the seller in whose favour an irrevocable credit is opened can ship goods in the absolute certainty that, barring the bank's insolvency, or fraud, he will be paid in accordance with the credit. If the court were to allow the payment obligation to be revoked, that certainty would be undermined. 'A letter of credit is like a bill of exchange given for the price of goods. It ranks as cash and must be honoured. No set off or counterclaim is allowed to detract from it'[4] and, just as the irrevocable letter of credit is 'the life blood of commerce', 'thrombosis will occur if . . . the courts intervene and thereby disturb the mercantile practice of treating rights thereunder as being the equivalent of cash in hand'[5].

Comments such as these must be treated with some care. As we will see, the opening of a documentary credit is only a conditional payment and so a documentary credit is not the equivalent of cash for all purposes; however, they do emphasise the separation of the credit from the underlying contract, and the reasons for it. The result is to reverse the balance of negotiating power between buyer and seller in the event of any dispute about the quality, etc, of the goods delivered. Instead of withholding payment, the buyer must pay and then bring proceedings to recover damages for any alleged breach.

The autonomy of the credit also means that the court will enforce payment even despite an order of a foreign court forbidding payment[6]. However, it has been held that it does not prevent the bank exercising a set off in respect of sums owed to it by the beneficiary[7].

Payment under the credit may be withheld only in two exceptional cases: first, where the credit itself is illegal or void, for instance on the grounds of mistake[8]; and second, where the claim for payment is affected by fraud. However, the fraud exception is narrowly interpreted: payment will only be restrained where there is clear evidence of fraud to which the beneficiary under the credit is a party[9]; and even such fraud will not prevent payment to an innocent third party such as a holder in due course of a bill of exchange drawn under the credit[10].

1   Article 3.
2   [1958] 1 QB 542.
3   [1975] 1 WLR 315.
4   Per Lord Denning MR in *Power Curber International Ltd v National Bank of Kuwait* [1981] 1 WLR 1233 at 1241.
5   Per Donaldson LJ in *Intraco Ltd v Notis Shipping Corpn, The Bhoja Trader* [1981] 2 Lloyd's Rep 256 at 257.
6   *Power Curber International Ltd v National Bank of Kuwait* [1981] 1 WLR 1233.
7   *Hong Kong and Shanghai Bank Corpn v Kloeckner & Co AG* [1990] 2 QB 514 [1989] 3 All ER 513.
8   *PowerCurber International v National Bank of Kuwait SA* [1981] 1 WLR 1233. There is some authority that the credit may be rendered illegal where the underlying contract is illegal and the credit is tainted by that illegality: see *Group Josi Re v Walbrook Insurance Co Ltd* [1994] 4 All ER 181; affd [1996] 1 All ER 791 at 803, per Staughton LJ.
9   *United City Merchants (Investments) Ltd v Royal Bank of Canada* [1983] 1 AC 168, below 34.2.4.
10 *Discount Records Ltd v Barclays Bank Ltd* [1975] 1 WLR 315.

34.2 Stages in the transaction

Having examined some essential characteristics of the documentary credit we must now consider some of the stages in the documentary credit transaction in more detail.

34.2.1 *The opening of the credit*

Where the contract of sale requires the buyer of goods to pay by documentary credit it is the buyer's duty to open a credit in accordance with that contract. The contract will specify the type of credit required. The buyer does so by instructing a bank to open a documentary credit in favour of the seller. The bank may be nominated in the contract of sale: if so, that bank must be used; if not, the buyer may choose any bank, provided that the terms of the credit conform to the sale contract. The buyer's instructions to the bank form the basis of a contract between the buyer and the (issuing) bank, and are normally given on the bank's standard form. It is essential that the buyer's instructions to the bank are clear and unambiguous, and this is confirmed by the UCP[1]. The instructions will set out the documents to be presented by the seller in order to obtain payment under the credit; they will also contain an undertaking by the buyer to repay the amount of the credit, unless the buyer has put the bank in funds prior to payment, and will generally grant the bank a charge or hypothecation over the goods to be delivered[2]. The buyer will, of course, have to pay the bank its fee for opening the credit.

The credit must be opened in accordance with the contract of sale. The time for opening of the credit may cause difficulties. If the sale contract fixes a date for opening the credit, then the credit must be open by that date. If the credit is to be opened 'immediately', it must be opened within such time as it would take a reasonably diligent person to open a credit[3]. Where no time for opening the credit is fixed, the credit is generally required to be opened before the time fixed by the contract for shipment of the goods; where a single shipment date is fixed, the credit must be open a reasonable time before the shipment date[4]; however, where the contract allows shipment within a period, the credit must be open by the beginning of the shipment period, but it is not clear if it must be open a reasonable period before then[5].

If the sale contract is expressed to be 'subject to credit', the opening of the credit is a condition precedent to the contract coming into being[6]. More commonly, the requirement for the buyer to open a credit conforming to the terms of the sale contract will be a condition of the contract, precedent to the seller's liability to ship the goods. Thus if a credit is not opened in accordance with the sale contract, the seller is not obliged to ship the goods, and may terminate the contract and claim damages[7]. It is irrelevant that circumstances beyond the buyer's control prevent him opening the credit[8]. It seems that the damages are not limited by the market price rule in s 50(3) of the Sale of Goods Act 1979 but may extend to the seller's lost profits provided they were not too remote under the rule in *Hadley v Baxendale*[9].

The seller is not obliged to terminate the contract. If he ships the goods although the credit is not open, he may be taken to have waived the breach, or to have agreed to a variation of the contract. The distinction between a waiver and a variation may be difficult to draw, but it has great practical significance: if the seller has waived the requirement to open the credit, he may generally nevertheless reinstate the requirement on giving the buyer reasonable notice[10]. However, if the contract is varied, it is impossible for the seller unilaterally to restore the original position.

In *W J Alan & Co Ltd v El Nasr Export and Import Co*[11] the contract called for the opening of a documentary credit payable in Kenyan shillings. A credit was opened for payment in sterling, and the seller initially made no objection. However, following devaluation of sterling, the seller claimed damages for the difference between the two currencies. The claim failed; the majority of the Court of Appeal held that the contract had been varied; since sterling could (in theory) move either up or down relative to the Kenyan shilling, either party could benefit from the variation, so there was consideration. Lord Denning, however, held that the seller had waived the original requirement and was now estopped from reasserting it, regarding the doctrines of waiver and 'equitable estoppel' as aspects of the same general principle.

Once the credit is opened, the bank will arrange for the seller to be notified of that fact. Generally, the issuing bank will instruct an advising bank to notify the seller; and where the contract calls for a confirmed credit, the advising bank will be asked to add its confirmation. The instructions to the advising/confirming bank form the basis of a contract between it and the issuing bank and constitute the mandate of the advising/confirming bank, and again the instructions must be clear. If they are not, the confirming bank is entitled to act on a reasonable interpretation of the instructions, unless there is time to seek clarification from the issuing bank[12]. The advising bank will obviously charge the issuing bank for its services.

1   Article 5.
2   See below 34.2.7.
3   *Garcia v Page & Co Ltd* (1936) 55 Ll L Rep 391.
4   *Plasticmoda Societa per Azioni v Davidsons (Manchester) Ltd* [1952] 1 Lloyd's Rep 527, CA.
5   *Pavia & Co SpA v Thurmann Nielson* [1952] 2 QB 84; *Ian Stach Ltd v Baker Bosley Ltd* [1958] 2 QB 130, [1952] 1 All ER 492, CA; contrast *Sinason Teicher Inter-American Grain Corpn v Oilcakes and Oilseeds Trading Co Ltd* [1954] 1 WLR 1394, CA.
6   *Trans Trust SPRL v Danubian Trading Co Ltd* [1952] 2 QB 297, [1952] 1 All ER 970, CA.
7   See *Glencore Grain Rotterdam BV v Lebanese Organisation for International Commerce* [1997] 4 All ER 514, CA.
8   *A E Lindsay & Co Ltd v Cook* [1953] 1 Lloyd's Rep 328.
9   *Trans Trust SPRL v Danubian Trading Co Ltd* [1952] 2 QB 297, [1952] 1 All ER 970, CA.
10 *Panoutsos v R Hadley Corpn* [1917] 2 KB 473, CA.
11 [1972] 2 QB 189, [1982] 2 All ER 127.
12 See *Credit Agricole Indosuez v Muslim Commercial Bank Ltd* [2000] 1 All ER (Comm) 172.

34.2.2   *Presentation of the documents*

Once notified that the credit is open, the seller can ship the goods in confidence that he will be paid. He will probably already have prepared an invoice and arranged insurance (where necessary); on shipment he should receive the appropriate shipping document – traditionally a bill of lading but often today a combined transport document or other document – and so will be in a position to present the documents to the bank for payment.

The documents will generally be presented to the advising bank. Its capacity and duties on presentation depend on the terms of its contract with the issuing bank. When it acts only as an advising bank, it acts as the agent of the issuing bank and, if it pays the seller, it does so on behalf of the issuing bank. If it has confirmed the credit, it will pay on its own behalf and then seek reimbursement from the issuing bank in accordance with the contract between them. When documents are presented to the issuing bank, it acts in a similar capacity to a confirming bank: it accepts or rejects the documents, and pays the presenter, on its own behalf, and then seeks reimbursement from its client under the terms of the contract between them.

On presentation, the bank must decide whether to take up the documents and pay the seller. The bank is not concerned with the state of the goods and, provided that the documents presented are in order, it is obliged to pay the seller. We have already seen that the contracts between the issuing and confirming banks and the seller are independent of the contract of sale, and that provided the documents are in order, payment may not be withheld on the grounds that the goods themselves are defective. As the UCP provide[1], 'in Credit operations, all parties deal with documents, and not with goods . . .' If the credit contains conditions without specifying the documents to be presented to satisfy them, the bank will ignore them[2]. However, the bank will scrutinise the documents carefully to ensure that they comply with its instructions. The advising bank will have a lien on the documents until it is paid by its principal, the issuing bank, which in turn will take the documents from the advising bank and have a lien until paid by its client, the buyer. Should either principal refuse to pay, the bank will have to realise its security by selling the goods using the documents; it is therefore in the bank's own interests that the documents be readily marketable. Furthermore, the advising bank and issuing bank are only entitled to be reimbursed sums they pay out in accordance with their instructions[3] and if a bank accepts non-conforming documents, its principal may refuse to take up or pay for the documents, leaving the bank to dispose of the goods.

Conversely, if the documents are on their face in apparent good order and comply with the terms of the credit, the bank may accept them and is entitled to be reimbursed[4]. Moreover, the bank owes its client a duty of care to scrutinise documents carefully[5], for even though the buyer may reject goods which do not conform to the contract, his bargaining position will be weak if the seller has been paid and the goods have been delivered, and the bank may therefore be liable to compensate its client for any losses suffered as a result of its failure to take reasonable care. Provided, however, that the bank has taken reasonable care, it will not be liable to its customer if the documents turn out to be forged[6].

The UCP provide that the bank:

> 'shall . . . have a reasonable time, not to exceed seven banking days following the receipt of the documents, to examine the documents and determine whether to take up or refuse the documents and to inform the party from which it received the documents accordingly'[7].

It seems clear that the seven-day period, which was introduced for the first time in the 1993 Revision, is a maximum and that in appropriate cases the time for the bank to make its decision will be shorter. In deciding what is a 'reasonable time' for a bank to take to examine documents and make its decision, account must be taken of the current practice of local banks operating in the same market and of the nature and complexity of the documents and the amount of technical language contained in them[8]. Thus in *Bankers Trust Ltd v State Bank of India*[9] there was evidence that London clearing banks would normally make and notify a decision in three working days. It has also been suggested that the court may take account of 'subjective' factors such as the size and expertise of the particular bank and the linguistic abilities of its staff[10], so that a bank which takes longer than the norm will not automatically be found to have taken an unreasonably long time.

The bank is required to make its decision whether to accept the documents 'on the basis of the documents alone'[11] but this means only that the bank is not concerned with alleged breaches of contract or other matters not apparent on the face of the documents. The Court of Appeal held in *Bankers Trust Ltd v State Bank of India* (decided under the previous revision, UCP 400) that if the bank discovers any discrepancies or inconsistencies in the documents, it may consult its customer in order to ascertain whether the customer is nevertheless willing to accept the documents and waive the discrepancy[12], but that it is not entitled to pass the documents to its customer for him independently to carry out the checking process: the decision whether to accept or reject the documents is for the bank. This seems commercially unrealistic: if the customer discovers and notifies the bank of discrepancies not discovered by the bank, it can hardly be expected to ignore that fact. The majority of the Court of Appeal[13] held that the time required to consult the customer on any discrepancies discovered by the bank could be taken into account when deciding if it had completed its examination within a reasonable time, but that any additional time taken by the customer carrying out an independent examination would be excluded from calculation of the 'reasonable time'. The UCP[14] now expressly permit the bank to approach the applicant for the credit for a waiver of any discrepancies, and add that 'This does not, however, extend the period [for notification of the bank's decision]', but it seems that this means that consultation with the applicant will not extend the maximum seven-day period, not that it cannot be taken into account in assessing a 'reasonable' time.

If having completed its examination of the documents the bank decides to reject them, it must give notice to the person from whom it received them indicating the reasons for rejection, so that the beneficiary may have an opportunity to retender[15]. Notice must be given 'by telecommunications or, if that is not possible, by other expeditious means, without delay but no later than the close of the seventh banking day following the day of receipt of the documents'[16]. In *Seaconsar Far East Ltd v Bank Markazi Jomhouri Islami Iran*[17] the Court of Appeal held that the effect of this provision is that the bank has up to seven working days to decide whether to accept or reject the documents, but once it has decided to reject them it must notify its decision 'without delay', even if the seven day period has not expired. A second issue arose in that case. The bank had notified its decision to reject documents to the beneficiary's sales manager, who was present at the bank's premises, in person. It was argued that that was not an effective under the UCP. The Court of Appeal held that the UCP require the bank to notify rejection by telecommunications if possible and, if not, by other expeditious means, and, in any case, without delay. It went on to hold, however, that there is an implied term that where the beneficiary or its authorised representative is present at the bank, the bank may notify its decision in person.

The bank's notice of rejection must specify the bank's reasons for rejecting. The bank cannot later justify rejection of the documents on other grounds not stated in its notice. If the bank does not give notice of discrepancies within the period allowed by the UCP, it is precluded from claiming that the documents are not in compliance with the terms of the credit[18].

It should be noted that an advising/confirming bank has no contract with the applicant for the credit (the buyer of the goods). It may be that, in accepting documents, the advising/confirming bank owes a tortious duty of care to the applicant, but such a duty has never been established. Moreover, under art 18(a) of the UCP, the issuing bank accepts no liability for the acts of the advising/confirming bank which are said to be 'for the account and at the risk of the Applicant'. This is an extremely wide exclusion of liability. It was given a restricted interpretation in *Credit Agricole Indosuez v Generale Bank (No 2)*[19], where it was held that it prevents the issuing bank being liable to its customer for the negligence of the advising/confirming bank but that where the advising/confirming bank negligently accepts non-conforming documents, art 18(a) does not entitle the issuing bank to claim reimbursement from its customer.

1 Article 4.
2 Article 13.
3 See *Banco Santander SA v Bayfern Ltd* [2000] 1 All ER (Comm) 776, below 34.2.4. See UCP, art 14(a).
4 UCP, art 14(b).
5 *Gian Singh v Banque de l'Indochine* [1974] 2 All ER 754, [1974] 1 WLR 1234, reflected in UCP, art 13(a).
6 See UCP, art 15.
7 Articles 13(b), 14(d).
8 *Bankers Trust Ltd v State Bank of India* [1991] 2 Lloyd's Rep 443; see Bennett [1992] LMCLQ 169; *Hing Yip Hing Fat Co Ltd v Daiwa Bank Ltd* [1991] 2 HKLR 35; see Murphy [1992] LMCLQ 26.
9 *Bankers Trust Ltd v State Bank of India* [1991] 2 Lloyd's Rep 443. The documents in this case ran to some 967 pages.
10 *Bankers Trust Ltd v State Bank of India* [1991] 2 Lloyd's Rep 443; *Hing Yip Hing Fat Co Ltd v Daiwa Bank Ltd* [1991] 2 HKLR 35.
11 UCP, art 14(b).
12 This is now confirmed by UCP, art 14(c).
13 Lloyd LJ dissented.
14 UCP art 14(c). In *Bayerische Vereinsbank Aktiengesellschaft v National Bank of Pakistan* [1997] 1 Lloyd's Rep 59 at 68, Mance J seems to have taken the view that the bank may reject documents on the basis of discrepancies identified by its customer.
15 UCP, art 14(d).
16 UCP, art 14 (d)(i).
17 [1999] 1 Lloyd's Rep 36.
18 UCP, art 14(e). See *Credit Agricole Indosuez v Generale Bank (No 2)* [1999] 2 All ER (Comm) 1016.
19 [1999] 2 All ER (Comm) 1016.

34.2.3 *The rule of strict compliance*

We have seen that the bank is only concerned with the documents presented to it, but that it is only entitled to accept documents which comply with its instructions. The corollary of this is that the bank is entitled to reject documents which do not exactly correspond with the requirements of the credit. This rule is strictly applied at common law. Thus where a credit called for a bill of lading in respect of 5,000 bags, the bank was entitled to reject a bill which covered 4,997 bags[1]. Similarly, the description of the goods in the documents tendered to the bank must exactly correspond with the credit: in *J H Rayner & Co Ltd v Hambros Bank*[2] the credit referred to 'coromandel groundnuts'. The seller presented a bill of lading referring to 'machine shelled groundnut kernels' and the bank refused payment. It was held that the bank was entitled to reject the documents even though it was well known in the trade that 'coromandel groundnuts' and 'machine shelled groundnut kernels' were the same thing. The bank could not be expected to be expert in all the trades its customers might deal in. Similarly, where the credit required a certificate of quality issued 'by experts', it was held that the bank should have rejected documents which included a certificate issued 'by expert'[3]. In addition, the documents must all be consistent with each other[4], otherwise it will be impossible to be sure that they all refer to the same goods. In *Bank Melli Iran v Barclays Bank (Dominion, Colonial and Overseas) Ltd*[5] a credit was opened for payment for '100 new Chevrolet trucks' against documents including a delivery order and a government certificate that the trucks were new. The delivery order presented referred to 'new-good' trucks, the invoice to 'trucks in new condition' while the government certificate described them as '100 new, good Chevrolet trucks'. It was held that none of the documents described the goods in accordance with the contract and the bank was entitled to reject them. The bank has to make a decision whether or not to accept the documents in a short time: 'There is no room for documents which are almost the same, or which will do just as well'[6]. Thus the modern, non-technical approach taken to the construction of commercial contracts generally is not applicable when determining whether documents presented to the bank conform to the credit[7].

The strict compliance rule is modified in some respects. The UCP provide that bills of lading will be accepted provided that the quantity of goods shipped is within a tolerance of plus or minus 5% of the quantity stated in the credit[8]; and the documents may be read together so that, provided that the goods are correctly described in the invoice, errors of description in the other documents will not be grounds for rejection, provided that the documents all refer to the same goods[9]. Errors which are clearly typographical or similar mistakes will not justify rejection[10]. Moreover, where the bank is unsure about documents presented to it, it may seek instructions from its client in order to clarify the situation[11]; alternatively, it may pay the seller 'under reserve', allowing it to reclaim the money so paid if its client refuses to take up the documents[12]. Nevertheless, over 50% of documents presented to banks under documentary credit transactions are rejected on first presentation[13], leading at best to a delay in the seller receiving payment and nullifying much of the benefit the credit was intended to provide.

Whilst a requirement of strict compliance is commercially convenient and enables banks to make speedy decisions about the documents presented to them, it may lead to documents being rejected for insubstantial discrepancies. It may be argued that it also facilitates and encourages bad faith rejection of documents. Where documents are discrepant the bank may now approach its customer to seek a waiver of the discrepancy. Where the market has fallen, the buyer may be unlikely to waive even an insignificant discrepancy if it offers a means of escaping an unprofitable contract.

Essentially, the issue here is the familiar one of striking the balance between certainty and fairness. The Court of Appeal's decision in *Kredietbank Antwerp v Midland Bank plc*[14] illustrates the point. The credit in that case required the beneficiary to tender an 'original insurance policy'. The document tendered had been produced by a word processor and laser printer on the insurer's watermarked and embossed headed paper. However, art 20(b) of the UCP states that:

> 'banks will also accept as an original document(s) a document(s) produced or appearing to have been produced:
> (i) by reprographic, automated or computerized systems;
> (ii) as carbon copies
> provided that it is marked as original and, where necessary, appears to be signed.'

The document was accepted by the confirming bank but rejected by the issuing bank which argued that since it had been produced by a word processor it fell within art 20(b) and, since it was not marked 'original', did not conform to art 20(b) or to the credit. In an earlier case, *Glencore International AG v Bank of China*[15] the Court of Appeal had held that where the seller presented a signed photocopy of a document produced on a word processor it was required to be marked 'original' in accordance with art 20(b), even though for commercial purposes, being signed, it was to all intents the 'original' copy of the document. Moreover, certain comments in *Glencore* appeared to suggest that any document produced by any of the methods specified in art 20(b) would have to be marked 'original' in accordance with that article in order to be acceptable. The result of that would be that a document produced by word processor would have to be marked 'original' in order to be accepted, whereas the same document produced by an electric typewriter would not. The Court of Appeal in *Kredietbank* rejected that interpretation and, distinguishing *Glencore*, held that art 20(b) does not require a document to be marked 'original', even if produced by computer or other means, if it clearly is an original and not a copy of another document. There was abundant evidence on the facts of the case from which it could be inferred that the document presented by the beneficiary was an original, and it was therefore unnecessary for it to be marked.

Strictly speaking, *Kredietbank* was concerned with the interpretation of the UCP rather than with strict compliance, and may be seen as an example of the court adopting a 'commercial common sense' approach to that task. However, the court clearly saw the issue as closely linked to 'strict compliance and Evans LJ observed that:

'the requirement of strict compliance is not equivalent to a test of exact literal compliance in all circumstances and as regards all documents. To some extent, therefore, the banker must exercise his own judgment whether the requirement is satisfied as regards the documents presented to him'[16].

This is perhaps an echo of the UCP, which provide that documentary compliance is to be determined 'in accordance with international standards of banking practice as reflected in these Articles'[17]. The precise meaning of this phrase is unclear. In particular, it is not clear if the words 'as reflected in these Articles' limits the preceding words or whether the bank is also required to take account of practice not reflected in the UCP but which is evidenced in opinions of the ICC Banking Commission and/or can otherwise be established[18]. It does, however, suggest that the standard of compliance required by the UCP is not an absolutely strict one.

The decision in *Kredietbank* does illustrate the problem of relaxing the strict compliance doctrine. On the one hand, the court's decision is eminently sensible and takes account of modern commercial practice. On the other hand, it may be argued that it undermines the very certainty which the strict compliance rule seeks to promote. *Glencore* established a 'bright line' rule according to which if a document appeared to have been produced by one of the specified means it could be rejected unless marked 'original'. After *Kredietbank*, a bank faced with an unmarked document which appears to have been word processed must ask itself if the document is, on its face, an original which does not need marking. It may be argued that, given that the UCP apply worldwide, in the interests of consistency in documentary credits practice a bright line rule would be preferable[19].

1 *Moralice (London) Ltd v ED and F Man* [1954] 2 Lloyd's Rep 526.
2 [1943] KB 37, [1942] 2 All ER 694, CA.
3 *Equitable Trust Co of New York v Dawson Partners Ltd* (1926) 27 Ll L Rep 49, HL.
4 UCP, art 13(a).
5 [1951] 2 Lloyd's Rep 367.
6 Lord Sumner in *Equitable Trust Co of New York v Dawson Partners Ltd* (1926) 27 Ll l. Rep 49 at 52, HL.

811

 7 *Mannai Investments Co Ltd v Eagle Star Assurance Co Ltd* [1997] 3 All ER 352 at 380, per Lord Hoffmann; see 2.2.5.5.
 8 Article 39(b). Expressions such as 'about' or 'approximately' allow a margin of plus or minus 10%: see art 39(a).
 9 *Midland Bank Ltd v Seymour* [1955] 2 Lloyd's Rep 147; *Guaranty Trust v Van den Berghs* (1925) 22 Ll L Rep 447.
10 See eg *Hing Yip Hing Fat Co Ltd v Daiwa Bank Ltd* [1991] 2 HKLR 35, where a discrepancy in the name of the applicant for the credit between 'Cheergoal Industries Ltd' and 'Cheergoal Industrial Ltd' was held not to be significant.
11 Under UCP, art 14(c), above.
12 *Banque de l'Indochine et de Suez SA v J H Rayner (Mincing Lane) Ltd* [1983] QB 711.
13 See the Foreword to UCP 500. It is sometimes suggested that the figure is considerably higher than 50%.
14 [1999] 1 All ER (Comm) 801.
15 [1996] 1 Lloyd's Rep 135.
16 [1999] 1 All ER (Comm) 801 at 806.
17 Article 13a.
18 In the event of a dispute, such practice would have to be proved, for instance, by expert evidence.
19 See Johnson [1999] JIBL 287. In July 1999 the ICC published a decision which effectively adopts the *Kredietbank* interpretation of art 20(b) and goes some way to clarifying the position by setting out details of what may, and what may not, be considered an 'original' for this purpose.

34.2.3.1   *Electronic credits*

As explained in the previous chapter, there are commercial advantages to be gained by seeking to replace paper documentation with electronic equivalents, capable of instantaneous transmission. The BOLERO project has shown that it may be possible to replicate electronically the functions of a bill of lading. As it stands, however, electronic documentation would not be acceptable to a bank under a credit governed by the UCP, unless special provision were expressly made for it in the credit. The UCP do make limited provision for certain instructions and notifications to be given by teletransmission[1], but require the presentation of paper documents. It is expected that, in light of the development of 'electronic bills' amendments will be made to permit electronic presentation of documentation[2].

At present, documents are checked manually. Once documents can be presented electronically, it may also be possible, in principle, for them to be checked electronically, with potential speed gains. However, electronic checking would almost certainly have to operate on the basis of a very strict or absolute standard of compliance. A two-stage process might be appropriate, using suitable computer software, programmed with details of the documents required, to carry out initial checking and identify discrepancies, which could then be considered by a member of the bank's staff to determine whether they justify rejection.

1   See art 11(a).
2   In May 2000 the ICC Commission on Banking Techniques and Practice established a working group to consider the issues raised by the electronic presentation of documents.

34.2.4   *The fraud exception*

The one exceptional case where the bank is entitled to reject documents which appear on their face to conform to the credit is where the documents are forged or their presentation is affected by fraud. In that case, the buyer may be able to obtain an injunction to prevent the bank paying the seller, or to prevent the seller drawing on the credit. The fraud exception is, however, narrowly construed. In the leading case of *United City Merchants (Investments) Ltd v Royal Bank of Canada*[1] the contract and the credit called for a machine to be shipped by 15 December 1975. The sellers presented a bill of lading showing that it had been shipped on 15 December but, unknown to them, the bill had been fraudulently altered by the shipping brokers and shipment had actually taken place on 16 December. The defendant bank refused to accept the documents. The House of Lords emphasised that the documentary credit is separate from the contract of sale and held that the bank was in breach: the documents were good on their face and conformed to the credit and it was irrelevant that the buyer would be entitled to reject the goods for breach of contract. The bank would only be entitled to reject the documents if the beneficiary was party to the fraud affecting them or fraudulently presented documents which he knew to contain untrue statements of fact.

The result of *United City Merchants* is severely to restrict the cases where a bank can refuse payment on the grounds of fraud. If the documents are good on their face, the bank may only reject them where there is compelling evidence of a fraud to which the beneficiary (or its agent) is party or (possibly) where the documents are forged so as to amount to a nullity (which was not the case in *United City Merchants*). Suspicion of fraud is insufficient to justify non-payment[2]. Nor will the bank be entitled to refuse payment on the grounds that there is evidence from which a reasonable banker would infer fraud[3]. However, the court will not require the bank to prove fraud beyond reasonable doubt: the bank must be able to satisfy the court at trial that there was fraud; and the court will conclude that there was fraud if the beneficiary has been given the opportunity to explain the situation and has been unable satisfactorily to do so, or where that is the only realistic inference[4]. On the other hand, if the bank's customer produces compelling evidence of fraud before the time when payment is due under the credit the bank will pay at its own risk. If it does so it will not be entitled to be reimbursed by its client. In *Banco Santander SA v Bayfern Ltd*[5] a confirming bank discounted its own payment undertaking in favour of the beneficiary some five months before payment was due under the credit, taking an assignment of the beneficiary's rights under the credit. Before the date for payment arrived, the issuing bank produced evidence of fraud by the beneficiary. It was held that the bank was not entitled to reimbursement: although at the time when it paid the beneficiary it was ignorant of the fraud, that payment was not under the credit but was for its own benefit. By the time payment was due under the credit it had notice of the fraud.

Normally, the bank is happy to pay and the account party seeks to prevent it doing so by seeking an injunction either to prevent the bank paying or to prevent the beneficiary drawing on the credit. The case law shows that such an application is unlikely to succeed[6]. The court will not grant an injunction preventing the bank from paying unless there is evidence of fraud to the standard described above. The same test is applied if the account party seeks an injunction to restrain the beneficiary from drawing on the credit[7]. Moreover, in practice the account party seeking an injunction will face a further obstacle. The application will normally be made at a pre-trial hearing, without consideration of all the evidence. An injunction will only be granted at this stage if the applicant establishes that it is seriously arguable that the only reasonable inference is that the claim for payment is fraudulent, *and* that the balance of convenience favours the grant of an injunction[8]. This last requirement means that an injunction will rarely be granted. In *Czarnikow-Rionda Sugar Trading Inc v Standard Bank London Ltd*[9] Rix J reviewed the case law and concluded that the basis of the court's jurisdiction to grant an injunction against the bank to prevent it paying in cases of fraud is to prevent a breach of contract by the bank. On this basis he concluded that the balance of convenience will almost always favour refusing the injunction. If the claim of fraud is valid, the customer will have a claim against the bank for damages for breach of contract if it pays the beneficiary, which will provide him with an adequate remedy, whereas if the claim is invalid there are no grounds for the grant of an injunction. There are cases which suggest that the court's jurisdiction to restrain payment is based on broader grounds of preventing fraud, and therefore does not depend on a breach of contract by the bank. However, the balance of authority favours the view taken by Rix J. In any case, even if he was wrong on this point the balance of convenience will still normally favour the refusal of an injunction on the grounds that its grant will undermine the integrity of the documentary credit system. The applicant can be protected to some extent by obtaining a 'freezing', or 'Mareva' injunction to restrain the beneficiary from dealing with the proceeds of the credit.

A similar approach has been taken in relation to performance bonds and similar instruments, and, indeed, cases on bonds are cited in credits cases and vice versa. This strict approach is said to be justified by the need to protect the certainty of documentary credit and bond transactions, and thus it is argued the approach facilitates commerce by maintaining the integrity of the system, but arguably these cases go too far. Their effect is to place the buyer in a very weak position: in a case such as *United City Merchants* he may have a claim against the seller for breach of contract, but he will be unable to reject the documents; the seller will have been paid, and the bank will be entitled to be reimbursed by the buyer. The seller is deemed to accept that risk by agreeing to pay by documentary credit. A 'freezing' order does not give the buyer the same protection as an injunction restraining payment. The significance of the courts' approach is demonstrated by the financial amounts involved – in *Credit Agricole Indosuez v Generale Bank (No 2)*, for instance, the sum was $1.6m; in *Banco Santander SA v Bayfern Ltd* it was over $20m. The jurisdiction to restrain payment in cases of fraud originated in the United States[10] where apparently the courts are more willing to exercise it.

1   [1983] 1 AC 168, [1982] 2 All ER 720.
2   *Discount Records Ltd v Barclays Bank Ltd* [1975] 1 All ER 1071, [1975] 1 WLR 315.
3   *Society of Lloyd's v Canadian Imperial Bank of Commerce* [1993] 2 Lloyd's Rep 579.
4   *United Trading Corpn v Allied Arab Bank* [1985] 2 Lloyd's Rep 554n, CA.
5   [2000] 1 All ER (Comm) 776.
6   There are only two reported cases in which an application has succeeded, both concerned with performance bonds: *Themehelp Ltd v West* [1995] 4 All ER 215 and *Kvaerner John Brown Ltd v Midland Bank plc* [1998] CLC 446.
7   *Group Josi Re v Walbrook Insurance Co Ltd* [1994] 4 All ER 181; affd [1996] 1 All ER 791, CA; cf *Themehelp Ltd v West* [1995] 4 All ER 215, CA.
8   See 36.1.2.1.
9   [1999] 1 All ER (Comm) 890.
10   In *Sztejn v J Henry Schroder Banking Corpn* 31 NYS 2d 631 (NY SC 1941).

34.2.5   *The effect of acceptance*

We have seen that where documents are presented to a bank which acts only as an advising bank, it accepts or rejects them as agent for the issuing bank. In that case, its acceptance of the documents will bind the issuing bank provided it acts within the scope of its authority: ie provided it is authorised to accept documents and the documents presented conform to its instructions. It is then entitled to reimbursement and the issuing bank must take up the documents.

However, where the documents are presented to a confirming bank or to an issuing bank (either directly or through an agent), the bank accepts the documents and pays as principal, in accordance with its obligations to the seller under the terms of the credit. Thus acceptance by a confirming bank does not bind the issuing bank which can refuse to take the documents from the confirming bank; but does bind the confirming bank so that it cannot return the documents to the seller. Similarly, acceptance by the issuing bank prevents the return of the documents to the confirming bank or seller, but does not bind the buyer to take them from the issuing bank unless they conform to its instructions to the issuing bank[1].

Further, acceptance of documents by the bank does not prevent the buyer rejecting the goods themselves if they prove defective on arrival, and, since the issuing bank acts as principal when taking up the documents, it seems that in theory the buyer could reject the goods even for defects apparent on the face of the documents[2]. However, in practice this is unlikely to happen. If serious defects are apparent on the face of the documents, the buyer will normally refuse to take up the documents from the bank, leaving it to dispose of the goods. If the buyer is bound to take up the documents, because of some error in his instructions to the bank on arranging the credit, he could in theory reject the goods, but that would leave him in a weak position vis-à-vis the seller, pursuing a claim for a refund against an overseas defendant already paid.

1   See *Credit Agricole Indosuez v Generale Bank* [1999] 2 All ER (Comm) 1009 and *(No 2)* [1999] 2 All ER (Comm) 1016.
2   Goode, *Commercial Law* (2nd edn, 1995) p 990.

34.2.6   *Rejection and non-payment*

If the bank rejects the documents on presentation, the seller will be notified of the reason and will normally have an opportunity to put right any defect and re-present the documents, provided there is time to do so in accordance with the contract of sale and the credit. Alternatively, the seller may contact the buyer direct and ask him to instruct the bank to accept the documents; but having agreed to payment by documentary credit, the seller may not 'short circuit' the agreed procedure and present the documents direct to the buyer for payment[1].

However, the credit is generally regarded only as a conditional payment. The effect of this is that if the bank fails to pay, for instance due to insolvency, the buyer's obligation under the sale contract to pay for the goods revives, and the seller may then seek payment direct from the buyer[2]. This general rule is excluded if the circumstances show that the seller accepted the opening of the credit as absolute payment: in that case, the seller is only entitled to seek payment from the bank.

1   *Soproma SpA v Marine and Animal By-Products Corpn* [1966] 1 Lloyd's Rep 367.
2   Per Lord Denning MR in *W J Alan & Co Ltd v El Nasr Export and Import Co* [1972] 2 QB 189, [1972] 2 All ER 127, CA.

34.2.7   *Release of the goods*

We have seen that, provided the bank pays against documents which conform to its instructions, the buyer is obliged to take up the documents, reimburse the bank and pay it for its services. Where the buyer has put the bank in funds, the bank will simply debit the buyer's account in accordance with its mandate. Until it is paid, the bank has possession of the bill of lading which gives it constructive possession of the goods and operates as a pledge of the goods. If the buyer fails to pay, he cannot obtain the release of the goods and the bank may realise its security by selling them. However, the buyer will often be dependent on reselling the goods to obtain funds to pay for them. The goods must then be released to the buyer to enable him to sell them. Normally, such release would destroy the bank's security: a pledge is dependent on the pledgee retaining lawful possession vis-à-vis the pledgor, and although the bank would still have the benefit of any hypothecation agreed in the application for the credit, such a hypothecation agreement will require registration under the Bills of Sale Acts 1878–1882 in order to bind third parties, or, if the buyer is a company, under the Companies Act 1985 in order to be effective if the buyer becomes insolvent[1]. This difficulty is avoided by the bank releasing the goods under the terms of a 'trust receipt', under which the buyer acknowledges that he has received the goods to realise them as trustee on behalf of the bank and holds the goods and their proceeds in that capacity. The effect of this is to preserve the bank's possessory security under the pledge of the documents; moreover, the trust receipt does not require registration as a bill of sale since the bank's rights derive not from the agreement but from the original pledge[2], and does not create a registrable charge in the case of a company[3]. The bank is thus protected against the buyer becoming insolvent; however, a bona fide purchaser of the goods from the buyer will obtain a good title under s 2 of the Factors Act 1889[4].

1　See 22.0.3.
2　*North Western Bank v Poynter* [1895] AC 56, HL.
3　*Re David Allester Ltd* [1922] 2 Ch 211.
4　*Lloyds Bank Ltd v Bank of America* [1938] 2 KB 147, [1938] 2 All ER 63, CA.

34.3　Other performance guarantees

The documentary credit is ideal as a payment guarantee, particularly in contracts of sale. However, other breaches may take place: the seller may fail to deliver, causing extensive losses to the buyer. Or the buyer may be required to make an advance payment or deposit, for instance in the case of shipbuilding or construction contracts. The sums involved in such contracts may be huge. The 'buyer' may want some guarantee of performance. The documentary credit is unsuitable for use in such cases but some form of 'guarantee' from a creditworthy third party is needed.

A simple personal guarantee could be used, but a simple guarantee carries none of the certainty offered by a documentary credit. A guarantor offers only a secondary undertaking, dependent on the contract of the primary debtor. Thus a guarantor, unlike the bank in a documentary credit transaction, can dispute liability to pay by raising defences available to the principal debtor[1]. The great advantage of the documentary credit is its autonomy from the contract of sale: it is that which provides the seller with the certainty of payment. Moreover, under English law, contracts of guarantee must be evidenced in writing to comply with the Statute of Frauds[2].

In recent years the commercial community has developed a number of guarantee arrangements which share some of the features of the documentary credit and which can be used to secure performance of obligations other than the payment of money. Mention has already been made of the standby credit[3] under which a bank undertakes to make a payment to the beneficiary if the bank's customer, who arranges the credit, defaults in performance of some obligation. Standby credits developed in the US where banks are legally prohibited from giving guarantees; in reality the standby credit has much more in common with a guarantee than with a documentary credit. A number of similar instruments have now been developed including the following.

(a)   Performance bonds/performance guarantees/first demand guarantees

These names tend to be used almost interchangeably[4]. Under these arrangements, a bank is required to give an undertaking on behalf of its client (the account party[5]) to a beneficiary that the bank will make a payment if the account party defaults in performance of an obligation and other conditions are fulfilled.

(b)   Tender bonds

A party submitting a tender to obtain a contract, for instance to carry out construction work or to supply goods, may be required to arrange a bond to show that the tender is serious. If the tender is awarded but the tenderer fails to perform, the beneficiary can call on the bank to pay under the bond to cover its losses.

(c)   Advance payment bonds

Where a contracting party makes advance or stage payments it will wish to recover them if the other party fails to perform. It may therefore require the other party to arrange for a bank to provide a bond guaranteeing repayment.

Despite the different terminology, these arrangements share many characteristics and it is convenient to use the generic term 'performance bonds' to describe them all. Under all of them a contract between the account party and the beneficiary requires the account party to arrange the performance bond. As with a documentary credit, the account party instructs the bank to provide the bond, indicates in what circumstances payment is to be made, and undertakes to reimburse it sums paid out under the bond. In turn, the bank may instruct a correspondent bank in the beneficiary's own country and undertake to reimburse it. Although the performance bond is used to secure the account party's performance of a contractual or other obligation, the bank's liability is a principal and is separate from the underlying contract between account party and beneficiary; it is not a guarantee[6]. As Professor Goode puts it, the bond is 'secondary in intent' but 'primary in form'. The bank, of course, charges the account party for providing the service. In most cases the expectation, and the result, will be that no call will be made under the bond: in effect the bank rents out its creditworthiness to its client. In 1991 the ICC published a set of Uniform Rules for Demand Guarantees (URDG) which will cover most of the arrangements under consideration here, although, like the UCP, the rules will only apply where they are incorporated into the bond[7]. An UNCITRAL Convention on Independent Guarantees was completed 1995 and came into force on 1 January 2000. It has, however, been ratified by only five states, not including the UK.

More important than the different names are the conditions upon which the bond becomes payable. Under some, payment is only due from the bank if the account party is in default under the primary contract. Such arrangements are unsatisfactory from the point of view of the bank, since it is only entitled to debit the account of the account party if the conditions of the bond are fulfilled: ie if it actually is in default. Thus the bank may be drawn into disputes under the main contract. To avoid this, the bond may provide for payment to be made on production of a certificate of judgment or arbitration award, or a certificate from a third party such as a surveyor. In these cases the bank is protected provided that the correct documentation is produced, and the arrangement is closely analogous to a documentary credit. However, the most attractive arrangement for the beneficiary is the most controversial, under which payment is due 'on demand' by the beneficiary.

Under a demand bond the bank is required to pay if the beneficiary makes a demand. There is no need to prove a breach of the underlying contract, and the bank is therefore insulated against disputes arising under that contract. The arrangement clearly exposes the account party to unjustified demands by the beneficiary. These are relatively new commercial arrangements and the courts are still working out their response to them. However, in a number of cases the courts have had to consider whether to restrain payment under the bond where a demand has been made but the account party alleges it is unjustified. In general, it seems that the attitude of the courts is to equate performance bonds with documentary credits and thus preserve the separation between the bond and the underlying contract. Thus in *Edward Owen Engineering Ltd v Barclays Bank International Ltd* [8] sellers entered into a contract to deliver glasshouses to a Libyan customer. They were required to open a demand performance bond, and did so. The buyers were required to open a confirmed credit, but failed to do so. The sellers therefore refused to ship the goods. The buyers made a demand under the bond, and the sellers sought to restrain the bank from paying, arguing they were entitled to refuse performance. The Court of Appeal refused the injunction. The sellers had agreed to payment being made on demand, and could not now object if a demand was made. Had they wished to limit the bond to cases of default, it should have been so worded. Lord Denning MR explained that the performance bond –

> 'stands on a similar footing to a letter of credit. A bank which gives a performance [bond] must honour that [bond] according to its terms. It is not concerned in the least with the relations between the supplier and the customer; nor with the question whether the supplier has performed his contractual obligations or not; nor with the question whether the supplier is in default or not'[9].

Like the documentary credit, the performance bond is regarded as separate from the underlying contract which gives rise to it, in the interests of certainty in commercial affairs. Where the bond is payable on demand, however, it is in many ways analogous to a promissory note payable on demand[10].The autonomy principle is affirmed in the URDG:

> 'Guarantees by their nature are separate transactions from the contract(s) or tender conditions on which they may be based and Guarantors are in no way concerned with or bound by such contract(s) or tender conditions . . .'[11]

Since *Edward Owen* a series of similar attempts to prevent payment have met a similar fate[12]. The only exception recognised by the courts, again on analogy with the documentary credit cases, is where the claim is fraudulent. As with claims under a documentary credit payment will only be restrained where there is clear evidence of fraud, and will rarely be granted. An injunction to restrain payment was granted on this basis in *Kvaerner John Brown Ltd v Midland Bank plc*[13], which concerned a standby credit given to secure performance under a construction contract. It provided that the beneficiary was entitled to demand payment on supplying a written certificate that (a) the account party was in breach of contract and (b) that it had given notice of its call on the bond to the account party. An injunction was granted to restrain the bank from paying when it was established that the beneficiary had not given notice of its demand as required so that its certificate was false and the claim fraudulent.

In *Kvaerner* the bond was conditional on the beneficiary's certificate. In such a case there may be scope for the fraud exception to operate (although it should be noted that the account party's victory in such a case may be empty if, as in *Kvaerner*, it is open to the beneficiary immediately to rectify its earlier default by serving notice as required and making a fresh call on the bond). In other cases the requirements of the fraud exception may be difficult to satisfy. Where the bond is payable simply on demand it will be almost impossible to establish fraud. The effect of this approach is that the beneficiary obtains payment and the bank is entitled to debit its customer, the account party. The account party who wishes to challenge the beneficiary's entitlement to payment must then bring separate proceedings for damages under the original supply contract or an action for money had and received. Since the defendant beneficiary will be overseas, the account party is placed at a disadvantage in any such proceedings, although it may be possible to obtain a freezing, or Mareva, injunction to prevent the beneficiary disposing of the proceeds of the bond[14]. Such an injunction is not limited to assets within the jurisdiction[15].

In drafting the URDG, some thought was given to the problem of fraudulent calls on bonds. An earlier set of rules had provided that the beneficiary would only be entitled to payment on production of a court judgment or arbitration award, but they had proved popular neither with beneficiaries nor with banks. The URDG therefore merely require the beneficiary to include in the demand a written statement that the principal (account party) is in breach of contract and to specify the nature of the breach[16]. The guarantor is then required to transmit the demand to the principal without delay[17], thereby providing the principal with knowledge of the demand and an opportunity to take action to restrain it. Given the reluctance of the courts to intervene in bonds, however, one may doubt whether this will really provide effective protection.

The 1995 UNCITRAL Convention takes a different approach. Having asserted the autonomous nature of bond undertakings by describing them as 'independent commitments' and confirmed the bank's obligation to pay on the bond's conditions being fulfilled, it then provides that in making a demand the beneficiary is deemed to certify that his demand is made in good faith[18], and provides that the guarantor may withhold payment if 'it is manifest and clear that: (a) any document is not genuine or has been falsified; (b) no payment is due on the basis asserted in the demand and the supporting documents; or (c) judging by the type and purpose of the undertaking, the demand has no conceivable basis'[19]. Examples are given of circumstances in which a demand has 'no conceivable basis'. However, there is considerable uncertainty in these provisions. Their combined effect appears to be substantially to undermine the autonomy principle and to require a bank or other guarantor to explore the circumstances underlying a demand in order to determine if it is justified. This is hardly likely to be attractive to bond providers.

Although bonds are treated as analogous to documentary credits and to promissory notes, Lord Denning recognised in *Edward Owen* that an on demand bond may well operate in a way similar to a liquidated damages or penalty clause[20]. What saves bonds from being invalidated on this basis is that, although the beneficiary is entitled to call on the bond without proof of loss, it will normally be an implied term of the bond that there should at some stage be an accounting between the parties to determine their rights and obligations and the beneficiary will be permitted to retain only so much of the amount paid as is necessary to compensate him for losses actually suffered[21]. Where the bond exceeds the amount of his loss, he must account to the beneficiary for the excess. Conversely, if his actual loss, exceeds the amount paid under the bond he is entitled to bring a claim for damages for the balance. The duty to account can be excluded, but clear words will be needed. Thus a provision in a bond provided under a sale contract that in the event of breach by the seller the buyer would be entitled to 'forfeit' the bond, was held not to exclude the duty to account[22].

The effect of a bond is therefore not to determine the final rights of the parties but to affect the 'tempo' of parties' obligations, in the sense that when an allegation of breach of contract is made (in good faith), the beneficiary can call the bond and receive its value pending the resolution of the contractual disputes. He does not have to await the final determination of his rights before he receives some moneys.[23] It is therefore a manifestation of a principle which is familiar in international transactions, of 'pay now, argue later'[24]. Nevertheless, where the beneficiary has made a call on the bond the account party will be in a weak negotiating position.

The approach of the courts, especially to on demand bonds, has been criticised. It is not clear that the analogy with documentary credits is justified[25]. First, the two instruments perform different functions. A documentary credit is provided by way of performance of the buyer's primary obligation to pay for the goods. The bank's undertaking is a primary one, not dependent in any way on the buyer's default. A performance bond, in contrast, although primary in form, is essentially a secondary undertaking, provided to guarantee the account party's performance Secondly, under a documentary credit the bank is presented with documents which amount to a certificate of performance provided by a third party. Under a demand bond the bank is required to pay simply on the beneficiary's own say so. The courts' approach is justified on the basis of the need to avoid embroiling banks in disputes about contractual performance, and on the grounds of freedom of contract: the account party having agreed to a demand bond cannot then object to a demand being made or the bank paying. This, however, ignores the reality that in order to do business with contract partners in some parts of the world, the account party may have no alternative but to provide a bond. In theory, the account party will pass on to the beneficiary the costs of the bond, including the risk of unjustified calls, by increasing the contract price[26]. As Ackner LJ put it in one case:

'The plaintiffs took a commercial risk that the performance bonds might be called in dishonestly . . . If, as is apparent, the plaintiffs were prepared to run the obvious risk, then they should have provided for those risks in the contract prices'[27].

It is, however, far from clear that commercial pricing is so sophisticated. Nevertheless, even in light of the obvious risks, a performance bond may be more attractive than the possible alternatives, such as depositing funds in the hands of a third party stakeholder or a joint account with the other contract party, and thus interrupting cashflow. Moreover, the account party may be able to pass on the risk of an unjustified call by insurance: such insurance is provided by the Government under the Export Credit Guarantee Scheme and in certain cases the Export Credit Guarantee Department may agree to provide a bond on terms that it will reimburse the exporter if an unjustified call is made. Exports are, after all, in the national interest.

1 See ch 23.
2 See 23.1.1.3.
3 Above 34.1.1.
4 Strictly speaking, a 'bond' is a guarantee undertaking contained in a deed: see 23.0.4.
5 In the ICC's Uniform Rules for Demand Guarantees the account party is referred to as 'the principal'.
6 See eg *Wahda Bank v Arab Bank plc* [1994] 2 Lloyd's Rep 411.
7 [1992] LMCLQ 190.
8 [1978] QB 159, [1978] 1 All ER 976.
9 [1978] QB 159 at 171, [1978] 1 All ER 976 at 983.
10 See Lord Denning in *Edward Owen* [1978] QB 159 at 170, [1978] 1 All ER 976 at 983.
11 URDG, art 2(b).
12 The older cases are discussed by Coleman, 'Performance Guarantees' [1990] LMCLQ 223. Eveleigh LJ suggested in *Potton Homes Ltd v Coleman Contractors Ltd* (1984) 28 BLR 19 that there might be circumstances short of fraud where the court would grant an injunction to prevent the beneficiary drawing on the bond; see *Royal Design Studio v Chang Development* [1991] 2 MLJ 229, noted by Hsu [1992] LMCLQ 297.
13 [1998] CLC 446. See also *Themehelp Ltd v West* [1995] 4 All ER 215, CA.
14 *The Bhoja Trader* [1981] 2 Lloyd's Rep 256.
15 See *Derby & Co Ltd v Weldon* [1989] 1 All ER 469; *Republic of Haiti v Duvalier* [1990] 1 QB 202, [1989] 1 All ER 456, CA.
16 URDG, art 20.
17 URDG, art 21.
18 Article 15.
19 Article 19.
20 At 170, 982.
21 *Cargill International SA v Bangladesh Sugar and Food Industries Corpn* [1996] 4 All ER 563; affd [1998] 2 All ER 406, CA; see McMeel [1999] LMLQ 5. See also *Comdel Commodities Ltd v Siporex Trade SA* [1997] 1 Lloyd's Rep 424, CA.
22 *Cargill International SA v Bangladesh Sugar and Food Industries Corpn* [1996] 4 All ER 563; affd [1998] 2 All ER 406.
23 Per Morrison J in *Cargill International SA v Bangladesh Sugar and Food Industries Corpn* [1996] 4 All ER 563 at 568.
24 See McMeel, above note 21.
25 See Debattista [1997] JBL 289.
26 See per Lord Denning MR in *Edward Owen* [1978] QB 159 at 170, [1978] 1 All ER 976 at 982.
27 *United Trading Corpn SA v Allied Arab Bank Ltd* [1985] 2 Lloyd's Rep 554n at 566, CA. See also *Kvaerner John Brown Ltd v Midland Bank plc* [1998] CLC 446 at 449, per Cresswell J.

Part VI

Protecting the Transaction

Chapter 35

Insurance

35.0 Introduction: commerce, risk and insurance

Commercial activity necessarily involves risk: the buyer may not pay; the seller may not deliver; the goods may be delivered, but be defective, or fail to do the job they were bought for; goods may be delayed, lost or damaged in transit; a new product line may prove unsuccessful, or defective, exposing the producer to extensive product liability.

A business may seek to minimise those risks by using appropriate terms in its contracts with trading partners to allocate particular risks between the contracting parties. For instance, a clause in a contract of sale excluding the seller's liability for damage caused by the goods throws the risk of such loss onto the buyer, protecting the seller; similarly, a manufacturer's guarantee under which the manufacturer undertakes to repair defects appearing during the guarantee period, throws the risk of such defects onto the manufacturer. The rules as to the passing of risk in supply contracts, including any express contract terms, allocate the risk of accidental loss of or damage to the goods.

In some cases the law restricts the reallocation of risks between contracting parties. This is the case where the law prohibits or restricts the use of exclusion clauses: for instance, a manufacturer cannot exclude liability under the Consumer Protection Act 1987 for damage or injury caused by defective products[1]. In effect, the law stipulates that, as between a manufacturer and an injured party, the risk of injury caused by defective products is allocated to the manufacturer. In general, however, even where the law allocates the risk as between two parties in this way, there is nothing to prevent the party on whom the risk is imposed agreeing that some third party should bear the risk, by entering into an agreement for the third party to indemnify him. An indemnity may be contained in a term in a contract, as, for instance, where a retailer who sells goods requires his supplier to indemnify him against any liability he incurs to consumers as a result of selling the goods, or in a wholly separate agreement, as where a sea carrier of goods delivers goods to a person without production of a bill of lading but in return for an indemnity against liability[2]. The most common means of guarding against risk, however, is by insuring against it. A contract of insurance is effectively a contract by which a person pays someone else – the insurer – to bear a risk to which he is exposed.

Insurance is sometimes regarded as a risk-sharing device: the premium a manufacturer pays for product liability insurance will be an overhead of his business, and will therefore be reflected in the price of his product. The cost of claims is then shared between all purchasers of that particular manufacturer's products, allowing the risk to be distributed more widely. Moreover, if he has a bad claims record, his premiums, and therefore the price of his products, will increase, so that the price of his products may reflect their true social cost. However, this depends on premiums accurately reflecting the individual manufacturer's claims record: in many cases it seems that the calculation of premiums is far less sophisticated, being based on the records not only of the individual business, but of businesses engaged in similar activities.

Many of the risks of commercial activity can be covered by insurance, and a prudent business will therefore insure against them. Indeed, it is compulsory to carry certain types of insurance. Thus any person who uses a motor vehicle on a road must carry compulsory insurance against potential liability to third parties for death or personal injury[3] and employers must carry insurance against their potential liability to employees injured at work[4]. Certain types of business are required by statute[5], or by rules of professional conduct[6], to carry additional insurance cover. Furthermore, a business will normally carry insurance against many other types of risk, including property insurance, product liability insurance, bad debt insurance; it may also provide health insurance for employees, or take out 'key person' insurance to guard against the loss of vital senior personnel.

Insurance therefore plays a vital role in commercial activity. In addition, the courts may take into account the availability of insurance cover when making a decision which may have the effect of allocating loss between contracting parties. The courts rarely advert openly to the insurance position; however, under the Unfair Contract Terms Act 1977 the court is expressly directed to take the availability of insurance into account in assessing the reasonableness of clauses which impose a financial limit on liability[7]. Of course, many policies of insurance are unrelated to commercial activity: for instance, many individuals insure their property and, in particular, may take out life insurance[8]. Moreover, the contract of insurance is itself an important commercial transaction. In the last two decades a number of new forms of insurance have been developed. In particular, forms of insurance are now commonly used as investment devices. However, there is not space in the present work to examine the law of insurance in detail, and we are primarily concerned with the use of insurance in the context of other commercial activity. What follows is therefore a brief examination of the general principles of insurance law in that context[9].

1   Consumer Protection Act 1987, s 7; however, in some circumstances the manufacturer may require his immediate customer to indemnify him against product liability claims: see 2.6.4.1.
2   See 32.4.
3   Road Traffic Act 1988; such insurance has been compulsory since the Road Traffic Act 1930.
4   Employers' Liability (Compulsory Insurance) Act 1969.
5   Eg Nuclear Installations Acts 1965–69; Riding Establishments Act 1964.
6   Eg for solicitors under the Solicitors Indemnity Rules 1989.
7   Unfair Contract Terms Act 1977, s 11(4)(b); see eg *Salvage Association v CAP Financial Services Ltd* (9 July 1993, unreported) above 2.6.4.4.
8   Strictly 'life assurance' but the terminology is no longer used consistently.
9   For more detailed coverage of the subject the reader is referred to Professor Birds' excellent *Modern Insurance Law* (4th edn, 1997).

35.0.1   *Classification of risk and insurance*

Insurance may be classified by reference to the nature of the risk. Some risks may be regarded as 'pure' risks, in that they relate to events which, if they occur, can only produce a loss: for instance, insurance of buildings against fire and bad debt insurance protect against pure risks. However, many of the risks which may arise in the course of commercial activity are speculative risks, in that, depending on the course of events, they may produce a profit or a loss (or neither): for instance, the launch of a new product may result in a loss, but it may also result in a profit. In general, insurance is not available against speculative risks.

A distinction may also be drawn between first and third party insurance. Typically, insurance on property will be first party, whilst liability insurance will be third party. However, the two types of cover may be combined in a single policy, as is commonly the case with motor insurance: a 'fully comprehensive' policy provides (compulsory) third party cover and also provides the vehicle owner with first party cover against damage to the vehicle itself. Where the holder of a third party liability policy becomes insolvent, any rights he has against his insurer under the policy are transferred to the third party to whom liability was incurred[1], so that a third party injured by the insured prior to the insolvency can claim directly against the insurer. He is therefore protected from being merely an unsecured creditor in the insolvency. However, recent decisions have revealed limitations to this protection: in particular, where the insured is a company, the claim must be made before the company has been wound up and its name removed from the register of companies[2].

A further distinction is between indemnity and contingency insurance. Under a policy of indemnity insurance, the insurer undertakes to indemnify the insured against the loss insured against, by paying the amount of the loss. Examples include liability insurance, such as product liability insurance, and property insurance. Under a contingency insurance, the insurer undertakes to pay a fixed sum of money if the contingency insured against matures: the best example is a policy of life insurance, under which a fixed sum is payable on the death of the insured.

All policies of insurance share certain common features. The risk insured against must be uncertain: in cases of indemnity insurance, there is no certainty that the event insured against will ever occur; in cases of life insurance, although death is ultimately certain to occur, its timing is uncertain. Thus a policy on goods will normally not be construed as covering wear and tear. Further, the risk insured against must be outside the control of the insurer; there is no requirement that it be outside the control of the insured, otherwise it would be impossible to obtain insurance against third party liability. As a general rule, however, policies will be construed as not covering loss caused by wilful conduct of the insured, nor loss resulting from inherent vice in the subject matter of the insurance.

1   Third Parties (Rights Against Insurers) Act 1930, s 1.
2   *Bradley v Eagle Star Insurance Co Ltd* [1989] AC 957, [1989] 1 All ER 961, HL. The effect of the decision is somewhat mitigated by the power to apply to have the name of the company restored to the register in order to bring a claim; however, where the claim is for damages for property damage, as opposed to personal injury or death, the application must be made within two years of completion of the winding up: Companies Act 1985, s 651. The Law Commission has provisionally recommended extensive changes to the 1930 Act: see Law Commission Consultation Paper 152, January 1998.

35.0.2   *Definition of insurance*

In view of the wide range of risks which may be covered by insurance, the utility of seeking a definition of 'insurance' might be questioned. However, for certain purposes a definition may be useful. First, persons carrying on an 'insurance business' are subject to regulatory control, currently under the Insurance Companies Act 1982[1] or, in the case of life assurance, the Financial Services Act 1986, However, in much the same way that there is no comprehensive definition of 'banking'[2], neither Act defines 'insurance'[3]. Secondly, other statutory provisions refer to 'insurance contracts': for instance, certain provisions of the Unfair Contract Terms Act 1977 do not apply to a 'contract of insurance'[4]. Thirdly, although the contract of insurance is a contract, and is therefore governed by the general law of contract, a number of special rules apply to such contracts at common law. Most notably the contract of insurance is a contract *'uberrimae fidei'* – of the utmost good faith. Extensive duties of disclosure are imposed on the parties to such a contract at common law[5]. In order to decide whether the special rules applicable to contracts of insurance apply to a particular contract, a court must first decide if the contract in question is a contract of insurance.

In *Fuji Finance Ltd v Aetna Life Insurance Ltd*[6] it was necessary to decide whether a particular contract was a contract of life insurance. The case concerned an investment contract between an insurance company and an investor under which a lump sum was payable on the death of a named person but the investor was permitted to withdraw its investment at any time. The sum payable to the investor on withdrawal was the same as the sum payable on death. Nicholls V-C, at first instance, concluded that a contract of insurance is one 'under which a sum of money becomes payable on an event which is uncertain as to its timing or as to its happening at all'[7] and therefore concluded that the contract was not one of insurance: although a sum was payable on death, the same sum was payable on demand at any time. The Court of Appeal unanimously reversed this decision. Recognising that many new forms of insurance contract have been developed in the last 20 or so years, and that life insurance is often now used as a form of investment, they concluded that it was not fatal to the classification of the contract as one of life insurance that the same benefits were payable on death as on surrender, provided that the event upon which the policy sum was payable was sufficiently life- or death-related. It was therefore sufficient that the contract would come to an end and the policy value become payable on the death of the policy holder.

It is suggested that, for more general purposes, a contract of insurance can be defined more fully as a contract under which one party (the insurer) agrees in return for a consideration, to assume the risk of an event, the occurrence or timing of which is uncertain, to which the other party (the insured) is exposed and in which the insured has an interest, and agrees that on the occurrence of the event insured against, he will pay the insured a sum of money, or provide some other benefit with a monetary value[8]. However, whilst this definition may suffice for certain purposes, including the application of regulatory control, it may be that a different definition will be appropriate for different purposes[9].

---

1   See 35.0.4. See eg *Fuji Finance Inc v Aetna Life Insurance Ltd* [1994] 4 All ER 1025; revsd [1996] 4 All ER 608, CA.
2   See 29.0.2.
3   Once the Financial Services and Markets Act 2000 is brought into force all forms of insurance will be regulated by the Financial Services Authority under that Act, but the Act contains no definition of 'insurance'.
4   Schedule 1, para 1.
5   See 35.3.
6   [1994] 4 All ER 1025; revsd [1996] 4 All ER 608, CA.
7   [1994] 4 All ER 1025 at 1031, following *Prudential Insurance Co v IRC* [1904] 2 KB 658.
8   It seems that it is not necessary that the insurer should pay money, but that the provision of some valuable benefit will suffice: see *Department of Trade and Industry v St Christopher Motorists'*

Association [1974] 1 All ER 395, [1974] 1 WLR 99 (provision of chauffeur service to members disqualified from driving). However, the insurer must be obliged to provide the benefit: see *Medical Defence Union v Department of Trade* [1980] Ch 82, [1979] 2 All ER 421. See also Birds, *Modern Insurance Law* (4th edn, 1997) pp 14–18; *Chitty on Contracts* (28th edn, 1999) para 41-001.
9   See Birds, *Modern Insurance Law* (4th edn, 1997) p 19.

35.0.3   *Marine insurance*

We have already noted the importance of insurance in international commercial transactions[1]. Where goods have to be carried by sea they will almost always be insured against the perils of the sea and, indeed, the principle of insurance was first developed to guard against maritime perils. Under a CIF contract, a policy of marine insurance is one of the documents which the seller must tender in order to perform the contract[2].

Marine insurance is now governed by the provisions of the Marine Insurance Act 1906. However, the 1906 Act, which, like the Sale of Goods Act 1893 and Bills of Exchange Act, was drafted by Sir Mackenzie Chalmers, merely codified the pre-existing common law, and many of its provisions are reflected in the general law or applied, even today, by analogy to other, non-marine insurances[3]. Marine insurance is often effected at Lloyd's.

A policy of marine insurance is 'a contract whereby the insurer undertakes to indemnify the assured . . . against marine losses, that is to say the losses incident to marine adventure'[4]. There is a marine adventure where:

'(a)   any ship goods or other moveables are exposed to maritime perils;
 (b)   the earning or acquisition of any freight, passage money, commission, profit or other pecuniary benefit, or the security for any advances, loan, or other disbursements, is endangered by the exposure of insurable property to maritime perils;
 (c)   any liability to a third party may be incurred by the owner of or other person interested in or responsible for insurable property, by reason of maritime perils'[5].

'Maritime perils' are widely defined to include:

'perils consequent on or incidental to the navigation of the sea, that is to say, perils of the seas, fire, war perils, pirates, rovers, thieves, captures, seisures, restraints, and detainments of princes and peoples, jettisons, barratry and any other perils, either of the like kind or which may be designated by the policy'[6].

The result is that a policy on goods carried by sea is clearly a marine insurance policy. Moreover, a policy of marine insurance may be extended to cover loss on inland waterways or land risks which may be incidental to any sea voyage[7].

Although many of the principles of marine insurance law are similar to those of the general law of insurance, some aspects are highly specialised. This chapter will concentrate on the general principles of insurance law; the reader seeking full coverage of marine insurance law must consult one of the specialist texts on the subject[8].

1   See generally Pt V.
2   See 33.2.6.
3   See eg *Lambert v Co-operative Insurance Society Ltd* [1975] 2 Lloyd's Rep 485, CA, applying the statutory test of materiality, and *Highlands Insurance Co v Continental Insurance Co* [1987] 1 Lloyd's Rep 109n, following *Container Transport International Inc v Oceanus Mutual*

Underwriting Association (Bermuda) Ltd [1984] 1 Lloyd's Rep 476, CA; see below 35.3.2; *PCW Syndicates v PCW Reinsurers* [1996] 1 All ER 774.
4   Marine Insurance Act 1906, s 1.
5   Marine Insurance Act 1906, s 3(1).
6   Marine Insurance Act 1906, s 3(2).
7   Marine Insurance Act 1906, s 2.
8   See eg Arnould, *The Law of Marine Insurance and Average*; Ivamy, *Marine Insurance*; Bennett, *The Law of Marine Insurance* (1996).

35.0.4   *History and development*

Like much of banking law, the modern law of insurance has its origins in the practice of Italian merchants in the fourteenth century, who would arrange to insure their vessels and cargoes against the risks of sea travel. Merchants would agree, in return for a fee, to undertake a share of the risk of their fellow merchants' trading ventures, and, indeed, this practice was adopted as the basis of insurance business at Lloyd's in the eighteenth century and still provides the model for insurance effected through Lloyd's of London today.

Initially, disputes arising out of contracts of insurance were decided according to the custom and practice of merchants. The law of insurance therefore formed part of the lex mercatoria, and, as with many other aspects of commercial law, and, in particular, the law relating to banking and bills of exchange, it was only in the eighteenth century that insurance contracts came under the jurisdiction of the common law courts. Perhaps, as a result, the law relating to contracts of insurance is, in many ways, idiosyncratic and the principles of contract law are sometimes modified in their application to contracts of insurance.

Moreover, the early law of insurance developed out of the practice of merchants and was primarily concerned with marine insurance. Today, of course, marine insurance represents only one special type of insurance business, and many contracts of insurance are taken out by individuals for domestic purposes. However, principles developed in the context of marine insurance continue to be applied to insurance generally. Once again, the question arises whether principles developed in the context of commercial transactions are appropriate for application to modern 'consumer' or small business contracts[1].

There has been regulatory control of insurance businesses since 1870[2]. In general, legislation has been passed in response to individual insurance scandals and company failures which have revealed loopholes in the protection of the customers of insurance companies. The current controls are under the Insurance Companies Act 1982 and regulations made under it and, in the case of life insurance, the Financial Services Act 1986. Under the 1982 Act, a person can only carry on an insurance business if authorised by the Secretary of State for Trade and Industry. However, certain persons are exempted from the requirement of authorisation; most notably, members of Lloyd's are not required to be authorised. In general, only companies can be authorised[3], and the Secretary of State must refuse authorisation if persons in the applicant company are not fit and proper persons to hold their positions[4]. The Act also imposes continuing obligations on insurance businesses. In particular, there are detailed regulations designed to ensure that insurance businesses maintain adequate financial reserves and solvency[5].

The aim of many of these provisions is to protect clients of insurers against the insurer becoming insolvent. If an insurer does become insolvent, further protection is provided by the Policyholders Protection Acts 1975 and 1997, which established a Policyholders Protection Board, financed by a levy on insurers. The Board can provide financial assistance to insurance businesses in financial difficulties, and, in the event of an insurer becoming insolvent, ensures that policyholders receive at least 90% of the sums to which they are entitled under their policies.

This regulatory scheme will be replaced when the Financial Services and Markets Act 2000 (FSMA 2000) is brought into force. All forms of insurance, including life insurance and, for the first time, insurance effected at Lloyd's, will be subject to the regulatory regime of the Act under the supervision of the Financial Services Authority. The provision of insurance, including by way of investment, and participation at Lloyd's are regulated activities under the Act, which will require authorisation from the FSA. It will be illegal to engage in regulated activities without authorisation. The FSA has extensive powers under the Act to determine the conditions of authorisation and to make rules and issue codes of conduct to govern the performance of regulated activities by authorised persons[6]. The Policy Holders' Protection scheme will be replaced by a general Financial Services Compensation Scheme under FSMA 2000[7], which may include power to continue policies of long-term insurance entered into by an insurer who is unable to satisfy claims[8].

Although there is now an extensive system of supervision and regulation of insurance businesses, there is at present relatively little regulation of the terms of individual contracts of insurance, even though they are almost always made using standard forms, on terms largely or even wholly dictated by the insurer. Instead, the relationship between insurers and their clients has been left, on the whole, to be governed by self-regulation. This has been achieved by adoption of voluntary Statements of Practice and undertakings: for instance, insurance contracts were excluded from the ambit of the Unfair Contract Terms Act 1977 in return for the insurers' agreement to adopt a Statement of Practice[9]. Insurance contracts are, however, subject to the Unfair Terms in Consumer Contracts Regulations 1999.

In 1981 the Insurance Ombudsman Bureau was established to deal with disputes between insurers and their private (non-business) customers. The scheme is voluntary but most, although not all, insurers are members[10]. Once the Financial Services and Markets Act comes into force, the Bureau will be abolished and insurers authorised under the Act will be required to participate in the Financial Services Ombudsman Scheme established under that Act[11].

1 There are signs that the courts recognise this and that certain principles are applied differently to marine and non-marine insurances. In 1997 the National Consumer Council published a report recommending a number of reforms to the law as applied to consumer insurance.
2 Life Assurance Companies Act 1870.
3 Insurance Companies Act 1982, s 7.
4 Section 7(3). There is power for the Secretary of State to revoke authorisation in certain circumstances: s 11.
5 Section 32.
6 It is anticipated, however, that at least in the first instance the conditions for authorisation will be much as they are at present, not least because many of them are derived from EC Directives.
7 FSMA 2000, s 212.
8 FSMA 2000, s 216.
9 Statement of Insurance Practice 1977, revised and replaced by Statement of Insurance Practice 1986. For a discussion of some of the agreements and of the issues raised by this form of regulation see Lewis (1985) 48 MLR 275.
10 The IOB has no jurisdiction over life insurance matters which are handled by the Personal Investment Authority Ombudsman under the Financial Services Act 1986.
11 See 36.3.1.

35.1 Insurable interest

It is a fundamental requirement of modern insurance law that the insured must have an insurable interest in the event insured against. There was no such requirement at common law, but in contracts of indemnity insurance it has always been necessary that the insured should have an interest at the date of loss, since his right to recover under the policy is limited to an indemnity against the loss he has suffered. In certain cases there is now a statutory requirement under the Life Assurance Act 1774 that the insured have an insurable interest at the date of entering into the contract, and, in the absence of such interest, the policy is void and illegal[1]. The reason for this requirement is to prevent 'a mischievious kind of gaming'[2] which might follow if the insured could insure an event in which he had no interest. Even where the statutory requirement of insurable interest does not apply, the Gaming Act 1845 will apply and the contract will be void as a contract of wager if at the time of the contract the insured has no interest in the event insured against. However, it is easier to satisfy the requirements of the Gaming Act than those of the Life Assurance Act.

1   Life Assurance Act 1774, s 1.
2   Life Assurance Act 1774, s 1.

35.1.1 *Definition of insurable interest*

It is difficult to provide a comprehensive definition of insurable interest which can be applied to the many different classes of insurance contract. Essentially, it seems that the insured has an insurable interest in an event if its occurrence will cause him a financial loss, either due to the imposition of legal liability or by adversely affecting any right of his recognised by law.

> 'Where the assured is so situated that the happening of the event on which the insurance money is to become payable would, as a proximate cause, involve the assured in the loss or diminution of any right recognised by law, or in any legal liability, there is an insurable interest to the extent of the possible loss or interest'[1].

Where an insurer successfully argues that the insured has no insurable interest, the effect will be to provide the insurer with a defence to any claim on the policy. Moreover, the insured will generally not be entitled to recover any premiums. Where the policy is valid, there is no ground for refunding the premiums; where it is covered by the 1774 Act, the contract will be illegal, and recovery will generally be prohibited[2]. Thus it has been said that:

> 'it is the duty of a court always to lean in favour of an insurable interest, if possible, for it seems to me that after underwriters have received the premium, the objection that there was no insurable interest is often, as nearly as possible, a technical objection and one which has no real merit, certainly not as between the assured and the insurer'[3].

1   *McGillivray and Parkington on Insurance Law* (9th edn, 1997) para 1-45.
2   Except where the parties are not in pari delicto: see *Hughes v Liverpool Victoria Legal Friendly Society* [1916] 2 KB 482, CA.
3   Per Brett MR in *Stock v Inglis* (1884) 12 QBD 564 at 571, CA.

35.1.2 *Insurable interest in life assurance*

The Life Assurance Act 1774 clearly applies to contracts of life assurance, and requires the insured under a policy of life assurance to have an insurable interest in the life assured[1]; in the absence of such an interest the policy is illegal[2]. It is now settled that the Act merely requires that the insured have an interest at the time the policy is effected, not at the time of a claim on the policy[3].

In general the insured must have a financial interest in the life insured. Thus a creditor has an insurable interest in the life of his debtor, and an employer may have an insurable interest in the life of an employee[4]. However, this principle is modified in two situations: a person has an insurable interest in his own life, even though he clearly has no financial interest, and spouses each have an interest in the other's life.

In order to prevent evasion of the requirements of the Act, it further provides that the name of the person for whose benefit the policy is made shall be inserted in the policy, and that failure to do so makes the policy illegal[5]. However, it seems that in many cases this requirement serves little useful purpose; provided the insured has an interest at the time the policy is made, he may assign the benefit of the policy to another person, and it has been suggested that s 2 could be repealed[6].

1 Life Assurance Act 1774, s 1.
2 Section 1 actually states that the policy is void, but it has been held that the policy is illegal: *Harse v Pearl Life Assurance Co* [1903] 2 KB 92.
3 *Dalby v India and London Life Assurance Co* (1854) 15 CB 365.
4 In theory, the interest, and therefore the right of recovery, is restricted by the value of the interest (*Hebdon v West* (1863) 3 B & S 579) but the point is rarely taken in practice. See, however, *Fuji Finance Inc v Aetna Insurance Co Ltd* [1996] 4 All ER 608. A company had taken out a policy on the life of its controller. The policy was effectively an investment vehicle. It was calculated that, had it run its course, its value would have been equal to the gross domestic product of the UK for 460,000 years – which was held to be somewhat in excess of the insured's interest in the life assured!
5 Life Assurance Act 1774, s 2.
6 See Birds, *Modern Insurance Law* (4th edn, 1997) pp 46–47.

35.1.3 *Insurable interest in indemnity insurance*

The insured under an indemnity policy is required at common law to have an insurable interest in the subject matter of the policy at the time of loss. In addition, the Gaming Act applies to all such contracts, and requires the insured to have sufficient interest at the time the policy is effected to prevent the contract being one of wager. However, the requirements of the Gaming Act are less strict than the requirements of 'insurable interest', and the contract will be a contract of insurance, rather than a wager, provided that the insured has an interest in, or an expectation of acquiring an interest in the subject matter of the contract. Moreover, the common law requirement of interest at the date of loss can be waived by clear words in the policy[1]. In order to decide if a strict insurable interest is required at the time of the contract, it is necessary to decide if the Life Assurance Act 1774 applies to the contract.

The 1774 Act is expressly stated not to apply to insurance on 'ships, goods, or merchandise'[2] but its application to other types of insurance is unclear. Modern English cases favour the view that the Act does not apply to insurance of real property, although there are conflicting authorities[3], and in *Siu Yin Kwan v Eastern Insurance Co Ltd*[4] (a case concerned with s 2 of the Act) the Privy Council approved that view and held that the Act does not apply to any form of indemnity insurance.

Lord Lloyd, giving the opinion of the Committee, observed that the preamble to the Act indicates that it was intended to prevent certain transactions which amounted to a 'mischievious kind of gaming' and that 'by no stretch of the imagination could liability insurance be described as a mischievious kind of gaming'[5].

In any case, the insured must have an interest at the date of loss in order to satisfy the common law indemnity requirement. The classic definition of 'insurable interest' in relation to property insurance was given by Lord Eldon in *Lucena v Crauford*[6], when he defined it as 'a right in the property, or a right derivable out of some contract about the property, which in either case may be lost upon some contingency affecting the possession or enjoyment of the party'. This is a narrow definition: in approving it the House of Lords rejected a wider test which would recognise a person as having an insurable interest in an event whenever he has a factual expectation of loss on the happening of that event[7].

The difference between the two tests is illustrated by the decision in *Macaura v Northern Assurance Co Ltd*[8]. M was the sole shareholder and also a major creditor of a company which owned a quantity of timber. The timber was stored on M's property and M took out a policy of insurance on the timber, in his own name. It was held that he had no insurable interest and so was not able to maintain a claim on the policy when the timber was destroyed by fire. M was clearly at risk of prejudice if the timber, a major asset of the company, was destroyed, but he had neither proprietary nor contractual rights in it[9].

It is clear that a person who owns property, either in law or equity, and either solely or jointly, has an insurable interest in it. Similarly, a person who may be exposed to legal liability as a result of an event has an insurable interest in it, so that the bailee of goods has an insurable interest in them, as does a person who bears the risk of loss. Thus a buyer to whom risk, but not property, has passed under a contract of sale of goods has an insurable interest in the goods[10]. An unpaid seller who retains possession of goods has an insurable interest to the extent of his lien over the goods[11]. It is also clear that the nature of the interest required may vary according to the type of insurance. A person who has insufficient interest to insure property against loss may have sufficient interest in it to insure against losses arising from its loss[12]. So, for instance, a person who has contracted to buy goods but to whom neither risk of loss of, nor property in, the goods has passed, has insufficient interest in them to insure them against loss; but if he has contracted to resell them as specific goods he may have sufficient interest in them to insure against loss of the expected profits arising from the anticipated sale. Similarly, a manufacturer who may be exposed to product liability claims has sufficient interest to insure against that liability.

However, where the insured has only a limited interest in property, such as a co-owner of property, or a bailee, his right to recover from the insurer is limited to the extent of his own interest, unless the contract on its true construction waives the need for insurable interest, or extends to cover the interests of other persons interested in the property.

1   *Prudential Staff Union v Hall* [1947] KB 685.
2   Life Assurance Act 1774.
3   See *Mark Rowlands Ltd v Berni Inns Ltd* [1986] QB 211, [1985] 3 All ER 473, CA; cf *Re King* [1963] Ch 459, [1963] 1 All ER 781, CA. The application of the Act was not considered in *Lonsdale & Thompson v Black Arrow Group plc* [1993] Ch 361, [1993] 3 All ER 648. In *Davjoyda Estates Ltd v National Insurance Co of New Zealand* (1965) 69 SRNSW 381 the court followed the line in *Re King* and held that the Act does apply to real property insurance. See generally Birds, *Modern Insurance Law* (4th edn, 1997) pp 69–71.
4   [1994] 2 AC 199, [1994] 1 All ER 213; see Birds [1994] JBL 386.

5 [1994] 1 All ER 213 at 224, approving *Mark Rowlands Ltd v Berni Inns Ltd* [1986] QB 211, [1985] 3 All ER 473, CA.
6 (1806) 2 Bos & PNR 269 at 321, HL.
7 It was expressed by Lawrence J in *Lucena v Crauford* at 302 and adopted by the Canadian Supreme Court in *Constitution Insurance Co of Canada v Kosmopoulos* (1987) 34 DLR (4th) 208.
8 [1925] AC 619, HL.
9 He could have insured his shares.
10 *Inglis v Stock* (1885) 10 App Cas 263, HL.
11 Sale of Goods Act 1979, s 41, see 18.3.1.
12 *Glengate-KG Properties Ltd v Norwich Union Fire Insurance Society Ltd* [1996] 2 All ER 487.

35.1.4 *Insurable interest in marine insurance*

In marine insurance, 'every person has an insurable interest who is interested in a marine adventure'[1] including where he stands in any legal or equitable relation to the adventure 'or to any insurable property at risk therein'[2]. It is sufficient that the insured has acquired an interest by the time of loss, provided that at the time the policy was effected he had an expectation of acquiring an interest[3].

1 Marine Insurance Act 1906, s 4.
2 Marine Insurance Act 1906, s 5.
3 Marine Insurance Act 1906, s 4(2).

35.1.5 *Insurance of interests of third parties*

Where a policy of insurance is effected by a person without any interest, or only a limited interest, in the subject matter, the question arises whether third parties with an interest in the policy can take the benefit of it. The problem arises in relation to property insurance, and a distinction must be drawn between insurance of real property and other property. It may be particularly significant in the context of commercial operations: for instance, a bailee or carrier of goods may insure them, and it may be necessary to decide if that policy covers the interest of the owner of the goods. A similar question may arise where the seller of goods remains in possession after property has passed to the buyer and the goods are damaged without fault on the part of the seller: in many cases the goods may not be covered by the buyer's insurance, and it may be important to decide if the buyer is protected by the seller's insurance.

   In the case of insurance on goods it is clear that the insured who has an interest in the property can recover to the extent of his interest. Thus, for instance, a bailee, such as a warehouseman or carrier, can claim on a policy on the goods for any damage to goods bailed with him for which he is liable in law. However, if damage is caused wholly accidentally, the insured bailee will have no interest which will justify recovery. In that case the question arises whether the owner of the goods can recover for the loss. The answer will depend on whether, on the proper construction of the policy, it extends to the owner's interest. In *North British and Mercantile Insurance Co v Moffatt*[1] it was held that a warehouse company's policy on goods in their possession which covered goods 'in trust or on commission for which they are responsible' only covered the bailee's own interest. The crucial words were 'for which they are responsible' and, in contrast, in *Waters and Steel v Monarch Fire and Life Assurance Co*[2] a policy held by a bailee covering goods 'in trust or on commission' was held to cover the owner's interest. Similarly, the owner's interest was covered by a carrier's policy in *Hepburn v A Tomlinson (Hauliers) Ltd*[3], where the carrier had an interest and the owners of the goods were expressly named in the policy. The terms of the policy were held to be consistent with it being a goods policy, rather than a mere liability policy.

Even if the insured has no interest, he may be able to recover on the policy provided the requirement of insurable interest is waived[4].

Similar issues arise in the context of large-scale construction and engineering projects, when a main contractor seeks to effect insurance on the whole of the contract works to protect itself and sub-contractors working on the project[5]. Difficult questions then arise if a breach of contract by one of the sub-contractors causes a loss covered by the policy to one of the other contractors and the insurer, having compensated the victim of the breach, seeks to exercise rights of subrogation against the sub-contractor in breach[6].

If the policy is construed to cover the interest of the third party as well as of the insured, there is a second question: can the third party enforce the contract himself, or can he require the named insured to enforce the policy for his benefit? If the insured does claim, he will hold the proceeds for the third party, either on trust, or subject to a duty to account.

Prior to 1999 the third party could only enforce the contract by invoking agency principles. The third party may now be able to enforce the policy without invoking agency reasoning on the basis of the Contracts (Rights of Third Parties) Act 1999.

It is well established that the third party can enforce a contract of insurance made in his name and with his prior authority, in accordance with straightforward agency reasoning. This is a simple case of disclosed, authorised agency[7]. The third party will often not be named in the policy, but it seems that this will not be fatal to his intervention and, provided that he can establish that he authorised the named insured to obtain cover on his behalf, the third party will be able to enforce the contract either as an unnamed or an undisclosed principal. In *Siu Yin Kwan v Eastern Insurance Co Ltd*[8] the Privy Council held that a contract of insurance is not so personal as to preclude the intervention of an undisclosed principal. The third party will therefore be entitled to take the benefit of the policy unless excluded by its terms[9]. In some cases this may be a commercially convenient result and it was probably correct on the facts of *Siu Yin*[10]. Allowing the intervention of an undisclosed principal on a contract of insurance could, however, give rise to difficult questions: the contract of insurance is of the utmost good faith and requires the insured to make full disclosure of all material facts[11]: in many cases the identity of the insured party is likely to be a material fact.

If the third party did not authorise the first insured to contract on his behalf he may be able to take the benefit of the insurance by ratifying it. To do so he must establish that the named insured purported to act on his behalf and, if he is not named in the policy, that he was identifiable as a member of a class of persons protected by and referred to in the policy[12]. Even if these requirements are satisfied, the third party will generally not seek to ratify until he wishes to rely on the policy. In *Grover & Grover v Matthews*[13] it was held that that a policy of insurance other than marine insurance[14] cannot be ratified after the loss insured against has occurred but more recently, in *National Oilwell (UK) Ltd v Davy Offshore Ltd*[15] it was said, obiter, that there is no general rule prohibiting ratification after loss. This would be commercially convenient and it is to be hoped that this line will be upheld.

The third party will now be able to enforce the policy without invoking agency reasoning if he can rely on the Contracts (Rights of Third Parties) Act 1999. There is no doubt that the Act applies to contracts of insurance; several of the examples of its anticipated operation given by the Law Commission were of insurance contracts[16]. The Act will allow the third party to enforce a policy made for his benefit if either (a) the policy expressly provides that he is to be able to enforce or (b) the policy purports to confer a benefit on him, unless it appears on its proper construction that it was not intended that he should be entitled to enforce it[17]. He must be identified in the policy by name, description or as a member of a class. So a works policy taken out by a contractor and expressed to be for the benefit of all sub-contractors, employees and agents would be enforceable by a sub-contractor, unless it is established that it was not intended that the sub-contractor should be able to enforce it[18].

The position now is therefore that the third party can enforce the policy:

(a) under the 1999 Act if he is identified in the policy and it expressly provides for him to be able to enforce;
(b) on the basis of agency if the insured acted with his prior authority, regardless of whether or not he is identified in the policy;
(c) under the 1999 Act even though the policy does not expressly provide for him to be able to enforce, unless it is established that it was not intended that he should be able to enforce;
(d) by ratifying, even though the insured did not have his authority and he is not identified in the policy, provided that the insured purported to act on his behalf.

Subject to the difficulties which may arise where the third party intervenes as an undisclosed principal, the first two situations are relatively straightforward. The second two may give rise to difficult questions of construction. It has been suggested earlier that the fact that the insured purports to contract as agent for the third party may exclude the operation of the 1999 Act[19]. However, it will generally be more advantageous for the third party to rely on the 1999 Act rather than on ratification since under the Act there is no equivalent to the rule precluding ratification after loss.

There may still, however, be cases where the third party is not entitled to enforce. In *DG Finance Ltd v Scott*[20] a finance company let a trailer to a haulage contractor under a contract of hire purchase. The contract required the hirer to insure the trailer for its full value and to notify the insurer of the company's interest. The hirer insured the trailer but failed to notify the company's interest as required. It was held that the finance company had no right to enforce the policy. There was no agency as the hirer had not intended to insure for their benefit. Since they were not identified in the policy, they were not entitled to ratify. The case was decided before the passing of the 1999 Act but it is submitted that the result would now be no different. The company was not identified in the policy and would therefore be unable to rely on the 1999 Act.

1 (1871) LR 7 CP 25; but contrast *Petrofina (UK) Ltd v Magnaload Ltd* [1984] QB 127, [1983] 3 All ER 35.
2 (1856) 5 E & B 870.
3 [1966] AC 451, [1966] 1 All ER 418, HL.
4 See *Williams v Baltic Insurance Association of London* [1924] 2 KB 282.
5 See *Petrofina (UK) Ltd v Magnaload Ltd* [1984] QB 127, [1983] 3 All ER 35; *Stone Vickers Ltd v Appledore Ferguson Shipbuilders Ltd* [1991] 2 Lloyd's Rep 288; revsd [1992] 2 Lloyd's Rep 578, CA.
6 See 35.7.2.
7 See 5.1.
8 [1994] 2 AC 199, [1994] 1 All ER 213; see Birds [1994] JBL 386.
9 See 5.3.2.
10 The facts seem closer to a case of an unnamed rather than undisclosed principal but the judge at first instance found that the principal was undisclosed.
11 See 35.3.1.
12 *National Oilwell (UK) Ltd v Davy Offshore Ltd* [1993] 2 Lloyd's Rep 582. Colman J added that it must be shown that the person making the contract intended to act on behalf of the party seeking

to ratify but this is inconsistent with general agency principles (see 4.7.1), and it seems that the judge was concerned with the question whether, on its true construction, the contract purported to be made on behalf of the party seeking to ratify.

13   [1910] 2 KB 401.
14   Marine Insurance Act 1906, s 6.
15   [1993] Lloyd's Rep 582.
16   See Law Commission 242, Cmnd 3329, *Privity of Contract: Contracts for the Benefit of Third Parties*, July 1996, paras 7.31–7.35.
17   Contracts (Rights of Third Parties) Act 1999, s 1; see 2.7.2.
18   Compare *Trident General Insurance Co Ltd v McNiece Bros Pty Ltd* (1988) 80 ALR 574; see Law Commission 242, Cmnd 3329, *Privity of Contract: Contracts for the Benefit of Third Parties*, July 1996, para 7.50.
19   See 4.7.4.
20   [1999] Lloyd's rep IR 387, CA.

35.1.5.1   *Life Assurance Act 1774, s 2*

The insurance of third party interests is further complicated by the Life Assurance Act 1774. As already noted, the scope of application of the Act is not clear. If it applies, the Act makes the policy void unless the insured has an interest in the property, and requires any other person for whose benefit the policy is made to be named in it. In *Siu Yin Kwan v Eastern Insurance Co Ltd*[1] managing agents had purported to effect an employer's liability policy on behalf of the owners of a ship; however, the policy named the agents as 'proposer' and made no mention of the owners. The insurer therefore argued that the policy was void by virtue of the 1774 Act. The Privy Council held that the Act does not apply to indemnity insurance. If correct, this removes an obstacle to allowing third parties to enforce contracts of insurance intended to protect them; however, as already noted, there are authorities which suggest that the 1774 Act does apply at least to policies of insurance on real property. In *Davjoyda Estates Ltd v National Insurance Co of New Zealand*[2] it was held that the effect of the 1774 Act on real property insurance is to require the insured either to have an interest or, if he makes the policy on behalf of a third party, to name that party in the policy. If this approach is correct, it means that where the insured has a limited interest in the property, for instance as a tenant, he may insure for the full value of the property, and his right to recover beyond the value of his own interest will depend on the principles discussed above. Where the insured has no interest, the person with an interest must be named in the policy; if not, the policy is illegal; if he is named he will generally be able to rely on the 1999 Act and/or to establish an agency.

1   [1994] 2 AC 199, [1994] 1 All ER 213.
2   (1965) 69 SRNSW 381. See Birds, *Modern Insurance Law* (4th edn, 1997) pp 69–71.

35.1.6   *Transfer of property and insurance*

Where a person who has insured property disposes of it, several difficult questions may arise if the property is subsequently damaged or destroyed. It is well settled that the sale of insured property does not per se transfer to the purchaser the benefit of any insurance on the property[1]. Moreover, if the transferor parts with all interest in the insured property, the policy lapses[2]. However, the benefit of a policy is assignable[3], provided the requirements of s 136 of the Law of Property Act 1925, including giving notice to the insurer, are satisfied.

Often compliance with those requirements may be impracticable. In the case of real property, s 47 of the Law of Property Act 1925 may be relevant. In that case, if the insured property is damaged after the exchange of contracts, at which point risk passes to the buyer, the buyer is entitled to the benefit of any moneys recovered by the seller. The section is applicable to contracts for the sale of goods, but it will rarely be relevant: if property and risk have passed to the buyer at the time of damage, the seller will be unable to recover as he will no longer have any insurable interest, while if risk has not passed to the buyer, he may reject the goods.

There is, in theory, no reason why the policy of insurance itself should not be assigned. However, as a personal contract, the consent of the insurer is required. Moreover, the policy must be assigned at the same time as the assignment of the insured property.

These restrictions mean that assignment of the benefit of the policy, or of the policy itself, is of little practical value in commercial transactions. However, there clearly are situations in which assignment of the policy will be commercially desirable. For instance, life assurance policies are often used as security for loans; and, as we have seen, the transferability of marine insurance policies is essential to the free flow of international trade. There are therefore special statutory rules facilitating the assignment of such policies.

The benefit of life policies may be assigned under s 136 of the Law of Property Act, but a more favourable system is provided by the Policies of Assurance Act 1867. Consideration of its provisions is outside the scope of this book. The assignment of marine insurance depends on the provisions of the Marine Insurance Act 1906, which provides that a policy of marine insurance is assignable unless it contains terms expressly prohibiting assignment[4]. Clearly, where goods are to be resold, a policy forbidding assignment will be unacceptable to the insured, or to his buyer. The Act allows a policy to be assigned after loss, so that a CIF seller can assign the policy, allowing the buyer to recover, even after the goods are lost[5]. However, since the policy lapses when the insured parts with all interest in the goods, an assignment after transfer of property and risk will normally be ineffective[6], unless it is made in pursuance of an agreement made while he still had an interest[7].

1   *Rayner v Preston* (1881) 18 Ch D 1, CA.
2   *Rogerson v Scottish Automobile and General Insurance Co Ltd* (1931) 48 TLR 17, HL.
3   For assignment of contractual rights see 27.3 above.
4   Marine Insurance Act 1906, s 50.
5   See 33.2.6.
6   *North of England Oil-Cake Co v Archangel Insurance Co* (1875) LR 10 QB 249, confirmed by Marine Insurance Act 1906, s 51.
7   Marine Insurance Act 1906, s 51.

35.2   Form and formation

All contracts of insurance are subject to the general law of contract, and thus there will only be a valid contract if the legal requirements for the creation of a valid contract are satisfied. In particular, the parties must have reached agreement on all the essential terms of the contract – the premium, the nature of the risk and the duration of the policy – and there must be an effective offer and acceptance. However, there is generally no requirement for contracts of insurance to be in any particular form. There are exceptions: notably, contracts of marine insurance must be contained in a policy, containing certain terms stipulated by statute[1].

Provided that the requirements of offer and acceptance are satisfied, there is therefore no reason why a valid contract of insurance could not be concluded wholly orally. In practice, however, a standard formation procedure tends to be followed. The applicant for insurance fills in a proposal form, providing information about the risk to be insured, on which the insurer will base its decision whether or not to insure, and, if so, at what price. The proposal will normally be regarded as an offer, which the insurer is free to accept or reject. If it 'accepts' the proposal subject to conditions, for instance by providing that the insurance is not to come into force until the first premium is paid, the insurer probably makes a counter-offer, so that no contract comes into force until the first premium is paid, accepting the counter-offer. However, the proposal will normally be construed as an offer to enter into a contract on the insurer's standard terms, so that they will be incorporated into the contract[2]. In most cases the proposal form will expressly refer to them.

In accordance with the general law of contract, acceptance by either party will only be effective when communicated to the other. However, there are exceptions: if the insurer issues a policy under seal, the contract is immediately binding. Where the offer is made by the insurer, the insured may accept by acting on the offer, for instance by an insured driving a car in reliance on a cover note issued by an insurer[3], or, in some cases, by doing nothing at all but merely retaining the policy without rejecting it[4].

Once the requirements of offer and acceptance are satisfied, there will be a binding contract, although in certain cases a 'cooling off' period is prescribed by statute in order to protect consumers[5].

In some cases, especially motor insurance, the insured is initially issued with a temporary cover note pending consideration of the proposal. A cover note is a full binding contract, although normally only effective for a limited period. Where a cover note is issued in response to a proposal by the insured, it operates as an acceptance, or counter-offer, by the insurer. Where, as commonly happens, a cover note is issued on expiry of an existing policy, it operates as an offer by the insurer, which the insured is free to accept or reject. Cover notes normally expressly incorporate the insurer's standard terms; if not, the terms are not impliedly incorporated[6].

A different procedure is adopted where contracts of insurance are made at Lloyd's. The proposer instructs a broker, who prepares a slip containing details of the insurance required, and circulates this to underwriters. An underwriter who wishes to accept part of the risk does so by initialling the slip, indicating the amount of the risk he is prepared to undertake. It seems that each underwriter is bound as soon as he initials the slip[7].

Most indemnity policies are for a fixed term. On renewal a new contract is formed, so that there must be a fresh offer and acceptance. Generally, the insured is not required to complete a fresh proposal, and the offer for the new contract is made by the insurer; until the contract is renewed by the insured accepting the insurer's offer, it seems that he is not covered, although the practice of insurers is to allow a limited number of 'days of grace' so that the policy is renewed if the insured pays the renewal premium during the days of grace. In contrast, a life assurance policy is probably an entire contract, so that there is no question of renewal; however, the policy will normally be expressed to lapse if the premium is not paid. Again, the policy will normally allow a period of grace for payment, and it is clear that, provided the premium is paid during the days of grace, the policy remains in force[8].

1   Marine Insurance Act 1906, s 22. There are also statutory requirements for insurers to provide prospective insureds with certain pre-contract information: see Insurance Companies Act 1982, Sch 2E. Contracts of life insurance are subject to statutory rights of cancellation under ss 75–77 of the 1982 Act and/or the Financial Services (Cancellation) Rules 1989.

2   *General Accident Insurance Corpn v Cronk* (1901) 17 TLR 233.
3   *Taylor v Allon* [1966] 1 QB 304, [1965] 1 All ER 557.
4   *Rust v Abbey Life Assurance Co Ltd* [1979] 2 Lloyd's 334, CA (insured retained policy for seven months without dispute).
5   Insurance Companies Act 1982, ss 75–77; Financial Services Act 1986, s 51; Financial Services (Cancellation) Rules 1989.
6   *Re Coleman's Depositories Ltd and Life and Health Assurance Association* [1907] 2 KB 798, CA.
7   *General Reinsurance Corpn v Forsakringsaktiebolaget Fennia Patria* [1983] QB 856, CA.
8   *Stuart v Freeman* [1903] 1 KB 47, CA.

35.3   Misrepresentation and non-disclosure

Since the insurer's decision whether or not to insure, and, if so, on what terms, is based on the information supplied in the proposal form, the insured's statements in the proposal are particularly important. The proposal form may include a term converting all such statements into important terms of the contract[1]: if so, any false statement will be a serious breach, entitling the insurer to repudiate the contract. According to the Statement of General Insurance Practice[2], such 'basis of the contract' clauses should not be used in contracts for non-business insurance. However, any false statement in the proposal, even if it does not become a term of the contract, will be a misrepresentation, and the insurer is entitled to avoid the contract if the insured makes any material misrepresentation during negotiations for the contract[3]. Although the insurer's right to avoid for misrepresentation is put on a statutory basis for contracts of marine insurance, it is broadly equivalent to the right to rescind for misrepresentation in the law of contract[4]. A material representation is one which would influence the judgment of a prudent insurer in fixing the premium or deciding whether to accept the risk[5], and a misrepresentation may be a statement of fact, expectation or belief[6]. However, a statement of expectation or belief is true if made in good faith[7]. Thus it has been held that when an insured makes a statement of opinion or belief, all that is required is that he should be honest; there is no requirement that there be reasonable grounds for his belief[8]. There seems no reason in principle why the insurer should not also be entitled to claim damages where the misrepresentation is fraudulent or negligent, in accordance with general principles[9], but in practice the insurer will normally seek only to avoid the contract and thus escape liability under it. Similarly, the contract will be voidable in accordance with general principles if the insured is induced to enter into the contract by any misrepresentation by the insurer.

In practice the insurer's right to rescind for misrepresentation is of relatively little significance because, unlike most other commercial contracts, a contract of insurance is a contract *uberrimae fidei* and the parties therefore owe each other a duty of the utmost good faith. This is a mutual duty[10] but in practice its impact on the insured is much greater than on the insurer. It applies throughout the contract and involves a duty not to make fraudulent claims on the contract[11]. Its most important aspect, however, is that it imposes a duty of disclosure on the parties.

1   Confusingly, important terms in contracts of insurance are called 'warranties': see 35.4.1.
2   Paragraph 1(b).
3   Marine Insurance Act 1906, s 20(1).
4   See 2.4.2.1.
5   Marine Insurance Act 1906, s 20(2).
6   Section 20(3).
7   Section 20(5).

8 See *Economides v Commercial Union Assurance plc* [1997] 3 All ER 636, CA. On the facts it could have been argued that the insured did have reasonable grounds for his belief: see the comments of Sir Iain Glidewell (at 655).
9 See 2.4.2. However, the court will generally not exercise its discretion under s 2(2) of the Misrepresentation Act 1967 to award damages in lieu of rescission in relation to a contract of insurance: see *Highlands Insurance Co v Continental Insurance Co* [1987] 1 Lloyd's Rep 109n.
10 See *Banque Financière de la Cite v Westgate Insurance Co Ltd* [1991] AC 249, [1990] 2 All ER 947, HL, below.
11 *Black King Shipping Corpn v Massie, The Litsion Pride* [1985] 1 Lloyd's Rep 437; *Manifest Shipping & Co Ltd v Uni-Polaris Insurance Co Ltd & La Réunion Européene, The Star Sea* [1997] 1 Lloyd's Rep 360; *Galloway v Guardian Royal Exchange (UK) Ltd* [1999] Lloyd's Rep IR 209.

35.3.1 *Nature of the duty of disclosure*

The parties to the contract of insurance are under a mutual duty to disclose all material facts relating to the insurance. As noted above, although the duty applies equally to both parties, the duty on the insured is particularly important. A failure to disclose material facts will make the contract voidable at the instance of the insurer, in the same way as for misrepresentation.

The justification for the rule, as explained by Lord Mansfield in the leading case of *Carter v Boehm*[1], is that the information upon which the insurer evaluates the risk, and decides whether to insure and, if so, on what terms, 'lie most commonly in the knowledge of the insured only'. Thus:

'As the underwriter knows nothing and the man who comes to him to ask him to insure knows everything, it is the duty of the assured . . . to make a full disclosure to the underwriter without being asked, of all the material circumstances'[2].

The duty is not limited to disclosing facts about which express questions are asked in the proposal form, although the fact that specific questions are asked may be construed as waiving the requirement to disclose other information[3].

The rule has been applied stringently; the insured may be in breach of duty even though he acts in good faith and accurately answers all the questions put to him by the insurer, and it may be doubted whether the rule is still justified, especially in view of the ease of modern communications and the extensive use by insurers of standard form proposal forms, which enable them to ask specific questions about matters relevant to the contract. In 1957 the Law Reform Committee and in 1980 the Law Commission proposed reform to the disclosure rule[4]. The proposed reforms have not been implemented; instead, insurers have effectively restricted the disclosure rule by adopting a voluntary statement of practice. This requires the insurer to draw the duty of disclosure to the attention of the insured in the proposal form[5], to ask specific questions about matters which 'insurers have found generally to be material'[6] and not to repudiate liability to indemnify the insured on the grounds of non-disclosure of a fact which the insured could not reasonably be expected to have disclosed[7]. However, this statement of practice only applies to non-business insurance; in the context of policies relating to business and commercial operations, the common law duty of disclosure will apply with its full rigour.

The insured's duty of disclosure is said to derive from the nature of the insurance contract as one of 'the utmost good faith'. It is clear, however, that to the extent that non-disclosure may enable an insurer to avoid a policy on a relatively trivial ground, its effect is often to sanction what one would otherwise consider 'bad faith' conduct by the insurer. There are signs in recent cases that the courts have recognised the potential harshness of the non-disclosure rule and are willing to limit its scope at least in relation to private and small business insurance. As Staughton LJ recently put it:

> 'Avoidance for non-disclosure is a drastic remedy. It enables the insurer to disclaim liability after, and not before, he has discovered that the risk turns out to be a bad one; it leaves the insured without the protection which he thought he had contracted for'[8].

1   (1766) 3 Burr 1905 at 1909.
2   Per Scrutton LJ in *Rozanes v Bowen* (1928) 32 Ll L Rep 98 at 102, CA.
3   See *Schoolman v Hall* [1951] 1 Lloyd's Rep 139. Contrast *Hair v Prudential Assurance Co Ltd* [1983] 2 Lloyd's Rep 667, where it was held that a warning on a proposal form of the need for disclosure had the effect of limiting the proposer's duty to answering the question on the form.
4   Law Commission 104: *Insurance Law: Non-disclosure and breach of warranty* (Cmnd 8064).
5   Statement of General Insurance Practice, para 1(c)(i), (ii).
6   Paragraph 1(d).
7   Paragraph 2(b)(i).
8   *Kausar v Eagle Star Insurance Co Ltd* (1996) [2000] Lloyd's rep IR 154 at 157. See also *Economides v Commercial Union Assurance plc* [1997] 3 All ER 636.

35.3.2   Nature of the duty

The insured is required to disclose all material facts known to him. According to s 18(1) of the Marine Insurance Act 1906, the insured must disclose facts of which he has constructive notice: 'the assured is deemed to know every circumstance which, in the ordinary course of business ought to be known by him'. It has been held that the same rule applies to non-marine insurance[1]. It does not, however, apply to insurance by private individuals, since a private individual acting in a non-business capacity cannot know anything 'in the ordinary course of business'[2]. A private individual therefore satisfies the duty of disclosure if he acts honestly and discloses material facts known to him, provided that he does not deliberately shut his eyes to obvious facts. It has been held that a principal is not required on this basis to disclose frauds committed against him by his agent[3] – of which he could hardly be expected to know – but where an insurance is effected through an agent, the agent must disclose 'every material circumstance' known to him, including information which, in the ordinary course of business, he ought to know or which ought to have been communicated to him[4].

The Marine Insurance Act 1906 provides that a fact is material if it 'would influence the judgment of a prudent insurer in fixing the premium or determining whether he will take the risk'[5] and this definition of 'materiality' has been held to be generally applicable, since the 1906 Act merely codified existing common law[6]. The House of Lords considered the statutory definition of 'materiality' in *Pan Atlantic Insurance Co Ltd v Pine Top Insurance Co Ltd*[7] and, by a bare majority, held that a fact is material if it is one which would have an effect on the mind of a reasonably prudent insurer considering whether or not to accept the proposed risk, even if it would not have altered his actual decision. In effect, therefore, a material fact is one which a reasonably prudent insurer would want to know when making an assessment of the risk. This test, which confirms earlier authority[8], has been criticised as too favourable to the insurer[9]. The House of Lords did qualify it, however, by going on to hold that the insurer can only avoid a policy on the grounds of non-disclosure of a material fact if the non-disclosure did actually induce him to enter into the contract. The result is that the right to avoid a policy for non-disclosure depends on a two-stage test; however, the second stage is purely subjective. Provided that the fact in question would have 'influenced' the decision of a reasonably prudent insurer in the sense recognised by the House of Lords, it is irrelevant that it would have made no difference to the actual decision of such an insurer if it did in fact induce the entry into the contract of the actual insurer. Moreover, it seems that the second stage requires only that the non-disclosure should have been *an* inducement for the insurer, not necessarily the decisive inducement, and that in an appropriate case once it is shown that the fact not disclosed was material, the insurer may be able to rely on a presumption of inducement without adducing evidence of the effect of the non-disclosure on him[10].

The remedy for non-disclosure is avoidance of the contract, and this is so even if, had it been disclosed, the insurer would have accepted the risk but at a higher premium. It is thus irrelevant that the insured did not think the fact material: 'it seems that a fact may be material to insurers . . . which would not necessarily appear to a proposer for insurance, however honest and careful, to be one which he ought to disclose'[11]. Whether or not a fact is material is a question of fact, and the trial judge will normally be guided by expert evidence from insurers[12].

In general, it seems that facts will be regarded as material if they affect either the physical or moral hazard involved in the insurance. Thus, for instance, the construction of a building would be relevant to the physical hazard in a fire policy on the building; similarly, the nature and value of the goods would be material to a policy covering goods against theft[13], and in a contract covering goods carried by sea, whether the cargo is to be carried on deck would be material.

Facts relating to the moral hazard are those relating to the insured, or his family and associates, themselves. Thus facts relating to the insured's previous insurance history, including both claims and refusals of insurance[14], will be material as relating to the moral hazard. Similarly, if the insured has a criminal record, facts relating to that record may be material. Clearly, the fact that the insured has been convicted of an offence related to the subject matter of the insurance will be material, but serious offences may be material even if they are unrelated to the subject matter of the insurance, especially if they were offences of dishonesty[15]. The only limitation seems to be that there will be no duty on the insured to disclose convictions which are spent under the Rehabilitation of Offenders Act 1974. However, even under that Act, convictions resulting in sentences of more than two and a half years' imprisonment can never be spent.

The only limitations on the duty of disclosure are that the insured is not required to disclose facts of which he is not aware[16], which diminish, rather than increase the risk, which are already known to the insurer or his agent[17], which are covered by any express or implied warranty in the contract, or whose disclosure is waived by the insurer[18].

The duty continues up to the time of formation of the contract. Thus if the material facts change between the completion of the proposal and its acceptance by the insurer, the insured must disclose the change[19]. The insured is under no duty to disclose changes of material facts during the currency of the contract[20] unless either the change is so fundamental as to change the nature of the insurance[21] or there is an express contractual requirement to do so[22]. Some policies, especially for insurance against fire, do include such 'increase of risk' clauses. However, renewal of insurance involves the formation of a new contract; the duty of disclosure therefore arises anew when the contract is renewed, even though there may be no proposal form on a renewal.

1 *PCW Syndicates v PCW Reinsurers* [1996] 1 All ER 774, CA.
2 *Economides v Commercial Union Assurance plc* [1997] 3 All ER 636. See Clarke [1988] JBL 206.
3 *PCW Syndicates v PCW Reinsurers* [1996] 1 All ER 774, CA; *Arab Bank plc v Zurich Insurance Co* [1999] 1 Lloyd's Rep 262.
4 Marine Insurance Act 1906, s 19.
5 Section 18(2).
6 *Lambert v Co-operative Insurance Society* [1975] 2 Lloyd's Rep 485, CA.
7 [1995] 1 AC 501, [1994] 3 All ER 581; see Birds and Hird (1996) 59 MLR 285.
8 See *Container Transport International Inc v Oceanus Mutual Underwriting Association (Bermuda) Ltd* [1984] 1 Lloyd's Rep 476, followed in *Highlands Insurance Co v Continental Insurance Co* [1987] 1 Lloyd's Rep 109n. Contrast the view taken in Australia in *Barclays Holdings (Australia) Pty Ltd v British National Insurance Co Ltd* [1987] 8 NSWLR 514; see *Yeo Hwee Ying* [1990] JBL 97.
9 See eg Clarke [1988] JBL 298; [1993] LMCLQ 297; [1994] LMCLQ 473; Hird [1994] JBL 194; Birds and Hird (1996) 59 MLR 285.
10 *St Paul Fire and Marine (UK) Ltd v McConnell Dowell Constructors Ltd* [1996] 1 All ER 96, CA; see Hird [1995] JBL 608.
11 Report of the Law Reform Committee (Cmnd 62) (1957).
12 The judge is not necessarily bound by such opinions: see *Roselodge Ltd v Castle* [1966] 2 Lloyd's Rep 113; *Reynolds v Phoenix Assurance Co* [1978] 2 Lloyd's Rep 440.
13 See *Anglo-African Merchants v Bayley* [1970] 1 QB 311, [1969] 2 All ER 421.
14 *Glicksman v Lancashire and General Assurance Co* [1927] AC 139, HL.
15 See *Lambert v Co-operative Insurance Society* [1975] 2 Lloyd's Rep 485, CA; see also *Woolcott v Sun Alliance and London Insurance* [1978] 1 All ER 1253, [1978] 1 WLR 493 (conviction for robbery material in application for fire insurance).
16 *Joel v Law Union and Crown Insurance Co* [1908] 2 KB 863, CA.
17 Including facts which are matters of common knowledge, or which an insurer 'in the ordinary course of his business as such' ought to know.
18 Marine Insurance Act 1906, s 18(5). See *Marc Rich & Co AG v Portman* [1997] 1 Lloyd's Rep 225.
19 *Locker & Woolf Ltd v Western Australia Insurance Co Ltd* [1936] 1 KB 408, CA.
20 *Pim v Reid* (1843) 6 Man & G 1.
21 *Kausar v Eagle Star Insurance Co Ltd* (1996) [2000] Lloyd's Rep IR 154.
22 *Kausar v Eagle Star Insurance Co Ltd* (1996) [2000] Lloyd's Rep IR; *New Hampshire Insurance Co v Mirror Group Newspapers Ltd* [1996] CLC 1696.

35.3.3 The insurer's duty

As noted above, the duty of utmost good faith, and the duty of disclosure it includes, are mutual duties, so that they apply equally to the insurer as to the insured. This was recognised in *Carter v Boehm* itself:

> 'The policy would equally be void against the underwriter if he concealed; as if he insured a ship for voyage which he privately knew to be arrived: and an action would lie to recover the premiums'[1].

The existence of a duty on the insurer was confirmed in *Banque Financière de la Cité v Westgate Insurance Co Ltd*. However, the decision in that case also revealed serious limitations on the utility of the duty. The Court of Appeal[2] held that the insurer owed the insured a duty to disclose 'all facts known to him which are material either to the nature of the risk sought to be covered or the recoverability of a claim under the policy which a prudent insured would take into account in deciding whether or not to place the risk for which he seeks cover with that insurer'[3]. However, the only remedy for breach of that duty was to rescind the contract; the insured was not entitled to damages. In most cases of non-disclosure by the insurer, the right to rescind will be practically worthless. The decision was confirmed by the House of Lords[4] on other grounds, but Lord Templeman expressly confirmed the view of the Court of Appeal that breach of the duty by the insurer does not give rise to a claim for damages.

The limitations on the insurer's duty are highlighted by the decision in *Norwich Union Life Insurance Co Ltd v Qureshi*[5]. NU marketed a scheme for Lloyd's names to guarantee the names' liabilities at Lloyd's. Under the scheme the names were required to take out endowment policies with NU and then to assign the policies, and charge other property to NU as security for sums paid under the guarantee. Subsequently, the names suffered heavy losses at Lloyd's and it was discovered that, at the time of marketing the scheme, NU had known that some Lloyd's syndicates were about to suffer heavy losses. The names argued that had that information been disclosed they would never have entered into their contracts with NU but would have ceased to underwrite Lloyd's business. They therefore claimed that, in accordance with the duty of good faith, NU should have disclosed the information, and claimed damages. The Court of Appeal rejected the claim on two grounds. The duty of disclosure is limited to facts material to the risk underwritten. The insurance policies here were the life endowment policies taken out by the names. NU was therefore only obliged to disclose information material to the life risk insured. The non-disclosed information related not to that risk but to the decision to enter into the scheme as a whole and was not covered by the duty. Evans LJ recognised that 'the law is unattractive if it restricts the scope of [the duty of disclosure] to part only of what was, for both parties, a composite transaction' but concluded that it was not open to the Court of Appeal to hold that the duty 'goes beyond facts which are relevant to the insurance contract'. In any case, even if a claim were made out it would not entitle the names to damages.

1   (1766) 3 Burr 1905 at 1909, per Lord Mansfield.
2   [1990] 1 QB 665, [1989] 2 All ER 952.
3   Per Slade LJ at 772, 990.
4   [1991] 2 AC 249, [1990] 2 All ER 947. See also the decision of the Court of Appeal in *The Good Luck* [1990] 1 QB 818, [1989] 3 All ER 628.
5   [1999] 2 All ER (Comm) 707.

35.4   The terms of the contract

The contract of insurance will contain a number of terms, derived either from the policy, or from the proposal form. Most will impose obligations on the insured. The effect of breach of any of the terms by the insured will depend on the classification of the term in question. Confusingly, the terminology used to describe terms in contracts of insurance differs from that used in the general law of contract, and important terms are classified as 'warranties', whereas less important terms are labelled 'conditions'. Moreover, even this terminology is not used consistently, and the contract may contain a third category of term, the term 'descriptive of the risk'.

As explained elsewhere, there has in recent years been a change in the approach of the courts to the interpretation of contracts, in favour of a 'purposive' or 'commercial common sense' approach[1]. According to that approach, words are to be interpreted in their contractual and broader commercial context, in order to give effect to the overall purpose of the contract, and the court will lean against an interpretation which would produce absurd or unreasonable results. There is no doubt that that approach is as applicable to contracts of insurance as to other types of contract; indeed, several of the leading cases in which the 'new' approach has been propounded have been concerned with contracts of insurance[2]. The same approach applies to the classification of contract terms, and one consequence of the 'new' approach is that a court will not necessarily be bound by the description or classification of a term in the contract[3].

1 See 2.5.5.
2 See *Deutsche Genossenschaftsbank v Burnhope* [1995] 4 All ER 717; *Charter Reinsurance Co Ltd v Fagan* [1997] AC 180, [1996] 3 All ER 46.
3 See *Kler Knitwear Ltd v Lombard General Insurance Co Ltd* [2000] Lloyd's Rep IR 47.

35.4.1 *Warranties*

Major terms in insurance contracts are called 'warranties'. Until recently, it was widely thought that a warranty in a contract of insurance was the equivalent of a 'condition' in general contract law, so that a breach of warranty by the insured would give the insurer the right to terminate the contract. However, in *The Good Luck*[1] the House of Lords had to consider the effect of a breach of warranty in a contract of marine insurance. Section 33(3) of the Marine Insurance Act 1906 provides that:

> 'A warranty is a condition which must be exactly complied with whether it be material to the risk or not. If it be not so complied with . . . the insurer is discharged from liability from the date of breach the warranty, but without prejudice to any liability incurred by him before that date'.

Their Lordships therefore concluded that the effect of a breach of warranty in a contract of marine insurance is that the insurer is automatically discharged from liability, without the need for any positive action on his part to terminate the contract, because fulfilment of the warranty is a condition precedent to the insurer's liability.

Although strictly the decision in *The Good Luck* is concerned with the interpretation of the 1906 Act and warranties in marine insurance, it is clear that the same rule will apply to warranties in non-marine insurance[2]. However, the application of this principle to non-marine cases may pose some difficulties and a number of older cases may have to be reconsidered[3]. For instance, in *West v National Motor and Accident Insurance Union*[4] it was held that on a breach of warranty an insurer had either to terminate or affirm the contract as whole: he could not merely repudiate liability for an individual claim and lost his right to terminate if he insisted on a right under the policy to take a dispute to arbitration[5]. In *The Good Luck* Lord Goff made it clear that the effect of a breach of warranty is not to terminate the policy as such but to discharge the insurer from liability so that the remainder of the policy remains in force. Applying *The Good Luck*, the insurer in *West* could therefore have repudiated the particular claim while insisting on arbitration.

Although breach of warranty automatically discharges the insurer from liability, the Marine Insurance Act[6] and general insurance law both recognise that the insurer can waive the breach and he may be held to have done so if, for instance, he continues to accept premiums[7] or renews the policy, after becoming aware of the breach[8].

The precise effect of a breach of warranty will depend on whether it is a warranty of past or existing fact, or a continuing promissory warranty relating to the future. A statement in the proposal may be construed as a warranty merely of facts existing at the time the contract is made. If it is false at that time, there is a breach at that time and the insurer will automatically be discharged from liability: in effect, the risk under the policy will never attach, unless on discovering the breach the insurer waives it. Assuming that the insurer discovers the breach some time later but does not waive it, he will have to refund any premiums paid. The effect of breach of warranty of past or existing fact is therefore much like that of rescission for misrepresentation. However, provided a warranty of existing fact is true when made, there is no breach even if circumstances later change, although the policy may impose a duty on the insured to notify the insurer of the change in circumstances[9].

Conversely, if the warranty is construed as a continuing promissory warranty, the insured is treated as promising that the warranted state of affairs will continue to exist, so that any change will be a breach of warranty, discharging the insurer from liability as from the date of breach. In *The Good Luck* itself, a contract for the insurance of a ship contained a warranty that the ship would not go into certain prohibited high risk areas in a war zone. The warranty was broken and the insurer discharged from liability when the ship entered the prohibited area. In general, a warranty will only be interpreted as continuing, so that it relates to the future, if the language used clearly relates to the future. Thus in *Woolfall and Rimmer v Moyle*[10] a warranty that all the insured's plant and machinery 'are properly fenced and guarded' was held not to be a continuing warranty. There was therefore no breach, since the statement was true when made. However, the position may be different if the circumstances show that, even though the present tense is used, the warranty can only sensibly relate to the future. In *Beauchamp v National Mutual Indemnity Insurance Co Ltd*[11] the insured, a builder, undertook a contract to demolish a mill. He had never done any demolition work before and sought insurance in respect of the demolition contract. The proposal form asked 'Are any explosives used in your business?', to which the insured replied 'No'. It was held that this statement must be construed as relating to the future.

It now seems that a court will be reluctant to interpret a warranty as continuing unless it is in clear terms. For instance, in *Hussain v Brown*[12] the proposal form asked 'Are the premises fitted with any kind of intruder alarm?' and then asked for details of the system. The proposer answered 'Yes' and provided details. The Court of Appeal held that the statement gave rise only to a warranty of existing fact. It was not warranted that the premises would continue to be alarmed, or that the alarm would be kept in working order. As Saville LJ observed, if the proposer had answered 'No' to the question in the proposal form, he could not have been taken to be warranting that no alarm would ever be fitted. It had been argued that warranties relating to such matters as security and alarm systems in contracts of fire and burglary insurance must be interpreted as continuing as a matter of common sense, as they would otherwise be of no value to the insurer. The court in *Hussain* rejected this view: even a warranty of existing fact would have value for the insurer as showing what kind of person the insured was.

It is common for the proposal form, or the policy itself, to contain a provision which provides that the insured's answers to the questions on the proposal form shall form 'the basis of the contract'. The effect of this provision is to convert all of the insured's answers into warranties, allowing the insurer to terminate the contract if they prove false, regardless of whether or not they are material to the risk insured, and it may operate very harshly against the insured. In *Dawsons Ltd v Bonnin*[13] a proposal form for insurance of a lorry asked where the lorry was to be garaged, and contained a basis of the policy clause. The insured gave an incorrect address. It was held that the insurer could terminate the policy, and thus avoid liability for loss, even though the inaccurate statement was immaterial and unconnected to the loss. The result is that:

'by making the questions and answers and declarations on a proposal form the basis of the contract, and providing that in the event of any untruth the contract could be voidable, insurers succeeded in equipping themselves with a potential defence to an action on the policy much wider than that arising by virtue of the duty of disclosure'[14].

In light of the decision in *The Good Luck* the result is that, where the proposal contains a 'basis' clause, any false statement in the proposal automatically discharges the insurer from liability as from the moment of contract formation. The position of private policyholders is somewhat ameliorated by the Statement of General Insurance Practice, which provides that neither the proposal form nor the policy shall contain any term converting statements about present or past facts into warranties[15], but this protection is not available to business insureds.

The courts have recognised the potential harshness of classifying a term as a warranty.

'A continuing warranty is a draconian term . . . the breach of such a warranty produces an automatic cancellation of the cover, and the fact that a loss may have no connection at all with that breach is simply irrelevant . . . If underwriters want such protection then it is up to them to stipulate for it in clear terms'[16].

They therefore attempt to mitigate the effects of construing a clause as a warranty. In particular, warranties will be construed strictly contra proferentem: 'if there is any ambiguity, since it is the [insurers'] clause, the ambiguity will be resolved in favour of the assured'[17]. So, for instance, where a policy in several sections provided insurance against several different risks, including fire and theft, a warranty in the theft section that all burglar alarms at the premises would be fully operational when the premises were closed for business was construed as applying only to the theft section of the policy. The insurer was therefore not able to avoid liability for a claim for fire damage on the grounds that the burglar alarms at the premises were not functioning at the time of the fire[18].

1 *Bank of Nova Scotia v Hellenic Mutual War Risks Association (Bermuda) Ltd* [1992] 1 AC 233, [1991] 3 All ER 1; see Birds (1992) 108 LQR 540; Bennett [1992] JBL 592.
2 See especially per Lord Goff ([1991] 3 All ER 1 at 16), approving Kerr LJ in *State Trading Corpn of India Ltd v Golodetz Ltd* [1989] 2 Lloyd's Rep 277; and see *Hussain v Brown* [1996] 1 Lloyd's Rep 627; *Printpak v AGF Insurance Ltd* [1999] 1 All ER (Comm) 466.
3 See Birds, 'Insurance Contracts' in Birds, Bradgate and Villiers (eds), *Termination of Contracts* (1995).
4 [1955] 1 All ER 800, [1955] 1 WLR 343, CA. The Law Commission recommended the reversal of the rule in *West*: Law Com 104, paras 6.6 and 6.23.
5 The decision in *West* would in any case appear to be inconsistent with the general principle that an arbitration clause is treated as severable from the contract in which it appears so that even if the main contract is terminated, the arbitration clause will survive: *Heyman v Darwins Ltd* [1942] AC 356. See 36.2.5.3. The point was not argued before the Court of Appeal.
6 Section 34(3).
7 *Ayrey v British Legal and United Provident Assurance Co* [1918] 1 KB 136.
8 The explanation seems to be that the insurer is discharged from legal liability, but may choose to continue to accept the risk under the policy. Compare the position in the law of sale of goods, where a breach of condition by the seller discharges the buyer from the duty to perform the contract by accepting the goods, but the buyer may nevertheless choose, or be taken to have chosen, to accept and thus perform: see 12.2.1.
9 See above 35.3.2.
10 [1942] 1 KB 66, [1941] 3 All ER 304, CA.
11 [1937] 3 All ER 19.
12 [1996] 1 Lloyd's Rep 627; see Hird [1996] JBL 404; cf *Hales v Reliance Fire and Accident Insurance Co Ltd* [1960] 2 Lloyd's Rep 391.
13 [1922] 2 AC 413, HL.
14 Birds, *Modern Insurance Law* (4th edn, 1997) p 139.

15   Paragraph 1(b).
16   *Hussain v Brown* [1996] 1 Lloyd's Rep 627 at 630, per Savill LJ.
17   Per Somervell LJ in *Houghton v Trafalgar Insurance Co Ltd* [1954] 1 QB 247 at 249, CA.
18   *Printpak v AGF Insurance Ltd* [1999] 1 All ER (Comm) 466.

35.4.2   *Clauses descriptive of the risk*

The harshness of the warranty doctrine may also be mitigated by construing a clause, not as a warranty, but merely as a clause descriptive of the risk covered by the policy. If a clause is descriptive of the risk, the insurance cover is suspended whilst it is not complied with. Thus in *Farr v Motor Traders' Mutual Insurance Society*[1] the plaintiff insured two taxis with the defendants, stating in answer to a question in the proposal form that the taxis would only be used for one shift each day. For a short time one of the taxis was used for two shifts. It was subsequently damaged when only being used for one shift per day, but the insurers sought to terminate the contract and avoid liability on the basis that the insured had been guilty of a breach of warranty. It was held that the clause was merely descriptive of the risk; since the accident occurred whilst the clause was being complied with, the insurers were liable.

The interpretation of a clause as descriptive of the risk depends on the construction of the contract, and it may be possible to interpret a clause as descriptive of the risk even if the insured is said to 'warrant' its truth[2]: 'there is no magic in the word "warranty"'[3].

1   [1920] 3 KB 669, CA.
2   *De Maurier (Jewels) Ltd v Bastion Insurance Co* [1967] 2 Lloyd's Rep 550; *CTN Cash & Carry Ltd v General Accident Fire and Life Assurance Corpn plc* [1989] 1 Lloyd's Rep 299 (where construction of the clause as descriptive of the risk benefited the insurer).
3   *McGillivray and Parkington on Insurance Law* (6th edn) at p 264, cited with approval by Lambert J in *Case Existological Laboratories Ltd v Century Insurance Co of Canada, The Bamcell II* [1986] 2 Lloyd's Rep 528n, per Lambert J; see also *Kler Knitwear Ltd v Lombard General Insurance Co Ltd* [2000] Lloyd's Rep IR 47 at 50, per Morland J.

35.4.3   *Conditions*

The policy may also contain a number of other terms, described as 'conditions', stipulating duties to be performed by the insured. Many of these will relate to claims procedures – for instance, requiring the insured to notify the insurer of claims within a certain period. Policies of liability insurance will generally include conditions requiring the insured to take reasonable care to avoid liability, and not to make any admission of liability.

The effect of a breach of a condition will depend on its classification. In general, conditions will be described as conditions precedent to liability. It will be necessary then to construe the contract to determine to what the condition is precedent, but a court will probably be reluctant to interpret a condition as precedent to all liability under the contract[1], especially where the condition relates to ancillary matters such as claims procedures. It is more likely that compliance with a condition will be interpreted as precedent to a particular liability, so that the insurer may avoid liability for a particular claim if the condition is not complied with. Of course, some conditions cannot be conditions precedent to liability: for instance, a condition may impose obligations to be fulfilled by the insured after a claim has been satisfied; the insurer's remedy for breach of such a condition is a claim for damages.

If a condition is not stated to be precedent to liability, breach will generally only entitle the insurer to claim damages. The insurer will be entitled to set off any claim for damages arising from such breach against the insured's claim on the policy, and where the insured's breach of condition has led to the loss in respect of which the insured claims the insurer's loss will be the amount of the claim and thus cancel it out. The Court of Appeal has, however, recently recognised that terms in insurance contracts may be classified as 'innominate' terms, just as they can in contracts generally. Where a term thus classified as 'innominate' is broken, the insurers' rights will depend on the seriousness of the breach. Where the term relates to an individual claim under the policy, the insurer will always be entitled to damages but if the consequences of the breach are sufficiently serious the insurer will also be entitled to repudiate liability for that particular claim[2].

1   See *Kazakstan Wool Producers (Europe) Ltd v Nederlandsche Credietverzekering Maatschappij NV* [2000] 1 All ER (Comm) 708, CA.
2   *Alfred McAlpine plc v BAI (Run-Off) Ltd* [2000] 1 All ER (Comm) 545, [2000] Lloyd's Rep IR 352. See 2.5.6. There seems no reason why this approach should not be extended to recognise that there may be innominate terms relating to the policy as a whole, so that a serious breach may amount to a repudiation of the whole policy.

35.5   Agents in insurance

Most insurance business is, necessarily, conducted through intermediaries, including independent 'brokers'[1] and employees and canvassing agents working for the insurer. An insurance policy effected at Lloyd's must be effected through the agency of a Lloyd' s broker. In general, the legal consequences of dealing with such agents depend on general principles of agency law[2]; however, in some respects the normal principles are modified and their application is not always clear. It will often not be clear, but may be vital to decide whether the agent is the agent for the insured or the insurer, particularly in deciding, in the context of the insured's duty of disclosure, the effect of disclosure of information to the agent, and in deciding to whom the agent's fiduciary duties and duty of care are owed.

It is well established that information known to the agent may be imputed to the agent's principal if the agent has actual or apparent authority to receive such information[3]. Thus if the agent is acting for the insurer, disclosure of material facts to the agent will satisfy the duty of disclosure[4], and if the agent knows that a statement in the proposal is false, his knowledge may be imputed to the insurer who may therefore be held to have waived any breach of warranty[5]. However, whilst canvassing agents and employees of the insurer are clearly agents of the insurer, brokers are normally regarded as agents for the insured, so that disclosure by the insured to the broker will not satisfy the duty of disclosure. If the insured discloses information to the broker and the latter fails to pass it on to the insurer, the insured will be in breach of his duty of disclosure but will have a claim against the broker for breach of duty[6]. However, whilst this is the general rule, it seems that a broker or other agent may be deemed to be the agent of the insurer to issue cover notes or to receive information if the facts are such as to suggest that he has authority to do so[7].

On the other hand, if the agent completes the proposal form on behalf of the insured, it seems that the insured will generally be bound by the contents of the form, even though the agent would normally be regarded as the agent of the insurer, for instance because he is an employee of the insurer. Thus if the proposal contains a false statement warranted to be true, the insurer will be entitled to repudiate the policy, even though the agent may know that the statement is false. In *Newsholme Bros v Road Transport and General Insurance Co*[8] a canvassing agent completed a proposal form on the basis of information supplied by the insured but for some reason deliberately included a false statement in the proposal form. The insured signed the form, which contained a clause by which the insured warranted the truth of its contents. It was held that, in completing the form, the agent was acting as the agent of the insured, and that his knowledge of the true facts could not be imputed to the insurer. The reasoning of the Court of Appeal is not clear, but one reason offered by Scrutton LJ was that the agent had no authority from the insurer to complete proposal forms. In reaching its decision, the court distinguished the earlier case of *Bawden v London, Edinburgh and Glasgow Assurance Co*[9], where the agent completed a proposal for an insured who was illiterate. The Court of Appeal distinguished *Newsholme* in the later case of *Stone v Reliance Mutual Assurance Society*[10], where the proposal was completed by a claims inspector. The court held that the inspector had authority to complete proposal forms.

The application of agency principles in this area is rather confused. The decision in *Newsholme* does not coincide with the natural expectation of the insured, and it would seem that, given the common practice, which was recognised by Scrutton LJ in *Newsholme*, of the insurer's agents completing proposal forms, it might be argued that such agents do have apparent authority to complete proposals. However, consideration of the agent's authority to complete proposals seems to be a red herring. The position might be better explained on the basis that the insured who signs the proposal form is bound by its contents unless the facts are such as to entitle him to claim non est factum. Liability for breach of warranty then depends on whether the agent had authority to receive information about the true facts, and therefore notice that the warranty in the policy has been broken. If so, the agent's knowledge of the true facts will be imputed to the insurer and the insurer will be held to have waived the breach if he accepts premiums. On this basis it may be that the agent in *Newsholme* had no authority to receive notice of breach[11].

The agent will owe the normal duties of an agent to his principal. He will thus be liable if he fails to take reasonable care, or is in breach of his fiduciary obligations and, since the agent is normally a paid agent, for failing to carry out his instructions[12]. Thus an agent acting for the insured may be liable if he negligently fails to disclose material facts, with the result that the policy is voidable[13], or if he fails to ask for material information[14] or, perhaps, if he fails to advise the insured on the suitability of a particular insurer[15].

---

1   The term 'broker' may only be used by a broker registered with the Insurance Brokers Registration Council, established under the Insurance Brokers (Registration) Act 1977, which has drawn up a government approved code of conduct for brokers covering such matters as minimum capital and solvency requirements, the separation of client and broker's funds and the maintenance of professional indemnity insurance.

2   See Pt II.

3   However, knowledge of the agent's fraud against the principal is not attributed to the principal: see *PCW Syndicates v PCW Reinsurers* [1996] 1 All ER 774, CA; *Group Josi Re v Walbrook Insurance Co Ltd* [1996] 1 All ER 791, above 35.3.2.

4   *Ayrey v British Legal and United Provident Assurance Co* [1918] 1 KB 136; *Woolcott v Excess Insurance Co Ltd* [1979] 1 Lloyd's Rep 231, CA.

5   *Wing v Harvey* (1854) 5 De GM & G 265.

6 The insured's cause of action arises at the time when the policy is effected: *Iron Trade Mutual Insurance Co Ltd v J K Buckenham Ltd* [1990] 1 All ER 808; *Islander Trucking Ltd v Hogg Robinson & Gardner Mountain (Marine) Ltd* [1990] 1 All ER 826.

7 See *Stockton v Mason* [1978] 2 Lloyd's 430; *Woolcott v Excess Insurance Co Ltd* [1979] 1 Lloyd's Rep 231, CA. This may result in the agent being the agent of both parties for different purposes: see Birds, *Modern Insurance Law* (4th edn, 1997) pp 176–177.

8 *Newsholme Bros v Road Transport and General Insurance Co* [1929] 2 KB 356, CA.

9 *Bawden v London, Edinburgh and Glasgow Assurance Co* [1892] 2 QB 534.

10 See *Stone v Reliance Mutual Insurance Society* [1972] 1 Lloyd's Rep 469, CA.

11 It is worth noting that there was little evidence of any waiver on the facts of *Newsholme*.

12 See ch 6.

13 *Iron Trade Mutual Insurance Co Ltd v J K Buckenham Ltd* [1990] 1 All ER 808; *Islander Trucking Ltd v Hogg Robinson & Gardner Mountain (Marine) Ltd* [1990] 1 All ER 826. The agent is required to disclose material facts known to him: Marine Insurance Act 1906, s 19: see 35.3.2 above.

14 *McNealy v Pennine Insurance Co* [1978] 2 Lloyd's Rep 18, CA.

15 *Osman v J Ralph Moss* [1970] 1 Lloyd's Rep 313, CA.

35.6 Claims and cover

In the event of loss caused by the risk insured against, the insured is entitled to enforce the policy and claim the benefit promised by the insurer. Normally, the insured will be entitled to monetary payment, but in certain circumstances the insurer may have the option of repairing or replacing damaged property[1], and there seems no reason why a valid contract of insurance cannot provide for the insurer to provide some benefit other than cash payment[2].

The policy is likely to impose obligations on the insured in relation to claims under the policy, including, for instance, a requirement that the insured notify the insurer of any claim under the policy, and, under a liability insurance, that the insured should not make any admission of liability. In order to enforce the insurer's obligation to pay under the policy, the insured must comply with those obligations. The policy will normally provide that such obligations are conditions precedent to the insurer's liability under the policy, so that if the insured fails to comply, the insurer may be able to avoid liability for the particular claim.

In order to mitigate the impact of such conditions on the insured, the courts tend to construe them strictly against the insurer; they will be construed as mere conditions, giving rise only to a right to claim damages, or possibly now innominate terms[3], rather than as conditions precedent to the insurer's liability, unless clear words are used. Moreover, it has been held that a condition requiring the insured to give full particulars of an accident under a third party liability policy was satisfied provided that the insurer received full particulars within the time limit fixed by the contract, even though the particulars were provided by someone other than the insured[4]. Even if the insured is guilty of a breach of condition, the insurer may be unable to escape liability under the contract if his conduct can be interpreted as waiving the breach. Thus if, for instance, the insurer takes steps, such as asking for more information, to process a claim made outside the time limit fixed by the contract, he may be held to have waived the breach of condition[5].

1 See 35.7.

2 See *Department of Trade and Industry v St Christopher Motorists' Association Ltd* [1974] 1 All ER 395, [1974] 1 WLR 99, above 35.0.2.

3 See *Alfred McAlpine plc v BAI (Run-Off) Ltd* [2000] 1 All ER (Comm) 545, [2000] Lloyd's Rep IR 352 above 35.4.3.

4 *Lickiss v Milestone Motor Policies* [1966] 2 All ER 972; the case was distinguished in *Cox v Orion Insurance Co* [1982] RTR 1, CA.

5 *Lickiss v Milestone Motor Policies*.

35.6.1 *Fraudulent claims*

The duty of good faith continues after the policy is concluded. The duty requires the insured to make full disclosure of all material circumstances when making a claim under the policy. The insured therefore commits a breach of the duty if he makes a fraudulent claim under the policy[1], as, for instance, where he conceals or misrepresents the circumstances of a loss or exaggerates the value of property for which he claims[2]. According to s 17 of the Marine Insurance Act 1906, breach of the duty of good faith allows the insurer to avoid the contract, and it has been held that this means that the contract may be avoided ab initio[3]. Since the 1906 Act codified the existing common law, the same principle should apply to other policies of insurance; if correct, this means that a fraudulent claim allows the insurer to escape liability even for a valid claim made before the fraudulent claim, although there is no authority to that effect.

It has been said that there is no breach of duty unless there is 'substantial fraud'[4] but this means only that the breach of duty must be material. Thus if the insured makes an exaggerated claim under the policy the whole claim is tainted by fraud. It is not necessary that the fraudulent element be a substantial proportion of the whole claim, provided that the value of the fruadulent part itself is not insignificant[5]. If, as seems to be the case, a fraudulent claim allows the insurer to avoid the whole policy, the consequences for the insured of a fraudulent claim are drastic. Millett LJ has justified this approach to fraudulent claims as follows.

> 'The making of dishonest claims has become all too common. There seems to be a widespread belief that insurance companies are fair game, and that defrauding them is not morally reprehensible. The rule which we are asked to enforce today may appear to some to be harsh, but it is in my opinion a necessary and salutary rule which deserves to be better known to the public. I for my part would be unwilling to dilute it in any way.'[6]

1   *Manifest Shipping & Co Ltd v Uni Polaris Insurance Co Ltd and La Réunion Européene: The Star Sea* [1997] 1 Lloyd's Rep 360; see Clarke [1998] LMCLQ 465.
2   See *Galloway v Guardian Royal Exchange (UK) Ltd* [1999] Lloyd's Rep IR 209.
3   *Black King Shipping Corpn v Massie, The Litsion Pride* [1985] 1 Lloyd's Rep 437.
4   *Orakpo v Barclays Insurance Services Co Ltd* [1994] CLC 373.
5   *Galloway v Guardian Royal Exchange (UK) Ltd* [1999] Lloyd's Rep IR 209, per Millett and Mummery LJJ.
6   [1999] Lloyd's Rep IR 209 at 214.

35.6.2 *Cover*

In order to claim under the policy the insured must establish that he has suffered a loss caused by the risks covered by the policy. However, where the policy contains exceptions to the cover, the burden is on the insurer to prove that the insured's loss was caused by one of the excepted risks. It is important for the insured to ensure that he has adequate cover: for instance, a product liability policy may cover the insured against liability for damages paid to compensate third parties for loss or damage caused by defective products, but will not normally cover such other items as, for instance, the costs of recalling a batch of defective products.

Whether or not a particular risk is covered by the policy depends on the construction of the particular policy. We have already seen that a policy will not ordinarily be construed as covering loss caused by inherent vice in the property insured[1], or wilful misconduct of the insured[2]; loss caused by the insured's negligence may be covered by an accident or 'all risks' policy[3] but the policy may contain a condition requiring the insured to take reasonable care to avoid loss. Taken literally, the effect of such provisions would be that, where the insured is negligent, the insurer is entitled to avoid liability on the grounds of breach of condition and they would therefore deprive the insured of cover in situations where it is most required. However, in a recent case the Court of Appeal held that a requirement in a policy that the insured should take 'all reasonable steps' to safeguard property covered by the policy would not be broken if the insured was merely negligent but only if the insured recklessly failed to safeguard the property[4].

   Subject to presumptions such as those mentioned above, words in insurance policies describing the insured risks are construed in accordance with the purposive, commercial commonsense approach to contract interpretation described earlier. However, the wording of insurance policies is often complicated and may be difficult for the ordinary individual insured to understand. Insurance policies are generally standard form contracts, prepared by the insurer. Unlike many other standard form contracts, their contents have, in the past, been subject to little legal control. However, the General Statement of Insurance Practice provides that 'Insurers will continue to develop clearer and more explicit proposal forms and policy documents whilst bearing in mind the legal nature of insurance contracts'[5]. Moreover, insurance contracts with consumers are subject to the Unfair Terms in Consumer Contracts Regulations 1999. Many of their more important terms, including those which define the risk accepted by the insurer, may avoid being assessed for fairness by the exclusion from the regulations and the underlying directive of those terms which 'define the main subject matter of the contract' or concern 'the adequacy of the price or remuneration', but they are exempt from control on this basis only in so far as they are expressed in plain and intelligible language[6]. Policies in general will have to comply with the requirement to be expressed in plain language and where there is doubt about the meaning of any provision it will be given the meaning most favourable to the insured[7].

   On occasions the courts have provided a measure of protection to the insured by interpreting policies strictly contra proferentem. For instance, where a motor insurance policy excluded liability if the car was carrying 'any load in excess of that for which it was constructed', it was held that the insured was covered when the car was carrying six persons, even though it was designed only to carry five: passengers were not 'load'[8]. However, other rules of interpretation, less favourable to the insured, may also be used and in some cases the approach of the courts has been excessively technical. In particular, where words with a technical legal meaning are used, they will be interpreted according to that meaning[9], even though that may be contrary to the expectations of the insured. Thus, for instance, where a business policy covered loss or damage caused by 'theft' involving 'entry or exit . . . by forcible or violent means', it was held that 'violent' must mean something other than 'forcible'. The insured argued that it meant merely 'unlawful' but it was held that, since theft must always be unlawful, 'violent' must mean something more here in order to add something. Thus where a burglar gained entry to the premises by means of a stolen set of keys there had been a theft, but the loss was not covered by the policy because, although the entry was forcible (the turning of the key in the lock was held to involve a use of force), it was not violent[10]. In the same way, a policy which covers against loss by 'theft' will not cover losses caused by other offences of dishonesty, so that if the insured is deprived of property by deception, he will not be covered[11].

Similarly, a policy which provides cover against 'loss' will only apply where the property is 'lost'. Clearly, property which is totally destroyed is 'lost', as are goods which are mislaid and cannot be found[12]. In *Webster v General Accident Fire and Life Assurance Corpn Ltd*[13] the plaintiff's car was insured against 'loss' caused by theft. The car was stolen, and later discovered in the hands of a third party; it was not clear if the third party had acquired a good title to the car[14]; however, it was held that the car was 'lost', and the insured was not required to sue to recover it[15]. In contrast, in *Eisinger v General Accident Fire and Life Assurance Corpn Ltd*[16], the insured sold his car and took a cheque in payment. The cheque was dishonoured, but it was held that the insured could not claim for loss of the car: he had parted with the car voluntarily, and his loss was the value of the cheque.

In marine insurance there may be an actual or constructive loss. There is an actual loss if the subject matter of the insurance is destroyed or if it is so damaged that it ceases 'to be a thing of the kind insured', or if the insured is irretrievably deprived of it[17]. In addition, the insured is entitled to abandon goods or a vessel if the circumstances are such that total loss appears unavoidable, or where total loss can only be avoided by expenditure of a greater sum than the property would be worth after being saved. In that case there is a 'constructive total loss', and the insured may give notice of constructive total loss to the insurer and treat the situation as if there were a total loss[18].

1 *British and Foreign Marine Insurance Co v Gaunt* [1921] 2 AC 41, HL. The same rule is applied to marine insurance: Marine Insurance Act 1906, s 55(2)(c); however, if on its proper construction the policy covers inherent vice, the court will give effect to it: *Soya GmbH Mainz v White* [1983] 1 Lloyd's Rep 122, HL.
2 *Slattery v Mance* [1962] 1 QB 676, [1962] 1 All ER 525.
3 *Harris v Poland* [1941] 1 KB 462, [1941] 1 All ER 204, where the insured hid jewellery in a fire grate and then, forgetting the jewellery, lit the fire.
4 *Sofi v Prudential Assurance Co Ltd* [1993] 2 Lloyd's Rep 559. See also *Hayward v Norwich Union Insurance Ltd* [2000] Lloyd's Rep IR 382. Cf *Port-Rose v Phoenix Assurance Co Ltd* [1986] NLJ Rep 333, where Hodgson J held that the insured had not been negligent.
5 Paragraph 5.
6 Unfair Terms in Consumer Contracts Regulations 1999, SI 1999/2083, reg 3(2); see 2.6.5. The DTI originally proposed that insurance contracts should be wholly exempt from the regulations but were ultimately persuaded that they are (probably) caught by the directive.
7 Unfair Terms in Consumer Contracts Regulations 1999, SI 1999/2083, reg 7(2).
8 *Houghton v Trafalgar Insurance Co Ltd* [1954] 1 QB 247, [1953] 2 All ER 1409, CA. See also *Hayward v Norwich Union Insurance Ltd* [2000] Lloyd's Rep IR 382, where an exclusion in a policy of motor insurance where keys were 'left in the car' was construed as only applying where the keys were left unattended in the car.
9 See *Deutsche Genossenschaftsbank v Burnhope* [1995] 4 All ER 717 ('theft').
10 *Dino Services Ltd v Prudential Assurance Co Ltd* [1989] 1 Lloyd's Rep 379.
11 See *Dobson v General Accident Assurance Corpn* [1990] 1 QB 274, [1989] 3 All ER 927, where the Court of Appeal went to great lengths to interpret the facts as a case of theft. But insurance against theft will also cover loss of property due to robbery: see *Hayward v Norwich Union Insurance Ltd* [2000] Lloyd's Rep IR 382.
12 *Holmes v Payne* [1930] 2 KB 301.
13 [1953] 1 QB 520, [1953] 1 All ER 663.
14 Under one of the exceptions to the nemo dat rule: see ch 17.
15 There would be nothing to prevent the insurer suing to recover the car, relying on its right of subrogation, or by virtue of an assignment of the right of action. See *National Employers' Mutual General Insurance Association Ltd v Jones* [1990] 1 AC 24, [1988] 2 All ER 425, HL (above 17.4.2) where this happened.

16   [1955] 2 All ER 897, [1955] 1 WLR 869.
17   Marine Insurance Act 1906, s 55(1).
18   Marine Insurance Act 1906, ss 60–63.

35.6.3   *Causation*

In order for the insured to succeed in a claim on the policy, the insured risk must be the 'proximate' cause of the loss[1]. Where property is damaged in an attempt to avoid an imminent peril covered by the policy, the damage can be treated as caused by that peril, so that the insured is entitled to recover on the policy[2]. However, expenses incurred in an attempt to avoid a peril running are not recoverable because the event insured against has not occurred[3].

Difficult questions of causation may arise where events not covered by the policy intervene between the occurrence of the event insured against and the loss in respect of which the insured claims. It is not necessary that the insured risk be the last cause of the ultimate loss, but it must be the dominant or effective cause. This test may be difficult to apply in practice and many of the cases are difficult to reconcile. Where there are two causes of loss, the original cause will generally be regarded as operative unless the subsequent event can be regarded as breaking the chain of causation. For instance, a policy covering loss caused by fire would probably cover loss caused by water used to extinguish a fire, but not loss caused by a mob who come to watch the fire[4].

Where two separate causes are equally responsible for the loss but only one is covered by the policy, the insured will not be able to recover. In *Wayne Tank and Pump Co Ltd v Employers' Liability Assurance Corpn Ltd*[5] the policy excluded liability for damage caused by the 'nature and condition of any goods . . . supplied by' the insured. The insured supplied and installed equipment at a factory for a customer. The equipment was defective, and one of the insured's employees left it turned on, unsupervised, overnight. The equipment caused a fire which destroyed the customer's factory. The Court of Appeal held that the employee's negligence did not break the chain of causation between the defect in the goods and the fire, so that the fire was caused by an excepted risk. However, the court added that even if the case were regarded as one where there were two causes of loss – the defective nature of the goods, and the negligence of the employee – the insurer would be entitled to rely on the exception: the loss would not be caused solely by the insured peril.

1   The same rule applies to Marine Insurance by s 55(1) of the Marine Insurance Act 1906.
2   See *Symington & Co v Union Insurance Society of Canton* (1928) 97 LJKB 646.
3   *Yorkshire Water Services Ltd v Sun Alliance & London Insurance plc* [1997] 2 Lloyd's Rep 21.
4   See *Marsden v City and County Assurance* (1865) LR 1 CP 232.
5   [1974] QB 57, [1973] 3 All ER 825, CA.

35.7   Principles of indemnity

Where the insured makes a claim under the policy, the question arises how the amount recoverable is to be assessed. Under a contingency insurance, such as a life policy, the amount the insured is entitled to recover is fixed by the terms of the policy. However, under an indemnity policy the insured is essentially entitled to be compensated for the amount of loss he suffers as a result of the event insured against. The terms of the policy may place a ceiling on the amount recoverable, but they will not necessarily define the amount.

The basic principle of indemnity was described by Brett LJ in *Castellain v Preston*[1] as follows:

> 'The contract of insurance is a contract of indemnity and of indemnity only and . . . this contract means that the assured, in case of a loss against which the policy has been made, shall be fully indemnified, but shall never be more than fully indemnified. That is the fundamental principle of insurance and if ever a proposition is brought forward which is at variance with it, that is to say, which will either prevent the assured from obtaining a full indemnity or which will give the assured more than a full indemnity, that proposition must certainly be wrong'.

This essential principle, that the assured is entitled to a full indemnity, no more and no less, is embodied in three groups of rules: those concerned with the measure of loss, the rules concerning the insurer's rights of subrogation, and the rules concerned with double insurance. The insurer's right to contribution in cases of double insurance is not directly linked to the indemnity principle, but it arises where there is double insurance and is linked to the doctrine of subrogation, and so it is examined below.

1   (1883) 11 QBD 380 at 386, CA.

35.7.1   *The measurement of loss*

Even in a policy of indemnity insurance, the amount recoverable by the insured is governed by the terms of the contract. In particular, the maximum amount recoverable by the insured depends on the amount of cover provided by the policy, and if the amount of loss exceeds the sum insured, the insured must bear the extra loss himself. The policy may contain an excess clause: if so, the effect is that the insured must bear the first part of the loss in person: for instance, if a policy has an excess of £100, the insured must bear the first £100 of any loss himself. If the loss is not more than £100, the insured must bear the whole of the loss. A marine insurance policy may contain a franchise clause. The effect of such a clause is to relieve the insurer of liability for any loss below the figure fixed by the clause; however, if the insured's loss exceeds the franchise figure, the insurer is liable for the whole of the loss.

If a valid claim is made, the insurer is obliged to satisfy it. If he fails to do so, he is in breach of contract, so that a claim by the insured to enforce the policy is a claim for damages for breach of contract. The measure of the insured's damages is prima facie the amount of the claim and the Court of Appeal has recently held that the insured cannot claim additional damages for losses caused by delay in payment[1]: there is no claim for damages for late payment of damages at common law[2]. The insurer may be in breach of an implied term that claims should be processed with reasonable diligence but the court held that there was no remedy in damages for breach of such a term.

Under a third party liability policy, such as a public liability policy, the amount payable to the insured is the amount required to indemnify him against the third party's claim, subject to the ceiling fixed by the policy and any excess or franchise payable. However, in a case of first party insurance on property, the valuation of loss may be more difficult. The principles applicable may differ according to whether the property is goods or realty, and whether the claim is for total or partial loss.

(a) Total loss

In the case of goods, the measure of loss in a case of total loss is the market value of the goods at the time of the loss. Thus, unless the goods are new at the time of loss, the insured will not recover sufficient to buy new goods, unless the policy provides for replacement on a 'new for old' basis. A higher premium will be charged for such cover.

In the case of buildings insurance the situation may be more difficult. As a result of building costs inflation, the market value of the premises at the date of loss may be considerably less than the cost of rebuilding the premises. If the insured is only given the market value of the premises, he may be forced to move, or to recover less than his real loss. It therefore seems that the insured is entitled to recover the cost of reinstating the premises, subject to the ceiling fixed by the sum insured, if he genuinely intends 'for any reason that would appeal to an ordinary man in his position' to reinstate so that the claim for reinstatement is not 'a mere pretence'[3].

(b) Partial loss

In cases of partial loss, where goods or premises are damaged but not destroyed, the position is more complicated. Essentially, the measure of loss then, for both goods and premises, is the cost of repair, subject to a deduction for betterment if the result of repair is to leave the property better than it was before the loss: the insured is entitled to be restored to the position prior to loss. Again, the sum insured fixes a ceiling on the amount recoverable by the insured; however, provided that the amount of the loss is less than the sum insured, the insured is prima facie entitled to recover the whole of his loss, even if the property is insured for less than its full value.

Since premiums for property insurance are normally fixed by reference to the value of the property and therefore the sum insured, the insured may be tempted to insure the property for less than its full value in order to reduce the premium payable. He will not be fully protected if the property is wholly lost, but since total loss is relatively unlikely, that may appear to be a risk worth taking. In order to guard against under insurance and encourage the insured to insure property for its full value, a commercial policy on goods is likely to contain an average clause[4]. In that case, the insured who under insures will not recover the full amount of his loss, even if the amount of loss is less than the sum insured. Instead, he will recover the proportion of his actual loss which bears the same relationship to his actual loss as the sum insured bears to the actual value of the property. For instance, if goods worth £1,000 are insured for £500, and suffer damage which would cost £300 to repair, the insured will only recover 50% of his actual loss – £150. A similar principle applies by statute to contracts of marine insurance[5].

Where there is an average clause in the policy it is therefore important to ensure that property is insured for its full value. In addition, since the value of property is a material fact, if property is insured for less than its full value, the insured may be guilty of misrepresentation or non-disclosure, and if that comes to light the insurer will be entitled to avoid the policy ab initio[6]. Alternatively, the policy may contain a provision by which the insured warrants the value of the goods. If the valuation is inaccurate at the time of the policy, the insured is then guilty of breach of warranty. If the property increases in value after the policy is made, there is no breach of warranty unless the warranty is promissory, or the policy includes a further warranty requiring the insured to notify the insurer of increases in value or maintain the insurance at the value of the property.

(c)   Valued policies

It has been assumed so far that the policy is a simple indemnity policy. However, insurance on property may be effected by means of a valued policy. In such a case the parties agree a value for the property and agree that that sum will be payable in the event of total loss. Valued policies are common in marine insurance, and are perfectly binding, provided that the valuation is not so excessive as to amount to a breach of the duty of good faith.

In the event of total loss, the valuation works in the same way as a liquidated damages clause in a contract, or the sum assured in a contingency policy: the insured is entitled to recover the agreed value[7]. However, in the event of partial loss, the insured will be able to recover the proportion of the cost of repair which bears the same relation to the cost of repair as the policy value bears to the actual value of the property prior to loss[8].

(d)   Reinstatement

An indemnity policy normally requires the insurer to pay the insured a sum of money; it is for the insured to decide how to spend it. However, the insurer may be entitled, or required, actually to replace or reinstate lost or damaged property, either under a term of the contract, or under statute.

There is no objection to the policy itself giving the insurer a contractual right to repair or replace the insured property, and such a clause may be attractive to insurers as a means of guarding against fraud or inflated claims. If the insurer elects to reinstate, the effect is as if the policy had always been a contract to reinstate. The insurer must then reinstate the property, regardless of the cost of reinstatement, even though it may exceed the sum insured under the policy. In addition, where a building is damaged by fire, any person 'interested' in the property has a statutory right to require the insurer to use the policy monies to reinstate the premises[9].

1   *Sprung v Royal Insurance (UK) Ltd* [1997] CLC 70, where payment was made three years later than it should with reasonable diligence have been made. See Birds [1997] JBL 368, Hemsworth [1998] LMCLQ 154. See also *The Italia Express (No 2)* [1992] 2 Lloyd's Rep 281; cf *Grant v Co-operative Insurance Society Ltd* (1983) 134 NLJ 81.
2   *Lips Maritime Corpn v President of India* [1987] 3 All ER 110.
3   See *Reynolds v Phoenix Assurance Co Ltd* [1978] 2 Lloyd's Rep 440; contrast *Leppard v Excess Insurance Co* [1979] 2 All ER 668, [1979] 1 WLR 512, CA, where evidence showed that the insured had no intention of occupying the premises but intended to sell.
4   An average clause may be implied in such a policy: *Carreras v Cunard Steamship Co* [1918] 1 KB 118.
5   Marine Insurance Act 1906, s 81.
6   But see *Economides v Commercial Union Assurance plc* [1997] 3 All ER 636: a valuation will normally involve a statement of opinion or belief in which case the insured will not be liable for misrepresentation so long as he honestly believes it to be true and does not deliberately shut his eyes to the truth.
7   Marine Insurance Act 1906, s 27.
8   *Elcock v Thomson* [1949] 2 KB 755, [1949] 2 All ER 381.
9   Fires Prevention (Metropolis) Act 1774, s 83. The Act also gives the insurer a right to use the proceeds in this way if it suspects fraud or arson.

35.7.2 *Subrogation*

Where the insurer has indemnified the insured under a policy of indemnity insurance, the insurer is entitled to exercise rights of subrogation. The principle of subrogation is not limited to insurance; it is part of the law of restitution and applies wherever one person, A, has 'unofficiously conferred a benefit on another, B, . . . and where it is just in all the circumstances' that in order to prevent B being unjustly enriched, A should have the benefit of B's rights or property[1]. In such cases, it allows A to be substituted for B and to take over B's property, or to exercise B's rights, in order to recoup the amount of the benefit provided to B[2].

Subrogation in insurance involves two elements: first, in accordance with the general principle of indemnity described in *Castellain v Preston*[3], that the insured should not be over-compensated for his loss; and, secondly, that where the insured suffers loss as a result of the wrongful action of some third party, the insurer should be able to exercise any rights of action the insured may have against the third party. Thus, for instance, if the insured's goods are damaged at sea by the negligence of the carrier, the insurer may be subrogated to the insured's right to sue the carrier.

The first aspect of subrogation means that if, after being fully indemnified by his insurer, the insured receives further sums referable to the loss, he is accountable for such sums to the insurer. The simplest example of this principle will arise where an insured's property is damaged by a third party and the insured successfully claims for the damage on his own insurance. If the owner recovers compensation for the damage from the third party, he must account to his insurers for that sum. In *Castellain v Preston*, O, the owner of property, contracted to sell it to P. However, between exchange of contracts and completion, when the property was at P's risk, the property was damaged. It was held that, nevertheless, P was obliged to complete the transaction, and it was therefore held that O's insurers were entitled to recover from O the sum paid by P. The duty to account extends to include voluntary payments made by third parties, provided that they are intended as compensation for the damage covered by the insurance.

However, the duty to account only arises where the insured has received a full indemnity under the policy. Equally, since the purpose of subrogation is to prevent the insured being unjustly enriched at the expense of the insurer, the insurer is only entitled to claim such sums as will recoup the amount he has paid out. Any excess over the sum paid by the insurer belongs to the insured[4]. This does not necessarily mean, however, that the insured will be fully compensated for all his losses: where there is an excess on the policy the insured will have to bear some of his losses unless he can recover from the third party enough to repay the insurer and his uninsured losses. The effect on subrogation rights of an excess in a policy was explained by the House of Lords in *Napier and Ettrick v Kershaw*[5]. Where a policy contains an excess, the insured has, effectively, agreed with the insurer to bear the first part of any loss, up to the amount of the excess, himself. If, therefore, the insurer has indemnified the insured, subject to the excess, in respect of damage caused by a third party, the insurer is entitled to claim sums recovered from the third party before the insured may recover the amount of his excess. Suppose, for instance, that A's property is insured by B under a policy with an excess of £100. C negligently damages A's property, causing damage worth £250. A is indemnified by B, subject to the excess, and recovers £150. B is now entitled to claim any moneys recovered from C in priority to A, in order to reimburse the amount paid to A. Suppose, therefore, that A sues C and recovers £180. A must account to B for £150 and may retain only £30, leaving A out of pocket by £70.

Conversely, if the insurer's liability is limited to a maximum amount, the insured is entitled to recover the amount by which his loss exceeds the limitation before the insurer can claim subrogation rights. Thus, if in the example just given A's policy with B limits B's liability to £100 on any one claim, A will recover only £100 from B. Having recovered £180 from C, he is entitled to retain £50 from the amount recovered from C before accounting to B for £100 by way of subrogation; he is entitled to retain the balance of £30 from the sum recovered, which reduces the amount of his excess loss. In both cases A's net loss, after recovering compensation from C, is £70 but, as against B, A has agreed to bear the first £100 of any loss and must therefore bear the whole of his net loss. Now suppose that in the example there is no excess on the policy but that B's liability is limited to £150. A recovers £180 from C, and is entitled to retain the first £100, to compensate for his uninsured losses, leaving only £80 for B. In this situation the net loss is still £70 but as between A and B, B has agreed to bear the first £150 of any loss.

The insurer is entitled to an equitable charge or lien over any sums recovered from a third party to protect his subrogation interest[6].

In practice, the second aspect of the insurer's right of subrogation is the more important. It allows the insurer to bring proceedings in the name of the insured against any person responsible for the insured's loss, and many of the cases examined earlier in this book, particularly in the context of international trade, involved disputes between insurers.

Again, the right only arises where the insured has been fully indemnified under the policy, and if the insured has not received a full indemnity, he is entitled to bring proceedings on his own behalf[7]. Moreover, if the insurer fails to sue, the insured may do so, although he will hold any moneys recovered for the insurer under the first aspect of subrogation. The insured must not do anything to prejudice the insurer's right of action, and if he refuses to allow his name to be used in proceedings, the insurer may commence an action in his own name, joining the insured as a second defendant. However, subject to that, the insurer's right of action is identical to that of the insured. The insurer therefore can be in no better position than the insured, and his claim is subject to any defences available in an action by the insured. For the same reason the insurer cannot sue the insured even if he was responsible for the loss, since the insured cannot sue himself. This may be important where insurance is effected by a person with a limited interest for the benefit of other interested parties, especially in the context of construction and engineering projects. In *Petrofina (UK) Ltd v Magnaload*[8] a policy taken out by the main contractors on a construction project was held to protect sub-contractors working on the project. Thus the insurers, having paid the main contractors, could not sue the sub-contractors who had negligently damaged the insured property. The result depends, however, on the extent of the cover granted to the sub-contractor by the policy. It is possible for co-insureds under one policy to be insured for different interests and the insurer may be able to assert subrogation rights against the sub-contractor in breach where the subrogated claim relates to a loss in respect of which the sub-contractor is not insured[9].

In practice, the insurer's rights of subrogation are often supplemented by express terms of the policy allowing the insurer to take and defend proceedings in the name of the insured, and requiring the insured to provide assistance to the insurer. The right of the insurer to be subrogated to the insured's right of action operates in the same way as an implied assignment of the right of action. The policy may supplement the right by requiring the insured to make an express assignment of the right of action. In that case the insurer will bring proceedings in his own name, and will be entitled to retain all that he recovers.

It can be argued that, in the context of insurance, subrogation is inefficient. Where property is damaged by the negligence of a third party, the owner is entitled to claim an indemnity in respect of that damage from his own insurer. However, by exercising rights of subrogation the insurer is then entitled to sue the third party, and in order to guard against that potential liability, the third party must carry liability insurance. As a result, the same property is effectively insured twice over. This may be particularly important in the context of commercial disputes, where litigation in respect of damage to goods may often be between two insurers: for instance, the insurer of the owner of goods covered by a marine insurance policy, and the insurer of the carrier. Indeed, the owner's insurer is most unlikely to pursue his right of subrogation unless the party responsible for the damage is insured. Some commentators have therefore suggested that subrogation in this context is wasteful and should be prohibited. It encourages not only double insurance, but also litigation.

However, the difficulty stems not from the doctrine of subrogation itself, but from the preference for third party liability in tort over first party insurance. Moreover, it may be argued that, even where there is double insurance, the effect of allowing the person responsible for causing damage to be sued, even by means of subrogation, is to throw the cost of negligent damage, in the form of increased insurance premiums, onto the party at fault, which may possibly have the effect of promoting higher standards of care. Essentially, therefore, the argument is about the justifiability of fault-based liability.

In fact, in one of the most common situations where subrogation rights might be relevant, they are often not exercised. In the context of motor insurance, insurers have entered into 'knock-for-knock' agreements with each other[10]. Under such agreements, where two vehicles involved in a collision are both insured on a fully comprehensive basis, each insurer will pay its own insured and not exercise its rights of subrogation, regardless of the responsibility of the two drivers for the accident. This is beneficial for the insurers, since it avoids the need to investigate claims and bring proceedings in many cases, and each insurer's gains and losses will balance out in the long run. However, knock-for-knock agreements may prejudice the individual insured, who may be treated as having made a claim on his policy, and therefore lose any no claims bonus to which he would otherwise be entitled, as a result of an accident for which he was not responsible.

1 Goff and Jones, *The Law of Restitution* (5th edn, 1998) p 120.
2 The rights of an indorser who pays a bill of exchange arise under a form of subrogation: see 28.4.5.
3 (1883) 11 QBD 380, above 35.7.
4 *Yorkshire Insurance Co v Nisbet Shipping Co* [1962] 2 QB 330, [1961] 2 All ER 487; see Marine Insurance Act 1906, s 79(2).
5 [1993] AC 713, [1993] 1 All ER 385.
6 [1993] AC 713, [1993] 1 All ER 385.
7 *Commercial Union Assurance Co v Lister* (1874) 9 Ch App 483.
8 [1984] QB 127, [1983] 3 All ER 35. The sub-contractors were held to have an insurable interest in the whole of the works. See also *Stone Vickers Ltd v Appledore Ferguson Shipbuilders Ltd* [1991] 2 Lloyd's Rep 288; revsd [1992] 2 Lloyd's Rep 578.
9 *National Oilwell (UK) Ltd v Davey Offshore Ltd* [1993] 2 Lloyd's Rep 582; see *Deepak Fertilisers & Petrochemicals Corpn v ICI Chemicals and Polymers* [1999] 1 Lloyd's Rep 387, where the co-insured's interest was limited in time.
10 See Lewis (1985) 48 MLR 275.

35.7.3   *Salvage*

In addition to the right of subrogation, the insurer also enjoys the right of salvage in respect of the insured property. The right of salvage derives, like subrogation, from the indemnity principle. If the insurer indemnifies the insured for his total loss in respect of the insured property, the insured must abandon his interest in it. Thus if the property is subsequently recovered, the insurer is entitled to it. In marine insurance the principle applies not only in cases of actual loss, but also in cases of constructive total loss where the insured gives notice of abandonment[1]. However, whilst the principle of salvage is most commonly applied in marine insurance, it is applicable to all insurance.

1   See 35.7.1.

35.7.4   *Double insurance and contribution*

It may happen that the same risk is covered by two or more policies of insurance. This may come about because the insured insures the same risk twice with two different insurers. However, it is more likely to occur where the same item is covered by two separate policies: for instance, a business might take out specific insurance on an expensive piece of equipment which is also covered by a general policy covering factory contents, or effect specific product liability insurance in addition to general public liability insurance. Alternatively, the same item may be insured by two different insureds. For instance, if O stores goods in B's warehouse, the goods may be covered by both O's and B's insurance.

   To allow an insured to recover twice for the same loss would contravene the basic indemnity principle, and so the law precludes double recovery. If the same risk is covered by two or more insurances, the insured can recover up to the full amount of his loss (subject to any ceiling fixed by the particular policy) from any individual insurer; he may not make a further claim for the same loss from any other insurer. The insurer forced to pay may then claim a contribution from any other insurer liable for the same loss. The principle is the same as that which requires contribution between two or more sureties of the same debt[1]. In practice, however, the position is again likely to be modified by the terms of the policy, which will normally include a rateable proportion clause. The effect of such a clause is to prevent any one insurer being required to pay more than his 'share' of the loss, forcing the insured to pursue separate claims against each insurer for a proportionate contribution.

   There will only be double insurance in law where the same liability or property is covered by two separate policies in respect of the same risk. In *North British and Mercantile Insurance Co v London, Liverpool and Globe Insurance Co*[2], O deposited goods with B, a bailee, for storage. O insured the goods as owner; B insured the goods as bailee. The goods were lost as a result of B's negligence, and B therefore claimed from their insurers. They in turn claimed a contribution from O's insurers, arguing that there was double insurance. It was held that there was no double insurance in these circumstances: B's policy covered them against the risk of loss for which they were responsible, whilst O's policy covered them against the risk of accidental loss. If O's insurers had paid for the loss, they would have been subrogated to O's rights to claim against B, and therefore against B's insurers.

   Where there is double insurance, any insurer who is required to pay is entitled to claim a contribution from any other insurer liable in respect of the same loss. It is then necessary to decide the proportions in which they should contribute. Normally, contribution is dealt with by agreement between insurers, and two different bases of apportionment are adopted. If a case does go to court, the court is likely to follow the practice of insurers and adopt one of those two bases of apportionment.

The 'maximum liability' basis of contribution requires the insurers to contribute in the same proportion as the ratio of the sums insured under the two policies: for instance, if A and B both insure the same property, for £20,000 and £10,000 respectively, they will contribute to any loss in the ratio 2:1. The 'maximum liability' basis is appropriate where premiums are based on, and proportionate to, the value of the property insured, and is therefore the normal method for property insurance.

However, in cases of liability insurance it has been held that the 'independent liability' basis should be used[3], because the sum insured under an indemnity policy is not intended to reflect the value of insured property but simply to fix a limit on the insurer's potential liability. This requires the insurers to contribute in the ratio of the amounts they would each pay for the particular loss if there was no double insurance. Thus if A and B both insure I against public liability, for £20,000 and £10,000 respectively, and I suffers a loss of £10,000, A and B contribute equally, because each of them would be fully liable for the claim independently of the other. However, if I suffers a loss of £15,000, A would be liable for the whole loss, whilst B would be liable only for £10,000. The insurers therefore contribute in the ratio 15:10. If the loss is £20,000 or more, the insurers contribute in the ratio 2:1. It seems that this basis should be used wherever the maximum liability basis would be inappropriate.

Application of contribution principles become difficult if one of the insurers is entitled to avoid liability to the insured. In *Legal & General Assurance Society Ltd v Drake Insurance Co Ltd*[4] the majority of the Court of Appeal held that contribution depended on the rights of the insurers at the date of the loss so that where an insurer was entitled to repudiate a claim because of the insured's failure to notify the claim in accordance with the policy, the insurer was nevertheless liable to contribute. However, this approach has been criticised[5] and has subsequently been doubted by the Privy Council, holding that an insurer who would be entitled to resist a claim from the insured, including on the basis of a breach of condition occurring after loss, is not liable to make a contribution[6]. In order to enable the insurer to exercise his right to claim a contribution in cases of double insurance, the policy will normally contain express provisions requiring the insured to notify the insurer if he effects double insurance. If such a provision is a warranty, failure to notify will entitle the insurer to terminate the contract for non-compliance[7].

1 See 23.2.2.
2 (1877) 5 Ch D 569.
3 *Commercial Union Assurance Group v Hayden* [1977] QB 804, [1977] 1 All ER 441.
4 [1991] 2 Lloyd's Rep 36.
5 See Birds [1992] JBL 98.
6 *Eagle Star Insurance Co Ltd v Provincial Insurance plc* [1994] 1 AC 130, [1993] 3 All ER 1. The point is somewhat academic for the Court of Appeal recognised in *Drake* that if there is a ratable proportion clause in a policy, an insurer who pays more than his ratable proportion of the loss is not entitled to recover any contribution from any other insurer, on the grounds that any sum paid in excess of the ratable proportion is paid voluntarily and contribution is only available in respect of compulsory payments. In practice such clauses are almost universal and the problem under consideration only arises where one insurer, unaware of the existence of the other insurance, pays the whole of the claim.
7 But see *Steadfast Insurance Co v F & B Trading Co* (1971) 46 ALJR 10, where it seems to have been assumed that non-compliance made the policy automatically void.

Chapter 36

Resolution of Commercial Disputes

36.0 Introduction

Given the nature and complexity of commercial activity, it is inevitable that disputes arise, especially where transactions involve large amounts of money. Disputes use up valuable resources in terms of money, management time and loss of trade. They may also damage trading reputations and relationships. It is therefore essential, in the interests of justice and the efficient use of economic resources, that machinery be provided for their speedy resolution.

Businesses will normally seek to minimise the potential for conflict by taking steps to prevent disputes arising and establishing procedures for speedily resolving any which do arise. Potential suppliers and customers may be investigated to determine their commercial reputation and creditworthiness. Careful planning and drafting of contracts may minimise the scope for disputes, by ensuring that they comply with relevant legal and regulatory requirements, are clearly expressed, fulfil the business's needs and provide, so far as possible, for those eventualities which may arise. Suitable provisions will be included to discourage disputes and to facilitate their speedy resolution. These may include provisions requiring payment of deposits; provision for the exercise of self-help remedies such as rights to withhold performance and/or terminate the contract or to recover goods under reservation of title clauses; arbitration or similar clauses defining the procedures to be adopted for resolving disputes; and provisions enabling the business to take advantage of simple and efficient procedures if litigation is resorted to, such as, for instance, clauses excluding or restricting rights of set-off or providing for payment of liquidated damages in the event of breach. A long-term contract may contain mechanisms allowing it to be varied in order to meet new contingencies as they arise.

No matter how much care is taken in the drafting of contracts, however, disputes will still inevitably arise, as is shown by the volume of litigation generated by the commodity trades and shipping industry, despite the widespread use of carefully drafted and well-known standard form contracts. In general, it may be said that disputes are likely to arise where one party seeks to act opportunistically, by taking advantage of a change in circumstances or uncertainty in a contract or in the law. Even the best drafted contract cannot provide with absolute certainty for every eventuality. There must therefore be mechanisms for resolving those disputes. The simplest, and most beneficial, is for the parties to seek themselves to resolve the dispute by negotiation, and most disputes are in fact settled by negotiation, generally without the intervention of lawyers[1]. Failing settlement, however, they may resort to litigation, to formal arbitration or to one of the many developing alternative dispute resolution (ADR) mechanisms.

1 See Beale and Dugdale, 'Contracts Between Businessmen' (1975) 2 BJLS 45. Cf Deakin, Lane and Wilkinson, *Contract Law, Trust Relations and Incentives for Co-operation: A Comparative Study* in Deakin and Michie (eds) *Contracts, Co-operation and Competition: studies in economics and management* (1997), who found a relatively high likelihood that small English firms in their survey would resort to litigation, especially to recover unpaid debts.

36.1 Litigation

In general, businesses tend to prefer to avoid litigation if at all possible. It may be costly and time consuming, generate bad publicity and damage a trading relationship. Above all, many business people are suspicious of lawyers who, they often suspect, do not understand their needs. Thus a survey of businesses' attitudes to contracts in 1975 confirmed that:

'Lawyers and legal remedies . . . tend to be avoided as being inflexible; lawyers are thought not to understand the needs of commerce and those firms who had consulted solicitors were not at all satisfied'[1].

The English adversarial system of litigation has often been thought to be inappropriate to the needs, especially, of commercial litigants. In the past, the system allowed the parties themselves, or rather their legal representatives, largely to control the progress of the litigation and thus provided considerable scope for them to engage in procedural manoeuvring in order to obtain tactical advantages. As a result, litigation could often be protracted and expensive. In contrast, the civil law inquisitorial system, under which the court exerts much greater control over the proceedings, was often said to possess many advantages. In 1987 Sir Jack Jacob, a Master of the Supreme Court, observed that:

'the English adversary system has many inherent failings, which are manifested in practice more often than is generally realised. Since it is the lawyers who choose when and what procedural steps should be taken or resisted, which they think would best serve their respective interests, it is a hit and miss system, sometimes producing the right result and sometimes not. The . . . system inevitably creates avoidable delays and increases both the labour and the costs. It introduces an element of sportsmanship or gamesmanship into the conduct of civil proceedings . . . [I]t prejudices the litigant who is unable to engage lawyers with an adequate resource base and skills to match his opponents. The true casualties of the adversary system are the litigants themselves, who are frustrated in their search for justice'[2].

Similarly, in 1980, Mr Justice Kerr (as he then was) wrote that: 'In long and complex cases the Continental inquisitorial procedure is often more effective than our adversary system'[3]. The defects of the English civil litigation system were recognised by Lord Woolf in his 1995 Report, *Access to Justice*. Lord Woolf recommended a number of changes to the system, designed to improve its efficiency, reduce costs and increase the speed with which cases are dealt with. The Woolf proposals received a generally favourable response and they have been implemented, in part, by the introduction of new Civil Procedure Rules (CPR), designed to simplify and speed up litigation. The new rules state that their 'overriding objective' is to 'enable the court to deal with cases justly'[4]. This involves, so far as possible,

- ensuring that the parties are on an equal footing,
- saving expense,
- enabling the case to be dealt with in a way which is proportionate to
  - the amount of money involved,
  - the importance of the case,
  - the complexity of the issues raised and
  - the financial position of each party
- ensuring that it is dealt with expeditiously and fairly; and
- allotting to it an appropriate share of the court's resources, while taking into account the need to allot resources to other cases.

The court is required to give effect to the 'overriding objective' when exercising any power under the rules or interpreting any rule, and the parties are under a duty to help the court further the overriding objective.

One of Woolf's main proposals was that judges should exercise a much greater degree of control over the proceedings in order to prevent the sort of procedural manoeuvring criticised above, with power to 'knock litigants' heads together' with a view to promoting a settlement. To this end, the new rules impose on the court a duty to actively manage litigation in order to further the overriding objective. 'Active management' involves encouraging the parties to co-operate with each other, identifying issues at an early stage, disposing summarily of issues where possible, encouraging settlement of all or part of the claim and fixing timetables and controlling the progress of the case[5].

Implementation of the Woolf reforms and the new CPR should reduce the adversarial nature of litigation and make litigation generally quicker and cheaper. Certainly, it should henceforth be more difficult for a litigant to use procedural tricks to spin out litigation and delay resolution of a dispute. Nevertheless, in many cases litigation will, inevitably, remain a hazardous and expensive business. Moreover, there is often simply no alternative to litigation; indeed, in recent years the volume of litigation has increased and the increase shows no sign of slowing down. Some of this increase is attributable to the fact that society is increasingly more litigious, some to the economic conditions of recent years. The increased availability of legal fees insurance and the legalisation of the use of contingency fees, permitting lawyers to take cases on a 'no-win, no-fee' basis[6] are likely to increase the growth in the volume of litigation. Just, therefore, as the substantive law has developed rules to facilitate commercial activity and meet the special needs of business, special procedures have been developed in an attempt to meet those needs.

1   See Beale and Dugdale, 'Contracts Between Businessmen' (1975) 2 BJLS 45; see also Wheeler, *Reservation of title clauses: impact and implications* (1991) ch 6, especially p 161 examining the attitudes of businesses to the role of lawyers in retention of title disputes.
2   *The Fabric of English Civil Justice* (1987) p 16.
3   The Hon Mr Justice Kerr, 'International Arbitration v Litigation' [1980] JBL 164 at 180.
4   CPR, Pt 1.
5   CPR, Pt 3.
6   Courts and Legal Services Act 1990, s 58, as amended by the Access to Justice Act 1999.

36.1.1 *Commercial litigation*

A dispute arising out of a commercial transaction may be heard in the county or the High Court. The county court has unlimited jurisdiction to hear cases involving claims in contract and tort, and cases involving less than £15,000 must be commenced in the county court. Many commercial disputes, including simple debt cases, will therefore fall within its jurisdiction. The more important commercial cases, however, will be heard in the High Court and generally in the Queen's Bench Division, although the Chancery Division hears cases concerned with companies and with insolvency. Some types of action may be brought in either division: retention of title litigation, for instance, may arise in the Queen's Bench Division if a supplier sues for wrongful interference with his goods, or in the Chancery Division, especially if the matter is brought before the court by a receiver or liquidator.

It has long been recognised that the commercial community should have a special forum to hear its disputes. As we saw in Chapter 1, even in medieval times there were special fora to deal with disputes within the mercantile community. In the eighteenth century Lord Mansfield held court sittings in the Guildhall in the City of London to hear commercial cases, assisted by panels of merchant jurymen to provide commercial expertise. However, during the nineteenth century the commercial community became increasingly reluctant to use the law courts to resolve disputes and in 1865 the Guildhall sittings were discontinued. Thereafter, commercial cases had to be heard by the ordinary common law courts. This seems to have been unpopular with the commercial community. Litigation was often protracted as a result of procedural delays and the judges were not conversant with the needs and practices of the commercial community. Perhaps as a result, there was at this time a significant increase in the use of arbitration to resolve commercial disputes. In 1892 the Council of Judges resolved that there should be a special court to hear commercial cases and in 1895 a special commercial list was established in the Queen's Bench Division, in order to provide speedier procedures for the resolution of commercial disputes and persuade the commercial community to continue to use the court[1]. In 1970 a separate Commercial Court was formally established within the Queen's Bench Division[2].

The jurisdiction and procedure of the Commercial Court are defined by Pt 49 of the Civil Procedure Rules and relevant Practice Direction. It has jurisdiction in relation to commercial claims, defined as including:

> 'any case arising out of trade and commerce in general including any case relating to –
> (i)   a business document or contract;
> (ii)   the export or import of goods;
> (iii) the carriage of goods by land, sea, air or pipeline;
> (iv) the exploitation of oil and gas resources;
> (v)   insurance and reinsurance;
> (vi)   banking and financial services;
> (vii) the operation of markets and exchanges;
> (viii) business agency; and
> (ix)   arbitration'[3].

The purpose of the Commercial Court is to provide a forum where there is familiarity with commercial disputes and procedures to enable them to be settled speedily and effectively without undue legal formality.

'The Commercial Court prides itself upon being as much a part of the City of London as it is of the machinery of the law'[4].

To this end, the court is staffed by specialist judges with particular expertise in commercial matters and adopts simplified procedures designed to make the court more suitable to the needs of commerce. On the whole, the Commercial List and subsequently the Commercial Court have been a great success. Although use of the Commercial List declined in the years after the Second World War, procedural reforms in the 1960s restored its popularity, which has continued to grow ever since. One factor contributing to the success of the court has been the high reputation of its judges, who have included some of the most highly respected members of the judiciary. A specialist Commercial Court Committee exists to monitor and review the procedures of the court, in consultation with representatives of users of the court, such as the Commercial Bar Association (COMBAR), the City of London Law Society and representatives of arbitrators, banks, commodity traders and insurers. The Committee publishes *The Commercial Court Guide,* which contains a complete guide to the practice of the court, updated from time to time. As the *Guide* observes:

'The success of the Court's ability to meet the special problems and continually changing needs of the commercial community depends in part upon a steady flow of information and constructive suggestions between the Court, litigants and professional advisers'[5].

The court is subject to the general Civil Procedure Rules, except as modified by the special procedures contained in its own rules and relevant Practice Direction. Indeed, its procedures have been used as a model for many of the reforms to general civil procedure arising out of Lord Woolf's proposals. The court is therefore subject to the overriding objective of the CPR. However, the court has its own special procedures, designed to meet the special needs of commercial people and their advisers and, above all, to enable disputes to be resolved as speedily as possible.

'The Commercial Court has since it was first established sought periodically to adapt its procedure to the continually changing needs of the commercial community'[6].

Thus, for instance, interlocutory applications are heard by the judge in charge of the list, not by a Master.

'The advantage of having access to the judge direct is not merely or mainly that it eliminates a set of proceedings before the Master; it is that in dealing with interlocutory matters the parties are in the presence of the judge who may be conducting the trial. Most schemes for reducing the costs of legal proceedings recognise the advantage of having someone who can in the early stages . . . knock the parties' heads together'[7].

Particulars of claim and defence are usually required to be kept short and simple; there is power for the court to order trial without service of particulars and procedures for the early disclosure of evidence. In addition, applications can be heard outside normal court hours and cases are generally given a fixed date for hearing.

'In principle, and the resources available to the Court permitting, the trial or other hearing of a case should take place at the earliest date for which the parties can be ready'[8].

As a result, the Commercial Court attracts a large volume of commercial litigation, much of it between parties neither of whom is English but who choose to litigate their disputes in London before the Commercial Court, making it 'almost certainly the most widely used single court for international commercial litigation'[9]. In recent years, however, the objectives of the Commercial Court have to some extent been frustrated by the volume of cases coming before it, resulting in increasing delays in cases coming to trial[10]. In order to reduce the burden on the court, a series of Practice Notices have therefore provided for the hearing of commercial cases outside London by establishing 'Mercantile Lists' in Liverpool and Manchester[11], Birmingham[12], Bristol[13], Leeds and Newcastle[14], Cardiff and Chester[15]. These are not, strictly, branches of the Commercial Court but their procedures are clearly modelled on those of the Commercial Court. 'Mercantile claims' are defined in the same way as 'commercial claims' but with the addition of claims relating to 'the customs and practices of particular trades, businesses and commercial organisations; commercial fraud; professional negligence in a commercial context; and arbitration applications'[16]. They are governed by a separate Mercantile Courts and Business Lists Practice Direction[17] and it is intended in due course to produce a 'Mercantile Courts and Business Lists Guide', but in the meantime practitioners responsible for cases listed in the mercantile lists are required to use the Commercial Court Guide.

1 For a description of the creation of the Commercial Court, see Mackinnon, 'The Origin of the Commercial Court' (1944) 60 LQR 324; see also Veeder (1994) 110 LQR 292.
2 By the Administration of Justice Act 1970, s 3; see now Supreme Court Act 1981, s 6. There is also a separate Companies Court which forms part of the Chancery Division.
3 CPR, Pt 49 and Practice Direction 49. Compare the previous rather archaic definition, in r 72 of the Rules of the Supreme Court: 'any case arising out of the ordinary transactions of merchants and traders and without prejudice to the generality of the foregoing words, any cause relating to the construction of a mercantile document, the export or import of merchandise, affreightment, insurance, banking, mercantile agency and mercantile usage'. The definition in r 72 was little changed from that in the Notice as to Commercial Causes of 1895 which first established the Commercial List.
4 Devlin, 'The relationship between commercial law and commercial practice' (1951) 14 MLR at 250.
5 *Commercial Court Guide*, para A6.1.
6 Paragraph A3.1.
7 (1951) 14 MLR at 261.
8 *Commercial Court Guide*, para A4.1.
9 The Hon Mr Justice Kerr, 'International Arbitration v Litigation' [1980] JBL 164 at 178.
10 Delay in an actions coming to trial in the Commercial Court has been held not to be sufficient reason to justify transferring the action to the Chancery or Queen's Bench Division: *Zakhem International Construction Ltd v Nippon Kokan KK* [1987] 2 Lloyd's Rep 661; *Morgan Guaranty Trust Co v Hadjantonakis (No 2)* [1988] 1 FTLR 107.
11 [1990] 1 All ER 528.
12 [1993] 4 All ER 381.
13 [1993] 4 All ER 1023; [1999] 2 All ER 1024.
14 [1997] 2 All ER 223.
15 [2000] 1 All ER (Comm) 384.
16 Practice Direction 49H.
17 Practice Direction 49H, para 5.6.

36.1.2   *Pre-trial procedures*

Only a small percentage of commercial cases in which litigation is commenced actually come to trial. The great majority are either settled by mutual agreement or come to a premature end as a result of procedural steps taken by one of the parties. There are a number of procedural devices which may be used to force an early conclusion. In most cases these will require one of the parties to apply to the court before a full trial of the case for an order requiring the other party to do, or debarring the other party from doing, something. Applications for pre-trial orders are generally made to a Master in cases before the High Court in London, or to the District Judge in proceedings in the High Court outside London or in the county court. In the Commercial Court, however, as we have seen, they will often be heard by the judge in person.

In an action to recover a simple debt, such as the price of goods delivered, the claimant may be able to obtain default judgment because the defendant simply fails to file or serve a defence to the claim. All that is required is the completion of the appropriate form: there is no hearing.

If the defendant indicates that he intends to defend the claim, it has long been possible for the claimant to seek summary judgment. The summary judgment procedure is a particularly powerful one by which the claimant seeks to persuade the court that there is no real defence to the claim and that the court should give judgment without a full trial. Under the new Civil Procedure Rules, the court's power to give summary judgment has been considerably extended. Either party can now apply for summary judgment, in any type of proceedings, and on an application the court can give judgment for either party on the whole claim or on a particular issue so as to narrow the range of issues which need to be considered at a full trial. The application is made on the basis of written evidence and the court will grant summary judgment if it is satisfied that the claimant has no real prospect of succeeding on, or the defendant has no real prospect of successfully defending, the claim or issue, as the case may be, and that there is no other reason why the issue should be disposed of at a full trial[1]. An application might be made where, for instance, the claimant seeks payment for goods delivered and there has been no indication by the defendant of any complaint about the goods before commencement of proceedings; or where the contract requires the buyer to pay in full without deduction or set-off; or where the claimant makes a claim on a bill of exchange, where the court will not permit claims based on the underlying contract to be used as a basis to resist payment[2]. A successful application for summary judgment may therefore enable the applicant to avoid the delay and expense of protracted proceedings and a full trial. Even if the court feels that there is an issue to be tried, it may grant leave to defend or proceed with a claim subject to conditions, such as that the defendant pay the amount of the claim into court or the claimant provide security for the defendant's costs.

Other tactics may be used to try to force a settlement. The claimant may apply to the court for an interim payment: if the court is satisfied that the claimant is likely to succeed at trial, it may order the defendant to make an interim payment on account of damages. Alternatively, either party may put pressure on the other by making an offer to settle the whole claim or a particular issue. The availability of this procedure has also been extended by the Civil Procedure Rules. It is now possible for either party to offer to settle any type of claim by making a written Part 36 Offer (although where the defendant offers to settle a money claim, he must make a payment into court, known as a Part 36 payment, of the amount offered in settlement). The significance of such offers is that the court has power to penalise by an award of costs and/or interest a party who refuses to accept such an offer. Where a Part 36 offer or payment is made, the offeree may accept it and end the proceedings, or discontinue the particular issue to which the offer relates. The offer may be accepted up to 21 days before the commencement of the trial. If the offeree chooses not to accept the offer, the case will proceed to trial, where the judge will not be told of the offer until after judgment. If the offeree fails to obtain a judgment more favourable than the offer, the court may order him to pay the costs of the offeror from the latest date when the offer could have been accepted. Since costs escalate dramatically as litigation proceeds and, especially, at the time of preparation for and during the hearing itself, a party who refuses a Part 36 Offer or Payment runs a considerable risk. In addition, if a defendant refuses a claimant's offer to settle a money claim and the court at trial awards the claimant more than he offered to settle for, the court may order the defendant to pay interest on the sum awarded from the latest date when the offer could have been accepted.

Other steps, too, may be taken to force the pace or to put pressure on the other party. Applications may be made for orders to strike out particulars of claim or defence, or requiring further particulars, although such procedural manoeuvres are frowned upon and discouraged in proceedings in the Commercial Court.

1   CPR, Pt 24
2   See 28.1.2 above.

36.1.2.1   *Interim measures*

Partly as a result of the delays involved in preparing the case and in making and opposing pre-trial applications, it may often take years for a case to come on to a full trial. In some cases, however, urgent steps may have to be taken to protect a business' interests – for instance, where it is feared that the defendant may destroy evidence, or remove assets outside the jurisdiction of the court in order to prevent enforcement of any judgment, or that the defendant may resell assets alleged to be subject to a retention of title clause. In such cases the court must be able to act promptly. The court therefore has wide powers to grant interim measures including injunctions – temporary orders, granted during proceedings, before a full trial in order to maintain the status quo pending trial.

Such orders will often be made, in the first instance on the application of one party without notice to the other. The principles governing the grant of such orders were established by the House of Lords in *American Cyanamid Co v Ethicon Ltd*[1] and are now confirmed in the Civil Procedure Rules[2]. Subject to the overriding objective of the rules, an order will be granted if (a) the claimant shows that there is a serious issue to be tried and (b) the balance of convenience favours the grant of an injunction. This test will often favour the grant of the injunction[3].

When the order is made without the court hearing both parties, it will normally be granted for only a limited period until a further hearing at which the court can hear both parties and decide whether to continue or to discharge the injunction. Moreover, a claimant who seeks an injunction without notice to the defendant will normally be required to give an undertaking to compensate the defendant by paying damages for any losses caused by the injunction if it is ultimately decided that it should not have been granted. Nevertheless, interim injunctions can often have a devastating effect on a business and may force a party to the negotiating table.

Two types of interim injunction deserve special mention, because they demonstrate the willingness of the courts to devise new procedures to meet the special needs of commercial disputes. In 1975 the Court of Appeal recognised that the court could grant an order restraining a defendant from dealing with some or all of his assets, or from disposing of or removing them from the court's jurisdiction[4], and the court's power to grant such orders is now confirmed by statute[5]. Such orders, which effectively freeze the defendant's assets, were formerly known as 'Mareva injunctions' after one of the early cases in which such an order was made[6]. They are now known as 'freezing injunctions'.

Mareva/'freezing' injunctions have proved highly effective and the jurisdiction to grant them has gradually been extended. A freezing injunction may now be made at any stage of the proceedings, before or during the trial or even after judgment, and may be made in support of proceedings in a foreign jurisdiction[7]. Its purpose is to protect the plaintiff against the defendant thwarting any judgment by dissipating assets or removing them beyond the reach of the court. The injunction may cover a wide range of assets, including personal and real property and bank accounts, and may extend to property outside the jurisdiction of the court[8]. It binds not only the defendant against whom it is made but also any third party who has notice of it, such as the defendant's bank, and the order may be supported by further orders requiring the defendant or others to disclose the whereabouts of assets. However, the order does not give the claimant any proprietary or security interest in the assets it covers or affect the order of priority of distribution of assets if the defendant becomes insolvent[9]. Breach of the order amounts to a contempt of court for which the offending party may be fined or imprisoned.

A freezing injunction may have a devastating impact on a defendant's business. In practice, an order is often sought at a pre-trial stage without notice to the defendant – indeed, often before or at the same time as the commencement of substantive proceedings. In order to protect the defendant against abuse of the process, the court will require the claimant applying for an injunction to show that he has a good arguable case and that there is a real risk that the defendant will try to dissipate assets, or remove them from the jurisdiction. As a condition of obtaining the order, the claimant will have to give undertakings, including one to compensate the defendant for any loss caused by the grant of the order if his claim ultimately fails at trial and one to indemnify third parties against any expense incurred in complying with the order, and the order will be limited to the amount required to satisfy the claimant's claim and will provide for the defendant to draw reasonable living and legitimate trading expenses; it may even permit the defendant to dispose of assets in the ordinary course of business. Moreover, because of their impact on business, freezing injunctions will not normally be granted against banks[10]. Nevertheless, despite these safeguards, the freezing injunction has become a highly potent weapon in commercial litigation.

A second type of order developed in the mid-1970s was the 'Anton Piller order', named after the case in which such an order was first granted[11], and now known as a 'search order'. This is an order requiring the defendant to permit the claimant's representatives to enter his premises and inspect or remove documents or other property specified in the order. Its purpose is to prevent the destruction of evidence. Typically, it will be used where it is alleged that the defendant has infringed the claimant's intellectual property rights or interfered with his business – for instance, if an agent has wrongfully diverted business or income from his principal. It is not a civil search warrant – it does not empower anyone to enter premises – but requires the defendant to allow the claimant's representative to have access to premises and to examine and remove evidence. Failure to comply with the order will be a contempt of court. Like the freezing injunction, the search order is now granted pursuant to statutory powers[12] but was initially developed by the court.

A search order is almost always sought without notice to the defendant – the element of surprise is essential to its effectiveness – and often before the service of proceedings on the defendant. Like the freezing injunction it may have a devastating effect on the defendant's business. The removal of documents may paralyse the business; their disclosure could give the claimant access to confidential or secret commercial information. The courts have therefore been concerned to prevent the abuse of such orders. The claimant seeking an order is required to make full and fair disclosure of all relevant facts and must show: (a) that he has a strong prima facie case (the order cannot be used as a means of searching for evidence to see if there is a case); (b) that the defendant's activities pose a serious risk of actual or potential harm to his interests; and (c) that there is clear evidence that the defendant possesses the documents or evidence covered by the order and that they will be removed or destroyed if an inter partes application or notice is made. The claimant will be required to give undertakings, including one to compensate the defendant for any losses caused by the order if it is shown to have been improperly obtained, and the claimant's solicitor will normally be required to give further undertakings, including one to explain the order to the defendant, to inform the defendant of the right to seek legal advice before complying with the order, to make a list of any items removed, not to use them for any purpose other than the litigation in which the order is granted, and to return them to the defendant after copying them. In order to guard against oppressive use of the order, it will normally contain further restrictions on the time at which and the persons by whom it may be executed: for instance, the execution of the order will normally have to be supervised by an independent solicitor[13]. An order will not normally be made which will require the defendant to incriminate himself[14]. An order may be set aside, and the claimant ordered to pay damages, if it is obtained improperly.

Although the power to grant freezing injunctions and search orders is now confirmed by statute, both were first developed by the courts, providing striking examples of the power of the courts to develop new remedies to meet the needs of commercial litigants. Lord Denning described the development of the Mareva (freezing) injunction as 'the greatest piece of judicial law reform in my time'[15] and the Anton Piller (search) order as 'an innovation which has proved its worth time and time again'[16]. On the other hand, his successor as Master of the Rolls, Lord Donaldson, pointed out that the making of such orders involves the exercise of a 'draconian power which should only be used in a very exceptional case'[17] and described Mareva injunctions and Anton Piller orders as 'the law's two "nuclear" weapons'[18]. The use of search orders was even challenged as being contrary to the European Convention on Human Rights, but was upheld so long as the order is not used oppressively and is accompanied by adequate safeguards[19]. The courts must therefore be vigilant to prevent their abuse, but provided that the use of such orders is accompanied by appropriate and adequate safeguards, they are an immensely useful tool in commercial litigation and a significant contribution by the law of procedure to commercial law.

1 [1975] AC 396.
2 CPR, Pt 25
3 This test may not be appropriate where the grant of an injunction would effectively determine the issue between the parties: see *Cambridge Nutrition Ltd v BBC* [1990] 3 All ER 523 and the general statement of principles in CPR, Pt 25.

4   *Mareva Compania Naviera SA v International Bulkcarriers SA* [1975] 2 Lloyd's Rep 509.
5   Supreme Court Act 1981, s 37(3); Civil Procedure Rules, Pt 25; Practice Direction 25.6.
6   *Mareva Compania Naviera SA v International Bulkcarriers SA* [1975] 2 Lloyd's Rep 509; the first case in which such an order was granted was *Nippon Yusen Kaisha v Karageorgis* [1975] 2 Lloyd's Rep 137.
7   Civil Jurisdiction and Judgments Act 1992, s 25(1).
8   See eg *Babanaft International Co Ltd v Bassatne* [1990] Ch 13; *Republic of Haiti v Duvalier* [1990] 1 QB 202; *Derby & Co Ltd v Weldon* [1990] Ch 48.
9   *Capital Cameras Ltd v Harold Line Ltd* [1991] 3 All ER 389.
10 *Polly Peck International plc v Nadir (No 2)* [1992] 4 All ER 769.
11 First granted in *Anton Piller KG v Manufacturing Processes Ltd* [1976] Ch 55.
12 Civil Procedure Act 1997, s 7; Civil Procedure Rules, Pt 25; Practice Direction 25.6.
13 See *Universal Thermosensors Ltd v Hibben* [1992] 3 All ER 257.
14 *Rank Film Distributors Ltd v Video Information Centre* [1982] AC 380; *Tate Access Floors Inc v Boswell* [1991] Ch 512; cf *IBM United Kingdom Ltd v Prima Data International Ltd* [1994] 4 All ER 748.
15 *The Due Process of Law* (1980) p 134.
16 *Rank Film Distributors Ltd v Video Information Centre* [1982] AC 380 at 406.
17 Per Donaldson LJ in *Yousif v Salama* [1980] 1 WLR 1540 at 1544.
18 Per Lord Donaldson MR in *Bank Mellat v Nikpour* [1985] FSR 87 at 92.
19 *Chappell v United Kingdom* (1989) European Court of Human Rights Series A, no 132-A, [1989] FSR 617.

36.2   Arbitration[1]

Arbitration has long been a popular method of settling business disputes arising out of contractual relationships. The parties may agree to refer a dispute to arbitration after the dispute has arisen, but often the contract itself will provide for any disputes which arise out of it to be referred to arbitration. In particular, the standard forms of contract commonly used for international and commodity trading, shipping and construction and engineering contracts generally provide for disputes to be referred to arbitration, but individual contracts prepared for particular parties or transactions may also include arbitration clauses.

There are a number of well-established bodies providing an arbitration service, including the Court of Arbitration of the International Chamber of Commerce, the London Centre of International Arbitration and the American Arbitration Association. The provision of arbitration services can be highly lucrative and a number of other regional centres have been established in international trade centres. Moreover, a number of international and domestic trade associations provide arbitration services for their members. A contract which requires disputes to be referred to arbitration will often provide for reference to one of these centres or bodies, but it is not uncommon for a contract to provide simply for ad hoc arbitration by a single arbitrator or a panel of arbitrators to be appointed by the parties as and when a dispute arises.

Arbitration is essentially a consensual process, the parties in dispute agreeing to refer that dispute to an independent third party for adjudication on the basis of evidence and arguments to be presented to him and that that adjudication shall be binding upon them. The arbitrator's decision thus acquires its binding force from the parties' agreement. In the past, the courts tended to be suspicious of arbitration, fearing that arbitration agreements might be used to oust the jurisdiction of the court. However, in recent years the courts have treated arbitration with much less suspicion than hitherto, recognising that:

'Courts and arbitrators are in the same business, namely the administration of justice. The only difference is that the courts are in the public and the arbitrators in the private sector of the industry'[2].

It is increasingly recognised, therefore, that where parties have freely agreed to refer disputes to binding and final arbitration, their agreement should be respected and they should be held to it and, since 1979, the power of the English courts to intervene in a dispute referred to arbitration pursuant to a valid arbitration agreement has been much restricted. Different considerations apply to consumer contracts where consent to arbitration may not be freely given and arbitration clauses in consumer contracts are therefore subject to strict controls.

1   What follows is only an outline of some of the more important features of arbitration: the reader seeking more detailed coverage should refer to one of the standard works on the subject such as Mustill and Boyd, *The Law and Practice of Commercial Arbitration in England* or Redfern and Hunter, *The Law and Practice of International Commercial Arbitration.*
2   *Bremer Vulkan Schiffbau und Maschinenfebrik v South India Shipping Corpn Ltd* [1981] AC 909 at 921, per Donaldson J.

36.2.1   Advantages of arbitration

Arbitration is often thought to have a number of advantages over litigation. In particular, it is often thought to be quicker and cheaper than litigation. Proceedings are held in private, enabling parties to avoid publicity for their dispute. It may be particularly attractive in an international context where each party may be unwilling to submit to the jurisdiction of the other's national courts, but be prepared to agree to arbitration by an independent third party. As Professor Schmitthoff observed:

> 'In international disputes the parties are sometimes disinclined to go to the national courts. They prefer their dispute to be settled by persons with an international outlook'[1].

Moreover, the parties can choose their own arbitrator(s) and thus may refer their dispute to a person with special experience or expertise in the relevant area. The proceedings may be less formal than litigation and the parties may give the arbitrator extensive powers. Finally, it is thought that arbitration may be less confrontational, and therefore less damaging to a commercial relationship, than litigation and may therefore be preferred where the parties wish to preserve their trading relationship.

In fact, these advantages may sometimes be more perceived than real[2]. In particular, arbitration can often be at least as time consuming as litigation; a dispute may raise complex issues of fact or technical points of fact or law which require considerable time to be set aside for argument. Moreover, arbitration can be expensive, especially where the reference is to more than one arbitrator. The arbitrators will generally be experienced professional persons whose time must be paid for; they may also have to be paid expenses to travel to and attend hearings. Some of the institutional arbitration schemes may be particularly expensive. Conversely, delay and expense may be increased unless the parties have taken care to define the procedures to be adopted and the powers of the arbitrator. Although the court's powers to intervene in arbitration proceedings are now limited, they are not wholly excluded and in some circumstances the parties may need to invoke the court's assistance, for instance, to enforce an award, or to resolve unforeseen procedural problems.

In the past, a particular disadvantage of arbitration has been that an arbitrator's powers to make interim orders have been much more limited than those of the court. Until 1990, arbitrators had no power to dismiss an application for delay in prosecution; a party to a dispute could therefore use reference to arbitration to 'kill' the dispute by delaying taking necessary steps in the proceedings, allowing the arbitration to 'go to sleep'. The courts attempted to control such delaying tactics by finding a mutual duty on parties to arbitration proceedings to co-operate in the arbitration[3] or that the behaviour of the parties amounted to an agreement to abandon the arbitration[4], but both approaches proved unsatisfactory[5]. Since 1990, however, arbitrators have had power to dismiss a claim for want of prosecution[6], and under the Arbitration Act 1996 they now have extensive powers, including the ability to order a party to provide security for costs, and to give directions for such matters as the inspection, preservation, sampling etc of property, the preservation of evidence and the examination of witnesses. However, their powers are still less extensive than those of the court.

In many cases, therefore, arbitration may be no more advantageous than litigation in the Commercial Court. Nevertheless, it is widely favoured and some of its advantages are real. In particular, for reasons explained below, in the context of international disputes it may sometimes be easier to enforce an arbitration award in another country than it would be to enforce a court judgment.

1   Schmitthoff, 'Why arbitration is the favoured method of dispute settlement', *Financial Times*, 4 October 1985.
2   See generally The Hon Mr Justice Kerr, 'International Arbitration v Litigation' [1980] JBL 164.
3   *Bremer Vulkan Schiffbau und Maschinenfebrik v South India Shipping Corpn Ltd* [1981] AC 909. The parties are now under a similar duty by virtue of s 40 of the Arbitration Act 1996.
4   *The Leonidas D* [1985] 2 All ER 796.
5   See per Lord Goff in *Food Corpn of India v Antclizo Shipping Corpn* [1988] 2 All ER 513 esp at 515 and 521; see also the Departmental Advisory Committee on English Arbitration Law, 'Report on Delay: Striking out Claims in Arbitration' (1988) 4 Arb Int 160-1.
6   Arbitration Act 1950, s 13A, inserted by Courts and Legal Services Act 1990, s 102; see now Arbitration Act 1996, s 41(3).

36.2.2   *Harmonisation of arbitration law*

The procedure of an arbitration is governed by the arbitration law of the state in which the arbitration has its 'seat', the place where it has its juridical base (not necessarily the place where it is geographically based) and there may be significant differences between national arbitration laws. If arbitration is to be an effective means of resolving international disputes, the arbitration process must have international respect. If, say, an English company and an American company enter into a contract and agree to refer any disputes arising from their contract to arbitration in New York, their agreement will be frustrated if either party can subvert the agreed procedure by referring a dispute to a court instead. It is therefore not enough for the agreement to be respected by the English courts; it must also be respected by the US courts. Similarly, an arbitral award may be useless unless it is recognised and can be enforced in other countries. Moreover, just as the parties to an international contract may be reluctant to submit to each other's national courts, each may be reluctant to submit to the other's domestic arbitration law. It has therefore been recognised that harmonisation of arbitration law is just as important as harmonisation of substantive law.

Two international conventions, the Geneva Convention of 1924 and the New York Convention of 1950, provide for the mutual recognition of arbitration awards. Thus an award made in one state party to either convention will be recognised and can be enforced in another convention state, provided that the award conforms to the appropriate convention rules. The UK is party to both conventions.

Further progress towards harmonisation of arbitration law has been stimulated by UNCITRAL, which has produced a set of Arbitration Rules and a model arbitration law. The UNCITRAL Arbitration Rules are widely used and may be adopted by the parties to an arbitration. A number of states, including Scotland and several common law jurisdictions in the Commonwealth and the United States, have adopted the Model Law as the basis for their domestic arbitration laws.

Where contracting parties distrust each other's arbitration systems, they may agree to submit to arbitration subject to the law of a 'neutral' third party state. It is partly for this reason that London is such a popular arbitration centre. An alternative is for them to agree to arbitration by one of the bodies established to provide an international arbitration service, such as the Court of Arbitration of the International Chamber of Commerce. This is probably the most commonly used of the international arbitration bodies. It has been described as 'the most truly international of all arbitral systems'[1] and it has a set of detailed arbitration rules which 'provide a code that is intended to be self-sufficient in the sense that it is capable of covering all aspects of arbitrations conducted under the rules, without the need for any recourse to any municipal system of law or any application to the courts of the forum'[2].

1   Per Steyn J in *Bank Mallet v GAA Development and Construction Co* [1988] 2 Lloyd's Rep 44 at 48.
2   Per Kerr LJ in *Bank Mallet v Helsinki Techniki SA* [1984] QB 291 at 304.

36.2.3   *Arbitration in English law*

The essence of arbitration is that the parties agree to refer disputes, actual or potential, to the decision of a third party or parties, and to be legally bound by the decision of that party or parties. The arbitrator's decision therefore derives its binding force from the agreement of the parties. However, as with any other agreement, an arbitration agreement will only be legally binding if it is recognised and enforced by the law. Moreover, again as with any agreement, the parties to an arbitration agreement are unlikely to anticipate and provide for every eventuality. If some unprovided-for circumstance should arise, they may need to seek the assistance of the court to resolve it. Arbitration therefore needs the sanction and the support of the law.

The attractiveness of arbitration as a means of resolving commercial disputes has required most developed systems of commercial law to evolve a set of rules governing arbitrations. England, and especially the City of London, has long been a major arbitration centre and the English law of arbitration dates back at least as far as 1698 when the first statute on the subject was passed[1]. The primary source of the English law of arbitration is now the Arbitration Act 1996. Prior to the passing of the 1996 Act, however, the law was contained in four statutes – the Arbitration Acts 1950, 1975, 1979 and the Consumer Arbitration Agreements Act 1988 – and a mass of case law.

Publication of the UNCITRAL Model Law prompted the DTI to establish a Departmental Advisory Committee, initially chaired by Lord Mustill, to review the English law of arbitration and consider whether to adopt the Model Law in its place. In 1989 the Committee reported and recommended that the Model Law should not be adopted, on the grounds that it was not a complete code and would therefore need to be supplemented in order to replace the whole of the existing domestic law and that, in any case, English law was superior in some respects. However, using the Model Law as a 'yardstick by which to judge the quality of

. . . existing arbitration legislation'[2], the Committee also concluded that English law was in need of revision, modernisation and rationalisation. A major weakness of the existing domestic law was that it was 'spread around a hotchpotch of statutes and countless cases'[3]. The Committee recognised that what was needed in its place was a modern statute comprising 'a statement in statutory form of the more important principles of the English law of arbitration, statutory (and to the extent practicable) common law'[4], set out in a logical order and expressed so far as possible in non-technical language so as to make the law accessible to the ordinary lay user.

The result, after a long gestation period, was the 1996 Act[5]. Its purpose, as its long title states, is to restate and improve the existing law. As the Advisory Committee recommended, the Act does not adopt the Model Law, but follows its structure and has adopted a number of provisions from it[6] and where appropriate the courts may refer to both the Advisory Committee Report and to the Model Law in interpreting its provisions[7]. The Act also draws on the pre-existing English law. However, the Act is not intended to be a complete codification or restatement of the existing law, it being felt that that would have tended to freeze the law and hamper its future development. Nor would it have been practicable to codify the mass of pre-existing case law in some areas. Instead, some issues have been left to be developed in case law. As a result, according to one commentator, 'the English law of arbitration might have a strong claim to be the most well-developed and sophisticated system in the world'[8].

Section 1 of the Act contains a statement of the general principles on which it is based and in accordance with which it is to be construed. It states that:

'(a) the object of arbitration is to obtain the fair resolution of disputes by an impartial tribunal without unnecessary delay or expense;
 (b) the parties should be free to agree how their disputes are resolved, subject only to such safeguards as are necessary in the public interest;
 (c) in matters governed by this Part the court should not intervene except as provided by this Part.'

The core philosophies of the Act can therefore be said to be respect for party autonomy and support for the arbitration process, and these themes are developed throughout the Act. Thus, for instance, it extends the powers of arbitrators to make orders relating to procedural matters such as security for costs, reducing the need to involve the courts in the arbitral process, whilst restricting the rights of parties to appeal to the courts against arbitral decisions.

English law has not always shown such respect for arbitral autonomy. In the context of arbitration two principles collide: respect for freedom of contract and the public policy that the jurisdiction of the court should not be ousted. Particularly during the first half of the twentieth century the courts were often deeply suspicious of arbitration and jealously guarded their right of supervision. Thus in 1922 Scrutton LJ emphasised the supervisory authority of the court, observing that the courts –

'do not allow the agreement of private parties to oust the jurisdiction of the King's Courts . . . There must be no Alsatia in England where the King's writ does not run'[9].

In some areas this suspicion continued until relatively recently. In more recent times, however, this attitude has changed. London is an important arbitration centre, especially for disputes arising out of commodity and shipping contracts, and many disputes are referred to arbitration in London, even where neither party is English. Arbitration is therefore a valuable 'invisible export'. During the 1970s concern grew that the ease with which a party dissatisfied with an arbitral decision could have it reviewed by the court might undermine the advantages of arbitration and lead parties to remove their arbitral business from London to other centres more willing to respect arbitral autonomy[10]. The 1979 Arbitration Act was therefore passed to restrict the right of a party dissatisfied with an arbitration decision to refer it to the courts, and the courts followed suit by establishing restrictive principles governing the grant of leave to appeal from an arbitral decision[11]. In *Channel Tunnel Group Ltd v Balfour Beatty Construction Ltd*[12] the parties had agreed that disputes should be referred in the first instance to a panel of experts and, following that, to arbitration. The House of Lords held that the statutory power to order a stay of court proceedings could be exercised where, as here, some procedure other than arbitration was itself a condition precedent to arbitration and that the court had an inherent jurisdiction to order a stay in order to support the parties' chosen method of dispute resolution. Lord Mustill emphasised that the parties were 'large commercial enterprises, negotiating at arm's length in the light of a long experience' and that the court proceedings should therefore be stayed –

> 'in accordance . . . with the presumption . . . that those who make agreements for the resolution of disputes must show good reasons for departing from them [and] with the interests of the orderly regulation of international commerce'[13].

However, as recently as 1994 concern was expressed that the willingness of the courts to interfere in the arbitral process by ordering security for costs[14] might prejudice the status of London as a leading arbitral centre. By affirming and reinforcing the principle of party autonomy the 1996 Act should help to assuage those concerns.

1   9&10 Will III c 13.
2   Steyn (1994) 10 Arb Int 1.
3   Lord Savile [1997] LMCLQ 501 at 504.
4   Report of the Departmental Advisory Committee.
5   The process of preparation of the Act is described by Lord Savile [1997] LMCLQ 501.
6   For a general comparison of the Act and the Model Law, see Davidson [1997] JBL101.
7   See *Patel v Patel* [1999] 1 All ER (Comm) 923 at 926 (Model Law); *Azov Shipping Co v Baltic Shipping Co* [1999] 2 All ER (Comm) 453 (DAC Report).
8   Davidson [1997] JBL 101 at 129.
9   *Czarnikow v Roth Schmidt & Co* [1922] 2 KB 478 at 488.
10   See Sir Anthony Lloyd, 'The Bill of Lading: do we really need it?' [1989] LMCLQ 47 at 58.
11   In *The Nema, Pioneer Shipping Ltd v BTP Trioxide Ltd* [1982] AC 724; see below 36.2.3.5.
12   [1993] AC 334, [1993] 1 All ER 664; cf *Halifax Financial Services Ltd v Intuitive Systems Ltd* [1999] 1 All ER (Comm) 303.
13   [1993] AC 334 at 353, [1993] 1 All ER 664 at 678.
14   In *Coppée Lavalin SA/NV v Ken Ren Chemicals and Fertilizers Ltd* [1995] 1 AC 38.

36.2.3.1   *Arbitration Act 1996*

The 1996 Act is in four parts. Its main provisions are in Pt I, which applies to arbitrations generally. Part II contains special provisions applicable to 'domestic' arbitrations and to arbitration agreements with consumers. For reasons explained below, those relating to 'domestic' arbitrations have not been, and will not be, brought into force. Part III contains provisions on the recognition and enforcement of foreign arbitration awards.

Most of the provisions in Pt I of the Act apply automatically only where the 'juridical seat' of the arbitration is in England and Wales – that is to say, where the law of England and Wales is the law governing the arbitration procedure. Consistent with the principle of autonomy, the Act provides that the parties may designate the seat of the arbitration, or may authorise any arbitral or other institution (such as the ICC), or the arbitral tribunal itself, to do so. In the absence of such designation, the seat is to be determined 'having regard to the parties' agreement and all the relevant circumstances'[1].

The Act draws a distinction between 'mandatory' and 'non-mandatory' provisions. Again, in accordance with the principle of autonomy, most of its provisions are 'non-mandatory', meaning that the parties may modify or exclude them by agreement. In effect, therefore, most of the Act's provisions operate as 'default rules', much like the provisions of the Sale of Goods Act in relation to a commercial sale contract, which govern those aspects of the arbitration for which the parties have not provided expressly or impliedly, or by adopting the rules of an institutional arbitration scheme.

Prior to 1996 a distinction was drawn in English law between 'domestic' and 'international' arbitrations. Essentially, an arbitration was 'domestic' when all the aspects of the arbitration were connected with one country. This distinction was particularly important in relation to the court's jurisdiction to grant a stay of judicial proceedings brought in breach of an arbitration agreement and the power of a party to the arbitration to appeal to the court against an arbitrator's decision. In both cases the court had greater freedom to intervene in a domestic than an international arbitration. The Advisory Committee recommended the abolition of this distinction but in the Act as passed it was preserved by the inclusion of special provisions applicable to domestic arbitrations[2]. However, in 1996 the Court of Appeal held that to apply different rules to arbitrations involving UK nationals and nationals of other EU member states would be contrary to EC law, as unlawful discrimination and an impermissible restriction on the freedom to provide services[3]. To have extended to international arbitrations the rules applicable to domestic arbitrations would have put the UK in breach of its obligations under the New York Convention governing the international recognition and enforcement of arbitration awards. The decision was therefore taken to abolish the distinction by not bringing into force the provisions relating to domestic arbitrations.

1   Section 3.
2   Sections 85–87.
3   *Philip Alexander Securities and Futures Ltd v Bamberger* [1996] CLC 1757.

36.2.3.2   *Arbitration agreements*

An agreement can only be referred to arbitration with the consent of both parties. The foundation of any arbitration is therefore the parties' agreement, which confers jurisdiction on the arbitrator and may define much of the arbitration procedure. The agreement may relate either to an existing dispute or to future potential disputes which may arise out of the parties' relationship. In the former case the agreement will obviously be a free-standing agreement, known as a 'submission' or 'compromis'. Commercial contracts often contain an arbitration clause, or 'clause compromissoire', by which the parties agree to refer future to arbitration disputes arising out of their contract. The Arbitration Act applies to both types of agreement.

The agreement may contain provisions covering in detail such matters as the constitution of the arbitral tribunal, the procedure to be followed and so on, or may be quite simple. A distinction is drawn between 'ad hoc' and 'institutional' arbitration. An ad hoc arbitration is governed by procedural rules adopted for the particular dispute or contract. Those rules may either be drafted by, or for, the particular parties, or may be derived from the rules of an arbitral organisation. An institutional arbitration is administered by one of the established arbitral organisations, such as the ICC which provides the procedural rules for the arbitration.

At common law an arbitration agreement could be in any form. The Arbitration Act 1996, however, only applies to arbitration agreements which are in writing[1]. Section 5 of the Act defines 'writing' in wide terms for this purpose, making special provision, inter alia, for the use of modern technology[2]. There is no need for the agreement to be signed by the parties and the requirement of writing is satisfied by:

- an exchange of communications in writing;
- a written record evidencing a prior agreement[3], produced with the authority of both parties by either of them or by a third party[4];
- an exchange of written submissions in arbitral proceedings or litigation in which an arbitration agreement is alleged by one party and not denied by the other[5].

The Act further provides that 'references to anything being written or in writing include its being recorded by any means'[6]. It seems clear, therefore, that fax and telex messages would qualify as 'writing' for this purpose. So, too, it is submitted, would a computer record, including e-mail. On its face the section would also appear to cover recordings made by tape or video recording, as, for instance, where a telephone conversation in which the parties agree to refer a dispute to arbitration is recorded by one of them, or an agreement is recorded in an exchange of voice mail messages. However, it is not clear that this was intended[7].

Given the widespread use of standard terms, an important question is whether the requirement of writing is satisfied by an arbitration clause contained in a set of standard terms. The answer under the 1996 Act is that it is. It provides that 'Where the parties agree otherwise than in writing by reference to terms which are in writing, they make an agreement in writing'[8]. Thus where parties orally agree to contract by reference to a set of standard terms including an arbitration clause there is a written arbitration agreement for the purposes of the Act[9].

A related question which has given rise to a considerable volume of litigation is whether, where a contract between A and B refers to and purports to incorporate the terms of a separate contract between B and C on which it depends, an arbitration clause included in the B-C contract is incorporated by the reference into the A-B contract. This question has typically arisen where bills of lading issued under a charterparty purport to incorporate the terms of the charterparty, which include an arbitration clause, but it may arise in other circumstances where one contract is dependent on another. Thus, for instance, the same question has arisen in relation to contracts of reinsurance and similar problems could arise in relation to construction contracts where a sub-contract is made on the same terms as the main contract. The answer which emerges from the charterparty cases is that everything depends on the wording of the two contracts[10]. It is not necessary for the B-C contract to refer specifically to the arbitration clause; the normal rule, however, is that a general reference in the B-C contract to the terms of the A-B contract will not incorporate an arbitration clause from the A-B contract[11] unless that clause, on its face, applies to disputes arising under the B-C contract[12].

In short, general words of reference will not normally be sufficient to incorporate into a contract an arbitration clause from a separate contract.

Although it may be argued that bills of lading, being transferable, are a special case, the same rule has been extended and applied to other classes of contract[13]. The rule has been explained on the basis that the arbitration clause is, strictly speaking, in law a separate contract from that in which it appears. It seems, however, that the rule has its roots in judicial hostility to arbitration and the feeling that a contractor should not be deprived of his right to refer disputes to the courts without his clear assent.

The 1996 Act does not resolve this problem. Section 6(2) provides that:

> 'The reference in an agreement to a written form of arbitration clause or to a document containing an arbitration clause constitutes an arbitration agreement if the reference is such as to make that clause part of the agreement'.

In *Trygg Hansa Insurance v Equitas*[14] it was held that the pre-1996 case law should be used to determine whether a reference to the terms of a contract which contains an arbitration clause 'is such as to make that clause part of the agreement'. A contract of reinsurance provided that 'this policy is to follow the same terms, exclusions, conditions, definitions and settlements as the Policy of the Primary Insurers'. The primary insurance contained an arbitration clause. It was held that, following the rules established prior to 1996, general words of reference are normally insufficient to incorporate an arbitration clause, and that therefore the arbitration clause in the primary insurance was not incorporated into the reinsurance contract.

It may now be possible in some circumstances for a person to take the benefit of and be bound by an arbitration agreement to which he is not party by virtue of the Contracts (Rights of Third Parties) Act 1999. That Act enables a person, in certain circumstances, to enforce a term in a contract to which he is not a party[15]. The Law Commission originally proposed that arbitration agreements should be excluded from the legislation, on the grounds that the 1999 Act generally only entitles a third a party to take the benefit of, but not to be subject to obligations under, a contract to which he is not party, whereas arbitration agreements are bilateral agreements, binding both parties to use arbitration. However, concern was expressed that this could produce difficulties. If A and B were to enter into a contract conferring a benefit on C and providing for disputes arising out of the contract to be referred to arbitration, the intention of the contracting parties that disputes should be referred to arbitration would be defeated if C were to be entitled to enforce the benefit but not to be bound by the arbitration clause. A late amendment was therefore introduced into the legislation to ensure that, in such cases, C's acceptance of the benefit under the contract is conditional on his acceptance of the arbitration clause. The Act provides that where third party beneficiary, C, has a right under the 1999 Act to enforce a substantive term of a contract between A and B, and that term is subject to a term providing for the reference of disputes to arbitration, C is to be treated for the purposes of the Arbitration Act as a party to the arbitration agreement as regards disputes relating to the enforcement of the substantive term[16]. He will therefore take the benefit of, and be bound by, the arbitration agreement. Suppose, therefore, that A and B enter into a construction contract which contains (i) provisions for A to make certain payments to C and (ii) a requirement for all disputes relating to such payments to be referred to arbitration. If C is entitled under the 1999 Act to enforce the term providing for payment, his right to do so is subject to the arbitration clause and if he commences court proceedings to enforce his right A may seek a stay of proceedings to require him to refer the dispute to arbitration.

In addition, where under the 1999 Act C has a right to enforce an arbitration agreement between A and B, if C exercises that right he is treated for the purposes of the Arbitration Act as a party to the arbitration agreement and is therefore bound by it[17]. Thus, suppose that A contracts with B for A to do work on C's property, and the contract provides for the reference to arbitration of disputes between A and B, or between either of them and C, arising out of performance of the contract. If the contract confers on C no right to enforce any of its substantive terms, C is not bound by the arbitration clause. Thus if A negligently damages C's property, C can bring a tort claim against A by means of court proceedings. However, if C takes the benefit of the arbitration clause in the contract, for instance by commencing arbitration proceedings against A, he is then treated as being a party to the arbitration agreement for all purposes and is therefore bound by it.

1   Section 5. The Act also requires any other agreement as to any other matter – for instance, to refer a question to the court, to be in writing.
2   The section is based on, but goes further than, the UNCITRAL Model Law. The New York Convention on the Mutual Recognition and Enforcement of Arbitral Awards also applies only where the arbitration agreement is in writing.
3   Section 5(2)(c).
4   Section 5(4).
5   Section 5(5).
6   Section 5(6).
7   The Advisory Committee Report thought that the section would be limited to agreements recorded as text rather than speech: see p 14, para 43. It is equally not clear whether speech recordings would qualify as 'writing' for the purposes of the UNCITRAL Model Law, art 7.2, which refers to an exchange of letters, telex, telegrams or other means of telecommunication which provide a record of the agreement. See Hill [1997] ICLQ 274 at 284.
8   Section 5(3).
9   See also *Zambia Steel v James Clark* [1986] 2 Lloyd's Rep 225. This goes further than the Model Law, which permits an arbitration clause to be incorporated into a contract by reference but requires the contract itself to be in writing: art 7(2).
10 See generally Todd [1997] JBL 331
11 *T W Thomas & Co Ltd v Portsea Steamship Co Ltd* [1912] AC 1.
12 *The Merak* [1965] P 223; *The Annefield* [1971] P 168.
13 See eg *Aughton Ltd v M F Kent Services Ltd* (1991) 57 BLR 1 per Megaw LJ; *Excess Insurance Co Ltd v Mander* [1995] LRLR 358.
14 *Trygg Hansa Insurance Co Ltd v Equitas Ltd* [1998] 2 Lloyd's Rep 439.
15 See 2.7.2.
16 Contracts (Rights of Third Parties) Act 1999, s 8.
17 Contracts (Rights of Third Parties) Act 1999, s 8.

36.2.3.3   *The arbitrator's jurisdiction*

It has long been settled that the termination of a contract as a result of breach or frustration did not prevent reliance on an arbitration clause. Thus if A terminates a contract with B, alleging that B has committed a repudiatory breach, and B commences an arbitration relying on an arbitration clause in the contract, A cannot resist the arbitration by arguing that the termination brings the arbitration clause to an end together with the substantive contract[1]. For some time, however, there was doubt whether in English law an arbitration clause could empower an arbitrator to decide questions relating to the initial validity of the contract in which it appeared, as where it was alleged that the contract was void, voidable or illegal. In *Harbour Assurance Co (UK) Ltd v Kansa General International Insurance Co Ltd* [2] the

Court of Appeal accepted the principle, already established in most other jurisdictions, that as a matter of law where an arbitration clause is incorporated in a contract it gives rise to a contract separate from that in which it appears. The arbitration clause is therefore not invalidated by the invalidity or illegality of the contract in which it appears. This principle of the separability of the arbitration clause is now confirmed by s 7 of the 1996 Act. An arbitrator is therefore not deprived of jurisdiction under an arbitration clause simply because it is alleged that the contract in which the clause appears was void, voidable, illegal or did not come into existence.

This does not mean that the arbitrator necessarily has jurisdiction to determine questions relating to the initial validity of the main contract. Whether he does will depend on the proper construction of the arbitration clause itself. Thus, for instance, it has been held that a reference to 'all disputes or differences arising out of this agreement' was sufficient to enable the arbitrator to determine questions of initial validity[3]. On the other hand, a reference to 'disputes arising under this agreement' was held not to cover claims relating to misrepresentation, negligent misstatement or breach of collateral warranty, which did not arise *under* the main contract[4]. A formula such as 'all disputes or differences arising out of or in connection with this agreement' probably would be effective to cover such claims[5].

A separate, but related, question is whether the arbitrator can determine questions relating to his own jurisdiction. This question is now resolved by s 30 of the 1996 Act. In furtherance of the principle of upholding arbitral autonomy, s 30 provides that:

> 'Unless otherwise agreed by the parties, the arbitral tribunal may rule on its own substantive jurisdiction, that is, as to—
> (a) whether there is a valid arbitration agreement;
> (b) whether the tribunal is properly constituted; and
> (c) what matters have been submitted to arbitration in accordance with the arbitration agreement'.

The arbitrator may therefore rule on questions relating to the existence and scope of his own jurisdiction, a power sometimes referred to in German as 'Kompetenz-Kompetenz'. He may make such a ruling either as part of his final award or in a special preliminary ruling as to jurisdiction. Clearly, though, the arbitrator cannot have the last word on the subject. The Act permits a party dissatisfied with the arbitrator's ruling as to jurisdiction to challenge it either by appeal in the arbitral process, or by applying to the court to review the ruling[6]. However, the right to apply to the court for a review of a ruling as to jurisdiction is subject to a number of restrictions. In particular, the Act requires a party who objects to the arbitrator's taking jurisdiction to raise his objections at the earliest possible time after they arise[7]. If he continues to participate in the proceedings without raising the objection, he may be barred from subsequently raising that objection before the tribunal or the court[8]. A party thus cannot 'wait and see', fighting the case on the merits and only raising an objection to jurisdiction if the substantive issue is decided against him. In any case, no application to the court can be made until all internal review and appeal procedures within the arbitral process have been exhausted[9].

One of the features which distinguishes arbitration from other dispute resolution methods, such as conciliation and mediation, is that the arbitrator decides the dispute in a judicial manner. It is well settled that the system of law which governs an arbitration need not be the same as the system applicable to the substantive dispute covered by the arbitration. Thus an arbitration governed by English law may provide for a dispute to be decided by the arbitrator applying (say) German law or US law. However, parties might wish to give an arbitrator power to decide their dispute according to wider considerations than strict legal rules. Indeed, one of the reasons for preferring arbitration over litigation might be to enable the arbitrator to take account of wider considerations than could be considered by a court, for instance in interpreting a contract. In other jurisdictions it has long been accepted that an arbitrator may be authorised to decide a dispute '*ex aequo et bono*' or as '*amiable compositeur*'. Such a provision enables the arbitrator to depart from strict legal rules. Prior to 1996 the status of such provisions in English law was unclear. In some cases the judges appeared extremely hostile to such arrangements, expressing the view that it would be contrary to public policy to uphold an agreement which permitted an arbitrator to decide a case not in accordance with the law:

> 'but in accordance with some other criteria, such as what the arbitrators consider to be fair and reasonable . . . arbitrators must in general apply a fixed and recognisable system of law . . . and cannot be allowed to apply some different criterion such as the view of the individual arbitrator or umpire on abstract justice or equitable principles, which, of course, does not mean 'equity' in the legal sense of the word at all'[10].

One reason for this attitude might be that it would be difficult for a court to supervise and review a decision of an arbitrator made on such a basis. In some more recent cases there were signs of a greater willingness to uphold such arrangements[11]. For instance, in *DST v Raknoil*[12] the Court of Appeal held that it would not be contrary to public policy to enforce an arbitration award made under an agreement subject to Swiss law which permitted the arbitrator to decide in accordance with 'internationally accepted principles of law governing contractual relations'. The effectiveness of 'equity' clauses in English law nevertheless remained unclear at best[13]. However, s 46 of the 1996 Act now seems to have settled the question and to have considerably liberalised English law. It provides that:

'(1) The arbitral tribunal shall decide the dispute—
　　(a) in accordance with the law chosen by the parties . . . ; or
　　(b) if the parties so agree, in accordance with such other considerations as are agreed by them or determined by the tribunal'.

It therefore seems that the parties may now authorise the arbitrator to decide the dispute in accordance with English or any other national law, or in accordance with other principles, including by acting *ex aequo et bono* or as *amiable compositeur*, or by applying other more general principles. Thus, for instance, a clause might authorise an arbitrator to decide a dispute in accordance with an international convention not yet in force (such as the Vienna Sales Convention), general statements of legal principles, such as the UNIDROIT Principles of Interpretation of Commercial Contracts or the Lando principles, or '*lex mercatoria*', which might encompass such principles and other material such as the Uniform Customs and Practice for Documentary Credits and commercial custom and practice in general. Any dispute as to the content or meaning of such practice would, presumably, be for the arbitrator to decide. It is even possible for the parties to authorise the arbitrator to determine the considerations to be applied[14].

1   *Heyman v Darwins* [1942] AC 356.
2   [1993] QB 701, [1993] 3 All ER 897.
3   *Harbour Insurance Co (UK) Ltd v Kansa General International Insurance Co Ltd* [1993] QB 701, [1993] 3 All ER 879.
4   *Fillite (Runcorn) Ltd v Aqua Lift* (1989) 26 Con LR 66, CA.
5   *Woolf v Collis Removal Service* [1948] 1 KB 11; *Ashville Investments Ltd v Elmer Contractors Ltd* [1989] QB 488. Since the proper construction of a clause will depend on its context, there is no guarantee that a form of words held to be effective in one case will be effective in another.
6   Section 30(2), s 67: see below 36.2.3.5.
7   Sections 31(1), 31(2).
8   Section 73.
9   Section 70.
10 Megaw J in *Orion Compania Espanola de Seguros v Belfort Maatschappij Voor Algemene Verzekgringeen* [1962] 2 Lloyd's Rep 257 at 264.
11 See eg *Eagle Star Insurance Co Ltd v Yuval Insurance Co* [1978] 1 Lloyd's Rep 357, CA; *Home Insurance Co and St Paul Fire and Marine Insurance Co v Administratia Asigurarilor de Stat* [1983] 2 Lloyd's Rep 674.
12 *Deutsche Schachtbau und Tiefbohrgesellschaft mbH v Ras Al Khaimah National Oil Co* [1987] 2 All ER 769. See also *Channel Tunnel Group Ltd v Balfour Beatty Construction Ltd* [1993] AC 334, [1993] 1 All ER 664 where the agreement provided for the contract to be interpreted in accordance with principles common to English and French law and, in the absence of such common principles, 'by such general principles of international trade law as have been applied by national and international tribunals'.
13 See *Home and Overseas Insurance Co Ltd v Mentor Insurance Co (UK) Ltd* [1990] 1 WLR 153; see generally Yu [1999] Int A LR 2(2) 43.
14 Section 46(1)(b).

36.2.3.4   *Conduct of the proceedings*

In accordance with the principle that arbitration is a consensual process, the parties enjoy a large degree of freedom to define the arbitration procedure, either by drawing up a detailed agreement for ad hoc arbitration or by adopting the rules of institutional arbitration scheme. In the absence of such agreement, however, the 1996 Act contains default provisions governing the conduct of the arbitration and defining the powers of the tribunal.

In all cases the tribunal is under a mandatory general duty in all aspects of its conduct of the arbitration to:

'(a) act fairly and impartially as between the parties, giving each party a reasonable opportunity of presenting his case and dealing with that of his opponent, and [to]
(b) adopt procedures suitable to the circumstances of the particular case, avoiding unnecessary delay or expense . . . '[1].

Alongside this we may note that the arbitrator is not liable for anything done or omitted in the discharge of his function unless the act or omission is shown to have been in bad faith[2].

Subject to the general duty just referred to, and to any agreement of the parties, the arbitrator is given a broad discretion to decide all procedural and evidential matters relating to the arbitration, including when and where to hold the proceedings, the language to be used in the proceedings, whether written statements of claim and defence should be used, whether there should be discovery of documents, whether to apply the strict rules of evidence and whether to adopt an accusatorial, inquisitorial or hybrid procedure[3]. There is a general right to legal representation in the proceedings unless the parties (not the tribunal) agree otherwise[4].

Unless otherwise agreed by the parties, the tribunal has a number of further powers, including the power to order a party to provide security for costs, to make directions as to the examination, preservation etc of property and to direct that a party or witness be examined on oath[5]. If the parties so agree, the tribunal also has power to make provisional awards – eg for the payment of money.

The tribunal must have a means of ensuring compliance with its orders. In the past arbitration was often used as a means of 'side-tracking' a dispute, by commencing an arbitration but not proceeding with it and thus using the reference to arbitration as a means of preventing the commencement of court proceedings. This should no longer be possible. Both parties are under a general duty to do 'all things necessary for the proper and expeditious conduct of the arbitral proceedings', including complying with orders and directions of the tribunal[6]. If a party fails to comply with an order or direction of the tribunal, the tribunal may make a peremptory order, fixing a time limit for compliance. Non-compliance with a peremptory order may be penalised in various ways, including by an order for costs. In addition, the court may order compliance with a peremptory order. However, perhaps the most important of the tribunal's powers over the parties is the power to dismiss a claim if satisfied that there has been 'inordinate and inexcusable delay on the part of the claimant in pursuing his claim' which gives rise to a substantial risk that it is not possible to have a fair resolution of the issues, or causes serious prejudice to the respondent[7]. It should therefore no longer be possible to use arbitration as a means of freezing potential claims.

The parties have a general freedom to define the tribunal's remedial powers but, in the absence of any contrary agreement, the tribunal has wide general powers, equivalent to those of the court, to order the payment of money in any currency, to make declarations, order a party to do or refrain from doing anything, order specific performance of a contract or order rectification of a deed or document[8]. In addition, the tribunal has a wide discretion – in some respects greater than that of the court – to award actual or compound interest[9], and to allocate the costs of the arbitration as between the parties[10].

1 Section 33.
2 Section 74.
3 Section 34(2).
4 Section 36.
5 Section 38.
6 Section 40.
7 Section 42(3).
8 Section 49.
9 Section 49.
10 Section 61.

36.2.3.5 *Intervention of the court*

We have seen that one of the principle reasons for agreeing to arbitration is to avoid litigation. That purpose is frustrated if parties who have agreed to arbitration may ignore their agreement and resort, instead, to litigation before the court if disputes arise. There is, of course, no reason why the parties should not ignore their arbitration agreement and resort to the court if both agree. There will also be situations in which the court's assistance is needed to ensure that the arbitration proceedings work effectively – for instance, where the parties are unable to agree on an arbitrator, or where interlocutory orders beyond the scope of the arbitrator's own jurisdiction are required. However, if the objectives of the arbitration agreement are not to be frustrated, neither party should be permitted to resort to court proceedings in preference to arbitration without the agreement of the other. Moreover, the arbitration proceedings themselves must, so far as possible, be final, for the purpose of the arbitration agreement would also be frustrated if a party dissatisfied with the outcome of arbitration could then challenge it in the court. The parties cannot, however, oust the jurisdiction of the court altogether. The court must retain a general supervisory jurisdiction to be invoked where, for instance, a decision is manifestly wrong or in the event of improper behaviour by the arbitrator, for the parties cannot have intended to agree to the decision being improperly made, or the law being wrongly applied.

The law must therefore strike a balance between upholding the autonomy of the arbitral process and maintaining effective supervision of it. The general trend of both statutory and common law developments in recent years has been to bolster the autonomy of the arbitral process. The 1996 Act continues this trend by extending the powers of arbitrators to make interim orders in the arbitration, thus reducing the need to seek the assistance of the court, and further restricting the powers of the court to interfere in the process. The court has a general power to stay court proceedings brought by a party to an arbitration agreement, and the right to appeal to the court against an arbitrator's decision is limited.

(a)   Staying court proceedings

If one of the parties to an arbitration agreement seeks to litigate rather than to pursue the arbitration, the other may apply to the court to have the court proceedings stayed. Under the 'old law' a distinction was drawn for this purpose between 'domestic' and 'non-domestic' arbitrations. In relation to domestic arbitrations the court had a discretion[1] to stay the proceedings in certain circumstances. In relation to 'non-domestic' arbitrations the court had a more restricted discretion and was obliged to grant a stay of court proceedings unless satisfied that the arbitration agreement was void, inoperative or incapable of being performed or that there was no dispute within its terms[2].

The right of a party to an arbitration agreement to seek a stay of court proceedings is now contained in s 9 of the 1996 Act. The section also applies where the reference to arbitration is only to be made after exhaustion of other dispute resolution procedures[3]. The distinction between 'domestic' and 'non-domestic' arbitrations has been abolished[4]. The party seeking a stay must first have acknowledged the legal proceedings commenced against him, but must have taken no steps to answer the substantive claim[5]. However, provided that these requirements are satisfied, the court must now grant a stay of proceedings in all cases, unless satisfied that the arbitration agreement is null and void, inoperative or incapable of being performed[6].

It will be noted that the court's discretion to refuse a stay is now even more restricted than under the 1975 Act, the power to refuse a stay where there is no dispute having been omitted from the new Act. Prior to the 1996 Act the courts had developed a practice of refusing a stay on this basis in certain circumstances. A claimant who felt that he had an undeniable claim – for instance, for an unpaid debt – might prefer to commence proceedings rather than arbitrate, in order to take advantage of the court's power to grant summary judgment and prevent his debtor using procedural tricks in the arbitration to delay payment. If in such a case the debtor sought to have the proceedings stayed, the court would hear the application for the stay at the same time as the application for summary judgment. If it found that there was in fact no defence to the claim, it would refuse a stay on the grounds that there was no 'dispute' between the parties, and grant summary judgment. This practice was commercially useful in so far as it prevented a debtor using the arbitration as a means to delay payment. However, it could be argued that it undermined the principle of arbitral autonomy and in *Halki Shipping Ltd v Sopex Oils Ltd* [7] the Court of Appeal held that this course of action was no longer available under the 1996 Act. Where there is no dispute, the arbitrator will normally not have jurisdiction. However, there will be a dispute unless liability is admitted[8]. Provided, therefore, that the debtor withholds payment in such a case, there is a 'dispute' for the purposes of the arbitration agreement, over which the arbitrator has jurisdiction. The court must therefore grant a stay under s 9 (unless one of the surviving grounds for refusing a stay under that section is made out). Although there may thus be a risk that in some cases debtors may be able to use the arbitration proceedings as a means of delaying payment, the arbitrator now has extensive powers to award interest and to make interim payments, which should to some extent protect the creditor against abuse.

(b)   Orders in support of the arbitration

The court has limited powers under the 1996 Act to make orders in support of the arbitration. However, maintaining the policy of upholding arbitral autonomy, these powers are generally exercisable only at the request of the arbitral tribunal or with the consent of both parties, and only where the tribunal is unable to act. Thus the court may (unless the parties agree otherwise): order a party to comply with a peremptory order of the tribunal[9]; make orders for witnesses to attend before the tribunal and give evidence or produce documents[10], for the taking of evidence, the preservation of evidence, the inspection, preservation, sampling etc of property; and grant interim injunctions[11]. There is also power for application to be made to the court to determine a point of law which arises in the proceedings[12]. However, this power may be excluded by the parties, and is deemed to be excluded if the parties have agreed to dispense with a reasoned award, and the court may only consider an application made by one of the parties if (a) the tribunal consents and (b) the court is satisfied that determination of the question is likely to produce substantial costs savings and that the application was made without delay.

(c)   Challenges to the tribunal's decision

A decision of an arbitral tribunal may be challenged before the court on three grounds: lack of substantive jurisdiction; procedural irregularity; and error of law. All three are subject to tight restrictions in the interests of supporting arbitral autonomy. A party wishing to challenge an award on any of the three grounds must first exhaust any internal appeal procedure available under the arbitral process[13] and must bring the application to the court within 28 days of the award[14]. In addition, a party who continues to participate in an arbitration without raising any objection based on lack of jurisdiction or procedural irregularity may be precluded from subsequently raising that objection either before the tribunal or the court[15].

(i)   Lack of jurisdiction

Either party may, on notice to the other and to the tribunal, challenge a decision of the tribunal as to its own jurisdiction, or challenge a final award of the tribunal on the grounds that the tribunal lacked substantive jurisdiction[16].

(ii)   Procedural error
Either party may, on notice to the other party and to the tribunal, challenge any
award of the tribunal on the grounds of a serious procedural irregularity affecting
the tribunal, the proceedings or the award[17]. The Act sets out an exhaustive list of
the types of procedural irregularity which may provide grounds for a challenge.
It includes failure by the tribunal to comply with the general duty to act fairly and
impartially and to adopt appropriate procedures; the tribunal's exceeding its powers;
failure to conduct the proceedings in accordance with the agreed procedure;
uncertainty or ambiguity in the award; and the award's being obtained by fraud or
in a manner contrary to public policy[18]. In any case, the irregularity will only be
considered a serious irregularity if the court considers that it has caused, or will
cause, substantial injustice to the party challenging the award.
    The underlying rationale of this ground of challenge is that it is contrary to the
parties' reasonable expectations – and therefore outside the scope of their agreement
– for the tribunal to make a decision on the basis of a serious procedural error.
If the court upholds the challenge it may remit the award to the tribunal for further
consideration, or, if satisfied that it would be inappropriate to remit the award, set
it aside or declare it to be of no effect, in whole or in part.

(iii)   Error of law
Either party may, on notice to the other and to the tribunal, appeal to the court
against a decision of a tribunal on a point of law[19]. However, the power of the
court to intervene on this basis is very limited. A central principle of the 1996
Act is that the court should respect the will of the parties by upholding the
arbitration agreement. One aspect of that is that the arbitrator's decision should,
so far as possible, be final. A party disappointed by the award should not be able
to have a second bite at the cherry by re-opening the dispute before the court,
especially since an appeal to the court may be used simply to delay enforcement
of an award. It should be borne in mind, too, that one reason for encouraging the
use of arbitration is to reduce the workload of the courts. That objective will be
undermined if the right of appeal is too readily available. On the other hand, it is
assumed that parties who agree to arbitration expect the arbitrator to decide in
accordance with the law, and the court must retain some supervisory jurisdiction
over arbitration to ensure that the law is applied. The law must therefore strike a
balance between these two policies.
    Prior to 1979 it was relatively easy for a party disappointed with an arbitrator's
decision to seek to have it reviewed by the court. In order to maintain the
attractiveness of England as an arbitral centre, the Arbitration Act 1979 Act restricted
the right to appeal by requiring the consent of all the parties or the leave of the
court before an appeal could be brought, and allowed the parties to exclude the
right of appeal altogether in certain circumstances. Nevertheless, applications
for leave were frequently made and, it was felt, leave was too frequently granted.
In *The Nema*[20] the House of Lords therefore laid down guidelines as to the exercise
of the court's discretion to grant leave to appeal.
    Under the UNCITRAL Model Law the right of appeal to the court is wholly
excluded. The 1996 Act does not go that far but continues the trend of restricting the
right of appeal to the court by further restricting the right of appeal and, in effect,
putting the *Nema* guidelines on a statutory basis. A party to an arbitration can appeal
on a point of law against the arbitrator's decision either (a) with the consent of the
other party or (b) with the leave of the court. The court will only give leave if satisfied
that:

'(a) determination of the question will substantially affect the rights of at least one of the parties;

(b) the question is one which the tribunal was asked to determine;

(c) on the basis of the tribunal's findings of fact either the tribunal's decision is obviously wrong *or* the question is one of general public importance and the decision of the tribunal is open to serious doubt; and

(d) notwithstanding the parties' agreement to resolve the question by arbitration, it is just and proper in all the circumstances for the court to determine the question'[21].

The restriction in (c) above means that leave will more readily be granted in relation (say) to questions arising from the interpretation of standard form contracts. Leave will only rarely be given in 'one off' cases. Moreover, the parties may agree to exclude the right of appeal altogether, and are taken to have done so if they agree to the arbitrator giving an unreasoned award. An appeal from the court's decision to grant or refuse leave needs the leave of the court.

If the court grants leave to appeal it may confirm the award, vary it, remit it to the tribunal for reconsideration or, if satisfied that it would be inappropriate to remit it, set it aside in whole or in part[22]. An appeal against the court's substantive decision needs the leave of the court, which will only be given if the court is satisfied that the question is one of general public importance or that there is some other special reason for its being considered by the Court of Appeal[23].

1 Under s 4 of the Arbitration Act 1950.
2 Arbitration Act 1975, s 1.
3 Section 9(2), confirming the decision of the House of Lords in *Channel Tunnel Group Ltd v Balfour Beatty Construction Ltd* [1993] AC 334, [1993] 1 All ER 664, where the parties had agreed that disputes should be referred in the first instance to a panel of experts and, following that, to arbitration.
4 See above 36.2.3.1.
5 Section 9(3). A party will not be precluded from seeking a stay unless he takes some step in the court proceedings which may be taken as representing that he does not intend to enforce the arbitration agreement: *Patel v Patel* [1999] 1 All ER (Comm) 923.
6 Section 9(4).
7 [1998] 2 All ER 23.
8 See *Wealands v CLC Contractors Ltd (Key Scaffolding Ltd, third parties)* [2000] 1 All ER (Comm) 30.
9 Section 42.
10 Section 43.
11 Section 44. See *Re Q's Estate* [1999] 1 All ER (Comm) 499 (freezing order).
12 Section 45.
13 Section 70(2).
14 Section 70(3).
15 Section 73.
16 Section 67; see above 36.2.3.3.
17 Section 68.
18 Section 68(2).
19 Section 69.
20 *Pioneer Shipping Ltd v BTP Trioxide Ltd* [1982] AC 724. See also *The Antaios, Antaios Cie Naviera SA v Salen Redierna AB* [1985] AC 191.
21 Section 69(3).
22 Section 69(7).
23 Section 69(8).

36.2.3.6   *Enforcement of the award*

Once an award has been made the court's assistance may be required to enforce it. The successful party may sue on the award as a contract debt or, with the leave of the High Court, enforce it as if it were a judgment of that court[1].

Where an arbitration arises out of an international transaction the award may have to be enforced outside the UK. In the ordinary way the enforcement of judgments outside the jurisdiction can be problematic, although the enforcement of court judgments in other European countries is facilitated by the EEC Convention for the Reciprocal Recognition and Enforcement of Judgments and in some other countries enforcement may be possible by virtue of reciprocal treaties. The enforcement of foreign arbitration awards is made possible by the 1958 New York Convention on the Recognition and Enforcement of Arbitral Awards, which is given effect in the UK by the 1975 Arbitration Act, and by the 1924 Geneva Convention on the Execution of Foreign Arbitral Awards. The New York Convention has now been widely adopted and as a result 'in most of the main trading countries of the world, arbitration awards are more easily enforceable than judgments, which of course in itself supplies a great spur to arbitration'[2]. The UK is a party to both conventions. The New York Convention is given effect by Pt III of the 1996 Act. The Geneva Convention is given effect by Pt II of the 1950 Act[3].

1   Arbitration Act 1996, s 66.
2   The Hon Mr Justice Kerr 'International Arbitration v Litigation' [1980] JBL 164 at 167.
3   Continued in force by s 99 of the 1996 Act.

36.2.3.7   *Consumer arbitration agreements*

Many trade associations operate arbitration schemes to resolve disputes between their members and consumers. However, although arbitration clauses which commit the parties to arbitration rather than litigation are relatively unobjectionable in commercial contracts, where they may offer both parties advantages described earlier, the position is different where an arbitration clause is included in a consumer contract. Although arbitration may be quicker and cheaper than litigation, it may offer a number of disadvantages to the consumer. The consumer may be anxious, for instance, to obtain publicity for a complaint in order to put pressure on the business to settle the dispute, or to provide a warning to other consumers. Moreover, a consumer may be suspicious of an arbitration scheme operated by the business's own trade association. Many arbitration schemes provide for 'documents only' arbitration, where evidence is given only in writing, or allow for an oral hearing only on payment of an increased fee. Such schemes may deprive the consumer of a 'day in court' and a chance to present a claim in an oral hearing. Furthermore, the cost of referring a dispute to some institutional arbitration schemes may be considerably higher than that of bringing a small claim in the County Court. An arbitration clause requiring consumer disputes to be referred to such a scheme might therefore effectively preclude the bringing of claims and thus deny the consumer access to justice.

The Consumer Arbitration Agreements Act 1988 therefore restricted the enforceability of arbitration agreements against consumers making them enforceable against a consumer only if the consumer agreed, in writing, to arbitration after the dispute had arisen, or if the consumer actually submitted to the arbitration, or the court made an order allowing enforcement of the agreement.

The 1996 Act repealed the 1988 Act and replaced it with a much simpler scheme[1]. An arbitration agreement between a supplier of goods or services and a consumer is now subjected to the Unfair Terms in Consumer Contracts Regulations 1999[2] and is conclusively presumed to be unfair, and therefore unenforceable against the consumer, if the amount in dispute does not exceed £5,000[3]. 'Consumer' is given an extended meaning for this purpose and includes any natural *or legal* person acting for purposes which are outside his trade, business or profession[4].

1 Sections 89–91.
2 See 2.6.5.
3 Unfair Arbitration Agreements (Specified Amount) Order 1999, SI 1999/2167.
4 Section 90.

36.3 Alternative dispute resolution

In recent years there has been growing interest in a number of systems for alternative dispute resolution (ADR). Some are merely variants on arbitration or litigation but in certain circumstances they may offer advantages over both for the resolution of commercial disputes, enabling the parties to save time and money, avoid publicity and preserve their trading relationship and commercial reputation.

Among the most popular mechanisms in the commercial context are conciliation and mediation. The objective of both is to enable the parties with the aid of an independent third party to seek an amicable settlement to their dispute without resort to more formal and potentially antagonistic proceedings. They differ in that a conciliator merely seeks to find common ground between the parties and encourage them to find a settlement, whereas a mediator may play a more active role in bringing the parties together, offering a solution of his own. In addition to the advantages listed above, the mediator or conciliator may be able to propose remedial solutions not available through court proceedings or arbitration. Unlike arbitration, they do not lead to a legally enforceable award, but a consensual solution reached through mediation or conciliation is more likely to be honoured by the parties in its own right.

There is no statutory regulation of conciliation or mediation, equivalent to the Arbitration Act. There are therefore no legal default rules to govern the applicable procedure, so that it is important for the parties to define the procedure to be followed, either expressly or by adopting the scheme of one of the established suppliers of mediation and conciliation services. UNCITRAL has produced a set of Conciliation Rules which parties may adopt, and the ICC, long a provider of commercial arbitration services, has also drawn up Conciliation Rules.

Another form of ADR is the 'mini-trial', in which representatives of each party make short presentations to a panel made up of executives drawn from each party and an independent chairman. A decision of the panel can be embodied in a written agreement and thus made contractually enforceable.

It might be thought that the courts would be jealous of these alternatives to litigation. In fact, they are keen to encourage them. Under the CPR the court is required to encourage parties to consider the use of ADR[1], and the court has jurisdiction to stay proceedings, at the request of the parties or of its own initiative, to facilitate the use of ADR[2]. ADR is similarly encouraged in the Commercial Court. A 1996 Practice Direction, now reproduced in the *Commercial Court Guide*, noted that whilst 'the Commercial Court will remain an entirely appropriate forum for resolving most of the disputes which are commenced before it', ADR could offer the parties the advantages listed above, whilst also being 'likely to make a substantial contribution to the more efficient use of judicial resources'[3]. In order to assist parties interested in making use of ADR, the Commercial Court keeps a list of bodies offering ADR services.

The court does not, however, have any statutory power to stay proceedings commenced in breach of an agreement to refer disputes to ADR equivalent to the power under the Arbitration Act to stay proceedings in favour of an arbitration agreement. The court could exercise its inherent jurisdiction to stay proceedings in such a case, but the non-enforceability of agreements to negotiate may be an obstacle to a party seeking a stay. In *Halifax Financial Services Ltd v Intuitive Systems Ltd*[4] the parties had entered into a contract which contained a structured dispute resolution procedure. It provided, in the first instance, for negotiation and required representatives of the parties to meet 'in good faith' to attempt to resolve the dispute. If such informal negotiations proved unsuccessful, either party could call for 'structured negotiations' with a neutral adviser. If those failed, either party could refer the dispute to the court unless both agreed to resort to arbitration. When one of the parties commenced court proceedings Mackinnon J refused to grant a stay of proceedings to allow the procedure to be invoked, observing that there was nothing in the agreement to make the procedure a condition precedent to litigation and, of more concern, that the procedure unlike that in the *Channel Tunnel* case[5], would not lead to a legally binding result. In effect all that the parties had done was to agree to try to negotiate an agreement to settle prospective disputes and it is established that an agreement to negotiate in good faith is not legally binding[6]. Thus even had the agreement made the procedure a condition precedent to litigation, it would not have been binding. Mackinnon J also refused to adjourn proceedings to permit negotiations: lengthy informal negotiations had already failed to produce a settlement and an adjournment would therefore not promote a speedy settlement but would delay resolution of the dispute.

On the facts of the case the result seems reasonable: moreover, in light of established case law on the enforceability of 'agreements to agree', the decision appears to be correct in law. It does, however, indicate the limits of ADR: if one party chooses to ignore the agreed procedure the other will be able to do nothing to hold him to it.

1   CPR 1.4.
2   CPR 26.4.
3   [1996] 3 All ER 383; Commercial Court Guide, para G1.2.
4   [1999] 1 All ER (Comm) 303.
5   *Channel Tunnel Group Ltd v Balfour Beatty Construction Ltd* [1993] AC 334, [1993] 1 All ER 664; see 36.2.3 above.
6   *Walford v Miles* [1992] 2 AC 128, [1992] 1 All ER 453, see 2.3.3.

36.3.1   *Ombudsman schemes*

Under the encouragement of the Director General of Fair Trading, a number of trade associations have produced codes of practice, many of which include conciliation and/or arbitration schemes for resolution of disputes between members of the association and consumers. A number of professional and business organisations have introduced ombudsman schemes to enable individuals with complaints to pursue them with the ombudsman rather than through the courts.

The first such scheme was the Insurance Ombudsman Bureau, established in 1981. It was followed in 1986 by the Banking Ombudsman scheme. A similar scheme for building societies was established under the Building Societies Act 1986.

Ombudsman schemes may offer consumers some advantages over formal litigation or arbitration, especially if reference to the ombudsman is free and does not preclude litigation if the complainant is dissatisfied with the ombudsman's decision. They can suffer from a number of weaknesses, however, especially where, as in the case of the insurance and banking schemes, membership of the scheme is voluntary.

By 1999 there were eight separate ombudsman schemes covering different branches of the financial services industry. The Financial Services and Markets Act 2000 creates a single regulatory structure covering all aspects of the financial services industry, including banks, building societies, insurance companies, credit unions, friendly societies, investment advisers, Lloyd's and so on. One of the professed objectives of the Act is consumer protection and, to this end, it will, when brought into force, replace all of the existing ombudsman schemes in the financial services industry with a single Financial Services Ombudsman Scheme which, it is predicted, will be the largest such scheme in the world.

In November 1999 the Financial Services Authority and the Financial Services Ombudsman Scheme Ltd jointly published a consultation paper[1] setting out details of the proposed new scheme. Membership of the scheme will be compulsory for firms regulated by the FSA. The scheme's objective will be to provide a free, informal and accessible forum, as an alternative to the courts, for the resolution of consumer complaints against regulated firms, to resolve disputes quickly and with a minimum of formality. The scheme will be open to consumers (private individuals) and, following the model of some of the existing schemes, small businesses, which are expected to be defined as businesses with a turnover of less than £1m per annum *and* less than five employees. The scheme will not be available for claims by regulated firms against customers.

The ombudsman will have authority to decide cases in accordance with what he considers 'fair and reasonable', taking account not only of law but also of codes of practice and, it is proposed, 'good industry practice'. It is anticipated that this may result in the ombudsman taking a more 'pro-consumer' line than would be justified by application of strict law. The existing Insurance Ombudsman has adopted a similar approach in recent years and in a number of cases has been prepared to deviate from the strict law in resolving disputes in favour of consumers. The ombudsman will have power to award compensation up to a maximum of £100,000, and his decisions will be binding on the firm, but not on the customer who will retain the option of pursuing a claim before the court if dissatisfied with the ombudsman's decision.

1   Consumer Complaints and the New Single Ombudsman Scheme, CP33.

36.4   Conclusion

There is now general acceptance of the validity and desirability of party autonomy and of dispute resolution methods other than litigation, including, but not limited to, arbitration. This can only be reinforced by the new Civil Procedure Rules, which require judges to encourage litigants to consider alternative dispute resolution, including mediation and mini-trials. The courts, too, seem much more willing than previously to recognise such methods.

It is generally recognised that parties to a dispute, especially commercial parties, need speedy, effective and informal methods of resolving their disputes. The Commercial Court has long attempted to serve the needs of the commercial community by providing suitable and effective procedures. More general civil procedure, and English arbitration law, have not always served the needs of litigants and disputants. However, with the introduction of the Arbitration Act 1996 and the new Civil Procedure Rules both arbitration and civil litigation are better attuned to those needs. As Lord Woolf, the architect of the new civil procedure regime, recognised, both regimes are based on the same general principles – the fair and effective resolution of disputes without unnecessary delay or expense[1].

In many ways the Arbitration Act 1996 is a paradigm of the legal response to the needs of commerce. It is intended to be accessible to and comprehensible by the commercial people affected by it. In many ways it appears to be in the tradition of the great Victorian commercial codifying statutes. Interestingly, many of the criticisms which were levelled at arbitration law prior to 1996 – that the law was a confused hotch-potch of statutes and case law, difficult to locate and with no obviously discernible underlying principles – might also be levelled at many other areas of commercial law, including sales law. It is perhaps too much to hope that the Arbitration Act might provide a model for the more general reform and rationalisation of other areas of commercial law.

To return to the issue of dispute resolution, the existence, side by side, of so many different dispute resolution procedures should be no surprise: given the wide range of transactions which fall within the broad definition of 'commercial law' it is unlikely that any one scheme could ever meet the needs of all parties to all disputes in all circumstances. The aims of the various dispute resolution schemes, including litigation, are essentially the same: to resolve disputes quickly, cheaply, in a commercially sensible way and with the minimum of damage to trading relationships. In many ways the needs of the commercial community which they seek to meet are the same as when the lex mercatoria was administered by the Courts of Pie Powder. Indeed, with revitalisation of arbitration and the development of ADR schemes whereby commercial disputes are decided in a pragmatic way by commercial people it may be that commercial law has come full circle. What is clear, however, is that unless the law continues to be alert and responsive to the needs of commerce, both in its substance and in the procedures it offers for the resolution of disputes, the commercial world will look elsewhere for solutions to its problems.

1   See *Patel v Patel* [1999] 1 All ER (Comm) 923 at 926.

Index

References are to paragraph number.

Index

Index

CONSUMER CREDIT ETC
AGREEMENTS—*contd*
negotiations, 'antecedent', 26.2.1-26.2.3,
26.4
'representation' made during, 26.2.3
non-commercial agreements, 25.3
offer and acceptance, 26.2
orders, 26.7
penalties, 26.6.4
policy considerations/balance of interests,
21.3
private agreements, 25.3
protection order, 26.7
quotations, 26.0.2
regulated agreements, 25.0 *et seq,* 26.0 *et seq*
remedies. *See* 'termination' *below*
rental agreement. *See* RENTAL CONTRACT
restricted/unrestricted-use credit, 25.1.1.2,
25.1.1.3
revolving, 21.1, 21.1.1, 21.1.3.1
running account, 23.0.3, 25.1.1.1, 25.1.2
security, 28.1.2
enforcement, 26.6.6
signature, 26.1.2, 26.1.3
small agreements, 25.3
termination, 26.6
debtor's default, on, by creditor, 26.6.4
early discharge by debtor, 26.6.1
hire agreement, by hirer, 26.6.2
hire purchase/conditional sale, return of
goods, 26.6.3
notice from creditor, 26.6.6
repossession of goods, 26.6.5, 26.6.7
repudiatory or non-repudiatory breach,
26.6.4
time order, 26.7
unfair terms regulation, 26.1.2, 26.7.2. *See
also* UNFAIR CONTRACT TERMS
withdrawal, 26.2, 26.2.2
CONSUMERS' ASSOCIATION
enforcement powers, unfair contract term,
2.6.5.4
CONTAINERISATION, 32.5.3
CONTRACT HIRE, 8.2.4.4
CONTRACT LAW, 2.0 *et seq*
agency, contract of, 6.0, 6.2, 6.3.1.1. *See
also* AGENCY
agreement, elements of, 2.3
acceptance. *See* ACCCEPTANCE
agreement to agree, 2.3.3
formalities, 2.3.6
intention to create legal relations, 2.3.5,
8.1
letter of intent, 2.3.4
lock-out agreement, 2.3.3
offer. *See* OFFER
voluntary entry, 2.3, 2.4, 2.4.3
assignment of rights, 2.7.1, 27.3.1
background and changes in, 2.0.1

CONTRACT LAW—*contd*
breach of contract, 2.5.1, 2.5.6
anticipatory, 2.9.3, 2.10.3.3, 9.1
condition, breach of, 2.9.3, 12.3
discharge of party, 2.9.3
'fundamental breach' doctrine, 2.6.2
innominate term, 2.5.6
parties agreeing consequences, 2.5.6
remedies, 2.10. *See also* DAMAGES;
TERMINATION OF CONTRACT
repudiatory. *See* REPUDIATION
sale of goods contract. *See* SALE OF
GOODS
businesses, and,
'business efficacy', term implied for,
2.5.4
commercial expectations, 2.1.1
overview, 2.1
practical approach, 2.1.1
cancellation, 2.3.7. *See also* CANCELLATION
caveat emptor rule, 2.4.1, 11.0.1, 11.2
caveat venditor, shift to, 11.3.1
consideration, 2.2
commercial contract, in, 2.2.1
discharge by agreement, for, 2.9.1
doctrine of, 2.2, 2.8.1
fresh promise, for, 2.2.1
goods or services, 8.2.3
guarantee, for, 23.1.1
'money', sale of goods, 8.1.3, 8.1.3.1
new/varied term, for, 2.2.1, 2.8.1
none, transfer by deed, 8.2
past, examples of, 2.2.1
performance of existing duties, 2.8.1
total failure, recovery of money, 2.10.4
voucher, 8.2.3
'contract', definition, 2.2, 2.3
defect in formation, 2.4-2.4.3
effect of, general, 2.4
discharge. *See* DISCHARGE OF PARTY TO
CONTRACT
duress, 2.4.3
enforcement of incomplete agreement,
2.3.3, 2.3.4, 2.3.5
exclusion of liability. *See* EXCLUSION CLAUSE
formation and formalities. *See* 'agreement,
elements of' *above*
'freedom of contract', 2.0.1, 2.4.3, 2.5.3
frustration. *See* FRUSTRATION DOCTRINE
implied contract, 2.0, 2.2.1
implied term. *See* TERMS OF CONTRACT
insurance contracts. *See* INSURANCE
letter of comfort, status of, 2.3.5
letter of intent, 2.3.4
misrepresentation. *See* MISREPRESENTATION
mistake, 2.4.1, 16.2, 16.2.4
negotiations, 2.3.4
non-interventionist approach, 1.1.2, 1.3.1,
2.0.1, 11.1.3

910